Universal- und kulturhistorische Studien. Studies in Universal and Cultural History

Series Editors

Alberto Bernabé Pajares, Madrid, Spain

Sebastian Fink, Innsbruck, Austria

Ann C. Gunter, Evanston, USA

D. T. Potts, New York, USA

Robert Rollinger, Innsbruck, Austria

Kai Ruffing, Kassel, Germany

Mit der Krise des Nationalstaates am Ende des 20. Jahrhunderts und der Erfahrung einer zusehends vernetzten und globalisierten Welt gewinnt auch eine neue Perspektive in den Geschichtswissenschaften an Bedeutung. Dieser neue Blick auf die Vergangenheit macht den Weg frei für eine innovative und interdisziplinäre Annäherung an das Phänomen einer vernetzten Weltgeschichte, in der Europa nicht mehr das Zentrum der Welt darstellt, von dem aus „Historie" vermessen wird. Dieser universale Blick auf die Geschichte soll durch die neue Reihe befördert werden. Die Reihe umfasst alle Weltregionen und alle Epochen der Menschheitsgeschichte. Sie will vergleichende und auf dem neuesten Stand der Forschung gewonnene Einblicke in das Laboratorium der Weltgeschichte gewähren und befördern. Die Reihe versteht sich als eine peer-reviewed series, die sowohl für Monographien wie für Sammelbände offen ist.

With the crisis of national states at the end of the 20th century and the experience of a highly interconnected, globalized world, a new perspective in historical studies has emerged, which critically analyzes those concepts and methodologies formed under the influence of national consciousness. This intellectual framework fosters an innovative, strongly interdisciplinary approach to world history, seeking to transcend a regional focus in the writing of history. This series figures within these developments, which it endeavors to promote through the publication of new research. The new series aims to encourage a universal view of historical phenomena, broadly defined both geographically and chronologically. Its scope embraces all world regions and all periods of human history. The peer-reviewed series will publish both monographs and edited volumes.

D. T. Potts
Editor

Agreeable News from Persia

Iran in the Colonial and Early Republican American Press, 1712-1848

Volume II

Editor
D. T. Potts
New York University
New York, USA

ISSN 2524-3780　　　　　　ISSN 2524-3799　(electronic)
Universal- und kulturhistorische Studien. Studies in Universal and Cultural History
ISBN 978-3-658-36033-7　　　ISBN 978-3-658-36032-0　(eBook)
https://doi.org/10.1007/978-3-658-36032-0

© The Editor(s) (if applicable) and The Author(s), under exclusive license to Springer Fachmedien Wiesbaden GmbH, part of Springer Nature 2022
This work is subject to copyright. All rights are solely and exclusively licensed by the Publisher, whether the whole or part of the material is concerned, specifically the rights of translation, reprinting, reuse of illustrations, recitation, broadcasting, reproduction on microfilms or in any other physical way, and transmission or information storage and retrieval, electronic adaptation, computer software, or by similar or dissimilar methodology now known or hereafter developed.
The use of general descriptive names, registered names, trademarks, service marks, etc. in this publication does not imply, even in the absence of a specific statement, that such names are exempt from the relevant protective laws and regulations and therefore free for general use.
The publisher, the authors and the editors are safe to assume that the advice and information in this book are believed to be true and accurate at the date of publication. Neither the publisher nor the authors or the editors give a warranty, expressed or implied, with respect to the material contained herein or for any errors or omissions that may have been made. The publisher remains neutral with regard to jurisdictional claims in published maps and institutional affiliations.

This Springer VS imprint is published by the registered company Springer Fachmedien Wiesbaden GmbH, part of Springer Nature.
The registered company address is: Abraham-Lincoln-Str. 46, 65189 Wiesbaden, Germany

Preface and Acknowledgements

This study owes its origin to a curious accident. About 4 years ago, I stumbled upon a notice referring to Mansfield Tracy Walworth's (1830–1873) novel *Delaplaine*.[1] While far from a literary masterpiece, *Delaplaine* has two striking features. To begin with, much of it is set in the Second Russo-Persian War (1826–1828) and contains remarkable details of individual battles. Secondly, the Qajar crown prince 'Abbas Mirza, son of Fath 'Ali Shah, features prominently in the novel. As Walworth lived in Utica, New York, I began to wonder what sources on contemporary Persian history were available to him when he wrote his book. Certainly he could have accessed some studies of Qajar and Russian history from the eighteenth and the early nineteenth century in American libraries, as well as the *Annual Register*, which gave a yearly synopsis of political and military history. This led me to inquire into the extent to which contemporary Iranian affairs featured in the American press and to examine newspapers published in America at the time of the Second Russo-Persian War.

To my surprise, the quantity of material on the conflict in American newspapers was prodigious. Databases like *America's Historical Newspapers*, *NYS Historic Newspapers* and T.M. Tryniski's *Old Fulton New York Post Cards* have made available literally millions of pages of searchable, digitized newspapers. Coincidentally, one copy of the *National Intelligencer and Washington Advertiser* from 9 December 1826, containing Nicholas I's Declaration of War against Persia, bears the signature of Walworth's father, Reuben Hyde Walworth of Saratoga Springs, New York, confirming how well-informed readers in a small, upstate New York town with a population of less than 10,000[2] were at that time. Fascinated by this unexpected discovery, I became equally curious about the period before the Second Russo-Persian War, extending my inquiry back to the very earliest newspapers in America, and carrying my searches through the reigns of Fath 'Ali Shah and Mohammad Shah. Because of the wealth of material from the mid- and the late-nineteenth century (principally the reign of Nasr al-Din Shah), and because the advent of

---

[1] Walworth (1871).
[2] Anonymous (1900: 15).

the telegraph in the 1840s changed news dissemination radically, I decided to use the death of Mohammad Shah as a cut-off point for the present inquiry.

The result of this research is an annotated collection of 2767 newspaper articles concerning Persia, published in 650 different American newspapers between 1712, soon after the establishment of the first regular newspaper in the colonies, the *Boston News-Letter*, and 1848, the year of Mohammad Shah's death. The names of these newspapers and their places of publication are listed after this Preface. Historians of Safavid and Qajar Iran have not, to my knowledge, exploited contemporary newspaper accounts of current events in Iran to any great extent. Yet, despite the exigencies of communication by land and sea, and the time it took for couriers from Constantinople to reach St. Petersburg, or letters on board ships from Smyrna to arrive in Venice and proceed overland to Amsterdam, Hamburg or London, the rapidly unfolding sequence of events involving Safavid, Afghan, Afsharid, Zand and early Qajar Persia featured on an almost daily basis in British and Continental European newspapers, copies of which were conveyed regularly to America. Thanks to the willingness of innumerable ships captains who arrived at Boston, New York, Philadelphia, Charleston and other American ports bearing newspapers by then 6 weeks or more old,[3] an enormous quantity of reportage on contemporary events in Iran—the fall of the Safavid dynasty, the Afghan occupation, the wars with the Ottomans and Russians, the diplomatic involvements of France and Britain, the rise and demise of Nader Shah, the struggle for supremacy in the Zand period and the reigns of the first three Qajars—reached newspaper offices scattered up and down the eastern seaboard of the American colonies and, later, the United States. After their initial publication in America, these stories were recycled and republished in many more newspapers scattered far and wide.[4] The market for such news was clearly an expanding one. At the end of the American Revolution, there were only 35 newspapers in the thirteen American colonies, whereas by 1833, that figure exceeded 1200.[5]

For the most part, these news articles were either taken verbatim from their British or European sources or lightly rewritten. They came from many news outlets. Letters from

---

[3] Schwarzlose (1989: 13) cites as unusual and innovative the visitation of ships arriving in Boston and New York by two local newspaper editors in the late eighteenth century in order to acquire news and intelligence, but countless examples quoted in the entries below show clearly that the provision of foreign newspapers to American editors by the captains of vessels arriving at American ports, many of whom are named as the providers of those newspapers, was a far older and more widespread practice than Schwarzlose suggests.

[4] Benjamin Russell's *Columbian Centinel*, for example, founded in Boston in 1784, was described by North 1884:37 as 'a vehicle of useful and accurate intelligence...superior to that of any other American newspaper. Russell had a peculiar mode of condensing and arranging the contents of foreign journals and presenting in the most readable shape all the incidents then (1790–1815) agitating Europe. Through the whole of this period, and for some years afterward, the Centinel was an indispensable source of news for the country printers, every one of whom relied upon it for matter to fill up the news department of his paper'.

[5] Copeland (1997b: 556).

correspondents in Isfahan, Tabriz, Tiflis, Constantinople, Smyrna, Moscow, St. Petersburg, Venice, Genoa, Naples, Hamburg, Vienna, Amsterdam, Lemberg, The Hague, Paris, London and elsewhere were published in British and European newspapers, providing first hand, often contradictory information. Reading these it is clear just how difficult a task reporting was when battlefields were distant and communication slow. Statements expressing doubt regarding the outcome of a battle, such as the following, are common: 'It is said that there has been an engagement between the Russians and Persians near Caucasus, in which the Persians were terribly beaten. This account, however, is not confirmed' (7.43). Moreover, intentional disinformation can be detected, as this example shows: 'the Turks lost most of their men, and their Reinforcement of 3000 Men were most of them cut to Pieces. But the Porte fearing the Fury of the Populace, has given out that the Army of the Schach Nadir was put to Flight' (5.119).

In general, little attempt was made by European and American newspaper editors to editorialize, although comments were sometimes appended querying a report or warning the reader that the news just reported could not be confirmed, such as 'the Persian News by Way of Constantinople is so variable, there's no being positive in any Particular' (1.14). In the main, however, the editorial policy seems to have been one of making everything that passed through the editors' hands available to readers, presumably in the belief that, as reports could not be confirmed or refuted by editors sitting in New York or Boston, there was no point in trying, and if something was inaccurate, it would be corrected sooner or later by a more authoritative account.

Not infrequently, one newspaper pre-dating another arrived in America, and its content was excerpted and printed days after a later newspaper's contents had already appeared, giving a contradictory account of an event. News travelled at variable rates. It was late May, 1725, for example, before the first account was published in America of the death of Peter the Great, on 8 February. In some cases, editors clearly dipped back into old newspapers for content, perhaps because they needed copy to fill the columns of their papers. It is not uncommon, therefore, to find an article reappearing a couple of years, even a decade, after its original publication. One of the more extreme cases of this practice is an article first published on 27 November 1740 in *The American Weekly Mercury* (4.206) that was reprinted on at least four occasions in 1789, as though it were a record of contemporary events.

The material collected here contains much that is not found in conventional, synthetic histories, particularly modern studies of the twentieth and twenty-first centuries. The names of individual Russian and Ottoman military commanders, Persian diplomats in St. Petersburg and foreign envoys in Constantinople; the movements of Mahmud and Ashraf Ghalza'i, Tahmasp Mirza, Nader Shah, Karim Khan, Agha Mohammad Shah or 'Abbas Mirza; the size of the opposing forces facing each other at Erivan, Kars, Baghdad and Mosul; the number of victims from earthquakes at Tabriz, Shiraz and Kazerun; or cholera outbreaks in Qazvin and Tehran—these and a host of other details featured on an almost daily basis in the early American press.[6] Yet, although this study has brought to light several thousand newspaper articles relevant to the Safavid through early Qajar periods in Iran, it makes no pretence to completeness. Generally, articles were identified through keyword searches for terms like 'Persia', 'Tauris', 'Ghilan', 'Derbent', 'Kasben', 'Ispahan', 'Thamas', 'Sophi', 'Nadir', etc., and their variants, but not infrequently searches have failed to identify articles that had already been excerpted and it is clear that, because of the indistinctness of some of the scanned print images, and the illegibility of some letters or letter combinations, such searches cannot be assumed to capture every attestation of a keyword. Be that as it may, enough material has been found, it would seem, to suggest that no major historical events have escaped inclusion using this method.

Most studies of the Colonial and Early Republican American press have stressed its contribution to the formation of a new national identity and its relationship to political parties—particularly in the context of Federalists vs. anti-Federalists—and to the development of American political institutions.[7] Yet even a cursory examination of early American newspapers reveals that a staggering amount of foreign content was published in them that had nothing to do with nascent Americanism, and everything to do with maintaining a strong connection to the rest of the world. Not only does this cast the literate public of the American colonies and early United States in a new light. It reveals how global the world was at a time when we tend to think of globalism largely in terms of international trade and trans-oceanic or trans-continental wars. In fact, political events, the comings and goings of royalty and aristocracy and military developments in Europe and Asia, presented with extraordinarily fine-grained detail, were sifted over and over again in the course of successive daily and weekly newspapers.

For convenience, this work is divided into 15 chapters, spread across three volumes as follows. The first volume covers the period from the reign of Shah Soltan Hoseyn to the death of Agha Mohammad Shah; the second volume is concerned solely with events during the reign of Fath 'Ali Shah and the third volume examines the reign of Mohammad Shah. While somewhat arbitrary, the chapter divisions were deemed necessary to make the mass of material presented here more intelligible. The chapters are not divided strictly according to years or decades, but rather according to major historical events, such as the death or accession of a ruler. Invariably there is some overlap between chapters, given the time lag in the printing and reprinting of some pieces, such that articles that might have reported a momentous event in the autumn of one year, continued to appear sporadically into the spring and summer of the next. Each article excerpted below, with its title or byline, has been given a unique identifying number. For the most part, the articles are bulletins of current events—political, military, economic and social. These are presented in

---

[6] It is also important to note that there are curious lacunae, sometimes lasting years, in which no content concerning Iran seems to have been published. Whether this is a genuine reflection of newspaper coverage, or an artefact of the keywords used in searches for this work, is unclear.

[7] See, e.g., Humphrey (1996), Copeland (1997a), Alexander (1998: 168).

chronological order, regardless of the fact, noted above, that some articles with a later dateline may have appeared in print before articles that predated them in the European press.

Articles that concern matters outside the stream of current events—reports on Persian customs, books related to Persia, vignettes drawn from Persian poetry, prospects for trade, earthquakes, cholera outbreaks and so forth—have been grouped at the end of each chapter, in chronological order, under the heading 'Miscellaneous'. Their titles are all listed in the Table of Contents. A further clarification is needed regarding Chap. 14 which concerns the activities of the American Presbyterian missionaries at Urmia. Chronologically, the material in this chapter overlaps that found in Chaps. 13 and 15. As much of the content ignores contemporary political events, however, it was felt that readers interested primarily in the American Mission would find it convenient to have all of the articles pertaining to it gathered in one chapter.

Pre-modern spellings, capitalization and italics have been maintained, as they appeared in the original, printed articles. Every attempt has been made to identify people, places and foreign terms that appear in these articles, with explanations given in the footnotes. Where an unfamiliar name appears without any further clarification, that is because none could be found. Obvious misspellings are indicated by [sic], and spelling variants are clarified where necessary. Given the range of subject matter in these articles, users of this book may come from widely disparate fields, from British Colonial and Indian history, to American, Russian, Ottoman, French, Austrian, Persian and Central Asian studies. Names, even ones with corrupted or variant spellings, that may be easily recognized by specialists in one field, may be wholly unintelligible to those in another.[8] Therefore, variant spellings of names in the eighteenth and the early nineteenth century English, French, German, Turkish or Russian orthography, which often differ from the twentieth and the twenty-first century conventions, are given in a Glossary just before Chap. 1.

It is probably accurate to say that few students of eighteenth and nineteenth century Iranian history would have expected to find the full texts of treaties between Persia and the Ottoman Empire, or Persia and Russia, on the front pages of newspapers in colonial and early Republican America; let alone realized that bulletins on the progress of the wars between Persia and the Porte and Persia and Russia during the eighteenth century and the early nineteenth century appeared almost daily in the American press. It will be all too apparent to specialists in one or another field—Safavid, Qajar, Ottoman, Russian, British, American and other branches of history—that much more remains to be said by way of

---

[8] Following the advice of a colleague who is expert in all matters of Safavid and Qajar, I have opted not to include diacritics where a stricter, philological presentation of names and terms would have called for them. Scholars possessing competence in Persian and Arabic will know where they should be, while other users of this book will not particularly care, so long as they can read a given name. Needless to say, wherever I have quoted directly from another work, I have retained any diacritics given in the original Personal names, too, present a challenge, and I trust that the use of Ahmed, rather than Ahmad, or Mehmed rather than Mehemet, will not cause undue trouble for the reader.

providing additional context or explication of events, motivations of personalities and consequences of developments alluded to in the articles presented here. Beyond providing explanatory notes and a brief introduction to each chapter, the work of achieving this is better left to the experts, however, who now have an additional corpus of contemporary evidence with which to work, differing from that found in eighteenth and the nineteenth century scholarly books and articles. It is my hope that this material, with all its flaws, will henceforth be exploited as a valuable source for the *Zeitgeschichte* of eighteenth and early nineteenth century Iran. It is salutary to consider that the trials and tribulations of the people of Iran, in many walks of life, engrossed the early American reading public, even if they seem to us a world away. With this body of material, historians and anyone interested in Iranian history can get some sense of what it was like, in real time, to live through the tumultuous eighteenth and early nineteenth century. Access to such a lens for the better understanding of any historical epoch ought to enrich the experience of research and appreciation, bringing a distant period that much closer to our own experience of the often messy, contradictory, rapidly evolving situations reported in the news media.

Before closing this Preface, I want to thank my wonderful wife Hildreth Burnett Potts who has lived with this work for the past 4 years, listening to countless anecdotes of the historical characters found on these pages and asking probing questions that improved the work immeasurably. I would also like to thank my friend and colleague Willem Floor, whose mastery of Safavid and Qajar history is second to none. He has answered many questions and been a valuable sounding board, particularly regarding the organization of the present work.

Finally, I dedicate this work to my grandchildren who may find it amusing, when they are old enough to use this book, to think that their grandfather went down so many rabbit holes when he was trying to identify the distant people and places whose unfamiliar names confronted early American newspaper readers in the eighteenth and the early nineteenth century.

New York, USA
29 June 2021

D. T. Potts

Contents

8 The Early Career of Fath 'Ali Shah (1798–1804) 699
    8.1 Miscellaneous 746
           Anticipating the Publication of Olivier's Voyages Dans l'empire
           Othoman 746
           The Wahhabis 747
           Persian Yeast 749
           Hafez 750
           Hormuz Island 751
           The Caspian Sea Fishery 753
           Persian Viticulture 754
           Hot Winds 755
           The Persian Gulf Pearl Fishery 755
           Sir William Ouseley's Goals in Persia 755
           The Tabriz Earthquake of 1780 757
           A Curious Coin from Ohio 758
           Virtues of the Plane Tree 761
           A Description of Isfahan 762
           A Brief History of Persia 764
           Distemper 768
           Commerce of Astrakhan and Persia 768
           Blending Fact and Fiction in Persian Affairs 769
           Smallpox 770
           D'Ohsson's Tableau Historique de l'Orient 771

**9 The First Russo-Persian War and British, French and Persian
    diplomacy (1804–1816)** 773
    9.1 Miscellaneous 884
           Some Aspects of Persian Geography 884
           Russian Perspectives on Persian Trade 888
           A Summary of Recent Persian History 889

	John Malcolm's Uniform	891
	Persian Chiefs and Raiding	893
	Sir William Ouseley's Manuscript Collection	895
	Rev. Henry Martyn's Persian Translation of the New Testament	895
	An Excerpt from Pietro Della Valle	897
	Rev. Robert Pinkerton	898

10 From 1816 to the End of the Turco-Persian War (1816–1825) ... 903

10.1	Miscellaneous	1063
	A Brief Review of Morier's Travels	1063
	Persian Wheat in New York	1064
	Persian Rice in New England	1065
	Mirza Abu'l Hasan Khan Shirazi in England	1065
	Persian War Trophies in St. Petersburg	1069
	'Abbas Mirza and the Garden Wall	1070
	Persian Manners Described by J.J. Morier	1071
	Rev. Henry Martyn's Persian Translations of Scripture	1074
	The Persian Gulf and its Principal Islands	1076
	Oil on the Absheron Peninsula near Baku	1081
	Résumé of Diplomatic Relations with Persia	1085
	Excerpts from Morier, et al.	1090
	Captain Gordon in Russia	1090
	Rev. Henry Martyn in Shiraz	1094
	The Alleged Conversion of Fath 'Ali Shah	1095
	A Scottish Cloak (Tartan?) for Fath 'Ali Shah	1096
	Missionaries from Basel	1096
	The Danish Orientalist Rasmus Rask	1097
	The Destruction of Kermanshah by Earthquake	1097
	The Persian Language	1098
	Marble from Azerbaijan	1098
	A Persian Meal	1099
	Morier's Quarters in Tabriz	1101
	Lancashire Meets Persia	1103
	Fath 'Ali Shah's Questions for Sir Harford Jones	1103
	Fath 'Ali Shah's Family	1104
	The Destruction of Shiraz and Kazerun by Earthquake	1104
	The Plague	1109
	Christian Jews	1109
	Persians at the Leipzig Messe	1109
	'Abbas Mirza's Horsemanship	1110
	Persian Women and Infants	1111
	A New School for Tabriz	1112

11	**The Second Russo-Persian War and the Treaty of Torkmanchay (1826–1828)**	1115
11.1	Miscellaneous	1285
	Persian trade	1285
	Chevalier Gamba's Travels	1286
	A Prince Prepares for Blindness	1287
	Uniting the Atlantic Ocean and the Black Sea	1288
12	**From the Murder of Griboyedov to the Death of Fath 'Ali Shah (1829–1835)**	1289
12.1	Miscellaneous	1345
	A Persian translation of Herodotus	1345
	Caspian Sea trade	1346
	General Devaux, in the service of Mohammad 'Ali Mirza	1346
	A Persian poet	1348
	Members of Fath 'Ali Shah's family make a pilgrimage to Mecca	1348
	Sir John Malcolm and Madame de Staël	1349
	Rumored visit of Mirza Abu'l Hasan Khan Shirazi to the United States	1349
	Cholera and plague	1350
	Rev. Joseph Wolff	1355
	A 'Persian' ambassador and the Reform Bill	1355
	Seeds of Persian cultivars sent to America	1356
	Cashmere shawls	1361
	Hydraulic works at Shushtar	1363
	Lithography in Persia	1363
	Philosophy	1364
	Byron's brass buttons	1364
	The Death of Sir John Malcolm	1365
	Descriptions of Isfahan	1367
	Astrologers	1369
	Fath 'Ali Shah's crystal bed	1370
	Fath 'Ali Shah's plate	1371
	The Persian discovery of wine	1372
	The Dasht-e Kavir	1372
	Raiding in Persia	1373
	Execution	1376
	The security of Persian pilgrims	1377
	James Baillie Fraser on Persian history	1378
	A Persian view of the West	1388
Index-2		1389

Contents for Volume 1

1 **From the Reign of Shah Soltan Hoseyn to the Accession of Shah Ashraf (1712–1726)**..... 1
   1.1 Miscellaneous..... 113
      The Death of Sir John Chardin..... 113
      Provision of Wells Along a Caravan Route Linking Persia and Turkey..... 114
      Death of an English Physician in Isfahan..... 114
      Destruction of Tabriz by Earthquake in 1721..... 115
      Portuguese Assistance for the Persians Against the Omanis..... 118

2 **From the Accession of Shah Ashraf to His Death (1726–1730)**..... 121
   2.1 Miscellaneous..... 159
      Abbé Raynal's Account of the Late Revolution in Persia..... 159

3 **From the Rise of Tahmasp Qoli Khan to the Coronation of Nader Shah (1730–1736)**..... 185
   3.1 Miscellaneous..... 292
      Persian Gulf piracy..... 292
      Tahmasp Qoli Khan's real origins..... 293
      The Anglo-Russian Commercial Treaty and Persia..... 295

4 **The Career of Nader Shah, Up to and Including the Conquest of India (1736–1741)**..... 297

5 **Nader Shah's Last Years (1741–1748)**..... 393
   5.1 Miscellaneous..... 512
      The Value of the Booty Taken by Nader Shah from India..... 512
      Russian Efforts to Mitigate the Spread of the Plague..... 513

6	**From 'Adel Shah to the Death of Karim Khan Zand (1748–1779)**	515
	6.1 Miscellaneous	608
	The Destruction of Kashan by An Earthquake in 1755	608
	The Plague	609
	Khorasan archers to aid the British army against the Americans	611
7	**From the Demise of the Zand Dynasty to the Death of Agha Mohammad Shah (1783–1797)**	613
	7.1 Miscellaneous	660
	The Destruction of Tabriz by an Earthquake in 1780	660
	Two 'Persian' Visitors to London	661
	The Caspian Sea Trade	661
	Anachronistic References to the Reign of Karim Khan Zand and Mir Muhanna	662
	Joseph Beauchamp in Baghdad and Iran	665
	An Elephant Given by Nader Shah to the Ottoman Sultan Makes its Way to Naples	666
	Nader Shah's Tent	667
	Once more on the Value of Nader Shah's Booty	668
	Mistaken Identity – William Francklin Mistaken for Benjamin Franklin's Son	670
	The Tale of a Diamond	670
	Francklin's Description of the Women of Shiraz	671
	The Caspian Sea Trade	673
	Nader Shah's Cruelty	673
	Wahhabism	674
Index-1		677

Contents for Volume 3

13	**Civil War, the Accession of Mohammad Shah and the Persian Retreat from Herat (1834–1839)**		1411
	4.1 Miscellaneous		1474
	Bastinado		1474
	Persian Musical Instruments		1475
	An end to harems?		1477
	Diplomatic Etiquette		1479
	Persians as 'Zoroastrians'		1480
	The plague		1480
	Ascent of the Karun River		1480
	A Persian newspaper		1481
	Fath 'Ali Shah's wives		1482
14	**The American Mission at Urmia (1833–1848)**		1485
	5.1 Miscellaneous		1723
	Rock and water samples from Persia		1723
	A Yankee cooking stove for Mohammad Shah		1725
	New England rum in Persia		1728
	Temperance societies in Persia		1728
	Cholera and the American Mission		1728
15	**From the Aftermath of Herat to the Accession of Naser al-Din Shah (1839–1848)**		1731
	6.1 Miscellaneous		1832
	Royal Orders from Mohammad Shah		1832
	French Lazarists		1833
	Tobacco Use in Persia		1835
	Catherine I and the Shah of Persia		1836
	A Napoleonic Anecdote		1837
	Earthquakes		1838
	Fowler's Three Years in Persia		1839

Fath 'Ali Shah's Crystal Bed, Again 1844
The Death of Sir Robert Ker Porter 1845
Rev. Wolff Again 1846
More on the Karun Route for Commerce 1857
The Power of Prayer 1858
Voskoboynikov's Mining Explorations 1858
Ambassador Rush's Anecdote of Mirza Abu'l Hasan Khan Shirazi
in London 1859
Mohammad Shah Blinds his Brothers 1861
Haji Mirza Aqasi 1862
The Baha'i Faith 1863
Muslim Schools in Paris 1864
Asafoetida 1865
Cholera 1866
A Persian Poet 1879
Turquoise Mines near Nishapur 1880
An American Painter and a Persian Prince 1880
A Persian Dick Whittington 1881
Persian Watermelon 1882
American Cotton for Persia 1882
A Russian Lake 1883
Dervishes 1883
George III's Letter to Fath 'Ali Shah 1884
The Persian Slave Trade 1884
Mohammad Shah's Gift to Queen Victoria 1888
The Death of Xavier Hommaire de Hell 1889

Bibliography 1891

Index-3 2009

Abbreviations

BAI	Bulletin of the Asia Institute
BSO[A]S	Bulletin of the School of Oriental [and African] Studies
CHI	Cambridge History of Iran
CRAIBL	Comptes-rendus de l'Académie des inscriptions et belles lettres
DNB	Dictionary of National Biography
EnIrOE	Encyclopaedia Iranica Online Edition
GJ	The Geographical Journal
IJMES	International Journal of Middle East Studies
IrSt	Iranian Studies
JA	Journal Asiatique
JAOS	Journal of the American Oriental Society
JESHO	Journal of the Economic and Social History of the Orient
JRAS	Journal of the Royal Asiatic Society
JRGS	Journal of the Royal Geographical Society
MES	Middle Eastern Studies
MH	The Missionary Herald
PRGS	Proceedings of the Royal Geographical Society
SEER	The Slavonic and East European Review
StIr	Studia Iranica
ZDMG	Zeitschrift der Deutschen Morgenländischen Gesellschaft

American Newspapers Excerpted in This Work

Title	Place of Publication
L'Abeille	New Orleans, LA
The Age	Augusta, ME
Albany Argus	Albany, NY
The Albany Chronicle	Albany, NY
Albany Evening Journal	Albany, NY

Albany Gazette	Albany, NY
The Albany Register	Albany, NY
The Albion	New York, NY
Alexandria Advertiser and Commercial Intelligencer	Alexandria, VA
Alexandria Gazette [*& Daily Advertiser*]	Alexandria, VA
The Alexandria Herald	Alexandria, VA
The American	New York, NY
American Advocate [*& General/Kennebec Advertiser*]	Hallowell, ME
American Apollo	Boston, MA
The American Beacon and Commercial Diary	Norfolk, VA
American Beacon and Norfolk & Portsmouth Daily Advertiser	Norfolk, VA
American [*&*] *Commercial Daily Advertiser*	Baltimore, MD
American Citizen [*and General Advertiser*]	New York, NY
American Federalist Columbian Centinel	Boston, MA
American Freeman	Prairieville, WI
The American Journal	Ithaca, NY
The American Journal and General Advertiser	Providence, RI
American Patriot	Portland, ME
The American Minerva [*and the New-York Advertiser*]	New York, NY
American Repertory	St. Albans, VT
American Repertory & Advertiser	Burlington, VT
American Sentinel	Middletown, CT
American Telegraphe	Bridgeport, CT
American Traveller	Boston, MA
American Watchman [*and Delaware Advertiser*]	Wilmington, DE
The American Weekly Mercury	Philadelphia, PA
The Amherst Journal and the New-Hampshire Advertiser	Amherst, NH
Andrews's Western Star	Stockbridge, MA
The Argus, or Greenleaf's New Daily Advertiser	New York, NY
Argus of Western America	Frankfort, KY
Arkansas Intelligencer	Van Buren, AK
Arkansas State Gazette	Little Rock, AK
The Atlas	New York, NY
Auburn Journal and Advertiser	Auburn, NY
Augusta Chronicle and Georgia Advertiser	Augusta, GA
Augusta Herald	Augusta, GA
Aurora General Advertiser	Philadelphia, PA
The Balance, and Columbian Repository	Hudson, NY
The Balance, & New-York State Journal	Albany, NY
Ballston Spa Gazette, and Saratoga Farmer	Ballston Spa, NY

Abbreviations

The Baltimore Daily Intelligencer	Baltimore, MD
Baltimore Gazette and Daily Advertiser	Baltimore, MD
Baltimore Patriot & Mercantile Advertiser	Baltimore, MD
Baltimore Republican and Commercial Advertiser	Baltimore, MD
Bangor Register	Bangor, ME
The Baptist Advocate	New York, NY
Barre Gazette	Barre, MA
Barre Patriot	Barre, MA
Bartgis's Maryland Gazette, and Frederick-Town Weekly Advertiser	Frederick, MD
Bay State Democrat	Boston, MA
The Bee	New London, CT
Bellows Falls Gazette	Bellows Falls, VT
The Berks and Schuylkill Journal	Reading, PA
Berkshire County Whig	Pittsfield, MA
The Berkshire Chronicle	Pittsfield MA
Berkshire Gazette	Pittsfield, MA
The Berkshire Reporter	Pittsfield, MA
Binghamton Courier	Binghamton, NY
Black River Gazette	Lowville, NY
Boston Courier	Boston, MA
Boston Daily Advertiser [& Patriot]	Boston, MA
Boston Daily American Statesman and City Register	Boston, MA
The Boston Daily Atlas	Boston, MA
The Boston Evening-Post	Boston, MA
The Boston-Gazette, and Country Journal	Boston, MA
The Boston-Gazette [or, Weekly Journal]	Boston, MA
The Boston-Gazette, and Weekly Republican Journal	Boston, MA
Boston Intelligencer & Evening Gazette	Boston, MA
The Boston [Weekly] News-Letter, and New-England Chronicle	Boston, MA
Boston Patriot & Mercantile Advertiser	Boston, MA
Boston Press and Post	Boston, MA
Boston Recorder	Boston, MA
The Boston Semi-Weekly Atlas	Boston, MA
Boston Weekly Messenger	Boston, MA
The Boston Weekly Post-Boy	Boston, MA
Brattleboro' Messenger and Farmers and Manufacturers' Public Journal	Brattleboro, VT
The Bristol County Register	Warren, RI
The Brooklyn Daily Eagle and Kings County Democrat	Brooklyn, NY

The Broome Republican	Binghamton, NY
The Brunswick Gazette	New Brunswick, NJ
The Burlington Advertiser or Agricultural and Political Intelligencer	Burlington, NJ
Burlington Hawk-Eye	Burlington, IA
Camden Gazette and Mercantile Advertiser	Camden, SC
Carey's United States' Recorder	Philadelphia, PA
The Carlisle Gazette, and the Western Repository of Knowledge	Carlisle, PA
Carolina Centinel	New Bern, SC
The Carolina Gazette	Charleston, SC
The Cayuga Patriot	Auburn, NY
The Centinel of Liberty, and George-Town and Washington Advertiser	Georgetown, DC
The Charleston Courier	Charleston, SC
Chelsea Courier	Norwich, CT
Chittenango Herald	Chittenango, NY
Christian Herald	Exeter, NH
The Christian Intelligencer	New York, NY
Christian Messenger	Middlebury, VT
The Christian Mirror	Portland, ME
Christian Observer	Philadelphia, PA
Christian Reflector	Worcester/Boston, MA
Christian Register	Boston, MA
Christian Secretary	Hartford, CT
Christian Watchman	Boston MA
Christian Witness and Church Advocate	Boston, MA
Chronicle Express	New York, NY
Christian Witness	Boston, MA
The Cincinnati Daily Gazette	Cincinnati, OH
City Gazette and/or [the *Commercial*] *Daily Advertiser*	Charleston, SC
City of Washington Gazette	Washington, DC
Claypoole's American Daily Advertiser	Philadelphia, PA
Cleveland Daily Plain Dealer	Cleveland, OH
The Columbia Washingtonian	Hudson, NY
Columbian Centinel [*& Massachusetts Federalist*]	Boston, MA
Columbian Courier, or Weekly Miscellany	New Bedford, MA
Columbian Gazette	Utica, NY
The Columbian Herald or, the New Daily Advertiser	Charleston, SC
The Columbian Herald or the Patriotic Courier of North-America	Charleston, SC

Columbian Minerva	Dedham, MA
Columbian Museum & Savannah Advertiser	Savannah, GA
Columbian Register	New Haven, CT
Columbian Reporter	Taunton, MA
The Columbian Star	Washington, DC
The Commentator	Frankfort, KY
Commercial Advertiser	New York, NY
Concord Gazette	Concord, NH
Concord Observer	Concord, NH
Connecticut Courant [*and, Weekly Intelligencer*]	Hartford, CT
Connecticut Gazette	New London, CT
The Connecticut Gazette, and the Commercial Intelligencer	New London, CT
The Connecticut Gazette, and the Universal Intelligencer	New London, CT
Connecticut Journal [*and New-Haven Post-Boy*]	New Haven, CT
Connecticut Mirror	Hartford, CT
Connecticut Observer	Hartford, CT
The Constitution	Middletown, CT
The Constitution	Washington, DC
The Constitutional Gazette	New York, NY
The Constitutional Telegraphe	Boston, MA
The Country Journal and the Poughkeepsie Advertiser	Poughkeepsie, NY
The Corrector	Sag-Harbor, NY
The Courier	Norwich, CT
The Courier	New Orleans, LA
Courier des États-Unis	New York, NY
Courier of New Hampshire	Concord, NH
The Daily Advertiser [*Political, Historical and Commercial*]	New York, NY
The Daily Chronicle	Philadelphia, PA
Daily Chronicle & Sentinel	Augusta, GA
Daily Commercial Bulletin	St. Louis, MO
Daily Democrat	Rochester, NY
Daily Georgian	Savannah, GA
Daily Herald	New Haven, CT
Daily National Intelligencer	Washington, DC
Daily National Journal [= *National Journal*]	Washington, DC
Daily Ohio State Journal	Columbus, OH
The Daily Picayune	New Orleans, LA
The Daily Sanduskian	Sandusky, OH
Daily Sentinel and Gazette	Milwaukee, WI

The Dayspring	Boston, MA
Dedham Gazette	Dedham, MA
The Delaware & Eastern Shore Advertiser	Wilmington, DE
The Delaware Gazette	Delhi, NY
The Delaware Register	Wilmington, DE
The Democrat	Boston, MA
The Democratic Press	Philadelphia, PA
The Diary or Loudon's Register	New York, NY
Dundee Record	Dundee, NY
Dunlap's American Daily Advertiser	Philadelphia, PA
Dunlap's Pennsylvania Packet; see *The Pennsylvania Packet*	
The Dutchess Observer	Poughkeepsie, NY
The Eagle of Maine	Kennebunk, ME
The Eastern Argus	Portland, ME
The Eastern Herald [and Gazette of Maine]	Portland, ME
Eastern State Journal	White Plains, NY
Easton Gazette	Easton, MD
Easton Star	Easton, MD
Eastport Sentinel	Eastport, ME
Edes' Kennebec Gazette	Augusta, ME
Edwardsville Spectator	Edwardsville, IL
The Emancipator	Boston, MA
The Emancipator	New York, NY
The Emporium	Trenton, NJ
The Enquirer	Richmond, VA
Epitome of the World	Bennington, VT
Essex Gazette	Haverhill, MA
The Essex Gazette	Salem, MA
The Essex Journal and [Merimack Packet, or,] the Massachusetts and New-Hampshire General Advertiser	Newburyport, MA
Essex Patriot	Haverhill, MA
Essex Register	Salem, MA
The Evening Gazette	Boston, MA
The Evening Journal	Albany, NY
The Expositor	Geneva, NY
Exchange Advertiser	Boston, MA
Farmers' Cabinet	Amherst, NH
Farmer's Gazette	Barre, MA
The Farmer's Library: Or, Vermont Political & Historical Register	Rutland, VT

Abbreviations   xxv

Farmer's Museum, or Lay Preacher's Gazette	Walpole, NH
Farmers' Museum, or Literary Gazette	Walpole, NH
The Farmers' Register	Chambersburg, PA
Farmers' Register	Troy, NY
Farmer's Repository	Charles Town, WV
Federal Galaxy	Brattleboro, VT
The Federal Gazette	Baltimore, MD
The Federal Gazette and Philadelphia Daily Advertiser	Philadelphia, PA
Federal Orrery	Boston, MA
Federal Spy	Springfield, MA
Fincastle Mirror	Fincastle, VA
The Floridian	Tallahassee, FL
Frankfort Argus	Frankfort, KY
Franklin Gazette	Philadelphia, PA
Franklin Gazette and Public Advertiser	Greenfield, MA
Franklin Post and Christian Freeman	Greenfield, MA
Federal Intelligencer, and Baltimore Daily Gazette	Baltimore, MD
Federal Republican	Baltimore, MD
Fredonian	Chillicothe, OH
Freedom's Sentinel	Schenectady, NY
Freeman's Friend	Portland, ME
The Freeman's Journal	Cooperstown, NY
The Freeman's Journal or The North-American Intelligencer	Philadelphia, PA
The Free Press	Auburn, NY
The Friend	Salem, MA
The Gazette	Syracuse, NY
The Gazette	Portland, ME
Gazette Française	New York, NY
Gazette of Maine	Portland, ME
Gazette of Maine Hancock Advertiser	Buckstown, ME
Gazette of the United States, and [Philadelphia] Daily [Evening] Advertiser	Philadelphia, PA
The General Advertiser [and Political, Commercial, Agricultural and Literary Journal]	Philadelphia, PA
The Genesee Farmer	Rochester, NY
Geneva Advertiser	Geneva, NY
The Geneva Gazette [and General Advertiser]	Geneva, NY
Geneva Palladium	Geneva, NY
The Genius of Liberty	Leesburg, VA
The Georgetown Gazette	Georgetown, SC

Georgia Courier	Augusta, GA
Georgia Gazette	Savannah, GA
Georgia Journal	Milledgeville, GA
The Georgian	Savannah, GA
The Georgia Telegraph	Macon, GA
The Globe	Washington, DC
Greene County Republican	Catskill, NY
The Greenfield Gazette & Franklin Herald	Greenfield, MA
Greenfield Gazette. Or, Massachusetts and Vermont Telegraphe	Greenfield, MA
Greenleaf's New Daily Advertiser	New York, NY
Greenleaf's New York Journal and Patriotic Register	New York, NY
The Green Mountain Patriot	Peacham, VT
Green & Russell's Boston Post-Boy & Advertiser	Boston, MA
Greensburgh Gazette	Greensburgh, PA
The Groton Balance	Groton, NY
Guardian of Freedom	Haverhill, MA
Hallowell Gazette	Hallowell, ME
Hampden Federalist & Public Journal	Springfield, MA
Hampden Patriot [and Liberal Recorder]	Springfield, MA
Hampden Whig	Springfield, MA
Hampshire Federalist	Springfield, MA
Hampshire Gazette	Northampton, MA
Hampshire Sentinel	Belchertown, MA
The Harbinger	New York, NY/Boston, MA
The Hartford Times	Hartford, CT
Haverhill Gazette, and Essex Patriot	Haverhill, MA
The Herald	Greenfield, MA
The Herald	Sandy-Hill, NY
The Herald; A Gazette for the Country	New York, NY
The Herald of Liberty	Washington, PA
Herald of the United States	Warren, RI
Herald of the Valley	Fincastle, VA
Hillsborough Recorder	Hillsborough, NC
Hingham Patriot	Hingham, MA
Hornet	Frederick, MD
The Hudson River Chronicle	Ossining, NY
Illinois Intelligencer	Vandalia, IL
Impartial Herald	Newburyport, MA
Impartial Herald	Suffield, CT
The Independent Advertiser	Boston, MA

Independent American	Georgetown, DC
Independent Chronicle & Boston Patriot	Boston, MA
The Independent Chronicle [and the Universal Advertiser]	Boston, MA
The Independent Gazetteer; or, the Chronicle of Freedom	Philadelphia, PA
Independent Journal	New York, NY
Independent Statesman	Portland, ME
The Indiana State Sentinel	Indianapolis, IN
Ithaca Journal & General Advertiser	Ithaca, NY
The Jamestown Journal	Jamestown, NY
The Jeffersonian	Portland, ME
Jeffersonian Republican	New Orleans, LA
Jenks' Portland Gazette	Portland, ME
Kalamazoo Gazette	Kalamazoo, MI
The Kennebec Gazette	Hallowell, ME
Kentucky Gazette	Lexington, KY
Kinderhook Herald	Kinderhook, NY
Kline's Carlisle Weekly Gazette	Carlisle, PA
The Ladies' Weekly Museum, or Polite Repository of Amusement and Instruction	New York, NY
Lancaster Journal	Lancaster, PA
Lexington Gazette	Lexington, KY
The Liberator	Boston, MA
The Liberty Hall and Cincinnati Gazette	Cincinnati, OH
The Lincoln Intelligencer	Wiscasset, ME
Litchfield Monitor	Litchfield, CT
The Litchfield Republican	Litchfield, CT
Literary Cadet, and Saturday Evening Bulletin	Providence, RI
The Livingston Register	Geneseo, NY
Livingston Republican	Geneseo, NY
The Long Island Farmer [and Queens County Advertiser]	Jamaica, NY
The Long Island Star	Brooklyn, NY
Louisiana Advertiser	New Orleans, LA
Louisiana Courier	New Orleans, LA
The Lutheran Observer	Baltimore, MD
The Lynchburg Virginian	Lynchburg, VA
Lyons Advertiser	Lyons, NY
Macon Georgia Telegraph	Macon, GA
The Madisonian	Washington, DC
The Mail; or, Claypoole's Daily Advertiser	Philadelphia, PA
Maine Cultivator and Hallowell Weekly Gazette	Hallowell, ME

Maine Intelligencer	Brunswick, ME
Manufacturers and Farmers Journal	Providence, RI
The Maryland Gazette	Annapolis, MD
Maryland Herald	Easton, MD
The Maryland Herald and Elizabeth-Town Advertiser	Hagerstown, MD
The Maryland Journal [and Baltimore Advertiser]	Baltimore, MD
The Massachusetts Centinel [and the Republican Journal]	Boston, MA
The Massachusetts Gazette/ And Boston News-Letter/and the Boston Post-Boy and Advertiser	Boston, MA
Massachusetts Mercury	Boston, MA
The Massachusetts Spy [and/or Worcester County Advertiser/Worcester Gazette]	Worcester, MA
The Maysville Eagle	Maysville, KY
Mechanics' Press	Utica, NY
The Medley or Newbedford Marine Journal	New Bedford, MA
Mercantile Advertiser	New York, NY
The Mercury	New York, NY
The Mercury and New-England Palladium	Boston, MA
Metropolitan	Georgetown, DC
Michigan Herald	Detroit, MI
The Middlesex Gazette [or, Federal Adviser]	Middletown, CT
Miller's Weekly Messenger	Pendleton, SC
Milton Gazette and Roanoke Advertiser	Milton, NC
Milwaukee Sentinel and Gazette	Milwaukee, WI
Milwaukie Journal	Milwaukee, WI
Milwaukie [Daily] Sentinel	Milwaukee WI
Miners' and Farmers' Journal	Charlotte, NC
The Miner's Journal, and Schuylkill Coal & Navigation Register	Pottsville, PA
The Minerva	Dedham, MA
The Minerva & Mercantile Evening Advertiser	New York, NY
The Mirror	Concord, NH
The Mirror	Russellville, KY
Mirror of the Times, & General Advertiser	Wilmington, DE
Mississippi Free Trader	Natchez, MS
Mississippi Herald & Natchez Gazette, Extra	Natchez, MS
The Mohawk Courier	Little Falls, NY
The Mohawk Sentinel	Schenectady, NY
The Moral and Political Telegraphe: or, Brookfield Advertiser	Brookfield, MA

Morning Chronicle	New York, NY
Morning Courier and New-York Enquirer	New York, NY
Morning News	New London, CT
Nantucket Inquirer	Nantucket, MA
The Nashville Gazette	Nashville, TN
The National Advocate	New York, NY
National Ægis	Worcester, MA
The National Era	Washington, DC
National Gazette and Literary Register	Philadelphia, PA
The National Intelligencer and Washington Advertiser	Washington, DC
National Journal	Washington, DC
National Messenger	Georgetown (Washington, DC)
The National Register	Washington, DC
The National Republican, and Ohio Political Register	Cincinnati, OH
National Standard	Middlebury, VT
Newark Daily Advertiser	Newark, NJ
New-Bedford Gazette & Courier	New Bedford, MA
New-Bedford Mercury	New Bedford, MA
New-Bedford Register	New Bedford, MA
New Brunswick Fredonian	New Brunswick, NJ
Newburyport Herald [*and Country Gazette*]	Newburyport, MA
The New-England Courant	Boston, MA
New-England Galaxy & Masonic Magazine	Boston, MA
New England Puritan	Boston, MA
The New-England Weekly Journal	Boston, MA
The New-Hampshire and Vermont Journal: Or, The Farmer's Weekly Museum	Walpole, NH
New-Hampshire Gazette	Portsmouth, NH
The New Hampshire Gazette and Republican Union	Portsmouth, NH
The New Hampshire Gazetteer	Exeter, NH
New-Hampshire Inelligencer	Haverhill, NH
New-Hampshire Patriot and State Gazette	Concord, NH
New-Hampshire Repository	Concord, NH
New-Hampshire Sentinel	Keene, NH
New-Hampshire Statesman and Concord Register	Concord, NH
The New-Haven Gazette [*and the Connecticut Magazine*]	New Haven, CT
The New-Jersey Journal [*and Political Intelligencer*]	Elizabethtown, NJ
New London Democrat	New London, CT
The New-London Gazette [*and General Advertiser*]	New London, CT
Newport Mercury	Newport, RI

New-York Advertiser	New York, NY
New-York American [for the Country]	New York, NY
The New-York Columbian	New York, NY
New-York Daily Gazette	New York, NY
New-York Evangelist	New York, NY
New-York Evening Post	New York, NY
New-York Gazette [revived in the Weekly Post-Boy]	New York, NY
The New-York Journal, or the General Advertiser	New York, NY
The New-York Morning Herald	New York, NY
New-York Observer [and Religious Chronicle]	New York, NY
The New-York Packet	New York, NY
New-York Spectator	New York, NY
New-York Weekly Journal	New York, NY
Niles' Weekly Register	Baltimore, MD
Norfolk Advertiser [and Independent Politician]	Dedham, MA
The Norfolk Democrat	Dedham, MA
Norfolk Gazette and Publick Ledger	Norfolk, VA
The North American	Philadelphia, PA
The North American and Daily Advertiser	Baltimore, MD; Philadelphia, PA
North American and United States Gazette	Philadelphia, PA
The North-Carolina Journal	Halifax, NC
The North River Times	Haverstraw, NY
North Star	Danville, VT
The Northern Budget	Lansingburgh, NY
Northern Light	Ogdensburgh, NY
Northern Post	Salem, NY
The Northern Standard	Clarksville, TX
[The] Northern Whig	Hudson, NY
Norwalk Gazette	Norwalk, CT
Norwich Courier	Norwich, CT
The Norwich Packet and the Connecticut, Massachusetts, New-Hampshire, and Rhode-Island Weekly Advertiser	Norwich, CT
The Norwich-Packet, or The Country Journal	Norwich, CT
The Norwich Republican and Stonington Telegraph	Norwich, CT
The Observer	Cortland, NY
The Observer	Haverhill, MA
Ohio Monitor	Columbus, OH
The Ohio Observer	Hudson, OH
The Ohio State Journal and Columbus Gazette	Columbus, OH
Old Colony Memorial	Plymouth, MA

Olive Branch	Sherburne, NY
Oneida Observer	Rome, NY
Oneida Whig	Utica, NY
Onondaga Register	Onondaga Hollow, NY
Onondaga Register & Syracuse Gazette	Syracuse, NY
Ontario Repository	Canandaigua, NY
L'Oracle	Charleston, SC
L'Oracle and Daily Advertiser	New York, NY
The Oracle of Dauphin [and Harrisburgh Advertiser]	Harrisburg, PA
The Oracle of the Day	Portsmouth, NH
Orange County Patriot; or, The Spirit of 'Seventy Six	Goshen, NY
Oriental Trumpet [or the Town and Country Gazette]	Portland, ME
Orleans Gazette and Commercial Advertiser	New Orleans, LA
Osborne's New-Hampshire Spy	Portsmouth, NH
Oswego Palladium	Oswego, NY
Otsego Herald: or, Western Advertiser	Cooperstown, NY
Painesville Telegraph	Painesville, OH
The Palladium of Liberty	Morristown, NJ
Patriot	Utica, NY
Pawtucket Chronicle [and Rhode-Island and Massachusetts Register]	Pawtucket, RI
The Pennsylvania Chronicle, and Universal Advertiser	Philadelphia, PA
Pennsylvania Correspondent, and Farmers' Advertiser	Doylestown, PA
The Pennsylvania Gazette	Philadelphia, PA
Pennsylvania Inquirer and Daily Courier	Philadelphia, PA
Pennsylvania Inquirer and Morning Journal	Philadelphia, PA
Pennsylvania Journal, or, Weekly Advertiser	Philadelphia, PA
The Pennsylvania Mercury, and Universal Advertiser	Philadelphia, PA
The Pennsylvania Packet, and Daily Advertiser	Philadelphia, PA
The Pennsylvania Packet, and/or the General Advertiser	Philadelphia, PA
Pennsylvania Telegraph	Harrisburg, PA
The Pennsylvanian	Philadelphia, PA
Pensacola Gazette [and Florida Advertiser]	Pensacola, FL
The People's Advocate	New London, CT
The People's Friend & Daily Advertiser	New York, NY
The People's Friend & Gazette	Little Falls, NY
Peoria Register and North-Western Gazetteer	Peoria, IL
Perry Democrat	Bloomfield, PA
Petersburg Intelligencer	Petersburg, VA
The Phenix; Or, Windham Herald	Windham, CT
The Phenix	Westfield, NY

Phenix Gazette	Alexandria, VA
The Philadelphia Gazette, and Commercial Intelligencer	Philadelphia, PA
The Pilot	Cazenovia, NY
The Pittsfield Sun	Pittsfield, MA
The Plattsburgh Republican	Plattsburgh, NY
Plebeian	Kingston, NY
The Plough Boy	Albany, NY
Political Barometer	Poughkeepsie, NY
Political Calendar [and Essex Advertiser]	Newburyport, MA
Political Gazette	Newburyport, MA
Political Observatory	Walpole, NH
Portland Advertiser [and Gazette of Maine]	Portland, ME
Portland Gazette	Portland, ME
The Portsmouth Journal of Literature & Politics	Portsmouth, NH
The Portsmouth Journal and Rockingham Gazette	Portsmouth, NH
Portsmouth Oracle	Portsmouth, NH
The Post-Boy, and Vermont & New Hampshire Federal Courier	Windsor, VT
Poughkeepsie Eagle	Poughkeepsie, NY
Poulson's American Daily Advertiser	Philadelphia, PA
Providence Gazette [and Country Journal]	Providence, RI
The Providence Journal, and Town and Country Advertiser	Providence, RI
Providence Patriot Columbian Phenix	Providence, RI
Providence Patriot	Providence, RI
The Providence Phoenix	Providence, RI
The Public Advertiser	New York, NY
Public Intelligencer	Savannah, GA
Public Ledger	Philadelphia, PA
The Recorder	Boston, MA
The Red-Lander	San Augustine, TX
The Reflector and Schenectady Democrat	Schenectady, NY
Relfs Philadelphia Gazette, and Daily Advertiser	Philadelphia, PA
Religious Intelligencer	Providence, RI
Religious Intelligencer	New Haven, CT
Religious Reporter	Middlebury, VT
The Reporter	Brattleboro, VT
The Reporter and Democratic State Journal	Harrisburg, PA
The Reportory	Boston, MA
Repository and Observer	Concord, NH
The Republican	Cortland Village, NY

The Republican	Ellicottville, NY
Republican Advocate	Frederick, MD
Republican Advocate	New London, CT
The Republican Advocate	Batavia, NY
The Republican Agriculturalist	Norwich, NY
The Republican or, Anti-Democrat	Baltimore, MD
Republican Chronicle	Ithaca, NY
Republican Crisis	Albany, NY
The Republican & Eagle	Cortland, NY
Republican Farmer	Danbury, CT
Republican Farmer	Bridgeport, CT
Republican Gazette and General Advertiser	Frederick, MD
Republican Monitor	Cazenovia, NY
Republican Spy	Northampton, MA
Republican Star, and [or Eastern Shore] General Advertiser	Easton, MD
Republican Watch-Tower	New York, NY
Rhode-Island American, and General Advertiser	Providence, RI
Rhode Island American, Statesman and Providence Gazette	Providence, RI
The Rhode-Island Gazette	Newport, RI
Rhode-Island Republican	Newport, RI
Richmond Enquirer	Richmond, VA
Richmond Whig and Public Advertiser	Richmond, VA
The Rising Sun	Keene, NH
Rochester Republican	Rochester, NY
Rondout Freeman	Kingston, NY
The Rural Repository	Leominster, MA
[Supplement to] Rivington's New-York Gazetteer	New York, NY
Rutland Herald	Rutland, VT
Salem Gazette	Salem, MA
The Salem Mercury; Political, Commercial, and Moral	Salem, MA
Salem Observer	Salem, MA
The Saratoga Advertiser	Ballston Spa, NY
Saratoga Sentinel	Saratoga Springs, NY
Saturday Morning Transcript	Boston, MA
Savannah Georgian	Savannah, GA
The Schenectady Cabinet	Schenectady, NY
The Schoharie Observer	Schoharie, NY
The Scioto Gazette	Chillicothe, OH
The Semi-Weekly Eagle	Brattleboro, VT

The Sentinel of Freedom [*and New Jersey Advertiser*]	Newark, NJ
South-Carolina Gazette, and General Advertiser	Charleston, SC
South-Carolina State Gazette, and Columbian Advertiser	Columbia, SC
The Southern Chronicle [*and Camden Literary Gazette and Political Gazette/Register*]	Camden, SC
Southern Churchman	Richmond, VA
Southern Religious Telegraph	Richmond, VA
The Southern Patriot [*and Commercial Advertiser*]	Charleston, SC
The Spectator	New York, NY
The Spirit of 'Seventy-Six	Washington City [DC]
Spirit of the Times	Bridgeport, CT
Spirit of the Times & People's Press	Batavia, NY
Spooner's Vermont Journal	Windsor, VT
State Gazette	Trenton, NJ
The State Gazette of South-Carolina	Charleston, SC
The Statesman [*& Advertiser for the Country*]	New York, NY
St. Albans Messenger	St. Albans, VT
St. Lawrence Gazette	Ogdensburgh, NY
St. Lawrence Republican	Ogdensburgh, NY
Suffolk County Recorder	Sag Harbor, NY
Suffolk Gazette	Sag Harbor, NY
The Sun	Pittsfield, MA
The Sun	Dover, NH
The Sun	Baltimore, MD
The Supporter and Scioto Gazette	Chillicothe, OH
Susquehanna Centinel	Montrose, PA
Tablet of the Times	Bennington, VT
The Telegraph	Gloucester, MA
Telegraph and Texas Register	Houston, TX
The Time Piece	New York, NY
The Times, and Alexandria Advertiser	Alexandria, VA
The Times and District of Columbia Daily Advertiser	Alexandria, VA
The Times and Dover Enquirer	Dover, NH
The Times, and Weekly Adviser	Hartford, CT
Thomas's Massachusetts Spy, or Worcester Gazette	Worcester, MA
The Torch Light and Public Advertiser	Hagers-Town, MD
Trenton Federalist	Trenton, NJ
Tri-Weekly Ohio Statesman	Columbus, OH
The True American	Lexington, KY
True Republican	Norwich, CT
Trump of Fame	Warren, OH

Trumpet and Universalist Magazine	Boston, MA
The Truth Teller	New York, NY
The Union Herald	Cazenovia, NY
The United States Chronicle [Political, Commercial, and Historical]	Providence, RI
The United States Gazette	Philadelphia, PA
United States' Telegraph	Washington, DC
United States' Weekly Telegraph	Washington, DC
The Universal Gazette	Philadelphia, PA
The Vergennes Gazette and Vermont and New-York Advertiser	Vergennes, VT
Vermont Centinel	Burlington, VT
Vermont Chronicle	Windsor, VT
Vermont Gazette [an Epitome of the World]	Bennington, VT
Vermont Intelligencer and Bellows Falls Advertiser	Bellows Falls, VT
The Vermont Journal [and the Universal Advertiser]	Windsor, VT
Vermont Patriot and State Gazette	Montpelier, VT
Vermont Phoenix	Brattleboro, VT
Vermont Precursor	Montpelier, VT
Vermont Republican [& American Yeoman]	Windsor, VT
Vermont Temperance Herald	Woodstock, VT
Vermont Watchman and State Gazette	Montpelier, VT
Village Messenger	Amherst, NH
Village Register and Norfolk County Advertiser	Dedham, MA
The Virginia Argus	Richmond, VA
Virginia Chronicle, & General Advertiser	Norfolk, VA
The Virginia Gazette	Williamsburg, VA
The Virginia Herald	Fredericksburg, VA
The Virginia Journal and Alexandria Advertiser	Alexandria, VA
Wabash Courier	Terre Haute, IN
The Wachusett Star	Barre, MA
Waldo Patriot	Belfast, ME
Washington County Journal	Union-Village, NY
Washington Expositor	Washington, DC
Washington Gazette	Washington, DC
Washington Reporter	Washington, PA
Washington Review and Examiner	Washington, PA
Washington Whig	Bridgeton, NJ
The Watch-Tower	Cooperstown, NY
The Wayne Sentinel	Palmyra, NY
The Weekly Advertiser	Reading, PA

Weekly Aurora	Philadelphia, PA
The Weekly Herald	New York, NY
The Weekly Messenger	Boston, MA
Weekly Monitor	Litchfield, CT
The Weekly News-Letter	Boston, MA
The Weekly Rehearsal	Boston, MA
Weekly Visiter	Kennebunk, ME
Weekly Wanderer	Randolph, VT
Western Budget	Schenectady, NY
Western Centinel	Whitestown, NY
Western Herald & Steubenville Gazette	Steubenville, OH
Western Intelligencer [*Religious, Literary, and Political*]	Cleveland, OH
Western Reserve Chronicle	Warren, OH
The Western Star	Westfield, NY
Western Star and Lebanon Gazette	Lebanon, OH
Western Sun & General Advertiser	Vincennes, IN
The Western World	Frankfort, KY
The Wilmingtonian, and Delaware Advertiser	Wilmington, DE
Windham Herald	Windham, CT
Wisconsin Democrat	Madison, WI
The Witness	Litchfield, CT
Der Wöchentliche Philadelphische Staatshofe	Philadelphia, PA
Woodstock Observer. Windsor & Orange County Gazette	Woodstock, VT
The World	Bennington, VT
Yeoman's Gazette	Concord, MA
Zion's Herald	Boston, MA

Glossary of Corrupted or Archaic Spellings of 1. Anthroponyms, 2. Titles, 3. Ethnonyms, 4. Toponyms and Hydronyms, and 5. Nouns

1. Anthroponyms

Variants	Modern form
Abbaz/Abbes/Abbos/Abbot/Abbus	'Abbas
Abolfut Kan/ Abdul-fat-Chan/ Abdul-Fut-Khan	Abu'l-Fath Khan Zand
Abdul Lateef Khan	Mir Abdul Latif Khan Shustari
Abdul Rezek Khan	Abdul Rezak Khan
Abool Hassan	Mirza Abu'l Hasan Khan
Aboul-Kasem	Abu'l-Qasem
Achehof/Acheroī	Ashraf
Achmet/e	Ahmet/Ahmad
Adil-Nadir	Adel Shah
Addul Fat Kan	Abu'l-Fath Khan Zand
Aga Mahmoud Khan	Aqa Mohammad Shah
Aga Nubber Khaun	Mohammad Nabi Khan
Aga Yhacoub	Khoja Mirza Yakub Markarian
Agha Mahmood	Aqa Mahmud
Agha Mahomed Jaffer Terahnee	Aqa Mohammad Jaf'ar Tehrani
Ahmat Chah/Ahmeed Shah	Ahmad Shah
Ala Khan	'Ata/'Ataollah Khan Shahsevan
Alaiar Khan	Allah Yar Khan-e Qajar Devehlu
Ali Kennee	Haji Molla 'Ali Kani
Ali Koulican/ Aly Cooly Khan	'Ali Qoli Khan
Ali Mahummed Mirza	Mohammad Mirza [Shah]

Ali Pasha	Ḥaji Moḥammad 'Ali Ridha Pasha
Alisar Khan/Ali Yankhan/Al-Khae/Allair Khan/ Allaya Khan/Alliar Khan/Alli Yar Khan/Alluya Khan	Allah Yar Khan-e Qajar Devehlu
Alli Shah	'Ali Shah Mirza
Allum	Alam
Ally	'Ali
Amir Chan	Amir Khan
Amurat/Amurath	Murad
Andriff	Andreev
Arbas	'Abbas
Arenski	Valensky
Arungzebe	Aurangzeb
Ashraff	Ashraf
Asker Chan	'Askar Khan-e Afshar Orumi
Aslan Caun	Aslan Khan
Aszraff	Ashraf
Atchmet	Ahmad
Aubel/Audel	Adel
Baba-Khand/Babi Khan	Baba Khan, i.e. Fath 'Ali Shah
Bageur	Baqir Khan
Baha Khan	Baba Khan, i.e. Fath 'Ali Shah
Baki Cham	'Abd al-Baqi Khan Zangana
Bekewick	Bekovich-Cherkassky
Benkendoff/Benkendorff	Benckendorff
Bulcacow/Bulhakow	Bulgakov
Buquer Kan	Baqer Khan
Caffi	Safi
Carem Khan	Karim Khan
Carini Caan	Karim Khan
Casa Osman, Oglon Aga	Carosman Oglu
Cautimir	Cantemir
Ceporly	Köprülü
Chadschi-Ibrahim	Haji Ibrahim
Chah-Nazaroff	Mirza Neriman Melik-Shah-Nazarov
Cham Tefterkam	Cham Tatar Khan

Glossary of Corrupted or Archaic Spellings... xxxix

Chan Azad	Azad Khan Afghan
Chahrokh/Charok	Shahrokh
Chasan	Hasan
Cherim Khan	Karim Khan
Cherecphana	Ashraf
Chiek Dervich	Shaykh Darvish Montafeq
Chosereff/Chosrew Mirza	Khosrow Mirza
Chrouk-Scach	Shahrokh Shah
Cosseim Beg	Qasem Beg
Cuperly/Cuporly	Köprülü
Dalion	d'Alion
Dand/Daud-Aga Żādūr/Mir David Zadour	Dawud Khan Malekshah Nazar/Mir Dawud/ Dawoud-Zadour de Melik Chah-Nazar
Davidow	Davydov, Denis Vasilyevich
Deveaux	Devaux
Dgaissar Chan	Ja'far Khan
Dolborucki/ Dolgoronsky/Dolgorouki	Dolgorukov
Duncan/Dunka	Denḥa
Durtad	Trdat/Tiridates
Enverri Effendi	Enveri Efendi
Eresa Guli	Reza Qoli [Mirza]
Eschreff/Esref/Eshref/Esreff/Ezref	Ashraf
Espiriesz	Espiries
Ezad Chan	Azad Khan Afghan
Fat-Ah/Ali-Kan	Fath 'Ali Khan
Fata Aly Shah/Fatali/Fathali Char/Fathali-Sha/Fatali-Schah/ Feth-Ali-Chah/Feth-Ali-Shak/Fethaly Schach/Feth Aly Schah/Fetti Ali Shah/Futeh Allee Shah/Futtee Ali Shah/ Futteh Ali Khan/Futty Ali Schah	Fath 'Ali Shah
Freyganch	Freygang
Galitzin/Galliczin/Galliezin/Gallitzin/Gallizin	Golitsyn
Galowski	Kalushkin
Gardanne/Gardaune	Gardane
Gaschim Khan	Hashim Khan
Geigen/Giegen	Yeken
Geybydoff	Griboyedov
Giafar Han/Khan	Ja'far Khan Zand
Gibojadow	Griboyedov

Goloskin	Golovkin
Gourko	Gurko
Gouseff	Gusev
Grebayadoff	Griboyedov
Gretoff/Grotoff	Grekov
Gribjedoff/Gribojedoff/ Gribojidoff/Griboyedoff/Grybydoff	Griboyedov
Hajabi	Muḥammad b. ʿAbd al-Wahhāb
Hadji-Mirza-Agas/si/Hadjti Mizra Agassi/Hadjj Mirza Agassi/Hajee Meerza Agasee/Hajee Meerza Aghasei/Haji Mirza Aghassi	Haji Mirza Aqasi or ʿAbbas-e Erevani
Hali/y	ʿAli
Hassad Chan	Mohammad Hasan Khan Qajar
Hassan Allee Meerza/ Hassan Alli Mirza/Hassed Ulie Mirza	Hasan ʿAli Mirza
Haujee Khaliel/Khuleel Khann/Haujee Khuleel Khann/Haujee Khuleel Khaun	Haji Khalil Khan
Havouza/Hazouza, Prince	Huwaizah/Hoveyzeh
Hazee Sayed Mohammed	Haji Seyyed Mohammad-Baqer Shafti Rashti
Helmadoff/Helmandoff	Ermolov
Hir/Hit-Timur Kan	Mir Timur Khan
Hoernly	Hoernle, Christian Gottlieb
Hoolakoo Meerza	Holagu Mirza
Hoosein Ali Mirza/Hussein Alli Mirza	Hoseyn ʿAli Mirza Farman-Farma
Hoossein Booroojerdee	Hoseyn Borujerdi
Hosreff Mirza	Khosrow Mirza
Humaioon	Homayun
Hussein Khan	Hoseyn Khan Develu Qajar
Hussein Khan Seidar	Mohammad Hoseyn Khan Sardar Qazvini
Hussein Kouli Khan	Hoseyn Qoli Khan
Illowaisky/Illowwaisky	Ilovaysky
Imaum Seyd Sultaun	Imam Sayyed Soltan
Ivanoff	Ivanov
Jachi/y Kan/Khan	Zaki Khan
Jaffar/Jaffer/Jafier Kan/Khawn	Jaʿfar Khan Zand
Jaffier Kooli Khan	Jaʿfar Qoli Khan

Glossary of Corrupted or Archaic Spellings... xli

Jalaladdin Pacha	Çelaleddin Pasha
Jarmoloff/Jermoloff	Ermolov
Jusapow	Yusupov
Jusef/Jussuf/Jussuff	Yusif/Yūsuf
'Kaem Makom'/'Kaimacan'	Mirza Abu'l-Qasem Qa'em Maqam
Kamili Pacha	Halil Kâmili Paşa
Kardoff	Karpov
Karini Khan	Karim Khan
Kassim-Chan	Qasem Khan
Kerim Kan/Kerim-kan	Karim Khan
Kham Baul/Kham Ran	Kamran
Kherin Chan	Karim Khan
Kiamelli Pacha	Halil Kâmili Paşa
Kiupergli/Kiuperly/Kuperli	Köprülü
'Koem Makem'	Mirza Abu'l-Qasem Qa'em Maqām
Koslowsky	Kozlovsky
Kourschid	Khurshid
Kuly Mirza	Reza Qoli Mirza
Kurreem Khan	Karim Khan
Kusakin	Kurakin
Lewaschew/Lewashau	Levashov
Loffali Kahn/Lolf Ali Kan/ Lolf Alikan/Lutf Ally Khan	Loṭf 'Ali Khan
Machamet-Ismail	Mohammad Ismail
Machmur	Mahmud
Madatoff/Madatow/Madstoff	Madatov
Mahomed Ali Mirza	Mohammad 'Ali Mirza
Mahomed Houssain Khan	Mohammad Hoseyn Khan Qajar
Mahomed Rahun Khan	Mohammad Rahim Khan of Khiva
Mahomed Shah	Mohammad Shah
Mahomet Ally	Mohammad 'Ali Chakhmaqsaz
Mahomet Han	Agha Mohammad Khan
Malek Kasim/Kassem Meerza	Malek Qasem Mirza
Malek Mansoor Meerza	Malek Mansur Mirza
Malttitz	Maltitz
Maltzoff	Mal'tsev

Meerza Mahmood Andermanee	Mirza Mahmud Andarmani
Mehemet Ali	Mohammad 'Ali Mirza
Mehemet Fat Aly Kan	Agha Mohammad Khan Qajar
Mehmed Mirza	Mohammad Mirza
Mehmet Chan/Kan	Agha Mohammad Khan Qajar
Mehemed-Veli-Mirza	Mohammad Vali Mirza
Mehomed Husn Khan	Mohammad Hoseyn Khan
Meli Koff	Melikov, Melikichvili
Melzoff	Mal'tzov/Mal'tsev
Menchikoff/Mensicoft/Menzikof/Menzikoff/Menzikow	Menshikov
Meriveis	Mir Wais
Mereweis/Meriweis/Meri-weys/Meryweys	Mir Wais
Mervabis	Mir Wais
Merza Ally Acbor	Mirza 'Ali Akbar
Minziaky	Minciacky, Matei
Mirabuma	Mir Muhanna
Mirmiaux	Mir Muhanna
Miriweis/Miriweys/Miri-weys/Miri-Weys/Miriwey/Mirriweis	Mir Wais
Mirmabuna/Mirmaduna/Mirmana	Mir Muhanna
Mirza Abdoul/Abdul Hassan Kan/Mirza Abool Hassan	Mirza Abū'l-Hasan Khan Shirazi
Mirza Abdool Wehab/Mirza Abdoul-Wehab	Mirza 'Abd ol-Vahhab-e Esfahāni
Mirza Abul Kausim	Mirza Abu'l-Qasem
Mirza Buzurk Caimaquam	Mirza Bozorg Qa'em Maqam-e Sadarat-e'Ozma
Mirza-Hassan-Khan	Mirza Abu'l Hassan Khan
Mirza Ishafer	Mirza Jaf'ar Khan
Mirza Kouli Khan	'Abbas Qoli Khan
Mirza Mahomet Saulat/Mirza Mahomed Sauhl/Saulit	Mīrza Saleh Shirazi
Mirza Mahommed Sheffi/Mirza Sheffea	Mirza Shafi'
Mirza-Méhémet-Ali	Mirza Mohammad 'Ali
Mirza Mussan Khan	Musa Khan
Mirza Taki	Mirza Taqi-ye Farahani (Amir Kabir)
Mistchenko/Mitzchenko	Mitchenko

Glossary of Corrupted or Archaic Spellings...   xliii

Miza-Albas	Mirza 'Abbas, i.e. 'Abbas Mirza
Metoski	Matyushkin
Modatow	Madatov, Valerian Grigoryevich
Molitz	Maltitz, Franz Friedrich Freiherr von
Moravioff	Muraviev/Murav'ev
Mostopha	Mustapha
Murat Kan	'Ali Morad Khan Zand
Myr Mana	Mir Muhanna
Muhamed Chasan-Khan	Mohammad Hasan Khan Qajar Qoyunlu
Muhamet-Saidal	Mohammad Saidal Khan
Murza Sheffea	Mirza Shafi'
Musteff Fiel Chassa Mirsa	Mustapha Kaza Mirza
Nadyr	Nader
Nasa-Moll Molla	Nizamu'l-Mulk
Neplief/Nepluet/Nieplief	Neplyuyev
Nesser-ud-Deen-Shah	Naser od-Din Shah
Nezib Pacha	Najib Pasha
Novoziltzoff	Novosiltsev
Obesnoff/Obreskoi	Obrescov
Omer	'Omar/'Umar
Osmin	Osman
Palowitsch	Pavlovich
Pana-Kan	Panah Khan Javanshir
Paschewitz/Paskeetch/Paskevitch/Paskewitch/Paskewitsch/Paskiwitsch/Paskewitz	Paskevich
Pir Kouli Kan Kiagar	Pir Qoli Khan Qajar Shambayati
Quarraman	Qahramān
Rehman Kuli Khan	Rahman Qoli Khan of Khiva
Reschid Pacha	Rashid Pasha
Revandooz Bey	Revanduz Beyi, Mehmed Bey or Paşa
Risa Kulachan/ Riza Kauli Khan	Riza Qoli Khan
Riza Kouly Mirza	Reza Qoli Mirza
Romanshoff/Romanzoff/Romanzow	Rumyantsev
Rujut/Runjeck/Runjeet/Runjut Sing/h	Ranjit Singh

Saboft	Zubov
Sader/Sadi-Chan/Sadik Kan	Sadeq Khan-e Shaqaqi
Sadick	Sadeq
Saduk Khan	Sadeq Kan-e Shaqaqi
Said Morad	Sayyid Morad Khan Zand
Salim	Selim
Salsuchin	Suchtelen
Samoiloff	Samoilov
Santharim	Zand Karim [Khan]
Scofer	Schorer
Schach Nadyr	Nader Shah
Schach-Thamas	Shah Tahmasp
Schah Kouh	Shahrokh
Schaffkoff/Schaffirof	Shafirov
Schekali Mirza	Shaykh 'Ali, i.e. 'Ali Naki Mirza
Schon Kour Khan	Shükür Khan
Schultz	Schulz
Sebactagi	Sebüktegin
Sedi-Chan/Sedi-Khann/	Sadeq Khan-e Shaqaqi
Sermoloff	Ermolov
Sevi	Safi
Shah Soejah/Shah Sooja/Ool Moolk	Shah Shujah ol-Molk
Sharug	Shahrokh
Shawroke/ Shawrook/Shawrooke/Shawrouk/Shawrouke/ Shawruck	Shahrokh
Shah Aly Mirza	Shah 'Ali Naki Mirza
Sheick Nassir	Shaykh Naser Al Mazkur/ Matarish
Sherbatoff	Shcherbatov (Щербатов)
Shimoun	Shimon
Sidy-Khan	Sadeq Khan-e Shaqaqi
Sied Mahomed	Aqa Seyed Mohammad
Simelin	Simolin
Sizianoff	Tsitsianov
Skworzolo	Skvortzov
Sleeva	Sliwa
Soliman Bey	Solayman Agha, a.k.a. Büyük Solayman Pasha
Soliman-Chiab	Salman of the Banu Ka'b

Glossary of Corrupted or Archaic Spellings...   xlv

Sourkay	Surchai
Suboff/Subor/Subow	Zubov
Suwarow/Suwarrow	Suvorov
Syfe Byn Mahomen	Saif Bin Mohammad
Syiad Khan	Sadeq Khan-e Shaqaqi
Synd Moraud Khan	Sayyid Morad Khan
Tachma [Sib]/ Tachmas/Tahmar/Tamas	Tahmasp
Tachmach Culicam/ Tahmas Couli-Kan/Thomas Couli-Kan/ Thamas Kouli Kam/Thomas Kouli Kam	Tahmasp Qoli Khan (Nader Shah)
Tahi-Khan	Mohammad Taqi Khan
Thamar	Tahmasp
Thamas	Tahmasp
Thirky	Turki
Timour Schah	Timur Shah Durrani
Tippoo	Tipu Sultan Fath 'Ali Khan of Mysore,
Tiutschkof	Sergei Alekseyevich Tuchkov
Tochmas	Tahmasp
Tolsti	Tolstoi
Usseihn	Hoseyn
Vetteran	Wattrang
Vicovich	Vitkievich/Witkiewicz/Vitkevičius
Voliensky	Voljensky
Voskoboinikof	Voskoboinikov
Wahabee/Wahaggee/Whabis/ Wechabite	Wahabi
Weljaminow/Williaminoff	Velyaminov
Wisniakow	Vishnyakov/Veshnjakov
Witkewitch	Vitkievich
Woskoboinikoff	Voskoboinikov
Yarmaloff	Ermolov
Yeghen	Yeken
Yermaloff/Yermohoff/Yermoloff/Yermouloff	Ermolov
Youdine	Yudin
Zakikam/Zakee Khan	Zaki Khan Zand
Zamain Shah	Zaman Shah
Zancharim Chan	Karim Khan Zand
Zemaun	Zaman
Zendi Kerim Kan	Karim Khan Zand

Zerberdert/Ziberdert — Zabardast
Zguria Khan — Ugurlu Khan
Zizianow — Tsitsianov
Zochaniki Ali Pacharo — Ispinakchi Mustafa Pasha
Zukee Khan Zund — Zaki Khan Zand

---

2. Titles

Variants	Modern form
Ameen-a-Doolah	Amir od-Doula
Ameer	Amir
Assadou Doulah/Assafed Dewlet/Assefout-Dovle	Asaf od-Doula
Bashaw/Bassa/Bassau/Bassaw	Pasha
Begler Begee/Beglerbeye/Beglier-Bey	beglerbeg
Cadhi	Qadi
Caimaken	Qa'em-maqam
Califf	Caliph
Catirdji	katirji
Caun	Khan
Captain Bashaw	Kapudan pasha
Chadschi	Haji
Chalif	Caliph
Chanhal	Shamkhal
Char	Shah
Chawadars	Muleteers
Chean	Khan
Chiek	Shaykh
Chulesa	Kholafa
Cogan	qaghan/khagan
Elmatta Dowla	i'timad al-dawlah
farady basheer/Feraj Bashi	farrash-bashi
Iman/Imaum	Imam
Iktamadoulet	i'timad al-dawlah vazir-e divan-e 'ala
Imam-e Toomah	Emam-e Jom'a
Kaem Makom	Qa'em-maqam
Kahn/Kan	Khan
Kaim Makaum	Qa'em-maqam
ketkhodeh	kadkhuda

Glossary of Corrupted or Archaic Spellings... xlvii

Kaimakan	Qa'em-maqam
Khawn	Khan
Kiaja/Kiaya	kiayabeg
Kislar Aga	Kızlar Ağa
Knees	knyaz/kniaz/knez,
Koem Makem	Qa'em-maqam
memendar	mehmandar
Merza/Meerza/Mirsa/Mirtz/Myrza	Mirza
Moabi/r Bashy	mo'ayyer-bashi
mooshtebed/mooshtehed/moostahid/mushtakeid	mojtahed
muezzins	mu'adhdhin, mu'azzin
Nalbus Salthanet/ Naibus Solthanet	Na'eb os-Saltanat,
Pacha/Pascia/Pashaw	Pasha
Sahbelzaman/Sahebelzaman	sahib al-zaman
Sarief	Sharif
Sasalar	sepahsalar
Scach/Schach/Schack/Scah/Sciach	Shah
Sedar/Seidar/Serdar/Serdar/Surdar/Surder	sardar
Seich	shaykh
Selou Sultan	Zell os-Soltan
Seraskier	sar 'askar
Sschiech	shaykh
Sha/Shack/Shagh	Shah
Schaksadi/Shah Rade/Shahsade	shahzadeh
Shaugh/Shaw	Shah
Sherick	shaykh
Sidar	sardar
Sied	Seiyed
Sirdar	sardar
Sophi/a/y	Safavid shah
spahi	soldier
Surdar	sardar
Umeer	Amir
Wakeel	vakil
Wallee	Vali
Wuzeer	vezir
Xeriff	Sharif
Yoos Bashi	yüzbaşi
Zileh/Zillah/Zill Sultan/Zzil-us-Southan	Zell os-Soltan

3. Ethnonyms

Variants	Modern form
Adjaline	Ajirli
Affshars	Afshars
Aghuans/Aguans/Auganizes/Avogans	Afghans
Agliuans	Afghans
Anezian	'Anayzah
Bactrians	Bakhtiyari
Barukzyes/Baruykzyes/Baruykzees	Barakzais
Baskiers	Bashkirs
buchares	Bukharans
Bucktiari	Bakhtiyari
Cadjar	Qajar
Calmucks/Calmugues	Kalmyks/Kalmuks
Cefevi	Safavi
Curds/Curde/	Kurds
Dooranee	Durrani
Eelaut	ilat (nomadic tribes)
Gellaleez	Jelali Kurds
Grusians	Georgians
Herattees	Heratis
Kadjar/Kajar	Qajar
Kiab	Banu Ka'b
Koords/Kourds	Kurds
Kozacks/Kozaks	Cossacks
Kujar/Kujur	Qajar
Lasians/Lekzan/Lesgees/Lesgintzes	Lezgins
Lores	Lurs
Ophgoon	Afghan
Oozebecks	Uzbeks
Oss	Ossetians
Sckaksevan	Shahsevan
Seiks	Sikhs
Sekaksevan	Shahsevan
Shiratians	Shirazis
Sieks	Sikhs
Skiekans	Chechens
Sudoogehees	Suddozai/Sadozai
Tschetschenzes	Chechens
Usbech/Usbeck	Uzbek

Glossary of Corrupted or Archaic Spellings... xlix

4. Toponyms and Hydronyms

Variants	Modern form
Aberan	Aparan, Armenia
Aborkoh	Abarkih
Abelaiae/Abelaise	Abkhazia
Abeheron	Absheron
Abucker	Aboukir
Abu Sherer/Abushir/Abushire	Bandar-e Bushehr
Abzirhijan	Azerbaijan
Achisca	Akhaltsikhe
Achsebiuk	mountain in Armenia
Ackermann	Bilhorod-Dnistróvskyi
Ada/Adah	Adeh
Aderbigian/Aderheian/Adirbeitzan	Azerbaijan
Adrianople	Edirne
Adzerbaldjane/Adzerbijan	Azerbaijan
Afcheir	Afshar
Afsharon	Absheron
Agar	Agarakadzor
Aghistan	Daghestan
Agraham	Agrahan
Agvan	Afghanistan
Aiglanlon	Aglenlu
Airak	Arak
Akerman/Akkerman	Bilhorod-Dnistróvskyi
Akh-Uglan	Akoglan
Akoucha	Akusha
Akouglane	Akoglan
Akseri	Aksaray
Akstapha	Aghstafa
Akzebeouk/Aksibijuk/Akziuk	mountain in Armenia
Alazan	Alazani
Alderbesan	Azerbaijan
Alburs	Alborz
Alexandrette	İskenderun
Algezirah	Al-Jazirah
Alkalsike	Akhalzik (Turk.); Akhaltsikhe (Georg.)
Alvorkoh	Abarkuh
Aly Shah	Alishah

Glossary of Corrupted or Archaic Spellings...

Alzirbijan	Azerbaijan
Amadan/Amedan	Hamadan
Andreof/Andreoff/Andreofka/ Andrewka/Andriff	Endirey
Anselly	Bandar-e Anzali
Araks/Arras Arax/Araxe/ Araxes/Araxis/Araxus	Aras
Aran	Arran
Arderum	Erzurum
Ardishai	Ordushahi
Arkevan	Erkivan
Arminia	Armenia
Arpascai/Arpatchai	Arpačay
Arrarat	Ararat
Artevel	Ardabil
Asebgan	Azerbaijan
Asfangas/Aslangas	Aslanduz
Asoph	Azov
Asterbat/Astrabat	Astarabad, mod. Gorgan
Astracan/Astrican	Astrakhan
Axerbijan/Azerbeyan	Azerbaijan
Azium	Erzerum
AzerbajanAzerbidgan/Azerbidjan/Azerbija/Azudbejan	Azerbaijan
Babelabwab	Bab al-Abwab
Baccow/Bacha/Bacow/Bacu	Baku
Baden	Bender
Bagdat	Baghdad
Bahrem	Bahrain
Bahu	Baku
Baiazeth	Doğubayazit
Bajadad/Bajdat	Baghdad
Bajazed/Bajazid	Doğubayazit
Baka/Bakee/Bakou	Baku
Balck	Balkh
Balfousk	Balfrush, mod. Babol
Balikloo	Baliklu
Balk	Balkh
Balla Hor	Balahor
Balruth	Balfrush
Balsora/ Bassarais/Bassaro/Bassaroah/Bassera/Bassora/ Bassorati/Bastra	Basra
Bareck	Khark
Bashire	Bandar-e Bushehr

Glossary of Corrupted or Archaic Spellings... li

Bastra	Basra
Batavia	Jakarta
Bayezend	Doğubayazit
Bebaham	Behbehan
Becht	Rasht
Bendar Abassi/Benderabassi	Bandar 'Abbas
Bendar-Braiher/Bender Braiker	Bandar-e Bushehr
Benderik	Bandar-e Rig
Benderbukhir/Bonderburkhur	Bandar-e Bushehr
Beyroot	Beirut
Bias	Baz/Bazi
Bockhara	Bukhara
Bolgarou	Bolgaru
Boson	Basra
Boujdnourd	Bojnord
Boukara/Boxhara	Bukhara
Bozobdal	Besobdal
Breshire	Bushehr
Broosa/Brussa	Bursa
Bucharey/Bucharia	Bukhara
Bunder Abassi	Bandar 'Abbas
Bushier/Bushire	Bushehr
Bussora/h	Basra
Byzied	Doğubayazit
Cabardie	Kabardia
Cabool	Kabul
Cabulistan	Kabulistan
Cabul/l	Kabul
Cabus	Gonbad-e Qabus
Cachan	Kashan
Cachetie	Kakheti
Cadestan	Kurdistan
Calat	Kalat
Candahar/Candahor	Kandahar
Candaliar	Kandahar
Candia	Crete
Candus	Kunduz
Caplantic (mountains)	Kafilan Kuh/Kaflankuh
Carabagh/Carabah/Carabak/Carabat	K/Q/Gharabagh
Caradac	Qaradagh
Carassan	Khorasan

Carek	Khark
Carelsbad	Karlovy Vary
Cashmere	Kashmir
Cassana	Kashan
Carek	Khark
Cars/Carsa	Kars
Carskozelo	Tsarskoe Selo
Casan	Kazan
Cassana	Kashan
Casben/Casbin	Qazvin
Caswin/Caswira	Qazvin
Caubul	Kabul
Cazernoon/Cazeroon	Kazerun
Chalis	Al Khalis
Chamachy	Shamakhi
Chamagni	Shamakhi
Chamodam	Hamadan
Chamora	Shamkhor/Shamkura
Charack	Khark
Charmehal	Chahar Mahal
Charon	Karun
Chatul, Arabian	Shatt al-Arab
Chekiue	Sheki
Chenate	Khanate
Chenfe	Ganja
Cherman	Kerman
Chervan	Shirvan
Chesi	Sheki,
Chilan	Gilan
Chio	Chios
Chiras	Shiraz
Chirvan/Chirwan	Shirvan
Chislar	Kizlyar
Chiva	Khiva
Choczim/Choczin/Chockzyen	Khotyn
Choi	Khoy
Choras	Shiraz
Chorasan/Chorassan/Chorazan	Khorasan
Chorour	Sharur
Chudoperin	Khoda Afarin
Chuhr/Chur	Kur

Glossary of Corrupted or Archaic Spellings...

Churegel	Shoregel/Shuragel
Chusistan	Khuzestan
Chuznee	Ghazni/Ghazna
Ciaharbag	Chahar Bagh
Clanhora	Shamkhor/Shamkura
Corassan	Khorasan
Corbin	Qazvin
Corosen	Khorasan
Cosveen	Qazvin
Couban	Kuban
Coubla	Quba
Cronstadt	Kronstadt
Cuban	Kuban
Cuhistan	Kuhistan
Cuamchalil	Shamshadil
Cundabar	Candahar
Cundistan/Curdistan	Kurdistan
Cura	Kur
Curadac	Karadagh
Cutaga	Kütayah
Cyrus	Kur
Daghestun/Dagistan/ Daglostan/Daguestan	Daghestan
Daraourte	Dara Yort/Dala-Urt
Daria	Amu Darya
Deghastan	Daghestan
Dekhargane	Deh Kurgan
Delhy/Dely/Delly	Delhi
Derbant/Derbent	Darband
Desful	Dezful
Dezeh Khaleel	Diza Khalil
Diabekir/Diarback/ Diarbeck/Diarbeker	Diyarbakir
Dilem	Dailam
Dilly	Delhi
Diddeen	Diyadin
Dimascus	Damascus
Diurbekir	Diyarbakir
Djavat	Javad
Djikoir	Jekir
Doria/Dosia	Amu Darya
Driebuker	Diyarbakir
Dschajawak/Dschawat	Javad

Durozzo/Durazzo	Durrës,
Dzumalesk/Dzumulesk	Çölamerk, mod. Hakkâri
Elborz	Alborz
Elis/zabethpol	Ganja
El Koosh	Alqosh
Engeli/Ensejeli/Enzelli	Bandar-e Anzali
Erdabit	Ardabil
Ergerum	Erzurum
Erivan/Eriwan	Yerevan
Ersereum/Erserum/ Ertz Roum/Erzerom/Erzeroom/Erzroom	Erzurum
Ervel	Erbil
Erwan	Yerevan
Eschkuarski	Etchmiadzin
Esdom/Esserom/Esserorn	Erzurum
Etchmaidzine/Etchmiadsin/Etchmiadzine/Eutch Relaser	Echmiadzin
Evrezuma	Erzurum
Fabirez	Tabriz
Fahetchivan	Nakhchivan/Naxçivan
Farebat	Farabad/Farahabad
Faristan/Farsistan	Fars
Gailistan	Gulistan
Galivan	Gavlan, Iran
Gamberoon/Gambroon/Gameron	Bandar 'Abbas
Gangea/Gangi/Gangia/Gangis/Gantcha/Genghe/Genscha/Ghencia/Ghenza	Ganja
Gannshin/Gannshiu	Ganja
Gavalan	Gavlan
Geag/Geg Tapa	Gök/Gug/Guy Tappeh
Gehran	Tehran
Geog Tapa/Tupa	Gök/Gug/Guy Tappeh
Ghillan/Gilham/Gilhan	Gilan
Ghizny/Ghuzni/Gizny	Ghazni/Ghazna
Ginges	Ganja
Ginghen	Yegen
Girrumseer	*garmsir* ('warm region')
Gokcha/Gokchah/Goktcha/Goktscha/Goukcha/Goukha	Gökçe (Lake Sevan)
Gombra/Gombroon/Gomron	Bandar 'Abbas
Gomeri	Gyumri
Goolisten/Goulestan	Gulistan
Greag Tapa	Gök/Gug/Guy Tappeh
Grusien/Grusija/Grusnia/Grussinie	Georgia

Glossary of Corrupted or Archaic Spellings... lv

Guenge	Ganja
Guerrcha	Ganja
Guesilar	Güzelhisar, mod. Aydın
Gufferale	Julfār
Guilan	Gilan
Guira/Guriel/Gurier	Guria
Gulestan	Gulistan
Gumry	Gyumri, Armenia
Guselisar	Güzelhisar, mod. Aydın
Guyez	G/Juz
Hakary	Hakkari, Turkey
Hamadam	Hamadan
Haramooz	Hormuz
Hasenbath	Hasanabad
Hassan Colleh/Kulaah	Hasankale, mod. Pasinler
Havadan	Hamadan
Hazadara, Hazaadara	Hezar-dereh
Hendeza	Hendijan, Iran
Heraut/Herot	Herat
Hierac	'Irāq 'Ajami
Hindustdan	Hindustan
Hirat	Herat
Hispahan	Isfahan
Houveth	Huwaizah/Hoveyzeh
Huveis	Huwaizah/Hoveyzeh
Hyrant	Herat
Immanetta	Imereti
Indostad/n	Hindustan
Irac-Arabia	Iraq-e Arab
Irewan/Irvan	Yerevan
Isharetta	Imereti
Ispaham/Ispahan	Isfahan
Jamalava	Jovlan/Jowlan
Jassy	Iași
Jediboulouk	Yedi Balük
Jehan Numah	Baghi Jahan Numa
Jessetten	Yazd
Jolvan	Holwan
Joolamerk	Çölemerik, mod. Hakkâri
Jorgan	Gorgan
Juster	Shushtar

Jullabad	Jalalabad
Jutpha	Julfa
Kaabasch	K/Q/Gharabagh
Kaboul	Kabul
Kachum	Kasikumük, mod. Kazikumukhsky
Kaeese	Kish or Jazirat al-Qeys
Kaghizmann/Kagzetnan	Kağızman
Kaketia	Kakheti
Kala	Kalat
Kalan	Holwan
Kalay	Qale-ye
Kallarasch	Călăraşi, Romania
Kalouga	Kaluga
Kam	Qom
Kampschatka/Kamschatka	Kamchatka
Kandeith	Khandesh
Kapanaktchay/Kapanktchay	Kapan çay
Kara Aineh	Siah Cheshmeh
Karabag/Karabak/Kara Bang/Karabasch/Karabaugh/ Karabog/Karabosch/Karapagh	K/Q/Gharabagh
Karak	Khark
Karaklis/Kara-Kelissiah/Kara Keloseh	Kara Kilisse/Qara Kelisa
Karassou/Karasu	Kara Su
Karee/Karek	Khark
Kareklissia	Kara Kilisse/Qara Kelisa
Karis/Karz	Kars
Karoon	Karun
Karrack/Karrak/Karric/Karvik	Khark
Kasbin/Kasvine	Qazvin
Kazasch/Kazask	Kasatcha/Kazachia
Kazroon	Kazerun
Kebrabath	Gabarabād
Keirmann	Kerman
Keish	Kish (Jazirat al-Qeys)
Kelar	Kalat
Keleeseh	Kelisa
Kendolan	Khaldan
Kenn	Kish (Jazirat al-Qeys)
Keraddaz	Darrah Gaz, mod. Dargaz
Kerbela/h/Kerbelay/Kerbella	Karbala'

Glossary of Corrupted or Archaic Spellings... lvii

Kerkoud/Kerkuck/Kerkut	Kerkuk
Kermanchah/Kermencha/Kermanshaw	Kermanshah
Kertch	Kerch
Khaboosdan	Khabushan
Khannat	Khanate
Khars	Kars
Khess	Kish (Jazirat al-Qeys)
Khiara/Khiwa	Khiva
Khonartueta	Konartakhteh
Khoee	Khoy
Khorasen/Khorason/ Khorassann/Khorassen	Khorasan
Khosrova	Khosrowabad
Khudaperim	Khoda Afarin
Khumsa	Khemseh
Kiew	Kyiv
Kilan	Gilan
Kirhoot/Kirkiut/Kirkut	Kerkuk
Kirs	Kars
Kischme/Kishme/Kishum	Qeshm
Kohraisan	Khorasan
Kokan	Kokand
Kolomenskoi	Kolomenskoye
Kol-Sanschak	Koy Sanjaq
Koom	Qom
Korassan/Korazan/Korisan	Khorasan
Kormava	Kamara
Kosilusan	Kisil-osun
Koupoperinisk	Khoda Afarin
Kour/Koura	Kur
Koy	Khoy
Kuba	Quba
Kubela	Karbala'
Kulpekin	Golpayegan
Kuoth	Kuba
Kutaja	Kütahya
Kuttum	Kutuma
Kuveer	Dasht-e Kavir
Lacki	Laçin
Lahoer/Lahor	Lahore
Lahr	Lar
Lahristan	Laristan

Glossary of Corrupted or Archaic Spellings...

Lankaron	Lankaran
Larristan	Luristan
Lattaquie	Latakia
Leghorn	Livorno
Leipsic	Leipzig
Lemberg/Lembergh	Lviv/Lvov/Lwów
Lenkoran	Lankaran
Loresten	Luristan
Lory	Lori
Macandamur	Mazandaran
Mached	Mashhad
Machor	Mahshahr/Ma'shur (Bandar-e)
Mahine	Mahé, Mayyazhi
Mailian	Maraljan
Maliz/Malz Ghird	Malazgirt
Mana	Mianeh
Maraga	Maragha/eh
Marundarum	Mazandaran
Masagha	Maragha/eh
Mascar/Mascate	Muscat
Maschat	Mashhad
Masenden/Masenderan	Mazandaran
Masked	Mashhad
Massagna	Maragha/eh
Massagong	Mazagaon
Matelino	Mytiline (Lesbos)
Mazandarn/Mazandran/ Mazandumir/Mazenderan/ Mazinderan	Mazandaran
Meca/Meccha	Mecca
Mechat	Mashhad
Mendeli/Menduli/Menouli	Mandali, Iraq
Merend/a	Marand
Merve	Merv
Mesched	Mashhad
Meschkine	Meshkin
Meshed/Meshid	Mashhad
Messagong	Mazagaon, India
Messendheran	Mazandaran
Meudoli	Mandali, Iraq
Mezanderan	Mazandaran

Glossary of Corrupted or Archaic Spellings... lix

Mian/Miana	Mianeh
Michet	Mashhad
Misandron	Mazandaran
Mischer	Mashhad
Missendroon	Mazandaran
Mocran	Makran
Mogan/Mongan	Mughan
Mohamra	al-Muhammarah, mod. Khorramshahr
Monghaw	Mughan
Moorhia	Merv
Moosul/Moussoul/ Mussul/Musul	Mosul
Morra	Morea, i.e. Peloponnese
Moshatt/Mushat	Mashhad
Mousel	Mosul
Mursch/Musch	Muş
Mushed	Mashhad
Mynunnal	Mynunnah, mod. Maymana
Naakyn	Nanjing
Nakchevan/Nakhetchevan/Nakhitchevan/Nakman/ Nakhtchiwan/Nakshivan	Nakhchivan/Naxçivan
Nantz	Nantes
Nauhivan	Nakhchivan/Naxçivan
Neister	Dniester
Nemirow/Nimirow	Nemyriv
Nepaul	Nepal
Nezib	Nizip
Nicomedia	İzmit
Nigaristan	Bagh-e Negarestan
Nimirow	Nemyriv
Nishapoor	Nishapur
Nooshky	Nushki
Oczakow	Ochakiv
Odinabazar	Adina Bazar
Okotsk	Okhotsk
Olonitz	Olonets
Ooramah/Oormiah/Ooromania Ooroomiah	Urmia
l'Orient	Port l'Orient
Orfa	Urfa, Turkey
Oristan	Luristan

Ormus	Hormuz
Osquitise	Etchmiadzin
Oude	Oudh
Oudian	'Udjani
Ouleonguerd	Borujerd
Oural	Ural
Ourmiah	Urmia
Panjeb	Punjab
Pera	Beyoğlu
Peshamer/Pishaws	Peshawar
Poloria	Lori
Precop	Perekop
Pshiad	Pshada
Punjaub	Punjab
Purneah	Purnia
Rachan	Kashan
Ragdachana	Rudkhaneh
Randeish	Khandesh
Rascht/Rash	Rasht
Ratisbon	Regensburg
Razroon	Kazerun
Reirsth/Reschd/Rescht	Rasht, Iran
Revan	Yerevan
Revel	Tallinn
Rhest	Rasht
Riaschtsche/Riatscha/Riatsche	Rasht
Rivan	Yerevan
Romelia	Eyalet-i Rum-eli
Rungpoor	Rangjpur
Salimanieh	Sulaymaniyah
Sallian	Salyan
Salvate, Mount	Sabalan/Savalan
Samache/Samanske	Shamakhi
Samarad	Samara
Samarcand	Samarkand
Samboor	Sambur
Samnune	Semnan
Sanderut	Zayandarud
Sanga	Hrazdan
Sangan	Zanjan
Sarakamyche	Sari-Gamish

Glossary of Corrupted or Archaic Spellings... lxi

Sardar Abad	Nor Armavir
Sauvidgeboulogh	Savojbolagh
Schamakha/Schamachia/Schimachy	Shamakhi
Schamshadil	Shamshadil
Schekin	Sheki
Schildin	Childir
Schiras/Schirez	Shiraz
Schirmanshach	Kermanshah
Schirus	Shiraz
Schirvan/Schirwan	Şirvan
Schivas	Shiraz
Schouchi	Shusha
Schuragalskoi/Schuragei/Schuragel	Shoregel/Shuragel
Schuscha	Shusha
Scind/Scindea	Sind
Scivas	Sivas
Scorpoot	Serhetabat (?)
Scutari/Scutaria	Üsküdar
Sebastopal	Sevastopol,
Selissawatopol	Elizabethpol
Sengilabat/Sengliabat	Zanjilabad
Seraz	Shiraz
Serekha	Serakhs
Serireddhehab	Sarir ad-Dahab
Servan	Şirvan
Servia	Serbia
Shamakhoo/Shamaki	Shamakhi
Shamcur/Shamkoor	Shamkhur
Sheerauz	Shiraz
Sheerwan	Şirvan
Sheesha	Shusha
Shekey	Sheki
Sheraz/Shiraauz/Shirauz	Shiraz
Sherei Baee	Shahr-e Babak
Shirean/Shirvin	Şirvan
Shishawan	Shishvan
Shizan	Borazjan
Shoosh/Shouchi/Shuse	Shusha
Shusteer	Shushtar
Shyrass/Shyrus	Shiraz
Sina	Sanandaj

Sirwan	Şirvan
Sizistan	Sistan
Skyras	Shiraz
Smirna/Smyrna	İzmir
Soleimania/Soolimanieh	Sulaymaniyah
Soultanieh	Soltaniyah
Spahan/Spahaun/Spahawn	Isfahan
Staraja Schamokha	Old Shamakhi
Suabia	Swabia (Schwaben)
Suleimaniah/Sulimanje/Sullimania/Sullimanieh	Sulaymaniyah
Sultanea/Sultani/Sultania/Sultanie	Soltaniyah
Surias	Shiraz
Suttledge	Sutlej
Taaoeeran	Teheran
Tabaris/Tabreez/Tabreeze/Tabries/Tabriez	Tabriz
Taheran/Tahiran/Tairan	Tehran
Taiquie	Tarkhi/u
Tairberan	Tabarsaran
Talidje/Talischin/Talish/Tallish/Talyche/Talychine/Talyschyne	Talysh
Tanki	Tarkhi/u
Tarbarassan	Tabarsaran
Tarbrizi	Tabriz
Tarbut	Torbat-e Jam
Tauris/Taurus	Tabriz
Tchoudouv	Khoda Afarin
Tebriz	Tabriz
Teeheran	Tehran
Tefflies/Teffleez/Teflis/Tefis/Tiffes/Tiffis/Tiffles/Tiflis	Tbilisi
Teheren	Tehran
Tejan	Tedzhen/Tejen
Tekhoma	Tkhuma
Temeswar	Timişoara
Tenzumer	Tergawar
Teminschanski	Temirchanshura, mod. Buynaksk
Teran/Terheran	Tehran
Terki	Tarkhi/u
Terrack Agemi	'Iraq 'Ajami
Tertus	Tartus
Tewris	Tabriz

Glossary of Corrupted or Archaic Spellings... lxiii

Tiffis	Tbilisi
Thebisand	Trabzon
Theran	Tehran
Tobrao-Kelah	Toprakkale
Tokarestian	Tocharistan
Toopruck Kullat	Toprakkale
Toorhish	Torshiz, Iran
Tourkmantscha/Tourkmantschal	Turkmanchy
Transilvania	Transylvania
Trebizende/Trebizond/Trechismont	Trabzon
Treflis/Triflees/Trifflis/Triflis	Tbilisi
Treorzond	Trabzon
Tripolizza	Tripoli/Tripoliçe
Tschargab	Chahar Bagh
Turkmantschi	Turkmanhay
Tygris	Tigris
Uch Keleeseh	Üç Kelisa
Udjoam	'Udhaim/'Adhaim
Ukrania	Ukraine
Urumea	Urmia
Verenitz/Veronitz	Voronezeh
Vosneseusk	Voznesensk
Wahlsiat	Wahlstatt (Legnickie Pole)
Wan	Van
Widdin/Widin	Vidin,
Wladikawkask	Vladikavkaz
Wolga	Volga
Woronege	Voronezh
Yavshamly	Yushanlu,
Yedibouloob	Yazdabad
Yerack	'Iraq 'Ajami
Yerski	Tarkhi/u
Zaardam	Zaandam
Zablestan	Zabulistan
Zainderood/Zendera/Zenderhend	Zayandarud/Zayanderorud
Zambour	Sambur river
Zarabah	Zharabad/Zarabad
Zarskojasselo	Tsarskoye Selo
Zebreez	Tabriz
Zeheran	Tehran
Zerenge	Zaranj

Zeyva	Zeiva, Seiva/Siewa/Zuivan River (Gulistan)
Zinzili	Bandar-e Anzali
Zoprak-Kaleh	Toprakkale,
Zorabah	Zharabad/Zarabad
Zulpha	Julfa

5. Nouns

Variants	Modern form
Cailleau	*Qalyan* (water pipe)
Charbass	*Zarbaf* (gold brocade)
Fursak	*Farsakh* (unit of distance)
Hadschi	*Haji* (one who has made the Haj)
Kalcoore/kalioun	*Qalyan* (water pipe)
Kelkodapesend	*Kadkhoda pesand* (type of silk)
Taktrawan	*Takht-ravan* (litter)

List of Figures

Fig. 8.1	Fath 'Ali Shah, by Mihr 'Ali, 1815. Watercolor and gold on paper. Gift of Laura L. Barnes, David Ellis, Mr. and Mrs. Alfred H. Otto, Mabel Reiner, and anonymous gifts, by exchange. Brooklyn Museum, CC0 1.0 Universal	702
Fig. 8.2	Antoine-Isaac Silvestre de Sacy. Lithograph by François-Séraphin Delpech after a portrait by Antoine Maurin. Yale University Art Gallery, CC0 1.0 Universal	716
Fig. 9.1	Pierre-Amédée-Émilien-Probe Jaubert, engraving by E. Ducrocq. Bibliothèque National de France, CC0 1.0 Universal	797
Fig. 9.2	James Rennell, 1794, possibly by George Daniel. CC0 1.0 Universal. After E.T. Thackeray, *Biographical Notices of Officers of the Royal (Bengal) Engineers*. London: Smith, Elder, & Co., 1900, between pp. 10 and 11	837
Fig. 10.1	'Mr. Willock. Camp at Mt. Ararat,' by James Justinian Morier. Pencil on paper. Balliol College Archives Morier-N03–04-145	927
Fig. 10.2	Mirza Abu'l Hasan Khan Shirazi, by Sir Thomas Lawrence, 1810. Oil on canvas. Harvard Art Museums/Fogg Museum, Bequest of William M. Chadbourne, CC0 1.0 Universal	1069
Fig. 11.1	Prince Valerian Grigoryevich Madatov, by George Dawe, 1820. Oil on canvas. Military Gallery of the Winter Palace, CC0 1.0 Universal	1160
Fig. 11.2	'Capt.[n] Monteith, of the E.C. Artillery serving in Persia. 1813,' by James Justinian Morier. Pencil on paper. Balliol College Archives Morier-N03-04-051	1192
Fig. 12.1	Alexander Sergeyevich Griboyedov, by Ivan Kramskoy, 1873. Oil on canvas. Tretyakov Gallery, CC0 1.0 Universal	1293
Fig. 12.2	'Mirza Buzurk, Minister to Abbas Mirza,' by James Justinian Morier. Pencil on paper. Balliol College Archives Morier-N03-04-119	1298

The Early Career of Fath 'Ali Shah (1798–1804)   8

As early as 1794 Agha Mohammad Shah, a eunuch with no children of his own, had designated his nephew Fath 'Ali Khan, whom he always referred to as Baba Khan, as his successor. After a brief period of resistance by Fath 'Ali Khan's uncle, Sadeq Khan Qajar Devehlu, who had been one of Agha Mohammad Shah's military commanders, Fath 'Ali Shah mounted the throne. One of his first acts was to send conciliatory messages to St. Petersburg, indicating that he had no intention of pursuing his uncle's policy of expansion in the southern Caucasus.

By the autumn of 1798 Napoleon had emerged on the world stage and although fears in the English press of an invasion of India via the Red Sea were quickly voiced another thought took hold almost immediately, namely the necessity of securing Fath 'Ali Shah's cooperation in thwarting any planned movement of French troops overland, through Persia, towards the EIC's domains in India. To that end, Capt. John Malcolm was sent by the EIC to Tehran in late December, 1799. Proceeding by sea to Bushehr, the mission travelled via Shiraz and Isfahan to Fath 'Ali Shah's capital. Among other things, this resulted in the Anglo-Persian Commercial Treaty of 1801.

Meanwhile, tensions with Russia simmered and although Fath 'Ali Shah attempted to restore some of Persia's Georgian holdings through peaceful means, this was not always successful. In the summer of 1802 trouble arose on a completely different front when Haji Khalil Khan-e Koroghlu Qazvini, whom Fath 'Ali Shah had sent to India to reciprocate Malcolm's embassy, was brutally and unexpectedly murdered, along with members of his suite, in his residence at Bombay. This led to a flurry of diplomatic activity and protestations on the part of the Governor-General, Lord Wellesley, of deep mortification and regret, including the payment of a lifetime pension to the victim's son, Mohammad Isma'il Khan. The shocking incident was widely covered in the press.

© The Author(s), under exclusive license to Springer Fachmedien Wiesbaden GmbH, part of Springer Nature 2022
D. T. Potts, *Agreeable News from Persia*, Universal- und kulturhistorische Studien. Studies in Universal and Cultural History,
https://doi.org/10.1007/978-3-658-36032-0_8

While this was going on reports in the American press covered a much wider, more diverse array of incidental topics concerning Persia than ever before. These ranged from discussions of the rising Wahhabi power in Arabia, and its implications for Persia and the Persian Gulf, to stories about the pearl fishery, viticulture, the Caspian Sea fishery and Persian yeast. Thanks to scholars like Sir William Jones and Sir William Ouseley, Persian literature and history were becoming much better known, and it is clear that their works were enjoying wide distribution.

Several non-political stories stand out, including notices of the introduction of smallpox vaccine, and vaccination trials at Bandar-e Bushehr on the Persian Gulf coast of Iran, involving EIC surgeons. Another EIC-related story that was solely American, and not derived from the Continental European or British press, concerned the discovery of a coin near the banks of the Ohio River that was shown by its discoverer, a Yale graduate, to the theologian and educator Timothy Dwight IV who mistook the script on it for Middle Persian (Pahlavi). Another reader who saw an engraving of the coin, however, was able to correctly identify it as an EIC coin from Bengal datable to 1776.

8.1 'Fresh convulsions in Persia,' *Aurora General Advertiser* (Saturday, 3 March, 1798) and 'Fresh convulsions in Persia,' *City Gazette and Daily Advertiser* (Saturday, 31 March, 1798): 'Since the murder of the Eunuch Mehmet Chan,[1] who had usurped the crown of Persia, that country is a victim to all the disorders of an interregnum, which, whilst the leaders of the different parties are fighting in the field for the Sovereignty, will last until one of the pretenders shall grow powerful enough to subdue his rival, and render himself master of the empire. It is said, that Sedi-Chan, one of the generals of the late usurper,[2] who commanded against the Russians, had the best prospect to obtain the preponderance.'[3]

8.2 'Bombay Courier, April 1, 1797,' *The Daily Advertiser* (Saturday, 17 March, 1798): 'The Russians, including those who invaded Daghestan, the Armenians, Daghestans, Turks, Georgians and others, have just formed a junction with the Grand Army in

---

[1] Agha Mohammad Shah.

[2] As Markham (1874: 356) put it, 'Agha Muhammad had murdered almost every relation who was at all likely to dispute the throne; but there was one uncle left, named Sâdik Khân, who rose in rebellion.' In Malcolm (1829/2: 203) we read, 'this ambitious nobleman [Sadeq Khan Qajar Devehlu] not only afforded them [the assassins] protection, and accepted the crown jewels which they brought him, but, having assembled his tribe, endeavoured to seat himself on the throne of Persia.'

[3] Leaving Shisha, Sadeq Khan proceeded towards Qazvin where his family was. By this time Fath 'Ali Shah, Agha Mohammad Shah's chosen successor, was already in Tehran. The gates of Qazvin remained closed to him however, and his brothers had been defeated by the governor of Khoy, from whom they fled. Fath 'Ali Khan's forces defeated Sadeq shortly thereafter. See Watson (1866: 108–109).

neighbourhood of Tauris, from whence they will continue their route to the Eastward, to contend the fate of Persia with Aga Mahomet Khan, in Tairan,[4] from whence they may easily penetrate into Korassan, where the inhabitants in crowds demand their protection.'[5]

8.3 'Latest European Intelligence from Hamburgh papers. Persia, Oct. 26,' *Aurora General Advertiser* (Saturday, 5 May, 1798), 'Late Foreign Intelligence. Persia, Oct. 26,' *The Philadelphia Gazette and Universal Daily Advertiser* (Saturday, 5 May, 1798), 'Persia, October 26,' *Carey's United States' Recorder* (Tuesday, 8 May, 1798), 'Foreign Articles. Persia, October 26,' *Gazette of the United States, and Philadelphia Daily Advertiser* (Tuesday, 8 May, 1798), 'Foreign Intelligence. Persia, Oct. 26,' *The Universal Gazette* (Thursday, 10 May, 1798), 'Asia. Persia, Oct. 26,' *The Independent Chronicle and the Universal Advertiser* (Thursday-Monday, 10–14 May, 1798), 'Foreign Intelligence. Asia,' *The Oracle of the Day* (Saturday, 19 May, 1798) and 'European Intelligence. Persia, October 26,' *Norwich Packet* (Tuesday, 22 May, 1798): 'The disturbances which arose on account of the succession to the throne were of but short duration, and Persia again begins to enjoy the blessings of peace. Baba-Chan, nephew of the late Eunuch,[6] whose memory is vowed to everlasting execration, met but few obstacles in ascending the throne. Supported by an army of 60,000 men, and master of immense riches, which he inherited from his uncle, he has hitherto triumphed over all his rivals: Sadi-Chan, the most formidable among them, laid down his arms, having been twice defeated, and submitted. Baba-Chan made him governor of an important province.[7] All unite in commending Baba-Chan our new sovereign.' (Fig. 8.1).

---

[4]Tehran.

[5]This first appeared in in the *Calcutta Gazette* on 14 January, 1797. See Seton-Karr (1865: 478).

[6]Baba Khan, i.e. Fath 'Ali Shah. As Schlechta-Wssehrd (1864a: 21) noted, 'Sein eigentlicher Name war Fethali, doch pflegte ihm sein verstorbener Oheim [Agha Mohammad Shah], dessen Liebling er war, die zärtliche Benennung Baba (Väterchen) beizulegen die ihm auch bis zu seiner Thronbesteigung verblieb.' According to the Qajar chronicle used by MacGregor (1871: 107), 'In the year 1794 A.D., Aga Mahamad proclaimed his nephew, Fateh Alī Khān, commonly called Bābā Khān, successor to the throne, and appointing him to the government of Persia Proper sent him to reside at Shīrāz.' As Malcolm (1827/2: 140) noted, 'his cruel but able uncle, Aga Mahomed, had destroyed all who were likely to dispute his possession of the crown. "He had," to use his own words, "raised a royal palace, and cemented it with blood, that the boy Bâbâ Khan (the name he always gave his nephew) might sleep within its walls in peace."' After the death of Lutf 'Ali Khan, 'Baba Khan was appointed to the government of Fars.' See Scott Waring (1807: 304–305). According to Malcolm (1829: 205), Agha Mohammad Shah 'used often to exclaim, when speaking of his successor, the present King of Persia, "I have shed all this blood, that the boy, Bâbâ Khan, may reign in peace."'

[7]Watson (1866: 101) related that, Agha Mohammad Shah's murderers 'seized the crown jewels, and handed them over to Sadek Khan Shekaki, one of the generals of the army, who afforded the assassins protection.' Further, he wrote, 'Sadek Khan, who had carried the crown and the royal jewels away with him from the field of Kasveen, was enabled by their means to make his peace with the king, who appointed him governor of a province.' See Watson (1866: 112). Later, however, he joined a conspiracy against Fath 'Ali Shah and when this collapsed as a result of strife among the conspirators,

Fig. 8.1 Fath 'Ali Shah, by Mihr 'Ali, 1815. Watercolor and gold on paper. Gift of Laura L. Barnes, David Ellis, Mr. and Mrs. Alfred H. Otto, Mabel Reiner, and anonymous gifts, by exchange. Brooklyn Museum, CC0 1.0 Universal

8.4 'Political Miscellany. Persia,' *The Newburyport Herald and Country Gazette* (Tuesday, 17 July, 1798), 'Persia,' *The Philadelphia Gazette and Universal Daily Advertiser* (Wednesday, 18 July, 1798), 'Political Summary. Persia,' *The Courier* (Thursday, 19 July, 1798), 'Persia,' *The Albany Centinel* (Friday, 20 July, 1798), 'Persia,' *Federal Gazette & Baltimore Daily Advertiser* (Friday, 20 July, 1798), 'Summary. Persia,' *The*

Sadeq Khan sought the Shah's mercy, was detained and transferred to Teheran. See Watson (1866: 115). When called upon to provide troops for a planned invasion of Khorasan, in response to Zaman Shah Durrani's request for Khorasan to be surrendered to him as part of the Afghan kingdom, Sadeq Khan was sent for 'and condemned to be bricked up in a room at Tehran, and there left to starve to death,' in accordance with Fath 'Ali Khan's former promise never to shed Sadeq Khan's blood. See Watson 1866: 125. According to Markham 1874: 357, 'Sâdik Khân surrendered himself a prisoner, trusting to the sacred oath of his nephew that no violence should be used against him. The cruel Kájar, imitating the treachery of his predecessor, shut him up in a room, closed up the doors and windows, and left him to die of starvation. When the doors were opened, some weeks afterwards, it was found that the wretched man had dug deep into the earth with his hands, and swallowed the clay to assuage his hunger.' For the Persian custom of eating clay, see Laufer (1930: 150–153).

Mirror (Tuesday, 24 July, 1798), 'Survey of Universal Politics. Persia,' *The Farmer's Register* (Wednesday, 1 August, 1798), 'Persia,' *Hampshire Gazette* (Wednesday, 1 August, 1798) and 'Persia,' *The Otsego Herald or Western Advertiser* (Thursday, 2 August, 1798): '[Persia] is an Empire, subject to superstition and military despotism; could it be cursed with more! Yes, it is.—For many years it has been in anarchy and confusion. It has had civil wars with the Russians and Turks. These concern us little, and we know as little of their events.'

8.5 'Late Foreign News. London, July 23,' *Commercial Advertiser* (Monday, 1 October, 1798), 'July 23,' *Gazette of the United States, and Philadelphia Daily Advertiser* (Tuesday, 2 October, 1798), 'London, July 23,' *The Salem Gazette* (Friday, 5 October, 1798), 'Continuation of Foreign Intelligence, received by the Fanny, Braine, arrived at New-York, from Greenock. London, July 23,' *The Times, and Alexandria Advertiser* (Saturday, 6 October, 1798), 'England. London, July 23,' *The Albany Register* (Monday, 8 October, 1798), 'England,' *The Newburyport Herald and Country Gazette* (Friday, 12 October, 1798) and 'By Saturday's Mails. Foreign Articles,' *Oriental Trumpet, or the Town and Country Gazette* (Thursday, 18 October, 1798): 'A peace between Russia and Persia has been signed at Tiflis,[8] but a Russian corps of twenty thousand men remains at Kur; the Turks have likewise established an army of observation on the Persian frontier.'

8.6 'London, July 27,' *The Philadelphia Gazette & Universal Daily Advertiser* (Friday, 12 October, 1798), 'London, July 27,' *Gazette of the United States, and Philadelphia Daily Advertiser* (Friday, 12 October, 1798), 'London, July 27,' *The Telegraphe and Daily Advertiser* (Tuesday, 16 October, 1798), and 'England. London, July 27,' *New-Jersey Journal* (Tuesday, 16 October, 1798; minor typos and variations): 'According to the latest advices from Mount Caucasus, peace has been concluded and signed at Tiflis, between Russia and Persia. The Treaty is tolerably advantageous to the Persian Monarch,[9] the Court of Russia having given up the conquests which its troops made on that side, except some villages and portions of territory on the Caspian Sea, and particularly Derbent and

---

[8] No such treaty was signed but as Atkin (1979: 64–65) noted, 'The new Shah opened the way for improved relations with Russia by sending several friendly messages to Paul sometime in 1798 or early 1799....Paul addressed the new Shah in a letter—not intended to sound hostile—by his precoronation name, Bābā Khan, and the title *sardār* (general)....The tsar certainly gave up nothing to Fath 'Ali in matters considered important to Russia's interests—the security of Georgia and environs and freedom for Russian merchants to do business throughout Iran. Nonetheless, he did not exploit the Shah's supposed weakness by treating him as an inferior....His lack of condescension of the Shah was evidenced by his countermanding various measures which displeased Iranians, such as the plan to build a fort to protect Russian commercial interests in the Iranian port city of Anzali. The tone of his letter to the Shah, the freeing of several Iranian merchants imprisoned in Russia, the relaxation of commercial restrictions, and a variety of other actions all showed Paul's desire to win the Shah's good will.'

[9] Fath 'Ali Shah.

Baccow,[10] which have been already ceded by former treaties. Notwithstanding this peace, a body of 20,000 men remains posted along the river Cyrus.[11] It appears that this little army has given umbrage to the Porte, since orders have been [given] by the latter to assemble an army of observation in the neighbourhood.'

8.7 'Nouvelles politiques. Londres, 27 Juillet,' *Gazette Française* (Friday, 12 October, 1798): 'D'après les dernières lettres du Mont-Caucase, il parait que la paix a été conclue entre la Russie & la Perse. Le traité est assez avantageux pour le roi de Perse, la cour de Russie ayant abandonné toutes les conquêtes que ses troupes ont faites de ce côté, excepté quelques villages & portions de territoire sur la mer Caspienne, particulièrement Derbent & Baccow,[12] qui avaient été cédées par des traités précedens. Malgré cette paix, un corps de 20,000 hommes reste campé sur la rivière Cyrus.[13] Il parait que cette petite armée a donné de l'ombrage à la Porte, puisque cette dernière a donné des ordres pour assembler une armée d'observation dans le voisinage.'

8.8 'Paris, November 9,' *The Bee* (Wednesday, 30 January, 1799), 'Late Foreign News. France. Paris, Oct. 25,' *The Oracle of the Day* (Saturday, 2 February, 1799), 'Latest Foreign News. Paris, October 25,' *The Centinel of Freedom* (Tuesday, 5 February, 1799), 'Paris, Nov. 12,' *New-Jersey Journal* (Tuesday, 5 February, 1799) and 'By the last Mail. October 25,' *The Herald of Liberty* (Monday, 11 February, 1799): 'If we may give credit to the letters which arrive from the banks of the Euphrates, Asia is not more tranquil than Europe; and Persia, the ancient enemy of the Ottoman Porte, is manifesting the most hostile dispositions. Buonaparte[14] being master of Suez, will advance towards the Persian Gulph, and will lend the Persians a strong support.'

8.9 'Vienna, November 11, *Claypoole's American Daily Advertiser* (Tuesday, 5 February, 1799), 'Latest Foreign Intelligence. Vienna, Nov. 11,' *Commercial Advertiser*

---

[10] Baku.

[11] Kur.

[12] Baku.

[13] Kur.

[14] On the spellings Buonaparte and Bonaparte, Scott (1827/3: 4, n. *) wrote, 'There was an absurd debate about the spelling of the name, which became, as trifles often do, a sort of party question. Buonaparte had disused the superfluous *u*, which his father retained in the name, and adopted a more modern spelling. This was represented on one side as an attempt to bring his name more nearly to the French idiom; and, as if it had been a matter of the last moment, the vowel was obstinately replaced in the name, by a class of writers who deemed it politic not to permit the successful General to relinquish the slightest mark of his Italian extraction, which was in every respect impossible for him either to conceal or to deny, even if he had nourished such an idea. In his baptismal register, his name is spelled Napoleone Bonaparte, though the father subscribes, Carlo Buonaparte. The spelling seems to have been quite indifferent.'

(Wednesday, 6 February, 1799), and 'Latest Foreign Intelligence. Vienna, Nov. 11,' *The Spectator* (Saturday, 9 February, 1799): 'A letter from Florence, dated the 21st of October, inserted in the [Austrian] Court Gazette of this day, contains the following intelligence: "The French Vice-Admiral, Blanquet,[15] who was obliged to surrender to the English in the battle of Abucker, has arrived here....Admiral Blanquet stated that Buonaparte had nothing left but to leave Egypt to penetrate through Syria, to cross the Tygris and the Euphrates, and to march through Persia to the East Indies, an enterprize which, however, it woiuld be necessary to attempt before the Turks could assemble in Syria, in sufficient numbers to oppose his passage.'

8.10 'Untitled,' *New-Jersey Journal* (Tuesday, 12 February, 1799) and 'Baltimore, Feb. 2,' *Impartial Herald* (Tuesday, 19 February, 1799): 'By European papers we find every thing still enveloped in doubts and darkness, ascertainable only by the vagueness of conjecture. Of Buonaparte, although letters have been received at Hamburgh as late as the seventh November, from Constantinople, nothing certain can be learnt, either as to his position, or his actual or intended operations—One account states his army to be encamped near Cairo, surrounded by Arabs, while another asserts that having driven the Beys and Mamelukes into Asyssinia! he is making rapid strides, some say for Constantinople, others for the Tigris, and that the Khans of Persia viewing his rapid approach, have offered him men and necessaries to overthrow the British possessions in the east. What the real operations and intentions of this general may eventuate in, time only can reveal. At present it is in vain we look for any thing like truth and authenticity in our accounts respecting him.'

8.11 'The Foreign News,' *The Gazette* [Portland ME] (Monday, 18 February, 1799): 'The foreign news, is so imperfect and contradictory as to afford nothing certain or satisfactory as to present or future operations. The last news from the continent of Europe, leaves every thing enveloped in darkness, and the most important events are mentioned without authority. Something authentic, it is hoped, will shortly transpire to clear up our doubts.

Of Buonaparte, although letters have been received at Hamburgh as late as November 7, from Constantinople, nothing certain can be learnt, either as to his position, or his actual or intended operations—One account states his army to be encamped near Cairo, surrounded by Arabs, while another asserts that having driven the beys and mamelukes into *Abyssinia!* he is making rapid strides, some say for Constantinople, others for the Tigris, and that the khans of Persia viewing his rapid march, have offered him men and necessaries to overthrow the British possessions in the east. What the real operations and intentions of this would-be Alexander may eventuate in, time only can reveal.'

---

[15] Armand Simon Marie Blanquet du Chayla (1759–1826), 'né à Marvéjols (Lozère)...se distingua pendant la guerre d'Amérique, puis à Aboukir, où il commandait une division de la flotte française; quitta le service en 1803; reçut de Louis XVIII le titre de comte.' See Wimpffen (1900: 19, n. 1).

8.12 'From the Aurora,' *Supplement to the Commercial Advertiser* (Tuesday, 19 March, 1799), 'From the Aurora,' *The Spectator* (Wednesday, 20 March, 1799), 'Untitled,' *The Universal Gazette* (Thursday, 21 March, 1799), 'Untitled,' *The Centinel of Liberty, and George-Town and Washington Advertiser* (Tuesday, 26 March, 1799), 'From the Aurora,' *The Salem Gazette* (Tuesday, 26 March, 1799), 'From the Aurora,' *American Mercury* (Thursday, 28 March, 1799), 'March 22d,' *The Herald of Liberty* (Monday, 1 April, 1799) and 'Philadelphia, March 18,' *City Gazette and Commercial Daily Advertiser* (Saturday, 6 April, 1799): 'Letters have been received in this city from Hamburgh, of date the 12th of January—which contain particulars of a very interesting nature concerning the grand expedition under Buonaparte, who, it appears, had in November complete and undisturbed possession of Egypt and Syria....That the communication with Persia had been opened, and two Wakeels[16] had arrived at Cairo from the Sultan of Mysore.[17] That war had commenced in India between the natives and the British, and that French officers had been sent to Randeish/Kandeith[18] and the countries bordering on the Caspian sea to lead a vast army into Hindustan.'[19]

8.13 'Miscellaneous and Informing. England,' *The Newburyport Herald and Country Gazette* (Tuesday, 3 September, 1799), 'Official. Operations of Buonaparte,' *Thomas's Massachusetts Spy, or Worcester Gazette* (Wednesday, 4 September, 1799), 'Miscellaneous and Informing. England,' *The Providence Journal, and Town and Country Advertiser* (Wednesday, 4 September, 1799), 'Miscellaneous and Informing. London, July 2,' *The Philadelphia Gazette & Universal Daily Advertiser* (Thursday, 5 September, 1799), 'Miscellaneous and Informing. London, July 2,' *United States Chronicle* (Thursday, 5 September, 1799), 'England,' *Federal Galaxy* (Monday, 9 September, 1799), 'Latest Foreign Intelligence. London, July 2,' *New-Jersey Journal* (Tuesday, 10 September, 1799), 'Miscellaneous and Informing,' *Berkshire Gazette* (Wednesday, 11 September, 1799), 'Late Foreign News,' *The Oracle of the Day* (Saturday, 14 September, 1799) and 'By the last Mail...London July 2,' *The Herald of Liberty* (Monday, 16 September, 1799; second paragraph only): ['July 2.—The dispatches received overland from India to which we alluded yesterday, are dated Bombay, sixth March, and contain letters from Benares, dated the 15th January....] Zemaun Shah, who for some time had been in a hostile

---

[16] Persian *vakil*, i.e. viceroy, deputy, representative of the ruler and sometimes head of finance. Cf. 6.130 and 6.143 for Karim Khan Zand's use of this title.

[17] Tipu Sultan (1753–1799), ruler of Mysore (Mysuru). For his life see Brown (1849: 33ff).

[18] Kandeish, a district in the Bombay Presidency. 'To the Eastward of Surat and Southward of Malûa is the province of Kandish, to which that of Berar is found to be annex'd....Berar is to the Eastward of Kandish....Brampur, the capital of Kandish, is a great town, near the head of the river Tapti.... One of the two roads leading from Surat to Agra, passes through Brampur.' See Herbert (1759: 37).

[19] Much has been written of Napoleon's designs on British India. See e.g. the long chapter entitled 'Napoléon Ier et ses projets sur l'Hindoustan' in Gaffarel (1908: 349–424).

8 The Early Career of Fath 'Ali Shah (1798–1804)

position, and seemed to threaten some of the company's possessions,[20] had altered his situation, and retreated on the fourth of January from Lahore into his own country,[21] Persia. He seems to have been induced to take this step from his two brothers[22] having appeared in arms in the neighborhood of Herat, which rather disconcerted him.[23]

---

[20] Zaman Shah Durrani (r. 1793–1800) of Afghanistan. For his career see e.g. Elphinstone (1815: 564ff). As Kaye (1856/1: 90) noted, 'The invasion of Zemaun Shah, the weak and ambitious ruler of the country now known as Afghanistan, was at that time an old bugbear. Year after year had the Douranee [Durrani] monarch threatened a descent upon Hindostan; but his expeditions, which rose in blustering pomp, had ever set in ludicrous failure. The danger was great in our eyes; but only because it was remote and shadowy.'

[21] As Milburn (1813: lxxxiii) noted, 'The empire of Hindostan being threatened with invasion by Zemaun Shah, an embassy was sent from Bengal to Persia, which was received with honour, and succeeded in the principal objects of its mission. The King of Persia was not only induced to attack Khorosan, which had the effect of withdrawing Zemaun Shah from his designs upon India, but entered into treaties of political and commercial alliance with the British Government, which, while they completely excluded the French nation from Persia, gave the English every benefit which they could derive from the connexion.' Similarly, in his biographical sketch on Malcolm, Philippart (1823: 470–471) observed, 'Shortly after the termination of the Mysore war [4 May, 1799; see Hamilton (1828: 271)], and the arrangements of the conquered territory were completed, it was deemed expedient that a mission should proceed from the Supreme government of India to Baba Khan [Fath 'Ali Shah], in order to ascertain the intentions and power of that prince, and more particularly of Zemaun Shaw; and, under the apprehension that the latter was meditating the invasion of Hindostan, to engage the court of Persia to act with vigour and decision against either him or the French, should either attempt to penetrate to India through any part of the Persian territories.' Elphinstone (1815: 568–569) noted of Zaman Shah, 'In his foreign policy, his first object ought to have been to defend Khorassaun' from Persian attempts to reconquer it, but instead he 'made no serious effort to save Khorassaun; and his ill-directed and ill-timed attempts at Indian conquest, tended only to frustrate that favourite object of his ambition. . . . The rest of Shauh Zemaun's reign was spent in attempts to invade India, from which he was always recalled by the pressure of the dangers which he had left unprovided for in the west.'

[22] One of Mehdi 'Ali Khan's goals on his embassy from the Governor of Bombay to Fath 'Ali Shah (see below) had been 'to hurry the advance upon Affghanistan of Prince Mahmoud and Prince Ferooz-shah, two brothers of the monarch of Cabul, who were at that time refugees seeking the aid of Fetteh Ali against their relative.' See Watson (1866: 123–124).

[23] According to Malcolm, 'Zemaun Shah. . .was necessitated to retreat, to prevent the threatened attack of Mahomed Khan, Khujjur [Agha Mohammad Shah], on the province of Herat. Since that we have received accounts that Mahomed Khan has fallen under the blow of an assassin. If this prove true, it will leave the Candahar Prince much at liberty to execute his favorite projects.' See Kaye (1856: 90). Is this a confusion for Mohammad, Zaman Shah's brother? According to Watson (1866: 120), 'Prince Mahomed, the brother of Zeman Shah of Cabul, and the grandson of the founder of the Affghan kingdom, had taken refuge in Persia. He now wrote [to Fath 'Ali Shah] to ask for help in recovering the government of Herat, which province he offered to hold under the orders of the Shah, whom he further offered to serve in extending his dominion in the direction of Turkestan. The Shah accordingly gave him the troops he required, and with their aid he succeeded in establishing himself at Herat.'

It is thought by many well informed people, that Buonaparte's next object,[24] had he succeeded immediately on his reaching Egypt, would have been not to have sailed down the Red Sea, as was for some time talked of, but to have marched an army into Persia, which would have been joined by Zemaun Shah, who had for some time been making preparations to facilitate the approach of the expected French army.'

8.14 'From the Madras Courier. June 8,' *Gazette of the United States, and Philadelphia Daily Advertiser* (Saturday, 9 November, 1799), 'From the Madras Courier. June 8,' *Connecticut Journal* (Thursday, 14 November, 1799), 'From the Madras Courier. June 8, *The Centinel of Liberty, and George-Town and Washington Advertiser* (Friday, 15 November, 1799), 'From the Madras Courier. June 8,' *The Maryland Herald and Elizabeth-Town Advertiser* (Thursday, 21 November, 1799), 'East-Indies. Madras, May 15,' *The Vergennes Gazette and Vermont and New-York Advertiser* (Thursday, 28 November, 1799) and 'Madras, June 2,' *City Gazette and Daily Advertiser* (Thursday, 28 November, 1799): 'By the Arab ship Suffenutal Nubec, arrived [at Madras] on the sixth inst. in eleven days from Muscat, we learn that when she left that port, some Dows had arrived there from a port or ports of Tippoo's[25] coast,[26] with three Elephants and a casket of jewels, intended to be offered by that prince to the present Regent or king of Persia[27]; and, thro' the same channel of intelligence, we learn that Tippoo's agents had spread a report at Muscat of his having given a very serious defeat to our army, as, in his hyperbolical language, to have made it fly for many coss.[28] These circumstances afford, were it

---

[24] In Napoleon's *Commentaries*, written during his captivity on St. Helena, he wrote, 'The invasion of India from Egypt is worked out with detail, and the attempt is made to treat the entire Expedition to Egypt as in the nature of a preparatory move toward an ultimate destination beyond the Indus.' See Dennis (1901: 209).

[25] Tipu Sultan.

[26] The coast of Karnataka, west of the capital Mysuru.

[27] Fath 'Ali Shah. Ekbal (1982a: 40) suggested that, at almost the exact moment as Malcolm was travelling to Tehran, representatives of Zaman Shah and Tipu Sultan were in Tehran in order to forge a unified anti-English front. Whether this was Zaman Shah's intention is doubtful. According to Watson (1866: 124), 'Zeman Shah...caused his vizeer to send an officer to Haji Ibraheem, the prime minister of Persia, with a request that Fetteh Ali would make over to Affghanistan the province of Khorassan,' but Fath 'Ali Shah 'instructed his minister to reply that it was his intention to restore the south-eastern limits of Persia to the condition in which they had existed in the time of the Sefaveean Shahs: that is, he proposed to overrun, and to retain possession of, Herat, Merve, Balkh, Cabul, Candahar, Thibet, Kashgar and Seistan. Nor was this meant to be an idle threat; for orders were at once given for the royal forces to assemble at Tehran.'

[28] Anglo-Indian term, 'The most usual popular measure of distance in India, but like the mile in Europe, and indeed like the mile within the British Islands up to a recent date, varying much in different localities.' It corresponded to c. 2 mi. in the Bengal Presidency, 2.25 mi. in Madras and 4 mi. in Madras. See Yule and Burnell (1903: 261).

necessary, additional proofs of the vigilance of our late enemy, and of his inveterate animosity to the British name.'

8.15 'No. 1 of a Brief History, of the Political State of the World, at the last dates. Asia,' *Columbian Centinel & Massachusetts Federalist* (Saturday, 16 November, 1799), '[No. 1.] Brief History of the Political State of the World, at the last dates. Asia,' *The Daily Advertiser* (Friday, 22 November, 1799), 'No. 1 of a Brief History, of the Political State of the World, at the last dates. Asia,' *The Philadelphia Gazette & Universal Daily Advertiser* (Friday, 22 November, 1799), 'No. 1 of a Brief History, of the Political State of the World, at the last dates. Asia,' *Greenfield Gazette* (Saturday, 23 November, 1799), 'No. 1 of a Brief History, of the Political State of the World, at the last dates. Asia,' *The Connecticut Courant* (Monday, 25 November, 1799), 'No. 1 of a Brief History, of the Political State of the World, at the last dates. Asia,' *Farmers' Museum, or Lay Preacher's Gazette* (Monday, 25 November, 1799), 'No. 1 of a Brief History, of the Political State of the World, at the last dates. Asia,' *The Middlesex Gazette* (Friday, 29 November, 1799), 'No. 1 of a Brief History, of the Political State of the World, at the last dates. Asia,' *New-Hampshire Sentinel* (Saturday, 30 November, 1799), 'No. 1 of a Brief History, of the Political State of the World, at the last dates. Asia,' *Columbian Minerva* (Thursday, 5 December, 1799), 'Brief History, of the Political State of the World, at the last dates. Asia,' *The Green Mountain Patriot* (Friday, 6 December, 1799) and 'No. 1 of a Brief History, of the Political State of the World, at the last dates. Asia,' *The Spectator* (Saturday, 7 December, 1799): 'Of Persia, and its extensive Provinces, we know but little which we can give in abstract; nor is it essential to our plan, we should know much.'

8.16 'Asiatic Intelligence. Jan. 29,' *Massachusetts Mercury* (Friday, 1 August, 1800): 'On the 29th ultimo [29 December, 1799], departed from Bombay,[29] Captain John Malcolm,[30] on his Embassy to the Court of Persia.[31] Captain Malcolm with his suite[32] embarked on the

---

[29] There is some confusion regarding the date. The date of departure given here is also the date given in Kaye (1856/1: 105). However, according to Anonymous (1801a), Malcolm and his mission departed on board the *Bombay* 'on the fourth of January last.'

[30] John Malcolm (1769–1833). He sailed from Scotland to India at the age of only 13, joining the Madras Establishment as an ensign in 1781 and rising to Major-General in 1819. See Philippart (1823: 469, n. *).

[31] According to Watson (1866: 126), the success of Mehdi 'Ali Khan's embassy to Fath 'Ali Shah in provoking a Qajar attack on Zaman Shah 'had not been known at Calcutta when the Earl of Mornington selected Captain Malcolm for the purpose of proceeding to the Court of Tehran.' Lord Mornington appointed Malcolm as 'Envoy to the Court of Persia,' in early August, 1799. See Kaye (1856/1: 89).

[32] Malcolm's suite included Capt. William Campbell, First Assistant; Lt. Charles Pasley and Mr. Richard Strachey, Assistants; Lt. John Colebrooke, commander of the escort; Mr. Gilbert Briggs, surgeon; and Mr. William Hollingbery, writer. See Kaye (1856/1: 105).

Honorable Company's frigate the *Bombay*,[33] under the salute of the garrison; and the same compliment on their going on board.'

8.17 'Asiatic News,' *The Salem Impartial Register* (Monday, 4 August, 1800) and 'By the *Perseverance*, Capt. Wheatland, from *Calcutta*,' *Windham Herald* (Thursday, 7 August, 1800): 'Jan. 30. On the 29th Dec. [1799] Capt. Malcolm, left Bombay, on his embassy to the Court of Persia. He and his suite embarked in the Bombay frigate.'

8.18 'Latest Foreign Intelligence. London, June 10,' *Commercial Advertiser* (Wednesday, 6 August, 1800) and 'Untitled,' *Gazette of the United States, and Daily Advertiser* (Thursday, 7 August, 1800): 'We are informed by late private letters from Bengal, that captain Malcolm, formerly one of the Secretaries to the Commissioners for the affairs of Mysore,[34] had been deputed on an Embassy to the Court of Persia, accompanied by Mirza Ally Khan.[35] It is reported that this deputation is sent thither in consequence of Zemaun Shah's evacuation of the Panjeb.'[36]

8.19 'Foreign. August 1,' *Connecticut Gazette, and the Commercial Intelligencer* (Wednesday, 24 September, 1800): 'It appears by a private letter lately received from the East-Indies, that Zemaun Shah retired into Persia on the 3d of November last. The cause of relinquishing his hostile intentions in Hindostan is attributed solely to the remonstrances made by our government to the court of Persia. Col. Malcolm, it is further said has been entrusted with an important mission to the court of Persia, which has for its object the future tranquility of Asia.'

---

[33] Commanded by Capt. William Selby, the *Bombay* was escorted by the brig *Harrington* and left Bombay on 29 December 1799. See Kaye (1856/1: 105).

[34] Malcolm, at the time Assistant to Capt. James Achilles Kirkpatrick, the Resident at Hyderabad, was appointed jointly with Capt. Thomas Munro Secretary on the Commission including Sir Arthur Wellesley and Col. Barry Close 'to settle finally the Mysore Government' as well as the 'division of the territories of Mysore, and the investiture of the young Rajah with the government of that country.' He received news of this on 30 May 1799. See Kaye (1856/1: 87); Philippart (1823: 469).

[35] Mirza Mehdi 'Ali Khan Khorasani. In a letter of 23 August 1799 to Jonathan Duncan, Malcolm requested that 'such parts of the correspondence of Mr. Manesty, Mr. Jones, Mehedi Ali Khan, and others, relating to Persia, as you conceive would be useful to me, to be extracted for my perusal.' According to Kaye (1856/1: 94, n. *), 'Mehedi Ali Khan was a Persian, long employed in the Company's service, whom Mr. Duncan had despatched to Persia with letters to the King.' On his mission, see Kaye (1856/1: 114–115, 513–515); Busse (1972: 91).

[36] 'Captain Malcolm was charged to make some arrangement for relieving India from the annual alarm occasioned by the threatened invasion of Zeman Shah; to counteract any possible designs which the French nation might entertain with regard to Persia; and to endeavour to restore to somewhat of its former prosperity a trade which had been in a great degree lost.' See Watson (1866: 126–127).

8.20 'Untitled,' *Gazette of the United States, and Daily Advertiser* (Saturday, 22 November, 1800), 'Untitled,' *Mercantile Advertiser* (Tuesday, 25 November, 1800), 'Untitled,' *The New York Gazette General Advertiser* (Wednesday, 26 November, 1800), 'Foreign Articles,' *Jenks' Portland Gazette* (Monday, 8 December, 1800) and 'Untitled,' *Maryland Herald* (Tuesday, 9 December, 1800): 'A singular character has lately appeared in Paris. He calls himself the son of Charok Shaw,[37] late king of Persia, Governor of the Province of Guilan, and brother of the reigning King, who took possession of the Throne in the room of his father, who had become blind through illness.—The Orientalists of Paris have pronounced him an impostor, as they assert that Charok Shaw, who was the grandson of Nadir Shaw, and who reigned nearly fifty years in the Chorassan, never was King of Persia, never lost his eyes, nor ever was succeeded by a son.'[38]

8.21 'Bombay, March 3. Colonel Malcolm's Embassy to the Court of Persia,' *Poulson's American Daily Advertiser* (Wednesday, 10 December, 1800), 'Bombay, March 3. Colonel Malcolm's Embassy to the Court of Persia,' *The Philadelphia Gazette* (Saturday, 13 December, 1800), 'Bombay, March 3. Colonel Malcolm's Embassy to the Court of Persia,' *The Centinel of Freedom* (Tuesday, 16 December, 1800), 'Bombay, March 3. Colonel Malcolm's Embassy to the Court of Persia,' *The National Intelligencer, and Washington Advertiser* (Wednesday, 17 December, 1800), 'Bombay, March 3. Colonel Malcolm's Embassy to the Court of Persia,' *Washington Federalist* (Thursday, 18 December, 1800) and 'Bombay, March 3. Colonel Malcolm's Embassy to the Court

---

[37] Nader Mirza, 'the son of Shahrukh, and the great-grandson of Nadir Shah. That prince, on the occasion of the visit of Aga Mahomed to Khorassan, had taken refuge with the Affghans, and on the death of the first Kajar Shah he had returned to Khorassan, and assembled troops about his person.' When it was clear that he was no match for Fath 'Ali's forces, which had already stormed Nishapur and Turbat, 'The disconcerted prince tendered his submission, received the Shah's pardon, and gave his daughter in marriage to a Kajar general; by which alliance the feud between the two princely houses was put an end to.' See Watson (1866: 121). According to Hasan-e Fasa'i, 'When the royal army arrived in the vicinity of Mashhad, Nāder Mirzā, ruler of Khorasan, son of blind Shāhrokh Shāh, son of Reżā Qoli Mirzā, son of Nāder Shāh, fled to Afghanistan, deserting his blind father.' See Busse (1972: 69). 'After the death of the shah...Nāder Mirzā went from Herāt to Mashhad without being disturbed by anybody. The inhabitants of Mashhad accepted his authority....After the royal army marched off from Nishāpur, the shah [Fath 'Ali Shah] gave orders to encamp outside Mashhad, Nāder Mirzā sitting behind the fortifications and the rampart of the town.' After the entry of caravans with food had been blocked, 'a group of Reżavi seiyeds, ulema and sheikhs came out of the town to ask for pardon on behalf of themselves and of Nāder Mirzā...The shah...accepted Nāder Mirzā's request, and allowed them to return. Nāder Mirzā was pardoned and given the robe of honor befitting such an occasion.' This occurred shortly before 17 August 1799. See Busse (1972: 89, 91).

[38] Nader Mirza was certainly never in Paris, but his father certainly was king of Persia, albeit in a truncated fashion; did have his eyes put out; and in a sense Nader succeeded Shahrokh in the government of Khorasan. Cf. Malcolm (1829: 55–56), Watson (1866: 94–95) and some of the articles cited above on Shahrokh Shah. Nader Mirza was arrested in late March, 1803 and, 'After a trial he and some of his brothers were executed.' See Busse (1972: 105).

of Persia,' *Kline's Carlisle Weekly Gazette* (Wednesday, 24 December, 1800): 'Yesterday afternoon[39] anchored in the harbour [of Bombay], the Hon. Company's frigate the Bombay, captain Selby,[40] last from Abu Sherer.[41] The frigate had a tolerable good passage to Muscat, at which place she arrived on the eighth of January [1800], the Imaum[42] was not present, having proceeded on a military expedition to Ormus.[43] Syfe Byn Mahomen, the governor,[44] paid Colonel Malcolm a visit, which was returned with the requisite ceremony; and on the 12th, after taking in a supply of water and fresh provisions, they sailed for Ormus,[45] at which once celebrated island they arrived on the 14th, after a quick and agreeable passage of two days. This place has lately received considerable repairs from

---

[39] The original article (Anonymous 1800b) is from a letter dated 'Bombay, March 5,' hence 'yesterday afternoon' ought to be 4 March 1800, not 2 March, as would be implied by the datelines in the American press. 'March 3' is a misreading of 'March 5.'

[40] William Selby 'of the hon. Company's marine of this establishment [Bombay]' and sometime 'commodore on the Surat station.' See Anonymous (1803a).

[41] Bandar-e Bushehr.

[42] The Al Bu Sa'id ruler Seyyid Sultan ibn Ahmed (r. 1792–1803; see Markham 1874: 426). Busse (1972: 317) gives the name as 'Seiyid Solṭān.'

[43] According to Kelly (1968: 70), 'Saiyid Sultan was away, cruising in search of Qasimi pirates in his frigate Gunjava at the entrance to the Gulf.' As Badger (1871: lvi) noted, in the EIC treaties of 1798 and 1800 'Sultân is styled "Imaum," as well by his own as by the British representative. I can only account for this fact on the supposition that both parties believed him to be virtually possessed of the implied authority; but it is certain, nevertheless, that the title [Imam] is never given to him in the author's [Salil ibn Razik] narrative of his regency. He is uniformly referred to as "the Seyyid Sultân."'

[44] Sayf bin Mohammad. As Miles (1919/2: 292–293) noted, 'On anchoring in the harbour the *Bombay* was visited by the Governor of the town, Saif bin Mohammed, who came to call on Captain Malcolm, and stated that Sultan was absent on an expedition against the Attoobees ['Utub] and that his return was uncertain. Captain Malcolm returned the Governor's visit the following day, and then having landed Dr. Bogle and installed him in his appointment set sail for Hormuz in search of Sultan.' According to Kaye (1856/1: 106), 'The Governor (Syfe Ben Mohamed) was a man of intelligence and experience, who knew the English and their Government well; he had made thirty-six voyages, of which sixteen had been to Bombay, and one to Calcutta; and he had sense enough to estimate the magnitude of our resources, and the advantages, both political and commercial, to Muscat of an alliance with so powerful a state.'

[45] As Kaye (1856/1: 108–109) noted, after visiting Sayf bin Mohammad, Malcolm and his suite 'took ship again and set off in pursuit of the Imaum, whom he had expected to find at Ormus. But when he reached that island, he found that the Prince, after reducing the neighbouring island of Kishm [Qeshm], had sailed for Jalfa [Julfar], on the Arabian side of the Gulf. Malcolm, however, once on the track, was not likely to give up the pursuit; so, after exploring on foot a great part of the "once celebrated island," and collecting all the information that could be gathered, re-embarked on board the *Bombay*.'

the Imaum of Muscat,[46] who obtained possession of it about four years ago—.[47] What is peculiarly remarkable is that not a single spring of *fresh* water is to be found in the Island, which is 15 miles in circumference. Streams of *salt* water[48] are seen running in every direction from the mountains, on the banks of which the finest salt grows in thick flakes, having much the appearance of frozen snow. Many of the hills seem composed entirely of salt, and the whole soil of the island is strongly impregnated with that and sulphur,[49] which occasions the intense heats so prevalent there.—After quitting Ormus, the Bombay frigate proceeded to Kishum,[50] where Col. Malcolm had an interview with the Imaum of Muscat, on board his ship the Ganjava, of 32 guns.[51] After their departure from that place, they had

---

[46] Seyyid Sultan bin Ahmad. See Badger (1871: 213ff). Several decades later, as Berghaus (1832: 47) observed, the fort was 'in leidlichem Zustande.' Moreover, Stiffe (1874: 16) noted, that after gaining possession of Hormuz from the Portuguese in 1622, 'The place was utterly ruined by the Persians, who wished to transfer the trade to their new port, Bandar 'Abbasi, and has since remained in the same state. Even the building material appears to have been carried away and used for the new settlement at Bandar 'Abbasi.' Kleiss (1978: 172–173) noted a second and third phase of construction, following the original building of the fort, which he could not date. Perhaps the last of these represents the Omani repairs referred to here.

[47] According to the chronicle of Salil bin Raziq, sometime prior to 1799, 'Sultân attacked...el-Kásum [Kishm], and reduced it. Then, after a reconciliation was effected betwixt him and the Benu-Mâîn, the people of el-Kásum, he attacked it again; he also attacked Hormûz, the port of which island belonged to Mullah Hásan, el-Mâîny, and took both places. These successes increased his renown and whetted his thirst for conquest.' See Badger (1871: 226). Cf. Ross (1883: 24). As Miles (1919/2: 287) noted, after seizing control of Chabahar, 'Sultan next sent an expedition against the Beni Naeem of Kishm and Hormuz, who had given him much provocation. This enterprise he commanded in person and with such skill that his conquest of the islands was complete.'

[48] Cf. Pedro Teixeira's description of Hormuz [orig. Jarun] from 1587, 'Es gibt auf dieser Insel drei ausdauernde Quellen, die am Fuße der Bergkette an verschiedenen Orten liegen; daraus gehen drei Bäche mit klarem reinem Wasser hervor, dieses ist aber so salzig wie Meerwasser.' See Schwarz (1914: 536).

[49] Teixeira wrote, 'There is plenty of good rock-salt, and very pure sulphur, whereof, during my stay, there were found mines, and much got out of them.' See Sinclair (1902: 164).

[50] Qeshm.

[51] Cf. Hollingbery (1814: 10), who called it 'the Gunjava of 32 guns.' According to Phipps (1840: 178), the Gunjava was built at Rangoon in 1786 and 'broken up at Calcutta' in 1820. Malcolm (1827/1: 13) described the incident recorded here as follows: 'we had been introduced to him [Saiyid Sultan, Imam of Muscat] on board the Ganjava, his flag ship, of a thousand tons burthen, and carrying forty guns.' Kelly (1968: 70) wrote that, because Seyyid Sultan was absent from Muscat chasing al-Qasimi pirates, 'Malcolm followed him, and on 17 January he fell in with Sultan off Hanjam Island. He had a long conversation with him, in which he dwelt insistently upon the extent of British power in India, enhanced now by the defeat of Tipu. Sultan, in reply, made the most cordial professions of friendship for the British. Malcolm then introduced to him Surgeon Archibald Bogle, of the Bombay establishment, expressing the hope that Sultan would accept him as the Company's agent at Muscat. Sultan had not taken up the offer made to him by Jonathan Duncan in 1798 of the services of "a regular bred surgeon", but he had lately been reported as desiring to have an English physician by him. Sultan now accepted Bogle without demur, both as private physician and as political agent, and the arrangement

an untoward wind for some time, which however, became more favourable, and enabled them to run as far as Karrack,[52] as the breeze was too fresh to permit of their anchoring in Bushire. At Karrack they stayed only one day,[53] and next morning, the wind becoming moderate, the whole of the embassy arrived in safety at Abu Sherer,[54] from which place the frigate was dispatched. Every arrangement having been made for the suite of the embassy, Col. Malcolm was expected to move without loss of time, to fulfil the object of the embassy—the costly presents and baggage were immediately sent forward under a strong escort.'[55]

8.22 'Asiatic Articles,' *The Mercury and New-England Palladium* (Friday, 9 January, 1801), 'Foreign Intelligence. From Asia,' *The Observer* [Haverhill MA] (Friday, 16 January, 1801), 'Asiatic Articles,' *The Courier* (Wednesday, 28 January, 1801) and 'Untitled,' *Federal Gazette and Baltimore Daily Advertiser* (Tuesday, 10 February, 1801): 'Col. Malcolm, has been sent by the English East India Company on an embassy to the Court of *Persia*. In proceeding in a ship to *Abu Sherer*, from which he was to commence his journey, he stopped at the island of *Ormus*; of which a person who was with him, observes, "It is peculiarly remarkable, that not a single spring of *fresh* water is to be found in the island, which is 15 miles round.—Streams of *salt* water are seen running in every direction from the mountains, on the banks of which the finest salt grows in thick flakes, having much the appearance of frozen snow. Many of the hills seem composed intirely of salt, and the whole soil of the island is strongly impregnated with that and sulphur, which occasions the intense heat so prevalent there."

8.23 'Untitled,' *Federal Gazette & Baltimore Daily Advertiser* (Thursday, 12 February, 1801), 'Untitled,' *The Virginia Argus* (Tuesday, 24 February, 1801) and 'New London, March 4,' *Connecticut Gazette, and the Commercial Intelligencer* (Wednesday, 4 March, 1801): 'A late London paper says—The trade expected to be opened with Persia is likely to be very lucrative. That country—(once the most florishing [sic] and powerful in the world,

---

was confirmed in an agreement drawn up and signed on 18 January 1800.' According to this document, an 'English gentleman of respectability, on the part of the Honourable Company, shall always reside at the port of Máskat, and be an agent through whom all the intercourse between the states shall be conducted.' See Badger (1871: lvi).

[52] Khark.

[53] Kaye (1856/1: 110) makes no mention of a stop at Khark, noting only that after Malcolm concluded his negotiations with Seyyid Sultan, 'Malcolm steered his course for Bushire' and 'On the first of February he entered that port.'

[54] Bushehr.

[55] As noted above, Malcolm and his suite did not succeed in leaving Bushehr until the latter part of May and thus spent almost four months there before proceeding to Shiraz. Nor were the presents and baggage sent on. Rather, when 22 May arrived and Malcolm was ready to proceed, the party included, as pack animals, 27 camels and 346 mules. As Kaye (1856/1: 116, n. ‡), observed, 'The presents alone found employment for a large proportion of the camels and mules.'

though now little known beyond the route of travellers going to or coming from the East-Indies)—abounds in gold and silver mines, which have not been worked for a number of years, owing to the want of fuel.'[56]

8.24 'Latest from Europe. From London papers to the ninth of February, received by the ship Liberty, Woodham, from Liverpool. January 27,' *Mercantile Advertiser* (Tuesday, 24 March, 1801), 'Latest Foreign Intelligence. Further Details of News received by the Ship Liberty, Captain Woodham, in 38 days from Liverpool. January 27,' *American Citizen and General Advertiser* (Wednesday, 25 March, 1801), 'Further Foreign Intelligence. [By an arrival at New-York with London dates to February 9.] England. London, Jan. 27,' *The Albany Centinel* (Tuesday, 31 March, 1801), 'Latest Foreign News. By arrivals at Boston, and New-York. January 27,' *Connecticut Gazette, and the Commercial Intelligencer* (Wednesday, 1 April, 1801), 'Foreign Articles. Madrid, Jan. 27,' *The Salem Impartial Register* (Monday, 6 April, 1801) and 'Late & Important Foreign Intelligence. [Further—by an arrival at Newyork, with London dates to February 9.]. London, Jan. 27,' *Weekly Wanderer* (Saturday, 11 April, 1801): 'It is reported that a very plended [sic, splendid] embassy from the French Republic to the King of Persia[57] is to take place in the course of this year. A brother of the Chief Consul[58] is said to have the appointment of ambassador;[59] but citizen[60] de Sacy, the celebrated Persian scholar,[61] is to prepare the way

---

[56] Cf. Tavernier (1678: 143), 'There are also some Mines of Gold and Silver in *Persia*, wherein it appears that they have anciently wrought. *Sha-Abas* also try'd again, but found his expence to be more than his profit: whence it is become a Proverb in *Persia*, *Nokre Kerven dehkrarge nohhassel*; The Silver-Mine of *Kerven*, where they spend ten to get nine, which is the reason that all the Gold and Silver of *Persia* comes out of Foreign Countries.' Cf. Tavernier (1718: 619–620), 'Il est constant qu'il y a eu anciennement en Perse des mines d'or & d'argent, dont il paroît encore des marques en quelques endroits dans de grands bouleversemens de terres & de rochers: Mais depuis que l'or & l'argent se sont rendus communs, par la quantité d'or qui sort du Royaume des Abyssins, de l'Isle de Sumatra, de la Chine & de plusieurs autres lieux, comme je diray au discours des Mines dans mes relations des Indes; & par les flotes d'argent qui viennent du Perou, & celuy que le grand commerce des soyes fait sortit du Japon, d'où l'on tire aussi une bonne quantité d'or; depuis ce temps-là, dis je, les Persans ont negligé de rechercher des mines dans leurs païs, & se contentent des especes d'or & d'argent qui leur viennent de l'Europe, dequoy j'ay parlé amplement dans le discours des monnoyes.' For sources known in the nineteenth century see e.g. Tietze (1879: 648–650); Houtum-Schindler (1881: 178–180)

[57] Fath 'Ali Shah.

[58] Napoleon Bonaparte, titled 'First Consul' during the brief First Republic (1799–1804).

[59] Napoleon's older brother Joseph Bonaparte (1768–1844) who, in 1800 and 1801 undertook diplomatic missions involving the United States, Austria and Great Britain. He did not, however, go to Iran.

[60] For the title 'citizen' in France during and after the French Revolution, see Gross (1999: 73–76).

[61] Antoine-Isaac Silvestre de Sacy (1758–1838), renowned French Orientalist.

Fig. 8.2 Antoine-Isaac Silvestre de Sacy. Lithograph by François-Séraphin Delpech after a portrait by Antoine Maurin. Yale University Art Gallery, CC0 1.0 Universal

by setting out some months before.[62] This embassy is to be joined at Petersburgh by one equally magnificent from the Emperor Paul[63]; and both are to proceed by the usual rout [sic, route] of Allracan [sic, Astrakhan] and the Northern Provinces of Persia to the residence of the King.'[64] (Fig. 8.2).

8.25 'Foreign Articles. Collected from Papers received by arrivals sometime since. England. London, Jan. 27,' *The Mercury and New-England Palladium* (Friday, 3 April, 1801) and 'Foreign. London, Jan. 27,' *The Salem Impartial Register* (Thursday, 9 April,

---

[62] Silvestre de Sacy made no such journey. According to Dehérain 1918: 33, 'Jamais Silvestre de Sacy n'alla dans les pays orientaux. L'épisode de son exploration des archives de Gènes [a department of the French Empire with its capital at Genoa] en 1805 mis à part, toute sa vie s'écoula sous le ciel de l'Ile-de-France, à Paris l'hiver et l'été à Ognes, près de Nanteuil-le-Haudouin.'

[63] No such Russian diplomatic mission was sent by Paul I to Persia. For his diplomatic efforts in Asia see Atkin (1979); Tsvetkova (2017).

[64] Tehran, Fath 'Ali Shah's capital.

1801): 'By the late mission from Bombay to Shiras, the commercial relations between the Company and Persia, have been extended and strengthened, and the King,[65] in manifestation of the close and friendly connection thus promoted, has enjoined all his subjects, and particularly Imaum Seyd Sultaun,[66] who had been suspected of favoring the interests of France,[67] under severe penalties to abstain from all intercourse commercial or political with the enemies of England.'[68]

8.26 'On British Ambition,' *New-Jersey Journal* (Tuesday, 21 April, 1801) and 'On British Ambition,' *American Mercury* (Thursday, 30 April, 1801): 'We have reason to suppose…that the time is not far distant, when the tyranny of Great-Britain over those countries [in India] will be destroyed. The lightning is ready to fall.—The pride and avarice of England will probably force Russia to wage a ferious [sic, ferocious] war, and India will soon be torn from her present masters. A Russian army organized near *Astracan*, may easily descend to Astrabad, the southmost point of the Caspian, and crossing part of Persia, fall on the British settlements.—The way is marked and well known; for so early as the fourteenth century, the Venetians and Genoese drew by means of the Caspian to Asof and Caffa,[69] the rich produce of Persia and India. It is also well known, that towards the latter end of *Peter's* reign, he marched a considerable army into Persia and seized on that immense tract of country extending along the eastern and southern coasts of the

---

[65] Fath 'Ali Shah.

[66] The designation of Seyyid Sultan as a 'subject' stems from the fact that Fath 'Ali Shah, c. 1796–1799, had leased Bandar 'Abbas and the nearby islands (Qeshm, Larak, Hormuz) to the Omani ruler. As Floor (2011a: 61) noted, however, 'Despite the customs farm, Sayyed Soltan did not behave as someone who was but a customs farmer, but rather as the right-out owner of the customs jurisdiction. For on 12 October 1798 Sayyed Soltan concluded a treaty with the EIC that states, inter alia, "In the port of Bandar Abbas (Gombroon) the English shall be disposed to establish a factory, making it as a fort.'

[67] As Lorimer (1915: 171) noted, 'A letter from Bonaparte to the Sultān of 'Omān, written at Cairo in January 1799, was intercepted by the British at sea.' However, previously, on 12 October 1798, 'an agreement was obtained from the Sultān…binding him to the British side in the Anglo-French contest, excluding the French from his territories during its continuance, and granting the British a right to settle at Bandar 'Abbas, which he held on lease from Persia. See Lorimer (1915: 172). In fact, the governor of Muscat had informed Malcolm that 'a little more than a twelvemonth ago the French had stood much higher in the Imaum's favor than the English—a circumstance to be accounted for by the paying him more attention, and sending him presents of cannon, &c.; but that they had lately captured one of his vessels, and he had since that period been very violent against them, and as strong in his expressions of partiality for the English.' See Kaye (1856/1: 106, n. *).

[68] As Markham (1874: 426) noted, 'In January 1800, Sultân concluded a…treaty with Sir John Malcolm, by which it was arranged that a British Agent should reside at Máskat.'

[69] Mod. Feodosia, an important Genoese trading settlement on the Crimean peninsula founded in the 1270s. See e.g. Bent (1881: 113ff); Khvalkov (2018).

Caspian.[70]—The Russian Government is possessed of precious documents on the situation of *Hindostan*; and although the British may cover the Indian seas with their numerous fleets they cannot oppose the invasion of a Russian army, assisted by the inhabitants.[71] We may expect, therefore that the avarice and ambition of England will be duly punished, and its government incapacitated from disturbing any longer the peaceful intercourse of nations.'

8.27 'India,' *Federal Gazette & Baltimore Daily Advertiser* (Thursday, 23 April, 1801): 'By the able exertions of Mehnide Ali Khan, the commercial resident at *Bushire*[72] (in the gulph of Persia) the trade thither has greatly increased, and the late consignments have been most advantageously disposed of....

Accounts from India state the successful issue of the late mission from Bombay to Schiras, (capital of Persia.) The commercial relations between the company and Persia, have been essentially extended and strengthened, and the king,[73] in manifestation of the close and friendly connexion thus happily promoted, has enjoined all his subjects, and particularly Imauna Seyd Sultaun, who has been suspected of favoring the interests of France, under severe penalties to abstain from all intercourses, commercial or political, with the enemies of England.

The present annual consumption of Indian commodities in Persia, is estimated at about 2,000,500 rupees, and the exports exclusive of copper, about 960,000.

British subjects of all descriptions, as likewise the company's dependants in India, are prohibited from trading with Persia in woollens, metals, and a variety of other articles hitherto constituting the ordinary investments for that country....

---

[70] As Atkin (1979: 69) noted, 'At the end of February 1801, an invasion force of fewer than twenty-three thousand men set out for India via Central Asia and met with a series of difficulties: first, there were terrible winter storms, then an early thaw, which broke up the ice on the rivers and forced the troops to alter their route several times. They ended up in unfamiliar territory where food for men and horses were scarce. At this point, word reached the commander that Paul was dead and Alexander had recalled the expedition.'

[71] See in general Strong (1965).

[72] Nawab Mirza Mahdi 'Ali Khan Bahadur (c. 1760–1805), the Native Resident at Bandar-e Bushehr. It was he who in 1798 negotiated the agreement, confirmed in 1800 by Malcolm, with Seyyid Sultan. See Anonymous (1906: 12). As Onley (2007: 87) noted, 'From 1798 to 1803 Mahdi 'Ali Khan served as Britain's first and only Native Resident in Bushire and Envoy to the Persian court. Mahdi 'Ali Khan began his career with the East India Company twelve years before when he joined the staff of the Political Residency in Benares under Jonathan Duncan. He served initially as a munshi and later as the Native Agent in Ghazpur. In 1795, the Company appointed Duncan Governor of Bombay and Mahdi 'Ali Khan went with him. When Duncan appointed Mahdi 'Ali Khan Resident in Bushire in 1798, he invested him with the full authority and responsibility held by all previous Residents.'

[73] Fath 'Ali Shah.

8 The Early Career of Fath 'Ali Shah (1798–1804)

It is reported that a very splendid embassy from the French Republic to the King of Persia is to take place in the course of this year. A brother of the Chief Consul[74] is said to have the appointment of ambassador; but citizen de Sacy, the celebrated Persian scholar, is to prepare the way by setting out some months before. This embassy is to be joined at Petersburgh by one equally magnificent from the Emperor Paul; and both are to proceed by the usual route of Astrakhan and the Northern Provinces of Persia, to the residence of the king.'

8.28 'London. Monday, April 13,' *Poulson's American Daily Advertiser* (Thursday, 21 May, 1801): 'All obstacles to the commercial intercourse between the India company's territories and Persia, have at length been completely removed, and trade has revived in a manner that promises the highest advantage.'

8.29 'Late Foreign Intelligence. London, April 22,' *Poulson's American Daily Advertiser* (Friday, 12 June, 1801; second paragraph only), 'Untitled,' *The Times and District of Columbia Daily Advertiser* (Wednesday, 17 June, 1801) and 'London, April 27,' *The Carolina Gazette* (Thursday, 2 July, 1801; second paragraph only): 'We find the following among the evidences of the authenticity of the royal prints:

"The King of Persia,[75] in testimony of his attachment to Great-Britain, and to prevent the introduction of Jacobinism[76] into his dominions, has offered a considerable reward for the apprehension of any Frenchman who may be found therein."[77] Whether the name of

---

[74] Joseph Bonaparte.

[75] Fath 'Ali Shah.

[76] Distinctly associated with the French Revolution, Barruel (1797: iii), 'Sous le nom désastreux de *Jacobins*, une secte a paru dans les premiers jours de la Révolution Françoise, enseignant que *les hommes sont tous égaux & libres*; au nom de cette égalité, de cette liberté désorganisatrices, foulant aux pieds les autels & ls trônes; au nom de cette même égalité, de cette même liberté, appellant tous les peuples aux désastres de la rebellion, & aux horreurs de l'anarchie.' For the pejorative connotations of the term 'Jacobin' and the many difficulties attending the definition of Jacobinism, see Scrivener (2010: 27). In this case, preventing the introduction of Jacobinism in Persia is a veiled reference to Napoleon's plans of using Persia as a bridgehead in a future assault on India. To achieve this, the EIC established a Residency in Baghdad. Harford Jones was chosen as its first Resident and, as Yapp (1967: 326) wrote, 'He was given letters to Sulaymān Pasha from [Henry] Dundas and the Secret Committee [of the Board of Control, which oversaw the EIC] warning the Pasha against French Jacobinism.'

[77] In fact, the treaty concluded by Malcolm with Fath 'Ali Shah pledged British support in the 'expulsion and extirpation' of any French forces attempting 'to settle with a view of establishing themselves on any of the islands or shores of Persia,' and further, 'if ever any of the great men of the French nation express a wish or desire to obtain a place of residence or dwelling on any of the islands or shores of the kingdom of Persia that they may there raise the standard of abode or settlement, such request or representation shall not be consented unto by the high in rank of the State encompassed with justice (the government of Persia), and leave for their residing in such a place shall not be granted.' See Hurewitz (1956: 69).

Jacobinism was ever heard in Persia or not is a matter of no importance; a Persian would find it difficult to articulate the sound; but there is a preposterous ignorance in talking of a king of Persia; as if there was such a king. Persia has been for an age divided into a number of petty sovereignties, without any general head; the Khan's [sic] each at enmity with the other.'

8.30 'Persian Embassy,' *The National Intelligencer, and Washington Advertiser* (Friday, 25 September, 1801), 'Persian Embassy,' *City-Gazette and Daily Advertiser* (Saturday, 10 October, 1801), 'Italy. Milan, July 20. Persian Embassy,' *Thomas's Massachusetts Spy, or Worcester Gazette (*Wednesday, 14 October, 1801), 'Italy. Milan, July 20. Persian Embassy,' *United States Chronicle* (Thursday, 22 October, 1801), 'Persian Embassy,' *The Albany Centinel* (Friday, 30 October, 1801), 'Persian Embassy,' *Otsego Herald, or Western Advertiser* (Thursday, 12 November, 1801) and 'Persian Embassy,' *Vermont Centinel* (Thursday, 12 November, 1801): 'An English Ambassador[78] was sent last year to the court of Persia, and the following letters are from the pen of one of the gentlemen[79] who accompanied him. They afford some information respecting a country not a little distinguished both in ancient and modern times, which still possesses considerable power and importance in the East, and which will soon excite greater attention should the English revive the trade which was once carried on with it, or the French retain possession of Egypt.

Shiraz, August 29 [*Albany Centinel* '28,'] 1800

In a former letter I mentioned to you the Embassy having left Abu Shiher, commonly called Bushire, for this place; we travelled in the most splendid style with respect to our equipment and attendants, and were treated with the utmost attentions and respect throughout the whole of our journey. The different governors of the respective provinces through which our route lay, came out to receive and welcome the Envoy, conducting him to his tents, under a continual discharge of fire arms, with a grand display of military evolutions. The early part of our journey we moved extremely unpleasant, on account of the excessive heat, until we arrived at Cazeroon[80]; having then passed, or rather ascended, two ranges of exceeding high mountains, we experienced a very sensible alteration in the climate. We halted at Cazeroon ten days after our fatigue, regaling ourselves with plenty of different ices, great quantities of snow being brought from the surrounding mountains.

On our leaving Cazeroon, we ascended two more ranges of mountains before we reached Shiraz, with the sight of which we were at length gratified on the 13th of June. Captain Malcolm, the Envoy, made his public entry the following day,[81] and was received

---

[78] John Malcolm.
[79] Possibly William Hollingbery. See Hollingbery (1814).
[80] Kazerun.
[81] According to Malcolm's own diary, the mission arrived on 13 June. See Malcolm (1827/1: 122). For some reason, Kaye (1856/1: 117) wrote, 'On the 15th of June the Embassy reached Shiraz.'

with the highest and most flattering distinction. Five noblemen of the higher order, attended by a retinue of upwards of a thousand horses, came out to receive him on his arrival, and conducted him to where his tents had been pitched, which was on a lofty terrace, under the walls of the garden called Johan Numa,[82] and within a few hundred yards of the tomb of the celebrated Hafiz; and the stream of Rochnabad,[83] so famed in his poems, does us the honor of running through our camp; it is at present not a very mighty stream, being no more than two feet wide, but the pureness of its waters justly deserve all the praises they have received.[84] The bower of Mosella[85] is also close at hand, but which has suffered from time, nothing now remaining of that formerly much admired place, but the ruins of an old brick wall.

Our stay here has altogether been extremely pleasant, particularly the latter part of our time; the first six weeks we were continually entertained with feasting, feats in wrestling, rope-dancing, and fire works.—Soon after our arrival we quitted our tents, and took up our residence in a Palace, situated in the centre of the delightful garden of the Jehan Numa. Since our arrival we have seen the Prince Regent[86] two or three times; he is a very handsome boy about 12 years old. I suppose our stay at this place will not now exceed eight or ten days; when we shall begin our journey to Ispahan, from whence you may expect again to hear from me. I profess I cannot help feeling a particular degree of veneration for the place we are now in, and conceive that I am treading classic ground.

Ispahan, September 23.[87]

Agreeable to my promise, I transmit you a short account of our journey from Shiraz to this place. We left Shiraz on the fourth inst. and the roads and country through which we passed were excellent, generally leading through large entensive plains, of a rich soil; but the traces of industry or the cultivating hand of the farmer, were evidently wanting, owing

---

[82] As Markham (1874: 324–325) noted, 'In the vicinity of the city are numerous beautiful gardens. The most famous is the Jahân Numa, or "Epitome of the World"—where the cypress-trees, which line the walks are the tallest and largest that were anywhere to be found. Intermixed with these are broad spreading chenars (plane trees), all manner of fruits, and abundance of roses and jessamine.'

[83] Cf. Sir William Jones' translation of Hafez, 'A stream so clear as Rocnabad/A bow'r so sweet as Mosellây.' See Jones (1771: 138) and Jones (1774: 59).

[84] As Markham (1874: 325) noted, 'Close to this garden [Jahān Numa] flows the classic stream of Roknabâd' and n. 1, 'General Monteith says it is only two or three feet wide, but it is a perennial stream of clear water.'

[85] A popular garden in Hafez's lifetime, where he was later buried. Cf. Nott (1787: 85), 'In the preceding note, Mosella is mentioned, as a chapel near Shiraz, by the learned orientalist [Sir William Jones] I have quoted; but I apprehend, it was only the name of a pleasantly-situated and sacred spot of ground, in the time of Hafez, after whose death, a chapel and monument were built there by Mohammed Minai.'

[86] Hoseyn 'Ali Mirza was born on 1 September 1789 and thus was almost exactly 12 years old when Malcolm met him. See Malcolm (1827/1: 122); Busse (1972: 36 for his birthdate and 91–92). He was Fath 'Ali Khan's fifth son and Farman Farma of Fars. See Anonymous (1873: 715).

[87] Malcolm's suite only arrived at Isfahan on 23 September. See Kaye (1856/1: 127).

probably to the scarcity of water, but still more so from the want of population. On our way from Shiraz we visited the ruins of the once celebrated city of Persepolis, but as we only continued there one day, we had but a very cursory view of it, yet still sufficient to forcibly impress on the mind an idea of its former grandeur. Our reception at Ispahan was truly magnificent[88]; the Beglerbeg's[89] brother, and son,[90] attended by nearly ten thousand troops marched out the distance of 8 miles to meet us, and if I may be permitted to judge from appearances, there must have been not less than 30,000 spectators assembled to witness the novelty of such a sight.[91] We have not yet paid a visit to the city, but it appears to be of immense extent, and its whole appearance denotes the capital of a great and extensive empire. One of the palaces of the Seffeiran Monarchs[92] is fitted up for our reception, and we shall take possession of it to-morrow or next day[93]; at present we are encamped on the banks of the river Zainderood, to the westward of the city. The Beglerbeg, Hajy Mahomed Hussian [sic, Hussain] Khan, has just paid us a visit; he is a remarkable pleasant old man, said to be extremely rich, and made an elegant and shewy appearance in his dress and equipage.[94]

---

[88] On 9 October Malcolm wrote to his friend Neil Benjamin Edmonstone, 'The entertainment given me yesterday by the Begler Bey exceeds all I have yet seen. The illuminations and fireworks were very grand; and, to crown all, when we were seated in an elegant apartment, one side of it, which was chiefly formed of mirrors, opened, and a supper laid out in the English style, with tables and chairs, presented itself to our utter astonishment, for we little expected such apparatus in the middle of Persia. The difficulty of feasting us in our own style made the compliment the greater.' See Kaye 1869/1: 211. For the life and career of Edmonstone (1765–1841), who held various important posts in Calcutta, ranging from Chief Intelligence Officer of the EIC and Secretary of the Secret, Foreign and Political Department to Acting Governor-General on two occasions and Professor of Persian at the College of Fort William, see Chancey (2003) and Tritton (2019).

[89] Haji Mohammad Hoseyn Khan (1758–1823). See Busse (1972: 100).

[90] 'Abdollah Khan. See Ouseley (1823: 22).

[91] In his memoirs Malcolm made no mention of this reception but in a letter written at Isfahan on 27 September to his uncle, John Pasley, he wrote, 'Nothing can exceed the attention I receive. I was met eight miles from this town by all the great men, ten thousand troops and about twenty thousand inhabitants.' See Kaye (1856/1: 127).

[92] Safavid.

[93] Malcolm wrote to Pasley that, after being greeted by the great throng of thousands outside of Isfahan, he was 'conducted to my tents, which I have since left to occupy one of the finest palaces, which has been prepared for my reception.' See Kaye (1856/1: 127).

[94] As Walcher (2001: 117–118) noted, 'Hajji Muhammad Husayn Khan [1758–1823] has been credited with the initial revitalization of Isfahan at the beginning of the century. He began his career as a warehouse manager (*anbardar*), rising to become headman (*kadkhuda*) of a city quarter. In 1210/ 1795–96, he was named governor of Isfahan, Qum, and Kashan and in 1221/1806, he was appointed mustawfī al-mamālik and given the title "Amin al-Dawla." Seven years later, the title "Nizam al-Dawla" was also confrred on him. In 1234/1818 on the death of Mirza Shafi'Mazandarani he was appointed to the position of *ṣadr-i a'ẓam* which he held until his death in 1239/1823. By the end of his life he was one of the richest men in Persia.' Without naming him Gardane (1809a: 57), wrote, 'Visite au Beglierbey d'Ispahan. Ce Seigneur est immensement riche; on dit qu'il a 3000 domestiques.' Ouseley (1823/3: 22) noted, 'We had not been many hours in this Persian Elysium

8 The Early Career of Fath 'Ali Shah (1798–1804)

We propose to leave this in about ten days, and expect to be at the Imperial Stirrup[95] in about three weeks afterwards at farthest.'

8.31 'Foreign News. London, August 16,' *The New-York Gazette and General Advertiser* (Tuesday, 29 September, 1801), 'London, August 16,' *Gazette of the United States, and Daily Advertiser* (Wednesday, 30 September, 1801), 'Foreign Intelligence. London, August 16,' *The Albany Centinel* (Tuesday, 6 October, 1801) and 'Latest Foreign Intelligence. London, August 16. *The Sun* [Pittsfield MA] (Tuesday, 13 October, 1801): 'The King of Persia[96] has undertaken a journey to Tauris, a distance of 300 miles from Ispahan.[97] This place carries on a prodigious trade in cotton, cloth, silks, gold and silver brocades, and fine shawls. It is seated in a delightful plain, surrounded by mountains, whence a stream proceeds, which runs through the city.—The King's visit is said to be occasioned by some commercial matters which require regulation.'

8.32 'Untitled,' *The National Intelligencer, and Washington Advertiser* (Monday, 26 October, 1801): 'The present sovereign of Persia[98] is devoting himself with success to revive the trade of his empire, and has caused several large vessels to be built on the Caspian and Persian Seas. The alarm excited by the movements of the Russians having subsided, the cities of Gangi and Tiflig [sic, Tiflis], which had been nearly deserted, are again in a flourishing state; and Aggai Mahommed Khan[99] having retreated from Masshad, the capital of Kohraisan,[100] to Tabran [sic, Tehran], tranquility is restored. The emperor, in compliment to the English, has prohibited the sale of horses throughout the Persian dominions, for exportation, to any others than the agents of the India company.'[101]

8.33 'Conspiracy to murder the Emperor of Persia,' *City-Gazette and Daily Advertiser* (Tuesday, 9 February, 1802): 'A plot was lately discovered, which had for its object the murder of Baba Khan, the present Sovereign of Persia,[102] and which, involving many of the

---

[Isfahan] before the Ambassador received a visit from Háji Muhammed Husein Khán…the *Amín ad douleh*…second minister of the Empire and ruler of that extensive region, which lies between *Amínábád* and *Tehrán*.'

[95] For the Persian idiom *rasmi rikab*, 'paying attendance at the imperial stirrup, at court, &c,' see Steingass (1963: 584 s.v. *rikab*, 'A stirrup').

[96] Fath 'Ali Shah.

[97] The distance is closer to 569.3 miles (916.2 kms).

[98] Fath 'Ali Shah.

[99] An anachronism, as Agha Mohammad Khan had died in 1797 and Fath 'Ali Shah had already reigned for four years.

[100] Khorasan.

[101] The commercial treaty between Fath 'Ali Shah and Great Britain of 28 January 1801 makes no mention of the horse trade. See Aitchison (1892: 37–41); Hurewitz (1956: 69–70).

[102] Fath 'Ali Shah.

most distinguished officers of the state, has excited the strongest sensation throughout the empire. An officer who had been instrumental in advancing the Prince to the throne, conceiving himself neglected, formed a project to depose him, and won over to his purpose the prime minister Elmatta Dowla,[103] by promising to advance him to the sovereignty: by like means he engaged nineteen persons of the first rank in the empire to embark on the plot, and Mulam Alli,[104] the favorite and constant attendant of the Emperor in his retirement, was bribed to assassinate him. The scheme wore the most promising aspect, and in order to [?...our] the intended change, troubles were excited in various quarters; but on the eve of its execution, the treason was discovered by means of a letter to the prime minister, which was by chance intercepted. Elmatta Dowla, and fourteen of his associates, were immediately apprehended and put to death in dungeons of the palace, and such other steps were taken as have effectually crushed the conspiracy.[105] Elmatta Dowla was a decided friend of the English; he materially contributed to the success of our late embassy to the court of Persia, and is spoken of by capt. Malcolm in terms of high respect.'[106]

8.34 'Untitled,' *Salem Gazette* (Friday, 9 April, 1802): 'Letters were received last week, overland from Bombay, dated the 20th of August [1801], which state in confident terms the

---

[103] Haji Ibrahim Khan I'temad od-Doula, the 'grand vizir.' See Busse (1972: 94). For the title see e.g. Floor and Faghfoory (2007: 20).

[104] No friend of Fath 'Ali Shah's by this name is mentioned by Hasan-e Fasa'i.

[105] Hasan-e Fasa'i gave a very different account of the alleged plot against Fath 'Ali Shah, noting that 'every day courtiers and other people submitted false accusations and mendacious indictments to the shah with regard to Haji Ebrahim,' but when letters were produced – allegedly sealed with Haji Ebrahim's seal - addressed to the Shah's brother Hoseyn Qoli Khan and other high-ranking officials, inviting them to join a conspiracy to overthrow the empire, Haji Ebrahim and his family were arrested. Despite his protestations of innocence, Haji Ebrahim had his eyes blinded and his tongue cut out and he and many members of his family, 'his brothers, sons, and relatives, everybody at his respective place, were either killed or deprived of their sight.' See Busse (1972: 98–99). As Watson (1866: 128–129) noted, 'The Itimad-ed-Dowleh, Haji Ibraheem, the prime minister of Persia, had acquired such a degree of influence throughout the country as gave his enemies' statements the appearance of reasonableness, when they whispered to the Shah that it was the intention of his minister to depose him. There is no ground for believing that Haji Ibraheem actually did harbour any such design....But Haji Ibraheem was too powerful to be openly attacked. Nearly the half of Persia was governed by his some or other relatives, who would at his command have at once raised the standard of revolt against the Shah. An order was therefore issued that, on a given day, the prime minister and all his kindred should be seized or put to death.' Cf. Wheeler (1871: 36–37).

[106] While in Tehran Malcolm in fact was housed in the palace of Haji Ibrahim Khan. See Busse (1972: 94). According to Malcolm (1829/2: 309, n. s), 'The late Hajee Ibrahim, during the whole period that he was prime minister to Aga Mahomed Khan, presided over every department of the state.' Haji Ibrahim Khan's seal was affixed to the treaty concluded by Malcolm with Fath 'Ali Shah. See Kaye (1856/1: 144).

8 The Early Career of Fath 'Ali Shah (1798–1804)

death of the King of Cabul,[107] early in the month of April [1801], while on an expedition to Candahar. . . . It is stated, that several Chiefs who composed Zemaun Shah's army at the time of his entering Hindostan, and who were active in the subsequent undertaking against the Seiks[108] at Lahore, had assembled at Candahar, for the purpose of assisting in a revolution, said to be in agitation in that country.[109] The King, some months prior to his death, concluded a treaty, offensive and defensive, with the Seik Government.'[110]

---

[107] Zaman Shah Durrani (r. 1793–1800) was deposed and blinded. As Kaye (1851: 23) noted, 'Between a blind king and a dead king there is no political difference. The eyes of a conquered monarch are punctured with a lancet, and he de facto ceases to reign. They blinded Shah Zemaun, and cast him into prison; and the Douranee Empire owned Shah Mahmoud as its head. . . . He survived the loss of his sight nearly half a century; and as the neglected pensioner of Loodhianah, to the very few who could remember the awe which his name once inspired, must have presented a curious spectacle of fallen greatness. . . He died at last full of years, empty of honours, his death barely worth a newspaper-record or a paragraph in a state paper. Scarcely identified in men's minds with the Zemaun Shah of the reigns of Sir John Shore and Lord Wellesley, he lived an appendage, alike in prosperity and adversity, to his younger brother, Soojah-ool-Moolk.' Cf. Beale 1894: 427, 'He was blinded by his younger brother, Mahmūd Shāh of Herāt, about the year A.D. 1800, and confined in the Bālā Hisār. When, in the year A.D. 1839, the British Government placed Shāh Shujāa on the throne of Kābul, Zamān Shāh was proclaimed king by the Afghāns in January A.D. 1842.'

[108] Sikhs.

[109] This was what Sykes (1940/1: 381) termed 'the conspiracy of the chiefs.' According to Burnes et al. (1839: 52–53), 'Shah Zemán during the early part of his reign, listened to the counsels of his minister Ramatulla Khan, and wasted his power in ill timed invasions of India. It was this king that raised Runjeet Singh to consequence in the Punjab, having created him viceroy there. Shah Zemán previous to one of his invasions of India rejected his brother Hamayoon from Candahar, and taking him prisoner with him to Bhag, there blinded him; he also imprisoned Abbas and secured Peshawer. On his return from one of his latest campaigns, having detached the Shaheeuchee-bashee with a force against the Sikhs (who was killed at Guzerat) his Vizier Ramatulla Khan persuaded him that his nobles had entered into a conspiracy to dethrone him, and that they held their counsels at the house of a learned and pretendingly pious man Myan Ghulam Mahammed. Among the nobles, was Penda Khan the father of the present Affghan Chiefs, who received the title of Sirfraz Khan from Timoor Shah for his brave conduct in the battle of Multan; Shah Zeman had him with several others of the principle nobles put to death in Candahar. His wife with her eldest son Fatteh Khan fled to Mahmood who was in retirement in Persia; they collected a force, and took Herat, while Shah Zeman was in a campaign in the Punjab, from his sons Princes Naseer and Hyder: this news brought Shah Zeman, from Hindoostan; Mahmood had in the interval taken Candahar from Prince Kaisar, and a battle took place between the two rivals at Mukud, which ended in the defeat of Shah Zeman, who fled to Cabool, where, however, he could not keep his position, but retired to Peshbulak, almost alone and took refuge in the house of a mulla named Ashuk, who betrayed him to a party that Mahmood had sent in pursuit of him; by whom he was taken a prisoner to Cabool, where his eyes were put out, and his Vizier Ramatulla Khan after being paraded through the streets on an ass, was beheaded.' The death of Ramatullah may have caused the confused report of Shah Zaman's death.

[110] Although no such treaty was ever made, Shah Zaman did deal with a Sikh uprising in Lahore against the Afghan garrison and governor, who was killed, and 'Upon reaching the capital, which the Sikh rebels had abandoned upon his approach, he received the homage of the Chiefs, among whom was Ranjit Singh. He then agreed to their petition that the Governor of Lahore should be selected from

8.35 'Late from Europe,' *The Salem Gazette* (Tuesday, 31 August, 1802), 'Latest from Europe,' *Commercial Advertiser* (Wednesday, 1 September, 1802), 'Late from Europe,' *The New-York Evening Post* (Wednesday, 1 September, 1802), 'Late from Europe,' *The Courier* (Wednesday, 1 September, 1802), 'Latest from Europe. July 17,' *American Mercury* (Thursday, 2 September, 1802), 'Latest from Europe. Boston, August 30,' *Philadelphia Gazette* (Thursday, 2 September, 1802), 'Boston, August 30,' *The Gazette of the United States* (Thursday, 2 September, 1802), 'Boston, Aug. 30. Late from Europe,' *New-York Herald* (Saturday, 4 September, 1802), 'Boston, Aug. 30. Late from Europe,' *American Commercial Daily Advertiser* (Saturday, 4 September, 1802), 'August 30,' *Alexandria Advertiser and Commercial Intelligencer* (Monday, 6 September, 1802), 'August 30,' *Columbian Advertiser; and Commercial, Mechanic, and Agricultural Gazette* (Monday, 6 September, 1802), 'Latest from Europe. Boston, August 28,' *The Republican or, Anti-Democrat* (Monday, 6 September, 1802), 'Massachusetts. Boston, August 30. Late from Europe,' *The Sun* (Monday, 6 September, 1802), 'July 17,' *The Centinel of Freedom* (Tuesday, 7 September, 1802), 'Boston, Aug. 30. Late from Europe,' *The Connecticut Centinel* (Tuesday, 7 September, 1802), 'Boston, August 30. Late from Europe,' *The Commercial Register* (Friday, 10 September, 1802), 'Summary of European News, to the 17th of July, Received, via Halifax, Boston and N. York,' *The Virginia Argus* (Wednesday, 15 September, 1802) and 'Boston, August 30,' *Middlebury Mercury* (Wednesday, 15 September, 1802): 'Hostilities have broken out between the Russians and Persians, the former of whom have already penetrated into the province of Ghilan.[111] Some violence offered to the Russians at Asterbat is mentioned as the cause of these hostilities.[112] Persia

---

among the Sikh Chiefs to the exclusion of the unpopular Afghans. Zaman Shah thereupon appointed Ranjit Singh, who, although only nineteen years of age, had already acquired a great reputation for courage and statesmanship.' See Sykes (1940/1: 380–381). Cf. Burnes et al. (1839: 52).

[111] As Atkin (1979: 67) noted, 'As late as 1802, Iranian efforts to recapture Georgia were limited to small-scale, ineffectual raids that were justified as the defense of Bagration [on whom see below] claims. Fath 'Ali Shah also tried to obtain his ends through peaceful methods by upholding his case in letters to Paul and Russian officials in the Caucasus.' The war did not properly begin until the Russian conquest of Ganja in 1804.

[112] Cf. Anonymous (1802a: 243), 'Of the war between Russia and Persia there is yet no farther information, than that the new regent of the latter, Baba Khan, has collected a considerable body of troops, in order to meet the Russian army, which has penetrated from the corner of Astracan, through Derbent to the Persian province of Ghilan. The circumstance which gave occasion to these hostilities is, that all the Russian subjects resident in the states of the said Regent were driven from their possessions, under a pretence that Russia acted unjustly in taking under its protection the provinces of Georgia and Mingrelia. It is apprehended that this dispute will be attended with a great deal of bloodshed.' A translated letter of 8 May, 1802 (or 1801?), to Lord Castlereagh [Robert Stewart] (sender unknown), reported that, according to 'letters and persons...arrived from Reshd [Rasht], the whole of the Russian craft at Enzelleh [Bandar-e Anzali] have been ordered to return to Derbend and Baku, and that they are preeparing for their departure....There are persons arrived from Baku...who openly say that there are 14,000 Russian troops at Derbend, and that others are following them, and

and European Turkey open a rich prospect to the desiring eyes of Austria, Russia, and France.'

8.36 'Turkey,' *The Salem Register* (Thursday, 2 September, 1802), 'Foreign Articles. Turkey,' *The Eastern Herald & Maine Gazette* (Monday, 6 September, 1802) and 'Boston, Aug. 31. Turkey,' *New-Jersey Journal* (Tuesday, 7 September, 1802): 'The Russians have commenced hostilities against the Persians—and have already taken one of their towns.'

8.37 'General Summary of Foreign and Domestic News,' *The Eagle of Maine* (Thursday, 9 September, 1802): 'Russia, has commenced the further disturbance of peace she having cast a wistful eye upon some of the fine provinces of Persia.'

8.38 'Untitled,' *The Salem Register* (Thursday, 9 September, 1802): 'The state of Russian affairs, in regard to the southern neighbors of the Empire in Persia, is unexplained.'

8.39 'Postscript,' *The Daily Advertiser* (Monday, 20 September, 1802): 'Letters from Constantinople state, that Russia is at war with Persia, and that she has actually occupied Georgia.[113]—The Porte is extremely alarmed at these operations[114]; for if Russia should be able to render Persia tributary to her, the Empire of Constantinople would be surrounded by that immense power.'

8.40 'Constantinople, May 30,' *The Gazette of the United States* (Wednesday, 22 September, 1802), 'Foreign Articles. Constantinople, May 30,' *The Salem Register* (Thursday, 30 September, 1802), 'Foreign Articles. Constantinople, May 30,' *The*

---

these persons also say that there is a considerable number of vessels belonging to Government coming from Astrachan to Derbend and Baku.' See Vane (1851: 171–172).

[113] Paul I had incorporated Georgia into the Russian Empire in 1800, an act that was confirmed by his successor Alexander, who 'sent General Zizianoff [Prince Pavel Dimitriyevich Tsitsianov (1754–1806)], a Georgian by birth or extraction, as Governor General and Commander in Chief into the provinces beyond the Caucasus.....He had no sooner arrived at Tiflis than he marched a force to Mingrelia, which submitted without resistance, and was immediately occupied by Russian troops.' See McNeill (1836: 56). Cf. Low (1881b: 243). As Ingram (1973: 511–512) observed, after annexing Georgia, 'The Russians immediately discovered...that it was impossible to administer Georgia without controlling the surrounding Mahometan Khanates, partly to safeguard Georgia from the Persians. In consequence, in the autumn of 1802, Alexander I sent Prince Tsitsianov to impose Russian rule upon the whole of the south eastern Caucasus.'

[114] The Earl of Elgin, British ambassador in Constantinople, wrote to Harford Jones in Baghdad on 21 October 1801 noting, 'The Porte seem well apprized of the conduct of the Russians on the banks of the Caspian Sea at Tiflis and Rumbec, and at Kars. They consider these operations as directed certainly against the interests of Persia, but not on any extensive scale or ambition, or as likely to be carried beyond their present progress. Explanations on these matters have passed between Russia and Turkey, which leave no apprehension on the minds of the Ottoman Government.' See Vane (1851: 165).

Providence Phoenix (Tuesday, 5 October, 1802) and 'Foreign Articles. Constantinople, May 30,' *The Virginia Argus* (Wednesday, 6 October, 1802): 'The Porte appears much alarmed at the occupation of Georgia by the Russians, and at the war which they have undertaken against Persia. Georgia, Mingrelia, and Guriel[115] had claimed the protection of Russia, against Mahomet Khan.[116] A Russian army has marched upon Astracan, passed the Debent, and entered the province of Ghilan. Cabar [sic, Baba] Khan, the new Emperor of Persia, has marched with a numerous army to encounter the Russian army. If Russia should be able to render Persia her tributary, the empire of Constantinople will be surrounded by that immense power.'

8.41 'Foreign Articles,' *Jenks' Portland Gazette* (Monday, 18 October, 1802) and 'Foreign. London, Aug. 26,' *Edes' Kennebec Gazette* (Thursday, 21 October, 1802): 'Hostilities have commenced between Russia and Persia. The Russians have obtained advantages over some troops which were sent by Baba-Khand [sic, Khan] to encounter them.'

8.42 'Political. Present Situation of the Turkish Empire,' *The Green Mountain Patriot* (Wednesday, 3 November, 1802) and 'The Present Situation of the Turkish Empire. [From a Rotterdam paper.],' *The Commercial Register* (Wednesday, 17 November, 1802): 'Hostilities have commenced between the Persians and Russians; and should the latter

---

[115] Guria, region in southwest Georgia, bordering the Black Sea. It is divided from Mingrelia by the river Rion. See Boyes (1877: 208).

[116] This is not an anachronistic reference to Agha Mohammad Shah, but rather to Fath 'Ali Shah's envoy, Mohammad Hoseyn Khan Qajar Qoyunlu. As Brosset (1857: 267–268) noted, in 1798, after Giorgi succeeded his father Erekle II as king, 'Chah-Baba-Khan envoya au roi Giorgi son chef des pages, Mahmad-Khan Qadjar, pour l'inviter à se soumettre à lui et demander un des fils de ce prince, qui resterait auprès de sa personne, moyennant quoi il promettait de lui donner Chaki et le Chirwan, ainsi qu'Erivan et Gandja....Entendant ses propositions, le roi Giorgi, alors à Thélaw, dans le Cakheth, expédia son beau-père Giorgi Tzitzichwili, général du Gaghma-Mkhar, chargé de promettre qu'il ferait tout ce qui lui était demandé, si le chah, de son côté, lui livrait tous les captifs enlevés de Tiflis par son oncle [Agha Mohammad Shah]. Lorsque Giorgi Tzitzichwili et Mahmad-Khan, l'envoyé du chah, arrivèrent à Phambac, ils y apprirent la nouvelle d'un mouvement en Perse. En effet Baba-Khan, étant venu dans l'Aderbidjan et se trouvant à Khoï, fut informé de la défectionn de son frère Ouséin-Qouli-Khan, qui régnait dans l'Iraq ['Iraq 'Ajami], ce qui le força lui-même à aller dans ce pays. Sur ce, Giorgi Tzitzichwili revint d'Erivan et laissa Mahmad-Khan se rendre auprès du chah....L'empereur Paul en fut informé et fit sur-le-champ promettre par écrit au roi Giorgi, afin de l'empêcher de se joindre aux Persans, qu'il le secourrait et lui accorderait tou ce qu'il voudrait....le roi se mit de nouveau sous la protection russe, aux termes de l'arrangement ou traité de 1783, conclu entre l'Impératrice Catherine et le roi Iracli.' For the text of that treaty see Boulger (1879/1: 345–348). This 'Mahmad-Khan Qadjar,' identified here as 'chef des pages,' was presumably Mohammad Hoseyn Khan Qajar Qoyunlu, who had been Aga Mohammad Shah's chamberlain. See Busse (1972: 75).

carry on the war in earnest, and finally prevail, what might not then become of the Turkish Empire, enfeebled and inert as it is?'

8.43 'Bombay, August 15, 1801,' *The Carolina Gazette* (Thursday, 25 November, 1802): 'An ambassador from Persia[117] landed here [Bombay] this morning [15 August, 1801], and was received with much ceremony and military parade. He is a wealthy merchant at Bushire, and arrived here two days since in a ship of his own, commanded by an Englishman, and under convoy of a frigate; but could not come on shore sooner, waiting for a *lucky day*.[118] His being rich, is said to have been one motive with his master[119] for giving him the appointment, as he is to bear most of his own expences.'[120]

8.44 'India News,' *New-York Evening Post* (Tuesday, 11 January, 1803) and 'From the Calcutta Gazette Extraordinary of August 11-12,' *Salem Register* (Friday, 20 January, 1803): 'Fort-William,[121] August 11.—On the ninth inst. His majesty's frigate La Chiffonne,[122] Capt. stuart,[123] arrived in the river [Hooghly] from Bombay, with dispatches from that Presidency to his Excellency the most noble the Covernor-General [sic] in Council,[124] containing the afflicting intelligence of the death of his Excellency Haujee

---

[117] Haji Khalil Khan-e Koroghlu Qazvini, who was *malek ot-tojjar*, 'alderman of the merchants,' was 'appointed envoy to India in the name of the Persian government. Carrying befitting gifts and presents from the Persian government, he departed from Tehran at the end of Ramażān of that year [1215, i.e. 1800/1801] in the company of the ambassador, Sir John Malcolm,' according to Hasan-e Fasa'i. See Busse (1972: 95).

[118] An unwavering belief in astrology and in waiting for a propitious day to do something important is frequently found in literature on Safavid and Qajar history. As Scott Waring (1807: 9) noted, 'The Persians are firmly persuaded of the truth of judicial astrology, and seldom undertake any business without consulting their astrologers; the most lucrative profession in all Persia. It is useless to attempt convincing them of the fallacy of their belief.' Cf. Fraser (1825: 64, n. *), 'no one will commence any undertaking, however trifling, without consulting their oracle for a fortunate day or hour.'

[119] Fath 'Ali Shah.

[120] Risso (1989: 388) described him as 'a tax farmer and also...the port's [Bandar-e Bushehr] chief merchant (malik-i tujjar)... Hajji Khalil...along with his brother-in-law and son, established a network between Iran and India that lasted well into the nineteenth century.' His purpose, following Malcolm's visit, was 'to pay the compliment of a return mission, and to arrange for the ratification and interchange of the treaty.' See Rawlinson (1849: 11, n. *).

[121] As Low (1877/1): noted, 'In 1698 the Company obtained a grant of the towns of Chattanuttee, Govindapore, and Calcutta, and constructed Fort William, when the station was constituted a Presidency.'

[122] As its name suggests, the *Chiffonne*, 36 guns, was originally a French frigate. It was captured by HMS *Sibylle*, 38 guns, Capt. C. Adam, on 19 April 1801 in the Seychelles and 'added to the British navy under her French name.' See Cust (1862b: 102–103). In 1809–10, HMS Chiffonne took part 'in the expedition against the pirates' in the Persian Gulf. See Horsburgh (1817: 408).

[123] Henry Stuart. See Steel (1802: 5).

[124] Richard Wellesley (1760–1842), Earl of Mornington and Governor-General of India (1798–1805).

Khuleel Khann, Ambassador to the British Government on the part of His Majesty the King of Persia.[125] In the afternoon of the 20th ultimo, a dispute unfortunately arose between the Persian servants of the Ambassador and the Sepoys[126] of the Corps of Bengal Volunteers composing his Excellency's honorary guard, at the house assigned for his residence near Massagong.[127] An affray ensued, and both parties resorted to arms. At the commencement of the disturbance, his Excellency the Ambassador, with his nephew Aga Hoossain,[128] and his attendants, descended into the Court for the purpose of quelling the tumult, and while his Excellency was exerting his endeavours with the utmost degree of humanity and firmness for that purpose, he received a wound from a musket which instantly proved mortal. His Excellency's Nephew was severely wounded in several places. Four of the Ambassador's servants were killed, and five more wounded.—Tranquility however was speedily restored, and medical assistance was immediately procured for the relief of the

---

[125] Scott Waring heard conflicting accounts of his death while travelling back to India from Basra in 1802. He wrote (Scott Waring 1807: 134–135), 'On the fifth of October I left Bassora on my return to India...and on the seventh, in the evening, we anchored off Bushire. It was here I learnt the melancholy fate of Hajee Khuleel Khan, the Persian ambassador to his excellency the most noble the Governor General of India. The accounts which were given me of this unfortunate event, differed very inconsiderably from the real facts; and the whole of the people appeared fully impressed with the notion, that this accident was as sudden and unforseen, as the catastrophe was deeply and feelingly lamented....Hajee Khuleel Khan was a shrewd sensible man; but as his origin was obscure, he was not much respected by the chief families in the empire. His influence with the king excited their envy, and his riches and prosperity confirmed the sentiments they entertained concerning him. He was a successful and an extensive merchant; but his economy, I fear, will not escape the imputation of excessive avarice. He has left an only son, of about eleven years of age, who has been most nobly and liberally provided for by the British government in India.'

[126] Persian *sipah*. 'Generally written and pronounced *Sepoy* in India; a soldier....This is the same word as the Turkish *Spahi*, which occurs so often in the English prints.' See Kirkpatrick (1785: 70).

[127] Mazagaon, where the house assigned to the Persian ambassador was located, effectively a suburb of Bombay. It was famous for its mangos. See Crawfurd (1867: 263). According to Hasan-e Fasa'i, 'One day at sunset two or three of the ambassador's servants shot at the birds which were sitting on the roof and trees, killing some. As the Indians hold the life of animals sacred, they tried to stop the shooting. Upon this a quarrel arose, the rest of the servants came out of the palace and there was fighting between the soldiers and the servants. Haji Khalil Khān, coming out of the palace to settle the dispute, was struck by a ball and killed.' See Busse 1972: 106. For the early Qajar state record's account see Brydges (1833: 210–213).

[128] Agha Mohammad Hoseyn. Described by Abu Talib Khan, who met him in Bombay, as 'a sensible and genteel young man...not quite recovered from the effects of five or six wounds which he received' during the attack that led to his uncle's death. He was 'waiting at Bombay, in expectation of being appointed Ambassador, in the room of his deceased uncle, and, in consequence, received a liberal pecuniary allowance from the [East India] Company. He lived in a handsome style, and frequently invited me to his parties....A short time before I quitted Bombay, he received intelligence that Aga Abd al Nubby [Mohammad Nabi Khan; see Busse 1972: 132], the Bussora [Basra] merchant, was appointed to fill the station of his uncle; which very much mortified him, and he was obliged to return to Persia.' See Stewart (1810: 392–393).

surviving sufferers. The most active and judicious exertions were successfully employed by the acting President at Bombay, J.H. Cherry Esq.[129] and by the Civil and Military Officers under his authority, for the purpose of restoring order, and of tranquilising the minds of the attendants and followers of the deceased Ambassador, as well as of securing the means of bringing to justice the perpetrators of this atrocious act. A Court of Enquiry has accordingly been instituted at Bombay, for the purpose of investigating, with due deliberations and solemnity, all the circumstances of the case. The Governor General in council has adopted measures for affording to the relations and followers of the late Ambassador, all the relief and consolation which can be administered them under the pressure of this severe calamity. As a testimony of the public regret for the death of the late Ambassador, and of a deep sense of sorrow for the calamitous event which occasioned it, and as a mark of public respect for the high station of the deceased Ambassador and for the Sovereign whom he presented, his Excellency the Governor General in Council has been pleased to direct, that minute guns be fired on this melancholy occasion, at five o'clock, this afternoon, from the Ramparts of Fort William.—By command of his Excellency the most noble the Governor General in Council.

N.B. Edmonstone,[130]
Secretary to Govt. Sec. Pol. & For. Depts.'

8.45 'Untitled,' *Mercantile Advertiser* (Tuesday, 11 January, 1803) and 'January 11,' *Alexandria Advertiser and Commercial Intelligencer* (Sunday, 15 January, 1803): 'Captain Blakeman, arrived here yesterday from Calcutta, informs us, that previous to his sailing a riot had taken place at Bombay between the guard of honour of the government and the

---

[129] John Hector Cherry (1763–1803), 'who died Member of Council, Bombay.' He is buried in the cemetery of St. George's Cathedral, Madras (Chennai). See Cotton (1905: 93). Brydges (1833: 211, n. ll) noted, 'Mr. Duncan was at this time Governor of Bombay, but was absent from Bombay, and the late amiable John Hector Cherry was in charge of the Government.'

[130] Neil Benjamin Edmonstone (1765–1841). In addition to his position as Secretary to Government, he was 'Professor of the Persian Language and Literature' in the College of Fort William in Bengal. See Anonymous (1805a: 237). For his career and enormous influence, see Chancey (2003); Tritton (2019). His name appears as translator on many official documents, e.g. letters of Tipu Sultan written in Persian. According to Kaye (1869/1: 352–353, n. *), 'the more I study the history of India, in the transactions of the first twenty years of the present century, the more convinced I am that, among the many eminent public servants who helped to build up the great *Raj* of the Company, he had not a superior and scarcely an equal. He was the great political foreman of a succession of Governors-General. It was his lot to be, ostensibly, little more than the mouthpiece of others. Seen in official records, therefore, the merit of his best work belongs to others; and it is only by men who have access to those best materials of history—the rough-hewings, as it were, of great measures, traceable from their first inception to their final formal execution—that the measure of his greatness can be justly estimated.'

attendants of Haujee Khullel Khan, ambassador from the King of Persia[131]: and that whilst the ambassador was endeavouring to quell the tumult, one of the Sepoys shot him dead on the spot.'

8.46 'Untitled,' *Morning Chronicle* (Tuesday, 11 January, 1803) and 'Untitled,' *Chronicle Express* (Thursday, 13 January, 1803): 'In a Calcutta paper of the 26th August, received by the ship Citizen, arrived yesterday, we find an account of the death of *Haujee Khaliel Khann*, Ambassador from his majesty the king of Persia,[132] to the British government in the East. He arrived at Bombay on his way to Calcutta, where he was killed in a scuffle which took place between his attendants and the guard of honor of the government at that place.'

8.47 'Untitled,' *The Spectator* (Saturday-Wednesday, 8–12 January, 1803), 'Untitled,' *The Courier* (Wednesday, 26 January, 1803) and 'Foreign Herald,' *The Otsego Herald or Western Advertiser* (Thursday, 27 January, 1803): 'We have received a Calcutta paper of the 26th, of August, by the ship Citizen, Capt. Blakeman, arrived here this day. It contains an account of the death of *Haujee Khaliel Khann*, Ambassador from his majesty the king of Persia,[133] to the British government in the East. He arrived at Bombay on his way to Calcutta, where he was killed in a scuffle which took place between his attendants and the guard of honor of the government at that place.'

8.48 'New-York, January 15. Eastindia News,' *American and Commercial Daily Advertiser* (Friday, 14 January, 1803): 'In the Calcutta Gazette of the 26th August, is a declaration of the governor general,[134] relative to the assassination of Haujee Khuleel Khaun, late ambassador to the governor general in council, which, if we have room, shall appear to-morrow.'

8.49 'Bombay Courier Extraordinary, July 18,' *American and Commercial Daily Advertiser* (Friday, 14 January, 1803): 'A few days since we published an account of the assassination of the Persian ambassador,[135] at Messagong,[136] near Bombay, which event, it appears, had excited, in a particular manner, the regret and interest of the English government in the East. The following is the declaration of the governor general on that subject:—.

---

[131] Fath 'Ali Shah.
[132] Fath 'Ali Shah.
[133] Fath 'Ali Shah.
[134] Richard Wellesley (1760–1842), Earl of Mornington.
[135] Haji Khalil Khan-e Koroghlu Qazvini.
[136] Mazagaon.

Declaration of his excellency the most noble the governor general, &c. &c. &c.— Addressed to the surviving relations[137] and attendants of the deceased Haujee Khuleel Khaun, late ambassador from his Persian majesty to the Governor General in Council.[138]

The solicitude of the British government of India to strengthen and improve the relations of amity and honourable alliance with his majesty the king of Persia,[139] has been manifested by the most signal acts of systematic policy, and has been publicly acknowledged by all the states of Asia. The peculiar splendour of the embassy which conveyed the testimonies of my respect and attachment to his majesty's presence, the extraordinary honors with which his majesty's ambassador was received, under my express orders, on his excellency's arrival in the British territories; the zeal and assiduity displayed by the government of Bombay, and by all ranks of British subjects at that settlement, to conciliate the good will of the Persian ambassador; and the public preparations, conducted under my immediate and personal direction, for his excellency's reception with the most distinguished solemnity at the seat of the Supreme British Authority in India, afford sufficient demonstrations to the world of my high consideration for the dignity of the Persian monarch, and of my uniform intention to evince that unalterable sentiment towards the accredited representatives of his Royal Person.

Reviewing these incontrovertible testimonies of my anxiety to establish a friendly and honorable alliance with the power of Persia on the most solid foundation, his majesty and all the states of Asia will anticipate the deep affliction and anguish of mind with which I have witnessed the sudden interruption of our bright and happy prospects by a disaster, which as far eluded the scope of human prudence and foresight, as it surpassed the ordinary extent of human calamity, and the common vissisitudes [sic] of fortune. To this awful dispensation of providence, I submit with resignation, but not without hope.

In the most painful moments of my disappointment and grief, I have derived consolation from the reflection, that as I have hitherto assiduously employed every possible effort to cultivate a lasting friendship and harmony of interests between his Persian majesty and the British government, my amicable sentiments have been uniformly returned with equal cordiality by the auspicious disposition of that illustrious sovereign.

A dreadful, unforeseen, & uncontroulable calamity has intervened to afflict both states with mutual sorrow and consternation, and to retard the completion of their reciprocal wishes; but not to suspend their established friendship by groundless jealousy and unjust suspicion; not to frustrate the natural and propitious result of their united counsels; not to destroy the fruits of their mature wisdoim and justice; nor to dissolve those sacred

---

[137] Principally his son Mohammad Isma'il Khan. See Busse (1972: 106). In a listing of 'Pensions and Charitable Allowances' paid out in the fiscal year ended 30 April 1854, i.e. over half a century later, by the EIC, 'Aga Mahomed Ishmael Khan (Son of Hajee Khalil Khan)' received a pension of £1312. See Anonymous (1856a: 26).

[138] The identical text is included in the publication of Marquess Wellesley's papers. See Martin (1836: 669–671).

[139] Fath 'Ali Shah.

engagements, by which they had cemented the foundations of durable concord, secured the channels of free intercourse and beneficial communication, and enlarged the sources of their common safety, prosperity, and glory.

Entertaining a due sense of the value and importance of those engagements to both States, I shall pursue, with unabated confidence and perseverance, the policy on which the subsisting Treaties are founded, and the amicable and earnest exertions, by which they were obtained. The pursuit of this coarse [sic, course] cannot ultimately fail to attain success. The calamity which we have suffered is a just subject of lamentation; but its consequences are not irretrievable. From the reciprocal condolence of the two States may arise new motives of combined interest and additional securities of amity and alliance. A zealous interchange of the offices of humanity, a concurrent sense of common sorrow, and the conscious certainty of mutual sincerity and good faith may lead to a more intimate union of sentiments and views: and the temporary suspension of this important Embassy may tend to ensure and improve the benefits of our actual connection.

Supported by these hopes, and relying on the justice and integrity of the principles and motives which have actuated the British Government, I trust that the progress of our renewed intercourse with your illustrious Sovereign will gradually obliterate the remembrance of this fatal and unparallelled disaster, and will amply compensate to my mind for its actual distress by the final accomplishment of the same salutary plans of policy which had rendered a personal interview with your lamented master the object of my most anxious expectation.

To repair the severe loss sustained by his untimely decease; to demonstrate my sincere respect for his memory, & my unfeigned regret that he should have fallen by a violent death, within the British Dominions, and in the immediate exercise of functions, which the laws and usages of all civilised Nations have rendered sacred, it is my primary duty to administer to his surviving relations and attendants every office of humanity and friendly compassion, every attainable comfort and alleviation of their just grief, and every possible compensation for the injuries which they have suffered.[140]

---

[140] According to Hasan-e Fasa'i, Haji Khalil's surviving son Mohammad Isma'il Khan, 'was paid an indemnity of 50,000 toman, and in addition to this he received a monthly advance. For many years he lived in a prosperous condition in Paris and London, always clad in the Persian style. All his life he wore the high headgear of black lambskin, the long-sleeved coat, the cloak, the short padded coat, the wide trousers, and shoes of shagreen leather with high heels. He died in Paris about the year 1280 [1863/4].' See Busse (1972: 106–107). Cf. Sykes (1915: 399), who wrote, 'The English authorities, who were much upset at the untoward occurrence, made the most handsome amends, and the Shah is said to have observed that more ambassadors might be killed on the same terms' and in n. 1, 'Ismail Khan, son of the envoy, was granted a pension of two thousand rupees a month for life. He lived to enjoy this annuity for sixty-five years, and died in Paris, where he attended every performance of the opera during a period of fifty years.' Cf. Lang (1948: 330), n. 31 who wrote the same thing almost word for word without attributing it to Sykes.

In endeavouring to discharge this dutey, I have selected an officer, who was recently vested with the honorable character of Envoy, from this government to the court of Persia, and who now occupies the most confidential station in my family.[141]

That Officer is directed to proceed immediately to Bombay, and to afford to you, in my name, such effectual aid and assistance, and such testimonies of affectionate commisseration, as may tend to mitigate your suffering, and to console your affliction.

With the same view, I have provided the most speedy means of offering to your Royal Sovereign the respectful expressions of my sincere condolence on this disastrous event, and of concerting with his Majesty such measures, as may conduct the Embassy to its original purpose, accelerate the favourable issue of every depending question, and confirm the subsisting relations between the two states, in the conciliatory spirit of the recent negociations, and on the basis of the Treaties already concluded.

(Signed) WELLESLEY.

Fort William, August 17, 1802.'

8.50 'Untitled,' *The Albany Centinel* (Saturday, 21 January, 1803) and 'Untitled,' *Weekly Wanderer* (Tuesday, 15 February, 1803): '*Haujee Khulleel Khaun*, Ambassador from the King of Persia[142] to the English Presidency of Bombay, was murdered at Massagong, in an insurrection of the natives, in August last. The British Governor, *Wellesley*, has addressed a letter of condolence to the relatives of the Ambassador, and taken measures to apprehend and punish the murderers.'

8.51 'Extracts from a letter of a gentleman in India to a gentleman in this city. Bombay, September, 1802,' *City-Gazette and Daily Advertiser* (Saturday, 19 March, 1803): '"The most important incident which has happened here, is the extraordinary murder of the ambassador[143] from the king of Persia,[144] who resided here pro tempore, until the necessary preparations were adjusted for his conveyance to, and accomodation at the seat of the supreme government. I mentioned to you his pompous reception, and the same degree of assiduous attention and respect was shewn to him on all occasions. Unluckily, the military guard which was stationed as a mark of honor at his house, consisted of Bengal sepoys,

---

[141] None other than John Malcolm who occupied the position of private secretary to the Governor-General while Henry Wellesley, the Governor-General's brother, was away on a special mission to Oudh [Avadh/Awadh]. As Kaye (1869/1: 214) observed, 'Whenever any difficulty arose, it occurred to Lord Wellesley at once to send Malcolm on a special mission to set it right. So when, in July, 1802, the Persian Ambassador, who had come to India about the ratification of the treaties, was unhappily shot in an affray at Bombay, Malcolm was despatched to that Presidency to endeavour to make the best of so untoward an occurrence.'

[142] Fath 'Ali Shah.

[143] Haji Khalil Khan-e Koroghlu Qazvini.

[144] Fath 'Ali Shah.

lately brought thither from the Egyptian expedition,[145] who regard themselves as of a *high cast*, are bigoted and insolent—and as the attendants of the ambassador were also of the proudest sect of mussulmen, equally ignorant and equally bigoted to their own manners, they were ill calculated to associate near each other. The scarcity of Bombay troops was one reason for the Bengalees being placed on this duty. It is supposed that much ill-blood subsisted between the parties for some time before it broke out into violence; but from whence it arose, is not clearly known, I believe, to those who have taken official pains to investigate it; amongst the public a number of different stories were told, but all so vague or contradictory, that I have never been able, though on the spot, to learn any thing respecting it. The immediate cause of the unfortunate event that followed, is generally said to have been a dispute between a centinel at the gate and one of the servants, who probably drew his sword, when the sepoys of the guard, about 30 or 40 in number, as if by a general impulse, flew to their arms, and being unaccountably supplied with ammunition, fired indiscriminately on all the ambassador's people; and, as some assert, surrounded the house and shot at those who were in the apartments thro' the windows. When the affray commenced, the ambassador was sitting on the terraced roof with a gentleman attached particularly to his person as an interpreter, and to communicate on all occasions between him and government, who, in the apprehension of losing his life, instantly fled, and the ambassador coming down, in hopes that his presence might prevent or put a stop to the mischief, received a wound from a ball, which almost immediately deprived him of life, four of his servants were killed, and his nephew, with five more, severely wounded. It is not certain that any of his people had fire arms, and I believe none of the sepoys were hurt.

"This disagreeable and uncommon accident has much agitated our government. All the guard, the European officers* [*A Jamaldar (non-commissioned officer) is said to have declared in his own justification, that he only obeyed the orders he received from an European officer, of whom there were three—a captain and two subalterns.] as well as the sepoys, have been under close confinement ever since,[146] (the 20th July) as I believe it is not yet determined what mode of trial or punishment it is best to adopt. Our papers were not suffered to make mention of this transaction until after it was first published in Calcutta by

---

[145] As per the 'Memo (Most Secret) of the court of Directors, as to order for a force to be sent from India to cooperate in expelling the French from Egypt, to Bombay Government, 7 October 1800,' cited by Bandyopadhyay (1990: 712, n. 27). Given the fact that British naval resources in the Mediterranean were not overly strong and British land forces in England were needed to thwart a potential French invasion, 'it was thought urgent, as desired by the British Diplomats and merchants, to conquer Egypt with the help of the Indian Sepoys from Bombay. On the fourth March 1801 seven ships laden with arms and ammunition and carrying 2901 sepoys including followers...sailed from Bombay towards Suez commanded by 70 European officers. After the expulsion of the French and the restoration of the dominant British influence in Egypt in collaboration with the Anglo-Turkish troops despatched from Turkey the Indian Sepoys were sailed back to Bombay in July 1802.' See Bandyopadhyay (1990: 708–709).

[146] According to Hasan-e Fasa'i, 'The governor of Bombay had all the soldiers and the officers imprisoned and reported the affair to the governor general of India.' See Busse (1972: 106).

official authority; addresses of condolence from the principal inhabitants here were sent to the governments at this place and at Bengal. Public prayers were offered up in the English church for the recovery of the wounded Mussulmen, at which all the Europeans on the island were invited to assist, by proclamation—an extraordinary phenomenon in church history; and a salute of 21 guns was fired on the 40th day from the ambassador's death, as a compliment, after the custom of Mahometans of rank. In the overland dispatch which conveyed the intelligence to England, all the letters from individuals were returned, unless they made oath that they contained nothing on the subject of politics.'"

8.52 'Latest Foreign Intelligence. London, March 7,' *Morning Chronicle* (Friday, 15 April, 1803), *Morning Chronicle* (Friday, 15 April, 1803), *Chronicle Express* (Monday, 18 April, 1803), 'Accounts have been received from Bombay dated the first of January, by which we learn, that the King of Persia[147] had received the intelligence of the accidental death of his ambassador,[148] with great distress; but that his majesty was perfectly satisfied with the explanations which were given by our Government in India on the occasion.[149] The ambassador's nephew,[150] who was wounded, is so far recovered as to be able to ride abroad.'

8.53 'Foreign Articles. Extracts from English Papers,' *The Farmer's Cabinet* (Thursday, 16 June, 1803): 'The Turkish Empire appears to be, in some sort, taken possession of by the French. French Engineers *alias* Commercial Agents, have been stationed in all the sea ports, and indeed, in all other places of defence.[151]—Divers rumours are afloat as to the

---

[147] Fath 'Ali Shah.

[148] Haji Khalil Khan-e Koroghlu Qazvini.

[149] As Kaye (1869a/1: 214–215) noted, Malcolm 'wrote letters of explanation and condolence to the Shah and his Ministers; and made such liberal grants of money to all who had suffered by the mischance, that it was said afterwards in Persia that the English might kill a dozen Ambassadors, if they would always pay for them at the same rate.'

[150] Agha Mohammad Hoseyn.

[151] 'By a treaty between France and Turkey…Napoleon, then Chief Consul, acknowledged the sovereignty of the Porte over Egypt and its other dominions in full integrity; and the Sultan renewed the ancient privileges which the French had, under their kings, enjoyed in Turkey. The old policy of France, in seeking the friendship of the Ottoman Court, was now revived: and before long, the skill of Napoleon's ambassadors, Generals Brune and Sebastiani, restored the French influence at Constantinople.' See Creasy (1856/2: 345). For the text of the treaty, concluded on 25 June 1802, with ratifications exchanged on 8 September in Paris, see Hurewitz (1956: 71–72). Article 3 stipulates, 'The French Republic shall enjoy in the Ottoman districts adjacent to the Black Sea, as much for its commerce as for the agents and commissioners of commercial relations which might be established in those places where French trade would render such establishment necessary, the same rights, privileges and prerogatives enjoyed by France before the war in other parts of the states of the Sublime Porte, by virtue of the old capitulations.' As Puryear (1951: 2) observed, 'The search for added profits made Bonaparte insist on penetrating the Black Sea for the first time.'

particular acts of encroachment, which the Consul[152] has in view[153]; but none of these acts seem to be decidedly fixed, and we will venture to say, that they cannot, without the concurrence of Russia. The most probable conjecture is, that France will make use of all her power and her policy to obtain the re-possession of Egypt, in which object, maugre the arrangement, made through the mediation of Lord Elgin,[154] we are fully persuaded she will succeed, upon condition of winking at an equivalent acquirement on the part of Russia. The fate then of Turkey, and eventually of India, will depend, as far, at least, as present appearances allow us to calculate, on the disposition of Russia. If that power is, as we formerly observed, under the guidance of ambition, if her projects with respect to Persia and India are revived, our Empire in the East must be placed in an uncertain, not to say a dangerous situation, especially when we recollect that Cochin and the Cape of Good-Hope are at the command of the French,[155] to which latter place the armament under Decaen[156] and Linois[157] is certainly gone.'

---

[152] Napoleon.

[153] The first step, after the ratification of the treaty, was to dispatch maréchal Guillaume Marie-Anne Brune (1763–1815) as ambassador to the Porte. Brune left Paris on 22 Octdober 1802 and arrived at Pera on 6 January 1803. 'L'intention du Premier Consul est que l'ambassadeur de la République à Constantinople reprenue par tous les moyens la suprématie que la France avait depuis deux cents ans dans cette capitale.' See Coquelle (1904: 55).

[154] Thomas Bruce, seventh Earl of Elgin (1766–1841), Ambassador Extraordinary and Minister Plenipotentiary to the Porte from 1799 to 1803. See Cumming Bruce (1870: 306–308).

[155] As Anonymous (1803b: 756) noted, 'After one year and sixteen days of peace, or rather of suspended hostilities, war has again begun, France having during the interval, received from us, all the conquests we had made (the Island of Malta excepted), and having, since the signature of the Preliminaries [on 1 October 1801], and even in *consequence thereof*, gained an immense acquisition of power and of territory, on the Continent of Europe. Holland, from the whole tenor of our complaints as well as from the well-known fact itself, can now be regarded as neither more nor less than an appendage of the Republic of France. The Cape, therefore, Cochin, Demerara, Surinam, Essequibo, and every other spot of earth, which we have restored to the Dutch, have, in reality, been surrendered to France.'

[156] Charles Mathieu Isidore Decaen (1769–1832), named by Napoleon governor 'de nos colonies dans l'Océan Indien.' According to Gaffarel (1908: 310), 'Les instructions du Premier Consul étaient d'ailleurs très nettes. Decaen se savait appelé à un poste de combat, et il était résolu à s'y maintenir. "Vous pourvoierez avec l'activité qui vous distingue particulièrement, lui était-il dit, à toutes les dispositions de défense qu'exigera la sûreté des iles. Vous savez qu'elles son le boulevard de la France dans la mer des Indes; que de tout temps elles furent considérées comme le point militaire le plus essentiel pour balancer, inquiéter, combattre la puissance anglaise.'

[157] Charles Alexandre Léon Durand Linois (1761–1848), Rear Admiral of the French fleet sent to the Indian Ocean in 1803. The division of labor between Decaen and Linois was left very vague by Napoleon. As Gaffarel (1908: 314) noted, 'On avait eu le tort à Paris de ne pas préciser les attributions de l'amiral et du général: aussi se prétendaient-ils égaux, et, s'ils consentaient à contribuer à une œuvre commune, ils entendaient bien ne se subordonner en rien l'un à l'autre. Il résulta de ce manque de clarté des froissements et bientôt des conflits.'

8.54 'Late Foreign Intelligence. Paris, June 13,' *The New Hampshire Gazette* (Tuesday, 23 August, 1803), 'Foreign Intelligence. Paris, June 13,' *The Gazette of the United States* (Thursday, 25 August, 1803), 'Paris. (*France*) June 13,' *The Albany Centinel* (Friday, 26 August, 1803), 'Paris, June 13,' *Republican Advocate* [Frederick MD] (Friday, 2 September, 1803), 'Paris, June 13, 1803,' *New-Hampshire Sentinel* (Saturday, 3 September, 1803) and 'Paris, June 13, 1803,' *The South-Carolina State Gazette and Columbian Advertiser* (Friday, 16 September, 1803): 'The General commanding in the Isles of France and of the Reunion, to the First Consul of the republic,[158] 15th Pluviose 11th year [4 February 1803].

Citizen First Consul,

Of all the colonies, that of the Isles of France and of the Reunion[159] are the most indebted to you; they proclaim you as their saviour, and the day on which they learned your magistracy for life, wass to them a day of festivity and enthusiasm.

The affairs of the English in India assume the most unfavourable appearance. Being too far extended, they cannot face danger on all sides; and their sceptre, which is become burdensome in proportion to the extent of its sway, has increased the discontents of the nations over which it domineers. *They have just lost an important battle against the Marattas.*[160] The ashes of Tippoo are rekindling, and the *murder* of the Persian Ambassador[161] at Bombay, has done them the more harm in the minds of the different nations, as they have been informed that he had been sent to reclaim, in the name of his government, the sum that the English government had engaged, by a signed convention, to pay to the King of Persia[162] on condition of his not favouring the passage of the Army of Egypt.

It does not belong to me to look into futurity; but I have foundation for thinking, from all the information I receive, that the epoch approaches wherein the oppression of the English, their usurpations in India, the mass of power and possessions they have accumulated, and the weakness of their physical means to support themselves upon such an extent of country, must bring on great and sudden revolutions in this quarter of the world.

---

[158] Napoleon.

[159] Abandoned by the Dutch in early 1712, Mauritius was renamed Isle de France by order of Louis XV on 20 September 1715, by Guillaume Dufresne, sieur d'Arsel (1668- c. 1730), captain of *Le Chasseur*. Réunion was named Isle de Bourbon in 1657 by Étienne de Flacourt (1607–1660), the governor of Madagascar. See Grant (1801: 29, 147); Cunat (1857: 306–308); d'Épinay (1890: 73, 75).

[160] It is not immediately clear what engagement is being referred to in the long-simmering conflict between the Mahrattas and the British in the first few years of the nineteenth century. For a year by year account see Grant Duff (1918).

[161] Haji Khalil Khan-e Koroghlu Qazvini.

[162] Fath 'Ali Shah.

(Signed) Magallon-Lamorliere.[163]
June 15.'

8.55 'Foreign Articles,' *Charleston Courier* (Tuesday, 25 October, 1803): 'We have great pleasure in stating, on the authority of a letter just received from the Presidency of Bombay, that the harmony which subsisted between our government and the King of Persia,[164] previous to the death of his Ambassador, the Khan,[165] has been happily renewed; and that the object of this important mission has been fulfilled in all its political relations, which promise to our government the most consequential advantages, in respect to an exclusive and unlimited trade with the Persian Empire.—The exports and imports are to be received in a reciprocal proportion; but the balance of the commercial intercourse cannot fail to give the greatest energy and spirit to our merchants in the Eastern part of the globe.'

8.56 'From Calcutta Papers, received at the Office of the Morning Chronicle. From the Calcutta Monthly Journal,' *Morning Chronicle* (Thursday, 26 January, 1804) and 'From the Calcutta Monthly Journal,' *Charleston Courier* (Monday, 13 February, 1804): 'Yesterday afternoon having been fixed upon, by the honorable the Governor,[166] to pay a visit of ceremony to Aka Hussen,[167] the nephew of the late Persian ambassador[168]; and to deliver to him the dispatches from Bengal; his majesty's 86th regiment having formed from the government house towards the secretary's office, a royal salute from Hornby's battery,[169] at a little after three announced the departure of the honorable the Governor from his town residence. A number of beautiful led horses, very ricly [sic, richly] caparisoned led the procession, they were followed by the governor's peons in their proper uniforms, his aid-de-camps mounted, came next and immediately preceded his carriage which conveyed

---

[163] François Louis Magallon, comte de La Morlière (1754–1815), Général de Division, Gouverneur Général des deux Iles, *par interim*, appointed 29 July 1800, based on Mauritius, and succeeded on 26 September 1803 by Decaen. See Fairfield (1880: 113). The date 'June 15' beneath the signature here is puzzling, since the letter appears to be dated to 4 February 1803 in the address above.

[164] Fath 'Ali Shah.

[165] Haji Khalil Khan-e Koroghlu Qazvini.

[166] Jonathan Duncan (1756–1811). He was 'a member of the Bengal Civil Service, and for many years Resident at Benares,' and 'afterwards Governor of Bombay, from 1795 to his death on 11th August 1811. He died at Bombay, and was buried in the Cathedral.' See Mandlik (1877: xi). For a short account of his life and achievements see Anonymous (1812b).

[167] Agha Mohammad Hoseyn.

[168] Haji Khalil Khan-e Koroghlu Qazvini.

[169] Battery on the south side of the Bombay Castle, 'mounting upwards of 20 guns.' See Eastwick (1859: 274). It was named after William Hornby (1723–1803), Governor of Bombay from 1771 to 1784. For his colorful career see Douglas (1893: 434–438).

8 The Early Career of Fath 'Ali Shah (1798–1804)

himself, the Recorder,[170] and his council: the commanding officer of the forces with his staff, and the rest of his majesty's and the honorable company's, naval, military, and civil servants, heads of departments, whose attendance were requested at the ceremony, followed in their carriages.

On the procession reaching the avenue which leads from the Parell road to the residence of the late Persian ambassador, it was complimented by a royal salute from four field pieces stationed there with a company of artillery for the purpose. The procession then moved through a street formed by the 2d battalion of the first regiment of native infantry, under the command of major Holmes,[171] towards the residences of the embassy.

The Governor, with the officers who accompanied him, having approached the residence of the embassy, were received at the gate by its principal officers, and conducted into a hall where Aka Mohammed Hussen had been, for the first time, able to sit upright on a couch, although still unable to remain in an erect posture:—after the civilities of coffee and the houka had been gone through, whilst the royal music of Persia and that of the regimental bands played alternately the national airs of their respective countries, the Governor delivered standing with all the rest of the company, (excepting only Aka Hussen, whose debility precluded his joining in this part of the ceremony), the letter and declaration from his excellency the most noble the Governor General,[172] and the Persian original of the latter, was thereupon read aloud to the company:—after which Aka Hussen pronounced a short suitable reply, which follows here in the English language.

Aka Hussen's Reply

Translation of the verbal answer by Aka Mohammed Hussen, upon hearing read the declaration of his excellency the most noble the Governor General.

Praise to the bountiful disposer of events, that whatever I and those along with me, (being all of us the devoted servants of the shadow of God, his majesty the King of Persia), had conceived and thoroughly relied on; respecting the permanency of the friendship and unity between the two nations, hath, from the magnanimous and benign disposition of his excellency the most noble the Governor general, been in the terms of his Excellency's present declaration confirmed and realized; and since from the kind attention of Mr. Duncan, the Governor here, and the skilful care of the excellent surgeons that have attended me, my wounds are now so far advanced in their cure, that I have recovered strength to address by my own hand an arzee[173] to his excellency the most noble marquis

---

[170] This must have been an interim Recorder, for the previous Recorder, Sir William Syer, who had served since 20 February 1798, died on 7 October 1802, and his replacement, Sir James Mackintosh, did not arrive in Bombay until 26 May 1804. See Haydn (1851: 272); Mackintosh (1835: 210).

[171] Maj. George Holmes had shortly before commanded the second Battallion first Native Infantry, under General Sir David Baird, in Egypt. See Anonymous (1817a: 95–96). Cf. 1803.8 reporting the deployment of Sepoys in Egypt.

[172] Richard Wellesley, Earl of Mornington.

[173] 'An address from an inferior; a petition.' See Rousseau (1805: 23).

Wellesley, the eminent and renowned governor general of India; in answer to his lordship's favorable communication, now directed to me; I shall accordingly soon have the happiness, to prepare and deliver the same for transmission to his excellency.

I have also great pleasure in the present opportunity of expressing my fullest sense of the humane and consolatory care bestowed on me during my confinement, by Mr. Cherry whilst acting president, in the interval of the arrival of governor Duncan from the northward.

(Signed) *Mohammed Hussen*.

The honorable the Governor, after a short time passed in conversation with the Aka Hussen, took his leave, and returned to the government house in town, in the same order as distinguished his departure.

The entertainment announced to be given at Parell house,[174] by Abdul Lateef Khan,[175] in testimony of his respect, towards the British Society as well as for the members of the Persian embassy, who et together on this social occasion, took place on Monday evening last, attended by a numerous assemblage of ladies and gentlemen. If, where so many were conspicuous, it may be permitted to allude to a comparatively small number, it is but justice to say, that the recent arrivals from Europe, equally contributed to the beauty, and enlivened the gaiety which distinguished the party. Ever thing which taste and elegance could supply was amply displayed to render the scene splendid and attractive. Parell avenue was lined with lamps for the approach of the company, and the court or area of the house, was ornamented with well disposed illumination in the form of festoons. The dancing commenced at half past nine, and continued with unabated spirit till a grand display of fire works, soon after twelve, called attention to a new and yet more brilliant scene of amusement. Supper was announced at one, and the repast was animated by a variety of the most select Persian airs sung by natives of that country, of the beauty of which those only could taste completely, who were familiar with that sublime and highly descriptive language. Bands of instrumental music filled up the pauses of vocal harmony. After supper one of the gentlemen of the governor's staff proposed the health of the king of

---

[174] The Governor's mansion of Bombay, 'a handsome and commodious building, having excellent and extensive gardens and grounds attached to it. It was formerly a Portuguese church, and was connected with a monastery. Being purchased by a former Governor of Bombay, he added a beautiful upper story to it; which has this peculiarity, that the floor is raised in the centre, like the quarter-deck of a ship.' See Harvard (1823: 129). It was considered the Governor's 'country residence,' in contrast to 'the old Government House within the Fort walls.' Sir James Mackintosh, who saw Parell House when he was in Bombay (1804–1811), described it as 'a large, airy, and handsome house, with two noble rooms, situated in the midst of grounds, that have much the character of a fine English Park.' See Mackintosh (1835: 210).

[175] Mir Abdul Latif Khan Shushtari (1758–1805), described as, 'A gentleman descended from a very ancient Persian family, and distinguished, amongst the learned, as the author of the *Tohfit al Aalum* (The Rarity of the World).' See Stewart (1810: 392). For the significance of his autobiographical work detailing his journey to India, see Dabashi (2019: 26–46). For his transmission of ideas on modernity, especially science, in the West, see Tavakoli-Targhi (2011: 267–268).

8 The Early Career of Fath 'Ali Shah (1798–1804)

Persia, which was drank with enthusiasm by all present;—those of the king, queen, and royal family, Aka Hussen, the members of the Persian embassy, and the most noble the Governor General of India, followed in succession; and the last toast, which conveyed the pleasing intelligence that the favourite amusement of the ladies was again to be resumed, recalled them to its enjoyment, which appeared to have acquired fresh charms by the cessation. The assembly at length broke up, regretting only the unwelcome, though unseasonable, approach of day.[176]

Among the other *divertisements* of the evening, the successful exertions of a *fire-eater* to excite astonishment, cannot be passed over in silence. This person, a native of Persia, after extinguishing a number of lighted torches in his mouth, and swallowing several pounds of blazing cotton, seemed only to *burn* with increased *ardor*, to prove his contempt for what is generally thought the most irresistible of all elements; accordingly, having taken various pieces of live charcoal from a flaming chaffing dish, he placed them, if we may use the expression, *coolly* in his mouth, and then blew forth *sparks* in such abundance as might have exhibited a poetical image of a votary of *Cupid*, realizing the flames which consumed his breast.'

8.57 'Foreign Intelligence. Bombay, Oct. 10 [1803],' *The Philadelphia Evening Post* (Friday, 30 March, 1804) and 'Hindustan News,' *Aurora General Advertiser* (Friday, 27 April, 1804).: 'We understand, a Memander[177] arrived from the court of Persia at Abushir on the tenth ult. [10 September 1803] who is to accompany Jonathan Lovett, Esqr.[178] and Lieut. Charles Pasley, to the court of Persia[179]; it is supposed they will take

---

[176] Aga Mohammad Hoseyn 'embarked on his return to Persia on the Faz Rebany, captain Henderson, under a salute of seventeen guns,' on 3 December 1803. See Campbell (1806: 85).

[177] Persian *mehmandar*, 'official in charge of visitors to the court.' See Busse (1972: 491).

[178] Jonathan Henry Lovett, 'a good linguist and one of the few civil servants at Bombay fluent in Persian. He was torn away from the compilation at Fort William of a Maratha dictionary for the government of Bombay, to be dumped in an outpost in the Persian Gulf and given political and diplomatic tasks for which he lacked aptitude and inclination.' Following the accidental death of Haji Khalil Khan in Bombay, 'Wellesley and Malcolm expected Lovett to re-establish the British reputation for good conduct easily and quickly.' See Ingram (1995: 73).

[179] Charles William Pasley (1780–1861), 'an intelligent officer, who is also a writer of no common merit, began his service in the army as second-lieutenant of artillery, in 1797, removed into the royal engineer corps in 1798, and rose to be lieutenant-colonel of engineers, in December, 1814.' He was knighted and ended his career as a General, having written a number of influential works on both military and non-military subjects. See Anonymous (1823e: 103–104); Tyler (1863); Vetch (1895). Pasley was John Malcolm's cousin on his mother's side. See Philippart (1823: 469, n. *); Ingram (1981: 294). In a letter to Charagh 'Ali Khan-e Nava'i, vizier of Fars (Busse 1972: 452), Malcolm wrote, 'Mr. Lovett, a gentleman of rank and respectability, has been nominated Resident at Bushire, and he has been particularly appointed to take charge of the letter from his Excellency the most noble the Governor-General to the King.' However, in a postscript Malcolm added, 'After writing this letter, I have been induced, by the severe illness of Mr. Lovett and the fear of detaining for a longer period his Lordship's letter to the King, to send that letter with an Urzee ['petition or humble

their departure as early as possible before the winter set in too severe, which would make travelling both unpleasant and difficult.'

8.58 'Further Extracts, From Foreign papers, received by the late arrivals. Feb. 27,' *New-York Commercial Advertiser* (Tuesday, 3 April, 1804), 'Latest Foreign Articles. February 27,' *Aurora General Advertiser* (Thursday, 5 April, 1804), 'Latest Foreign News,' *Jenks' Portland Gazette* (Saturday, 7 April, 1804) and 'Foreign. London, February 26,' *The Repertory* (Friday, 13 April, 1804): 'The King of Persia[180] has resumed his preparations for establishing himself in the government of the Panjah [sic, Punjab]. The fortifications of Lahoer [sic] are in consequence strengthening, and the walls, ditch, &c. surrounding the city, are undergoing extensive repairs.'[181]

8.59 'Calcutta,' *The Daily Advertiser* (Friday, 22 June, 1804): 'The expences of the late embassy to Persia were incredible; upwards of 250,000 l.[182] The murder of the Persian

---

representation either oral or in writing;' see Yule and Burnell (1903: 959)] from myself and several letters to the nobles of the Government, by Mr. Pasley, who will, till the arrival of Mr. Lovett, fulfill his duties.' See Kaye (1856: 193). Cf. Ingram (1995: 74) who noted that, because he was ill when he arrived at Bandar-e Bushehr, Lovett tried to persuade the government of Fars 'to allow Pasley to deliver Wellesley's letter. They refused, owing to Pasley's junior rank...Nothing Lovett could say would persuade the Qajars that he was not an ambassador.'

[180] Fath 'Ali Shah.

[181] Although Fath 'Ali Shah never threatened Lahore or the Punjab, this may be a mistaken reference to the long perceived threat of an invasion by Shah Zaman or his successor Shah Shuja'. See Elphinstone (1815: 585–592). Lahore at this time was firmly under the Sikh ruler Ranjit Singh's control. See Anonymous (1858).

[182] The enormous cost of the sumptuous presents given to Fath 'Ali Shah has been commented on many times. Sutherland (1837: 30) noted, 'We have wasted vast treasures to obtain the support of Persia against the invasion of the French and the Afghauns.' Rawlinson (1849: 9) inveighed, 'Captain Malcolm's Treaty was not, perhaps, the most objectionable feature of his mission; his prodigality left a more lasting impression, and that impression, in the ratio of its original force and effect, has operated ever since to our prejudice. So lavish was his expenditure, that he was popularly believed to have been granted a premium of 5 per cent. on all the sums he could disburse; while the more intelligent, who rejected an explanation savoring so strongly of the "Arabian Nights," could only draw, from his profusion, an exaggerated estimate of the wealth of England, or an inordinate appreciation of the value which we placed upon the Persian alliance. Money, we know, in the moral world, is much like opium in the physical. The stomach, once drugged, is insensible to milder stimulants; and thus, ever since we administered the first fatal dose, to create an influence, or to persuade the Persians of our really being in earnest in seeking for their friendship, we have had to follow the same pernicious treatment, with a merely temporary effect upon the patient, but to the ever active depletion of our Indian store, from which the prescriptions have been drawn.' The gifts made to Fath 'Ali Shah included, 'Watches glittering with jewels; caskets of gold beautifully enamelled; lustres of variegated glass; richly chased guns and pistols of curious construction; marvels of European science, as air-guns and electrifying machines; besides a diamond of great value, and the mirrors, which had been brought up with so much toil.' See Kaye (1856: 132–133). Kaye (1856:

8 The Early Career of Fath 'Ali Shah (1798–1804)

ambassador[183] was notoriously accidental; and the measures taken by Lord W.[ellesley] have been so satisfactory to the court, that instead of diminishing, it will, probably, increase the amity subsisting between the two countries.'

8.60 'Late Foreign Intelligence. Paris, July 20,' *The United States Gazette* (Saturday, 29 September, 1804) and 'Late Foreign Articles. Paris, July 25,' *Hornet* (Tuesday, 9 October, 1804): 'There is a kind of fraternity between the English troops in India, and the Russian troops in Persia. While the former defeat defenceless Mahrattas and Hindoos, the latter no less brave conquer and disperse some disarmed friends of liberty in Georgia.[184] The province Imiretia has been occupied by the Russian soldiers without resistance,[185]

134, n. *) also noted, 'As the extravagance of Malcolm's mission, especially in the matter of presents, has been commented upon by some writers (myself among the number), it is only right that his own recorded justification should be given... "I had good grounds," he wrote in his journal, "to conclude that my conduct on this point will establish me an influence that would enable me to carry both the Political and Commercial objects of my mission, without subjecting the Government to any heavy engagements."' He then went on to enumerate how this expense had saved money, e.g. in the willingness of Fath 'Ali Shah to campaign in Khorasan if necessary as a check on Zaman Shah; in its being 'almost out of the power of an European nation to rival it in a country where so much depends on show and expense;' and in the value of presents to be sent in return; and in truncating the mission by some two months, 'a circumstance which, if it takes place, will meet the additional expense.'

[183] Haji Khalil Khan-e Koroghlu Qazvini.

[184] As Baddeley (1908: 65–66) noted, 'The refusal of the free Djáro-Bielokáni tribesmen to deliver up those of the Georgian princes who had taken refuge amongst them was made the excuse for an expedition resulting in the annexation of their territory, thereby to some extent guaranteeing Georgia against the raids of the Daghestan mountaineers. Severe punishment meted out to those of the latter who had settled in the neighbourhood of Akhaltsikh kept them in check until the following year, when, to the number of 600, they were disarmed and sent back to their native fastnesses....Western Georgia now breathed more freely, and Tsitsiánoff's next step was to annex Mingrelia.'

[185] The occupation of Imeritia was not entirely pacific. Baddeley (1908: 66) wrote, 'the rulers of Imeritia carried on perpetual warfare with their western brothers, and at last, instigated, no doubt by Tsitsiánoff himself, the dadian [Mingrelian ruler], following the example of Georgia, sought Russian protection, and Mingrelia was formally proclaimed a Russian province. Imeritia was now isolated, with the Russians on either side, and could no longer hope to maintain its independence. With a very bad grace the Tsar Solomon submitted to the inevitable, and his kingdom likewise was annexed by Russia on the 25th April 1804. Thus the ancient Iberian monarchy, broken up by the testamentary dispositions of the Tsar Alexander I. of Georgia four hundred years previously, was at last reunited under the sceptre of Alexander I.' According to Brosset (1857: 276–277), 'En 1803 Tzitzianof invita le roi Solomon à venir et à s'allier avec les Russes. Le roi étant venu, on lui fit prêter serment de fidélité, et on lui promit qu'il jouirait de l'indépendance sa vie durant. On lui demanda aussi qu'un petit corps de Russes résidât à Kouthathis. Le roi ayant consenti à tout, on lui donna l'ordre de Nevski en brillants. Il envoya aussi comme ambassadeur à la cour de Russie le thawad Solomon, fils de Léon, qui fut bientôt congédié, parce que le roi avait fait alliance avec les Osmanlis. Depuis lors il y eut, entre la Russie et l'Iméreth, rupture et dissentiment.' And further, 'Comme Solomon, roi d'Iméreth, ne cessait de faire des prisonniers dans l'Odich et dans le Letchkhoum, et de perséuter le dadian

under the pretence that its mountainous situation was favourable as a refuge for robbers; when in fact it was the last refuge for liberty in the Persian empire; as for thirty centuries before, no soldier of a despot, ever dared to pollute it with his presence. The great distances of those countries, causes Europeans to lose sight both of their real and relative value and consequences; and while we are combatting and intriguing for some few towns, villages, or rivers, of no significance, the English and Russians are conquering provinces in the East, the revenues of which are greater than those of most kingdoms in Europe. We are butchering each other for pebbles while they are decorating themselves with real diamonds. The yearly revenue of the late English conquests in India is greater than those of the kingdoms of Prussia, Naples, Sweden and Denmark together and the revenues of the Russian usurpation in Persia amount to more than those of the Swedish and Danish monarchs. We have only one hope, that those destroyers of the human race and enslavers of mankind will finally quarrel among themselves, and that his majesty our emperour[186] will be called on as an umpire to settle their disagreements.

[*Journal des Defenseurs.*]

8.1 Miscellaneous

Anticipating the Publication of Olivier's Voyages Dans l'empire Othoman

8.61 'Untitled,' *Commercial Advertiser* (Saturday, 21 July, 1798), 'Untitled,' *The Spectator* (Wednesday, 25 July, 1798), 'Untitled,' *The Daily Advertiser* (Friday, 27 July, 1798) and 'Untitled,' *The Rutland Herald* (Sunday, 13 August, 1798): 'Oliver,[187] a traveller sent into Persia by the French government, has transmitted from Constantinople a large and curious collection of antiquities, medals and objects of natural history, which he has

---

Grigol [of Mingrelia], celui-ci n'eut plus d'autre ressource que de se mettre sous la protection russe, et fit connaître ses intentions à Tzitzianof, que cette nouvelle combla de joie. Comme il désirait abattre le roi d'Iméreth et s'emparer de ce pays, il fit tout ce que voulait le dadian.' See Brosset (1857: 278).

[186] Napoleon.

[187] Guillaume-Antoine Olivier (1756–1814). For his voyage see Olivier 1801–1807; Bernard (1997). As Watson (1866: 99) noted, 'The object of this mission appears to have been twofold: in the first place, to ascertain whether or not a profitable interchange of commodities could be established between France and Persia; and in the second place, to endeavour to unite the Persians with the Ottoman Porte in a combination against Russia. Satisfactory replies were given on both points by the prime minister, but the difficulties which lay in the way of the establishment of a trade between Persia and France appeared to be too great to be overcome. Two treaties had at an anterior period been concluded between the two countries; but it did not seem worth while to the French negotiator to propose to renew them, nor to obtain protection as formerly for French establishments at Ispahan and Sheeraz and on the shores of the Persian Gulf.'

collected in the East. The account of his travels is impatiently expected by the literary world.'

The Wahhabis

8.62 'Untitled,' *The Newburyport Herald and Country Gazette* (Tuesday, 25 December, 1798), 'Copious Details of the Latest Foreign News. Translations,' *The Oracle of the Day* (Saturday, 29 December, 1798) and 'Latest Foreign News...Paris, Oct. 3,' *The Philadelphia Gazette & Universal Daily Advertiser* (Friday, 4 January, 1799): 'A revolution in religion had begun in Persia. The Persian prince, Mahabee[188] is determined to introduce another religion instead of Mahometanism, upon purer morals, and more simple doctrines. The ceremonial is to be more conformed to the ancient institutes. It is to be called simply, The Religion, or the divine gift of peace. Mahabee acknowledges the existence of one God, calls himself the servant of God, and admits the immortal existence of man, but not agreeably to the Mahometan doctrine.'

8.63 'Translated for this Gazette, from a Paris paper,' *City Gazette and Daily Advertiser* (Wednesday, 22 January, 1800), 'Translated for this Gazette, from a Paris paper,' *The Carolina Gazette* (Thursday, 23 January, 1800), 'Translated for the Charleston Gazette, from a Paris paper,' *Claypoole's American Daily Advertiser* (Monday, 17 February, 1800), 'New Religion. Translated for the Charleston Gazette, from a Paris paper,' *The Independent Chronicle and the Universal Advertiser* (Thursday-Monday, 20–24 February, 1800), 'Translated from a Paris paper,' *The Georgetown Gazette* (Saturday, 22 February, 1800), 'Translated for the Charleston Gazette, from a Paris paper,' *The Constitutional Telegraphe* (Wednesday, 26 February, 1800), 'New Religion. Translated for the Charleston Gazette, from a Paris paper,' *The Newburyport Herald and Country Gazette* (Friday, 28 February, 1800), 'New Religion. Translated for the Charleston Gazette, from a Paris paper,' *The Eastern Herald and Gazette of Maine* (Monday, 3 March, 1800), 'New Religion. Translated for the Charleston Gazette, from a Paris paper,' *Oriental Trumpet, or the Town and Country Gazette* (Thursday, 6 March, 1800), 'Translation from Paris Papers,' *Vermont Gazette* (Thursday, 6 March, 1800), 'New Religion. Translated from a late Paris paper,' *The Bee* (Wednesday, 12 March, 1800) and 'Foreign Intelligence. Translated from a late Paris paper,' *The Oracle of Dauphin and Harrisburgh Advertiser* (Monday, 17 March, 1800): 'It is now a matter of notoriety, that the French government has for a long time past, and for several years prior to Buonaparte's expedition, held a political correspondence with the chiefs of certain Arabian tribes that occupy the country between Mecca and the Gulf of

---

[188] Muhammad b. 'Abd al-Wahhab.

Persia.[189] A Scheick of those parts, named Hajabi,[190] has for six or seven years back been fomenting a religious solecism, the basis of which is simple Deism, the adoration of the Deity without churches or temples, in the open air....Father Hajabi, who is yet alive, and near one hundred years old, is the author, or rather restorer, of this new code of religion, which he first instituted in his own family, afterwards throughout his tribe, and which has been successively adopted by many other tribes in Arabia Felix. Prodigious multitudes of people have also embraced it along the western side of the Gulf of Persia, from Mascate to Bassora....We have undoubted information also, that this new sect of religion, thus collected in different parts of Arabia, are organizing an army, which is possessing itself of the shores of the Euphrates and Tigris, above Bassora; and it was suspected, they meditated a descent upon Persia.'

8.64 'Untitled,' *The Salem Register* (Thursday, 20 May, 1802): 'A new alarm has arisen upon the borders of the Persian Gulph. It is said that the Bedowin Arabs have excited alarm at Bagdad,[191] and in those countries thro' which it has been anticipated that commerce would again convey its riches. It is confessed by all writers that we have very imperfect maps both of Arabia and Persia, after all the learned labours bestowed upon these countries.

---

[189] After his conquest of Egypt, in August, 1798, Napoleon was known to have written to the Sharif of Mecca, the Imam of Muscat, the Sultan of Darfur and later the chief mullah of Damascus. See Dennis (1901: 191). The Porte, however, had declared a *jihad* against the French and Ghalib Sharif (1788–1813), at Mecca, was urged by other tribal chiefs in Arabia and north Africa to join it. He was, however, too disdainful of the Ottomans and too preoccupied with the Wahhabi threat to his own position to follow the call. See Abir (1971: 192–193).

[190] Muhammad b. 'Abd al-Wahhab.

[191] While this statement is vague, it probably relates *inter alia* to Wahhabi raids around Basra 'and in 1801, the lamentable business at Kerbela...which spread a gloom over the Mahommedan world, ' referring to the Wahhabi capture of Kerbela. See Brydges (1834/2: 27). According to Longrigg (1925: 217), 'On the evening of April 2 the alarm had spread in Karbala that Wahhabi forces were in sight....The Wahhabis, judged to number some six thousand camelriders and four hundred horsemen, dismounted, pitched tents, and divided their forces into three parts. From the shelter of a khan they assaulted the nearest gate, and forced an easy entrance while the inhabitants, unled and panic-stricken, ran as terror directed. Forcing their way into the court of the shrine, the ferocious Purists began their task in the very Tomb. The rails, then the casings, then the huge mirrors of the shrine were torn down. Offerings of Pashas, Princes, and Kings of Persia, walls and roofing plated with gold, candlesticks, rich carpets and hangings, bricks of copper, doors studded with precious stones—all were seized and dragged forth. Within the Tomb nearly fifty persons were massacred, in the courtyard five hundred more. In the town the raiders murdered without restraint, looted every home, spared neither age nor sex from brutal ill treatment or captivity. The sum of the dead was computed by some at a thousand, by others at five times the number.' As Rousseau (1809: 193–194) wrote, 'Ce qui acheva de consolider leur renommée, ce fut le saccage horrible qu ils firent, en 1801, de *Kerbela*, autrement nommé *Imam-hussein*, ce lieu si vénéré par les *Kezelbaches* qui pleurent encore ses malheurs et sa profanation.' For a vivid description of the massacre of the worshippers at the shrine of Imam Hoseyn and the pillage of its treasures, see also Corancez (1810: 27–28). For the Persian perspective see Busse (1972: 101–103).

It was hoped that Niebuhr[192] would accompany his valuable work[193] with a map. These Bedowins, as they are named in Europe, are not so inconsiderable in number and power, as the general description of wanderers would lead us to suppose. They are divided into several religious sects. They who are in Persia, named Belludijes [Baluchis], and classed among the Bedowins, are found to be Sunnites, an important Mahomedan sect, and trade much in the Persian gulph. Bagdad, better known as not very far from the ancient site which tradition assigns to Babylon, than by any correct history, is situated on the Tigris. The Tartars, Persians, and Turks have successively held it. It was taken by Sultan Morad, III [sic, IV],[194] in 1638, and the Turks hold it. Its population is given at 150,000 inhabitants.[195] Ana, which is the most eastern possession of the Arabs of the desert, as they are called, has 5000 inhabitants, and is nearly the same latitude upon the Euphrates. The western bank of the Euphrates, and the western part of Ana is still inhabited by the trading Arabs. How far the troubles extend we do not learn. This whole country will probably undergo great changes in a short time from the nature of the European commerce which will be employed in it. While south of the Caspian troubles arise, the troubles continue north of the Hellespont.'

Persian Yeast

8.65 'Copy of a receipt for making Yeast, taken many months ago from an English paper,' *The Philadelphia Gazette & Universal Daily Advertiser* (Thursday, 15 August, 1799), 'Copy of a receipt for making Yeast, taken many months ago from an English paper,' *The Maryland Herald and Elizabeth-Town Advertiser* (Thursday, 22 August, 1799), *Maryland*, 'Copy of a receipt for making Yeast, taken from an English paper,' *The Universal Gazette* (Thursday, 22 August, 1799), 'Copy of a receipt for making Yeast, taken many months ago from an English paper,' *Maryland Herald* (Tuesday, 3 September, 1799), 'From a late Jamaica Paper. Copy of a receipt for making Yeast, taken many months ago from an English Paper,' *Columbian Courier* (Wednesday, 11 September, 1799) and 'Copy of a

---

[192] Carsten Niebuhr (1733–1815), German surveyor who undertook an important exploratory expedition in the service of the Danish king Frederik V.

[193] Niebuhr (1778) contains maps of southern Iraq (the Euphrates above and below Basra; the area north and south of Baghdad) but not of 'Arabia and Persia' as the writer complains.

[194] During the Ottoman-Safavid War Murad IV (r. 1623–1640) captured Baghdad. See Longrigg (1925: 69–72).

[195] This figure is probably much too high. As Olivier 1801/4: 324 noted when visiting Baghdad in April/May, 1796. 'Les habitans de Bagdad font monter la population de leur ville à plus de cent mille ames; mais le cit. [citoyen] Rousseau, depuis long-tems commissaire des relations commerciales, un négociant italien, nommé Liony, établi depuis plus de quarante ans dans ces contrées, ainsi que le supérieur du couvent des Carmes [Joseph de Beauchamp], dont nous avons déjà parlé, ne l'évaluent qu'à quatre-vingt mille.'

receipt for making Yeast, taken from an English paper,' *The Oracle of Dauphin and Harrisburgh Advertiser* (Wednesday, 25 September, 1799): 'Yeast.—This useful article, of which there is so frequently a scarcity in this country, is thus prepared in Persia:—Take a small tea-cup or wine glass full of split or bruised peas, pour on it a pint of boiling water, and set the whole in a vessel all night on the hearth, or any other warm place; the water will have a froth on it top the next morning, which will be good yeast. Mr. Eton,[196] when in Persia, had his bread made with this yeast, and in the English manner, of good wheat flour. In our cold climate, especially in a cold season, it should stand longer to ferment, perhaps four and twenty hours. Of all methods of making yeast hitherto known, this is by far the most simple and commodious.'[197]

Hafez

8.66 'Untitled,' *Farmer's Museum, or Lay Preacher's Gazette* (Monday, 26 August, 1799) and 'Untitled,' *The Philadelphia Gazette & Universal Daily Advertiser* (Friday, 30 August, 1799): 'Pray, reader, have you ever read the works of the poet Hafez? He is the Horace of Persia,[198] and, from the elegant translation of Sir William Jones,[199] many of his odes in praise of love, indolence and wine, are in the very tone of Anacreon's Greek.[200] The

---

[196] William Eton, long resident in Russia and Turkey, he was 'British consul first in Russia and then in Turkey in the 1790s,' who 'favored Greek liberation under the auspices of Russia.' See Speake (2003: 512). Cf. Eton (1798). As Ingram (1995: 37) noted of Eton, 'Employed in his youth at Basra, ...he knew as much about conditions in the Ottoman empire as anyone.' In fact, he had served as Dutch consul at Basra. See Ingram (1984: 174, n. 15). According to Christie (1971: 391, n. 23), Eton 'entered into a trading partnership at Constantinople in 1776, and was beginning to explore the possibilities of trade in the Black Sea lands...Samuel Bentham met him in St. Petersburg in 1780.' Bentham told his brother that Eton 'understands everything very well but can do nothing...a man of a great deal of learning, but very little of the knowledge of the world.' Cf. Schiffer (1999: 371–372).

[197] Originally published in Anonymous (1798: 269). The description also appears in Eton (1798: 237–238).

[198] Good (1801: 521) stressed 'the resemblance beteween Hafiz and Horace.' Cf. Macaulay who called 'Hafiz, the Horace of Persia' in his review of *Memoirs of the Life of Warren Hastings, first Governor-General of Bengal*, published in 1841. See Montague (1903: 75, n. 1). According to McCarthy and McCarthy (1901: 352), Hastings 'had a vision in his mind of a new scholarship, to be called into being by the generosity of the East India Company. He thought of Englishmen becoming...as intimate with the Ghazels of Hafiz as with the Odes of Horace.' Cf. Sherlock Holmes' concluding line in 'A case of identity,' 'There is as much sense in Hafiz as in Horace, and as much knowledge in the world.' See Conan Doyle (1891: 259).

[199] Jones (1791) by Sir William 'Oriental' Jones (1746–1794). Thus Beale (1881: 99), 'At the head of the English translators, stand Sir W. Jones, Messrs. Richardson and Carlyle.' Cf. Robins (1987).

[200] The comparison between Anacreon and Hafez began with Sir William Jones who called 'Hafiz, the Anacreon of Persia.' Cf. John Nott (1751–1825) in his translation of select poems by the Persian poet, 'In this ode, which is truly bacchanalian, and might alone entitle our poet to the appellation of

Asiatics still hallow the remembrance of this charming bard. The stream of Rocknabad,[201] and the bower of Roseliay are still haunted by the Persian youth, singing the mellow odes of Hafez, and lamenting that his lyre and his life, should be wrenched from him, by the ruthless hand of the warrior.'

8.67 'Incidents Abroad. Literary,' *Farmers' Museum, or Literary Gazette* (Monday, 1 September, 1800): 'The lovers of Oriental literature will be pleased to hear, that a translation of several odes by Hafiz, the Anacreon of Persia,[202] is now almost ready for publication;—The literal version is accompanied by a poetical paraphrase, and prefaced by a biographical and critical account of this celebrated poet; compiled from the best authorities, both manuscript and printed, by the Rev. Mr. Hindley of Manchester.'[203]

Hormuz Island

8.68 'Island of Ormus,' *Poulson's American Daily Advertiser* (Wednesday, 4 February, 1801), 'Island of Ormus,' *The Philadelphia Gazette and Daily Advertiser* (Friday, 6 February, 1801), 'Island of Ormus,' *Thomas's Massachusetts Spy, or Worcester Gazette* (Wednesday, 11 February, 1801) and 'Island of Ormus,' *Alexandria Advertiser and Commercial Intelligencer* (Thursday, 12 February, 1801): 'A gentleman in the suite of Colonel Malcolm,[204] who was lately deputed by the Supreme Government of India, as Ambassador to the Court of Persia, gives the following account of the once celebrated island Ormus, in a letter lately received the the last ships.

---

the Anacreon of Persia, Hafez concludes each distich in the original by calling for wine.'. See Nott (1787: 8–9). Cf. Blake (1859: 549), 'a celebrated poet, the Anacreon of Persia;' and Beale (1881: 99), 'From his frequent celebration of love and wine in his odes he has not improperly been denominated, by some Orientalists, the Anacreon of Persia.'

[201] Cf. the description by Ker Porter (1821/1: 686) who noted, 'It is now diminished to a mere rivulet, still, however, retaining its singular transparency, and softness to the taste; but the Arcadian scenery which embanked it, is vanished away; nothing now distinguishes the spot, so often the them of Hafiz, but the name of the river, and the brilliancy of its wave.'

[202] As noted above (n. 200), this epithet was first applied to Hafez in Jones (1771: 45). It was used by several later writers, e.g. Nott (1787: 8–9); Hindley (1800: 39) ('the polished *Anacreon* of *Irán*'); Kinneir (1813: 62) ('the Anacreon of the East'); Malcolm (1814: 23); Malcolm (1815/1: 447); Blake (1859: 549) and Beale (1881: 99).

[203] John Haddon Hindley (1765–1827), published as Hindley (1800). Hindley was librarian of the Chetham Library in Manchester which possessed a number of Persian manuscripts. He dedicated it 'to William Ouseley, Esquire, an able and zealous restorer of Oriental literature in Great Britain at the close of the Eighteenth Century.'

[204] Presumably William Hollingbery whose *Journal of observations* recounts his experiences in Malcolm's mission. See Hollingbery (1814). Although the cited text in the article is not quoted verbatim from Hollingbery's account, and the order of statements is different, it nevertheless seems to derive from his work.

"The Portuguese, under [Afonso de] Albuquerque,[205] took possession of this island in 1507, and were expelled by Shah Abbas, with the assistance of the English, in 1622.[206] It was at that time the emporium of the East, and was supposed to be the richest mart in the world; it shortly, however, fell into decay in the hands of the Persians; and when [Jean de] Thevenot visited it in 1665, it was a place of little or no importance.[207] When we arrived here on the 14th of March,[208] the appearance of the place was an oblong fort,[209] which was built by the Portuguese,[210] and has lately received considerable repairs from Imaum of Muscat, who obtained possession of it about four years ago.[211] It is situated on a narrow neck of land jutting into the sea, by which the walls are washed on the northern and eastern fronts. To the east and south it has a ditch, about eight feet deep, and fifteen yards broad, which is filled by the tide.[212]

"On the outside are a few straggling huts, forming a Pettah,[213] round which they are at present building a slight wall, flanked by round towards, at equal distances. A chain of hills run across the island, at the distance of about a mile and a half from the fort; the whole ground is one continued ruin; and from all appearance, there has been formerly a large city, from four to five miles in circumference, of which not a single house is standing.—What is

---

[205] For his career see e.g. Earle and Villiers (1990). For his 'Commentaries,' in English translation see Birch (1875–1884).

[206] For a contemporary account see Boxer (1930) and more generally Boxer (1935). Stiffe (1874: 13–14) also discusses the Anglo-Persian campaign to dislodge the Portuguese in some detail.

[207] After sketching a bit of the Portuguese history of Hormuz and its loss to Shah 'Abbas, with English aid, Thevenot (1674: 266) observed, 'presentement il n'en reste plus de marque, & il n'y a que la forteresse qui soit habitée.'

[208] The month given here is inccorect, since the delegation did not arrive anywhere on 14 March 1800. As noted above, Malcolm's mission had left Bombay on 29 December 1799. The *Bombay* entered Muscat harbor on 8 January, 1800; was becalmed off of Qishm on 16 January; and reached Bušehr on 1 February. There Malcolm and his suite remained until 22 May when they prepared to depart, reaching Shiraz on 15 June. See Kaye (1856/1: 105, 109, 110, 116, 117). Rather, the date, according to 8.21 above, should be '14 January,' where the *Bombay* arrived 'after a quick and agreeable passage of two days.'

[209] Oblong is an inaccurate way to describe the Portuguese fort on Hormuz. Stiffe (1874: 13) called it 'a quadrilateral bastioned fort, about 750 feet long by 620 feet broad.' Kleiss (1978: 171) made it 260 × 176 m.

[210] More precisely it was begun by Albuquerque on 24 October 1507, immediately after the Portuguese conquest of the island, and improved considerably in 1559/60. See Lizardo (2001) and particularly Campos (2011) for the construction history.

[211] 'The Seyyid Sultân rented el-Kishm [Qeshm], Hormûz, Bandar 'Abbâs, and the sulphur mines of Khamir from the Shâh of Persia.' See Markham (1874: 426).

[212] As Berghaus (1832: 47) noted, 'Auf der Nordseite der Insel liegt das Fort.'

[213] From Tamil *pēṭṭai*, 'The extramural suburb of a fortress, or the town attached and adjacent to a fortress.' See Yule and Burnell (1903: 702).

peculiarly singular is, that not a spring of fresh water is to be found in the island, which is fifteen miles in circumference; every house had formerly a cistern,[214] which caught the rain as it fell from the clouds."

The Caspian Sea Fishery

8.69 'Fishery of the Caspian Sea, from Pallas,'[215] *The Salem Impartial Register* (Monday, 16 February, 1801): 'It would be difficult to find in the whole world, a more abundant Fishery, except on the banks of Newfoundland, or one more advantageous to the government, than those of the Volga and Caspian Sea united. During the fast of the Greek church and the weekly fast days, which amount to a full third of the year, it may be said that this fishery affords the principal food to the whole European part of Russia, and its populous capitals. Many thousand of individuals are employed, and acquire wealth, either by fishing, or conveying the fish on rafts or sledges, or by the sale of this article.

The whole value of the different kinds of Sturgeon, caught in the waters of Astrakhan and the Caspian Sea, amounts to an annual sum of 1,760,405 rubles, according to the average price. It may hance be concluded in what incalculable numbers these large fish, so rich in caviare are continually produced in the depths of the Caspian Sea....Their superabundance may be still more clearly conceived, from what has been related to me by an eye witness, respecting the fishery of Sallian[216] in Persia. As the Persians eat no sturgeons,[217]

---

[214] In 1662 John Nieuhoff visited Hormuz and described 'a large plain, where the inhabitants used to have their cisterns together and keep rain-water in, which were always locked up; for not only hereabouts, but also all over the island the ground is brackish, which makes the rainwater which is kept in these cisterns much better than what is gathered from the pools or ponds.' See Churchill (1744: 186). Cf. Stiffe (1874: 13) on the 'fine large underground water cistern, with a groined roof, supported by rows of pillars,' inside the Portuguese fort. For a photograph of this cistern see Kleiss (1978: Abb. 7). It measured 15.3 × 5.8 m., and was over 3 m. deep. Thus, it had a 265 m³ capacity. See Kleiss (1978: 172).

[215] Peter Simon Pallas (1741–1811), distinguished Prussian scientist who worked extensively on zoological and botanical matters in Russia for decades. See e.g. Pallas 1799 and 1801. This article is a paraphrased translation of Pallas (1799: 183–184).

[216] Salyan in the 'The Delta of the Kur,' (McNeill 1836: 14), between Lenkoran and Baku in what is today the Republic of Azerbaijan. Eichwald (1834: 423) wrote, 'Den 7 März 1825 ritt ich nach Ssallian, um den Fischfang anzusehen, der so eben seinen Anfang genommen hatte.' Further, according to Eichwald (1834: 400), 'Von Fischen wurde aus Ssallian der Lachs (*Salmo salar*) und der Schamaï (*Cyprinus chalcoides*) gebracht.'

[217] The assertion that the Persians did not eat sturgeon is interesting, but not always true. Thus, e.g. while at Darband in 1475, Ambrogio Contarini noted that, 'Sturgeon...are caught in' the Caspian 'in very great numbers.' See Stanley (1873: 145). The anonymous Italian merchant who was in Iran from c. 1511–1520 noted that, at Tabriz, 'To this place there are...brought many sturgeon, smaller than those of the Mediterranean, but still excellent. There is delicious caviar also, which, as well as the sturgeon, is brought from the Caspian Sea, nine days' journey distant from this place.' See Grey

the speculator in the sturgeon fishery have rented the river at an annual sum, which of late years, has been raised to 24,000 rubles,[218] (as many dollars.) In the usual season of migration, there are sometimes taken with the hook, about 15,000 sturgeon of different kinds in one day.[219] The Persian fishery,[220] established only a few years ago, with the rent, amounts to an expence of 80,000 rubles, and is said to produce 200,000 rubles. The fishermen by preserving the fish as well as the air bladders for isinglass[221] might render it still more lucrative.[222] Besides the sturgeon, the small fish and seals taken in the Caspian, yield half a million of rubles.'

Persian Viticulture

8.70 'Extract from "The present state of the Cape of Good Hope, 1731," by Peter Kolben,' *The Times and District of Columbia Daily Advertiser* (Thursday, 19 February, 1801): 'The Europeans were a long time at the Cape of Good Hope before they could see a good vineyard planted among them, though from the time of their arrival they had bestowed all the pains and expence they could in the procuring and planting of vines. They procured some quantities of vine stock from the Rhine, and some by the way of Batavia from

---

(1873: 171). Tavernier (1678: 146) noted that, 'The Province of *Media* is well stor'd with Sturgeon from the mouth of the River *Araxes*.'

[218] Malte-Brun (1822: 60) wrote, 'The Kur, after being augmented by the junction of one of its branches with the Aras, becomes navigable. The sturgeon fisheries at its mouth, near Sallian, bring in 20,000 rubles (or L.3000) to the khan of Kouba, who lets it out to the Russians.'

[219] While the figures are impossible to convert, 200 tons of caviar were cured in one month at Astrakhan in 1829 according to Monteith (1833: 19).

[220] By the nineteenth century most if not all of the sturgeon caught off the coast of Mazandaran was also destined for Russian consumption. Morier (1818: 376) noted that, at Astarabad, 'On the coast they have a fishery, which is frequented by the Russians only, who pay to the Governor of Asterabad 100 tomauns annually for the liberty. Seven or eight small ships are employed in this fishery, which consists of sturgeon, from which they extract the caviar.' Similarly, Fraser 1826: 74 mentioned 'a small establishment formed for the purpose of catching sturgeon, and curing them for the Russian market,' near Farahabad. Cf. Napier (1876: 93) who noted that, near Farahabad, in the estuary of the T river, was 'one of the principal sturgeon fisheries on the coast, farmed with the other fisheries of the province to a Russian company for the annual sum of 68,000 tomans.' Similarly, Markham (1874: 345–346) noted that, along the coast of Mazandaran, 'Sturgeon and salmon, besides smaller fish, are caught in immense quantities.'

[221] Isinglass, derived from the bladders of the sturgeon, was used as a 'clarifying or fining agent (for coffee, wines, and beer)' but more importantly to manufacture gelatine. See Pereira (1857: 769).

[222] In a similar vein Fraser (1834: 344, n. *), wrote of the Caspian sturgeon, 'The writer…has seen these fish lying in thousands upon the banks of the Suffeidrood [Sefid Rud] in Ghilan, having been caught by the Russian fishers merely for the caviare and isinglass; after extracting which, the carcasses were thrown away to rot, and tained the air to a great distance round.'

Persia[223]; these they planted and cultivated in the ordinary way; but none being able to procure, from either of those places vine-stocks sufficient for a plantation that might deserve the name of a vineyard, vines for many years made but a very inconsiderable figure at the Cape; and the vintages there were nothing....The vine-stocks they afterwards imported from Persia and from Europe, were only for the sake of variety.'[224]

Hot Winds

8.71 'From a London Paper of January 4,' *The Spectator* (Saturday, 14 March, 1801) and 'From a London Paper of January 4,' *Alexandria Advertiser and Commercial Intelligencer* (Thursday, 19 March, 1801): 'The samel[225] or hot winds, have, during the late summer, been particularly fatal in Persia, more especially on the borders of the desert where vast numbers of persons have perished.'

The Persian Gulf Pearl Fishery

8.72 'Salem, Thursday, April 16, 1801,' *The Salem Impartial Register* (Thursday, 16 April, 1801): 'In Persia, in the East, we hear the Pearl Fishery at the Isle of Balhern [sic, Bahrain] is renewed.[226] There is a continual intercourse between Persia and Russia.'

Sir William Ouseley's Goals in Persia

8.73 'Persia,' *The Salem Impartial Register* (Monday, 4 May, 1801), 'Persia,' *The Times and District of Columbia Daily Advertiser* (Friday, 8 May, 1801), 'Persia,' *American*

---

[223] As Jullien (1856: 485) noted, a grape variety 'nommé *haenapop*...a été apporté de Schiras en Perse, et...produit un vin de liqueur [dessert wine] excellent.' Cf. Estreicher (2014: 517). According to Thudichum and Dupré (1872: 718), 'The Haenapop (has-no-pip) is easily recognized as the Persian vine, yielding the stoneless Sultana raisins; such raisins are...made in large quantities at the Cape.'

[224] This text was taken from Kolben (1731/2: 75–76).

[225] Ar. *shamāl*, lit. 'north.'

[226] For the pearl trade on Bahrain at this time see Kelly (1968: 28–30). The year 1801 was not exactly peaceful in and around Bahrain for, as Miles (1919/2: 294) noted, 'In 1801 the island of Al-Bahrain, which has ever been, on account of its rich pearl-fishery, the chief bone of contention for the peoples round the shores of the Persian Gulf, was again the object of Sultan's [Seyyid Sultan bin Ahmed] ambition, and was invaded, this time successfully, by a grand naval expedition from Muscat, the Attoobees ['Utub] being driven out and the island occupied by the Omani troops, and Saif bin Ali, who had already done good service on the Mekran coast, was appointed Governor and Commandant....Nor did Al-Bahrain remain long in the possession of Muscat; a few months later it was retaken from Salim bin Sultan, then a boy of twelve, who had replaced Saif bin Ali, by the Attoobees, who succeeded in surprising the garrison.'

Citizen and General Advertiser and *Republican Watch Tower* (Wednesday, 13 May, 1801), 'Persia,' *The Eastern Herald & Maine Gazette* (Monday, 18 May), 'Persia,' *The Herald of Liberty* (Monday, 18 May) and 'Persia,' *Vermont Centinel* (Thursday, 11 June, 1801): 'The king of Persia,[227] to whose court captain Malcolm has been sent with some other officers by the East India company, resides in the northern provinces of the empire, leaving his son to govern in the south.[228] Captain Malcolm was to wait upon him at Tahiran,[229] a town in the vicinity of Ria, the ancient Rageia of the Greeks,[230] and not far from the banks of the Caspian Sea. Sir William Ousley [sic, Ouseley],[231] who proposes visiting those places in the course of the present year,[232] is preparing for the Persian monarch a present which cannot fail of being welcome—it is a map of Persia on an immense scale, with the names of places written in the Arabic or Persian characters, and containing many hundred towns, villages, mountains, rivers, &c. not to be found in any other map, inserted from original manuscript authorities. Such errors or defects as may appear, Sir William intends to correct from local observation; so that his Persian majesty will probably receive from an European traveller, the only accurate delineation of his own dominions that he has ever seen, as the Asiatic geographers are very deficient in science and exactness, and inelegant in the execution of their maps.'[233]

---

[227] Fath 'Ali Shah.

[228] While Fath 'Ali Shah resided at Tehran, in the north, his son, Hoseyn 'Ali Mirza, was governor in Fars at the time of Malcolm's visit. See Busse (1972: 91–92).

[229] Tehran.

[230] Rayy. Described in Isidore of Charax's *Parthian Stations* (§7), dating to the first century AD, as 'the greatest of the cities in Media.' See Schoff (1914: 7, 29). For the mediaeval Arabic and Persian sources see Le Strange (1905: 214–217).

[231] Sir William Ouseley (1771–1842), younger brother of Sir Gore Ouseley (for their relationship see M'Cullagh [1906: 10–11]; Kelly [1910: 138]). As Conder (1830: 336), observed, Sir William Ouseley 'explored the country with all the zeal of a learned and accomplished antiquary.' As testimony to his keen collecting see, among his many publications of Persian and Arabic works in his own collection, the broader vademecum which he wrote on Persian manuscripts, Ouseley (1795). For his life and activities as a collector of manuscripts see Avery (2004). It has been said since the 1820s that Ouseley was born in Monmouthshire, Wales, e.g. Anonymous (1823e: 70); cf. Avery (2004). The authority of Richard J. Kelly, however, seems undeniable. He was 'Assistant Legal Land Commissioner, and a gentleman well known in Limerick, where for many successive years he was our popular Assistant Revising Barrister. In this notice of the Ouseley family with which Mr. Kelly is so closely connected, and in which he draws upon some family papers we read much that connects the Ouseleys with Limerck and the city with the name.' See Anonymous (1910).

[232] In fact Ouseley did not succeed in visiting Iran until 1810 when he served as his brother Gore Ouseley's secretary on the latter's mission as ambassador to the court of Fath 'Ali Shah. See Avery (2004).

[233] That Ouseley was working on an important new map of Persia was widely known. For example, noting that Ouseley had pronounced a map by S.F.G. Wahl in his *Altes und neues Vorder- und Mittel-Asien* (Leipzig, 1795) 'very excellent,' von Zach (1801: 384–385) wrote, 'Gewiß ist *Sir William* dieses am besten zu beurtheilen im Stander, der selbst im Orient gereist, und nun seit zwei Jahren mit

8.74 'Untitled,' *Gazette of the United States, and Daily Advertiser* (Wednesday, 27 May, 1801), 'Untitled,' *American Citizen and General Advertiser* (Thursday, 28 May, 1801), 'Untitled,' *Philadelphia Gazette and Daily Advertiser* (Friday, 29 May, 1801), 'Untitled,' *The Times and District of Columbia Daily Advertiser* (Saturday, 30 May, 1801), 'Untitled,' *Washington Federalist* (Monday, 1 June, 1801) and 'Gleanings from late London Papers,' *The Providence Gazette* (Saturday, 13 June, 1801): 'Amongst the literary and antiquarian objects of Sir William Ouseley's proposed Expedition to Persia, one is, we understand, to obtain if possible, some ancient Greek and Hebrew Manuscripts,[234] of which that Orientalist has traced the vestiges through a series of writers from the tenth to the middle of the present century. They had escaped the troubles which agitated Persia under Nadir Shah, and were seen about fifty years ago by a contemporary of that Prince, who describes them as relics of immense antiquity, and preserved in one family for several generations with a religious care, although their contents were perfectly unintelligible to their possessors.'

The Tabriz Earthquake of 1780

8.75 'Destruction by Earthquakes, during the last century,' *The Balance, and Columbian Repository* (Thursday, 21 May, 1801), 'Destruction by Earthquakes—During the last Century,' *The Western Star* (Monday, 15 June, 1801), 'Destruction by Earthquakes, during the last century,' *Windham Herald* (Thursday, 2 July, 1801), 'Destruction by Earthquakes, in the last century,' *Weekly Wanderer* (Saturday, 1 August), 'Destruction by Earthquakes. During the last Century,' *The Constitutional Telegraphe* (Saturday, 8 August, 1801),

---

Entwerfung einer großen Karte von *Persien* beschäftigt ist. Sie ist nach einem so großen Maßstabe gezeichnet, daß sie einen Raum von 6 Engl. Fuß in der Länge, und 5 Fuß in der Breite einnimmt. Sie wird viele hundert Namen von Städten, Flüssen, Bergen, Ruinen, Denkmälern, Brunnen, *Rebats* und *Karavanserais* enthalten, welche alle aus Original-Handschriften eingetragen worden, und noch in keiner andern Karte dieses Reichs vorgekommen sind. Allein alle Namen sind auf dieser Karte in Persischer Sprache, und mit Persischer Schrift geschrieben, weil sie zu einem Geschenke für den Monarchen von Persien bestimmt ist. Man hat Hoffnung, daß *Sir William* diese Karte mit Europäischen Lettern wird stechen, und vielleicht zur Herausgabe der von ihm versprochenen Persischen geographischen Handschrift *Mesalek ú Memalek* wird dienen lassen.' Similarly, in a review of Arrowsmith's *Map of Asia*, it was noted that, 'the German critic [F.X. von Zach] is greatly deceived when he supposes that Mr. Arrowsmith derived any intelligence from the *intended* map by sir William Ouseley, as that learned gentleman never proceeded further in his design than the insertion of a dozen or two of names in Persia, the only country he endeavoured to delineate; and these names being written in Persian, Mr. Arrowsmith could not have read them if he even had had access, which he had not, to sir William Ouseley's sketch, or rather shadow of an outline of a sketch.' See Anonymous (1801b: 583).

[234] It is highly unlikely that this was one of Ouseley's chief goals. The vast majority of the manuscripts which he collected in Iran were Persian. See Ouseley (1831). In addition, he obtained some books printed in Hebrew and Greek, as well as 'a Hebrew phylactery, written on leather.' See Ouseley (1831: iii, n. * and viii).

'Destruction by Earthquakes During the last Century,' *Newburyport Herald, and Country Gazette* (Tuesday, 11 August, 1801), 'Destruction by Earthquakes, in the last Century,' *Haswell's Vermont Gazette* (Monday, 17 August, 1801), 'Destruction by Earthquakes during the last century,' *The Kennebec Gazette* (Friday, 21 August, 1801), 'Destruction by Earthquakes, During the last Century,' *American Mercury* (Thursday, 27 August, 1801) and 'Destruction by Earthquakes during the last Century,' *The Pilot* (Wednesday, 9 May, 1810; 'Fauris'): 'At Tauris in Persia, 15,000 houses were thrown down by an earthquake, and a great part of the inhabitants perished, A.D. 1780.'[235]

A Curious Coin from Ohio

8.76 'From the Connecticut Gazette,' *City-Gazette and Daily Advertiser* (Monday, 17 August, 1801): 'Messrs. Greens, The subject of the following letter is so interesting, and the sentiments which it contains are so just, that I am induced to transmit it to you for publication in your paper.

By a comparison of the characters on the fac simile with the Zend, or Old Persian Alphabet,[236] and with a specimen of Old Persian writing, copied from an engraving on paper, both published in the first volume of the Asiatic Researches,[237] I have satisfied myself that these characters are the Old Persian....

There are on the fac simile seventeen characters. Of these, nine may be fairly considered as perfect resemblances, if a very small difference in form may be allowed to different engravings....and all can be satisfactorily shewn to be contained in the Persian specimens.... T. Dwight. Yale College,[238] July 14, 1801.

Marietta, June 18, 1801.

Sir—through the politeness of governor St. Clair,[239] I am enabled to send you a model of a copper coin, lately discovered at a small distance from the Ohio [River], on the bank of the little Miami river,[240] at the depth of about four feet from the surface of the earth, in cleaning out a spring, in the neighbourhood of some ancient ruins. This coin is now in the

---

[235] Cf. 7.77.

[236] Zend/Zand, now known as Pahlavi, a form of Middle Persian. See West (1880: x-xi). It was identified as 'old Persian, or Zend' by Hastings (1788: 12), though not in the sense that Old Persian carries nowadays, i.e. as the language of some Achaemenid inscriptions written in modified cuneiform.

[237] Hastings (1788: Pl. 3).

[238] Timothy Dwight IV (1752–1817), professor of theology and eighth president of Yale College. For his life see Dwight (1874: 140–160).

[239] Arthur St. Clair (1737–1818). He was confirmed by the United States Senate as Governor of the North-western Territory, or 'the Territory north-west of the Ohio.' For his career see Smith (1882).

[240] A tributary of the Ohio River in Ohio which enters near Cincinnati. It is not navigable except for small craft like canoes. See Jones (1922: 260).

governor's possession; and we believe it to be as ancient as the ruins themselves; yet, on a comparison of its characters with the alphabetical tables of the east, delineated in the Encyclopedia, we have been able to discover no striking resemblance; and the milling on the edge, most strongly resembles that on the coins of Spain. . . .it is in all other respects so totally different, that we are convinced it could not have had an European origin. . . .

Was this coin brought over from Asia?. . . .I am convinced that this coin was not fabricated in America. . . .

These circumstances seem to point out to us an emigration from the old world, (probably it was an early one) of a few adventurers; who might bring this coin along with them. . . .

Unfortunate country! denied even the sad consolation of being remembered, like Carthage, in the annals of your conqueror! I am, sir, with respect, your humble servant,
Elijah Backus'[241]

8.77 'Philadelphia, August 25. The Pope not Infallible,' *The Virginia Argus* (Tuesday, 1 September, 1801), 'The Pope not Infallible,' *The Salem Impartial Register* (Thursday, 3 September, 1801) and 'From the Aurora. The Pope not Infallible,' *The Constitutional Telegraphe* (Saturday, 19 September, 1801): 'We conceived it proper to publish a few weeks since the letter of a Mr. Bakus [sic, Backus],[242] and the *very learned* conjectural criticism of Dr. Dwight,[243] concerning a coin found in the Western country—and which as a divine, and the head of a College,[244] is a just cause of regret; because after what Noah Webster said about New-England learning[245] the learned must laugh heartily at our

---

[241] Born in New Haven, Connecticut, Elijah Backus (1759–1811) attended Yale University before he 'removed to the Northwest Territory, and was Receiver of public moneys. He was elected to the Senate, and was considered a good lawyer. . . .He is said to have owned the first printing press west of the mountains.' See Backus (1889: 13). His diary of 1777, when he was a senior at Yale, was published as Larned (1895). In her introduction, Larned describes Backus as 'a sober, pains-taking youth, duly interested in current events.' See Larned (1895: 355). That the letter reprinted here was sent by Backus to Dwight is suggested by the fact that, while a student at Yale, Backus attended lectures 'upon history' by Dwight and 'read the Elements of Criticism before Mr. Dwight.' See Larned (1895: 357).

[242] Elijah Backus.

[243] Timothy Dwight IV.

[244] Yale.

[245] Noah Webster (1758–1843). In *Ten Letters to Dr. Joseph Priestly*, Webster wrote, 'The truth seems to be that in the Eastern States, knowledge is more diffused among the laboring people than in any country on the globe. The learning of the people extends to a knowledge of their own tongue, of writing and arithmetic sufficient to keep their own simple accounts; they read not only the bible, and newspapers, but almost all read the best English authors, as the Spectator, Rambler, and the works of Watts, Doderidge and many others. If you can find any country in Europe where this is done, to the same extent, as in New-England, I am very ill informed. But in the higher branches of literature, our learning is superficial, to a shameful degree. Perhaps I ought to except the science of law, which being the road to political life, is probably as well understood as in Great Britain; and Ethics and political science have been greatly cultivated, since the American revolution. . . .But as to classical learning,

colleges really. The coin, however, has fallen into hands, which, without the same motives or obligations to be learned, have learned enough for the illustration of this *wonderful discovery*.—Upon the first perusal of Dr. Dwight's remarks, we were satisfied that the *characters* with *square* and *round* points with occasional *stars* must be either Arabic or Persian, and the fact proves to be so.

This wonderful coin, however, boasts no high antiquity for its origin, but appears to be of *genuine British Manufacture*.

The coin is in Bengal of the value of *one thirty-second* part of a *Rupee*; a rupee being equal to a half a dollar of our money. The Inscription on one side gives the title *Shah Allum* (king of the World), and the date which appears to be of the same impression as one in a collection of coins in possession of the Editor's Son, the date of which is 1190 of the Hejra, or 1776 of the Christian era; that year of the Hejra commenced on the 21st Feb. 1776.'[246]

8.78 'Marietta, September 15, 1801' *Gazette of the United States, & Daily Advertiser* (Monday, 5 October, 1801): 'Mr. Wayne, Sir, In an attack upon the President of Yale College in the Aurora of August 25, I find myself accused of an attempt to "impose upon the public understanding," in an account of a certain copper coin, said to have been discovered in the western country. It will probably be recollected from the railings of the Aurora, that in my letter to that gentleman, after noticing certain facts relative to the discovery of this coin; I stated it as the common opinion here, that it was an ancient Asiatic one; and observed, that if this opinion should prove to be well grounded, it would afford a new evidence, that this country was peopled from Asia. This coin it seems is allowed by the Editor of the Aurora, to be an Asiatic, but, not an ancient one. What the truth was, I did not pretend to know.

Not having been bred in the family of Tamerlane; nor taken a degree in the British East India prison; I did not profess, as a scholar, to be acquainted, either with "S*hah Allum*" or the "*Bengal Coinage of 1776.*" But I have the most abundant evidence of having received my information, from a source too respectable, to admit, thus circumstanced, of my disbelief of the facts stated. This information, thus received, I was led to communicate, in a private letter, which I never expected would meet the public eye, to a gentleman whom, in early life, I had been taught to revere, having been educated under him, and let me add, whose opinion in this instance (as far as he has given one) is acknowledged to be correct.

History, civil and ecclesiastical, Mathematics, Astronomy, Chymistry, Botany and Natural History—excepting here and there a rare instance of a man who is eminent in some one of these branches,—we may be said to have no leaarning at all, or a mere smattering.—And what is more distressing to me, I see every where a disposition to decry the study of ancient and original authors, which I deem far superior to the moderns and from which the best modern writers have drawn the finest parts of their productions.' See Webster (1800: 22).

[246] Silver coins equal to 1/32 of a rupee, bearing the name of the last but nominal Mughal emperor Shah Alam II, were issued by the Bengal Presidency (East India Company). The mint was established in 1758. See Johnston (1903: 73).

It remains to be proved, hereafter, what this coin is, which has put the Editor of the Aurora in such a passion: but I cannot forbear to make this one remark, that if on *subjects of mere literature*, an unknown, and undesigning writer, who ventures, as a pupil to send a letter to his old master, however erroneous his conclusions may be, is to be the butt of this man's abuse, it may happen to be believed, that in America, among other strange things, an imported black-guard has been appointed door-keeper to the sciences.

I am Sir,
Your humble servant,
C. Backus'[247]

Virtues of the Plane Tree

8.79 'From the Albany Register. Button Wood,' *Mercantile Advertiser* (Monday, 26 October, 1801) and 'From the Albany Register. Button Wood,' *The Salem Impartial Register* (Thursday, 5 November, 1801): 'Sir, it is a melancholy circumstance, that men of the best meaning should introduce or propagate errors injurious to society. Witness your correspondent of the ninth instant, who sets on foot against my family the most wanton proscription. His recommendation of the wild cherry tree, cannot excite my jealousy; for every body knows it to be of all trees the most infested with caterpillars...But respecting myself, let your correspondent consult the works of historians, poets, philosophers and naturalists, from the remotest antiquity down to this day, and he will find that my wood has been always celebrated. What high store did not the Romans set on their *Platanus*, in English *Plane*, and here commonly called *Button Wood*?....

To conclude, sir, by a most authentic fact, tell the inhabitants of New-York, that the people of Ispahan (a capital town in Persia) cultivate the Button-Wood in their gardens and streets, for the very purpose of *preventing and destroying all sorts of contagion*.[248]

Thus, if the sickness which prevailed a few years ago is to be attributed (according to your correspondent's own observation, which is not improbable) to the cutting down of the trees in New-York, be pleased to ask him whether those trees were not chiefly of my family. Button Wood.'

---

[247] 'C.' is a misprint for 'E,' i.e. Elijah, as per 8.78 and Backus (1889).

[248] 'Les Persans pensaient que le platane (platanus orientalis L.) avait une vertu naturelle contre toute infection de l'air: ils croient que si Ispahan et autres villes de la Perse échappent à la contagion, elles en sont redevables aux fluides émanés de cete arbre, qu'on voit dans toutes les rues et jardins.' See Tavares (1823: 35). More generally, on the plane tree (*Platanus orientalis* L.) in Iran, see Potts (2018b).

A Description of Isfahan

8.80 'Account of Ispahan, the capital of Persia,' *The Times, and District of Columbia Daily Advertiser* (Friday, 30 October, 1801): 'Ispahan, the capital of Persia is thought by some, to be the finest city in the east.[249]—It stands in the middle of a plain, surrounded on all sides by mountains at three miles distance, and on a small river, called Sanderut,[250] which supplies almost all the houses with water. It is 20 miles in circumference,[251] with well-built houses and flat roofs, on which they walk, eat, and lie, in summer, for the sake of the cool air. Here are a great number of magnificent palaces; and that of the king is two miles and a half in circumference.[252] There are 160 mosques,[253] 1800 large caravanseries,[254] above 260 public baths,[255] a prodigious number of coffee houses, and very fine streets, in which are canals,[256] planted on each side with trees.—The streets are not paved; but always clean,[257] on account of the dryness of the air; for it seldom rains or snows here. The inhabitants were computed at above one million[258]; but this kingdom

---

[249] This is an almost verbatim copy of the entry 'Ispahan' in Walker (1795) (unpaginated; s.v. 'Ispahan'). Alternatively the second edition of 1798 could have been the source.

[250] Zayandarud.

[251] Cf. MacGregor (1871: 187), 'It was formerly surrounded by a wall 24 miles in circumference, but this was destroyed by the Afghans and now scarce a vestige of it remains.'

[252] MacGregor (1871: 189), 'The palaces of the King are enclosed in a fort of lofty walls, which may have a circumference of three miles.'

[253] Describing the situation in 1811, Ouseley (1823/3: 33) wrote, 'The hundred and sixty-one *masjeds*...or mosques, comprehended within this city's walls during the seventeenth century according to Chardin, are now reduced to sixty...and even of these...no more than forty are kept in a state of repair, the others having fallen to ruin.'

[254] Thus MacGregor (1871: 188) noted, 'The bazaars are very extensive, and it is possible to walk under cover in them for 2 or 3 miles together.'

[255] Ouseley (1823/3: 34–35) noted, 'Yet in another instance the recent calculation is considerably lower than Chardin's; according to notes which he had collected the publick baths of *Ispahán* amounted in his time to two hundred and seventy three. Mírzá Ján, who resided there in 1811, informs us that the city contains about eighty baths.... Mírzá Sáleh at the same time, inquired their number, and says that they amount to about one hundred. My own questions on this subject produced very vague information, fluctuating between eighty and a hundred and twenty.'

[256] MacGregor (1871: 189), 'The water-supply of Ispahān is excellent, coming, as it does, from numerous canals from the Zainderūd.'

[257] Cf. MacGregor (1871: 188), 'The streets of Ispahān are narrow, dirty, and mean, and not less than one quarter of the city is in ruins.'

[258] Certainly an exaggeration. Ouseley (1823/3: 24) estimated the population at under 200,000 in 1811. Cf. MacGregor (1871: 189).

having been long distracted by civil wars, the principal towns are greatly depopulated. Isaphan has three large suburbs, called Julfa,[259] Hasenbath[260] and Kebrabath.[261] Though at

---

[259] The well-known Armenian quarter of Isfahan.

[260] Olearius (1662: 302) wrote, 'The Suburbs of *Hasenabath* is the ordinary habitation of the *Tzurtzi*, that is to say, the *Georgians*, who are also *Christians*, and most of them Merchants, and wealthy men...as well by reason of the Trade they drive within the Kingdom, as in all other places abroad.' Kaempfer (1711: 167) referred to the Hassanabad gate ('Pyli Hassenabad'). Cf. Chardin (1711/8): 'Porte de Hassen abad.' Ouseley (1823/3: 24) visited 'the *Bázár* of Hassan Abád.' Hasanabad was also the name of one of the city's gates. See MacGregor (1871: 187).

[261] Between 1616 and 1625 'Gabr-abad' was visited by Pietro Della Valle who noted 'in dem vierten und letzten Winckel aber, gegen Hispahan, ligt Gabr-abàd, welches die Gauren bewohnen, und diese Heyden seyn.' See Della Valle (1674/2: 22). Cf. Don Garcia de Silva y Figueroa who visited in 1618 and noted that 'il n'y eust gueres plus de dix ans, que le Roy de Perse [Shah 'Abbas I] les eust contraints de quitter le lieu de leur naissance, pour venir demeurer auprés d'Ispahan.' See Wicqfort (1667: 179). Olearius (1662: 302) wrote, 'There is yet a noble part of the Suburbs towards the West-side of the Citie, named *Kebrabath*, deriving its name from a certain people called *Kebber*, that is to say, *Infidels*, from the *Turkish* word *Kiaphir*, which signifies a *Renegat*. I know not whether I may affirm they are Originally *Persians*, since they have nothing common with them but the Language.' Similarly, Daulier Deslandes (1673: 51) noted, 'Si vous voulez passer à un quart de lieuë de Julpha en tirant vers la montagne, vous verrez un beau village composé d'une longue ruë, il se nomme Guebrabad, c'est la demeure des Guebres ou Guavres, que l'on dit estre les anciens Perses qui adoroient le feu. Le Roy leur a donné ce lieu pour habiter; les ayans détruits en beaucoup d'autres endroits.' Chardin (1711/8: 227) called it the '*Bourg des Guebres*, qui sont les *Ignicoles*, parce qu'ils y étoient tous ramassez.' Further, Chardin (1711/8: 228–229) noted, 'Ce fut A*bas second* qui fit bâtir ce magnifique *Bourg*, après en avoir transporté les *Guebres*, ou anciens *Ignicoles*, qui y demeuroient auparavant comme je l'ai dit, & lesquels il logea au bout du bourg de *Julfa*.' Kaempfer (1711: 164) estimated the population at 500 families. According to Tavernier (1678: 157) 'The Habitation of the *Gaurs* is only a large Village, the first Houses whereof are but a little way from the River.' Otter (1748/2: 13) also visited the village, but noted 'Dans tous les endroits de ce Royaume où j'ai passé, je n'ai trouvé que le seul village de Guebrabad auprès d'Ispahan, où il y eût des Guebres reconnus pour tel.' By the time Ker Porter visited it was uninhabited. Discussing the remaining Zoroastrian population of Iran, he wrote, 'The liberal spirit of Shah Abbas tolerated their existence at Ispahan; where, afterwards, the Afghan Mahmoud gave them a mart, and enlarged their suburb, still called Guebrabad: but, like that of the Armenian colony from Julpha, it is fallen to decay; nothing now inhabiting its ruined streets, but houseless dogs and the refuse of the people.' See Ker Porter (1821/2: 46). Jackson (1906: 273) knew the reference in Olearius but could find no trace of the place. As he wrote, 'During my short stay in Isfahan I found time to inquire whether there were any Zoroastrians engaged in business there, as I thought this would be probable in so large a place. It seemed the more likely also because there once was a suburb of Isfahan called *Gabarabād*, "Settlement of the Gabars," to which the German traveller Olearius alluded, three centuriess ago, giving a picture likewise of the Tower of Silence (*dakhmah*) in the vicinity.' The *dakhmah* of Isfahan still stands and thus the village of Gabarabad was presumably nearby. Menant (1914: 149) noted, 'No trace of Gabrābād can now be found. Three hundred yards below the bridge of Julfa, and at about the same distance above the Pul-i-Khaj, the river is crossed by the Pul-i Jhubi, a brick bridge of fourteen arches...The suburb upon the southern bank at this spot was known as Gabristān because it was inhabited by the Zoroastrians; but the ground was cleared by 'Abbas II., who transformed the place into a royal residence...which was named Sadat Ābād, or "Abode of Felicity," where he kept his seraglio. The name alone has survived.'

a distance from the sea, it carries on a great trade, people of several nations resorting there for the sake of traffic. It is 260 miles N.E. of Bassarais,[262] and 1400 miles S.E. of Constantinople. Lon. 52 55 E. lat. 32 35 N.'

A Brief History of Persia

8.81 'Untitled,' *The Salem Impartial Register* (Monday, 16 November, 1801; second paragraph only) and 'Persia,' *The Independent Chronicle and the Universal Advertiser* (Monday-Wednesday, 23–25 November, 1801): 'In the anticipations of the progress of Bonaparte from Egypt to the East, much was said of Persia. This nation had seen with jealousy the power of the English in Hindostan. It is now said that the extent and resources of this ancient Kingdom, as well as its intentions, are examined with great care under the favorite name of negociation, and that we may expect that the profound researches of the East, which have illustrated so much of the history of these distant countries will extend to this country, and for which such encouragement has been given by the labours of sir W. Jones,[263] and of the men of genius who have enjoyed his patronage and his example. It is said the King of Persia[264] has gone to visit the northern part of his dominions, which extend towards the Caspian and Black Seas.

The attempts of the English to gain an influence over the Court of Persia, and the failure of success in establishing a minister,[265] make an enquiry into the condition of Persia interesting. We have not so late documents as we wish, but shall attend to the description of Asia,

---

Another 'Gabarabad' was located south of Kashan. See Conder (1826: 178); Curzon (1892/2: 16); d'Allemagne 1911: 24; and Weston 1921: 418 (map) and 463.

[262] Basra. The actual distance between Basra and Isfahan is over 440 mi. Cf. 6.117.

[263] Sir William Jones (1746–1794). For a contemporary appreciation of his achievements see Sir John Shore's discourse of 22 May 1794, Shore (1795).

[264] Fath 'Ali Shah.

[265] It is not correct to say that 'the English,' i.e. Malcolm, failed to establish a minister for as he wrote in his journal, 'On the political part of my mission I spoke with indifference, lest I should, by showing any anxiety, give an idea that the English would purchase the assistance of the Persian monarch. I told the Hadjee [Ibrahim], that if the King his master saw his advantage in entering into political engagements on principles of prudence and equity, that such I was authorised by the Governor-General to contract; but that if he was averse to such a measure, I should neither persist in it, nor enter into further explanation.' See Kaye (1856/1: 136, n. *). Similarly Kaye (1856/1: 135) observed, 'he told Hadjee Ibrahim that it was necessary, to the cultivation of the friendship of the two states, that a Commercial Treaty advantageous to the interests of both should be concluded; but that, as to the Political Treaty, although prudence would seem to recommend it, there appeared no immediate necessity for it on the part of either.' As Haji Ibrahim wanted both a political and a commercial treaty, one was signed but the political portion concerned principally Zaman Shah in Afghanistan, and the French, with no stipulation concerning the establishment of a British or EIC representative. As McNeil (1836: 58) noted, 'this was a special mission; no British minister was left at the Court, and no attempt was made to preserve the influence that had been acquired.'

8.1 Miscellaneous

as given with the late superb edition of the history of Nadir Chah in the works of Sir William Jones,[266] and take some of the most interesting particulars.—Iran, or the Empire we call Persia, is bounded by seas and rivers. It has the Indian sea on the south, and the Caspian opposite to it. The Persian Gulph, or, as the Asiatics call it, the Green Sea, the Tigris and Euphrates, the Cyrus and Araxes, the Oxus and Bactrus[267] and the five branches of the Indus, divide it on the other sides, from Arabia, from Syria, from Georgia, from Turkistan, and from India. On the south, Pars, or Persis, extends along the Gulph near three hundred leagues. On the north is a desert named Noubendigan.[268] On the border of this desert is the valley of Bavàn.[269] Its finest cities are Shiraz, Yezd and Firuzabad, all of which have given birth to celebrated writers. Having passed the desert you enter the province of Khorasan, the Bactriana of the Ancients. It is the most eastern kingdom of Iran. It is bounded on the north by the Oxus, on the west by a desert, and on the east by the mountains of Candahar, which separate it from India. Its principal cities have all, at different times, been the seats of Kings. To Balkh, the successor of Cyrus retired.[270] Herat was the Aria of the Greeks, and has been fully described by a learned Persian historian who was born in it.[271] It was ruined by the Tartars, as was Merushahjan.[272] Nishapur was built by Shapur,[273]

---

[266] Jones (1770).

[267] Name used e.g. by Quintus Curtius 7.4.31 and others (Strabo, Polyaenus) flowing at the foot of Mount Parapomisus and giving its name to the city of Bactra. Mod. Dehās. See Forbiger (1844/2: 556–557); Geiger (1896–1904: 392).

[268] Actually a town in Fars, attested as Nawbandajan/Nubandagan in the mediaeval geographical literature. 'This place, when Iṣṭakhrî wrote, was larger than Kâzîrun, the climate was hot and the date palm grew here. Muḳaddasî speaks of its fine markets, of the gardens with their abundant water-supply, also of its mosque. In Saljuḳ times Nawbandajân had fallen to ruin, but in the 5th (11th) century the town was rebuilt by the celebrated Atabeg, the Amir Châûli.' See Le Strange 1905: 264. Cf. Schwarz 1896–1935: 31. The ruins, which are today within the confines of Nurabad-e Mamasani and which the author visited on several occasions in 2003–2004, were described by de Bode (1843: 78) as 'heaps of stones and hillocks scattered over the plain: an eloquent lesson on the instability of human things, but wasted on the desert.'

[269] A valley between Nawbandajan and Kurjan according to Ibn Khurdadbih, noted for its beauty. See Schwarz (1896–1935: 173). Baron de Bode (1843: 79) called it 'Sha'b-beván (Tent-pole defile) and noted that it 'is said by the Arabian and Persian poets to be one of the four terrestrial paradises.'

[270] A reference to the Iranian mythical cycle concerning the Kayanid king Kai Khosro (Cyrus) whose son Lohrasp, according to Mirkhvand, abandoned Istakhr and retired to Balkh. See Ouseley (1821/2: 393).

[271] Both Mirkhvand and his son Kandamir, who completed his seven volume world history after his death, were born in Herat. See Szuppe (2012).

[272] Merv Shahjan, 'Merv the city of the king.' For the epithet in Yaqut's geographical dictionary see e.g. Barbier de Meynard (1861: 526).

[273] Shapur II (r. 309–379). Cf. Le Strange 1905: 383, 'In modern Persian the name is pronounced Nîshâpûr, the Arab form being Naysâbûr, which is from the old Persian Nîv-Shahpuhr, meaning "the good (thing, deed, or place) of Shâpûr," and the city is so called after the Sassanian king Shâpûr II, who had rebuilt it in the fourth century A.D., for Naysâbûr owed its foundation to Shâpûr I, son of Ardashîr Bâbgân.'

and Tus, now called Meshehed,[274] was made the capital of Khorasan in the past century. Segestan, or Sistan, the Drangiana of the Greeks, touches at its eastern boundary, the province of Multan, which makes a part of Sind. Its chief cities are Bosr [sic, Bust], Zerenge,[275] which was populous and commercial in the reign of the Suffrarian[276] princes. This Province and Zablestan,[277] the ancient Arachosia, were considered as one principal city by the old Persians. In Zablestan is Cabul, the Capital of Cabulistan, which is well known, Meimend,[278] celebrated for its gardens, Gazna,[279] conquered by the Persians, and Bamian which Genghiz took in 1224. Sind, next to Segestan, though generally considered as part of India, comprehends Mocran, and Multan, provinces of Persia,[280] and it is to be observed, the Easterns divide the Indian Empire into two parts, the Hind and Sind, in the last including the countries on each side of the Indus, and in the first the countries on the Ganges....Kerman or Carmana, bounds on the Persian Gulph. The soil is dry. Sirjan is watered by artificial canals,[281] Zerend,[282] and Hormuz, formerly on the continent, now on an island in the Gulph of Persia.[283] Its commerce was removed to the port of Abbas, or Gomron. To the west of Pars is Khuzistan, called by the Greeks Susiana, remarkable for its

---

[274] As Le Strange (1905: 388) noted, Mashhad was the capital of Khorasan 'and a few miles to the north of it may be seen the ruins of Ṭûs, the older city. Ṭûs, in the 4th (10th) century, was the second city of the Naysâbûr quarter of Khurâsân.'

[275] Destroyed by Timur, 'the ruins still remain, covering a considerable area of ground.' See Le Strange (1905: 335).

[276] Saffarid. For a history of the dynasty see Bosworth 1994.

[277] 'The highlands of the Ḳandahâr country, along the upper waters of the Helmund, were known as Zâbulistân.' See Le Strange 1905: 334.

[278] 'Maywand in Zâbulistân, half-way between Girishk and Ḳandahâr...Yâḳût...writes of Maymand (or Mîmand) of Ghaznah.' See Le Strange (1905: 425).

[279] Ghazna/h 'became famous in history at the close of the 4th (beginning of the 11th) century as the capital of the great Maḥmûd of Ghaznah, who at one time was master both of India on the east and Baghdâd on the west.' See Le Strange (1905: 348).

[280] To call Multan, in the Punjab (mod. Pakistan) a 'province of Persia,' is anachronistic and could only apply after Nader Shah's conquest of the Mughal empire. Le Strange (1905: 331) reckoned 'Al-Multân, the great city far up the affluent of the Indus called the Sindarûdh,' as belonging to mediaeval India.

[281] A reference to the fact that 'the water of the town was derived from two underground channels that had been dug in the 3rd (9th) century by 'Amr and Ṭâhir, sons of Layth the Ṣaffârid.' See Le Strange (1905: 301). Presumably two qanats are meant here.

[282] Briefly the capital of Kerman province after its takeover by the Saljuq Turks, Zarand was located a short distance to the northwest of Kerman. See Le Strange (1905: 305, 308).

[283] A reference to the fact that the original Hormuz, sometimes called Old Hormuz, was located on the mainland near mod. Minab, until it was abandoned in 1300 by Baha'-al-Din Ayaz and the population moved to the island of Jarun which became known as (New) Hormuz. Vosoughi (2009: 92–93).

plains. Tostar, or Shuster, the ancient Susa,[284] famous for its velvets,[285] is among its cities. Arabian or Babalonian Irak has Mesopotamia on the west, Bagdat is the capital of this province. The Tartars, Persians and Turks have been successively in possession of this city. It was taken in 1638 by the Sultan Morad III [IV], and continues to remain in the hands of the Turkish princes. Among its celebrated cities is Basra, well known to merchants. Persian Irak, or Cuhistan[286] is also a fine province. In it, is Ispahan, which the Sefi[287] formerly made the metropolis of their kingdom. Azarbigian, or Media, and Armena, Armenia are sometimes considered as one province. In Shirvan, are the cities of Bacu, on the Caspian, Shamakhi, well known to the Russians, and Derbend which commands the Cassian, and was considered as the boundary of the Persian Empire. Daghestan, the ancient Albania, extends to Russia. Dilem and Ghilan are described by Abulfeda, and are the country of the ancient Galæ.[288] Tabarestan and Mazenderan, were the ancient Thyrcania and Margiana. Khorezm lies on the Oxus. Badakhshan and Tokarestian lie towards the source of the Oxus. On the south is Candahar. Algezirah, or Country between the Tigris and Euphrates, a country well known in ancient history, is now divided into four cantons. The first period of the history of Persia extends till the Arabs became masters of Persia in the middle of the seventh century, who held it till it was taken by the Tartars in 1428.[289] In 1450 it was subject to the Turcomans,[290] and in the fifth period of its history it was subject to the Sefis in 1515. Nader Chah succeeded to the race of Sefis. A country so often conquered can afford us no favorable opinion of its political situation. But directed in its affairs by a brave conquerer, it may be formidable to its neighbors. Still the first glance assures us that an invasion by a disciplined army, would probably be followed by the same consequences as have already marked its history. Its favorite arts are in great perfection. It has produced excellent poets and historians, and has all the resources which an extended population and a fertile soil can give it.'

---

[284] The confusion of Susa (Shush) with Shushtar was common in the eighteenth and early nineteenth century. See Potts (1999 [2002]: 30) with a review of the literature.

[285] Velvet (*makhmal*) was produced in Shushtar (Grohmann 1993: 791) but it was most famous for its silk brocades (*diba-ye shushtari*). See Le Strange (1905: 235). Yazd, Kashan, Isfahan, Mashhad, Herat and Tabriz were noted centers of velvet production. See Floor (1999: 170).

[286] 'Iraq 'Ajami, lit. 'non-Arab Iraq,' in which Ajam/'Ajami particularly referred to Persians, also called al-Jibal, 'the mountains,' or, as Qazvini wrote in Persian, 'Kuhistān.' See Le Strange (1905: 185–186).

[287] Safavids.

[288] The Gelae of Strabo, Pliny, Cl. Ptolemy, located in the area southwest of the Caspian Sea, who gave their name to Gilan. For refs. See Forbiger (1844/2: 594).

[289] It is not clear what this date refers to. To say that the Arabs controlled Iran until the Tartars took it in 1428 ignores the Saljuqs, Mongols and Timurids. The Qara-qöyünlü inflicted a defeat on Temür's son Shahrokh in 1428, capturing Sultaniyah (Potts 2014: 215 with refs.), but this is unlikely to be the event implied here.

[290] The Aq Qöyunlü and Qara Qöyünlü were both Türkmen tribes. See Potts (2014: 215–220).

Distemper

8.82 'Latest Foreign Intelligence. London, March 6,' *Morning Chronicle* (Friday, 15 April, 1803), 'Latest Foreign Intelligence. London, March 6 and March 7,' *Chronicle Express* (Monday, 18 April, 1803), 'Intelligence. Transatlantic. England. London March 6,' *The National Aegis* (Wednesday, 27 April, 1803) and 'Untitled,' *Charleston Courier* (Tuesday, 3 May, 1803): 'An epidemic distemper, of uncommon virulence has, according to late accounts, committed horrid ravages in Caswin in Persia.'

Commerce of Astrakhan and Persia

8.83 'City of Astracan. From a foreign paper, under head of Copenhagen, Nov. 3, 1803,' *Columbian Courier, or Weekly Miscellany* (Friday, 10 February, 1804): 'The following details which have been published respecting the Asiatic town of Astracan, comprised in the vast provinces of Russia, and center of the commerce between that state and Persia,[291] by means of the Caspian sea, in the neighbourhood of which it is situated, given an idea of its importance, and of the prosperity to which it has risen by degrees. It possesses an establishment of silk-worms, eighty-four silk manufactories, eighty one cotton manufactories, five morrocco manufactories, seventy four dye-houses, twenty four brick-kilns, ninety two vineyard-plots, two hundred and twelve mills, &c. The commercial houses consist of eleven hundred and eighty Russians, five foreigners, eighteen Tartars[292] and four Hindoos. Amongst the inhabitants there are two thousand one hundred and eighty-two Persians, buchares and Hindoos. The town contains two thousand shops, six convents, fifty-seven churches, four of which are Armenian, two Catholic, one Lutheran, twenty seven Tartarian mosques, and a meeting house of Hindoos.'[293]

---

[291] Levesque (1800: 243) wrote, 'Le commerce de Perse procure à cette ville [Atrakhan] une nombreuse population; et l'on assure qu'elle ne mone pas à moins de soixante et dix mille hommes. Une assez grande partie est composée d'étrangers, Allemands, Français, Anglais, Italiens, Suédois, Arméniens, Géorgiens, Tatars de différentes nations, Grecs, Kalmouks et Indiens. Les plus riches maisons de commerce expédient des vaisseaux sur la mer Caspienne et sur le Volga. Plusieurs fabriques mettent en œuvre le coton et les soies de la Perse. On a transporté aux environs d'Astrakhan des vignes de Perse, qu'on enterre pendant l'hiver, et l'on y recueille de gros raisins d'un goût exquis.' And further Levesque 1800: 321, 'Dans la ville d'Astrakhan, sont établis des Tatars, des Juifs, des Indiens, des Tourkestaniens, des Arméniens, des Persans, tous faisant un grand commerce avec la Khive, la Boukharie et la Perse. Les principaux articles de ce commerce consistent en toile, cire, savon, fer, cuivre, plomb, or, argent, acier, mercure, couperose, cuirs de Russie.'

[292] According to Tooke (1800: 451), 'The present Astrakhan Tartars are for the most part Nogayans. They are distinguished into town, village, and tent Tartars. The first dwell in Astrakhan.'

[293] The 'foreign paper' from which this was taken was probably the Journal de Paris under a dateline of Russia, Pétersbourg, 1 October, not Copenhagen. The French article was followed by one with a dateline of 'Danemarck, Copenhague, 9 novembre,' and this was probably the source of the incorrect

Blending Fact and Fiction in Persian Affairs

8.84 'Genoa, Feb. 15,' *The Philadelphia Evening Post* (Wednesday, 2 May, 1804), 'Genoa, Feb. 14,' *Aurora General Advertiser* (Thursday, 3 May, 1804), 'Genoa, Feb. 15,' *Poulson's American Daily Advertiser* (Thursday, 3 May, 1804), 'Genoa, Feb. 15,' *Albany Gazette* (Thursday, 10 May, 1804), 'Genoa, Feb. 15,' *The Repertory* (Friday, 11 May, 1804) and 'Genoa, Feb. 15,' *Charleston Courier* (Saturday, 19 May, 1804): 'A letter received at Salonica, from an Armenian merchant, gives the following account of the present state of the Persian empire.

"The sons of the last Sophi, who was murdered by his wives,[294] in his seraglio last year, are combating against each other for the succession to the throne. There are three of them; two by the Sophi's sister, the third by Zirza,[295] famous for her beauty, whom the Sophi had carried off from her father, a Bonze[296] of Thibet.—She is still in the full bloom of her beauty, and is kept a prisoner by the two elder brothers her enemies, who watch her closely. Mevalek, her son, is master of Ispahan, and of three inland provinces. He has a great many elephants, and has an intelligent general, who has served under Paswan Oglu.[297] The two other brothers have nearly an equal force."'

---

date. This English translation contains an error in the number of silk manufactories in Astrakhan. 'Pour juger de l'accroissement de notre commerce, il suffit de jeter les yeux sur les établissemens qui se sont faits à Astracan, seulement depuis le règne d'empereur Alexandre. En voici l'état: 24 manufactures de soies, 81 de coton, 5 de maroquin, 74 teintureries, 24 briqueries, 92 vignobles, 212 moulins. Astracan, située dans une île du Wolga, est une ville d'environ 70 mille ames de toutes nations, Allemands, Français, Tartares, Persans, Arméniens, Indiens & Russes. La ville renferme 2000 boutiques, 6 couvens, 57 églises, 27 mosquées & une maison de prières des Indoux. La plupart des maisons sont en bois. Aussi fut-elle brûlée presqu'en entier en 1767. Elle s'est relevée de ses cendres.' See Anonymous (1803b).

[294] This is patently a fictional account blending elements of fiction (Zirza) with fact (Paswan Oglu).

[295] Zirza features as a Christian beauty in Voltaire's *Candide* (Voltaire 1764: 629–631) and as a French slave in the play *Arlequin esclave à Bagdad* (Vallier 1798).

[296] A Buddhist priest, normally in China or Japan. From Japanes *bonzō* via Portuguese *bonzo*. See Fennell (1892: 165).

[297] Osman Paswan Oğlu, pasha of Widdin (mod. Vidin) from 1798 to 1807. As Browne (1799: 419–420) wrote, 'Originally Aga of that city, that is, chief of the Janizaries and commandant, he formed a powerful opposition to the Pasha...By numerous intrigues and disputes the latter was gradually deprived of his authority, and Paswan Oglo usurped his place...The Porte, following its usual policy of rewarding where it cannot punish, of decorating the head which it wishes to strike off, confirmed Paswan in the Pashalik.'

Smallpox

8.85 'Kine Pock,'[298] *Political Calendar* (Thursday, 16 August, 1804), 'Kine Pock,' *Columbian Courier, or Weekly Miscellany* (Friday, 17 August, 1804) and 'Kine Pock,' *Kennebec Gazette* (Thursday, 30 August, 1804): 'Doctor De Caro,[299] now at Vienna, has received letters, which state, "that the Vaccine has met the greatest success in Persia. Doctor Milne,[300] and M. Jokes [sic, Jukes],[301] his correspondents at Bassors [sic, Basra],

---

[298] Cowpox. See e.g. Anonymous (1802b).

[299] Jean de Carro (1770–1857), Swiss physician, mainly active in Vienna (1794–1826), credited with introducing innoculation in Europe. See Anonymous (1857b: 504).

[300] Dr. John Milne (1775–1841) was Carro's correspondent in transmitting smallpox vaccine to India for the first time in 1802. In 1798 he was posted as EIC Surgeon to the Factory at Basra, where he remained until late 1803 or early 1804. See Smith (1871: 15–17). For his life, much of which was spent in Bombay, see Smith (1871) and Rodger (1893: 137–147). According to Colvill (1872: 68), 'The Bombay Medical Board, writing on first August, 1801, says...that the Board has made several attempts teo get vaccine lymph to India but without success, and now recommends the trial by Constantinople, Baghdad, and Busreh, performing vaccination at those places so as to send fresh lymph from them. Sir Harford Jones, Resident, writing 18th April 1802, says the operation of vaccination has been successfully performed at Baghdad with some matter received from Dr. de Carro at Vienna on the 30th ultimo, and he sends fresh vaccine lymph express to Busreh [Basra] for conveyance to India....The lymph arrives safely at Busreh April 25th, and on the fifth of May Dr. Milne sends fresh supplies by the "Alert" to Bushire, Muscat, and the Presidency. He again sends by four following vessels till September 1802, when the establishment of vaccination is publicly notified in the "*Bombay Courier*."' Cf. Bowers (1981: 22). On Milne's activity in Iraq before leaving for Bombay, see Elgood (1951: 433–434).

[301] Surgeon Andrew Jukes vaccinated at Bushehr in 1804 and was in charge of the Residency there from December, 1808 to May, 1809. See Tuson (1979: 184). In a letter to de Carro written at Bušehr on 4 March 1805, Jukes said, 'j'ai eu le plaisir de vous écrire une longue lettre de 6 février dans laquelle je vous faisois part du bonheur que j'avois eu de produire la vaccine à Bushire avec de virus que vous aviez eu la bonté de m'envoyer de Vienne; je ne dissimulois point ma vive espérance de réussir dans mes effots pour répandre le bienfait de la vaccination dans toute la Perse.' See de Carro (1805: 83–84). As Sir Harford Jones noted in his memoir on his mission to Fath 'Ali Shah, Lord Minto, the Governor-General of India, 'appointed Surgeon Jukes, of the Bombay Establishment, to take charge of the British interests at Tæheran, until the arrival there of General Malcolm,' i.e. the rival mission to Jones' own. See Brydges (1834/1: 345). However, although Jukes was going to Tehran 'to make explanations to the Shâh of Persia, and to represent our motives of action in the Gulf... he died on his way, of the plague, at Isfahân.' See Markham (1874: 432) (Wright 1998: 166 gave cholera as the cause of death). His travelling companion, James Baillie Fraser was with him at the time and gave a full description of Jukes' illness (Fraser 1825: 120–124). In fact Fraser ended up delivering 'the dispatches intended for the Persian court...into the hands of Henry Willock, Esq., chargé d'affaires to His Britannic Majesty.' See Fraser (1826: 1). Jukes is buried in the cemetery of the Armenian monastery of Surb Amenaprgich in Julfa, Isfahan. His epitaph reads, 'Sacred to the Memory of Andrew Jukes, Esq., Political Agent in the Persian Gulph, who departed this life at Isphahan on the tenth November 1821, Aged 43 and lies interred here.' See Kurdian (1939: 262). Jukes left his name at Persepolis in 1804 but did not die in that year, as stated by Simpson (2005: 10).

one of the most commercial cities of the empire, state, that all the Persians were desirous to have their children inoculated with the vaccine.'"[302]

D'Ohsson's Tableau Historique de l'Orient

8.86 'Chevalier Mouradgrad D'Ohsson,' *Morning Chronicle* (Saturday, 25 August, 1804) and 'Chevalier Mouradgrad D'Ohsson,' *Aurora General Advertiser* (Thursday, 30 August, 1804): 'Chevalier Mouradgrad d'Ohsson.[303]—late Swedish minister in Turkey, is now publishing at Paris, from the press of didot,[304] a new work, intitled, Tableau Historique de l'Orient, dedicated to the king of Sweden.[305] The two first parts contain every thing concerning the present situation of Persia,[306] and the other parts explain in a clear and distinct manner, the internal and relative situation of every power in India. Born at Constantinople, the author speaks all the oriental languages, and has passed ten years in travel in Persia and India. The work is spoken of in very high terms.'

---

[302] In a letter of 27 March 1804 written at Vienna, de Carro (1804a: 123) noted, 'Dr. Milne and Mr. Jukes write me from Bashire, on the 11th and 15th of January, that their first success has made the most powerful sensation in that town, which now carries on the greatest trade of any in the empire; and that the people flock to them to have their children vaccinated.' For Milne's extensive correspondence with de Carro see de Carro (1804b: 154–164). Jukes wrote to De Carro from Bandar-e Bushehr on 4 March 1805, 'depuis mon retour de ma dernière mission en Perse je quittai mon appartement dans la factorerie anglaise, et pris un logement dans une maison américaine [arménienne?], pour être plus tranquille, et suivre mes études avec plus de liberté. Ce changement de demeure me procura un beaucoup plus grand nombre de visites; comme je n'étois plus dans un lieu public, les femmes venoient me consulter en grand nombre; et comme elles m'amenoient toujours une quantité d'enfans, que je vaccinois, louin de les repousser, je les accueillois de mon mieux.' See de Carro (1805: 84–85). Cf. Floor (2004: 39). Unfortunately, in Jukes' next letter to de Carro of 26 May 1805, he explained that the Governor had visited him, indicating that he did not approve of the women of Bušehr visiting Jukes. 'Il chercha à me faire croire que son unique intention en défendant aux femmes de venir me consulter, avoit été la crainte qu'elles ne m'incommodassent par leur indiscrète affluence…Mais, le mal étoit fait; car, quoique le Gouverneur m'eût fait quelques excuses, la crainte de lui déplaire continua à empêcher les femmes de venir chez moi…Cet état de choses a achevé de détruire la vaccine.' See de Carro (1805: 88).

[303] Ignatius Mouradgea D'Ohsson (1740–1807). The reference is to D'Ohsson (1804). For the life and achievements of this Armenian-born Swedish subject see Findley (1998).

[304] 'The most important and successful printers in France during the eighteenth and early nineteenth centuries.' See Manheimer (1972: 207). D'Ohsson (1804) was printed and published by the Imprimerie de Didot jeune.

[305] Gustav IV Adolf (r. 1792–1809).

[306] In fact the first volume is entirely devoted to ancient Persian mythic history as represented in the *Shahnameh*, while the second treats the period from Alexander to the Islamic conquest.

The First Russo-Persian War and British, French and Persian diplomacy (1804–1816)

In December, 1804, American newspapers were suddenly flooded with reports of a crushing victory by Russian forces, commanded by Prince Pavel Tsitsianov, over the Persians near Yerevan in the preceding June. Thus began news coverage of the First Russo-Persian War. The often lengthy reports of the war were frequently based on official accounts from St. Petersburg containing details of troop movements, villages and towns in the battle zone, officers involved, size of combatant units, casualties suffered, and so forth. Misinformation or disinformation also flowed freely. Inflated reports of Persian victories, of numbers killed and wounded, and of war materiel seized were rife.

In 1805 Napoleon sent secret envoys (Jaubert and Romieux) to Fath 'Ali Shah with a view to establishing friendly relations and keeping Russia in check. In February, 1806, the war took an ugly turn when the Persian governor of Baku treacherously murdered Tsitsianov at what was meant to be a conference between the two sides. Napoleon's presence hovered in the background of the war and in February, 1807, a Persian ambassador met with him in Poland. An anti-Russian, Turco-French alliance was proposed as well. Coming so soon after Malcolm's embassy to the Persian court, Persia's friendly relations with France caused alarm in both the EIC and Whitehall. Although battle reports often mentioned Fath 'Ali Shah, it was clear now that Persian offensive operations were led by his son, Crown Prince 'Abbas Mirza. Although talks were held with an envoy sent by Yusuf Pasha, governor of Erzurum, the prospects of Turco-Persian cooperation, given the history of their relations, were slim. Napoleon urged close relations with Persia, and talk of French military advisers joining the Persian army was rumored. An embassy, led by General Claude Mathieu de Gardane, was sent by Napoleon to Tehran. However, the Treaty of Tilsit, signed by France and Russia in July, 1807, altered matters materially and removed the necessity of France securing Persia's cooperation for a projected invasion of India. Despite this, no attempt was made to abort Gardane's mission.

© The Author(s), under exclusive license to Springer Fachmedien Wiesbaden GmbH, part of Springer Nature 2022
D. T. Potts, *Agreeable News from Persia*, Universal- und kulturhistorische Studien. Studies in Universal and Cultural History,
https://doi.org/10.1007/978-3-658-36032-0_9

Speculation was rife in the press concerning the route which an invading French force might follow to reach India, and how Britain might best hinder the execution of Napoleon's plans and Fath 'Ali Shah's participation in them. Accordingly, Malcolm was once again sent on a mission to the Persian court in April, 1808. Independently, however, another embassy, led by Sir Harford Jones, was dispatched by Whitehall to counteract French influence. Malcolm never got further than Bushehr but Fath 'Ali Shah and his court, bending again towards Britain, Gardane left just as Jones was about to arrive in Tehran and Persia was once again brought under British sway. The consolidation of these ties was strengthened by the visit, in 1810, of Fath 'Ali Shah's ambassador, Mirza Abu'l Hasan Khan, to Britain, and the reciprocal visit of Sir Gore Ouseley to Tehran for the purpose of concluding a definitive treaty between Persia and Great Britain.

Meanwhile, the war in the southern Caucasus dragged on. In October, 1812, 'Abbas Mirza only narrowly escaped capture by Russian forces and it did not take long before Persia was beaten. Sir Gore Ouseley mediated the Treaty of Gulistan which was signed in October, 1813. By the terms of this treaty Persia ceded large portions of the southern Caucasus to Russia, as well as all rights to Caspian Sea traffic.

9.1 'London, October 19,' *New York Gazette* (Thursday, 20 December, 1804), 'Late Foreign Intelligence. London, Oct. 19,' *Aurora General Advertiser* (Saturday, 22 December, 1804), 'Late Foreign Intelligence. London, Oct. 19,' *Poulson's American Daily Advertiser* (Saturday, 22 December, 1804), 'Untitled,' *Columbian Centinel* (Wednesday, 26 December, 1804), 'Untitled,' *Newburyport Herald* (Friday, 28 December, 1804), 'Oct. 20,' *The Salem Gazette* (Friday, 28 December, 1804), 'Untitled,' *The Farmer's Cabinet* (Tuesday, 1 January, 1805), 'Untitled,' *Federal Spy* (Tuesday, 1 January, 1805) and 'Untitled,' *The Green Mountain Patriot* (Tuesday, 15 January, 1805): 'Letters from St. Petersburgh give an account of a great victory obtained by the Russians over the Persians.'

9.2 'Petersburgh, Sept. 19,' *The Spectator* (Saturday, 22 December, 1804), 'Petersburgh, (Russia) Sept. 19,' *Albany Gazette* (Monday, 31 December, 1804), 'Petersburgh, (Russia) Sept. 19,' *Political Calendar and Essex Advertiser* (Monday, 31 December, 1804), 'Petersburgh, Sept. 19,' *Spooner's Vermont Journal* (Tuesday, 1 January, 1805), 'Foreign. Russia. Petersburg, Sept. 19,' *Connecticut Gazette* (Wednesday, 2 January, 1805), 'Latest Foreign Intelligence. Petersburgh, Sept. 19,' *The Courier* (Wednesday, 2 January, 1805), 'Foreign Intelligence. Petersburgh, (Russia) Sept. 19,' *The Northern Post* (Thursday, 3 January, 1805), 'Untitled,' *New-York Commercial Advertiser* (Thursday, 3 January, 1805; with slight variations), 'Petersburgh, Sept. 19,' *Windham Herald* (Thursday, 3 January, 1805), 'Intelligence. Russia. Petersburgh, Sept. 19. Russian Victory,' *The Eastern Argus* (Friday, 4 January, 1805), 'Untitled,' *New-York Spectator* (Saturday, 5 January, 1805), 'Petersburgh, Sept. 19. Russian Victory,' *Federal Spy* (Tuesday, 8 January, 1805), 'Defeat of the Persian Army,' *Litchfield Monitor* (Wednesday, 9 February, 1805), 'Petersburg, Sept. 19,' *Vermont Centinel* (Friday, 11 January, 1805),

'Untitled,' *The Daily Advertiser* (Monday, 14 January, 1805), 'Petersburg, (Russia) Sept. 19,' *Republican Advocate* [Frederick MD] (Friday, 18 January, 1805) and 'Untitled,' *The Saratoga Advertiser* (Monday, 21 January, 1805): 'Our [or 'The Petersburgh] Court Gazette [Russian] contains a report[1] of a victory obtained by Prince Zizianow[2] over the Persians, upon the frontiers of Grusien[3] and Erivan[4] on the 20th of last June.[5] The engagement continued for 10 h. The enemy, after a most obstinate resistance, was finally defeated with great slaughter, and fled in confusion. On the 23rd the Persians had rallied some thousand cavalry, but made no attack. On the 25th some skirmishes took place, but the Russian army continued always to advance, and after pursuing the enemy over the river

---

[1] Extensive reports taken from the official Russian account appeared in French and German newspapers on 11, 12 and 13 October. See (1804b, c, d). An important point to note, not indicated in the present article, is Fath 'Ali Shah's provocation, from the Russian perspective. According to Anonymous (1804b), 'Le général d'infanterie prince Zizianow, commandant-général dans la Grusinie (Géorgie), reçut du visir de Babakhan [Fath 'Ali Shah], régent de Perse, une lettre remplie de menaces, & par laquelle il demandoit, que les troupes russes évacuassent la Grusinie, en ajoutant que le fils de Babakhan étoit déjà en marche vers ce pays, avec une armée nombreuse; que le régent lui-même le suivoit avec des forces encore plus considérables. Le prince Zizianow fit à cette lettre une réponse très laconique, portant qu'il étoit prêt à le recevoir.'

[2] Prince Pavel Tsitsianov (1754–1806), 'a Georgian of noble birth who had been brought up in Russia.' See Busse (1972: 107, n. 81). The transcription common in nineteenth century accounts, Tsitsianoff, is in fact closer to his Georgian name, Tsitsishvili. See Lang (1957: 167). Freygang and Freygang (1823: 159–160) noted, 'The Prince Czizianow, descended from a Georgian family, after having distinguished himself during many years in Russian service, was nominated in 1803 military governor of Georgia. He it was who gained by assault the fortress of Ganja, the name of which he changed to that of Elizabetpol: he took possession of several khanships, such as those of Schoucha and Karabagh, and was held in awe by the Persians, Turks and Lesgees, and by all the other tribes of these countries. To this very day his name is repeated as something dreadful, when the Persians wish to frighten their children.'

[3] Russian name [Грузия] (Grusija) for Georgia.

[4] As McNeill (1836: 56–57) noted, after Czar Alexander had sent Tsitsianov to the Caucasus, 'Mahommed Khan Kajar, then (1804) Governor of Erivan, having rebelled against his sovereign, and finding that the Shah was advancing with a considerable force to reduce him to obedience, invited the Russian General to advance to his relief, promising to deliver up the fortress, or to receive into it a Russian garrison. At this time there was no war between Russia and Persia ... Yet on the invitation of this rebel against his sovereign and feudal lord, tempted by the hope of profiting by his treachery, did the Russian army, while there was yet no war between the governments, advance for the purpose, seizing Erivan. Zizianoff had proceeded as far as the Armenian convent of Etzmiadzin, within a few miles of the fortress, when he encountered the Persian army advancing to oppose him; and an action was there fought, in which the Persians were defeated and forced to retire.' The Persian force was commanded by the crown prince, 'Abbas Mirza.

[5] The official Russian account of hostilities makes no mention of any occurrence on 20 June. Rather, a series of encounters between the two sides began on 21 June and ending on 11 July. See Anonymous (1804b).

Sanga,[6] drove them from the town of Erivan, which they had occupied. On the 30th, the Russian army crossed the river Sanga, near, the village Kavagera,[7] seven wersts[8] above Erivan, where the Persian camp was fixed, which was attacked. Five different times were the Persians repulsed, but they regained the heights in the vicinity, which they had fortified, when at last one of their strongest positions was forced with the bryonets [sic, bayonets] of forty Russian fusileers with the cry of *Huzza!* The enemy, 27,000 men strong, then took flight, and after much slaughter, the survivors saved themselves by swimming over the river. A number of guns, and a large quantity of ammunition, provisions &c. with several hundred dromedaries, fell into the hands of the victors.'

9.3 'Translations. From late French Papers, received at the Office of the Political Register, by the ship Portland, captain Wills, from l'Orient,' *Norfolk Gazette and Publick Ledger* (Friday, 4 January, 1805), 'France. Paris, Oct. 10,' *The Hive* (Tuesday, 8 January, 1805), 'France. Paris, Oct. 10, 1804,' *True Republican* (Wednesday, 16 January, 1805), 'Paris, October 10,' *Columbian Gazette* (Monday, 21 January, 1805) and 'Translations from late French papers, received at Philadelphia, by the ship Portland, from L'Orient,' *The Northern Post* (Thursday, 24 January, 1805): 'The Russians have obtained decisive advantages in Grussinie (Georgia) over the Persians, whom they have pursued beyond Erivan, the capital of Persian Armenia.'

9.4 'Petersburgh, September 19,' *City Gazette and Daily Advertiser* (Tuesday, 22 January, 1805): 'We are now involved in a war with the Persians. Respecting the cause of the war, and the battles which have taken place, our Court Gazette of this day [19 September, 1804] gives the following information:[9]—

"The Commander in Chief in Grusia (Georgia) the General of Infantry, Prince Zizianof, received a letter from the Vizier[10] of the Persian Baba Khan,[11] filled with threats, in which he demanded that the Russian troops should evacuate Grusia, and informed him that the son[12] of Baba Khan was already on his march to Grusia with a numerous body of troops which would be followed by Baba Khan himself, with a more numerous army. Prince

---

[6] The Hrazdan river; Turkish Zanga/i/u, Zengy. As Kotzebue (1819a: 125) noted, 'the Sanga … issues from the lake of Erivan [Lake Sevan], traverses the greater part of Armenia, and unites itself with the Araxes not far from the Caspian sea.' In Klaproth (1824: 258) it appears as 'Zanghi.' Brosset (1857: 280, n. 5), called it the 'Zanga.'

[7] Presumably the Armenian village of Kavakert, located between Yerevan and Echmiadzin. See Daghbaschean (1893: 8, 21), Hübschmann (1904: 440), Bournoutian (2004: 63).

[8] Roughly 7.5 kms. 1 verst = 1.06678 km. See Crawford (1893: xiii).

[9] English translation of the account published in (1804b, c, d).

[10] Mirza Shafi'-e Mazandarani. He had been appointed to this post after Haji Ibrahim Khan had been deposed and killed in the spring of 1801. See Busse (1972: 99). Cf. Brydges (1833: 199).

[11] Fath 'Ali Shah.

[12] Crown Prince 'Abbas Mirza.

Zizianof immediately returned a short answer, in which he stated, that he was ready to receive him. But as the Russian troops are not accustomed to wait for the arrival of the enemy, the Commander in Chief collected a detachment of 4000 men, and dispatched 2 days before them the Caucasian regiment of grenadiers, that they might pass with more convenience the mountainous districts and morasses which separate Grusia from the province of Erivan, after giving orders to their commander, major-general Tiutschkof,[13] to form a junction in the Schuragalskoi[14] Steppe with two battalions of the regiment of Teffis, which had marched for that place and to wait there for his arrival. The commander in chief set out himself on the first of June with the remainder of the troops; and on the 12th joined the troops above mentioned. He was here informed by major-general Tiutschkof, that on the 10th of that month he had fallen in with a detachment of above 4000 Persians, whom he attacked and put to flight. In this action 100 of the enemy were killed, and about the same number taken prisoners. A great many cattle also had fallen into his hands, and he rescued and set at liberty 4000 families, fugitives from Erivan, whom the Persians were carrying off by violence.

"On the 15th, the Russian troops again broke up their camp, and on the 19th arrived at the Armenian monastery named Etchmiadsian, the very extensive gardens of which were beset by the Persians. Here the enemy were driven back to the walls of the monastery by the Kozaks and Grusians. Next morning, that is on the 20th, at day break, numerous bodies of Persians were observed on the heights behind the monastery; some minutes after several columns of the enemy's cavalry appeared with an intention, as supposed, of attacking the Russian camp, and who divided themselves in order to surround it. The brave resistance, however, which they experienced and the strong and well directed fire of our artillery, made a great havoc among the enemy, and defeated their design. At length, after an obstinate engagement, which lasted 10 h, the Persians were obliged to retreat in great confusion. In this action our loss was trifling, while that of the enemy was very great; but nothing certain can yet be known in this respect, as the Persians, according to the principles of their religion, use every exertion not to leave any of their dead or wounded on the field of battle,

---

[13] Variously Tutschkow, Tutshkow, Tutshkov, Tuchkov, Toutchkow. Sergey Alexeyevich Tuchkov (1767–1839) 'was elevated ... to major general, and appointed chef of the Caucasus Grenadier Regiment on 22 November 1798. He remained in the Transcaucasia for the next 6 years, fighting the Chechens, Circassians, Turks, and Persians.' See Mikaberidze (2005: 411). Atkin (1980: 73) observed, 'Tuchkov believed that Tsitsianov deliberately provoked confrontations with Muslim rulers because he wanted the opportunity to impress Alexander. The accuracy of Tuchkov's comments about Tsitsianov might be questioned on the grounds that Tuchkov believed he was denied the honors due him because of Tsitsianov's spite. Although Tuchkov's memoirs contain some errors, the credibility of his judgments on his commander is strengthened by information derived from a variety of contemporary sources, including Tsitsianov's own letters.'

[14] Old Armenian Shirakavan, Shoregel/Shuragel. See Hübschmann (1904: 390). The capital of the 'Shuragel salient' was Gyumri. See LeDonne (2008: 35). This is referred to by Mahmudov (2010: 303) as the Shöreyel Sultanate.

and in this they have hitherto succeeded, as we had not a sufficient number of cavalry to pursue them.

"On the 21st, the day after the battle, no Persians were to be seen.

"On the 22d, and 23d, a corps of the enemy's cavalry, consisting of 12,000, made an attempt to attack our camp, but discouraged by the result of the first battle, they did not venture to approach nearer than within cannon shot, and returned without being able to accomplish their design. On the 24th, as they found their plan was defeated, they left the Russians at rest.[15]

"On the 25th, the Commander in Chief pushed forward twelve versts[16] with the whole army to the village of Saragarta, on the river Sanga,[17] situated at the distance of seven versts from the town of Erivan which was beset by the enemy, but they were driven from it, and made their escape by swimming.

"The Commander in Chief expresses the utmost satisfaction with the conduct of all the officers and soldiers who had a share in both these battles, and he praises in particular the artillery officers, as the victory on the 4th day was owing chiefly to the good effect produced by the artillery.

"At break of the day on the 30th of June, the Russian troops crossed the river Sanga at the village Kavagera, where a barricado of waggons had been left, formed themselves in order of battle into four squares, the chassuer [sic, chasseur] square[18] making the advanced guard, and in that manner marched forward to attack the Persian camp, which was established near the village Kanagria,[19] seven versts behind the fortress of Eriuan [sic,

---

[15] 'Beym berühmten Armenischen Kloster Etschmiadschin, etwa 30 Werste von Eriwan, wurde am 20. Junius das Russische Lager vom Georgischen Königssohne Alexander, mit 15,000 Persischen Soldaten, ohne Erfolg angegriffen, und der Feind genöthigt, sich aus der Ebene in die Gebirge zurückzuziehen.' See Klaproth (1812: 398).

[16] According to (1812: 398–399), 'Am 25sten rückte die ganze Armee 25 Werst weiter bis Kanagheri, am Ssangiflusse [Zanga] vor, wo in einer Wagenburg alles Schwere zurückgelassen ward. Am folgenden Tage ging sie über den Ssangi nach Eriwan und nahm das Persische Lager der unter Alexander stehenden Truppen, bey Karbuli, etwa drey Werst von Eriwan.' Kanagheri is a variant of Kavagera (Kavakert), mentioned further on in the article.

[17] Cf. Kavagera/Kavakert in 9.2 above. Anonymous (1804b, c, d), however, all have 'Sawagerta' which is *Cavakert* 'sur le bord du Hourazdan,' i.e. the modern Hrazdan, 'la Zanga de nos jours,' of Stephanos Orbelian's *History of the State of Sisakan* §37. See Brosset (1864: 101, n. 4). Bedrosian (2012–2015 unpaginated) transcribed the name as *Kawkert*. Cf. Hübschmann (1904: 440), s.v. *Kavakert*, 'am Fluß *Hurastan*' with the etymology 'von Lehm gemacht.' This is a typical Persian-Armenian toponym with the ending *-karta*, signifying 'built/made.' See Hübschmann (1876), Blau (1877), Nöldeke (1879).

[18] 'Carré de chasseurs,' a square formation made up of chasseurs. The term may denote either riflemen, i.e. light infantry, or light cavalry. See Willcox (1899: 75). The context here suggests the chasseurs in question were not mounted.

[19] Jean Ouoskherdjan called it the 'village arménien de Kanakhier.' See Klaproth (1824: 258). Cf. Kanagheri in Klaproth (1812: 398–399), who may have confused the movements of 25 and 30 June. Brosset (1857: 280, n. 5), called it 'Kanakir.'

Erivan], and which was protected in front by awful and dangerous cliffs. They continued their march for five versts in the Steppe in sight of the right side of the fortress, and beat, back all the detachments of the enemy sent to oppose them.—At last, having reached a plain surrounded by hills, and interpersed [sic] with eminences about four versts in circumference, Prince Zizianof gave orders to the chasseur-squareto commit their artillery and heavy baggage to the care of the next square, to disperse themselves over the heights, and to drive from them the enemy, who had taken post there in numerous groupes.

"Five times the Persians occupied the hills and eminences over the high road, and as often were they forced from them by the chasseurs. At length, after they had reached the absent of the steep and rocky mountain, the access to which was reduced more difficult by the resistance made by the enemy from the summit, Prince Zizianof detached the Colonel of the Caucasian grenadiers, Koslofski,[20] with the fusileer battalion of that regiment, to storm it. The colonel, notwithstanding the difficulty of this attempt, and the steepness of the mountain, advanced rapidly with 40 fusileers, having major Ossifof[21] at their head, put the enemy to flight, and thus opened a passage for the whole corps, which terminated the operations of the day.

"The enemy, thrown into great consternation abandoned their camp, and fled beyond Erivan. Their troops, amounting to 27,000 men, who were besieging it, swam in the utmost confusion across the River Araks, and dispersed themselves, leaving in our hands four standards, seven field pieces, 40 poods of gun-powder, a part of which was bruised, and a considerable quantity of copper, iron, and leaden shot, their rich and magnificent camp equipage, a great many dromedaries, and abundance of provisions.

"Prince Zizianof speaks in high terms of the bravery and good conduct of the whole army, and recommends in particular notice Colonel Zechanskoy, of the ninth chasseur regiment;[22] Lieut. Prince Bagration[23] of the body Guards, Hussar Regiment, &c.'"

---

[20] Also Koslowsky. Platon Timofeyevich Kozlovsky (1779–?) 'was promoted to colonel on 11 September 1802 and appointed commander of the Caucasus Grenadier Regiment on 4 May 1803. Kozlovsky took part in operations against Persians in Armenia and fought at Echmiadzin (received the Order of St. George, 4th class, 4 September 1804) and Erivan (wounded).' In 1807 he commanded the Mogilev Musketeer Regiment, part of the Fifth Division under Tuchkov (see above) against Napoleon at Eylau. See Mikaberidze (2005: 204–205).

[21] Also Ossipow. An Alexis Ossipow was attached to the Ministry of War in 1809. See Hassell (1809: 591). A Colonel Ossipoff (Osipov) fought in the Russo-Turkish War in 1829. See Anonymous (1829b). Similarly, the expedition of 1836 to the Taisingan Sands in the lower Urals was commanded by a Colonel Osipof. See Perofski (1867: 58).

[22] Also Zechansky. See Anonymous (1805b). Identified by Count Mikhail Vorontsov in a letter of 12 October 1804, sent from Tiflis to his father, where he wrote, 'Toute notre petite armée a pleuré après cela de la mort du digne colonel Цеханской, chef du 9-me régiment de chasseurs, devenu victime des maladies d'Érivan, et dont l'exemple et les manières nobles et militaires avoient donné un esprit invincible à tout son régiment.' See Bartenev (1890: 95).

[23] Peter Ivanovich Bagration (1765–1812), a great-nephew of Vakhtang VI (Hoseyn Qoli Khan), king of Kartli and an ally of Peter the Great's. See Lang (1957: 119). 'Einer der besten Befehlshaber der

9.5 'Monday, February 4, 1805,' *Salem Register* (Monday, February 4, 1805): 'It is said that the Russians are about to add to the places they already possess in Armenia, Nauhivan[24] and Koy. It was expected they would get possession of the principal places in that province, and then advance to Guilan. They increase their naval force on the Caspian, and were preparing to make a descent upon Mazanderan. They had in 1783 two fortresses in this quarter,[25] for the security of their trade. At Tauris the Persians had an encampment, and were collecting their forces under Fathali Char,[26] to check the Russians.'

9.6 'Latest News,' *Charleston Courier* (Monday, 11 March, 1805): 'The Russians are stated to have made themselves masters of all Georgia, and of several places of importance on the Caspian Sea, lately belonging to the Persians.'

9.7 'Late European News. Constantinople, November 12 [1804],' *The Carolina Gazette* (Friday, 15 March, 1805): 'According to intelligence which has been received, the Russians at this moment are masters of all Georgia, of a number of ports in the Caspian Sea, of Erivan, Guenge,[27] and several other considerable places. On the banks of the Araxes they lately defeated the Persians, commanded by the sons[28] of Fathali, and pursued them to the city of Taurus. Since this event, it is said, that a numerous army has been collected in the province of Mazanderan, which is commanded by the Persian monarch in person; and he purposes to march against the Russians with all possible expedition.'

9.8 'Foreign News,' *Columbian Gazette* (Monday, 1 April, 1805): 'The Russian troops had been successful against the Persians, and conquered a large district of country.'

9.9 'From Late London Papers,' *The Daily Advertiser* (Tuesday, 2 April, 1805), '(From a late London paper.),' *Aurora General Advertiser* (Saturday, 6 April, 1805) and 'From a late London paper,' *The Independent Chronicle* (Thursday, 18 April, 1805): 'The late accounts

---

Russischen Armee, von vielen Feldherrn-Talenten und der größten Unerschrockenheit in den verzweifeltsten Lagen. Er hat sich in der Schule Suwarows in den Pohlnischen Feldzügen von 1792 und 1794, und im Italiänischen Feldzüge von 1799 gebildet.' See Rittgräff (1813: 73). He was active in the Napoleonic Wars and was mortally wounded at the Battle of Borodino on 7 September 1812. See Anonymous (1881b). For his career see Pollock (2012: 93–103).

[24] Nakhchivan/Naxçivan.

[25] As Coxe (1785: 238) noted, 'The Russian ports and trading places upon the Caspian are, 1. Gurief; 2. Kislar. 1. Gurief is situated upon the mouth of the Yaik or Ural, at a little distance from a bay of the Caspian. It is a small, but strong fortress, which guards the frontiers of the Russian empire towards the territory of the Kirghees Tartars ... The fortress of Kislar stands near the Eastern coast, and covers the frontiers towards the limits of Persia.'

[26] Fath 'Ali Shah.

[27] Ganja.

[28] At this point in the war the only son of Fath 'Ali Shah's involved was 'Abbas Mirza. See Brosset (1857: 280, 282, n. 3, 285), Busse (1972: 107).

from India announce a severe action to have been fought on the banks of the Jumna,[29] between a strong corps of Holkar's[30] cavalry, which had been scouring the country, and an equal force of Scindea's;[31] the battle lasted nearly 2 h, and terminated in favour of the latter.

Holkar's army is stated to have suffered greatly from a want of provisions, and that vast numbers of his followers had been carried off by a flux.[32] He expected some French officers by way of Persia, but the Persian Monarch,[33] alarmed at the insurrections which French emissaries had excited at Cabul, and other parts of India,[34] issued an order for the apprehension of all persons coming under the denomination, throughout his Empire; several of the French Officers were in consequence taken into custody, and the passage of others, who intended to follow, has been prevented.'[35]

---

[29] Also Jamna and Yamuna, a major tributary of the Ganges running past Delhi and Agra.

[30] Yashwant Rao Holkar (r. 1799–1807, 1807–1811), Maratha prince and Maharaja of Maratha. See Beale (1881: 134).

[31] Daulat Rao Sindhia (r. 1794–1827), Maharaja of Gwalior who, in 1798, was said to have 'twenty thousand sepoys disciplined by Europeans or Americans. This was originally De Boigne's corps, and was then commanded by M. Perron, the subordinate officers being chiefly British.' See Torrens (1880: 135). Gaffarel (1908: 439) wrote, 'Grâce aux soldats enrégimentés et disciplinés par de Boignes et Perron, le Scindiah était … le plus puissant prince de la confédération Mahratte.' Cf. Beale (1881: 223).

[32] Dysentery. See Macaulay (1831: 220).

[33] Fath 'Ali Shah.

[34] The French would have liked to have done this, but it is not clear that they did more than sound out Fath 'Ali Shah via his friend Mirza Morteza, the Shaykh ol-Islam of Isfahan, whom the French commercial agent at Baghdad, Jean-François Xavier Rousseau, had met in Baghdad in 1794 when Mirza Morteza came on a pilgrimage to the tombs of 'Ali and Hoseyn. See Dehérain (1927: 365, n. 1). As Natchkebia (2015: 115–116) noted, 'Mirza Morteza confided the eagerness of Fath-'Ali Shah … to establish relations with Napoleon. The Shah was tired of vain promises from the English with regards to Russia and dissatisfied with the imperative request by England to join future expeditions against the Afghans, whom the Shah did not consider enemies. J.-F. Rousseau argued that it could be profitable to take advantage of the Shah's negative attitude towards the English and drew up a plan. He called for Napoleon to send a letter to the Shah, followed by an embassy to Tehran and Kandahar for secret negotiations to contract a tripartite alliance between France, Persia and Kandahar, with Fath-'Ali Shah as the mediator between Kandahar and France. The king of Kandahar would declare war on the English, due to the Afghans' hostility towards the English. The king of Kandahar would gather Afghan and 70,000 Sindhi cavalrymen, who should be joined by 2000–3000 French soldiers. In addition, the Marathas would join. These troops would pass through Delhi, Agra and Lahore and seize Benares and Patna … Finally, they would continue along the Ganges to conquer Bengal once and for all, and occupy all the places *suffering under the yoke*" of England.' It is not at all the case that, at this early date, Fath 'Ali Shah had turned against the French. For Rousseau's letter to Talleyrand of 20 October 1804, with his proposal to contact Mirza Morteza, see Dehérain (1930: 27). Subsequently, Alexandre Romieu travelled to Tehran with Napoleon's letter and presents for Fath 'Ali Shah which he delivered on 1 and 4 October 1805. See Dehérain (1930: 36–37).

[35] This seems to be a complete fabrication. In 'Extracts from a memorial and project of peace written by a French Diplomatic Agent in London in June 1801 translated from a manuscript copy of the

9.10 'Thursday [sic, Monday], April 8, 1805,' *Salem Register* (Monday, 8 April, 1805): 'From Petersburg, in December [1804], an account was given[36] of the great success of the Russians against the Persians. The Russians represent their losses as small, but that they have taken from the Persians seven standards,[37] heavy ordinance, and a great train of artillery, many dromedaries, and a rich camp which the Persians abandoned.'

9.11 'Egypt. Alexandria, Dec. 13,' *Charleston Courier* (Wednesday, 12 June, 1805): 'Intelligence has been received here, that the Russians have concluded a truce for 4 months with the Persians.[38] After the expiration of this term, Feth-Ali-Chah, who is employed in organizing a numerous army, will march in person against the enemies of his States. It appears, that the plan of the Russians is to possess themselves of the best provinces of Persia, and to establish themselves there by the same means which the English have used at Bengal, to secure their possessions in that country. It is a plan which they conceived since 1790, and have attempted to carry into execution at different times. It is very doubtful whether they will be able to carry it into effect in all its points. Besides, tho' a cowardly and indolent nation, like that of the Indians, may have been subjugated, the bravery of the Persians, the love of their country, and, above all, the experience and great resources of their present Sovereign, will always place obstacles in the way of the conquests which the Russians wish to add to that of Georgia, and of several other cities on the banks of the Caspian sea. The Russian troops, which were upon the banks of the Araxes, have retired to Teslis;[39] and Feth-

---

original,' the writer expressed a pessimistic view of the chances of any French expedition in conjunction with Fath 'Ali Shah when he wrote, 'To march through Persia in conjunction with a Russian army, for Russia would not let a French army march into that country alone, we would have to conquer and then organise a government in Persia before we could venture to cross the Indus: were it possible that a French and Russian Army could act in concert so long, to subdue and secure Persia would require at least 2 years; in the mean time the English would have exterminated our Friends in India as they did Typpo [Tipu Sultan]. In possession of all the passes from Cabul and Kandahar to the mouth of the Indus, and commanding the Gulph of Persia, the Red sea and the Mediterranean with her squadrons, from where could an army be procured and recruited that would dare to enter Hindostan? From Russia!—in that case we should be the auxiliaries, and as a consequence we would be the dupes if not the sacrifice in the end.' See 'Polybius' (1805: 82).

[36] This is the account in Anonymous (1805b), dated 14 December and labelled 'Extrait de la gazette de la cour.'

[37] The official Russian account mentions only four standards. See 9.5. According to (1805b) six Persian standards were captured.

[38] No such truce was concluded.

[39] As Baddeley (1908: 69) observed, 'Eriván held out, and a wet autumn, making transport difficult, coupled with other unfortunate circumstances, compelled the Russians to raise the siege and effect a perilous retreat to Georgia. Eriván then opened its gates to the Persians.' In the state record of the early Qajar period (to 1811) we read that Tsitsianov 'departed from the Fort of Erivan to Ashk; and, with burning sighs, from thence proceeded to Teflis.' See Brydges (1833: 209). A more plausible account is given in Anonymous (1805b) where we read, 'La manque de vivres joint aux nouvelles que le Prince Zizianow reçut des troubles fomentés par les peuples qui habitent les rochers du Caucase, et

Ali-Chah is at present at Casbin,[40] to attend the marriage of one of his Ministers, to whom he gives one of his near relatives.[41]

9.12 'Foreign Intelligence,' *The Repertory* (Saturday, 6 July, 1805), 'Foreign Articles,' *The Farmers' Cabinet* (Tuesday, 9 July, 1805), 'Foreign Intelligence. Egypt,' *Thomas's Massachusetts Spy, or Worcester Gazette* (Wednesday, 10 July, 1805), 'Foreign Articles,' *The Pittsfield Sun* (Saturday, 13 July, 1805), 'London, May 18,' *Aurora General Advertiser* (Tuesday, 16 July, 1805), 'Untitled,' *Mirror of the Times, & General Advertiser* (Wednesday, 17 July, 1805) and 'Foreign Herald,' *The Otsego Herald or Western Advertiser* [Cooperstown NY] (Thursday, 25 July 1805): 'The Moniteur[42] of the 30th ult. contains the following strong reflection upon the conduct of Russia.—"The preponderance of Russia in the Morra[43] continues to increase in an alarming manner. There is even a report of its obliging the Sublime Port to renew with it the scandalous treaty of 1798,[44] according

---

excités, tant par Baba-Chan que par les Princes Grusiniens, Julon, Parnaos et Alexandre (le premier est déjà pris) forcèrent le général en chef a [sic] assembler un conseil de guerre, dans lequel il fut décidé, à la pluralité des voix, que quoiqu'on eut des nouvelles certaines de la retraite de Baba-Chan, et que cette retraite livrât la forteresse d'Erivan à ses propres forces, qui devenoient insufisantes, il étoit cependant nécessaire, de remettre à un tems plus propice la prise de cete [sic] forteresse ainsi que la punition du perfide Mamut-Chan [Mohammad Khan Qajar], et de retourner à Teflis pour y rétablir l'ordre. Les troupes russes abandonnèrent en conséquence Erivan le 4 Septembre. Les ennemis tentèrent le même jour une nouvelle sortie de la forteresse, et Baba-Chan descendant des hauteurs parut dans la plaine, mais il se contenta de nous canonner. Le 15 Septembre, les troupes russes atteignirent les frontières de la Grusinie et furent envoyées en quartier d'hiver pour se délasser de leurs fatigues.' Cf. Hasan-e Fasa'i who says that the Russian withdrawal from Erivan started on 8 August 1804. See Busse (1972: 109).

[40] Qazvin.

[41] Hasan-e Fasa'i said that when Tsitsianov retired to Tibilisi, Fath 'Ali Shah repaired to Tehran which he reached on 22 September 1804. He made no mention of the wedding at Qazvin. See Busse (1972: 109). Similarly, the early Qajar history is silent on the matter of a wedding and says, 'As the season of campaigning had now terminated, and that of destruction to the vine-leaf had arrived, the wide-ruling monarch turned his face to the seat of empire; and the world-embellishing retinue, proceeding by way of imperial Tabreez, diffused musk-scented gales in the direction of Teheran, and on the 14th of Rejeb arrived at the centre of monarchy.' See Brydges (1833: 210). Brosset (1857: 183), on the other hand, said that 'Baba-Khan [Fath 'Ali Shah], ayant appris la nouvelle d'un soulèvement en Perse, battit en retraite et délivra par là de toute inquiétude Tzitzianof, qui plia bagage et partit pour Tiflis.'

[42] *The Gazette nationale ou Le Moniteur universel*, published in Paris was founded in 1789 by Charles-Joseph Panckoucke. It became the official newspaper of the French government in 1799 and remained so to the end of 1810. In 1811 it became simply *Le Moniteur universel* and continued as the official organ of government until 1868. It was published through 30 June 1901.

[43] Possibly Morran, var. Mormran, Mormrean, in Armenia. See Garsoïan (1970: 212*).

[44] The Russian-Turkish Treaty of 1798, signed 23 December 1798 (3 January 1799) in Constantinople, largely aimed at countering French aggression. It was renewed on 11 September 2005 in the Russo-Turkish Treaty of 1805 but this second treaty was never ratified by the Porte. See Hale (2013: 15–16).

to which, without any reciprocity, the Porte would alienate its political independence entirely in favor of Russia. Very different is the case between Russia and Persia: the Russians beaten at Araxe, have lost the fruits of a 2 year campaign in one day; and were compelled to retire with precipitations towards their own frontiers, with the loss of three parts of their artillery. The Emperor of Persia,[45] full of energy and resolution, defends his estate and his independence in person, he has sent Ambassadors to the Porte to solicit succor,[46] or at least its intervention; but that feeble Government has not only been deaf to his representations, but even pretended to doubt the authority of the messengers, and compelled them to leave Constantinople in an abrupt manner. Whatever may be the views and the ambition of the Russians; it is easy to see that they must yield to the cavalry and artillery of Fatali Schah.[47] Hostilities were to recommence on the 1st of April;[48] and it cannot be conceived what object the Russians can have in fomenting a division between the Porte and the Persians, its neighbors.'"

9.13 'Untitled,' *Poulson's American Daily Advertiser* (Friday, 12 July, 1805), 'Untitled,' *Alexandria Daily Advertiser* (Monday, 15 July, 1805), 'From the Salem Register,' *Pennsylvania Correspondent, and Farmers' Advertiser* (Tuesday, 23 July, 1805) and 'Untitled,' *Charleston Courier* (Tuesday, 30 July, 1805): 'While Russia has been busy in its attempts to force its troops into the northern parts of Persia, we are assured that the resistance has been worthy of better days, and that the Persians do not refuse the last defence of their country.'

---

[45] Fath 'Ali Shah.

[46] An apparent reference to the mission of Ossip Vassilovitz, an Armenian 'modestement habillé,' who, however, was sent to the French ambassador in Constantinople, Guillaume Marie-Anne Brune (in office 1802–1806), not to the Porte. He arrived on 12 December 1804 with a letter from the Shah suggesting a Franco-Persian alliance. See Dehérain (1930: 28–30). Cf. Amini (1999: 50–55). 'Instruit par le maréchal Brune des ouvertures de Feth Ali chah, l'Empereur [Napoléon] les accueille favorablement et, sans délai, fait acheminer vers Téhéran deux Envoyés: le secrétaire interprète Amédée Jaubert et l'adjudant commandant Alexandre Romieu.' See Dehérain (1930: 30), Puryear (1951: 43).

[47] According to Hasan-e Fasa'i, after the campaign of 1804, 'royal decrees were issued to the effect that a hundred pieces of artillery should be cast of copper and brass, with all the accessories, in the provinces of Ādherbāyjān and Fārs, and to be delivered after completion.' See Busse (1972: 109). Pierre Ruffin, the French diplomat in Constantinople, noted, after his interview with Vassilovitz, 'De ses dires, il résultait que le chah attendait principalement de la France le concours de techniciens, d'officiers, d'ingénieurs et de fondeurs de canons.' See Dehérain (1930: 30). The fact that this story appeared in the *Moniteur*, which did not shy away from publishing disinformation from the French Foreign Ministry (Puryear 1951: 46), is perhaps telling.

[48] Right after the Iranian new year (21 March), i.e. in spring. In fact, according to Hasan-e Fasa'i, Fath 'Ali Shah did not leave Tehran for Azerbaijan to renew the war with Russia until 24 May 1805. See Busse (1972: 110).

9.14 'Miscellaneous,' *Newburyport Herald* (Friday, 19 July, 1805), 'Foreign News. London, May 30,' *The Daily Advertiser* (Monday, 22 July, 1805), 'Untitled,' *The United States Gazette* (Monday, 22 July, 1805), 'Late Foreign Intelligence,' *Connecticut Herald* (Tuesday, 23 July, 1805), 'Miscellaneous Articles,' *The Farmers' Cabinet* (Tuesday, 23 July, 1805), 'London, May 30,' *Federal Gazette & Baltimore Daily Advertiser* (Tuesday, 23 July, 1805), 'Late Foreign Articles. London, May 27,' *Aurora General Advertiser* (Wednesday, 24 July, 1805), 'Untitled,' *Kennebunk Gazette* (Wednesday, 24 July, 1805), 'Foreign Intelligence. London, May 30,' *Thomas' Massachusetts Spy, or Worcester Gazette* (Wednesday, 24 July, 1805), 'From an English newspaper. Miscellaneous,' *Alexandria Daily Advertiser* (Thursday, 25 July, 1805), 'London, May 29,' *American & Commercial Daily Advertiser* (Thursday, 25 July, 1805) and 'Foreign News. London, May 27,' *The Sentinel of Freedom* (Tuesday, 30 July, 1805): 'The *Paris Moniteur* says that "an Ambassador from the King of *Persia*[49] had arrived at *Constantinople*, to complain of the conduct of the Pacha of Three Tails, who refused to supply with provisions a Persian army of 100,000 men, who were pursuing the Russians, while he had granted supplies to the Russians."[50] The *Moniteur* adds, "the Ambassador cannot obtain any thing from a corrupt and enervated Divan, who seem to be the only persons in the world that do not see or dare not look at the fate which attends *Turkey*: They dread to perceive that empire hasten to its ruin, and that those Ottomans, formerly so proud and brave, are on the eve of persisting without the honor of a war, so much are they pressed and surrounded by the Russians."'

9.15 'Syria. Aleppo, Dec. 20,' *Courier of New Hampshire* (Wednesday, 7 August, 1805): 'The latest letters from Persia appear to confirm the news of a signal advantage gained over the Russians by the Persians. It has been known here for some time, that about four months ago a Russian army, already master of Teflis, possessed itself of Erivan. Since that, Feth-ali-Chah himself, at the head of a strong army, has fought the Russians near that city, and completely defeated them. It is said, that he has taken Erivan, and even Teflis; and that before his return to Casbin, where he now is, he built a fort at the Three Churches,[51] for the purpose of opposing a barrier to new incursions on their part.—This intelligence has been confirmed by the Sardar of the Janissaries at Aleppo, who is a native of Teflis, and has

---

[49] The reference to an 'ambassador' (i.e. Vassilovitz) is interesting, but the use of the title 'king of Persia' is particularly intriguing. As Puryear (1951: 43) noted, as Napoleon's answer to Fath 'Ali Shah's letter was being formulated in Paris, 'the foreign ministry discussed the proper salutation. Everyone preferred a short and simple phraseology. Someone recalled that King Louis XIV had sent several letters to the "King of Persia," but emperor was decided upon to match Napoleon's own title.'

[50] This is a complete fabrication. While Russia and the Porte were nominally allies as a result of the treaty of 1798, there was certainly no aid forthcoming from Constantinople for Russian military adventures in the Caucasus, nor was the Porte supporting Fath 'Ali Shah.

[51] Üç-Kilise, lit. 'three churches,' i.e. the seat of the Armenian Catholicos, Echmiadzin.

delivered an account to that effect.[52] Although the details of the advantage gained by the Persians is called in question, the retreat of the Russians is not to be doubted. All the letters agree in stating, that they have retreated into Georgia. There are some reports even of a truce concluded between the Russians and the Persians.'[53]

9.16 'Foreign News. Answer to the Russian Note, declining to mediate for peace,' *New-England Palladium* (Tuesday, 17 September, 1805), 'Foreign Intelligence. End of the Russian Mediation,' *The Repertory* (Tuesday, 17 September, 1805), 'Foreign Intelligence. Berlin, July 15,' *The United States Gazette* (Wednesday, 18 September, 1805), 'Paris, July 25,' *Aurora General Advertiser* (Thursday, 19 September, 1805), 'Foreign Department,' *The Northern Budget* (Tuesday, 1 October, 1805), 'Answer to M. Novosiltzoff's Note. Paris, July 25,' *Middlebury Mercury* (Wednesday, 9 October, 1805), 'Important State Paper. Answer to M. Novoziltzoff's note. Paris, July 25,' *True Republican* (Wednesday, 9 October, 1805) and 'Answer to M. Novoziltzoff's Note,' *American Mercury* (Thursday, 17 October, 1805): 'Berlin, July 15. M. Novosiltzoff[54] left this capital yesterday for *St. Petersburgh*...The mission of that Russian Envoy was announced to all *Europe* several months before it commenced; and this was sufficient to render it abortive. It also became the subject of many discussions, calculations, and intrigues....[55]

If the object of his mission was to allay the coolness existing between *France* and *Russia*, he would probably have succeeded. What, indeed, have *France* and *Russia* to do with each other? ... If the Emperor of the French[56] exerts great influence in Italy, the Emperor of Russia[57] exerts a much greater influence on the Ottoman Porte and in Persia.... it [Russia] ought not to demand that the Emperor of the French should not see what becomes of the ancient and illustrious empire of Solyman and Persia; that he should not see that for 10 years past the whole Caucasus has been united with Russia, at the solitary request of a few families of that country... that ... obliging the Porte to suffer her

---

[52] Considering the fact that the Janissaries of Aleppo rebelled in 1805 this seems highly unlikely. For the political history of Aleppo in these years see Hathaway and Barbir (2013: 92–94).

[53] As noted above, no such truce was concluded.

[54] Baron Nikolai Nikolaievich Novosiltsev (1761–1838), distinguished Russian diplomat and confidante of Emperor Alexander I. On his life and career see LeDonne (2003).

[55] Cf. Anonymous (1805c), 'La Russie avait fait demander, par l'intermédiaire de la Prussie, des passeports pour un chambellan qu'elle désirait envoyer à Paris auprès de S. M. l'empereur. Les passeports ont été, comme cela devait être, accordés sans aucune explication. Depuis, les papiers anglais nous ont appris quelque chose de l'objet de la mission de M. Novoziltzoff. Apres beaucoup d'ordres & de contre-ordres, ce chambellan est arrivé à Berlin, puis retourné à Saint-Pétersbourg, & sa mission paraît terminée ... Tout bien consideré, dit le Moniteur, le contre-ordre qui rappele M. Novoziltzoff à Saint Pétersbourg, est probablement plus utile à la paix que l'ordre qui l'envoyait à Paris.'

[56] Napoleon.

[57] Alexander I (r. 1801–1825).

conquests, she has procured great advantages to herself for pursuing her conquests into the centre of Persia ... if a Russian Commissary, coming to Paris ... should say ... that a guarantee should be given for Persia and the Porte ... that the Phasis shall be evacuated and the Caucasus restored to the Shah of Persia, and that tranquility shall be given to that empire after so many years of internal wars and calamities: then it would be easy to conceive what would be the effect of such language; and although we are not in the secrets of the Cabinet of the Thuilleries, we dare say the Emperor of the French would be ready to meet so noble an agreement ... Whatever sacrifices he should make for the independence of the Porte and of Persia, he would still be a gainer; posterity, for which he labours, would acknowledge him its deliverer, and admire the acuteness of that reason which made him discover before hand that the Russians would be the oppressors of the whole world, even as they now oppress the North ... We have already declared, and once more repeat it, that if Russia evacuates the Bosphorus, Caucasus, Phasis, Georgia, &c. France will accede to any arrangements which can be required with respect to Italy.—But, unfortunately, it is too well known, that no one finds pleasure in sacrifices of this nature, and hence France must be allowed to indemnify herself so as to compensate for such advantages as are obtained by the other powers.'

9.17 'Untitled,' *Boston Courier* (Thursday, 19 September, 1805): 'The Moniteur (French government paper) has published a long answer to Novosiltzoff's note, under the appearance of a letter from Berlin; but what private disinterested individual in that city would prepare such an elaborate letter?—It shews little respect for the Emperor of Russia[58]—is not conciliatory—and says France has as much reason to be offended by the influence of Alexander in Turkey and Persia—as Russia has by the influence of Bonaparte in Italy.'

9.18 'Thursday, October 17, 1805,' *Salem Register* (Thursday, 17 October, 1805): 'In Asia, the Russians are supposed to have gained advantages which are not well known in Europe. In Turkey, the troubles do not appear to lessen. It is reported that the Grand Seignior[59] is determined to profit from the discipline of the European armies, especially when he sees the evils which the Persians experience in their wars with the Russians.'

9.19 'Translations from French papers to the 18th September. Paris, September 18,' *New-York Commercial Advertiser* (Thursday, 14 November, 1805), 'Extracts from the Moniteur, and from the Imperial Journal, or *Journal des Debats*, to the 18th of September,' *New-York Gazette & General Advertiser* (Thursday, 14 November, 1805), 'Extracts from the Moniteur, and from the Imperial Journal, or *Journal des Debats*, to the 18th of September,' *The United States Gazette* (Friday, 15 November, 1805), 'Extracts from the Moniteur, and from the Imperial Journal, or *Journal des Debats*, to the 18th of September,'

---

[58] Alexander I.
[59] Selim III.

Aurora General Advertiser (Saturday, 16 November, 1805), 'Extracts from the Moniteur, and from the Imperial Journal, or *Journal des Debats*, to the 18th of September,' *The Sentinel of Freedom* (Tuesday, 19 November, 1805), 'Untitled,' *Republican Farmer* [Danbury CT] (Wednesday, 20 November, 1805, with 'Fathili Shaw'), 'Extracts from the Moniteur, and from the Imperial Journal, or *Journal des Debats*, to the 18th of September,' *The Repertory* (Friday, 22 November, 1805) and 'Extracts from the Moniteur, and from the Imperial Journal, or *Journal des Debats*, to the 18th of September,' *The Post-Boy, and Vermont & New Hampshire Federal Courier* (Friday, 26 November, 1805: 'The King of Persia, Fathali-Sha, has gained a compleat victory over the Russians in Georgia, who were obliged to fly, leaving 6,000 of dead in the field.'[60]

9.20 'Constantinople, August 2,' *Alexandria Daily Advertiser* (Thursday, 14 November, 1805), 'Constantinople, August 2,' *New-York Evening Post* (Friday, 15 November, 1805), 'Constantinople, August 2,' *Aurora General Advertiser* (Friday, 15 November, 1805), 'Constantinople, Aug. 2,' *The United States Gazette* (Friday, 15 November, 1805), 'Constantinople, Aug. 2,' *The Daily Advertiser* (Saturday, 16 November, 1805), 'Constantinople, Aug. 2,' *New-York Spectator* (Saturday, 16 November, 1805), 'Constantinople, August 2,' *Plebeian* (Friday, 22 November, 1805) and 'Translations, from French Papers, received at Norfolk,' *Connecticut Journal* (Saturday, 27 November, 1805): 'Bagdad, Bassora, and the countries bordering on the Gulf of Persia, have a long time since freed themselves from the dominion of the Porte. Casa Osman, Oglon Aga of Natolia,[61] who has for thirty years past been accumulating immense riches, executes the decrees of the Grand Seignor[62] only when revolts costs more than obedience—he has made useless efforts (real or dissembled) to reduce the Pacha of Trebizende,[63] who is in full

---

[60]This seems to refer to Russian losses prior to their raising the siege of Erivan. As Hasan-e Fasa'i wrote, 'Ali Qoli Khan-e Shahsevan and Pir Qoli Khan Qajar Shambayati captured a Russian camp and with it '4000 Russians were either taken prisoner or killed.' See Busse (1972: 109). Judging by the official Russian account, this number is hugely inflated. 'Notre perte pendant toute cette campagne monte tant en morts qu'en blessés à 15 officiers et environ 300 soldats. L'ennemie a perdu plus de 5000 hommes y compris 3 Chans et plusieurs chefs de distinction.' See Anonymous (1805b).

[61]'The great Carosman Oglu, prince of Natolia' See MacGill (1808: 111). MacFarlane (1829: 321–322) called 'the great Carasman Oglu family ... that illustrious race, that held so long the whole of these wide regions of Asia Minor as their property, or their government, and who had maintained, to an astonishing degree, (for Turkey,) peace, justice, and happiness; who had improved the country and the condition of the people, and to whose comparative refinement of manners, and noble hospitality, all travellers at the time bore witness.' For the Karaosmanoğlu 'magnates' or 'notables' in 1805 see Yaycioglu (2016: 66, 314). For the rise of the Karaosmanoğlu dynasty see Hasluck and Hasluck (1929: 597–603).

[62]Selim III.

[63]Tajar Pasha. See Anonymous (1805d), 'Les différens survenus entre Tschapan-Oglou et Tajar, gouverneur de Trebisonde, deux des plus puissans Pachas de la Turquie asiatique, ont pris la tournure

insurrection. The Pacha of Evrezuma marches against him,[64] and leaves without defence Turkish Armenia, whilst the Russians penetrate into all parts of this fine country that belongs to the Persians, and assemble large forces on the side of d'Erivan.'

9.21 'Untitled,' *The United States Gazette* (Friday, 15 November, 1805): 'We have again received papers from Paris to a late date. They misrepresent the progress of affairs on the continent as usuel [sic]. The Russians are said to have raised the seige [sic] of Erivan in Persia.

9.22 'Aleppo, June 26,' *Newburyport Herald* (Friday, 22 November, 1805), 'Syria. Aleppo, June 26, 1805,' *Columbian Centinel* (Saturday, 23 November, 1805), 'Aleppo, June 26,' *New-York Commercial Advertiser* (Friday, 26 November, 1805), 'Syria. Aleppo, June 26,' *Thomas's Massachusetts Spy, or Worcester Gazette* (Saturday, 27 November, 1805), 'Latest Foreign Intelligence. Aleppo, June 26,' *Aurora General Advertiser* (Monday, 29 November, 1805), 'Foreign News. Aleppo, June 26,' *The Sentinel of Freedom* (Tuesday, 3 December, 1805), 'Aleppo, June 26,' *Connecticut Herald* (Tuesday, 3 December, 1805), 'Foreign Articles. Syria. Aleppo, June 26, 1805,' *The Farmers' Cabinet* (Tuesday, 3 December, 1805), 'Latest Foreign Intelligence. Received via Boston. Aleppo, June 26,' *The Courier* (Wednesday, 4 December, 1805), 'Aleppo, June 26,' *True Republican* (Wednesday, 4 December, 1805), 'Aleppo, June 26,' *Gazette of Maine. Hancock Advertiser* (Thursday, 5 December, 1805), 'Turkey. Constantinople, Aug. 15,' *The Enquirer* (Friday, 6 December, 1805), 'Foreign Intelligence. Syria. Alepppo, June 26,'

---

la plus sérieuse. Il y a eu une bataille décisive, dans laquelle les troupes de Tschapan-Oglou ont été complettement defaites. Angora, Tokat, Amasie et d'autres villes de moindre importance, ont subi la loi du vainqueur, et se sont soumises à Tajar-Pacha, qui s'est toujours montré ennemie juré de *Nizami-Gedid* et du nouveau systême militaire.'

[64]Erzurum. The pasha in question was Yusuf Pasha. See Anonymous (1805e), 'Le pacha de Trébisonde s'est révolté contre le grand-seigneur, et a pris les armes. Au premier avis de cette rebellion, l'ordre fut donné à Kallarman Oglou, gouverneur de la Natolie, de marcher contre le pacha séditieux; ce dernier lui-même [..?] à la rencontre de son adversaire, et il s'engagea [en] combat dont l'issue fut entièrement au désavantage de Kallarman Oglou, qui dut céder à la supériorité du nom...[?] et se retirer précipitamennt. La Porte, informée de ce malheureux événement, vient de rejoindre à Jussuf Pacha, gouverneur d'Erzerum, ci-devant grand visir, de réunir ses troupes à celles du gouverneur de la Natolie et d'agir de concert avec ce dernier pour réduire à obéissance le pacha de Trébisonde. Jussuf Pacha a saisi cette occasion de donner au grand-seigneur une nouvelle preuve de son attachement; il s'est mis aussitôt à la tête d'un corps nombreux, et s'est dirigé vers Trébisonde; il doit être joint en route par Kallarman-Oglou.' Cf. Neale (1818: 291). According to Creasy (1856/2: 359), 'in the early part of 1805 the influence of Russia over the Sultan was ... strikingly displayed on the south-eastern coasts of the Black Sea. The Porte consented that the Russians should have the free navigation of the river Phasis in Mingrelia, and erect fortresses, and place garrisons on its banks for the better security of their flotillas. The Pacha of Erzeroum was ordered to assist the Russians in establishing these posts, and in any other operations that might be of use to them, for the purposes of the war with Persia. in which Russia was then engaged.'

The Green Mountain Patriot (Tuesday, 10 December), 'Aleppo, June 28,' *Hornet* (Tuesday, 10 December) and 'Aleppo, June 26,' *Otsego Herald* (Thursday, 12 December, 1805): 'The Russians continue their preparations against the Persians; they are striving to procure auxiliaries among the Armenians. Their hostile designs seem to extend through the whole Peninsula between the Caspian and Black Seas ... Prince Zizianow has caused 60 of the principal inhabitants of Teflis to be arrested, while two sons of Prince Heraclius have been compelled to take refuge in Persia.'[65]

9.23 'Monday, November 25, 1805,' *Salem Register* (Monday, 25 November, 1805): 'The accounts respecting their [Russian] operations with the Persians are very contradictory. Had their success been uninterrupted, it is to be presumed that it would have been announced in the clearest manner.'

9.24 'Aleppo, April 10,' *Norfolk Gazette and Publick Ledger* (Wednesday, 4 December, 1805) and 'Foreign Articles. From a late French Paper. Aleppo, April 20. Affairs of Persia,' *Spooner's Vermont Journal* (Monday, 6 January, 1806): 'We have learnt here from authentick correspondence, that the troops which Fathali Shah marched against the Russians, to force them to raise the siege of Erivan, have entirely accomplished their object: the Russians were forced to renounce their enterprizes, and to fall back on Tefflis. We are assured they have lost many men in the different battles which took place, and it appears that they will not try any more irruptions into the neighbouring provinces of Georgia, the bad success of their arms would discourage them. It is certain that their

---

[65] Regarding the attempted defection of the Georgian princes, sons of Erekle II, Brosset (1857: 281) wrote, 'Informés de l'arrivé du chah [Fath 'Ali Shah] à Erivan, les princes Ioulon [Iulon] et Pharnaoz [Pharnavaz/Parnaos], qui étaient en Iméreth, partirent pour se rendre auprès de lui. Lorsqu'ils furent dans le petit bois d'Oulev, en Iméreth, un Imer informa les Russes, postés à Souram, de leur intention d'aller à Erivan. Alors une compagnie de chasseurs se mit en route sous la conduite du grand-chambellan Gogia Raminis-Chwili, qui avait assuré aux Russes qu'ils les prendrait. Les Russes arrivent, attaquent au point du jour, le 29 juin, fête des saints Pierre et Paul; ils ... s'approchent du prince Ioulon, pour lui donner la mort; mais Advid [sic, David] Abazadzé, le chef de ses pages, le couvre, et la baïonnette d'un Russe l'atteint lui-même et le blesse à la tempe. La vie du prince Ioulon fut sauvée, mais il tomba au pouvoir des Russes. Quant à ses fils, Léon et Louarsab, et au prince Pharnaoz, ils s'enfuirent. Léon et Pharnaoz allèrent à Atsqour, auprès des Lesguis, delà à Akhal-Tzikhé, puis auprès du sardar Pir-Qouli-Khan, à Phambac, où ils trouvèrent leur frère *et oncle* Alexandré, et leur neveu *et cousin* Théimouraz. Pour Louarsab, qui ètait d'un âge tendre, il alla chez Zourab Tséréthel, qui l'accueillit.' Cf. Fähnrich (2010): 'Im September schlossen sich die Bagratiden Iulon und Parnaos, die sich nach der fehlgeschlagenen Erhebung von 1802 nach Imeretien zurückgezogen hatten, dem Aufstand mit ihren Truppen an. Den Russen gelang es jedoch, Iulon gefangenzunehmen, während Parnaos nach Kachetien floh, wo er den Adel für seine Pläne gewann und mit Truppen nach Chewi zog, wo er die Führung des Aufstands übernahm. Iulon beabsichtigte, die Erhebung auf ganz Ostgeorgien auszuweiten, doch das mißlang. Die Russen zerschlugen nach und nach die einzelnen Aufstandsherde ... Mitte Oktober wurden die Truppen des Parnaos von neuen russischen Verbänden besiegt, die von Norden durch die Darial-Schlucht nach Georgien vorgedrungen waren. Die Führer des Aufstands gerieten in Gefangenschaft.'

force has considerably diminished, being reduced at the utmost to 7 or 8000 men, which are scarcely sufficient to keep Georgia in obedience.

On the other hand, the Georgians, disappointed in their hopes, and better informed of the real intentions of the Russians, already feel the weight of their yoke, and regret that of the Persians. The number of discontented daily augment in the province and we expect sooner or later to see a general insurrection.

Fathali Shah has addressed a circular letter[66] to his son, and to all the governours of provinces, announcing the complete victory which the Persian arms have gained over those of Russia. The following is a translation of this circular, from which we could not retrench the metaphorical ornaments used in the prolix and pompous language of the Orientals, and translate military terms according to European usages:

Translation of the Circular of Fathali Shah, king of Persia, addressed to his son Hussein Kuli Mirza [67] *at Icuran.*[68]

"August fruit of the royal tree, blossomed grove of the garden of the empire, Hussein Kuli Mirza, let it be known to you, that whilst our banners were floating triumphant in the plains of Sultania,[69] agitated by the Zephyrs of victory, the publick voice reaching the foot of our throne, informed us that the Russian troops, which had previously taken the town of Tefflis, and laid seige [sic] to Erivan. At the first report of the new enterprize of the enemy, our invincible cohorts, animated by a heroick courage, and inspired only by battles and vengeance, like clouds of vigorous eagles, spreading the wings of diligence, put themselves suddenly in motion to go to the relief of that place, and to save it from the danger with which it was threatened. As soon as the enemy's camp was perceived from afar at the foot of the ramparts at Erivan, the brave general who commanded our army gave orders to the cavalry to charge first, and immediately afterwards made the company of carbiners advance. The Russians at first sustained the shock of our squadrons; but almost at the same moment, the infantry having arrived, they could no longer resist, and yielding to the Persian valour, they abandoned their posts, and took refuge in an old Mosque at some distance, where they entrenched themselves, after having had 1500 men killed and wounded.

"Some days after this happy event, the enemy, flattering themselves that the star of success, by a nocturnal surprize, might efface the darkness of their shame, came to fall at

---

[66] 'A letter printed or written in the same form, which is sent round to any number of persons, to serve in the place of an advertisement.' See Crabb (1823: s.v. Circular).

[67] As Fath 'Ali Shah did not have a son named Hoseyn Qoli Mirza, the addressee was probably Hoseyn 'Ali Mirza, his fifth son and governor of Fars in 1805. See Anonymous (1873: 715), Busse (1972: 109).

[68] Tehran.

[69] 'A plain so ample that Napoleon's Grand Army, with which he invaded Russia, might have manœuvered in it with ease.' This is 'where the Shah of Persia usually encamps during the summer months to avoid the hot and unhealthy climate of Tehrān.' See MacGregor (1871: 570). For a lengthy description of Soltaniyeh and its history see Ker Porter (1821/1: 276–280). For the original Mongol capital sited there, visible as ruins in the nineteenth century, see Blair (1986).

night upon our victorious camp like bats that dare not quit their obscure residence but in the absence of the sun. But our warriours, protected by a fortune always vigilant, being warned of their silent march, advanced boldly to meet them, and gave them a reception calculated to make them repent of their temerity. The action was warm and bloody; and the Russians seeing themselves broken at all quarters, fled in disorder, being pursued to their entrenchment, and leaving upwards of 900 of their men upon the field, of whom about the half had received mortal wounds, and the rest were made prisoners.

"While this was passing, an escort of three hundred Georgians on horseback, who were conducting a considerable convoy to the enemy's camp, were attacked on the road, and cut to pieces by a detachment of our army that had been sent to cut them off. The provisions were seized, and more than one hundred Georgians made prisoners; the rest of their troops having fallen in the action.

"The Russian general having been informed that we had given to the valorous Pir Kouli Kan Kiagar,[70] our commission to go and re-establish order in the province of Georgia, sent one of his lieutenants against him with 400 men, in order to frustrate his object, or at least to retard him as much as possible on his march. Our general was overtaken in the environs of Pelenk,[71] where an obstinate battle took place; but the Russians were defeated, and 350 of them became food for the Persian sabres. After this victory Pir-Kouli Kan turned the reins of diligence towards a body of the enemy which was coming to join their army. Having joined, he charged them with vigour, and dispersed them like dust scattered by the wind. Their artillery, ammunition, and effects, all fell into the hands of the vanquishers.

"Impatient to complete the rout of the Russians, on the 9th of this month we caused to advance against them a chosen corps which we had hitherto kept in reserve. As they had time to rally their forces, they thought themselves able to face us, and waited our army with firmness. After some little skirmishes, the action became general and murderous. The first who signalized themselves by their bravery was the musqueteers, who by their smart and repeated fires, mowed down a great number of the enemy. Our cavalry performed prodigies of valour, overthrowing every thing which opposed it.—The Russians shewed themselves intrepid, but they could not withstand the Yranian [Iranian] impetuosity, they were routed, and our troops made such a dreadful carnage, that all the field of battle was strewed with their carcases, and with with streams of their blood.

---

[70] Pir Qoli Khan Qajar Shambayati. See Clark (2006a: 44). For his involvement in the early hostilities of 1804 against the Russians, see Brydges (1833: 206–208), Busse (1972: 109). According to Brosset (1857: 283), 'Baba-Khan envoya aussi dans le Phambac [mod. Pambak, Armenia] son sardar Pir-Qouli-Khan, avec un corps de 8000 hommes, pour attaquer Qaraklis [Kara Kilise], lieu fortifié par les Russes, qui y tenaient leur provisions de plomb et de poudre. Cette place fut donc attaquée par Pir-Qouli-Khan, sans qu'il réusait à la prendre, parce qu'il s'y trouvait une garnison de 200 Russses.' Later (1810/11) Pir Qoli Khan was charged with defending the Mughan frontier. See Brydges (1833: 423).

[71] Pers. and Turk. *pelenk* means tiger or leopard. See Jones (1771: 22), Kieffer and Bianchi (1835: 227). On the way from Shirwan to Tbilisi and Erzurum, via Gori, in 1578 George, the brother of the ruler of Imeritia, 'encamped near the castle Pelenk.' See von Hammer (1835a: 259). Brydges (1833: 207–208) refers to an encounter 'between Pambak and Erivan.'

"The two chiefs who commanded, Lewed and Dergon, with many other officers of distinction, and 6000 men, were killed and wounded.[72]

"This memorable victory gained us 34 pieces of cannon, and many other objects of warlike ammunition. Those of the Russians who escaped, precipitately abandoned their camp and baggage, and fled towards Georgia. But we have given the necessary orders to persue [sic] them, and we hope that they will sooner or later meet with the fate they merit.

"Wishing to circulate incessantly through our kigdom [sic], news of the general rout of the enemy's army, and to publish the splendid triumphs of our arms, we have dispatched couriers express to all our lieutenants and governors of provinces, to enjoin them to cause to be celebrated in their respective departments, by publick rejoicings, and solemn acts of grace, the signal victory which Heaven has accorded us.

"On the arrival of Mohemmed Hussein-Heg [sic, Beg], officer of our guard, who will transmit you this, you will hasten, on your peril, to fulfil exactly our intention, which are to order, in our capital, publick rejoicings and prayers, which are to be continued three days successively; and you will take care that they shall be accompanied with all the pomp and magnificence exacted by the circumstances and the place. Such is our supreme will.

"FATHALI SHAH."
(Signed)
And sealed with the Royal Seal.
The Cheban, 1219.'

9.25 'Thursday, December 12, 1805,' *Salem Register* (Thursday, 12 December, 1805): 'Among the French papers we notice one from the King of Persia[73] addressed to his son.[74] It is in the Persian manner, but we know not how much authority may be attached to it. It says, that the Russians lost 1500 men near Erivan, and in an attempt by night to force the Persian camp, left 900 on the field. That near Pelenk, in another action, they lost 350, and afterwards 6000 men, besides 34 cannon taken by the Persians. From this letter probably arose the reports of the ill success of the Russians. No dates are given for these events. Other accounts give success to the Russians, but the position of the Armies, and the attempts to turn the arms of the Armenians against the Persians, indicate that the Russians have not yet had the full success they have expected in the war with Persia.'

---

[72] As noted above, according to Anonymous (1805b), the official Russian account of the campaign, the Russians lost 15 officers and c. 300 regular soldiers. 'Lewed' and 'Dergon' do not resemble the names of any of the Russian officers who fought in this campaign and are mentioned e.g. by Brosset (1857). Lewed may be a corruption of *lewend*, 'irregular troops, militia, marines' (von Hammer 1815/2: 500; Morell 1854: 168; Kramers 1993) and *dragoons*, in which case the comma between 'commanded' and 'Lewed' is incorrect.

[73] Fath 'Ali Shah.

[74] Hoseyn 'Ali Mirza. Cf. 9.24.

9.26 'Constantinople, Sep. 1,' *The United States Gazette* (Thursday, 12 December, 1805): 'The Pacha of Bagdad has gained a complete victory over the rebel Abdulrahman, Pacha of Curdistan; the army of the latter was almost cut to pieces, and he himself obliged to fly to the Persian territory. The pacha of Bagdad has written to the king of Persia to engage him to give up this rebel.'[75]

9.27 'Late Foreign News. St. Petersburgh. Extract of a letter, Nov. 5,' *New-York Spectator* (Wednesday, 19 February, 1806), 'St. Petersburgh. Extract of a letter, Nov. 5,' *Salem Gazette* (Friday, 28 February, 1806), 'Foreign Inelligence. Russia. St. Petersburgh. Extract of a Letter, November 5,' *The Reporter* (Saturday, 1 March, 1806), 'Picture of Russia. Extract of a letter from St. Petersburgh in Russia, dated Nov. 5,' *The Balance, and Columbian Repository* (Tuesday, 4 March, 1806), 'Foreign Intelligence. London, Dec. 7. Extract of a letter from St. Petersburgh, (Russia,) dated Nov. 5,' *New-Jersey Journal* (Tuesday, 4 March, 1806) and 'Extract of a letter from St. Petersburgh, dated November 5, 1805,' *Connecticut Gazette* (Wednesday, 5 March, 1806): 'Russia … is a power immense in resources, defying a foreign enemy, because tangible in no quarter of attack … In Asia—Can France, excite the Porte against her?—No; the Porte subsists only on her pacific insignificance. In her Persian and Tartar borders she is equally secure. You can

---

[75] As Ateş (2013: 43–44) observed, 'the first Baban crisis in the Ottoman-Qajar period started in 1805 when the new governor of Baghdad, 'Ali Pasha (r. 1802–7), dismissed 'Abd-al-Rahman Pasha, the hereditary ruler of the Baban provinces. Defiant, 'Abd-al-Rahman Pasha routed forces from Mosul sent to unseat him, before being defeated by forces from Baghdad, at which point he took refuge in Sinne [Sanandaj], the capital of the wali of Ardalan, or Iranian Kurdistan … Fath 'Ali Shah asked the Baghdad governor for the reinstatement of the Baban pasha. The governor, inn turn, sent a representative to Tehran to request that 'Abd-al-Rahman be returned or resettled in the interior of Iran.' Corancez (1810: 96) noted, 'Au nord de Bagdad, sur les frontières orientales de la Turquie, et près des confins de la Perse, est le Kurdistan, région inégale et coupée de hautes montagnes. Ses abords difficiles, sa position aux extrémités des deux grands Empires de l'Orient, l'ont presque toujours rendue indépendante de l'un et l'autre. Elle est divisée en trois pachaliks qui relèvent du pacha de Bagdad … Abd-elrahman-Pacha, après avoir assassiné Mohammed, pacha de Suleïmanieh, le premier de ces pachaliks, s'étoit réfugié à Derbent [near Sulaimaniyah, not in the Caucasus]. Attaqué par Ali-Pacha en 1805, il avoit été battu et obligé de se réfugier à Sineh, auprès du khan de cette ville. Ali-Pacha exigea des Persans qu'on le remît entre ses mains. Refusé par le roi de Perse, il venoit de réunir ses troupes sur les frontières de cet Empire.'. As Eppel (2008: 241–242) noted, 'Abd al-Rahman was not trying to free himself of Ottoman rule, but rather to obtain independence from the vali of Baghdad. The threat to his rule resulted from attempts by Ali Pasha to oust him and replace him with his rival within the family, Khalid Baban … In the autumn of 1805, in view of the superiority of the Mamluk-Ottoman forces and his Kurdish rivals, headed by his own relative Khalid Baban, Abd al-Rahman was forced to flee froim Sulaymaniyya and seek asylum in Persia. The Shah of Persia, Fath Ali Shah, gave Abd al-Rahman his protection and pressured the Mamluk-Ottoman vali of Baghdad into returning Abd al-Rahman to Sulaymaniyya.' According to Longrigg (1925: 231) the Ottomans 'were completely defeated by the Kurd at Altun Kupri. 'Abdu 'l Raḥman looted the town, surveyed the corpses of a dozen Turkish commanders, and retired to fortify a position on the Darband pass in readiness for the inevitable army from Baghdad. It came, and he failed to withstand it: rapid flight to Sannah alone saved his life, his following was scattered, and his throne given to his kinsman Khalid.'

scarce collect an army of Persians to shew their face to a Russian soldier; you can scarcely tempt a horde of Tartars to rob the granary of a Russian peasant ... She is deterred by no foreign enemy; she is confident in her own people.'

9.28 'M. Jaubert. Constantinople, April 15,' *Relfs Philadelphia Gaette, and Daily Advertiser* (Monday, 21 July, 1806), 'Foreign Intelligence. Constantinople, April 15,' *The Daily Advertiser* (Thursday, 24 July, 1806, first two paras. only), 'M. Jaubert. Constantinople, April 15,' *The United States Gazette* (Thursday, 24 July, 1806, first two paras. only), 'Extracted from late London Papers, received at Philadelphia. Turkey. Constantinople, April 15. M. Jaubert,' *New-England Palladium* (Tuesday, 29 July, 1806), 'Constantinople, April 5,' *National Intelligencer, and Washington Advertiser* (Wednesday, 30 July, 1806), 'Letter from M. Jaubert to M. Ruffin,' *Kline's Carlisle Weekly Gazette* (Friday, 1 August, 1806, first two paras. only), 'M. Jaubert. Constantinople, April 15,' *Republican Advocate* [Frederick MD] (Friday, 1 August, 1806, first two paras. only), 'M. Jaubert. Constantinople, April 15,' *The Enquirer* (Friday, 1 August, 1806), 'Late Foreign Articles. M. Jaubert. Constantinople, April 15,' *The Democrat* (Saturday, 2 August, 1806), 'Foreign News. Constantinople, April 15. M. Jaubert,' *Connecticut Herald* (Tuesday, 5 August, 1806), 'Constantinople, April 15,' *City Gazette and Daily Advertiser* (Tuesday, 5 August, 1806, first two paras. only), 'Foreign Intelligence. Turkey. Constantinople, April 15,' *Newburyport Herald* (Tuesday, 5 August, 1806; first two paras. only), 'Foreign Intelligence. Constantinople, April 15,' *The Northern Post* (Thursday, 14 August, 1806; first two paras. only), 'Foreign News. Turkey. Constantinople, April 15,' *Concord Gazette* (Saturday, 16 August, 1806), 'Letter from M. Jaubert to M. Ruffin,' *The Western World* (Saturday 16 August, 1806, beginning 'From the Camp...'), 'Constantinople, April 15,' *Olive Branch* (Friday, 20 August, 1806; first two paras. only) and 'M. Jaubert. Constantinople, April 15,' *American Mercury* (Thursday, 25 September, 1806): 'M. Jaubert,[76] Secretary and Interpreter to his Majesty the Emperor of the French,[77] well known here for the several missions in which he has been employed to the Sultan,[78] had been sent by his sovereign to the king of Persia.[79] We had heard nothing of him for upwards of a year;[80] and no doubt was any longer

---

[76] Pierre Amédée Émilien Probe Jaubert (1779–1857), Orientalist and diplomat. For his biography see Biot (1848).

[77] Napoleon.

[78] Selim III.

[79] Fath 'Ali Shah. As Biot (1848: 75), wrote, Napoleon 'lui ordonna de se rendre secrètement auprès du shah de Perse et de reconnaître s'il était possible de lier avec ce souverain des relations amicales, afin de tenir de ce côté la Russie en échec.'

[80] Jaubert was imprisoned at Bayazid in eastern Turkey from 7 July 1805 until 19 February 1806. See Dehérain (1930: 38). On his imprisonment and release, Watson (1866: 152–153) wrote, 'this envoy, who had been sent from Paris, in consequence of a wish expressed on the Shah's part to the French ambassador at Constantinople that he might receive the support of France, was arrested near the Persian frontier, by the agents of the Pasha of Byazeed, and was conducted to that town, where he was for 8 months confined in a dry subterranean cistern. The Pasha of Byazeed died at the end of that time,

entertained of his death! at length, however, we have been informed of his situation. His letter to M. Russin [sic, Ruffin],[81] the French Charge d'Affaires, will convey some idea of the sufferings of this interesting young man.

When the Sublime Porte was informed of his mission to Persia, they gave him a firman to protect his passage. He arrived at the Court of the Persian Schah, who had dispatched a considerable escort to meet him.'[82] (Fig. 9.1)

Letter from M. Jaubert to M. Ruffin.
"From the Camp of the Vizer Josef,[83] 60 leagues south-west of Ertz Roum,[84] March 14, 1806.

---

and the news of the victory of Austerlitz, which penetrated into the heart of Turkey, was likely to give increased security to the agents of France; and when the crown-prince of Persia demanded the release of M. Jaubert, he was permitted to continue his journey.'

[81] Pierre Ruffin (1742–1824). For his career see Dehérain (1929, 1930). This article is a verbatim translation of Jaubert's letter to Ruffin in French which appeared in Anonymous (1806a, b, c, d, e, f). It is a mystery how the letter came to appear on 1 April, 1806, in *L'Abeille du Nord* (Anonymous 1806a) before appearing in the *Gazette Nationale* which printed official state documents from the Foreign Ministry (beneath the newspaper's banner were the words, 'A dater du 7 nivoise an 8, les Actes du Gouvernement et des Autorités constituées, contenus dans le Moniteur, *sont officiels*'). The English version published in America was presumably taken from *The Times* (London) of Wednesday, 4 June 1806 (Anonymous 1806g).

[82] The French original of this opening paragraph was printed in the *Mercure de France* (Saturday, 3 May, 1806 = Anonymous 1806b) and the *Gazette Nationale ou Le Moniteur Universel* (Tuesday, 21 May, 1806 = Anonymous 1806c) but not in *L'Abeille du Nord* (Tuesday, 1 April, 1806 = Anonymous 1806a). As Jaubert wrote to Ruffin on 20 June 1806, 'On y [Tehran] avait mis une pompe extraordinaire. Environ dix mille hommes étaient sous les armes; le roi et toute sa cour magnifiquement habillés. Ma lettre fut lue et ensuite le roi m'entretint sur les affaires de ma patrie, sur la grandeur de Bonaparte, sur son amitié pour la France et sur mes malheurs passés ... Trois jours après seconde audience et même cérémonial.' See Dehérain (1930: 39).

[83] Yusuf Pasha. Cf. 9.20. Jaubert (1821: 95) wrote, 'Youssuf pacha, quoique âgé de plus de soixante-dix ans, conservait une force d'esprit et de corps extraordinaire. Il était d'une grande stature, l'ensemble des traits n'était pas régulier; sa barbe était blanche et rare, son regard vif et pénétrant. Né en Géorgie, il avait été, dans sa première jeunesse, amené comme esclave à Constantinople. On lui avait donné une éducation toute militaire qu s'accordait parfaitement avec son caractère belliqueux, et il s'était élevé des derniers degrés de la milice aux plus hautes dignités de l'empire. Aussi habile à pénétrer les secrets du sérail que brave à la tête des armées, il avait su se concilier l'estime et la confiance du sultan Sélim, qu'il avait pour ainsi dire vu naître, et pour lequel il conservait autant d'attachement que de respect.' Cf. Tancoigne (1820: 49) who described Yusuf Pasha in 1807 as 'about seventy years of age, and by birth a Georgian: he has been twice grand vizier, and in that capacity commanded the Ottoman armies in Egypt and Syria. Although Yousouf lost an eye in his youth, at the game of djerid, this defect does not diminish the nobleness and expression of his countenance, ornamented with a long white beard. For two years past he has commanded at Erzerum with absolute power ... I should add, that Yousouf Pacha is very popular.'

[84] Erzurum.

Fig. 9.1 Pierre-Amédée-Émilien-Probe Jaubert, engraving by E. Ducrocq. Bibliothèque National de France, CC0 1.0 Universal

"Sir—Divine Providence, that watches over the destinies of France, has permitted me to survive the event which I have the honor to relate, and for the publication of which I am rather anxious. At the same time I request you will transmit it to his Majesty's government.

"I left Ertz Roum on the night of July 1, and continued my journey to the north-east of that place, without meeting any danger, but from two corps of Kurdish cavalry, from whom I escaped by the swiftness of my horse, and the obscurity of the night. The Russians being in the neighbourhood, have occasioned these hordes to over-run the whole country south of the Araxus. I traversed this river on the 4th, and on the following day I arrived at the principal source of the Euphrates, about 54 leagues from Ertz Roum.

"On the evening of the 5th, I was obliged to stop at Arzab, an Armenian village, two leagues from Bajazed,[85] a city where Mahmoud Pacha resides. This governor, hearing of

---

[85] Mod. Doğubayazit, Turkey.

me at the village, expressed his wish to see me, and sent some horsemen with orders to conduct me to his residence. Mahmoud Pacha is about 32 years of age, and is famous in this country for his tyranny, his vexatious spirit, and his riches. He received me with great coolness in his first interview, and having separated me from my people, questioned them concerning me; and while he affected a great deal of politeness on my account, he actually, as I was afterwards informed, put my guide to the torture, from whom, having extorted some equivocal acknowledgments, he afterwards had the man secretly assassinated. At the same time he formed the base project of robbing me, as much to satisfy his avarice, as to make himself agreeable to the Russians.

"You may go," said he to me, "to Erwan, which is but five leagues from hence, but fail not upon your return to pass through my province.

"I shall entrust you with some business at Constantinople, and with Jusef Pacha: you shall be escorted by my most faithful servants. When they arrive upon the frontier, they will deliver to you a passport. Your guide will rejoin you this evening."

"I suspected his treachery, but it was not in my power to avoid it. I left Bajazed with a considerable escort, and under the protection of a Vizier of the Sublime Port. I had a right, therefore, to consider myself in full security; but you will perceive how my confidence was rewarded.

"There is a stream[86] at the foot of Mount Ararat, that runs into the Caspian sea; this stream is a boundary between the territory of the Sublime Port and that of Persia. I passed it, and finding myself upon Persian territory, my guides invited me to alight from my horse; but, while I was thanking Heaven for having reached the Persian territory, at such a distance from my own country, I was surrounded, disarmed, and thrown with my face to the ground.[87] At this moment, Heaven is my witness, no unworthy thought once entered my mind:—my last wishes were for the prosperity of my sovereign's arms. I did not forget that I carried the Imperial Eagle, around which is engraved these words—*Honour our Country*;[88] the first my only guide, and the latter the object of all my affections.

"Thus surprised and accosted upon the Persian territory, I was dragged away by those persons whose duty it was to defend me from my enemies. In this situation I was left till the evening, night coming on, I was conducted over frightful precipices, quite out of the beaten road; and, after a short march of 3 h, I arrived at a lonely house some distance from Bajezed, where the Pacha, in disguise, waited my arrival. I complained bitterly of this want of good faith, and my firmness on this occasion saved my life, as well as the lives of those who accompanied me. This traitor, fearing the consequences of his attempt, said, with some

---

[86] The Aras/Araxes river.

[87] A slightly different version of this text, clearly reworked by the author, appears in Jaubert 1821: 37–38. Sections of it, such as the preceding paragraph, were reprinted in Dehérain 1930: 38.

[88] 'Honneur et patrie,' or 'Honour and (my) country,' the motto on the French Legion of Honor (Légion d'Honneur), created by Napoleon and continued to this day. See Washbourne (1841: s.v. Honneur et patrie). The obverse bore a portrait of Napoleon and the reverse the imperial eagle, clutching two thunderbolts, with the legend in exergue. See Jacomy (1859: 88).

embarassment, that he should write to Constantinople. He then caused me to be stripped naked, and I was dragged to the castle, where there is a subterraneous dungeon, an invention worthy of such a wretch.[89]

"About midnight, I was obliged to descend into this cavern by a rope, the Pacha giving orders to the Commandant of the Castle to keep me upon a small quantity of bread and water; to keep my confinement a profound secret; and not to allow me to have any light, for fear people should suspect the fact of some person being imprisoned there.

"I languished in this situation, and in the mean while the plague raged in the city. The heat of the weather was intolerable: I was without clothes, and without hopes of life; still I was in pretty good health, as were also the three persons who belonged to me. About the first of Vendemiaire, of the year 14,[90] the Pacha was affected with the plague, and in one of the intervals of his malady, he gave orders to have me assassinated; this the commandant of the Castle refused to execute; and this was not the only service done me by this venerable Musselman during the eight months I was in confinement. To him I owe my life and liberty.

"The Pacha died, the city was then divided into parties, respecting the choice of a successor. Atchmet Bey, his son, at length carried the cause. To me he seemed more dangerous than his father. One of my horses happened to be recognized, and he ordered it to be killed. He also removed my friend, the Commandant of the Castle, and seemed inclined to deprive me of the wretched existence he had for a while spared, just at the time he was seized by the plague, and, like his father, carried off. Ibrahim Bey still survived, and seemed more favorably inclined than his predecessors; still he suffered me to remain a captive: he did nothing more than order my place of confinement to be shifted, after the expiration of 34 days. During this interval, I found an opportunity of writing a few lines, and sending them into Persia, I have since received two answers, copies of which I have inclosed and sent to my Government.

---

[89] The castle was badly damaged in the Russo-Turkish war of 1828–1829 by Russian bombardment. As Brant (1840: 422) wrote, 'The ancestors of Behlúl Páshá have for several generations ruled the Páshálik of Báyazíd, nominally as a dependence on Erẓ-Rúm; but Maḥmúd, the father of the present Páshá, established a real independence, and was a powerful though lawless chief. He built the palace, and obliged the Kurds to bring him materials at their own charge. His former residence is situated on the opposite side of a ravine, in face of the new Palace: it is half excavated in the side of the mountain, and contains immense stores: it has also a battery of guns in an unserviceable state. The place is impregnable, except by the aid of artillery; and its position and character are well chosen for the residence of a chieftain like Maḥmúd Páshá, who might be considered rather as the head of a band of freeboters than a páshá governing a wide district. On the summit of the same mountain, on the side of which this stronghold is placed, are the remains of a more ancient castle, which I suppose to have been the last of the stations of the Genoese. It was in the more modern castle that M. Jaubert was confined.' Anonymous (1866a: 358), on the other hand, suggested that Jaubert was imprisoned in the old 'Genoese' castle, noting, 'There is also a Genoese castle here, in which M. Jaubert, the envoy of the Great Napoleon, was confined by the Turkish Pasha Mohammed, who hoped that his captive would die in the dungeon and leave him in possession of the valuable jewels he was taking to the Shah.' Brant, the eyewitness, is probably the more reliable source in this case.
[90] 22 September, 1805.

"The Vizier Jusef Bey having been informed of my history, gave orders for me to attend him. A Persian Officer arrived at the same time from Taurus, to claim me in the name of his Sovereign. The Bey caused me to be conducted here, and I cannot sufficiently praise the reception I have met with.—It is still my intention to deliver the letter (merely a friendly one) of which I am the bearer, to the King of Persia. The Sublime Porte will feel, I presume, that it cannot consistently deny me a passage. It is the interest of the Porte, and, above all, it is that of justice, not to abuse its power on my account or to take an advantage of my weakness. I speak in the name of a Sovereign whose name is revered through the universe. If the Sublime Porte wishes to preserve his friendship, let it give him this proof of its own amity. I request you will send a copy of this to the Minister for Foreign Affairs,[91] to whom I have not written, having almost forgotten my native language; excuse, therefore, the style of this letter. Tell him that he may assure the Emperor, I will not return without fulfillling my mission. Eight months passed without my seeing the light of the sun, have not abated my zeal. I shall not see Paris till I return from Ispahan with the answer of the Persian Schah.

"P. Amadez Jaubert.'"

9.29 'From the Paris Argus of May 29. Constantinople, April 9,' *National Intelligencer, and Washington Advertiser* (Friday, 25 July, 1806) and 'Foreign Intelligence. Constantinople, April 9,' *Political Barometer* (Tuesday, 5 August, 1806): 'The French agent Romieux, who was sent from hence [Constantinople] about the end of last summer, we now learn, had a mission to Fatali Scham [sic, Shah], the king of Persia; but upon his return he had the misfortune to be attacked and murdered not far from the Turkish frontier. The perpetrators are unknown.'[92]

9.30 'From the Salem Register,' *The Witness* (Wednesday, 24 September, 1806) and 'From the Salem Register,' *Relfs Philadelphia Gazette, and Daily Advertiser* (Monday, 29 September, 1806): 'Among the reports of the day, the most interesting are such as lead us to review the scenes through which the French Emperor[93] passed to his present glory . . .

---

[91] Charles Maurice de Talleyrand-Périgord (1754–1838), in office from 22 November 1799 to 9 August 1807.

[92] Antoine Alexandre Romieu (1764–1805). For his life and mission see Dehérain (1930: 35–37), Gotteri (1993), Amini (1999: 65–75). Romieu was not murdered on his return. He arrived in Tehran on 24 September 1805 and had two audiences with Fath 'Ali Shah, on 1 October, when he delivered Napoleon's letter of 30 March 1805, and 4 October, when he delivered the presents for Fath 'Ali Shah with which he had been entrusted. But, as Dehérain (1930: 37) noted, 'il était arrivé à Téhéran fort malade et le 12 octobre 1805 il succombait. Avant de mourir, il rédigea partiellement un mémoire sur la Perse, son souverain, son gouvernement et son état de faiblesse militaire, qui parvint à Talleyrand par l'intermédiaire de J.-F. Rousseau. En ordonnant pour Romieu le cérémonial d'obsèques en usage lors de décès des grands de sa cour, en faisant construire un tombeau surmonté d'une coupole, le chah voulut témoigner sa considération pour l'Envoyé de Napoléon.'

[93] Napoleon.

no doubt remains that the Emperor engaged warmly in the expedition against Egypt, and many things lead to the belief, that he has not abandoned this great object of his ambition ... But should the ambition of France not embrace the object of conquering or gaining Egypt, yet the intercourse of Europe with India, and the extending settlements of Russia, as well as the continued discoveries of travellers, lead us to expect that the communications by land cannot much longer remain obstructed ... Wht sound policy will not accomplish, daring ambition will achieve. Europe has not been without expectations that the Emperor of France will not overlook this great design, and after Russia has attempted in vain to secure itself against Persia, the narrow limits between the Black and Caspian Seas, that a French Emperor will dare to extend his dominion to the Southern ocean. We find the distances once terrible to enterprise, daily becoming less forbidding to private as well as national courage. By the researches, and the discoveries already made, we know the countries and the inhabitants who have so long prevented the visits of Europeans to the richest part of the Globe. Mr. Jackson, in 1797,[94] passed from the Persian Gulf by Bagdat, Mosul and Diabekir to the Black sea, and from thence to Constantinople, in a route which had not been attempted for a century by an European traveller ... The distance from the Persian Gulf to the Black Sea, does not exceed ten degrees of latitude, and lays between 30 and 40 degrees of N. latitude, and his route was in less than ten degrees of longitude. He passed over the mountains of Armenia. In 1784, Mr. Foster,[95] of whom Maj. Rennel[96] gives an account, passed from Bengal to the Caspian. From Calcutta to Moultan, according to Rennel, is about 1500 miles, and to Cabul and Candahar, about 1800 ... From Candahar to the Caspian, according to Foster, is 772 miles, giving about 2500 miles to Calcutta. The difference between Candahar and the Caspian, being about 15 deg. of long. and 4 of lat. In the latitude of Candahar, and within 15 deg. of longitude, lays Ispahan the capital of Persia, and Ispahan is within 7 degrees of Bagdat at the head of the Persian Gulf, not exceeding 1500 miles for the traveller. According to Page,[97] and many other modern travellers, from Bagdat to Syria, about ten degrees, the travelling, free from the plundering parties of the desert, by sufficient guards, might be easily performed. The distances from Egypt to the Red Sea, are inconsiderable in themselves, and as they have been, so they may again become the path of a rich and extensive Commerce.—We have long been disused to contemplate long journeys with horror, and the expeditions of Alexander and Cæsar, though

---

[94] John Jackson (d. 1807). His account was published in Jackson (1799).

[95] George Forster (1752–1791). The full account of his journey is given in Forster (1798). For his life see Franklin (2017).

[96] James Rennell (1742–1830). Rennell (1792) (first ed. 1788) contains some thirty references to Forster's 'accurate computations of distances, and especially his comments upon the course, navigability, and fordability of rivers.' See Franklin (2017).

[97] Pierre Marie François, vicomte de Pagès (1748–1793) travelled around the world from 1767 to 1771. See Pagès (1791–1792) (orig. French ed. 1782). His work was cited by Beauchamp. See Beauchamp (1784: 475).

in opposite directions, would not, in our days, have the glory which they secured to those immortal conquerors.'

9.31 'London, Sept. 7,' *New-York Commercial Advertiser* (Monday, 27 October, 1806), 'London, Sept. 7,' *New-York Spectator* (Wednesday, 29 October, 1806), 'London, Sept. 7,' *The Enquirer* (Friday, 7 November, 1806) and 'London, Sept. 7,' *Suffolk Gazette* (Monday, 10 November, 1806): 'The Persians intend to take Bassora; for which purpose Babi Khan[98] was in full march against it.'[99]

9.32 'Russia. Petersburg, Aug. 7,' *Newburyport Herald* (Tuesday, 28 October, 1806), 'Russia. Petersburg, Aug. 7,' *Portsmouth Oracle* (Saturday, 1 November, 1806) and 'Russia. Petersburg, Aug. 7,' *The Reporter* (Saturday, 8 November, 1806): 'A courier from the army in Persia has brought favorable news of its operations.'

9.33 'July 26,' *The Repertory* (Tuesday, 28 October, 1806) and 'July 26,' *Republican Spy* (Wednesday, 5 November, 1806): 'Letters from Bassora say, that the Persians have designs on Bassora. Baha Kahn[100] is in full march to seize on that place, on which he pretends to have legitimate claims.'

9.34 'London, Sept. 7,' *American Commercial Daily Advertiser* (Saturday, 1 November, 1806), 'Untitled,' *The Sentinel of Freedom* (Tuesday, 4 November, 1806; with minor variations), 'London, Sept. 7,' *The Enquirer* (Friday, 7 November, 1806; with slight variations), 'Political Review,' *Virginia Gazette, and General Advertiser* (Saturday, 8 November, 1806), 'London, Sept. 7,' *Spooner's Vermont Journal* (Monday, 10 November, 1806), 'London, Sept. 7,' *Suffolk Gazette* (Monday, 10 November, 1806) and 'London, Sept. 7,' *Vermont Gazette, an Epitome of the World* (Tuesday, 11 November, 1806; with slight variations): 'A letter from St. Petersburgh, of one day later date than the

---

[98] Baba Khan, i.e. Fath 'Ali Shah.

[99] Fath 'Ali Shah never threatened Basra but the idea may have arisen in the aftermath of the flight of 'Abd al-Rahman Pasha, the Persian proxy in Sulaimaniyah, to Persian territory and the demand made by 'Ali Pasha in Baghdad to the Shah for his return, as alluded to tersely in 9.26. As Corancez (1810: 96–97) noted, after these events, 'La guerre parut alors inévitable entre la Perse et le pacha de Bagdad. Les khans des frontières occidentales [of Persia] eurent ordre de prendre les armes, pour s'opposer à Ali-Pacha. Dans tout autre moment, l'inégalité des forces eût donné aux Persans tout l'avantage de cette querelle; mais leur position étoit à cette époque extrêmement fâcheuse. Attaqués par les Russes dans l'Abderbijan [sic, Azerbaijan], ils y éprouvoient chaque jour de nouveaux revers. La nécessité sembloit donc dicter impérieusement tous les sacrifices, plutôt que de s'attirer au midi une nouvelle guerre. Aussi les oulémas d'Ispahan supplièrent-ils Feth-Ali-Schah d'abandonner Abd-elrahman-Pacha à son mauvais sort.' Persuaded of the correctness of this strategy, Fath 'Ali Shah sent Haji Hoseyn Khan, who had a good rapport with 'Ali Pasha, to try to 'trouver quelques moyens de conciliation.'

[100] Baba Khan, i.e. Fath 'Ali Shah.

dispatches transmitted to government, state, that news had just reached that capital of a complete victory gained by the Russian army over the Persians, in which the latter were almost all killed or taken prisoners.[101] It appears, that the Russian officers had for some days previous to the battle been exciting their troops to take a dreadful revenge for the murder of prince Zizianoff,[102] and their efforts were of so much importance, that when the post came away, preparations were making to illuminate the Russian Capital.'

[101] This may be a reference to the victory of Major General Peter Feodorovich Nebolsin (d. 1809) described as follows by Baddeley (1908: 76), 'General Niebolseen, with only his own regiment and the battalions of Kariághin and Lissaniévitch, 1600 bayonets in all, totally defeated the Persians in the Khanashin defile; then marched on Noukhá, the capital of Shekeen, and took it by storm; while in no direction did the enemy gain any real success.' Cf. Brosset (1857: 288, n. 1), 'le général Nébolsin remportait un avantage signalé sur les troupes d'Abaz-Mirza, auprès du petit fort d'Askaran, sur la rivière Karaképek.' This victory occurred on 25 June. See von Bernhardi (1877: 229) who noted, 'General Glasenap, der den interimistischen Befehl in Grusien führte, konnte dem persischen Prinzen ['Abbas Mirza had crossed the Araxes with 20,000 men] nur 1700 Mann, bei denen sich aber Kotlärewsky [1782–1852] befand, unter einem General Nebolsin entgegensenden—und diese geringe Macht genügte bei Askeran (am 25. Juni 1806) einen glänzenden Sieg über Abbas Mirza davon zu tragen, und die Perser über den Araxes zurück zu treiben.' Alternatively, the article may be referring to the Russian capture of Derbend on 3 July 1806. See Pölitz (1826/2: 351) (or 22 June according to Baddeley (1908: 74). The dateline of the original report on which these articles were based is 7 August.

[102] The murder of Tsitsianov has been recounted many times. In the Georgian account given by Brosset (1857: 286–287), early in 1806 Tsitsianov resumed his campaign and, 'Ayant traversé le Chirwan, Tzitzianof vint à Bakou, avec l'intention de s'en emparer, pour faire venir par-là, d'Astrakhan, les provisions nécessaires à l'armée occupant la Géorgie, le pays n'en fournissant pas suffisamment aux besoins des Russes. Arrivé près de Bakou, il campa à un pharsang [parsang, farsakh] delà et écrivit au khan Ouseïn [Hoseyn Qoli Khan, governor of Baku; cf. Brydges (1833: 252), Busse (1972: 111)] de lui apporter les clefs de la ville. En vain le khan le conjura de lui épargner un affront aussi sensible que celui d'apporter de sa propre main les clefs de cette place; Tzitzichwili n'écoutait rien. Enfin le khan lui écrivit: "L'inquiétude m'empêchant de me rendre au sein de votre armée, je vous prie de vous approcher de la citadelle avec seulement deux personnes. Je viendrai moi-même avec deux de mes serviteurs, et dans notre mutuelle rencontre je vous présenterai les clefs." Tzitzianof partit donc avec deux Cosaques et Elishar éristhaw, fils d'Agha-Baba [Giorgi Evseevich Eristov; see Baddeley (1908: 71)], pour s'aboucher avec le khan. Celui-ci s'avança également avec deux serviteurs. Ils descendirent de cheval, s'embrassèrent, et lorsque le khan fit la remise des clefs, les deux serviteurs, faisant feu de leurs fusils zur Tzitzichwili, le tuèrent, ainsi qu'Elisbar, fils d'Agha-Baba éristhaw, le jeudi 8 février … On lui coupa la tête, qui fut envoyé au chah.' The early Qajar history identified Ibrahim Beg, son of the paternal uncle of Hoseyn Qoli Khan of Baku, as the shooter. 'At the moment Ashpukhdar [Tsitsianov] and Husain Kuly Khan had met, and made propositions for an interview, Ibrahim Beg, with Husain's permission, and without the prince's ['Abbas Mirza] sanction, slew him with a musket-ball; on which Pir Kuly Khan Kajar, Husain Kuly Khan and the other commanders, surrounded his escort: some of them were slain; others made prisoners; whilst such as survived, fled, and … embarked in their ships and proceeded to Saru [Sari]. These Khans directed Ashpukhdar's confused head, which he through pride and insolence rubbed against the solar diadem, to be cut off; and sent it by couriers to the seat of Government. The Prince Viceroy had, however, given express commands to those employed on the expedition to repel

9.35 'Parisian Review of Politics,' *Alexandria Daily Advertiser* (Friday, 7 November, 1806): 'Russia, too feeble in population to expect success in Europe and Asia at the same time, has adopted the policy which her interest and her glory required. At the very moment in which her peace with France ensures the repose of the West, a solemn embassy unites the court of Petersburgh with the court of Pekin; ships from Kamschatka explore the seas of Japan, and lay the foundation of a commerce which will civilize the North. Policy does not alone contribute to the prosperity of Russia—her armies have passed the Caucasus; spread over the plains of Persia, & are already under the walls of Ispahan; treaties will unite the Czar[103] to the Shah,[104] and from that moment the trade of India, lost to England, will abandon the vast ocean, and return to the seas and rivers that flow into it. That day will deprive Great Britain of her riches and her resources for loans—that day will turn against

---

this rash man in the field of battle, and not to slay him at the moment of interview; and therefore this sad present gave no pleasure to his noble mind.' See Brydges (1833: 252–253). Cf. According to von Bernhardi (1877: 229), Tsitsianov 'ritt an dem dazu bestimmten Tage (20. Februar) nur von zweihundert Mann begleitet bis an den Brunnen, eine halbe Werst vor der Stadt, wo ihn die "Aeltesten" derselben mit den Schlüsseln der Thore, und mit "Brod und Salz" erwarteten. Zizianow nahm dieses Symbol der Gastfreundschaft an, die Schlüssel gab er zurück. Nun nahte der Chan zu Pferde, mit einem Gefolge von fünf Reitern; Zizianow ließ seine Truppe am Brunnen zurück und eilte ihm entgegen, nur von dem grusinischen Fürsten Eristow und einem Kosaken begleitet; als er aber nahe herangekommen war, gab der Chan ein Zeichen, und seine Begleiter schossen Zizianow und Eristow nieder—nur der Kosak entkam. Von den Wällen Baku's wurde darauf ein lebhaftes Feuer auf die russischen Truppen eröffnet; Zizianow's verwaistes Heer wußte sich, ohne Führer und rathlos, nicht anders seiner gefährlichen Lage zu entziehen, als dadurch, daß es sich auf die Flotille einschiffte, die zum Glück herangekommenwar, und nun die Truppen über das Meer nach Astrachan brachte. Der Chan von Baku aber, den Zizianow als den harmlosesten aller dortigen Fürsten geschildert hatte, übersendete jetzt Zizianow's Kopf dem Schah von Persien als ein köstliches und ruhmreiches Siegeszeichen.' Baddeley (1908: 71) provided other details: Hoseyn Qoli Khan 'rode out with a mounted escort, and Tsitsiánoff advanced to meet him, accompanied only his adjutant, Prince Eristoff, and one Cossack. The little party had no sooner come within reach than the treacherous natives rushed at them, firing their pistols. In a moment all was over; Tsitsiánoff fell dead; Prince Eristoff met the same fate immediately after. The guns mounted on the walls of the town opened fire on the Russian army, and Zavaleeshin, upon whom the commanded devolved, for a second time showed his pusillanimity. Careless of Russian honour, he thought only of securing his own safety and that of his men; and instead of avenging the infamous murder of his chief, retreated by way of the Caspian, first to the Shamkhal's dominions, and finally to the northern Line. Tsitsiánoff's head and hands were cut off and sent in triumph to Teheran; his body was buried under the walls of Baku, to be disinterred later on when that city was finally captured by the Russians under Boulgákoff, and, eventually, in 1811 committed to its last resting-place with every circumstance of funeral pomp and solemnity in the venerable church of the Sion monastery in Tiflis.'

[103] Alexander I.
[104] Fath 'Ali Shah.

her the treasures she employs to agitate Europe, and the arms upon which she relies for the defence of her territory.'[105]

9.36 'Collection of Foreign Intelligence. Nov. 15,' *Vermont Precursor* (Saturday, 22 November, 1806): 'From London, Sept. 7th, we hear, that the Russians had lately obtained a complete victory over the Persians. The battle was occasioned by the murder of the Russian Prince Zizianoff by the Persians. In celebration of the victory, Petersburgh, the Russian capital has been illuminated.'

9.37 'London, January 9,' *The People's Friend & Daily Advertiser* (Tuesday, 3 March, 1807; has 'French' instead of 'Persian Ambassador'), 'Foreign Intelligence. Selected from London Papers to the 11th of January, Received by the British Packet, Manchester,' *The Public Advertiser* (Tuesday, 3 March, 1807), 'London, January 9,' *Poulson's American Daily Advertiser* (Thursday, 5 March, 1807), 'Foreign News. Selected from London Papers to the 11th of January, Received by the British Packet, Manchester,' *The Witness* (Wednesday, 11 March, 1807) and 'London, January 9,' *Norfolk Gazette and Publick Ledger* (Wednesday, 11 March, 1807): 'The Persian Ambassador, who arrived at Constantinople from Persia,[106] is, it is said, the bearer of very important political dispatches from the Emperor[107] to Napoleon, exclusive of many rich presents. An offensive and defensive alliance, between France and Persia, is said to be the chief design of this embassy. Many French officers, and other emissaries, have already gone to Persia, by way of Constantinople.[108] The Persian and Turkish languages are now being taught with great assiduity to a number of French officers at Paris, who are destined to go on expeditions to those countries.'

---

[105] This piece is attributed to 'B. Barrère,' more correctly the notorious Bertrand Barère de Vieuzac (1755–1841) who earned a reputation for political opportunism and cruelty during and after the French Revolution. For his memoirs see Carnot and David d'Angers (1842). In his scathing review of Barère's memoirs, Macaulay wrote, 'It is not easy to settle the order of precedence among his vices; but we are inclined to think that his baseness was, on the whole, a rarer and more marvellous thing than his cruelty.' See Macaulay (1853: 623).

[106] Mirza Mohammad Reza Qazvini. When Jaubert left Tehran for Constantinople, 'Mirza Muhammed Raza Cazviny, a noble and accomplished person from Cazvin, and Vizir to his royal highness Prince Muhammed Aly Mirza, was ordered to accompany him, by way of Islambul, as Ambassador to the French Government.' See Brydges (1833: 276). Mirza Mohammad Reza Qazvini arrived in Constantinople on 21 September 1806. 'Il fut reçu au Palais de France par le général Sébastiani, qui venait de remplacer [Pierre] Ruffin à la tête de l'ambassade. Pendant son séjour, le général ambassadeur et le conseiller prônent les avantages que vaudra à la Perse une alliance avec la France.' See Dehérain (1930: 41). For his mission see Amini (1999: 85ff).

[107] Fath 'Ali Shah.

[108] Certainly an exaggeration to say 'many' for at this point only Jaubert and Romieu, and his secretary-interpreter Georges Outrey (Gaffarel 1908: 394–395), had visited Fath 'Ali Shah. Gardane's mission was yet to come.

9.38 'Bade, Dec. 25,' *Salem Register* (Monday, 9 March, 1807), 'Bade, Dec. 25,' *The United States Gazette* (Tuesday, 17 March, 1807), 'Salem, March 9,' *American & Commercial Daily Advertiser* (Thursday, 19 March, 1807) and 'Bade, Dec. 25,' *Alexandria Daily Advertiser* (Tuesday, 24 March, 1807): 'What has been said of the treaty between Russia and Turkey, is false. The Mussulmans are alarmed at the movements of Russia, and the Russian commanders have demanded reinforcements. The Schah of Persia[109] is also said to intend to repulse the unjust aggressions of the Russians, and enter Georgia.'

9.39 'Breda, Dec. 25,' *The Friend* (Saturday, 14 March, 1807), 'Breda, Dec. 25,' *The United States Gazette* (Tuesday, 24 March, 1807) and 'Breda, Dec. 25,' *Fredonian* (Saturday, 18 April, 1807): 'Articles of a treaty between Russia and the Porte, have been published in all the papers. But the reports are false, and no treaty has been concluded.— The evils which Russia has caused the Porte, rally all Musselmen in the common cause. Already Michelsen[110] and Dolgoronsky,[111] who command the Russian army, have demanded succors. We learn also that the Shah of Persia[112] is preparing to repulse the aggressions of Russia, and to enter Georgia.'[113]

9.40 'Further Translations from French papers received at Marblehead. Paris, January 15,' *The United States Gazette* (Tuesday, 24 March, 1807) and 'Jan. 15,' *Republican Spy* (Wednesday, 8 April, 1807): 'Persia and the Porte have declared war against Russia.[114]

---

[109] Fath 'Ali Shah.

[110] Johann von Michelsohnen (Ivan Ivanovich Mikhelson (1740–1807), Estonian nobleman and general in the Imperial Russian army. For the earlier part of his career see Schoell (1834: 238).

[111] Prince Peter Petrovich Dolgorukov (1777–1806) was with Michelsohnen in Moldavia. 'Les cosaques qui sont dans nos murs semblent être de toutes nouvelles recrues. Leur chef, le général Michelsen, est attendu et il passe pour un officier de mérite. L'avant-garde, forte de 1800 à 2000 hommes, est commandée par un prince Dolgorouki, que l'on dit jeune, beau, très aimé des femmes,' See Wimpffen (1900: 233 and n. 1), 'Le même qui, aide de camp du Tsar, avait été envoyé en parlementaire à Napoléon, avant la bataille d'Austerlitz, pour lui porter l'injonction de quitter l'Allemagne. La réponse qu'il avait reçue de l'Empereur avait excité son ressentiment contre la France. Il mourut à Pétersbourg, peu de temps après son retour des principautés danubiennes.' For Napoleon's caustic account of his encounter with the 28 year old Prince Dolgorukov see Michajlowitsch (1902: 19).

[112] Fath 'Ali Shah.

[113] The French Foreign Minister Talleyrand wrote to Sébastiani, French ambassador in Constantinople, on 20 January 1807, as follows: 'Il faut aussi remuer la Perse et diriger ses efforts vers la Géorgie. Obtenez de la Porte qu'elle donne au pacha d'Erzeroum l'ordre de marcher sur cette province avec toutes ses forces. Maintenez les bonnes dispositions du prince des Abazes, et excitez-le à prendre part à la grande diversion contre l'ennemi commun. Que ce prince, le pacha d'Erzeroum, les Persans et la Porte attaquent en même temps la Géorgie, la Crimée et la Bessarabie.' See Testa (1865: 290–291).

[114] This sentence makes it sound as if the declaration of war had been coordinated, which was certainly not the case. 'Le 30 décembre [1806], la Porte avait déclaré solennellement la guerre à la Russie.' See Testa (1865: 291). This was done in response to the Russian invasion of the Danubian

Michelson attacks the Porte.[115] These two great empires, neighbours of Russia, are tormented by the unsteady politicks of the cabinet of St. Petersburg, who has for 10 years behaved to them, as it has for 50 years acted towards Poland.'[116]

9.41 'Monday, March 30, 1807,' *Salem Register* (Monday, 30 March, 1807): 'The Persians have long been prepared for such favourable events as may assist them to free themselves from the continued encroachments of the Russians. For several years the Russians have been interrupted at Retsch[117] in Ghilan, where they had for some time free communication, in their trade upon the Caspian.—They were treated in the same manner at Asterabad, near which the Russians had been permitted to have fortifications. To maintain their claims on the southern parts of the Caspian must be of the highest consequence to the Persians... Many causes have concurred to give internal strength to Persia. Sir Wm. Jones informs us that Hussein,[118] who reigned at the opening of the last century, was a weak prince; that in his reign the Afgans from the mountains poured into Persia; that Mahmud the usurper reigned in Ispahan. Several provinces threw off their allegiance, and Persia was filled with desolation and rapine. The history of Nader Chah has been immortalised by the pen of Sir Wm. Jones.[119] This hero perished by conspirators in 1747. Ali and Ibrahim succeeded to his power, as did Chahrokh, who was succeeded by

---

Principalities (Wallachia and Moldavia) in October, 1806, which in turn was a response to Turkey's increasingly warm relationship with France following the battle of Austerlitz and its deposing of the Hospodars of Wallachia and Moldavia without consulting Russia as it should have according to its treaty relations with the latter power. See Holland (1877: 13–14). Selim III's actions in Wallachia and Moldavia were instigated by Napoleon's ambassador General Horace Sébastiani and, as Creasy (1856/2: 365) noted, 'Such a war was then most desirable for Napoleon's purposes, as it was calculated to make an important diversion of part of the Russian forces from the great scene of conflict in Prussian Poland, where the Czar Alexander was striving to support King Frederick William of Prussia against the armies of victorious France.' As von Bernhardi (1877: 231) noted, 'Die althergebrachte Feindschaft zwischen Türken und Persern gestattete ihnen nicht übereinstimmend, nach einem gemeinsamen Plan zu handeln, ja die Paschas verschiedener türkischer Provinzen in dem asiatischen Theile des Reichs standen einander nicht selten feindlich gegenüber—und die kriegerischen Stämme im Kaukasus vollends, hatten gar kein Verständniß für umfassendere politische Combinationen; sie waren unfähig darauf einzugeben.'

[115] In 1806 Michelsohnen was commanding the Russian army on the Danube. For his actions against the Ottoman forces in southeastern Europe (Serbia, Moldavia, Rumania), see Yakschitch (1907).

[116] This is clearly based on the 'Message de Napoléon Ier lu au sénat par l'archichanceller de l'empire le 17 février 1807,' in which we read, 'L'empereur de Perse, tourmenté dans l'intérieur de ses états, coimme le fut pendant soixante ans la Pologne, comme l'est depuis vingt ans la Turquie, par la politique du cabinet de Pétersbourg, est animé des mêmes sentiments que la Porte, a pris les mêmes résolutions, et marche en personne sur le Caucase pour défendre ses frontières.' See Testa (1865: 298). A later article (below) gives a more exact English rendering of Napoleon's words.

[117] Rasht.

[118] Shah Soltan Hoseyn.

[119] Jones (1770) = Jones (1799/5).

Mehomed Husn Khan, of whom the Persians said, May his banners be exalted above the stars, so long as the heavens endure. Aga Nubber Khaun,[120] Ambassador from his present Majesty the King of Persia,[121] was publicly received at Fort William, Calcutta, on the 28th April, 1806, in the most honourable manner.[122] He proceeded in the Governor's carriage, and was received with the highest honours. The letter from his Majesty the King of Persia was brought in by the son in law of the Ambassador on a silver tray, and by the Ambassador was

---

[120] Mohammad Nabi Khan. According to Morier (1812: 23, n. †), 'He was originally a *Moonshee*, who got his bread by transcribing books and writing letters for money. He taught Sir Harford Jones, when a young man at *Bussora*, to read and write Arabic and Persian. He afterwards became a merchant, selling small articles in the *Bazar* at *Bushire*, and being fortunate in his early trade, extended his speculations still more largely and successfully: till, when an embassy to *Calcutta* was projected by the King of Persia, he was enabled to appear (according to the report of his countrymen) as the highest bidder for the office, and was consequently invested with it. Having enriched himself enormously by his mission, he has yet never failed to complain before the King, of the evil stars which, by leading him to accept such a situation, had reduced him to beggary.' According to Brydges (1834/1: 36), he was the brother-in-law of the murdered Persian envoy Haji Khalil Ibrahim, guardian of the latter's son, i.e. his own nephew and, in short order, third husband of the deceased ambassador's wife and consequently inheritor and executor of his estate. Brydges (1834/1: 37–38) noted, 'Considering to what point the embassy of Hajee Kheleel had arrived, there might be good policy, or there might be a necessity, that it should be carried to its close by his executor. Be this, however, as it may, Mohammed Nebee proceeded to Tæheran, and received the title of Khan, and his credentials to India, on the same terms as his late brother-in-law had formerly received them. If I am asked how I know this, I reply because he told me so. If I am asked what these terms were, I answer from the same authority, that the king of Persia was to be at no further charges on account of this mission, than those which have been already enumerated. The expense of the mission, and the advantage the ambassador was to derive from it, were, the one to be paid, and the other to be made from the ambassador being allowed to import and export throughout the British territories in India large quantities of merchandize duty free, and from the splendid allowance the ambassador expected, and actually did draw, from our government.' As Ingram (1973: 520–521) noted, Fath 'Ali Shah hoped that Jaubert's visit would incite the English to offer him more support against Russia, 'Simultaneously, therefore, he made a final appeal to the British through his ambassador to India, Aga Nebee Khan … the Persians wanted the British to intervene permanently to guarantee their frontier, not temporarily to evict the French. At this time the British would not have intervened for either reason, but in the eyes of the Briutish his manoeuvres discredited the shah. What was a serious question for the Persians, the security of their frontier, became concealed behind a trivial one for the British, the security of India from a European invasion overland. The British Government did not believe that there was any danger of the French invading India overland. By his appeal through Aga Nebee Khan the Shah was calculating that the government of India might.' According to Sykes (1915: 399), 'profound indifference concerning Persia prevailed at Calcutta, more especially after the disastrous ending to the French campaigns in Syria and Egypt, and Aga Nabi Khan returned home in January 1807 a disappointed man.' For his mission in general see Shadman (1944: 29).

[121] Fath 'Ali Shah.

[122] According to Sandeman (1865: 19–21) this date is incorrect. The Persian ambassador, accompanied by Dr. Jukes and Lt.-Col. Wilson, arrived in convoy aboard the *Jahangeer* from Bombay on 29 March; he landed on 11 April and 'entered his state palanquin … through Fort William towards the house which had been prepared for his reception.'

delivered to the Governor General.[123] The Ambassador returned in the Governor's carriage and was saluted with military honours. The kingdom of Persia which, on the north, bounds on Tartary, Russia, the Caspian sea, and Bucharey, and on the east, upon Hindostan, and on the south upon the Indian sea and Persian Gulf, and on the west upon Georgia, Turkey and Arabia, is of great extent, and can command great resources. The disposition to reclaim all the antient advantages of its own commerce, and to direct the government of the different parts of the kingdom, indicates the return of activity, strength and firmness to Persia.'

9.42 'Untitled,' *Salem Register* (Monday, 13 April, 1807): 'The greatest activity was maintained by the French Emperor.[124] He had received a courier from Persia, since he has been in Poland,[125] and kept a constant correspondence with the court of Turkey.'[126]

9.43 'From the Atlantic World. No. II. Observations concerning the politics of Europe, and particularly as they are connected with the Emperor of France, by "Americus",' *Vermont Centinel* (Wednesday, 15 April, 1807): 'The same motives and policy which induced Russia to divide Poland, to wage war against the state of Persia, would also induce her to seize upon Turkey, Austria, or Prussia, if a favorable opportunity had occurred ... What madness could induce the cabinet of London to place confidence in the designs of a power, which, with an empire extending from Lapland to Kamchatca, embrasing [sic] more than half the globe, with an empire more than eight times as extensive as the rest of Europe and 40 times as large as France, is still unsatisfied, and seems willing to push her conquests and acquisitions into the most flourishing parts of Asia? Persia has been dismembered and even India & China, might next dread the approaches of insatiable and savage ambition.'

9.44 'From the Imperial Camp at Warsaw, January 29, 1806,' *Salem Register* (Thursday, 16 April, 1807), 'Russia, Turkey and France,' *New-England Palladium* (Tuesday, 21 April, 1807; with very slight differences) and 'From the Imperial Camp at Warsaw, January 29, 1807,' *National Intelligencer, and Washington Advertiser* (Wednesday, 29 April, 1807): 'The Senate were to meet on the 17th of February, and the following is the adddress of the Emperor:[127]—Senators ... The Emperor of Persia,[128] vexed in his dependant states,

---

[123] Sir George Barlow (1762–1847), acting Governor-General from 10 October 1805 to 31 July 1807.

[124] Napoleon.

[125] An ambassador, not merely a courier. Fath 'Ali Shah's ambassador Mirza Mohammad Reza Qazvini left Constantinople in December, 1806, together with the Ottoman ambassador Emin Vahid Efendi, bound for Poland. When Marshal Berthier mentioned his impending visit in a letter to General Marmont of 29 January 1807 he said, 'Un ambassadeur de Perse et un de Constantinople se rendent à Varsovie, et, quand vous recevrez cette lettre, ils seront déjà arrivés à Vienne.' See Testa (1865: 292). Mirza Mohammad Riza had an audience with Napoleon at Warsaw on 28 February 1807. See Dehérain (1930: 42).

[126] For letters exchanged between Napoleon and Selim III during 1806 and 1807 see Testa (1865).

[127] Napoleon.

[128] Fath 'Ali Shah.

as Poland was for 60 years, and as Turkey has been for 20 years, by the policy of the Cabinet of Petersburg, is animated by the same sentiments as the Porte, has taken the same resolutions, and is marching in person upon the Caucasus to defend his frontiers.'[129]

9.45 *Salem Register* (Thursday, 16 April, 1807): 'We learn from the Address of the French Emperor[130] to his Senate, that Persia is seriously engaged in hostilities against the Russians[131] and that this period may be favourable to the restoration of that power in Persia, which has distinguished this portion of the globe in antient as well as modern times. In the last Century the population of Persia and its dependances was reckoned at 40 millions,[132] with 500 cities, and as many 1000 villages. The encroachments of the Russians, particularly on the Caspian, have been well known, and some late attempts to check them have occasioned the late ruptures.'

9.46 'Extracts from the 45th and 47th Bulletins of the French Grand Army, dated 27th and 30th December,' *The Orleans Gazette and Commercial Advertiser* (Monday, 20 April, 1807): 'Turkey and Persia have declared war, (according to the bulletins) against Russia,

---

[129] Napoleon's letter 'Donné en notre camp impérial de Varsovie, le 29 Janvier [1807], contains the statement which reads, in the original French, 'L'Empereur de Perse, tourmenté dans l'intérieur de ses états, comme le fût pendant soixante ans la Pologne, comme l'est depuis vingt ans la Turquie, par la politique du cabinet de Petersbourg, est animé des-mêmes sentimens que la Porte, a pris les mêmes résolutions, et marche en personne sur le Caucase, pour défendre ses frontières.' See Fischer (1808: 307), Testa (1865: 297).

[130] Napoleon.

[131] This refers to Napoleon's message to the senate of 17 February 1807. See Testa (1865: 297). In fact, according to von Bernhardi (1877: 231), 'Während Gudowitsch sich—1807—zu einem Angriff auf das türkische Gebiet in Kleinasien rüstete, verbrachten die Perser die Zeit mit Unterhandlungen über einen Waffenstillstand, und die Waffen ruhten längere Zeit, auch ohne daß er geschlossen war. Vielleicht wollte Abbas-Mirza, entmuthigt durch so manche schmachvolle Niederlage, nicht eher neue Kämpfe wagen, als bis die Lehren der französischen Offiziere seinen Truppen zu einer Haltung verholfen hätten, die Besseres hoffen ließ.' Moreover, Napoleon clearly considered Persia of secondary importance compared with Turkey. As he wrote to the Foreign Ministry on 3 March 1807 regarding a proposed Franco-Persian treaty, 'Quel traité faire avec la Perse? Comment voulez-vous que je réponde à cette question quand voius ne m'avez pas encore fait remettre le mémoire de M. Jaubert, qui me fasse connaître ce que c'est que la Perse? Ce traité, d'ailleurs, peut se faire à Paris, c'est le moins pressant. Cela est différent pour la Porte, mais, tant que vous ne me ferez pas connaître ce qu'elle veut, quel est le but de la mission de son ambassadeur, je ne puis vous envoyer d'instruction.' See Testa (1865: 298–299).

[132] Cf. Anonymous (1891a: 66), where we read, 'We have no certain information regarding the population of Persia ... In the seventeenth century the French traveller, Chardin, thought 40 millions not too high a figure. Recent travellers, however, reduced these sums to numbers varying from 15 to 8 millions.'

and (according to other reports) the Russian general Michelson, had taken the strong Turkish fortresses Baden[133] and Chockzyen,[134] and was advancing victoriously.'[135]

9.47 'Untitled,' *Salem Register* (Monday, 20 April, 1807): 'While every person is reading with great solicitude the bulletins of the French army, it will not be expected that we should attempt an abstract of their contents ... The apprehensions from Turkey, which may be thrown into the arms of France, are just, and they are serious to all Europe. The concurrence of Persia, which waits only an opportunity to be avenged upon its northern enemy; and the advantages from the situation of Persia to open a sure communication between the East and the West, are not things of little moment ... Turkey in arms, and Persia on the march, are not inconsiderable events, and the past campaign will challenge comparison with any on the Globe.'

9.48 'Sixty-fourth Bulletin of the Grand Army. Osterode, 2d March, 1807,' *New-York Evening Post* (Thursday, 23 April, 1807), 'Sixty-fourth Bulletin of the Grand Army. Osterode, March 2, 1807,' *The People's Friend & Daily Advertiser* (Friday, 24 April, 1807), 'Sixty-fourth Bulletin of the Grand Army. Osterode, 2d March,' *The United States Gazette* (Saturday, 25 April, 1807), 'Sixty-fourth Bulletin of the Grand Army. Osterode, March 2, 1807,' *The Democratic Press* (Monday, 27 April, 1807), '64th Bulletin. Ostreode, March 2,' *Newburyport Herald* (Tuesday, 28 April, 1807), 'French Grand Army Bulletins. No. 64. March 2,' *Thomas's Massachusetts Spy, or Worcester Gazette* (Wednesday, 29 April, 1807) and 'Sixty-fourth Bulletin of the Grand Army. Osterode, 2d March, 1807,' *National Intelligencer and Washington Advertiser* (Wednesday, 29 April, 1807): 'The Ambassadors of Constantinople[136] and of Persia[137] have entered ['reached,' *Newburyport Herald, Thomas's Mass. Spy*] Poland, and approach Warsaw.'[138]

---

[133] Bender/y, in Bessarabia, located today in Moldova.

[134] Also Choczim, mod. Khotyn, Ukraine.

[135] As Dumas (1826: 97) wrote, 'la guerre éclatait entre la Russie et la Porte ottomane ... La déposition des hospodars de Moldavie et de Valachie, que le dernier traité mettait sous la protection de la Russie, servit de prétexte. La satisfaction offerte par le divan, qui rétablit les hospodars, ne changea rien à la résolution du cabinet de *Saint-Pétersbourg*, d'envahier ces deux provinces. Le général Michelson y entra avec une armée russe d'environ trente-six mille hommes, formée de quatre divisions, le 23 novembre 1806, et ouvrit la campagne par la prise de *Choczim, Bender* et *Jassy*.' Elsewhere Dumas (1826: 267) put the size of Michelsohnen's forces at 40–50,000 and used the variant spelling *Choizim*. In a letter from Napoleon to Selim III of 1 December 1806 Napoleon had written, 'Fais marcher les troupes sur Choczim: tu n'as pas rien à craindre de la Russie.' See Testa (1865: 284).

[136] Emin Vahid Efendi.

[137] Mirza Mohammad Reza Qazvini. Cf. 9.37.

[138] Napoleon wrote to Selim III from Warsaw on 1 January 1807 as follows: 'J'attends votre plénipotentiaire: il me dira ce que vous avez fait, vos projets, vos ressources, et nous concerterons ensemble les opérations de la guerre.' See Testa (1865: 289). On 29 January 1807 Marshal Berthier

9.49 'Russia and Turkey,' *Newburyport Gazette* (Monday, 4 May, 1807) and 'Russia and Turkey,' *The Green Mountain Patriot* (Tuesday, 26 May, 1807): 'Russia, while contending against the French armies, is also at war with Persia and the Ottoman Empire. Of the course of events between her troops and the Persians we have no recent accounts.'

9.50 'From the Salem Register,' *Virginia Argus* (Saturday, 16 May, 1807): 'The Russians find the war opening with the Turks and Persians, and have provided to meet their southern enemies … Against the Persians, the Russians are collecting troops in their southern territories. The Persians have discovered a disposition to acquiesce in the plans proposed by the French, and it is expected will have assistance from the ambitious French officers which will engage in the Persian service.'

9.51 'Foreign Intelligence,' *The Expositor* (Wednesday, 3 June, 1807): 'We add another from Frankfort March 15. "For some days past there has been a report of a three-fold alliance between France, Persia and the Porte. Some say it is already signed by the two latter Powers, and that France will accede to it."'[139]

9.52 'Aleppo, Jan. 1,' *New-England Palladium* (Friday, 12 June, 1807), 'Aleppo, Jan. 1,' *The United States Gazette* (Tuesday, 16 June, 1807), 'Aleppo, Jan. 1,' *American Mercury*

---

wrote to General Marmont from Warsaw, 'Un courrier parti de Constantinople le 2 janvier arrive à Varsovie.' See Testa (1865: 291). In a letter of 6 March 1807 to his Foreign Minister Talleyrand, Napoleon wrote, 'Je vous répète, laissez l'ambassadeur ottoman à Varsovie encore quelque temps. Notifiez-lui, au reçu de cette lettre, qu'il m'attende à Varsovie. Vous ne me dites pas quels sont ses pouvoirs. Sa cour désire-t-elle que j'envoie 20,000 hommes pour couvrir Constantinople? S'il dit non, veut-elle que je les envoie pour balayer le Danube? Comment les traiterait-on? Qui en aurait le commandement? Enfin voyez s'ils ont songé à quelque chose et s'ils désirent quelque chose. S'il y avait un congrès, l'ambassadeur a-t-il des pouvoirs pour ce congrès? Que veut la Porte à la paix générale? Voilà des choses sur lesquelles il faut que vous m'éclairiez.' See Anonymous (1863: 383). As Driault (1904: 167–168) noted, 'Emin Vahid-Effendi, arrivé le 2 mars à Varsovie … voyagea presque en compagnie de l'ambassadeur persan, Mirza-Riza-Khan, et ne s'en montra point satisfait; car Turcs et Persans ne s'aiment point, coimme Talleyrand l'écrivait à l'Empereur; il y avait de continuelles querelles sur leurs frontières, et les Persans ne cachaient pas leur ambition de reprendre l'Irak-Arabi ou Mésopotamie. L'ambassadeur ottoman ne manquait pas de faire remarquer d'autre part que si les Persans ne sont pas les sujets de la Porte, ils sont au moins ses vassaux, et que l'empereur Napoléon accordait vraiment "trop d'importance à ces gens-là."' According to Gourgaud Mirza Mohammad Reza Qazvini arrived at Finkenstein on 25 April 1807. 'Le duc de Bassano fut chargé de négocier avec lui les conditions d'une alliance offensive et défensive entre la France et la Perse; et au bout de quelques jours, la négociation parvint à un heureux résultat.' See Ségur and Gourgaud (1825: 23). The Persian ambassador departed on 7 May and the Ottoman ambassador arrived three weeks later, on 27 May. See Ségur and Gourgaud (1825: 23).

[139] Napoleon's instructions to General Gardane clearly stipulated, 'Le général Gardane ne doit pas perdre de vue que notre objet important est d'établir une triple alliance entre la France, la Porte et la Perse, de nous frayer un chemin aux Indes et de nous procurer des auxiliaires contre la Russie.' See Dehérain (1930: 46).

(Thursday, 18 June, 1807), 'Aleppo, Jan. 1,' *National Intelligencer and Washington Advertiser* (Monday, 22 June, 1807), 'Continuation of Late Foreign News. Aleppo, January 1,' *Charleston Courier* (Friday, 26 June, 1807), 'Aleppo, January 1,' *The Republican; and Savannah Evening Ledger* (Thursday, 2 July, 1807), 'Aleppo, January 1,' *Miller's Weekly Messenger* (Tuesday, 16 July, 1807) and 'Alepo [sic], January 1,' *The Mirror* [Russellville KY] (Thursday, 18 July, 1807): 'The Persians make a common cause with the Turks, and attack, at once the Russians and the English. All the English factories have been seized,[140] and the correspondence from England with the East Indies by the way of Persia,[141] must at this moment be stopped.'

9.53 'Aleppo, January 1,' *New-York Evening Post* (Monday, 15 June 1807), 'Aleppo, January 1,' *New-York Herald* (Wednesday, 17 June, 1807), 'Aleppo, January 1,' *The United States Gazette* (Thursday, 18 June, 1807), 'Aleppo, January 1,' *Connecticut Herald* (Tuesday, 23 June, 1807), 'Aleppo, Jan. 1,' *The Courier* (Wednesday, 24 June, 1807) and 'Aleppo, January 1,' *Suffolk Gazette* (Monday, 29 June, 1807): 'The news from Persia is very satisfactory. The Persians make a common cause with the Turks, and attack in concert the Russians and English.[142]

The Prince Feth Aly Schah is a very active man, who comprehends perfectly the situation of Affairs. He has been often deceived by the intrigues of England, who never fails to sacrifice its friends to its interest. All the English decks have been seized,[143] and all the correspondence that they had established with the Indies through Persia is intercepted.

9.54 'Constantinople, March 7,' *The People's Friend & Daily Advertiser* (Wednesday, 17 June, 1807), 'Constantinople, March 7,' *New-York Herald* (Wednesday, 17 June, 1807), 'Constantinople, March 7,' *The Pittsfield Sun; or, Republican Monitor* (Saturday, 20 June, 1807; with minor variations), 'Constantinople, March 7,' *Connecticut Herald* (Tuesday, 23 June, 1807) and 'Constantinople, March 7,' *The Courier* (Wednesday, 24 June, 1807): 'We receive agreeable news from Persia.—The Russians have been forced by Prince Abbas Merza to evacuate a considerable extent of territory. They have experienced checks in many rencounters ['engagements' in *The Pittsfield Sun*]. The commanders, weakened by the detachments sent to the army of Poland, press for succours, to be able to withstand the Persians.'

---

[140] This is completely false.

[141] Communication between England and India did not proceed via Iran.

[142] As Napoleon's correspondence makes clear, the French solicited the involvement of both Turkey and Persia, but the two did not act in concert.

[143] This statement may relate to the successful Ottoman attack on the English fleet commanded by Admiral Sir John Duckworth (1748–1817) that had previously penetrated the Dardanelles on 19 February 1807 and destroyed a Turkish naval squadron using artillery refurbished and newly erected by French engineers, led by Colonel Antoine Juchereau de Saint-Denys, and deployed by Sébastiani. See Juchereau de Saint-Denys (1819), Creasy (1856/2: 367–368).

9.55 'Munich, April 17,' *The People's Friend & Daily Advertiser* (Tuesday, 16 June, 1807), 'Munich, April 17,' *The Public Advertiser* (Tuesday, 16 June, 1807), 'Munich, April 17,' *American and Commercial Daily Advertiser* (Friday, 19 June, 1807), 'Munich, April 17,' *Republican Watch-Tower* (Friday, 19 June, 1807), 'Munich, April 17,' *Farmers' Register* (Tuesday, 23 June, 1807), 'Munich, April 17,' *Connecticut Gazette* (Wednesday, 24 June, 1807), 'Munich, April 17,' *Hampshire Federalist* (Thursday, 25 June, 1807) and 'Munich, April 17, *City Gazette and Daily Advertiser* (Thursday, 2 July, 1807): 'Considerable advantages are reported to have been obtained by the Turks and Persians over the Russians....the Turks have entered the Crimea, and the Persians are seizing the most important passages of the Caucasus.'[144]

9.56 'Foreign Intelligence,' *The Expositor* (Wednesday, 17 June, 1807): 'Hamburgh, 13th March. The Persian embassy now on its way to the emperor Napoleon, may produce consequences most fatal to the British power.[145] It is through Persia alone, that England can conveniently carry on its communications by land with India, of which the king of Persia is the most powerful neighbor. Hyder Ally[146] had already endeavored to form an alliance with the Persians in order to destroy the dominion of the English in India, and Tippoo Saib[147] employed all his means to obtain from them auxiliary troops; but the civil wars which then rent that beautiful kingdom prevented the execution of his projects. Every thing

---

[144] This was, of course, wishful thinking.

[145] Cf. Popper von Podhrágy (1884: 30), 'Eine Expedition in Asien im grössten Massstab zur Erschütterung der Herrschaft der Engländer erschien bei der damaligen politische Sachlage, dem innigen Verhältnisse Frankreichs zu den Islamitischen Grossmächten, Persien und Türkei, im Lichte der Möglichkeit.'

[146] As Francklin (1788: 125) noted, 'Ambassadors from the famous Hyder Ali came to the court of Kerim Khan with rich presents, and expressed a desire of an amicable alliance.' As Milburn (1813: liv) observed, Hyder 'Ali 'usurped the government of the kingdom of Mysore in 1763, and in a short time extended his dominions so as to become formidable to his neighbours,' extending his conquests from 1767 to 1769 when he advanced on Madras before negotiating peace with the Madras Presidency (East India Company). Cf. M.M.D.L.T. (1848), Yazdani (2014).

[147] Tipu Sultan of Mysore, son of Hyder 'Ali. According to Conder (1827: 236, n. †), 'The attention of our Indian Government was first drawn to Persia by events occurring within its own sphere. When it was discovered that Tippoo Sultaun had sent an embassy to the Shah, it was deemed expedient to despatch a mission to counteract it; and Mehdee Ali Khan, a Hindoo gentleman of Persian extraction, was sent out in 1798, by Mr. Duncan, governor of Bombay. Neither party drew any result from these negotiations.' Cf. Watson (1866: 123), 'Shortly after the return of Fetteh Ali Shah from Meshed, he was informed of the coming of an envoy who had already opened diplomatic communication between the British authorities in India, and the court of Persia. This envoy was named Mehdi Ali Khan, and he had been deputed to Tehran by the Governor of Bombay. The object of his mission was to endeavour to persuade the Shah to attack Affghanistan, and thereby relieve, for the time being, the minds of the European rulers of India from the apprehension under which they laboured lest India should be invaded by Zeman Shah.'

has now changed, and since Fatali-Schah, after overpowering his rivals[148], has seated himself on the Persian throne; and an alliance between Turkey, France and Persia has given a new impulsion and another direction to the forces of that empire, the English may well have reason to dread for the future: the spirit too which animates the petty Indian princes, is well known; it is a fire which is constantly hid under the ashes, and which a neighbor such as the king of Persia, would have no great difficulty to rekindle.'

9.57 'Extract of a letter from M. Meriage, Adjutant Commandant to the Minister for Foreign Affairs,' *The National Aegis* (Wednesday, 17 June, 1807), 'Extract of a letter from M. Meriage, Adjutant Commandant to the Minister for Foreign Affairs,' *National Intelligencer and Washington Advertiser* (Monday, 22 June, 1807) and 'Extract of a letter from M. Meriage, Adjutant Commandant to the Minister for Foreign Affairs,' *The Sentinel of Freedom* (Tuesday, 23 June, 1807): 'The Turks here[149] assure me,[150] that a considerable army, commanded by Jussuf Pacha,[151] has entered the Crimea, seconded by a division of Persians in Georgia.'

9.58 'Turkish Affairs. London, May 5,' *Newburyport Herald* (Friday, 19 June, 1807), 'Affairs of Turkey,' *Portsmouth Oracle* (Saturday, 20 June, 1807), 'Affairs of Turkey,' *The Connecticut Courant* (Wednesday, 24 June, 1807) and 'London, May 6,' *Hampshire Federalist* (Thursday, 25 June, 1807; 'London'; minus the last sentence): 'The progress of the Russians against the Turks, is stated to have been arrested; and the Court of Vienna, according to a letter from Constantinople, has not only declared, that it will not be an idle spectator of the spoliation of Turkey by any power whatever, but permitted a French army to pass through her territory on its way to protect the Turkish dominions against the invasion of the Russians. The united Turks and Persians are reported to have obtained some signal advantages over the Russian army. But we do not credit the rumor.'

9.59 'Russia and Turkey,' *The Repertory* (Friday, 19 June, 1807): 'Of the progress of the war between the Russians and Turks, we have no satisfactory accounts. They vary,

---

[148] It was rather Agha Mohammad Shah who overcame his rivals, and whose efforts secured the Persian throne for his nephew Fath 'Ali Shah.

[149] As the citation in the next footnote makes clear Mériage was writing from Vidin, Bulgaria.

[150] Louis-Auguste-François Mériage (1767–1827). As Driault (1904: 164–165) noted, 'L'adjudant-commandant Mériage, envoyé par Napoléon en observation à Widdin et arrivé dans cette place le 20 février [1807], rend compte, dans ses rapports très détaillés, de cette situation.' Cf. Boppe (1886).

[151] Yusuf Pasha. He had previously intervened to release Jaubert from his captivity. Cf. 9.20, 9.28. According to Puryear (1951: 208), 'Before the news of Tilsit, Ottoman military officers had begun to take the Franco-Turkish alliance for granted, together with its implied joint effort with Persia against Russia. There is Yousef Pasha, generalissimo of the army of Asia, who wrote the French ambassador at Constantinople as late as September 2—apparently not yet crediting a Russo-Turkish armistice. He promised to concert with the Persians in a big offensive against Russia.'

according to the channel, through which they are received. The Porte has solicited aid of Bonaparte and has obtained the promise of an army and marine force.[152] Germany, it is said engages to be neutral, but she has consented to suffer a French army to pass through her dominions, to the aid of Turkey. The Russians have called their forces from the Crimea, to join General Michelson's army, which French accounts say has been driven, with loss, from Wallachia. The same accounts say the Turks have entered the Crimea, and the Persians have seized the most important passages of the Caucasus.'

9.60 'The Latest News from the Continent of Europe, Received by the John & Joseph Manning, 39 days from Antwerp,' *American and Comercial Daily Advertiser* (Saturday, 20 June, 1807), 'The Latest News from the Continent of Europe, Received by the John & Joseph Manning, 39 days from Antwerp,' *Alexandria Daily Advertiser* (Monday, 22 June, 1807), 'Latest from the Continent of Europe,' *New-York Commercial Advertiser* (Monday, 22 June, 1807), 'The Latest News from the Continent of Europe, Received by the John & Joseph Manning, 39 days from Antwerp,' *The Public Advertiser* (Monday, 22 June, 1807), 'Latest Foreign Intelligence. Baltimore, June 20,' *Poulson's American Daily Advertiser* (Tuesday, 23 June, 1807), 'From the Baltimore American of Saturday,' *Republican Crisis* (Tuesday, 30 June, 1807), 'From the Baltimore American of Saturday,' *The Balance, and Columbian Repository* (Tuesday, 30 June, 1807), 'From the Baltimore American,' *The Phenix* (Saturday, 4 July, 1807) and 'Latest from the Continent of Europe,' *New Hampshire Sentinel* (Saturday, 11 July, 1807): 'By a gentleman at present in this city [Baltimore], we were yesterday put in possession of the "*Journal du Commerce*" to the 9th of May inclusive, containing Paris dates to the 8th of that month ... Jussuf-Pacha, governor of Erzerom, who has been invested with all the powers of a Grand Vizier in Armenia and Colchis,[153] was advancing towards the Crimea for the purpose of attacking the Russians, in which the Persians were to join.'[154]

---

[152] As Driault (1904: 168–169) noted, to the Ottoman ambassador, 'Napoléon ... se dit le meilleur ami des Turcs; il leur garantit une indépendance absolue et durable: il les arrachera au sort de la Pologne; il déchiera les articles onéreux que leur ont imposés les Russes au traité d'Yassy; il leur rendra la Crimée, il leur rendra la Géorgie: la mer Noire redeviendra "la fille des sultans". Mais il faut qu'ils travaillent eux-mêmes à ce relèvement prochain, qu'ils le méritent, qu'ils opèrent de concert avec les Perses et les peuples du Caucase, que le pacha d'Erzeroum fasse sa jonction avec Abbas-Mirza, le fils du schah, que la flotte turque, au lieu de s'immobiliser à l'entrée des Dardanelles...que le grand-vizir francisse enfin le Danube, et se hâte en Valachie, en Moldavie, vers le Dniestr, où les Français lui donnent rendez-vous vers Kaminiec. Les circonstances sont critiques: que la Turquie se réveille enfin, et elle retrouvera son ancienne splendeur; sinon, elle sera livrée aux destinées impitoyables.'

[153] Classical name for the eastern end of the Black Sea in modern Georgia. Famously it was the object of Jason and the Argonauts' quest for the golden fleece. For refs. see Forbiger (1844/2: 439–445).

[154] According to the early Qajar history published by Brydges (1833: 298–302), 'Abbas Mirza, received an envoy (Mohammad Faiz Allah Efendi) from Yusuf Pasha at his camp and discussed a Persian-Ottoman entente. Later, after discovering that the Russian army was being resupplied from

9.61 'Latest from the Continent of Europe,' *New-York Commercial Advertiser* (Monday, 22 June, 1807; only source with the first paragraph), 'Warsaw, March 16,' *New-England Palladium* (Friday, 26 June, 1807), 'Warsaw, March 16,' *The Balance, and Columbian Repository* (Tuesday, 30 June, 1807) and 'Foreign Intelligence. Warsaw, March 16,' *The Maryland Herald, and Hager's-town Weekly Advertiser* (Friday, 3 July, 1807): 'The following article was presented to us in manuscript. It represents the Persians as carrying all before them:—

Warsaw, March 16

'The ambassador[155] of his majesty the emperor of Persia,[156] to his majesty the emperor of the French and king of Italy,[157] has received from Theran, the account of a brilliant success obtained by the arms of his sovereign.

The Prince, Abbas-Mirza, son of the emperor, and renowned in the East for his bravery, announced to him, under date of the 26th of December last, that prince Mehemed-Veli-Mirza, one of his brothers,[158] who commands in the Khorassan, has carried his victorious

---

Bayzaid and Van, areas within Yusuf Pasha's jurisdiction, he wrote to him as follows: "'If you pretend to sincere friendship with Iran, it is necessary to give up all such transactions with the Russians in the above districts: it is incumbent on you to be, to your friends, genial as the April showers are to the rose-garden, and blasting to your malignant foes as the lightning is to the harvest." After this, Yusuf Pasha despatched positive orders to the frontier-Pashas dependent on his authority, to abandon all intercourse with the Russians.' Brydges (1833: 317). In a footnote, however, Brydges (1833: 323, n. ‡) noted, 'Truth will out;—and it is, that Yusuf Pasha, tired of and seeing no end to the delays and excuses of the Persian Government, resolved to attack the Russians, without their assistance. It neither meets my conception nor belief, that a Turkish and Persian army can ever act cordially together. The very act of prayer in such a camp would put the soldiers together by the ears.' According to Brosset (1857: 289), in June 1807, Gudovich 'reçut de Qars la nouvelle que le général Névétaïef, envoyé par lui contre cette place, avec 4000 hommes, avait été vaincu par Ousouph-Pacha, et s'était retiré avec les débris de son monde dans la citadelle de Goumri, d'où il demandait du secours.' As he noted, 'le général ici nommé commandait un petit corps d'observation, posté près de la frontière et souvent exposé aux attaques des Turks. Notamment au commencement de juin 1807, Iousouph, séraskier d'Erzroum, avait fait une forte démonstration contre ce corps, trop faible pour tenir tête à une armée considérable.' See Brosset (1857: 289), n. 1. According to Monteith (1856: 52–53), 'In June 1807 the Seraskier Hadji Yusuf Pasha advanced from Kars towards Gumri, and the Persian army under Abbas Mirza marched to join him; but the hatred entertained for each other by these hitherto hostile nations rendered any cordial co-operation impossible; and the Seraskier, who would neither await the arrival of the Prince Royal nor listen to his advice, was totally defeated by General Goudowitch at the village of Tickniss.' Gudovich's victory followed the initial defeat of the Russians and for this he was made Field Marshal by Czar Alexander.

[155] Mirza Mohammad Reza Qazvini.

[156] Fath 'Ali Shah.

[157] Napoleon.

[158] Mohammad Vali Mirza, governor of Khorasan, was Fath 'Ali Shah's fourth son according to Anonymous (1873a: 715) or his third son according to von Hammer (1819: 281) and Hasan-e Fasa'i. See Busse (1972: 35).

arms even to Oxus, and that he had taken the city of Merve, belonging to the Tartars-Usbecks, situated about 5 days journey from Boukara. The governor of this country has sworn obedience to the emperor of Persia.[159]

Kaboul and Candahar are entirely subject to Feth-Ali-Shak. They make this day a part of the Persian empire, and many solemn embassies have been sent to the emperor, to assure him of the fidelity of the inhabitants of this country, even to the frontiers of India.

The prince Abbas-Mirza is in the Moghan and Carabagh, at the head of a formidable army, four day's journey from Tifflis. He has taken from his army forty thousand men, to march to Georgia. Ahmed-Ahan,[160] who commanded them, has already taken Churegel[161] and Penbeh,[162] where he found many pieces of artillery. All the Russians who defended those places have been killed or brought prisoners to prince Abbas-Mirza.[163] A great number of Russian deserters arrive every day at the Persian camp.[164] The Emperor

---

[159] The early Qajar chronicle considered 'one of the most distinguished victories gained during this period was that of Prince Muhammed Waly Mirza, Governor of Khorasan. In the beginning of Rabi-ul-akhir, pursuant to the royal command ... this prince turned his energies to the reduction of Herat, and the extermination of the Afghans of that region.' See Brydges (1833: 325–326).

[160] Ahmed Khan. Kinneir (1813: 156) noted that 'Ahmed Khan, a nobleman of the first rank, and for many years *Beglerbeg of Azerbijan*,' was chief of the 'Mukudum' (Moghaddam) tribe. According to Tancoigne (1820: 77–78), 'Ahmed Khan is an old man of seventy, who has preserved all the gaiety and animation of early youth: he is very partial to the French, and is said to be the first who gave the King of Persia the idea of entering into a correspondence with our court. By a peculiar privilege, and contrary to the ordinary custom of the Persians in advanced years, who dye their beards in order to spare a young prince the necessity of rising to receive an old man, this Beylerbey has preserved his, blanched as it is by age, in its natural colour. We found Ahmed possessed of more information than the rest of his countrymen; he is, however, accused of a fault, which has a deadly influence on his memory and mental faculties. He is one of those whom the orientals term, theriaki, or eaters of opium, and the abuse he makes of this dangerous drug, throws him into a kind of delirium which lasts for whole days. This pernicious habit has already caused his disgrace with the Chah Zade ['Abbas Mirza], who dismissed him from his employment some months ago; the grand vizir assured us that he had been reinstated in it a few days previous to our arrival, merely on account of his attachment to France.'

[161] Shoregel/Shuragel. Cf. 9.5.

[162] Persian *punbah/pembeh*, 'cotton.' See West (1880: 223), Jardin (1881: 28).

[163] This hyperbolic account is roundly contradicted by Monteith who witnessed some of the action in this campaign from the Persian side, for he had been seconded as 'second lieutenant of engineers,' and was at Tabriz before being deployed to Qarabagh. See Monteith (1856: 62). The defeat suffered by the Russians in trying again to take Erivan is described by Monteith (1856: 56).

[164] For Russian deserters around this time see Atkin (1980: 106) who noted, 'Desertion was a serious problem in the Russian army as a whole and especially in the Caucasus. This is not surprising considering that the rank and file was composed of peasant draftees forced to serve for a 25-year term and that morale in the Caucasus was particularly low ... There were a few officers among the deserters, including a lieutenant who was with Kariagin when Kariagin was nearly defeated by the Iranians in 1805 and a lieutenant-colonel who had been commandant at Elizavetpol' (Ganjeh) for several years before his defection in 1808.' During the First Russo-Persian War, a regiment of

of Persia, to recompence the brave Ahmed-Khan, has joined to his government that of Erwan. This train of success, obtained at every point of the empire, gives to Persia a new degree of splendor and of power. The Khorassan is no longer exposed to the incursions of the Tartars—the authority of Persia arrives even to the frontiers of the English possessions in India. The Russians are badly established in Georgia, and are attacked on all sides. The most perfect union exists in all the provinces of the empire, and Persia can bring new forces against her enemies.

The Russians have made propositions of accomodation. Feth-Ali-Schah has refused them.[165] He has stopped all kinds of commercial relations, and all communication with Russia; and has answered, that as long as the grand emperor [Napoleon], his friend and ally, shall carry on war against the Russians, they ought not to hope for peace, nor a cessation of arms from Persia.'

9.62 'From the Aurora,' *Republican Star or Eastern Shore General Advertiser* (Tuesday, 23 June, 1807): 'The war against the Russians and English is carried on with the utmost vigor by the Turks and Persians. Every sort of English property has been confiscated in the dominions of these powers, and all the English factories shut up.'[166]

Russians formed part of the guard of 'Abbas Mirza. According to Drouville (1819/2: 124), describing the situation in 1812–1813, 'Le régiment russe d'un bataillon était en entier composé de déserteurs de cette nation, et commandé par des officiers également russes; nommés par le Prince-Royal ['Abbas Mirza]. Il n'existe plus aujourd'hui: cerné par le corps du général Kotlérowski, il fut écharpé en partie, le reste fut rendu à la paix de 1813.' A decade later, in 1817, Johnson (1818: 213) estimated that there were 'nearly 1000 privates of the Russians and Georgians' in 'Abbas Mirza's service, 'who have from time to time deserted from their own, and have been received by him.' Russian deserters came to play an even more important role in the Second Russo-Persian War, see below.

[165] As Monteith (1856: 53) noted, 'General Goudowitch attempted to enter into negotiations with Persia, both directly, and indirectly through the agency of the French ambassador; but it was evident from the tone adopted by both parties that peace was impossible, and that the attempt had only been made on the part of Russia for the purpose of gaining time.'

[166] This was premature but anticipated French intentions. According to instructions received by Gardane in a letter of 26 August 1807 from the French Foreign Minister Champagny, 'L'objet auquel vous devez vous attacher avant tout, est de faire cesser tout commerce entre la Perse et l'Angleterre, de faire éloigner des ports de l'Empire tous les agents, tous les facteurs anglais, d'empêcher toute communication par votre résidence entre l'Angleterre et l'Inde; enfin de maintenir la Perse dans les dispositions qu'elle a déjà exprimées contre cette puissance, et de suivre à cet égard tout ce qui vous a été indiqué dans vos instructions.' See Gardane (1865: 319–320). Consequently, in a letter to Fath 'Ali Shah dated 11 February 1808, Gardane wrote, 'S.M. [Sa Majesté] l'Empereur demande que tout commerce cesse entre la Perse et l'Angleterre, que tous les agents, tous les facteurs de cette nation soient exclus des villes et ports de l'Empire, que toute la correspondance entre l'Angleterre et les Indes, par le territoire persan, soit interceptée.' See Gardane (1865: 147–148). Gardane (1809a: 21–22) encountered him at Erzurum and noted, 'Isouf-Pacha passe 65 ans: il a été Grand-Visir, a commandé l'Armée contre le Général Kléber, et n'est de retour de l'armée contre les russes que depuis quelques jours.' As Puryear (1951: 248) noted, 'Minister Gardane scored an initial success, and the shah broke relations with the English East India Company soon after his coming. On

9.63 'Foreign Intelligence,' *Portland Gazette and Maine Advertiser* (Monday, 29 June, 1807): 'French papers state the Persians have obtained some advantages over the Russians in Khorasen,[167] and the English papers inform, that the Turks are defeated in every encounter in the interior with the Russians.'

9.64 'Untitled,' *Farmers' Register* (Tuesday, 30 June, 1807): 'Accounts have been received of many brilliant victories obtained by the Persians over the Russians.'

9.65 'Untitled,' *New Hampshire Sentinel* (Saturday, 4 July, 1807): 'Napoleon has completely succeeded in preventing any accomodation between the Turks and Russians, and has instigated the Persians to commence hostilities against Russia.'

9.66 'French Grand Army. Seventy-third Bulletin,' *New-York Herald* (Tuesday, 16 July, 1807), 'French Grand Army. Seventy-third Bulletin,' *The Democratic Press* (Wednesday, 17 July, 1807), 'Latest Foreign Intelligence. LXXIIId Grand Army Bulletin,' *Newburyport Herald* (Wednesday, 17 July, 1807), 'French Grand Army. Seventy-third Bulletin,' *The People's Friend & Daily Advertiser* (Wednesday, 17 July, 1807), 'Foreign News. Seventy-third Bulletin of the French Grand Army,' *The Repertory* (Wednesday, 17 July, 1807), 'French Grand Army. Seventy-third Bulletin,' *The United States Gazette* (Wednesday, 17 July, 1807), 'French Grand Army. Seventy-third Bulletin,' *New-York Herald* (Thursday, 18 July, 1807), 'French Grand Army. Seventy-third Bulletin,' *Poulson's American Daily Advertiser* (Thursday, 18 July, 1807), 'French Grand Army. Seventy-third Bulletin,' *Alexandria Daily Advertiser* (Saturday, 20 July, 1807), 'Seventy-third Bulletin of the Grand Army,' *City Gazette and Daily Advertiser* (Saturday, 20 July, 1807), 'French Grand Army. Seventy-third Bulletin,' *Trenton Federalist* (Saturday, 20 July, 1807), 'French Grand Army. Seventy-third Bulletin,' *Connecticut Herald* (Sunday, 21 July, 1807), 'French Grand Army Bulletins,' *The Farmers' Cabinet* (Sunday, 21 July, 1807), 'French Grand Army. 73 Bulletin,' *American Mercury* (Tuesday, 23 July, 1807), 'The Latest Mails. Foreign. Seventy-third Bulletin of the French Grand Army,' *Hampshire Federalist* (Tuesday, 23 July, 1807), 'Foreign Department. Seventy-third Bulletin,' *Western Budget* (Thursday, 25 July, 1807), 'Foreign Intelligence. France. Paris, May 18, 1807. French Grand Army Bulletins,' *Political Observatory* (Saturday, 27 July, 1807), 'Foreign Intelligence. French Grand Army. Seventy-third Bulletin,' *The Albany Register* (Sunday, 28 July, 1807), 'Foreign Intelligence. French Grand Army Bulletin. No. 73,' *Concord Gazette* (Sunday, 28 July, 1807), 'Foreign Intelligence. French Grand Army. Seventy-third Bulletin,' *North Star* (Sunday, 28 July, 1807), 'Foreign Intelligence. French Grand Army.—73 Bulletin,' *The National Aegis* (Monday, 29 July,

---

December 24 the shah ordered all the English expelled from Persia, and he withdrew his envoy from Bombay.'

[167] Needless to say, the Russians were not present in Khorasan.

1807), 'Seventy-third Bulletin from the French Grand Army,' *Otsego Herald* (Tuesday, 30 July, 1807), 'Foreign Intelligence. Seventy-third Bulletin of the French Grand Army,' *Weekly Wanderer* (Monday, 3 August, 1807) and Foreign Intelligence. 73d Bulletin of the French Grand Army,' *The Expositor* (Wednesday, 5 August, 1807): 'Elbing,[168] May 8, 1807.

The Persian Ambassador has had his audience of leave.[169] He had been the bearer of very handsome presents to the Emperor[170] on the part of his master,[171] and has received in return the portrait of the Emperor enriched with diamonds. He proceeds for Persia direct. He is a very considerable personage in his own country, and is a man of spirit and sagacity.[172] It has been settled, that there shall be henceforward a numerous legation of Persians at Paris, and of Frenchmen at Terheran.'

---

[168] Elbing in former German Ost-Preußen is now Elbląg in northern Poland.

[169] Mirza Mohammad Reza Qazvini left Poland to return to Persia on 7 May 1807. See Ségur and Gourgaud (1825: 23). He had accompanied Napoleon to Tilsit and concluded a treaty, which was ratified by Napoleon three days before Mirza Mohammad's departure, on 4 May 1807. For the full text see Hurewitz (1956: 77–78). Prior to this time Napoleon had already signed the directive for the Gardane mission to Tehran on 12 April, although this was kept 'dans le carton des affaires secrètes juqu'au 1er juin.' See Gardane (1865: 25). James Justinian Morier saw and made a copy of the treaty in Teheran. He noted, 'In the evening, we went to the prime minister's, and were shewn the treaty with France, signed and ratified at Finkenstein by Buonaparte, in May, 1807. In [sic] was written on vellum, in a beautiful French hand, and inserted in a cover of black velvet, curiously and elegantly wrought with a spread eagle at each corner, and the initial N in the centre, in a wreath of gold embroidery. The great seal was pendant from it, inserted in a plain gold box. The treaty was countersigned by Talleyrand; and by Maret, the plenipotentiary appointed to treat with Mirza Reza, the Persian plenipotentiary. I copied this document (consisting of 14 articles) in the room, and as we went away, the minister sent the envoy the commercial treaty, which contained 28 articles.' See Morier (1812: 216–217). The First Russo-Persian War began in 1804 and the loss of Ganja, Qarabagh, Sheki and Shirvan in 1805 brought Russian forces to the Aras. After Baku and Darband were taken by Bulgakov and Glasenapp in 1806, Fath 'Ali Shah sent his ambassador to Napoleon with all haste. See Krahmer (1903: 19). As Demorgny (1916: 209) noted, however, 'L'empereur pensait plutôt à menacer les Anglais dans les Indes qu'à arrêter les progrès des Russes au Caucase.'

[170] Napoleon.

[171] Fath 'Ali Shah.

[172] He had formerly been the vizier of Mohammad 'Ali Mirza, governor of Fars and later Kermanshah, and son of Fath 'Ali Shah. See Busse (1972: 119); Ekbal (1982a: 42, n. 23). As Savary (1828: 49) noted, 'The Shah of Persia had sent an ambassador to the Emperor. He came from Constantinople to join our headquarters at Finkenstein. The Emperor took him to Dantzic to show him a European army; and the grave Persian could not understand why, as we were enemies, we did not cut off the heads of all the inhabitants of the town. He was very curious about every thing he saw. He inquired how the soldiers could be made to march together with so much precision; and he was particularly fond of the military bands. He requested the Emperor to give him some of the musicians, as though they had been so many slaves.' A more critical assessment of Mirza Mohammad Reza Qazvini was given by McNeill (1836: 59) who called him 'a person named Mirza Reza, a man of no note, but the only individual of education and intelligence who could be induced to undertake the journey.'

9.67 'Paris, May 12,' *Alexandria Daily Advertiser* (Monday, 29 July, 1807), 'Paris, May 12,' *True Republican* (Monday, 29 July, 1807) and 'Paris, May 12,' *The Western World* (Thursday, 13 August, 1807): 'The Persian ambassador[173] arrived on the 25th [26th in *The Western World*] of April in the castle of Finkenstein.[174] The following day he had an audience of the emperor,[175] who on the 27th shewed him 20 battalions of infantry of his guard, and ordered them to make several manœuvres, which the ambassador contemplated with the utmost astonishment.

On the 28th he had another audience of his majesty who conversed with him a considerable time on Persian literature & antiquities. He is a gentleman of much information, and assured the emperor that there exists in Persia, memoirs of the war between the Persians and Romans, & also a history of Alexander, which does not agree with ours. The interpreter having told the emperor that a copy of the above history exists in the library, he has ordered it to be translated.'[176]

9.68 'Foreign Summary. Russians and Turks,' *Portsmouth Oracle* (Saturday, 1 August, 1807), 'Boston, July 29. Russians and Turks,' *Connecticut Herald* (Tuesday, 4 August, 1807), 'Russians and Turks,' *The Enquirer* (Tuesday, 4 August, 1807), 'Russians and Turks,' *The Farmers' Cabinet* (Tuesday, 4 August, 1807), 'Russians and Turks,' *North Star* (Saturday, 8 August, 1807), 'Russians and Turks,' *Connecticut Centinel* (Tuesday, 11 August, 1807) and 'Russians and Turks,' *Vermont Precursor* (Friday, 14 August, 1807): 'The Persians ... were said to be in arms against the Russians, stimulated by French officers.'[177]

---

[173] Mirza Mohammad Reza Qazvini.

[174] As Hecht (1897: 225) noted of 'des dem Reichs- und Burggrafen zu Dohna gehörenden Schlosses und Parkes von Finckenstein ... Das im sogenannten Kasernenstil 1721 erbaute dreiflügelige Schloß blickt mit der Gartenfront über weite Plätze und durch breite Alleen nach dem kleinen, reich umschilften Gauden-See ... Noch merckwürdiger ist das Schloß als Hauptquartier Napoleons vor der Schlacht bei Friedland. Nach den vorhandenen Urkunden besetzten die Garden schon am 20. März Finckenstein, wohin Napoleon am 1. April das Hauptquartier verlegt hatte. Er bewohnte mit seinen Generalen die Zimmer des oberen Stockwerks im Nordflügel und nach der anstoßenden Gartenfront. Er selbst hatte 3 Zimmer nach der Gartenseite inne.' The castle was located in what was formerly Ostpreußen, and is today part of the town of Susz in north-central Poland. In January, 1945, it was destroyed by the advancing Red Army. See Vogt, Kricheldorff and Ostermeyer (1990: 114).

[175] Napoleon.

[176] Possibly a reference to Ferdowsi's *Shahname*.

[177] When Gardane's Mission reached Khoy, Gardane wrote in his journal, 'Nous trouvons ici Mr Bontems-Lefort et Mr Auguste de Nerciat. Ils sont dans la faveur d'Abbas-Mirza à qui ils ont été utiles dans la guerre contre la Russie.' See Gardane (1809a: 33). The first was an engineer ('Capitaine du Génie'; Gardane 1809a: 2) and the second an interpreter attached to the mission.

9.69 'From Europe. French and Russians,' *Portland Gazette and Maine Advertiser* (Monday, 3 August, 1807): 'Bonaparte has excited the Persians to make war against the Russians.'

9.70 'Latest Foreign Intelligence. Vienna, May 27,' *The Daily Advertiser* (Monday, 10 August, 1807) and 'Vienna, May 27,' *Poulson's American Daily Advertiser* (Friday, 14 August, 1807): 'M. Lablanche, the Secretary to the French Legation,[178] and Lieutenant-Colonel Pouton, have set out from Constantinople to Fethaly, Schach,[179] to conduct the operations of the Persians against Grusnia.'

---

[178] Xavier Olympe Hüe de la Blanche (1779–1848) was a nephew of Talleyrand's. See Gaffarel (1908: 396). According to an announcement dated Paris, 28 February, 1806, 'Le Ministre des Relations Extérieures propose à l'Empereur de nomme M. Lablanche à la place de deuxième secrétaire à Vienne et à sa place M. Viefville des Essarts troisième secrétaire.' See Masson (1899: 34). Anonymous (1806g) reported, 'M. Lablanche qui était arrivé ici [Constantinople] le 26 juin [1806], comme secrétaire de la légation française, fut présenté le 29 du même mois, par le chargé d'affaires M. Ruffin, au reiss-effendi; il remit à ce ministre une lettre de M. de Talleyrand (prince de Bénévent), ministre des affaires étrangères, pour le grand-visir. Cette lettre contenait la notification officielle de la nomination de M. le général Sébastiani, comme ambassadeur de S.M. l'empereur des français, roi d'Italie, près la Sublime-Porte ottomane.' According to Anonymous (1807f), 'Il fit, avec son frère Pierre Mathieu, ses preuves de noblesse devant Berthier: il se destinait à l'artillerie. La Révolution l'empêcha de donner suite à ce projet: il fut obligé de se cacher pour échapper aux fureurs du fanatisme politique et ce n'est qu'en 1828 qu'il put entrer dans l'administration. Il débuta par être conseiller de Préfecture à Lyon; puis, il obtint un poste de premier secrétaire d'ambasade d'abord en Perse, puis en Turquie, et fut même chargé d'affaires en Autriche, fonctions qu'il remplit avec honneur et qui lui valurent les brevets de chevalier des ordres de la Réunion de France, du Croissant de Turquie, du Soleil de Perse et de Léopold d'Autriche.' See du Mesnil (1885: 177). From 2 October 1813 he was First Secretary at the French embassy in Vienna. See Georgel (1869: 32).

[179] 'As the French Colonel Boutin is with the army of the Grand Vizier [then at Adrianople], M. Lablanche, Secretary of Legation, and Lieutenant Colonel Pouton, set off at the end of April to Teth-Aly Schah [sic, Fath], Sovereign of Persia, to take part in his attack upon Georgia.' See Anonymous (1807c). Anonymous (1807b) announced that 'M. Lablanche, premier secrétaire de légation française, se dispose à partir pour la Perse,' while Anonymous (1807c) reported, 'Le premier secrétaire, M. Lablanche, a reçu ordre de se rendre à Paris, pour y rendre compte lui-même de sa mission en Perse.' According to Anonymous (1807d), 'Le secrétaire de légation française, M. Lablanche, et le lieutenant-colonel Pouton, sont partis pour se rendre près du roi de Perse, Feth-Ali-Schah; ils prendront part aux opérations qui seront dirigées contre la Géorgie, M. Boutin, colonel français, se trouve, comme l'on sait, à l'armée du grand-visir.' Boutin is an error for Bontems. Anonymous (1807e) wrote that, 'Le secrétaire Lablanche gère instantanément les affaires près du schah.' According to Dehérain (1930: 44), Georges Philippe Auguste Andréa de Nerciat (1782–1847), who had arrivé in Constantinople in early 1803, 'se rendit assez promptement maître de la langue persane pour accompagner en mars 1807, comme interprète, le secrétaire d'ambassade La Blanche, chargé par le général Sébastiani de porter à Feth Ali chah une lettre de l'Empereur.' As for Hüe de la Blanche's return, Anonymous (1808b) reported, 'On écrit de *Constantinople*, que M. de la Blanche, secrétaire de l'ambassade de France auprès de la Porte, le même qui fut envoyé l'année dernière en Perse, a été arrêté, dépouillé, & maltraité par les Curdes, peuple d'Asie répandu dans

9.71 'From the Richmond Enquirer. An overland Expedition to India,' *Alexandria Daily Advertiser* (Monday, 17 August, 1807) and 'From the Richmond Enquirer,' *L'Oracle* (Tuesday, 25 August, 1807): 'It has been for some time believed that the French government meditated an overland expedition to the British dominions in India; but the difficulties which were in the way, tempted many persons to treat the question as a visionary project, plausible in the theory, but impossible in practice. The British government have hastened the question to maturity. The insolent demand made upon the Porte, induced the Sultan of Turkey[180] to strengthen the ties of friendship with France.[181] The army was immediately prepared for war, and every corps is organized and instructed by a French officer. It may therefore be concluded, that the expedition to India will receive not only the countenance of the government of Turkey, but aid from the people.

The great empire of Persia is situated between Turkey and India, it is therefore necessary to obtain the co-operation of that power. We have been advised that an alliance has been formed between the emperors of France and Persia, and now we perceive that a very distinguished French general, Gardanne,[182] has gone to Persia and is accompanied by three hundred French officers of different grades, and as many artillerists.[183] These officers and artillerists will be sufficient to organize an army of Persians, with which, without further aid, the British possessions in India might be attacked, but it is not likely that the emperor of France will depend upon that resource. He will send an army of Frenchmen thro' Turkey and Persia, and will obtain such assistance from each of those powers as may promote the object.

Nor is this all. The Russians and Persians are at war. By the means of the French officers and artillerists, the Persian armies will be better qualified to wage a successful war against

---

l'Arménie turque & persane, qui se tient dans l'indépendance, vit de brigandage & de son bétail, & peut être comparé aux Arabes du désert.' Anonymous (1808c) announced, 'M. de la Blanche, secrétaire de la légation française, est revenue de Perse par Bagdad. On attendoit sous peu de jours à Constantinople Asker-Han, ambassadeur persan qui se rend à Paris pour complimenter l'empereur sur l'arrivée du général Gardanne à Théheran.'

[180] Selim III was Sultan until 29 May 1807, after which he was succeeded by Mustafa IV, to whom this article probably refers.

[181] For the increasingly close ties between France and the Porte at this time see Creasy (1856/2: 363–365).

[182] General Claude Mathieu de Gardane (1766–1818). For his mission see e.g. Gardane (1809a, 1865), Delrieu (1854), Driault (1900/1, 1904), Héron de Villefosse (1966), Calmard (2000/2012). His name frequently appears as Gardanne.

[183] This is untrue. Cf. Anonymous (1811d: 202), 'Instead of 300 Frenchmen, as had been reported, it had been ascertained that there were only 30 at the court of Persia. Who they are, or of what rank or description, we have not been able to learn.' As Tancoigne (1820: 3) noted, 'We shall form a caravan of about 100 persons, including the Turkish muleteers and their kervandii-baschi, or chief of the caravan ... The General, finding so numerous a company sufficiently formidable in itself, has not considered it necessary to demand an escort; we are, in fact, all armed, as if we were going on a military expedition.' The official legation, including Gardane and his interpreters, secretaries, scholars, officers, a doctor and missionaries, numbered only 26. See Gardane (1809a: 1–2).

the Russians; and in this way, the emperor of France will weaken the Russian force, and, perhaps, curtail and circumscribe that mighty empire. Such will be the first fruits of the plan, and of course the first object of his care. While, therefore, the war between these two powers requires the employment of their forces against the common enemy of Europe and Asia, the expedition to India will be deferred; but whenever the Russian government shall from necessity or policy make a just and reasonable peace, the overland expedition to India may, and no doubt will be, successfully prosecuted.'

9.72 'From the Aurora. Speculative Views,' *Republican Star or Eastern Shore General Advertiser* (Tuesday, 15 September, 1807), 'From the Aurora. Speculative Views,' *Alexandria Daily Advertiser* (Friday, 18 September, 1807), 'Political Miscellany, &c. Speculative Views,' *The Bee* (Tuesday, 22 September, 1807) and 'Speculative Views,' *Virginia Argus* (Wednesday, 23 September, 1807):

'The Russian frontier will be reduced within narrow limits on the Caspian.
The Persians will become the allies and send ambassadors to France.
The Hindustan princes will form alliances with Persia.'

9.73 'Frankfort, July 4,' *Aurora General Advertiser* (Thursday, 17 September, 1807) and 'Frankfort, July 4,' *Epitome of the World* (Monday, 21 September, 1807): 'It is now thought possible that the Russians, united with the Turks may drive the English out of the Mediterranean; or assisted by the Persians, penetrate to the East Indies.'

9.74 'New Combinations. London, Aug. 17,' *Federal Gazette & Baltimore Daily Advertiser* (Friday, 2 October, 1807): 'In a letter from the Elbe of August 7, it is stated that one of the secret articles of the treaty of Tilsit[184] stipulates, that if England does not accept the mediation of Russia to make peace that Russia and Persia[185] are to attack the British

---

[184]The treaty between France and Russia, signed on 7 July 1807. Neither the 'articles séparés et secrets,' of the treaty, published in de Clercq (1864: 212–213), nor the additional 'traité secret d'alliance,' only a Russian copy of which exists (for the French translation see Tatistcheff 1891: 619–623) makes any mention of this stipulation. Nevertheless, Fath 'Ali Shah wrote on 13 February 1808 to Gardane as follows: 'Quant à l'interruption des rapports de la Perse avec les Anglais, Votre Excellence doit être instruite que, du jour même où l'union de nos deux trônes sublimes a eu lieu [i.e. the day on which the Treaty of Finkenstein was signed, 4 May 1807], l'on a fermé toute voie de communication entre les Persans et les Anglais; et notre ambassadeur qui avait été envoyé aux Indes, rappelé par nos ordres, est de retour en cette capitale. De plus, tous les Anglais, qui se trouvaient sur le territoire et dans les portes de notre domination, ont été chassés et renvoyés.' See Gardane (1865: 151).

[185]In fact, as Gardane emphasized to Fath 'Ali Shah, 'Sa Majesté déclare qu'il n'a rien été stipulé de relatif à la Perse dans le traité conclu à Tilsit … Sa Majesté n'ayant donc aucune donnée positive sur le cours futur de ses relations avec la Perse, n'a pas dû mettre en avant auprès de la Russie des liens qui n'étaient point encore consolidés.' See Gardane (1865: 145).

possessions in India; and that the Russian forces now in the Mediterranean, are to join the Turks to expel the British fleet from the Mediterranean.'

9.75 'Semlin,[186] Aug. 5,' *Suffolk Gazette* (Monday, 19 October, 1807): 'Letters from Jassy, written by christian merchants, affirm that the Duke of Richelieu[187] has received orders to join with his corps the army which was acting against Persia, and to cross that kingdom for the purpose of going to attack the English possessions in India.[188] The Persian monarch, Feth-Aly-Sha, is about being invited by an embassy, to make a common cause with Russia against England.'

9.76 'Salem, Monday, October 19, 1807,' *Essex Register* (Monday, 19 October, 1807): 'The public attention is again called to the East. The meeting of Ambassadours at Constantinople indicates some serious enquiries upon this subject. The Minister from Persia,[189] and the French minister from [sic, to] the Persian Court,[190] and the negociations with Russia are mentioned at Constantinople. The return of the French Ambassador from Persia will assist a knowledge of the state of the intermediate countries between Europe [and] the distant Indies.[191] When the Emperor of Russia[192] assures his subjects that he has

---

[186] This could refer to Semlin in Serbia or in Poland. The reference in 10.258 to the Pasha of Belgrade makes it, however, likely that the Semlin referred to here was the Serbian city.

[187] Armand Emmanuel Sophie Septimanie de Vignerot du Plessis, duc de Richelieu (1766–1822). No such order appears in *Le duc de Richelieu. Correspondance et documents, 1766–1822*. See Imperial Russian Historical Society (1886b).

[188] In fact, as Hurewitz (1956: 78) noted, 'The instructions to ... Gardane, head of the French mission to Persia, amply attest to the seriousness with which Napoleon viewed the Persian alliance—at the time of its signature. They also shed light on Napoleon's grand design for the conquest of India via the Ottoman Empire and Persia ... Yet once France unexpectedly entered into a competing alliance with Russia at Tilsit on 7 July 1807, Napoleon abandoned his plans for invading India with Ottoman and Persian collaboration. But Gardane, already *en route* to his post by then, was not recalled.'

[189] 'Askar Khan-e Afshar Urumi. As Brydges (1833: 333) noted, 'Askar Khan Afshar Arumy, a distinguished chief, was ... ordered, with complete equipments and appointments, to proceed as Ambassador to France, taking with him many precious commodities and beautiful objects as memorials of friendship; and charged also with Letters, both from his exalted Majesty and the Prince Viceroy, expressive of their friendship and good-will towards Napoleon.' On his return to Persia 'Askar Khan stopped in Vienna where he engaged in a little private business with some of the gifts he had failed to distribute in Paris, for which he earned the wrath of Fath 'Ali Shah. As von Hammer observed, 'Asker Chan verkaufte in Wien die Shawls, die er von Persien als Geschenke in Paris mitgebracht hatte und verfiel dafür später in Teheran in Ungnade.' See Bachofen von Echt (1940: 151). Previously, 'Askar Khan had served as a cavalry commander under Agha Mohammad Shah beginning in 1790/1, and against the Russians. See Kondo (1999: 546).

[190] More likely 'to the Persian Court,' indicating Gardane.

[191] Gardane arrived in Tehran on 4 December 1807 and left on 27 January 1809. He arrived back in Constantinople on 18 April 1809. See Gardane (1809a: 126–128).

[192] Alexander I.

finished a very important war assisted by the bravery of his troops, and promises himself additional territory, it is supposed that, his acquisitions towards Europe, are not his only expectations, though rich to him. The long contacts with Persia upon the southern parts of the Russian Empire, for advantages in Asia, may be finished with the quiet possession of those countries, if the Persians could extend their dominions in the countries beyond their present limits. From the combination of the four powers of Turkey, Persia and Russia with France, the greatest changes would be in their power in Asia, without the least apprehension of that formidable resistance which they might find, but which has been in vain in Europe.'

9.77 'Salem, November 17,' *New-York Evening Post* (Saturday, 21 November, 1807), 'Salem, November 17,' *The Democratic Press* (Monday, 23 November, 1807), 'Salem, November 17,' *Republican Watch-Tower* (Tuesday, 24 November, 1807), 'Salem, November 17,' *New-York Spectator* (Wednesday, 25 November, 1807) and 'Untitled,' *The World* (Sunday, 7 December, 1807): 'It was reported, that immediately after the peace between Russia and France, the Russians suddenly made a peace also with Persia, that the Russian army employed against the Persians had now formed a junction with them,[193] and thus combined, were marching toward the ancient Mogul Empire, now possessed by the British, and upon the borders of which they had arrived; that with the Persian army the French Emperor had numerous intelligent officers of artillery and engineers;[194] that the grand Bonapartean plan was to form two great *independent* kingdoms in India, stipulating with them a free trade with all the nations of the earth, *very cunningly excepting England*—Whatever may be the reality, this shews how rumour is busied.'

9.78 'From a late London Paper. Danger of the Empire in India, from Russia and Persia,' *The Daily Advertiser* (Wednesday, 2 December, 1807): 'What may be the final close of our greatness in India, and the termination of an empire springing from honourable motives of commerce, but which, in its progress, has been tarnished by every vice that ambition and despotism ever knew, will be a subject of serious contemplation . . . Our late governor-

---

[193] No such alliance, of course, ever existed.

[194] Notwithstanding the hyperbole of this report, Sir Harford Jones wrote, 'I have not the smallest doubt . . . but that Bonaparte designed to form . . . a point d'appui in Persia, from whence, when the time came, he might either persuade or force another great power to join him in the invasion of British India, and our allies there. For what other purpose can it be imagined, that General Gardanne carried out with him cannon founders, military artificers of all sorts, and inferior officers to drill and instruct the Persians in the military tactics of Europe? To those also were added engineers of some rank and celebrity in the French service.' See Brydges (1834/1: 222). In fact, according to Delrieu (1854: 195), 'L'opinion subissait en Perse, à cet égard, un mouvement d'enthousiasme si prononcé, qu'on regardait M. Fabvier, qui résidait à Ispahan, où sa fonderie de canons était établie, coimme le chef de l'avant-garde future de la grande armée d'invasion.'

general marquis Wellesley,[195] seems to have had ... ideas upon the subject[196] ... "It is not improbable, he observes, but that the British empire in India may experience a fate somewhat similar to that which precipitated the greatness of the Roman power.—A remote and an unknown enemy may burst upon our security; the savage hordes of the North East may rush down upon us, and the immense empire of Russia, which now almost touches upon our frontier, may [..?us] she is extending her conquests into Persia or China, be induced to turn aside to discovery what prey she may be able to seize in Hindostan."

This observation of the noble authors [sic] is of more value from some late hints which have been dropt in the Moniteur,[197] with respect to the mediation which Russia has offered between England and France—we are there told, in language tolerably plain, that if England refuses to accept this mediation, Russia is to confederate with France against us; that Persia is to be employed as one of the main instruments of aggression; and that an attack is to be immediately made upon our empire in the East.

This is certainly not improbable; we have seen the respect, not to say cajolery with which the Persian embassy has been received at Paris.[198] A deputation from that empire

---

[195] Richard Colley Wellesley, Earl of Mornington. Cf. 8.47. See also Torrens (1880: 132ff). For Wellesley's 'Gallophobia,' see Rawlinson (1849: 7).

[196] As Torrens (1880: 140–141) noted, 'That he burned with the ambition to set his mark indelibly on the system of British rule in the East, every line in his voluminous correspondence shows. But his hunger was for fame that would last, not for pelf that would perish. He coveted neither for his country or for himself mere acquisitions of money, jewels, or lands. His immediate if not his sole feeling of antagonism was to Jacobinical France, and to the Sultan of Mysore [Tipu Sultan] as her accessory in designs for the subversion of our power. In Asia as in Europe, this was the question of the day to which all others must give place.'

[197] The *Moniteur* was long considered the popular voice of the French government and an unofficial, i.e. non-diplomatic, venue for disseminating positions and policies. Thus, commenting on an apparent contradiction between Napoleon's actual attitude towards Prussia and the views of an article in the *Moniteur*, Anonymous (1804e) wrote, 'After all that we have been told, and truly told, about the French press ... after we have, for years, regarded the articles in the Moniteur as being all sanctioned, if not actually written or dictated, by persons in the French government; after all this, it will hardly be suggested, that the above article found its way into print without the consent or knowledge of that government. Indeed, the writer...proceeds upon the contrary supposition; for, he represents the article as the "growling and foaming" of Buonaparte himself.'

[198] A reference to Yusuf Bey, described by Gardane as 'a simple courier. He left Teheran in September, 1806, travelling by way of Aleppo,' who was, however, treated like a proper ambassador in Paris until Gardane informed his superiors of their mistake. See Puryear (1951: 321). Puryear (1951: 218) recounted this remarkable incident as follows: 'In mid-September Yousef Bey, presumably a second Persian envoy, arrived impressively with a suite of four persons. This individual, as we know, had come to Constantinople while Mirza Riza was still in Warsaw and had waited to learn where to go next. He delivered several letters which had been transmitted by General Sebastiani. Without asking questions, Napoleon thought that Yousef might be the expected resident ambassador from Persia. He and Chmpagny decided to play safe. In the state courtesies accorded Yousef they followed the precedents of 1715, when a Persian envoy had visited Paris, and of April, 1807, in entertaining Mirza Riza ... Yousef submitted no credentials—which should have aroused suspicions

was even entertained in the camp of Napoleon[199] whilst occupied in the last campaign; and though his motive was doubtless, at that period, to stir up an enemy against Russia, and invite the Persians to attack the possessions of that power, which lie between the Caspian and the Euxine,[200] it is not to be questioned but that his designs have changed with his circumstances, and that instead of employing Persia against England, his intention is now to employ her against India.

Whether Russia will co-operate in this hostility we know not; but weak, we had almost said despicable, as is the court of Alexander, there is much reason to fear that the temptation of a very slight booty will put aside every principle of honor and national justice.—*Bell's Weekly Messenger, Oct. 4.*'

9.79 'Persia,' *Washington Federalist* (Wednesday, 20 January, 1808), 'Miscellany. Persia,' *The Democrat* (Wednesday, 20 January, 1808), 'Miscellany. Persia,' *The Repertory* (Friday 22 January, 1808) and 'Persia,' *Charleston Courier* (Thursday, 4 February, 1808): 'Amongst the gigantic projects of French ambition, a passage to India thro' Persia is prepared. By accounts we learn that a military survey, by French officers,[201] had

---

but did not … Meanwhile, Yousef for several weeks did very well. That Napoleon blundered in entertaining a simple courier as an ambassador we shall see from Gardane's belated and blistering reaction from Teheran.' In fact, 'Yousef Bey, Persia's messenger in Paris, transacted no official business. That he found himself fêted as if a full-fledged ambassador … was due to a mistake on Napoleon's part. In December he stated that he felt called upon to request with vigor that replies be handed him to the letters he had delivered from the shah and the visir. Owing to his health he wished to return to Teheran, but he could not leave France without the replies. Napoleon accordingly, upon his return to Paris in mid-January [1808] wrote briefly to the shah. His letter stated that it would be delivered by Yousef, an individual who had been "treated as the envoy of a Prince who is dear to me and with whose actions I have been pleased."' See Puryear (1951: 248–249). In a letter sent by the Foreign Minister Champagny to Gardane, dated 10 November 1807, we read: 'Youssuf-Bey a été bien reçu de Sa Majesté. Elle a vue avec plaisir une personne qui pourrait lui parler de Feth-Ali-Chah, et qui avait part à l'estime et à la confiance de ce Prince. Tout ce qui peut concourir au maintien des relations amicales formées entre les deux pays, entre dans les vues de sa Majesté.' See Gardane (1865: 323).

[199] A reference to the Persian ambassador's visit to Napoleon at Finckenstein.

[200] The Black Sea.

[201] The Gardane Mission included 'Trezel, Capitaine Ingénieur-Géographe' and 'Bernard, Lieutenant Ingénieur-Géographe.' See Gardane (1809a: 2). They were chosen 'par le général [Nicola Antoine Sanson [1756–1824] parmi ceux du bureau topographique de la Grande Armée. Trézel était chargé de la détermination des points astronomiques et de la rédaction des mémoires militaires et statistiques; Bernard, des reconnaissances, des levés et dessins topographiques.' See (Berthaut 1902: 67). Bernard drew up the itinerary. As Berthaut (1902: 68) observed, 'L'ingénieur géographe Bernard fit un très bon itinéraire, à une ligne pour 100 toises, de la route de Constantinople à Bayazid. Ce fut son seul travail; il mourut de la fièvre quelques jours après son entrée en Perse, en arrivant à Khoï. Le général Gardanne le destinait à étudier plus tard les routes du Kachemyr.' According to Das, Gardane 'sent Trezel and Adrien Dupré ['Attaché à la Légation;' see Gardane (1809a: 2); for his own account see Dupré (1819)] to inspect the ports in the Persian Gulf. They surveyed Bandar Abbas and other places

commenced from Constantinople to the shores of the Indus: and a letter from Augsburgh informs us, that Jussuf Bey, attended by a French interpreter, had passed through that city on the 7th Sept. on his way to Paris, as ambassador from the Persian Court.[202] Under these circumstances the political philosopher will look with attention to the sources of information on the present state of Persia. This country from Hindostan, the eastern frontier, to the western mountains of Elwind,[203] is 1200 miles in length, and 1000 miles in breadth, from the deserts on the Indian Ocean, to the inhospitable districts bordering on the Sea of Aral. The authorities with which the learned are acquainted, are those of Strabo, Pliny, the historians of Alexander, and among the Arabian writers, Ebu, Houkal [sic, Ibn Hawqal], Edrisi, and the princely Abulfeda. All the most important authorities, on the coast extending from the Tigris and Euphrates, to the confines of the eastern peninsula, are given in the voyage of Nearenus [sic, Nearchus]; and the Periplus of the Erithrean [sic, Erythrean] Sea, by the learned Dean of Westminster.[204] The British government have not been wholly inatentive to this subject; and in 1774, a little squadron was equiped from Bombay, in order to explore the coast between the Indus and the Gulph of Persia,[205] of which there had been scarcely any account since the time of Alexander the Great. When the Romans obtained possession of Egypt, the Indian trade, which had been conducted by land to the Caspian Sea, and thro' the defiles of Mount Caucasus to the Euxine,[206] received a different direction, and the treasures of the east were conveyed to Europe by the Red Sea and the Mediterranean. The most curious document on the new channel of communication

---

on the Gulf and at Shiraz conferred with the envoys from Sind who were on their way back.' See Das (2016: 38). Berthaut (1902: 69) wrote, 'De son côté Trézel, après avoir reconnu la région de Tiflis et d'Érivan, où il fit quelques observations astronomiques, accomplissait un voyage également difficile au golfe Persique, puis une reconnaissance de Rescht à Astrabad, en suivant la mer Caspienne, destinée à se relier avec le travail de Truilhier dans le Khorassan.'

[202] Puryear (1951: 218) recounted the first news of Yusuf Bey as follows: 'At Paris, Champagny [Jean-Baptiste de Nompère de Champagny (1756–1834), French Foreign Minister (1807–1811)] was surprised when a rumor respecting Persia was fulfilled. Someone had reported "an officer" to have been touring Europe for three months and to have left Persia some five months earlier.'

[203] Alvand.

[204] William Vincent (1739–1815). See Vincent (1805).

[205] From 'in the year 1774,' to 'Gulph of Persia,' this sentence is taken verbatim from Vincent (1797: v–vi). The 'little squadron' consisted of three vessels: 'Fox, Lieutenant Robinson, Commodore. Dolphin, Lieutenant Porter. A Patamar boat [writing about the Deccan, Fryer (1698: 111) noted, '*patamars* were 'the only Foot-posts of this Country;' *patamar* boats were 'open boats carrying four or five tons; on account of their being excellent sailers, they are frequently employed in conveying letters and dispatches;' see Howell (1791: 10, n.*)], in which Mr. Blair and Mr. Mascall, volunteers, were occasionally employed. From the materials collected by these officers, Mr. Dalrymple constructed a chart, containing the Survey of Lieutenant Robinson, and accompanied it with a Memoir drawn up by Lieutenant Porter, which he prefaces with the following observation: "The coasts here described are so little known, that every particular must be acceptable, *as we have scarcely any account of them* since the time of Alexander the Great."'

[206] The Black Sea.

is Cosma's Iudicopleustes,[207] written A.D. 535, by which we learn, that the trade continued on the same footing from the reign of Claudius to the termination of the 5th century, and that in that period the island of Ceylon was considered as the grand emporium of oriental commerce.

The population of modern Persia is supposed to exceed ten millions; and the military force is estimated at 200,000.

The Persians never were a maritime people because some of the precepts in the laws of Zoroaster must be disregarded in long voyages. As the Mahometan religion is adverse to trade, here also, as well as in Turkey, commercial intercourse is conducted by foreigners. As in the one the Christians and Jews are traders, so here the natives of Armenia [*Washington Federalist* has 'America'] and Hindostan. The revenue of Persia is about 5 millions, of which three are derived from the eastern and two from the western monarchy.

Peter the Great once held the mountainous provinces adjacent to the Caspian sea. The alliance with Candanar [sic, Kandahar], or the eastern despot, in the present circumstances, would be of the greatest consequence to the security of British dominions in India. The nature of the country presents innumerable difficulties, which will require all the ardor of enterprise possessed by Bonaparte to overcome. Persia has been called by an intelligent writer (Chandin) [sic, Chardin][208] a country of mountains. In the contracted vallies there is little or no produce. No Asiatic country is so deficient in rivers, if we exclude the bladeless leefless regions of Arabia. Excepting in the north, and among some of the western mountains, not a single tree is to be found to shelter the weary traveller. Contemplating this country in a military point of view, it should not escape notice, that the horses of Persia are more beautiful than any other in the world—and that the camels are powerful and numerous. It is well known, that Tippo Saib constantly employed agents in Persia to provide horses for his cavalry.'[209]

9.80 'Salem, Wednesday, January 20, 1808,' *Essex Register* (Wednesday, 20 January, 1808): 'From the entire absence of late European information we are not able to add any late events. Various reports have been in circulation respecting the negociations between the Swedes and the French; and the reports respecting Russia and England have been repeated, that the commerce of Russia and England has been interrupted. If the Russians are seriously engaged, as the French would represent in the expeditions to the east, it is not to

---

[207] Cosmas Indicopleustes, a Christian (monk?) from Alexandria, Egypt, Cosmas wrote the *Christian Topography*, c. 547–550, a work containing important information on India, Sri Lanka (Taprobane) and the route to China. See e.g. Faller (2011).

[208] Cf. 1.190, 1.196.

[209] Rao, who was 'long in their employ,' makes no mention of Tipu's acquisition of horses in Persia. See Brown (1849). A letter 'To Meer Kâzim, *Commercial Consul, or Chief of the Factory at Muscat*,' states, 'Propose to the merchants of *Muscat*, (and get the *Imaum* to issue orders to the same effect,) to bring hither, on the empty *Dingies*, such horses as they may have for sale; which being sold to us, the owners can carry back the produce in rice.' See Kirkpatrick (1811: 6).

be doubted that a rupture must follow ... That many French officers have gone to Persia is universally admitted, and that they were accompanied with a Persian minister from Turkey. The reason of this first enterprise may be understood from the state of Persia. The account of the Persian military arrangements from a person on the Bengal establishment, who published his travels last year,[210] and who appears to have had every opportunity for information on the subject, is, that the Persian army consists chiefly of cavalry, well mounted, well cloathed, and well paid, but under very little discipline. That, of these troops the King[211] can collect in a very short time 60,000; with 20,000 of the guards, which attend his person. The latter are considered as the best troops of the Empire. They have higher pay, and more expensive uniforms. The infantry has but few arrangements. Sometimes they act at sieges, and with the artillery, but they have no instruction in the military art, from which they can deserve the name of discplined troops. At the time when this writer visited Persia, it was conjectured that the French might profit from the Persians against the Russians, and it was acknowledged that the French at that time had claimed to employ a powerful influence in the Persian court. To the French the state of Persia could not be a secret. The many provincial wars had not allowed the Persians to refuse all claim to courage, and all love of the military character. They needed discipline; and it is for discipline the French have made generous provision in the three hundred officers who are commissioned from France to instruct the courage of the Persians.'[212]

9.81 'Untitled,' *L'Oracle and Daily Advertiser* (Wednesday, 24 February, 1808) and 'Untitled,' *The Independent Chronicle* (Thursday, 3 March, 1808): 'If Bonaparte, during his stay in Poland, has actually engaged the Persians in his quarrel with England, if he has

---

[210] Edward Scott Waring (d. 1819; see Burke 1835: 504), of the Bengal Civil Establishment, who travelled from India to Shiraz in 1802. See Scott Waring (1807: 81–84) for the account on which this news story was based.

[211] Fath 'Ali Shah.

[212] This is a wild exaggeration. As Driault (1900/1901: 132–133) noted, 'Pendant que quelques-uns des officiers de Gardane, notamment Verdier et Lamy, entreprenaient l'instruction des troupes d'Abbas-Mirza et s'efforçaient de constituer peu à peu un noyau solide de troupes disciplinées, le lieutenant Fabvier fut chargé d'établier à Ispahan une fonderie, et de construire 50 canon semblables à celui dont le schah était si fier. Fabvier s'installa à Ispahan dès le comment de février [1808]. Il n'y trouva rien qui pût l'aider à accomplir sa tâche, aucun atelier, point d'ouvriers, point de matériaux, beaucoup de mauvaise volonté de la part des fonctionnaires royaux ... Il est incroyable qu'il ait pu vaincre tous ces obstacles et construire en cinq mois une vingtaine de canons.' De Rochechouart (1867: 97) noted, 'Les premiers essais d'armée régulière datent du règne de Feth-Ali-Chah, et ont été faits par son fils Abbas-Mirza; les premiers instructeurs furent des Français: MM. Trezel, Bernard, Lamy, Bontems, Fabvier, Reboul, Verdier; ils ont laissé un grand souvenir, et quelques-uns de leurs règlements sont encore en vigueur.' Of Lamy's contribution in particular, Berthaut (1902: 69) wrote, 'M. Lamy, officier du génie, était à la disposition du prince Abbas-Mirza, pour la construction d'un pont sur l'Arax et pour celle des fortifications de la place de Nackitschewan. Lamy forma des élèves, destinés à devinir des officiers du génie et d'état-major. Il eut aussi à s'occuper des reconnaissances entre le Kour et l'Arax.'

obtained from Alexander,[213] as one of the secret articles of the treaty of Tilsit, the privilege of marching a small French division through his territory; if he has had the artifice to conceal these motions from the English ministry; if his journey to Italy and the movements of his troops in Dalmatia tend to the accomplishment of this gigantic project, and if Oudinot[214] has finally arrived at Astracan,[215] it is a matter of impossibility to credit the sincerity of his propositions for peace. The blow which he meditates against the British government, is too important in its nature, and its success too probable, to allow us to harbor the idea of his relinquishing the undertaking.'

9.82 'From the London Morning Chronicle,' *The Enquirer* (Friday, 26 February, 1808):
'Mr Editor,

An emigrant died lately, at his furnished lodgings, in my neighborhood; & being acquainted with the landlady, I was desired to take an inventory of the effects of the deceased. Among his papers I found one so full of singular hints, that I requested, and obtained leave to make it public. I shall translate it here literally, with all its half sentences and breaks. To the words, within the parentheses, I could find no apposite English expressions.

"December 7th, 1806, sent a letter to T. with a sketch of my plans, rolled in Arbeuil's double leather boots—answer received in a small bale of cambric. 4th February, I was desired to be more explicit—Rhine to Danube—Danube across Black Sea to the Don—Don from river to river up to the Wolga—Wolga, through Caspian Sea—double Canal through Persia[216]—leave obtained—across: 14,000 men—Indus to Ganges—14,000 men

---

[213] Alexander I, of Russia.

[214] Nicolas Charles Oudinot (1767–1847), Duke of Reggio, Marshal of France and one of Napoleon's generals. For his life see Stiegler (1897).

[215] On 29 December 1807 a report originally published in a London newspaper stated, but picked up in a French daily, reported, 'Le bruit s'est généralement accrédité que le général Oudinot était arrivé, il y a deux mois, à Astrakan, avec son corps d'armée de 12 mille hommes. On assure que la nouvelle positive e ce fâcheux evenement est arrivée ces jours-ci à la compagnie des Indes. Nous espérons qu'on aura pris les mesures nécessaires pour déjouer l'objet de cette expédition. Two days later, on 31 December, 1807, Lord Brougham wrote to Lord Grey, 'You will perceive contradictory statements as to Oudinot's marching towards Astrakan; but I know it for a fact that the directors [of the EIC] believe he is. The deputy-chairman said so at Hertford College [Oxford] last week to Malthus, from whom I heard it. It is supposed Oudinot will settle matters in Persia for an attack upon India after some interval; and the probability is they will enter the peninsula by the Punjaub, for obvious reasons … If we lose India, there will be infinite clamour; but we shall be more frightened than hurt—thanks to the company's monopoly, which has so much stunted our commerce with that country.' See Brougham (1871: 396–397). Citing an article published in 1813, De Lacy Evans (1829: 9) confirmed that, after the Treaty of Tilsit, 'Nothing ever transpired as to the secret stipulations regarding Persia; but it was generally understood on the Continent, that Oudinot had been actually selected to proceed with a corps of 12,000 men, with all the baggage and equipments necessary for such an expedition.' In fact, Oudinot never undertook the mooted expedition to Astrakhan and on to Iran via the Caspian.

[216] While this is obviously a comic piece, it highlights a real anxiety about Napoleon's designs on India via Persia. Note that Gardane drafted a concrete plan for exactly how such an invasion might

on that parallel. Free transport for India goods, and cheaper than round the Cape of Good Hope. Add 14,000 men west of Persia, and will be effected within six years or even less—pioneers protected by 20,000 men, half Russians and half Persians, staff French officers. On account of my knowledge of the Persian, and other oriental languages, T. offers me 50,000 livres a year to be among the workmen, and a promise of the estate of C.C. at my return—agreed—tried the liquid, fired with a common pistol—tree on fire in less than 2 min, and burnt to the ground—timber cannot stand it—tried again in my room with an air-gun, and a ball rubbed with the liquid more than 3 weeks before, and left exposed to the air—fired at my trunk—in a blaze instantly—water had no effect on it—I grew frightened—put the fire out by throwing a blanket on the trunk—will do very well—the rowing boats must be flat with two large 24 pounders fore and aft (*bouchee evasee*)[217]—cannot try them among the hulls with safety, but I have promised to shew the effects to T. in presence of the little corporal—worth a hundred Trafalgars—B. bro't me a letter, 3rd April, in the little corporal's own hand writing with an ingot of gold worth 200 guineas—requested to send a full receipt of the composition—complied—sent a receipt in our private ink, by the thin Amazon (*meigre!*").

The remainder of the paper contains hardly any writing, but consists of drawn sketches which I cannot make out, I do not fully understand the hints; but T. seems to stand for *Talleyrand*, and every body knows that the French soldiers always call Bonaparte the *little corporal*. The plan seems to be for opening a communication between Europe and Asia, through several rivers, and the Black and Caspian Seas to the Indus and Ganges. This appears very romantic, and even extravagant; but, however the hint should not be totally neglected with a character so very enterprizing as Bonaparte is known to be. I am told that, since the peace with Russia, all the smiths near Neufchatel, and other places in Switzerland, have been employed in making spades and pick-axes of a peculiar form; and that they are forwarded with great expedition through Poland. Why this? Does it not look as if they had a mind to begin the canal scheme? It is to be hoped, that the present ministers will keep a good look out, and disappoint the schemers. What an useful and glorious thing; if they could contrive a secret expedition, and bring to English shores all those cursed spades and pickaxes! Heaven grant it."

Should you wish, Mr. Editor, to ask me any explanatory question, do it in your usual answer to correspondents, as I regularly read your paper, and most of the others, having little else to do than to walk about the streets, eat a good dinner, and play my game of *piquet* in the evening. I suppose that the *liquid* is intended for a trial to burn our fleets at sea; but as the thing is impossible, and as besides we have now ships more than enough, it matters not at all. There are some other whimsical papers in the poor emigrant's bundle; concerting schemes in the interior of France, which if you like to have, let me know. Correct any fault you please, as I write English but indifferently. Believe me more attached to you.

---

proceed across Iran. See Gardane (1865: 111–128), 'Idées du général Gardane sur une expédition dans l'Inde par Delhi et Patna en traversant la Turquie et la Perse,' sent to Paris on 24 December 1807.

[217] *bouchée, évasée*, said of a cannon when it is blocked up (*bouchée*) and no longer functional (*évasée*). See Mozin and Biber (1828: 159).

D.P.

Bedford-square.'

9.83 'Salem, Wednesday, March 16, 1808,' *Essex Register* (Wednesday, 16 March, 1808): 'According to the French papers, the news had reached Paris in December last, that Persia had declared war against England.[218] This report is in consent with all the declarations the French have made respecting their operations in the East, and is confirmed by the last news from England by an English agent from Calcutta, who was sent from India to Persia, but finding no hopes of success against the French influence in the Persian Court, he passed through Europe to England with information respecting the French operations. The public expectations are greater from the interest the French take in the expedition into Persia, than from any disposition which Persia can have to produce a revolution in Indian affairs. The English have not failed to profit from a correspondence with Persia, and its ministers have been received at Calcutta with the highest honours. Not only have the alarms of British power made a disposition for war more ready to discover itself, but the great changes in the internal affairs of India and the adjacent countries have dissolved all the establishments upon which the hopes of resistance to new changes could possibly rest. Sir Wm. Jones, after his successful attempt to give in the French language a History of Nadir Shah,[219] the Persian Conqueror, at the request of the King of Denmark,[220] promised to arrange materials for a history of Persia, from the foundation of the Kingdom to our own times. As an evidence of his attention to the work, he gave a table of the Persian Kings, in five periods. The first of the Caioumaras[221] embraces four dynasties. The second the 58 Califfs, for the Arabians were masters of Persia from the middle of the seventh beyond the middle of the thirteenth century of the Christian Æra. The third period cembraces the reign of the Tartars in two dynasties till 1450. The fourth period includes the reign of the Turcomans till 1515. The fifth period is of the Sefis[222] till 1734. Nadir Shah, Ali, Ibrahim and Shahrock, succeeded to the Sefis. From M. Rennels [sic, Rennell], the Geographer of India,[223] we learn that Nadir Shah died in 1747, and one of his Generals seized upon the Eastern part of his Empire. The Mahrattas profited from the confusion, and contemplated to

---

[218] As noted above, Fath 'Ali Shah wrote to Napoleon informing him that he had severed ties with Great Britain, but he did not declare war.

[219] Jones (1770).

[220] The title page of Jones (1770) bears the subtitle 'Traduite d'un manuscrit persan, par l'ordre de Sa Majesté le Roi de Dannemark.' The dedication reads, 'À Sa Majesté Chrétien VII. Par la Grace de Dieu Roi du Dannemark et de la Norwegue, des Goths, et des Vandales, duc de Slesvic, Hollstein, Stormarn, et Dittmarshen, comte d'Oldenbourg et Dellmenhorst. &c. &c. &c.'

[221] First king of the mythical Pishdadian dynasty as recounted in the *Shahname*. Gayomard in Zoroastrian sources. See e.g Cereti (2015).

[222] Safavids.

[223] Cf. 9.32.

restore the Hindoo government, but in the action of 1761, the Mahrattas suffered exceedingly, and Abdalla established his power at Delhi. The English, under Lord Clive, profited from this state of things, and in 1765 supported the nominal Emperor, who was not faithful to them, and so low was this Prince that in 1784, his son came to Mr. Hastings for relief from private distresses. This prince, Shah Allum,[224] died 19th November, 1806, and was succeeded by his eldest son, who takes the name of Acber Saunee.[225] Mr. Rennel speaking of these countries of Agra and Delhi, betweeen Persia and the English settlements, not 20 years ago, says they are in the most wretched state to be conceived. They have been the seat of continual wars for nearly half a century; the fear of pillage prevents cultivation, and nothing but the mildness of the climate could secure it any population. Let us suppose the Persians disciplined by the French, and marching into this Eastern part of their Empire, as they rendered it by conquest in the last century, and then having all Hindostan open to them, and what shall we oppose to their power. At Delhi they are not above 1000 miles from Calcutta, and about the same distance to Bombay. But should the French descend the Indies they might approach the English settlements by routs we have already noticed.[226] We more particularly notice these distances as we may [have] occasion to refer to them hereafter' (Fig. 9.2).

9.84 'Political Retrospect. Foreign Affairs,' *Washington Expositor* (Saturday, 16 April, 1808): 'War it is said has actually commenced in the East, between the Persians and the English:[227] an event long anticipated by those who have considered the possessions of the latter power in that country, not only as the source of her greatness, but as her Achillean heel, and who remembered the numerous and well trained officers which France has from time to time forwarded to the nations the most likely there to support her interests.'

9.85 'Calcutta, Nov. 25,' *The North American and Mercantile Daily Advertiser* (Wednesday, 4 May, 1808), 'The Travellers in Persia. Ansely, (on the Caspian Sea) June 25, 1807,' *L'Oracle and Daily Advertiser* (Wednesday, 1 June, 1808; from 'We entered Persia' to 'circuitous route of Persia'), 'Calcutta, Nov. 25,' *Charleston Courier* (Saturday, 4 June, 1808) and 'The Travellers in Persia. Ansely, (on the Caspian Sea) June 25, 1807,' *The Courier* (Wednesday, 8 June, 1808; from 'We entered Persia' to 'circuitous route of Persia'): 'In one of the late numbers of the Mirror, we had the honor to introduce our readers to a party of Gentlemen, travelling from Bombay over-land, by way of Persia, to England.[228] Our former account, dated the 14th of May [1807], left them at Bagdad,

---

[224] Shah 'Alam II, the Mughal emperor (r. 1760–1788, 1788–1806).

[225] Akbar Shah II, the Mughal emperor (r. 1806–1837).

[226] Cf. the full discussion of possible routes of invasion in De Lacy Evans (1829).

[227] Obviously a false rumor.

[228] Identified in the *Asiatic Annual Register* 10 (1811) as 'colonel Macquarrie, Dr. Thomas, and Lieut.-general Brande,' who were joined on 16 May 1807 by 'Major O'Neil, of his Majesty's

Fig. 9.2 James Rennell, 1794, possibly by George Daniel. CC0 1.0 Universal. After E.T. Thackeray, *Biographical Notices of Officers of the Royal (Bengal) Engineers*. London: Smith, Elder, & Co., 1900, between pp. 10 and 11

preparing to enter Persia. We have the satisfaction to learn that they have safely arrived at Anselly,[229] on the eastern shore of the Caspian, from whence we are favored with letters, dated the 25th of June, of which the following is an extract.

Anselly, June 25.

---

service.' See Anonymous (1811b: 179). Lachlan Macquarie later served as Governor of the colony of New South Wales, Australia (28 December 1809–21 December 1821). For the journey, from Macquarie's perspective, see Page (2009: 70.3–70.5). 'Dr. Thomas' was Assistant-Surgeon William Thomas (d. 1813). He is mentioned in a letter from the Court of Directors of the EIC to Bombay, dated 17 January 1810, noting that he 'had come to England on furlough as a prisoner of war on parole,' and 'had been exchanged.' See Crawford (1914: 203). 'Lieut.-general Brande' was George William Brande (1785–1854) who was, however, not a 'Lieut.-general' but rather a Lieutenant (he was 23 at the time of the journey described in this article). See https://www.mq.edu.au/macquarie-archive/lema/biographies/profiles/brandegeorge.html. 'Major O'Neil' was Major Robert O'Neil of the 56th (West Essex) Regiment of Foot.

[229] Bandar-e Anzali.

"We entered Persia on the 22d of May. In consequence of the Resident at Bagdad,[230] having previously written to the court of Persia, giving notice of our intended journey, orders were issued, permitting us to pass wheresoever we desired: but a Frenchman resident at the court as ambassador from Bonaparte,[231] hearing of our arrival, contrived to insinuate unfavorable suspicions of the motives of our travelling into Persia; and, in consequence a Khan was directed to conduct us to court. The Khan accordingly waited upon us, announcing himself as our Memender, and delivered a highly complimentary message, in the eastern stile, from the Vizier;[232] stating that his highness could on no account allow a party of English gentlemen to travel through his Majesty's Dominions, without having the pleasure of seeing them at court.

"At Bagdad we had been joined by an additional traveller, an Irish officer, a major,[233] a very pleasant though some what eccentric companion. On the morning succeeding the day, on which we were visited by the Khan, the major had unluckily parted from the Caravan, and could no where be found. This circumstance alarmed the Deputation, and raised a suspicion that the major had made his escape to avoid being carried to court, and that he had gone off with information of importance to the Russians, now at war with Persia.—Three days elapsed before the major was discovered. Having thoughtlessly strolled to a distance from the caravan, he was seized, robbed, stripped of his clothes, detained in captivity, and unceremoniously employed at hard work.—When discovered, he was actually at labor in a gravel pit.[234]

---

[230] W. John Hine, Acting Resident at Baghdad (1806–1808) in the absence of Harford Jones who had gone back to Britain and did not sail on his return voyage until 27 October 1807. See Brydges (1834/ 1: 17). Macquarie's correspondence makes it clear that Hine would have been the writer and was involved in the arrangements for the onward travel of Macquarie's party. See Ritchie (1986: 246).

[231] General Gardane. Cf. 9.73.

[232] Mirza Shafi'-e Mazandarani. Cf. 9.4. He became grand vizir in 1801. See Busse (1972: 99). For an assessment of his career see e.g. Behrooz (2013: 54–57).

[233] Maj. Robert O'Neil.

[234] Cf. Anonymous (1809a): 'Major O'Neil who accompanied Colonel Macquarie in his overland journey, met with the following singular and perilous adventure, in one of those little excursions which are not very dangerous perhaps in a flat country, but which are undoubtedly imprudent in a hilly one.—On the 5th of June, having travelled about two thirds of the distance between Bagdad and the Caspian Sea, he lost sight of the Caravan in one of those picturesque places, and wandered about the whole day without being able to find it again.—During this time repeated attempts were made to disarm and rob him by the lawless wretches who prowl about the country. At length about sun-set he was so suddenly attacked by four of them that before he could stand on his defence he was knocked down from his horse and disarmed.—The banditti then literally stripped him to the skin and shared the plunder amongst them, giving him a few of their own rags to defend him from the cold: after much ill treatment and repeated threats against his life they finally dismissed him.—In this forlorn condition he walked all night, and early the next morning was again attacked by three other men.—One of them who was well mounted and better armed than the others, after striking him several times, seized him and dragged him in the cruellest manner to his house; where for two days he obliged him by blows to work at the hardest labour. Making him pull grass for his cattle, dig gravel, and carry it home from the

"The major being fortunately recovered, and restored to our society, served to do away all suspicion as to the object of our journey. The Persians were fully convinced as to the truth of our account, that the Turkish war was the sole motive of our travelling to Europe by the circuitous route of Persia.

"It happened luckily at this time, that the king was on the road from the capital to his camp, and crossing our intended track, saved us the necessity of a long and tedious journey.[235] I shall say nothing further on political subjects, than that we have reason to believe that the king of Persia and his confidential advisers, discern the true character and object of the French propositions, and that they have already given a decided negative to the late overtures of Bonaparte; and have signified to his ambassador, that they can on no account, take any measure to disturb the good understanding that now subsists between G. Britain and Persia. The king is anxious to put an end to the war with Russia. Col. Macquarrie has letters both from the King[236] and the Vizier,[237] addressed to His Britannic Majesty[238] and to his Ministers, requesting, as we understand, the mediation of England, in effecting a peace between the two empires.

"In our journey through Persia, we have been occasionally entertained with princely splendor by the Governors of the cities through which we passed.—With apparent fertility, the finely diversified scenery of Persia, and its natural beauties we have been delighted. Very different must be our account of its inhabitants.

"The detention occasioned by the temporary loss of our fellow traveller; and the journey to court delayed our arrival here [Bandar-e Anzali] 10 days beyond the time expected. We

---

pit, and then pull up by the roots a weed of remarkably strong fibres, which overran the greater art of an adjacent tract of meadow ground.—Notwithstanding this insupportable degree of labour, the barbarian had not the humanity to give him any other food than bread and some milk diluted with water.—On the third day however he was liberated from this dreadful state of slavery by the gallantry of the chief driver of the caravan, who generously volunteered to go in search of him. Even after the Major was discovered by this brave and honest fellow, there was some difficulty in effecting his release; and nothing but the determined spirit of the driver, who threatened the ruffian with the immediate vengeance of the whole caravan, could have prevailed.—The feelings of Major O'Neil may be easily conceived.—He had little hopes of ever being discovered, the village being situated in a retired part of the mountains.—The night preceding his delivery he received a private hint that it was in contemplation to cut his throat unless he instantly make his escape.—This however, we are rather inclined to think was an indirect method of attempting to get rid of him; as the fellow who kidnapped him might have been alarmed by the inquiries making after his victim.'

[235] Cf. Page (2009: 70.4), 'A few days into their detour Macquarie was happy to find that Fath Ali Shah was making "an annual Summer Progress through his very extensive Dominions", and thus they would not have to travel all the way to Tehran (10 June 1807). Macquarie did not meet the Shah, but was greeted with "great kindness and politeness" by his ministers.'

[236] Fath 'Ali Shah.

[237] Mirza Shafi'-e Mazandarani.

[238] George III.

embark in a day or two upon the Caspian to proceed to Astracan—from thence we go post to Petersburgh, and still hope to reach England in September.'"[239]

9.86 'From our Correspondent,' *New-York Evening Post* (Tuesday, 10 May 1808) and 'Foreign Intelligence,' *The Expositor* (Wednesday, 25 May 1808): 'An article under the head of Petersburgh, 20th of February, mentions that several regiments of the army in Moldavia, have received orders to proceed to the Caspian sea, where the Russian army is to embark, in order to go through Persia for Hindostan; and that they have begun their march for this destination.

General Gardanne, the French Minister, arrived with his suite, at Teheren, in Persia, on the 4th of December, and was pompously received by its sovereign,[240] who lavished upon them the insignia of the order of the Sun.'[241]

9.87 'Intelligence. Constantinople, March 6,' *The Expositor* (Wednesday, 29 June 1808): 'A suspension of hostiities for the space of two months has been agreed upon between the Sublime Porte and Russia, for the purpose of negociating a treaty of peace.[242] Many difficulties will, no doubt be removed, indeed the principal points are already settled. Much, it is said, has been effected by the interference of the French Ambassador at our

---

[239] The author of this letter is not identified but as both Macquarie and O'Neil are mentioned in the narration, it must have been either Thomas or Brande.

[240] Fath 'Ali Shah.

[241] Gardane (1809a: 53) describes how, on 22 December 1807, 'nous parvenons au pavillon du Roi. Le Grand-Visit nous conduit l'un après l'autre au pied de son trône. Le Prince de la manière la plus gracieuse a donné aux Secrétaires de la Légation et aux Officiers l'ordre du Soleil. L'Ambassadeur avait reçu la veille le grand Ordre, dont la devise en lettres persannes dit: *Que le Roi élève l'Ambassadeur de poisson à la lune. Sur la croix ordinaire, on lit en vers persans: Marque de bienveillance d'un Prince qui chérit ses amis. Feth-Ali-Chah, Souverain, qui dissipe ses ennemis et les anéantit.*' For the Order of the Lion and Sun (*nešan-e šir o koršid*) see Wright (1981), Šahidi (1994).

[242] The dateline of the article is Constantinople, 6 March 1808. As Driault (1900/1901: 141) noted, 'Les hostilités entre les Persans et les Russes, d'ailleurs interrompues de fait depuis de longs mois, cessèrent officiellement au mois de Février 1808. Ce fut le premier résultat du traité de Finkenstein et de la mission de Gardane.' General Ivan Vasilyevich Gudovich (1741–1820) defeated the Ottoman forces near Gyumri, on the right bank of the Arpaçay river, on 18 June, whereupon he 'was rewarded with the rank of field-marshal, and such was the effect of the victory that the Shah, though nominally still at war with Russia, made haste to congratulate him. The ensuing negotiations for peace, however, took so unsatisfactory a course, in spite of the friendly efforts of Napoleon's envoy at the Persian Court, General Gardanne, that Goudóvitch in September 1808 made an attempt on Eriván.' See Baddeley (1908: 77). According to Driault (1900/1901: 145–146), 'Le 2 octobre, Goudowitch lève son camp et se transporte à Pembek. Le 3, il est à Anamlou, le 4 à Ortnan sur la frontière. Le 10, il établit ses troupes aux Trois-Églises [Echmiadzin], à trois lieues et en vue d'Érivan; il prépare l'attaque de la place.' Brosset (1857: 290), however, wrote that Gudovich's campaign to take Erivan began on 5 November.

[Turkish] Court.²⁴³ The influence of this ambassador is so great that he has obtained permission for a French army to march through the Turkish empire to Persia on its route to India.'²⁴⁴

9.88 'Foreign Intelligence. London August 15-16. Bombay, Feb. 21, 1808,' *Public Intelligencer* (Tuesday, 18 October, 1808) and 'East-Indies. Bombay, Feb. 21,' *Connecticut Gazette* (Wednesday, 19 October, 1808): 'It is said that the king of Persia²⁴⁵ has ceded Omus and Gombroon to the French, and that a squadroon which left this [Bombay] the other day, consisting of the Albion, 74, two frigates, Royal George, Mornington, and Ternate, are gone to intercept the French armament gone to take possession.²⁴⁶ We also hear of a French General,²⁴⁷ and 300 partizans, of all descriptions being arrived at Teheran, in Persia, with a view of getting on to India.'

9.89 'French Embassy to Persia,' *The Democrat* (Wednesday, 5 April, 1809), 'Foreign News. From London Papers. French Embassy to Persia,' *Spooner's Vermont Journal* (Monday, 17 April, 1809), 'Persia. Curious anecdotes from the late travels of M. Gardane in Persia,' *National Intelligencer & Washington Advertiser* (Friday, 5 May,

---

²⁴³ General Horace François Bastien Sébastiani de la Porta (1771–1851). His role at this time is extensively discussed in Delrieu (1854).

²⁴⁴ As Rawlinson (1849: 15) noted, 'It is . . . known that Sebastiani endeavoured to obtain permission from the Porte, that the French troops destined for the expedition should pass by Constantinople, and we have little doubt that Gardanne's principal instructions in his Persian Embassy referred to the same subject; but it is also notorious, that in spite of Mirza Reza's engagements, the project from the commencement found no favor with the Persian monarch, and that a very short experience of the Persian character and of the state of the relations of the Court with Russia, sufficed to convince Gardanne, not only of the impossibility of a tripartie alliance [France, Russia, Persia], but of the extreme difficulty of persuading the Shah to admit the presence in Persia of an auxiliary army of any European nation whatever.'

²⁴⁵ Fath 'Ali Shah.

²⁴⁶ As Ingram (1984: 123–124) noted, early in 1808, the British government in India 'were warned by the captain of an American merchantman, who had been given the information by the captain of a French privateer, later captured, that a French squadron of two ships of the line and up to six frigates had broken out of Rochefort [on the Atlantic coast of France] the previous June. If the information were true, the enemy might shortly be expedted in the Persian Gulf, either at Bandar Abbas or at a port higher up, like Bushire . . . Without waiting for new instructions from the governor-general . . . Captain Ferrier . . . had already taken steps to blockade the strait of Hormuz. He was urged on by the governor of Bombay, whom the news from the Middle East had thrown into a panic . . . At Bombay, Ferrier could make up a squadron of the *Albion*, HCS *Royal George* (36), which was an armed Indiaman, four frigates—*Fox, Pitt, Phaeton* (38), and *Dedaigneuse* (36)—and two Bombay Marine cruisers, *Mornington* and *Ternate*, which mounted 14 guns apiece. He also summoned HMS *Russell* (74) and the frigate San Fiorenzo (36) from the bay of Bengal. Then, on 4 February 1808, Ferrier sailed for Bandar Abbas.'

²⁴⁷ Gardane.

1809; from 'The politeness of the Persians' onward), 'Persia. Curious anecdotes from the late travels of M. Gardane in Persia,' *Farmer's Repository* (Friday, 12 May, 1809), 'Persia. Curious anecdotes from the late travels of M. Gardane in Persia,' *Boston Patriot* (Wednesday, 17 May, 1809), 'Persia. Curious anecdotes from the late travels of M. Gardane in Persia,' *The Bristol County Register* (Saturday, 20 May, 1809), 'Persia. Curious anecdotes from the late travels of M. Gardane in Persia,' *Vermont Republican* (Monday, 29 May, 1809), 'Persia. Curious anecdotes from the late travels of M. Gardane in Persia,' *Alexandria Daily Gazette. Commercial & Political* (Friday, 2 June, 1809), 'Persia. Curious anecdotes from the travels of the late M. Gardane in Persia,' *Boston Mirror* (Saturday, 3 June, 1809), 'Persia. Curious anecdotes from the late travels of M. Gardane in Persia,' *Salem Gazette* (Tuesday, 13 June, 1809), 'Persia. Curious anecdotes from the late travels of M. Gardane in Persia,' *Connecticut Herald* (Tuesday, 27 June, 1809), 'Persia. Curious anecdotes from the late travels of M. Gardane in Persia,' *New-York Weekly Museum* (Saturday, 8 July, 1809), 'Persia. Curious anecdotes from the late travels of M. Gardane in Persia,' *National Aegis* (Wednesday, 12 July, 1809), 'Politeness,' *The Eastern Argus* (Monday, 17 July, 1809; only the paragraph beginning 'The politeness'), 'Customs of the Persians,' *The Fredonian* (Tuesday, 17 April, 1810), 'Customs of the Persians,' *Concord Gazette* (Tuesday, 1 May, 1810), 'Customs of the Persians,' *The Berkshire Reporter* (Wednesday, 9 May, 1810), 'Customs of the Persians,' *Windham Herald* (Friday, 26 July, 1811), 'Persia. Curious anecdotes from the travels of M. Gardanne in Persia,' *Salem Gazette* (Tuesday, 14 February, 1826; last four paragraphs only), 'Curious anecdotes from the travels of M. Gardanne in Persia,' *Connecticut Herald* (Tuesday, 21 February, 1826) and 'Persia. Curious anecdotes from the travels of M. Gardanne in Persia,' *Georgetown Gazette* (Tuesday, 7 March, 1826): 'It is a matter of public notoriety, that two years ago the French gen. Gardane was sent on a mission to the Persian monarch,[248] avowedly with the intention of procuring his co-operation in a plan of attack upon our East India possessions. An octavo volume has just been published at Paris, giving on [sic] account of the progress of that embassy. It is entitled, *Travels in Turkey, Asia, and Persia, in the years 1807 and 1808; by M. Ange de Gardane, First Secretary of Legation.*[249] The following interesting observations on this work are extracted from one of the minor French papers:

---

[248] Fath 'Ali Shah.

[249] Referring to Gardane (1809a). No English translation by this title ever appeared. As Schwab (1876: 32) noted, 'Ce court Journal ne porte pas de nom d'auteur; mais il est évident, d'après l'avant-propos et les préliminaires, qu'il est de M. Ange de Gardane, attaché à la légation et frère de l'ambassadeur, et non, comme on l'a cru, du général Gardane lui-même.' The German translation, Gardane (1809b), bears Ange de Gardane's name on the titlepage. Debidour (1887: 314) wrote of Ange de Gardane, 'Né à Marseille le 2 mars 1765, mort dans la même ville le 8 janvier 1822. Il revint de Perse avant le général.' Jules Verne noted, 'Son frère, Ange de Gardane, qui lui avait servi de secrétaire, rapportait une assez courte relation du voyage—ouvrage qui contient quelques détails curieux sur les antiquités de la Perse, mais que devaient de beaucoup dépasser les ouvrages publiées

Travels written in the form of an itinerary are of great utility, in a geographical point of view, when the distances are given in a positive manner, and without any chasm. It is by a comparison of modern itineraries, with those which the ancient have left us that we discover the position of the places, an acquaintance with which is indisputably necessary for understanding history. It is a species of utility which even vulgar minds allow to comparative geography; but to philosophers, who are worthy of appreciating that science, it is in itself an interesting spectacle again called fourth [sic] into existence, upon a geographical map, those kingdoms, and those republics, whose annals we have learned by heart, whose legislators and heroes we admire, but with whose extent, physical resources, commerce, and revenues, history makes us but imperfectly acquainted. To confine ourselves to the countries of which M. Gardane treats, is it not much more interesting to know what means the nature of cirtain [sic] situations afforded the great Mithridates to resist, for so long a time, the conquerers of the world, than the precise date of all the battles which he fought with the Romans? Who could pretend to write the history of the wars between the Parthians and Romans, without having previously studied the physical geography of the tremendous mountains of Curdistan, where so many Romans, from Anthony to the Emperor Julian, were foiled in their attempts, and tarnished their glory?

Though much has been done to elucidate the geography of that part of the Asiatic Continent, through which M Gardane conducts his readers, still we think it not at all unlikely that the itineraries through ancient Phrygia which he has given, will induce geographers to alter some positions; but a discussion of this point would lead us into greater lengths than our limits will admit. We shall, therefore, merely point out to men of science, this merit in the itinerary of M. Gardane; but we think it our duty to direct the attention of the public in general to another kind of interest, which distinguishes the account of this traveller. We allude to those hasty sketches in which he delineates the manners and present state of the east.

The Persons composing the French embassy, paid a visit to the Pacha of Nicomecia [sic, Nicomedia]. The first objects that struck their view, were the dead bodies of two persons, one of whom had been hanged and the other beheaded, extended at the threshold of the door.[250] They reach Erzerum, the residence of the celebrated Jussuff Pacha; and here the

---

par les Anglais.' See Verne (1880: 61). The Gardane brothers belonged to a family that had occupied French diplomatic posts since the early seventeenth century and included Louis de Gardane, consul at Sidon (1611); his nephew Louis, consul at Marseille (1660); Ange de Gardane, grandson of Louis, consul general in Persia (1715); Ange-Nicolas, nephew of Ange, consul on Cyprus (1748) and at Tripoli (1755); Ange-Paul-Louis, son of Ange-Nicolas, secretary of General Gardane (1807) and his brother General Gardane (1807). See de Ribbe (1879: 191).

[250] In his journal, Gardane (1809a: 5) wrote, 'Visite au Pacha: un pendu et un décapité étendus sur le seuil de sa porte.' Cf. Tancoigne (1820: 6–7) who noted, 'A bin-bachi, or colonel of the Nizami Djedid, new troops trained in the European mode, came this morning to conduct us to the Pacha, who had taken the precaution of ordering the dead bodies of a man that was hanged, and another beheaded, which had been exposed in front of his palace, to be removed previous to the General's visit.'

ambassadors of France and Persia are presented with horses, covered with gold and pearls, to make their entry into that city.[251] Here they fell in with a horde of Curds, who attempt to plunder the caravan; there shepherds, worthy of ancient Arcadia, guide in the night track some of our travellers, who had lost their way. In the center of Asia Minor, Chapan Oglou[252] raised enormous contributions in his own name, and gives himself out to the inhabitants as their sovereign, while they dare neither to punish nor even to find fault with him. At Bagdad, the Pecha [sic] Soliman[253] respectfully receives the horse tails sent him by the Porte; but for a 120 years his ancestors and himself have held the same government from which the orders of the Grand Signior have not been able to remove them; or, in other words these Pachas are hereditary monarchs, who out of politeness, transmit intelligence to the Porte, of their accession to the throne. In short Turkey in Asia is in a state of anarchy, which predicts the same fate to the Ottoman empire as formerly befel that of the Chalifs. The conditions of the people differs [sic] according to the character of the Pachas; and the happiest provinces are those in which those Satraps have possessed themselves of hereditary power. But amidst the barbarism which pervades this portion of the world, may still be perceived some brilliant traces of ancient civilization. The people appear highly susceptible of a good legislation, and wherever any order or tranquility prevail, the inhabitants manifest an honest and hospitable disposition.

Persia exhibits a very different spectacle. It is now an empire regularly organized, and infinitely more civilized than Turkey. The court is magnificent; gold and diamonds glitter on the garments of those who compose it; you walk on nothing but carpets covered with embroidery in gold, or on some super Mossaic [sic] pavements; costly perfumes are kept burning in vessels of precious stone; the apartments are cooled by fountains of limpid water, which fall into basons [sic] of marble and porphyry. The people, who are extremely submissive, are engaged in useful works, pay their taxes, and supply the army with recruits. M. Gardane only observes, that the Persians are very slow, even in the most trivial affairs; that they pay no kind of respect to women; that in the audiences given by the Grand Vizer of Persia,[254] the nobles themselves remain on their knees at the threshold of the floor;

---

[251] On their arrival at Erzurum, Gardane's group was met by 'une escorte de 25 cavaliers commandés par un Officier qui présente, de la part d'Issouf-Pacha, aux Ambassadeurs de France et de Perse un cheval couvert d'une housse brodée en or et en perles, pour faire leur entré dans la ville.' See Gardane (1809a, b: 21).

[252] Émïn (1792: 153) called 'Chapan Oglu, a head of banditti, and a great robber.' Cf. Moltke (1854: 242), 'Tschapan-oglu (the Son of the Tiger), sprung from one of the noblest Asiatic families.' In fact the Chapanoğlu were a family. As Iorga (1908: 226) noted, 'In Kleinasien waren die stärksten Vertreter des Unabhänigkeitssinnes … die Kara-Osman-Oglus und Tschapan-Oglus, die … ausgedehnte Ländereien … besassen … Auf der Insel Slobozia wurde Ende 1811 auch Tschapan-Oglu … gefangengenommen und nach Rußland geschickt.' The headquarters of Chapanoglu were at Yozgat. See Hasluck and Hasluck (1929: 596).

[253] Solayman Küçük, 'Little Solayman,' appointed Pasha of Baghdad in the spring of 1808. See Longrigg (1925: 224).

[254] Mirza Shafi'-e Mazandarani. Cf. 9.4.

that mutilated carcases may be seen lying before the royal palace,[255] as in Turkey; that the officers of the army cannot read; in a word, that he found in the Persians, Orientals and not Europeans.—For the rest, says he, the difference of characters and manners does not prevent the Persians and French from entertaining reciprocal love and esteem for each other, and uniting their political interests. The name of Emperor, (Bonaparte) is there held in the highest veneration; the portraits and medallions of Napoleon appear to the Asiatics presents of inestimable value. The monarch of Teheran is so anxious to receive news from France, that he heard of the battle of Austerlitz, on the 45th day after it was fought.[256]

The politeness of the Persians is of a species perfectly Oriental. A nobleman, of high rank, went one day to the French Ambassador's, "to beg his pardon because the weather was bad in Persia."[257]

The diplomatic conferences at Teheran, are held in the same manner as in our dramatic exhibitions, with the doors open, and in the presence of a multitude of auditors. The Orientals cannot conceive the necessity of secrecy in conventions between states.

The women are kept as much enslaved in Persia,[258] as in the rest of the East. A Frenchman belonging to the suit [sic] of the ambassador, one day excited a great uproar at Teheran, for having ventured to cast some inquisitive looks at the garden of a seraglio. At the sight of a man, the women uttered screams of affright; some of them even snatched up arms, and prepared to repel ogles with musket balls.

M. Gardane one day asked a Persian nobleman how many children he had? "I don't know," said he, "enquire of my secretary." The secretary turned to his list, and answered, that his master had seventeen children.'[259]

9.90 'London. April 27,' *Federal Gazette & Baltimore Daily Advertiser* (Wednesday, 14 June, 1809): 'Substance of the Treaty of Commerce between the Courts of France and Persia, signed in January 1809.[260]

---

[255] As Gardane (1809a: 52) noted, 'Quatre cadavres dont on avait coupé la tête, sont étendus devant la porte du palais du Roi. Chaque passant ne manque pas de donner un coup de pied à ces têtes.'

[256] The Battle of Austerlitz took place on 2 December 1805.

[257] 'Neuf heurs trois quarts de Zing-hian [Zanjan] à Sultanié: 80 maisons. Vent très-froid. Un persan vient demander pardon à l'Ambassadeur de ce qu'il fait si mauvais temps.' See Gardane (1809a: 43).

[258] 'Chez eux une femme n'est qu'une esclave.' See Gardane (1809a: 57–58).

[259] Gardane (1809a: 36), 'Nous demandons à un grand Seigneur le nombre de ses enfans: il répond naïvement qu'il n'en sait rien, se tourne du côté de son Secrétaire et le lui demande; celui-ci répond: dix-sept.' This occurred at Tabriz while Gardane was a guest of 'Abbas Mirza.

[260] The 'Traité de commerce conclu entre les Cours de France et de Perse. En date du mois de Janvier 1808' was in fact signed a year earlier than stated here, i.e. prior to Gardane's departure from Tehran. For the text see Martens (1839: 132–140). The treaty consists of 23 articles, not all of which are referred to in this presentation, although the paragraphing does relate to the discrete articles of the treaty. Gardane was roundly criticized for his efforts. In a letter of 2 November 1808 Champagny 'reproche à Gardane d'avoir signé un traité de commerce sans instructions suffisantes; son projet d'ailleurs est moins avantageux que les traités de 1708 et de 1715.' See Driault (1900/1901: 145). For

When French merchants, or other French subjects, arrive either in the harbors or on the frontiers of Persia, no violence shall be offered them by the governors or magistrates of the country, who shall, on the contrary send them help and assistance in time of need.[261]

If the French consul general proposes to fix his residence at Ispaham, crown land [...?] for him that he may build a house upon it. The same with regard to other French merchants who may be likewise inclined: when they wish to remove, the authority of the country shall take care of their property, and restore the same to them the moment they claim it.[262]

The French ambassadors shall be treated with all honors due to the first of christian monarchs; & the consuls, envoys, & French merchants, shall take precedence above those of all other nations.[263]

When French merchants export or import merchandize, they shall pay duty according to a fair valuation of the goods, at the time being, and be allowed to pay the same either in specie or commodity.[264]

No duty shall be levied on servants of French merchants settled in Persia, either French, Americans [sic, Armenians], or Indians, until they amount to twenty; nor shall any duty be exacted on their Drogomans, or interpreters of the country.[265]

---

the full texts of the commercial treaties of 1708 and 1715 see Hauterive and de Cussy (1844: 376–410). As Delrieu 1854: 218 observed, 'Il faut dire que le général avait conclu son traité de commerce sans le soumettre préalablement à l'approbation du ministre; un attaché de la légation, M. Ange de Gardane, était parti, dès la fin de janvier 1808, pour le porter à Napoléon.'

[261] Article 1, beginning, 'Lorsque des négocians et autres personnes de la nation française arriveront, soit par mer, soit par terre, dan les ports ou sur les frontières de l'Empire de Perse, les Beyler-Beys, juges et gouverneurs de toute province...ne leur feront ni violence ni chicane.' See Martens (1839: 133).

[262] Article 2, beginning, 'Si le Consul général du commerce français qui arrivera en Perse, veut se domicilier à Ispahan, on lui donnera à louage un terrain, propriété de la Couronne de Perse, afin qu'il y construise une maison pour sa demeure.' See Martens (1839: 133).

[263] Article 3 in its entirety, 'Comme l'Empereur de France est devenue le vainqueur et le chef de tous les Monarques de la religion de Jésus, conformément au respect que lui portent ces Rois, si un Ambassadeur de France vient en Perse, l'on s'acquittera envers lui, avec la dernière exactitude, des tributs d'honneurs, d'égards et d'amitié que son caractère commande, et l'on donnera le pas aux Consuls, Envoyés et négocians français, sur les Consuls, Envoyés et négocians des nations étrangères.' See Martens (1839: 134).

[264] Article 5 in its entirety, 'Si des négocians français apportent des marchandises en Perse ou qu'ils en emportent de ce pays, on prendra le paiement de la douane d'après le juste prix que lesdites marchandises seront estimées vaoir à cette époque, et les Français auront le choix de payer cette douane soit en argent, soit en nature.' See Martens (1839: 134).

[265] Article 6, beginning, 'On n'exigera pas des Français qui seront en Perse, négocians...d'impositions relativement aux domestiques, jusqu'à la concurrence de vingt, soit Français, soit Arméniens, soit Indiens d'origine; l'on n'en demandera pas non plus des dragomans, c'est-à-dire des interprètes indigènes.' See Martens (1839: 134).

Governors shall give assistance to ships that may be wrecked, and cause the expence to be paid them accordingly; but they shall not, under any pretence, retain any articles belonging to the ship they may happen to have saved from the sea.[266]

During the space of 3 years from the date of the treaty, Frenchmen shall pay no duty (Custom-house.) The same with respect to Persian merchants in France.[267]

French merchants shall only once pay duty in Persia, for whatever merchandize they may import or export. The rate is three per cent. Persian gentlemen shall enjoy the same priviledge in France. Goods imported or exported by the way of Bagdad, to pay duty as at Ispahan.[268]

Consuls shall be permitted to build a church contiguous to their residence, and to display the French colours on the tops of their houses—at sea ports only.[269]

In case a French merchant should experience a reverse of fortune without having given security to any body, no other Frenchman shall be called upon to discharge his debts, but in the case of security being given, the same shall be executed.[270]

When agreements are entered into between French, Persians, and merchants of other countries, respecting partnership and insurances, such agreement must be submitted to the judge of the country, or to the French consul, and a copy of the same to be lodged with the latter, that it may be resorted to according to circumstances.[271]

---

[266] Article 7, beginning, 'Si des vaisseaux et bâtimens français, battus par la tempête, viennent à échouer, les gouverneurs des côtes leur porteront secours ... le gouverneur de la côte se fera rembourser de toutes les dépenses qu'il aura faites; mais quant aux effets du vaisseau que l'on aurait sauvés de la mer, et qui seraient tombés entre les mains de ceux qui auraient contribué à porter secours, on les restituera à qui de droit, en s'abstenant de tout sentiment de cupidité.' See Martens (1839: 134–135).

[267] Article 8, beginning, 'Pendant l'space [sic] de trois ans, à dater de l'époque où ce Traité a été conclu, les négocians français ne paieront point de douanes en Perse; même condition pour les négocians Persans en France.' See Martens (1839: 135).

[268] Article 9, beginning, 'Les négocians français ne paieront qu'une fois en Perse la douane d'une marchandise, soit qu'ils l'apportent, soit qu'ils l'exportent: le tarif est de trois pour cent. Les négocians persans en France jouiront du même privilège. Toute marchandise qui sera exportée ou importée par la voie de Bagdad, devra payer la douane à Ispahan.' See Martens (1839: 135).

[269] Article 10 in its entirety, 'Dans tout endroit que résidera un Consul, il lui sera permis de construire une église attenant à sa maison; si c'est dans un port, il pourra arborer le pavillon sur le toit de sa demeure; personne autre que le Consul ne pourra l'arborer, et il ne sera pas permis de le faire flotter en d'autres lieux que les ports.' See Martens (1839: 135).

[270] Article 12, beginning, 'Si un négociant français en Perse vient à éprouver des revers et à se trouver sans ressources, et qu'il n'ait donné de caution à personne, l'on ne pourra attaquer d'autres Français ni exiger d'eux la dette du Français ... Mais si ce négociant français a donné caution, il faudra que la caution s'exécute.' See Martens (1839: 136).

[271] Article 13, beginning, 'Si des conventions concernant le commerce, l'association et les assurances, se concluent entre des négocians français, persans et d'autres nations, il faudra que le contrat en soit passé à la connaissance du juge du pays et à celle du Consul français, et qu'une copie du contrat reste entre les mains du Consul et entre celles du juge, afin que, dans l'occasion, elle puisse servir

When a French slave shall fall into the hands of Persian subjects, and not having become a mussulman, signifies to the French consul that he demands his protection, no opposition shall be made to his being given up on paying for his ransom the sum that he had cost originally.[272]

With respect to the effects and goods belonging to Persian subjects embarked at the Persian ports on board of Turkish ships, market vessels bound to the Indies or elsewhere or loaded with India commodities for the return if during their double voyage the French vessels should have any difference with the above mentioned countries, & that their vessels should fall into their power, and that there should be found on board merchandize, the whole of their goods and effects shall be restored.[273]

It have been agreed upon between the agents of the Court of France and that of Persia, that the Island of Bareck [sic, Khark] shall be given to the former, there to establish a factory, immediately after the evacuation of Georgia and all other Persian Provinces by the Russians.[274]

If French merchants happen to be pillaged by robbers, Governors shall make inquires [sic], so as to seize the banditti, and restore the goods to the owners, who shall have to recompence the trouble to that effect.[275]

---

d'autorité.' See Martens (1839: 136). Note that the English version would have a copy of the contract lodged with the Persian judge or the French Consul, whereas the treaty clear stipulates that each shall receive and retain a copy, not merely the French Consul.

[272] Article 14, beginning, 'Si un esclave français tombe entre les mains des Persans, qu'il ne soit pas fait musulman, et qu'il prévienne le Consul français qu'il ... veut venir auprès de lui ... on ne s'y opposera pas, on rendra l'esclave, et on ne demandera pour sa rançon que ce qu'il a coûté d'achat.' See Martens (1839: 137).

[273] Article 16, beginning, 'Qu8\cr1ant aux effets et marchandises appartenant à des Persans, qui seraient embarqués dans les ports de Perse, sur des bâtimens turcs, maskatins, et destinés pour les Indes et autres contrées, ou bien chargés de l'Inde pour le retour, si pendant le double voyage, des vaisseaux français étaient en mésintelligence avec les nations susdites, et que ces navires tombassent en leur pouvoir et qu'on y trouvât des marchandises apparenant à des Persans, l'on restituera ces biens et effets en leur totalite.' See Martens (1839: 138). Note that the translator has misunderstood 'maskatins,' i.e. (vessels) of Muscat [Omani], and written 'market vessels.'

[274] Article 17, beginning, 'Les Agens de la Cour de France ayant manifesté le desir que la Cour de Perse leur fit dotation de l'île de Kharek, qui est une des îles de la dépendance des ports du Farsistan, afin qu'ils y puissent établir des comptoirs, il a été arrêté qu'après l'évacuation de la Géorgie et de toutes les provinces persanes par les Russes.' Martens (1839: 139).

[275] Article 20, beginning, 'Les juges et gouverneurs montreront la plus grande amitié aux Français qui viendront en Perse; et quand, en route, des valeurs se seront emparés de leurs biens, ils feront toutes les perquisitions en leur pouvoir, pour se saisir des brigands et des effets volés et les rendront à leurs propriétaires. Les gouverneurs ayant donné leurs soins pour retrouver les objets perdus, lesdits marchands ne défraieront pas ceux qui auront été à la recherche de ces effets, ni pour leurs dépenses, ni pour autre chose, si ces biens n'ont pas été retrouvés.' Martens (1839: 140).

When a French merchant fails, the remainder of his property shall be divided amongst his creditors, according to their respective and individual claims.'[276]

9.91 'Foreign Intelligence. Persia,' *The Pilot* (Wednesday, 28 June 1809): 'It is confidently said, that the embassy of Capt. Malcolm to the Perssan [sic, Persian] Court,[277] has been crowned with complete success.[278] A treaty of amity and friendship, it is asserted, has

---

[276] Article 22 in its entirety, 'Si des marchands français avaient, en Perse, des réclamations sur un individu, et si cet individu restait, après sa banqueroute, sans aucune ressource, on partagera ce que possède encore ce débiteur entre ses créanciers, conformément à leurs justes prétentions particulières.' Martens (1839: 140).

[277] Malcolm's second mission, by which time he was a Lieutenant-Colonel, although he 'received the rank of a Brigadier General before his departure for Persia.' See Minto with Kynynmound (1980: 126, n. 1). As Philippart (1823: 479–480) wrote, 'Intelligence of the French design of invading India through Persia, and that the invaders would probably be supported in it by the Turkish ad Persian states, reached the Gov.-Gen., Lord Minto, late in 1807; in consequence of which, his lordship appointed Lieut.-Col. M. [Malcolm] to be the Gov.-Gen.'s political agent, and to be vested with plenipotentiary powers in Persia, the Persian Gulph, and in Turkish Arabia. By this appointment, the powers of separate political agency possessed by the Residents at Bagdad, Bussorah, and Bushire, were suspended, and Lieut.-Col. M. was authorized, any time when he might judge it to be expedient for the benefit of the public service, to take upon himself the powers of Resident at any of those stations. He was also, in additions to his powers as political agent, furnished with credentials as envoy or ambassador to the court of Persia, and to the Pacha of Bagdad, in the event of his finding it practicable or expedient, to repair in person to either or both of those courts ... Lieut-Col. M., on the 17th April 1808, quitted Bombay for the Persian Gulf.'

[278] Quite the opposite is true. In fact, as is well-known, Malcolm's second mission from the Government of India crossed with Sir Harford Jones' deputation from the Crown, who was sent to Iran, in the words of Rawlinson (1849: 16), 'in October 1807, with ... full powers to conclude a direct treaty between the Shah of Persia and the King of England ... General Malcolm, who was allowed the initiative in this singular diplomatic combat, had no sooner arrived in the Persian Gulf in May, 1808, than, agreeably to his instructions, he opened trenches against the French position at Teheran. But Gardanne was then basking in the full sunshine of Court favor: he had given something, promised much, and led the Shah to hope for more; he was pleading earnestly to Russia for forbearance: his engineers were constructing fortifications: his officers were diplining the Persian troops: and, although the British Envoy resorted freely to his old strategy of a golden influence, and fairly offered to buy the French out of Persia, he found it impossible to make any way. A discomfiture, so signal and so unexpected, seems to have obscured the General's judgment, as much as it shocked his vanity. Without considering the causes of his failure, or duly weighing its probable effects, or even seizing upon an eligible remedy, he indignantly quitted the shores of Persia, "breathing reproach, defiance and invasion."' As Marshman (1893: 294–195) observed, 'On reaching Persia Colonel Malcolm, overlooking the paramount influence the French minister had acquired at the Court, assumed a dictatorial tone, and was forbidden to advance farther than Sheraz, where he was desired to place himself in communication with the king's son. Colonel Malcolm took umbrage at this proceeding, abandoned the mission, and, returning to the coast embarked with his suite for Calcutta.'

been concluded between the King of Persia[279] and our Indian government.[280] Should this prove true, one of the routs [sic, routes] to India, at least, is shut against Napoleon.'

9.92 'Summary of Foreign Reports,' *Thomas's Massachusetts Spy, or Worcester Gazette* (Wednesday, 28 June, 1809): 'The French Ambassador, in Persia, Gardanne, has tried by all possible means, solicitations, arguments, threatenings, &c. to get possession of the island of Ormus.[281] The Persians seem to have been suspicious of the Great Napolean, and the British government at Hindostan has had influence enough to circumvent the schemes

---

[279] Fath 'Ali Shah.

[280] This is completely incorrect. Gardane's presence in Teheran had prompted the British government to send Sir Harford Jones to counter French influence. But by the end of his stay, Gardane and Napoleon were no longer in high favor, and Fath 'Ali Shah was exasperated at the lack of French support for his interests in the Caucasus, specifically the reclamation of Georgia. Gardane left Tehran just before Harford Jones arrived and, as McNeill (1836: 62) put it, 'the inability of the French ambassador to perform the promises his master had made, secured to this mission [Jones'] a favourable reception.' Harford Jones and Mirza Shafi' negotiated a new treaty which was signed on 12 March 1809. For the text, see Aitchison (1892: 45–48). Malcolm finally caught up with Fath 'Ali Shah at his camp near Soltaniya on 23 June 1810 when he presented him with several pieces of artillery and several army officers to go with them, as a contribution to the war effort against the Russians. Malcolm then departed on 23 July and returned to India, but no additional treaty was signed. See Markham (1874: 375). As Kaye (1869a: 268) noted in his biography of Malcolm, 'The Company's [EIC] Government, in the person of their representative, were sufficiently lustrated; but as the management of our Persian relations was thenceforth intrusted to the King's Ministers, this was not of much importance.' For Harford Jones' account of his embassy, see Brydges (1834). Sir Harford Jones [on 4 May 1826 he adopted the name Brydges] (1764–1847) had previously served as Joint East India Company Factor at Basra and was a gifted linguist (for his very interesting correspondence with Sir William Jones see Franklin 2005). He was envoy at the Persian court 1807–1811.

[281] According to the commercial treaty (Art. 17) negotiated by Gardane, Khark was meant to become the site of a French trading station as soon as the French had assisted the Persians in reclaiming Georgia and all other formerly Persian provinces in the Caucasus from the Russians. See Martens (1839: 139), Hauterive and de Cussy (1844: 420). In addition, rumors concerning Hormuz and Qeshm abounded. Thus Anonymous (1809b) wrote, 'Dispatches from Governor Duncan at Bombay, dated the 30th October [1808], and 4th November [1808] last, state his apprehensions that Gen. Gardanne had induced, or would prevail on the King of Persia to cede to France, more than one important port or island in the Persian Gulph. It was not known with certainty what places were the objects of negotiation; but no doubt was entertained that the islands of Ormus and Kishmi were among the number.' It is also true that while Gardane was in Tehran, General Decaen ordered Commander Pierre Bouvet de Maisonneuve to transport a courier from Île de France to Hormuz or Bandar 'Abbas with dispatches for him. As Bouvet (1865: 40) wrote, 'Informé du séjour du général Gardanne près la cour de Perse, le général Decaen voulut correspondre avec ce diplomate, et me donna pour mission spéciale de transporter à Ormus ou Bender-Abassy un émissaire chargé de ses dépêches pour l'ambassadeur français à la cour de Téhéran.' Bouvet de Maisonneuve set sail on 4 October 1808 and, before heading to Muscat with dispatches for the Imam of Muscat, as he wrote, 'je mis le cap sur Ormus, et, le lendemain au matin, j'expédiai le commissionaire du capitaine général, à bord d'un bateau pêcheur du pays.' See Bouvet (1865: 43).

of Gen. Gardanne, at the Persian Court,[282] and it is said has executed a treaty with Persia. Gardanne could not prevail on the Persian or Arabian princes[283] to shut their ports against the English.'

9.93 'Defeat of the Russian Army by the Persians,' *National Intelligencer & Washington Advertiser* (Friday, 17 November, 1809),' London, Sept. 26. Curious Document,' *Newburyport Herald* (Friday, 17 November, 1809), 'Defeat of the Russian Army by the Persians,' *American Citizen* (Tuesday, 21 November, 1809), 'London, Sept. 28. Curious Document,' *Federal Republican & Commercial Gazette* (Tuesday, 21 November, 1809), 'London, Sept. 26. Curious Document,' *Connecticut Journal* (Thursday, 23 November, 1809), 'London, Sept. 20. Curious Document,' *Independent American* (Thursday, 23 November, 1809). 'Defeat of the Russian Army by the Persions [sic],' *Republican Watch-Tower* (Friday, 24 November, 1809), 'Defeat of the Russian Army by the Persians,' *Virginia Argus* (Friday, 24 November, 1809), 'London, Sept. 26. Curious Document,' *Federal Gazette & Baltimore Daily Advertiser* (Saturday, 25 November, 1809) and 'London, Sept. 25. Curious Document,' *Windham Herald* (Friday, 8 December, 1809): 'A Persian newspaper, containing an account of some of the principal occurrences which immediately preceded the departure of the ship *Rahimshaw* from Bushire,[284] has within

---

[282] As Rawlinson (1849: 18–19) wrote of Gardane's mission, when Sir Harford Jones arrived at Bushehr in 1808, 'He found that General Gardanne had overplayed his game, that a "reactionary" tendency was setting in against the French. The idea therefore occurred to him to propose England, instead of France, as the power which should protect Persia against the great Northern Leviathan, and time and circumstances both favoured the substitution: for as the French, in their early efforts to undermine British influence at Teheran, had been careful to instil into the minds of the Shah's ministers, that the enemy of Russia could be the only natural ally of Persia, and as by force of iteration this doctrine had now come to be received almost as a maxim of international policy; so when Sir Harford revived the argument ("fas est et ab hoste doceri") he obtained a ready—almost an anxious—hearing; and when he further urged its practical application, he had the satisfaction of finding that not only did the precept recoil upon the French, but that the recoil was doubled in effect by experience having proved in the interim thefolly of trusting to the feeble powers of mediation and good offices in dealing with such an enemy as the inexorable Czar. So effective indeed was the "coup," that lttle more remained for diplomatic handling, and that little was accomplished by the Envoy's personal friendship with the Persian ministers, and by the "prestige" which he enjoyed as the direct representative of the British King. He advanced in a sort of ovation to the capital, General Gardanne retiring on his approach, and Monsieur Jouannin, the Secretary, who still clung with a leech-like tenacity to the court, being fairly eclipsed by the rising luminary. A "pourparler" then ensued, not less remarkable for its brevity than for the importance of the matters discussed; and in March, 1809, was concluded the Preliminary Treaty, which, in spite of much Procrustean manipulation sustained during an interval of 40 years, continues in force to the present day as the basis of our Persian alliance.'

[283] Principally the Imam of Muscat.

[284] As Bulley (2000: 53) noted, 'In 1803 *Rahimshaw*, snow [a brig-rigged vessel with a try-sail 'carried by a small mast set just abaft of the mainmast;' Robinson and Dow (1922: 30–31)], 275 tons, owned by Aga Mahomed Nebee [Mohammad Nabi Khan, Fath 'Ali Shah's second ambassador to the East India Company in India] on the death of Haji Kaleel [the first ambassador whose death is

these few days, been received by a respectable Arab merchant, at present resident in Calcutta. Among other matters, of less importance, it communicates the details of the conflict between the Persian and Russian armies in Georgia; which, as relating to an event of which no authentic account had previously been received, will, doubtless, be perused by our readers with considerable interest. We give them pretty nearly in the terms of the original:—

"By the ship Rahimshaw we have received an account of the victory lately obtained by the warriors of Iran over the armies of Russia. This event happened towards the latter end of the month of Ramazad, in the year 1223 of the Hijiree, corresponding with the middle of Nov. 1808, of the Christian Æra. The following are the particulars. A large Russian force, well appointed and accoutred, & powerfully supported by a formidable artillery, having marched from Teffleez, for the purpose of reducing the fortress of Prawn [sic, Erivan], intelligence of their movements was communicated to Mahomed Houssain Khan, Kujjar of Cosveen Begler Begee, the High in Dignity.[285] Immediately on the receipt of this information, that Chieftain assembled together such troops of the victorious army as he had in readiness, and proceeded, by rapid marches, to meet the Russians. As soon as the two armies came within sight of each other, the enemy opened a heavy fire from their artillery, which destroyed a portion of the Persian troops. Upon this Mahomed Houssain, Khan, the renowned for bravery, calling to mind the words of the proverb (which may be translated—"The better part of valour is discretion")—had recourse to the warfare of flight.[286] He thus

---

described above], the Company's Agent at Bushire was granted an English Pass and permitted to use English colours although "according to our regulations she be not entitled to either".' Anonymous (1807a) referred to 'the Rahimshah,' as a 'small merchant brig.' The *Rahimshaw* was lost at sea in 1815. See Phipps (1840: 142).

[285] Mohammad Hoseyn Khan Qajar, *beglerbeg* [governor] of Qazvin, on whom see Busse (1972: 108).

[286] This is a description of a failed operation that took place in conjunction with the eventually unsuccessful siege of Yerevan. According to Monteith (1856: 54–55), 'General Goudowitch detached a force under General Portnagene [Semen Andreyevich Portnyagin; see Brosset (1857: 295, n. 2), Mikaberidze (2005: 309); he had distinguished himself on 7 June 1804 in the unsuccessful siege of Erivan; see Baddeley (1908: 69)], to drive off the Persian covering force, encamped 25 miles off on the banks of the Arras, from whence they impeded his operations. The Russians made a forced night march; but the Persians appear to have had early intelligence of the proposed attack, for when General Portnagene reached the place, the camp had been struck, and the troops, which were almost all cavalry, were drawn up on the plain. The general attempted a charge of cavalry with his regiment of heavy dragoons, but was deceived by the apparent flight of the enemy, who quickly rallied and surrounded his troops, many of whom fell from the fire of their active opponents: it was exactly the manœuvre so often described in ancient history as the Parthian mode of fighting.' Brosset (1857: 290) presents a very different view of the campaign, writing, '1808, le 5 novembre, le comte Goudovitch se mit en campagne pour prendre Erivan, avec ses troupes et un corps de Géorgiens. Etant venu et ayant pris la ville, il se posta à Kanakir. La citadelle d'Erivan était alors bien défendue, par un sardar persan. En effet le chah, lors de sa venue, avait emmené à Téhéran Mahmad-Khan et sa famille, et l'avait retenu depuis lors, parce que c'était un homme à double language et peu soumis. Comme donc le chah

inveigled the Russians to follow him and directed his way towards the fortress of Abomee,[287] where the tents of his soldiers were intermixed with the dwellings of the inhabitants. The pursuit was kept up by the enemy with much eagerness and precipitation, until they came within the range of the fortress: when the Persian artillery opened, and at the first discharge, a vast number of the Russian soldiers were consumed in the fire of mortality. At the same moment, the victorious troops of Mahomed Houssain Khan pushed, with drawn scimitars, among the ranks of the enemy, and completed their discomfiture. In the conflict which ensued, about 7 or 8000 Russians fell a prey to the remorseless sword, many of their chieftains were made prisoners, and a great part of their guns, arms, and accoutrements, fell into the hands of the conquering Persians. The Russian commander in Chief fled towards Teffleez.

"As soon as Mahomed Houssain Khan was completely assured of the defeat and flight of the enemy, he transmitted an account of this great victory to the *Prince of the World*, Abbas Mirza, who sits on the Throne of Royalty at Zebreez [sic, Tabriz]. At the same time Mahomed Houssian [sic] Khan himself proceeded towards Teffleez, in pursuit of the Russians.[288] When the intelligence reached the Prince Abbas Mirza, he immediately forwarded a detail of the circumstance of the victory to the King and taking the field in person, with a powerful army, also set out in the direction of Teffleez with a fixed determination, in his valiant mind, to extirpate the Russian nation!

"Mahomed Kurreem Khan Afshaar (a relation to the Prime Minister, Mirza Mahomed Shussee [sic, Shafi])[289] received instructions from the King, to spread abroad the tidings of this joyful event. Three dispatches upon the subject were accordingly sent from Taaoeeran [Teheran], one to the Prince of the World,[290] Ruler of Persia and Khokhalpoys, of all the

---

se méfiait de lui, il avait mis dans la citadelle une garnison de ses gens et donné le commandement d'Erivan à un de ses sardars.'

[287] 9.96 has 'fortress of Aroomee' which, while it recalls a common spelling (Aroumi/Aroomee) used for Urmia, much further south, is probably meant to render Erzurum. This city was not besieged in November, 1808, by Gudovich, however. Rather, Yerevan, was and it seems the author of the article has confused the names Aroomee/Erzurum and Erivan.

[288] In fact, if the Georgian account is correct, the erstwhile governor of Erivan took no part in the action. Rather, as Brosset (1857: 290) described matters, 'A la nouvelle des événements précédents Abas-Mirza, fils du chah, qui commandait dans l'Aderbidjan et résidait à Tauriz, se mit en campagne avec ses troupes, avec ceux des soldats réguliers, ouvellement instruits par les Français, et avec de l'artillerie. Arrivé à Nakhtchévan, pour secourir la place assiégée, il s'y arrêta. En ayant reçu avis, Goudovitch fit partir deux régiments, l'un de mousquetaires, de Troïtski, l'autre de chasseurs. Quand les Russes arrivèrent à Nakhtchévan, il s'ensuivit un combat acharné, où les Persans eurent un léger avantage, dû à la valeur des réguliers nouvellement instruits. Cependant Goudovitch ordonna aux soldats d'appliquer les échelles et de monter à l'assaut d'Erivan. Les soldats montèrent aux échelles, tandis que les Persans de la citadelle ouvrirent le feu de l'artillerie: les Russes furent vaincus et perdirent 2000 hommes.'

[289] Mirza Shafi'-e Mazandarani. Cf. Busse (1972: 99, 108, 117, 120, 131, etc.).

[290] 'Abbas Mirza.

Ravens and Shores,[291] and of the Land of Lhar, another to Mahomed Nubee Khan,[292] Lord of the Sea—and a third to the British Envoy.[293]

"As, moreover, it was manifest, that in this affair, the Russians had been the aggressors, it now occurred to the mind of the King,[294] that they must have acted under the influence of the French Ambassador, at present in attendance at the Court of Persia.[295] The dust of vexation, therefore, settled in the skirts of the Royal favor towards the French nation; and it became desirable in the eyes of the King, that the friendship subsisting with that people should be dissolved. He was inclined to dismiss the Embassy; and according to one report, has actually done so. According to another, however, which is considered as the more authentic of the two, he has postponed the execution of his purpose, until the arrival of the English Envoy."'[296]

9.94 'Summary of Foreign Reports,' *Thomas's Massachusetts Spy, or Worcester Gazette* (Wednesday, 22 November, 1809): 'Sir Harford Jones, the British Ambassador at the Court of Persia,[297] has, it seems, been successful in counteracting French influence there.—A Persian Newspaper received in Calcutta, gives an account of a battle, fought by the Persians and Russians, in November last, at the fortress of Aroomee [sic, Yerevan] in which the Russians lost 7 or 8000 men in killed, beside a great number of prisoners. The Persians supposed that the Russians were actuated by French influence, and in consequence, it was expected that the French Ambassador would be dismissed from the court of Persia.'

---

[291] The source of this article, Anonymous (1809c), has 'Ruler of Persia and Khokhalooya, of all the havens and shores.' Khokhalooya looks like a corruption of Kuhgiluyeh, the name of both a tribe and a district in Fars, sometimes written Kuh Kiluye, as in Laufer (1919: 249), or Kohkiluyeh, as in the 1966 *National Census of Population and Housing* cited in Loeffler (1976: 287).

[292] Fath 'Ali Khan's ambassador in India, Mohammad Nabi Khan. Cf. 9.41.

[293] Sir Harford Jones.

[294] Fath 'Ali Shah.

[295] Gardane.

[296] This final paragraph neatly expresses Fath 'Ali Shah's increasing disillusionment with Gardane and the French position, in the lead up to the arrival of Sir Harford Jones.

[297] Harford Jones (1764–1847), who took the surname Brydges in 1836. For his account of the embassy to Fath 'Ali Shah see Brydges (1834). For a brief sketch of his life see Perry (1989). As Yapp (1967: 325–326) noted, 'He was descended from two old-established and locally prominent families in Herefordshire and Radnorshire, the Harfords and the Jones. He had entered the East India Company's service as a writer on the Bombay establishment and had spent the whole of his career in the Gulf. Like Manesty he had supplemented his meagre pay and allowances with private trade and had established a relationship with an Armenian woman by whom he had three illegitimate children' although, on a trip to England, he married 'Sarah Whitcombe (née Gott), the widow of his cousin, Richard Whitcombe.'

9.95 'Latest Foreign News. London, October 23,' *American Watchman* [Wilmington DE] (after 10 January, 1810): 'We have already mentioned the arrival of Mr. Morier[298] with dispatches from Sir Harford Jones, the British Envoy to the Court of Persia announcing the complete overthrow of the French influence in that quarter,[299] and the conclutions of a treaty with that Power.

This treaty was concluded on the 15th of March, and it appears, that, in the execution of this important mission, Sir Harford Jones acquitted himself with great ability; but, that Ld. [Lord] Minto, the Gov. General in India,[300] has divested him of his public functions, and apprised the Persian Court that he is only to be considered as a private person. This conduct of Ld. Minto is supposed to have risen from the circumstance of Gen. Malcolm, who had been sent as ambassador by the Indian government, having been refused admittance in that character at the Persian Court.[301]

---

[298] James Justinian Morier (1780–1849). Born at Izmir (Smyrna), he was the second son of Isaak Morier, Consul General of the Levant Company in Constantinople. He attended Harrow and at the age of 27 accompanied Sir Harford Jones as his private secretary. For his life see Zeidler (1908: 39–40). Cf. Brydges (1834/1: 19). Morier arrived back in England on 25 November 1809. See Morier (1812: viii). His accounts of his journeys to Persia (Morier 1812, 1818) have been widely read for two centuries and his novels, particularly *The Adventures of Hajji Baba, of Ispahan*, earned him great notoriety. See Morier (1824, 1832), Amanat (2003/2012). For a comprehensive list of his published works see Bateson (1969: 410–411).

[299] Although Fath 'Ali Shah offered Jones the Order of the Lion and Sun, Jones declined this Persian quasi-knighthood 'on account of the circumstances attending its origin,' i.e. it had been created originally for Gardane. See Malcolm (1827/2: 163, n. *).

[300] Gilbert Elliot Murray Kynynmound (1751–1814), 1st Earl of Minto, Governor-General of India (1807–1813).

[301] According to Markham (1874: 373), 'Lord Minto, then Governor-General of India,' was 'annoyed at the interference of the Home Government in the affairs of Persia, which, in his opinion, belonged exclusively to India; he refused to honour Sir Harford's bills, which caused him great annoyance and embarrassment, wrote despatches in which he found fault with all he had done, and finally sent Sir John Malcolm as a rival Envoy to Tehran.' Minto's niece, however, suggested otherwise, when she wrote, 'It has been represented that the despatch of two missions to Persia had arisen from the jealousy entertained by the Indian Government of an Envoy from the Crown. This was not the case. The resolution to appoint an Envoy to represent both Crown and Company had been taken with Lord Minto's knowledge and participation, before he left England.' See Minto 1880: 130. For Jones' own account of the hostility against his mission expressed by Lord Minto, who ordered him 'to retire from the Persian territories,' see Brydges (1834/1: 127). At one point Jones noted, 'Lord Minto had certainly not given me any great reason to respect or admire him; but when Meerza Sheffee [Mirza Safi'], in his letter to me, told me, that on these dispatches being read to the Shah, he had publicly called the Governor-General *fool* and *madman*, I did feel…very sorry that *the dignity of the Company's Indian Government* should be spoken of in such terms.' See Brydges (1834/1: 345–346). For a full assessment of Lord Minto's policies via-à-vis Napoleon and Persia, see Das (2016). Rawlinson's critical view of the efforts of Minto and Malcolm vs Jones were noted above. Rawlinson (1849: 20–21) summed up his scathing assessment of this rivalry when he wrote, 'The best reply indeed to the charges which have been brought against Sir Harford Jones—that "he ignominiously purchased the protection of Persia for England;" that, "he saddled the Indian Government with a

The King of Persia[302] has declared his determination to adhere to the treaty, and has detained Sir Harford Jones until he receives intelligence from the Court of St. James, to which he has sent a Charge d'Affaires, with a formal complaint against the conduct of the government of India in the business. This person has accompanied Mr. Morier to England.'[303]

9.96 'Untitled,' *The Public Advertiser* (Wednesday, 14 February, 1810), 'Untitled,' *The Long Island Star* (Thursday, 15 February, 1810), 'Untitled,' *The Otsego Herald* (Saturday, 24 February, 1810), 'Persia and Russia,' *Freeman's Friend* (Saturday, 24 February, 1810) and 'Persia and Russia,' *Weekly Visiter* (Saturday, 24 February, 1810): 'Accounts have been received from India, of hostilities beteween the Persians and Russians, on which subject the French minister at the Court of Persia[304] is said to have presented a strong remonstrance.[305] It will require all the talent of Napoleon to produce even a temporary cordiality between Russia and Persia, which like all other powerful neighbors, are in a state of habitual jealousy and animosity.'

9.97 'Foreign,' *Portland Gazette, and Maine Advertizer* (Monday, 26 February, 1810): 'We are glad to hear that there is no prospect of Asia's being brought under the Corsican yoke.[306] The Persians have dismissed Bona[parte]'s Arch Devil (Gardanne), whom he had sent there to "expostulate and reason" with them.'

---

useless and extravagant debt, &c,"—is to be found in the fact that Lord Minto, who regarded his personal proceedings as actually mutinous, who by anticipation repudicated his possible negociations with the Shah, disavowed his diplomatic character, and ordered him summarily to leave the country, who went the length even of dishonoring the bills drawn by him on the public service—still did not hesitate, when furnished with a draft of the treaty, and while yet in ignorance of the feelings of the Home authorities, to accept all the pecuniary and military engagements which had been contracted in the name of His Britannic Majesty, with the proviso that their execution should be entrusted to an officer honored with His Lordship's confidence, and prepared to uphold the dignity of the Indian Government.' Lord Minto himself concluded, 'Notwithstanding the total failure of our views in Persia, the general tone of his (Lieut.-Col. M.'s) measures has vindicated the dignity and honour of the British government.' See Philippart (1823: 481).

[302] Fath 'Ali Shah.

[303] A reference to Fath 'Ali Shah's Envoy Extraordinary to the Court of St. James, Mirza Abu'l Hasan Khan on which much more will be found below. He travelled with Morier, and together they left Tehran on 7 May 1809. See Morier (1812: viii).

[304] Gardane.

[305] According to McNeill (1827: 162), 'The favourable reception of the mission of Sir Harford Jones, in 1808, and the consequent expulsion of the French agents from Persia, while she was still engaged in a war with Russia, put an end for the time to all competition for the friendship of the Shah, and laid the foundation of an alliance between the crowns of Great Britain and Persia, which was confirmed by a preliminary treaty.'

[306] An allusion to Napoleon's Corsican birth. In fact, Napoleon's relationship with his Corsican heritage was problematic throughout his life. To begin with, as Englund (2010: 17) observed, 'Had

9.98 'London, Dec. 2,' *Kentucky Gazette* (after 28 February, 1810): 'The Ambassador from Persia,[307] who has been for some time expected, has arrived at Plymouth, in the Formidable, from Malta.'[308]

9.99 'Calcutta, Dec. 22,' *Federal Gazette* (Wednesday, 2 May, 1810): 'By private letters from the neighborhood of Tabriz in Armenia, of date the 17th of Aug. [1809] we learn that Abbas Mirza, the heir apparent, and Mahomed Ali Mirza his brother, had marched at the head of 60,000 Persians to engage the Russians at Erivan.[309] The latter are said, in consequence of the alarm which this has excited, to have sent an ambassador[310] to treat with the king of Persia.'

Genoa not ceded Corsica to France,' the 9 year-old Napoleon 'would not be going anywhere at this point, for the Genoese did not give scholarships to minor Corsican noble sons. Perhaps, when he had been older, he would have gone to an Italian university, probably Pisa, as his father had done, or maybe Naples, where Paoli had studied.'

[307] Mirza Abu'l Hasan Khan Shirazi. For his career see e.g. Ekbal (1987), Cloake (1988), Eskandari-Qajar (2007), Sohrabi (2014) and many of the entries that follow here.

[308] As Morier (1812): viii noted, 'on the 7th May I quitted *Teheran* with Mirza Abul Hassan, the King of Persia's Envoy Extraordinary to the Court of London, with whom I reached Smyrna on the 7th September, and embarked there on board H.M.S. *Success*, Captain Ayscough. Having at Malta changed the Success for H.M.S. *Formidable*, we finally reached Plymouth on the 25th November, 1809.'

[309] As Monteith (1856: 57–58) noted, 'The Persians … emboldened by their success at Erivan, and encouraged by the apparent dissatisfaction existing in the provinces occupied by Russia, determined to make greater efforts than usual for a general attack upon Georgia. The King moved from Teheran early in May [1809], directing his eldest son Mahomed Ali Mirza, to join him with the army of the Bagdad frontier … he addressed his two sons, however, as rival candidates to the throne, and said he expected to see which of them would prove himself most worthy of it. Mahomed Ali Mirza's army consisted entirely of the old Persian troops, who looked upon the introduction of the new system with jealousy and dislike. There were neither regular infantry nor artillery among them, while Abbas Mirza's army was provided with both. In numerical strength they were about equal, each reckoning about 25,000 men … Both armies marched towards Erivan, but at some days' interval.' As Hasan-e Fasa'i wrote, 'On being informed that Tormasov [Alexander Tormasov (1752–1819)], commander in chief of the Russian troops, was encamping 1 parasang from Tiflis and that he had dispatched several detachments of his army to Karabagh, the shah after some deliberation sent Moḥammad 'Ali Mirzā, governor of 'Erāq and Kermānshāh, with 2000 horsemen and infantry to Tiflis, and Crown Prince 'Abbās Mirzā with a corps of his army to Ganja.'

[310] A reference to Lieutenant-Colonel Baron von Wrede. According to Brydges (1834/1: 357), 'on the 5th of February, Baron Wrede, dispatched on the part of General Tormesoff, the Russian Governor-General of Teflis and the regions of the Caucasus, arrived at Tauris.' This is incorrect, however, in that the Baron had been sent by Tormasov's predecessor, Gudovich, who was not replaced by Tormasov until September or October 1808. See Brosset (1857: 291, n. 1). As Gardane noted in a letter to Champagny dated Tehran, 2 June 1808, 'M. le baron de Wrede, lieutenant-colonel d'artillerie, a été envoyé à la cour de Perse par S. Exc. le feld-maréchal comte de Goudowitsch, commandant les troupes russes en Géorgie … Il m'a remis le 21 mai une lettre extrêmement amicale de M. le comte de Goudowitsch.' Although Gardane and von Wrede signed an armistice of one year

9.100 'From Charleston, May 26,' *New-Bedford Mercury* (Friday, 8 June, 1810), 'From the N. York Gazette, June 6,' *Philadelphia Gazette* (Friday, 8 June, 1810), 'Untitled,' *Federal Gazette and Baltimore Daily Advertiser* (Saturday, 9 June, 1810), 'Untitled,' *Poulson's American Daily Advertiser* (Saturday, 9 June, 1810), 'Untitled,' *New-Hampshire Patriot* (Tuesday, 12 June, 1810), 'Untitled,' *The Spirit of 'Seventy-Six* (Tuesday, 12 June, 1810), 'Untitled,' *Connecticut Gazette* (Wednesday, 13 June, 1810), 'Boston, June 6,' *Alexandria Daily Gazette* (Thursday, 14 June, 1810), 'Untitled,' *The Balance, & New-York State Journal* (Friday, 15 June, 1810), 'Untitled,' *Petersburg Intelligencer* (Friday, 15 June, 1810) and 'Untitled,' *The Geneva Gazette* (Wednesday, 4 July, 1810): 'A new and splendid embassy is preparing in *England* for *Persia*. Sir George Oussley [sic, Gore Ouseley] is appointed Minister,[311] is to have a large salary during his residence, and a liberal pension for life on his return. Mr. Morrier [sic, Morier] is appointed his Secretary.[312] He is a near relation of Mr. Morrier, who is named to succeed Mr. Jackson.'[313]

---

between Russia and Persia, this was rejected by the Czar. See Driault (1900/1901: 141). In the journal kept by Thomas Henry Sheridan, Political Assistant, of Sir Harford Jones' interactions during the mission, a uniformly negative view of Wrede is given. 'Abbas Mirza's vizir, Mirza Bozorg, told the British envoy, 'that in the course of conversation, the Baron [von Wrede] told him, that the Russians only waited the breaking up of the season to commence an attack on Constantinople; and that, in fact, he considered the attack as already commenced … The Meerza said Baron Wrede had told Fath Ally Khan, the Governor of Tauris, that the French in India had taken a large part of the English possessions there; which, on being asked whether he had said so or no, he positively denied. "This," the Meerza added, "has given me a very bad impression not only of the Baron's sense, but of his veracity."' See Brydges (1834/1: xxiv–xxv).

[311] Sir Gore Ouseley (1770–1844). He served as Ambassador Extraordinary and Plenipotentiary in Persia from 1811 to 1814. For his life see Reynolds (1846). For genealogical information, refuting the suggestion often found in the literature that William was the elder brother, see Kelly (1910: 137). They were, in fact, 'Irish twins.' Gore was born on 24 June 1770, William on 13 April 1771. For confirmation of the veracity of Kelly's information on the Ouseleys, see Anonymous (1910).

[312] Morier acted as 'secretary of embassy,' whereas Sir Gore Ouseley's 'private secretary' was his younger brother, the Orientalist Sir William Ouseley. See Ouseley (1819: 1–2).

[313] John Philip Morier (1776–1853), elder brother of James Justinian Morier, was being sent to the United States as the successor of the deeply unpopular British ambassador, Francis James Jackson (1770–1814). Thus, as Francis' brother Sir George Jackson noted in a letter of 30 March 1810, 'Sir Gore Ouseley … is going to Persia … He speaks the Persian language fluently, and was, in consequence, named to attend the Persian Minister. He is now appointed *King's* ambassador—for our present envoy, Sir H. Jones, is more a *Company's* [EIC] than a king's servant. Morier goes with him as secretary … P. Morier, the brother of the Persian secretary, is to go to America as secretary of legation, and is to remain as *locum tenens* when Francis leaves.' See Jackson (1873: 103). Jackson's departure was highly fraught as he had offended the American Secretary of State and indeed the entire government. So 'indecorous and insolent' did the Secretary of State find Jackson that Congress passed a 'A bill to prevent the abuse of the privileges and immunities enjoyed by Foreign Ministers within the United States' in early December, 1809, and it was decided not 'to hold any further communication with Mr. Jackson.' See Benton (1857: 169).

9.101 'Untitled,' *Commercial Advertiser* [New York NY] (Friday, 24 August 1810): 'His Excellency Mirza Abdul Hassan, the Persian Ambassador,[314] (says a London paper of June 29) will embark in a few days on board the Lion man of war, at Portsmouth, on his return to Persia.[315] His property, consisting of the best specimens of British mechanism,[316] is partly on board.—Since his Excellency has been in England, his attention has been chiefly directed to our useful inventions. He has constantly preferred articles of general utility, to those made for ornament and show; and his remarks on European goods in general, have proved him to be a man of strong discernment. Among a variety of articles in the upholstery and cabinet line, he has purchased portable bedsteads, dining tables, elegant chairs, dressing stands, sideboards, and chair beds, made on a new mechanical principle.[317]— He has also purchased a considerable number of newly invented instruments for producing

---

[314] As noted above Mirza Abu'l Hasan Khan Shirazi made a visit to Great Britain in 1810. Having travelled with J.J. Morier, 'delivering his credentials on 17 January, and presenting the Queen with three boxes of jewels, several shawls, and a carpet. A few days later he was introduced to the Prince Regent [George Augustus Frederick, later George IV], who presented him with a clock, invented by Congreve. He left England in July, accompanied by Sir Gore Ouseley and his secretary, James Justinian Morier.' See Aspinall (1938: 49). Mirza Abu'l Hasan was later Prime Minister and Minister for Foreign Affairs. See MacAlister (1910: 56). For the journal of his stay in England see Cloake (1988). For a recent analysis of him see Sohrabi (2014). Morier (1812: 220–223) describes his life and career up to 1809 when he met him. For a sketch of Mirza Abu'l Hasan during his first visit to Britain in 1809–1810 by William Waldegrave, 1st Baron Radstock see Waldegrave (1820).

[315] According to Toone (1834: 462), 'The Persian ambassador took leave of their Majesties, previous to his departure for Persia,' on 11 July 1810. Subsequently, 'the *Lion* man-of-war of 64 guns, Captain Heathcote having the command' (Reynolds 1846: xlviii) left Portsmouth on 18 July 1810. Cf. Ekbal (1987: 23). He was accompanied by Sir Gore Ouseley's mission. In order to avoid French warships in the Mediterranean, the embassy did not proceed by sea to Constantinople and from there overland. Rather, it sailed around the Cape of Good Hope and up to the Persian Gulf. In the Atlantic it made a stop in Brazil. See Ekbal (1987) for the Brazilian detour and the Persian ambassador's experience of the journey. The embassy arrived in Bombay in January, 1811, and landed at Bandar-e Bushehr on 5 March 1811. See Reynolds (1846: xlix).

[316] Such as the clock invented by Sir William Congreve (1772–1828) which, according to Aspinall (1938: 49), was given to him by the Prince Regent. As Britten (1899: 296–297) noted, 'In 1808 Sir William Congreve, of Garden Court, Temple, who had invented other curious clocks, patented a timekeeper in which a small steel ball rolled down grooves in an inclined plane, which was movable on its centre. The grooves were zigzag, forming a succession of V's, so that the ball, once started, traversed the whole surface of the plate by rolling down one groove and entering the next at the point of the V. On arriving at the lowest point of the inclined plane the ball had sufficient impetus to unlock the train, which thereupon reversed the inclination of the plane or table by the intervention of a crank and connecting rod, and the ball started on its journey in the other direction. Congreve clocks, as they are called, go fairly well if made with exactness and kept free from dust.' Cf. Anonymous (1808d).

[317] According to the original article on which this is based, all of these pieces of furniture were purchased from Morgan & Saunders [sic, Sanders]. See Cloake (1988: 276). The British Post Office directory of 1814 lists 'Morgan & Saunders, Patent Sofa-bed and Chair-bed Manufacturers, Upholsterers and Cabinet-makers, 16 & 17, Catherine-street, Strand.' See Critchett and Woods (1814): 227. Otherwise known as Morgan & Sanders, this was one of the most important furniture

instantaneous light. The best production of glass manufacture have been an object of great importance with him; and he has not neglected samples of cutlery ware. The arts, sculpture, and literature, also compose a great part of his selections. We understand that the articles are principally intended as presents for the Sultan [sic, Shah], his master.'[318]

9.102 'Foreign Articles,' *Kentucky Gazette* (after 10 September, 1810): 'The British East-India Company have presented the Persian Ambassador with a superb *dirk*, the handle set with precious stones, and the blade most ingeniously carved; the case to preserve it is of crimson velvet, the seams of which are covered with narrow gold lace.[319]—If Bonaparte conquers Turkey, *this dirk* will not prevent his "Overland Journey to India," or preserve the possessions of the East-India Company from his grasp.'

9.103 'Extract of a letter from an Officer attached to the English Embassy to Persia,' *New York Journal* (Saturday, 13 October, 1810), 'Persia. Extract of a letter from an Officer attached to the English Embassy to Persia,' *Alexandria Gazette, Commercial & Political* (Tuesday, 16 October, 1810), 'Persia. Extract of a letter from an Officer attached to the English Embassy to Persia,' *Republican Watch Tower* (Tuesday, 16 October, 1810) and 'Persia. Extract of a letter from an Officer attached to the English Embassy to Persia,' *Washington Advertiser* (Monday, 29 October, 1810): '"Tehran, May 22, 1810.

"In my last I[320] mentioned that we had commenced our journey towards the capital by easy stages. We arrived at Sheraz on the 30th December [1808], and on the road the highest

---

manufacturers in London during the first two decades of the nineteenth century. See e.g. Austen (1974), Shimbo (2016: 129–132).

[318] Among the presents brought by Mirza Abu'l Hasan Khan to Queen Charlotte, wife of George III, was a golden container with mumiah, a bituminous substance from the Dara mountain near Shiraz. It was so expensive that £8 (9 toman) reportedly bought only a walnut shell full of the substance and real mumiah was only extracted for the Shah. See Schweer (1919: 49). As noted by Petri (1810: 108), 'Ein Berg, nahe bei Schiras, liefert die kostbare Mumie, welche in ganz Asien so berühmt und eine Art Tropfpech ist, die binnen 24 Stunden alle Brüche, selbst die an starken Knochen, heilt. Sie tröpfelt von dem Felsen in eine Höhle, die immer sorgfältig bewacht wird, un man sammelt sie alle Jahre im September, gewinnt aber, und wenn die Lese noch so reich ist, nicht viel über 10 Unzen. Sie sieht schwarz aus, beinahe wie Pech, hat aber keinen Geruch. Man gewinnt auch in einigen Bergen fon Lar Mumie, diese ist aber weniger wirksam und daher nicht so geschätzt. Man bekommt die Unze für 2 Louisd'or, da hingegen die von Schiras, wenn man sie echt bekommt, 200 Louisd'or kostet. Etwas davon war immer mit unter den Geschenken, welche die Kaiser von Persien den benachbarten Mächten gaben; auch die Russische Kaiserin Katharina II. erhielt einst von Ali Murat Khan eine Unze davon in einer goldnen mit kostbaren Perlen besetzten Dose.' In return, Abu'l Hasan was presented with a miniature of Queen Charlotte painted by George III's miniaturist, George Engleheart, on 16 May 1810. See Williamson and Engleheart (1902: 34, 44).

[319] According to Toone (1834: 458), this occurred on 11 January 1810, when 'The directors of the East India company gave a splendid entertainment to the Persian ambassador.'

[320] Sir Harford Jones was accompanied by 'Major Smith, public Secretary,' Morier, Thomas Henry Sheridan, 'Political Assistant,' Capt. James Sutherland 'Surveyor,' Cornet Willock, who 'had been

honours were paid to the Representative of our Gracious Sovereign. Governors of provinces came out to meet and welcome us, dismounting from their horses, as a mark of respect on our near approach.

"We paid two visits[321] to the prince of Sheraz,[322] and had barely time to view the tombs of the poets Sadoe and Hasiz [sic, Sa'di and Hafez], which are in good preservation. The country seats in the environs of Sheraz are not fine houses with extensive pleasure ground, but small gardens with summer houses, some of which and especially those of the Europeans, are very pretty. Mr. Morier took sketches of the whole, which you will therefore probably see. A letter from the seat of government in India nearly put a stop to our hitherto successful enterprize.[323] Sir Harford taking all responsibility on himself, did

---

attached to General Malcolm's Mission, but left by him at Bombay,' and a Persian secretary. See Brydges (1834/1: 19–20). Morier is mentioned in the article and is therefore not the writer. The final paragraph refers to Fath 'Ali Shah inspecting 'my troop.' Although it would seem logical to assume that Major Smith, the highest ranking military officer in the Mission, was the officer who authored this letter ['Major L.F. Smith, late of the Mahratta service, accompanies Sir Harford Jones on his embassy to Persia, as secretary.' See Anonymous (1811c: 189)], it is more likely that the writer was 'Cornet Henry Willock, of the *Madras* cavalry, commander of the body guard,' or 'Lieutenant Blacker, of the *Madras* cavalry,' who joined the Mission. See Morier (1812: 1–2). As Brydges (1834/1: 337) wrote that, 'Sir Henry Willock had enough to do in superintending the troop and detachment of Sepoys,' and the author of the letter quoted in the present newspaper account mentions that, just before Jones' first audience with Fath 'Ali Shah, 'I was ready with the troop to salute,' it seems most likely that Willock was the writer of this account. Thomas Henry Sheridan's journal is quoted liberally in Brydges (1834) but, as Political Assistant, he is unlikely to have been the 'Officer attached to the English Embassy.'

[321] The first took place on 1 January 1810. See Brydges (1834/1: 98).

[322] Contrary to Sheridan's journal, quoted extensively by Jones, this was not Hasan 'Ali Mirza, Fath 'Ali's sixth son, who was governor of Tehran (Gardane 1809a: 52), but Hoseyn 'Ali Mirza Farman-Farma of Fars, his fifth son. See Anonymous (1873a: 715). Sheridan described him as 'a fine youth ... very handsome, and his manners very engaging.' See Brydges (1834/1: 100). Cf. Gardane (1809a: 76), 'Le cinquième, Hussein-Ali-Mirza, commande à Chiras.' According to Hasan-e Fasa'i, he was born on 1 September 1789 (Busse 1972: 36), making him about 20 years old when Jones met him.

[323] On 4 January 1810 Jones received a letter from Lord Minto, which he deferred opening until the following day, 'directing him to retire from the Persian territories, acquainting him that precautionary measures would be immediately taken, and that the Governor-General intended to seize on the island of Carrack [Khark], in the Persian Gulf ... I gave his Lordship ample proof at Bombay, by my conduct towards Malcolm, that before I really commenced the duties of my Mission, I was most willing, and most ready to make all my proceedings square with his—but now my position is materially changed, I am in Persia, and I am not only in Persia, but I am the king's accredited Minister in Persia, I have my Sovereign's honor and name to support, and these are things, which, if necessary, I will support with my life and fortune...I will not retire from Persia, for many reasons, but principally for this, that by doing so, at this moment, I should proclaim to the Persians, that the Governor-General is superior in power to the King; and this my Welsh blood will never suffer me to do.' See Brydges (1834/1: 127–128).

not comply with the wishes of the government for his return to India, but on the 12th January recommenced his journey.[324]

"On account of the report of general Malcolm coming up the Gulph, the Persians, suspicious of our designs, wished to detain us at Ispahan to see the event;[325] for several days we were agitated between hope and fear: Sir H. surmounted this difficulty as well as the former, and on the 7th we again moved,[326] and arrived at Tehran on the 14th; the distance we computed to be about 250 miles; this for eastern travelling, where you have no post chaises or mail coaches at command, is extremely fast—The former embassies took 5 months to go over the same ground which we performed in less than two. We should have arrived a day sooner; and it was so arranged out of compliment to the English Mission, that general Gardanne, with the whole of his train who had been detained for that purpose, were to have gone out of one gate of the city in disgrace,[327] while we entered in triumph at the other; but travelling in a most boisterous and dark dark night, our party, by some accident, separated and lost the road.

---

[324] As Jones noted, 'On the 11th, a Mehmandar was appointed to attend me to Isfahaun ... On the 12th, I caused our tents to be pitched about a mile out of Schyras; and, accompanied by most of the gentlemen, I privately repaired to them, as we were to commence our journey next morning.' See Brydges (1834/1: 145). Similarly, Sheridan's diary entry reads, 'January the 13th.—Commenced, at eleven, A.M. our journey to Isfahaun.' See Brydges (1834/1: 148).

[325] As Jones wrote, on 21 January he 'received a letter from Mr. Bruce, at Schyras, acquainting me that it was currently reported, and believed there, that I should be detained a month at Isfahaun.' See Brydges (1834/1: 159).

[326] Jones and his suite arrived at Isfahan on 1 February. See Brydges (1834/1: 166). Thus they remained only one week. According to Sheridan's diary, 'At one P.M. the bugle sounded, and the Mission was put in motion.' See Brydges (1834/1: 177).

[327] In a brief note to Mirza Shafi', Fath 'Ali Shah's Grand Vizir, dated 25 November 1808, Gardane wrote: 'Je déclare d'après l'audience qui a eu lieu avant-hier avec Sa Hautesse, que je dois à mon devoir et à l'honneur de mon auguste maître et de la grande nation, de quitter votre cour avec toute la légation dès l'instant que les Anglais seront admis sur votre territoire.' See Gardane (1865: 248). There is some discrepancy, however, concerning the date of Gardane's departure from Tehran. Gardane's own account says that he left Tehran on 27 January. See Gardane (1809a: 77). According to Driault (1900/1901: 152), however, after being informed that, on 4 February, Jones had received permission to proceed to Tehran, Gardane had a brief audience with Fath 'Ali Shah on 8 February and left Tehran for Tabriz on 13 February. This later date is confirmed by an extract from the journal of J.-M. Jouannin, the French Mission's interpreter, dated 6 February in which we read that Mirza Shafi' 'me fit entendre dans la suite de son discours que le Roi se décidait à ne pas arrêter l'Ambassadeur [Gardane] plus longtemps; que le général fit ses préparatifs.' See Gardane 1865: 353. On 21 January, while travelling from Shiraz to Isfahan, Jones had received a letter from Mirza Shafi' informing him 'that in approaching the capital, he will have the satisfaction to find that the French Ambassador will not be there, as General Gardanne is on the point of leaving Tæheran.' See Brydges (1834/1: 160). In fact, as Jones note, 'my entry into Tæheran, and General Gardanne's departure from it, had been fixed for the 13th.' Jones noted that, while approaching Tehran on 13 February, 'a messenger arrived, who acquainted me, that General Gardanne had left Tæheran yesterday,' and the Mission entered Tehran on 14 February. See Brydges (1834/1: 183–185), confirmed by Hasan-e Fasa'i, see Busse (1972: 126, n. 126).

"On the 17th, contrary to the Persian customs, as their mohorrum, or mourning, had commenced,[328] we paid our first visit to his majesty; Sir Harford bearing the King's[329] letter on a gold plate, and Mr. Morier the presents, to the outside of our house, where I was ready with the troop to salute; Sir H. then mounted. On arriving at the Palace Sir H. again bore the letter, and Mr. Morier the presents.[330] The Persian infantry, drilled by the French, were drawn up to receive us, they appeared to be very imperfect in their exercise. The King,[331] on account of the mourning, did not receive us in the public hall of audience: we parted close by it, it was not so grand as the old palace I before mentioned, built by Shah Abbas; in the private court a great many Persian Khans or Noblemen were ranged along the wall; we made several obeisances before we entered the apartments, and took off our slippers at some distance from the door; this was probably because they feared we might behave like the French, who never took off their boots in any houses of the Persians, which offenced them very much.[332] The King, on our entry, welcomed us; when Sir H. (having delivered the letter, and Mr. Morier the presents, to the Prime Minister for the King) made a short speech, which Jaffer Ali Khan,[333] our great assistant in the whole of the transaction, interpreted;[334] Sir H. then seated himself in a chair about 15 yards from the King; Mr. Morier on his right hand standing, and Jaffer Ali Khan on his left; the rest of the gentlemen stood against a wall in the rear of the Ambassador. His Majesty was very

---

[328] According to Sheridan's journal, quoted by Brydges, 'the room was so much purposely darkened, and his [Fath 'Ali Shah's] dress so nearly black, that I could not distinctly examine either the one or the other.' He explained this as follows: 'The reason why the King of Persia appeared with so little splendour to-day, is that it is the second day of the Moharrem, or mourning for the death, or rather murder, at Kerbela, of Imaum Hossein, one of the sons of Aly, by the Prophet's daughter Fatima. This mourning lasts 10 days, during which the Persians ordinarily decline to undertaake any kind of business. The King of Persia's consenting to receive the Mission at this period, and to order that negociations for a treaty should immediately commence, is regarded as something very wonderful and uncommon. But Sir Harford observes to me, that he considers this to be Meerza Bozurg's doing.' See Brydges (1834/1: 186, 188).

[329] George III.

[330] According to Sheridan's journal, 'Sir Harford...took the King's letter to the King of Persia in his hands, and holding it above his breast, he directed Morier to precede him with the presents, which consisted of a very large diamond, which Sir Harford valued to the Persians at £25,000; a gold-enamelled snuff-box, on the lid of which was the king's picture set round with large brilliants; and a small ebony box, on the lid of which a representation of the Battle of Trafalgar was beautifully cut in ivory; and some other smaller things which I forget.' See Brydges (1834/1: 186).

[331] Fath 'Ali Shah.

[332] Cf. the notorious visit by the Russian General Ermolov (see below), who refused to take off his boots in the presence of Fath 'Ali Shah and the visit of the comte de Sercey, the French envoy, over a decade later, who did the same.

[333] Ja'far 'Ali Khan. He was 'the acting English agent at *Shiraz*,' according to Morier (1812: 30). Cf. Brydges (1834/1: 101), who called him the 'British Agent.'

[334] According to Sheridan's journal, 'Sir Harford addressed the King in English, in a set speech, which, when finished, Jaafer Ally Khan repeated in Persian, having previously learnt the translation of it by heart.' See Brydges (1834/1: 187).

affable, and hoped his brother, the King of England, was in good health. He asked if the old or the young was reigning; Sir H. answered the old. The King then addressed the Prime Minister, Murza Sheffea,[335] and afterwards made several inquiries respecting England and Sir H's. health. After an audience of a quarter of an hour we took our leave. The King was in a dark corner of the room, so that we could not observe distinctly his person or dress. The pictures painted for him are very flattering.—The particular beauty of his person is a long beard which sweeps the ground. Six of his sons were present, standing on his right hand. The grandeur of the Court was much inferior to what we expected. The presents given by the King of England were very valuable; the diamond estimated at twenty five thousand pounds, was of finer water than any the Persian Monarch possessed. He had it immediately set, and wore it as a ring the next day. The city of Tehran is the dirtiest pig stye we have seen in Persia; there is scarcely a street where you can ride two a breast, and very dirty.

"I have been informed, that in a late interview, the Persian Monarch expressed himself in terms of great indignation against the insatiable ambition of the French emperor, and the atrocities he had recently committed.

"Since our arrival the foundery for cannon which the French established here,[336] has been put under the direction of an English officer. No foreigners are allowed to cast ordnance or to manufacture warlike stores without the approbation of Sir Harford.

---

[335] Mirza Shafi'-e Mazandarani. Fath 'Ali Shah's astonishment at this news is revealed in Sheridan's account. After Jones told him that 'His Majesty King George the Third is still on the throne.'— "What!" says the King of Persia, turning to Meerza Sheffee, "Have the French told us lies in this respect also? you know they said that King George the Third died in June last year."' See Brydges (1834/1: 188).

[336] The cannon foundry was established in Isfahan by two artillery lieutenants, Charles Nicolas Fabvier (1782–1855) and Lieut. Reboul. See Tancoigne (1819/2: 79), 'MM. Fabvier et Reboul viennent de créer une fonderie de canons à Ispahân. Sans autre secours que leur zèle et leurs talens, et quoiqu'ils aient eu long-temps à lutter contre quelques intrigues, ils sont parvenus, à force de soins et de persévérance, à mettre cet établissement sur un pied respectable, et Fèth-Ali-Châh, leur doit les premières pièces de campagne qu'on ait vues en Perse.' Isfahan was chosen by Fath 'Ali Shah as the site for the foundry because of its central location which 'paraissait offrir plus de sécurité que Téhéran aux établissements qu'il méditait.' See Debidour (1887: 329). As Gardane (1865: 43) noted, 'M. le capitaine Fabvier, de son côté, présentait au Sha de Perse vingt pièces de canon attelées, bien supérieures à tout ce qu'on avait encore vu en Perse.' Cf. Lacoin de Vilmorin (1894: 153, n. 1), 'M. le général Fabvier fut chargé par Feth-Ali-Schah de créer une artillerie de campagne. Il fonda à Ispahan un arsenal dont il dut faire jusqu'aux moindres outils, car les Persans ne possédaient aucun moyen de fabrication. Après mille peines et obstacles de tous genres, M. Fabvier réussit à monter quelques pièces sur leurs affûts. Ce fut le point de départ, le germe de l'artillerie légère que possède aujourd-hui le schah de Perse.' Adrien Dupré who was also a member of the Gardane mission and travelled separately to Iran from Constantinople along with the engineer-geographer, Capt. Camille Alphonse Trézel (1780–1860), observed, 'Les Persans ont des canons de tout calibre, presque tous coulés à froid. Une vingtaine de pièces prises sur les Russes, sont les meilleures qu'ils aient, à l'exception de celles que deux officiers français d'artillerie leur ont fondues à Ispahan.' See Dupré (1819/2: 296). For extracts from letters describing the establishment of the foundry and the many difficulties encountered, see Debidour (1887: 329ff). However, according to Fabvier's interpreter, 'Féth-Aly-Châh avait lui-même spécifié le calibre et la forme des pièces qu'il souhaitait, et qu'il

"Sir H. I think will remain in Persia much longer than he has any idea of himself. While the Persians have such powerful enemies as the French and Russians their ability to withstand them, and remain in peace with us, notwithstanding their great inclination to do so must necessarily be very precarious; and while affairs remain in this manner, the government will have great difficulty in finding a person so capable of fulfilling the

---

prescrivit le modèle des affûts qui devaient servir à les monter. Aucune des nombreuses observations que M. Fabvier fit pour en démontrer l'absurdité, n'eurent de crédit auprès de Sa Hautesse, influencée des Ministres aux gages de l'Angleterre. Pour comble de disgrâce, ces pièces furent fondues à Ispahane, dans le Gouvernement d'un Beylerbey entièrement dévoué au parti anglais. M. Fabvier ne pût obtenir ni les métaux, ni les bois convenables. Arslâne-Khâne, grand-maitre de l'artillerie, devait, par sa présence, faciliter l'exécution des ordres que M. Fabvier jugerait à propos de donner pour l'avancement de la chose; mais l'amour-propre blessé de cet homme inepte, et d'ailleurs plongé dans une ivresse continuelle, était intéressé à faire échouer l'entreprise. Par ses sourdes pratiques, les ouvriers, tous très-habiles, et d'une facilité de conception extraordinaire, étaient journellement, sous cent prétextes ridicules, distraits de leur occupation. Les agens du Beylerbey finirent par dégoûter la plupart de ces ouvriers, par des menacés et le refus de leur salaire. Lorsque les fourneaux furent construits (car il fallut que M. Fabvier fît tout), quand les matrices furent préparées, les difficultés devinrent plus grandes pour les charpentes de la machine à forer, et l'acier dont on devait composer les forets. M. Fabvier fut obligé de payer de sa bourse le peu d'artisans qu'il put engager à l'aider de leurs bras. Le bois des affûts et leurs ferremens, ensuite la fonte des boulets, donnèrent bien d'autres obstacles à lever. Malgré toutes ces entraves, malgré tous ces dégoûts, rendus plus sensibles par la privation de son interprète, M. Fabvier amena, dans le temps déterminé, vingt pièces d'artillerie à Théhérâne.' See de Nerciat (1825a: 227–228). Moreover, after it was completed, Fabvier's hard work was scarcely appreciated. As he wrote to his brother on 15 January 1809, 'On a éprouvé mes pièces, on a fait l'impossible pour les casser. N'ayant pu réussir, ils les ont enfermées dans des magasins et me voilà aussi avancé que si je n'eusse rien fait de toute cette année ... Ne va pas croire qu'on me traite mieux du côté des finances, bien loin de là; le gouverneur d'Ispahan ne payant pas mes ouvriers, il m'en a coûté environ quatre mille francs à moi pour avoir le plaisir de fonder un bel arsenal au roi de Perse. J'avais juré de réussir, j'ai réussi, mais c'est fini, on ne me décidera plus facilement à rentre en lice.' See Debidour (1887 343). This is confirmed by Nerciat (1825a: 228–229) who noted, 'On en fit l'essai devant le Roi et toute sa cour. Les boulets, également dirigés par cet excellent officier d'artillerie, portèrent tous, sans manquer, dans le but très-éloigné que l'on avait dressé. La malveillance et la jalousie furent seules mécontentes ... J'étais l'interprète de M. Fabvier, dans cette épineuse commission; et je dois convenir, que je ne pouvais lui être que d'un faible secours, puisqu'il fallait parler de choses qui m'étaient tout-à-fait étrangères, d'une part, et d'un autre côté, demander des objets dont on n'avait aucune idée en Perse. La langue persane manquait d'élémens pour la représentation d'une infinité de procédés et d'outils en usage dans cette opération compliquée. M. Fabvier, qui, après mon départ d'Ispahane, avait, en fort peu de temps, appris à parler le persan avec facilité, trouva dans son seul génie le moyen de subvenir à de si graves inconvéniens, même beaucoup mieux que n'eût pu le faire le meilleur interprète diplomatique. C'est lui qui créa toutes les fabriques, tous les instrumens, et qui forma tous les ouvriers.' Curiously Reboul is not mentioned once, either in this article or in Debidour (1904). Tancoigne (1819/2: 79, n. 1) wrote, 'Je crois que M. Reboul a été tué depuis en Espagne.' When he visited Isfahan Adrien Dupré stayed 'dans une partie de l'ancien palais du roi, qu'habitaient aussi trois officiers attachés à la légation de France en Perse,' noting, 'Ces officiers étaient MM. le colonel Fabvier, alors lieutenant d'artillerie, Reboulh, lieutenant dans la même arme, et Nerciat, second interprète de la légation française.' See Dupré (1819/2: 118 and n. 1).

situation Sir H. holds as himself; indeed he has so perfect a knowledge of the customs, manners, and language of the country, and has so completely the confidence of the King[337] and Ministers, that a great objection would be made on their side to his retiring.

"The King, after reviewing his own troops the other-day (when they performed a sham fight, in which one man and two horses were killed, from the disciplined soldiers having loaded their muskets with ball instead of blank cartridge) looked at my troop, and was much pleased with their performance; he intends to review them once more before he leaves the capital.'"

9.104 'Untitled,' *Essex Register* (Saturday, 3 November, 1810): 'It has been said that the Persians had appeared in arms against the Russians, but nothing is known beyond the usual attention to their frontiers, and the common jealousies which the late submission of the tribes beyond the Caspian to the Russians might occasion.'

9.105 'Untitled,' *New-York Gazette* (Monday, 2 December, 1811) and 'Untitled,' *New-York Herald* (Monday, 2 December, 1811): 'October 16. Advices have been received at the Admiralty of the loss of the Pomone frigate[338] coming through the Needles.[339] The length of the Gazette precludes our entering further upon particulars than merely to state, that no lives were lost, and that the Pomone brought home our Ambassador from Persia, Sir Harford Jones, who, it is said, was refused admission at the Persian Court.'[340]

9.106 'From the Dublin Evening Herald. Bonaparte's Speech to the Russian Ambassador,' *Federal Republican* (Monday, 2 March, 1812): 'At a court held June 12, 1811, the Emperor Napoleon successively addressed the different Envoys of the Confederation of the Rhine, with his usual affability. His majesty then whispered some words to the Prussian

---

[337] Fath 'Ali Shah.

[338] A 44-gun French frigate launched in 1785 and seized from the French in 1794 by a British squadron under Sir J.B. Warren off the Île de Batz. At the time it was considered 'the finest frigate afloat.' See Grocott (1997: 130). According to Anonymous (1907: 92), 'On 14 Oct. 1811 His Majesty's frigate, *La Pomone*, Capt. Robert Barrie, having on board Sir Harford Jones, our late minister at the court of Persia, struck on the Needle Rock, and was lost. The officers, crew, and passengers were all happily saved. Capt. B., his officers and crew, exhibited the utmost coolness and discipline on this distressing occasion. Capt. B. has been fully acquitted by a Court-martial, who have adjudged the master to be severely reprimanded, and a seman, who was intoxicated, to receive 50 lashes.'

[339] Off the Isle of Wight. The dangers of Bridge Reef and the three Needles Rocks which 'lead along the backbone of this dangerous reef,' are well-known. See Anonymous (1920: 240). Cf. Harford Jones' own account of the wreck in Brydges (1834: 457–462).

[340] Here Jones has been confused with Malcolm.

ambassador;[341] when turning to the Russian minister, he spoke as follows in a loud and resolute tone:—

"Well, Prince Kusakin [sic, Kurakin],[342] what is this I hear? What am I to understand?— What, your Emperor[343] then will make peace with the Turks; with those rascally Musselmen, who are like the enemies of their own, and of the other European government. He would fain be master, no doubt. Yes, a pretty master, to give up those rich provinces; those fine military positions, which formed such admirable defence on the left of his empire; and to abandon the system which was marked out for him by Peter the Great and the illustrious Catherine. I left him those possessions; and as I loved him would never have taken them away. My father-in-law of Austria saw this with pain, but I would have appeased and indemnified him, because I wished well to Russia. If your emperor concludes his projected peace my conduct towards him will be totally changed ... my brother of Persia[344] has sent back my ambassador,[345] to please the English, and has therefore exposed himself to my wrath. Prince Kusakin, no power can resist me. I am armed with a power to which all other powers must yield.'

9.107 'Untitled,' *Essex Register* (Wednesday, 1 July, 1812): 'the Russian commerce has been increasing in the Black sea ... The commerce of the Black sea and of the sea of Azoph, had been extended on the coasts of Anatolia. And so full of hopes were the Russians, that the project of a Canal to join the waters of the Kur, from the Caspian, with the branches of the rivers from the Black sea which interlock, has been seriously contemplated. The Persians are alarmed at this progress of the Russians, and have made some resistance at Derbend, without any thing decisive. The Emperor of Russia[346] has

---

[341] Major-General Baron Friedrich Wilhelm Ludwig von Krusemark (1767–1822), Prussian ambassador in Paris. For his role at this time see e.g. Cavaignac (1898).

[342] Prince Alexander Borisovich Kurakin (1752–1818), Russian ambassador to France (1809–1812), named Envoy Plenipotentiary by Alexander I. Together with Talleyrand he negotiated the Treaty of Tilsit. See Tatistcheff (1891: 161). As Bingham (1884: 135) noted of the impending rupture between France and Russia 'In August, 1811, Napoleon at a grand reception addressed the most violent reproaches to Prince Kourakine on the subject of the conduct of Russia—reproaches and invectives similar to those addressed to Lord Whitworth on the rupture of the treaty of Amiens, to Prince Metternich, on the eve of war with Austria, and to Cardinal Consalvi, over the Concordat, to the Portuguese ambassador at Fontainebleau, and to the Neapolitan ambassador at Milan. However, up to the very last moment, both Czar and Emperor denied that their intentions were hostile.'

[343] Alexander I.

[344] Fath 'Ali Shah.

[345] General Gardane.

[346] Alexander I.

lately appointed a Greek Bishop in Georgia,[347] and extends his plan to the whole government of these countries.'[348]

9.108 'Extracts,' *Boston Weekly Messenger* (Friday, 30 October 1812): 'Accounts have lately been received by government, announcing that a definitive treaty of alliance has been concluded[349] between this country and Persia by Sir G. Ously [sic, Ouseley]. The terms of the treaty[350] are represented as highly favorable to British interests, and as well calculated to unite the two countries in the bands of a lasting and advantageous connection. It has always been deemed a primary object to include the heir apparent, Mirza Abbas,[351] in the stipulations of any treaty between Persia and G. Britain. The French attempted to negociate a treaty on a similar footing, but in that attempt they have failed. Sir G. Ousely's endeavors have, however, been succesful, and his success is attributed principally to his personal

---

[347] This is probably a reference to the Armenian archbishop Narses (Narcissus). 'In 1811 Narses received from the Patriarch Ephraim the appointment of Eparchial Archbishop of Georgia: he introduced order and discipline into his diocese, and saved from its revenues a fund for establishing schools.' See von Haxthausen (1854: 301). On Narses' many achievements see e.g. Gamba (1826: 156ff). Anton II, '111e catholicos siégant dans la Géorgie' (Brosset 1857: 298), was 'unilaterally retired from his office by an Imperial decree of 11 July 1811, and immured in a monastery in Nizhnii Novgorod, where he remained until his death on 21 November 1828.' See Gvosdev (2000: 125). Anton was the brother of the late Georgian king Giorgi and one of the sons of Erekle II.

[348] As Neale (1850: 25) noted, 'The Diœcese of Georgia was originally under the Catholic of Mtsketh; it is now immediately under the Archbishop of Tiflis, and mediately under the Holy Governing Synod of Russia.' However, according to Gvosdev (2000: 125), 'As early as 1802, questions had been raised about his links to anti-Russian members of the royal [Georgian] family. Anton's brother was the same Prince Alexander who was threatening to enter Georgia at the head of a Persian force to restore the Bagratid house to power and his nephew was Prince Levani, who had escaped from deportation to Russia and was active among the Ossetian tribes. Levani was the son of Prince Iulon, the son of King Erekle [II] and Queen Darejan, who had been prevented from succeeding his brother Giorgi as king. While Antoni's personal loyalty to the Russian Emperor had never been openly challenged, he was very conscious of his role as Catholicos-Patriarch, a position which under old Georgian law made him the equivalent of the secular king. He was not prepared to submit meekly to the demands of the Russian government. As General Tormasov noted, "he [the Catholicos] is used to directing everything arbitrarily, by himself, to which local custom gives him the right, on account of his descent from the royal family, as he is the son of King Erekle and the brother of the last king." The Catholicos was not prepared to surrender any of his privileges and was a zealous defender of the old Georgian traditions and laws, and cited the very decrees of Emperor Alexander confirming Georgian autonomy and the independence of the Georgian Church.'

[349] The new treaty was signed on 14 March 1812. See Aitchison (1892: 52).

[350] For the text of the treaty see Aitchison (1892: 48–52).

[351] The attachment to the treaty entitled 'Form of His Royal Highness Abbas Mirza's ratification of the Definitive Treaty with England,' states, 'I have agreed to this same arrangement, and from this period to the end of time hold myself and my heirs, generation after generation, boiund to respect and hold sacred the terms and the Articles comprised in this happy Treaty concluded between the two great States.' See Aitchison (1892: 53).

influence with the king of Persia, arising, perhaps, from his intimate knowledge of the Persian language, manners, and customs, and from the guarded propriety of his conduct since the arrival of the embassy in Persia.'[352]

9.109 'Letters from Persia,' *The National Advocate* (Tuesday, 23 July, 1813) and 'To the Hon. Col Greville Howard[353] MP Grosvenor Place,' *Daily National Intelligencer* (Friday, 22 October, 1813 minus the preface, first letter only): 'As the fortune of war has thrown the following letters into our hands,[354] and as there is nothing in them which even the most scrupulous delicacy towards an enemy renders improper for publication, we have thought it right to give them to the public. They contain matter of a highly interesting nature, both scientific and political. It must be well known to our readers that the French and British governments have been long contending for the supreme influence in Persia. It seems the British ambassador thinks he has fixed that of his court upon an immoveable basis. Be this as it may, what is more worthy of our notice is to see a country, for which nature has done so much, wasted by the scourge of despotism, and of a despotism, too, which does not secure its victims against the horrors of anarchy. Every American ought to be thankful for the goodness of Providence, which has cast his lot in a land, where civilization, freedom, law and order, at once dispense their blessings.

---

[352] As McNeill (1827: 162) noted, 'In 1811, Sir Harford Jones returned to England, and the Persian ambassador, who had been sent to London with the ratification of the preliminary treaty, returned to Persia, accompanied by Sir Gore Ouseley in quality of Ambassador Extraordinary from the King of England .... A definitive treaty was concluded on the basis of the preliminary engagements entered into by Sir H. Jones, and immense presents were lavished on the Shah and his courtiers, to keep alive the friendly feeling which had happily been excited towards England.'

[353] Colonel Fulk(e) Southwell Greville Howard (1773–1846), British member of Parliament (1808–1832). He only took the name Howard after marrying Mary Howard, heiress of Richard Howard of Castle Rising, in 1807. See http://www.historyofparliamentonline.org/volume/1790-1820/member/howard-hon-fulk-greville-1773-1846.

[354] The War of 1812 (June, 1812–February, 1815). The version printed in Britain was entitled 'Some particulars respecting the present State of Persia. Communicated in a Letter to the Hon. Colonel Greville Howard,' with the note, 'Printed among intercepted correspondence in an American newspaper.' See Tilloch (1813: 422–424). More detail is given in Anonymous (1813d): 'A curious seizure has been made on board an American East Indiaman, captured by one of our cruizers. It is some correspondence from Sir Gore Ouseley, Sir James Gambier, and Mr. Stratford Canning, to our Government: which correspondence was found in a printed state. How it could have come into the hands of the Americans we know not. They no sooner obtained possession of it than they caused it to be printed.' It is difficult to determine when and where these letters were originally intercepted by, presumably, an American vessel. Soley (1888: 457–458) lists 18 'single ship actions,' involving British and American warships and privateers between 1812 and 1815. Given that this article is dated 23 July 1813, only a few of those, between August, 1812 and June, 1813, could possibly have resulted in the capture of letters and despatches. Since Ouseley was in Tehran, however, and since several of his letters were sent to Constantinople, it seems much more likely that his letters were transported by courier overland to the Ottoman capital, and from there conveyed on board a British vessel that may have been captured in the Mediterranean or off the Atlantic coast of Spain or France.

To the Honorable Colonel Greville Howard, M.P. Grosvenor Place.
Gehran [sic, Tehran], November 22, 1812.
My dear Howard,

I have just been made happy by the receipt of your letter of the 4th of July last, and, with my wife, beg you will accept our thanks for giving us the pleasure of knowing that Mrs. Greville Howard[355] and yourself are well.

Just after the despatch of my last letter to you, my business with the Shah[356] and his ministers commenced, and although I have travelled over a good deal of Persia since, I have been too constantly occupied with government affairs to have time to arrange what little research I have been able to make. I have not, however, been idle *entirely*, and I flatter myself that my journal and sketch-book will, one of these evenings by the fireside at Claremont, afford you and Mrs. Greville Howard a few hours occupation, if not amusement.

In March last, I concluded a Definitive Treaty with the Shah, by which the paramount influence of the English at this court is, I trust, ensured forever. Ere this, my brother, Sir William,[357] has reached England with it,[358] and he probably, before I reach home, will have given his researches to the world. I sent him into Mazinderan[359] on the banks of the Caspian, and gave him every opportunity whilst with me of rooting up such precious

---

[355] The former Mary Howard (1784–1877). See Causton (1862: 483). In the opinion of Bagot (1901: 141–142), 'No one who had once known Mrs. Greville Howard could ever forget her. There is nobody left like her now; it is an extinct type in England. Though she was a *grande dame* of the past, she nevertheless went with her day. All young people delighted in her, and found her a most sympathetic and interesting companion. She had had an excellent education, and had a man's understanding with a woman's tenderness, and the playfulness and simplicity of a child. Yet she was fine mouche as well, seeing through every one, and possessed of a great sense of humour. She was a good linguist, and an excellent water-colour artist, being one of De Wint's best pupils.'

[356] Fath 'Ali Shah.

[357] Sir William Ouseley. Cf. 9.4.

[358] 'In March the Ambassador and his suite were witnesses of the ceremony of the Núrúz, the New-Day, the first of the Persian year. The definitive treaty between England and Persia was, after long and annoying discussions, arranged and signed, and Sir Gore resolved that his brother should return home with it.' See Reynolds (1846): lxxvii. But as Monteith (1856: 105–106) noted, 'The treaty concluded by Sir Gore Ouseley, and sent to England by his brother Sir William Ouseley, was never confirmed; it was acted upon for some time, but in 1814 was returned unratified by the British government; and Mr. afterwards Sir Henry Ellis, in conjunction with Mr. Morris [sic, Morier; see Markham 1874: 379], who had been left as minister plenipotentiary after the departure of Sir Gore Ouseley, was directed to get the article rescinded, which promised the continuance of a subsidy till some restitution was made to Persia; he was also to have the officers withdrawn who had been left to discipline the Persian troops. It was clear both these clauses, however necessary they might have been at the time the treaty was made, when we were at war with Russia, had become very inconvenient under our altered circumstances, as they might cause our being in a state of war with Russia on one point, whilst we were allies on the other.'

[359] Mazandaran.

remains of antiquity as yet are allowed to exist by the present race of Barbarians. But I much fear that there is little to be seen in Persia which can properly be called antique, except the ruins of Persepolis, and of another ancient city (name unknown) near Murghat [sic, Murghab],[360] and the tomb of Solomon's mother.[361] The characters and sculptures in both the above are evidently coeval; the former, as yet undeciphered, are the arrow headed characters, delineated in Le Bruyn,[362] Kempfer,[363] Chardin,[364] and other travellers.

There are a set of sculptures and inscriptions to be found in Persia in tolerably good preservation, from 12 to 1500 years old, all appertaining to the Sassanian Dynasty of Persian Kings, cut on the native rock near Persepolis, at Shafur [sic, Shapur],[365] Bisitun, Gehran,[366] Shiraz and other places; but as far as I have been able to decipher them, they do not contain more than De Sacy has very ingeniously given to the world.[367] The language is the old Persian, and the character Pehlavi. The sculptures are very spirited; and as Shafur (Sapores) conquered the Roman Emperor Valerian,[368] it is more than probable that he made some of the captive Greeks or Romans exert their talents to immortalise him.[369]

---

[360] Mashhad-e Murghab, c. 6 mi. from Pasargadae. See Jackson (1906: 279).

[361] 'Ḳabr-e Mādar-i Sulemān,' see Weissbach (1894), Jackson (1906: 279), Herzfeld (1908: 1–2).

[362] Cornelis de Bruyn, or Corneille Le Brun (1652–1726 or 1727). An important Dutch painter whose drawings of Persepolis were among the most accurate made by any European traveller. For his career see Floor (1994/2011).

[363] Engelbert Kaempfer (1651–1716). A physician and botanist best known for his descriptions of Japan who, however, also spent time in Iran and left an important record. See Kaempfer (1711). For his career see Brakensiek (2002), Haberland (2009/2012) with refs.

[364] Sir John (Jean) Chardin.

[365] The city founded in Fars by Shabuhr I, generally known as Bishapur. See Le Strange (1905: 262).

[366] A reference to the no longer extant Sasanian relief at Rayy outside of Tehran. As Curzon (1892/1: 351–352) noted, 'This was a semi-obliterated bas-relief of a figure mounted on horseback and armed with a spear ... In the latter part of Fath Ali Shah's reign, however, this bas-relief, in the true spirit of Persian restoration, was effaced to make way for a sculpture representing the long-bearded monarch spearing a lion; and no one now seems to be aware of the history of this wanton palimpsest.' As Fraser (1838b/2: 49), who saw it in 1834 wrote, 'One half-executed sculpture of the Sassanian æra, cut on a tablet of rock, has been effaced to make room for an execrable bas-relief of the present king spearing a lion.' For an image of the Sasanian relief before it was defaced see Ouseley (1823: Pl. 65). For a description of it see also the account by William Price, Sir Gore Ouseley's Assistant Secretary, in Price (1825: 37).

[367] Antoine-Isaac Silvestre de Sacy (1758–1838), French Orientalist. See Silvestre de Sacy (1793).

[368] Valerian was not merely 'conquered' but *captured*, an event commemorated in no fewer than five of Shabuhr I's rock-reliefs. See Herrmann (1983). For the Persian perspective and Tabari's famous account, see Bosworth (1999: 29–30).

[369] This has long been suspected and continues to be treated as a serious likelihood. See e.g. the discussion in Canepa (2009: 66–67).

The more modern remains scarce deserve notice, except as proofs of the magnificence and power of the Changizian[370] Princes and those of the Cefevi[371] Dynasty. Some of the former of 6 and 700 years standing, surpass any structure of the present day, and might at a trifling expense be repaired. But unfortunately it is not the fashion to repair or finish the buildings of other Princes, and therefore the most beautiful Mosques, Palaces and Baths of Shah Abbas, Tahmas and others, are gradually giving way to the temporary structures of the Kajars built with sun-burnt bricks, and totally devoid of taste or convenience.

In short, the sun of Persia has set. Science is confined to the modest few. The Arts are totally lost, and there is not public spirit or munificence enough to encourage the revival of them. I have been greatly disappointed, as you may imagine, having conceived so much more exalted an idea of Persia from their own books, even after making every allowance for the favorite figure of the Persians, hyperbole. The climate, too, has disagreed with me and all the gentlemen of my mission; so that I have been obliged to solicit his royal highness the Prince Regent's gracious permission to allow me to return to England in the spring of 1814. In the interim I shall hope to hear from you often, and shall also write to you whenever any thing interesting occurs.

Lady Ouseley[372] joins me in kindest respects to Mrs. Greville Howard, and with best wishes for you both and kind remembrance to your brother,[373] I remain, my dear Howard, most faithfully and sincerely yours,

GORE OUSELEY.
To Sir James Gambier,[374] &c. &c.
Gehran, November 23, 1812

My dear Sir,

Lady Ouseley's letter to Lady Gambier[375] will have made you acquainted with our movements up to the commencement of last year. Since then I have often intended troubling you with a few lines, knowing the kind interest yourself and Lady Gambier are so good as to take in our welfare, but constant occupation, ill health, and a severe domestic affliction (the death of a beautiful little girl, with whom Heaven blest us last June twelve

---

[370] Mongol.

[371] Safavid.

[372] The former Harriet Georgina Whitelock (c. 1785–1848), whom he married on 12 April 1806. See Reynolds (1846: xxxviii).

[373] John Henry Upton, Viscount Templetown (1771–1846), elder brother of Fulke Greville who took the name Howard after his marriage. See Courthope (1838: 645–646).

[374] Son of Admiral James Gambier, Sir James (1772–1844) was briefly British Consul-General in Lisbon, in Brazil and, for many years, in the United Netherlands. See Anonymous (1844).

[375] Jemima Snell, married in 1797 to Sir James Gambier. See Agnew (1886: 401). She was described by Elizabeth Macquarie (1778–1835), wife of Lachlan Macquarie (see above) as 'one of the most elegant and pleasing women we had ever seen, and very handsome.' See Battersby (2010: 26).

month at Shiraz)[376] altogether conspired to prevent me from intruding on our friends with a list of grievances.

As the papers inform us that you are in London,[377] it is unnecessary for me to enter into a detail of my public operations here, as you can always hear of them at the Foreign Office. My friends flatter me by thinking that I have been successful beyond their most sanguine expectations, and I believe I have got over difficulties hitherto considered insurmountable, and gained points of great importance.

I have, however, been greatly disappointed with respect to Persia itself and its climate. The state of anarchy in which the country has been left since the death of Nadir Shah, has at length rendered it a complete desert; and I have often travelled 30 miles without meeting a single inhabitant. The far-famed climate too has induced a greater secretion of bile in all our party than even that of India, by which we have lost some valuable members of our very confined society. My own health has suffered so materially that I have been forced to solicit H. R. H. the Prince Regent's[378] gracious permission for my returning to England, where I hope for the happiness of seing you and Lady Gambier by the end of 1814.

With Lady O's and my kindest regards to Lady Gambier and yourself, I remain, my dear Sir, yours most faithfully and sincerely,

GORE OUSELEY.'

---

[376] Eliza Shirin Ouseley, born 13 June 1811 'at the Takt-i-Kajar, a palace lent to the Ambassador by the Prince-Governor,' in Shiraz, where she was christened by the Rev. Henry Martyn. 'The child afterwards died, and ws interred at Tahrán. The Ambassador upon this occasion received not the congratulations, but the condolence of the Persian authorities, at the birth of a daughter in the room of a son.' See Reynolds (1846: lxv). As William Ouseley noted, 'Early on the twenty-second [April, 1812], Eliza Shirín, the infant daughter of Sir Gore Ouseley, was relieved by death from the pains of a tedious illness; and in the evening was buried near some trees of the royal garden called *Sultán ábád*, between the *Cazvin* and the *Sháh abd al ázím* gates, within the city walls; a spot granted by the king for this particular purpose. Mr. Morier read the funeral service; and froim the design drawn by him, a little monument was, within 4 or 5 days, erected over the place of interment.' See Ouseley (1823: 349).

[377] Gambier and his family lived in Rio de Janeiro at this time. As Battersby (2010: 26) noted, 'Brazil was a key British trading partner and ally, especially once the cool relations between Britain and the United States descended into open warfare in 1812. Compounding British difficulties was the start of the protracted Latin American revolt against Spanish and Portuguese colonial rule … But skilful diplomacy, aggressive trading and selective use of the force of the Royal Navy enabled Britain to maintain a positive position in the turbulent world of Latin American politics and to exploit these relationships to counterbalance France and the United States. Sir James Gambier played a vital part in this balancing act, working with the Portuguese royal family in exile in Rio de Janeiro from 1808 until 1814.'

[378] George Augustus Frederick (1762–1830), son of George III, later reigned as George IV, was Prince Regent from 1811 to 1820.

9.110 'Intercepted Letters,' *The National Advocate* (Tuesday, 27 July, 1813), 'Intercepted Letters,' *Charleston Courier* (Monday, 9 August, 1813; first para. ends with 'publishing them'): 'Having lately given to our readers several interesting original letters from Persia, we now add others from that country and from Turkey; at the same time expressing our sense of the obligation which the public ought to feel to those who have thus liberally made us the instruments of publishing them. In these letters will be found some traits of British policy worth noting. This policy is the same in Europe, in Asia, in Africa, and in America. To acquire a "*paramount influence*" in every country of the world is the object to which it is directed. For this end all the arts of intrigue and corruption are set in motion. For this end they assumed the office of *keeping the peace* between Russia, and the Turks and Persians; so that the former power might be at full leisure to pursue the war against France. How well they succeeded, not only these letters, but the events of the last winter attest. And all this time, whilst the British pursuing their own sinister objects, and building up an empire in the East greater than that of NAPOLEON in Europe, they are crying out against his rapacity, and begging that other nations would submit to be insulted, plundered and murdered, for fear Great Britain should be conquered by the French Emperor!'

To the Right Honorable Lord Viscount Castelreagh,[379] *H.M. Principal Secretary of State for Foreign Affairs.*

No. 31—PRIVATE
GEHRAN [sic, Tehran], Nov. 22, 1812.

My Lord,— I consider it my duty to make your Lordship acquainted with the wishes, expectations and intentions of His Royal Highness Abbas Mirza, respecting his eldest son Mahommed Mirza, and to solicit your instructions for my guidance in this delicate affair.

It seems that H.R.H. has determined (as far as depends upon himself) to send his eldest son to be educated in England, and that he is under the idea of his wishes having been made known to and approved of by the government.[380] However, on examining the archives here, I cannot find more than a copy of a letter from Sir Harford Jones to H.M. Minister for Foreign Affairs, announcing the above intention; and as far as I can learn, no answer has been ever given to it.

The Prince Royal further wishes to send from 20 to 40 sons of Persian noblemen and chiefs with his son to England, and for a similar purpose.[381]—The expenses of these boys

---

[379] Robert Stewart, Viscount Castlereagh (1769–1822), Foreign Secretary (1812–1822).

[380] While 'Abbas Mirza may have considered sending one or more of his sons to England for their education, he did not in fact pursue this. Although Kotzebue (1819a: 161–162) wrote, 'he has sent two of his sons to England, to be educated there,' the unidentified translator of his work noted, 'Abbas-Mirza has sent two Persians to this country; but they are not his sons. One of them is studying surgery, and the other military engineering.'

[381] Cf. Anonymous (1834a: 323), 'Abbas Mirza sent some young men to be educated in England, and it was his wish that they should translate such works from the English into the Persian language, as were fitted to improve the knowledge and direct the taste of their countrymen.' The experiences of six

will be defrayed by their fathers or the Shah, but those of his son, he seems to think, will be paid by the English government.[382]

Having no instructions on this subject, either from his Majesty's government, or the British government of India, I felt considerably embarrassed in the Prince Royal's conversations on this subject, but endeavored to make my replies as general as possible, until I am honored with his Royal Highness the Prince Regent's commands.

The Prince Royal's last intimation on this subject was a request that I would acquaint your Lordship for the information of H.R.H. the Prince Regent, that his son should proceed to England when he had attained his ninth year. I conceive him to be at present about 6 years old.

With respect to the policy of the measure, it is generally conceived that having the eldest son of the acknowledged heir apparent of Persia in England, may ensure our paramount influence at this court for the ensuing 7 or 8 years, which is the utmost period that its vascillation could be injurious. On the other hand, as the Prince would expect to have an establishment for his son, and masters to attend him at his house or wherever he may reside, the expense to be incurred must also be a subject of consideration.

Praying your Lordship's early instructions on this very delicate point, I have the honor to be with great respect and consideration, my Lord, your Lordship's most obedient and faithful humble servant.

---

young Iranians sent to England by 'Abbas Mirza are recounted in Atai (1992), Green (2016). According to Dabashi (2019: 134) 'Abbas Mirza sent 'two in 1811 and five in 1815.' Although Ouseley's letter, written in late 1812, does not hint that he was aware 'Abbas Mirza had sent any students to England yet. the first two had accompanied Sir Harford Jones on his return to England. Brydges (1834/1: 397) noted, 'I will cut short my parting with Abbas Meerza; and confine myself to saying ... that he put under my care, to proceed to England, two Persian youths of good families, to be educated there and instructed; the one, in medicine and astronomy, the other, in painting;' Further he wrote, 'Lord Wellesley expressed himself greatly pleased with my having brought to England two Persian youths of good family for their education,—instantly gave the most liberal directions for the establishment of them under the care of Sir James Sutherland,—and a few days afterwards ordered me to present them to him at Apsley House, where he received them in the kindest manner.' Brydges (1834/1: 467). In fact, one of the two died not long after his arrival. According to Anonymous (1813c), 'Mahommed Kausim, one of the two Persian youths sent by his Royal Highness Prince Abbas Mirza to this country for education. He was the son of the painter to the prince, and was intended to succeed his father; for which the astonishing genius displayed by him in painting, aided by the scientific instruction he would have received in this country, must have eminently qualified him. He was a youth of very promising talents and pleasing manners, and his premature death is much regretted. He died at Major Sutherland's, Halfmoon-street, March 20.'

[382] In fact, unbeknownst to Ouseley, Jones had written to Castlereagh on 20 April 1821 to let him know that he had not discussed the subject of who would pay for the education of the two Persians, because 'it would have been unbecoming the dignity of His Majesty's Government or the character of the nation considering the great and eminent services the Prince Royal had rendered us in Persia.' See Atai (1992: 16 and n. 20).

GORE OUSELEY.

To Mr. Canning, late British Minister at Constantinople.[383]
PRIVATE.
GEHRAN, Nov. 26th, 1812

Dear Sir,—Now that I trust the danger no longer exits [sic, exists], I will honestly confess that when I wrote you last your brother[384] was in a very bad way indeed with the liver complaint. We gave him, however, calomel[385] enough to set him on his legs until our eratic mission to Aderbaijan was over, and as the weather is now cool he is to be immediately salivated,[386] which, with the precaution I mean to take in future to avoid the heats of summer, will completely cure him of that terrible malady.

The Turks and Persians are at their old work, and in consequence of the stupid pertinacity of the former in refusing the interference of Mr. [Robert] Liston[387] and myself,

---

[383] Sir Stratford Canning (1786–1880), Viscount Stratford de Redcliffe, Secretary of Embassy in Constantinople (1809–1812) and British Ambassador Extraordinary and Plenipotentiary to the Porte (1810–1812). For his life and career see Lane-Poole (1888).

[384] The Rev. William Canning, M.A., Canon of Her Majesty's Chapel of St. George, Windsor, known as 'the Parson,' had been Ouseley's chaplain. See Lane-Poole (1888/1: 235, n. 1). In fact, as Reynolds (1846: cxv) noted, in his diary, Ouseley 'frequently records expressions of devout gratitude towards the providence and goodness of God. He was, unfortunately,—although an Ambassador of such high rank, and deputed to originate precedents in Persia,—unaccompanied, at first, by a chaplain; an omission which must have conveyed to the Persians the impression, either that the English possessed no priesthood or rites, or that their knowledge of the doctrines, and fulfilment of the duties of their Church, rendered them superior to the aids of religious offices, ceremonies, or teaching. Mr. Canning was afterwards appointed chaplain, and accompanied Sir Gore Ouseley to St. Petersburgh.' As Markham (1874: 556) noted, 'The Rev. W. Canning, as chaplain to the Embassy, landed at Bushire in January 1812, and joined the Mission at Tehran.' Canning 'closed his days at Windsor, a canon of the royal chapel.' See Lane-Poole (1888/1: 5, n. 1).

[385] Mercury chloride, used as a cathartic in Western medicine since the sixteeth century. See Lysons (1771).

[386] According to Good and Cooper (1829: 408), 'The best internal medicine is calomel, in small doses, in union with some carminative for the purpose of keeping up the action of the stomach, a healthy state of which is of great importance. The calomel, however, should be employed rather as a stimulant or tonic, so as to excite the mouths of the torpid vessels to a return of healthy action, than as a purgative or with a view of producing salivation.'

[387] Sir Robert Liston (1742–1836), British Ambassador Extraordinary and Plenipotentiary to the Porte (1793–1796, 1812). He succeeded Sir Robert Aislie. Dry (1906: 432) described him as 'froid, réservé, flegmatique, mais homme distingué et de manières correctes.' In viewing some of the architectural sights of Constantinople with Liston, Sir Robert Ker Porter observed that 'his taste was awake to every note-worthy object, from the greatest to the least. See Ker Porter (1821/2: 756). For his service in Constantinople see Cunningham (1993).

Abdallah Pasha[388] has been obliged to pay £50,000 as a *paskkash* to the Shah,[389] and after all owes the saving of Bagdad to my influence here, for I had Mohammed Ali Mirza[390] recalled from the very gates of that city!!![391]

I hope very shortly to hear that the signal services which you rendered the state of Constantinople have been properly rewarded. How exactly you timed the conclusion of the negotiation between Russia and the Porte! for you had scarcely turned your back when Andreossi[392] appeared and set every engine at work to reverse the treaty, and although nothing as yet has taken place, Mr. Liston writes that he is not without fears for the future.

With best respects from Lady Ouseley and myself to Mrs. Canning[393] and your sister,[394] believe me to be with esteem and regard, dear Sir, very sincerely your obedient and faithful humble servant.

---

[388] The candidate consistently backed by 'Abbas Mirza to lead, as a Persian puppet, the Baban dynasty in Sulaimaniyah. See Longrigg (1925: 242–247).

[389] *pishkesh*, 'gift.' On the custom of 'voluntary gifts' to the Shah, made at Nowruz, see e.g. Morier (1812: 237), Lambton (1994), Ashraf (2016). Ker Porter (1821/2: 202) claimed that 'nearly 30,000 tomauns arrive annually as a peace-offering from the Pasha of Bagdad.' Similarly, Schlechta-Wssehrd (1864b: 54, n. 1), 'Von Bagdad aus nur schlecht unterstützt, musste Abdurrahman [Baban] zuletzt die Verzeihung Mohammad Ali Mirza's erflehen die auch, gegen Erlag bedeutender Summen und Stellung von Geisseln, gewährt wurde.' Longrigg (1925: 243, n. 2), however, wrote, 'His [Ker Porter's] assertion that the Pasha paid a regular tribute to Karmanshah cannot be accepted.' For the episode see Brydges (1833: 433–435).

[390] The eldest son of Fath 'Ali Shah by a Georgian slave, appointed governor of Kermanshah in 1807, the year in which Jean-Baptiste Louis Jacques Joseph Rousseau (1780–1831), French consul-general in Aleppo, met him (although Amanat (2011) says he was appointed governor in 1809, Rousseau's testimony contradicts this). Rousseau (1813: 86) noted, 'Muhammed Ali Mirza est agé de vingt-deux ans, il a une physionomie agréable, de l'énergie, du courage, de l'affabilité dansles manières et tous les talens nécessaires pour bien gouverner un état.' Buckingham (1830: 415, n. *) called him 'a high-spirited and aspiring character, and a great favourite of the nation.'

[391] Longrigg (1925: 243) suggested that, 'The Mirza was restrained, perhaps, by the reluctance of his father to break the peace, by the pressure of foreign diplomats in Teheran, and by large sums sent as hush-money to Karmanshah,' noting in n. 1, 'The British Ambassador in Persia persuaded the Shah to respect the 1639 frontier.' It is also surely relevant that on 14 April 1811 an Ottoman ambassador, Abdul Wahhab Efendi,

[392] Antoine François, comte Andréossy (1761–1828), distinguished soldier, diplomat and scholar, French ambassador to the Porte from 28 May 1812 to 13 August 1814. See Marion (1844: 9), Mullié (1852: 20).

[393] As Canning married Harriet Raikes (d. 16 June 1818) on 3 August 1816 (Lane-Poole 1888/1: 86), this 'Mrs. Canning' must be his mother, the former Mehitabel Patrick, 'daughter of a well-to-do Dublin merchant.' See Lane-Poole (1888/1: 4).

[394] His sister Elizabeth married George Henry Barnett, Esq. (Butler 1897: 26), 'head partner in the old banking-house of Barnett, Hoare & Co., by whom she had a numerous family.' See Lane-Poole (1888/1: 4, n. 1).

GORE OUSELEY.'

9.111 'London, Dec. 6,' *Boston Daily Advertiser* (Thursday, 10 February, 1814), 'London, Dec. 6,' *The Repertory* (Thursday, 10 February, 1814), 'London, Dec. 6,' *The Enquirer* (Wednesday, 23 February, 1814), 'London, Dec. 6,' *Charleston Courier* (Tuesday, 1 March, 1814) and 'Untitled,' *Argus of Western America* (Saturday, 19 March, 1814): 'The India Gazettes lately received, notice the arrival of despatches from Sir Gore Ouseley, the British Minister at the Court of Persia, with private communications from Tebreez to the 10th of January last [1813].[395] It appears from them that the war in Georgia, between the Russians and Persians, was still prosecuted on both sides with unabated rancour, but with various success;[396] and the British Officers in the service of the King of Prussia [sic, Persia] found themselves placed, by the continuance of hostilities, in a situation equally singular and embarrassing. They had no choice but to desert the cause which they had espoused, or to fight against the allies of their country.[397] A

---

[395] Ouseley and his suite were in Tabriz from 26 June to 7 September, 1812. See Reynolds (1846: lxxviii).

[396] Cf. Schlechta-Wssehrd (1864b: 56–57) who noted that, even after Ouseley's arrival, 'Indessen hatten die Feindseligkeiten mit Russland ununterbrochen fortgedauert. Doch bestanden dieselben, wie früher, eben nur aus Raubzügen, wobei es persischerseits mehr um Plünderung und Gewinn des auf Russenköpfe gesetzten Blutgeldes zu thun war, als um Erreichung eines höheren strategischen Zweckes. Der einzige ernstlichere Zusammenstoss fand anfangs des folgenden Jahres (Februar 1812) zu Sultanbud im Karabagh in der Nähe von Schuscha ['Sultan-boudá (Kerza-Kertchee, 50 miles from Shoushá); see Baddeley (1908: 83)] Statt und verdient desshalb nähere Erwähnung, weil er, ein selten gewordener Fall, für die Perser günstig ausging.'

[397] As Watson (1866: 164–165) noted, 'Sir Gore Ouseley ... had joined the prince's ['Abbas Mirza's] camp near the Araxes, in the hope of being able to act as mediator between his Royal Highness and the Russian commissioner ... In the meanwhile a report had reached Tabreez to the effect that a peace had been brought about between England and Russia, and as this report was in some degree confirmed by a letter from a Russian officer in the Caspian, Sir Gore Ouseley ordered the English officers with the Shah's army not to take any further part in the military operations against Russia. He further informed the Russian commissioner of his having issued this instruction.' Rawlinson (1849: 27) observed, 'In 1812 the reconciliation of England and Russia, which followed on Napoleon's rupture with the Czar, necessitated the withdrawal of the British officers from the battle field, and the inferiority of the Persian troops became at once apparent.' Similarly, as Wheeler 1871: 44 noted, 'The diplomatic complication of being engaged in a close and defensive alliance with two powers who were in active hostility to each other, naturally led to an attempt on the part of the British ambassador to reconcile the differences between the Courts of St. Petersburg and Teheran.' It is in light of this sudden alteration that Ouseley's testy exchange with 'Abbas Mirza over Major D'Arcy's return journey should be understood. As Ouseley noted, on 1 September 1813, in Tabriz, 'After a long and tolerably good-humoured discussion about a peace with Russia, I accidentally said that Major D'Arcy delayed his departure until I had accounts from Dr. Campbell about the prospect we might have of a peace, or otherwise, that I might give immediate intelligence to Lord Cathcart, the English Amassador at the Russian court.' 'Abbas Mirza protested that D'Arcy had better not travel via Tiflis to St. Petersburg, since he knew all of the strengths of the Persian forces and might prove to be a traitor.

regard to their own character, however, as well as the honour of the English name (which in the eyes of all the Persians would have been forever branded with infamy by a dereliction of their engagements at so critical a period), impelled them to embrace the latter alternative, painful as it must have been;[398] and it will be regarded as an anomaly in history that while Russia and Great Britain were manfully and conjointly maintaining in the North the greatest struggle that perhaps Europe ever witnessed in modern times, a body of British officers yielding precedence to none in fidelity and zeal to the cause of their country, were employed in the South, in an active and romantic contest against the Russian army.'[399]

9.112 'Persians and Russians,' *Connecticut Herald* (Tuesday, 22 February, 1814): 'The Persian camp (containing 14,000 men) was surprised in Oct. 1812, by the Russian army, on the banks of the river Arras.[400] The former lost 2000 killed, 500 wounded, and all their

---

Ouseley told him bluntly that this was an insult to D'Arcy's integrity as a British officer, and that, at any rate, as D'Arcy was no longer in Persian employ and was a free British citizen, he might travel however he wished. See Reynolds (1846: xciii).

[398] As Watson (1866: 165) noted, even after Ouseley terminated the secondment of the British military advisers to 'Abbas Mirza's service, 'On the entreaty, however, of the crown-prince and his ministers, the English ambassador permitted two of the British officers, with 13 sergeants, to remain in the Persian camp. These officers received no specific orders as to how they were to conduct themselves, but they thought that they were bound in honour not to refuse to fight for the prince under whom they were serving.'

[399] After Napoleon's invasion of Russia British policy changed 'and the British Ambassador became as anxious to bring about peace as he had formerly been to push on the war. The English officers were withdrawn from the Persian army; and it was only at the earnest entreaty of Abbas Mirza that Captain Christie and Captain Lindesay [Lindsay] were permitted to remain in the camp ... Orders had been given to the British officers to quit the Persian camp, if any forward movement should take place.' See Monteith (1856: 87–88). As Drouville (1819: 101–102, n. *) noted, Sir Gore Ouseley 'avait reçu depuis long-temps, par Mr. de *Vezelago* capitaine de haut bord et commandant les forces maritimes de S.M. L'Empereur [Alexander I], sur la mer Caspienne, la ratification officielle de la paix, entre cette dernière puissance et la Grand-Bretagne; il n'en continua pas moins à opposer les officiers anglais à l'armée Russe, malgré toutes les observations qui lui furent faites à cet égard, et desquelles il ne tint aucun compte. A l'époque dont je parle, et quand le Prince ['Abbas Mirza] voulut partir pour se rapprocher de l'*Araxe*, Messieurs L ... [Lindsay] et C ... [Christie] qui tenaient beaucoup au commandement de leur corps, furent chez leur Ambassadeur pour savoir de quelle manière ils devaient se conduire dans cette circonstance; celui-ci mis la main devant ses yeux, disant qu'il ne voulait rien voir, et qu'ils pourraient faire comme ils voudraient. Il savait bien que ces jeunes officiers n'auraient pas renoncé volontiers au commandement de leurs troupes, et encore moins aux énormes émolumens qu'elles leur rapportaient.'

[400] The battle of Aslanduz on 19 October 1812. As de Fonton (1840: 102–103) noted, 'Sous les généraux Paulucci et Rtistcheff, qui se succédèrent comme généraux en chef au Caucase, se développe la carrière brillante de Kotlarewski. Colonel en 1811, il se porte, à la tête de deux bataillons, sur Akhalkalaki [against the Turks], escalade ses murs malgré une résistance opiniâtre, et se rend maître de la place en moins de deux heures. Elevé pour ce haut fait au grade de général, il reçoit, après la paix avec la Porte, conclue à Bucharest, le commandement d'un détachement contre les Persans. Ce n'était qu'une poigné d'hommes, mais dont sa parole et son exemple avaient fait des

artillery but two pieces.[401] The Prince of Persia narrowly escaped being made prisoner.[402] Major Christie, an English officer, was killed.'[403]

---

héros. Les masses nombreuses qu'Abbaz-Mirza conduit à sa rencontre ne l'effraient pas. Il les rencontre à Aslanduz. Les Persans, au nombre de 20,000 hommes, occupaient la rive droite de l'Arax, Kotlarewski n'avait que 1500 hommes, 800 dragons et 6 pièces d'artillerie. Ayant franchi la rivière au-dessus de la position des Persans, il tombe sur leur aile gauche avec toute sa masse, l'enfonce, et met successivement en déroute le reste de l'armée persane.' Schlechta-Wssehrd (1864b: 60–61), gave a vivid account. Von Akoghlan her in Eilmärschen vorrückend, gelang es ihm [Kotlyarevsky], unter dem Schutze des Dunkels, die auf dem jenseitigen Ufer des Araxes aufgestellten spärlichen persischen Vorposten wegzufangen und ungehindert den Fluss zu überschreiten. Beim ersten Morgengrauen...stand er am Eingange des offenen Lagers dessen schlaftrunkene Vorwachen, im Glauben, es seien die erwarteten Wandertribus welche einträfen, sich hüteten Allarm zu schlagen. Erst der Anblick der plötzlich entfalteten feindlichen Standarten riss sie aus ihrem tödtlichen Irrthume. Panischer Schrecken und augenglickliches Drängen zur Flucht waren die natürlichen Folgen der Überraschung. Der Kronprinz allein bewahrte seine gewöhnliche Kaltblütigkeit. Das Erste war, dass er seiner Kameelartillerie gebot, Salven abzufeuern, um seine noch zum Theil schlummernden Soldaten zu wecken und die Erwachten zu sammeln. Dann warf er sich mit seiner nächsten Umgebung den ansprengenden Kossacken entgegen die er auch im ersten Anpralle zurückwarf. Von dem heftigen Kartätschenfeuer der Russen zurückgetrieben, wollte er hierauf dasselbe seinerseits erwiedern, aber die englischen Officiere welche die neue Artillerie commandirten, weigerten sich, gegen eine Macht, mit welcher ihre Regierung seither Frieden geschlossen hatte, den Kampf aufzunehmen. Sein langes orientalisches Gewand aufschürzend, versuchte daher Abbas Mirza das Feuer selbst zu leiten, indem er eigenhändig mehrere der Geschütze losbrannte. Aber die junge und kampfungeübte Mannschaft hielt nicht Stand und gar bald verwandelte sich der chaotische Zustand in wilde Flucht.'

[401] Baddeley (1908: 88) put the loss of human life at 10,000 Persians, 'the Russian loss being only three officers and 124 men killed and wounded.' As for ordinance, according to de Fonton (1840: 103), '9 pièces de canon, 36 fauconnets, toutes les munitions et un riche camp sont le butin de l'armée russe.' In contrast, Monteith (1856: 95) put the figure at, 'Twelve out of fourteen English guns were taken by the Russians, having fallen into the unfinished intrenchments.' According to Baddeley (1908: 89), 'Eleven cannon of English make were captured, bearing the inscription, according to the Russians, "from the King of Kings to the Shah of Shahs."'

[402] As Schlechta-Wssehrd (1864b: 62) wrote, 'Abbas Mirza selbst gerieth in die äusserste Gefahr. Sein Pferd stürzte im Getümmel und warf ihn in einen Graben. Die Meinung, er habe sich bei dem Falle getödtet, steigerte natürlicherweise den Schrecken seiner Begleiter. Nach einiger Zeit sich wieder aufraffend, glaubte er sich dennoch verloren, da sein Pferd zur Fortsetzung der Flucht untauglich geworden war. Mit geschwungenem Säbel stürzte er daher auf einen eben vorübersprengenden Reiter der ein, wie der Kronprinz glaubte, erbeutetes, Handpferd nach sich schleppte, um demselben dieses Mittel der Rettung abzukämpfen. Glücklicherweise erkannte er noch im letzten Augenblicke den vermeintlichen feindlichen Cavalleristen als einen seiner eigenen Stallleute dessen Handpferd er nun benützte, um sich in Sicherheit zu bringen.'

[403] Captain Charles Christie, 5th Bombay Native Infantry, had originally come to Persia as a member of Malcolm's second mission, travelling separately however from Bombay together with Ensign Henry Pottinger. See Kaye (1856: 512, n. *), MacAlister (1910: 30), Ekbal (1991/2011). As Pottinger (1816: 245) noted, 'Captain Christie having been selected by His Majesty's Envoy at the Court of Persia, as one of the officers to remain in that country, to fulfil that part of the treaty relative to organizing the Persian troops, he wrote out a hasty Memoir of his journey in the course of a halt of

9 The First Russo-Persian War and British, French and Persian... 881

9.113 'Russia and Persia,' *The Plattsburgh Republican* (Saturday, 11 June, 1814): 'A peace has been concluded, between Russia and Persia.[404] The following are the terms upon which it was made:

---

5 or 6 days made by General Malcolm at Muragha [Maraga] for the express purpose of affording him an opportunity to do so.' Kinneir (1813: 114) acknowledges referring to his journal. Goldsmid (1880: 159) referred to him as 'the highly distinguished officer who commanded Abbas Mirza's infantry.' His death occurred after the Persian camp was surprised on 30 October 1812. Although Christie's brigade 'had already been withdrawn by him' (Monteith 1856: 90), when Lindsay [Major Henry Lindsay Bethune , the artillery commander, see below] and a few of his men were threatened with capture while scouting for ammunition, their retreat 'was covered by some light infantry under Major Christie.' At midnight, however, the Russians launched a surprise attack. 'The Persian troops ... began, in the darkness and confusion, to fire at each other. The attack had been so sudden and unexpected, that the English officers had only the choice of fighting on the side of the Persians, or of abandoning in a situation of great difficulty the prince who had entrusted the men to their charge, and, above all, the soldiers whom they had long commanded, and who were devoted to them; and they determined to run every risk, even that of disobedience to their orders, in preference to leaving the troops when actually engaged with the enemy. Major Christie was shot in the neck, and more than half the battalion he had raised and disciplined himself fell in the attempt to bring him off ... Christie was discovered in the morning by a Russian party, who offered assistance; but he had determined never to be taken alive, and cut down the officer who attempted to raise him. A report was sent to General Kutlerousky that there was a wounded English officer who refused to surrender; orders were sent to disarm and secure him at all hazards. Christie, however, made a most desperate resistance, and is said to have killed six men before he was despatched, being shot by a Cossack.' See Monteith (1856: 93–94). A different account of the battle can be found in Drouville (1819: 102–103), according to whom 'le 1 Octobre à 10 heures du matin,' the Russian forces launched an attack on 'le flanc gauche et les derrières de l'armée persane. La confusion se mit partout, malgré les efforts du brave major Christie qui se battit fort bien, mais qui blessé et pris par les Kosaques qui le reconnurent pour Anglais, fut mis en pièces, d'aprés un manifeste de Monsieur de Kotlérowsky. Ce général avait su qu'au mépris de la nouvelle alliance qui unissait les deux nations, ces officiers étaient dans les rangs ennemis et il avait ordonné de les saisir morts ou vifs.' 1 October is probably a misprint for 31 October, for the attack which began on the night of 30 October lasted into 31 October, as confirmed by Pottinger (1816: 245, n. *), who wrote, 'Captain Christie was unfortunately killed in an attack made by a body of Russian troops on the Persian camp on the night of the 31*st of October*, 1812. No officer ever died more universally regretted, as none had ever lived more beloved and respected. His acquirements and talents were of the very highest order, and his untimely death was not only felt by his numerous friends to be an irreparable loss, but was justly considered such, in a public light, to his country and his employers.' According to Schlechta-Wssehrd (1864b: 62), 'Major Christie, der englische Militär-Instructor, fiel mit einigen der ihm beigegebenen englischen Soldaten, ohne sich zu vertheidigen, unter den ersten Streichen der Andringenden.' Dr. John Cormick's lengthy letter to Malcolm of 23 November 1812 explaining the circumstances of Christie's death as he understood them appears in Kaye (1856/2: 623–630). A memorial was raised to Christie in St. James's Gardens, London, bearing the text, "To the memory of Captain Charles Christie of the 5th Regiment, Bombay Native Infantry, killed in Persia by the river Aras, near Aslandus in Georgia in an attack made by a body of Russian troops on the Persian camp. 1st November 1812, aged 32 years."' Note that Aslanduz is on the Persian side of the Aras, not in Georgia.

[404]The Treaty of Gulistan, mediated by Sir Gore Ouseley and signed on 12 October, 1813. For the text of the treaty see Hurewitz (1956: 84–86). As McNeill (1836: 64) noted, 'The basis on which this

Persia cedes to Russia the government of Karabog,[405] Gannshiu,[406] Schekin,[407] Schirwan, Kuoth,[408] Baka,[409] Talischin,[410] & the whole of Daglostan.[411] Persia renounces besides, all its claims to Georgia, with the province of Schuragel[412] upon Immanetta,[413] Guira,[414] Mingrelia, and Abeleaise;[415] and gives up to Russia forever the sovereignty of all those countries.[416]

The Russian flag alone shall be allowed on the *Caspian Sea*, so that no other power shall be permitted to have ships of war or vessels on that sea.'[417]

---

treaty was negotiated, was that each party should retain the territory of which it was in possession when hostilities ceased; and Russia, by this arrangement, from her having a garrison in Lankeran, would become entitled to a considerable portion of the khanat or lordship of Talish.' Gulistan is mod. Gülüstan in the Republic of Azerbaijan.

[405] Qarabagh.

[406] Ganja.

[407] Sheki.

[408] Kuban, north of Baku.

[409] Baku.

[410] Talysh.

[411] Daghestan.

[412] Shoregel/Shuragel.

[413] Imeritia.

[414] Guria.

[415] Abkhazia.

[416] Article 2 of the treaty stipulates, 'The status quo ad presentem having been agreed on as the basis of treating in virtue of this arrangement, the several districts hitherto possessed by the respective States shall remain under their subjection.' See Hurewitz (1956: 84). Cf. Krahmer (1903: 21). Article 3 of the treaty reads, 'His Majesty the King of Persia, in demonstration of his amicable sentiments towards the Emperor of Russia, acknowledges in his own name and that of his heirs the sovereignty of the Emperor of Russia over the provinces of Karabagh and Georgia, now called Elizabeth Paul [Elizabetpol, i.e. Ganja], the districts of Shekie, Shiriwan, Kobek, Derbend, Bakoobeh, and such part of Talish as is now possessed by Russia, the whole of Degesten, Georgia, the tract of Shoorgil, Achook, Bash, Gooreea, Mingrelia, Abtichar, the whole country between the boundary at present established and the line of Caucasus, and all the territory between the Caucasus and the Caspian Sea.' See Hurewitz (1956: 85). But as Krausse (1899: 111) observed, 'Sweeping as were the clauses in the Treaty of Gulistan, they were so haltingly drawn and so vaguely worded, as to tend rather to add to the differences between the two countries. For thirteen years was the frontier a constant scene of squabbles and fighting.'

[417] As Krausse (1899: 111) noted, 'This treaty is remarkable for the number and extent of privileges it secures to Russia, while Persia gets nothing whatever … Russian men-of-war are permitted to navigate the Caspian, but no others … Despite the stringency of this treaty, which, it will be noted, forbids the Persians to have a fleet upon their own seaboard, it was signed without demur, for the reason that the Shah was not in a position to protest.'

9 The First Russo-Persian War and British, French and Persian ...

9.114 'Untitled,' *The Geneva Gazette* (Wednesday, 15 June, 1814): 'A Treaty of peace has been concluded between Russia and Persia.'[418]

9.115 'Translated from the Journal de Paris, for the Boston Daily Advertiser,' *New-York Herald* (Monday, 11 July, 1814): 'Petersburg, Feb. 20.—Our Gazette contains the conditions of the peace between Russia and Persia.—The following is the substance of them.

Persia cedes to Russia the Governments of Karabag, Gannshin, Schekin, Schirwan, Derbent, Kuban, Baku, Talischin, and all Daghistan. She renounces besides all her pretentions to Georgia, the province of Schuragei upon the Isharetta, Gurier, Mingrelia, and Abelaiae, and cedes to Russia forever the sovereignty of all these countries.

The Russian flag will command alone upon the Caspian Sea, as no other power can have any ship or other vessel in this sea.

The following regulations have been made concerning the commerce between the two powers.

Russian subjects may export their merchandize not only into Persia, but likewise into the neighbouring kingdoms. They pay only 5% on all that they import.[419] Russian subjects can be compelled to appear in commercial matters, only before the Russian consuls and other agents in the different towns of Persia.'[420]

9.116 'Untitled,' *The Geneva Gazette* [Geneva NY] (1 November, 1815): 'London, Aug. 5. A very elegant and admired stud of about 30 horses has arrived, in charge of Sir Gore Ousley, as a present from the Prince Royal of Persia[421] to his Royal Highness the Prince Regent.[422] Sir Gore's attention induced him to accompany the Horses on the journey from Persia to St. Petersburgh, and on the voyage from that port to this country in person.'[423]

---

[418] The Treaty of Gulistan. Cf. 9.116.

[419] Thus Article 9 notes, 'The duties on Russian merchandise brought to Persian ports shall be in the proportion of five hundred dinars (or 5%) on property of the value of one toman, which having been paid at one city the goods may be conveyed to any part of Persia without any further demand of duty being made on any pretence whatever.' See Hurewitz (1956: 86).

[420] According to Article 8, 'Merchants having occasion to complain of failure of payment or other grievances will state the nature of their cases to the mercantile agents; or, if there are none resident in the place, they will apply to the Governor, who will examine into the merits of their representations, and will be careful that no injustice be offered this class of men.' See Hurewitz (1956: 86).

[421] 'Abbas Mirza.

[422] George August Frederick, later George IV.

[423] In a letter from Sir Gore Ouseley to the Prince Regent dated Tehran, 20 March 1812, Ouseley noted, 'Your Royal Highness's Arab horse and some trifles, the produce of this country, will accompany the ratified Treaty to England.' See Aspinall (1938: 49–50). Cf. Anonymous (1812c: 83), 'On Tuesday, the 24th instant, were brought to town, from Portsmouth, where they were landed from on board his Majesty's ship Alceste, under the care of Mr. James Adkins, four beautiful Persian horses; two from the King of Persia, and one from Sir Gore Ouseley, our Ambassador, as presents to

9.117 'Foreign News. From late London Papers. London, Nov. 14,' *Poulson's American Daily Advertiser* (Friday, 5 January, 1816): 'It is said Sir George [sic, Gore] Ouseley is to receive a pension of 2000*l*. per annum for his mission to Persia,[424] in addition to any foreign grant, for having negociated a peace between the Russians and Persians—those two powers having been previously in a state of hostility for many years.'

9.1 Miscellaneous

Some Aspects of Persian Geography

9.118 'Monday, January 14, 1805,' *Salem Register* (Monday, 14 January, 1805), 'Untitled,' *Charleston Courier* (Tuesday, 5 February, and Monday, 18 February, 1805), 'From the Salem Register,' *Mississippi Herald & Natchez Gazette, Extra* (Saturday, 11 May, 1805) and 'Untitled,' *Poulson's American Daily Advertiser* (Monday, 27 May, 1805): 'Some late accounts assure us that the Russians are active upon their southern territories, and are encroaching upon their Persian neighbours. Whether these are repetitions of the same accounts which were brought last autumn, is uncertain; but the importance of all the movements of the extensive Empire of the North, is unquestionable, especially in regard to the extent of their southern possessions. To judge of the object, we have already noticed the position of the Persian Provinces towards which the Russians direct their armies, and shall now refer to the past history of the country which Russia has repeatedly attempted to gain. Georgia and Erivan fill part of the space between the Black and Caspian seas, and by these the Persians have an important navigation. The following is the history of Derbend, the sea-port of the Persian province of Erivan, as given by Sir W. Ousely [sic, Ouseley],[425] from the Oriental Geography of Ebn Staukal [sic, Haukal], a Traveller of the tenth century. Derbend[426] is a city built upon the shore of the sea [Caspian], on two banks of a bay, with

---

his Royal Highness the Prince Regent, and the fourth to the Marquis Wellesley, in consequence of the Treaty of Amity and Friendship concluded between the King of Persia and Great Britain.' Also Price (1832: 1), in which the author, who was Assistant Secretary to Sir Gore Ouseley, noted that on 1 July 1812 he set out with Sir William Ouseley, accompanied by 'several grooms in care of some horses, presents to the Prince Regent (now H M George IV,) and Marquis Wellesley.' Note the 2 year discrepancy in dates between these two sources.

[424] The figures of £2000 and £5000 per annum can be found in various sources. According to Kelly (1910: 138), Ouseley had received 'a pension of £5000 … in return for his eminent diplomatic services.' The same figure appears in Joyce (1896: 3) and M'Cullagh (1906: 14).

[425] Sir William Ouseley. Cf. 8.29, 8.31.

[426] From here the text is a direct quotation from Ouseley (1800: 158–159).

9.1 Miscellaneous

two walls so constructed as to render the navigation more convenient and safe, and a chain is drawn across the entrance, that ships may not enter or sail out without permission: and these two walls are formed of stone and lead: and this town of Derbend is situated on the coast of the sea [of] Taberistan.[427] It is larger than Ardebil, with many fields and meadows, and cultivated lands. It does not produce much fruit, but the people supply that from other quarters. A wall of stone extends from the city to the mountain; and another of clay, to hinder Caffres[428] from coming into the town. Part of this wall projects a little way into the sea, so that ships may not come too near the ramparts. This wall is a strong building, and was the work of Noushirvan Aadel (the just).[429] The city of Derbend is very large, and remarkable: it is surrounded by enemies, who have different languages. On one side of Derbend is a great mountain, called Adeib. On this mountain they assemble every year and kindle fires to terrify their enemies.[430] The sovereigns of Persia have considered the possession of this city as a matter of great importance, and have established a race of people called Tairberan,[431] to guard it. And there is another tribe called Heilabshar,[432] and another called Lekzan.[433] There are also two other tribes, the Leniran and Servan. The foot soldiers are most of these tribes; they have few horsemen. Derbend is the port

---

[427] 'Sea of Tabaristan' is here used as an alternative name for the Caspian.

[428] *kafir*. Pagan, idolater. Cf. Kāfiristān, 'country of Unbelief ... which had never heard of Muḥammad.' See Minorsky (1955: 70). In this case it probably refers to pagan Daghestanis.

[429] Xosrow I Anushirvan, 'Xosrow of the Immortal Soul.' As Minorsky (1958: 13–14) noted, 'Possibly already under the Achæmenids some measures were taken to protect the Caucasian passes against the invaders, but the memory of the fortification of the most important of them, Darband (in Armenian *Chʻor*, in Arabic *al-Ṣūl*, but usually *al-Bāb*) and of a series of "gates" (i.e. fortified passes), is traditionally connected with the names of the Sasanian kings Kāvāt (in Arabic: Qubādh b. Fīrūz, A.D. 488–531) and his famous son Khusrau (Chosroes, Kisrā) Anūshirvān (A.D. 531–79).' The same tradition is found in the *Darbandnama* for which see Kazem-Beg (1851).

[430] According to Qazvini, 'Seitwärts von der Stadt [Derbend] ist ein steiler hoher Berg, genannt *el-Dhib*, auf dessen Gipfel jedes Jahr viel Holz zusammengetragen wird, um damit Feuer anzuzünden, wenn man die Bewohner von Arran, Aserbaidschan und Armenien vor der Ankunft des Feindes zu warnen hat.' See Dorn (1847: 62).

[431] This correction was suggested by Dorn (1848: 557, n. 16). According to Razi, '*Sirehgheran* und *Terseran* [Taberseran?] sind zwei Gebiete seitwärts von Bab-el-abwab,' i.e. Derbend. See Dorn (1847: 82), Vockerodt (1758: 481). According to Sprenger (1841: 401), 'Tabasseran ... is the name of an ancient fortress, and of a province of Daghestán. It has with the Persians, also, the name ... Taberserán.' Minorsky (1937: Map xi), marked Tabasaran just to the southwest of Derbend.

[432] Neumann (1830: 80) compared this with 'Khailenturk,' 'one of the numerous tribes of Huns on the other side of the pass of Djor, or the Alanian-gate...mentioned by Elisæus,' i.e. the Armenian historian Elishe. Dorn (1848: 557, n. 17) considered it a corruption of Filbanan, another name for Tabarsaran. My thanks to Willem Floor for his help with this reference.

[433] Dorn (1875: 55), gives Lekzan in Nasr ed-Din Tusi as a variant of Lezgin. Cf. Minorsky (1937: 454, 1958: 181) with refs., s.v. Lakz.

town for Khozr,[434] and Serir,[435] and Gurkan,[436] and Taberistan,[437] and Kurge, and Kapchak;[438] and from it they send linen cloths to all parts of Arran[439] and Azerbaijan. Here they also weave tapestry, or carpets, and cultivate safron. Such is the accoiunt of this ancient Geographer.[440] In the French history of Nader Chah, given in the fifth vol. of the splendid edition of Sir William Jones's Works,[441] notice is taken of the operations of this Hero in this country in 1734. After this conqueror had quieted Tefflis, he prepared to pass to Derbend to chastise Khan Khouim.[442] This officer had received orders from the Ottoman Generalissimo to enter Persia by Derbend. In consequence Nader ordered Ali to throw himself into Derbend, and to wait his arrival. As fortune had conducted the rapid movements of this Hero of the age from success to success, his name everywhere excited admiration and terror. The Emperor of the Turks, observing how seasonably the Russians had made peace, by abandoning the provinces they had taken, and finding how many checks his troops had received, determined to appease Nader.[443] Khouim was ordered not to advance, and the limits of the Turkish and Persian empires were proposed as the basis of a treaty of peace. The messenger reached Nader while at Tefflis. His reply was, We will quench the fire, of dissention, by the liquid fire of death, and make our enemies drink

---

[434] Khos/zrek, south of Kumukh, scene of a victory over Sorkhay, khan of Qazi-Qomuq, by the Russian (Karabaghi) Major-General Prince Valerian Grigoryevich Madatov (1782–1829) in 1820. See Brosset (1857: 316), Baddeley (1908: 137). The name appears as Joserek in Gutierrez (1827: 397).

[435] *ard al-Sarir*, also called Avaristan, a mediaeval Christian kingdom populated by Caucasian Avars in northern Daghestan. Cf. Minorsky (1937: 447–450, 1958: 182) with refs., s.v. al-Sarīr (Avaria).

[436] A variant of Gorgan. See Forbiger (1844/2: 571, n. 16).

[437] 'The hilly part of western Mazanderân,' cf. the ancient Tapyroi. See Malte-Brun (1822: 264), Minorsky (1937: 134, 1958: 151–154).

[438] The Dasht-e Kapchak, 'a territory stretching from the Caspian Sea to Kazan.' See Michie (1864: 172).

[439] An archaic name for Karabagh. See Marquart (1901: 116–119). It 'is included in the great triangle of land lying to the west of the junction point of the rivers Cyrus and Araxes—the Kur and the Aras of the Arabs.' See Le Strange (1905: 177).

[440] This marks the end of the verbatim transcription from Ouseley (1800).

[441] Cf. 8.68, 8.81. Published as Jones (1770) and later republished as Jones (1799/5).

[442] 'Après que l'armée victorieuse eût demouré vingt jours à Teflis, elle se prépara à passer en Derbend, pour châtier Khan Khouïm. Voici les circonstances de cette affaire. Quand Abdalla Pacha Kiuprili Ogli fut nommée généralissime par la cour Ottomane, un ordre fût envoïé en même tems à Khan Khouïm d'assembler ses troupes de Tartares, & d'entrer en Perse par la route de Selak & de Derbend. Aussi-tôt que l'illustre conquérant en fût informé, il commanda à Ali Khan gouverneur de Chirvan, & au gouverneur d'Asterabad, de se jetter dans la ville de Derbend, & d'y faire ferme, mais de ne point livrer bataille, & d'attendre l'apparence splendide des banniéres toûjours victorieuses.' See Jones (1770/1: 219–20) = Jones (1799/5: 222).

[443] 'L'empereur des Turcs, voïant que les Russes avoient été trop heureux de faire la paix, en rendant les provinces qu'ils retenoient, et ses propres troupes aïant reçû tant d'échec, songea serieusement à appaiser Nader.' See Jones (1770/1: 220).

9.1 Miscellaneous

destruction instead of life. We are fixed.[444] Winter and all its horrours, snow topped mountains, and dangerous defiles did not oppose him; like the sun, says the Persian he looked with the same eyes on proud hills and humble vales, and like a Lion he killed, he sacked, he humbled at his will. To Derbend he sent families from Taberseran and Dagestan, and victory gave glory to the country, blessed with his protection.

We cannot refuse to give the account which follows, in the description of Asia.[445] The great cities of Aran and Armenia, are Gangia and Erivan, its capital, a large, but unpleasant town, without any fine edifice in it, or any other ornament than a number of gardens and vineyards. Some geographers place in Armenia, cities, which we consider as belonging to Georgia, Shamcur[446] and Tefflis, a city not large, but tolerably elegant. It is washed on the eastern side by the Cyrus. The cities of Shirvan are Bacu, a port on the Caspian, Shamakhi, a city well known to the Russians, and Derbend, or the Barrier, which stands at the foot of Mount Caucasus, and commands the Caspian. This place was called by the ancients *Caspiæ Portæ*, by the Turks, Demir Capi, or the gate of iron, and by the Arabs, Babelabwab, or the important passage. It was antiently considered as the boundary of the Persian Empire, and an old King of Persia built to the north of it a vast wall, like that of China, which has been repaired at different times, in order to prevent the incursions of the northern savages. Some ruins of this mound are still to be seen, and the cement of it is as hard as marble. This city was once thought so considerable, that the governor of it had the privilege of giving audience in a golden chair, whence the territory around it was called, Serireddhehab, or the throne of gold.[447] It has long been the purpose of Russia to possess this country, and no Nader is found in the Russian [sic, Persian] Empire to inject the necessary fears, which can retard the Russian arms.'[448]

---

[444] 'Nous étancherons le feu de la dissension avec la splendeur liquide de nos cimeterres, & nous ferons boire à nos ennemis la coupe de la destruction, au lieu de la liqueur sacrée qu'ils attendoient: notre résolution sur ce point es irrevocablement fixée.' See Jones (1770/1: 220–221).

[445] The text that follows, ending with 'throne of gold,' is taken from Jones' A description of Asia, according to the Oriental geographers.' See Jones (1799/5: 571–573).

[446] Shamkir, c. 40 km northwest of Ganja. In Le Strange (1905: 178–179) we read, 'the ruins ... still exist, and this town in the third (ninth) century was known as Mutawakkilîyah, from having been rebuilt by orders of the Caliph Mutawakkil in the year 240 (854).' In some periods it was 'the western frontier point (thaghr) of Ganja.' See Minorsky (1953: 26).

[447] According to Istakhri, 'Man sagt, dass dieser Thron (serir) einem Könige von Persien gehörte, aus Gold war, und das Dieses Serir, sagt man, war ein Thron, und zwar der goldene Thron einer der persischen Könige. Als die Herrschaft ihrem Hause entging, begab sich einer seiner Nachkommen dorthin, und nahm den Thron mit sich. Man sagt ferner, er sei ein Nachkomme der Behram Tschubin gewesen.' See Dorn (1847: 57) and the discussion in Vacca (2017: 8).

[448] This last sentence is presumably that of the writer of the article, since no other source can be found.

Russian Perspectives on Persian Trade

9.119 'Untitled,' *Salem Register* (Monday, 24 June, 1805) and 'Untitled,' *Alexandria Daily Advertiser* (Saturday, 6 July, 1805): 'The Russians regard, as their most interesting concerns, the conquest of that part of the Persian Empire which lays conveniently for their Trade. Ten years have given to the Russians the correct view of the size of Persia from the able investigation of Pallas.[449] The Persian trade had not been profitable. The tribute for the raw silk, especially in specie sent out of the Country; the rents for the Fisheries; the importation of raw and spun cotton and madder, and the galls which are not furnished from the few oak forests in their temperate southern climates. To these he adds that the manufactured goods, annually imported from Persia, may be reckoned at 100,000 rubles. Pallas then observes that the Russians made slow advances in their exports. That Cochineal was the most considerable and most lucrative.[450] From Astrican annually are exported a thousand pood, at 300 rubles a pood.[451] Indigo was formerly a good article, but since some conquests in Multan,[452] it had been brought from Lahor to Persia and thence to Astrican.[453] The exports in cloths may amount to 150,000 rubles, velvet from 15 to 20,000, and other articles to 40,000 rubles. Sugar is exported to the value of 20,000 rubles. He then observes, "As the balance, therefore, to trade with Persia is against us, it is worthy of investigation in what manner our commercial intercourse could be rendered, if not profitable, at least, less

---

[449] Peter Simon Pallas. Cf. 8.71.

[450] Red dyes have been made from several insect species throughout history, but the source of the 'cochineal' exported from Russia has been identified chemically as a member of the genus *Porphyrophora*, e.g. Polish cochineal (*Porphyrophora polonica*) and Armenian cochineal (*P. hamelii*). See Melo (2009: 7), Phipps (2010: 8–9), correct Donkin (1977: 853) who identified it as *Margarodes polonicus*. Cf. Fraser (1826: 370), 'Cochineal is an article of dyeing stuff greatly used in spite of its high price in Persia. Hitherto it has chiefly been sent by Russia, and has sold as high as 150 tomauns per pood of 40 lbs. (about 2*l*. to 1*l*. 6*s*. 8*d*. a pound English); it was as low as 100 tomauns when I was in the country.'

[451] 1 pood = 36.1128 lbs. or 16.3807 kg.

[452] It is unclear to what these conquests were. Ranjit Singh did not attack Multan until 1806, returning in 1807 and finally taking possession 1810, but in 1802 Muzaffar Khan, the governor of Multan, gave him gifts and friendly relations were established. See Griffin (1898: 183–184), Rodgers (1881: 83).

[453] Writing about Mashhad, Conolly (1834: 350) noted, 'The indigo that is brought from India into this country is of two qualities—that manufactured by the English, which is called neel-e-feringe, and a very inferior sort, made chiefly in Sinde, but which is most used. The price of English indigo, when we were at Meshed, was eighty Irâk reals for a Tabreez mun; we were told that it had been known to sell for a 100 and a 120, and, on one or two occasions, even for a 150 reals the mun: there is not an extensive demand for it, and it is only used to stain glass and the enameled tiles which are used in Persian buildings, for drawings, and perhaps to dye the best silks. The second sort, or, as it is called in India, the cutcha indigo, finds its way into Khorassaun from Sinde viâ Kandahar and Heraut, and also (I presume from the Punjaub) by the way of Caubul and Bokhara. Its cost at Meshed, when we were there, was twenty reals for a Tabreez mun.'

A Summary of Recent Persian History

9.120 'Untitled,' *Salem Register* (Thursday, 3 October, 1805), 'From the Salem Register,' *National Intelligencer, and Washington Advertiser* (Wednesday, 23 October, 1805), 'From the Salem Register,' *Alexandria Daily Advertiser* (Thursday, 24 October, 1805) and 'From the Salem Register,' *City Gazette and Daily Advertiser* (Monday, 28 October, 1805): 'From the French papers we have been able to obtain the outline of the history of Persia till the commencement of the war with Russia. After the death of Nadir Char, in 1737 [sic, 1747], Persia was divided between two usurpers. One held Chiras as his residence, and the other Isaphen [sic, Isfahan]. The contest for the supreme power was not immediate. The Khan of Daber[455] gave the first serious check to Dgaissar Chan[456] of Chiras, and he received a check from the brother of Aga Mahomet,[457] of Isphan. In 1787, Dgaissar was again in arms, and though he suffered a great defeat by Aga Mahemet he defeated Aga Mahamet in turn on the 10th August, 1788. The public wishes followed Dgaissar, who entered Isaphan in triumph in October of the same year.—Unfortunately for his power, he returned to his own capital to quiet some divisions among the inhabitants, and was assassinated.[458] Said Morad[459] was then proclaimed prince regent, at about 40 years of age. This revolution of 1789, did not free the prince from fears of the vengeance of the son of Dgaissar or his rival still living. The son gained Chiras, the capital, and punished the assassin, but the rival of his father yet remained. For a time he was able to repel this prince, but the affairs of his capital kept him at home. His rival, Aga Mahamet was employing this time in gaining reinforcements, with which he pushed for the capital of his enemy, & after several bloody battles victory declared for Aga Mahemet. Still possession of the capital was not gained till 4 years afterwards, in 1794. The son of Dgaissar[460] was obliged at last to retreat with a few friends, but was afterwards taken and after his eyes were put out, he was permitted to live on a pension granted to him. Aga Mahamet had now reached his 30th year, and held his residence at Chiras.

---

[454] This English translation of Pallas was published in Anonymous (1799: 533). For the German original see Pallas (1799, 1801).

[455] 'Ali Mardan Khan Shamlu.

[456] Ja'far Khan Zand.

[457] It may be assumed that these events occurred before 1787, as the next sentence begins 'In 1787.' This being the case, several brothers of Agha Mohammad Shah come into consideration, including Ja'far Qoli Khan and 'Ali Qoli Khan. Busse (1972: 25, 29).

[458] According to Hasan-e Fasa'i he was poisoned by a female slave. See Busse (1972: 31).

[459] Seyyid Morad Khan.

[460] Lotf 'Ali Khan.

It was after the submission of the son of Dgaissar, he turned his arms against Russia, and sacked Tefflis and massacred the Russians he found in that place. It was at this time that Catharine II. sent Count Subow[461] against him, as he had declared himself the enemy of Russia. He refused the treaties which claimed former privileges in exchange for the provinces conquered by Peter I. in the beginning of the last century. Count Subow, at Chislar,[462] discovered that the Persians had sent to seize upon Derbent, and began his march on the 29th of April, 1796, and united his troops before Derbent on the 10th of May, and carried the place on the 18th. The same Khan, aged 120, who gave the keys of Derbent to Peter I. delivered them to Count Subow.[463] The garrison was disarmed and the inhabitants left unmolested. The Russians soon convinced Aga Mahemet of his error in rousing so powerful an enemy, and sent an ambassador to Constantinople in 1797, either to obtain succours, or for assistance in restoring peace. He communicated freely his apprehensions, and the Porte gave vague assurances, but from the weakness of the prince and from fear of Russia, did nothing. The Russians continued to advance, and were preparing for a new campaign. Aga Mahemet perished by the hands of one of his generals, in July [sic, 17 June], 1797, after having rendered himself odious by his cruelty and tyranny. The Persian army at Tehran, afterwards proclaimed Baba Khan Serdat, called Fath Ali Chah, sovereign of Persia, in the place of his uncle. His first step to public favor was in lessening the public burdens. Another event soon contributed to the quiet possession of his power. A powerful army under Zeki,[464] from the southern provinces, was marching against his capital with great success, but the failure of his treasures, at the time, when he had the greatest expectations, obliged him to abandon his enterprize. The Russians have not abandoned the war. However justifiable the commencement of the war might have been, they persevere, though they have not yet penetrated far, and the Persians have not been without advantags in the numerous engagements with their northern neighbours.

The present prince of Persia, Fath Ali Chah, is said to be 36 years of age.[465] He is declared to possess a fine person, and military character, but is exceedingly voluptuous. He has many children, but he administers justice. Order reigns in his towns, safety is found on all his roads, and discipline live in his armies. His troops are good, but without European tactics. The success of the Whabis gave him great disquiet, after he learnt the massacre at Iman Hussein.[466] He put his court in mourning, and sent to the Pacha of Bagdat to reproach his neglect, and to enjoin upon him to march against them, or he would visit him after the

---

[461] Valerian Alexandrovich Zubov.

[462] Kizlyar, Daghestan.

[463] Cf. 7.63, 7.64.

[464] This seems to be a confused allusion to Zaki Khan Zand who, however, died in 1780 (Busse 1972: 9), long before Fath 'Ali Shah came to power.

[465] At the time of his death on 23 October 1834 Fath 'Ali Khan was variously said to have been 64 and 4 months, 67 or 70. One source gave his birth year as 1771/2. See Busse (1972: 229–230).

[466] The massacre at Karbala'.

9.1 Miscellaneous

conquest of the Whabi, by his own hand, with an army numerous as the stars in the firmament.[467] The French say that the English, who neglect no opportunities to extend their commerce, had applied to him to obtain two establishments for the English company at Bender Abana [sic, Abbas] & Herat. But that the English ambassador, Manesty,[468] had not accomplished this purposes, but had promised to enquirie [sic] into the nature of his request. The French say that Russians are extremely jealous of any the measures in Europe, which have Persia as their object. That in 1787, count Sauvebaeuf [sic, Sauveboeuf][469] went from Constantinople into Persia. He had been in Persia before, and had furnished useful information to this country. The Russian envoy at Constantinople, Bulhakow,[470] demanded of the court whether the count had been acknowledged by the court of Versailles. M. de Choiseul Gouffier[471] replied, that he was only a French merchant, induced by the views of private interest. But the Russian minister being dissatisfied, the French ambassador assured him that the count was not to meddle with political affairs, and that M. Simelin,[472] the minister of Russia, at Paris, had been notified of the undertaking. The Chah had discovered that the French had an agent at Trebisend, and as with the English, appeared to encourage their hopes. In '96, the Chah had no knowledge of the French revolution or of the wars in Europe, and it is affirmed that he had no knowledge of the names of the nations which inhabit Europe.'

John Malcolm's Uniform

9.121 'Oriental Sketches. Dress,' *The Farmers' Cabinet* (Tuesday, 14 August, 1810), 'From the Boston Repertory. Dress,' *Alexandria Gazette, Commercial & Political* (Saturday, 25 August, 1810), 'From the Repertory. Dress,' *Spooner's Vermont Journal* (Monday, 27 August. 1810), 'Dress,' *Windham Herald* (Friday, 7 September, 1810), 'From the Repertory. Dress,' *Vermont Centinel* (Friday, 21 September, 1810) and 'From the Salem Gazette,' *Middlesex Gazette* (Thursday, 15 February, 1821; with preamble: 'Mr.

---

[467] Hasan-e Fasa 'i discussed the massacre but made no mention of any such actions taken by Fath' Ali Shah in response to it.

[468] Samuel Manesty (1758–1812), EIC Resident at Basra, who because of Jonathan Lovett's illness (1804.3), agreed to take the letter from Wellesley, explaining the death of the Persian ambassador Haji Khalil in Bombay, to Tehran. In fact, Manesty made the outlandish offer to arrange an armistice between Persia and Russia. See Ingram (1973: 513–514). For the entire episode see Wright (1986).

[469] Louis François de Ferrières-Sauvebœuf (1762–1814). See Ferrières-Sauvebœuf (1790).

[470] Yakov Ivanovich Bulgakov (1743–1809), Russian ambassador in Constantinople (1781–1787). See Spuler (1936b: 439).

[471] Marie Gabriel Florent Auguste de Choiseul-Gouffier, French ambassador to the Porte (1784–1791). For his life and career ee Pingaud (1887).

[472] Ivan Matveevich Simolin (1720–1800), Russian ambassador to France (1784–1799). For his career in France, particularly during the French Revolution, see Mazour (1942).

Cushing—In looking over some of my old journals recently, I found the enclosed article, written in Calcutta in 1809. The gentleman who related the anecdote to me had it from Col. Malcolm's own mouth, and assured me it was in every circumstance a fact. Respectfully yours, Nauticus;' and with minor variation in the first sentence, 'About the year 1800, I am not certain as to the exact year, Lt. Col. John Malcolm was sent...'): 'In the year 1809 [sic, 1800], Lieut. Colonel John Malcolm was sent by the Marquis Wellesley as an Envoy Extraordinary to the court of Persia. Great preparations were made by the Persian Monarch to receive the English Minister in a style suitable to the dignity of his office, and the importance of his mission. Col. Malcolm, a fine military figure, presented himself for introduction to the king in full uniform,[473] accompanied by a suite splendidly attired in the staff dress of the Governor-General of India's household.—The Persian Ministers who were appointed to receive the Envoy, and to conduct him into the royal presence, on seeing him and his retinue, suddenly halted, and dispatched a messenger to inquire whether the representative of the British government was not ready to attend them. On being informed that Col. Malcolm was the person expected in that character, they deliberated among themselves for some minutes, and at length went to the palace for the picture of an ambassador who visited their court in the time of Queen Elizabeth, and shewing it to the Colonel, told him that his dress was not that of a Civilian, affirming at the same time, that it was impossible his master could ever suffer so strange a departure from established custom, as would be the case, were his servants employed in the diplomatic line, to assume the garb of military officers. So hard was it for them to conceive of the contrary, that the Colonel's intimate acquaintance with their language, his display of talents adapted to his employment, and the production of his credentials, were scarcely sufficient to overcome the scruples and objections that his dress afforded. However, notwithstanding his red coat, epaulets, whiskers and boots, he succeeded in convincing the Persians, that he was their Envoy, and to insinuate himself into the good opinion and confidence of the king, that he was completely successful in his negociations, and attained, without difficulty, every object of his mission. The grave Persians observed that the disposition of the British people must be very fickle, frivolous and inconstant, seeing that according to their minister's assertion they often changed the fashion of their garments—whereas, the steady, the wise and the truly noble, allowed of no alteration in their dress, but were proud of the garb of their fathers.'

---

[473] Malcolm's dress at his audiences with Fath 'Ali Shah was commented upon by Kaye (1856/1: 131) who noted, 'Conducted by the chamberlains, or masters of the ceremonies, Malcolm advanced, wearing the uniform of an English officer.' Earlier, the governor of Qazvin had 'sent Malcolm a dress of honor and some fine horses, and requested that he would wear the former and ride one of the latter to an entertainment he was about to give him. To this request Malcolm replied that he could not wear a Khelat [robe of honor; see Floor (1999: 290–295)] over his clothes from any person except the King, and therefore he hoped the Governor would not send it.' At one of several visits Fath 'Ali Shah 'presented Malcolm with a dress of honor, which the English gentleman wore over his uniform on the occasion of his next visit to the Shah.' See Kaye (1856/1: 130, n. * and 140).

Persian Chiefs and Raiding

9.122 'Miscellany from the Analectic Magazine. Account of the Persians. [From Kinnier's (sic) Memoir of the Persian Empire.],' *Trump of Fame* (Wednesday, 30 March, 1814), 'Account of the Persians. [From Kinnier's Memoir of the Persian Empire.],' *Lancaster Journal* (Wednesday, 11 June, 1817), and 'The Persians. From Kinnier's Memoir,' *Providence Gazette* (Monday, 10 January, 1820): 'Of the horses of this country, Mr. K.[474] speaks with admiration; also the sheep, the poultry and the game; but the beef is coarse, and is eaten by the lower classes only. The revenue does not much exceed three millions; the tax on land yields, probably, about two thirds of this sum; the remainder is derived from imposts, and duties on merchandize.[475] The military power is an undisciplined rabble, unfit to contend with regular European troops.

They seldom shed much blood in their engagements; and Mr Kinneir mentions a battle fought while he was in the country, that lasted *four days*, yet, although ten thousand men were engaged on each side, and the conflict terminated in a complete route [sic], the *whole* loss was about *five men* killed and wounded. Predatory excursions are the favorite warlike exploits of the Persians; what ravages they occasion may be conjectured, though but faintly, from the following instances. The first describes the manner of four Persian chiefs, who are brothers but at variance.

To enable the reader to form some faint idea of the detestable system which has reduced these fine countries to their present state of barbarism, I will here relate an anecdote of one of these chiefs, whom Mr. Monteith[476] and myself had occasion to visit, in our way from

---

[474] Lieutenant John Macdonald, of the Madras Native Infantry, afterwards Sir John Macdonald Kinneir (1782–1830). See Monteith (1856: 65). The work cited in the present article is Kinneir (1813). He was originally a member of Malcolm's second mission as Lieutenant Macdonald, 'supernumerary assistant.' See Kaye (1856: 512, n. *). He eventually began to use Kinneir, his mother's maiden name. He served as East India Company envoy to Fath 'Ali Shah from 1824 until his death from cholera at Tabriz in 1830.

[475] Cf. Brydges (1834: 402–403), who wrote, 'I have not attempted to give an estimate, much less an account of the Revenue of the Persian Empire, because I would not willingly mislead, and because Meerz Bozurg told me its amount varied every year very considerably. He also said, the accounts delivered into the Royal Treasury are so confused and perplexed, that were they even laid before me, I should not be able to come to an accurate, and consequently satisfactory, result.'

[476] William Monteith (1790–1864), long-serving officer in the Madras Engineers whose Persian service began in 1809/10 with Malcolm's first mission. Thereafter he stayed to help train 'Abbas Mirza's army, fought in the First Russo-Persian War and fulfilled various other roles as well. See Chichester (1894). In 1810, at the request of 'Abbas Mirza, Monteith and Kinneir were permitted by Malcolm 'to reconnoitre the Russian posts on the banks of the Arras [Aras] near Megeri.' Later, when 'Abbas Mirza went with his forces to Erivan, and ordered Hoseyn Khan, governor of Erivan, 'to proceed to Akhiska, and co-operate with the Pasha of that province. Lieutenant Monteith accompanied Hussain Khan on this expedition into Georgia.' When Ouseley revoked permission for most of the British military staff to continue to serve 'Abbas Mirza, apart from Christie and Lindsay, Monteith was allowed to remain 'with the Erivan force.' When Russian forces attacked the

Shushtar to *Shiraauz*, in the month of March, 1810,[477] at the time when the first crops were ready for the sickle. Our road lying through the district of Ram Homuz [sic, Hormuz], and not far from the villages of three of the brothers, we alternately became their guests.—On the second day, at the house of the youngest of the four, and just as we had finished our breakfast, he came into the room armed and equipped as if prepared to set out on an expedition. In the courseof conversation, he enquired how we had been treated by his relation the preceding day, and without giving us time to reply, added, that as he knew him to be a *scurvy dog*, and incapable of exercising the rights of hospitality, he would give us ample revenge, by loading our cattle (if we would allow them to accompany him in his intended excursion) with as much wheat and barley as they were able to carry. We thanked him for his generosity, but told him, that as we had no reason to complain of the manner in which we had been entertained by his brother, we could not possibly avail ourselves of his kind offer.—He shortly afterwards withdrew, and mounting his horse, issued forth at the head of his adherents. He was absent the greater part of the day, and returned towards the close of the evening, with an immense booty. The quarrels of these chiefs not unfrequently prove fatal to themselves and to their followers. They are, in that event, summoned to attend the tribunal of the *Beglerbeg of Bebaham*,[478] and he whose suit is sustained with the largest sum of money, is in no fear of loosing his cause.

Erivan region in March/April 1813, 'Lieutenant Monteith was in command of a battery of six guns, and some cavalry, at the ford of the Arras. Hussain Khan sent him orders to retire, but he refused to obey, as while he remained the Russians could not cross without being under fire ... During the years 1810 to 1813 there were four active campaigns, and during this time Lieutenant Monteith commanded a frontier force and the garrison of Erivan. He was engaged in many skirmishes, and was wounded in one at a place called Kulky Tippa.' When Ellis, Ouseley's successor, was instructed to negotiate a definitive treaty between Great Britain and Persia in 1814, Monteith served as his secretary. He received the Order of the Lion and Sun from Fath 'Ali Shah. In 1819 Monteith served in the expedition to reduce the Qawasim pirates in the Persian Gulf as aide-de-camp of Sir William Grant Keir. Following the peace treaty between Russia and Turkey, 'Monteith was appointed Commissioner to ascertain the limits of the respective countries.' Again, after the Second Russo-Persian War in 1828, he was 'appointed Commissioner for paying the indemnity, and part of the treasure was actually conveyed to the Russian camp by Captain Monteith ... During the payment of the contribution levied on Persia, Captain Monteith had a great deal of communication with Prince Paskiewitch ... It was thus Monteith's acquaintance with Prince Paskiewitch began, and he was afterwards on terms of considerable intimacy with him, which led to Monteith accompanying the Russian army to Tiflis, and being an eye-witness of part of the operations against the Turks,' as reported in Monteith (1856). See Vibart (1883: 113–122). Monteith finally returned to India in 1832 when he was appointed Chief Engineer of Madras; was promoted to Major-General in 1841; and retired in 1847. See 131.

[477] The article here has shifted to the first person, in the voice of Kinneir, and refers to the journey described in Monteith (1857: 108), which begins, 'In 1810, Lieut. M'Donald (afterwards Sir John M'Donald Kinneir) and myself were directed to proceed along the shores of the Persian Gulf to Bussorah.'

[478] Behbehan.

Such are the internal enemies of their own kin, and their own country; which the government is too weak or too slothful to punish!

The following are proofs that the external relations of this people, or at least of their border provinces, are in a state as barbarous as among the most savage tribes of the most savage nations.'[479]

Sir William Ouseley's Manuscript Collection

9.123 'Eastern Manuscripts &c.,' *The Geneva Gazette* (Wednesday, 6 September, 1814): 'The most valuable collection of Eastern Manuscripts ever brought to Europe by any individual, is said to be that of Maj. [Sir William] Ouseley. Besides Arabic, Persian, and Sanscrit books (amounting in number to nearly fifteen hundred)[480] there are several port folios of immense size, containing mythological paintings of the most ancient kind, splendidly illuminated, and procured at great expense from all parts of Hindostan, Tibet, Tartary, China, Ceylon, Ava, &c. with idols of stone, metal, wood, and other materials. Many of the volumes are filled with botanical paintings, executed in the most accurate manner; vast collections of natural history and mineralogy; original views and drawings taken on the spot in various parts of India; with a cabinet, of the most rare medals, gems, and other antiquities: A complete series of the coins struck by Mahometan Princes since the reign of Timour, with the armor, horse furniture, swords, spears, bows, arrows and all the weapons used in Persia, India, and other countries of the East; with various musical instruments, and songs set to music, by Maj. Ouseley, from the voice of Persian, Cashmeran, and Indian singers.'

Rev. Henry Martyn's Persian Translation of the New Testament

9.124 'Miscellaneous articles selected from a file of London Papers, to the 27th December,' *New-York Herald* (Saturday, 1 April 1815): 'By accounts from Persia of the 8th of May [1814?], we learn, that the Schah of Persia had written the following letter to the English Envoy, Sir Gore Ouseley:—

---

[479] The subsequent paragraphs are taken verbatim from Kinneir (1813) as follows: from 'The Persians are a remarkably handsome race' to 'change their linen = Kinneir (1813: 22–25): From 'The Persians are a remarkably handsome race of people' to 'the remainder is divided equally amongst his followers' = Kinneir (1813: 22–27); from 'The road from Cashan to Koom' to 'in as many days' = Kinneir (1813: 115–116); from 'The following account' to 'divided equally amongst his followers' = Kinneir (1813: 170–171, n*).

[480] Ouseley (1831) is a catalogue made by Sir William Ouseley of his own collection of manuscripts. Cf. Anonymous (1845a: 102). For the 419 works acquired by the Bodleian Library in 1844, 2 years after Sir William Ouseley's death, see Madan (1897: 664–673).

"In the name of God, whose glory is over all! It is our high will, that our dear friend, the worthy and respectable Sir Gore Ouseley, Envoy Extraordinary from his Majesty the King of Great Britain, be informed, that the book of the Gospels translated into the Persian tongue by the labors of Henry Martin [sic, Martyn],[481] of blessed memory, and which has been presented to us in the name of the worthy, learned, and enlightened Society of Christians,[482] who have united for the purpose of spreading the divine books of the teacher Jesus, to whose name, as to that of all the prophets, be inscribed honour and blessing, has been received by us, and merits our high acknowledgement.[483] For many years past the

---

[481] Rev. Henry Martyn (1781–1812), a hugely respected and revered British clergyman. For his life see e.g. Sargent (1819), Anonymous (1820b), Lee (1824).

[482] This could be a reference to either the Christian Missionary Society or the British and Foreign Bible Society, of which Ouseley was one of thirty vice-presidents. See Anonymous (1816c: vii).

[483] As M'Cullagh (1906: 12–13) noted, while in Bandar-e Bushehr and Shiraz, where he spent eleven months (Sargent 1819: 463), Martyn 'employed his time in translating the New Testament into the Persian language. He travelled to Teheran that Sir Gore Ouseley might present copies to the Shah and to his son and heir. The Shah was at an encampment, and Sir Gore, to be near him, was at Tabreez. There Martyn arrived more dead than alive. Sir Gore Ouseley received him as his own guest, and presented the copies of the Persian New Testament to the great Shah, Fateh Ali Khan, who was greatly pleased with the translation.' As Sargent (1819: 462–463) noted, 'On the evening of the 24th of May, one year after entering Persia, Mr. Martyn left Shiraz, in company with an English clergyman [Rev. William Canning], having it in intention to lay before the King his translation of the New Testament; but finding, that without a letter of introduction from the British Ambassador, he could not, consistently with established usage, be admitted into the Royal presence, he determined to proceed to Tebriz, where, at that time Sir Gore Ouseley, his Britannic Majesty's Minister, resided.' As Morier (1818: 224) noted, 'Mr. Martyn caused a copy of his translation to be beautifully written, and to be presented by the Ambassador to the King, who was pleased to receive it very graciously.' Cf. Sargent (1819: 491, n. *) who wrote, 'Sir Gore Ouseley presented Mr. Martyn's New Testament to the King of Peria, who, in a public rescript, expressed his approbation of the work. He also carried the MS. to St. Petersburgh, where, under his superintendance, it was printed and put into circulation.' In a letter from St. Petersburg dated 20 September 1814, the Rev. Robert Pinkerton wrote, 'His Excellency [Ouseley] related to me, that the King of Persia himself [Fath 'Ali Shah], had, at his recommendation, read Mr. Martyn's translation, and thought so much of the work, that he commanded several copies to be taken of it for his friends.—Yea, more, His Majesty has written a recommendation of Mr. Martyn's translation with his own hand, and sealed it with his own seal. This His Excellency [Ouseley] is bringing home with him, as a certificate to the British and Foreign Bible Society, that his Majesty is pleased with Mr. Martyn's labours.' See Pinkerton (1815: 318–319). Fath 'Ali Shah's letter was read before the first Annual Meeting of the Russian Bible Society on 28 September 1814. As Pinkerton observed, 'The King of Persia's letter was also read and heard with astonishment. Who in the Assembly could ever have expected to hear a letter read from a Mahomedan King, of the most encouraging nature, for the Russian Bible Society, in particular, at her first Anniversary, whose sphere of operation includes so many nations that are the votaries of Islamism? This is, indeed, the Lord's doing, and marvellous in our eyes!' See Pinkerton (1815: 321). In a later letter of 1 October 1814, Pinkerton clarified that, after ascertaining that the printing and proofing could be done, 'I brought the matter regularly before the Committee on the 28th inst.; all the Members were struck with the particulars respecting the great need there is in Persia of the Holy

four Gospels of Matthew, Mark, Luke and John, were known in Persian, but now the whole of the New Testament is completely translated, which event is a new source of satisfaction for our enlightened mind. With the grace of God the Merciful, we will direct those of our servants who are admitted into our presence, to read the said writings from beginning to end before us, that we may listen to their sentiments respecting the same. Inform the members of the above enlightened Society, that they receive as they merit, our loyal thanks.

Given at Reki, in the year of the Hegira, 1229.

"FARE [sic, FATH] ALI SCHAH."
(Signed)'

An Excerpt from Pietro Della Valle

9.125 'Miscellany. Singular custom among the Persians. From the Travels of Pietro della Valle,' *The Weekly Messenger* (Friday, 7 April, 1815): 'On Friday, the 5th of July, the Persians celebrated an anniversary, which I [Pietro della Valle] had never before seen, perhaps because the absence of the king had occasioned the ommission of the solemnities. They call it, in their own language, *Ab Pascian*,[484] but more elegantly in their books, *Abrizan*;[485] that is to say, the sprinkling of water. On the day of this anniversary, all the Persians, not excepting those of the highest rank, not even the king hiself, giving up all business, dress themselves in a short garment, after the manner of the *Mazanderans*, with an ordinary sort of bonnet, coming very close to the head (for their turbans, of which they are very careful, might receive some injury) with the sleeves of their robes turned up, and their arms naked, assemble on the edge of a river, or some other more agreeable place, where is a considerable quantity of water; and there, with vessels, which they bring with them, at a signal given by the king, they begin to throw water at one another, at the same time capering, dancing, jesting, and performing a thousand other tricks, which are pleasant

---

Scriptures, even among Christians, whom Dr. Buchannan reckons at 200,000; but they were still more surprised when they heard a Russian Translation read of the King of Persia's letter, regarding Mr. Martyn's Translation. It was therefore agreed unanimously, that we ought to lose no time in proceeding to print an edition of the same for the sake of the western provinces of Persia.' See Pinkerton (1815: 320–321). Martyn left Tabriz on 2 September 1812 but died in Armenia on 16 October. For his life see Martyn 1819.

[484] Persian '*āb-pāshān*, Name of a Persian festival, on which occasion each one sprinkles rosewater on his neighbour.' See Johnson (1852: 6).

[485] According to Benfey and Stern (1836: 157), 'eine Abkürzung von *Abrizegân*, *riz* ... heisst ausgiessen und *gân* bedeutet Fest ... Della Valle giebt eine ausführliche Schilderung dieses Festes, dessen wesentlichste Ceremonie darin besteht, dass sich die Perser alle ins Wasser werfen und darin allerlei Scherz treiben. Dieses Fest wird auch bei den Armeniern und vielen anderen christlichen Völkern gefeiert, so dass man es sogar für ein ursprünglich christliches Fest gehalten hat; ebenso haben es die Mahomedaner in Persien auf Mahomeds Taufe bezogen. Della Valle hat aber schon richtig eingesehen, dass es ein altpersisches Fest ist.'

enough in this exercise. They become at last so heated, that either through excess of anger or for some other cause, they cased aside their vessels, and using only their hands to throw the water, they begin to press one another, and to push each other into the river or pond, with so much violence, that it is seldom the sport is ended without the drowning of some one of the number. This year there were five in different places, who met this fate. At Ispahan, this holyday is celebrated upon the river, at the place where it crosses the beautiful street of Ciaharbag, passing under a superb bridge.

I was unable to learn the origin of this anniversary, or the reason of its institution and perhaps they are equally unknown to the Persians themselves. There are some, who suppose that it was introduced by the christians, in commemoration of the baptism of *St. John*; and they offer two reasons in support of this hypothesis. The first is, that the Armenian christians, and almost all those of Asia, have the same custom though not on the same day. Others would have it, that it is in honour of the *Epiphany*, when our Saviour was baptised by *St. John*, upon the bank of the *Jordan*, and that the Armenians, for this reason, put a cross into the river, and call the day *Cacciuciran, Carci* in the Armenian language signifying a cross, and *Givre*, water. The other reason, which seems more clear and satisfactory, to prove that this solemnity has been instituted in commemoration of the baptism of *St. John*, rather than of the Savior, is that it is celebrated on the eve, or on the day of his birth, although the Persians have delayed it to the fifth of July. But the most intelligent among them confess, that it has been deferred, because the king so ordered it; the true and proper time for it having been 12 days before, which would have brought it on the eve of his nativity, and on the day of the solstice. Other christians are of opinion, that it commemorates the day of Penticost. However, I cannot vouchsafe to you for the truth, one way or the other. I am inclined to think it a remnant of those feasts of the ancient idolators, which the christians have applied to a better use, and have preserved, to honor the memory of some saint, as we know to be the case in many other instances.'[486]

Rev. Robert Pinkerton

9.126 'Persia. Church Missionary Society. Letter from the Rev. Robert Pinkerton,' *The Recorder* (Tuesday, 3 December, 1816): 'The following Letter to the Secretary from the Rev. Robert Pinkerton[487] dated St. Petersburgh, Jan. 19, (O.S.) 1816, will illustrate the

---

[486] This entire passage is a direct translation of Della Valle (1674: 16–17) beginning 'Freytags den 5. Julii' and ending 'Gleich wie bey uns.'

[487] Robert Pinkerton (1780–1859) was a Scottish missionary, active in Karass in the northern Caucasus from 1805, thereafter in St. Petersburg. He functioned also as 'Foreign agent to the British and Foreign Bible Society (Pinkerton 1833) and was considered 'one of the most active Scottish missionaries in Russia.' See Kirimli (2004: 80).

9.1 Miscellaneous

importance of the plans which the [Church Missionary] Society[488] is pursuing with reference to the Mahomedans.

Rev. Sir,—It will doubtless afford you, and the other Members of the Committee of the Church Missionary Society, very great pleasure to hear that the excellent Translation of the New-Testament into Persian, by the much lamented Henry Martyn, is now published;[489] and that the most encouraging prospect opens for its speedy circulation, by means of the

---

[488] Founded in 1799 as the Church Missionary Society for Africa and the East. See Ward and Stanley (2019); https://churchmissionsociety.org/about/our-history/archives/.

[489] By the Russian Bible Society in St. Petersburg. The idea for doing this arose as a result of a conversation that Pinkerton had with Sir Gore Ousley on 19 September 1814. As he wrote, 'I yesterday waited upon the Ambassador [Ouseley], who received me with great kindness, gave me a number of interesting particulars in regard to the late Rev. Mr. Martyn, of whose abilities and conduct he spoke in the highest terms; and informed me, that he had two copies of Mr. Martyn's Persian traanslation of the New Testament with him. As soon as I heard this piece of joyful information, the western provinces of Persia, most of which are now subject to Russia, immediately rushed into my mind, as an open field for circulating this sacred book. I suggested to His Excellency the idea of printing an edition of Mr. Martyn's translation here [St. Petersburg] for the west of Persia. His Excellency not only highly approved of the proposition, but offered willingly to give a transcript of his manuscript, provided a person could be obtained to take it.' See Pinkerton (1815: 318). The project took roughly a year to complete. As Prince Alexander Golitsyn, the Society's president, noted in a letter to Pinkerton, 'The Committee of the Russian Bible Society, in its last sitting of the 23d of September [1815], perceived, with pleasure, that the edition of the Persian New Testament is now completed. This edition affords the Society a new means of making the inhabitants of those provinces which have been lately ceded to Russia, acquainted with the word of God, and also many thousands, in other quarters, who speak the Persian language … To you, my dear Sir, belongs the honour of having had the greatest labour in this edition. Your care about the correct and speedy printing of it, and your personal daily superintendency of this, made you a powerful instrument of the Grace of God toward the desired completion of this undertaking. In the correcting of the press you took part during the whole time of His Excellency Sir Gore Ouseley's residence here; and, after his departure, you had the chief superintendency of the work, and made a successful use of the talents given you by your knowledge of the oriental languages.' See Galitzin (1819: 214–215). In a letter of 1 October 1814, Pinkerton wrote that, 'Sir Gore Ouseley, Bart., is not only willing to grant us a transcript of the deceased Mr. Martyn's valuable Persian Translation, but has also promised to assist in correcting the press, so long as he remains here, in conjunction with a learned Persian, Mirza, whom I have found employed in the College for Foreign Affairs. I have also found very good Persian types in the Imperial Printing Office, the Master of which is willing to undertake the work.' See Pinkerton (1815: 319). Later, Pinkerton commented on Ouseley's involvement in a letter of 23 May, 1815: 'We are now advanced with the Persian to the end of the Acts of the Apostles. Sir Gore Ouseley has been unwearied in his exertions to render the edition correct, so far as it is printed; and now that he is just on the eve of leaving us, we have made such arrangements as, I hope, will bring it to a successful termination in the course of a few months … Even the Bucharian Ambassador himself, lately arrived in this city, has assisted one of his countrymen in copying part of the manuscript; and when Sir Gore leaves us, we expect the aid of the First Secretary of the Persian Ambassador to assist in correcting the press.' See Pinkerton (1819: 10). The secretary in question was Mirza Ja'far, who had accompanied the Persian ambassador Mirza Abu'l Hasan Khan Shirazi), who had previously been in London) there as his secretary. See Green (2012: 120).

Scotch Missionaries in Orenburg and Astrachan,[490] and the Correspondents of the Russian Bible Society in Georgia.[491]

Several thousand Persians visit Astrachan every year. Many of them have shewn an almost incredible desire to possess the New-Testament in their own language. The Missionaries there have distributed 300 Tartar New-Testaments within these few months: most of them among Persians.[492] A learned Effendi, lately arrived from Persia, having received a copy of the Tartar Testament offered to translate it into Persian, provided the Missionaries would print it. He was quite overjoyed at the information, that what he so much desired was already accomplished, and that, in a few weeks, he should receive a printed copy of the Persian Translation.

From Dr. Campbell, who arrived here a few days ago from Persia,[493] I was overjoyed to hear that the labors of Mr. Martyn in Persia had made a great impression; that the Tract

---

[490] The Edinburgh Missionary Society was represented at their Astrachan Station by 'Messrs. Mitchell and Dickson,' and in Orenburg, by 'Messrs. Fraser and Macalpine.' See Dickson (1816: 49).

[491] In a letter dated 1 October 1814, Pinkerton reported on a meeting with the Georgian Archbishop Dositheos, in part, 'to consult with the Archbishop about the possibility of establishing a Bible Society in Tiflis, the capital ... He said, that the number of Christians, who belonged to the Græco-Georgian Church in Georgia, Imeretta, and Mingrellia, was upwards of one million. That in Georgia Proper, there were nearly 900 churches or congregations; and in Imeretta and Mingrelia, 1,100. Notwithstanding which, the Archbishop affirmed, that there were not 200 copies of the Bible to be found in all these 2000 churches. There never has been but one edition of the Gruzian or Georgian Bible printed. This was executed in Moscow, in 1743, in a large folio volume ... His Grace agreed most heartily to promote the establishment of a Georgian Bible Society, on his arrival in Tiflis. He expressed a great desire for a number of copies of the Holy Scriptures in the Armenian, Persian, Modern Greek, Turkish, and Tartar languages; all of which are spoken by numbers in Georgia. We promised to furnish him with Modern Greek, Armenian, and Tartar Testaments, and informed him that we had great hopes of being able also to add Persian and Turkish in the course of some time.' See Pinkerton (1815: 319–320). Further, Pinkerton (1815: 321) noted that, 'we have every means for giving the edition a wide circulation through our numerous Armenian and Georgian Friends. The edition is to consist of 5000 copies in quarto, upon a good paper.'

[492] The Rev. David Dickson, in Astrachan, wrote that the 'Turkish or Tartar New Testament' was distributed 'chiefly among Persian Merchants; by whom they were received with uncommon eagerness, completely understood, and carried away with them to Derbent, Shirvan, and even to Ispahan. There is every prospect, therefore, that when the Persian New Testament, publishing by the Russian Bible Society, is ready for distribution, it will obtain an easy entrance into the Persian Dominions, and be gratefully received by the inhabitants. At Astrachan, also, the repugnance of the Tartars to the circulation of the New Testament, which at first was extremely great, appears to be considerably diminished.' See Dickson (1816: 49).

[493] Dr. James Drummond Campbell (1787–1818), of the Bombay Medical Service (1808–1818), went to Persia in Sir Gore Ouseley's mission and was appointed surgeon to 'Abbas Mirza. Ker Porter (1821/1: 301) described him as 'a man, in the bloom of life; full of the most eminent talents, not merely professionally, but pointing to every line of Asiatic literature. He had been some time attached to the British embassy in Persia; and his perfect knowledge of the language of the country, rendered him one of the most valuable members of the mission. Abbas Mirza held these public qualities in great consideration, but he more particularly esteemed Dr. Campbell for his amiable private virtues.'

9.1 Miscellaneous

which he wrote in Arabic, on the Mahomedan and Christian Religions,[494] had made much stir among the Learned; that a certain Molwee [molla] had taken in hand to answer it, but that, after his answer appeared, it was condemned by his learned brethren as quite inconclusive;[495] and that, since that time, some other learned Effendi had prepared another answer, with which, however, many seemed not quite satisfied.[496] Dr. Campbell has been about seven years in Persia, is an excellent scholar in the language, and is about to return in a few weeks. He says the Persians are much more tolerant than the Turks; and in general, are fond of religious argument; and that, as a proof of this, he had held an argument lately on the subject of religion with one of their learned men who called himself SUFFA (a Freethinker,) in the presence of the King himself, who hearkened attentively to the dispute; and that the Heir Apparent, in conversing with him, sometimes quotes the words of the Gospel in confirmation of what he is saying.

From these interesting facts, surely your Society has much encouragement to proceed with ts excellent plan of printing appropriate Religious Tracts for circulation among Mahomedans.—These, accompanied by the Holy Scriptures, will penetrate where Missionaries, as such, dare not yet go; and, by their means, many thousands may be called

---

Campbell accompanied Sir Gore Ouseley to St. Petersburg when he left Persia. See Reynolds (1846: cxviii, cxcix). On 18 May 1815 Sir Gore Ousley 'dispatched Dr. Campbell (from whom he parted with great regret) to Persia, with letters for the Prince Royal, Abbás Mírza, in which he endeavoured to tranquillize the mind of the Prince with respect to the dreaded consequences of Napoleon's return, and to urge upon him the expediency of refusing admission or audience to any French agent.' Ker Porter (1821/1: 330–331) described Campbell's death on 24 March 1815, noting, 'He was buried in the interior of the Armenian church at Teheran, not far from the altar . . . and no European, dying in these dominions, probably was ever more deeply regretted by the Persians, from the King himself to the humblest of his subjects.'

[494] As Morier (1818: 223–224) wrote, 'When he [Martyn] was living at Shiraz, employed in his translation, he neither sought nor shunned the society of the natives, many of whom constantly drew him into arguments about religion, with the intention of persuading him of the truth and excellence of theirs. His answers were such as to stimulate them to farther arguments . . . At length he thought that the best mode of silencing them was by writing a reply to the arguments which they brought both against our belief and in favour of their own.' Lee (1824: 80–160) gives English translations of three tracts written by Martyn in reply to Mirza Ibrahim's defence of Islam.

[495] As Morier (1818: 224) noted, 'His tract was circulated through different parts of Persia, and was sent from hand to hand to be answered. At length it made its way to the King's Court, and a Mollah of high consideration, who resided at Hamadan, and who was esteemed one of the best controversialists in the country, was ordered to answer it. After the lapse of more than a year he did answer it, but such were the strong positions taken by Mr. Martyn, that the Persians themselves were ashamed of the futility of their own attempts to break them down.' The first rejoinder was published in Lee (1824: 161–450) as 'rejoinder of Mohammed Ruza of Hamadan in reply to Mr. Martyn.'

[496] As Morier (1818: 224) related, 'after they had sent their answer to the Ambassador [Ouseley], they requested that it might be returned to them again, as another answer was preparing to be given,' to which Morier added in n. *, 'I have heard since my return to England that Mr. Martyn's tract has been sent to a Mollah of great celebrity residing at Bagdad, in the hope that he may be more successful in refuting it.'

to consider impartially themerits of the Christian Religion, and untimely be added to the Church of Christ.

Tracts, in three languages, are peculiarly requisite for Mahamedans—in Arabic, Persian, and Turkish. In all these languages, there are now abundant opportunities for their circulation: and it ought to be considreed, that not only every Testament and Bible, but every cogent Gospel Tract also, is a voice for the Saviour … Should you find any difficulty in procuring accurate translations of your Tracts into Persian, only have the goodness to send me a copy of each MS. and I will employ our Persian Corrector to translate it for you. The translation may then be sent to you, and stereotyped.

We hope you will have the goodness to send us a number of copies of all that you publish for the Asiatics … I remain, dear Sir, yours, &c.[497]

ROBT. PINKERTON
(Signed)'

---

[497] This is an excerpt of a longer letter by Pinkerton. The title of this article is identical to that of Pinkerton (1816a), whereas Pinkerton (1816b) gives the same letter but with an abbreviated title. This particular letter is not included in Pinkerton (1817) where, however, many of the same topics are discussed.

From 1816 to the End of the Turco-Persian War (1816–1825)

10

Although the Treaty of Gulistan was signed in 1813, it was only in 1817 that Lieutenant-General Alexei Petrovich Ermolov, commander-in-chief of Russian forces in Georgia, was sent to Tehran to settle the outstanding boundary issues. Numerous accounts, including lengthy excerpts from the letters of Captain Moritz von Kotzebue, a member of his staff, offer detailed insight into the progress of Ermolov's embassy. For his part, Fath 'Ali Shah sent Mirza Abu'l Hasan Khan Shirazi to St. Petersburg, heavily laden with valuable presents, including two elephants.

In 1819 Mirza Abu'l Hasan Khan was sent to London via Vienna and Paris. His diplomatic efforts were largely eclipsed by the beautiful Circassian concubine whom he brought along. Bulletins of the envoy's stays in Vienna, Paris and London described the presents he brought for the heads of state whom he saw and the sites he visited. French and British royals and aristocrats featured prominently in these accounts.

After Ermolov's mission Emperor Alexander sent Semyon Ivanovich Mazarovich to Tehran. Arrogant and openly disdainful of diplomatic convention, Mazarovich claimed that Russian troops would soon occupy Tabriz, that Persia's shahs would henceforth be chosen in St. Petersburg and that Persia should wage war on Turkey.

Unchastened by the disastrous losses of territory to Russia, Fath 'Ali Shah's sons, Mohammad 'Ali Mirza and 'Abbas Mirza, launched a two-pronged attack on the Ottoman East in 1821. While Mohammad 'Ali Mirza, the governor of Kermanshah, attacked Baghdad, his brother, based at Tabriz, targeted eastern Turkey. Russia looked on with interest, as a war between Persia and the Porte served Alexander's interests. Despite the assistance of French mercenaries like General Charles Devaux, Mohammad 'Ali Mirza's failed to capture Baghdad. Accounts of Persian victories appeared regularly in the press, but Ottoman forces held firm. It was even rumored that Alexander and Fath 'Ali Shah had come to an arrangement regarding the partition of the Ottoman empire once it had been defeated.

Then suddenly, in early 1822, just as the Persians seemed to be on the verge of capturing both Erzurum and Baghdad, the sieges of both cities were lifted. What appeared to be a coordinated ceasefire was, in reality, a retreat dictated by the outbreak of cholera in the Persian forces. Shortly thereafter, Mohammad 'Ali Mirza died. Passed over by his father as Fath 'Ali Shah's successor in favor of 'Abbas Mirza, Mohammad 'Ali Mirza had publicly vowed to contest his brother's succession, a stipulation guaranteed in 1813 by Article 4 of the Treaty of Gulistan, so that his death removed one trigger for wholesale instability in the country.

After the cessation of Turco-Persian hostilities, the British ambassador in Constantinople, Lord Strangford, attempted to act as mediator. Although his efforts were initially rebuffed by the Porte, he ultimately prevailed and in late 1823 reports in the press stated that peace was on the point of being concluded. In London, a new Persian ambassador, Mirza Saleh Shirazi, had arrived, as had a number of Persian students sent to learn useful trades. Reports appeared in the summer of 1825 alleging that Fath 'Ali Shah had decided to abdicate in favor of 'Abbas Mirza, but these proved false. As something of a celebrity, 'Abbas Mirza became the subject of numerous accounts extolling his progressiveness, his intelligence and his general character, all of which tended to express a hope that, with 'Abbas Mirza on the throne, a new day might dawn in Persia, bringing it more into line with Western sensibilities.

10.1 'Foreign and Domestic News,' *Ontario Repository* (Tuesday, 2 July 1816): 'An Embassy from the Sophi[1] at Persia, has arrived in France.'[2]

10.2 'From Persia. Ispahan, Sept. 21, 1815,' *Northern Whig* (23 July, 1816): 'Information has just been received that the Khans of Schiras, Ormus, Gombroon,[3] Teflis, and Erivan, have conspired together against the King,[4] and are now marching with a large army

---

[1] Fath 'Ali Shah.

[2] In a letter from the Russian ambassador to France, General Pozzo di Borgo, to Count Nesselrode, the Russian Foreign Minister, dated 22 May 1816, we read, 'Un envoyé de Perse, nommé Mir-Daoud-Zadour-el-Melik, chevalier de première classe des ordres du Soleil et du Lion, vient d'arriver ici, chargé d'une lettre de compliments pour le Roi. Il est sans aucune suite, et n'a pas même été présenté à la Cour en forme; M. de Richelieu m'a dit qu'il s'en retournera, porteur de la réponse d'usage. See Polovtsoff (1902: 518). For his observations on Persia see Schahnazar and Cirbied (1818). A decade later Daud Khan was in Constantinople, ostensibly 'to induce the Porte to join Persia against Russia.' See Anonymous (1826n). Later, in 1851, he undertook an embassy to Vienna on behalf of Naser al-Din Shah in order to engage six professors for the newly founded military academy in Tehran. See Polak (1876: 11–12).

[3] Bandar 'Abbas.

[4] Fath 'Ali Shah.

towards the capital.[5] All the royal treasures have been sent off, or thrown into the river Zenderhend,[6] and preparation is making to give the traitors a warm reception.'

10.3 'Curious if true,' *The Pilot* (Wednesday, 11 September 1816): 'The Persian Ambassador at Paris, (says the Providence Patriot), is an American [sic, Armenian][7] born, of the Christian, not of the Mahometan persuasion, of creditable talents, and unblemished private character. He has long been a resident in Persia.'

10.4 'Foreign News,' *New-York Evening Post* (Thursday, 12 September, 1816): 'Paris, July 27. The following is an accurate account of the present place of abode of the 38 persons mentioned in the Second Article of the Ordinance of the 24th of July, 1615 [sic, 1815], and driven from France by the law of the 12th of January, 1816....Lallemant, the elder, and Savary, have left Smyrna, on their way to Persia.'[8]

10.5 'From the Bengal Harkarra (Messenger.) Calcutta, Oct. 16,' *Farmer's Repository* (Wednesday, 2 April, 1817): 'The following is an extract of a letter which has just reached us from an intelligent correspondent at Bushire. It is dated the 25th August.

---

[5] This remarkable statement combines a disparate set of places. The entire notion is fanciful.

[6] Zayandarud. This river runs through the former Safavid capital, Isfahan, which is obviously confused here with the Qajar capital, Tehran.

[7] Dawud Khan Malekshah Nazar (Mir Dawud-Zadur or Mir Dawoud-Zadour de Melik Chah-Nazar), born in Isfahan. See Hellot-Bellier (2000). For other variants of his name, including Shahnazareants, and Dāwud ibn Dādūr az nasl i Malik Šāh-Naẓar az aulād i Šāpur, see Storey (1972: 151). As Storey noted, he 'was sent to France with letters' from Fath 'Ali Shah, 'Abbas Mirza and the prime minister Mirza M. Shafi"acknowledging a letter dispatched in 1815 by Louis XVIII (1814–24) to announce his accession to the throne.'

[8] General Charles François Antoine Lallemand (1774–1839) and General Anne-Jean-Marie-René Savary, Duke of Rovigo (1774–1833). Louis XVIII's 'Ordonnance du 24 Juillet 1815,' which became law on 12 January, 1816, reads, 'Voulant, par la punition d'un attentat sans exemple, mais en graduant la peine et limitant le nombre des coupables, concilier l'intérêt de nos peuples, la dignité de notre couronne et la tranquillité de l'Europe, avec ce que nous devons à la justice et a l'entiere sécurité de tous les autres citoyens sans distinctions, Avons déclaré et déclarons, ordonné et ordonnons ce qui suit: Art. 1er, Les généraux et officiers qui ont trahi le Roi avant le 23 mars, ou qui ont attaqué la France et le Gouvernement à main-armée, et ceux qui, par violence, se sont emparés du pouvoir, seront arrêtés et traduits devant les conseils de guerre compétens, dans leurs divisions respectives (3), savoir:...les deux frères Lallemant...Rovigo.' See Duvergier (1837: 14). One of Napoleon's stalwart associates, Lallemand was condemned to death in absentia by a Bourbon military tribunal but managed to get on board an English merchant vessel headed to Smyrna [Izmir]. 'There, after being rebuffed by the Sultan and evading arrest by French agents, Lallemand headed for Persia where he hoped to gain employment in the Shah's army. This and a subsequent attempt to enter the service of Egypt having failed, Lallemand decided to join his younger brother, Henri, in America' where he arrived on 11 May 1817. See Blaufarb (2005: 87). He was accompanied by another former aide of Napoleon's, and Napoleon's one-time Minister of Police, General Savary. See Blaufarb (2005: 258).

"Report says that one hundred thousand Russians arrived at Tifliz, that they are commanded by Constantine Palowitsch,[9] that they are resolved to make war with Persia, that this commander in chief is brother to Alexander the king, and is empowered to act as he pleases. Wallachia and Moldavia the Russians have taken from the Turks, and we may expect to hear that they will shortly make further advances eastward. Their ambition is well known, and now they are at peace with their neighbors, they must find out employ for their immense armies...."

The article above, concerning Persia, is probably from one of the *Ukbahrs* (or newspapers) of northern Hindustan, the writers of which are apt to anticipate the future, and give it an apparent reality in the present; these articles mix prophecy and fable so fantastically, yet commodiously, that they assume all the externals of absurdity while they cover warnings and counsels, the most grave and serious, such as the wise and the sagacious only can discern, and which are concealed from the vulgar, by their familiarity with extravagant and marvellous tales. It has been long foreseen that the Russian power would grasp some day at Persia; the distracted state of that ancient nation, renders it an object of no great difficulty to a power of such unity and resource as Russia, and which can without doubt at any time establish its dominion over the Persians, to whom the rule of such a predominant power would operate as a blessing compared with the multitude of assassins which assume authority over its torn and distracted province. The English are very apprehensive of the approaches of the Russians, and the pretext of resisting the intrigues of the French in the north of Asia, has offered very convenient opportunities to send missions into Kabul Persia, and the countries bordering on the Caspian sea. Asia is destined, before many years pass away, to undergo revolutions as stupendous as any in her long and eventful history.—Asia Minor, and China, will, probably, before half a century, be under European subjection, as Hindustdan is now.

10.6 'Untitled,' *New-Bedford Mercury* (Friday, 9 May, 1817), 'From the Boston Palladium May 6. From France,' *New-York Daily Advertiser* (Friday, 9 May, 1817), 'Gleanings by former arrivals,' *Newburyport Herald, Commercial and Country Gazette* (Friday, 9 May, 1817), 'From France,' *American Advocate and Kennebec Advertiser* (Saturday, 10 May, 1817), 'Foreign. From France,' *Essex Patriot* (Saturday, 10 May, 1817), 'From the Boston Patriot. From France,' *The National Advocate* (Saturday, 10 May, 1817), 'Unti-

---

[9] Grand Duke Constantine Pavlovich (1779–1831), younger brother of Alexander I. After the Duchy of Warsaw became part of Russia as a result of the Congress of Vienna, Constantine was appointed commander-in-chief of the army in Poland and remained there until 1820, a 'virtual dictator,' according to Hodgetts (1908: 65). He never undertook a campaign in Georgia against Persia. In fact, 'Constantine grew to identify himself with Poland, which he even placed at last above Russia in his affections. In Russia he now found nothing to admire, and he could be induced with difficulty to pay flying visits to St. Petersburg,' according to Hodgetts (1908: 68).

tled,' *Hallowell Gazette* (Wednesday, 14 May, 1817), 'From the Boston Palladium, May 9. From France,' *Lancaster Journal* (Wednesday, 14 May, 1817), 'Boston, May 6. From France,' *The American Beacon and Commercial Diary* (Friday, 16 May, 1817), 'Untitled,' *Plattsburgh Republican* and 'From the Boston Patriot. Frome France,' *Suffolk County Recorder* (Saturday, 24 May, 1817): 'Some skirmishes have taken place between the Turks and Persians on their respective frontiers.'[10]

10.7 'Salem—Wednesday, June 25, 1817,' *Essex Register* (Wednesday, 25 June, 1817): 'Some difficulties between the Turks and Persians on their frontiers have been settled.'

10.8 'Translations,' *New-York Evening Post* (Friday, 25 July, 1817), 'By an Arrival from France,' *The Geneva Gazette* (Wednesday, 6 August, 1817) and 'Late from France,' *Plattsburgh Republican* (Saturday, 9 August, 1817): 'Petersburgh, (Russia,) May 19. . . . The Count d'Yermoloff[11] has departed for Persia, to negotiate the cession of the Southern provinces on the Caspian[12]; and the free communication of the Russians with the Indies, through the Persian States.'

---

[10] This may be another reference to ongoing conflict related to control of Solaimaniyah and the Baban struggle with Baghdad. See Longrigg (1925: 243). Heude, who travelled through the area on his way from Baghdad to Mosul in March, 1817, made no reference to clashes between Persian and local forces at this time. See Heude (1819).

[11] Lieutenant-General Alexei Petrovich Ermolov (1777–1861), appointed commander in chief of the Russian army in Georgia on 24 May 1816 (Brosset 1857: 306, n. 1), was appointed ambassador to Iran and on 17 April 1817 set out for Persia 'pour mettre la dernière main au traité de paix perpétuelle et déterminer les limites de la Géorgie et de la Perse.' See Brosset (1857: 306).

[12] As McNeill (1836: 64) noted, during the negotiations that led to the signing of the Treaty of Gulistan, 'The basis on which this treaty was negotiated, was that each party should retain the territory of which it was in possession when hostilities ceased. . . .the Persian Plenipotentiary declined to accept the basis unless Talish should be excluded. General Ritescheff, then Governor General and Commander-in-Chief in Georgia, and Plenipotentiary, on this occasion objected, that his instructions made the adoption of that basis a sine qua non, but solemnly pledged himself, if the Persian Ambassador would accept it, to procure from his court the restitution of Talish as an act of grace from the Emperor; and deliberately held out the hope that other provinces also would be restored. The British Ambassador [Ouseley], cognizant of these transactions, and satisfied of the sincerity of Ritescheff, felt himself justified in confirming the confidence of the Persians, and undertaking that the good offices of his government should be exerted at the Court of St. Petersburgh to procure an adjustment of the stipulation respecting the territory.' It was the first priority of Mirza Abu'l Hassan Khan Shirazi, when sent to St. Petersburg, to finalize the cession of these provinces but as McNeill (1836: 65) noted, he got nothing. According to Monteith (1856: 101–103), 'At Tabreez he refused to enter into any discussion with Abbas Mirza, and, after passing a short time in a country palace belonging to the Prince Royal, was received at the royal camp of Sultanieh on the tenth September [Brosset (1857: 306) dates his arrival at Sultanieh to 20 July]. It soon became evident the negotiations would lead to no favourable result: the conferences lasted eleven days; but the ambassador constantly declared he had no orders to restore any part of the territory occupied by Russia; until Abbas Mirza, losing patience, observed to him, "Your mission appears to have had no object, except that of

10.9 'An Elephant's Gallantry. St. Petersburgh, (Rus.) April 2, 1817,' *The Ladies' Weekly Museum, or Polite Repository of Amusement and Instruction* (Saturday, 18 October, 1817), 'Foreign. St. Petersburgh, April 2, 1817. An Elephant's Gallantry,' *Hampshire Gazette* (Wednesday, 12 November, 1817), 'An Elephant's Gallantry. Petersburg, April 2, 1817,' *Spirit of the Times & Carlisle Gazette* (Monday, 17 November, 1817), 'St. Petersburgh, (Rus.) April 2,' *New-York Daily Advertiser* (Tuesday, 18 November, 1817), 'An Elephant's Gallantry. Petersburg, (Russia) April 2, 1817,' *Lancaster Journal* (Wednesday, 19 November, 1817), 'An Elephant's Gallantry. Petersburg, April 2, 1817,' *The American Beacon and Commercial Diary* (Monday, 24 November, 1817), 'An Elephant's Gallantry. Petersburg, April 2, 1817,' *Portland Gazette and Maine Advertiser* (Tuesday, 25 November, 1817), 'An Elephant's Gallantry. Petersburgh, April 2, 1817,' *Susquehanna Centinel* (Saturday, 29 November, 1817), 'St. Petersburgh, (Rus.) April 2,' *Connecticut Herald* (Tuesday, 2 December, 1817), 'St. Petersburgh, April 2,' *New Jersey Journal* (Tuesday, 2 December, 1817) and 'St. Petersburgh, (Rus.) April 2,' *Patriot* (Tuesday, 2 December, 1817): 'A wooden house has been built for the Elephant's [sic] with which the Emperor[13] has been presented by the Shah of Persia[14]: the male is seventeen feet high, and

---

presenting us with some glass and china."....The requisitions of the Russian embassy were without bounds, and greatly distressed the places they passed through. The demands for tea, sugar, coffee, wine, sweetmeats, and other articles only procurable in large towns, weighed heavily on the smaller cities and inferior governments...A bad feeling was excited against the Russians, by the enormous supplies required, though the integrity of General Yermoloff personally was above suspicion; in fact, he was on principle economical and careful in his own expenses....Whatever faults he may have had, avarice and corruption were certainly not among them.' Indeed according to Baddeley (1908: 100–101), 'It was Yermóloff's task to put an end once for all to Feth Ali's cherished desires, yet at the same time to establish, if possible, genuinely peaceful and friendly relations between the two courts....If some slight rectifications of the frontier were found compatible with Russia's interests, he might to that extent give way, but anything like restoration on a large scale was really out of all question, and any one less likely than Yermóloff to abandon an inch of territory already won it would have been difficult to choose.'

[13] Alexander I.

[14] Fath 'Ali Shah. As Morier (1818: 300–301) noted, 'In order to the conclusion of a definitive treaty [syntax as printed], it was necessary that an embassy should be sent to the Emperor of Russia, and Mirza Abul Hassan Khan being again appointed to represent His Persian Majesty, was accordingly nominated Ambassador Extraordinary and Plenipotentiary to that Court....Great preparations were made to give this embassy an imposing effect. The Ambassador was furnished with a large suite of servants, with splendid clothes and rich utensils of all sorts. Presents for the Emperor were collected from all parts. Arabian horses, Abyssinian slaves, pearls from Bahrein, shawls from Cashmere, brocades and silks from Ispahan, constituted the principal articles, to which were added two of the King's elephants, that had been sent as presents from Herat.' Cf. Melville (2013: 89, n. 76). Hasan-e Fasa'i wrote, 'The presents for the Russian emperor and the nobles of the empire handed over to the ambassador were: 10,000 toman in cash, 2 elephants, 10 select horses, 100 Kashmir shawls, 10 incomparable strings of pearls, several rubies from Badakhshān, pomegranate-colored hyacinths, swords from Khorasan, brocaded silk from Esfahan, boxes studded with jewels and filled with bezoar stones from Shabānkarā, and carpets from Herāt.' See Busse (1972: 146–147). According to an

is the same upon which the Persian monarch used to ride under an awning.—— Some Persians have remained here [St. Petersburg] to attend these animals. A very curious circumstance occurred a few days since. A lady who often came to see the Elephant, was accustomed to bring him bread, apples, &c. One day the animal, by way of shewing his gratitude, seized the lady with his trunk, and put her upon his back, on the place where the driver usually sits. The poor woman, terrified by this unexpected piece of gallantry, shrieked violently, and begged to be taken down; but the Persians assured her that it was far more prudent to remain where she was. She was, threrefore, obliged to wait till the Elephant laid hold of her again, and set her down as gently as he had before lifted her up.'

10.10 'From a Liverpool paper of Sept. 22d,' *The Northern Budget* (Tuesday, 25 November, 1817): 'Russia.—A Work has appeared in the last week, which has given rise to much speculation. It is "A view of the Political & Military strength of Russia in 1817," Sir R. Wilson.[15] It shows the vast increase of power which Russia has recently received by the impolicy of other states, by additions on the side Swedon [sic], Poland, Turkey, & Persia; notwithstanding which extension of territory, her frontier has become

---

anonymous letter sent from St. Petersburg to London on 7 October 1815 (Anonymous 1816a), 'I have seen the two elephants that were sent as a present from the King of Persia to the Emperor of Russia. They were conveyed from Persia by Sultan Kattegery [Katti Giray], who is a serious young man, a native of Tartary.' Katti Giray commanded a Cossack troop that accompanied Mirza Abu'l Hasan Khan for part of his journey overland to St. Petersburg. See Kırımlı (2004: 76), who noted, 'Throughout his military career, Katti Giray experienced quite colorful assignments. At one point, in 1815, he was commissioned by General N.F. Rtishchev, the Commander-in-chief of the Russian troops in Georgia, to command the Cossack detachment which accompanied the Persian envoy to St. Petersburg. He successfully performed his escort duty of the diplomatic convoy which also included two elephants and twenty-four stallions to be presented to the Tsar.' In describing the presents sent by Fath 'Alī Shah to St. Petersburg, Lyall (1825/2: 90–91) noted, 'I had an opportunity of seeing the grand procession which took place at the presentation of the presents of the Shach of Persia to the Emperor of Russia. The chief objects of curiosity were huge elephants with enormous black and red leathern boots, which were made on purpose, in order to preserve their feet from injury by the cold or the snow.' O'Flynn (2017: 400) mistakenly identified these elephants as having arrived with the embassy of Khosrow Mirza, Fath 'Ali Shah's grandson, who he says accompanied Sir Gore Ouseley on his visit to St. Petersburg, 'The diplomatic convoy included two elephants and twenty-four stallions, the gift of Fatḥ 'Alī Shāh to Alexander I, in part reparation for the slaughter of the Russian Minister Griboyedov and his entire staff in Tehran.' In fact, Griboyedov's murder and Khosrow Mirza's mission both occurred in 1829 (on the latter see Idesbald 1833) and O'Flynn has confused Khosrow Mirza with Mirza Abu'l Hasan Khan who travelled fourteen years earlier. Although Fath 'Ali Shah also asked Sir Gore Ouseley to travel home via St. Petersburg, Morier (1818: 301) explained that, 'as it would not have been convenient for both Ambassadors with their numerous suites, to travel together through that country [Russia], Sir Gore Ouseley departed first, and in about two months after was followed by the Persian Embassy.'

[15] Sir Robert Thomas Wilson (1777–1849). The correct title is *A sketch of the military and political power of Russia, in the year 1817*. See Wilson (1817). For his life see Glover (1978).

more unassailable....Sir Robert distinctly states that an expedition against our East India possessions was, at one period in contemplation;

"Whether Alexander will profit by the positions and present superiority of Russia, to accomplish other projects, long assigned to her system of policy, most interests all governments, not excepting the government of the East Indies: whose attention may also be more excited by the information, that general Yermoloff, the governor of the Caucasus line, who probably at this very moment has reached the capital of Persia on an embassy, is an officer of the highest merit, and capacity as an administrator as well as a soldier; and that he has gone assisted not only by the French officers employed by Napoleon, under Gardaune [sic, Gardane], in Persia, and whom Alexander with the exception of three engaged in the Russian service, but with the reports and maps sent by that mission to Napoleon and which, being carried into Russia at the time of the invasion, were found, during the retreat, in two abandoned tumbrils—These reports and plans had convinced Napoleon, that the expedition to India was practicable; and it is a positive fact, that he had resolved on sending an united Russian & French force on that expedition, in Case Russia had been compelled to make peace on his terms.'"[16]

10.11 'Summary,' *The Onondaga Register* (Wednesday, 21 January, 1818): 'The relations between Persia and Russia, appear to be extremely friendly. The Ambassador from the latter government,[17] had been received in the most gracious manner[18]; and the

---

[16] Taken from Wilson (1817: 152–153).

[17] Ermolov.

[18] Ermolov arrived at Fath 'Ali Shah's camp at Soltaniyeh on 20 July 1817. As Brosset (1857: 306–307) observed, 'il y trouva le chah qui le reçut en grande cérémonie, le 20 juillet; Iermolof lui offrit les présents susdits: le règlement des frontières et les conditions du traité avec les Russes furent ratifiés.' He had two audiences with the Shah. 'La première eut lieu le 31 juillet, elle fut toute politique: la seconde, le 3 août, jour du Baïram, avait pour but la remise des présents, dont l'arrivée avait souffert quelque retard. Je ne me rappelle pas où j'ai lu qu'une des plus grandes difficultés d'etiquette, pour la première audience, avait été de faire consentir l'ambassadeur russe à oter ses bottes pour entrer dans la salle où devait se trouver le chah. On sait que c'est un usage en Asie, fondé sur la nécessité de ménager les tapis étendus dans les appartements. Iermolof y consentit à la fin, mais en exigeant qu'on le laissât entrer avec la chaussure qu'il aurait sous ses bottes, et il se trouva qu'il s'était muni d'une autre paire de bottes en maroquin rouge, très fin, lui tenant lieu de bas. La cérémonial persan s'arrangea comme il peut de cette infraction.' As Baddeley (1908: 103–104) wrote, 'In the end Feth Ali, upon whom Yermóloff's strange personality seems to have made an extraordinarily favourable impression, and whose rule over the khanates in question had in reality been little more than nominal, suffered himself to be persuaded or cajoled. Russia retained all her conquests, and Yermóloff returned in triumph. But, going and coming, he had passed through Tabriz, the residence of Abbas Mirza; and his high-handed, not to say insolent treatment of that prince confirmed the latter in his hostility to Russia, and made him Yermóloff's bitterest enemy, a fact that had no little influence on coming events. Russia's improvised ambassador, however, fully satisfied with the immediate success of his mission, and caring not a jot for Abbas Mirza or his feelings

horses of the royal stud, placed as relays on the road, to facilitate his progress to the capitol.'[19]

10.12 'Actual Strength of Russia—Chimerical Apprehensions of Hostilities,' *St. Lawrence Gazette* (Tuesday, 3 February, 1818): 'A fourth acquisition is that of the provinces of Georgia and the Caucasus. In 1791, (says Sir Robert)[20] the Cuban river was the boundary; Russia has now passed this river, and ascended and descended the adjoining mountains of Caucasus....A fifth, and the last acquisition of Russia, is on the side of Persia, where a late treaty[21] has given her the two important Persian provinces of Daughistan and Shirvan, an acquisition which has rendered her mistress of the Caspian. Russia, (says Sir Robert) is thus within three hundred miles of the capital of Persia.'[22]

10.13 'From late London papers. [Received at N. York per the Importer.] Constantinople, Dec. 18,' *Franklin Gazette* (Friday, 20 March, 1818): 'Accounts received from Persia inform us, that the late Russian embassy to the sovereign of that country, has not been attended with the advantages which had been expected from it, and that the Persians, unable to forget the cessions made at the last peace, try every imaginable means to recover the ceded provinces, in order, by this, to recover from the precarious situation in which they are placed[23] by the

---

hastened to Tiflis, already determined in his own mind to reduce the khanates to Russian provinces, though constrained, first of all, to devote his attention to affairs on the northern Line.'

[19] As Kotzebue (1819a: 90) noted, on the 26th of April, 'An officer has already been here, to ascertain precisely the number of persons and horses in order to make preparations for us accordingly.' And further (Kotzebue 1819a: 128–129), he observed on 7 May, 'from the day when the Embassy entered the Persian territory, their conveyance and daily maintenance were defrayed at the sole expense of the king. Saddle-horses were provided for us, and our baggage was forwarded on mules and camels.'

[20] Sir Robert Wilson. Cf. 10.10.

[21] The Treaty of Gulistan.

[22] Tehran.

[23] Kotzebue (1819a: 145 and n). * noted, '*Persia* by the late treaty, made under the auspices of England, *is herself prostrate* at the *feet of Russia*. The British ambassador obtained the best terms he could; but his inability to procure better, corroborates the assertion of the text, with respect to the present helpless situation of Persia.' As McNeill (1836: 65) later wrote, both Mirza Abu'l Hasan Khan and Lord Cathcart, the British ambassador to Russia, '*were unable to procure from the Emperor [Czar Alexander] the relinquishment of one foot of ground*'; and the final answer was, that General Yermoloff, then appointed ambassador to Persia, and Governor-General and Commander-in-Chief in Georgia, would discuss the matter with the Persian ministers on his arrival at Tehran. When General Yermoloff arrived in Persia, he would restore nothing; and thus all the acquisitions of Russia remained in her possession.'

proximity of the Russian frontier to the royal residence of Taheran [sic, Tehran], which is scarcely fifty German miles[24] distant from them.'[25]

10.14 'Latest from England,' *The Geneva Gazette* (Wednesday, 25 March, 1818) and 'Latest from England,' *Otsego Herald* (Monday, 30 March, 1818): 'A letter from a French officer in Persia[26] states that a treaty is about to be concluded which will secure to Russia a

---

[24] The length of the German mile varied in space and time. Using a common figure of 7500 m/German mile, 50 x 7.5 km = 375 km or 234 miles. Ritter (1822: 985) reckoned 5 German miles = 1 English mile, which would make the 50 German miles mentioned here 250 miles.

[25] As Wilson (1817: 147) noted, 'To reach *Tchiran* [sic, Tehran], the capital of the Shah, the columns [Russian] have to march only *three hundred* miles; and by the navigation of the Caspian they can be disembarked within *one hundred!*'

[26] When Gardane left Persia, French officers seconded by their government ceased, under British pressure, to serve the Qajars. But as Wilson (1817: 146) noted, some '*French* officers, officers of the army of Napoleon *proscribed* by Louis [XVIII],' were serving in Persia in 1817, although most, like Louis-Philippe Aubrélique (Le Calloc'h 2002: 106) and Charles Devaux (see 10.71, 75, 79; 12.81; Bran 1829; Belge 1829; Anonymous 1830a), arrived later and worked for Mohammad 'Ali Mirza in Kermanshah, where intelligence related to India and is less likely to have circulated than in 'Abbas Mirza's establishment. Johnson (1818: 213) noted, 'The Persians, at this juncture [1817], were in great alarm concerning the intentions of the Russians; and finding that our Indian government will not allow any of their officers or men to remain and act hostilely in the Persian service, they were of course eager to give employ to our ancient rivals the French. At present, that is at the period of our journey, there were five officers of that nation, and four of Italy and Sicily, recently entertained by the Prince ['Abbas Mirza], who had directly appointed them to the command of battalions, &c.' According to Anonymous (1826d), a translation of a French newspaper report: 'A short time after the restoration [of the Bourbon monarchy, i.e. Louis XVIII], some French officers went and offered their services to foreign countries. Some of them having reached Persia, attached themselves to the eldest son [Mohammad 'Ali Mirza] of the present sovereign [Fath 'Ali Shah], and left the country on the death of that prince in 1822. Others, who were in greater number, entered the service of the hereditary prince, Abbas Mirza, for the purpose of training his troops in the European manner. They had all obtained a higher rank than they had in France. Their pay was pretty considerable, and they were in general satisfied with their situation...England paid to Fat'h Ali Shah the last part of a military contribution which was due to him. It annexed, as a condition, the discharge of all the French officers, without any exception, and this condition was immediately executed. Almost all the French officers then returned to Europe, by way of Tiflis and Constantinople. Two of them only, a former aide-de-camp to Marshal Brune, and another officer of Buonaparte, a native of the Duchy of Modena resolved to go and offer their services to the King of Cabul, or to Runjeet Singh, chief of the Seiks at Lahore....A long time elapsed without any news being received of those two officers: only a report was spread that, on reaching the dominions of Runjeet Singh, they had been given over by him to the English East-India Company, which, it was said, had orders to embark them for France. It is, therefore, with great surprise, that a letter has been received from Tiflis, in the hand-writing of M. Allard de Saint Tropés himself, in which he announces that he is in Lahore, with Mr. Ventura—that they are very happy, loved and esteemed, and have the rank of general, with a pay amounting to 6000 francs per month.' According to Victor Jacquemont, Jean-François Allard (1785–1839) was in 'Abbas Mirza's service for a year. See Mérimée (1867: 205). As Pearse (1898: 312) noted, 'The fatal day of Waterloo, and the murder of his patron, Maréchal Brune, dashed his hopes to the earth, and

free passage to India and the Persian Gulf.[27] A session [sic, cession] of some provinces bordering on the Caspian, had been agitated; an Armenian kingdom was to be re-established by the common consent of Persia, Russia and Turkey.'

10.15 'View of Persia. Extract of a letter from Capt. Moritz von Kozebue,[28] in the Imperial Russian General's Staff (attached to the Russian Embassy in Persia,) to his father,[29] dated from Sultanie, (the Summer residence of the Schach of Persia) the 11th of August, 1818,'[30] *Richmond Commercial Compiler* (Saturday, 20 June, 1818): 'Persia,[31] which has been imagined to be so beautiful, is, as far as we know it, a dreary desert, inhabited by famished and unhappy people. The best description of Persia is given by Chardin,[32] about one

---

after four years of hesitation and of half-hearted attempts to make a fresh start in the royal army, Allard decided to seek his fortune abroad. His first intention was to visit the United States, but a communication from his friend Colonel [Rubino (Gian Battista) Ventura [1794–1858] caused him to change his plans and accompany the latter to Persia, where they entered the service of Abbas Mirza, the heir-apparent. Here the friends were treated with kindness and respect, but their aspirations in the matter of salary were very far from satisfied; so in the fulness of time they took leave of Abbas Mirza and passed through Afghanistan into the Panjab.' According to Roy (1857: 5), 'En 1815, Allard quitta le régiment pour s'attacher en qualité d'aide de camp, au service du maréchal Brune. Après l'assassinat de ce maréchal, il voulait se rendre en Amérique.' Instead, he went to Egypt to offer his services to Mohammad 'Ali. 'N'ayant pas trouvé en Égypte un emploi convenable, il se rendit en Perse au-près d'Abbas-Mirza, qui lui accorda le grade et la solde de colonel dans ses armées. Allard aurait voulu un régiment à commander; mais, ne pouvant l'obtenir, il donna sa démission pour passer dans l'Afghanistan, d'où il gagna le royaume de Lahore. Il entra alors au service de Runjet-Sing, dont il parvint si bien à capter les bonnes grâces, que ce prince ne tarda pas à lui accorder une confiance illimitée.' Allard may have been in 'Abbas Mirza's service when the letter referred to in this article was written, and could have been its author, although this cannot be confirmed.

[27] Wilson (1817: 147) shrewdly observed, 'an army might sail from the *Baltic* through an internal navigation from Petersburgh to Astracan, and landing on the southern shore of the Caspian, pitch their tents within *four hundred* miles of the Persian Gulf; from whence the voyage to *Bombay* is only from *twenty-four* to *thirty* days, in both Monsoons; and to Madras, but *eight* or *ten* days longer in the S.W. Monsoon.'

[28] Moritz von Kotzebue (1789–1861). He accompanied Ermolov's embassy to Fath 'Ali Shah in 1817. See Kotzebue (1819a-b). The younger von Kotzebue grew up in Russia and hence pursued a military career there because his father accepted a position in St. Petersburg in 1781, which led to 'die ehrenvolle Stelle eines Präsidenten des Gouvernementsmagistrats der Provinz Esthland' in 1785. See Cramer (1820: 85, 108). He later served as Ermolov's Chief of Staff during the Second Russo-Persian War. See 11.99.

[29] August von Kotzebue (1761–1819), noted German playwright.

[30] The date has been misprinted here for in the original versions, e.g. Anonymous (1818b), it is 'the 14th of August, 1817.' Note that this American article appeared on 20 June and hence could not be quoting another article from 11 (or 14 August) 1818, but rather from 1817.

[31] This is the translation of a letter from Kotzebue to his father. The text is only generally similar to that found in Kotzebue (1819a).

[32] Cf. 1.142.

hundred and fifty years ago. It does not contain any thing remarkably interesting, but the splendor of the court was at that time unequalled in its kind. Now, an old man who is in every respect superannuated, seeks only to amass treasures in his coffers.[33]—The character of the nation seems to us to be rather unamiable. How should it be otherwise, since they not only do not value the women, but even despise them?

On the 17th of April[34] we left Tiflis in a heat of 25 degrees. The trees were already out of blossom: but after a march of three days, we came near the mountains, where nature was still in her winter's sleep. The highest mountain of this chain forms, with another which lies opposite to it, a kind of gate, which the inhabitants call the *Great Mouth*.—But we ourselves made *great eyes* (a Germanism for staring,)[35] when a whirlwind, which is very common in these mountains, seized the whole embassy, and almost obliged them to dance a waltz. It is sometimes so dreadful, that neither men nor horses can stand against it.

On the 25th we passed a cavern close to the road, which is large enough to afford shelter to some hundred cattle.—Not far from this frightful cavern stands a simple white tombstone on an eminence;—which is surrounded by several other graves.—Here rests a brave soldier, Col. Montresor,[36] who was in our service 18 years ago, when Prince Sizianoff

---

[33] Fath 'Ali Shah was born in 1781/2 (Busse 1972: 4, n. 20), making him only about 46 years old when this article appeared. He was noted for his avarice. Thus Fraser (1825: 193) wrote, 'the ruling passion and besetting sin of Futeh Allee Shah, which has proved more injurious to his country and his power than all the efforts of his enemies, is avarice, an insatiable desire of accumulating wealth.' Cf. Fraser (1838b: 50), 'as for the old king, he is too much blinded by his avarice to see or dread anything that leads to its gratification.' Similarly, Markham (1874: 382–383) observed, 'The avaricious old Shâh continued to devote his attention to the extortion of the greatest possible amount of revenue, and the destruction of the power of all those great chieftains whose followers formerly composed the flower of the Persian army.'

[34] Kotzebue's dates are all Old Style. See the translator's note in Kotzebue (1819a: 174, n. *).

[35] The German idiom 'große Augen machen,' 'to make big/great/large eyes.'

[36] Also Montrezor. Colonel Joseph (Jozef) Antonovich Montrésor (1767–1804) came from a family of French Huguenots. Part of them had fled from France to England where they established a family that was extremely distinguished for its military service and included, e.g. Col. James Montrésor who was named 'Chief Engineer of America' in 1775, and Col. John Montrésor who served under Wellington in India. See Scull (1882: 6–7). Joseph Montresor's family had emigrated to Kiev and Kursk. See https://en.topwar.ru/123265-eto-imya-dolzhno-byt-bessmertnym-mayor-montrezor-nastoyaschiy-geroy-rossii.html.death His death during Tsitsianov's unsuccessful assault on Yerevan was described e.g. in Rottiers (1829: 88–89, n. *), 'En 1804, le général Tsitsianoff...fit assiéger Érivan; il y employa 6000 hommes d'infanterie, 2000 hommes de cavalerie et un train d'artillerie de siège et de campagne. Il perdit la moitié de ses chevaux et au moins un tiers de ses soldats, tant par suite de maladies qu'à l'escalade qu'il fit tenter....Pendant le siége, le major Montrésor fut envoyé à Tiflis pour commander des vivres; il avait avec lui une compagnie d'infanterie et deux pièces d'artillerie: cette petite expédition fut surprise par les Persans à 12 werstes de Karaklis, et tous les hommes qui la composaient furent massacrés après une défense héroïque. Montrésor mourut sur l'un de ses canons. Le siége fut enfin levé.' Cf. Brosset (1857: 281),who wrote, 'Dans ce temps-là la famine se faisant sentir, Tzitzichwili [Tsitsianov] fit partir du côté de Phambac le major Montrésor,

10 From 1816 to the End of the Turco-Persian War (1816–1825)

blockaded Eriwan.—Provisions became scarce among the blockading troops, and the next magazine was in Karaklis,[37] one hundred and sixty wersts distant. The way was very mountainous and intersected, and swarming with enemies. Meantime it was necessary to send a detachment thither, and the prince appointed, for this purpose, Col. Montresor, with 200 grenadiers and a cannon.[38] Amidst incessant skirmishes the little troop approached the above-mentioned cavern within ten wersts of Karaklis, reduced to the half of its original, and with but one shot left in the gun of each soldier, which was reserved for the last necessity. Unluckily there was a Tartar among the troops, who escaped during the night, and betrayed Montresor's desperate situation to the Persians. They attacked him at

---

avec 200 soldats et un canon, pour amener delà des provisions, Baba-Khan, informé de ce départ, en donna avis à son général Pir-Qouli-Khan, posté à Phambac, et qui assiégeait le fort de Qaraklis, où étaient les provisions, le plomb et la poudre des Russes, et où s'étaient réunis les habitants du Somkheth, de Phambac et de la vallée de Loré. Pir-Qouli-Khan eut donc l'ordre de s'emparer du corps russe,' and in n. 1 wrote, 'Le major Montrésor partit avec sa petite troupe vers le 17 août [1805], et il périt avec presque tout son détachement dans une affaire contre plus de 6000 Persans, qui eut lieu le 21.' Anonymous (1893: 525) put the size of Montresor's unit at only 109. Cf. von Bernhardi (1877: 225) who wrote, 'Die Verbindung mit Tiflis war durch feindliche Heertheile unterbrochen—drückender Mangel stellte sich ein, und die südliche Sommerhitze rief Krankheiten hervor. Ein Transport Lebensmittel, der von Tiflis auf dem graden Wege über Karaklissa heranzog, konnte nicht zum Heer gelangen; eine Abtheilung von 350 Mann, die Zizianow ihm unter einem Major Montresor entgegensandte, wurde unterwegs von einer vielleicht zwanzigfach überlegenen Macht unter dem Zaréwitsch Alexander [son of Erekle II] angegriffen und vernichtet.' Montresor's death is also mentioned briefly by Monteith (1856: 40) and discussed by Mahmudov (2010: 301–302).

[37] Kara Kilise, mod. Vanadzor, c. 117 kms. From Yerevan.

[38] The description in Kotzebue (1819a: 80–82) is slightly different. 'Sizianoff made the necessary dispositions to defend himself: the Persians could make no impression on him, and he did not even alter his plan of attack. At last, however, he began to suffer from a scarcity of provisions; and it became necessary to draw supplies from Karaklissa, which, although at the distance of 160 wersts, was his nearest depôt. As his whole army consisted only of a few thousand men, he could not weaken it by detaching a large body. He therefore selected the brave Colonel Montresor, and gave him two hundred grenadiers and a field piece, with orders to fight his way to Karaklissa, and return to the army with provisions and reinforcements. Montresor passed the Persian line during the night, and by dawn of day had considerably got the start of the enemy; and although he was pursued by a strong body of Persians, amounting to *several thousand* men, yet he retreated with so much ability, that he repelled their attacks throughout the whole of that day. In the night he gained a small height, which he speedily intrenched with stones, so as to secure the position against surprise. Early on the following morning he fought his way through the Persians who had already surrounded him, and continued to effect his retreat; but on account of the continual skirmishing, he found it impossible to get beyond this unlucky case. It was evening when he posted himself here, and he learned that his men had only one round of ammunition left. To add to his misfortune a Tártar deserted to the Persians in the night, ad acquainted them with his desperate situation. The Persians, informed that they had onlyone discharge of musketry to receive, overwhelmed the little band of heroes on all sides, and soon cut them down. In the mean time, the firing had been heard at Karaklissa, and a body of troops was dispatched to the assistance of their countrymen,—but they arrived too late. Thus fell Montresor, with the laurels of victory almost within his grasp. His own modest tomb is encircled by the graves of his brave companions in arms.'

daybreak with the more boldness, and sustained the single fire, and after a desperate resistance the Russians were all cut to pieces just as relief came from Karaklis, (where the firing had given notice of their approach) but alas! only to bury those that had fallen. I have been made acquainted with several examples of bravery, of which Georgia was the theatre; but the distance is so great, the European papers have made no mention of them. In order to obtain glory, much depends upon the place where glorious actions are performed.

On the 29th we reached the Persian frontier, and for the first time saw mount Ararat. Here we were received by Asker Chan, (formerly ambassador at Paris)[39] at the head of some thousand men on horseback, who introduced himself to the ambassador as our Momendar [sic, memandar], that is, as our purveyor, during our stay in Persia.[40] This, however, costs the government nothing, because all the villages on the road must furnish us gratis with what we want; if they fail, the peasants get beat or have their ears cut off. We had till now slept in our kibitki (carriage); we now received handsome tents.

A day's journey from Eriwan, we put up at a splendid and extremely rich Armenian convent, where the patriarch[41] resides.[42] The convent must pay dear to the government for its protection; it is squeezed and pressed on every occasion, and sighs of its deliverance. It is said; that on this spot Noah planted his first vine. We were magnificently entertained, and it must be confessed that the wine we drink does honor to Noah's memory. On the 3d of May, we went in state to Eriwan. About halfway 4000 cavalry met us, and manoeuvered before us. Some thousand infantry, with cannon, paraded near the city, in spite of violent rain, by which we here were surprised.[43]

---

[39] 'Askar Khan-e Afshar Urumi (d. 1855). For his time in Paris see e.g. Tancoigne (1820: 252–253, 318); Driault (1900/1). He is considered the 'first Iranian of significance known to have become a freemason.' See Atai (1992: 214). He was initiated into a Paris lodge while there as Fath 'Ali Shah's envoy. See Algar (1970: 276–277). He served under Agha Mohammad Shah in the Kerman and Georgian campaigns of 1790/1 and commanded an Afshar cavalry unit in the First Russo-Persian War. See Brydges (1833: 333); Kondo (1999: 546); Potts (2017b: 253, n. 50). Considered an enemy of the American missionaries who came to Urmia in the 1830s, he was 'assassinated in his own tent by a Koordish chief, Dec. 18th,' 1855. See Fiske (1868: 311).

[40] As Kotzebue (1819a: 91) noted, 'On our way we met Asker-Chan, formerly ambassador at Paris, accompanied by several thousand horsemen, who came to welcome the Ambassador [Ermolov] in the name of the King, and at the same time to announce that he was appointed memandar to the Embassy. A memendar is a functionary charged to receive an embassy, or a person of distinction, and to provide for their maintenance, and wants. The Persian government could, certainly not show a greater mark of civility than that of appointing to the Russian Embassy a memendar who had himself filled the station of ambassador plenipotentiary.'

[41] Yeprem (Estremus) I, who resided at Echmiadzin. See Anonymous (1818c: 92–94).

[42] 'It is the celebrated Jatshmiasin [Etchmiadzin], the residence of the Armenian patriarchs.' See Kotzebue (1819a: 96).

[43] As Kotzebue (1819a: 103–104) wrote, 'On the road between Jatshmiasin and Erivan, Hassan-Chan, brother to the commander of the province, advanced at the head of four thousand cavalry, to meet the Ambassador. The greater part of the troops consisted of Kurdins, who are known to be a very brave people, serving in Persian pay....After the Ambassador had said much to Hassan-Chan in their

10 From 1816 to the End of the Turco-Persian War (1816–1825)

The governor of the province (Sedar)[44] received us at the gate.[45] This man is accused of various *peccadillos*: for example that a short time before our arrival, he had a merchant hung up by the legs, in order to obtain possession of his money and wife, (a beautiful Armenian.) Such things are said to happen daily. I cannot vouch for them; only so much I know, that he not only is lodged well, drinks well, and is richly dressed, but to my astonishment, that he sleeps very well. Our quarters were the best in the town, yet wretched. We dined with the Serdan [sic], where everything was in abundance; but I sought in vain for the celebrated Asiatic magnificence. Three little tumblers danced themselves out of breath, and performed various feats to amuse us. On the second day we entertained each other in a newly erected summer-house, where our music, our punch, our ice, and our liquors, illuminated the Persian heads. The doctor of the governor had chosen a little corner for himself where he enjoyed himself at his ease.—The Serdan is said to be in secret a great friend to Bacchus; at least, he asked the embassador for eight bottles of liquors,[46] which he most likely emptied in the company of his sixty wives and twenty-four * * * * * *.

After we left Eriwan, the heat increased considerably, but the nights were insupportably cold, and occasioned every kind of sickness. On the 13th of May, we passed the celebrated river Araxes, which is now remarkable for nothing, except that, as they say, the plague never extends beyond it.

On the 15th we arrived at Meranda, where it is said that Noah's mother is buried.[47] The good old lady, I fear, does not enjoy much rest in her grave, for there is a public school built

---

praise, the troops formed a circle, and we went forward with the usual manœuvres. Not far from the river Sanga a dreadful shower overtook us, which was the more unwelcome, as we had our gala uniforms on, and intended to make a solemn entrance, with music, into Erivan.'

[44] Kotzebue (1819a: 105), referring to Hoseyn Qoli Khan Qazvini, 'the tyrant of Jatshmiasin,' as 'the sardar (commander-in-chief) of Erivan.'

[45] In his diary Ermolov wrote, 'At my first step on Persian ground, I demanded, that on my entrance into Erivan, the Serdar should come out to meet me. This distinguished grandee, a man who is intimately attached to the Shach, who was esteemed in his younger years for his bravery, and who had been looked up to for a long time only for his riches, certainly did not expect such a proposition; but I insisted with firmness on its execution.' See Lyall (1825/2: 94). In contrast to Kotzebue, Ermolov wrote, 'The Serdar himself came out a verst to meet me,' and 'endeavoured as much as possible to conceal his disagreeable feelings.' See Lyall (1825/2: 96).

[46] According to Kotzebue (1819a: 110–111), 'We had fine weather on the third day [in Yerevan]. At ten o'clock in the morning the sardar came to visit the Ambassador. He seated himself rather awkwardly in a chair, smoked a good deal, said little, and scarcely moved his head when we were presented to him; but in defiance of the laws of Mahomet he eagerly drank the liqueurs that were offered to him. Indeed he makes no secret of his love of spirituous liquors, and openly declares that he cannot live without them.' In his diary Ermolov wrote, 'That which surprised us was, that the governor said he could not live without the aid of spirituous liquors.' See Lyall (1825/2: 97).

[47] Marand is located approximately halfway between Julfa on the Aras and Tabriz. northeast of Lake Urmia. Cf. Cl. Ptolemy 6.2.9, Μορουνδα. See Hewsen (1982: 145). For the Armenian and Arabic refs. See Hübschmann (1904: 346–347). Kotzebue (1819a: 146) wrote, 'Maranda signifies, in the Armenian language, "the mother lies here."' Murad (1901: 64) noted, 'Bekanntlich beziehen die

upon it. On the 19th we arrived at Tauris, the residence of Abbas Mirtz [sic, Mirza], Crown Prince of Persia. A mile from the town we were received by 1000 troops, besides artillery.[48] It is well known that Persia, *with the help of the English*, has lately introduced regular troops. It is scarcely possible to refrain from laughing on seeing the long headed awkward Persians, in half English costume,[49] presenting their arms, while "God save the king" is played. Some English officers followed our suite at a distance; among them was major Lindsey[50]; a kind of war minister to Abbas Mirza. Fainting with the sultry heat, and

---

Armenier die Namen mehrerer Ortschaften in der Umgegend des Masis durch willkürliche Umformungen und Deutungen derselben auf Noah und die Sintflut....der Name der Stadt Marand...wird aus "Mayr-and", d.h. "die Mutter dort", erklärt, weil daselbst die Begräbnisstätte von Noahs Frau liege...Daß diese Volksetymologien späte Erfindungen sind, ist klar und allgemein zugegeben.' Cf. Hübschmann (1904: 451) who dismissed the Armenian folk etymology *mair and (ay)*, 'die Mutter ist dort...weil Noahs Frau dort begraben sein soll,' as 'Natürlich unsinn.' Three years later Stahl (1907: 122) misrepresented the tradition as an etymology of Noah's wife's name when he wrote, 'Marand ist schon im grauen Altertum bekannt gewesen, und die Einwohner leiten den Namen von der Frau Noahs ab, die angeblich hier begraben sein soll.' This seems to be a variant of the tradition recounted by Tavernier (1678: 16), 'They say...that his [Noah's] Wife has a Tomb at *Marante* upon the Road to *Tauris*.' Morier (1818: 302), 'Marand is a large straggling village, overlooked on one side by a small hill fort....The idle report that it is the repository of the remains of Noah's mother, led us to the spot, where we found two ignorant Mollahs, who took us to the corner of a mosque and told us, that tradition had pointed that out as the place, but upon what grounds or pretensions they were not able to inform us.' Cf. Godard (1956: 56).

[48] The figure 1000 here is presumably a misprint for 8000. According to Kotzebue (1819a: 148–149), 'When the Embassy approached the right wing, the commander of the troops saluted, the guns were fired, and the whole line presented arms. The right consisted of forty-eight pieces of horse-artillery, eight squadrons of organized cavalry, and eight thousand regular infantry, together with bodies of Kurdins and militia.'

[49] In Kotzebue (1819a: 162) the description was far different. 'The infantry, as well as the cavalry, are lightly and appropriately dressed. The former have blue and also red jackets of English cloth; the latter have blue jackets trimmed with cotton lace: the officers have gold or silver lace, and wear red silk sashes, such as are used in the English army.'

[50] Lieutenant (later Major) Henry Lindsay, afterwards Maj.-Gen. Sir Henry Lindsay Bethune (1787–1851), 'or *Linji*, as the Persians called him' (de Bode 1845: 62). As Goldsmid (1880: 158–159) noted, 'through the exertions of Lieutenant Lindsay, of the Madras Army, the Prince ['Abbas Mirza] found himself possessed of a corps of disciplined artillery in addition to other troops. The story goes that, notwithstanding the large authority vested in the English Commandant by royal mandate, this Officer never could get over the national antipathy to shaving the chin exhibited by all ranks of his men. One day, however, the chance explosion of a powder-horn in the hands of a gunner carried off the better part of the holder's beard, and Lindsay availed himself of the circumstance to gain his end. Thenceforward the shaved chin became an established rule for artillerymen.' Further, Sheil (1856: 380–381) noted, 'The artillery was placed under Lieutenant Lindsay, afterwards Major-General Sir H. Lindsay. This officer acquired extraordinary influence in the army, and in particular among the artillery. He brought this branch of the forces in Azarbaijan to such a pitch of real working perfection, and introduced so complete a system of esprit de corps, that to this day his name is venerated, and traces of his instruction still survive in the artillery of that province, which even now preserves some degree of efficiency.' Lindsay later played an important role in securing power for

suffocated by the dust, we arrived at Tauris, where the first minister had given up his house for our abode.[51]

After the visits of ceremony, the Crown Prince gave a display of fireworks,[52] in honor of the embassy and also reviewed several thousand cavalry. One afternoon we drank tea in a newly erected summer-house, when he pointed out to us a small habitation, which projected into the garden, and disfigured it very much, but which the possessor would not sell on any terms, and Abbas Mirza, would not take it from him by force. This indeed

---

Mohammad Mirza (Shah) after the death of his father, Fath 'Ali Shah. See e.g. Fraser (1840: 254–260); von Tornau (1849: 4); MacGregor (1871: 504–505). As Kotzebue (1819a: 155) wrote, 'The officers of the English East India Company, residing at Tauris, came to visit the Ambassador, and were invited to dinner. Among them were, Major Lindsay, Major Mackintosh, Captain Hart, Captain Monteith (who had accompanied General Malcolm to Persia), Dr. Cormick, and Lieutenant [George] Willock. Captain [Henry] Willock, the chargé d'affaires of England, and Dr. Campbell, were attending the King at Teheran.' In 1820 Jean-François Gamba (1763–1833), the French Consul at Tiflis, met Lindsay, 'officier d'artillerie, au service du prince Abbas-Mirza, avoit formé à Tauris une école d'artilleurs. Le prince lui avoit fait présent d'une Géorgienne prise dans son harem, et il en avoit eu trois enfants. Deux étoient restés avec la mére, et il emmenoit avec lui le troisième. Il retournoit en Angleterre pour la succession d'un de ses oncles de la famille illustre de Béthune, et en devoit prendre le nom.' Further he wrote in a footnote, 'J'ai logé à Tiflis dans la même maison que cette Géorgienne; elle étoit belle, et paroissoit fort attachée au major Lindsey. Au moment où je la vis, elle avoit à déplorer l'éloignement de son amant et la mort de sa mère. Emmenées par les Persans en 1795, elle fut élevée dans le harem de Feth-Ali-Châh, et transportée ensuite dans celui du prince héréditaire. Revenue à Tiflis avec le major Lindsey, elle s'informe de la demeure de sa mère, dont le souvenir n'étoit pas sorti de sa mémoire, et se présente chez elle sans précaution: la mère expire de joie en retrouvant une fille chérie, dont, depuis long-temps, elle pleuroit la perte.' See Gamba (1826: 6–7 and n. 1).

[51] Thus Kotzebue (1819a: 150), 'The house belongs to the first minister in Tauris, Mirza-Bejurk [Bozorg], who bears also the title Kaimakan, corresponding to vice-chancellor of the kingdom. He has been assigned as an assistant to the King's heir....His house is, like all Persian residences of persons of distinction, an endless labyrinth of courts and small apartments.'

[52] Kotzebue (1819: 173–174) wrote, 'A number of rockets, of a large size, were first let off, after which, through some mistake, the last row of fire-works was lighted first, upon which wheels and cascades began to set up a dreadful noise. Owing to the narrowness of the court, the fire-works were so huddled together that the last row, which had been lighted too early, set fire to the adjoining combustibles; these communicated with the remainder, and the whole works went off at once, with continual reports of mortars, producing a tremendous clatter and confusion, answering to the most poetical description of the infernal regions, &c. &c. Every thing flew about, spitting fire and spreading confusion in all directions: the people rushed down from the walls of the houses; and our apothecary, who had never seen any thing of the kind, exclaimed with astonishment that the battle of Leipzig was a pop-gun compared to this. Thus the entertainment, which had been calculated to last an hour, was over in ten minutes; and Mirza-Bejurk, who was at first rather disconcerted, told us, with his natural adroitness, that the whole of the fire-works had been purposely lighted at once, in order that the precious moments of the Ambassador might not be wasted by such trifles. The noise was still ringing in our ears when we reached home.' According to Lyall (1825/2: 108), the fireworks were 'prepared by French and Italian refugees.'

does him great honor. He is in general highly spoken of, for the good qualities both of his mind and heart, and it is to be hoped that he will one day make Persia happy.

Though we were allowed to walk freely about the city, yet the importunities of the beggars on one hand, and insults on the other caused us to refrain from such indulgences. When, indeed a fellow who had insulted us was taken, he was half beat to death; but this gave us no pleasure, and we therefore remained at home. We received from Teheran the unpleasant intelligence, that in consequence of the fast (of Ramasan),[53] the Schach could not receive us till the expiration of two months: on the other hand, he would welcome us in Sultanie which lies ten marches nearer to Tauris.[54] As we longed for the fresh air, being as it were, shut up in Tauris, Abbas Mirza offered us his own country house, for which we joyfully departed on the 25th, and took possession of our new habitation on the 28th.[55]

Persia is altogether dreary and mountainous, and one rejoices like a child at seeing some green trees. It very seldom rains, but constant winds fill the air with clouds of dust. The villages and towns have a melancholy appearance; the mode of building is miserable; the low houses are made of kneaded clay and some chopped straw mixed up with the clay, that they may not fall to pieces in the first rain, or the wind blow away a whole village. After every rain, there is a general patching of houses throughout Persia. The country seat of the Abbas Mirza is an exception, owing to its being built with the help of the English. The whole is very pretty, only the trees are yet very small, and in this month the winds blow too

---

[53] Ramadan, the ninth month of the lunar year, when Muslims fast from sunrise to sunset. According to Sura 2188–195 of the *Koran*, Ramadan was the month 'wherein the Koran was sent down to be a guidance to the people, and as clear signs of the Guidance and the Salvation, So let those of you, who are present at the month, fast it; and if any of you be sick, or if he be on a journey, then a number of other days.' See Arberry (1969: 52).

[54] The situation was presented differently in Kotzebue (1819a: 175) where we read, 'the Ambassador received a letter from Teheran, addressed to him by the Prime Minister Mirza-Jeffi [Shafi'], who announced, that on account of the insufferable heat of the weather in that city, it was the King's intention to receive the Embassy as his country residence of Sultanie.' Ermolov's own account is different again. Lyall (1825/2: 108) quoted Ermolov's own diary as saying, 'An officer arrived from Teheran, with intelligence from the Grand Vizier, that after the marriage of two of his sons, the Shach would set out for Sultania, his summer palace. By him I also received an invitation to go there, if I could not arrive at Teheran in time for the weddings. It was difficult to succeed in this, and therefore it was arranged that the journey should be performed leisurely, and it was resolved to quit Tabreez.'

[55] 'Abbas-Mirza offered us, in the mean time, the use of his own palace at Udgani [Awjan/Ujan; see Le Strange (1905: 163). Cf. Johnson (1818: 208), Oojaun; von Hammer (1819: 248), Odschan; Lyall (1825/2: 115), Udjani], in case we found the heat intolerable at Tauris. This obliging offer was accepted, more with a view to enjoy freedom from the restraint of daily etiquette with which the Ambassador had been already so much plagued at Tauris, and our departure was fixed for the following day.' See Kotzebue (1819a: 175). Johnson (1818: 208–209) noted that, 'This palace was built for His Majesty to retire to in the hottest weather, Oojaun being considered the coldest part of Persia.'

cold to inhabit it with pleasure.—We however remained there till the fifth of June,[56] and then went two marches farther, to the village of Sengilabat,[57] where water fit for drink, and shady trees, are found.[58] Here, to our great joy, there arrived a convoy from Tiffis, which brought our own wine; for it is very difficult to get wine here,[59] and yet it is indispensable, on account of the bad water. In Persia a place which has good water, is famed far and wide.

The surrounding villages were soon cleared of provisions. We left Sengliabat on the 20th, made several short day's journeys, and passed the town of Miana on the 24th, which is celebrated for its bugs, the bite of which proves mortal in a few hours, but is said not to affect the inhabitants. They only show themselves by night, are of an ash colour, quite flat,

---

[56] Lyall (1825/2: 108–109) noted that both Mirza Bozorg and 'Abbas Mirza 'keenly endeavoured to persuade the ambassador to remain a while at his country castle, called Udjani, and assigned different reasons with respect to the General's comfort for pressing this plan upon him. For two days, negotiations were continued about this business, when the extreme anxiety manifested for his delay, led him to suppose that they had some concealed design. "I therefore," says Yermólof, "told them determinately that, without fail, I should set off, and that I had reasons for so doing. To oppose me they could not; to stop me they dared not. The day before my departure, Abbas Mirza sent to ask me to ride out of town with him. I excused myself, because I was to depart on the following day; and said, that to-day I intended to take care of my eyes, which pained me, and therefore that I could not have the pleasure of seeing him. I begged leave, however, to send one of my officers to present my grateful acknowledgements to the heir-presumptive for his gracious and kind reception, and his attention. I added, that I ought to have had a farewell audience; but, as I had not been received by him in a convenient manner in the court, I did not reckon it necessary.'" According to Kotzebue (1819a: 191–192), 'When we had been several days at Udgani, intelligence arrived that it would not be possible that the King could receive the Embassy before the month of August, as the nation was celebrating the religious festival of the Bairam, during which not only no business is attended to, but from sunrise to sunset people are forbidden to taste anything, even water, or to smoke. As this Bairam lasts two months, we had the agreeable prospect of remaining at this wretched place during the whole of that period.'

[57] Mod. Zanjilabad. Johnson (1818: 199) has Shaingulabad. It is located between Tabriz and Ardabil.

[58] Here 'we found our tents most agreeably placed close to the stream, under the shade of old poplars and apricot trees, which seemed as if they were joined together by garlands of roses.' See Kotzebue (1819a: 194–195).

[59] As Kotzebue (1819a: 197–198) noted, 'We found ourselves rather ill off with respect to wine under the Persian management, for none is made except in Armenia, and that only for the use of the people themselves. They were, therefore, obliged to hunt for it in every village, far and wide; and it was generally so bad, that nobody could drink it. It would have been a very easy matter for the Persian government to have procured some from Grusia [Georgia], since they had undertaken to maintain us in Persia at their own expense, in return for the reception which their embassy had experienced in St. Petersburgh, where they drank the best wine, and were gratuitously provided with every thing that they could want. As that was not done, the Ambassador had too high a sense of delicacy to ask for Grusian wine; but His Excellency ordered a supply from Tiflis, which arrived here to our great satisfaction, and was issued to us in daily portions....As the Persians did not seem to have any objection to the matter, we subsequently received two further supplies of wine from Tiflis.'

and have eight feet.—They are not mentioned in any natural history.[60] We have taken some of them in spirits. We quickly passed through this town of bugs, and did not stop till we reached a large and beautiful bridge, built by Schach Abbes, 5 wersts further.

The following day we passed over the Caplantic mountains,[61] and enjoyed the beautiful prospects, among which I particularly remarked the Virgin's Castle, which was built by Artaxerxes,[62] and is said to have received this name from a beautiful but haughty virgin, who was here imprisoned. Beyond the mountains we met with another handsome bridge over the river Kosilusan.[63] Every thing worth seeing with respect to architecture, is from the time of Schach Abbas the Great. His successors have ruined much, but built little.

The country now became more desolate, the heat greater, and we thanked God when we arrived on the 30th in the town of Sangan, where Abdul [sic, Abdullah] Mirza, another son of the Schach's governs.[64]—The people here seemed less shy than those in Tauris. We saw many women, though wrapped up in veils; yet they knew how to throw them aside on accasion [sic, occasion]. But they would have done better to have let it alone, for then we

---

[60] *Argas persicus* (Oken 1818), the fowl or poultry tick. Fraser (1838a: 377–378) noted, 'The people of the place indeed, declare that the bug which abounds at Miana does bite strangers, and that its bite produces much inconvenience, and sometimes death: yet such instances are so rare, that none of those of whom I inquired regarding it, could say they recollected a case. No pain is felt at the time, and its effects are said to be first evinced by languor and weakness, which increase till death ensures. The cure consists in a milk diet and abstinence from animal food. The truth I believe is, that Miana being a marshy, unhealthy district, strangers are frequently attacked in it by the low fever peculiar to such situations, and as the place does happen to abound with a particular sort of bug, the fever is attributed to its bite. This insect is somewhat larger than a common bug, and frequents old buildings, bazars, and caravanserais, which are commonly ill swept and dirty. For my own part, I neither saw nor felt any.' MacGregor (1871: 330) noted, s.v. Miāna, 'This town is noted for a particular kind of bug, the bite of which is exceedingly poisonous, producing severe fever. The native remedies for it are various and ridiculous.' For an early study of the species see Fischer de Waldheim (1823). He received specimens from the Russian ambassador Mazarovich (see below).

[61] The Kafilan Koh (MacGregor 1871: 200–201), often written Kaflankuh. See e.g. von Hammer (1819: 239); Hassel (1821: 611); Brugsch (1862: 130).

[62] Most probably a Qaleh Dokhtar built by or attributed to Ardashir I (180–242 AD), founder of the Sasanian empire.

[63] Pol-e Dokhtar or Pol-e Kaflankuh which spans the Kisil-osun or Kizl Ozan of MacGregor (1871: 265), mod. Kizil Uzun. For a lithograph of the bridge ('Pont du Kizil-Hauzen') see Flandin (1851 [Planches]: Pl. 8).

[64] Kotzebue (1819a: 220) is more accurate, and gives 'Avdula-Mirza.' This is 'Abdollah Mirza, governor of Khamsa. See Busse (1972: 152). He was the eleventh son of Fath 'Ali Shah. See Anonymous (1873a: 716.) Lumsden (1822: 131) reported seeing 'Abdullah Mirza, one of the princes of the blood, who had just arrived from Zunjaun.' His image appears in the rock relief of Fath 'Ali Shah at Shah 'Abdul Azim. See Savage-Landor (1903/1: 244).

should still have fancied them beautiful; we thought their large black eyes handsome, although they have more of a savage than a feeling expression.—Their dress, especially their pantaloons, spoils their figure. Our habitation was close to that of the prince, whose women appeared every evening on a tower, to hear our evening music; but the tower was so high, that we could see nothing but painted eye brows.

On the fifth of July, we left Sangan, and encamped 5 miles further on, near the ruins of the village, where we had good water and cool breezes. We were now ten wersts distant from Sultanie, and the embassador determined to wait here for the Schach. The second minister[65] came to compliment us. During our stay here, I took a ride to Sultani, and found the palace miserable,[66] the neighborhood dreary and desolate, but covered [with] most magnificent ruins, such as are no where else to be found, except at Persepolis. I have myself counted the trees round the country seat; there are no more than fifteen.

---

[65] Mirza 'Abd ol-Vahhab Isfahani (1761/2–1829). According to Hasan-e Fasa'i, 'Mirzā 'Abd ol-Vahhāb Mo'tamad ed-Doula was sent to the province of Khamsa to prepare lodgings upon the Russian ambassador's arrival, a parasang from the pasture of Solṭāniya, and to entertain him and inquire into his opinions.' See Busse (1972: 152). According to Lyall (1825/2: 125), Ermolov 'had been previously informed, that Abdool Wehab was authorised by the Shach to open the preliminaries, so that, by the time of His Majesty's arrival, as much information as possible might be obtained from him. But the ambassador made a pretence of slight indisposition, and for some days avoided frequent meetings. This measure only seems to have increased the impatience of the minister to commence negotiations before the arrival of the Grand Vizier, Mirza Sheffi [Shafi'].' On 9 July, when Mirza 'Abd ol-Vahhab 'sent his credentials from the Shach, which authorised him to commence negotiations with the ambassador, and soon afterwards...followed himself,' Ermolov wrote, 'I informed him that not yet having had an audience with the Shach, I could not negotiate with any body....An explanation of four hours' duration followed, when General Yermólof informed the minister, that he had not come to Persia to seek the friendship of the Shach for his sovereign by the sacrifice of provinces, whose inhabitants flew to the protection of Russia, and whose allegiance he valued; and after assigning many reasons, or pretences, he ended by telling him finally, that it was impossible to cede any territories to the Shach. The discussions were carried on with frankness and all possible moderation on both sides; and after separation, the General returned the unopened credentials of Abdool Wehab.' See Lyall (1825/2: 127).

[66] As Kotzebue (1819a: 229–230) described the scene, 'I went to the castle, where I found a number of workmen employed in repairing broken windows and floors, whitening the walls, cleaning and placing the whole castle in a state fit for the reception of the sovereign of Persia. With the exception of the audience chamber, which forms the open side of the palace, and from which there is a very tolerable prospect, there was not one apartment which looked like the chamber of a palce. It is, however, necessary to state, that the King passes only a few months here, perhaps, once in four years.'

On the 19th of July, the Schach came with 10,000 men,[67] and two Englishmen, (Wilok [sic, Willock][68] and Campbell.)[69] On the 26th we repaired to a great camp, half a werst from the palace.[70] On the 31st we had the first audience, when the ambassador received an honor, which is is said was never before conferred in Persia, namely a chair was placed for him, and we all appeared in boots.[71]—[Here the writer gives an account of the audience, in substance the same as that which has already appeared in the newspaper.]

The scene was in a great tent at the bottom of the mountain, on which the palace stands; round about was an open space surrounded with curtains, on which were *painted* some thousand of Persian soldiers.[72] From hence to the tent stood the persons of distinction, in two rows, broiled by a sun in 23 degrees heat. At the entrance of the tent, stood a long

---

[67] In fact the group was even larger for Mohammad 'Ali Mirza 'had joined his father with 15,000 cavalry, which closed the procession.' See Kotzebue (1819a: 245).

[68] Henry (later Sir Henry) Willock (1791–1858). Cf. 9.103. In 1804 he went to India as a cavalry cadet on the Madras Establishment and later served as interpreter and escort commander for Sir Harford's Jones, and Persian Secretary for Sir Gore Ouseley, on their Missions to Tehran. He was chargé d'affaires of the British Mission from 1815 to 1826, and was knighted in 1827. He resigned from the service in 1834 and in 1835 was elected a Director of the East-India Company, later serving as deputy-chairman (1845–1846) and chairman (1846–1847). See Anonymous 1859a: v-vii. As Kotzebue (1819a: 155) noted, 'Captain Willock, the chargé d'affaires of England, and Dr. Campbell, were attending the King at Teheran;' hence they now returned together. Thus, this refers to Henry, not George Willock.

[69] Dr. James Drummond Campbell. Cf. 9.126.

[70] As Kotzebue (1819a: 226) noted, since Fath 'Ali Shah travelled very slowly from Tehran to Soltaniyeh, 'as his astrologers had named an auspicious day, before which time he would not dare to come to Sultanie, we remained twenty days in camp at Samanarchie.' Thereafter, as Lyall (1825/2: 134–135) noted, 'After the king had been six days at Sultania, he is said to have been surprised that the ambassador remained at Samanarchié; and, it is concluded, that he was ignorant of the fact, that his minister had not appointed rooms and other conveniences for the embassy, the expences of which, nevertheless, were thrown upon the nobles. . . .On the 26th the Shach sent an officer, named the Safer Khan, to conduct the embassy to Sultania.'

[71] According to Kotzebue (1819a: 265), 'His Majesty requested the Ambassador to seat himself on a chair, which was placed opposite the throne; an honour which, as well as the permission to appeaer in boots, has never yet been shown to any other person.' Ermolov himself wrote, 'The ceremony for me was different from that which had been in use on all similar occasions. All preceding foreign ambassadors had put on red stockings, and were conducted without slippers. I entered in ordinary boots, and was received with peculiar regard.' See Lyall (1825/2: 141). As the English translator of Kotzebue (1819a: 265, n. *) noted, however, 'Sir Harford Jones and Sir Gore Ouseley, the British Ministers, both sat in chairs opposite the King's throne.'

[72] According to Kotzebue (1819a: 266), 'After waiting perhaps a quarter of an hour in the outer tent, Mahmud-Chan invited us to the audience. We passed through the door of the curtain, having an immense dragon painted on it, and entered the first court, which was lined with Persian soldiery and Kurdins. The door of the second court was guarded by a numerous body of men, among whom was one with a silver staff. On entering this, at the extremity of which stood the King's tent, it appeared to me as if the square was filled with soldiers; but this was merely the first impression, produced by paintings on the curtains.'

bearded fellow with a thick silver staff. The form of the throne resembles our old arm chairs.[73] At the right side of the Schach stood one of his sons a child, by whose appearance it might be judged that his elegant dress was too heavy for him.[74] Seventeen older sons had nothing particular in their physiognomy.

When the ambassador was personally presented to the Schach, he paid us all the compliment of saying, that we were now as good as in his service, as eternal friendship was made with our monarch. To young count Samoiloff,[75] he said, he was a handsome boy; and to our doctor, that he should now be his doctor.[76] He always spoke in the third person; and to me he said, when he heard that I had sailed round the world,[77] "The Schach congratulates you, now you have seen every thing." He then mentioned, that as our emperor was a friend to travelling, he should expect him in Persia. "I will even go and meet him!" cried he repeatedly very loud.[78]

---

[73] Fath 'Ali Shah 'sat upon a golden throne, richly ornamented with real stones. It was shaped like one of our old-fashioned chairs. On the first step there was worked a bas relief of a tiger in gold.'

[74] This was later revised for Kotzebue (1819a: 270) wrote, 'Immediately adjoining the throne, was a handsome youth, said to be a nephew of the King, who stood in waiting near a carpet worked with genuine pearls, and upon which lay a round cushion, with tassels adorned with pearls of an enormous size.'

[75] Lieutenant Count Nikolai Alexandrovich Samoilov (1787–1848), one of Ermolov's aides-de-camp. See Kotzebue (1819a: 68). Ermolov had been an adjutant to the Count's father, General Prosecutor Alexander Nikolayevich Samoilov (1744–1814), a veteran of the Russo-Turkish war (see Brosset 1857: 250–251) and one of the signatories of the Treaty of Jassy. See Creasy (1856/2: 499). Ermolov's father, in turn, had been the head of Samoilov's chancellery.' See Mikaberidze (2011: 2).

[76] 'To Dr. Muller [sic, Müller; see Kotzebue 1819a: 67] he said, "You are now my physician."' See Kotzebue (1819a: 268). He is identified in Kotzebue (1819c: 46) as 'Hofrath Müller, Arzt der Gesandtschaft.' Kotzebue (1819a: 69) remarked that 'Dr. Müller...had resided several years in Grusia,' whereas Kotzebue (1819c: 47) says he lived there many years ('viele Jahre hier in Grusien ausgeharret').

[77] Both Moritz and his older brother Otto von Kotzebue took part in the Russian mission, led by Capt. Adam Johann von Krusenstern, that circumnavigated the Earth from August, 1803 to August, 1806. At the time Moritz was 14 and his brother 15. As Krusenstern (1810: 12) noted, 'Der Kollegienrath von Kotzebue wünschte, daß seine zwey Söhne, welche im Cadetten-Corps erzogen wurden, auf meinem Schiffe diese Reise mitmachen sollten. Sein Gesuch deshalb beym Kaiser ward ihm sogleich zugestanden. So schwer der Entschluß dem Vater seyn mußte, sie in dem Alter von 14 und 15 Jahren eine so gefahrvolle Reise unternehmen zu lassen; so hat der Erfolg ihn hinlänglich für dieß Opfer der väterlichen Zärtlichkeit entschädigt. Sie haben mit vielem Nutzen die Reise gemacht, und sind als gebildete und kenntnißvolle junge Menschen zurück gekommen.'

[78] Fath 'Ali Shah 'mentioned the custom which now prevails among the Sovereigns of Europe, of visiting each other. "I should be glad," he said, "if the Emperor of Russia would come and visit me: I should certainly go and meet him." See Kotzebue (1819a: 268).

Among the presents, a large toilet glass[79] pleased him so much, that he said "If any body was to offer the Schach his chooice between 500,000 (most likely pieces of gold) and this looking glass, he would choose the latter."

A great saloon is to be built at Teheran, purposely for this glass, and the first who brings the welcome news of its safe arrival is to have a reward of 1000 Tuman, (2500 ducats.) But on the contrary, whoever breaks any of the presents, is to have his ears cut off.[80] It is not yet settled when we shall return home. The Schach goes daily a hunting, and very often sends us game, which he has shot with his own royal hand. We made the whole journey on horseback, and have suffered very much from the heat. I endured the most from the astronomical watches[81] which I have in my care, and which will absolutely not bear the horse to go more than a walking pace.' (Fig. 10.1).

10.16 'Articles of Intelligence, by the last Mails. From the *Morning Chronicle*, London, 21 May,' *Onondaga Register* (Wednesday, 15 July, 1818), 'Untitled,' *St. Lawrence Gazette* (Tuesday, 21 July, 1818) and 'A prospect of another "HOLY ALLIANCE",' *Lexington Gazette* (Friday, 14 August, 1818): 'A suspicion is hinted that the Ottoman Court and Persia, are about to form a species of federation, to protect them against the European Powers.'

10.17 'The formidable attitude of Russia,' *St. Lawrence Gazette* (Tuesday, 21 July, 1818): 'In a sketch of the military and political power of Russia, in 1817, ascribed to the pen of Sir Robert Wilson,[82] the writer states, that since Alexander came first to the throne the population of Russia has risen, by increase and acquisition, from *thirty-six to forty-two millions* of people; that her territory has been extended on almost every side…that Persia is at her feet; that a Russian army might sail from the Baltic through an internal navigation from Petersburgh to Astrican, and landing on the southern shore of the Caspian, pitch their

---

[79] This was presumably the 'toilette mirror, of one piece, three yards in length, with candelabres, supported by two bronze figures of angels. The Persians were greatly surprised to see these figures, and enquired whether there were, in our country, people who had wings.' See Kotzebue (1819a: 251). Writing of the presents, Lyall (1825/2: 145) noted that Fath 'Ali Shah 'is said to have been *ravished* by them, especially by the large looking-glasses, and the crystal.' After Ramadan, when Fath 'Ali Shah had all of the Russian presents displayed in a tent where they could be expected, 'His Majesty now came, and, perhaps for the first time in his life, saw a full length reflection of his own figure. "These mirrors," said he, "are dearer to me than all my treasures."' See Kotzebue (1819a: 274).

[80] According to Kotzebue (1819a: 277), 'he commanded the minister instantly to dispatch a courier to Teheran, with orders to build a saloon expressly for the reception of the presents; adding, "He who shall be the first to bring intelligence of their safe arrival, shall receive a reward of one thousand tumanes; but he who disregards my commands, shall be answerable for his neglect with his head."'

[81] As Milham (1923: 255) noted, an astronomical watch 'indicates not only the time,' but may also show 'the tides, the moon's age, the place of the moon, the position of the sun, the sun's declination, the month, the date, and other things as well.'

[82] Wilson (1817).

Fig. 10.1 'Mr. Willock. Camp at Mt. Ararat,' by James Justinian Morier. Pencil on paper. Balliol College Archives Morier-N03-04-145

tents within four hundred miles of the Persian gulf...." The fact is, says the writer, "that Russia, after posting...thirty thousand on the frontier of Armenia, as many in Persia and leaving a reserve of one hundred thousand men to sustain these armies, possesses still a disposable force of above two hundred thousand infantry, eight thousand cavalry, and one thousand two hundred guns better horsed for service than any artillery or cavalry in the world.'

10.18 'Summary of Political News,' *City of Washington Gazette* (Friday, 24 July, 1818): 'Letters from Constantinople of a late date, says that negociations between the Porte and Russia are inactive.[83] There are reports that a union will be reciprocally entered into between the Turks and Persians for the preservation of their respective countries from invasion of the christian powers.

We cannot but believe that the cabinet of Great Britain, incites the sons of the Sun and the Crescent to an alliance for the purpose of rendering an access to the oriental Indies difficult to Russia.'

10.19 'Russian Embassy to Persia—1817. Extract from the Inedited Journal of Captain Moritz von Kotzebue,' *New-York Daily Advertiser* (Saturday, 15 August, 1818), 'Russian Embassy to Persia—1817. Extract from the Inedited Journal of Captain Moritz von Kotzebue,' *Poulson's American Daily Advertiser* (Monday, 17 August, 1818), 'Russian Embassy to Persia—1817. Extract from the Inedited Journal of Captain Moritz von Kotzebue,' *Commercial Advertiser* (Thursday, 20 August, 1818), 'Russian Embassy to Persia; 1817. Extract from the Inedited Journal of Captain Moritz von Kotzebue,' *Richmond Commercial Compiler* (Friday, 21 August, 1818), 'Russian Embassy to Persia—1817. Extract from the Inedited Journal of Captain Moritz von Kotzebue,' *New-York Spectator* (Friday, 28 August, 1818) and 'Russian Embassy to Persia—1817. Extract from the Inedited Journal of Captain Moritz von Kotzebue,' *Hampden Federalist* (Thursday, 3 September, 1818): 'On the third day after our arrival at Erivan,[84] the weather was fine; at ten o'clock in the morning the Sardar (or Governor)[85] paid a visit to the Ambassador.[86] He threw himself rather awkwardly on a chair, smoked a great deal, spoke little, and scarcely nodded his head when we were presented to him; but enjoyed the liquor in spite of the prohibition of Mahomet. The climax is, that he makes no secret of it, but declares openly that he could not live without spirituous liquors. After a good half hour he took his leave and invited us all to dinner. At 12 o'clock we proceeded with much pomp to the fortress, which is only inhabited by the Sardar.

---

[83] For an assessment focusing mainly on trade and economic considerations see Kühne (1818).

[84] The origin of this excerpt from Kotzebue's diary is unclear. It is slightly different than the English text of Kotzebue (1819a: 110–120), with minor alterations in word order and vocabulary, e.g. 'declares openly' rather than 'openly declares;' 'We formed a handsome procession,' rather than 'Our procession made a good display.' As the German, French and English versions of Kotzebue's account all appeared in 1819, it is impossible that the text of this article was based on Kotzebue's published report, but the language of this article suggests it must derive from the unnamed English translator of Kotzebue (1819a) who, as the footnotes in the book indicate, had a knowledge of, e.g. the missions undertaken by Sir Gore Ouseley and Sir Harford Jones.

[85] Hoseyn Qoli Khan Qazvini. Cf. 10.15.

[86] Ermolov.

10 From 1816 to the End of the Turco-Persian War (1816–1825)

We formed a handsome procession; a detachment of cossacks went first; then came our military band[87]; then the Ambassador and his suite, with another detachment of cossacks to close the procession. The people had never before seen any thing like it, and pressed on us dreadfully from all sides; the police officers threw great stones, beat back the crowd with clubs, and particularly one of them, who absolutely marched before the Ambassador, after the music, and who was provided with a club of metal, with which he laid about him most unmercifully on the heads of the people. I believe they would have killed many, had not the Ambassador out of compassion begged them to desist.

When we came to the gate of the fortress, the people were obliged to leave us. We rode thro' narrow streets, and alighted from our horses at the entrance of the house of Sardar. After we had passed many courts, which were all surrounded with armed men, we entered one in the middle of which there was a large marble bason [sic, basin], and several fountains: the Sardar came to the door to meet us, and led us into a large saloon, the open side of which was towards the court, in which the most distinguished persons of Erivan stood assembled, and nobody was permitted to enter, except the brother of the Sardar, and our Menander.* [*The person whose charge it was to provide for the embassy.] Opposite to the open side of the saloon, the building forms a great niche, in which there is a beautiful bason of white marble, with some fountains. This side can also be opened, and affords the most beautiful prospect into a newly laid out garden; the river Sanga flows close under the window; the banks are adorned with fine trees, a beautiful stone bridge of several arches is thrown across it, and the horizon is bounded by Mount Ararat. Certainly no house can be better contrived for a summer residence: there is constantly the fresh water from the fountains, a gentle current of air, and even the sight of the eternal snow upon Mount Ararat must produce a degree of coolness.

After we had all taken our seats, kallion† [† The tobacco-pipe, to smoke through water] was presented, and then a small table placed before each of us, with sherbet and confectionary. The latter is made with sheep's fat, so that it may be imagined with what appetite we ate of it, particularly before dinner. Nobody could get down a morsel, and this prelude to dinner was taken away. Hereupon a number of servants appeared with table cloths of white India cloth, here and there ornamented with flowers; in the corners were some suitable sentences in the Persian language, printed in black letters; as, for example, "All the fruits and provisions here presented to you are good, and given with a good will," &c. &c. But so much was given with a good will, that a thousand people might have dined upon it. I will only mention what stood on the table before me and Dr. Muller alone, and this will give an idea of the rest—a great pancake, which not only covered the whole table, but hung over half an ell all round; the Persians call it tschuruck, and make use of it both as bread and as a napkin; half a sheep, a leg of beef, two dishes of different kinds of roast meat, five dishes of various ragouts with saffron, two dishes full of boiled rice, two do[?] with boiled

---

[87] See Mohammadi (2016: 64–65) for the performances of Ermolov's military band both *en route* to and in Iran.

fowls, two dishes of roasted fowls, two dishes of roasted geese, two dishes of fish, two dishes of sour milk, a great dish with sherbet, and four pitchers of wine; and for all these no knife, no fork, and no spoons.

All these were piled upon one another with the greatest rapidity, so that I and Muller[88] suddenly sat behind a wall of meat, which deprived us of the prospect to the court, and could not see our opposite comrades except through little embrasures in these ramparts of cookery. I attempted to see through a little opening in my wall of dishes, what the Sardar did. The left hand resting upon a dagger, because the Persians never use the left hand in eating, he slowly put his right in the dishes full of fat rice, kneaded with three fingers a good portion together, and put this with much dexterity into his mouth, so that the beard and whiskers seldom showed any traces of it. After he had repeated this several times, he tore a peace [sic] off from the gigantic pancake, wiped his fingers in it, and swallowed this also happily down. He then put his finger according to his fancy in different dishes which pleased his taste, and performed every time the same manœuvre; he at last took the sherbet, drank part of it, and looked pleased on his amazed guests. As scarcely any body had touched any thing of his dinner, for many things could not be pulled out of the middle, for fear of upsetting the whole pile, signal was made to bear off, and the servants as well as the gentlemen, standing out and envying us, took us to be very genteel, because it is the fashion in Persia at great dinners, that the less you eat, the more fashionable you are.

After our redoubts were all happily destroyed we could take a mouthful of fresh air, and the servants presented water to wash the hands, but without towels; the Persians dry their hands in the air; we were obliged to dry them on our pocket-handkerchiefs. Scarcely was this work finished, when, to our terror, another army of dishes was brought in; but this time we escaped better, because they contained fruit and confectionary, and happily only one dish stood before every one, or else we should have seen nothing of the dancers who just entered, and placed themselves at the door. The music was composed of a guitar, a kind of violin with three strings, and two drums, and also a singer, who with dreadful grimaces and real convulsions, screamed with all his might, but happily, according to their custom, often covered his face with a piece of paper, not to shew to the public his wide opened jaws. The music kept time indeed, but altogether sounded like the mewling of cats.

Three pretty boys in long dresses, to which silk ribbons of different colours were fastened, were so inspired by this squeaking music, together with the screaming of the singer, that they at first danced, and at last performed summersaults. They had in their hands little metal castanets, with which they beat time to the movements of the dance. I believe that two of them represented women, as their movements were slower and more decent; but the one in the middle threw himself about as if he were mad, and turned himself alternately to the one and then to the other. The drollest was, when the music suddenly became very loud, the singers began to scream without mercy, the three dancers tumbled along the whole saloon, performing their summersaults, and at last stood still on both sides

---

[88] Dr. Müller, the embassy's physician. Cf. 10.15.

in a graceful attitude, while the middle one, standing upon his head, presented a couple of naked feet, which had before been hid by the long pantaloons. One thing these dancers performed with great dexterity; they were able to throw themselves heels over head several times in the air without touching the ground with their hands on their head.

With full ears and empty stomachs, we at last broke up. The Ambassador took leave of his liberal host; and we returned home in the same parade, to—get our dinner.'

10.20 'Kotzebue's Journey into Persia. Narrative of a Journey into Persia, in the suite of the Imperial Russian Ambassador, in the year 1817. By Moritz von Kotzebue Captain in the Staff of the Russian army &c. Translated from the German. London, 1819,' *Daily National Intelligencer* (Thursday, 11 November, 1819), 'Persian Customs. From Kotzebue's Travels in Persia,' *City of Washington Gazette* (Saturday, 8 January, 1820; from 'The houses of Persia'), 'From Kotzebue's Travels in Persia. Persian Customs,' *Poulson's American Daily Advertiser* (Tuesday, 11 January, 1820), 'From Kotzebue's Travels in Persia. Persian Customs,' *The Berks and Schuylkill Journal* (Saturday, 22 January, 1820), '[From Kotzebue's Travels in Persia.] Persian Customs,' *Thomas's Massachusetts Spy, or Worcester Gazette* (Wednesday, 26 January, 1820), 'Persian Customs. From Kotzebue's Travels in Persia,' *The Scioto Gazette* (Thursday, 27 January, 1820) and 'From Kotzebue's Travels in Persia. Persian Customs,' *Providence Gazette* (Thursday, 3 February, 1820): 'It is scarcely possible to make a book of travels uninteresting, though so many travellers have tried the experiment. When a person has passed through a country, and designs to give an account of his journey, it is generally found expedient to make a huge quarto; not only to shew that the author was very observant, but to secure an ample remuneration for his trouble and expense. His packet-book is accordingly put into the hands of some professed book-maker, who straightway collects all the works which have already appeared on the same subject, and, by dint of extracts and abstracts, contrives to swell out his scanty materials, and conglomerate the volume required. We mention this circumstance merely to say that the work before us is a shining exception to this general rule. The English embassy to China has already produced three thick quarto's[89]; and how many more are yet to be inflicted on the community, we know not. The Russian embassy was equally fertile of original incident; and yet here is only a thin octavo of between 3 and 400 loose pages. The reason of this difference is, that Captain Kotzebue, instead of compiling a book from the materials of his predecessors, has confined himself to an honest account of what he himself saw and felt.[90] The narrative is, indeed, drawn up by his brother [sic, father] Augustus[91]: but it has undergone in his hands nothing

---

[89] Actually two volumes. See Ellis (1817). In addition to taking part in the China mission as Third Secretary, Henry Ellis also served as British Ambassador in Persia, jointly with Morier (November, 1814-July, 1815) and on his own (November, 1835-August, 1836). See Markham (1874: 556).
[90] Kotzebue (1819a-c).
[91] August von Kotzebue. Cf. 10.15.

more than an improvement of its style. The author appears to be a sensible, jolly officer: proud to be employed upon arduous service: retaining his good humor under the severest hardships and privations; with a keen eye for the observation of men and things: and withal, a talent of communicating his impressions in the most precise and graphic phraseology. He is a little too prone, we think, to see things in a ridiculous light; his liveliness sometimes borders upon flippancy; and his descriptions now and then degenerate into caricature. But, with this slight exception, Captain Kotzebue will be found a most amusing, and even instructive companion; and we could wish that a man so liberal and tolerant in his views might travel over the whole surface of the globe.

The embassy consisted of Lieutenant General Jermoloff, the ambassador; two privy counsellors, a marshal, a secretary, a treasurer, a physician, four diplomatists, four aids-de camp, a painter, a superintendant of police, an apothecary, a confessor, and other gentlemen, officers, and soldiers, to the amount in all, of 300.[92] The account of their progress to Persia is replete with "moving incidents by flood and field;"[93] but, in the few extracts which we can afford to make, we must confine ourselves chiefly to that portion of the volume which is devoted to Persia itself.[94]

The party were frequently obliged to climb up steep hills, covered with snow, merely to slide down on the other side in the "most ridiculous postures;" and the following short extract will at once give the reader an idea of their journey, and of the manner in which this book is written: "The day happened to be the anniversary of the battle of Leipzig,[95] and we did not fail to celebrate it. Notwithstanding that we were up to the middle of our bodies in snow, we crawled up to the cross on the summit of the mountain, taking with us a few bottles of wine, and there, in a boisterous wind, that would have thrown us down had we not stuck so fast in the snow, we drank with three huzzas the health of the Emperor Alexander, then the allied armies, and afterwards the ambassador."

---

[92] For the complete list of members of the mission, see Kotzebue (1819a: 67–68).

[93] A variant of 'moving accidents by flood and field,' from Shakespeare's *Othello*, Act 1, Sc. 3, where the protagonist says, 'I spoke of most disastrous chances, Of moving accidents by flood and field; Of hairbreadth 'scapes in th' imminent deadly breach.'

[94] According to Wilson (1817: 153), Ermolov benefited greatly from access to intelligence previously gathered by Gardane's mission, noting, 'he has gone assisted not only by the *French* officers employed by Napoleon, under Gardanne, in Persia; and whom Alexander [I, ruler of Russia], with the exception of three, engaged in the Russian service, but with the Reports and maps sent by that mission to Napoleon, and which being carried into *Russia* at the time of the invasion, were found during the retreat, in two abandoned tumbrils.'

[95] 16–19 October 1813. Writing of Napoleon's defeat in this encounter by a Coalition of Austrian, Prussian, Swedish and Russian forces, Wilson (1817: 45) noted that, 'The...battles comprised under the name of the battle of Leipzig, were the most memorable in the history of the war, from the number of the troops engaged, the efforts made by the whole, and the magnitude of the prize in conest.'

10 From 1816 to the End of the Turco-Persian War (1816–1825)

The following extract is, we think, almost a model of narrative description. The author passes from one thing to another by an easy and natural association, and, in the compass of a few lines, runs through the whole domestic economy of a Persian—*Philad. Union.*

"The houses of Persia are very slightly constructed, and generally consist of but a few rooms, mostly open towards the north; that is to say, instead of a wall there is a window, with panes of variegated colors. It is shut during the night, but left open during the day. In the rooms are a number of cornices and niches, which the poor people generally paint white, but the rich decorate with beautiful flowers and gilding. In every room there is a chimney-piece, generally opposite the window; the floor is of stone, and covered with carpets by the affluent, and with mats by the poor. Such, in a few words, is the description of Persian houses. Their rooms are provided with neither chairs, tables, mirrors, nor any article of furniture whatever. The Persians sit cross-legged on the ground; they leave their slippers at the doors of their apartments. Their meals are served upon trays; and if a gentleman does not retire for the night to his harem, a pillow is bro't to him, and he sleeps on the same spot. To take a walk is considered highly ridiculous, and even vulgar. When the Persians see a person walk backwards and forwards, they conclude it must be on business, or they look at him with astonishment, and even think him out of his senses. According to their notions, a man should be on horseback as soon as he passes the door of his house. At home he must sit with due gravity near the window, rest his left hand on his dagger, and pompously waving the right, be loudly calling out, every quarter of an hour, "Kallion,"* [Kallion is the well known glass pipe, by which the smoke is passed through the water, and cooled before it comes to the mouth. As it is the business of the attendants to light the kallion, the finest flavor of the her has all been extracted before the master receives it.] to the gaping attendants, who stand on the outside the whole of the day. When he invites company, many of these Kallions are brought in: some of which are ornamented with gold, and even with diamonds. At intervals, confectionary, prepared with mutton fat, is offered to the guests, together with sherbet and fruit. The company assure the master of the house that he looks as red as his apples, as brilliant as the sun, as placid as the moon; and they take leave with the wish that the roses of happiness may ever bloom in the garden of his destiny. The host returns thanks with a friendly nod, laments that he must from that moment be unhappy, as they had accustomed his ear to the sweet tone of nightingales: he then resumes his former posture, yawns and waits for sun set, that he may perform his devotions, and be able to say that he has smoked away another day. In the mean while, the retiring guests look for their slippers in the anti-chamber, and courteously consume a quarter of an hour in deciding which shall go first: the most opulent, or the most distinguished at last generally yields condescendingly, and gracefully remounts his horse, with a profusion of bows. Twenty or more of his idle attendants form a circle found him, take his horse by the bridle, and obsequiously lead the great man to his home. The higher ranks are generally actuated by a furious disposition to plunder, and are particularly apt to speak ill of each other, which is their principal source of recreation. They frequently assemble in large numbers at the Prince's, and other great men, where they stand in the courts gaping at their excellencies, and then return happy to their homes, often without having been honored with the slightest notice by them. The towns in Persia consist of narrow lanes, of which the sides are walls, with little doors in them. In the gardens nothing is seen but espaliors of vines and fruit trees.'"[96]

10.21 'Salem, Wednesday, Feb. 11,' *Essex Register* (Wednesday, 10 February, 1819): 'The accounts are still uncertain how far the Persians, Turks, and Russian hordes are known to each other in the supposed troubles of the more distant parts of Russia. We can have no definite character of these troubles, till these relations are known.'

10.22 'Salem, Wednesday, March 17,' *Essex Register* (Wednesday, 17 March, 1819): 'In the East the Persians have still their friendship for the English and some have even travelled to the West, to England itself. The Persians have appeared at the Court of Constantinople, and with presents for other European princes.'

10.22 'East-India Intelligence. Calcutta, Oct 26,' *New England Palladium & Commercial Advertiser* (Friday, 2 April, 1819): 'The Herat frontier[97] has been the scene of hostilities between the troops of Mahomed Shah[98] and the Persians, in which the former are said to have been defeated and to have taken refuge under the Vizier[99] at Herat.'[100]

---

[96] Taken from Kotzebue (1819a: 106–110).

[97] As Longworth Dames (1888: 327) noted, 'Herāt was retained by Mahmūd Shāh after he had lost the rest of his dominions till 1829 (A.H. 1245), and his son Kāmrān maintained himself there till 1842 (A.H. 1258).'

[98] Mahmud Shah Durrani, king of Afghanistan r. (1801–1803; 1809–1829). See Longworth Dames (1888: 341).

[99] Wazir Fath Khan Barakzai. As Long White (1896: 279) noted, after the death of his father, Painda Khan, in 1799, formerly chief of the Barakzai clan, 'Fatteh Khān, who was the eldest son, fled with his brothers to Mahmūd Shāh in Persia,' where the latter had sought asylum. After Mahmud Shah reclaimed the kingship of Afghanistan from his elder brother Zaman Shah Durrani, Fath Khan became his Wazir and was 'better known as Wazīr Fatteh.' Ferrier (1858: 147) observed, 'This remarkable man united to a superior genius a great aptitude for governing and for war. . . .he struck hard, but he was generous after the victory was gained, and shone by his excessive liberality: always in the midst of combats, he still found time to direct the helm of state, and was ready for everything,— in activity he had no equal.'

[100] As Ferrier (1858: 151) observed, since 1800 Haji Firuz Eddin ruled as 'prince of Herat,' much to the outrage of Fath 'Ali Shah, 'who laid claim to the principality as having once formed part' of the Persian kingdom. 'But up to this period Hadji Firooz Eddin had paralyzed his efforts, sometimes by repelling the Persians by force of arms, but more frequently by paying a small tribute which was exacted from him; nevertheless, he had always protested against the pretensions of the Persian monarch, and declared that Feth Ali Shah had no more legitimate claim upon Herat than he had upon the other countries which had emancipated themselves from the dominion of Persia during the last century...In support of these arguments, Hadji Firooz Eddin sent detachments of troops across the frontier to the assistance of some chiefs in Khorassan whom Feth Ali Shah had not yet been able to bring under his rule.' This provoked Fath 'Ali Shah to send Hoseyn 'Ali Mirza against Haji

10.23 'Untitled,' *New-York Daily Advertiser* (Saturday, 3 April, 1819) and 'Foreign News,' *The Geneva Gazette* (Wednesday, 14 April, 1819): 'The Persian ambassador Mirza Abdoul Hassar Kan, arrived at Vienna on the first Feb. on his way to London. He brings with him a beautiful Circassian girl,[101] a present from the grand Vizier of Turkey.'[102]

10.24 'Summary,' *The Albany Argus* (after 6 April, 1819), 'Untitled,' *Northern Post* (Thursday, 8 April, 1819), 'Argus Summary,' *The Pilot* (Wednesday, 14 April, 1819), and 'Untitled,' *The Onondaga Register* (Wednesday, 14 April, 1819): 'A Persian ambassador[103] has arrived at Vienna,[104] on his way to London, having a beautiful Circassian girl,

---

Firuzuddin, but in the meantime the Wazir Fath arrived, deposed his brother Haji Firuzuddin in late 1816 (Sykes (1915/2: 415) dated this action to 1818 which seems more consistent with this newspaper report), and 'After these measures...marched against the enemy, encamped in front of the town of Kussan, about sixty miles from Herat.' Although the Afghans gained the ascendancy, Fath Khan was struck by a bullet in the mouth and given up for dead by his forces, 'losing at once all the courage they had so recently displayed...The first fugitives who arrived at Herat spread terror through the city...wher Fethi Khan arrived very à propos to restore confidence, for his wound was not a serious one, and he was always able to direct the affairs of government. The Persians retreated with scarcely a halt as far as Meshed, and were not a little astonished to learn a few days after their defeat that the Afghans believed that they were the victors, in spite of their having lost their artillery and baggage, which were not, it is true, taken possession of by their adversaries until nine days after the battle.' See Ferrier (1858: 154–155).

[101] The subject of many articles given below, and a full study (Eskandari-Qajar 2007), she was called Dilaram, 'heart's ease,' the wild pansy (*Viola tricolor*). See Kay (1838: 306); Granville (1874: 193).

[102] In his diary entry for 23 November 1819, at Carajular in Turkey, Ker Porter described 'standing out...enjoying the clear freshness of the air, when a band belonging to my old acquaintance, Abul Hassan Khan, (then Persian ambassador in London,) approached the village. The people were on their return from England to Teheran; and with them in charge, mounted on a sorry post-horse, was the celebrated fair Circassian! His Excellency had purchased her at Constantinople, in his way to the west.' See Ker Porter (1821/2: 721). There is a problem with the date, however, for according to other sources, Mirza Abu'l Hassan Khan only left Dublin on 20 November 1819. See Greene (2011: 4425). In fact, he did not leave England for good until 2 April 1820. See Tooke (1834: 549). Perhaps Ker Porter mistook someone else for the fair Circassian? Alluding to her slave status, Auguste de Nerciat wrote, 'What, for instance, can be more silly or more out of place than what has been published respecting his slave?' See Anonymous (1819g).

[103] Mirza Abu'l Hasan Khan.

[104] According to Joseph von Hammer-Purgstall's memoirs, Mirza Abu'l Hasan Khan's first reception at Schwechat, outside of Vienna, was by 'zwei Beamte mittleren Ranges der Staatskanzlei, kein Hofrat & kein Staatskanzleirat, sondern die beiden Hofsekretäre, Freiherren Brettfeld & Ottenfels.' See Höflechner, Wagner and Koitz-Arko (2018: 1291). He arrived in Vienna on 1 February 1819 with a letter and gifts for the Austrian Emperor. See Miruss (1847: 194). Among the gifts were a dozen shawls. 'A translation of the list sent with twelve shawls, which Mirza Abul Hassan Khan presented, in the name of the Schah of Persia, to her Majesty the Empress of Austria,' included '(1) Kaschmire shawl, Tirmeh, i.e. Moondart; (2) Risagt. white, with a wide border; from the manufactory of Dervish Mahommed; (3) Tirmeh, resembling linen. Moondart, or summer month, (for Tirmeh, or Tirmah, is

guarded by 3 black eunochs [sic, eunuch],[105] intended as a present, we presume to the Prince Regent!'[106]

10.25 'Latest from England,' *Connecticut Courant* (after 26 April, 1819) and 'Foreign and Domestic News. Latest from England,' *Lansingburgh Gazette* (Tuesday, 4 May, 1819): 'The Ambassador from Algiers has presented the Prince Regent with four elegant Arabian horses[107]; and the Persian Ambassador, sixteen of the finest horses of Persia.'[108]

---

the name of the first Persian summer month) with an apricot border; (4) White Risaji, with a chain border; (5) Musk-coloured Risaji, with leaves and chain; 6. Risaji, of the colour of the heavenly water, with a chain border; 7. Emerald Risaji, with roses in the corners; 8. Ditto; 9. White Risaji, with roses in the corners; 10. Garlick-coloured Risaji, bordered; 11. White shawl (Abreh.); 12. Ditto, with willow branches.' See D.V. (1831: 252). In his memoirs Viscount Castlereagh wrote, 'The Austrian Court was apprised of the PersianAmbassador having a letter and presents from his Sovereign to the Emperor of Austria, and had already given instructions to its Minister at Constantinople, if possible, in friendly and civil terms to set the mission aside; but that, if the Ambassador persisted in proceeding through Germany, a positive refusal to receive him was not to be given, but that he was clearly to understand that the country through which he was to pass was not to defray his expenses, or that the Austrian Government should bear any share of the expenses of his stay. The Ambassador expressed his readiness to continue his progress on these conditions.' See Vane (1853: 117). For the 'Anreden' and 'Antworten' spoken during his audience with the Emperor and Empress of Austria and Count von Metternich, see von Hammer (1818).

[105] Kay (1838: 304) wrote that, on 28 April 1819, when Mirza Abu'l Hasan Khan entertained Sir Gore Ouseley, Lord Castlereagh and Lord Walpole at dinner, she 'was constantly guarded by two of the four black eunuchs, with sabres by their sides, who were her only attendants.' For her fame and the stir she caused in London society see Eskandari-Qajar (2007).

[106] George Augustus Frederick (George IV)
British Prince Regent. That the celebrated Circassian beauty who accompanied Mirza Abu'l-Hasan Khan on his embassy was certainly not brought as a present to the Prince Regent is shown by the fact that, five years later, in 1825–26, when J.E. Alexander saw Mirza Abu'l-Hasan Khan, the 'fair Circasssian' was 'still an inmate of his harem at Tehran.' See Alexander (1827: 203).

[107] Anonymous (1819h) noted, that shortly after Mirza Abu'l Hassan Khan was received by the Prince Regent, 'A trois heures et demie, l'envoyé d'Alger est arrivé à Carlton-House, et a été admis à une audience du prince-régent, à laquelle il a été introduit par lord Bathurst et conduit par sir R. Chester. Pendant cette réception, les six beaux chevaux envoyés en présens par le dey [an Algerian title] d'Alger au prince-régent étaient dans la cour de Carlton-House, richement équipées.' For the history of Anglo-Algerian relations at this time see Grammont (1887: 376–383).

[108] According to Joseph Planta, Permanent Undersecretary of State for Foreign Affairs and previously Lord Castlereagh's secretary, '[George] Willock…came over with the horses.' See Vane (1853: 112). From the 'Memorandum on the Expenses of the Persian Embassy,' written by Planta for Lord Castlereagh, we find a reference, 'to the horses, eighteen in number, which are intended as a present to the Prince Regent,' not sixteen. See Vane (1853: 116–117). On the other hand, according to Anonymous (1819b), when Mirza Abu'l Hassan Khan arrived in Vienna, 'il a 18 chevaux arabes très-beaux, dont 6 sont destinés pour notre cour, pareil nombre pour la cour de France, et les 6 autres pour celle de Londres.' Additionally, we learn that it was Sir Robert Liston, British Ambassador in Constantinople, who 'authorised Mr. George Willock, under whose charge the horses have been placed, to draw for the expenses incurred in pursuance of that object.' See Vane (1853: 117–118).

10   From 1816 to the End of the Turco-Persian War (1816–1825)   937

10.26 'Items of Foreign News. From the Mercantile Advertiser,' *The Albany Argus* (Thursday, 27 April, 1819), 'Items of Foreign News,' *The Onondaga Register* (Wednesday, 5 May, 1819) and 'From the Mercantile Advertiser,' *The Geneva Gazette* (Wednesday, 12 May, 1819): 'The Persian Ambassador, now at Vienna, continues to view every thing worthy of inspection in that capital.[109] He was lately at the theatre, to which an immense crowd was attracted, in order to see him. It seems this assemblage of gazers became intolerable to his Excellency in one of the saloons, where, to the astonishment of the Austrians, he and his suit [sic, suite] began to lay about them on all sides among those who surrounded him. The writer of the article sagely remarks, that it is very likely his excellency and suit[e] were accustomed in their own country to have plenty of room made for them. It seems the physician attached to the embassy is also the Ambassador's chief cook, and it is his duty to ascertain the salubrity of the victuals served up at the table of his master. His excellency was to leave Vienna on the 20th ult.'[110]

10.27 'From the Mercantile Advertiser,' *The Geneva Gazette* (Wednesday, 12 May, 1819) and 'Diplomatic Etiquette,' *The Plattsburgh Republican* (Saturday, 15 May, 1819): 'The Persian ambassador has not had an audience of the French king[111] --- because he required as a sine qua non, that his majesty should depart from the constant etiquette, and receive him *standing* instead of sitting.'[112]

---

[109] Among the sites visited by Mirza Abu'l Hasan Khan was a porcelain factory. Thus, according to Anonymous (1819d), 'In der Porcellain-Fabrik wählte er sich einiges Porcellain von mäßigem Werthe. Man sagte ihm, Sr. Majestät der Kayser habe befohlen, ihm Alles, was er hier auswählen würde, ohne Bezahlung zu überlassen. Nun änderte er seine Wahl und nahm von dem Besten, das ihm war vorgelegt worden.'

[110] Mirza Abu'l Hasan Khan had his audience of leave with Count von Metternich on 5 February 1819, Joseph von Hammer acting as translator. According to Anonymous (1819a), 'Der nach London bestimmte Persische Bothschafter hielt gestern seine feyerliche Auffahrt bey Sr. Durchl. dem Fürst v. Metternich. Ueblichermaßen ward er in zwey Prachtwagen Sr. Durchl. des Fürsten eingeholt. Vor dem sechsspännigen Wagen, in welchem der Botschafter allein, und der K.K. Hofdollmetscher, Hofrath von Hammer, ihm gegenüber saß, ritten mehrere Bothschafts-Officiers in ihren eigenthümlichen Persischen Prachtschreibern. Der letzte, dessen Pferd von zwey Lakayen geführt ward, hielt mit feyerlichen Gebehrden ein Kissen in den Händen, auf welchem das Beglaubigungsschreiben des Bothschafters lag. (Bekanntlich hegen die Perser vor jeder Unterzeichnung des Schah eine so tiefe Ehrfurcht, daß des Kaysers Ramenszug, der in feyerlicher Form die Größe eines Tellers hat, knieend entgegen genommen wird) Die Audienz, in welcher die Unterredung mittelst des Hofraths von Hammer geführt ward, währte eine Viertelstunde; dann nahm der Bothschafter einige Erfrischungen ein und unterhielt sich mit dem Fürsten in Englischer Sprache.' Abu'l Hasan Khan left Vienna on 25 February 1819. See Miruss (1847: 195).

[111] Louis XVIII (r. 1814–1824).

[112] According to a letter from Joseph Planta to Lord Castlereagh dated 12 March 1819, Mirza Abu'l Hasan Khan arrived in Paris on 7 March 1819. See Vane (1853: 112). This is contradicted by Simond (1900: 427) according to whom Mirza Abu'l Hasan Khan arrived in Paris on 10 March and was presented to Louis XVIII on 30 March 1819. He was meant to have been presented on 20 March, but,

10.28 'From a Paris paper of March 31,' *Plattsburgh Republican* (Saturday, 22 May, 1819): 'Yesterday, after mass, the king,[113] seated on his throne, surrounded with the princes and princesses of his family received in public audience the Persian ambassador.[114] Three of the royal carriages, drawn by 8 horses, in which were the dignitaries appointed to conduct the ceremony of introduction, proceeded to his excellency's hotel, and accompanied him to the palace. The marquis Desolles[115] received his excellency at the entrance of the gallery Diana, and conducted him to the foot of the throne.—The ambassador saluted his majesty; the king returned his salutation, and then covered his head. His excellency offered as presents, six shawls, a scimitar, which formerly belonged to Ismael, one of the most valorous sovereigns of Persia,[116] and a precious stone, affirmed to be a panacea for all complaints.[117] The ambassador addressed the king, the substance of which was that "his sovereign prayed for the continuance of his dynasty." His majesty replied, "that he was sensible of his kind wishes, and that he thanked the emperor of Persia for the choice of his ambassador." After making a profound reverence, which was returned by the king, his excellency withdrew. His excellency has sent some very superb cachemires to the duchesses d'Angouleme[118] and de Berri.'[119]

10.29 'Foreign Articles,' *Franklin Gazette and Public Advertiser* (after 25 May, 1819): 'The Persian Ambassador, in passing through Vienna, on his way to England, presented the

---

'La réception de l'ambassadeur persan n'a point eu lieu hier. Les préparatifs qu'on avait faits dans la galerie de Diane ont été provisoirement enlevés. On assure que des difficultés nées de la différence du cérémonial des Orientaux avec le nôtre ont causé cet empêchement, qui n'est peut être que momentané.' See Anonymous (1819d).

[113] Louis XVIII.

[114] According to Planta, writing of Mirza Abu'l Hasan Khan, 'at Paris he appears to have been splendidly treated.' See Vane (1853: 120).

[115] Jean-Joseph Paul Augustin, marquis Dessolles, A highly decorated officer under Napoleon who, in 1817, had been named President of the Council of Ministers and, upon retirement, received the honorific title 'Ministre honnête homme.' See Mullié (1852: 427–428). He was Prime Minister of France from 29 December 1818 to 18 November 1819) For his early life see Anonymous (1816/1817: 390–393).

[116] Shah Isma'il (r. 1501–1524).

[117] Several candidates for this stone exist, e.g. chrysolite which, 'Powdered, and taken in drink...was held a panacea for all complaints of the chest and bowels,' according to King (1865: 168); the ruby which, 'Bruised in water...was a panacea for all complaints;' or 'Powdered agate...an infallible remedy for "all the ills that life is heir to,"' according to Mackintosh (1879: 276). Later, when the ambassador took his formal leave from Louis XVIII, he was given 'des présents magnifiques en armes de forme orientale, fabriquées à la manufacture royale de Versailles,' for Fath 'Ali Shah. See Michaud (1855: 844).

[118] Marie-Thérèse (1778–1851), daughter of Louis XVI, wife of Louis Antoine, duc d'Angoulême. For her life see Barghon-Fortrion (1858).

[119] Marie-Caroline de Bourbon-Sicile, duchesse de Berry (1798–1870). The duchesse d'Angoulême was her sister-in-law. For her life see Becquet and Malandain (2013).

Emperor of Austria[120] with several new poems, one of which consists of 11,000 stanzas.'[121]

10.30 'The Circassian Lady,' *Poulson's American Daily Advertiser* (Friday, 28 May, 1819), 'The Circassian Lady,' *Orange County Patriot; or, the Spirit of 'Seventy Six* (Tuesday, 1 June, 1819), 'The Circassian Lady,' *Boston Daily Advertiser* (Wednesday, 9 June, 1819), 'The Circassian Lady,' *The Albany Argus* (Tuesday, 15 June, 1819) and 'The Circassian Lady,' *The Republican* (Thursday, 24 June, 1819): 'The Gazette de France contradicts the ungallant observation of the other Paris Papers, as to the beauty of the fair stranger[122] who has been brought into Europe by the Persian Ambassador.[123] It describes her as possessing a very white skin and cheerful temper. Her beauty, according to the journal, appears to be according to the accounts we have received, of a nature to be prized among all people who think that beauty consists in perfect harmony of feature and the exactness of proportion. Large blue eyes, long black hair, a slender youthful figure, are advantages with which no one can be deemed ugly in France. But still she assuredly must

---

[120] Francis I (r. 1804–1835).

[121] Cf. Tschischka (1847: 465), 'Doch wir wenden uns nach Wien zurück. Am 8. Februar 1819 hatten dessen Bewohner das seltene Schauspiel des feierlichen Einzugs von Mirsa Abul Hassan Chan, persischen Botschafters, zur Audienz bei JJ. MM. dem Kaiser und der Kaiserin. Unter anderen Geschenken welche er darbrachte befanden sich auch: das Portrait des Schahs, auf einer Platte aus Milch-Chalcedon emallirt, mit Spinellen rund herum besetzt und ein Kranz großer Perlen, dem Medaillon zur Einfassung dienend; ferner ein von Timurleng auf Schah Abbas, und von diesem auf den regierenden Schah gekommener Damascener (Kara Chorassan), in einer mit Edelsteinen besetzten Scheibe; und das Schehinschahname, d. i. das Buch des Königs der Könige, als Seitenstück zu dem alten persischen Heldenbuch Schahname, von dem dermaligen Dichterfürsten und gefürsteten Dichter Persiens, dem der Schah seinen eigenen Namen beigelegt, nämlich Feth Ali Chan, in 80,000 Distichen verfaßt, das die Heldenthaten der regierenden Familie von der Zeit des Nadirschah bis auf die heutige Zeit beklingt.'

[122] Dilaram. Cf. 10.23, 10.24.

[123] The 'ungallant observation' regarding the Circassian originated at a reception given on 30 March 1819. As Rain (1919: 365) wrote, 'Réception aux Tuileries de l'ambassadeur persan Mirza Abdul Hassan Khan, lequel est ancien ambassadeur en Russie; c'est entouré des princes de sa famille, des grands dignitaires de la couronne des ministres, des maréchaux et de tout le corps diplomatique que le roi l'a reçu dans la salle du trône. L'ambassadeur extraordinaire était revêtu d'un bonnet orné d'une aigrette de diamants, d'une robe de cachemir blanc brochée d'or, une ceinture maintenant un poignard garni de pierreries. Le duc d'Escars a donné à l'envoyé persan un dîner de quarante quatre couverts. La chronique raconte que la circassienne qu'a amenée le Khan a eu plus de succès de curiosité que celui-ci même, quoiqu'on "ait trouvé que sa beauté ressemblait plus à celle des négresses qu'à celle des femmes grecques."' Among the guests was Lady Frances Shelley. See Edgcumbe (1912: 200) who noted that, after dining with the Duke of Wellington and attending the opera with him, 'We afterwards went on to Madame d'Escars, at the Palace of the Tuileries. In a garret, at the top of the Palace, an immense number of people were assembled. It was very hot, and everybody stood about, as they do at an English assembly. We had rather good fun with Madame de R—and the Persian Ambassador.'

excite a strong interest among us. A slave[124] without any family, without a country, her life in our capital, as every where else, is passed in the most profound seclusion. Exiled to her chamber inaccessible to all the world, she does not even appear at her window, without being covered with a large veil, and she is not relieved from this restraint except when her master is out with his people. She then walks about in her apartment without meeting any one save the females of the hotel, or the two persons charged to watch her. If she chances to meet the females, she becomes quite joyous with spirits—she plays with them—romps with them—caresses them; but on the least noise she disappears and shuts herself up in her cabinet. Some Ladies, among them Lady Somerset,[125] solicited the Ambassador to permit the interesting stranger to pass an evening at their houses; but their entreaties were all to no purpose.'

10.31 'Postscript: Latest from Europe,' *New-York Gazette* (Wednesday, 9 June, 1819), 'Foreign Compendium. Latest from England,' *Boston Intelligencer & Evening Gazette* (Saturday, 12 June, 1819), 'Latest from Europe,' *Essex Register* (Saturday, 12 June, 1819), and 'Latest from England,' *New-Hampshire Gazette* (Tuesday, 15 June, 1819): 'The Ambassador from Persia has reached London, and his Circassian is not surpassed in beauty by any female of the United Kingdom.'

10.32 'Arrival of the Persian Ambassador and the Fair Circassian. Dover, April 25,' *The New-York Columbian* (Thursday, 10 June, 1819), 'Arrival of the Persian Ambassador and the Fair Circassian,' *New-York Daily Advertiser* (Thursday, 10 June, 1819), 'Arrival of the Persian Ambassador and the Fair Circassian,' *Franklin Gazette* (Friday, 11 June, 1819), 'Arrival of the Persian Ambassador and the Fair Circassian,' *The American* (Saturday, 12 June, 1819), 'Arrival in England of the Persian Ambassador and the Fair Circassian,' *Boston Patriot and Daily Chronicle* (Tuesday, 15 June, 1819), 'Arrival of the Persian Ambassador and the Fair Circassian,' *The Centinel of Freedom* (Tuesday, 15 June, 1819), 'Arrival of the Persian Ambassador and the Fair Circassian,' *American Beacon and Norfolk*

---

[124] On the Circassian slave trade see Wagner (1856/2: 268–169), amongst the passengers on the boat from Trabzon to Constantinople, 'were thirty slaves, closely veiled...from Colchis and Circassia.... the best looking...were dressed in better stuffs, were allowed more delicate food, and even coffee.... Girls of less personal attractions, from twelve to sixteen years old' were valued at 'two to three thousand piastres. The latter came principally from the mountainous parts of Circassia; and being daughters of poor (Pschilt) serfs, had been sold by their parents, from poverty, or by the (Work) noblemen to whom they belonged, for gain.'

[125] Lady FitzRoy Somerset, née Emily Wellesley-Pole, daughter of William Wellesley-Pole, the third Earl Mornington, and niece of the Duke of Wellington. Her husband Lord FitzRoy Somerset was the youngest son of the Duke of Beaufort and was, inter alia, secretary to the Duke of Wellington. He lost his right arm from a gunshot wound at Waterloo. In 1852 he was created Lord Raglan and later Field-Marshal and commanded the British forces in the Crimean War, when he died. See Bagot (1909: 71). Lord and Lady Somerset accompanied Mirza Abu'l Hasan Khan to the Louvre on Tuesday 16 March 1819. See Anonymous (1819d).

& *Portsmouth Daily Advertiser* (Wednesday, 16 June, 1819), 'Foreign Intelligence. Extracts from late English papers, received at this office. Dover, April 25.—Arrival of the Persian Ambassador,' *Boston Daily Advertiser* (Wednesday, 16 June, 1819), 'Arrival in England of the Persian Ambassador and the Fair Circassian,' *Independent Chronicle & Boston Patriot* (Wednesday, 16 June, 1819), 'Arrival of the Persian Ambassador and the Fair Circassian, in England,' *Providence Patriot Columbian Phenix* (Wednesday, 16 June, 1819), 'Dover, April 25.—Arrival of the Persian Ambassador,' *The Repertory* (Thursday, 17 June, 1819), 'Dover, April 25. Arrival of the Persian Ambassador,' *National Messenger* (Friday, 18 June, 1819), 'Arrival in England of the Persian Ambassador and the fair Circassian,' *Vermont Republican* (Monday, 21 June, 1819), 'Arrival of the Persian Ambassador and the Fair Circassian,' *Augusta Chronicle & Georgia Gazette* (Wednesay, 23 June, 1819), 'Arrival of the Persian Ambassador and the Fair Circassian,' *Dedham Gazette* (Friday, 25 June, 1819), and 'Dover, (Eng.) April 25. Arrival of the Persian Ambassador,' *Hampden Federalist & Public Journal* (Wednesday, 30 June, 1819): 'About three this afternoon, H.M. schooner Pioneer,[126] arrived in the Roads, and very shortly after, the boat belonging to the Customs put off from her under a salute. She had on board the Persian Ambassador and suite, who on landing were greeted with another salute from the guns at the heights. As the schooner had been seen for some time before her arrival, there was an amazing concourse of people assembled on the beach, and the novel nature of the arrival of ten or a dozen persons, habited in silks and turbans, with daggers and long beards, in no small degree attracted the attention of the inhabitants, whose curiosity had been raised to the highest pitch by the different accounts of the beauty of the fair Circassian[127]; and had not a coach been provided at the water's edge, I much doubt if his Excellency and suite would have reached the inn without considerable difficulty. The crowd followed to Wright's Hotel[128] nearly as fast as the carriage, it being reported by some that the fair

---

[126] Described as 'a vessel employed in the preventive service,' by Huish (1821: 817). The service was constituted to enforce the Smuggling Prevention Acts. See Hansard (1822: 215–217).

[127] The term 'fair Circassian' appears in many newspaper articles in reference to the Persian ambassador's Circassian slave, and the epithet is undoubtedly an echo of Samuel Croxall's poem of this name, based on the Song of Songs, which appeared in 1720 (Croxall 1721; de Maar 1924: 84) and Samuel Pratt's 1781 play *The Fair Circassian*, on which see Brown (1947: 64–65).

[128] 'Wright's Hotel and Ship Inn, on the Quay, the front of which is towards the harbour, and the back-front in Strond-street; Timothy Wright.' Seee Horn (1817: 125). An article containing advice on travelling between England and France, published in New York, offered the following assessment of Wright's Hotel, from which coaches departed both for London and the ferry to France: 'At Dover, let him avoid the second-rate houses; Wright's Hotel has a high name, and persons complain of high charges; but at the York Hotel, which is on a scale of comfort and elegance equal to Wright's, the charges are very moderate.' See Anonymous (1828d). As Chambre (1858: 229) noted, 'The Brothers Wright had a monopoly of the road in these days—one had a house at Dover, another at Canterbury, another at Siggingbourne, and one more at Rochester. They were all good inns, and no one went very far wrong who took up his quarters in either of them. A sad change has come over them now, however.'

female was in a mask, under the habit of a male attendant, while others stated that she would not be landed till the middle of the night. In about half an hour, however, after the arrival of the first boat, a second boat came into the harbor, and landed the Circassian Beauty! She was attended from the schooner, by Lieut. Graham, of the preventive service,[129] and two black eunuchs. She was scarcely seen; for the instant she landed she was put into a coach which conveyed her to the inn. She had on a hood, which ccovered the upper part of her head, and a large silk shawl screened the lower part of her face, across the nose, from observation; therefore her eyes, which are truly beautiful, and part of her forehead, were the only part of her beauties that could be seen. She is of the middle stature, and appeared very interesting. Her look was languid from illness, arising from a rough passage. She was conducted to a bed-room on reaching the inn, but no one was allowed to attend her but eunuchs.'

10.33 'Foreign. Great Britain,' *The National Register* (Saturday, 12 June, 1819) and 'Abstract from Late London Papers,' *City of Washington Gazette* (Wednesday, 23 June, 1819): 'The Persian Ambassador, who has lately arrived at the Court of St. James' in London, accompanied by a Circassian female, possessing uncommon beauty, is the universal topic of conversation: his turban, his beard, his diamond hilted dagger, his magnificent Cashmere shawl and crimson satin dress studded with diamonds, and his display of horsemanship in which he appears ostentatious—all seem to engross the attention of the Metropolis of John Bull,[130] who seems quite *taken* with the dazzling stranger.

As for the Circassian beauty, she is described by an officer of the customs, the only being who had a peep at her,[131] two black eunuchs, excepted who guard her, with drawn sabres in their hands) as having the upper part of her head covered by a hood, the lower part of her face screened by a silk shawl tied across the nose, so that her eyes, which are beautiful, and part of her forehead, were the only part of her charms visible. She appeared of the middle size.

---

[129] The domestic British naval force meant to prevent smuggling along the coasts of Britain. See Hansard (1822: 215–217).

[130] The allegorical representation of Britain in a series of pamphlets published in 1712 by John Arbuthnot (1667–1735) and later reprinted together as *The History of John Bull*. For the text see Bower and Erickson (1976) and on the work more generally and its author see e.g. Mayo (1930); Taylor (1992).

[131] According to the *Durham County Advertiser* of 3 April 1819, 'An order has been sent to the Custom-House at Dover to pay the most respectful attention to the Persian Ambassador and his suite; so the Fair Circassian who accompanies him, enclosed in a Cabinet, will avoid search, and will not even be visible.' See Anonymous (1820a: 52). Cf. Anonymous (1819e).

Already the papers teem with puffs, announcing the "Genuine Circassian Soap;" "The Circassian Hat, made of tissue [sic, tissu] de paille;"[132] "The Persian Turban, for the ladies;" and many other nonsensical articles, which the mania of the day has given rise to, and have been invented to gratify the cocknies.'

10.34 'From the Advocate. Persian Ambassador,' *American & Commercial Daily Advertiser* (Thursday, 17 June, 1819), 'From the National Advocate. Persian Ambassador,' *Boston Intelligencer & Evening Gazette* (Saturday, 19 June, 1819), 'Persian Ambassador, vs. The Press,' *Kentucky Gazette* (Friday, 16 July, 1819; from 'The following translation') and 'Persian Ambassador,' *Orleans Gazette* (Friday, 6 August, 1819): 'The Europeans require something to talk and write about in these "piping times of peace,"[133] and if the public mind can be interested, it is of little consequence what the object is. John Bull was kept several weeks in countenance by two Cossacks from the Don,[134] whose

---

[132] Strawcloth.

[133] The phrase goes back to the early third century in Tertullian's *De Pallio* (*On the Pallium* 1), 'Men of Carthage, ever princes of Africa, ennobled by ancient memories, blest with modern felicities, I rejoice that times are so prosperous with you that you have leisure to spend and pleasure to find in criticising dress. These are the "piping times of peace" and plenty.' It also appears much later in Shakespeare's *Richard III* (Act 1, Sc. 1), 'Why, I in this weak piping time of peace, have no delight to pass away the time, unless to see my shadow in the sun.'

[134] As Anonymous (1813a) noted, on 9 April 1813, 'Two post chaises and four arrived on Friday April 9, at the General Post-office. In the first of them was an English officer of the artillery in full uniform, accompanied by two officers of distinction from the Russian Court, also in full uniform: and in the second chaise was a Cossack, with his beard, and in the full costume of his profession, with a tremendous long spear placed between his legs, reaching from ten to twelve feet out of the carriage window. It was shod with iron about six inches, and quite sharp, like our boarding pikes. By the side of the Cossack sat a Don Cossack, also in full costume. The Cossack had a most warlike appearance, very strong features, seeming about the age of forty. The Don Cossack was much younger, not looking above twenty...After waiting about ten minutes, they set off to the West end of the town, amidst the acclamations of multitudes of spectators. They came by the way of Heligoland [in the North Sea]. They drove to the house of the Russian secretary, Count Lieben, in Harley-street, Cavendish-square.' Five days later they appeared on the Royal Exchange, 'of which public notice had been given,' attracting 'an immense assemblage of spectators. The Exchange was literally crammed before one o'clock, and all the avenues completely filled.' There they were received by the Lord Mayor.. See Anonymous (1813b). A play was even staged in London in 1814 entitled *The Don Cossack in London*, author unknown. See Nicoll (1970: 452). The Don Cossacks were fêted in London because of the part they played in defeating Napoleon. Thus Anonymous (1813b), 'The name of the Cossack is Alexander Wittishendst, he is in his 54th year, and had been allowed to retire from the service nearly *fifteen years*, with a pension, the reward of his courage and good conduct. When he heard of the invasion of his country by the French, he quitted his retirement, and voluntarily enrolled himself and his two sons in defence of native independence....To a question put to him by Mr. Grant, at the desire of several gentlemen, whether he had killed any of the enemy, he answered with great naiveté,—"Three officers, besides *the fry*."' Cf. the satirical Anonymous (1814) where we read, 'the more thinking people asked, "What is a Don Cossack?"—"Why, don't you know?" replied the knowing ones; "he is a fellow, that, having neither money nor provender in his own country, leaves it

bushy beards, long javelins, and remarkable attachment to lamp oil and tallow candles, afforded much speculation and admiration also. The present rage is the Persian ambassador. The character, who partakes of all the qualities of a rigid musselman has been sent by his master the Schaw,[135] or if our East India friend in Philadelphia will permit us to call him so, the Sophy of Persia, to peep into the several courts of Europe, and ascertain what can be made out of them. In a national point of view, the mission can be of little permanent benefit, because information is seldom sought after, except it is coupled with interest—for the Persians bestow no thought on a nation, which is so remote as to create no fears of invasion, and no advantages of alliance. The English and Russians are the only two powers with whom it is the interest of Persia to be on the best terms. The present tranquil state of Europe was probably the motive in sending this mission to the several courts, and like all these eastern embassys, the minister and his suit are considered in the light of splendid beggars— that is, they have rich clothes, greasy shawls, lean horses[136] and scymetars, studded with brilliants, and with a remarkable condecension, they permit each court they visit to defray the contingent expenses of the mission, and accept likewise of any presents which may be offered. It is not however the ambassador and his long beard which are particular objects of interest—It is a beautiful Circassian slave which his excellency has with him, strictly guarded and closely veiled in the oriental style. The wags, say that he intends the lady as a present to the Prince Regent, who, though pretty well striken [sic, stricken] in years,[137] and afflicted with sundry twinges of the gout and rheumatism, is still a man of taste and

---

to plunder others; and, cutting off Frenchmen's ears, he toasts them with his lance for his food. You hear how he has slain them by scores.'" A caricature of the two Cossacks was published by George Cruikshank in *The Satirist* of 1 May 1813, entitled 'John Bull and the Cossacks.' See Douglas (1903: 247); Broadley (1911: 322–323).

[135] Fath 'Ali Shah.

[136] The reference to 'greasy shawls' and 'lean horses' echoes a report of the ambassador's gifts to Josef von Hammer who acted as his interpreter in Vienna. According to Anonymous (1819c), 'Als er [Mirza Abu'l Hasan Khan Shirazi] abreisen wollte, beschloß man, ihn auch auf der Reise bis an die Gränze freyzuhalten und zu begleiten. Wie man ihm von diere Begleitung sagte, wollte er einen General an ihrer Spitze haben, höchstens sich mit einem Obersten begnügen; doch es blieb bey einem Officier mit Lieutenants-Rang. Vor seiner Abreise beschenkte er die Dienerschaft, die ihm war zugegeben worden und die sehr zahlreich war, in Bausch und Bogen mit 100 Gulden; eine Gabe, welche die Beschenkten sogleich dem Armenfonds zuwiesen, und die ihnen vom Hofe durch eine angemessenere vergütet wird. Hr. von Hammer erhielt von dem Bothschafter einen mit Fettflecken versehenen Shawl und ein unansehnliches Pferd zum Präsent; so daß ein Spaßvogel die Bemerkung machte; Herr von Hammer habe von dem Persischen Bothschafter einen fetten Shawl und ein mageres Pferd zum Geschenk bekommen.' Cf. D.V. (1831b: 252), 'A very beautiful Fermaisch [striped shawl], striped with red and yellow, was presented by the Persian ambassador, Mirza Abul Hassan Khan, in 1819, to the court interpreter at Vienna, together with a very lean Persian steed, on which a wit observed, *"Que l'ambassadeur avait régalé un cheval maigre et un shawl gras."*' For von Hammer's own account of Mirza Abu'l Hasan Khan's visit to Vienna see Bachofen von Echt (1940: 187–193).

[137] The Prince Regent (1762–1830), who became George IV, was 56 years old in 1819.

gallantry—when his toilet is made—but we expect to hear of no such generous act from the Persian ambassador; the extent of his liberality may be a cashmere shawl and a live ostrich.—However, all the world is in motion to get a peep at this extraordinary beauty; and this curiosity distresses his excellency, who cannot imagine why his fair slave should excite so much interest; he has got out of Austria and France safe with her as yet, and has just landed in England, where, if he does not look sharp, his fair charge will give him the slip if she is so disposed, and if she does, her recovery is hopeless in a country where there are no harems, mutes and black eunuchs. It was once suggested in Barbary, to send a pretty Circassian to Mr. Jefferson[138] as a present, but certain constitutional objections intervened, as the President cannot accept of any present from a foreign potentate, and besides, it did not correspond with the habits and pursuits of this venerable patriot.

The following translation of a letter written by the Secretary of the Persian Ambassador, relates to the many newspaper paragraphs respecting his Circassian, and he has a very good idea of the character which the press should assume, though somewhat pettish and uneasy at the constant attention betowed [sic, bestowed] upon his concealed beauty. It is addressed to the Editor of the Gazette de France.

"Sir—His Excellency the Ambassador of the King of Persia expects from your justice and good sense, that you will insert the following observations.—His Excellency admires, for many reasons, the establishment of public newspapers; he intends even to have them established in Persia, where, by his means, printing has been introduced, and is brought into a state of perfection; but he will particularly recommend the Persian Editors, not to admit with that frivolity, as is the case in France, stories, scarcely worth repeating to a nation, which prides itself for its wit, taste and politeness. What can be more insipid, for example— what more out of place, than the stories which have been put in circulation and printing respecting his slave? One should suppose that politics, science, and the arts, are mines sufficiently fertile to furnish materials to public writers, for the purpose of satisfying the various tastes of their readers, and that they did not stand in need of inserting trash. I am, &c.

(*Signed*) Auguste Andrew de Nerciat,[139]
Secretary, &c.'

---

[138] Thomas Jefferson (1743–1826), third president of the United States.

[139] Auguste Andréa de Nerciat (1782–1847). The son of writer Robert Andréa de Nerciat, he arrived in Constantinople on 6 January 1803 and in 1807 served as Hüe de la Blanche's secretary when he was sent by Sébastiani to deliver a letter from Napoleon to Fath 'Ali Shah. See Dehérain (1930: 44). He also served as 'second Drogman,' i.e. translator, on Gardane's mission to Fath 'Ali Shah. See Gardane (1809: 1). As noted above, he served for awhile as Charles Nicolas Fabvier's interpreter while that officer established the cannon foundry in Isfahan. Cf. Nerciat (1825a: 228–229).

10.35 'London, May 12. The Fair Circassian,' *New-York Spectator* (Tuesday, 22 June, 1819), 'London, May 12. The Fair Circassian,' *Providence Patriot Columbian Phenix* (Wednesday, 23 June, 1819), 'London, May 12. The Fair Circassian,' *Alexandria Gazette & Daiily Advertiser* (Wednesday, 23 June, 1819), 'London, May 1. The Fair Circassian,' *Berkshire Star* (Thursday, 24 June, 1819), 'London, May 12. The Fair Circassian,' *New-Bedford Mercury* (Friday, 25 June 1819), 'Foreign Compendium. Latest from England. The Fair Circassian,' *Boston Intelligencer & Evening Gazette* (Saturday, 26 June, 1819), 'Foreign & Domestic. London May 12. The Fair Circassian,' *Vermont Republican & American Yeoman* (Monday, 28 June, 1819), 'Foreign. London, May 12—The Fair Circassian,' *American Beacon and Norfolk & Portsmouth Daily Advertiser* (Tuesday, 29 June, 1819), 'The Fair Circassian. London, May 12,' *City of Washington Gazette* (Wednesday, 30 June, 1819), 'London May 12, The Fair Circassian,' *Augusta Chronicle & Georgia Gazette* (Friday, 2 July, 1819), 'London, May 12. The Fair Circassian,' *Kentucky Gazette* (Friday, 16 July, 1819), 'Deferred Articles. The Fair Circassian,' *The Nashville Gazette* (Saturday, 17 July, 1819): 'His excellency the Persian Ambassador, with great politeness, has acceded to the wishes of our female nobility and gentry. The Fair Circassian may now be seen daily by those properly introduced. It is necessary to state that this *fair curiosity* receves some trifling present from every one admitted to her presence, and she is already highly gratified with a variety of pleasing ornaments to decorate her person.'

10.36 'Foreign Items,' *The Geneva Gazette* (Wednesday, 23 June, 1819): 'The Persian ambassador, and his fair Circassian, have arrived in London.'

10.37 'Untitled,' *The Alexandria Herald* (Friday, 25 June, 1819), 'Untitled,' *Plattsburgh Republican* (Saturday, 26 June, 1819): 'Of the numerous paragraphs in French & English papers, respecting the Circassian Girl, who accompanies the Persian Circular Envoy,[140] only one has hinted she was to be given to the Prince Regent. The story is probably a joke on Royalty.'

10.38 'The Fair Circassian,' *The New-York Columbian* (Monday, 28 June 1819; minus last two sentences), 'London, May 13. The Fair Circassian,' *Providence Patriot Columbian Phenix* (Wednesday, 30 June, 1819; minus last two sentences), 'Medley. The Fair Circassian,' *National Standard* (Wednesday, 14 July, 1819; minus last two sentences), 'Mirror of Life. The Fair Circassian,' *Boston Intelligencer & Evening Gazette* (Saturday, 17 July,

---

[140] Mirza Abu'l Hasan Khan Shirazi.

1819; minus last two sentences), 'From Bell's London Messenger. The Fair Circassian,' *Mercantile Advertiser* (Saturday, 24 July, 1819; minus last two sentences), 'Miscellaneous. The Fair Circassian,' *Vermont Intelligencer and Bellows Falls Advertiser* (Monday, 26 July, 1819; minus last three sentence), 'From Bell's London Messenger. The Fair Circassian,' *Augusta Chronicle & Georgia Advertiser* (9 August, 1819), 'From Bell's London Messenger. The Fair Circassian,' *Baltimore Patriot & Mercantile Advertiser* (Wednesday, 11 August, 1819), 'The Fair Circassian,' *South-Carolina State Gazette, and Columbian Advertiser* (Tuesday, 24 August, 1819), 'The Fair Circassian,' *Edwardsville Spectator* (Saturday, 28 August, 1819; minus last two sentences): 'The above much talked of female was, by permission of her keeper, His Excellency the Persian Ambassador, introduced on Monday last to upwards of twenty ladies of fashionable distinction, friends of his Excellency. The introduction took place between one and two o'clock in the front drawing-room at his Excellency's residence in Charles-street, Berkeley-square. The fair stranger was elegantly attired in the costume of her country; her dress was a rich white satin, fringed with gold, with a bandeau round her head and wreaths of diamonds. She received her visitors with graceful affability, and they were highly pleased with her person and manners. She is not, as has been represented, short and slender, she is of the middle stature, of exquisite symmetry, rather *en bon point*: her complexion is of a brownish cast, her hair a jet black, with beautiful arch black eye-brows, handsome black penetrating eyes, her features regular, and strikingly handsome. The ladies were highly gratified, and passed great encomiums on the elegance of her person. Among the ladies present were lady Augusta Murray,[141] and daughter[142]; lady Radstock[143]; lady Arden[144]; Countess

---

[141] Lady Augusta Murray (1761–1830), married to Prince Augustus-Frederick, Duke of Sussex (1773–1843), son of William IV. See Markham (1851: 496).

[142] Augusta Emma d'Este (1801–1866), generally known as Princess d'Este and later as Baroness Truro. She was married to Thomas Wilde, first Baron Truro, who became Lord Chancellor in 1850.

[143] Cornelia Jacoba van Lennep (1753–1839), who married Admiral William Waldegrave, later first Baron Radstock of Castletown, G.C.B. (1753–1825), in 1785. See Lodge (1839: 404). Anonymous (1819i: 73) called her, 'Lady Radstock, the wife of the religious bible-mad Admiral.' Lord Radstock became very good friends with Mirza Abu'l Hasan Khan during his first visit to Britain in 1809/1810. He wrote, for example, 'I have visited the Ambassador every day since his arrival, excepting one, when in the evening he told Mr. James Morier that "his heart was sick, as he had not seen his friend Lord Radstock during the whole day." I sometimes call upon him twice a day, and I have dined with him five times. ... I accompanied his Excellency the other night to the opera for the second time.' See Waldegrave (1820: 32).

[144] Margaretta Elizabeth Perceval (1768–1851), who married Charles-George Perceval, second Baron Arden, in 1787. See Lodge (1839: 25).

Westmeath[145]; the Misses Waldegrave,[146] Mrs. Malcolm, Mrs. Majoribanks.[147] &c.— Lady August Murray presented the fair Circassian with a beautiful nosegay, with which she seemed highly pleased.'

10.39 'Latest from Europe,' *New-York Evening Post* (Wednesday, 30 June, 1819), 'Latest from Europe,' *Connecticut Courant* (after 30 June, 1819), 'Untitled,' *Albany Gazette* (Monday, 5 July, 1819), 'Latest from Europe,' *Lansingburgh Gazette* (Tuesday, 6 July, 1819), 'Untitled,' *The Otsego Herald* (Monday, 12 July, 1819), 'Untitled,' *Geneva Gazette* (Wednesday, 14 July, 1819), 'Summary,' *Onondaga Register* (Wednesday, 14 July, 1819) and 'Untitled,' *The Plattsburgh Republican* (Saturday, 17 July, 1819): 'Among the magnificent presents presented to the Prince Regent of England, by the Persian ambassador, at a late court,[148] were carpets of cashmere shawls, composed of four distinct pieces; the

---

[145] Emily Anne Bennett Elizabeth Nugent (1789–1858), who married George-Thomas-John Nugent, Marquis and Earl of Westmeath, in 1812. See Lodge (1839: 511). Anonymous (1819i: 73) noted, 'I am not astonished to find her there, and dare say she found herself quite at home.' Countess Westmeath and her husband separated in June, 1819, just a few weeks after the visit described in this article. See Nichol (1827: 3).

[146] According to Anonymous (1819i: 73), these were not her Lady Radstocks' daughters but her two nieces. 'The Misses Waldegrave will be able to give a new impulse to the Dandyzettes, who will forthwith mount the Circassian eyebrows, and we shall have them displaying an arch of the Southwark Bridge over each eye in ghastly stile.' Dandyzettes were female 'dandies.'

[147] Anonymous (1819i: 73) observed, 'As for *Mrs. Malcolm*, and *Mrs. Majoribanks*, their connection with eastern nations and knowledge of modes and manners peculiar to those ladies who are *trained* in India, made them a great acquisition to the committee, as in all likelihood they were the interpretesses.' Both the 'connectionn with eastern nations' and the reference to India raise the possibility that Mrs. Majoribanks was Catherine Jane, wife of Campbell Majoribanks (1765–1840), Chairman of the East India Company in 1819. See Anonymous (1905: 111). Mrs. Malcolm, on the other hand, is unlikely to have been the wife of Sir John Malcolm, Isabella (née Campbell) as she should have been referred to as Lady Malcolm.

[148] Held at Carlton House on Thursday, 20 May 1819. As an account published two days later noted, 'The Prince Regent having been pleased to appoint this day for the ceremony of the public audience of His Excellency Mirza Abul Hassan Khan, Ambassador Extraordinary from His Majesty the King of Persia, the Marquess of Headfort, one of the Lords of His Majesty's Bedchamber, and Sir Robert Chester, the Master of the Ceremonies, were appointed to conduct His Excellency from his residence in Charles Street, Berkeley-Square, to Carlton-House.

Order of Procession.

A troop of Cavalry.

A leading coach and six of the Prince Regent, conveying the Ambassador's Secretary, and His Excellency's credentials.

A leading coach and six of the Prince Regent, conveying presents from the King of Persia.

A leading coach and six of the Prince Regent, conveying more presents from the King of Persia.

Eight Persian horses, richly caparisoned, presents from the King of Persia, led in single file, by the Prince Regent's grooms on one side, and the Persian grooms on the other.

A leading coach and six of the Prince Regent, conveying some of the Ambassador's attendants.

A leading coach and six of the Prince Regent, conveying more of the Ambassador's attendants.

principal carpet is in length 17 Persian yards, breadth 9 yards. They were manufactured for the king of the Afghans,[149] who sent them to the Shah,[150] and who, without hesitation, sent them, as a present, as the greatest rarity he possessed, to the Prince Regent. In Persia they are inestimable, such a specimen of manufacture being there hitherto unknown.

A gold enamelled looking glass, opening with a portrait of his Persian majesty; the object of which was to exhibit, at one view, the portraits of two sovereigns; the one in painting, the other by reflection; and around which were poetical allusions.

A gold enamelled box.

A magnificent costly sword, celebrated in Persia for the exquisite temper of its blade; the sheath ornamented with emeralds, rubies, and diamonds.

A string of Pearls.

Two carpets of Herat.

A large painting of his Persian majesty.

Ten magnificent cashmere shawls, of various sizes and denominations.

The Arabian horses brought by his excellency to England as a present to the Prince Regent, were drawn up in the court-yard.'[151]

10.40 'From late London Papers,' *The Otsego Herald* (Monday, 5 July, 1819): 'The Persian Ambassador has been received with very great distinction in London. The fair Circassian who accompanied him from Persia, has also received the attention of the curious in the metropolis, many ladies of the first distinction having visited her, and presented her many presents. She is represented to be of small stature, her skin of a yellow tinge, of regular features & expressive countenance.

On the 29th of April, many persons of distinction, and some of the foreign ministers, visited the ambassador. Among the latter was Mr. Rush,[152] the American minister, and Mr. Adams Smith,[153] the secretary of legation. In the afternoon of the same day, the

---

Cavalry

A state coach and six of the Prince Regent, conveying the Ambassador, who was accompanied by the Lord in Waiting, the Master of the Ceremonies, and Mr. Morier, His Excellency's Mehmander.' See Anonymous (1819j).

[149] Mahmud Shah Durrani is presumably meant here. Cf. 10.41.

[150] Fath 'Ali Shah.

[151] Cf. Anonymous (1819h), 'Les présens que S. Exc. a présentés, de la part de son maître, étaient étalés dans une pièce voisine. Ils consistent en une superbe épée, une boëte d'or émaillée, des schals de cachemire de diverses dimensions, des tapis de même étoffe, des perles et autres pierres précieuses, un portrait du roi de Perse. etc. Les chevaux arabes, envoyés aussi par le roi de Perse, étaient dans la cour d'entrée du palais.'

[152] Richard Rush (1780–1859), American Ambassador in London (1817–1825). The visit is not mentioned in Rush's memoirs. See Rush (1873).

[153] John Adams Smith (1788–1854), son of William Stephens Smith and Abigail Adams (II), grandson of John and Abigail Adams (I), and nephew of John Quincy Adams. See Levenson et al. (1982: 251).

Ambassador, accompanied by Mr. Gore Onsley [sic, Ouseley], and Mr. Willock, his secretary, mounted upon three of the Persian horses, took a ride through Hyde Park.[154] His excellency rode a beautiful grey horse, with a Persian saddle and bridle, and was dressed in his national costume, in rich crimson satin, and a fine large sash of the same color, with a highly finished dirk, with a large diamond in the centre of the hilt.'

10.41 'The Persian Ambassador,' *Boston Commercial Gazette* (Monday, 5 July, 1819): 'On the 20th of May the Prince Regent held a Court at Carlton House,[155] for the purpose of receiving Mirza Abul Hassen Khan, the Persian Ambassador. It was determined by the Prince that the Ambassador's introduction to him should be signalized by every attention possible, not only from himself and his Court, but also from the civil and military powers of the country, who were assembled in as great force as when the foreign Sovereigns were on a visit to England. After the procession had reached Carleton House, the Minister was introduced into the hall of audience: the Prince was standing under the canopy of the throne, with Lord Castlereagh[156] on his right hand, and the other ministers and nobles of the Court surrounding him in a group. The approach of the Ambassador to the Throne was after the eastern style of etiquette. He was dressed in a rich embroidered robe, his turban ornamented with jewels, and in his hand a silver stick or staff.—On his approaching the person of the Regent, the latter descended from the step of the throne, and advancing two or three paces, received him with his usual dignity and affability. The Ambassador in good English,[157] made an appropriate speech, which was answered by the Prince Regent in terms calculated to gain his confidence. After the audience, the Prince Regent and his Excellency, went into the next apartment, where the presents were laid out; they consisted of—.

A Gold Enamelled Looking Glass, opening with a Portrait of his Persian Majesty; the object of which was to exhibit, at one view, the portraits of two Sovereigns; the one in painting, the other by reflection; and around which were poetical allusions.

A Gold Enamelled Box.

---

[154] Lt. George Willock (1793–1870), of the 47th Madras Infantry, who commanded 'thirty privates of Indian cavalry, forming a body guard' for Sir Gore Ouseley (Morier 1818: 24), 'came over with the horses' to England, i.e. the horses intended as a present to the Prince Regent. Cf. 10.25. He was Henry Willock's brother. Hunter (1908: 258) described him as 'an excellent Persian scholar,' who 'served his country with credit in the East.'

[155] Originally 'the palace of Frederick, Prince of Wales, the father of George III., and subsequently for many years the residence of George I., when Prince of Wales....The building was modernised at a vast expense in the year 1788, and in 1815 further alterations were made in the interior.' It was demolished in 1828. See Walford (1870: 87).

[156] Robert Stewart, Viscount Castlereagh (1769–1822), long-serving British foreign secretary (1812–1822).

[157] In May, 1819, Lord Sheffield [John Baker Holroyd] wrote to Lord Colchester, 'I suppose you know that the Ambassador speaks English very well; and that when the Emperor Alexander and he met some time ago, the only language through which they could communicate was English.' See Abbot (1861: 77).

A magnificent costly Sword, celebrated in Persia for the exquisite temper of its blade; the sheath ornamented with emeralds, rubies, and diamonds.

A String of Pearls.

Carpets of Cashmere Shawls, composed of four distinct pieces; the principal Carpet is in length 17 Persian yards, breadth, 9 yards.—They were manufactured for the King of the Afghans,[158] who sent them as a present to the Shah,[159] and who, without hesitation, sent them as the greatest rarity he possessed, to the Prince Regent. In Persia they are inestimable, such a specimen of manufacture being there hitherto unknown.

Two Carpets of Herat.

A large Painting of his Persian Majesty.

Ten magnificent Cashmere Shawls, various sizes and denominations.

The Arabian Horses brought by his Excellency to England as a present to the Prince Regent, were drawn up in the Court Yard.

After his Royal Highness had examined the various presents, he re-conducted the Ambassador to the Hall of Audience, where his Excellency took his leave.'

10.42 'Weekly Summary,' *The Plough Boy* (Saturday, 10 July, 1819): 'The Fair Circassian, brought to England by the Persian Ambassador, excites great curiosity in the British metropolis. She is not, it seems, among the presents to the Prince Regent, as was formerly represented. The ladies of London, who visited her, were delighted with her beauty and gracefulness. It is not every Ambassador that carries abroad such an *irresistible* [sic, irresistible] credential!'

10.43 'Untitled,' *Franklin Gazette and Public Advertiser* (after 20 July, 1819): 'The Persian ambassador has presented his presents to the prince regent and considering the general parsimony of these Asiatic princes, they were splendid and valuable. The English, however, prosecute a favorable trade with them to the gulf and over land; their friendship is worth purchasing. His excellency has permitted several ladies of quality to visit his Circassian slave, and have a good long stare at her; she was dressed very elegantly on the occasion and showed all her movements and accomplishments to the best advantage; the ladies were highly pleased with her, and the Chronicle gravely tells us that lady Augusta Murray gave her a nosegay at parting—"Prodigious!" The prince regent has not yet paid her a visit of ceremony; he will no doubt; and probably incog if the ambassador has no objections.'

10.44 'Latest from England,' *Kentucky Gazette* (Friday, 23 July, 1819): 'Philadelphia, July 1. The ship Juno, at New York from Liverpool, has supplied the editors of the Franklin Gazette with London papers to the 21st may, 8 or 9 days later than before received....The

---

[158] Mahmud Shah Durrani. Cf. 10.39.

[159] Fath 'Ali Shah.

Persian ambassador, was introduced to the Prince Regent, at Carlton house, May 20, made a speech, with which the court were delighted, and some splendid presents to the prince.'

10.45 'From Bell's London Messenger. Persian Ambassador and the Fair Circassian,' *Mercantile Advertiser* (Saturday, 24 July, 1819), 'Fashionable Intelligence. Persian Ambassador and the Fair Circassian,' *New-England Galaxy & Masonic Magazine* (Friday, 30 July, 1819), 'From Bell's London Messenger. Persian Ambassador and the Fair Circassian,' *Alexandria Gazette & Daily Advertiser* (Monday, 2 August, 1819), 'From Bell's London Messenger. Persian Ambassador and the Fair Circassian,' *Augusta Chronicle & Georgia Advertiser* (Monday, 9 August, 1819), 'From Bell's London Messenger. Persian Ambassador and the Fair Circassian,' *Baltimore Patriot & Mercantile Advertiser* (Wednesday, 11 August, 1819), 'Miscellaneous. From Bell's London Messenger. Persian Ambassador and the Fair Circassian,' *Camden Gazette and Mercantile Advertiser* (Thursday, 19 August, 1819), 'From Bell's London Messenger. Persian Ambassador and the Fair Circassian,' *South-Carolina State Gazette, and Columbian Advertiser* (Tuesday, 24 August, 1819): 'During the residence of the Persian Ambassador in Paris, he was so great an object of public curiosity, that he could not leave his hotel without being surrounded by a multitude of gazers. When he attended fashionable parties, the eagerness evinced by the ladies to gain a sight of him, subjected him to a degree of embarrassment, the more insupportable, as the people of the east entertain notions very unfavorable to that kind of female curiosity. We extract the following from the French Journals:—"The Persian Ambassador, on returning one day from a ride, found his apartments crowded by ladies, all elegantly dressed, though not all equally beautiful. Astonished at this unexpected assemblage, he inquired what these European Odalisques could possibly want with him. The Interpreter[160] replied, that they had come to look at his Excellency. The Ambassador was surprised to find himself an object of curiosity among a people who boast of having attained the summit of civilization; and was not a little offended at conduct which in Asia would have been considered an unwarrantable breach of good breeding: he accordingly revenged himself by the following little scheme. The illustrious foreigner affected to be charmed with the ladies; he looked at them attentively, alternately pointing to them with his finger, and speaking with earnestness to his interpreter, who he was well aware would be questioned by his fair visitors, and he therefore instructed him in the part he was to act. Accordingly the eldest of the ladies, who, in spite of her age, probably thought herself the prettiest of the whole party, and whose curiosity was particularly excited, after his Excellency had passed through the suite of rooms, coolly inquired, what had been the object of his examination? "Madam," replied the Interpreter, "I dare not inform you,"—"I wish particularly to know, Sir,"—"Indeed, Madam, it is impossible."—Nay, Sir, this reserve is vexatious—I desire to know."—Oh! since you desire, Madam—know then that his Excellency has been valuing you."—"Valuing us—how Sir?"—"Yes, ladies, his

---

[160] Auguste Andréa de Nerciat. Cf. 10.34.

Excellency, after the custom of his country, has been setting a price upon each of you."—"Well, that's whimsical enough; and how much may that lady be worth, according to his estimation?"—"A thousand crowns."—"And the other?"—"Five hundred crowns."—"And that young lady with fair hair?—"Three hundred crowns."—"And that Brunette? "The same price."—"And that lady who is painted?"—"Fifty crowns."—"And pray, Sir, what may I be worth in the tariff of his Excellency's good graces?"—"Oh, Madam, you really must excuse me, I beg—"—"Come, come, no concealments." "The Prince merely said, as he passed you—" "Well! what did he say?"—"He said, Madam, that he did not know the small coin of this country."'

10.46 'Untitled,' *Northern Post* (5 August, 1819): 'Paris, June 19. . . .A few days since, the Persian Ambassador being present at a debate in the Chamber of Deputies, a gentleman who accompanied him happened to observe, that "the progress of Persia was considerably behind the light of the age."—His excellency replied, "My master is cousin german[161] to the sun, and uncle to the moon; he is content with the light of the family."'

10.47 'Foreign. Latest from England,' *Kentucky Gazette* (Friday, 20 August, 1819): 'The Persian Ambassador continue [sic, continues] to receive the greatest attention in London.[162] The Prince Regent had invited him and his fair Circassian to spend time at

---

[161] First cousin.

[162] Relations were not always smooth as a diary entry of Charles C.F. Greville shows: '*June 25th.*—The Persian Ambassador has had a quarrel with the Court. He wanted to have precedence over all other Ambassadors, and because this was not allowed he was affronted and would not go to Court. This mark of disrespect was resented, and it was signified to him that his presence would be dispensed with at Carlton House, and that the Ministers could no longer receive him at their houses. On Sunday last [20 June] the Regent went to Lady Salisbury's [Emily Cecil, Marchioness of Salisbury (1750–1835)], where he met the Persian, who, finding he had given offence, had made a sort of apology, and said that illness had prevented him from going to Court. The Regent came up to him and said, "Well, my good friend, how are you? I hope you are better?" He said, "Oh, sir, I am very well, but I am very sorry I offended your Royal Highness by not going to Court. Now, sir, my Sovereign he tell me to go first, and your Congress, about which I know nothing, say I must go last; now this very bad for me (pointing to his head) when I go back to Persia." The Regent said, "Well, my good friend, never mind it now; it does not signify." He answered, "Oh yes, sir; but your Royal Highness still angry with me, and you have not asked me to your party to-morrow night." The Regent laughed and said, "I was only going to have a few children to dance, but if you like to come I shall be very happy to see you." Accordingly he went to Carlton House, and they are very good friends again.' See Reeve (1875: 21). Another anecdote from the same party at Lady Salisbury's is worth recording. According to Lady Isabel Burton, Sir Richard Burton's wife, 'I can remember, at a reception at Lady Salisbury's, the Persian Ambassador and his suite following Richard about the whole evening, and when I joked them about it, they said, "It is such an extraordinary thing to us, to see any foreigner, especially an Englishman, speaking our language like ourselves. He might have never been out of Teheran; he even knows all the slang of the market-place as well as we do."' See Burton (1898: 111).

his palace, while he (the Prince) was absent—The Duke of Wellington[163] also gave a grand dinner to his excellency, at which a number of distinguished personages were invited.'

10.48 'Foreign Articles. Extracts from late English and French Papers,' *Franklin Gazette and Public Advertiser* (after 23 August, 1819) and 'Untitled,' *The Geneva Gazette* (Wednesday, 25 August, 1819): 'The Persian Ambassador opened his residence in Charles street on Tuesday evening[164] with a grand assembly. The interior was brilliantly illuminated, particularly in those parts where the whole length portraits of Persia appeared. The Sovereign[165] in his robes of office, occupied the principal situation in a leading drawing room, encircled by a canopy of rich Cashmere Shawls. In the banqueting room was a similar picture of the heir apparent. The apartments displayed all the costly luxury of Eastern splendor. The kind of throne was enriched with the most precious gems in diamonds and pearls. The fair Circassian retired to rest, at 10 o'clock, before the arrival of the company. The ambassador received the guests with the most polished demeanor, and accomodated them with sherbet and liquors peculiar to the Persian court.'

10.49 'For the Patriot. Politics No. 6,' *Hampden Patriot* (Thursday, 12 August, 1819): 'As it respects the ambitious designs of Russia, the English cabinet is not insensible of its *danger*. It may be indeed true, as you have intimated, that she will one day threaten our empire in India. She must however, first conquer the Turks. At least Turkey will continue to be the favorite theater of her arms and intrigues....In the Seraglio, England will continue to give the law, as long as Turkish *avarice* can be touched by British *gold*. We can at our *leisure* embroil her [Russia] in a war either with the Sublime Porte or the king of Persia, should the interests of England, render hostilities, between her and either of those powers *expedient*. As the Ottomans and Persians are a century behind the Russians in the *art of war*, it is easy to foresee the result of hostilities between those powers and the Russian empire.—Russia will conquer and appropriate their provinces to her own use.'

10.50 'From the National Advocate. Persia,' *American & Commercial Daily Advertiser* (Tuesday, 2 October, 1819), 'From the National Advocate. Persia,' *The Northern Whig* (Friday, 5 October, 1819), 'From the N.Y. National Advocate, Sept. 29,' *City Gazette and Daily Advertiser* (Monday, 8 October, 1819), 'From the National Advocate. Persia,' *Rochester Telegraph* (Thursday, 2 November, 1819), 'Miscellany. Persia,' *Middlesex Gazette* (Saturday, 4 November, 1819) and 'Persia,' *Lansingburgh Gazette* (Thursday, 16 November, 1819): 'From the remote situation of this kingdom, and its limited

---

[163] Arthur Wellesley, first Duke of Wellington (1769–1852).

[164] Given on 15 June 1819, the party was attended by Richard Rush, American Ambassador in London (1817–1825), who wrote in his diary, 'June 15. Dined at the Russian Ambassador's [Christoph Heinrich von Lieven]....Went next to a rout at the Persian Ambassador's in Charles Street, Berkeley Square, where five hundred were present.' See Rush (1873: 78–79).

[165] George III, although the Prince Regent seems more probable.

connexion with christian powers, it was supposed that no event could possibly occur, which would render the friendship and alliance of Persia an object of deep interest to any European state. For several years past, the British government have been particularly anxious to cultivate the friendship of Persia, as well as to obtain the most authentic information as to the resources and character of the people. And the intelligence which has been afforded the British by Sir George Ousley [sic, Gore Ouseley], Mr. Morier,[166] and others, has determined the cabinet, to draw closer the ties of interest and attachment. The reception of the Persian ambassador in England, and the particular attention shown him by all parties, were sufficient indications of the object in view. It now appears that a treaty of alliance is on foot, and the British, as usual, stipulate to furnish munitions of war, and, in addition, to supply the Persians with experienced British officers. There is but one distinct object in this alliance, and that is to check the progress of Russia. Peter the Great maintained, that the Swedes taught the Russians to fight and conquer; and Alexander,[167] with equal truth can assert, that Great-Britain developed the resources of Russia; and if this development is eventually to opperate [sic] against the interest of Great Britain, as it assuredly will, the cabinet of St. James' must, as a set off barrier, strengthen some neighboring power, to remedy the evils growing out of the original error—Persia presents herself as a suitable barrier; bordering on Russia on the one side, and the Indian Ocean on the other, the plans of Russia to reach India, and divert the commerce of that rich portion of the globe, will be frustrated, unless Russia can acquire secure passage through Persia with her armies, which depends much on the disposition of the Persians, for it is clearly and manifestly the interest of Persia, in point of situation and internal security, to cultivate an alliance with Russia, in preference to England, because the commerce of Persia can be very little benefitted by the English, except it is done to the injury of their possessions in India; and certainly in point of defence, Russia has more facilities at hand than Great-Britain, for a mere boundary line divides the two kingdoms, and Russia, from the borders of the Black and Caspian Seas, can pour into Persia a very considerable force. If Russia had the commercial enterprize of the British, and would keep a respectable naval force cruizing in the Arabian Sea, and menace Persia at the same time by land, it would not be long before she would acquire a great portion of the India trade; and by conveying India and China goods by water up the Persian Gulph, the intercourse would be materially facilitated, and render useless those tedious caravans which at present make a circuitous journey from India to Moscow.

---

[166] James Justinian Morier.

[167] Alexander I.

At all events, Great-Britain has much to fear from Russia; and the cabinet, foreseeing what may arise, have taken the only steps in their power, to prevent the evil, by negociating a treaty of alliance with Persia.'

10.51 'Economy and Manufactures,' *The Republican Agriculturalist* (Sunday, 7 October, 1819) and 'Latest from England,' *Lexington Gazette* (Friday, 15 October, 1819): 'It has been recently rumored in the political circles, that the British government has entered into a very close alliance with the court of Persia, and has not only engaged to supply the munitions of war, but to permit many British officers peculiarly selected for abilities, knowledge and experience, to engage in the Persian service. The chief object of the reported treaty,[168] is said to be, to form a check upon the ambition of Russia, and to interpose Persia as a barrier against any designs which Russia may hereafter meditate upon India.'

10.52 'Persia,' *Plattsburgh Republican* (Saturday, 23 October, 1819): 'It is stated that the British government are negociating a treaty, offensive and defensive, with the King of Persia,[169] by which the former is to furnish the latter with munitions of war and a number of experienced British officers. The object of this treaty and these liberal donations, to speak more properly *subsidies* is to check the power of Russia and frustrate her supposed views upon British India, the empire of Persia being the only intervening barrier to the progress of Alexander's ambitious views towards the British possessions in India, which he might invade by marching a powerful army through Persia. Whether Alexander will quietly wait the consummation and *practical operation* of this treaty, time will shew. The real interests of Persia would lead her to form a connection with Russia rather than with Great Britain, and she would probably do so, unless duped or overreached by the latter, and dazzled by her all-powerful and corrupting gold and splendid promises.'

---

[168] The Treaty of Teheran, signed on 25 November, 1814. 'By it Great Britain was bound to pay to Persia a subsidy of 200,000 tomans annually; to maintain troops in the event of her being attacked by any power at war with England; and should she be attacked by any nation at peace with England, we engaged to use our mediation towards an amicable adjustment of their differences, but, should it fail, to a pay a subsidy as above mentioned. Persia, on her side, engaged to obstruct any Power seeking to pass through her country for the purpose of invading India.' See MacAlister (1910: 31). For the text of the treaty see Markham (1874: 534–536); Hurewitz (1956: 86–88).

[169] Fath 'Ali Shah.

10.53 'Untitled,' *Plattsburgh Republican* (Saturday, 30 October, 1819): 'St. Petersburgh, Aug. 13. The Russian Embassy[170] which has been sent to Persia has arrived at the place of its destination, and has been received in the most friendly manner.'

---

[170] A reference to the arrival in Tehran of Semyon Ivanovich Mazarovich (c. 1784–1852). Previously he had participated in Ermolov's mission as one of two doctors (Natchkebia 2012: 206). See Kotzebue (1819a: 67). A letter written by Ermolov on 7 January 1817, while he was in Tibilisi, mentioned that at the time Mazarovich lacked nothing but a knowledge of Persian. See Stcherbatow (1890: 14). Mazarovich and his suite departed for Tehran on 28 January and arrived in the first week of March 1819. See Kneip (1976: 49–50). According to Lesur (1820: 665) they arrived on 13 August 1819, 'La légation russe envoyée en Perse pour y résider, est rendue à sa destination, et elle a reçu le meilleur accueil. A son arrivée à Tabris, qui est la résidence d'Abas-Mirza, prince héréditaire de Perse, on lui a fait beaucoup de prévenances. Pour le déjeuner, on lui donna des chaises et des tables, ce qui en Perse est une politesse exquise; et lors de l'audience que ce prince donna à la légation, il était debout, vêtu d'un habit de cérémonie, et portait le sabre au côté; c'est un honneur que les Perses n'accordent jamais aux Turcs, et qu'ils font rarement aux grands du royaume. Le schah de Perse fait inviter fréquemment les personnages de la légation aux fêtes de la cour à Teheran, aux revues de troupes, etc. Dans toutes les occasions, ce monarque, qui s'entretient familièrement avec M. Mazarewitch chargé d'affairs, ainsi qu'avec les autres personnes de la légation; ce qui est contraire aux mœurs orientales, et prouve en même temps que la bonne intelligence qui règne entre les deux états s'affermit de plus en plus.' Breton, the translator of the French translation of Kotzebue's memoir noted, 'Au moment où on imprime ce passage, les gazettes de Pétersbourg sont remplies des détails de la réception qui vient d'être faite, en 1819, à l'ambassadeur actuel, M. Mazarewitch. La saison a permis de le recevoir à Téhéran, et l'on assure que, contre l'ancien usage du pays, il jouit fréquemment d'entretiens familiers avec le schah.' See Kotzebue (1819b: 214, n. 1). According to Henry Willock, Mazarovich was recalled in 1820 for overstepping the bounds of his position. As he noted, 'In the year 1820, I obtained a letter written by M. Mazarowich, the Russian Chargé d'affaires at Teheran, urging the Persian Ministry, in the most undisguised language, to make war against Turkey. This letter was sent by her Majesty's Government to St. Petersburg, and M. Mazarowich, an excellent public serant, was recalled, and has never since been employed.' See Willock (1858: 35). In fact, according to MacAlister (1910: 51), 'Mr. Mazarowitch, the Russian Envoy, was away on leave from January, 1823, till July, 1824, Mr. Ambourger acting in his stead.' Cf. Markham (1874: 557).

10.54 'From London Papers,' *The Delaware Gazette* (Thursday, 10 February, 1820): 'The Persian Ambassador has been on a tour through Ireland[171] and Scotland.'[172]

---

[171] This report is misleading since Mirza Abu'l Hasan Khan visited Scotland *before* moving on to Ireland. Mirza Abu'l Hasan Khan arrived In Dublin on 8 November 1819. According to Anonymous (1819l), the ambassador slept one night in Dublin 'and left that city the following day for Mount Stewart, the seat of the Marquis of Londonderry. Thence he intends to proceed on a visit to the Marquis of Downshire [Arthur Hill],at Hillsborough.' Cf. Anonymous (1820a), 'The Persian Ambassador arrived on the ninth Inst. at Mount Stewart, in Ireland, the seat of the Marquis of Londonderry.' When he returned to Dublin, Mirza Abu'l Hasan Khan stayed at Bilton's Hotel where 14 year old William Rowan Hamilton went to seek him out, sending a letter he had composed in Persian (which he had been studying, along with Hebrew, Arabic and Sandkrit since the age of 10) up to his room, and had an interview with George Willock, who complimented him 'on the style and composition,' in which he 'observed no mistakes.' Sadly the ambassador himself had 'a bad headache' and could not receive guests.' The date of Hamilton's attempted visit is uncertain but it may have been on 22 November, the date of a letter to his Uncle James in which he reported the incident. Additionally, Hamilton noted in his letter that Willock 'could give me only a short audience,' as he 'was actually packing up.' See Graves (1882: 73). Mirza Abu'l Hasan attended a concert on 19 November billed as 'By special desire and under the immediate patronage of His Highness, Prince Mirza Abul Hassan Khan, the Persian Ambassador.' See Greene (2011: 4425), who is wrong, however, in suggesting that the ambassador left Dublin the next day, on 20 November 1819. In fact, on 20 November, at the Crow Street Theatre, 'the famous Miss [Eliza] O'Neill [later Lady Eliza Becher],' who would later act in Drury Lane, London, 'performed the role of "Mrs. Beverly" in the "Gamester," by special desire of Prince Mirza Abul Hassan Khan, the Persian Ambassador, who visited the Theatre in oriental style. The receipts in cash for this night were £437, the largest sum ever received there for one stock performance, with the exception of the benefit of the noted clown [Robert] Bradbury, when the house was said to have yielded £600.' See Gilbert (1903: 141, 153–154). The large size of the audience is confirmed in a report published on 22 November 'of a particularly distressing crush of patrons for this performance.' See Greene (2011: 4426). Eliza O'Neill (d. 1872) was one of the most beloved actresses of her day, although she retired soon after her performance for Mirza Abu'l Hasan Khan when she married Sir William Wrixon Becher on 18 December 1819. See Montgomery (1896: 243–244); Gilbert (1903: 154). The Crow Street Theatre performance included 'Prince Mirza Abul Hassan Khan's March,' which was 'composed for the occasion by O'Rourke and played by the band.' See Greene (2011: 4426). 'O'Rourke' may have been the Crow Street stage-manager, Anthony Rock (O'Ruarc). See Gilbert (1903: 144). A month earlier, on 25 October 1819, a performance of *The Gamester* with many of the same actors was staged in Kilkenny. See Anonymous (1825h: 117). Lennon (2008: 130) was thus mistaken when he wrote that Mirza Abu'l Hassan Khan never visited Ireland.

[172] According to Kay (1838: 307–308), Mirza Abu'l Hasan Khan 'arrived at Dumbreck's Hotel, Edinburgh, on Saturday the 30th of October.' Anonymous (1819k) dated his arrival to 29 October/ Simond (1815: 360) observed, 'Dumbreck's hotel at Edinburgh is the most convenient, the quietest, the cheapest, and, at the same time, the most creditable of any establishment of this sort we have seen anywhere in Great Britain.' Shortly thereafter he moved to the Royal Hotel.' While there he visited Parliament House and 'viewed with much interest the Courts of law, the Library of the Faculty of Advocates, and the Signet Hall;;' as well as the Palace of Holyrood House, the Castle and a number of other sites. Thomas Moore told the following anecdote of Mirza Abu'l Hasan Khan's visit to Edinburgh. 'Told of the Provost of Edinburgh showing the curiosities of that city to the Persian ambassador; impatience of the latter, and the stammering hesitation of the former. "Many pillar, wood

10   From 1816 to the End of the Turco-Persian War (1816–1825)   959

10.55 'Latest from England,' *The Delaware Gazette* (Thursday, 25 May, 1820): 'The Persian Ambassador has left England for the continent.'[173]

10.56 'Untitled,' *The Freeman's Journal* (Monday, 3 July, 1820): 'At a grand entertainment given by the British Ambassador at Paris,[174] the chief object of attention was a magnificent diamond collar about the neck of the Persian Envoy—a present to his Oriental Excellency from the King of England, George IV, "by the grace of God." A portrait of "the Defender of the Faith."[175] set in diamonds, was attached to the collar.'[176]

10.57 'From the Boston Daily Advertiser, August 3. Latest from England,' *The New-York Evening Post* (Monday, 7 August, 1820): 'The Schah of Persia[177] is dangerously ill.'

---

pillar? stone pillar, eh?" "Ba-ba-ba-ba," stammered the Provost. "Ah, you not know; var. well. Many book here: write book? print book, eh?" "Ba-ba-ba-ba." "Ah, you not know; var. well." A few days after, on seeing the Provost pass his lodgings, threw up the window and cried, "Ah, how you do?" "Ba-ba-ba." "Ah, you not know; var. well;" and shut down the window.' See Russell (1860: 394). From Edinburgh, the ambassador departed on 4 November for Hamilton Palace to spend several days with Alexander, tenth Duke of Hamilton, after which he 'proceeded through Kilmarnock and Ayr on his way to ireland.' See Anonymous (1819k); Kay (1838: 308–309). According to Anonymous (1819k), the ambassador proceeded from Hamilton Palace to Portpatrick. This harbor town 'stands directly opposite the Irish port of Donaghadee, on the coast of the county Down, at the distance from it of only 21 miles; and, occupying the spot of British ground which is nearest to Ireland, and whence a passage can at any time be made without obstruction, it has acquired importance as a great international ferry-station between the two great insular sections of the United Kingdom.' See Anonymous (1856c: 561).

[173] According to Toone (1834: 549), 'His Excellency the Persian ambassador left London on his return to Persia' on 2 April 1820.

[174] Sir Charles Stuart (1779–1845), served on this occasion from 26 March 1815 to c. 3 November 1824. See Bindoff, Malcolm-Smith and Webster (1934: 50).

[175] *Fidei Defensor*, title first conferred by Pope Leo X (r. 1513–1521) upon Henry VIII as a personal title. See Brown (1875: 16). After his excommunication, Henry was enabled, on dubious legal grounds, to continue using the title by an act of Parliament, after which it came to be considered hereditary. See Brown (1880: 247).

[176] A notice in the *Asiatic Journal* for 1 July 1819 reads, 'The Persian Ambassador had not long arrived at Carlton House on the evening of the Fancy Ball, given by H.R.H. the Prince Regent, when the Duke of Montrose [James Graham] was sent to him on the part of his Royal Highness the Prince Regent, requesting his attendance in a separate room, where his Royal Highness presented his Excellency with his Royal Highness's portrait, most richly set in diamonds, which he placed with his own hands round the Ambassador's neck, suspended by a dark blue riband. The Ambassador felt a national as well as personal satisfaction at the manner in which this distinguished token of esteem and favour was conferred.' See Anonymous (1819h: 199). The portrait could not have been George IV whose coronation did not take place until 19 July 1821. Nor is it likely to have been a portrait of George III who was superseded by his son the Prince Regent from 1811 until his death on 29 January 1820 due to mental illness.

[177] Fath 'Ali Shah.

10.58 'Persia and Russia,' *Essex Patriot* (Saturday, 4 November, 1820), 'From late English Papers,' *Weekly Aurora* (Monday, 6 and Monday, 13 November, 1820), 'Extracts from late English papers, received at the Office of the National Advocate,' *The National Advocate* (Wednesday, 8 November, 1820; to 'came to the Indies?') and 'Persia and Russia,' *Augusta Herald* (Friday, 17 November, 1820): 'Interesting dispatches have been received in England from Persia, which announce the intrigues of the Russian agents in that country, and indicate the designs of the Court of St. Petersburgh. The footing they have obtained is so firm, that they no longer consider it necessary to disguise their projects. On the death of the reigning monarch,[178] who is in the last stage of decline, they consider it as certain that they will possess complete control. The Russian Charge d'Affairs [sic, d'affaires] at Tehran[179] declared publicly, that in future the Persians must be content to receive their sovereigns from Russia; to which he added, England could not reasonably object, as she gave away kingdoms every day in India.—The regular army of Russia, now in Georgia, and on the line of Caucasus, is upwards of 100,000 men, and of which 30,000 are part of the late army of occupation in France. They have been actively in the field for the last two years against the Skiekans and Daughistanies.

The Russian Charge d'Affairs at a dinner which he gave to the British officers in the Persian service, said openly that General Yarmaloff, Governor-General in Georgia, would be in Tabries in less than four months. Six days march, he said would bring their infantry and artillery to Tabries, after which what was there to stop them till they came to the Indies; the Russians have taken possession of a place on the Caspian, near Astarabad, and have a clever man of the name of Moravioff,[180] amongst the Turcomans.[181] He belongs to the Quarter-Master-General's department. It is the opinion of the British officers in the service of Persia, that there is a secret understanding between the Court and the Russians—for the

---

[178] Fath 'Ali Shah.

[179] Mazarovich. Cf. 10.53. See Wilkes (1823: 691); Kelly (2006: 40, 58); Behrooz (2013: 62). Ermolov refused to ratify Mazarovich's proposal for the settlement of the boundary (arising from the Treaty of Gulistan), 'alleging that the Russian minister had exceeded his instructions.' See Alexander (1827: 272). As noted above, according to Henry Willock, Mazarovich was removed from his post as a result of a letter 'urging the Persian Ministry, in the most undisguised language, to make war against Turkey.' See Willock (1858: 35).

[180] Nikolai Nikolaevich Muraviev/Murav'ev (1794–1866). In 1819 he became the first Russian officer to reach Khiva. For the account of his 'Journey to Turcomania and Chiva,' see Nazaroff, Eversmann, Jakovlew and Mouraview (1823: 61–112); Muraviev (1823); Murawiew (1824); and Muraviev (1871).

[181] Mentioned by Fraser (1825: 59) as Captain Moravief, author of *Voyage en Toorkomanie* (Muraviev 1823) and described as 'an officer in the military service' of Russia 'who was intrusted with the charge of a mission to Mahomed Raheem Khan, of Khyvah [Kiva]' but 'was a prisoner closely confined, and jealously guarded, during the time of his stay in the territories of Khyvah, and could personally have seen but little, while what he heard must have been through channels not the most likely to be free from prejudice.'

10   From 1816 to the End of the Turco-Persian War (1816–1825)   961

army of his Royal Highness Abbos Merza,[182] Prince Royal of Persia, has been suffered to dwindle to almost nothing. The infantry amounts only to 11,742 men, of all ranks upon paper; but they have scarcely ever been mustered or drilled—are ill paid, fed and clothed; and indeed, completely abandoned.'

10.59 'Persia and Russia,' *Norwich Courier* (Wednesday, 8 November, 1820), 'Persia and Russia,' *Maine Intelligencer* (Friday, 10 November, 1820), 'Persia and Russia,' *New Hampshire Sentinel* (Saturday, 11 November, 1820), 'Untitled,' *Dutchess Observer* (Wednesday, 15 November, 1820) and 'Persia and Russia,' *Bangor Register* (Thursday, 16 November, 1820): 'Interesting dispatches have been received from Persia, which announce the intrigues of the Russian agents in that country, and the designs of the Court of St. Petersburgh. The Russian Charge d'Affaires,[183] at Teran, declared publicly, that on the death of the reigning Monarch,[184] who is in the last stage of a decline, the Persians must be content to receive their future Sovereigns from Russia; to which he added, England could not reasonably object, as she gave away kingdoms, every day, in India. The regular army of Russia, now in Georgia, and on the line of the Caucasus, is upwards of 100,000 men, of which 30,000 [*Maine Intelligencer*, '50,000'] are part of the late army of occupation in France. The Russians have taken possession of a place on the Caspian, near Asterabad. It is the opinion of the British officers in the service of Persia, that there is a secret understanding between the Court and the Russians.

London paper.'

10.60 'Untitled,' *Hallowell Gazette* (Wednesday, 8 November, 1820), 'Affairs of Russia. London, Oct. 6,' *Providence Patriot Columbian Phoenix* (Wednesday, 8 November, 1820), 'Untitled,' *New-Bedford Mercury* (Friday, 10 November, 1820), 'Affairs of Russia. London, Oct. 6,' *Village Register and Norfolk County Advertiser* (Friday, 10 November, 1820) and 'Foreign Articles. London, Oct. 6,' *Vermont Journal* (Monday, 13 November, 1820): 'Letters from Persia, announce that the Russian Minister[185] at Tetan [sic, Tehran] has intimated pretty broadly, that as soon as the present Persian Monarch[186] is no more—and he was in nearly the last stages of a decline—the Persians must be content to receive their future rulers from Russia. The Russian forces on the border of Persia exceed 100,000 men. If the Emperor[187] has, as some have supposed, a hankering after our rich

---

[182] 'Abbas Mirza.
[183] Mazarovich.
[184] Fath 'Ali Shah.
[185] Mazarovich.
[186] Fath 'Ali Shah.
[187] Alexander I.

possessions in India, the capture of Persia will undoubtedly be one of his preparatory steps.'

10.61 'Russia,' *New-York Evening Post* (Wednesday, 2 May, 1821), 'Postscript. Late and Important from England,' *The Long Island Farmer* (Thursday, 3 May, 1821), 'Russia,' *Lansingburgh Gazette* (Tuesday, 8 May, 1821), 'Foreign News,' *Geneva Palladium* (Wednesday, 9 May, 1821) and 'Foreign Intelligence,' *Oswego Palladium* (Friday, 18 May, 1821): 'It is said, that there are not less than 120,000 Russian troops assembled in Georgia, ready for the field. The Ambitious designs of Russia become daily more apparent, and we must not be surprised to see shortly that court openly avow its views on Turkey and Persia.'

10.62 'Russia and Turkey,' *Onondaga Register* (Wednesday, 19 September, 1821): 'New York, *September* 13. The Amity, arrived yesterday, brought London papers to July 31st and Liverpool to the 2d of August, two days later than were received by the Falcon at Boston…The following is an extract of a private letter from Paris, dated July 28.

"It appears decided that war is declared between Russia and Turkey[188]; but what seems very singular is, the rupture has originated with the Grand Seignior.[189] Russia is at present under no alarm with respect to Persia, having fifty-four thousand men along that part of her frontiers which borders upon that kingdom. It may be remembered that while the French occupied Moscow, that the last treaty of peace was signed between Russia and Persia."'

10.63 'Foreign News. Latest from Europe. Paris, Oct. 28,' *The Schoharie Observer* (Monday, 26 November, 1821), 'Foreign News,' *The New-York Evening Post* (Tuesday, 11 December, 1821), 'Latest from Europe. Paris, Oct. 28,' *National Advocate* (Tuesday, 11 December, 1821), 'Paris, Oct. 28,' *New-York Spectator* (Friday, 14 December, 1821), 'Paris, Oct. 28,' *Independent Chronicle and Boston Patriot* (Saturday, 15 December, 1821), 'Late Foreign News. [From the New York papers],' *Washington Gazette* (Saturday, 15 December, 1821), 'Paris, Oct. 28,' *American Mercury* (Monday, 17 December, 1821), 'Paris, Oct. 28,' *The Boston Commercial Gazette* (Monday, 17 December, 1821), 'Paris, Oct. 28,' *Connecticut Gazette* (Wednesday, 19 December, 1821), 'Foreign & Domestic. From the Evening Post. Latest from England,' *Hampshire Gazette* (Wednesday, 19 December, 1821), 'Paris, Oct. 28,' *Norwich Courier* (Wednesday, 19 December, 1821), 'From the New-York Evening Post, Dec. 14. Foreign News,' *Thomas's Massachusetts Spy or Worcester Gazette* (Wednesday, 19 December, 1821), 'Persia,' *The Freeman's Journal* (Monday, 24 December, 1821), 'Foreign Intelligence. From the New-York Evening Post, Dec. 11,' *Farmers' Weekly Messenger* (Monday, 24 December, 1821), 'Foreign News. Extracts from late English Papers. Paris, Oct. 28,' *Washington*

---

[188] War was not declared at this time.
[189] Mahmud II.

Reporter (Monday, 24 December, 1821), 'Latest from England. Paris, Oct. 28,' *American Repertory* (Tuesday, 25 December, 1821), 'Foreign News. Persia. Paris, Oct. 28,' *Portland Gazette* (Tuesday, 25 December, 1821) and 'Untitled,' *American Advocate and General Advertiser* (Saturday, 29 December, 1821): 'A report prevailed yesterday that Persia had declared war against Turkey, that hostilities had commenced, and that the Persians had obtained the first advantages.'[190]

10.64 'European Politics,' *The Delaware Gazette* (Wednesday, 12 December, 1821) and 'Politics in Europe,' *Onondaga Register* (Wednesday, 12 December, 1821): 'The following birds-eye view of the political views and relations of the European governments is copied from the Boston Patriot: Extract of a letter from an American gentleman in London, dated Sept. 20, 1821. "If Russia spreads out her gigantic arms over the Ottoman, Europe will be *in flames*. She will be growing too dangerous a next door neighbor, for Prussia and Austria to remain idle. England, as the favorite at present of the Persian Court, barely maintains her rebellious Rajahs of India in surly subjection. The Turkish power once subdued by Russia, the Court of Persia, is also at her mercy and opens the door for her to the British Possessions, whenever she commands it; and when she does so, she and the native Princes will reduce the British empire in India to the limits of '57.[191] This is *the Key of the Politics of Europe*, at this moment."'

10.65 'Latest from England,' *The Long Island Farmer* (Thursday, 27 December, 1821), 'Very late from England. November 4,' *Alexandria Gazette & Daily Advertiser* (Thursday, 3 January, 1822), 'Latest from England,' *American Journal* (Wednesday, 9 January, 1822) and 'Foreign,' *Plattsburgh Republican* (Saturday, 12 January, 1822): 'The last advices from Constantinople confirm those which had previously announced hostile movements on the part of Persia against the Porte. It appears that one of the sons[192] of the Schah[193] has marched against the Pachalik of Bagdad, with a force of 60,000 men.'[194]

---

[190] As Jouannin and van Gaver (1840: 395) noted, with the Greek war going on, 'Au milieu de tous ces désordres, l'empire ottoman est menacé d'une invasion des Persans; et, le 15 Novembre 1821, la guerre éclate entre ces deux puissances musulmanes.' The causes of the war were very different in the north, where 'Abbas Mirza was, and in the south, where Mohammad 'Ali Mirza was. See Anonymous (1866a): 357–358.

[191] 1757 is conventionally considered the year that the creation of 'British India' began with the capitulation of the Nawab of Bengal to the East India Company following Clive's victory in the battle of Plassey on 23 June. See Low (1877/1: 267); Beale (1881: 262).

[192] Mohammad 'Ali Mirza.

[193] Fath 'Ali Shah.

[194] While 'Abbas Mirza attacked in the north (Kurdistan), his brother Mohammad 'Ali Mirza launched an assault on Daud Pasha at Baghdad, from his base in Kermanshah. See Busse (1972: 166); Longrigg (1925: 242–245). Of Mohammad 'Ali Mirza Markham (1874: 389–392), noted, 'Haughty and impetuous to a degree, but, at the same time...enterprising, gallant, and generous. He had loudly protested against being excluded from succession to the throne....His province was

10.66 'From the New-York Daily Advertiser, December 27,' *Geneva Gazette* (Wednesday, 16 January, 1822): ['The following is a summary of the principal news contained in the London papers, received by the British sloop of war Hind....Accounts from Constantinople mention that Persia was in hostile movement against the Porte. One of the sons[195] of the Shaik [sic, Shah][196] had marched against the Pachalike of Bagdad with 60,000 men.'

10.67 'From an English paper,' *The Geneva Gazette* (Tuesday, 22 January, 1822) and 'Miscellaneous Selections. From foreign papers received at the office of the New-York Statesman and Evening Advertiser,' *The Statesman & Advertiser for the Country* (Monday, 25 February, 1822): 'The following account of Persia is extracted from the Hamburgh Journal:—"The population of Persia, very much diminished by the civil war of 1722, (the epoch of the overthrow of the dynasty of Ismael Sophi,)[197] and of 1743, (the year of the assassination of the celebrated Schah-Nadir,) is estimated at 22 millions of souls. The number of provinces is 58. The reigning sovereign ascended the throne in 1797. He is called Feth-Ali-Schah, and is about 53 years of age. He is reckoned a good poet.[198] He has 65 sons and as many daughters.[199] His third son, Abbas Mirza, is destined to succeed him, although Prince Ali Mirza,[200] who is rejected by this choice, is distinguished by great personal qualities. In the peace concluded with Russia, the 13th of October, 1813,[201] the emperor Alexander agreed to a stipulation by which both himself and his successor are bound to maintain by force on the throne, should it be necessary, the prince who is destined to succeed, in order that no foreign power shall interfere in the internal concerns of Persia."'[202]

---

bounded on the west by the Pashálik of Baghdâd....In the year 1821, a war broke out between Persia and Turkey, arising from the insults offered to Persian pilgrims going to Mekkah. Muhammad 'Aly Mirza led his army, consisting chiefly of Kurds who had been disciplined by French officers, to the invasion of the Baghdâd Pashâlik.' However, as Jouannin and van Gaver (1840: 395), 'La mort du prince Muhammed-Ali-Mirza, frappée par le choléra-morbus, arrêta bientôt les opérations de son armée contre Bagdad, qu'il voulait soumettre aux armes persanes, jaloux de la gloire de réunir à l'empire d'Iran une ville aussi célèbre, qui, depuis deux siècles, en avait été violemment séparée.'

[195] Mohammad 'Ali Mirza

[196] Fath 'Ali Shah.

[197] The Safavid dynasty (1501–1722), founded by Shah Ismail.

[198] Cf. 10.29 for a poem of 80,000 distichs allegedly composed by Fath 'Ali Shah and given to the Austrian Emperor Francis I.

[199] See Anonymous (1873a: 715–716) on the family of Fath 'Ali Shah.

[200] Mohammad 'Ali Mirza.

[201] The Treaty of Gulistan. According to Hurewitz (1956: 84) the treaty was signed on 12 October 1813.

[202] Article 4 of the treaty reads, 'His Majesty the Emperor of Russia, actuated by similar feelings towards His Majesty of Persia, and in the spirit of good neighbourhood wishing the Sovereign of Persia always to be firmly established on the throne, engages for himself and heirs to recognise the

10.68 '(From the Moniteur of Friday.),' *City Gazette and Commercial Daily Advertiser* (Wednesday, 30 January, 1822) and '(From the Moniteur of Friday,),' *Daily Georgian* (Saturday, 2 February, 1822): 'According to letters from Constantinople, dated October 27, the Sultan, upon learning the invasion of the Persians, sent one of his officers[203] to the Court of the Schah,[204] to implore him to avert the storm. The Pachas on the frontiers, at the same time, received orders to make every possible effort to repulse the attack.[205] The troops of Asia, which recently arrived in the Ottoman capital, have continued their march towards Greece, in order to prove that the Porte despises the attack made by the Persians.'

10.69 'Untitled,' *City Gazette and Commercial Daily Advertiser* (Wednesday, 30 January, 1822) and 'Late Foreign News,' *Carolina Gazette* (Saturday, 2 February, 1822): 'We have received this morning two Flanders Mails, bringing Brussels Papers to the 30th ult. [October, 1821] The following extract relates to the affairs of Turkey, in connection with the Persian war, and is deserving of consideration. The Ottoman Government is indeed in a perilous condition at this moment:—.

"Constantinople, Oct. 28.

"The uncertainty with respect to Russia continues, and the embarrassment of the Divan is increased by the news which was received on the 19th of October, that the Hereditary

---

Prince who shall be nominated heir-apparent, and to afford him assistance in case he should require it to suppress any opposing party. The power of Persia will thus be increased by the aid of Russia. The Emperor engages for himself and heirs not to interfere in the dissensions of the Prince, unless the aid of the Russian arms is required by the King of the time.' See Hurewitz (1956: 85). Later Alexander (1827: 275–276) considered Russian support for 'Abbas Mirza's pretentions to the throne to be at the root of the Russian Minister M. Amburger's influence at his court in Tabriz, despite the fact that 'the Prince...secretly entertained a dislike to Russia and a regard for the British.' Andreas Amburger was consul in Tabriz from 1828 to 1830. See Bitis (2006: 11). For his life career see Amburger (1986: 85ff).

[203] According to Hasan-e Fasa'i the Ottoman ambassador, Najib Efendi, did not arrive in Tehran until 16 February 1824. See Busse (1972: 169). The reference here may rather be to Ahmed Efendi, who was sent by Khosrow Mohammad Pasha, *seraskar* of Erzurum, to 'Abbas Mirza when he learned that 'Abbas Mirza had marched from Tabriz to Khoy, having been authorized by Fath 'Ali Shah to commence hostilities against Turkey. See Anonymous (1866a: 358).

[204] Fath 'Ali Shah.

[205] As Anonymous (1866a: 358) noted, 'The Turkish Pashaliks which border on Azurbáiján, the province of which Abbás Mirza was governor, are those of Bayazid and Ván. Abbás Mírza sent Hasan Kuli Khan [sic, Hoseyn Qoli Khan Qazvini], to invade the first-named Pashalik in advance of himself, and this officer marched to Toprák Kil'ah, a strong village of 200 houses, half way between the Persian frontier and Erzeroum, where he had heard the Turkish forces were concentrating.... Meantime Abbás Mírza had invested Bayazíd, the capital of the Pashalik, and situated at its north-eastern angle within sight of Mount Ararat.'

Prince of Persia[206] had entered Armenia, near Kars, at the head of 100,000 men,[207] and that he has already occupied Erzeum [sic, Erzurum], the capital of that province.[208]

---

[206] 'Abbas Mirza.

[207] This number is wildly inflated, if the numbers given by Anonymous (1866a: 358) for different troop movements of 'Abbas Mirza's commanders (2000; 8000; 10,000) at this time are anything to go by. Markham (1874: 392–393) suggested that Mohammad 'Ali Mirza's attack on Baghdad, allegedly to avenge wrongs done to Persian pilgrims to Mecca, was the motivation for 'Abbas Mirza to launch his assault in the north. He wrote, 'Jealous of the successes of his brother, 'Abbâs Mîrza invaded the Turkish territory with his highly disciplined army, and in 1821 besieged and took Bayazid. The Turkish army advanced to a small fort, called Topra Kala, and drew up in order of battle, with the Pasha of Vân on the right and the Sar'-Askar in the centre. The Persian army was led by the Prince in person, with the Sirdar of Erivan on the right. The *sarbâz* or "infantry" of Azerbaijan stormed a hillock in front of the Turkish position in gallant style. The Turks fled in confusion, and were pursued by the Persian cavalry; 2500 of them were killed, and all their camp equipage and baggage fell into the hands of the victors.' On the other hand, Watson (1866: 197) claimed that 'Abbas Mirza launched hostilities because, 'a dispute arose between the frontier Persian and Turkish authorities—between the Prince-Governor of Azerbaeejan and the Seraskier of Erzeroum—on accoiunt of two wandering tribes claimed by the former as Persian subjects, and to which the latter afforded his protection. The Seraskier was recalled, but his successor showed himself to be even more unfriendly towards the Persians, imprisoning an agent sent by the governor of Tabreez to remonstrate on the subject of some grievances. After this insult the Shah's Government became convinced that friendly relations were no longer possible between the frontier authorities, and Abbass Meerza was accordingly instructed to invade the Turkish dominions.' The critical reviewer of Watson's work (Lord Strangford?) wrote, however, in Anonymous (1866a: 358), that the situation was far more complex. As he noted, 'The two "wandering" tribes were the Haideránlu and the Sebiki, sometimes written Zebeki, and they were not wandering at all, but had their summer-quarters in the Pashalik of Ván, at the north-eastern corner of the great lake, and their winter-quarters in the adjoining district of Chaldarán, belonging to Persia. Nevertheless, one half the tribe of Haideránlu, about 2000 tents, were Persian subjects, and were forcibly sent back after the war, and acknowledged so to be. It is only fair to the Persian Government to say that their chief avowed to an English consul that they were better treated in Persia than in Turkey, and preferred the Persian Government, but that the supply of water was more abundant in Turkey, and that was what led them to change their allegiance. Abbas Mirza sent Hasan Khan Kazvíni [sic, Hoseyn Qoli Khan Qazvini, commander at Yerevan] to bring back the tribes by persuasion and mild measures, but this envoy was attacked by Salím Pasha, and obliged to retreat into Persia. Abbás Mírza then sent Alí Beg, the Mayor of Tabríz, who was, with a shameful disregard of international law, imprisoned by Khusrau Mohammed Pasha, who had been appointed Saraskar, or Commander-in-Chief of Erzeroum, in place of Háfiz Mohammed Pasha. Abbás Mirza being now convinced that redress could not be obtained by conciliatory measures, and being authorized by the Shah to use force, proceeded from Tabríz to Khoi, and after a fruitless conference with Ahmed Effendi, an envoy from the Saraskar, determined on war.' Jouannin and van Gaver (1840: 395) downplayed the Persian victories, noting only that, 'Les hostilités n'eurent, pendant cette année, d'autres résultats que la prise de quelques places, tells que Kars et Toprak-Kal'è.'

[208] This is incorrect. As Buchholz (1824: 403) noted, 'Der Kronprinz Abbas Mirza hatte gegen Ende des Juli [1821] die persische Gränze verlassen, und war auf Erzerum marschirt. Sein Heer bestand aus 30,000 Mann, mit welchen er am 3ten August auf ein türkisches Heer von 52,000 Mann stieß, das von mehreren Pascha's befehligt wurde. Nichts desto weniger griff der persische Kronprinz muthig an, und der Zufall wollte, daß die Türken auf die ersten Kanonenschüsse der Perser auseinander liefen.

"The Persians will not find much difficulty in occupying the whole of Asia, because all the troops have been sent for to Europe. This news has caused an extraordinary sensation in the Divan. The Hereditary Prince of Persia is a sworn enemy to the Turks. The Armenians, who profess the Greek religion, make no resistance.

"Diplomatic letters avow the embarrassment of the Porte, with respect to Persia, but they express the hope that the attack of the Persians will force the Porte to accept the conditions proposed by Russia in favour of the Greeks.

"It has been long known at Constantinople, that Persian troops were assembling on the frontiers; but the system of terror which reigns there had prevented our correspondents from mentioning it in their letters. This event is considered as deeply implicating the existence of the Ottoman Empire; and every thing indicates that it is on the eve of a crisis, the more terrible, as being attacked at once by a formidable Persian army, and by the Greeks[209]; it is also menaced by Russia, so that it was never in so critical a situation.'"

10.70 'Frankfort, November 25,' *City Gazette and Commercial Advertiser* (Wednesday, 30 January, 1822),.: 'Very considerable corps of the Russian army have arrived in the provinces, where they will take up their winter quarters. All the troops in general, of this Empire will be cantoned.—The army of the south, and that of observation, commanded by General Yermoloff, will remain on war footing, in order to be ready to act at the first signal.'

10.71 'Frankfort, Nov. 23. Extract of a letter from Constantinople, Oct. 23,' *National Advocate* (Thursday, 31 January, 1822), 'Frankfort, Nov. 23.—Extract of a letter from Constantinople, Oct. 23,' *New-York Spectator* (Friday, 1 February, 1822), 'Frankfort, Nov. 23.—Extract of a letter from Constantinople, Oct. 23,' *American Mercury* (Monday, 4 February, 1822), 'Frankfort, Nov. 23. Extract of a letter from Constantinople Oct. 23,' *Connecticut Journal* ('Frankfort') (Tuesday, 5 February, 1822), 'Frankfort, Nov. 23. Extract of a letter from Constantinople Oct. 23,' *Richmond Enquirer* (Tuesday, 5 February, 1822), 'Frankfort, Nov. 23. Extract of a letter from Constantinople, October, 23,' *Massachusetts Spy* (Wednesday, 6 February, 1822), 'Frankfort, Nov. 23. Extract of a letter from Constantinople, October, 23,' *Norwich Courier* (Wednesday, 6 February, 1822) and

---

Diesen Zufall zu erklären, ist hinterher behauptet worden, daß, gleich beim ersten Beginnen der Schlacht, Selim-Pascha, ein kurdischer Rebell, welcher erst vor Kurzem Verzeihung erhalten hatte, zu den Persern übergegangen sei. Wie es sich auch damit verhalten mochte: der ganze Krieg war durch diese kurzweilige Schlacht beendigt; denn, als der persische Kronprinz bei weiterm Vorrücken die Entdeckung machte, daß die Cholera Morbus sich bei seinem Heere einstellte, ging er eiligst nach Bajasid zurück.' Erzurum was not besieged by the Persians until August, 1822, but because of the outbreak of cholera among his troops, 'Abbas Mirza was forced to lift the siege. See Kennedy (1832: 211) and the discussion below.

[209] As Busse (1972: 166, n. 273) noted, 'While Turkey, from 1820 onward, was engaged on the Balkan [peninsula] in fighting the Greek revolution, 'Abbās Mirzā undertook a successful campaign on the Kurdish frontier; the war ended with the peace treaty of Erzerum,' concluded on 28 July 1823.

'Frankfort, Nov. 23,' *Saratoga Sentinel* (Wednesday, 13 February, 1822): 'Hostilities have commenced between the Turks and Persians. It is added, that the Turks have been beaten, and that the Persians were on the point of entering Bagdad.[210] This circumstance will prevent the Asiatic troops from coming into Europe. The day before yesterday [21 October, 1821] the government sent thirty persons into the different provinces of Turkey in Asia, to make levies which are to march against the Persians.'[211]

10.72 'Foreign News,' *New-York Evening Post* (Thursday, 31 January, 1822), 'Latest from Europe,' *Lansingburgh Gazette* (Tuesday, 5 February, 1822), 'London, Dec. 3. Important news from Paris,' *Connecticut Journal* (Tuesday, 5 February, 1822), 'Important news from Paris,' *The Freeman's Journal* (Monday, 11 February, 1822) and 'Foreign News,' *Geneva Gazette* (Wednesday, 13 February, 1822): 'The situation of affairs in the east of Europe has assumed a very different aspect from what we expected. Persia, according to private letters, has not only declared war against Turkey, but has actually commenced hostilities in Asia against the Turks. The fact is stated positively, and it is inferred that this would not have been done without some previous concert or communication with Russia, and that Russia will put her armies in motion against Turkey as soon as military operations can be undertaken from the banks of the Pruth.'

---

[210] According to Bran (1829: 461), 'Im Jahre 1818 erklärte dieser Prinz, ohne Beistimmung seines Vaters, der Türkei den Krieg. Devaux wurde zum Generalissimus der Armee ernannt. Daud-Pascha von Bagdad, erhielt von der Pforte eine Verstärkung von 6000 Mann nebst sechzehn Stücken Geschützes. Bald standen nun die Armeen einander gegenüber. Mohamed Ali Mirza fing an, die Verwegenheit seiner Unternehmung zu bereuen, als er erfuhr, die Türken wären 22,000 Mann stark, da er, mit Inbegriff der irregulären Truppen, kaum 14,000 Mann hatte. Es wurde Kriegsrath gehalten, in welchem Alle das Gefährliche der Unternehmung geltend machten, und es wurde daher beschlossen, die Schlacht nicht zu liefern. Devaux behauptete kräftigst die entgegengesetzte Meinung, und sagte zu dem Prinzen, daß, wenn man ihn unbeschränkt walten ließe, er in einer Stunde sich der Kanonen des Feindes bemächtigt haben werde.' This is exactly what he did, engineering a famous victory. Cf. Bardin and Oudinot (1851: 3532). The Persians, however, retreated from Baghdad due to the cholera outbreak in their ranks which eventually claimed the life of Mohammad 'Ali Mirza. See below.

[211] According to Longrigg (1925: 244), Daud Pasha informed the Porte of the threat posed by 'Abbas Mirza and Mohammad 'Ali Mirza, and 'His dispatch arrived just after news of the invasion of 'Abbas Mirza in the north. The Sultan replied in terms of war. Baghdad was to be strengthened, the army prepared, and Persia invaded as fast and far as might be. Immediate reinforcements of 5000 Albanian "Haitahs" were ordered out, of whom some portion reached Baghdad.' Belge (1829: 350) differed, noting that 'Daoud pacha, vice-roi de Bagdad, reçut de la Porte un renfort de 6000 hommes avec 16 pièces d'artillerie.' These forces were in place by September, 1821. In fact, Mohammad 'Ali Mirza and his troops suffered greatly from a cholera outbreak and came to an early accomodation with Daud Pasha. Not long after he retired with his forces Mohammad 'Ali Mirza died at Kerend. See Longrigg (1925: 245).

10.73 'The Foreign News,' *Daily Georgian* (Saturday, 2 February, 1822; 'The Foreign News'): 'The intelligence, upon the whole, as relates to the cause of Greek freedom, appears to us to be of a favorable nature. The declaration of war against Turkey, by Persia, which is repeated from different sources, is an event of the utmost importance. With the Persians in Asia, and the Greeks in Europe, in connection with the threatening stand maintained by Russia, the Sublime Porte must find himself in a critical situation—When to this is added the rebellious conduct of the Janissaries, and the dissatisfaction of his officers, the chances of success on the part of the Greeks, appears to be much increased. If the Turkish empire escape whole from its present difficulties, it will indeed be indeed wonderful.'

10.74 'Russia and Turkey,' *National Advocate* (Saturday, 2 February, 1822): 'The late intelligence from Europe, far from inducing us to change our opinion as to the designs of Russia on Turkey, has tended to confirm the views we have already given of this subject, and of the political relations of the European sovereigns. Even the London ministerial journals, particularly the Courier,[212] the most active and decided of the whole in attempting to mislead the public, now acknowledge, that "the situation of the affairs in the east of Europe has assumed a *very different aspect* from what we expected."

Alexander, in the whole of this business, has played a deep game. While secretly exciting the Greeks to revolt,[213] and, by splendid embassies to Persia,[214] inducing that power to commence hostilities against the Turks, the Emperor of Russia completely succeeds in deceiving his "august allies" as to his ulterior views, by holding, in official notes, the most pacific language, and ordering his troops into winter quarters. Great Britain, in particular, seems to have been more effectually cajoled than any other power. Her Embassador[215] was permitted to exercise the most unlimited influence at Constantinople; he dined with the Sultan,[216] an honor seldom or never permitted to the minister of a foreign

---

[212] A London newspaper published as *The Courier and Evening Gazette* (1798–1804) and *The Courier* (1804–1848).

[213] As Ustrialow (1840: 448) observed, Prince Alexander Ypsilanti, son of the former hospodar of Moldavia, whose death Sultan Mahmud had ordered, found both refuge and high military rank in Russia. 'Im Jahre 1821 erschien er in den Moldau, sammelte eine kleine Schaar und verkündigte in einem pomphaften zu Jassy erschienenen Manifest den Griechen, daß die Stunde ihrer Freiheit heranrücke, daß Rußland bereit sey, ihnen die Hand zur Hülfe zu reichen, und daß er die Stelle eines obersten Anführers im Kampfe für Glauben und Freiheit übernehme. Es erfolgte, was man erwarten mußte: in Morea und auf den Inseln des Archipels brach die Bewegung aus.'

[214] Probably a reference to the Ermolov embassy of 1817.

[215] Percy Clinton Sydney Smythe, sixth Viscount Strangford (1780–1855), Ambassador Extraordinary to Constantinople at this time.

[216] Mahmud II.

power.[217] Even the representative[218] of the Emperor Francis[219] was not admitted to so familiar an intercourse. Thus occupying the ground almost exclusively, and commanding the ear at all times of the Ottoman chief, the ministers of George IV appear not to have been aware, that this seeming advantage, given them by Alexander, was a snare laid to entrap them, and to conceal from them the secret workings of the determined enemy of the Porte. A new light seems, all at once, to have burst upon the cabinet of St. James'; the actual commencement of warlike operations by the Persians has served to remove the veil, which concealed from their sight the ambitious projects and the cunning diplomacy of the Russian court. Hence the reluctant admission, that the situation of the affairs in the east of Europe had assumed a *new aspect*.'

10.75 'Postscript. Latest from England,' *Boston Commercial Gazette* (Monday, 4 February, 1822), 'London, Dec. 24,' *Newburyport Herald* (Tuesday, 5 February, 1822), 'Boston, Feb. 4. Latest from England,' *Massachusetts Spy* (Wednesday, 6 February, 1822), 'From the Boston Gazette of Monday Last. Latest from England,' *Rhode-Island Republican* (Wednesday, 6 February, 1822), 'Still Later. From the Boston Gazette of Monday,' *Independent Statesman* (Thursday, 7 February, 1822), 'Foreign Advices,' *Essex Patriot* (Saturday, 9 February, 1822, with minor variations), 'Latest from England,' *New-Hampshire Sentinel* (Saturday, 9 February, 1822, with minor variations), 'London, Dec. 24,' *New-Hampshire Patriot & State Gazette* (Monday, 11 February, 1822), 'Latest from England,' *Vermont Republican* (Monday, 11 February, 1822), 'Late Foreign Intelligence,' *Hallowell Gazette* (Wednesday, 13 February, 1822), 'Postscript. From the Boston Patriot, February 4. Latest from Europe,' *Pittsfield Sun* (Wednesday, 13 February, 1822) and 'Foreign Intelligence. From the (Boston) Commercial Gazette. Latest from England,' *Berkshire Star* (Thursday, 14 February, 1822): 'Asiatic Turkey is trampled, with little opposition, by the Persians.—The Prince of Persia[220] is said to have entered Bagdad, with great pomp.'[221]

---

[217] As Schiemann (1904: 307–308) noted, at this juncture, 'Offenbar bereitete sich England vor, an die Seite der Pforte zu rücken. Als Lord Strangford danach am 18. Mai [1821] seine Antrittsaudienz beim Sultan hatte, hatte er König Georg III. ami und allié Mahmuds [the Ottoman Sultan] genannt, und, was keiner der andern Gesandten getan hate, von dem Interesse des Königs an der Integrität der Türkei gesprochen. Die türkischen Staatsmänner meinten daraus den Schluß ziehen zu dürfen, daß England im Fall eines russischen Krieges sie nicht im Stich lassen werde.'

[218] Rudolf Graf von Lützow (1780–1858), Internuncio or Imperial Austrian ambassador in Constantinope from 1818 to 1822. Previously he had served in Munich, Stuttgart and Copenhagen. See Kacir (2015: 46, n. 178).

[219] Francis I, of Austria.

[220] Mohammad 'Ali Mirza.

[221] A false rumor. As Belge (1829: 352) noted, after an initial victory outside the walls of Baghdad, Devaux cried, '*Profitons de la victoire...à l'exemple de mon ancien empereur* [Napoleon]; *marchons sur la capitale, et bientôt Bagdad sera en notre pouvoir*. On était en marche pour cette nouvelle expédition, lorsque Mohammed Ali Mirza tomba malade et mourut. Les Persans n'en poursuivirent

10 From 1816 to the End of the Turco-Persian War (1816–1825)

10.76 'Turkey, Russia, &c.,' *City Gazette and Commercial Daily Advertiser* (Monday, 4 February, 1822), 'Late Foreign News,' *New-York Evening Post* (Monday, 4 February, 1822; with minor variations, to 'before the Persian army'), 'Foreign News,' *Geneva Gazette* (Wednesday, 13 February 1822) and 'Brussels, Dec. 19,' *Connecticut Journal* (Tuesday, 19 February, 1822; from 'The Persians'): 'An account from Leghorn, of the 28th November, states:—"We have received here from the Levant, the important news that the Prince of Persia[222] has made his entry into Bagdad at the head of 10,000 cavalry, and that the Turks every where fly before the Persian army".... The Persians had advanced one side to Bagdad (which some state they have taken;) and, on the other, to Erzerum.[223] All the

---

pas moins leurs succès; ils étaient déjà sous les murs de Bagdad, lorsqu'ils reçurent du visir de Kirmanchah l'ordre de se retirer.' Cf. Jouannin and van Gaver (1840: 395), 'La mort du prince Muhammed-Ali-Mirza, frappé par le choléra-morbus, arrêta bientôt les opérations de son armée contre Bagdad, qu'il voulait soumettre aux armes persanes, jaloux de la gloire de réunir à l'empire d'Iran une ville aussi célèbre, qui, depuis deux siècles, en avait été violemment séparée.' The Georgian sources conflated 'Abbas Mirza and Mohammad 'Ali Mirza, as though only one Persian general, in this case Mohammad 'Ali Mirza, had been responsible for prosecuting the war in both the north (Kars, Erzurum) and the south (Baghdad). Thus, we read, 'La même année [1821] la guerre ayant éclaté entre les Turks et les Persans, ceux-ci prirent Baghdad, Van, Erzroum et Trébisonde, sous la conduite de Mahmad-Ali-Mirza, fils de Baba-Khan, général distingué et d'une rare bravoure, puis bientôt ils se rapprochèrent, grâce à la médiation de l'Angleterre. Dans ce temps-là Mahmad-Ali-Mirza, fils de Baba-Khan, qui conduisait la guerre contre les Turks, fut tué [sic, died of disease] à Baghdad. Quoique sa mort eût considérablement affaibli son armée, Baba-Khan ne ratifia pourtant pas le traité de paix. Il prit Baghdad, força le pacha à se soumettre et garda la ville, malgré le vif mécontentement des Anglais, et expulsa de Perse tous ceux de cette nation qui s'y trouvaient.' See Brosset (1857: 320).

[222] Mohammad 'Ali Mirza.

[223] It is important to stress that there was no coordination between the campaigns of the rival brothers, Mohammad 'Ali Mirza and 'Abbas Mirza. Regarding the latter, the author of Anonymous (1866a: 358) described 'Abbas Mirza's deployments at this time. After the victory at Toprakkale, in which 4000 Turkish troops were said to have been killed by an army led by Hassan Khan, the remainder of the Ottoman forces, under Khosrow Mohammed Pasha, retreated to Erzurum. Some of the troops at Erzurum were sent out under Bahlul Pasha to support Bayazid, then under siege by 'Abbas Mirza, but 'Bahlúl was captured by Aslan Khan, a Persian officer, and Bayazid soon afterwards surrendered to Abbás Mírza, who found there sixteen guns and great store of arms. After this success the Persian prince sent Mohammed Zamán Khan, Hasan Khan and Abdullah Khan Demavendi, with 2000 infantry and 8000 horse, to drive the Turks out of the southern districts of the Pashalik of Bayazíd, while he himself marched against Malasgird, a fort within three marches of Lake Ván. A variety of operations followed, which ended in the complete reduction of the two Pashaliks of Bayazíd and Ván. Salím Pasha, the Wali of Armenia, having surrendered to Abbás Mírza, was reappointed by him, and his brother, Mohammed Beg, was intrusted with the command of 10,000 fresh horse, raised by the Persian prince, who, after a campaign of three months, returned to Tabríz, having captured 48 guns, 5000 prisoners and 200,000 cattle and sheep. The forts of Bayazíd, Abishgar, Dayadin and Malasgird to the north of Lake Ván, Aklot, Adiljavas…on the shore itself of the lake, Mush and Bidlís to the west, Archis and Khindis, and several others remained in possession of the Persians.' However, Erzurum itself was not captured. 'The Prince ['Abbas Mirza]…advanced upon Erzurum, the Armenian capital, which he would probably have occupied with very little resistance, had not an

Governors of Asia Minor are called upon to assemble troops, to stop the progress of the Persians.'

10.77 'Petersburgh, Nov. 29,' *New-York Evening Post* (Monday, 4 February, 1822), 'Postscript. Latest from England,' *National Advocate* (Monday, 4 February, 1822), 'Very Late from England,' *Norwich Courier* (Wednesday, 6 February, 1822), 'New-York, Jan. 4. From England,' *Boston Daily Advertiser* (Thursday, 7 February, 1822, with minor variations), 'St. Petersburgh, Nov. 29,' *Richmond Enquirer* (Saturday, 9 February, 1822), 'Brussels, Dec. 13,' *American Mercury* (Monday, 11 February, 1822), 'Untitled,' *Connecticut Mirror* (Monday, 11 February, 1822; with minor variations), 'European Advices. Petersburg, Nov. 29,' *Daily National Intelligencer* (Monday, 11 February, 1822), 'Foreign. Russia & Turkey. Petersburg, Nov. 29,' *Republican Gazette and General Advertiser* (Saturday, 16 February, 1822) and 'Brussels, Dec. 13,' *Republican Gazette and General Advertiser* (Saturday, 23 February, 1822; with minor variations): 'It is rumored in this capital [St. Petersburg], that a considerable division(s) of our forces will march into Asiatic Turkey, to act in concert with the Persians.'[224]

---

unexpected stroke arrested him. The army was seized with a pestilential disorder of so rapid and terrible a character, that its movements were completely paralysed, and it was unable, during all the rest of the campaign, to effect any thing important.' See Anonymous (1824a: 334). The fact that the writer possessed details not found elsewhere suggests he must have been a near observer, possibly a diplomat. It cannot have been Henry Willock, who was British *chargé d'affaires* in Tehran from 1815 to 1826, as he died in 1858 and Anonymous (1866a) is a review of Watson (1866); similarly it cannot have been William Monteith who died in 1864; or Sir Henry Rawlinson who is referred to in the text. In view of an allusion to William Napier's *History of the Peninsula War*, it seems highly probable that the author was Lord Strangford, ambassador in Constantinople at the time of the Ottoman-Persian hostilities, for he had written 'Observations' on Napier's work which provoked a rejoinder. See Napier (1828). As Kennedy (1832: 211) observed, 'In the beginning of August, 1822, the Persian troops under the command of Prince Abbas Mirza, amounting to 30,000 or 40,000 men, obtained a victory over an equal body of Turks, which was encamped within a few days' march of Erzeroum. A short period previous to the engagement, the cholera had appeared amongst the Persians, and some persons had fallen victims. Notwithstanding the extension of the malady, the prince persisted in pursuing the retreating enemy, and, favoured by the fatigues of marching, the pestilential inroad suddenly assumed so decisive a character, that in a few days it destroyed 2000 of his army. The increasing mortality left such an impression on the survivors, that a precipitate retreat was commenced towards Byzied, from which place the whole army dispersed without orders.'

[224] After the Turks began slaughtering Greeks, including the Greek Patriarch himself, the Russian ambassador in Constantinople, Count Grigori Alexandrovich Stroganov (1770–1857), remonstrated before the Sultan in the strongest terms, and delivered an ultimatum regarding the restoration of the property and rights of the Christian minority. When the deadline was past, he then left Constantinople and sailed to Odessa. As Ustrialow (1840: 449) noted, 'Der Kaiser billigte alle Schritte des Baron Stroganow, und gab Befehl an den Südgränzen des Reichs ein Heer zusammenzuziehen. Ein Krieg mit der Türkei schien unvermeidlich. Rußland wartete mit Ungeduld darauf, es kam aber anders.' In reaction to representations made by London and Vienna, 'Der Kaiser der die allgemeine Ruhe aufrichtig wünschte, willigte ein, die Unterhandlungen mit der Türkei zu erneuern, in der Hoffnung,

10.78 'Six days later from London,' *New-York Evening Post* (Tuesday, 5 February, 1822), 'Greece, Turkey, Persia, and Russia,' *The Long Island Farmer* (Thursday, 7 February, 1822) and 'Foreign News,' *The Massachusetts Spy* (Wednesday, 13 February, 1822): 'An article from Constantinople, dated Nov. 27 [1821], says "War against Persia has been solemnly proclaimed in this capital."'[225]

10.79 'St. Petersburgh, Dec. 7,' *New-York Evening Post* (Tuesday, 5 February, 1822), 'St. Petersburgh, Dec. 7,' *Baltimore Patriot & Mercantile Advertiser* (Thursday, 7 February, 1822), 'St. Petersburgh, Dec. 7,' *New-York Spectator* (Friday, 8 February, 1822), 'St. Petersburgh, Dec. 7,' *National Advocate* (Saturday, 9 February, 1822), 'European Advices. St. Petersburgh, Dec. 7,' *Daily National Intelligencer* (Monday, 11 February, 1822), 'St. Petersburgh, Dec. 7,' *Boston Daily Advertiser* (Tuesday, 12 February, 1822), 'St. Petersburgh, Dec. 7,' *The Repertory* (Tuesday, 12 February, 1822), 'St. Petersburgh, Dec. 7,' *Independent Chronicle and Boston Patriot* (Wednesday, 13 February, 1822), 'St. Petersburg, Dec. 7,' *Richmond Enquirer* (Thursday, 14 February, 1822), 'Two days later from England,' *City Gazette and Commercial Daily Advertiser* (Saturday, 16 February, 1822), 'Foreign. Russia & Turkey. St. Petersburg, Dec. 7,' *Republican Gazette and General Advertiser* (Saturday, 16 February, 1822), 'St. Petersburg, Dec. 7,' *American Mercury* (Monday, 18 February, 1822), and 'St. Petersburgh, Dec. 7,' *The Watch-Tower* (Monday, 18 February, 1822): 'Accounts have lately been received from Lieutenant-General Weljaminow, Governor of Georgia,[226] dated Tiflis, November 7 [1821], according to which the Persians have invaded Asiatic Turkey, had really made

---

alle Streitigkeiten auf eine friedliche Weise beizulegen....Die Unterhanglungen wurden mit ihr durch den englischen Gesandten in Konstantinopel, Lord Strangford geführt.' Never, however, was the point of a Russian invasion to assist the Persians in their war with the Porte.

[225] 'Au milieu de tous ces désordres [the Greek uprising], l'empire ottoman est menacé d'une invasion des Persans; et, le 15 novembre 1821, la guerre éclate entre ces deux puissances musulmanes.' See Jouannin and van Gaver (1840: 395); Williamson (2008: 95–98).

[226] Alexei Alexandrovich Velyaminov (1785–1838), previously Ermolov's chief-of-staff and second-in-command at Tiflis. See Brosset (1857: 314). As Baddeley (1908: 109) noted, 'no history of the conquest of the Caucasus would be complete without a biography, however brief, of this remarkable man, who was chief of the staff to Yermóloff during his ten years' command, and, as the latter himself said, his *alter ego*. Russian military writers, even Yermóloff's eulogists, confess that it is difficult, impossible in fact, to distinguish the merits and services of the two, so perfect was their friendly collaboration. But it may safely be said that while Yermóloff was the greater man, the more commanding personality, Veliameenoff surpassed him in ability, culture, and military knowledge. One year younger than Yermóloff, he never achieved one-tenth of the latter's popularity or fame; yet his career was almost equally brilliant, and his merits in some respects greater.' Similarly, Whittock (1959: 55) wrote, 'Ermolov's chief of staff, Velyaminov, was an organizer of genius and a military thinker of some originality: cold, severe, and withdrawn where his chief was bluff and hearty, Velyaminov inspired the respect rather than the affection of his subordinates, but he was indispensable, by virtue of his amazing grasp of the terribly complex social, political, economic and military aspects of the Caucasian situation.'

themselves masters of the important city of Erzerum, after defeating the Pacha of Bagdad,[227] who attempted, in vain, to defend it. It is said that there were many French officers in the Persian army,[228] with which Prince Mirza,[229] the second son of the Schah, has undertaken this expedition.'

10.80 'Augsburg, Dec. 9,' *Baltimore Patriot & Mercantile Advertiser* (Tuesday, 5 February, 1822): 'Letters from St. Petersburgh state, that a Russian agent,[230] charged with an extraordinary mission, has been sent to the Schah of Persia.[231] There is no doubt that most interesting negociations are on foot between the two powers, and that they will

---

[227] Daud Pasha. See Longrigg (1925: 244ff).

[228] Despite the agreement by treaty for Britain to supply military officers which, even after the death of Christie (discussed above) still included Capt. Hart and Capt. Lindsay, 'a number of French officers were taken into the Persian service.' See Monteith (1856: 109). When Lt.-Col. John Johnson passed through Tabriz in 1817, 'The Persians, at this juncture, were in great alarm concerning the intentions of the Russians; and finding that our Indian government will not allow any of their officers or men to remain and act hostilely in the Persian service, they were of course eager to give employ to our ancient rivals the French. At present, that is at the period of our journey [1817], there five officers of that nation, and four of Italy and Sicily, recently entertained by the Prince, who had directly appointed them to the command of battalions, &c. For a short time, the English mode of drill and exercise was ordered; but of late it has been neglected.' See Johnson (1818: 213). French officers were also in the service of Mohammad 'Ali Mirza. Flandin (1851/2: 520) noted, 'A la fin du règne de Fet-Ali-Châh, le gouverneur de Kerman-Châh qui n'est qu'à dix journées de marche, s'avança vers Bagdad avec quelques bataillons; il recontra et mit en fuite les troupes du Pacha, et, si un exprès du roi n'avait apporté au Châh-Zadèh *Mehemet-Ali-Mirza*, l'ordre de se retirer, Bagdad serait infailliblement tombée cette fois au pouvoir de ce prince. Persans et Turcs se souviennent encore que le succès de cette journée fut dû à un officier français, M. Devaux, instructeur dans l'armée du prince gouverneur de *Kerman-Châh*.' In the opinion of the author of Anonymous (1866a: 358), who was clearly well-informed (Lord Strangford?), Mohammad 'Ali Mirza 'raised a body of troops that, disciplined and trained by excellent French officers, such as [Claude Auguste] Court [1793–1861] and Devaux, were a match for any soldiers in Asia.' Cf. Ferrier (1856: 24), 'The Kurds, who serve in considerable numbers in Mohamed Ali Mirza's army, are a warlike race, and possessed of every quality that belongs to a good soldier. They were trained by excellent French officers, such as Messrs. Court and Devaux, and would well bear comparison with the troops of Abbas Mirza, who were trained by English officers sent to him by the East India Company.' Aubin (1908: 329), writing of Mohammad 'Ali Mirza, said, 'il organisa le pays et rebâtit la ville actuelle [of Kermanshah]. Deux officiers français, MM. Court et Devaux, furent chargés de l'instruction des troupes.' On Devaux see Belge (1829); Bran (1829). For Court see Gray (1929: 148). A third French officer who served Mohammad 'Ali Mirza was Louis-Philippe Aubrélique (b. 1789) on whom see Gobineau (1931: 342–345).

[229] Mohammad 'Ali Mirza.

[230] Mazarovich.

[231] Fath 'Ali Shah. As noted above, Mazarovich and his mission left Tiflis for Tehran on 28 January 1819. See Kneip (1976: 49).

10 From 1816 to the End of the Turco-Persian War (1816–1825)

have an important influence on the destiny of the Ottoman Empire,[232] and perhaps, on the future relations of Russia with the East Indies.'

10.81 'Frankfort, Dec. 14,' *Baltimore Patriot & Mercantile Advertiser* (Tuesday, 5 February, 1822), 'Frankfort, Dec. 14,' *Boston Daily Advertiser* (Tuesday, 5 February, 1822), 'From the Mercantile Advertiser of Feb. 4. Very late from Europe. Frankfort, Dec. 14,' *Connecticut Courier* (Wednesday, 6 February, 1822), 'Frankfort, Dec. 14,' *Middlesex Gazette* (Thursday, 7 February, 1822), 'Frankfort, Dec. 14,' *The Times, and Weekly Advertiser* (Tuesday, 12 February, 1822; with 'manifesto of a son of the Schah') and 'Frankfort, Dec. 14,' *Edwardsville Spectator* (Tuesday, 5 March, 1822; with 'manifesto of a son of the Schah'): 'Letters received here from Constantinople, state the taking of Bagdad by the Persians; the Turkish garrison, and the greater part of the population were put to the sword; the Christians, alone, it is said, were spared in conformity with a manifesto for the Schah.'[233]

10.82 'Paris, Dec. 20,' *Boston Daily Advertiser* (Tuesday, 5 February, 1822) and 'Paris, Dec. 20,' *Baltimore Patriot & Mercantile Advertiser* (Tuesday, 5 February, 1822; with minor variations): 'The publication of a firman of the Grand Seignior,[234] announcing to his

---

[232] As Baddeley (1903: 141–142) noted, 'in 1821, her [Russia's] intriguing agent, Mazaróvitch, against the will, indeed, of the Tsar, succeeded, thanks to misplaced zeal, in bringing about an armed conflict between Persia and Turkey. Yermóloff was away, and Mazaróvitch, meantime, received his instructions from far-off St. Petersburg only, his information sometimes from nearer sources. He knew of the strained relations beween Russia and Turkey, and learning through a sure channel that the Tsar had withdrawn his ambassador from Constantinople, he concluded, naturally enough, that a declaration of war would speedily follow. In these circumstances, thinking to render his country a signal service, he pushed Abbas Mirza into war with the Turk....Now, a conflict between Persia and Turkey would only have suited Russia, at this time, in the event of her declaring war against the latter Power; but Alexander I., so far from being desirous of such a contingency, was bent on averting it if possible. The withdrawal of his ambassador was meant as a warning, and as such had the desired effect. The Porte gave way, the peace was not broken. Meantime, Abbas Mirza's proceedings came singularly mal à propos, and seriously embarrassed the Court of St. Petersburg, which hastened to instruct its agents accordingly....The British Government, on the information of its representative, [Henry] Willock, complained through Prince [Christoph von] Lieven [Russian ambassador in London, 1812–1834] of Mazaróvitch's conduct, and Alexander I., while professing disbelief in the accusations brought against him, wrote to Yermóloff, who had meantime returned to Tiflis, to the effect that it would be as well to make some inquiry. Yermóloff, who had much reason to be grateful to Mazaróvitch, made a vigorous though far from convincing defence, and the matter was allowed to drop. But we have Mazaróvitch's own naïve admission that he had egged on the Persians, and there can be little doubt that he was mainly responsible for the outbreak of hostilities.'
[233] Fath 'Ali Shah.
[234] Mahmud II.

subjects that the Schah of Persia[235] had declared war against him, had produced great sensation, and had still more contributed to the exasperation of the Turks.'[236]

10.83 'Constantinople, Nov. 10,' *Boston Daily Advertiser* (Tuesday, 5 February, 1822), 'Constantinople, Nov. 10,' *The Repertory* (Tuesday, 5 February, 1822), 'Constantinople, Nov. 10,' *Essex Register* (Wednesday, 6 February, 1822), 'Foreign Intelligence. Constantinople, Nov. 10,' *Boston Weekly Messenger* (Thursday, 7 February, 1822) and 'Extracts from two private letters received by a respectable house in the City,' *New-Bedford Mercury* (Thursday, 7 February, 1822): 'Persia has declared war formally against the Turks, and the Persians are marching. They consist of 120,000 men in three columns.[237] Bagdad is now besieged by one of their columns. It is said that Trebizond has been taken by another column.[238] All the Persians that could not escape from Constantinople have been put in prison.'[239]

10.84 'From the Vistula, Nov. 20,' *Boston Daily Advertiser* (Tuesday, 5 February, 1822), 'From the Vistula, Nov. 20,' *Essex Register* (Wednesday, 6 February, 1822), 'Farther Extracts from Foreign Papers. From the Vistula, Nov. 20,' *Newburyport Herald* (Thursday, 7 February, 1822) and 'Foreign,' *Palladium of Liberty* (Thursday, 14 February, 1822; with minor variations): 'The movements of the Persians seem to be connected with a general

---

[235] Fath 'Ali Shah.

[236] The formal declaration of the Turko-Persian war of 1821–1823. See Williamson (2008). The declaration of war was discussed by Strangford in a letter to Castlereagh dated 21 November 1821. See Prousis (2010: 270).

[237] Williamson (2008: 94) put the size of Mohammad 'Ali Mirza's force at something closer to 25,000 in total, but Belge (1829: 350) says that in the advance on Baghdad the Persian army number barely 14,000, whereas Daud Pasha, the Turkish commander, had 22,000. As noted above, however, there was no coordination between the armies of 'Abbas Mirza and Mohammad 'Ali Mirza.

[238] The capture of Trabzon is also mentioned by Brosset (1857: 320). However, Anonymous (1822c), citing the *Austrian Observer*, wrote, 'It appears that the report of the Persians having invaded Armenia is not true, and that the mistake originated in some disturbances which broke out in Trebisond.'

[239] Cf. 10.89, 10.93, 10.94, 10.95, 10.101, 10.114 and 10.121. According to Anonymous (1821e), 'Die Pforte hat seit Ausbruch der Unruhen an der Persischen Gränze alle Waarengüter der hier befindlichen Handelsleute dieser Nation in Beschlag genommen, ihre Magazine versiegelt, die Kaufleute selbst aber und andere Persische Unterthanen gefänglich eingezogen. Der hießige Agent der Familie Tschapan Oglu, Hadscha Mustapha Bey, soll zum Liquidirungs-Commissair der Schuld-Forderungen Ottomannischer und anderer Unterthanen an gedachte Handelsleute ernannt worden seyn.' A different story is told in the *Annual Register* for 1822, according to which 'when some Persian students arrived at Constantinople, on their return to Tabriz from England, the grand seignor and his vizir furnished them with passports, to protect their books, instruments, medicines, and the other contents of their baggage, from impost or search; yet, on their reaching Azzarroon [sic, Erzurum], the passports were disregarded, their baggage was ransacked, and contributions were attempted to be exacted by way of duty.' See Anonymous (1823d: 278).

plan of attack which has been formed against the Porte, and in which none of the possible objects has been overlooked. The Crown Prince of Persia,[240] who has made himself quite independent of the Schah his father,[241] is recognised as Sovereign of the finest and richest half of Persia,[242] commands a considerable part of the Persian army, and is, as it is believed, provided, with respect to his conquests, with all the guarantees that can be desired. By these operations of the Persians, all the Asiatic caravans are interrupted in their way to Constantinople, which must have a great influence both on the provisioning of the capital and on the revenue of the State. These extensive Asiatic plains are precisely calculated for the Persian Prince to display the whole strength of his excellent cavalry, and enable him to destroy in few actions those swarms of infantry, composed of peasantry and artisans, hastily collected.'

10.85 'Vienna, Dec. 2,' *The Repertory* (Tuesday, 5 February, 1822), 'Vienna, Dec. 2,' *Boston Daily Advertiser* (Tuesday, 5 February, 1822), 'Greece, Turkey, Persia and Russia,' *New-York Spectator* (Tuesday, 5 February, 1822; to 'Pachaliks') and 'Vienna, Dec. 2,' *Boston Weekly Messenger* (Thursday, 7 February, 1822): 'The *Austrian Observer* states, that on the first of Nov. the Reis Effendi,[243] at Constantinople, was suddenly dismissed and exiled to Scivas,[244] in Asia Minor. He had been succeeded by Sadick Effendi.[245] Important changes had also been made in several Pachaliks. The Persians, it is stated, have taken the fortress of Zoprak-Kaleh,[246] and that they menace Etzerum [sic, Erzurum] on one side, and Bagdad on the other.'

10.86 'From the New-York Gazette of yesterday. Postscript,' *Centinel of Freedom* (Tuesday, 5 February, 1822), 'Constantinople, Nov. 10,' *The Repertory* (Tuesday, 5 February, 1822; second paragraph), 'London Corn Exchange, Dec. 24,' *The Eastern Argus* (Friday, 8 February, 1822; second and third paragraphs only), 'Untitled ['the Persians'],' *Connecticut Mirror* (Monday, 11 February, 1822; fifth paragraph) and

---

[240] 'Abbas Mirza.

[241] Fath 'Ali Shah.

[242] Azerbaijan, of which 'Abbas Mirza had been governor since 1805. See Busse (1972: 110).

[243] Hamid Bey.

[244] Sivas in central Turkey, roughly halfway between Erzurum and Ankara.

[245] Sadeq Efendi. According to 1821e, 'Es war am 1sten dieses [1 November 1821], als der Reis-Effendi Hamid Bey plötzlich seines Postens entsetzt und nach Siwas (in Klein-Asien) verwiesen wurde. Sadik Effendi, der unter Salih Dschanid Effendi Untersecretair des Departements der auswärtigen Angelegenheiten gewesen, erhielt seine Stelle.' Cf. Nichols (1971: 49, n. 35).

[246] For the capture of Toprakkale see Watson (1866: 198); Anonymous 1866a: 358); Jouannin and van Gaver (1840: 395). This occurred in May 1822. See Williamson (2008: 95). When Abbott visited it in 1837, he wrote, 'Toprak Kaleh has a small fort crowning the rock on which the tower stands. The place may contain 150 to 200 houses, of which about 50 belong to Armenians.' See Abbott (1842: 219).

'Foreign Intelligence. Twenty-one Days Later. New York, February 4,' *The Supporter, and Scioto Gazette.* Wednesday, 20 February, 1822; fifth paragraph): 'The Court Gazette of the Russian capital...says, "A report is in circulation here, that a considerable part of our troops will march into Asiatic Turkey, in order to act in concert with the Persian army....

The Grand Seignor[247] had published a firman, announcing the declaration of war by Persia; it produced a great sensation, and still more contributed to the exasperation of the Turks.

The city of Bagdad was reported to have fallen. The Crown Prince of Persia[248] was said to have entered the city at the head of 10,000 cavalry, and that the Turks every where fly before the Persian army. The Turkish garrison and the greater part of the population were put to the sword.

Letters from St. Petersburg state that a Russian agent,[249] charged with an extraordinary mission, had been sent to the Schah of Persia. It is said, that they will have an important influence on the destiny of the Ottoman Empire, and perhaps on the future relations of Russia with the East Indies.... the Persians had advanced on one side to Bagdad, and on the other to Erzeium [sic, Erzurum].'

10.87 'Foreign Intelligence. From the New-York Statesman. Persia,' *Centinel of Freedom* (Tuesday, 5 February, 1822; first paragraph only), 'Persia,' *Berkshire Star* (Thursday, 7 February, 1822), 'Persia,' *The Farmers' Cabinet* (Saturday, 9 February, 1822) and 'Persia,' *American Journal* (Wednesday, 13 February, 1822): 'Reports had reached London, to which the Courier gave credit, that Persia had declared war against the Turks, and that hostilities had actually commenced. A letter from Constantinople, dated October 23d [1821], states that a battle had been fought between these new belligerents, in which the Persians were victorious, and were on the point of entering Bagdad.[250] The latter adds, "This circumstance will prevent the Asiatic troops from coming into Europe. The day before yesterday the government sent thirty persons into the different provinces of Turkey in Asia to make levies which are to march against the Persians."

Persia is supposed to be under the influence of Russia, and the declaration of war was believed to be a measure dictated by Alexander.[251] Should this intelligence prove correct,

---

[247] Mahmud II.

[248] A confusion here between the Crown Prince, 'Abbas Mirza, and his brother, Mohammad 'Ali Mirza, who besieged but never captured Baghdad, as noted above.

[249] Mazarovich.

[250] As Williamson (2008: 100) noted, 'In October 1821, after overcoming the Ottoman army in Kurdistan, the Persian army was encamped within a day's march of Baghdad.'

[251] Emperor Alexander I, of Russia. As Keçeci (2016: 160) noted, 'In 1821 General Ermolov was in fact on leave in European Russia and Mazarovich was for the most part receiving his orders from St. Petersburg, and to a significant degree beyond anyone's full control. Learning from Istanbul that

10 From 1816 to the End of the Turco-Persian War (1816–1825)   979

the civil war of Greece will extend to the heart of Asia, and the Ottoman empire must be shaken to its centre.'

10.88 'From the N.Y. Daily Adv. Jan. 31. Latest from England,' *Connecticut Journal* (Tuesday, 5 February, 1822), 'By the Mails. New-York, Jan. 31. Latest from England,' *Massachusetts Spy* (Wednesday, 6 February, 1822), 'Foreign Intelligence. New-York, Jan. 31. Latest from England,' *Norwich Courier* (Wednesday, 6 February, 1822), 'Untitled,' *Farmers'Weekly Messenger* (Monday, 11 February, 1822; first paragraph only) 'By the Last Mails. Foreign Intelligence, Latest from England,' *Nantucket Inquirer* (Thursday, 14 February, 1822): 'It is now confidently stated that Persia, supposed to be under the influence of Russia, has declared war, and commenced hostilities, against the Turks; and that Russia was only waiting for the time when military movements on the Pruth could be undertaken, to begin warlike operations against the Sublime Porte itself. On what ground the Persians have entered into the war the accounts do not state. It is a curious fact however, that the followers of Zoroaster, in Asia, should attack the seat of the Prophet's followers,[252] and exert their power to aid in the overthrow of the Mahometan empire, whilst Christian, and even Protestant nations of Europe, should shew a disposition to uphold that antichristian power.[253]

If this account is to be relied upon and the Courier comes to give it credit, the affairs of the eastern border of Europe may soon assume an interesting aspect. Attacked in his Asian dominions, the Grand Seignior[254] will find himself placed in a situation of extreme difficulty and peril between Persia and Russia.'

10.89 'Turkey. London, Dec. 26,' *Daily Georgian* (Tuesday, 5 February, 1822): 'The accounts from Armenia are alarming. The Persians have gained considerable advantages over the Turks, who have, however, opposed a brave resistance to them. The force of the Persirns [sic, Persians] has been very much exaggerated: it consists, according to Turkish accounts, of about 50,000 men, of whom 30,000 advance against Erzerum, and the rest against Bagdad. The Crown Prince[255] is with the first. The Turks are inferior in force in those parts. It is generally believed in Constantinople, that the Persians, supported by the

---

the Tsar had withdrawn his ambassador, Mazarovich concluded that a declaration of war would speedily follow. A messenger from the Porte also informed the Iranian government at that time of the prospect of an immediate war between Russia and the Ottoman empire. The Russian agent strongly urged 'Abbās Mīrzā to enter the war against the Ottomans, and even offered the Prince a loan of thirty-thousand tumans.'

[252] Here the Shi'a Persians are identified as 'followers of Zoroaster,' while the Sunni Turks are 'the Prophet's followers.'

[253] Great Britain is the Protestant nation supporting Persia.

[254] Mahmud II.

[255] 'Abbas Mirza.

discontented Armenians, may make great conquests without encountering any considerable obstacle. All the Persians here [Constantinople], and many Armenians, have been thrown into prison.[256] The changes of the Ministry and the Pachas, show sufficiently the embarrassments of the Divan.'[257]

10.90 'London, Dec. 30,' *National Advocate* (Tuesday, 5 February, 1822), 'London, Dec. 30,' *The Repertory* (Saturday, 9 February, 1822), 'Brussels, Dec. 19,' *Connecticut Journal* (Tuesday, 12 February, 1822), 'London, Dec. 30,' *Norwich Courier* (Wednesday, 13 February, 1822), 'London, Dec. 30,' *Republican Advocate* (Wednesday, 13 February, 1822), 'London, Dec. 30,' *Boston Weekly Messenger* (Thursday, 14 February, 1822), 'Brussels, Dec. 19,' *Carolina Centinel* (Saturday, 16 February, 1822) and 'Brussels, Dec. 19, *Connecticut Journal* (Tuesday, 19 February, 1822): 'Letters received from Vienna yesterday state, that there have been more changes among the Ministers at Constantinople. The Captain Pacha has been made Pacha of Brussa,[258] and is succeeded by the Capitana Bey.[259] The Persians are represented to have had several successes, and in some places, the Turks had revolted and joined the Persian Prince.'[260]

10.91 'Salem, (Ms.) Feb. 2. Latest from the Continent of Europe,' *Newburyport Herald* (Tuesday, 5 February, 1822) and 'Untitled,' *The Repertory* (Tuesday, 5 February, 1822): 'The Turks have a new enemy[261] in the Persians, and the hereditary prince[262] is said to have

---

[256] Cf. 10.83, 10.93, 10.94, 10.95, 10.101, 10.114 and 10.121.

[257] For the reshuffling of high officials at this time see Jouannin and van Gaver (1840: 396).

[258] Bursa.

[259] The Capitana (Kapudan) Bey was second-in-command of the Turkish navy under the Captain (Kapudan) Pasha. Nasuhzade 'Ali, generally known as Kara 'Ali, was Capitana Bey in October 1821 when his fleet, supplemented by Egyptian and Algerian squadrons, scored a famous victory in the Gulf of Corinth over the Greek rebels, and carried off 34 Greek vessels. According to Jouannin and van Gaver (1840: 394), 'La flotte ottomane, sous les ordres de Kara-Ali-Pacha, sétait dirigée sur Samos, sans oser rien entreprendre contre cette île; le kapoudan-pacha se réunit ensuite aux escadres de Tunis, d'Alger et d'Égypte; et, quoique poursuivi et harcelé par la flottille d'Ipsara et d'Hydra, il parvint néanmoins à ravitaliser les places de la Morée encore occupées par les musulmans, à incendier la ville de Galaxidi, et à s'emparer d'une trentaine de petits navires grecs.' As Finlay (1861: 275) wrote, 'He [Kara 'Ali] entered the port of Constantinople in triumph, towing his thirty-five Galaxidhiot prizes, and displaying thirty prisoners hanging from the yard-arm of his flag-ship. The sultan considered the results of this naval campaign as extremely satisfactory...Kara Ali, who had hitherto only held the rank of capitan-bey, was rewarded with that of capitan-pasha.'

[260] It is unclear whether this refers to 'Abbas Mirza or Mohammad 'Ali Mirza.

[261] 'New' only in the sense that, as Jouannin and van Gaver (1840: 395) noted, in the midst of Turkey's attempt to battle the rebellion in Greece, new troubles suddenly erupted with the Persian invasion in the east.

[262] 'Abbas Mirza.

10   From 1816 to the End of the Turco-Persian War (1816–1825)   981

entered near Kars in Armenia at the head of 100,000 men, and already occupies Erzerum, a town 35 leagues from the Black Sea, and 80 from the frontier of Persia.'

10.92 'Latest from Europe,' *The Repertory* (Tuesday, 5 February, 1822): 'Persia, it is said, in letters from Constantinople, dated Oct. 23d and 25th, has declared war against Turkey, and has pushed an army into her territory. It is even said that the Persians have gained a battle of the Turks, and were on the point of entering Bagdad. It was surmised that Persia was acting in concert with Russia, and even asserted that the army of the latter was on the point of entering the Ottoman territory.'

10.93 'Postscipt,' *The Repertory* (Tuesday, 5 February, 1822) and 'London, Dec. 22,' *The Portsmouth Journal of Literature and Politics* (Saturday, 9 February, 1822): 'A letter from Leghorn, dated Nov. 28, says "we have received here from the Levant, the important news that the Prince of Persia[263] has made his entry into Bagdad at the head of 10,000 cavalry, and that the Turks every where fly before the Persian army. Another account says the Persians had advanced in another quarter to Erzerum, and that all the Governors in Asia Minor are called upon to assemble troops, to stop their progress. All the Persians in Constantinople had been ordered to be thrown into prison.'[264]

10.94 'Turkey. Constantinople, Oct. 25,' *The Salem Gazette* (Tuesday, 5 February, 1822): 'the embarrassment of the Porte is increased by the news the Divan received on the 19th inst. [October, 1821][265] that the hereditary prince of Persia[266] has entered Armenia near Kars at the head of a hundred thousand men, and already occupies Erzerum, a city 35 leagues from the black sea, and 80 from the Persian frontier, containing 25,000 inhabitants. The Armenians will offer no resistance. All the Persians in Constantinople had been ordered to be thrown into prison.[267]

It is the son of Schah, who, with Gen Yermoloff, has established a good understanding between Russia and Persia.[268] If ever the situation of the Porte was critical, it is, without doubt, now. Many consider this circumstance a manifestation of divine justice, to punish

---

[263] Mohammad 'Ali Mirza.

[264] Cf. 10.83, 10.89, 10.94, 10.95, 10.101, 10.114 and 10.121.

[265] War was only declared on 15 November 1821. See Jouannin and van Gaver (1840: 395).

[266] 'Abbas Mirza.

[267] Cf. 10.83, 10.89 10.93, 10.95, 10.101, 10.114 and 10.121.

[268] The abridged translation of Ermolov's diary, given in Lyall (1825/2), makes it clear that the Russian envoy did not exactly hold 'Abbas Mirza in high esteem. He wrote, for example, 'No opportunities, no circumstances, present themselves, in which the Persians do not deem it necessary to demonstrate their pride; and I can imagine their surprise, when, in return, they are treated with still a greater degree of pride, and even contempt. In such a manner did I conduct myself towards them.' See Lyall (1825/2: 108).

the Mussulmen for the innocent blood which they have spilt: and regard as certain the speedy destruction of the Ottoman domination.

Diplomatic letters have been received acknowledging the embarrassment of the Porte in regard to Persia; but contain hope that the attack of the Persians will force the Porte to accept the conditions proposed by Russia, in favour of the Greeks.'

10.95 'Greece, Turkey, Persia and Russia,' *New-York Spectator* (Tuesday, 5 February, 1822), 'Greece, Turkey, Persia and Russia,' *Baltimore Patriot & Mercantile Advertiser* (Wednesday, 6 February, 1822), 'Vienna, Dec. 1,' *American Mercury* (Monday, 11 February, 1822; 'from 'The Persians' to 'himself''), 'Vienna, Dec. 1,' *Connecticut Mirror* (Monday, 11 February, 1822; 'from 'The Persians' to 'himself''), 'The Russians—Greeks—Persians and the Turks. Frankfort, Dec. 15,' *Connecticut Mirror* (Monday, 11 February, 1822), 'Greece, Turkey, Persia, and Russia,' *Ontario Repository* (Tuesday, 12 February, 1822), 'Greece, Turkey, Persia, and Russia,' *Onondaga Register* (Wednesday, 13 February, 1822), 'Greece, Turkey, Persia and Russia,' *The Schenectady Cabinet* (Wednesday, 13 February, 1822), 'Vienna, Dec. 1,' *Saratoga Sentinel* (Wednesday, 13 February, 1822), 'Foreign,' *Palladium of Liberty* (Thursday, 14 February, 1822; from 'The Persians' to 'himself''), 'Foreign Intelligence,' *The Pilot* (Thursday, 14 February, 1822; from 'The Persians' to 'himself''), 'Greece, Turkey, Persia and Russia,' *New-Hampshire Patriot & State Gazette* (Monday, 18 February, 1822; from 'The Persians' to 'himself''), 'Greece, Turkey, Persia and Russia,' *The Vermont Journal* (Monday, 18 February, 1822; from 'The Persians' to 'himself'') and 'Greece, Turkey, Persia and Russia,' *North Star* (Thursday, 21 February, 1822; from 'While the Greeks'): 'A Vienna paragraph of the first Dec gives the following information relative to the critical state of the Ottoman government....The Persians had advanced on the one side to Bagdad (Which some say they have taken) and on the other to Erzerum. Some persons are already alarmed for Treorzond [sic, Trabzon], on the Euxine,[269] whence a communication might easily be made to Sebastopal in the Crimea. All the governors in Asia Minor are called upon to assemble troops, to stop the progress of the Persians. The severe measures ordered by the Porte, to throw into prison all the Persians at Constantinople,[270] is a proof that the invasion was ordered by the Schah[271] himself....While the Greeks are...rigorously maintaining themselves against their oppressors, the fury of the latter has been greatly increased by the unexpected hostilities of Persia, whose operations, according to Vienna dates to the seventh of December, have been far more important than was believed. It is now ascertained to be a completely organized invasion. The different corps of the Persian troops have entered the dominions of the Porte at the same time by Bassorah, Mosul, and

---

[269] The Black Sea.
[270] Cf. 10.83, 10.89, 10.93, 10.94, 10.101, 10.114 and 10.121.
[271] Fath 'Ali Shah.

Cars[272]; that one of these corps has already passed the Euphrates, and that another is advancing to the Tigris; that Trapezunt, Erzerum, and other places are already in the hands of the Persians.

The accounts which have come to the Greek merchants, and which they receive from their correspondents in the Morea,[273] and also from Alexandria, in Egypt, maintain that an alliance has been formed between Russia and Persia; according to which an army of the Schah is to advance to Asia Minor, and occupy the south coasts of the Black Sea, while a Russian army is to proceed to Constantinople, along the west shores of that sea.[274] The Persian army which has passed the Euphrates, will enter Syria, &c.'

10.96 'New-York, January 31. Russia,' *The Times, and Weekly Adviser* (Tuesday, 5 February, 1822), 'Foreign News,' *Dutchess Observer* (Wednesday, 6 February, 1822) and 'New-York, January 31. From England,' *Providence Patriot* (Wednesday, 6 February, 1822): 'By accounts received in London, on the 3d December, it...appears, that the Persians have actually commenced hostilities in Asia against the Turks. The fact, says the London Courier, of that date, is stated positively, and it is inferred that this would not have been done without some previous concert or communication with Russia, and that Rusisa will put her armies in motion against Turkey as soon as military operations can be undertaken from the banks of the Pruth. The situation of affairs in the east of Europe (observes the same paper) has assumed a very different aspect from what we expected.'

10.97 'Very late from Europe. Greece, Turkey, Persia and Russia,' *The Spectator* (Tuesday, 5 February, 1822), 'From the Commercial Advertiser. Greece, Turkey, Persia and Russia,' *Poulson's American Daily Advertiser* (Wednesday, 6 February, 1822) and 'Important Compend. Greece, Turkey, Persia and Russia,' *Boston Commercial Gazette*

---

[272] As noted above, there is no evidence of coordination between Mohammad 'Ali Mirza and 'Abbas Mirza in the southern and northern Turkish fronts.

[273] The Peloponnese in Greece.

[274] While the Russians and the Persians may have had similar designs on Ottoman territory, and Mazarovich certainly incited the latter to take action against Turkish Iraq, they never acted in concert. As Baddeley (1908: 141) noted, 'On the rare occasions when, as in 1808–9, she [Russia] fought both at once, it was not for long, nor was there any effective co-operation against her.' Monteith (1856: 155) observed, 'The Persians, at no time willing to join or act with the Turks, were more inclined to assist Russia than to act against her; in fact, so great is the distaste of these two great Mahomedan powers for each other. that the only means of inducing them to act effectually in a common cause would be to assign different lines of attack to their armies. The rehearsal of the Mahomedan prayers would suffice to set the two armies fighting. When I served with the Persian army, at a time when the Persians and Turks were both at war with Russia, it was always found necessary that the two encampments should be at some distance from each other, and even that was not always sufficient to prevent quarrels and bloodshed.'

(Monday, 11 February, 1822): 'General Yermoloff is appointed to the command of the Russian army on this side of Persia.'[275]

10.98 'European News. From the Vistula, Nov. 20,' *Boston Daily Advertiser* (Tuesday, 5 February, 1822; second para. Beginning 'the movements;' minus final sentence), 'European News. From the Vistula, Nov. 20,' *The Repertory* (Tuesday, 5 February, 1822; second para. Beginning 'the movements;' minus final sentence), 'Greece, Turkey, Persia and Russia,' *New-York Spectator* (Tuesday, 5 February, 1822; from 'A letter...', minus the last sentence), 'Greece, Turkey, Persia and Russia,' *Baltimore Patriot & Mercantile Advertiser* (Wednesday, 6 February, 1822; from 'A letter...', minus the last sentence), 'Foreign Intelligence. From the Vistula, Nov. 20,' *Boston Weekly Messenger* (Thursday, 7 February, 1822; second para. Beginning 'the movements;' minus final sentence), 'Greece, Turkey, Persia, and Russia,' *The Long Island Farmer* (Thursday, 7 February, 1822), 'Foreign,' *Palladium of Liberty* (Thursday, 14 February, 1822), 'Greece, Turkey, Persia and Russia,' *The Vermont Journal* (Monday, 18 February, 1822), 'Greece, Turkey, Persia and Russia,' *North Star* (Thursday, 21 February, 1822) and 'November 20,' *Vermont Gazette* (Tuesday, 26 February, 1822; from 'second para. 'the movements' to 'collected'): 'While the Greeks are...rigorously maintaining themselves against their oppressors, the fury of the latter has been greatly increased by the unexpected hostilities of Persia, whose operations, according to Vienna dates to the seventh of December, have been far more important than was at first believed. It is now ascertained to be a completely organized invasion. The different corps of the Persian troops have entered the dominions of the Porte at the same time by Bassorah, Mosul, and Cars; that one of these corps has also passed the Euphrates, and that another is advancing to the Tigris; and that Trapezunt, Erzerum, and other places, are already in the hands of the Persians. The accounts which have come to the Greek merchants, and which they receive from their correspondents in the Morea, and also from Alexandria, in Egypt, maintain that an alliance has been formed between Russia and Persia; according to which, an army of the Schah[276] is to advance to Asia Minor and occupy the south coasts of the Black Sea, while a Russian Army is to proceed to Constantinople, along the west shores of the sea. The Persian army, which has passed the Euphrates, will enter Syria, &c.

A letter dated "from the Vistula,[277] November 20," says the movements of the Persians seem to be connected with a general plan of attack, which has been formed against the Porte, and in which none of the possible objects have been overlooked. The Crown Prince

---

[275] Ermolov had in fact been nominated as the seventh commander-in-chief in the Caucasus on 24 May 1816. See Brosset (1857: 306); Gammer (2003: 177).

[276] Fath 'Ali Shah.

[277] The longest river in Poland, the Vistula rises near the border of Poland and the Czech Republic and flows north for over 1000 kms, emptying into the Baltic Sea.

of Persia,[278] who has made himself quite independent of the Schah, his father, is recognised as Sovereign of the finest and richest half of Persia, commands a considerable part of the Persian army, and is, as it is believed, provided, with respect to his conquests, with all the guarantees that can be desired. By these operations of the Persians, all the Asiatic caravans are interrupted in their way to Constantinople, which must have a great influence both on the provisioning of the capital and on the revenue of the State. These extensive Asiatic plains are precisely calculated for the Persian Prince to display the whole strength of his excellent cavalry, and enable him to destroy in few actions, those swarms of infantry composed of peasants and artisans, hastily collected....Gen. Yermoloff is appointed to the command of the Russian army on this side of Persia.'

10.99 'From Europe. Frankfort, Dec. 14,' *Baltimore Patriot & Mercantile Advertiser* (Tuesday, 5 February, 1822), 'European News. Frankfort, Dec. 14,' The Repertory (Tuesday, 5 February, 1822), 'Untitled,' *Daily Georgian* (Wednesday, 6 February, 1822; with minor variations incl. 'Prince Royal' instead of 'Son of the Shah'), 'Frankfort, Dec. 14,' *Boston Weekly Messenger* (Thursday, 7 February, 1822; 'Letters...of 11th of December'; and minor variations), 'Frankfort, Dec. 14,' *Washington Whig* (Monday, 11 February, 1822; with minor variations incl. 'Prince Royal' instead of 'Son of the Shah') and 'Foreign News. Frankfort, Dec. 14,' *Connecticut Herald* (Tuesday, 12 February, 1822): 'Letters from Constantinople of Nov. 11th, announce that the celebrated city of Bagdad, which had no other defence than a single wall of no strength, had been taken by storm. The Persians are said to have put to the sword the whole of the Turkish garrison, and most of the inhabitants who followed the doctrine of Omar.[279] The Christians alone had been spared, conformably to the Manifesto published by the Prince Royal of Persia.'[280]

10.100 'Important Foreign News,' *Onondaga Register* (Wednesday, 6 February, 1822), 'Greece, Turkey, Persia, and Russia,' *The Long Island Farmer* (Thursday, 7 February, 1822) and 'Foreign News,' *Plattsburgh Republican* (Saturday, 9 February, 1822): 'The following intelligence was received at the office of the N.Y. Spectator, by the Packet ship Amity, which sailed from Liverpool on the sixth Dec....Private letters announce, on the authority of the London Courier, that Persia has not only declared war against the Turks, but actually commenced hostilities.—The same letter adds that Russia had put her armies in motion for the commencement of hostilities against the Porte also. The latter story we are inclined to doubt.'

---

[278] 'Abbas Mirza.

[279] The Turkish Sunni 'followed the doctrine of Omar.'

[280] This is completely untrue. Busse (1982) makes no mention of a manifesto. This is perhaps a confusion with Fath 'Ali Shah and the translation of the Gospels by Martyn which pleased him so much. See 1815.1.

10.101 'War between Persia and Turkey. Extracts of Letters,' *American Federalist Columbian Centinel* (Wednesday, 6 February, 1822), 'Foreign News. War between Persia and Turkey. Extracts of Letters,' *Boston Recorder* (Saturday, 9 February, 1822), 'Constantinople, Oct. 23,' and 'Vienna, Dec. 1,' *Providence Patriot* (Saturday, 9 February, 1822; first and third paragraphs), 'Vienna, Dec. 1,' *American Mercury* (Monday, 11 February, 1822; from 'the Persians' to 'himself') and 'Vienna, Dec. 1,' *Connecticut Mirror* (Monday, 11 February, 1822; from 'the Persians' to 'himself'): '"Constantinople, Oct. 23. War has commenced between the Turks and Persians. The Porte has sent 30 messengers to the Asiatic provinces to raise levies to reinforce the army acting against the Persians."

Later. "Brussels, Dec. 16. Leghorn letters of the 28th [ul]t. announce, that news has been received there, that the Prince of Persia had made his entry into Bagdad [*The most important Turkish frontier city, not far, on the Tigris, from the boundary line of the two empires*,] at the head of 10,000 cavalry; and that the Turks were every where flying before the Persian army."

Vienna, Dec. 1. By the mail from Turkey, we learn, that the Persians have advanced, on one side to Bagdad (which some say they have taken) and on the other to Erzerum:—That some persons were alarmed for Trebizond, on the Euxine,[281] whence a communication might easily be made with Sebastopal, in the Crimea. All the Governors of Asia Minor are called upon to stop the progress of the Persians. The Porte has ordered all the Persians in Constantinople to be imprisoned[282]; which is a proof that they consider the invation [sic] as having been ordered by the Schah[283] himself, and not by his son."'[284]

10.102 'Foreign News,' *Dutchess Observer* (Wednesday, 6 February, 1822): 'The Persians have...waged war with the Turks; in this we discover the finger of Alexander.[285] After suffering the Persians, Turks, and Greeks to exhaust each other, the Russian Autocrat[286] will probably place the iron hand of power upon the whole.'

---

[281] The Black Sea.

[282] Cf. 10.83, 10.89, 10.93, 10.94, 10.95, 10.114 and 10.121.

[283] Fath 'Ali Shah.

[284] 'Abbas Mirza is almost certainly meant here, not his brother Mohammad 'Ali Mirza.

[285] Alexander I.

[286] As Golovine (1846: 171) wrote, 'In this Government the Emperor is everything: all moves and lives only through him. From the colour of a dress and the button of a coat, to the most complex law-suit; everything passes, or is supposed to pass through his hands, and nothing can be done without his orders or his sanction. His interests ought to be the rule and the primary duty of every person in his service, and the Russian Government has the simplicity to write at the head of its legislation: the Emperor of all the Russias is an autocrat monarch, whose power is unlimited. God himself orders all to obey his supreme will, not only from fear, but from conviction.'

10.103 'Foreign. Latest from Europe,' *Independent Chronicle and Boston Patriot* (Wednesday, 6 February, 1822), 'By a later arrival,' *New-Hampshire Patriot & State Gazette* (Monday, 11 February, 1822) and 'Postscript. From the Boston Patriot, February 4. Latest from Europe.' *Pittsfield Sun* (Wednesday, 13 February, 1822): 'Of the progress of the Persians, the accounts are very contradictory. Under date of Constantinople, Nov. 10, we find the following:

"The Porte does not seem to attach much importance to the difference with Persia. The Divan displays, at least, great coolness on this subject.

"Every day there are reports of the taking of Bagdad. Erzerum, and even of Trebizond, but these rumors obtain no confirmation. Constantinople is tranquil.'

10.104 'London, Dec. 26,' *Republican Advocate* [New London CT] (Wednesday, 6 February, 1822) and 'New-York, Jan. 4,' *The Repertory* (Saturday, 9 February, 1822; with minor variations): 'The St. Petersberg papers speak less cautious than formerly. One of them says, "A report is in circulation here, that a considerable part of our troops will march into Asiatic Turkey, in order to act in concert with the Persian army."'

10.105 'Augsburg, Dec. 9,' *Republican Advocate* [New London CT] (Wednesday, 6 February, 1822): 'Letters from St. Petersburgh state, that a Russian agent,[287] charged with an extraordinary mission, has been sent to the Shah of Persia.'[288]

10.106 'Paris, Dec. 20,' *Republican Advocate* [New London CT] (Wednesday, 6 February, 1822): 'Letters from Constantinople of the 19th Nov. have been received. The publication of a firman, announcing that the Shah of Persia[289] had declared war against Turkey, had produced a great sensation among the Turks. The Persians had captured Bagdad, and put the Turkish population to the sword.'

10.107 'From the Boston Gazette of Monday Last. Latest from England,' *Rhode-Island Republican* (Wednesday, 6 February, 1822), 'London, Dec. 22,' *The Portsmouth Journal of Literature and Politics* (Saturday, 9 February, 1822) and 'Late Foreign Intelligence,' *Hallowell Gazette* (Wednesday, 13 February, 1822): 'The Persian army, now in the field against Turkey, is said to amount to nearly 150,000 men. This unexpected force, greatly superior to what was expected,[290] has created a very strong sensation in Constantinople.'

10.108 'From the New York Commercial Advertiser, February 5. Six Days Later from Europe,' *Baltimore Patriot & Mercantile Advertiser* (Thursday, 7 February, 1822), 'Latest

---

[287] Mazarovich.
[288] Fath 'Ali Shah.
[289] Fath 'Ali Shah.
[290] As noted above, this is a gross exaggeration.

from Europe. From the New-York Commercial Advertiser, of Tuesday last. Six Days Later from Europe,' *Essex Register* (Saturday, 9 February, 1822), 'Late from Europe,' *Newport Mercury* (Saturday, 9 February, 1822; to 'confirmed'), 'Foreign,' *Palladium of Liberty* (Thursday, 14 February, 1822), 'Greece, Turkey, Persia and Russia,' *The Vermont Journal* (Monday, 18 February, 1822) and 'Foreign Intelligence. Six Days Still Later. New-York, Feb. 5,' *The Supporter, and Scioto Gazette.* Wednesday, 20 February, 1822): 'The Persians continue to advance victoriously. The news that Bagdad had fallen into their hands is confirmed, and it is again said that they have taken Trebison, and totally destroyed a Turkish corps posted near Erzerum.'

10.109 'Foreign Summary, From English papers to the 28th December, received at the office of the *Georgian*,' Daily *Georgian* (Thursday, 7 February, 1822): 'Accounts from Vienna say, the first news of the invasion of Turkey by the Persians was received by the English Embassy at Vienna.'

10.110 'Persia,' *The Palladium of Liberty* (Thursday, 7 February, 1822), 'Frankfort, Dec. 15,' *American Mercury* (Monday, 11 February, 1822; second and third paragraphs) and 'The Russians—Greeks—Persians and the Turks. Frankfort, Dec. 15,' *Connecticut Mirror* (Monday, 11 February, 1822; 'The Russians'): 'Persia is supposed to be under the influence of Russia, and the declaration of war was believed to be a measure dictated by Alexander. Should this intelligence prove correct, the civil war in Greece will extend to the heart of Asia, and the Ottoman Empire must be shaken to its centre. The Grand Seignor[291] had published a firman, announcing the declaration of war by Persia; it produced a great sensation, and still more contributed to the exasperation of the Turks. The city of Bagdad was reported to have fallen. The Crown Prince of Persia[292] was said to have entered the city at the head of 10,000 cavalry,[293] and that the Turks every where fly before the Persian army. The Turkish garrison and the greater part of the population were put to the sword.

.... the Persians had advanced on one side to Bagdad, and on the other to Erzeium [sic, Erzurum].'

10.111 'Constantinople, November 27,' *Rhode-Island American, and General Advertiser* (Friday, 8 February, 1822), 'Constantinople, Nov. 27,' *American Federalist Columbian Centinel* (Saturday, 9 February, 1822), 'Constantinople, Nov. 27,' *Richmond Enquirer* (Saturday, 9 February, 1822), 'Constantinople, Nov. 27,' *Independent Chronicle and Boston Patriot* (Saturday, 9 February, 1822), 'The foreign News,' *New-Hampshire Patriot*

---

[291] Mahmud II.

[292] Mohammad 'Ali Mirza is meant, though he was not crown prince, nor had he entered Baghdad.

[293] A confusion between the crown prince, 'Abbas Mirza, who was fully occupied in the north, and Mohammad 'Ali Mirza, who was responsible for the siege of Baghdad. Baghdad, as noted above, never fell to the Persians due to the cholera outbreak that ended Mohammad 'Ali Mirza's life.

& *State Gazette* (Monday, 11 February, 1822; to 'Kerkuk'), 'Constantinople, Nov. 24,' *Centinel of Freedom* (Tuesday, 12 February, 1822), 'Constantinople, Nov. 27,' *Connecticut Herald* (Tuesday, 12 February, 1822), 'Constantinople, Nov. 27,' *The Times, and Weekly Advertiser* (Tuesday, 12 February, 1822), 'Constantinople, Nov. 24,' *American Repertory & Advertiser* (Tuesday, 19 February, 1822), 'Miscellaneous Foreign Selections. London, Dec. 31,' *City Gazette and Commercial Daily Advertiser* (Tuesday, 19 February, 1822), 'Constantinople, Nov. 27,' *Pittsfield Sun* (Wednesday, 20 February, 1822), 'Constantinople, Nov. 24,' *North Star* (Thursday, 21 February, 1821; to 'activity') and 'London, Dec. 31,' *Carolina Centinel* (Saturday, 2 March, 1822; to 'retreat'): 'The news from Persia is alarming to the Turks. The Persians had taken, on the Euphrates, the city of Musch,[294] and approached Erzerum. On the side of Bagdad, they had advanced to Kerkuk, but they had been repulsed by the inhabitants, and had thrown themselves into the villages of the neighbourhood. The Persian Prince,[295] who commanded the troops, had announced that he had received orders from his father to retreat.[296] In the meantime the Pacha of Bagdad[297] did not trust him, had formed his defence with the greater activity. It is generally believed here [Constantinople] that Bagdad is in a state not to fear any attack.[298] By news from Aleppo, it would appear, that the treachery of Kiaja,[299] Chief of the Turkish troops, his secret desire to supplant the Pacha, and to succeed to his honours, were the causes of the late irruption of the Persians on the Ottoman territory.'

10.112 'Late from Europe,' *Village Register and Norfolk County Advertiser* (Friday, 8 February, 1822): 'The Greeks persevere in their struggle for independence, and the Persians proceed in their war against the Turks.'

10.113 'Of Turkish Affairs,' *American Federalist Columbian Centinel* (Saturday, 9 February, 1822) and 'Of Turkish Affairs,' *New-Hampshire Sentinel* (Saturday,

---

[294] Muş, in Turkey, c. 200 kms. South of Erzurum.

[295] Mohammad 'Ali Mirza.

[296] An outbreak of cholera forced Mohammad 'Ali Mirza's retreat, not orders from his father.

[297] Daud Pasha (c. 1767–1851). He held this office from 1816 to 1831. See Longrigg (1925: 235–237) for the controversy surrounding his appointment.

[298] As Longrigg (1925: 245) noted, 'Daud Pasha had stocked and fortified his capital for a siege.... Daud had a full treasury, copious stores, adequate manpower, and little fear of treachery within. The attacking forces were ample for an extended raid, but scarcely formidable in the siege of a great walled city. The trial was not made. Cholera was raging in the Persian army,' and as noted above, a peace settlement was made between the two sides, the Persian army turned and headed for Kermanshah, and Mohammad 'Ali Mirza died at Kerend before he reached home.

[299] Mohammad Agha. See Longrigg (1925: 244–245) for the history of this 'renegade Kahya.' This is a corruption of *kahya/kiaja* (*kiyabeg*), 'In general, steward, warder, high officer: in particular, the chief Minister (for all purposes) in a provincial Government under the Pasha.' See Longrigg (1925: 354). Here the title has evidently been mistaken for a personal name.

16 February, 1822): 'Constantinople, Oct. 29. The Sultan[300] has made known by a firman, that the Persians have declared war against him.

Nov. 10. The Divan displays a great coolness and apparent indifference with respect to the conduct of Persia.'

10.114 'Foreign Advices,' *Essex Patriot* (Saturday, 9 February, 1822): 'Persia has declared war against Turkey, and the hereditary prince[301] has already entered the dominions of the Grand Seignior[302] at the head of an army of from 100 to 150,000 men. This event has thrown the Divan into great consternation. All the Persians in Constantinople were ordered to be imprisoned.'[303]

10.115 'Odessa, Nov. 28,' *Independent Chronicle and Boston Patriot* (Saturday, 9 February, 1822), 'Odessa. Nov. 28,' *Newport Mercury* (Saturday, 9 February, 1822), 'Odessa, November 28,' *Providence Gazette* (Saturday, 9 February, 1822), 'Odessa, Nov. 23,' *Centinel of Freedom* (Tuesday, 12 February, 1822), 'Odessa, Nov. 28,' *The Times, and Weekly Advertiser* (Tuesday, 12 February, 1822), 'Odessa, Nov. 23,' *Connecticut Herald* (Tuesday, 12 February, 1822), 'Odessa, Nov. 28,' *Connecticut Gazette* (Wednesday, 13 February, 1822), 'Odessa, Nov. 28,' *Essex Patriot* (Saturday, 16 February, 1822), 'Odessa, Nov. 28,' *American Repertory & Advertiser* (Tuesday, 19 February, 1822), 'Odessa, Nov. 28,' *Pittsfield Sun* (Wednesday, 20 February, 1822) and 'Odessa, Nov. 28,' *Vermont Gazette* (Tuesday, 26 February, 1822): 'Letters from Constantinople of the 24th of this month [November, 1821], state, that a Turkish corps had been defeated at Erzerum by the Persians, and that it lost all its artillery. One of these even affirms that the Persians are masters of Trebisond, on the Black Sea.'

10.116 'Nuremberg, Dec. 17,' *Independent Chronicle and Boston Patriot* (Saturday, 9 February, 1822), 'Persia and Turkey,' *Essex Patriot* (Saturday, 16 February, 1822; begins 'Of the operations of the Persians, accounts are very obscure, and from sources of doubtful credit. A Nuremburg article says: "Every thing relative to the war with Persia is kept quite secret. It is known, however, that the Persians have been hitherto victorious, and that the Porte has not a sufficient force to oppose them; it is now said, however, that great armaments are making in Asia."'

10.117 'Foreign News,' *Independent Chronicle and Boston Patriot* (Saturday, 9 February, 1822), 'Foreign,' *Village Register and Norfolk County Advertiser* (Friday, 15 February, 1822) and 'Foreign & Domestic. Boston, February 9,' *Vermont Republican* (Monday,

---

[300] Mahmud II.
[301] Given the size of the force involved, even allowing for exaggeration, 'Abbas Mirza is meant here.
[302] Mahmud II.
[303] Cf. Cf. 10.83, 10.89, 10.93, 10.94, 10.95, 10.101 and 10.121.

10 From 1816 to the End of the Turco-Persian War (1816–1825)

18 February, 1822): 'Under date of Constantinople, Nov. 27, it is said, war has been solemnly proclaimed in this capital against the Persians.'

10.118 'Frankfort, Dec. 23,' *National Advocate* (Saturday, 9 February, 1822), 'Frankfort, Dec. 23,' *Dutchess Observer* (Wednesday, 13 February, 1822), 'Frankfort, Dec. 23,' *Daily Georgian* (Friday, 15 February, 1822), 'Frankfort, Dec. 23,' *American Mercury* (Monday, 18 February, 1822), 'Frankfort, Dec. 23,' *Republican Advocate* [New London CT] (Wednesday, 20 February, 1822), 'Frankfort, Dec. 25,' *North Star* (Thursday, 28 February, 1822) and 'Frankfort, Dec. 23,' *Carolina Centinel* (Saturday, 2 March, 1822; with minor variations, e.g. '17th Nov'): 'On the 16th Nov. the day when the war against the Persians was proclaimed, at Constantinople, the Ottoman Government received the news that the Persians after a bloody battle, had taken possession of Musch,[304] and advanced by forced marches against Erzerum—almost at the same time it was informed, that the Greeks had taken Tripolizza by assault.'

10.119 'Later News from Europe,' *The Portsmouth Journal of Literature and Politics* (Saturday, 9 February, 1822), 'Late from Europe,' *Hampden Federalist and Public Journal* (Wednesday, 13 February, 1822), 'Constantinople, Nov. 27,' *Essex Patriot* (Saturday, 16 February, 1822; with slight variations): 'The Persians have taken the city of Mursch,[305] on the Euphrates, and had approached Erzerum.—On the side of Bagdad, they had advanced to Kerkuck, but had been repulsed.'

10.120 'Foreign Advices,' *Providence Patriot* (Saturday, 9 February, 1822): 'Advices from Constantinople to November 27th indicated great disturbances in that capital. . . .The Persians have made a serious impression on the Asiatic provinces, and distrust, rebellion and confusion pervaded the whole. Reports state that, on the 27th or 28th, the Sultan[306] was beheaded by the Janissaries.'[307]

10.121 'Frankfort, Dec. 15,' *American Mercury* (Monday, 11 February, 1822; first two paragraphs), 'The Russians—Greeks—Persians and the Turks,' *Connecticut Mirror* (Monday, 11 February, 1822; first two paragraphs), 'Greece, Turkey, Persia, and Russia,' *Boston Commercial Gazette* (Monday, 11 February, 1822; third paragraph beginning 'The Persians'), 'Brussels, Dec. 19,' *Connecticut Journal* (Tuesday, 12 February, 1822; third paragraph from 'The Persians' to 'the Persians'), 'Foreign Intelligence,' *The Pilot* (Thursday, 14 February, 1822) and 'From the New-York Gazette. 21 Days Later,' *Washington Review and Examiner* (Monday, 18 February, 1822; to 'East Indies'): 'The

---

[304] Muş.

[305] Muş.

[306] Mahmud II.

[307] A false rumor.

Grand Seignior[308] had published a firman, announcing the declaration of war by Persia; it produced a great sensation, and still more contributed to the exasperation of the Turks. The city of Bagdad was reported to have fallen. The Crown Prince of Persia was said to have entered the city at the head of 10,000 cavalry,[309] and that the Turks every where fly before the Persian army. The Turkish garrison, and the greater part of the population were put to the sword....Letters from St. Petersburg state, that a Russian agent,[310] charged with an extraordinary mission, had been sent to the Shah of Persia.[311] It is said that they will have an important influence on the destiny of the Ottoman Empire, & perhaps on the future relations of Russia with the East Indies....

Vienna Dec. 1. The mail from Turkey arrived yesterday evening with letters to tenth of November, but without any news decisive either of peace or war....The Persians had advanced on the one side to Bagdad (which some say they have taken) and on the other to Eazerum....All the governors in Asia Minor are called upon to assemble troops, to stop the progress of the Persians. The severe measure ordered by the Porte, to throw into prison all the Persians in Constantinople,[312] is a proof that the invasion was ordered by the Schah himself.'

10.122 'Foreign. Boston, Feb. 4, 1822. Late from Europe,' *New-Hampshire Patriot & State Gazette* (Monday, 11 February, 1822): 'The Turks, it is said, have been attacked by the Persians. If, however, they are left to themselves by the European powers, they will probably exhaust each other for some time and then by mutual consent remain *in statu quo ante bellum*.'

10.123 'The Foreign News,' *Connecticut Journal* (Tuesday, 12 February, 1822) and 'New York, February 5,' *Hampden Federalist and Public Journal* (Wednesday, 13 February, 1822) and 'By the Sloop Convoy, Captain Tuthill, arrived at Newbern from New-York. New-York, Feb. 5,' *Carolina Centinel* (Saturday, 16 February, 1822): 'Russia and Turkey are now confessedly in the most interesting situation of all the European nations. It would seem next to impossible that a war should be avoided by them. Every thing, by the latest advices, appeared to indicate speedy hostilities; and the preparations for such a state of things were of a formidable description. The declaration of war against the Grand Seignior [sic, Shah] of Persia,[313] and the connection which is understood to exist between the latter power and Russia, bespeaks something more in the undertaking than a mere diversion in favor of the latter. It is said that the Persians have taken Bagdad, which

---

[308] Mahmud II.

[309] The common confusion of 'Abbas Mirza with Mohammad 'Ali Mirza. Cf. 10.110.

[310] Mazarovich.

[311] Fath 'Ali Shah.

[312] Cf. 10.83, 10.89, 10.93, 10.94, 10.95, 10.101 and 10.114.

[313] Fath 'Ali Shah. Note the title given to the Ottoman Sultan has been used here instead of Shah.

was entered by the Prince of Persia[314] at the head of his troops; and it is added that the Turks generally retreat before the Persians in their warfare against the Asiatic dominions of Turkey. With this powerful attack on her eastern side, and the still more threatening one from Russia at home, the Sublime Porte will be placed in a situation from which it will require all her means and all her energy to extricate herself.'

10.124 'Latest from Turkey,' *The Repertory* (Tuesday, 12 February, 1822): 'We are indebted to Mr. Topliff[315] for a file of *Le Spectateur Oriental*, to Nov. 24, published by the Franks at Smyrna[316]. ...It is stated in this paper that Constantinople was tranquil—that the Persians were advancing into Armenia.'

10.125 'Latest from Europe,' *The Times, and Weekly Advertiser* (Tuesday, 12 February, 1822), 'From the New-York Daily Advertiser, Feb. 9. Latest from Europe,' *Norwich Courier* (Wednesday, 13 February, 1822), 'New-York, February 9. Latest from Europe,'

---

[314] Mohammad 'Ali Mirza.

[315] Samuel Topliff (1789–1864), proprietor of the Merchants Reading Room and its successor, the Merchants' Hall News Room, in Boston. As Bolton (1906: 9) noted, 'From 1818 on, newspaper after newspaper contains items of intelligence "from Mr. Topliff's correspondent" at Gibraltar or Smyrna, or some other distant port. Apparently a large part of the foreign news came through his correspondents, so that he might be said to be the forerunner of the Associated Press in New England.' Schwarzlose (1989: 14–15) observed, 'Samuel Topliff, whose bold and lucrative activities in Boston harbor have been the starting point for several historians of newsbroking, enters the picture in 1811. ...News room enterprises such as Topliff's provided local newspaper editors with substantial amounts of generl news—a clearing house or brokerage for harbor news, weather reports, and a scattering of general foreign and national news items.'

[316] *Le Spectateur Oriental de Smyrne* began appearing at Smyrna [Izmir] on 24 March 1821, generally three times per month. See Isambert (1823: 41). As Raynal (1826: 296–297) noted, 'Les grands événemens qui signalèrent les ving-cinq premières années de ce siècle leur firent concevoir de nouvelles espérances; l'esprit public se forma, la haine pour leurs tyrans multiplia le nombre des partisans d'un inévitable révolution. Quelques écrivains courageux fortifièrent ces heureuses dispositions d'une manière plus ou moins directe; nous citerons entre autres le Spectateur oriental qui s'imprimait à Smyrne, et dont le redacteur, M. Raffanel, nourrissait en secret le désir de voir la liberté triompher, sans oser encore en prononcer le nom. "L'existence de ce journal, qui était en quelque sorte un phénomène en Turquie, dit cet auteur estimable, n'est due qu'à une grande considération: il était de l'intérêt même des Grecs que l'Europe connût leur sort; le récit de leurs malheurs ou de leurs exploits devait intéresser vivement en leur faveur...Un journal seul pouvait remplir un pareil but; mais dans l'empire ottoman et sous le glaive du despote, un journal qui eût osé se constituer l'apologiste de l'insurrection eût, à coup sûr, en exaspérant les Turcs, attiré de nouveaux maux sur la tête des Hellènes, et eût compromis le rédacteur."' Several sources, e.g. Hatin (1866: cvi) are therefore incorrect when they assert, 'Le créatur du journalisme en Turquie fut un Français, M. Alexander Blacque, qui vint, au commencement de 1825, à Smyrne, où il fonda le *Spectateur de l'Orient*....Le *Spectateur de l'Orient*, qui ne tarda pas à prendre le nom de *Courrier de Smyrne*, fut donc la première feuille périodique et politique qui parut en Turquie.' Cf. Anonymous (1854b: 155). Rather, the *Spectateur* originated four years earlier.

The Berks and Schuylkill Journal (Saturday, 16 February, 1822) and 'Foreign. New-York, February 9. Late from Europe,' *Edwardsville Spectator* (Tuesday, 12 March, 1822): 'The Turks appear to be in rather a perilous situation. On the one side a numerous army of Persians pursues its march; a Russian army bounds the frontiers of Europe; while the Greeks have become masters of Patras,[317] &c.'

10.126 'Untitled,' *Woodstock Observer, and Windsor & Orange County Gazette* (Tuesday, 12 February, 1822): 'Some articles give assurances of continued peace between Russia and Turkey and others intimate the expectation of war in the spring. The Persians, as heretofore mentioned, have commenced hostilities against the Turks.'

10.127 'Russia and Turkey,' *The Delaware Gazette* (Wednesday, 13 February 1822): 'It is stated in letters from Leghorn, of 28th November, that the important intelligence had been received there of the Prince of Persia[318] having entered Bagdad at the head of 10,000 cavalry, and that the Turks every where fled before the Persian army. The greater part of the inhabitants were put to the sword. Only Christians were spared. Negociations, are said in letters from St. Petersburgh, of a most interesting nature, to be going on between the Schah of Persia[319] and the Russian court, which will have an important influence on the destiny of the Ottoman empire, and perhaps on the future relations of Russia with the East Indies.'

10.128 'Important news from Europe. Russia and Turkey,' *Ballston Spa Gazette, and Saratoga Farmer* (Wednesday, 13 February, 1822): 'The accounts from this quarter are still of a contradictory nature; however, from these accounts, we are led to the belief, that the cause of the Greeks is assuming a more favorable appearance. The Persians have already declared war against the Grand Seignior,[320] and from the connexion which is said to exist between the former and Russia, we conclude there is every reason to believe that the Greeks will ultimately be delivered from the Turks—the most barbarous and cruel nation on the face of the earth.'

10.129 'Late Foreign Intelligence,' *Hallowell Gazette* (Wednesday, 13 February, 1822): 'Persia has declared war against the Porte and invaded the Turkish dominions. There is no evidence, however, of any concert between Russia and Persia.'

---

[317] Pouqueville, the French consul at Patras, wrote an account of the Greek insurrection there, led by the Archbishop Germanos, which resulted in the expulsion of the Turks. See Pouqueville (1843: 80–82).

[318] Mohammad 'Ali Mirza.

[319] Fath 'Ali Shah.

[320] Mahmud II.

10.130 'Turkey,' *Norwich Courier* (Wednesday, 13 February, 1822), 'Later from Europe. Turkish Affairs, &c.,' *Essex Patriot* (Saturday, 16 February, 1822; beginning 'It now') and 'Turkey,' *Augusta Chronicle* (Monday, 25 February, 1822): 'The red flags had been hoisted[321] at Belgrade. The firman for the war against Persia was the cause for this circumstance.... It now appears certain that the Persians have invaded Asiatic Turkey, and captured Erzerum, after defeating the Pacha of Bagdad.'

10.131 'Extract of a letter received in Baltimore, dated Smyrna, 26th Nov. 1821,' *Baltimore Patriot & Mercantile Advertiser* (Thursday, 14 February, 1822), 'Turkey. Extract of a letter received in Baltimore, dated Smyrna, 26th Nov. 1821,' *Independent Chronicle and Boston Patriot* (Wednesday, 20 February, 1822), 'Extract of a letter received in Baltimore, dated Smyrna, 26th Nov. 1821,' *Richmond Enquirer* (Thursday, 21 February, 1822), 'Turkey. Extract of a letter received in Baltimore, dated Smyrna, 26th Nov. 1821,' *Village Register and Norfolk County Advertiser* (Friday, 22 February, 1822), 'From Smyrna. Extract of a letter received in Baltimore, dated Smyrna, Nov. 26,1821,' *Daily Georgian* (Monday, 25 February, 1822), 'Extract of a letter received in Baltimore, dated Smyrna, Nov. 26, 1821,' *The Supporter, and Scioto Gazette* (Wednesday, 27 February, 1822), 'Intelligence. Extract of a letter received in Baltimore, dated Smyrna, Nov. 26, 1821,' *Woodstock Observer* (Tuesday, 5 March, 1822) and 'Extract of a letter received in Baltimore, dated Smyrna, Nov. 26, 1821,' *Nantucket Inquirer* (Thursday, 7 March, 1822): 'the Persians have declared war against the Turks, and the Russians, who are no doubt at the bottom of all this, it is to be expected will not much longer put up with the insolence and insults of the Musselmen.'

10.132 'Translated from the Oriental Spectator. Smyrna, Nov. 24,' *Boston Weekly Messenger* (Thursday, 14 February, 1822) and 'Boston, Feb. 12. Translated from the Oriental Spectator. Smyrna, Nov. 24,' *Alexandria Gazette* (Monday, 25 February, 1822): 'a great sensation is produced in the capital by the Persian war. They are advancing into Armenia and are thought to be already under the walls of Erzerum.—They have gained a very considerable advantage over the Turks near Bagdad.—This victory if it is real, will render the Persians masters of the Irac-Arabia,[322] before any opposition can be made to their invasion. Regiments are forming in Asia to march upon the Euphrates. This new war is very disagreeable to the Turks at a time when they have to make head against so many enemies.'

---

[321] A traditional signal to commence hostilities, used by both land and sea forces. See e.g. Corbett (1908: 257).
[322] Arab Iraq as opposed to Persian Iraq, 'Iraq 'Ajami, i.e. western Iran. For the areas belonging to each see e.g. Le Strange 1905.

10.133 'Foreign Intelligence. Russia,' *Oswego Palladium* (Friday, 15 February, 1822): 'By accounts received in London, on the 3d December [1821], it also appears, that the Persians have actually commenced hostilities against the Turks. The fact, says the London Courier, of that date it is stated, and it is inferred that this would not have been done without some previous communication with Russia, and that Russia will put her armies in motion against Turkey as soon as military operations can be undertaken from the banks of the Pruth.'

10.134 'From the London Courier, December 27,' *Daily National Intelligencer* (Saturday, 16 February, 1822): 'every thing tends to embarrass the affairs of Turkey. On one side a numerous army of Persians pursues its march, and already occupies Bagdad; a Russian army, bounds the frontiers of Europe; the Greeks masters of Patros [sic, Patras],[323] the garrison of which they have put to the sword.'

10.135 'Later from Europe. Turkish Affairs, &c.,' *Essex Patriot* (Saturday, 16 February, 1822): 'The Persian invasion proceeds victoriously. The news of their successes and those of the Greeks, causes bands of the assassins, among whom are many Jannissaries and Asiatics, to run up and down the streets of Constantinople, and to give themselves up to the most unheard of atrocities. The ministers of the christian powers begin to make preparations to facilitate the escape of their families in case of necessity. The nearer the crisis approaches, the more the fanaticism of the Turks increases; it has risen to a height of which it is impossible to form an idea.

It now appears that the Persians have invaded Asiatic Turkey and captured Erzerum, after defeating the Pasha of Bagdad.'[324]

10.136 'St. Petersburgh, Nov. 21,' *American Repertory & Advertiser* (Tuesday, 19 February, 1822): 'By an ukase, addressed to the Senate, his majesty the Emperor[325] has commanded the establishment of a Russian General Consulate in Persia.'[326]

---

[323] Cf. 10.125.

[324] Daud Pasha.

[325] Alexander I.

[326] Russian *ukaz/ukase*. Given the dateline of this article, this may be a reference to Emperor Alexander's edict of 8 October 1821 regarding transit trade through the Caucasus to Europe, which involved exports from Persia. As Gamba (1826/1: 1–2) noted, 'L'empereur Alexandre venoit, par un ukase en date du 8–20 octobre 1821, de rouvrir aux peuples de la Méditerranée la plus courte et la plus ancienne route du commerce de l'Assie. Cette mesure, dont déjà il est permis de prévoir les vastes résultats, ayant été adoptée d'après les représentations du général en chef Yermoloff, sur les mémoires et les plans que j'avois soumis aux ministres de S. M. I.' For the text of the *ukaz* see Gamba (1826/1: 355–360). It did not, however, call for the establishment of a Russian consulate at Tehran and between April, 1819, and January, 1823, there was no Russian representation there. See Markham (1874: 557).

10 From 1816 to the End of the Turco-Persian War (1816–1825)

10.137 'Constantinople, Oct. 29,' *American Repertory & Advertiser.* Tuesday, 19 February, 1822): 'The force of the Persians is estimated at 150,000 men. It is not supposed that Erzerum can hold out long. This war has been made known to the people by a firman of the Sultan.'[327]

10.138 'Constantinople, Nov. 2,' *American Repertory & Advertiser.* Tuesday, 19 February, 1822): 'The day before yesterday a general council was held of all the great officers of the empire. The Reis Effendi was dismissed yesterday, and sent into exile to Asia.[328]—Some believe that this is only a covert measure of sending a negotiator to treat with the Persians.'

10.139 'Foreign News. French Papers,' *Connecticut Journal* (Tuesday, 19 February, 1822) and 'Brussels, Dec. 13,' *Republican Gazette and General Advertiser* (Saturday, 23 February, 1822; with minor variations), 'The French papers of Sunday and Monday contain a report...): 'The Moniteur contains a report which had been brought to Vienna.... that the Persians continue to advance into the Asiatic provinces of Turkey, and that a corpse [sic, corps] of Turks has been cut to pieces.'

10.140 'Foreign. From the New-York Commercial Advertiser of Monday Last. Latest from France,' *Rhode-Island American, and General Advertiser* (Friday, 22 February, 1822), 'New-York, February 18. Latest from France,' *The Watch-Tower* (Monday, 25 February, 1822), 'Latest from France,' *The Eastern Argus* (Tuesday, 26 February, 1822) and 'From the Commercial Advertiser. Latest from France,' *Berkshire Star* (Thursday, 28 February, 1822): 'Since the hostile attitude of the Persians, couriers passed more frequently between Constantinople and St. Petersburgh[329]; but war was believed to be inevitable notwithstanding.'

10.141 'Russia and Great Britain,' *National Advocate* (Saturday, 23 February, 1822), 'From the National Advocate. Russia and Great Britain,' *American Mercury* (Monday, 4 March, 1822) and 'Foreign. From the National Advocate. Russia and Great Britain,' *Republican Gazette and General Advertiser* (Saturday, 16 March, 1822): 'It is amusing to observe, of late, the altered tone of the ministerial English journals, when alluding to the policy of the Emperor Alexander....No sooner...was it discovered, that Russia cherished designs not in exact accordance with the plans of the British ministry, than the press under its influence immediately assailed the motives and conduct of the man they had so recently

---

[327] Mahmud II.

[328] Sadeq Efendi. Cf. 10.85.

[329] Couriers between these two cities are mentioned frequently around this time. A note to a a letter from the Russian ambassador in Vienna to Count Nesselrode, for example, says, 'Diese Privatkorrespondenz ist stets durch russischen Kurier oder durch sichere Gelegenheit befördert worden.' See Schiemann (1904: 572, n. 1).

idolized....the hostile movements of the Persians against Turkey, which, with the Greek insurrection, are attributed to the intrigues of Alexander, has created in England a despondency....It is known to be the wish of Alexander to lessen, if not to destroy the political influence of England on the continent of Europe. His attack upon Turkey is considered as the first step towards this. Having succeeded in making an ally of Persia, nothing can prevent him marching his forces on Hindostan, after he has subdued the Musselmen.'

10.141 'From Niles' Register. Foreign Articles. Turkey,' *Washington Reporter* (Monday, 25 February, 1822): 'The Persians were advancing victorious. The disasters of the Turks has caused them, according to custom, to vent their rage on the unprotected and unoffending—hence extensive slaughters of the Greeks and others at Constantinople, &c.'

10.142 'Russia,' *Daily Georgian* (Tuesday 26 February, 1822): 'Alexander has been playing an artful game. He has completely foiled the sharp sighted ministry of England, by the impenetrable veil which he has cast over his feelings and intentions. Even now the Autocrat, with the most consummate political coquetry, whilst he is strengthening his frontier, organizing his army, and making every preparation for war, keeps up the appearance of a desire for peace, and whilst he excites the Persians to an attack against his enemy, waits a pretext which will soon be furnished for pouncing upon him.'

10.143 'Banks on [sic, of] the Vistula, Nov. 29,' *Vermont Gazette* (Tuesday, 26 February, 1822): 'The invasion of the Persians appears to be part of a general plan of attack against the Porte.'

10.144 'Foreign,' The Onondaga *Register* (Wednesday, 27 February, 1822): 'An arrival at New-York has brought Paris papers to the fourth ult. The intelligence as to the affairs of the continent, and the Russians and Turks in particular, is not very important. Since the hostile attitude of the Persians, couriers passed more frequently between Constantinople and St. Petersburgh; but war was believed to be inevitable notwithstanding.'

10.145 'Latest from the Continent of Europe,' *The Geneva Gazette* (Wednesday, 27 February, 1822) and 'Latest from the Continent of Europe,' *The Pilot* (Thursday, 28 February, 1822): ['The ship Frederick, which arrived on Saturday, sailed from Havre on the sixth of January. We have received from our correspondent, Paris papers to the fourth of that month, inclusive...They contain St. Petersburgh dates to the ninth December....The intelligence is not decisive, but goes to confirm the prospect of a war between Russia and Turkey. The last advices from St. Petersburgh say, that since the commencement of hostilities between Turkey and Persia, the interchange of couriers between the latter power and Russia have become more frequent, and but little doubt remains as to what will be the final result.'

10.146 'Persia,' *Independent Chronicle and Boston Patriot* (Wednesday, 27 February, 1822): 'The Journal of Hamburg, under the head of Vienna, contains several statistical details concerning Persia, of which the following is an extract: The population of Persia is much diminished by the civil wars of 1722, (epoch of the overturning of the dynasty Ismail Sophi) and of 1743 [sic, 1747], (year of the assassination of the celebrated Nadir Schah,) is computed at twenty millions, spread over fifty eight provinces. The present sovereign mounted the throne in 1797, his name is Teth [sic, Fath] Ali Schah, of the family of Cadjar; he is fifty three years old and passes for a good poet; he has sixty fine sons and as many daughters; his third son Abdas [sic, 'Abbas] Mirza is destined to succeed him on the throne although the prince Ali Mirza[330] who finds himself excluded by this choice, is distinguished by great personal qualities. In the peace concluded with Russia, the 12th October, 1813, the Emperor Alexander engaged for himself and his successors to lend his power, if necessary, to support on the throne the Prince who is destined to fill it, so that no foreign power shall interfere in the internal concerns of Persia.'

10.147 'From late foreign papers. Persia,' *Norwich Courier* (Wednesday, 13 February, 1822) and 'Intelligence. From an English paper,' *The Geneva Gazette* (Wednesday, 6 March, 1822): 'The population of Persia, very much diminished by the civil wars of 1722 (the epoch of the overthrow of the dynasty of Ishmael Sophi) and of 1743 (the year of the assissination of the celebrated Scha Nadir) is estimated at twenty-two millions of souls. The number of provinces is 58. The reigning sovereign ascended the throne in 1797. He is called Feth-Ali-Schah, & is about 53 years of age. He is reckoned a good poet. He has 65 sons, & as many daughters—His third son, Al das [sic, 'Abbas] Mirza, is destined to succeed him, although Prince Ali Mira,[331] who is rejected by this choice, is distinguished by great personal qualities. In the peace concluded with Russia, the 12th of October, 1813, the emperor Alexander agreed to a stipulation by which both himself and his successors are bound to maintain by force on the throne, should it be necessary, the prince who is destined to succeed, in order that no foreign power shall interfere in the internal concerns of Persia.'

10.148 'Extracts. From Liverpool papers received at Savannah by the ship Emily. London, Jan. 2,' *Baltimore Patriot & Mercantile Advertiser* (Saturday, 9 March, 1822): 'War against Persia, it is said, has been formally declared by the Porte. An article from Petersburgh, dated the seventh ult. [December, 1821] states, on the authority of a letter from a General officer in Georgia, that the Persians have occupied Erzerum after having defeated the Pacha of Bagdad.[332] The Austrian Observer, which probably is as good an authority, disputes this fact. The capture of Erzerum and Bagdad, is not improbably a

---

[330] Mohammad 'Ali Mirza.
[331] Mohammad 'Ali Mirza.
[332] Daud Pasha.

groundless rumour,[333] and there is not much probability of its being realised. It was indeed extravagant to suppose, that so ill appointed and ill-supplied an army could make permanent conquests.'

10.149 'Foreign News. From London papers received at this Office. London, Jan. 19,' *New-York Spectator* (Tuesday, 12 March, 1822), 'From the N.Y. National Advocate, March 11. Latest from England,' *Baltimore Patriot & Mercantile Advertiser* (Wednesday, 13 March, 1822), 'London, Jan. 21,' *The Nantucket Inquirer* (Thursday, 14 March, 1822), 'Latest from England. London, Jan. 19,' *Alexandria Gazette* (Friday, 15 March, 1822), 'From Europe,' *Essex Patriot* (Saturday, 16 March, 1822), 'Foreign News,' *The Portsmouth Journal of Literature and Politics* (Saturday, 16 March, 1822), 'Latest from England. Greek War,' *Vermont Republican* (Monday, 18 March, 1822), 'London, Jan. 19,' *The Watch-Tower* (Monday, 18 March, 1822), 'Latest from England. Greek War,' *American Repertory* (Tuesday, 19 March, 1822), 'London, Jan. 19,' *The Times, and Weekly Adviser* (Tuesday, 19 March, 1822), 'Foreign News,' *Republican Advocate* [New London CT] (Wednesday, 20 March, 1822), 'By Mail. Boston, March 14. Latest from England. Greek War,' *Rhode-Island Republican* (Wednesday, 20 March, 1822), 'Foreign. Boston, March 18. Latest from England. Greek War,' *New-Hampshire Sentinel* (Saturday, 23 March, 1822), 'London, Jan. 19,' *Carolina Centinel* (Saturday, 23 March, 1822) and 'Foreign and Domestic Intelligence. London, Jan. 21,' *North Star* (Thursday, 28 March, 1822): 'The Nuremburgh Correspondent repeats the report that the Persians had gained an important victory over the Pacha of Bagdad.'[334]

10.150 'Greeks and Turks. From the Mount Zion (Ga.) Missionary,' *Boston Recorder* (Saturday, 16 March, 1822), 'From the (Georgia) Missionary. Greeks and Turks,' *New-Hampshire Repository* (Sunday, 1 April, 1822), 'Greeks and Turks. From the Mount Zion (Ga.) Missionary,' *American Repertory* (Monday, 2 April, 1822) and 'Greeks and Turks,' *Onondaga Register* (Wednesday, 24 April, 1822): 'But Turkey has other causes of alarm besides those which relate to her disaffected, or her blood-thirsty subjects. Persia is already in arms upon one of her borders—and if we may credit recent reports, a skirt of the empire has felt the footsteps of her victorious armies. Against Persia, war has been formally declared by the Porte, and published at Constantinople; while the news of Persian victories has spread consternation through the city. It is certainly in the power of the Persians to make destructive inroads upon the eastern part of the Empire. A determined foe from this quarter must be an unwelcome visitor to his *Sublime Highness*,[335] especially when the very pillars of the throne appear to be crumbling, and the government, in all its departments, is violently shaken by the storms of internal contention'.

---

[333] As noted above, the rumors were indeed groundless. Neither city was captured by the Persians.
[334] Daud Pasha.
[335] Mahmud II.

10 From 1816 to the End of the Turco-Persian War (1816–1825)

10.151 'Late from England,' *The Geneva Gazette* (Wednesday, 20 March, 1822) and 'Latest from England. Greeks, Turks and Russians,' *Catskill Recorder* (Wednesday, 20 March, 1822): 'By the arrival yesterday of the Robert Edwards, Capt. Sherburn, from London, the editors of the New-York Daily Advertiser have received files of London papers to the 22d, and London shipping lists to the 19th January, inclusive....The Persian war is said to be at an end.—Nothing was known at the court of Teheran, beyond the irruption of Prince Mohammed Ali Minza [sic, Mirza], into the Pashalick of Bagdad; it is said no orders were given for this irruption.'

10.152 'Gibraltar, Jan. 17,' *Daily Georgian* (Thursday, 21 March, 1822): 'The red flag had been effectively hoisted at Belgrade, and this circumstance gave some weight to the sinister reports spread upon the Austrian frontiers; but the firman of war against the Persians, which had been solemnly issued at Constantinople, was the sole cause of the measure taken at Belgrade, and of the disquietude evinced by the inhabitants on that account.'

10.153 'From the Kentucky Argus. Turkey and her Neighbors,' *St. Louis Enquirer* (Saturday, 23 March, 1822): 'The Persians with great force have entered the [Ottoman] Empire on the East, and having defeated the Turkish army in that quarter have already occupied Bagdad and Erzerum. This invasion is said to have been made simultaneously with three armies, one at Bagdad, a large city on the lower part of Tigris, one at Mosul towards the head of the same river and the other near the heads of the Euphrates in the vicinity of Erzerum....The circumstance of their putting to death the Turks and sparing the Christians at Bagdad, indicates that they act in concert with Russia.

It is stated by travellers, that within the last half century the military character of the Persians has been undergoing a rapid change. The Turks are too bigotted to be instructed; but the Persians, on coming in contact with the Russians in the countries between the Euxine[336] and Caspian seas, soon discovered that their tactics and arms were altogether inferior to those of their enemies. Like wise men, their princes immediately commenced a change; they adopted the Russian arms, uniform and discipline, attempting like Peter the Great, to learn wisdom from their enemies. It is probable, that in these particulars they approach the perfection of European armies; but by the exertions of the able prince who has for many years directed the military affairs on the frontiers of Turkey and Russia, much has doubtless been effected.

This invasion would not endanger the existence of the Turkish Empire, but for the revolt of the Greeks and the policy of Russia. The revolt of the Greeks drew the chief part of the Turkish troops into Europe and left the frontiers in Asia so destitute of defence that their principal towns have become an easy conquest. But it is the permanent policy of Russia which will probably give a lasting and important effect to this Persian invasion....Do not

---

[336] The Black Sea.

all these circumstances render it probable, that Alexander and the Schah of Persia[337] have agreed to divide the greater part of Turkey between them?

….That the Persians have invaded Turkey, taken Bagdad and beat the Turks near Erzerum is not doubtful. They are led by the celebrated Abbas Mirza, heir to the throne of Persia.'[338]

10.154 'Foreign News,' *New-York Evening Post* (Monday, 26 March, 1822), 'New-York, New-York, March 26. Latest from England,' *Newport Mercury* (Friday, 30 March, 1822), 'From the N.Y. Evening Post, March 25. Foreign News,' *Washington Reporter* (Sunday, 8 April, 1822) and 'Miscellaneous Items,' *The Supporter, and Scioto Gazette* (Wednesday, 10 April, 1822): 'Accounts from Vienna to January 14 says, the Porte had received intelligence that the Persians had entirely ceased hostilities, and peace might be considered as concluded between the two powers.

The Cholera Morbus has broken out in Bagdad and neighborhood, and carried off about 1000 persons in a few days.'[339]

10.155 'Postscript. Vienna, Jan. 14,' *New-York Spectator* (Monday, 26 March, 1822), 'From Europe. Vienna, Jan. 14,' *Baltimore Patriot & Mercantile Advertiser* (Tuesday, 27 March, 1822), 'Vienna, Jan. 24,' *The Palladium of Liberty* (Wednesday, 28 March, 1822), 'Vienna, Jan. 14,' *Essex Patriot* (Friday, 30 March, 1822), 'Vienna, Jan. 14,' *The Watch-Tower* (Sunday, 1 April, 1822), 'Vienna, Jan. 14,' *Richmond Enquirer* (Monday, 2 April, 1822), 'Vienna, Jan. 14,' *Connecticut Gazette* (Tuesday, 3 April, 1822), 'Vienna, Jan. 14,' *Boston Weekly Messenger* (Wednesday, 4 April, 1822) and 'Vienna, Jan. 14,' *Woodstock Observer, and Windsor & Orange County Gazette* (Tuesday, 9 April, 1822): 'The Porte has received intelligence that the Persians have entirely ceased hostilities, and peace may be considered as concluded between the two powers. In the vicinity of Bagdad and the neighbouring countries, the cholera morbus had carried off 1000 victims in a few days.'

---

[337] Fath 'Ali Shah.

[338] As noted above, 'Abbas Mirza was busy in the north while Mohammad 'Ali Mirza led the assault on Baghdad.

[339] According to *Niles' Weekly Register*, 'English papers of the first of Feb.', 1822, with news from Constantinople dated 11 January, reported on this loss of 1000 to cholera at Baghdad. See Anonymous (1822d). According to Macnamara (1876: 60–64), the entire western coast of India suffered from cholera by 1820, from which it seems to have been spread by Indian and European troops to Oman, by March, 1821, whence it was transmitted to Bandar-e Bushehr by 20 August and from there to Basra and Baghdad. Cf. Kelsall (1866: 60) who dated the appearance of cholera in Baghdad to August, 1821. More specifically, according to Ozanam (1835: 260), 'vers la fin d'août, il envahit Bagdad, 'où il enleva 3000 personnes.' Kennedy (1832: 211) wrote, 'Before the autumn of 1823, the contagion had spread throughout Asiatic Turkey, from Bassora and Bagdad to Erzeroum and Antioch.'

10 From 1816 to the End of the Turco-Persian War (1816–1825)

10.156 'Foreign. New-York, March 26. Latest from England,' *Alexandria Gazette* (Friday, 30 March, 1822), 'Foreign. New-York, March 26,' *American Mercury* (Sunday, 1 April, 1822), 'Foreign News. Latest from England,' *Connecticut Journal* (Monday, 2 April, 1822), 'New-York, March 2?. Latest from England,' *Massachusetts Spy* (Tuesday, 3 April, 1822), 'Foreign Intelligence. New-York, March 26. Latest from England,' *Norwich Courier* (Tuesday, 3 April, 1822) and 'Untitled,' *Daily Georgian* (Thursday, 11 April, 1822, from 'the inhabitants'): 'The war between Persia and Turkey is closed, though the inhabitants of Bagdad have had to encounter a new enemy since hostilities with the Persians have ceased. The Cholera Morbus had carried off 1000 persons in a few days.'[340]

10.157 'Untitled,' *Essex Register* (Friday, 30 March, 1822), 'Foreign News,' *Independent Statesman* (Wednesday, 4 April, 1822) and 'Foreign Articles,' *The Lincoln Intelligencer* (Thursday, 11 April, 1822): 'The Persians are said to have discontinued their war against Turkey.'

10.158 'Continuation of Foreign News,' *Daily Georgian* (Friday, 30 March, 1822), 'Foreign. Late from England. Charleston. March 27,' *Easton Gazette* (Friday, 6 April, 1822) and 'Persia and Turkey,' *Richmond Enquirer* (Friday, 12 April, 1822): 'The Porte had received the following intelligence from Bagdad:—"The Persians have entirely ceased hostilities, and peace may be considered as concluded between the two powers.—This notice was brought by a Tartar, who left Bagdad on the tenth November. The Persian troops had repeatedly attacked the palaces nearest the city, but had always been repulsed with loss by the Pacha's troops. Both parties, weary of his [sic, this] state of war, without any object, which had continued for a considerable time, joyfully accepted the mediation of a Sheik, who is highly esteemed by the Turks of that province, and also by Shasade[341] Mahomet Ali Mirza, Governor of Kermanshah. An amicable arrangement, removing every misunderstanding, was immediately concluded, according to which the two Pachas of the Curd are not to be removed from their posts.[342]

---

[340] As noted above, this was the same spread of cholera that took the life of Mohammad 'Ali Mirza. It also struck Tabriz where it was responsible for the Rev. Henry Martyn's death, as noted above, and halted 'Abbas Mirza's attack on Erzurum. Cf. Fraser (1826: 307, 315); Alexander (1827: 216); Kennedy (1832: 211).

[341] Persian *shahzadeh*, lit. 'king born,' used for princes of the blood but also of female offspring of the shah. See Ouseley (1819: 2, n. 1).

[342] As Longrigg (1925: 245–247) noted, 'His illness and the wish to avoid a long and indeterminate campaigned induced the Mirza [Mohammad 'Ali Mirza] to suggest terms. A Shi'i 'alim was sent in to negotiate. Daud Pasha replied by the mission of two ambassadors not less reverend. Settlement was quickly reached: Sulaimaniyyah was to be given to 'Abdullah Pasha' [the Persian candidate].... Meanwhile in Shahrizor the death of Muḥammad 'Ali Mirza had restarted the tedious rivalries of the Baban family. Maḥmud Pasha, by a bold march and a costly battle, regained Sulaimaniyyah. Persian and Ardalan troops drove him from it. 'Abdullah, accepted for the moment by both Baghdad and Karmanshah, held the throne until Maḥmud, abandoning Turkish for Persian allegiance, replaced him

"Abdulah Pacha[343] will remain in Sulimanje and Mahmond [sic, Mahmud] Pacha[344] in Kol-Sanschak.[345] Neither of them can be removed from his post or deposed, without the joint consent of the Pacha of Bagdad[346] and the Governor of Kermanshah.[347] The Persians engaged immediately to leave the Ottoman territory, and to make good, without delay, the damage they had done. According to later accounts, Mahomet Ali Mirza had fallen ill, and was unable to sign the convention with the Pacha of Bagdad, and his First Minister was obliged to do it. This circumstance, and the extraordinary haste with which the Persian troops made their retreat, gave some credit to the report that the Prince, who is considered as the real author and promotor of the hostilities with the Porte, was really dead.'"[348]

10.159 'From England,' *The Delaware Gazette* (Wednesday, 3 April, 1822): ['The ship James Cropper, which sailed in company with the Cadmus, and left Liverpool on the fourth of February, arrived here yesterday; but owing to the vessel not having any communication with the shore for three days previous to her sailing, no London papers have been received by this conveyance later than the 29th January, or from Liverpool beyond the first February.] Things remained in *statu quo* respecting Russia and Turkey; and it cannot be expected that either of the parties would take the field until the weather was favorable for action. We see nothing to induce us to believe that the Russian and Turks will be able to adjust their differences without an appeal to the sword.—The report of hostilities on the part of Persia is confirmed, and there is nothing new respecting Greece.'

10.160 'Latest from England,' *National Advocate* (Tuesday, 3 April, 1822), 'From the N.Y. National Advocate, of April 3. Latest from England,' Baltimore *Patriot & Mercantile*

---

with the consent of both. The mission of Aḥmad Beg, brother of Daud, to assume the direct government of the State sent Maḥmud hot-foot to Peria, and brought Baghdad troops to Kirkuk. That they were accompanied by 'Abdullah Pasha—time after time the Persian candidate—cannot surprise students of these intrigues remarkable for the absence of any consistent loyalty any humane principle, any end but the crudest self-interest. Peace descended only when, by arrangement of the two powers, Maḥmud was restored to Sulaimaniyyah and 'Abdullah to Keui [Khoy].'

[343] 'Abdollah Pasha Baban. See Longrigg (1925: 236ff).

[344] Mahmud Pasha Baban, who was accused of 'guilty correspondence' with Mohammad 'Ali Mirza. See Longrigg (1925: 243).

[345] Koysinjaq, a small town between Erbil and Sulaimaniyah.

[346] Daud Pasha.

[347] Mohammad 'Ali Mirza. For the complicated political history of this period and the shifting alliances involving Baghdad and Persian interests see Longrigg (1925: 225ff).

[348] The precise date of Mohammad 'Ali Mirza's death is unclear and is not given e.g. in Amanat (2011). Jouannin and van Gaver (1840: 395) gave 15 November 1821 as the beginning of Mohammad 'Ali Mirza's invasion, while Anonymous (1822a) noted, 'Des lettres d'Odessa, du 2 Janvier, confirment la nouvelle de la fin tragique du prince persan Mouhamed-Ali-Mirza, qui a été trouvé mort dans sa tente.' This suggests his death occurred in late November or December, 1821.

Advertiser (Thursday, 5 April, 1822), 'Russia, Turkey and Greece,' *New-York Spectator* (Thursday, 5 April, 1822; to 'cholera morbus'), 'Latest from England,' *Richmond Enquirer* (Tuesday, 9 April, 1822), 'Foreign Articles. From the National Advocate, April 3,' *Dutchess Observer* (Wednesday, 10 April, 1822), 'Greeks and Turks,' *Providence Patriot* (Wednesday, 10 April, 1822), 'Foreign. New York, April 3. Latest from England,' *Republican Gazette and General Advertiser* (Saturday, 13 April, 1822; from 'Mahomed' to 'morbus') and 'Foreign & Domestic. From the National Advocate,' *Vermont Republican* (Monday, 15 April, 1822; to 'morbus'): 'Letters from Constantinople are up to the first of January. The Persians, as already known, had ceased hostilities with the Porte. They had had several skirmishes with the Turks, in which they were defeated. Mahomed Ali Mirza, the Schah,[349] is dead—poisoned, as 'tis thought[350]; and nearly 7000 Persians had been swept off by the cholera morbus....Dutch papers to the 30th ult. Arrived yesterday. An article from Leghorn, dated the tenth January, states, that....Great doubts... "are entertained respecting the sudden death of the Persian Prince."'

10.161 'Postscript. Latest from England,' *Daily Georgian* (Wednesday, 4 April, 1822) and 'Charleston, April 2. Latest from England,' *The Southern Chronicle and Camden Gazette* (Thursday, 11 April, 1822): 'The Persian Prince Mahomet Ali Mirza, commander of the forces which invaded Turkey, was found dead in his tent. The Persians retreated in consequence,[351] and the Greeks are disappointed in that quarter.'

10.162 'Epitome of Late Intelligence. Foreign. Great Britain,' *The Palladium of Liberty* (Thursday, 11 April, 1822): 'Great doubts are entertained as to the cause of the death of the Persian Prince[352]; he is supposed to have been poisoned.—Upwards of 7000 Persians are said to have fallen victims in a few days to the cholera morbus.'

---

[349] Mohammad 'Ali Mirza was obviously not the shah, but a son of Fath 'Ali Shah's.

[350] All other sources concur in identifying the cause of Mohammad 'Ali Mirza's death as the cholera contracted during his Baghdad campaign.

[351] This report is contradicted by e.g. Belge (1829: 352) who noted that, after Mohammad 'Ali Mirza's general Devaux had his initial success capturing the Ottoman artillery, he encouraged his master to press on to Baghdad. 'On était en marche pour cette nouvelle expédition, lorsque Mohammed Ali Mirza tomba malade et mourut. Les Persans n'en poursuivirent pas moins leurs succès; ils étaient déjà sous les murs de Bagdad, lorsqu'ils reçurent du visir de Kirmanchah l'ordre de se retirer.' Cf. Bran (1829: 458–459).

[352] Mohammad 'Ali Mirza.

10.163 'Latest from Europe,' *Spirit of the Times* (Friday, 12 April, 1822): 'The war between Persia and Turkey had ended; and the conduct of the Persian prince who invaded the dominions of the Porte, had been disavowed by the Schah.'[353]

10.164 'Foreign News. Russia, Turkey and Greece,' *Farmers' Weekly Messenger* (Monday, 15 April, 1822): 'Upwards of 7000 Persians are said to have fallen victim in a few days to the cholera morbus.—N.Y. Com. Adv.'

10.165 'From India,' *The Long Island Farmer* (Thursday, 18 April, 1822): 'The ship George, arrived at Salem from Calcutta, brings accounts from India to the 26th December-....The papers brought by this conveyance, confirm the accounts previously received of the terrible ravages committed in Persia, and different other places in Asia, by the Cholera Morbus.'

10.166 'Odessa, January 24,' *City Gazette and Commercial Daily Advertiser* (Friday, 19 April, 1822): 'We are assured that notwithstanding the death of the son[354] of the Schah of Persia,[355] (which appears certain) war still continued between the Turks and Persians, and that the Schah had given an answer, by no means satisfactory to propositions of mediation made to him by the English agent[356] accredited at his court.'

10.167 'Odessa, Jan. 24,' *Daily Georgian* (Saturday, 20 April, 1822): 'It appears certain, that notwithstanding the death of the son[357] of the King of Persia,[358] which is now confirmed, war will continue between the Turks and Persians; and that the King of Persia has given an answer very little satisfactory to the propositions of mediation which have been made by the British Charge des Affairs[359] at that Court.'

10.168 'Latest from England,' *The Repertory* (Friday, 18 April, 1822), 'Late from Liverpool,' *New-York Evening Post* (Saturday, 20 April, 1822), 'Latest from England,' *Newport Mercury* (Saturday, 20 April, 1822), 'Latest from England,' *Portsmouth Journal of Literature and Politics* (Saturday, 20 April, 1822), 'Russia and Turkey,' *Baltimore Patriot & Mercantile Advertiser* (Tuesday, 23 April, 1822), 'Russia and Turkey,' *The Sentinel of Freedom* (Tuesday, 23 April, 1822), 'Russia and Turkey,' *New-York Spectator* (Tuesday, 23 April, 1822), 'Foreign News. Latest from England,' *Connecticut Journal*

---

[353] Fath 'Ali Shah.
[354] Mohammad 'Ali Mirza.
[355] Fath 'Ali Shah.
[356] Henry Willock.
[357] Mohammad 'Ali Mirza.
[358] Fath 'Ali Shah.
[359] Henry Willock.

(Tuesday, 23 April, 1822), 'Late from England,' *Washington Gazette* (Tuesday, 23 April, 1822), 'Late from Liverpool,' *The Dutchess Observer* (Wednesday, 24 April, 1822), 'Foreign. Latest from England,' *Hampden Federalist & Public Journal* (Wednesday, 24 April, 1822), 'Late from England,' *Boston Weekly Messenger* (Thursday, 25 April, 1822), 'Gleanings,' *Connecticut Mirror* (Monday, 29 April, 1822), 'Russia and Turkey,' *Ontario Repository* (Tuesday, 30 April, 1822), 'Russia and Turkey,' *City Gazette and Commercial Daily Advertiser* (Tuesday, 30 April, 1822), 'Foreign and Domestic Intelligence. Latest from England,' *Onondaga Register* (Wednesday, 1 May, 1822), 'Latest from England,' *The Delaware Gazette* (Wednesday, 1 May, 1822), 'Late Foreign News,' Pittsfield Sun (Wednesday, 1 May, 1822), 'Latest from England,' *Plattsburgh Republican* (Saturday, 4 May, 1822), 'Russia and Turkey,' *Washington Reporter* (Monday, 6 May, 1822) and 'Foreign Intelligence. Latest from Europe,' *The Supporter and Scioto Gazette* (Wednesday, 8 May, 1822): 'A letter from Odessa states that the Schah of Persia[360] has refused the intervention of the English minister, and has issued a formal declaration of war against the Porte.'

10.169 'Latest from England,' *New-York Evening Post* (Monday, 22 April, 1822): 'By the ship Parthian from Liverpool, and last from Milford Haven, we have received London papers ten days later than were brought by the Herald. We are indebted to Capt. Mackay for a regular file of London papers to March 21....It is said also that letters from Constantinople confirm the event of the conclusion of peace with Persia.'[361]

10.170 'Foreign and Domestic Intelligence. Most Important Intelligence. Received late last night from our correspondent at Paris,' *The Onondaga Register* (after 22 April, 1822), 'Most Important Intelligence received late last Night from our Correspondent at Paris,' *The Greenfield Gazette & Franklin Herald* (Tuesday, 23 April, 1822), 'Most Important Intelligence Received late last night from our Correspondent at Paris,' *The Pilot* (Thursday, 25 April, 1822), 'Latest from England,' *The Freeman's Journal* (29 April, 1822), 'From England and France,' *The Geneva Gazette* (Wednesday, 1 May, 1822) and 'Most important Intelligence. Received lat last night from our Correspondent at Paris,' *Plattsburgh Republican* (Saturday, 4 May, 1822): 'It is rumored that an alliance is forming between Persia and Russia.'

10.171 'Ten Days later from Europe. Russia and Turkey,' *New-York Spectator* (Tuesday, 23 April, 1822), 'Foreign Intelligence. Ten Days Later from Europe. Russia and Turkey,' *Centinel of Freedom* (Tuesday, 30 April, 1822), 'Russia and Turkey,' *Ontario Repository* (Tuesday, 30 April, 1822) and 'Russia and Turkey,' *American Journal* (Wednesday,

---

[360] Fath 'Ali Shah.
[361] This refers to the accomodation between Mohammad 'Ali Mirza and Daud Pasha, not to the Treaty of Erzurum which was signed on 28 July 1823.

1 May, 1822): 'The two sons[362] of the Schah of Persia,[363] in consequence of the death of their father,[364] had raised the seige of Bagdad, and were now contending who had the best right to the throne. Letters from Constantinople speak confidently of peace having been concluded with the Persians.'

10.172 'Latest from England,' *Oswego Palladium* (Friday, 26 April, 1822): ['New York, April 12. By the arrival of the regular packet ship Columbia, Capt. Rogers, in 37 days from Liverpool, we have received our files of London and Liverpool papers to the 3d of March....Nothing farther has transpired in relation to the affairs of Russia and Turkey....The war in Persia, it was asserted, had not been terminated, and, we shall not know what the final determination of Russia may be until the spring.'

10.173 'Untitled,' *Washington Whig* (Monday, 29 April, 1822): 'The Persians continue their war against the Porte, and it is supposed is entering into an alliance with the Russians against them.'

10.174 'Forign Articles. From Niles' Weekly Register, March 30,' *The Arkansas Gazette* (Tuesday, 7 May, 1822): 'Constantinople was tranquil on the 11th Jan. but the prospect of an adjustment with Russia remained as uncertain as ever. A report prevailed that the Persians has [sic] ceased hostilities, and made peace with the Turks. The cholera morbus was raging dreadfully at Bagdat—1000 persons were carried off by it in a few days.'

10.175 'Foreign News,' *The Geneva Gazette* (Wednesday, 8 May, 1822): 'The Shah of Persia[365] is dead. His two sons besieging Bagdad had raised the siege, and repaired to Persia to contend for the throne.'[366]

10.176 'Rusia [sic],' *Lexington Gazette* (after 11 May, 1822), 'Untitled,' *The Albany Argus* (after 27 May, 1822) and 'Latest from Europe,' *The Pilot* (Thursday, 30 May, 1822): 'The Court of Persia, it is mentioned refuses to make peace with Turkey unless Armenia is ceded to the Schah.[367] Rusia [sic] is said to have made a treaty with Persia, a secret article of which assures to the Schah the possessions of Armenia, as soon as the Turks shall be expelled from it.'

---

[362] Mohammad 'Ali Mirza (already deceased) and 'Abbas Mirza.

[363] Fath 'Ali Shah.

[364] A false rumor. Fath 'Ali Shah did not die until 1834, and of his two sons—Mohammad 'Ali Mirza and 'Abbas Mirza—only the former attacked Baghdad.

[365] Fath 'Ali Shah.

[366] Everything here is incorrect. Fath 'Ali Shah did not die; and Mohammad 'Ali Mirza succumbed to cholera; hence, he did not contest the throne with his brother 'Abbas Mirza.

[367] Fath 'Ali Shah.

10 From 1816 to the End of the Turco-Persian War (1816–1825)

10.177 'Foreign Intelligence. Russia & Turkey,' *The Long Island Farmer* (Thursday, 23 May, 1822): 'An article in the Austrian Observer, of the first April, says, "It is thought that the Russians will attempt a descent in the immediate neighbourhood of Constantinople, as the least expensive, and perhaps the only means of reaching that capital. The Russian army has still its great magazines at Kalouga,[368] above 200 leagues from Odessa. The struggle between the Russian and Diplomatic Agents at the Courts of Persia, is extremely spirited."'

10.178 'Latest from Europe,' *National Advocate* (Wednesday, 5 June, 1822): 'It is remarkable, that notwithstanding so many rumours, and so much disquietude relative to a war in Europe, the Porte, up to this moment, has made no preparations either by sea or land which would lead to the expectation of such a war. The military measures at Constantinople are exclusively directed against the Greek insurgents on the one hand, and against the Persians on the other. The armament against Persia has had this happy result, that the capital has been suddenly cleared of a great number of turbulent spirits, discontented Janissaries, and other evil-minded persons, inclined to every species of excess.'

10.179 'Russia and Turkey,' *The Long Island Farmer* (Thursday, 6 June, 1822): 'Our accounts from Constantinople are of the 27th March....Notwithstanding the numerous statements of an opposite tendency, it now appears that the differences between the Porte and Persia have not been adjusted. The negotiations with the Court of Teheran are stated to have been broken off, and the Schah[369] had set out in person with a large army to enter Asiatic Turkey. The army commanded by the eldest son[370] of Prince Ali,[371] who died last year, it is added, had commenced hostilities with the Pacha of Bagdad.[372]—Much obscurity, however, exists as to the actual state of matters between the two powers.'

---

[368] According to Anonymous (1822e), 'The *Leipsic Gazette* of the 30th ult. [March, 1822] contains the following article:—"Orders have been given in Russia for the formation of an army of reserve to assemble in the environs of Kalugâ [Russia], and for the establishment of very considerable magazines. The reserve of artillery will also be established at Kaluga, until a new destination be given to it. The army of the expedition against the Turks will be carried, if the war should break out, to 250,000 men.'

[369] Fath 'Ali Shah.

[370] Mohammad Hoseyn Mirza, 'un prince faible et pusillanime, toujours au milieu de ses femmes, et gouverné par un mauvais ministre.' See Belge (1829: 353). Cf. Bran (1829: 461). Keppel (1827/2: 24) met him *en route* from India to England in 1824. At the time Devaux was still employed by the prince. As for Hasan Khan, the 'mauvais ministre' who controlled Mohammad Hoseyn Mirza, he was described by Keppel (1827/2: 53–54) as blind and 'about sixty years of age.'

[371] Mohammad 'Ali Mirza.

[372] Daud Pasha.

10.180 'Russia and Turkey,' *Plattsburgh Republican* (Saturday, 8 June, 1822): 'The Algemeine Zietung [sic, Allgemeine Zeitung], a paper of great political note, states.... Persia will formally declare war against the Sultan.'[373]

10.181 'Foreign News. From the New-York Daily Advertiser,' *Connecticut Journal* (Monday, 1 July, 1822), 'From England,' *The Nantucket Inquirer* (Tuesday, 2 July, 1822), 'From the N.Y. Daily Advertiser,' *Hampden Federalist and Public Journal* (Wednesday, 3 July, 1822), 'Foreign. Affairs of Greece,' *Hampshire Gazette* (Wednesday, 3 July, 1822), 'Foreign News. From the New-York Daily Advertiser,' *Farmers' Weekly Messenger* (Monday, 8 July, 1822) and 'Untitled,' *Louisiana Courier* (Monday, 29 July, 1822): 'Intelligence from Constantinople, states that the Sultan[374] had not ratified the treaty concluded between the Pacha of Bagdad[375] and the Prince Kerman Shah,[376] and had sent 14,000 men against the Persians.'

10.182 'Foreign Intelligence. Turkey,' *The Freeman's Journal* (Monday, 8 July, 1822): 'On the 3d of April war was expected at Constantinople, and 14,000 troops had been recently sent into Asia, from whence it was inferred that war with Persia also, was not impossible. The Sultan[377] had not ratified the treaty concluded between the Pacha of Bagdad[378] and the Prince Kerman Shah.'[379]

10.183 'Untitled,' *New-York Evening Post* (Saturday, 13 July, 1822): 'Accounts from the Turkish frontiers assert that Persia insists upon the cession of Armenia; but that the Porte avoids giving any reply, in the hope that existing differences may be adjusted, through the mediation of England.'[380]

---

[373] Mahmud II.
[374] Mahmud II.
[375] Daud Pasha.
[376] Mohammad 'Ali Mirza.
[377] Mahmud II.
[378] Daud Pasha.
[379] Mohammad 'Ali Mirza.
[380] As Baddeley (1908: 147–148) noted, after Mazarovich had incited 'Abbas Mirza to go to war with Turkey, 'England...intervened with decisive effect. Her emissary found his way to Abbas Mirza's camp, and succeeded in persuading the latter that Russia was not in a position to declare war against Turkey without the consent of the European Powers, who in this matter were at one with England. The prospect of fighting Turkey single-handed, against the will of both England and Russia, alarmed the Persian prince, or, at least, his advisers, and the Persian army retired to its own side of the border.' This did not occur, however, until the campaigns described above against Bayazid and Van had been conducted.

10.184 'Seven Days Later from England. Persia,' *Centinel of Freedom* Tuesday, 16 July, 1822), 'From the New-York Commercial Advertiser. Persia,' *Rhode-Island American, and General Advertiser* (Tuesday, 16 July, 1822), 'Seven Days Later from England. Persia,' *New-York Spectator* (Tuesday, 16 July, 1822), 'Seven Days Later from England. New-York July 13. Persia,' *The Alexandria Herald* (Wednesday, 17 July, 1822), 'Latest from Europe. Persia,' *Rhode-Island Republican* (Wednesday, 17 July, 1822), 'New York July 13. Seven Days Later from England. Persia,' *Alexandria Gazette* (Wednesday, 17 July, 1822), 'Summary of News. Foreign. Persia,' *Religious Intelligencer* (Friday, 19 July, 1822), 'Foreign Intelligence. Seven days later from England. Persia,' *The Berks and Schuylkill Journal* (Saturday, 20 and 27 July, 1822), 'Foreign News. Received at New York, by the last arrivals. Persia,' *Washington Whig* (Monday 22 July, 1822), 'Foreign Intelligence. NewYork July10. Late from England. Persia,' *The Watch-Tower* (Monday 22 July, 1822), 'Persia,' *The Delaware Gazette* (Wednesday, 24 July, 1822), 'Persia,' *Onondaga Register* (Wednesday, 24 July, 1822), 'Intelligence, Foreign and Domestic. Seven days later from England. New York July 13. Persia,' *North Star* (Thursday, 25 July, 1822) and 'From the N. York Commercial Adv. July 13. Latest from England,' *Washington Reporter* (Monday, 29 July, 1822): 'It is asserted, in advices from the Turkish frontiers, that the Persians insist upon the cession of Armenia, but that the Porte had avoided giving any reply, in the hope that existing differences might be adjusted through the mediation of England. According to other accounts, said to rest on good authority, the Porte had ordered the Pacha of Bagdad[381] to continue the war with Persia, and not to listen to any proposals for peace.'

10.185 'From the Baltimore Morning Chronicle, July 15,' *The Freeman's Journal* (Monday, 29 July, 1822) and 'From the Baltimore Morning Chronicle, July 15,' *The Delaware Gazette* (Wednesday, 31 July, 1822): 'The last intelligence from the European continent, presents us with nothing so far as regards the Turks and the Russians, but a political chequer board of contraditions.—We meet alternately with the words peace and war, displayed alternately along in column after column, so that we are left to take which rumour we please, all which serves to show the profound and impenetrable mystery with which the negociation has been conducted.—Facts, however, are not such equivocal evidences....Whatever the English writers may say on this subject, and however they may affect to disbelieve the probability of a war, their own ministry know better—France knows better—Germany knows better—or why are all these powers exerting their confederated strength, to *prevent* the Russian monarch from entering into this war? They have couriers, employed by all these parties at Saint Petersburgh, and why is every effective engine short of the sword's point, exerted by themselves to defeat the plans of the Russian monarch?[382] Why have they not all been enabled to obtain from the Russian

---

[381] Daud Pasha.
[382] Alexander I.

Monarch, an explicit declaration, that war was not his object? The answer to all this, is, why does Alexander delay? To this we reply, that we know not—perhaps he is providing funds—perhaps magazines—perhaps, and he evidently is, stimulating the Persian court, to become a party with him in this war. He may have a thousand motives for delay, of which we on this side of the Atlantic know nothing, and yet be firmly resolved upon war.'

10.186 'Foreign Articles. New-York, June 27,' *The Arkansas Gazette* (Tuesday, 20 August, 1822): 'It is said that the Sultan[383] has refused to ratify the treaty between the Pacha of Bagdad[384] and the Prince Kerman Shah,[385] and that he has sent 14,000 men against the Persians.'

10.187 'Latest from England,' *Boston Daily Advertiser* (Wednesday, 28 August, 1822), 'Latest from England,' *Boston Weekly Messenger* (Thursday, 29 August, 1822), 'Foreign News,' *New-York Evening Post* (Friday, 30 August, 1822), 'From England,' *The Alexandria Herald* (Monday, 2 September, 1822), 'From England,' *New-York Spectator* (Tuesday, 3 September, 1822) and 'New-York, August 30. From England,' *Charleston Courier* (Monday, 9 September, 1822): 'There are some contradictory accounts of the progress of hostilities between the Turks and Persians. It is said that the Persians are advancing in Armenia, and threaten Kars and Erzerum. On the other hand it is stated that the Turks have gained a great victory in the Pashalick of Bagdard [sic, Baghdad] and have retaken Suleimaniah.'

10.188 'Russia and Turkey. Constantinople, June 11,' *National Advocate* (Wednesday, 28 August, 1822), 'Constantinople, June 11,' *Baltimore Patriot & Mercantile Advertiser* (Thursday, 29 August, 1822), 'Constantinople, June 11,' *Washington Whig* (Monday, 2 September, 1822), 'Constantinople, June 11,' *Richmond Enquirer* (Tuesday, 3 September, 1822), 'Constantinople, June 11,' *Dutchess Observer* (Wednesday, 4 September, 1822), 'Constantinople, June 11,' *Republican Chronicle* (Wednesday, 4 September, 1822), 'From France. From the New-York American of the 26th inst.,' *Daily Georgian* (Saturday, 7 September, 1822), 'Foreign. From the New York Commercial Advertiser of August 28. Five days later from England. Constantinople, June 11,' *Republican Gazette and General Advertiser* (Saturday, 7 September, 1822) and 'Foreign Articles. Constantinople, June 11,' *Vermont Journal* (Monday, 23 September, 1822): 'It is said that the Persians have gained a battle near Erzerum, where 3 Pachas, among whom is the Pacha of Trebisond, have been made prisoners. . . . The battle against the Persians, renders the

---

[383] Mahmud II.
[384] Daud Pasha.
[385] Mohammad 'Ali Mirza.

whole of this news suspicious: for it is the thirtieth time, at least, within these six months, that this battle has been talked of.'[386]

10.189 'From Niles' Weekly Register of July 20,' *The Arkansas Gazette* (Tuesday, 3 September, 1822): 'It now seems that the Persians are still, but feebly, prosecuting the war against the Turks in Asia—and advancing slowly.'

10.190 'Postscript. Latest from England. From the London Courier, July 30,' *National Advocate* (Friday, 6 September, 1822) and 'From the London Courier, July 30,' *The Hampden Patriot and Liberal Recorder* (Wednesday, 11 September, 1822): 'Letters from Constantinople were received in town [London] yesterday morning, which give a variety of versions of an engagement said to have taken place in the neighbourhood of Bagdad, between the Turkish troops under the command of the Viceroy of Bagdad,[387] and the Persians, in which the latter are stated to have been completely routed. The accounts are extremely confused and contradictory, but it seems quite certain that an engagement has taken place, in which the Turks were decidedly the victorious party; the number of killed and wounded, however, on either side, does not appear to have been very great.'

10.191 'Untitled,' *American Advocate & General Advertiser* (Saturday, 7 September, 1822): 'The Persians and Turks are again said to be engaged in hostilities.'

10.192 'From the Commercial Advertiser of Friday. Six days later from England. London, 29 July,' *Centinel of Freedom* (Tuesday, 10 September, 1822), 'Late from England. London, July 29,' *Daily National Intelligencer* (Tuesday, 10 September, 1822), 'London, July 29,' *New-York Spectator* (Tuesday, 10 September, 1822), 'London, July 29,' *City Gazette and Commercial Daily Advertiser* (Monday, 16 September, 1822), 'Foreign. From the New York Commercial Advertiser, of September 6. Six days later from England. London, July 29,' *Washington Whig* (Monday, 16 September, 1822), 'Latest from England,' *Ontario Repository* (Tuesday, 17 September, 1822), 'London, July 29,' *Saratoga Sentinel* (Tuesday, 17 September, 1822) and 'London, July 29,' *Vermont Gazette* (Tuesday, 17 September, 1822): 'Advices have been received from Constantinople, which asserts that an important victory had been obtained by the Turks, under the command of the Pacha of Bagdad,[388] over the Persian troops, a short distance from Bagdad. The victory is

---

[386] According to Brosset (1857: 320), in the spring of 1822, 'Le chah Baba-Khan [Fath 'Ali Shah] ayant recommencé la guerre contre Bagdad et l'Anatolie, les armées persanes vinrent à Erzroum et furent attaquées par les Ottomans. Dans un grand combat qui eut lieu, ils tuèrent trois pachas, ceux de Cars, d'Erzroum et de Trébisonde.'

[387] If this does not refer to Daud Pasha himself, it may refer to Haji Talib Agha, Mohammad Agha's successor as Daud Pasha's deputy, who enjoyed some success against the Persian forces of Mohammad Hoseyn Mirza. See Longrigg (1925: 246).

[388] Daud Pasha.

said to have been complete, the Persians being compelled to retire, with the loss of 4000 men killed, and 700 prisoners. The Prince of Persia[389] was at Erzerum. A strong fortress had been taken by the Turkish troops. This news must be received with some hesitation.'

10.193 'Foreign,' *Hampshire Gazette* (Wednesday, 11 September, 1822): 'It was reported that a battle had been fought between the Turks and Persians, near Bagdad, in which the Persians were defeated with a loss of 4000 killed and 700 prisoners.'

10.194 'London, July 29,' *Norwich Courier* (Wednesday, 11 September, 1822): 'Letters from Constantinople mention that a victory had been obtained by the Turks over the Persians in the vicinity of Bagdad. The loss of the latter is stated to be 4000 men killed, and 700 prisoners. There had also been a fortress captured by the Turks. The Prince of Persia was at Azium [sic, Erzurum].'

10.195 'New-York, Sept. 7. From Europe,' *New-Bedford Mercury* (Friday, 13 September, 1822), 'New-York, September 7. From Europe,' *Rhode-Island American, and General Advertiser* (Friday, 13 September, 1822), 'Latest from Europe. New York, Sept. 7,' *Boston Recorder* (Saturday, 14 September, 1822) and 'Foreign. New-York, Sept. 7. From Europe,' *New-Hampshire Repository* (Monday, 16 September, 1822): 'The Turkish army in Bagdad was reported to have gained a complete victory over the Persians who were besieging that city, killing 4000, and making 700 prisoners.'

10.196 'Foreign News. From the London papers of the 24th July. Turks and Greeks,' *Western Herald & Steubenville Gazette* (Saturday, 21 September, 1822): 'Many Turkish troops are arriving at Smyrna from the interior of the Asiatic provinces...It seems that the Persians are still at war with the Turks, and it is reported that they have lately gained a battle near Erzerum.'

10.197 'Europe,' *The Plattsburgh Republican* (Saturday, 28 September, 1822): 'Paris, July 22....Extract of a letter from St. Petersburgh:—"For some time there has been a very active correspondence between Sir Charles Bagot, the British Ambassador to our Court,[390] and H. Willock, esq. His Britannic Majesty's Charge d'Affaires, at the Court of Persia. Frequent dispatches are likewise received by Sir Charles from Lord Strangford.[391] The communications of his excellency Sir Charles to Count Nesselrode[392] are continual."'

---

[389] 'Abbas Mirza.

[390] Sir Charles Bagot (1781–1843) was British ambassador to Russia at this time (1820–1824).

[391] Percy Clinton Sydney Smythe, sixth Viscount Strangford (1780–1855), British ambassador to the Ottoman Porte (1820–1824).

[392] Karl Robert Reichsgraf von Nesselrode-Ehreshoven (1780–1862), Foreign Minister of the Russian Empire. For the record of his ministry at this time see Nesselrode (1904/6).

10 From 1816 to the End of the Turco-Persian War (1816–1825)

10.198 'Late Foreign News,' *The Lyons Advertiser* (Wednesday, 2 October 1822), 'Latest from Europe,' *The New-York Statesman* (Wednesday, 2 October 1822), 'New-York, Oct. 3. Latest from Europe,' *The Emporium* (Saturday, 5 October, 1822; 'French paper says'), 'Latest from Europe,' *Connecticut Mirror* (Monday, 7 October, 1822; 'French paper says'), 'Late Arrivals from Europe. New-York, Oct. 3,' *Connecticut Herald* (Tuesday, 8 October, 1822) and *The Ontario Repository* (Tuesday, 8 October, 1822), 'From the New-York Statesman. Latest from Europe,' *Vermont Gazette* (Tuesday, 15 October, 1822) and 'New-York, October 2,' *The Arkansas Gazette* (Thursday, 26 November, 1822): 'A French paper asserts, that the English ambassador, at the court of Persia, had demanded his passports and left that residence.'[393]

10.199 'Untited,' *National Advocate* (Thursday, 3 October, 1822), 'From the New York Commercial Advertiser. Four days later from England,' *Baltimore Patriot & Mercantile Advertiser* (Friday, 4 October, 1822), 'European News,' *New-York American* (Saturday, 5 October, 1822), 'Latest Foreign News. From the N.Y. Commercial Advertiser, Oct. 2,' *American Watchman and Delaware Advertiser* (Tuesday, 8 October, 1822), 'From the National Advocate. Europe,' *The Dutchess Observer* (Wednesday, 9 October, 1822), 'Foreign News. New York, Oct. 2,' *The Supporter, and Scioto Gazette* (Wednesday, 16 October, 1822), 'Latest from England. New York, Oct. 4,' *Milton Gazette and Roanoke Advertiser* (Thursday, 17 October, 1822): 'The English Ambassador at the Court of Persia,[394] is stated in the Paris papers to have demanded his passports and left that residence.'

10.200 'Latest from England,' *National Advocate* (Thursday, 31 October, 1822): 'Reports proceeding from Constantinople say, that the Pacha of Bagdad[395] has defeated the Persians; but nobody can tell where the battle took place.'

10.201 'Extract of a letter from a gentleman in Russia, to the Intrepid in Portland, dated Cronstadt, Aug. 1,' *The Albany Argus* (Thursday, 19 November, 1822) and 'Extract of a letter from a gentleman in Russia, to the Intrepid in Portland, dated Cronstadt, Aug. 1,' *The Freeman's Journal* (Monday, 25 November, 1822): 'Yesterday, the Emperor Alexander arrived at this place [Kronstadt].[396] The Commandant wished for 2 ships, the one English, the other American, to lie off the Mole head with the yards manned to give the great man

---

[393] Henry Willock, *chargé d'affaires* at the Court of Persia. Cf. his letter to Lord Londonderry, in which he described how 'Abbas Mirza threatened him with death unless he advanced him funds to cover a gambling debt, whereupon Willock wrote to say he could no longer perform his duties in Persia and had therefore determined to leave the country. See Willock (1822).

[394] Henry Willock.

[395] Daud Pasha.

[396] A major ship-building center with the Imperial Naval Academy and brisk commercial shipping traffic. See Willcocks (1832: 107, 333).

three cheers. The St. Peter, Capt. Holland, of Boston was selected for the Americans. The yards being manned, with the crews of other ships, the sailors sung out bravely *hurra* for the Emperor. Alexander, in his boat, took off his cap, and gave three cheers in return. Among the distinguished personages who visited the St. Peter, while in port, was the Persian Ambassador.'[397]

10.202 'Greece,' *Baltimore Patriot & Mercantile Advertiser* (Sunday, 22 November, 1822), 'Postscript. Latest from England. Greece,' *New-York Spectator* (Sunday, 22 November, 1822), 'Latest from Europe. Constantinople, Sept. 6,' *Daily National Intelligencer* (Monday, 23 November, 1822), 'Greece,' *The Alexandria Herald* (Monday, 25 November, 1822), 'Constantinople, Sept. 6,' *American Mercury* (Monday, 25 November, 1822), 'Foreign Intelligence. From the N. York Commercial Advertiser. Latest from Europe. Greece,' *Alexandria Gazette* Tuesday, 26 November, 1822), 'Foreign Intelligence. Latest from England. Greece,' *Centinel of Freedom* (Tuesday, 26 November, 1822), 'Foreign. Greece,' *Portland Gazette* Tuesday, 26 November, 1822), 'Foreign Intelligence. Constantinople, Sept. 6,' *The Repertory* Tuesday, 26 November, 1822), 'Greece,' *Saratoga Sentinel* (Tuesday, 26 November, 1822), 'Constantinople, Sept. 6,' *Connecticut Gazette,* 'From the N.Y. Commercial Advertiser. Turks & Persians,' *Hampshire Gazette* (Wednesday, 27 November, 1822), 'Latest from Europe. Greece,' *Providence Patriot* (Wednesday, 27 November, 1822), 'Constantinople, Sept. 6,' *Middlesex Gazette* (Thursday, 28 November, 1822), 'Constantinople, Sept. 6,' *Boston Weekly Messenger* (Thursday, 28 November, 1822), 'Foreign News. New-York, Nov. 23. Late from Europe. Greece,' *Newport Mercury* (Saturday, 30 November, 1822), 'Foreign. Turkey. Constantinople, Sept. 6,' *Portsmouth Journal of Literature and Politics* (Saturday, 30 November, 1822), 'Constantinople, Sept. 6,' *Vermont Journal* (Monday, 2 December, 1822), 'From Europe. From the N.Y. Commercial Advertiser,' *Washington Review and Examiner* (Monday, 2 December, 1822), 'Greece,' *The Watch-Tower* (Monday, 2 December, 1822), 'Foreign News. (By late arrivals at New-York.) Greece,' *The American Journal* (Wednesday, 4 December, 1822) and 'Foreign News. Latest from Europe. Greece,' *The Supporter, and Scioto Gazette* (Saturday, 7 December, 1822): 'On the 20th [of August or September, 1822] a considerable train of artillery, with a large supply of ammunition departed for Erzerum. In that quarter the Persians have recently obtained considerable advantages over the Turkish troops, commanded by Jalaladdin Pacha.[398]

---

[397] Mirza Saleh Shirazi. According to Anonymous (1822i), 'In Tchernigow [Chernigov, i.e. Chernihiv, in northern Ukraine] (1159 Werste von St. Petersburg) traf am 19. Juny [1822], auf der Straße von Ekatharinoslawl [Ekatarinoslav, mod. Dnipro, Ukraine], der persische Gesandte Mursa Selagio, ein und setzte denselben Tag seine Reise nach St. Petersburg fort, wo er seitdem auch angekommen ist.' Anonymous (1822j) reported, 'A St. Petersburg paper of July 20, has the following paragraphs...The Persian ambassador, Mizra Saleb [sic, Mirza Saleh], has arrived in this city.'

[398] Celaleddin Pasha, governor of Erzurum. See Ateş (2013: 50); Keçeci (2016: 151).

These advantages are the consequence of the defection of Selim Pacha, a Kurdish rebel, who, on the condition of receiving his pardon, had promised to join the Turkish army with 15,000 men, but who, instead of fulfilling his engagement, went over to the Persians.'[399]

10.203 'Postscript. By This Morning's Mail. Ten days later from Europe,' *Essex Register* (Monday, 23 November, 1822) and 'From Europe,' *Essex Patriot* (Monday, 30 November, 1822): 'The Persians had recently obtained considerable advantages over the Turks. Selim Pacha, with 15,000 men, had deserted from the Turks to the Persians.'

10.204 'From Madras,' *The Pilot* (Thursday, 28 November, 1822): 'Mr. Willock, the British Charge d'Affairs in Persia, had refused to pay the usual tribute, and demanded his passports. On their being refused he declared he should no longer act in a diplomatic capaciy: but leave the Court, unless forcibly detained. This produced a report, that there was a probability of a rupture between England and Persia. A good understanding is said to have been afterwards restored, and Mr. Willock left the Persian Court in an amicable manner, to proceed to England to consult his Government on an important point.'

10.205 'Foreign Summary,' *Village Register and Norfolk County Advertiser* (Friday, 29 November, 1822), 'Foreign. Latest from Europe,' *Connecticut Herald* (Tuesday, 3 December, 1822), 'Foreign Summary,' *Metropolitan* (Tuesday, 3 December, 1822) and 'Foreign Summary,' *Norwich Courier* (Wednesday, 4 December, 1822): 'The Persians are said to wage a successful war against the Turks, and to be joined by many deserters.'[400]

---

[399] Selim Pasha, *mütesellim* of Muş. See Ateş (2013: 50); Keçeci (2016: 148, 151); Koç (2021). Prior to defecting, however, he had led at least one successful attack on 'Abbas Mirza's forces. According to Anonymous (1822k), 'Selim Pacha, who commanded in Musch, had made an attack in the night on the Persian camp, on which occasion he took not only much booty, but many prisoners of distinction, who were expected soon to arrive at Constantinople.' In a document dated 29 August O.S. 1821, the Russian envoy Mazarovich noted, 'The Pacha of Moosh seduced from their allegiance to Persia the Hyderanloo and Sebekee Curds, and regardless of the obligations resulting from the amity of the two States [Turkey, Persia] afforded the protection. Hussun Khan who marched into Turkey for the purpose of bringing back these Tribes, and considered himself in the Territory of a friendly State was attacked by the troops of the Pacha of Moosh, and was placed under the necessity of defending himself. Selim Pacha derived no advantage from this attack, but the object is to shew that those who disturb the friendly relations of the two States are honoured and distinguished by the Turkish Government. The Pachas in reward for the opposition offered to Hussun Khan was created Sir Asker [*seraskar*].' See Costello (1967: 61, n. 28). For more on Selim Pasha see Jaba (1860: 44–45). According to Anonymous (1866a: 358), 'Salím Pasha, the Wali of Armenia, having surrendered to Abbás Mírza, was reappointed by him and his brother, Mohammed Beg, was intrusted with the command of 10,000 fresh horse, raised by the Persian prince.' According to Anonymous (1823d: 279), 'The Persians were subsequently joined by Selim Pacha, a Kurdish rebel, by whose aid they were enabled to obtain considerable advantages.'

[400] Amongst the 'deserters' were not merely Kurdish groups that switched sides periodically, but large numbers of Russians (*bagaderan*; see Williamson 2008: 96; Keçeci 2016: 202, n. 42) were in the

10.206 'Summary of News. Foreign,' *Boston Recorder* (Saturday, 30 November, 1822), 'Latest from England. Boston, Nov. 29,' *American Mercury* (Monday, 2 December, 1822), 'Boston, Nov. 28, 1822,' *The Times, and Weekly Adviser* (Tuesday, 3 December, 1822), 'Vienna, Oct. 3,' *The Alexandria Herald* (Wednesday, 4 December, 1822), 'Foreign Minutes,' *Connecticut Gazette* (Wednesday, 4 December, 1822), 'Foreign. Boston, Nov. 28. Latest from England,' *Rhode-Island Republican* (Wednesday, 4 December, 1822), 'Foreign. Latest from England,' *Bangor Register* (Thursday, 5 December, 1822) and 'Intelligence, Foreign and Domestic. Latest from England,' *North Star* (Thursday, 5 December, 1822): 'The Hamburg papers, to the 12th of Oct. again assert the discomfiture of the Turks, in the Morea, and its consequent evacuation by them. The loss of 50,000

---

service of 'Abbas Mirza, who had been sent as a 15 year old to fight the Russians. 'Ce fut à cette époque que le Roi [Fath 'Ali Shah] envoya en Azerbidjan son second fils Abas-Mirza, quoique fort jeune encore, pour diriger les opérations militaires, et dès ce moment tout prit une face nouvelle. Le prince mit le plus d'ordre possible parmi les soldats irréguliers, qui étaient pour ainsi dire les seuls dont il pouvait disposer. Il accueillit tous les déserteurs russes, les chargea de former plusieurs corps et d'exercer les hommes.' See Drouville (1819: 96). By the time of Gardane's mission, Tancoigne (1820: 316–317) noted, 'Abbas Mirza has incorporated about one hundred and fifty Russian deserters, with his own troops, and also a major of that nation. He required that they should be subjected to the same discipline, and adopt the French tactics.' During the years 1817–1820, for example, Ker Porter (1821/2: 588) noted 'a grenadier battalion, consisting of 800 men, formed of Russian deserters from the different military posts along the northern frontier. The officers of this body are all either Georgians, or made from Russian under-officers also deserters.' Mazarovich wrote to Ermolov on 18 December 1820, 'nos soldats désertent plus que jamais.' See Baddeley (1908: 311). On 20 June 1824 Keppel (1827/2: 169–170) remarked, 'we reached Aher, a fortified town, commanded by Yusuf Khan and garrisoned by three thousand Persians who are organized on the European millitary system, by Russian deserters, fifty-seven of whom are at present in the town. One of them told me that the greater part of his countrymen had been here since the battle of Kertch, which took place in 1812, when the Persians gained a vitory over the Russians on the banks of the Araxes.' In 1828, near the end of the Second Russo-Persian War, Armstrong (1831: 112), that at Tabriz, 'There is a battalion of Russian deserters, commanded by their own officers, in the service of Abbas Mirza. . . .Their ranks will be greatly increased on their return, by the numbers who daily flock here from the army now in Turkey.' As Kneip (1976: 55–56) observed, 'One of the most vexing problems confronting the tsarist authorities in Georgia was the army's steady loss of men through desertion. Conditions of service were difficult in the Caucasus; over the years a sizeable number of Russian soldiers had fled to Persia, attracted there by easier conditions of life and the chance to earn relatively good pay as military instructors. Abbas Mirza had long recognized the value of Russia's well-trained veterans: the most combat-worthy unit in his army at this time was the elite "Russian battalion," which had been organized entirely out of deserters and prisoners-of-war by an ex-sergeant major of the Nizhnii Novgorod Dragoons named Samson Iakovlev Makintsev. . . .A provision calling for the return of all prisoners-of-war and deserters was included in the Treaty of Gulistan, but all attempts at implementation had been to no avail, since the Persians were unwilling to part with such experienced veterans.' Some years later Sheil (1838: 55) noted, 'Selmás is. . .home for many of the Russian deserters in the service of Persia. Here they marry and settle when they are worn out and unfit for service and form a sort of colony.' Cf. Atkin (1980: 106–107); Cronin (2012); Keçeci (2016: 201–202, n. 42). In addition, deserters from the Ottoman forces are also attested. See 10.224.

10 From 1816 to the End of the Turco-Persian War (1816–1825)

Turks in killed and prisoners, is also mentioned as having taken place in the vicinity of Thebisand,[401] in a conflict with the Persians.'

10.207 'Text of a letter from Smyrna, Sept. 30,' *National Advocate* (Tuesday, 10 December, 1822), 'The Greeks,' *New-York Spectator* (Tuesday, 10 December, 1822), 'The Greeks,' *Daily National Intelligencer* (Thursday, 12 December, 1822), 'The Greeks,' *Baltimore Patriot & Mercantile Advertiser* (Friday, 13 December, 1822), 'The Greeks,' *Newport Mercury* (Saturday, 14 December, 1822), 'From the N.Y. Spectator, Dec. 9. The Greeks,' *Vermont Gazette* (Tuesday, 17 December, 1822), 'New-York, Dec. 9. The Greeks,' *City Gazette and Commercial Daily Advertiser* (Wednesday, 18 December, 1822), 'The Greeks,' *Augusta Chronicle and Georgia Advertiser* (Saturday, 21 December, 1822) and 'New-York, Dec. 9. Latest from England. The Greeks,' *Painesville Telegraph* (Wednesday, 25 December, 1822): 'it appears, that the Persians had defeated the Ottoman army of 12,000 men, and were actually near Erzerum.'

10.208 'Extract of a letter from Smyrna, Sept. 30, 1822,' *Massachusetts Spy* (Wednesday, 11 December, 1822), 'Extract of a letter from Smyrna, Sept. 30, 1822,' *The National Gazette and Literary Register* (Thursday, 12 December, 1822), 'The Extract. Extract of a letter from Smyrna, Sept. 30, 1822,' *Alexandria Gazette* (Saturday, 14 December, 1822), 'The Greeks and Turks. Extract of a letter from Smyrna, Sept. 30, 1822, received in Boston,' *Providence Patriot* (Saturday, 14 December, 1822), 'The Extract. Extract of a letter from Smyrna, Sept. 30, 1822,' *New-Hampshire Repository* (Monday, 16 December, 1822), 'The Extract. Extract of a letter from Smyrna, Sept. 30, 1822,' *Albany Argus* (Tuesday, 17 December, 1822), 'Extract of a letter from Smyrna, Sept. 30, 1822,' *The Times, and Weeky Advertiser* (Tuesday, 17 December, 1822), 'Extract of a letter from Smyrna, Sept. 30, 1822,' *Connecticut Gazette*, 'The Extract. Extract of a letter from Smyrna, Sept. 30, 1822,' *The Hampden Patriot and Liberal Recorder* (Wednesday, 18 December, 1822), 'From the Boston Centinel. From Smyrna,' *Republican Advocate* (Wednesday, 18 December, 1822), 'By the Mails. The Greeks and Turks. Extract of a letter from Smyrna, Sept. 30, 1822, received in Boston,' *Rhode-Island Republican* (Wednesday, 18 December, 1822) and 'The Extract. Extract of a letter from Smyrna, Sept. 30,' *Republican Chronicle* (Wednesday, 25 December, 1822): 'We have news here from the Morea, that the Greeks have the upper hand of the Turks, and completely destroyed their army of 22,000 men near Corinth. Equal success has attended the Persians, who are actually near Erzerum, after defeating the Turkish troops 12,000 in number. Such events cannot but prolong the termination of existing evils.'

10.209 'From London Papers. Received at the Office of the Commercial Advertiser,' *New-York Spectator* (Friday, 13 December, 1822): 'The Divan has not received any

---

[401] Trabzon, on the Black Sea coast of Turkey.

favourable news from Asia. It is now certain that the Persian army has conquered the greatest part of Armenia, but the Turks have still possession of Erzerum. Trebisond is also in their power. The Persians have made little progress on the side of Syria, so that the Pacha of Bagdad[402] has succeeded in protecting Bassora. It is, however, certain that the Turks have not acted on the offensive on any one point.'[403]

10.210 'Latest Foreign News. Greeks and Turks,' *New-Hampshire Sentinel* (Saturday, 14 December, 1822) and 'Latest Foreign News. Greeks and Turks,' *American Repertory & Advertiser* (Tuesday, 17 December, 1822): 'On the eastern side of the Turkish Empire, the Persians are said to have defeated the Turks, in a great battle.'

10.211 'Smyrna, Aug. 2. Persian Operations,' *American Federalist Columbian Centinel* (Saturday, 21 December, 1822), 'From the Boston Centinel. Persian Operations. Smyrna, Aug. 2,' *Hampshire Gazette* (Wednesday, 25 December, 1822), 'Persian Operations,' *New-Bedford Mercury* (Friday, 27 December, 1822), 'Smyrna, Aug. 2,' *Essex Patriot* (Saturday, 28 December, 1822), 'Persian Operations,' *New-York American* (Saturday, 28 December, 1822), 'Persian Operations,' *New-Hampshire Repository* (Monday, 30 December, 1822), 'Smyrna, Aug. 2. Persian operations,' *Vermont Journal* (Monday, 30 December, 1822), 'Persian Operations,' *The Charleston Mercury, and Morning Advertiser* (Tuesday, 31 December, 1822) and 'Persian Operations,' *The Southern Chronicle* (Wednesday, 8 January, 1823; scan cuts off at 'united to them those...'): 'It is now known, that the Persians have marched towards our Asiatic provinces, in three *corps d'armee*—one directed towards Erzerum; another towards Curdistan and Bassora; and the third towards Bagdad. It is presumed that the objects of two of these corps are the capture of Bassora and bagdad. Because, at two days march from the latter place are situated the tombs of *Ali*, and *Iman Hussein*,[404] the two most venerated Prophets [sic, martyrs] of the Persians; the

---

[402] Daud Pasha.

[403] As Longrigg (1925: 246) noted, 'Muḥammad 'Ali Mirza was succeeded by his son Muḥammad Ḥusain, whom revenge and ambition led to contemplate an invasion of 'Iraq on a large scale. Ḥaji Ṭalib had barely reached Zuhab when the Persian general, who had levied an army of 40,000, crossed the frontier at numerous points. At Mandali his forces massacred five hundred Turks [as noted above, in retaliation for a prior Turkish massacre of the garrison there]. Moving on Qizil Rubaṭ, he compelled the Kahya to give way. A conference of Turkish captains resolved on retreat; but the Persians, advancing into Shahroban and the Khaliṣ area, were simultaneously harassed by tribesmen, who cut up their scouts and burnt all crops on their line of march. A Shammar force eight hundred strong under Sufuk decoyed and then engaged and roundly defeated a large force of Persians—a feat soon copied by other tribal contingents. Cholera was again rife among the Persian troops. They retired, looting as they went. The frontier was crossed, the second invasion was finished and had failed.'

[404] 'Ali b. Abi Talib, the fourth Caliph and first Imam, a cousin and son-in-law of the Prophet Mohammad, was assassinated as he left the mosque at Kufa in 661; and his son Hoseyn was attacked and killed at Karbela in 680. 'Ali's tomb is at Najaf while Hoseyn's is at Karbela. Both became sites of pilgrimage, particularly for Iranian Shi'ites. See e.g. Petrushevsky (1985: 219–220). 'The tragedy

repossession of which by them, has long been desired. The mosques in which are these tombs are very rich, and becoming continually more so by the offerings which the Persians in their annual pilgrimages, bring to them. The Persians have long complained of being obliged to visit these tombs in a country under a foreign domination; and where these holy depositories of the treasures with which Persian Piety enriches them, enjoy but an equivocal protection, and precarious tenure. The Persians, therefore, though unquestionably urged to war by ambitious motives, unite to them those of a religious nature.

The Schah of Persia,[405] who leads one of his armies is considered a warlike monarch; and his son, Prince Arbas Myrza,[406] has great credit as a soldier. He is now heir apparent to the throne, his elder brother[407] having died at the time when hostilities ceased,[408] and brought the peace which the Grand Seignor[409] refused to ratify.'

10.212 'From the Philadelphia National Gazette, Dec. 20. Latest from Europe. Frontiers of Moldavia, Oct. 5,' *New-York Evening Post* (Saturday, 21 December, 1822), 'Latest from Europe. Frontiers of Moldavia, Oct. 5,' *New-York Daily Advertiser* (Monday, 23 December, 1822), 'Latest from Europe. Frontiers of Moldavia, Oct. 5,' *Alexandria Gazette* (Tuesday, 24 December, 1822), 'Latest and Interesting from Europe. Greece. Frontiers of Moldavia, Oct. 5,' *Daily National Intelligencer* (Wednesday, 25 December, 1822), 'Philadelphia, Dec. 20. Latest from Europe. Frontiers of Moldavia, Oct. 5,' *Dutchess Observer* (Wednesday, 25 December, 1822), 'Frontiers of Moldavia, Oct. 5,' *Essex Register* (Wednesday, 25 December, 1822), 'Frontiers of Moldavia, Oct. 5,' *Independent Chronicle and Boston Patriot* (Wednesday, 25 December, 1822), 'Frontiers of Moldavia, Oct. 5,' *Boston Commercial Gazette* (Thursday, 26 December, 1822), 'Frontiers of Moldavia, Oct. 5,' *Richmond Enquirer* (Friday, 27 December, 1822), 'Frontiers of Moldavia Oct. 5,' *Connecticut Gazette* (Wednesday, 1 January, 1823), 'Foreign. From England. Frontiers of Moldavia, Oct. 5,' *Bangor Register* (Wednesday, 1 January, 1822), 'From the N.Y. American. Latest from Europe. Greece,' *The Pilot* (Thursday, 2 January, 1823; from 'Selim Pacha'), 'Frontiers of Moldavia, Oct. 5,' *North Star* (Thursday, 2 January, 1823) and 'Frontiers of Moldavia, Oct. 5,' *Pittsfield Sun* (Thursday, 2 January,

---

of Kerbelā left a deep mark on contemporary Islam, and led the Shī'ites to make a regular cult of their third Imam, saint and marty, whose presumed tomb became a principal holy object and place of pilgrimage.' See Petrushevsky (1985: 37). The looting of the tombs by Wahhabi raiders in 1801 was reported on above. See 1802.3.

[405] Fath 'Ali Shah.

[406] 'Abbas Mirza.

[407] Mohammad 'Ali Mirza.

[408] 'Abbas Mirza was not named heir apparent as a result of the death of his elder half-brother, Mohammad 'Ali Mirza. He had been selected by his father to be his successor in 1799, largely because his mother was a high-born Qajar, whereas his elder brother's mother was a Georgian slave. See Busse (1982/2011).

[409] Mahmud II.

1823; 'latest' instead of 'last' letters): 'The last letters from Odessa confirm the account that Selim Pacha,[410] with 15,000 men, had gone over to the Persians; that several actions ensued, in which the Turks were totally defeated, and lost all their artillery.'

10.213 'Latest from Europe,' *National Advocate* (Monday, 23 December, 1822), 'From Europe,' *Providence Patriot* (Saturday, 28 December, 1822) and 'New-York, Dec. 23. Latest from Europe,' *American Mercury* (Tuesday, 31 December, 1822): 'to add to the Turkish reverses, Selim Pacha, with 15,000 men had joined the Persians, and every thing in that quarter was destructive to the prospects of the Turks.'

10.214 'Foreign News. Philadelphia, Dec. 21,' *Richmond Enquirer* (Tuesday, 24 December, 1822): 'Letters from Odessa confirm the accounts that Selim Pacha with 15,000 men had gone over to the Persians, and that several actions ensued in which the Turks were totally defeated.'

10.215 'Constantinople, Sept. 25,' *National Gazette and Literary Register* (Tuesday, 24 December, 1822), 'Constantinople, Sept. 25,' *Essex Register* (Saturday, 28 December, 1822), 'Constantinople, Sept. 25,' *Washington Whig* (Saturday, 28 December, 1822), 'Constantinople, Sept. 25,' *Massachusetts Spy* (Wednesday, 1 January, 1823), 'Constantinople, Sept. 25,' *Rhode-Island Republican* (Wednesday, 1 January, 1823), 'Constantinople, Sept. 25,' *Rochester Telegraph* (Monday, 6 January, 1823; from 'The news'), 'Constantinople, Sept. 25,' *Vermont Gazette* (Tuesday, 7 January, 1823) and 'Foreign Summary,' *The Supporter, and Scioto Gazette* (Saturday, 11 January, 1823): 'If the events of the Morea began to attract more attention, the news which the Porte has received from Mesopotamia and Armenia is still more afflicting for it, and has caused a great sensation among the Musselmen. The news bro't by the Couriers is, that on the 12th of Sept. the Turks, to the number of 50,000, had been defeated at Trebisond, and that the Persians had in consequence entered the town—that all Mesopotamia and the greater part of Armenia, were actually in their power, and that a Persian army was advancing in Anatolia; finally that the greater part of the towns of Armenia along the Black Sea, had revolted. If the Porte does not quickly succeed in making peace with Persia, the result of all these events may be very important.'

10.216 'Latest and Interesting from Europe,' *New-York Spectator* (Tuesday, 24 December, 1822), 'Latest and Interesting from Europe,' *The Schenectady Cabinet* (Wednesday, 25 December, 1822), 'Latest Foreign Intelligence,' *Essex Register* (Wednesday, 25 December, 1822), 'New York, Dec. 21. Latest and Interesting from Europe,' *Hampshire Gazette* (Wednesday, 25 December, 1822), 'From the New-York Commercial Advertiser of Saturday evening last. Latest and Interesting from Europe,' *Providence Patriot*

---

[410]Cf. 10.202, 10.203.

10 From 1816 to the End of the Turco-Persian War (1816–1825)   1023

(Wednesday, 25 December, 1822), 'New-York, Dec. 21. Late and Interesting from Europe,' *Rhode-Island Republican* (Wednesday, 25 December, 1822), 'Foreign Articles. London dates to Oct. 28 via Philadelphia. London, Oct. 26,' *Boston Commercial Gazette* (Thursday, 26 December, 1822), 'Untitled,' *Vermont Republican* (Monday, 30 December, 1822; first sentence only), 'Late and Interesting from Europe,' *Portland Gazette* (Tuesday, 31 December, 1822), 'From the Commercial Advertiser. Latest from Europe,' *The Rochester Telegraph* (Tuesday, 31 December, 1822), 'Foreign & Domestick News. New-York, Dec. 21. Latest and Interesting from England,' *Saratoga Sentinel* (Tuesday, 31 December, 1822), 'From the N. York Spectator, Dec. 24. Latest and Interesting from Europe,' *Vermont Gazette* (Tuesday, 31 December, 1822), 'Foreign News. Latest and Interesting from Europe,' *The American Journal* (Wednesday, 1 January, 1823), 'Intelligence, Foreign and Domestic. Latest and Interesting from Europe,' *North Star* (Thursday, 2 January, 1822), 'Foreign Articles. London, Oct. 26,' *Vermont Journal* (Monday, 6 January, 1823), 'Foreign Summary,' *The Supporter, and Scioto Gazette* (Saturday, 11 January, 1823) and 'New York, December 13,' *The Arkansas Gazette* (Thursday, 18 February, 1823): 'Fifteen thousand Turks are stated to have gone over to the Persians,[411] and that the latter had been successful in several engagements with the Ottoman troops. Great uneasiness prevailed at Constantinople, and the Sultan[412] had resorted to rigorous measures in order to obtain money, his treasury having become exhausted by the unexpected demands which the defeat of his armies had occasioned.'

10.217 'From England,' *American Federalist Columbian Centinel* (Wednesday, 25 December, 1822), 'From England,' *New-Hampshire Patriot & State Gazette* (Monday, 30 December, 1822) and 'From England,' *Connecticut Courant* (Tuesday, 31 December, 1822): 'Of the war between Turkey and Persia, the Greek accounts say, that the Persians, after beating the Turks in several battles, and taking their artillery, were joined by Selim Pasha, with 15,000 men. Most of the accounts from Asia Minor, &c. are not later than those received here [London] from Smyrna.'

10.218 'Hamburgh, Oct. 17,' *Essex Register* (Wednesday, 25 December, 1822), 'Hamburgh, Oct. 17,' *Independent Chronicle and Boston Patriot* (Wednesday, 25 December, 1822), 'Hamburgh, Oct. 17,' *Middlesex Gazette* (Thursday, 26 December, 1822), 'Constantinople, Sept. 20,' *Columbian Register* (Saturday, 28 December, 1822), 'Hamburgh, Oct. 14,' *New-Hampshire Gazette* (Tuesday, 31 December, 1822), 'Hamburgh, Oct. 17,' *North Star* (Thursday, 2 January, 1823) and 'Hamburg, Oct. 17,' *Pittsfield Sun* (Thursday, 2 January, 1823): 'Great uneasiness prevails here [Constantinople]; the Turks have been defeated by the Persians near Erzerum.'

---

[411] A reference to the troops of Selim Pasha who were Kurds, not Turks.
[412] Mahmud II.

10.219 'Russia and Turkey,' *Baltimore Patriot & Mercantile Advertiser* (Thursday, 26 December, 1822), 'Constantinople, Sept. 25,' *Middlesex Gazette* (Thursday, 26 December, 1822), 'Latest from England. Russia and Turkey,' *New-York Spectator* (Friday, 27 December, 1822), 'Russia and Turkey,' *Essex Register* (Saturday, 28 December, 1822; 'Russia'), 'Constantinople, Sept. 25,' *Columbian Register* (Saturday, 28 December, 1822), 'Foreign Items,' *Independent Chronicle and Boston Patriot* (Saturday, 28 December, 1822; with minor variations), 'Constantinople, Sept. 25,' *Centinel of Freedom* (Tuesday, 31 December, 1822), 'Constantinople, Sept. 25,' *Newburyport Herald* (Tuesday, 31 December, 1822), 'Constantinople, Sept. 25,' *The Times, and Weekly Adviser* (Tuesday, 31 December, 1822; from 'The Persians'), 'Constantinople, Sept. 25,' *Connecticut Gazette* (Wednesday, 1 January, 1823; from 'The Persians'), 'Latest from England. Turkey,' *Hampshire Gazette* (Wednesday, 1 January, 1823), 'Foreign Items,' *Providence Patriot* (Wednesday, 1 January, 1823), 'Russia and Turkey,' *Massachusetts Spy* (Wednesday, 1 January, 1823), 'Latest from Europe,' *Independent Statesman* (Thursday, 2 January, 1823), 'Constantinople, Sept. 25,' *New-Hampshire Intelligencer* (Friday, 3 January, 1823) 'Latest Foreign News,', *New-Bedford Mercury* (Friday, 3 January, 1823; with minor variations), 'Foreign. New York, Dec. 24. Latest from England. Russia and Turkey,' *Easton Gazette* (Saturday, 4 January, 1823), 'Constantinople, Sept. 25,' *New-Hampshire Sentinel* (Saturday, 4 January, 1823), 'From the New-York, Commercial Advertiser of December 24. Latest from England. Russia and Turkey,' *Washington Reporter* (Monday, 6 January, 1823), 'Foreign Intelligence. New-York, Dec. 27. Latest from England. Russia and Turkey,' *The Watch-Tower* (Monday, 6 January, 1823), 'Russia and Turkey,' *Vermont Gazette* (Tuesday, 7 January, 1823), 'Constantinople, Sept. 25,' *New-Hampshire Intelligencer* (Wednesday, 8 January, 1823) and 'Latest Foreign News. Russia and Turkey,' *Albany Argus* (Tuesday, 14 January, 1823): 'The latest accounts from Constantinople are of the 27th of Septem....The Persians had advanced on one side to Erzerum, and on the other to Salimanieh.[413] Bagdad defended itself with great vigour, but its capitulation was considered certain.'[414]

---

[413] Sulaimaniyah, in Iraqi Kurdistan.

[414] As Longrigg (1925: 246–247) summarized the constantly changing situation, 'in Shahrizor the death of Muḥammad 'Ali Mirza had restarted the tedious rivalries of the Baban family. Maḥmud Pasha, by a bold march and a costly battle, regained Sulaimaniyyah. Persian and Ardalan troops drove him from it. 'Abdullah, accepted for the moment by both Baghdad and Karmanshah, held the throne until Maḥmud, abandoning Turkish for Persian allegiance, replaced him with the consent of both. The mission of Aḥmad Beg, brother of Daud [Pasha], to assume the direct government of the State sent Maḥmud hot-foot to Persia, and brought Baghdad troops to Kirkuk. That they were accompanied by 'Abdullah Pasha—time after time the Persian candidate—cannot surprise students of these intrigues remarkable for the absence of any consistent loyalty, any human principle, any end but the crudest self-interest. Peace descended only when, by arrangement of the two powers, Maḥmud was restored to Sulaimaniyyah and 'Abdullah to Keui [Khoy].'

10 From 1816 to the End of the Turco-Persian War (1816–1825)   1025

10.220 'Smyrna, July 13,' *New-Bedford Mercury* (Friday, 27 December, 1822, omitting the second paragraph), 'Smyrna, July 13,' *New-York American* (Saturday, 18 December, 1822), 'Smyrna, July 13,' *New-Hampshire Repository* (Monday, 30 December), 'Smyrna, July 13,' *Vermont Journal* (Monday, 30 December), 'Smyrna, July 13,' *The Charleston Mercury, and Morning Advertiser* (Tuesday, 31 December, 1822), 'Smyrna, July 13,' *Independent Statesman* (Thursday, 2 January, 1823) and 'Smyrna, July 13,' *The Southern Chronicle* (Wednesday, 8 January, 1823): 'The accounts of the war operations on the side of Persia wear various phases. We have had reports of Turkish successes in some quarters; but it appears by the most authentic accounts, that the Persians have obtained some advantages on the side of Kars. There is no truth in the report, that the Persians have taken Erzerum. [This is an important city to the empire, being the capital of Armenia, and containing 270,000 souls. It is calculated to stand a long siege, having double walls round it, and being defended by square towers.] It is still reported, that the Persians have been beaten between Kermanshah and Sullimanieh, to the northeast of Bagdad.'

10.221 'Smyrna, Aug. 2,' *New-Bedford Mercury* (Friday, 27 December, 1822), 'Smyrna, Sept. 11,' *Village Register and Norfolk County Advertiser* (Friday, 27 December, 1822), 'Smyrna, August 2,' *New-York American* (Saturday, 28 December, 1822), 'Persian Operations,' *Essex Patriot* (Saturday, 28 December, 1822), 'Smyrna, Aug. 2,' *New-Hampshire Repository* (Monday, 30 December, 1822), 'Smyrna, Aug. 2,' *The Charleston Mercury, and Morning Advertiser* (Tuesday, 31 December, 1822), 'August 2,' *Independent Statesman* (Thursday, 2 January, 1823) and 'Smyrna, August 2,' *The Southern Chronicle* (Wednesday, 8 January, 1823): 'Advices from Constantinople confirm the accounts before received of a victory gained by the Turks over the Persians to the N.E. of Bagdad.'

10.222 'Latest from Europe,' *Rhode-Island American, and General Advertiser* (Friday, 27 December, 1822) and 'Latest from Europe,' *Newport Mercury* (Saturday, 28 December, 1822): 'The Turks are stated to have experienced great loss in their war with the Persians.'

10.223 'Summary of News. Foreign,' *Boston Recorder* (Saturday, 28 December, 1822): 'A Smyrna paper of July 13th, observes, that the account of the war operations on the side of Persia, wears various phases. We have had reports of Turkish success in some quarters; but it appears by the most authentic accounts, that the Persians have obtained some advantages. The probability is, that nothing decisive has been achieved on either side.'

10.224 'Foreign. Boston, Dec. 24. Latest from England,' *New-Hampshire Sentinel* (Saturday, 28 December, 1822) and 'Foreign News. From the Boston Palladium, Dec. 24,' *Connecticut Journal* (Monday, 30 December, 1822): 'The Porte is...unfortunate in its contest with the Persians, who are stated to have gained several important victories, and been strengthened by 15,000 deserters, including a Pacha.'[415]

10.225 'The Greeks,' *Western Herald & Steubenville Gazette* (Saturday, 28 December, 1822): 'the Persians are stated to have defeated a Turkish army of 12,000 men.'

10.226 'Smyrna Papers. Translated for the Boston Centinel from a file of Smyrna Papers, to September 28, 1822. War Between Turkey and Persia,' *New-York American* (Saturday, 28 December, 1822), 'Translated for the Boston Centinel from a file of Smyrna Papers, to September 28, 1822. War Between Turkey and Persia,' *The Charleston Mercury, and Morning Advertiser* (Tuesday, 31 December, 1822), 'Smyrna Papers. Translated for the Boston Centinel from a file of Smyrna Papers, to September 28, 1822. War Between Turkey and Persia,' *The Southern Chronicle* (Wednesday, 8 January, 1823): '[Remark.— The information on this topic has been loose and contradictory. The war was declared by Persia at a time when the affairs of the Porte and Russia were very threatening to the former. The Turkish governors of the provinces bordering on Persia were taken unawares; but they soon rallied a force sufficient to induced [sic] the Persians to propose a treaty of peace, in the negociation of which the Persian Schah[416] declared that the war and invasion were undertaken by his son,[417] without his knowledge or consent. The treaty was negociated by the Turkish Beglerbeg[418]; but the Grand Seignior[419] refused to ratify it, and the war has continued. Particulars follow: Advices from Constantinople confirm the accounts before received of a victory gained by the Turks over the Persians to the N.E. of Bagdad. Particulars follow:]

10.227 'Foreign. Rome, Oct. 12,' *Relf's Philadelphia Gazette, and Daily Advertiser* (Wednesday, 8 January, 1822), 'Foreign Intelligence. Rome, Oct. 12,' *Poulson's American Daily Advertiser* (Wednesday, 8 January, 1822), 'Foreign News. Translated for the N.Y. Daily Advertiser, from Paris papers. Rome, Oct. 12,' *Connecticut Journal* (Tuesday, 14 January, 1823) and 'Translated for the N.Y. Daily Advertiser, from Paris papers. Rome, Oct. 12,' *City Gazette and Commercial Daily Advertiser* (Thursday, 16 January, 1823): 'The Persians are making great exertions to reach the Black Sea, and to secure some port there for their subsequent operations.'

---

[415] Selim Pasha.

[416] Fath 'Ali Shah.

[417] 'Abbas Mirza.

[418] Mehmed Emin Rauf Pasha (1780–1859). Named in the 'Treaty of Peace between Turkey and Persia,' signed at Erzurum on 28 July 1823, as 'the Illustrious Mohammed Emin Raauf Pasha, Seraskier, Governor of Erzeroom, and *Wallee* (Lieutenant) of the Eastern Provinces of the Ottoman Empire.' See Hertslet (1891: 164). Previously he had served as Grand Vizir from 1815 to 1818. See Somel (2010: lxxxii).

[419] Mahmud II.

10 From 1816 to the End of the Turco-Persian War (1816–1825)

10.228 'Foreign Intelligence. Frontiers of Italy, Oct. 26,' *The Repertory* (Thursday, 16 January, 1823) and 'The Greeks. Frontiers of Italy, Oct. 26,' *Hampshire Gazette* (Wednesday, 22 January, 1823): 'Accounts have just been received that the Pacha of Egypt[420] recals [sic] his troops from Candia[421] to Alexandria.—Every thing seems to indicate that this extraordinary man has great undertakings in view, and is preparing every thing to put them in execution. He is again at variance with the Divan, because he has refused to send troops to Asia to support the Turks, and because he does not keep down the Wechabites,[422] whose Chiefs, in strict alliance with the Persians,[423] are preparing to issue from Arabia. The latest accounts from Alexandria affirm that Bagdad is closely besieged by the Persians, and cannot long hold out.—Nuremburgh Correspondent, Oct. 31.'

10.229 'Continuation of Foreign News,' *The Pilot* (Thursday, 23 January, 1823): 'Paris, Nov. 27 [1822]....In the course of October and during the first, couriers were dispatched to Teheran. Russia is actively cementing her relations with Persia.'[424]

10.230 'Odessa, Nov. 9,' *City Gazette and Commercial Daily Advertiser* (Saturday, 25 January, 1823): 'Accounts from Tifflis of 29th Sept. say, the Persians are negotiating with the Turks, and that the treaty of peace is on the point of being concluded. Col. Wright, of the English army,[425] lately passed through this country on his return from Persia. He brought the same intelligence, but as nothing is yet known of it at Constantinople, it does not appear to be certain.'

---

[420] Mehemet 'Ali Pasha (1769–1849). His career in Egypt ran from 1805 to 1848. See Fahmy (1998. Cf. 10.249).

[421] Heraklion, Crete.

[422] Wahhabis.

[423] No such alliance existed and the Wahhabis, who had sacked the Shi'ite shrines in southern Iraq in 1801, considered the Persians heretics.

[424] In 1823, Brosset (1857: 321) recorded that, 'Le chah Baba-Khan ayant envoyé à l'Empereur 15 chevaux, par Mahmad-Ali, un de ses khans.'

[425] George Wright. In 1818 'Lieut.col. Wright, of the royal engineers, is appointed to the command of the royal engineer department in the island of Ceylon' [Sri Lanka]. See Anonymous (1818d: 660). There he delivered several scientific papers on geological and meteorological topics to the Ceylon Literary Society. See Wright (1822a-b). This was presumably the 'Lieut. Col. Wright of the royal engineers, who lately came over land from India' bringing with him scientific samples (geological and botanical) from Persia. See Tilloch and Taylor (1823: 75) and Don (1832: 2). On 3 February 1824 the Linnæan Society received 'a collection of plants made in a journey through Circassia, Persia, and Georgia, by Lieut.-Col. Wright, of the Royal Engineers.' See Anonymous (1824d: 380). Lieut. Col. Wright was promoted to full Colonel on 29 July 1825. See Anonymous (1825e: 505). A notice from 1822 reported that 'A considerable number of new roads have been already completed in Ceylon, by the indefatigable exertions of Lieut.-Col. Wright, and the Officers of Royal Engineers in that island.' See Anonymous (1822c).

10.231 'Greece,' *City Gazette and Commercial Daily Advertiser* (Saturday, 25 January, 1823), 'Late from England,' *Alexandria Gazette* (Tuesday, 4 February, 1823) and 'Latest from England. Greece,' *Washington Review and Examiner* (Monday, 10 February, 1823): 'The reverses which the Turks have sustained in their engagements with the Persians must have a favourable influence on the future struggle of the Greeks; and, by dividing the attention and employing the troops of the Porte, will greatly increase the difficulty of collecting another army for the invasion of Greece.'

10.232 'Foreign News,' *New-York Evening Post* (Monday, 27 January, 1823)), 'Latest from Europe,' *National Advocate* (Monday, 27 January, 1823), 'From the National Advocate. Two Days Later from Europe,' *Dutchess Observer* (Wednesday, 29 January, 1823), 'Foreign Intelligence,' *The Repertory* (Thursday, 30 January, 1823), 'Latest from Europe,' *Independent Chronicle and Boston Patriot* (Saturday, 1 February, 1823), 'Paris, Dec. 7,' *New-Hampshire Patriot & State Gazette* (Monday, 3 February, 1823), 'Latest from Europe,' *American Repertory & Advertiser* (Tuesday, 4 February, 1823), 'Paris, Dec. 6,' *Connecticut Courant* (Tuesday, 4 February, 1823), 'Postscript,' *Nantucket Inquirer* (Tuesday, 4 February, 1823; with minor variations), 'Untitled,' *The Pilot* (Thursday, 6 February, 1823), 'Foreign Intelligence,' *Boston Weekly Messenger* (Thursday, 6 February, 1823) and 'Foreign. Paris, Dec. 6,' *American Advocate & General Advertiser* (Saturday, 8 February, 1823): 'Brussels Papers to the sixth inst. Have arrived this morning. It is stated, on the authority of letters from Tiffles, dated Sept. 20, that the Persians are negociating a treaty of peace with the Turks.'

10.233 'Postscript. By this morning's mail. From the Palladium. From Smyrna. Smyrna, Nov. 15,' *Salem Gazette* (Tuesday, 28 January, 1823), 'From the Boston Palladium. Smyrna, Nov. 15,' *National Advocate* (Friday, 31 January, 1823), 'From the Boston Palladium, Jan. 28. From Smyrna. Smyrna, Nov. 15,' *Baltimore Patriot & Mercantile Advertiser* (Saturday, 1 February, 1823), 'From Smyrna. Smyrna, Nov. 15,' *The Alexandria Herald* (Monday, 3 February, 1823) and 'From Smyrna. Boston, Jan. 28,' *Middlesex Gazette and General Advertiser* (Thursday, 6 February, 1823): 'According to the last news from Bagdad, the Persians were but 10 hours march from that city, upon which they advanced rapidly. They suffered some from the cholera morbus.'

10.234 'Two Days Later from England,' *New-York Spectator* (Tuesday, 28 January, 1823), 'New York, Jan. 27.—noon. Two Days Later from England,' *Baltimore Patriot & Mercantile Advertiser* (Wednesday, 29 January, 1823), 'Latest Foreign Intelligence. Received at New York by the ship Acasta, in 43 days from Liverpool,' *National Gazette* (Thursday, 30 January, 1823), 'Latest from England,' *The Alexandria Herald* (Friday, 31 January, 1823), 'Latest from Europe,' *Salem Gazette* (Friday, 31 January, 1823), 'Two Days Later from England,' *Alexandria Gazette* (Saturday, 1 February, 1823), 'Foreign News. New-York, Jan. 27. Latest from Europe,' *Newport Mercury* (Saturday, 1 February, 1823), 'Latest from England. New-York, January 27,' *Trenton Federalist* (Monday,

3 February, 1823), 'Two Days Later from England. New-York, Jan. 27,' *The Watch-Tower* (Monday, 3 February, 1823), 'From the New-York Spectator Jan 28. Latest and Important from Europe,' *Vermont Gazette* (Tuesday, 4 February, 1823) and 'New York, Jan. 27. Two Days Later from England,' *Hampshire Gazette* (Wednesday, 5 February, 1823): 'The Persians are stated/said to be negociating a treaty of peace with Turkey.'

10.235 'From the Boston Centinel,' *Newburyport Herald* (Friday, 31 January, 1823), 'From Europe,' *Haverhill Gazette, and Essex Patriot* (Saturday, 1 February, 1823), 'Foreign Intelligence. Latest from Europe. From Smyrna,' *New-Hampshire Repository* (Monday, 3 February, 1823), 'From Smyrna,' *Connecticut Courant* (Tuesday, 4 February, 1823) and 'From the Boston Centinel, Jan. 29. From Smyrna,' *Pittsfield Sun* (Thursday, 6 February, 1823): 'The war between Persia and Turkey continued active, and it was said the Persians were within a few hours march of Bagdad.'

10.236 'Revolutions,' *Oswego Palladium* (Friday, 31 January, 1823) and 'From the New-York Comm. Advertiser,' *Haverhill Gazette, and Essex Patriot* (Saturday, 1 February, 1823): 'Among the great Revolutions of the Ages, there is none more wonderful than that the modern Greeks and Persians should be employed in tearing to pieces the Turkish Empire....There is no instance in history of a great and learned nation, once "fallen from its high estate,"[426] that has resumed its ancient rank and character.—Persia makes the nearest approach to it, as it has long been gradually rising in the scale of Nations.'

10.237 'Latest Foreign News. The Greeks,' *Providence Patriot* (Saturday, 1 February, 1823) and 'Untitled,' *Bangor Register* (Thursday, February 6, 1823): 'The Persians were near Bagdad and advancing upon the city.'

10.238 'From Niles Register. Foreign News,' *St. Louis Enquirer* (Saturday, 1 February, 1823): 'The war with Persia still goes on—a Turkish army, of 50,000 men, had been defeated near Trebisond, which had been entered by the Persians, who are also said to be in possession of Mesopotamia, Armenia, &c. It was reported that they were advancing on Anatolia, and that many Turkish towns on the Black sea had revolted.'

10.239 'Twenty Days Later from England,' *New-York Spectator* (Tuesday, 11 February, 1823), 'Persia,' *The National Gazette and Literary Register* (Saturday, 13 February, 1823), 'Persia,' *The Long Island Farmer* (Saturday, 13 February, 1823), 'Persia,' *Providence Gazette* (Monday, 15 February, 1823), 'London, Dec. 29,' *American Mercury* (Thursday, 18 February, 1823; from 'By letters'), 'Persia,' *Vermont Gazette* (Thursday, 18 February,

---

[426] A popular phrase taken from John Dryden's (1631–1700) *Ode on St. Cecilia's Day* (IV.77–79), 'Fallen, fallen, fallen, fallen,/Fallen from its high estate,/And weltering in its blood!' This was said of the Achaemenid king Darius I (r. 522–486 BC). See Warton (1811: 340).

1823), 'Persia,' *Connecticut Gazette* (Friday, 19 February, 1823), 'Foreign. New-York, Feb. 10,' *Rhode-Island Republican* (Friday, 19 February, 1823; first sentence only), 'Persia,' *Haverhill Gazette, and Essex Patriot* (Monday, 22 February, 1823) and 'Persia,' *Washington Whig* (Monday, 22 February, 1823): 'Accounts through various channels, and even from Constantinople, concur in stating that the Persians have gained advantages over the Turks. By letters from Persia, dated Tabriz, 27th of August last [1822], it appears that on the first of July, the Persians, under the command of the Prince Royal,[427] marched from that city and attacked the Turks on the third of August, who in less than an hour, were completely defeated, with the loss of their tents and baggage, ten 4 pounders, two 12 pounders, one 14 pounder, one 16 pounder, and one mortar. The Persians pursued them to within two days march of Azzaroom,[428] which place would have fallen into their hands, but the *cholera morbus* afflicting the victorious troops, and fatigue rendering the disease mortal, the Prince Royal and his army returned to Tabriz with the spoils they had taken.'[429]

10.240 'From the New-York American,' *The Pilot* (Thursday, 20 February, 1823): 'Advices from the frontiers of Persia, state that the Pacha of Erzerum,[430] who had experienced some repulses, had been superseded, and that his successor,[431] endowed with greater capacity, after having re-established order in the Ottoman army, and received reinforcements, surprised a Persian camp and made himself master of it.'

10.241 'From the National Gazette. Foreign News,' *New-York Commercial Advertiser* (Saturday, 8 March, 1823), 'The Foreign News,' *The National Gazette and Literary Register* (Saturday, 8 March, 1823), 'From England,' *The Alexandria Herald* (Monday, 10 March, 1823), 'Late From England,' *Baltimore Herald & Mercantile Advertiser*

---

[427] 'Abbas Mirza.

[428] Erzurum.

[429] According to Markham (1874: 393), 'The Persian army was led by the Prince in person, with the Sirdar of Erivan [Hoseyn Qoli Khan Qazvini] on the right. The sarbâz or "infantry" of Azerbaijan stormed a hillock in front of the Turkish position in gallant style. The Turks fled in confusion, and were pursued by the Persian cavalry; 2500 of them were killed, and all their camp equipage and baggage fell into the hands of the victors. The cholera, that terrible scourge, which now first appeared in Persia, and which had already carried off Prince Muhammad'Aly [Mohammad 'Ali Mirza], put a stop to the Turkish war. It broke out with terrible violence in the victorious Persian army, and the Prince retreated in terror and confusion to Khoi, where the troops rapidly began to disperse.'

[430] Hafız 'Ali Pasha.

[431] Khosrow Mohammad Pasha. According to Anonymous (1866a: 358), 'Khusrau Mohammed Pasha…had been appointed Saraskar, or Commander-in-Chief of Erzeroum, in place of Hafiz Mohammed Pasha.' This may be an error for Hafez 'Ali Pasha. This was not the well-known Husrev Mehmed Pasha, who in 1822 was named *Kapudan Pasha*, suggesting either that we are dealing with a homonymous individual, or that the report of 1866 is incorrect. See İnalcik (1979:35–36); Çakir (2013: n. 22).

(Monday, 10 March, 1823), 'From English Papers,' *National Advocate* (Monday, 10 March, 1823), 'From the National Gazette. March 6. The Foreign News,' *Alexandria Gazette* (Tuesday, 11 March, 1823), 'Late Foreign News. From the Philadelphia National Gazette, of March 6,' *Daily National Intelligencer* (Tuesday, 11 March, 1823), 'From the National Gazette. Foreign News,' *New-York Spectator* (Tuesday, 11 March, 1823), 'Philadelphia, March 5,' *Connecticut Courier* (Wednesday, 12 March, 1823), 'English Articles,' *Boston Commercial Gazette* (Thursday, 13 March, 1823), 'Foreign,' *Albany Argus* (Friday, 14 March, 1823), 'Foreign. From the Philadelphia National Gaz. March 6,' *Easton Gazette* (Saturday, 15 March, 1823), 'Foreign News. From the National Advocate,' *Dutchess Observer* (Wednesday, 19 March, 1823), 'Late & Important from Europe!,' *North Star* (Thursday, 20 March, 1823), 'Untitled,' *The Pilot* (Thursday, 20 March, 1823), 'Foreign News. Philadelphia, March 6,' *The Supporter, and Scioto Gazette* (Saturday, 22 March, 1823) and 'English Articles,' *Bangor Weekly Register* (Thursday, 27 March, 1823): 'The Persians were rapidly approaching Bagdad at the latest advices.'

10.242 'Untitled,' *The National Gazette and Literary Register* (Thursday, 13 March, 1823), 'From the N. York Commercial Adver. March 11. Highly Important—War in Europe,' *Baltimore Patriot & Mercantile Advertiser* (Friday, 14 March, 1823), 'Selected Items of Intelligence,' *Daily National Intelligencer* (Friday, 14 March, 1823), 'Tuesday, March 11. Highly Important—War in Europe,' *New-York Spectator* (Friday, 14 March, 1823), 'Late Foreign News. War in Europe. [Extracts from Foreign Papers, received by the last arrivals at New-York.],' *Albany Argus* (Tuesday, 18 March, 1823), 'Foreign Intelligence. From the Com. Adv'r of Tuesday. Highly Important—War in Europe,' *Centinel of Freedom* (Tuesday, 18 March, 1823), 'From the New-York Commercial Advertiser,' *Rhode-Island American, and General Advertiser* (Tuesday, 18 March, 1823), 'Foreign,' *Providence Patriot* (Wednesday, 19 March, 1823), 'Foreign. From the N.Y. Com. Advertiser of the 11th inst. Highly Important—War in Europe,' *Rhode-Island Republican* (Wednesday, 19 March, 1823), 'Untitled,' *Richmond Enquirer* (Friday, 21 March, 1823), 'Foreign Intelligence. From Europe,' *Haverhill Gazette, and Essex Patriot* (Saturday, 22 March, 1823), 'Paris. Jan. 26,' *New-Hampshire Sentinel* (Saturday, 22 March, 1823), 'War in Europe! From the New York Commercial Advertiser of March 11. Highly Important,' *Washington Review and Examiner* (Saturday, 22 March, 1823), 'Latest from Europe,' *The Freeman's Journal* (Monday, 24 March, 1823), 'Greece & Turkey,' *Vermont Gazette* (Tuesday, 25 March, 1823), 'Foreign News. By the late arrivals at New-York,' *The American Journal* (Wednesday, 26 March, 1823) and 'Foreign Articles,' *The Arkansas Gazette* (Tuesday, 13 May, 1823): 'A letter from Persia dated Taberiz [sic, Tabriz], Sept. 20, gives the particulars of a great battle between the Persians and Turks, in which the army of the latter amounting to 52,000 men, was totally defeated.'

10.243 'Foreign News,' *New-York Spectator* (Friday, 14 March, 1823) and 'The Foreign News. From the New York Commercial Advertiser,' *Daily National Intelligencer*

(Wednesday, 19 March, 1823): 'It will be seen that the Persians, numerous and victorious, are crowding upon the Turks, which must create a strong diversion in favor of the Greeks, whether the Muscovite should step in to their assistance or not.'

10.244 'From London Papers. [By the New-York.] Received at the Office of the Commercial Advertiser. London, Jan. 20. Persian Affairs. Extract of a letter from Persia, dated Tabriz, Sept. 20, 1822,' *New-York Spectator* (Friday, 14 March, 1823) and 'Extract of a letter from Persia, dated at Tabriz, Sept. 20, 1822,' *The Watch-Tower* (Monday, 24 March, 1823): 'My letter[432] in July last [1822] acquainted you that the Persian army was then on the frontiers of Turkey. They crossed in at the latter end of that month, and advancing to Byzied,[433] remained there some days, in hopes than an accomodation might take place, to prevent a renewal of hostilities. The Prince Royal, Abbas Mirza, though anxious to make peace, at length found it necessary to advance with his army towards Toopruck Kullat,[434] where the Turkish army was encamped, consisting of 52,000 men. On the last day's march, his Royal Highness pushed forward, with a small body of irregular troops until within cannon shot of the enemy, to reconnoitre their position, and to inspect that portion of his army under Hussian [sic, Hussain] Khan's charge, which had halted within one fursang (about three miles and a half English) of the enemy's camp. The Prince having accomplished these objects, was engaged in pitching the camp colours for his army, when the enemy attacked and beat back his advanced detachment; however, he contrived to keep them in play until the main body came up. The Nackshewan[435] and Erivan battalions commenced the attack on the left, but were put into confusion by a charge from the Delhibash cavalry,[436] or mad-heads, who took one of the Prince's guns: fortunately, the two battalions of Tabreezies, under Cosseim Beg[437] and the Merandies,[438] arrived, and threw in two such effective vollies, that put the enemy in turn into confusion; this being immediately followed by the bayonet, put their left wing entirely to the rout.—The right wing held out until four twelve pounders came up and put them into disorder;—and they

---

[432] Although the author of this letter is unknown, it is likely to have been one of 'Abbas Mirza's English officers, such as Henry Lindsay (Bethune), particularly in view of the remarks about the Persian infantry and artillery which make it clear the writer was present during the attack described.

[433] Mod. Doğubayazit.

[434] Toprakkale. Cf. 10.85.

[435] Nakhchivan/Naxçivan.

[436] The *delibaşi* was a cavalry commander, but the term was used widely for 'cavalry' (deli) by nineteenth century Western writers. Pushkin published a lyric poem in 1829 entitled 'Delibash' (Делибаш). See Kalinowska (2004: 161).

[437] For the role of '*Surteer* (Colonel) Hajee Qassem Khan' in the battle of Toprakkale see Williamson (2008: 96). It is uncertain, but probable, that this is the same Qasem Khan, identified as 'commander of the Special Detachment (*fauj-e khass*) at Tabriz,' who was later sent as ambassador to Constantinople. See Busse (1972: 169).

[438] Troops from Marand in Azerbaijan.

then took to their heels, leaving in the hands of the Persians their whole camp, (which by all accounts took up about eight miles of ground) with 14 pieces of artillery, an enormous quantity of ammunition and stores of every kind. The Persian army certainly did not consist of more than 30,000 men, whilst, by papers found in the Turkish camp, their army proves to have been upwards of 52,000 strong. I am certainly amazed at the cowardly conduct of the Turks, and was in hope they would have tried the mettle of our Surbazies (Persian soldiers)[439] which has hitherto proved good. The Persians lost about thirty killed and wounded—the loss of the enemy must have been severe, as the Prince's cavalry followed them upwards of six fursangs. The whole affair was over in about fifteen minutes, and the more I hear of it, the more I am astonished. The only troops engaged were the battalions before mentioned—the irregulars lost but one man, Ali Khan Katoob, a very brave fellow. Some days previous to this affair, the cholera morbus, or spasmodic cholera of India, made its appearance among the Persian troops, and from six to twelve men daily had fallen victims to it; yet the Prince persisted in following the enemy torwards Erzroom. On the second day after the battle, his Royal Highness was about to enjoy the rich consequences of his victory by the plunder of that place, which, in all probability would have disposed the Turks to treat for peace, but the disorder suddenly assumed so decisive a character, that in a few days it destroyed 2000 of his army. The troops become [sic] terrified and in despair, commenced a precipitate retreat towards Byzied,[440] from which place the whole army dispersed without orders, and returned to their respective homes, leaving the Prince and his Minister almost alone.[441]

As far as regards the battle, I am very well satisfied with the result; although, in my opinion, the Seraskier and his half dozen Pachas, ought to lose their heads, or at least their tails,[442] for behaving so unmanfully. The Prince Royal returned to Khoe,[443] and after remaining there a few days, a messenger arrived from the Seraskier of Erzroom,[444] suing

---

[439] Alexander (1827: 281) referred to them as the '*Surbaz* (resolute), or disciplined battalions.' As H. Lindsay was deeply involved in training 'Abbas Mirza's army, the reference to 'our Surbazies' suggests he may have been the anonymous author of this report.

[440] Doğubayazit, Turkey.

[441] Mirza Bozorg (Mirza 'Isa-ye Farahani, Qa'em Maqam-e Sadarat-e 'Ozma). He died later that year from plague. See Busse (1972: 166). This was obviously the source used by Moreau de Jonnès 1831: 262 who noted, 'Au mois de juillet, le prince royal de Perse, Abbas-Mirza, ayant attaqué l'armée turque, la força de se retirer dans Erzéroum; mais le lendemain de sa victoire le choléra, qui quelques jours avant avait éclaté parmi ses troupes, et qui jusqu'alors n'avait enlevé que 6 à 12 soldats par vingt-quatre heures, redoubla tout à coup de violence, et en fit périr 2000 dans une seule marche. L'armée, épouvantée, battit précipitamment en retraite vers Bizied, et se dispersa malgré le prince et ses ministres, qui restèrent seuls, et furent forcés de se retirer à Khoé, où la suspension des hostilités fut convenue à la suite d'une négociation.'

[442] A reference to the horse-tails which were signs of high office in the Ottoman regalia.

[443] Khoy.

[444] Mohammad Emin Rauf Pasha. Cf. 10.226.

that hostilities might cease, and that the Prince would despatch an authoritated agent to negotiate a peace. Mirza Thirky[445] is at Erzroom, for that purpose. I sincerely hope that all enmity between the two nations may cease, for, notwithstanding the facility of this year's victory, by which the Prince has gained a great name and character, such decisive advantages are not always to be calculated upon.

Last year the cholera morbus made its appearance in Muscat, Bushira,[446] Bussorah, Bagdad and Shiraz. This year it has visited every city in Azerbaijan, and is now raging at Teheran, and as far as Erivan westward. The people of Tabriz have suffered severely; about 4800 of them died in less than five and twenty days.[447] You will be sorry to hear that the excellent and venerable Kaem Makom was one of the last of its victims; in him the English have lost a steady, and indeed, their best friend. His son, Mirza Abul Kausim a very different man from his father, is now factotum.'[448]

10.245 'England and Persia,' *Hampshire Gazette* (Wednesday, 19 March, 1823): 'It appears from a London paper, that an envoy[449] has recently arrived in England from Persia, in order to obtain satisfaction from the British government on several subjects.[450] Russia it is said has by unwearied exertions and considerable expense acquired a preponderating influence over the Persians, while the influence of England is much diminished and the British charge d'affaires had left the Persian court, on account of an affront offered to him by the Persian minister.[451] The friendship of the Persians is so important to England, both on account of their proximity to her India possessions and because they form a sort of barrier against the ambitious designs of Russia in that quarter,

---

[445] The identity of this person is unclear. The eventual treaty names 'Mirza Mahomed Alli Mustofee' as Plenipotentiary on this occasion. See Hertslet (1891: 164). It was certainly not Mirza Taqi Khan who was only 15 years old at this time and was employed in Mirza Bozorg's stables. See Algar (1989/2011).

[446] Bandar-e Bushehr.

[447] Moreau de Jonnès (1831: 263) noted, 'Un témoin oculaire évalue à 4800 le nombre des habitans de Tauris, qui périrent pendant les vingt-cinq jours que dura l'irruption. Cf. Macnamara (1876: 63).

[448] This letter was written at Tabriz on 20 September 1822. As Hasan-e Fasa'i noted, 'that year Mirzā 'Isā-ye Farāhāni, known by the name of Mirzā Bozorg and the title "Qā'em Maqām-e Ḥadārat-e 'Ozmā," died from plague. His office and title were conferred upon his son, Mirzā Abu'l-Qāsem.' See Busse (1972: 166).

[449] Mirza Saleh Shirazi. Cf. 10.201.

[450] As Kelly (2006: 268) noted, 'In 1822, Mirza Saleh returned to London, entrusted with diplomatic tasks of some delicacy by Abbas Mirza. On this occasion, he stayed for ten months, being sent to buy arms and stores. He was also to secure the arrears of Britain's subsidy to Persia, and to get Captain Willock replaced by an ambassador. Canning agreed about the subsidies being overdue, and in 1823 Mirza Saleh returned with Canning's decision: the Indian Government would be appointing a "new arrangement of the Mission to Persia". The Indian nominee would be Colonel John Kinneir Macdonald of the 24th Madras Infantry, who would arrive in 1826.'

[451] Henry Willock. Cf. 10.198.

that it was supposed the Persian minister would find little difficulty in accomplishing the object of his mission. The trade of Persia is now in the hands of the English who have depots of goods and agents at Bushire, Bussora, and Bagdad, but should a serious misunderstanding take place, this trade will immediately be transferred to the Russian merchants.—The London editor says that Russia seems to meditate the annexation of Persia to her already enormous territory. Russia has now the sole command of the Caspian sea; she has 130,000 troops in Georgia; she is cultivating the friendship of the tribes between the Caspian sea and Hindoostan, and already has the power of annoying the British India possessions when she pleases.'

10.246 'Persia and Turkey,' *Hampshire Gazette* (Wednesday, 19 March, 1823; 'Persia'): 'A letter from Tabriz in Persia, published in a London paper, describes a battle fought beteween 30,000 Persians and 52,000 Turks, in August last. The Turks were routed in a few minutes after the commencement of the action and fled in confusion, leaving in the hands of the Persians their whole camp which took up 8 miles of ground, 14 pieces of artillery, and an enormous quantity of ammunition and stores. The Persian prince royal, Abbas Mirza, pursued the Turks towards Erzroom and had advanced his army near that city, when the cholera morbus, which had made its appearance among his troops before the battle, suddenly became very mortal and destroyed 2000 of his army in a few days.—The troops became terrified, commenced a hasty retreat, and without orders dispersed and returned to their respective homes. In September last the cholera morbus was raging in many cities of Asiatic Turkey and Persia. In Tabriz 4800 had died in 25 days.'

10.247 'Foreign News.' *The Corrector* (Saturday, 29 March, 1823): 'A letter from Persia, dated Tabriz, Sept. 20, 1822, gives an account of a battle between the Turks and Persians, in which the former were defeated. After the left wing of the Turks had been routed, the account says, "the right-wing held out until four twelve pounders came up and put them into disorder; and they then took to their heels, leaving in the hands of the Persians their whole camp, (which by all accounts took up about eight miles of ground) with 14 pieces of artillery, an enormous quantity of amunition [sic] and stores of every kind.—The Persian army certainly did not consist of more than 30,000 men, whilst, by papers found in the Turkish camp, their army proves to have consisted of 52,000 men."'

10.248 'French Papers,' *Alexandria Gazette* (Thursday, 3 April, 1823): 'The Aga of the Janissaries, has been exiled from Constantinople,[452] because the Jannissaries would not march against the Persians, saying they would only march against the Russians.'

---

[452] The identity of this Aga is unclear for 'between 1808 and 1822 Mahmud II changed the Janissary commanders seventeen times.' See Kirca (2010: 100). On 23 February 1823 the Janissary Aga was removed by Mahmud II and replaced by Hüseyin Aga who began 'to remove dissidents in the corps by dismissal, forced retirement, and banishment.' See Shaw and Shaw (1977: 7). The rampant dissent

10.249 'Turkey,' *New-York Commercial Advertiser* (Monday, 14 April, 1823), 'Turkey,' *New-York Spectator* (Tuesday, 15 April, 1823) and 'Foreign. Turkey,' *Providence Patriot* (Saturday, 19 April, 1823): 'A letter from Ancona, of Jan. 18 says that the Persians have refused the offers of large sums of money to retire from the neighborhood of Bagdad, and that at Alexandria, it was believed that they already occupied Bagdad. Their progress is regarded with a favorable eye, and the Pacha of Egypt[453] is said to be on the eve, should they continue successful, to declare himself independant [sic].'

10.250 'Paris, March 12,' *Alexandria Gazette* (Tuesday, 29 April, 1823) and 'Paris, March 12,' *Independent Chronicle and Boston Patriot* (Wednesday, 30 April, 1823): 'The Persians were said to have retreated from Erzerum, after having been completely defeated by the Turks. The Cholera Morbus had been arrested by the rain and the cold, and was rapidly disappearing. At Orfa it had entirely ceased.'[454]

10.251 'Aleppo, Dec. 20,' *The Repertory* (Tuesday, 29 April, 1823), 'Aleppo, Dec. 20,' *New-York American* (Wednesday, 30 April, 1823), 'Aleppo, Dec. 20,' *Boston Weekly Messenger* (Thursday, 1 May, 1823), 'Aleppo, Dec. 20,' *Baltimore Patriot & Mercantile Advertiser* (Friday, 2 May, 1823), 'Aleppo, Dec. 20,' *New-Bedford Mercury* (Friday, 2 May, 1823), 'Aleppo, Dec. 20,' *New-York Spectator* (Friday, 2 May, 1823), 'Aleppo, Dec. 20,' *Columbian Register* (Saturday, 3 May, 1823), 'Aleppo, Dec. 20,' *The National Gazette and Literary Register* (Saturday, 3 May, 1823), 'Aleppo, Dec. 20,' *American Mercury* (Tuesday, 6 May, 1823), 'Aleppo, Dec. 20,' *Richmond Enquirer* (Tuesday, 6 May, 1823) and 'From Egypt. Aleppo, Dec. 20,' *Argus of Western America* (Friday, 21 May, 1823): 'The Persian army, which had retired from the neighborhood of Bajdat,[455] is fortified at some distance from their first encampment, and it appears that the Persians intend to pursue their designs against Bajdat. Our Pacha Bahram[456] is preparing to go to the assistance of this city, at the head of the troops which he is collecting, and which now amount to 7 or 8000 men.'

10.252 'Untitled,' *Boston Daily Advertiser* (Wednesday, 30 April, 1823), 'Untitled,' *The Repertory* (Thursday, 1 May, 1823), 'From the Boston Daily Advertiser, April 30,' *New-York Evening Post* (Friday, 2 May, 1823), 'Latest from Turkey,' *Newburyport Herald*

---

at this time amongst the Janissaries had nothing to do with the Persian war. On this period see Sunar (2006).

[453] Mehemet 'Ali Pasha.

[454] According to Maclean (1824: 432) cholera appeared at Urfa in October, 1822.

[455] Baghdad.

[456] The dateline of this article is Aleppo and the reference is to Bahram Mohammad Pasha, who replaced Mustafa Pasha there, in 1822. See Meriwether (1999: 42). As Bodman (1963: 136) noted, 'the city was in the hands of a provisional governor, Bahram Muhammad Pasha. Shortly thereafter he was appointed wali, only to gather troops and depart for Baghdad.'

10 From 1816 to the End of the Turco-Persian War (1816–1825)

(Friday, 2 May, 1823) and 'Untitled,' *Connecticut Courant* (Tuesday, 6 May, 1823): 'The cholera morbus has appeared at Aleppo.[457] In the beggining [sic] of December, the deaths were a hundred a day. The Consuls of Naples, Austria and Prussia, and many European merchants, had in consequence left the place.[458] This disease had overrun all Syria, and made frightful ravages at Mossoul, Orsa,[459] Biri[460] and Bagdad. The Persians have retired to Menduli where they have fortified themselves.'[461]

10.253 'Aleppo, Dec. 30,' *Connecticut Courant* (Tuesday, 6 May, 1823): 'The Persian army, which was repulsed before Bagdad, have made a fortified encampment, and propose, in the spring to recommence their operations.'

---

[457] According to Needham (1833: 122) cholera 'reached Aleppo in November, 1822.'

[458] Cholera appeared in Aleppo in November, 1822, but although the consuls of Naples, Austria and Prussia left the city, 'M. de Lesseps, the French Consul, took refuge, with all the Franks who chose to accompany him, in a garden surrounded by a wall and moat, and situated in the vicinity of the town. He remained there during the whole irruption. Two doors only were kept open, the one for ingress and the other for egress. Although the number of persons thus sequestrated consisted of about 200, and notwithstanding the variety of their constitutions, habits, ad manners, not one was attacked by the Cholera, which raged all around them.' See Needham (1833: 122). Cf. Macnamara (1876: 64).

[459] Urfa.

[460] Birecik on the Euphrates, in southeastern Turkey.

[461] Mandali was on the Ottoman side of the frontier, c. 160 kms northeast of Baghdad. See Alexander (1827/2: 30). Stein (1824: 178) simply noted, '3. Jan. Persisch-türkisches Treffen bei Menduli. Niederlage der Türken.' The attack, however, was in no way meant to avenge Mohammad 'Ali Mirza's death, which was due to cholera, but rather to avenge the Turkish massacre of the garrison left at Mandali when Mohammad 'Ali Mirza's forces, under General Devaux, had advanced on Baghdad, which had formally surrendered. According to Belge (1829: 352–353), 'Devaux avait laissé dans Mendeli, petite forteresse, une garnison de 300 hommes sous le commandement d'un officier persan qu'il avait lui-même formé, et qu'il affectionnait beaucoup. Mendeli, pressé de près, fut obligé de se rendre; mais aux termes de la capitulation, la garnison devait se retirer en Perse. Mais à peine sortie de la ville, elle fut passée au fil de l'épée. Révolté d'une pareille barbarie, le général Devaux demanda avec instance qu'on lui permit de reprendre la place; dans un nouveau conseil de guerre, on lui allégua, comme un obstacle puissant, la chaleur excessive, le vent empoisonné du désert, et les renforts qu'attendaient les Turcs. Devaux insista vivement, et ce ne fut qu'après avoir promisde payer de sa tête la non réussite, qu'il lui fut permis de partir à la tête de ses bataillons. Ce fut pendant la nuit qu'on arriva devant la place. Les troupes, dans le plus grand silence, se divisèrent pour l'attaquer sur trois points à la fois. Un coup de canon devait donner le signal de l'assaut. Devaux alla avec deux bataillons du côté de la porte qu'il croyait regarder Bagdad, car il faisait une nuit profonde. En effet, un Arabe vint annoncer qu'on était à quatre cents pas de la ville, qu'il en avait lui-même touché les murailles. Enfin, les étoiles commencèrent à pâlir et le général en chef braqua lui-même la pièce d'artillerie qui annonça le moment de l'attaque. Les troupes persannes escaladaient déjà les remparts et enfonçaient les portes, que les Turcs éperdus n'avaient pas même pu se rallier sur les murailles. On en fit un massacre affreux.'

10.254 'Magnesia, Feb. 18,' *Boston Daily Advertiser* (Wednesday, 14 May, 1823), 'Magnesia, Feb. 18,' *The Repertory* (Thursday, 15 May, 1823), 'Magnesia, Feb. 18,' *National Advocate* (Saturday, 17 May, 1823), 'Magnesia, Feb. 18,' *The Oracle of Dauphin* (Saturday, 24 May, 1823), 'Magnesia, Feb. 18,' *Saratoga Sentinel* (Tuesday, 27 May, 1823) and 'Magnesia, Feb. 18,' *Argus of Western America* (Wednesday, 4 June, 1823): 'An order has reached here[462] from the Porte for forming a body of 600 men, destined to march against the Persians.'

10.255 'Untitled,' *New-York American* (Monday, 9 June, 1823): 'The Boston Daily Advertiser contains Smyrna dates to the 21st March, from which we learn that....the war between the Porte and Persia was daily assuming a more serious character. After an action between the troops of the two powers, the Turks retreated, and the Persians fortified themselves at Menduli.'[463]

10.256 'Odessa, April 3,' *New-York American* (Wednesday, 11 June, 1823), 'Odessa, April 3,' *New-York Evening Post* (Wednesday, 11 June, 1823), 'Odessa, April 3,' *Independent Chronicle and Boston Patriot* (Saturday, 14 June, 1823), 'Odessa, April 3,' *Providence Patriot* (Saturday, 14 June, 1823), 'Odessa, April 3,' *City Gazette and Commercial Daily Advertiser* (Friday, 20 June, 1823), 'Odessa, April 3,' *Carolina Gazette* (Saturday, 21 June, 1823), 'Odessa, April 3,' *New-Hampshire Patriot & State Gazette* (Monday, 23 June, 1823) and 'Odessa, April 3,' *Augusta Chronicle and Georgia Advertiser* (Wednesday, 25 June, 1823): 'The last letters from Constantinople mention...some advantages gained by the Persians; in consequence of which great armaments are preparing.'

10.257 'Aleppo, Feb. 6,' *Boston Weekly Messenger* (Thursday, 12 June, 1823), 'Aleppo, Feb. 6,' *Herald of the Valley* (Friday, 20 June, 1823) and 'Aleppo, Feb. 6,' *New-Bedford Mercury* (Friday, 20 June, 1823): 'Yesterday a Tartar[464] arrived here [Aleppo] bearing despatches from Darud [sic, Daud] Pacha to Bagdad, to demand assistance.[465] The Turkish troops after a battle with the Persians have retreated. The latter have fortified themselves at Menduli/Menouli. This war becomes every day more serious. It is said that terrible tempests prevail which have occasioned incalculable losses.'

---

[462] Magnesia, mod. Manisa, in western Turkey.

[463] Mandali. Cf. 10.252.

[464] As Koelle (1882: 133) noted, 'In the course of time the name Tartar...acquired the meaning of "fast messenger, postman;" because these Nomads, the owners of countless camels and horses, as acquainted with the roads and accustomed to travel, were the most suitable persons to be employed for distant missions and messages requiring speed. In Turkish...Tatari = "the Tartarian," is still the name for a letter-carrying or post pigeon.'

[465] Cf. 10.251.

10 From 1816 to the End of the Turco-Persian War (1816–1825)

10.258 'Semlin, April 10,' *The National Gazette and Literary Register* (Saturday, 14 June, 1823), 'Semlin, April 10,' *Boston Daily Advertiser* (Monday, 16 June, 1823), 'Semlin, April 10,' *The Repertory* (Tuesday, 17 June, 1823) and 'Semlin, April 10,' *Boston Weekly Messenger* (Thursday, 19 June, 1823): 'The Pacha of Belgrade[466] has received certain news from Erzerum that the Turkish army in Armenia was destroyed by the Persians in the commencement of the month of March. The loss amounted to 25,000 men. This has redoubled the warlike preparations at Constantinople.'

10.259 'From Europe. Constantinople,' *Oswego Palladium* (Friday, 20 June, 1823): 'Proposals of peace had been made from Persia. The Port [sic, Porte] wishes the negociations to be carried on at Erzerum.'[467]

10.260 'Postscript. Latest from Europe. Bagdad, Jan. 9,' *National Advocate* (Friday, 20 June, 1823; from 'The Ottoman'), 'Eight Days Later from Europe,' *New-York Spectator* (Tuesday, 24 June, 1823), 'Foreign News. From the National Advocate, June 20. Latest from Europe. Bagdad, Jan. 9,' *Dutchess Observer* (Wednesday, 25 June, 1823; from 'The Ottoman'), 'From the N.Y. Commercial Advertiser,' *Providence Gazette* (Wednesday, 25 June, 1823) and '[From the New York Commercial Advertiser.] Greece,' *Richmond Enquirer* (Friday, 27 June, 1823): 'If the Persian war against the Sultan[468] should continue, it will create a powerful diversion in favor of the Greeks. At present, the news is favorable. An article from Bagdad, January 9, says: The Ottoman troops here [Baghdad] have experienced a new check from the Persians who are fortifying themselves in the province of Chalis[469] the environs of Menduli. The fate of Cordistan is very problematical, and the discontent of the resident of Bussora against the Government here, gives reason to fear a new rupture. A regular cruise of English ships is established in the Persian Gulf, to protect the commerce of India and secure the principal points of the Gulf, such as the Island of

---

[466] Abdurrahim/Abdurrahman Pasha held the position of Muhafiz of the Belgrade Fortress and Mutessarif of the Smederevo Sanjak,' with the rank of pasha, from 1821 to 1827. See e.g. Savić (2020: 261).

[467] The treaty negotiated at Erzurum and concluded on 28 July 1823. See Hurewitz (1956: 90–92).

[468] Mahmud II.

[469] Mod. Al Khalis, an area located northeast of Baquba between the Tigris and the Diyala rivers. See Billerbeck (1893: 90). It took its name from that of a canal running through the area which was itself part of the ancient Nahrwan canal. See Schweiger-Lerchenfeld (1875: 33); Banse (1919: 293). In all likelihood the name is cognate with Χαλα (Chala) and Χαλωνῖτις (Chalonitis) of Isidor of Charax, on which see Schoff (1914: 27–28); Herzfeld (1948: 48).

Djezan,[470] or Kischme.[471] The English vessels also watch the Arabian Chatul,[472] a river formed by the waters of the Tigris and Euphrates.'

10.261 'Semlin, April, 11,' *Louisiana Courier* (Monday, 30 June, 1823): 'Our pacha [of Belgrade][473] has received news from the frontiers of Persia, which state that the Turkish army was completely routed by the Persians in the beginning of March. The number of the dead is computed at 25,000 men. Since, the greatest war preparations have been going on at Constantinople and in Asiatic Turkey.'

10.262 'Pacha of Egypt,' *The National Gazette and Literary Register* (Thursday, 10 July, 1823), 'London, May 30. Pacha of Egypt,' *The Repertory* (Saturday, 12 July, 1823), 'London, May 30. Pacha of Egypt,' *Portland Gazette* (Tuesday, 15 July, 1823), 'Foreign Intelligence. London, May 30. Pacha of Egypt,' *New-Bedford Mercury* (Friday, 18 July, 1823) and 'Pacha of Egypt,' *Trenton Federalist* (Monday, 4 August, 1823): 'We have been favoured with the following interesting Extract from the journal of a gentleman[474] who has just returned from Egypt, which will enable our readers to form some idea of the nature and extent of the improvements of the present Pacha, and of the character of this wonderful man. . . .Jan. 7, 1823, at Cairo.—Visited the Pacha (Mahomed Ally),[475] a most intelligent countenance, and about 50 years of age. He asked many questions about the force of the Persians in regulars, and the news from Bagdad.'

10.263 'Further Extracts From our English and Irish papers by the Mary-Catherine. London, May 21,' *Charleston Courier* (Saturday, 12 July, 1823): 'Accounts from Bagdad of the ninth January state, that the Ottoman troops of that city have been again defeated by the Persians, who become stronger in the province of Chalis,[476] and the environs of Menduli.'

---

[470] Jizan, one of the Farasan islands, is in the Red Sea. This may be an error for 'Jarun,' the old name of Hormuz island.

[471] Qeshm.

[472] Shatt al-'Arab.

[473] Abdurrahim/Abdurrahman Pasha. Cf. 10.258.

[474] The identity of the writer is unknown but he was definitely an Englishman as the full article from which this excerpt was taken (Anonymous 1823a) attests. The first port described is Mocha in Yemen, visited on 21 November 1822, and the writer refers to 'the company,' suggesting he was an EIC employee sailing back to Britain from India.

[475] Mehemet 'Ali Pasha. Cf. 10.228, 10.249.

[476] Cf. 10.260.

10.264 'Late from Europe. Constantinople, April 10,' *The Corrector* (Saturday, 12 July, 1823): 'The negociations with Persia are not near to a determination. The Porte is said even to have declined the mediation of Lord Strangford.'[477]

10.265 'Turkey, Greece, and Persia,' *New-York Evening Post* (Friday, 18 July, 1823), 'Foreign News. From the N.Y. Evening Post, July 16. Ten days later from England,' *Dutchess Observer* (Wednesday, 23 July, 1823) and 'Turkey, Greece and Persia,' *The Geneva Gazette* (Wednesday, 30 July): 'The negotiations between Persia and the Porte had broken off, and both parties were preparing with great vigor to take to the field. The latter calculated on intestine divisions among the Persians; while the former was fearlessly assembling its armies to penetrate into the Turkish territory.'

10.266 'Postscript. Latest from Europe. Marseilles, May 14,' *National Advocate* (Friday, 18 July, 1823), 'Greeks, Turks and Persians,' *Baltimore Patriot & Mercantile Advertiser* (Monday, 21 July, 1823), 'Greeks, Turks, and Persians,' *Daily National Intelligencer* (Tuesday, 22 July, 1823), 'Greeks, Turks and Persians,' *New-York Spectator* (Tuesday, 22 July, 1823), 'Marseilles, May 14,' *Independent Chronicle and Boston Patriot* (Wednesday, 23 July, 1823), 'Greeks, Turks and Persians,' *Richmond Enquirer* (Friday, 25 July, 1823; with minor variations), 'Marseilles, May 14,' *Saratoga Sentinel* (Tuesday, 29 July, 1823) and 'Greeks, Tubks [sic, Turks] & Persians,' *Fincastle Mirror* (Friday, 1 August, 1823; with minor variations): 'We have received news here [Marseilles] that the negotiations between Persia and the Porte are broken off, because the latter absolutely refuses to cede the districts formerly belonging to Persia, and which it seized during the internal troubles in that kingdom. It seems that the Divan, in resolving not to yield this point, depends on fresh intestine divisions in Persia; but the latter Court does not seem to be uneasy, and has given orders to prosecute the war with fresh vigour. Its southern army, which has been considerably reinforced, was expected near Bagdad, the Pacha being too weak to resist: he has applied to all quarters for aid, but has received very few reinforcements. It seems that the southern Persian army is destined to penetrate to Syria, and the northern to take possession of Armenia. A general levy against the Persians is expected in Turkey in Asia.'

10.267 'Important News from Europe,' *Rochester Telegraph* (Tuesday, 22 July, 1823): 'With regard to the affairs of Persia, nothing can be said with precision; as the negociations are far from being concluded.'

10.268 'Greeks and Turks,' *Baltimore Patriot & Mercantile Advertiser* (Thursday, 21 August, 1823), 'Greeks and Turks,' *New-York Spectator* (Friday, 22 August, 1823) and 'New-York, August 19. From France,' *Charleston Courier* (Tuesday, 26 August,

---

[477] Cf. 10.74, 10.197.

1823; with minor variations): 'By a letter from Alexandria in Egypt we learn that the Viceroy[478] has received an order from the Sultan[479] to place himself at the head of all his troops, and to march to Bagdad to stop the progress of the Persians, but a portion of the troops stationed in the Delta having revolted, it appears that the Pacha found it impossible to obey the mandate of his Highness. He had in effect already given orders to the Egyptian fleet not to sail until the commotion should be quieted.'

10.269 'Turkey and Greece,' *The National Gazette and Literary Register* (Thursday, 21 August, 1823), 'France and Spain,' *Vermont Journal* (Monday, 1 September, 1823) and 'Turkey and Greece,' *Augusta Chronicle and Georgia Advertiser* (Wednesday, 3 September, 1823): 'Accounts from Alexandria in Egypt state, that the Turkish forces stationed in the Delta had revolted, and refused to march against the Persians, who were making inroads into the Turkish empire. The Pacha of Egypt,[480] who had received orders to proceed with his army to Bagdad, found it impossible to move in consequence of this revolt; and, as a precautionary measure he had interdicted the sailing of the Turkish fleet until the commotion should be quited. Add to this, that the plague was raging at Alexandria, Constantinople, Janina, and other places in the Turkish empire,[481] and the affairs of the Porte will appear in no very flattering condition.'

10.270 'Latest from France,' *New-York Spectator* (Friday, 22 August, 1823), 'Latest from France,' *Boston Commercial Gazette* (Monday, 25 August, 1823), 'Latest from France. New York, August 19,' *Republican Star and General Advertiser* (Tuesday, 26 August, 1823), 'Foreign News. New-York, August 19. From France,' *Cayuga Republican* (Wednesday, 27 August, 1823), 'Latest from France,' *The New-London Gazette and General Advertiser* (Wednesday, 27 August, 1823) and 'Foreign Intelligence. New York, August 19. Late from France,' *Hampshire Gazette* (Wednesday, 27 August, 1823): 'Accounts from Egypt, speak of a revolt of the troops in the Delta of the Nile,[482] which prevents the Viceroy[483] from marching, as ordered by the Sultan,[484] to arrest the progress of the Persians.'

---

[478] Mehemet 'Ali Pasha.

[479] Mahmud II.

[480] Mehemet 'Ali Pasha.

[481] See e.g. Prus (1846: 928).

[482] According to Fahmy (1998: 156), 'The decision to conscript the *fallahin* had repercussions that posed a serious threat to Mehemet 'Ali's authority. Immediately after conscription was introduced in Lower Egypt in 1823 a big revolt erupted in the province of Minuffiya in the Delta and the Pasha had to go there in person, guarded by his own palace troops and assisred by six field cannons, to subdue the revolt.'

[483] Mehemet 'Ali Pasha.

[484] Mahmud II.

10 From 1816 to the End of the Turco-Persian War (1816–1825)

10.271 'Latest from France,' *Alexandria Gazette* (Saturday, 23 August, 1823),' Foreign. Latest from France,' *Independent Chronicle and Boston Patriot* (Saturday, 23 August, 1823), 'Turkey and Greece,' *City Gazette and Commercial Daily Advertiser* (Tuesday, 26 August, 1823; with minor variations), 'Persians and Turks,' *Newburyport Herald* (Tuesday, 26 August, 1823) and 'Extract from a Marseilles paper, June 23,' *North Star* (Tuesday, 2 September, 1823): 'They write from Alexandria that the Viceroy of Egypt[485] has received orders from the Sultan,[486] to march at the head of his army to Bagdad, to arrest the progress of the Persians; but a part of the troops of the Delta have revolted, and the fleet is ordered to remain until the insurrection shall be suppressed.'

10.272 '"A year in Europe,"' *New-York Evening Post* (Saturday, 23 August, 1823): 'The following is the account Mr. Griscom[487] gives of his visit to Sir Joseph Banks[488]....Sir Joseph's house is pleasantly situated at one corner of Soho Square....The levees are held in the evening of the first day of the week....Among the most distinguished foreigners whom I met in Soho Square, was Cuvier, the celebrated naturalist of Paris[489]....At the same meeting were two young Persians,[490] who have resided some time in London, for purposes of science. Their enquiries, I am informed, are chiefly medical. They were dressed in the costume of their own country, in silk mantles and turbans. They spoke English tolerably, and appeared to be men of some acuteness of observations.'[491]

10.273 'Great Britain,' *Evening Post* (Tuesday, 26 August 1823; to 'subsistence'), 'Very Late from France,' *Newburyport Herald* (Friday, 29 August, 1823), 'Summary. Latest from Europe,' *Salem Gazette* (Friday, 29 August, 1823; to 'taxation'), 'From the French papers. Paris, July 18,' *American Federalist Columbian Centinel* (Saturday, 30 August, 1823; to 'religious freedom'), 'Constantinople, June 15,' *American Mercury* (Tuesday, 2 September, 1823; to 'taxes'), 'Untitled,' *The Lyons Advertiser* (Wednesday, 3 September 1823; to 'exemption from taxes'), 'Constantinople, June 15,' *Charleston Courier* (Thursday, 4 September, 1823), 'Latest from Europe. London, July 12,' *Augusta Chronicle and Georgia Advertiser* (Saturday, 6 September, 1823; to 'exemption from taxes') and 'Miscellany,' *The Nantucket Inquirer* (Tuesday, 16 September, 1823): 'Mirza Mahomet

---

[485] Mehemet 'Ali Pasha.

[486] Mahmud II.

[487] John Griscom (1774–1852), 'Professor of Chemistry and Natural Philosophy in the New-York Institution.' On a visit to Sir Joseph Banks, during a trip to Britain and Europe in 1818/1819, he met both Baron Cuvier and Sir Humphrey Davy. See Griscom (1859: 145).

[488] Sir Joseph Banks (1743–1820), internationally renowned botanist and Enlightenment figure who sailed on the *Endeavour* with Capt. James Cook. For his life see Suttor (1855).

[489] Georges, baron Cuvier (1769–1832), world famous French naturalist and statesman. For his life see Lee (1833).

[490] Probably Haji Baba and Mirza Reza. See Green (2016: 119).

[491] This description is quoted verbatim from Griscom (1824: 53, 55).

Saulat,[492] Persian minister at London, on leaving England, published an official invitation from the Prince Royal of Persia[493] to the people of England and to the European powers, inviting foreigners to go and reside in the kingdom of Abzirhijan,[494] the capital of which is Tabaris,[495] offering them land, houses, and every thing necessary for their subsistence. The prince is of a most liberal and enlightened mind, and will allow to all strangers religious freedom and exemption from taxes/taxation.

Upon this subject the Constitutionnel,[496] makes the following just reflections.

What a singular contrast does the political world now present. Proscriptions in civilized Europe, toleration in Asia, which is still barbarous. Switzerland forced to become inhospitable, and Persia offering lands free from taxes to all who are willing to fly thither. At Madrid it is audaciously published, that the religion of Jesus Christ is intollerant [sic], and fanatic voices solicit the re-establishment of the Inquistion. At Ispahan, a prince of the sect of Ali proclaims that he respects the liberty of all modes of worship and faith. . . .in servile Persia, a Mahometan appeals to generous ideas, and proudly declares, that he is religious without bigotry; that he does not persecute in the name of his God; and that he glories in his liberalism.'

10.274 'Persia,' Columbian *Register* (Saturday, 30 August, 1823), 'Persia,' *Connecticut Mirror* (Monday, 1 September, 1823), 'A new point of Emigration. From late French and English Papers. Persia,' *Washington Gazette* (Tuesday, 2 September, 1823), 'London, July 11.—Persia—,' *The Repertory* (Tuesday, 2 September, 1823), 'From London Papers. Received at the office of the Commercial Advertiser. Persia,' *New-York Spectator* (Friday, 5 September, 1823), 'Foreign Intelligence. London, July 11. Persia,' *New-Bedford Mercury* (Friday, 5 September, 1823), 'Persia,' *The Charleston Courier* (Friday, 5 September, 1823), 'Persian Notification,' *Alexandria Gazette & Advertiser* (Saturday, 6 September, 1823; different introductory paragraph, 'The Persian Minister in London, published the following notification on the eighth July last,' and minus the last paragraph) and 'Persia,' *Christian Watchman* (Saturday, 20 September, 1823): 'The Persian Minister, Mirza Mahomed Sauhl,[497] having effected the object of his mission to England, and made the necessary arrangements for his departure for Russia, in the Jasper sloop of war, has issued,

---

[492] Mirza Saleh Shirazi.

[493] 'Abbas Mirza.

[494] Azerbaijan. For an analysis of the motives behind and implications of this letter see Shahvar (2020).

[495] Tabriz.

[496] According to the writer of Anonymous (1846b: 75), 'The "Constitutionnel" was, about twenty or twenty-five years ago, (i.e., from 1820 to 1825.) the most successful and flourishing, and certainly one of the best conducted papers in France. It had then a greater circulation than any paper in Paris.'

[497] Mirza Saleh Shirazi.

10 From 1816 to the End of the Turco-Persian War (1816–1825)

as his last public act, an official notification from the Prince Royal of Persia[498] to the people of England, and the several other European nations of which the following is a copy:—.

"As many families from European countries have lately resorted some to America and New Holland,[499] and others to Georgia and Daghistan, as settlers; his Royal Highness Abbas Mirza, the Prince Royal of Persia, through the medium of his Minister at the Court of Great Britain, personally assures all those who may be inclined to take up their residence in his kingdom of Adzerbijan, of which the capital is Tabriz, that on their arrival in the district of Sauvidgeboulogh,[500] he will immediately assign to them portions of land, with residences attached, and every requisite for their comfort and subsistence. The soil will yield abundant crops of wheat, barley, rice, cotton and every species of fruit or grain they may choose to cultivate; and the natural produce of the country exceeds that of any other quarter of the globe. Besides receiving grants of land, such settlers shall, as long as they reside in Persia, be exempt from all taxes or contributions of any kind; their property and persons held sacred under the immediate protection of the Prince himself, who further engages, that they shall be treated with the greatest kindness and attention, and, as is the custom of Persia, be at full liberty to enjoy their own religious opinions and feelings, and to follow, without controul [sic] or interruption, their own mode of worship. As all travellers who have visited Persia agree that it is the best climate under the sun, it is only necessary to state, by way of exemplification, that it is the usual place of resort for persons whose health has been impaired by a residence in India, and it rarely happens that such invalids do not speedily become convalescent from the change.

His Royal Highness, in issuing his commands to give publicity to these sentiments, is prompted by an ardent desire naturally to promote the welfare of settlers and the improvement of his country; which he is convinced from past experience would be greatly advanced in knowledge, and materially benefitted in every point of view, by a more extended and familiar intercourse with Europans and especially with those whom he has ever felt pleasure in designating his 'English friends.'

The undersigned, in thus promulgating the views and wishes of his Prince, in obedience to the positive commands with which he has been honoured, scarcely conceives it necessary to offer any observations upon the assurances given in this paper, as the character of his Royal Highness is so well understood, and has been so duly appreciated by the subjects of Great Britain who have for years been domiciled in Persia, and to which many authors both of that and other countries have added their testimony; but for the satisfaction of such individuals as may not have the facility of obtaining information upon this point, the Prince's devoted servant and humble representative begs leave to state, that his Royal Master has ever been characterized as amiable, just, benevolent, and honourable in the

---

[498] 'Abbas Mirza.

[499] Australia. The name was given by the Dutch explorer Abel Tasman. See Barrington (1808: 2).

[500] Savojbolagh.

highest degree; though dignified in his deportment, extremely affable; proverbially of a liberal, enlightened and magnanimous mind; possessing great intellectual powers, which are nobly applied; a strenuous advocate for pure morality, and religion without bigotry; the friend of the oppressed and needy; uniformly administering strict and impartial justice, but at the same time exercising his high prerogative with the most merciful consideration; ardent in his endeavours to cultivate the mind, and improve the condition of all classes of his subjects, as far as the circumstances in which he is placed will admit; indeed, it may be said with truth, that he is pre-eminently distinguished for every virtue that is estimable in civilized society, or that can adorn and dignity the Monarch or the man.

Mahomed Sauhl.

No. 25, Great Coram street, London, July 8″.

[On the above singular paper, a London paper remarks

"For the general interests of this country, we need not say how desirable it might be to encourage the migration of some of her most enterprising citizens to a state at present so liable to an influence not the most friendly to the British nation. With regard, however, to the individuals themselves who may feel disposed to act upon these offers, we shall not risk any judgment at all. To plunge at once into the heart of Asia—to exist under a despotism, of the unlimited nature of which there is no model to be found at this moment throughout Christendom, and of which there can be no likeness until the Holy Alliance shall have achieved the consummation of its benevolent schemes—to be placed by the fierce and unchangeable Mahometan next in order of degradation the Guebre,[501] the most vile of created beings—these perhaps may be tests of constancy too severe for an English spirit. The Prince, to be sure, is much lauded by his Ambassador; but who and what will be the successor of Abbas Mirza?].'

10.275 'Emigration to Persia,' *City Gazette* (Friday, 5 September, 1823): 'The Persian Minister in England, Mirza Mahomed Sauhl, previous to his leaving London, published a notification to the European nations, inviting them to migrate to the country of his master[502]; which he describes as one of the most delightful under heaven, resorted to by invalids for the recovery of their health, and producing wheat, rice, barley, cotton, and every species of fruit and grain in abundance. He promises them in the name of the Prince Royal,[503] land, residences, and necessaries for subsistence, gratuitously, with aid in the means of transportation to the assigned territory. A London paper doubts the propriety of encouraging emigration to a country where christians are despised as infidels, and the most horrible despotism may succeed to the present ruler who is so highly lauded by his ambassador.'

---

[501] Zoroastrian.

[502] Fath 'Ali Shah.

[503] 'Abbas Mirza.

10 From 1816 to the End of the Turco-Persian War (1816–1825)   1047

10.276 'Untitled,' *The National Intelligencer* (Saturday, 6 September, 1823) and 'Untitled,' *The Herald* [Greenfield MA] (Tuesday, 16 September, 1823): 'The Persian Ambassador,[504] on leaving England a short time ago, published an official paper, in which, in the name of the Prince Royal of Persia,[505] he invited foreigners from any part of Europe to settle in the province of Alzirbijan, promising them religious freedom and exemption from taxes. The design of the Prince in making this liberal proposal is to extend more widely among his people a knowledge of the agriculture, manufactures, and economical institutions of Europe. We think the plan must excite the attention both of the Irish Catholics and the French Protestants. These oppressed people, in escaping from the conscientious restraint of *His most Christian Majesty*[506] and of the *Defender of the Faith*[507] may possibly find christian conduct, if not christian principles in the heart of Asia. It is a little remarkable that while Switzerland, an ancient abode of freedom, is reposing restraints upon the liberty of the press[508] and preventing as far as possible the settlement of foreigners in her territories; while England perseveres in the intolerance of the sixteenth century; while a numerous faction in Spain—free Spain—is clamouring for the last oration of the Inquisition, a free press should be established in Egypt, and religious freedom in a province of Persia. If the Sovereigns of Europe do not catch something more of the spirit of the times, they will either reduce their people to Asiatic ignorance and degradation, or the People will borrow a lesson from the East, and execute on them retributive justice, possibly by a summary process not unfrequent in Turkey.'

10.277 'Turks and Persians,' *Boston Recorder* (Saturday, 13 September, 1823; to 'peace'), 'Turks and Greeks,' *New Brunswick Fredonian* (Thursday, 18 September, 1823) and 'Turks and Persians,' *Edwardsville Spectator* (Saturday, 11 October, 1823; to 'peace'): 'The war between the Turks and Persians wears an aspect favourable to the former. The Persian monarch,[509] tired of the war, was pressing negociations for peace at Erzerum.'

10.278 '[From Our Correspondent.] Office of the Daily Advertiser, Boston, Sept. 15. Latest from Europe,' *Charleston Courier* (Thursday, 25 September, 1823): 'The English brig Jasper, arrived at Copenhagen on the 20th of July, having on board the Persian Ambassador, Mirez [sic: Mirza] Mahommed Saulit,[510] who was on his return home, by way of St. Petersburgh.'

---

[504] Mirza Saleh Shirazi.

[505] 'Abbas Mirza.

[506] Title borne by the French kings, at this time Louis XVIII (r. 1814–1815, 1815–1824). Cf. 5.74.

[507] George IV. Cf. 10.51.

[508] For the restrictions on freedom of the press in Switzerland at this time see Jungk (1947).

[509] Fath 'Ali Shah.

[510] Mirza Saleh Shirazi.

10.279 'Turks and Persians,' *Boston Recorder* (Saturday, 27 September, 1823): 'A vessel which left Constantinople on the 2d of July, announces that the negociations between the Porte and Persia had been broken off, and hostilities have commenced afresh.'

10.280 'Gibraltar, Aug. 22,' *National Advocate* (Saturday, 4 October, 1823), 'Gibraltar, Aug. 22,' *New-York Commercial Advertiser* (Saturday, 4 October, 1823), 'From Gibraltar,' *New-York Spectator* (Tuesday, 7 October, 1823), 'Untitled,' *Independent Chronicle and Boston Patriot* (Wednesday, 8 October, 1823), 'From Gibraltar,' *Providence Gazette* (Wednesday, 8 October, 1823), 'Gibraltar, Aug. 25,' *American Advocate & General Advertiser* (Saturday, 11 October, 1823; 'French [sic, fresh] hostilities'), 'Gibraltar, August 22,' *Charleston Courier* (Monday, 13 October, 1823), 'From Gibraltar,' *Vermont Gazette* (Tuesday, 14 October, 1823) and 'Untitled,' *St. Louis Enquirer* (Monday, 17 November, 1823): 'A vessel arrived at Trieste, from Constantinople, which she left on the 2d inst. [August] brought intelligence, that fresh hostilities had commenced between the Persians and the Porte.'

10.281 'Untitled,' *Baltimore Patriot & Mercantile Advertiser* (Monday, 6 October, 1823), 'From Gibraltar,' *The National Gazette and Literary Register, New-York Spectator* (Tuesday, 7 October, 1823), *Independent Chronicle and Boston Patriot* (Wednesday, 8 October, 1823), 'The Persians,' *New-Hampshire Sentinel* Friday, 10 October, 1823), 'The Persians,' *New Bedford Mercury* (Friday, 10 October, 1823), 'The Persians,' *Boston Recorder* (Saturday, 11 October, 1823), 'Intelligence. The Persians,' *Connecticut Herald* (Tuesday, 14 October, 1823), 'From Gibraltar,' *Vermont Gazette* (Tuesday, 14 October, 1823), 'The Persians,' *Charleston Courier* (Saturday, 18 October, 1823), 'The Persians,' *Washington Whig* (Saturday, 18 October, 1823), 'Untitled,' *Argus of Western America* (Wednesday, 22 October, 1823) and 'Untitled,' *St. Louis Enquirer* (Monday, 17 November, 1823): 'The Austrian Observer, of the 20th ult. Announces that the Kinja[511] of Daud Pacha, at the head of 5000 men, has gained a decisive victory over the Persians at Mendeli, a town five leagues from Bagdad, which the latter had captured from the Turks.[512] The garrison having made a sally, was repulsed with a loss of 1000 men, and the Persian commander was made prisoner. The Turks found considerable booty in the fortress.'

10.282 'Turkey and Greece,' *New-York Evening Post* (Tuesday, 7 October, 1823) and 'Foreign News. From the N.Y. Evening Post, Oct. 7,' *Dutchess Observer* (Wednesday, 15 October, 1823): 'Peace between the Turks and Persians is stated to have been on the eve of being concluded.'

---

[511] Haji Talib Agha. Cf. 10.190.
[512] Cf. 10.252.

10.283 'Latest from England,' *The Freeman's Journal* (Monday, 13 October, 1823): 'Peace between Turkey and Persia was on the point of being concluded.'

10.284 'Greece and Turkey,' *National Advocate* (Monday, 13 October, 1823), 'The Greeks and Turks. From the Baltimore American, Oct. 9,' *New-York Commercial Advertiser* (Monday, 13 October, 1823), 'New-York, Oct. 13. From Smyrna,' *The New-London Gazette, and General Advertiser* (Wednesday, 15 October, 1823), 'From Smyrna,' *American Sentinel* (Wednesday, 15 October, 1823), 'Smyrna Papers,' *Southern Patriot, and Commercial Advertiser* (Thursday, 16 October, 1823), 'Greeks & Turks,' *Essex Register* (Thursday, 16 October, 1823), 'From Smyrna,' *Middlesex Gazette and General Advertiser* (Thursday, 16 October, 1823), 'Smyrna Papers,' *Albany Argus* (Friday, 17 October, 1823), 'Miscellaneous News. Smyrna Papers,' *Newburyport Herald* (Friday, 17 October, 1823), 'Greeks and Turks,' *Saratoga Sentinel* (Tuesday, 21 October, 1823), 'A Constantinople date of July 21, says,' *The Times, and Hartford Advertiser* (Tuesday, 21 October, 1823) and 'Foreign. New York Oct 14. Latest from England,' *Edwardsville Spectator* (Saturday, 15 November, 1823): 'From several extracts from Bagdad, it would appear the Turks have taken Menduli, and repulsed the Persians.[513] The latter, after an action in which the former were said to have the advantage, were compelled to retreat several leagues. We have witnessed the arrival of a great number of bags filled with heads and ears, distressing but too eloquent proofs of the report.'

10.285 'Extracts from the Papers,' *New-Hampshire Patriot & State Gazette* (Monday, 13 October, 1823): 'The German accounts in these papers announce a decisive victory obtained by the Turks over the Persians near Bagdad.'[514]

10.286 'Smyrna Letters Smyrna, 19th August,' *American Federalist Columbian Centinel* (Wednesday, 15 October, 1823), 'Smyrna Letters. Smyrna, 19th August,' *The Farmers' Cabinet* (Saturday, 18 October, 1823), 'From Smyrna,' *National Advocate* (Saturday, 18 October, 1823), 'Smyrna Letters. Smyrna, 19th August,' *New-York Commercial Advertiser* (Saturday, 18 October, 1823), 'Smyrna Letters. Smyrna, 12th Aug.,' *Albany Argus* (Tuesday, 21 October, 1823), 'Smyrna Letters. Smyrna, 19th August,' *The National Gazette and Literary Register* (Tuesday, 21 October, 1823), 'Smyrna Letters. Smyrna, 19th August,' *New-York Spectator* (Tuesday, 21 October, 1823), 'Smyrna, 19th Aug,' *Middlesex Gazette and General Advertiser* (Thursday, 23 October, 1823), 'Smyrna Letters. Smyrna, 19th August,' *Easton Gazette* (Saturday, 25 October, 1823), 'Smyrna Letters. Smyrna, 19th August' *City Gazette* (Monday, 27 October, 1823) and 'Greece,' *Charleston Courier* (Tuesday, 28 October, 1823): 'We have accounts today that the Persians have made peace with the Turks.'

---

[513] Cf. 10.281.
[514] The victory at Mandali. Cf. 10.281, 10.284.

10.287 'Greeks & Turks,' *Essex Register* (Thursday, 16 October, 1823), 'Miscellaneous News,' *Newburyport Herald* (Friday, 17 October, 1823), 'From the Boston Centinel. Smyrna,' *City Gazette* (Monday, 27 October, 1823), 'Greece,' *Charleston Courier* (Tuesday, 28 October, 1823), 'Greece,' *Vermont Gazette* (Tuesday, 28 October, 1823) and 'Peace between Turkey and Persia,' *Geneva Gazette* (Wednesday, 29 October, 1823; with minor variations): 'A letter from Smyrna to a gentleman in this city [Boston], dated 17th of Aug. mentions that intelligence has been received from Constantinople to the 12th, when peace had been concluded with Persia, and the treaty was signed.'

10.288 'Greeks,' *Hampshire Gazette* (Wednesday, 22 October, 1823): 'The Turks, having made peace with the Persians, will, unfortunately for the Greeks, be less embarrassed in their war against them. Before the peace, the Turks had taken Menduli, and sent to Constantinople several bags filled with heads and ears[515] to be counted by the Grand Seignior.'[516]

10.289 'Missions in Russia and Persia,' *Boston Recorder* (Saturday, 25 October, 1823): 'The indefatigable Missionaries of the Scottish [Missionary] Society are proceeding in their arduous undertaking of converting the Tartars to Christianity, amidst alternate discouragements and hopes.[517] At one village they are derided, insulted, driven away, and threatened with expulsion, and even death, whilst in an other, the bigoted Mahomedan inhabitants after listening to them for a while, turn away, from the evident fear of an impression these strange doctrines might make. They will not hear, lest they should repent and be saved; yet at some few places, the people hear them gladly, and evidently remember what they hear. With the Persians, the prospect of success seems not quite so distant, as the scripturse are very widely circulated amongst a people who can read them, which few of the Tartars can. The exertions of the mission attract considerable notice, not only at Ispahan, but throughout Persia, for whilst priests and laymen visiting the former place, frequently seek out the agents, to dispute with them on the comparative merits of the Christian and Mahomedan systems, they were lately surprised at a request made through a merchant for a copy of the scriptures in Arabic, for the use of one of the chief Mollahs of Ispahan. This request was of course gladly complied with, as far as they possessed the ability to do so, for the Psalms and the New Testament were all they had in Arabic, though they added to them a Persian Testament.'

---

[515] Cf. 10.284.

[516] Mahmud II.

[517] Founded in February, 1796, originally as the Edinburgh Missionary Society. 'This Society was more highly favoured than any other that had entered Asiatic Russia, and remained longer in the country than any other.' See Aikman (1860: 115–116). The Scottish Missionary Society had tmissionaries at three stations in 'Russian Tartary,' viz. Karass (1802–1833), Astrakhan (1814–1825), Orenburg (1814–1825), and at Bakhchysarai in the Crimea (1821). See Anonymous (1846f: 106); O'Flynn (2017: 408).

10 From 1816 to the End of the Turco-Persian War (1816–1825)

10.290 'The Ship Canada,' *Richmond Enquirer* (Tuesday, 11 November, 1823): 'Peace has been concluded between the Persians and the Turks, an event, that is said to have been brought about by the agency of the British Minister.[518] But, to all appearance the Greeks are not disheartened by this intelligence—they are making the greatest exertions for the struggle, that is shortly to take place.'

10.291 'Untitled,' *Daily National Intelligencer* (Wednesday, 12 November, 1823) and 'Foreign Intelligence,' *The Long Island Farmer* (Thursday, 13 November, 1823): 'It appears by the late accounts from Odessa, that the peace between the Turks and the Persians, has been brought about by the exertions of the British Government, through the influence of Lord Strangford. The English agent endeavored to lessen the impression which was made on the Greeks by the news of the peace with Persia, by proclaiming that Lord Strangford had received instructions by a courier in 23 days from London, according to which England insists on the immediate independence of the Morea, &c. Persons who pretend to be well informed, assert, however, that the instructions alluded to relate wholly to the differences with Persia. This is the most probable conclusion; for as yet we have been able to perceive no sort of disposition on the part of any of the European governments to favor the Greeks. Strange that the influence of christian governments should be exerted to heal a quarrel between two nations of barbarians, while not a particle of sympathy has been manifested for a nation of Christians, struggling for their very existence, with the fact staring them in the face that defeat will be certain death!'

10.292 'Foreign Intelligence. Turkey and Persia,' *Ithaca Journal* (Wednesday, 19 November, 1823): 'It is stated that a treaty of peace between these two powers was signed at Ergerumon[519] the 15th of July last.'[520]

10.293 'Nuremberg, Oct. 23,' *National Advocate* (Wednesday, 10 December, 1823): 'During the negotiation between the Court of Teheran and the Porte, the Ottoman troops, under the Pacha of Bagdad,[521] suddenly attacked, and made themselves masters of the town of Meudoli,[522] in which there was a Persian garrison; such an event is calculated to rekindle the war between the two Empires.'

---

[518] Lord Strangford. As Frary (2015a: 505) noted, 'Strangford helped end the war by mediating between the Qajar Crown Prince and the Ottoman Divan and by deflecting Russian efforts to incite a Persian attack on Baghdad....Strangford's intervention prevented the peace agreement from evolving into an anti-Russian military alliance, thereby offsetting some very dangerous consequences.'

[519] Erzurum.

[520] The treaty was concluded at Erzurum on 28 July 1823. See Hertslet (1891: 164).

[521] Daud Pasha.

[522] Mandali.

10.294 'Continuation of Foreign Extracts. Mischief Brewing,' *The Northern Budget* (Tuesday, 16 December, 1823): 'Some persons who pretend to be well informed upon the subject, affect to say that the interview of the two Emperors on the frontiers of Poland,[523] has for its object the concerting of means to diminish the influence of England in the States of the Porte and of Persia....the Potentates of the North, they say, have a grand plan of detaching altogether the European Continent from English preponderance, which will be a prelude to the extinction of that power in India. Those persons to whom we allude found their opinions, on the one hand, on the efforts of Russia to extend its relations, in the New World; its desire to found new colonies on the expedition of Capt. Kotzebue[524]; and on the other, on the measures of England to place bounds to the ambition of Russia, as may be seen from its care in establishing peace between Persia and the Porte, and by the protection which it has afforded to the Greeks and the Pacha of Egypt.[525]—*Swabia Mercury*.'

10.295 'Extract of a letter from an American to the Editors of the Commercial Advertiser. Smyrna, Sept. 29,' *New-York Commercial Advertiser* (Wednesday, 17 December, 1823), 'Smyrna, 29th Sept. 1823,' *Baltimore Patriot & Mercantile Advertiser* (Thursday, 18 December, 1823), 'From the N.Y. Commercial Advertiser, Dec. 16. Good News from the Greeks,' *The National Gazette and Literary Register* (Thursday, 18 December, 1823), 'Latest from the Greeks. Extract of a Letter. "Smyrna, 29th Sept. 1823",' *Daily National Intelligencer* (Friday, 19 December, 1823), 'The Greeks. Extract of a letter from an American to the Editors of the N.Y. Commercial Advertiser. Smyrna, Sept. 29,' *Independent Chronicle and Boston Patriot* (Saturday, 20 December, 1823), 'Good News from the Greeks. New York, Dec. 16,' *Alexandria Gazette* (Tuesday, 23 December, 1823), 'Good News from the Greeks,' *Centinel of Freedom* (Tuesday, 23 December, 1823), 'Smyrna, Sept. 29,' *Richmond Enquirer* (Tuesday, 23 December, 1823), 'Smyrna, 29th Sept. 1823,' *Eastern Argus* (Tuesday, 23 December, 1823), 'The Greeks. Extract of a letter from an American to the Editors of the N.Y. Commercial Advertiser. Smyrna, Sept. 29,' *Dutchess Observer* (Wednesday, 24 December, 1823), 'From the N.Y. Commercial Advertiser. The Greeks,' *Hampshire Gazette* (Wednesday, 24 December, 1823), 'New-York, Dec. 16. Good News from the Greeks,' *Charleston Courier* (Thursday, 25 December, 1823), 'The Greeks. Extract of a letter from an American to the Editors of the N.Y. Commercial Advertiser. Smyrna, Sept. 29,' *Village Register and Norfolk County Advertiser* (Friday, 26 December, 1823), 'From the N.York Com. Advertiser, Dec, 16. Good News from the Greeks,' *The Oracle of Dauphin* (Saturday, 27 December, 1823), 'Good News from the

---

[523] Alexander I and the Austrian emperor Francis I met at Czernowitz (mod. Chernivtsi, Ukraine) in October, 1823. On the meeting see Metternich (1881: 84–91).

[524] Captain Otto von Kotzebue (1787–1846), captain in the Imperial Russian Navy. For the expedition referred to here, which took him from the Baltic, around Cape Horn, across the Pacific, up to Kamchatka, and back, see Kotzebue 1830.

[525] Mehemet 'Ali Pasha.

Greeks,' *Washington Review and Examiner* (Saturday, 27 December, 1823), 'Greece,' *The Watch-Tower* (Monday, 29 December, 1823), 'Good News from the Greeks. Extract of a letter from the Correspondent of the New-York Commercial Advertiser, dated Smyrna, 29th Sept. 1823,' *Ithaca Journal* (Wednesday, 31 December, 1823), '"The Greeks are doing well.",' *American Repertory* (Thursday, 1 January, 1824), 'From the N.Y. Commercial Advertiser. Good News from the Greeks,' *Kentucky Gazette* (Thursday, 1 January, 1824) and 'Latest from the Greeks. Extract of a Letter. "Smyrna, 29th Sept. 1823.",' *Edwardsville Spectator* (Tuesday, 13 January, 1824): 'It is reported that the Russians and Turks have arranged their differences; and as the Persians, (who are said to be entirely under the influence of Russia,) have made peace with the Turks, I am inclined to believe this report.'

10.296 'Turkey and Greece,' *The Arkansas Gazette* (Tuesday, 23 December, 1823): 'The Turks and Persians have made peace, under the influence of the British ambassador.'[526]

10.297 'Turkey & Greece,' *New-York Evening Post* (Friday, 2 January, 1824): 'The Divan is said, in accounts from Constantinople, to have expressed to Lord Strangford some disquietude on account of the renewal of negociations between Russia and Persia.'

10.298 'Description of the population of Constantinople. The Persians,' *North Star* (Tuesday, 13 January, 1824): 'Of these [Persians] there are so few at Constantinople that their existence disappears in the crowd, and any [?] characterization is hardly possible from the few specimens of observation. They are chiefly merchants, or dervizes, intent on gain, the one by commerce, the other by begging. As Shuis [sic, Shi'a], or heretics, they cannot lift up their heads and are more hated by the fanatical Sunnis, or orthodox, than even the Jews; for the Turks have a proverb, that at the last day, the Persians shall serve as asses for the Jews to ride to hell upon: Thus treated, no wonder they have recourse to that lying and cheating of which they are frequently accused.'[527]

---

[526] Lord Strangford.

[527] This is an English translation a paragraph from von Hammer (1822) that first appeared in Anonymous (1822f: 336). For the original see von Hammer (1822: 390), 'Derselben sind in Constantinopel so wenige, dass ihr Daseyn in dem unermesslichen Völkergewoge verschwindet, und dass die Charakterbezeichnung derselben nach den wenigen, hier angesiedelten Individuen, eine schwierige und missliche Aufgabe bleibt. Es sind meistens nur Kaufleute und Derwische, beyde auf Gewinn, jene durch Handel, diese durch Betteln erpicht. Als *Schiis*, d. i. Ketzer, dürfen sie nirgends ihr Haupt erheben und sind als solche vom fanatischen *Sunni* d. i. Rechtgläubigen noch mehr gehasst, als die Juden, denn nach einer türkischen Volkssage werden die Perser am jüngsten Tage die Lastesel abgeben, auf denen die Juden zur Hölle reiten werden. Aus so schlechtem Gesichtspuncte betrachtet, können sich dieselben wohl des Rufes von Lug und Trug, in welchem dieselben stehen, nicht los und ledig machen.' On Persians in the Ottoman empire more generally, see Masters (1991).

10.299 'Untitled,' *The National Gazette and Literary Register* (Saturday, 17 January, 1824): 'The text of the treaty between Turkey and Persia, is given in the French papers of 3d December. In the preamble, it is alleged that the interests of the *religion of Islam* commanded a reconciliation between the two countries.[528] The treaty was brought about by the agency of England! The sovereign of Persia[529] is styled—"the king of kings, the sultan, the son of a sultan, the conqueror, the ruler of Persia, &c."[530]—and the Turkish monarch[531]—"the Protector of the Faith, Ruler by sea and land, the sultan, the son of a sultan, the conqueror, the emperor of the Ottomans," &c.'[532]

10.300 'Latest from England,' *The Georgian* (Monday, 9 February, 1824): 'A treaty of peace, has been concluded between the Persians and Turks.'

10.301 'Untitled,' *Salem Gazette* (Tuesday, 9 March, 1824), 'Very late from Europe,' *Independent Chronicle and Boston Patriot* (Wednesday, 10 March, 1824), 'Corfu, Jan. 6,' *The Statesman* (Friday, 12 March, 1824), 'Untitled,' *Vermont Journal* (Monday, 15 March, 1824), 'Very late from Europe,' *Connecticut Herald* (Tuesday, 16 March, 1824), 'London, Feb. 18,' *Republican Advocate* (Wednesday, 17 March, 1824), 'Corfu, Jan. 6,' *Vermont Gazette* (Tuesday, 23 March, 1824) and 'Foreign. Very late from Europe,' *The Southern Chronicle* (Wednesday, 24 March, 1824): 'The Persians, it is reported, have declared war against the Turks.'[533]

10.302 'Miscellaneous,' *New-York Evening Post* (Thursday, 11 March, 1824): 'The Sultan of Persia[534] had ordered the war to be continued against the Turks, in consequence of the treaty of peace not having been ratified.'[535]

10.303 'Foreign,' *The Schenectady Cabinet* (Tuesday, 16 March, 1824), 'Untitled,' *The Northern Budget* (Tuesday, 16 March, 1824), 'The Greeks,' *Plattsburgh Republican*

---

[528] According to the Preamble, 'The interests of the religion of Islam required a reconciliation.' See Hertslet (1891: 164).

[529] Fath 'Ali Shah.

[530] The Preamble styles Fath 'Ali Shah 'His Majesty the King of Kings, the Hakan son of a Hakan, the Conqueror Feth Alli Shah, the Sovereign of Persia.' See Hertslet (1891: 164).

[531] Mahmud II.

[532] The Preamble styles the Sultan 'His Majesty, the Protector of the Faith, the Guardian of the Holy Cities, Sultan of the Sea and Earth, the Sultan, son of a Sultan, the Conqueror Mahmood Han, Emperor of the Ottomans.' See Hertslet (1891: 164).

[533] A false rumor.

[534] Fath 'Ali Shah, not a sultan but a shah.

[535] On the contrary, the treaty was ratified. Qasem Khan was sent to Constantinople in company with the Ottoman envoy, Najib Efendi, and returned with the copy sealed 'with the seal of the sultan' See Busse (1972: 169).

(Saturday, 27 March, 1824) and 'Foreign,' *Plattsburgh Republican* (Saturday, 10 April, 1824): 'Persia had refused to ratify the treaty with Turkey.'

10.304 'From England,' *National Advocate* (Monday, 19 April, 1824): 'The intelligence from Constantinople is to the 27th of January, the latest received. The situation of the Turks is by no means enviable; they have war without, and disaffection and trouble within...The Persians it...appears were moving towards the Turkish frontiers; this no doubt is the work of Russia, in consequence of the hesitancy on the part of Turkey to evacuate Moldavia and Wallachia according to the stipulation of the treaty.'[536]

10.305 'Turkey,' *Baltimore Patriot & Mercantile Advertiser* (Monday, 19 April, 1824), 'Turkey,' *The Cabinet* (Tuesday, 20 April, 1824), 'Later still from Europe. Turkey,' *Centinel of Freedom* (Tuesday, 20 April, 1824), 'Latest from Europe. Turkey,' *New-York Spectator* (Tuesday, 20 April, 1824), 'From the N.Y. Commercial Advertiser. Latest from Europe. Turkey,' *Hampshire Gazette* (Wednesday, 21 April, 1824), 'Foreign. From the N.Y. Commercial Advertiser. Latest from Europe. Turkey,' *New Brunswick Fredonian* (Thursday, 22 April, 1824), 'Foreign. Latest from Europe. Turkey,' *Richmond Enquirer* (Friday, 23 April, 1824), 'From the Boston Patriot, April 16. Latest from London. Turkey,' *The Oracle of Dauphin* (Saturday, 24 April, 1824), 'Foreign Intelligence. New-York, April 7. Latest from Europe. Turkey,' *The Watch-Tower* (Monday, 26 April, 1824), 'News— Foreign & Domestic. Latest from Europe. Turkey,' *North Star* (Tuesday, 27 April, 1824), 'Foreign. Turkey,' *Middlesex Gazette* (Wednesday, 28 April, 1824) and 'General Summary,' *The Supporter, and Scioto Gazette* (Thursday, 6 May, 1824): 'Letters from Constantinople, dated January 27, speak positively of the disastrous situation of the Turks.... It is also confirmed that the Persians in the neighbourhood of Bagdad have made hostile movements.'

10.306 'Turkey,' *New-York Evening Post* (Friday, 23 April, 1824): 'it is again said that all doubt relating to peace with Persia had vanished; and that the Porte having received official intelligence of the Persian Ambassador's[537] having passed the Euphrates on his way to Constantinople [damaged: had given an?]....order to the Turkish Envoy[538] at Bagdad to set out to meet him.'

---

[536] Ottoman recalcitrance over its withdrawal from Moldavia and Wallachia was a thorn in the side of Russia, and a precondition for the return of a Russian minister to Constantinople. Strangford was deeply involved in negotiations with the Porte to bring this about. See e.g. Lloyd (1826: 252–255); Wellesley [Wellington] (1867: 453–457); Florescu (1961).

[537] Qasem Khan. See Busse (1972: 169). Cf. 10.244.

[538] Najib Efendi. Cf. 10.68. As Hasan-e Fasa'i noted, Busse (1972: 169), after the peace treaty was signed at Erurum, 'it was handed over to Qāsem Khān...who was appointed ambassador to Istanbul. Together with Najib Efendi he travelled to Turkey.'

10.307 'Untitled,' *Portland Advertiser* (Saturday, 24 April, 1824), 'Untitled,' *Boston Commercial Gazette* (Monday, 26 April, 1824), 'Untitled,' *Daily National Intelligencer* (Tuesday, 27 April, 1824), 'Foreign. Late from England. Boston, April 23,' *Hampden Journal* (Wednesday, 28 April, 1824), 'Untitled,' *New-Bedford Mercury* (Friday, 30 April, 1824), 'Latest from Gibraltar,' *Village Register* (Friday, 30 April, 1824) and 'Untitled,' *Connecticut Mirror* (Monday, 3 May, 1824): 'George Bethune English, Esq.[539] who came passenger in the brig Herald which arrived at Boston on Thursday, in 71 days from Smyrna, reports that when he left Constantinople, peace had been made between the Turks and the Persians and Russians.'

10.308 'Boston, April 23. From Smyrna,' *New-Hampshire Patriot & State Gazette* (Monday, 26 April, 1824), 'Boston, April 23. From Smyrna,' *The National Gazette and Literary Register* (Tuesday, 27 April, 1824), 'Latest from Europe. Boston, April 22. Late from England,' *Hallowell Gazette* (Wednesday, 28 April, 1824), 'By the Mails. Boston, April 24,' *Massachusetts Spy* (Wednesday, 28 April, 1824), 'Foreign. From Smyrna,' *Providence Patriot* (Wednesday, 28 April, 1824), 'From Smyrna,' *Boston Weekly Messenger* (Thursday, 29 April, 1824), 'From Smyrna. Boston, April 23,' *Alexandria Gazette* (Saturday, 1 May, 1824), 'Foreign. From Smyrna. Boston, April 23,' *Richmond Enquirer* (Thursday, 6 May, 1824) and 'From the Boston Daily Advertiser. From Smyrna,' *Washington Reporter* (Monday, 10 May, 1824): 'We are indebted to a friend for a file of the Spectateur Oriental, received by the Herald, which arrived at this port [Boston] yesterday from Smyrna, to Feb. 6. . . .We do not find any intelligence of the restoration of peace, after the recent rupture, between the Porte and Persia, mentioned in the late English papers. It is mentioned under the date of Guselisar,[540] Jan. 17, that the Persians were marching in three corps, one of which, after an action, had entered into Chom,[541] and another had occupied Bagdad without firing a gun. These statements, however, appear to be doubtful. Preparations for this war were making at Constantinople as well as for that with the Greeks.'

10.309 'Turkey and Persia,' *New-York Spectator* (Tuesday, 27 April, 1824) and 'Turkey and Persia,' *The Long Island Farmer* (Thursday, 29 April, 1824): 'An extraordinary courier from Constantinople, had arrived at Paris, with information that all doubts relative to peace with Persia begins to clear up—the Porte has received official accounts that the Persian

---

[539] George Bethune English (1787–1828), Harvard College A.B. '07 (member of both the Porcellian and Hasty Pudding Clubs), A.M. 1811, soldier of fortune and noted convert to Islam who was Mehemet 'Ali's chief of artillery in his Nile expedition of 1820. See English (1822); Dunn (2006: 124). He later became a diplomat, and was sent to Constantinople in April, 1823, by John Quincy Adams and James Monroe with the goal of negotiating a trade agreement with the Porte. See Bergquist 1983: 361.

[540] Güzelhisar (mod. Aydın, ancient Tralles), inland from Izmir/Smyrna.

[541] Erzurum?

10   From 1816 to the End of the Turco-Persian War (1816–1825)

Envoy, on his way to Constantinople has passed the Euphrates and arrived at Erivan. Immediately the Turkish Envoy at Bagdad set off for Teherar [sic, Tehran]. Minziaky[542] has not as yet been able to deliver the despatches with which he is charged to the Reis Effendi, on account of the indisposition of that minister.[543] It appears the Sultan[544] has given orders that the former Reis shall provisionally take his situation, so as not to delay the answer to the propositions of the Russian Envoy.'[545]

---

[542] Matei Minciacky (a Romanian; for his full name see Lăzărescu 1995: 275) served as Russian Chargé d'Affaires while Constantinople was without a full-fledged ambassador. Technically, he was appointed 'to head an "economic mission" at Constantinople.' See Florescu (1961: 483). He arrived on 22 January 1824. 'Er öffnete daher s. Kanzlei erst im März und bloß als russ. Kanzleichef. Nun erst begann die Pforte ihre Truppen aus den Fürstenthümern [Moldavia and Wallachia] zu ziehen, und Alexander [I] ernannte den Geh. Rath v. Ribeaupierre am 27. Aug. 1824 zu s. Gesandten bei der Pforte. Endlich erfolgte die Räumung der Fürstenthümer in den letzten Monaten des Jahres, worauf Herr v. Minziaky sogleich am 11. Dec. 1824 sein Beglaubigungsschreiben als Geschäftsträger überreichte. Dadurch ward die diplomatische Verbindung zwischen Rußland und der Pforte wiederhergestellt.' See Anonymous (1827d: 527). According to Lane-Poole (1888/1: 410), 'M. Minziaki, who conducted the affairs of the Czar pending the full restoration of diplomatic relations with the Porte by the arrival of an ambassador, was "a sensible quiet well-conducted man, up to his business and void of pretension."' Little seems to be recorded about Minziaki. According to a notice from Vienna dated 23 October 1823, 'Both Count Nesselrode and M. Tatischeff are at Lemberg with Prince Metternich, as well as M. Minziaky, who is to fill the post of Russian Chargé d'Affaires at Constantinople, and who, after the Congress at Verona, was appointed Consul in Moldavia and Wallachia.' See Anonymous (1823d).

[543] Sadeq Efendi. According to Anonymous (1824b), 'Nachrichten aus Constantinopel vom 26. Jan. zufolge war unser Generalkonsul v. Minziaky am 17. Jan. Abends dort eingetroffen. Sobald seine Ankunft angezeigt wurde, kam ein Beamter aus dem Ministerium des Auswärtigen, um ihn im Namen des Reis-Effendi—der übrigens in den letzten Zügen liegen soll—zu bewillkommen. Es wurden ihm sogleich, als Beweis von Aufmerksamkeit, Blumen und eingemochte Früchte überreicht. Die Gesundheitsumstände des Reis-Effendi haben sich so verschlimmert, daß der Sultan seinem Leibarzte bey seiner Ungenade (das heißt in der Türkey: bey Verlust des Kopfes) befahl, ihn dem Tode zu entreißen. Der Leibarzt soll bey Verkündung, dieses Befehls ein wenig in Schrecken gerathen seyn.' Cf. Anonymous (1824c), 'D'après les lettres de Constantinople, du 7 février, lord Strangford à notifié l'arrivée de M. de Minziaky à tous les ministres ottomans. Celui-ci n'a déployé que le titre de conseiller d'État de la Russie. Mais, puisque le nouveau reis-effendi, Saada Effendi, qui est le canal ordinaire des communications diplomatiques, est malade, et que le Sultan ne s'est pas encore empressé de le remplacer sur-le-champ, ni le grand-vizir, ni les autres ministres n'est encore répandu à cette notification. Il paroît cependant que lord Strangford presse le Divan, et l'on annonce, en ce moment, que le dernier reis-effendi a été chargé de faire les démarches officielles usitées.'

[544] Mahmud II.

[545] It had fallen to Strangford 'die Pforte um den nöthigen Firman zur Reise des Hrn. v. Minziaky zu bitten, welcher mit einem förmlichen Beglaubigungsschreiben des Grafen Nesselrode an den Reis-Effendi versehen seyn soll.' See Anonymous (1823c). Eventually Minciacki delivered his note with the Czar's message on 5 April and received a reply from the Sultan in early May. For the texts of these communiqués see Lesur (1827: 93–97).

10.310 'The Greeks and Turks,' *New-York Evening Post* (Wednesday, 28 April, 1824) and 'From the National Advocate, April 29,' *Republican Advocate* [Frederick MD] (Friday, 30 April 1824 or later): 'Advices from Odessa of the 25th Feb. mention that the Schah[546] on the sixth January signed the ratification at the Divan of the treaty between Persia and the Porte. Some dispute appears to have arisen in Georgia between the Russian General Jarmoloff, & the Persian Prince Abbas Mirza, respecting the determination of the frontiers; but it was thought the Prince would give way.'[547]

10.311 'Foreign News,' *Independent Statesman* (Friday, 30 April, 1824): 'By an arrival from Smyrna, we have advices to Feb. sixth, affording some particulars from the Oriental Spectator, relating to the condition of the Morea.

The Editor of the Daily Advertiser, who has received a file of newspapers observes, that no intelligence of the restoration of Peace between the Turks and the Persians is contained in the Spectator. On the contrary, it is mentioned, under date of Guesilar,[548] Jan 17, that the Persians were marching in three corps, one of which, after an action, had entered Chom, and another had occupied Bagdad without opposition. Whatever doubts may be attached to this information, it appeared that preparations for this war were going on at Constantinople.'

10.312 'Untitled,' *The Nantucket Inquirer* (Monday, 3 May, 1824): 'George B. English Esq.[549] arrived at Boston on the 22d ult. [April] from Constantinople. Peace had been concluded between the Turks, Persians, and Russians.'

---

[546] Fath 'Ali Shah.

[547] As McNeill (1836: 76–77) noted, 'The treaty of Goolistan had not defined the line of frontier between Persia and Russia so distinctly as to leave no room for cavil, and the appointment of commissioners to effect the final demarcation was delayed on various pretexts, till the fresh impressions of what was really meant by the less definite terms of the treaty had become faint and imperfect. When commissioners, therefore, were at length appointed, numberless disputes arose, and the government of Georgia pressed their claims to insignificant patches of land as urgently as if the existence of their national power had depended on possessing them. These disputes gave rise to angry discussions...Various lines of frontier were successively proposed by one party, and rejected by the other...and agents were sent by the Prince Royal ['Abbas Mirza] to Teflis; and instructions transmitted to the Russian chargé d'affaires at Tabreez, without any progress being made towards the accomplishment of this object. At length all appeared to be arranged, and a proposal made by the Russian chargé d'affaires was accepted by the Prince Royal, who was charged with the affairs of the frontier. But the Russian agent had exceeded his instructions, and General Yermoloff refused to ratify the engagements which M. Mozarovich had contracted.'

[548] Güzelhisar, mod. Aydın. Cf. 10.308.

[549] Cf 10.307.

10 From 1816 to the End of the Turco-Persian War (1816–1825)

10.313 'Greece,' *The Freeman's Journal* (Monday, 3 May, 1824), 'Untitled,' *Connecticut Mirror* (Monday, 3 May, 1824) and 'Foreign Intelligence. Greece,' *Ithaca Journal* (Wednesday, 5 May, 1824): 'Accounts from Constantinople, to Feb. 12th, contradict the report of Peace having been ratified with Persia, & state that the Turkish army had recently been completely defeated in the neighborhood of Bagdad.'

10.314 'Untitled,' *The Schenectady Cabinet* (Tuesday, 4 May, 1824): 'Letters from Constantinople of the 3d of February, announce that the Emperor of Persia has ratified the peace with the Porte.'

10.315 'Latest from England,' *The Georgian* (Tuesday, 4 May, 1824): 'The Dutch Journals contain reports that...hostilities had again commenced between the Turks and Persians. The latter had invested Bagdad, and were advancing.'

10.316 'Foreign Items. Greece,' *Ithaca Journal* (Wednesday, 12 May, 1824): The Scah of Persia,[550] signed on the sixth of Jan. the ratification of the Divan of the Treaty between Persia and the Porte.'

10.317 'Greece and Turkey,' *Geneva Palladium* (Wednesday, 12 May, 1824): 'There appears to be no reason to doubt that Persia had concluded a treaty of amity with the Porte.'

10.318 'Turkey,' *Rochester Telegraph* (Tuesday, 8 June, 1824): 'On the 17th of March, Kassim-Chan the Persian Ambassador to the Sublime Porte,[551] made his entrance into the capital. The Porte has assigned as his residence a hotel in the quarter d'Akseri.'[552]

10.319 'Postscript. Nine days later from England,' *New-York Evening Post* (Thursday, 24 June, 1824): ['By the regular packet ship Euphrates, which left Liverpool on the 24th, we have received our usual files of London papers to the 22d ult]....The stipulations of the treaty between Turkey and Persia, were gradually carrying into effect.'

10.320 'Nuremberg, May 12,' *New-York American* (Friday, 25 June, 1824), 'Russia and Turkey,' *New-York Spectator* (Monday, 29 June, 1824) and 'Russia and Turkey,' *The Long Island Farmer* (Thursday, 1 July, 1824): 'The stipulations of the Treaty of Peace between Turkey and Persia, are now gradually carrying into execution. The Persian troops that were in the Pachalic of Bagdad have evacuated it, and withdrawn to the Persian frontiers; but it is affirmed that they were previously guilty of various excesses. Plenipotentiaries are to be

---

[550] Fath 'Ali Shah.
[551] Cf. 10.306. See Busse (1972: 169).
[552] Aksaray 'in the centre of the old city....was once a pleasant crossroads and market square.' See Freely (2000: 184).

appointed by both parties to regulate the frontiers. All Armenia has been long since evacuated by the Persians. The commercial intercourse between the subjects of the two Empires has likewise recommenced.[553] Many Persian merchants have gone to Turkish ports, especially to Constantinople and Smyrna, to make purchases, and more are expected.[554] The Armenian merchants, on their side, again venture into Persia, where they meet with a good reception.'

10.321 'Gibraltar Papers,' *New-York Spectator* (after 27 July 1824): 'Malta, April 30.— Warlike preparations continue to be made in Constantinople for the most vigorous prosecution of the war against the Greeks. The Porte, at peace with Russia and Persia, appears to be in earnest to bring the war to an issue this campaign. The sailing of the first squadron of its fleet has already been announced, and the second squadron, under the High Admiral,[555] will sail on the 20th. To bring the war with Persia to a close, the Porte ceded the conquest made by the Shah[556] to that power.'

10.322 'From Gibraltar,' *New-York Evening Post* (Monday, 11 October, 1824): 'The Persian envoy at Constantinople[557] was said to be about to leave that city in consequence of a disagreement with the Turkish government.'[558]

---

[553] According to Eugène Desbassayns de Richemont (1800–1859), writing at Tabriz and quoted in Bélanger (1838: 425), 'la route de Constantinople ayant été fermée au commerce pendant la guerre avec la Turquie, les marchands persans étaient allès faire leurs achats à Tiflis...aussitôt après le rétablissement de la paix, ils avaient quitté cette ville pour reprendre la route de l'Asie-Mineure et revenir à leurs anciennes relations.' Moreover, the same writer observed, 'Dans la dernière guerre avec la Turquie, la Perse ayant obtenu, pour ses marchandises, de ne payer aux douanes turques que 4 p. 100 une fois pour toutes et l'exemption du droit de passage dans le Kurdistân et dans les différentes villes de l'Asie-Mineure, ces avantages auraient dû accroître son commerce avec Smyrne et Constantinople. Cependant, un effet tout contraire a eu lieu. Le fermage des douanes de l'Adzerbaïdjân, qui avait été payé, les années précédentes, 12,000 tomans, ne l'a été que 10,500 en 1824, et, cette année [1825], on n'en aurait pas retiré plus de 7000 tomans, ce qui a obligé le prince à les mettre en régie. Ce fait prouve d'une manière incontestable le décroissement du commerce de cette province, et particulièrement la diminution progressive des rapports de la Perse avec Constantinople.' See Bélanger (1838: 432).

[554] As Desbassayns de Richemont observed, quoted in Bélanger (1838: 431), 'Les principales marchandises que les Persans envoient à Constantinople sont des châles de Cachemire et du Kermân, de l'indigo de l'Inde, quelques soies du Ghilân, un peu de noix de galle, du tabac, des peaux de Boukhara, des tuyaux de pipe et quelques drogueries. Ils en rapportent en échange, en fait d'objets européens, des indiennes, de toiles peintes, des draps légers, des soieries, des velours, des moires, des brocards, des galons, des paillettes, de la quincaillerie, de la poterie et de la faïence, etc.'

[555] Khosrow Mohammad Pasha. See Prousis (2018: 98, 101).

[556] Fath 'Ali Shah.

[557] Qasem Khan.

[558] Whether or not any disagreement occurred, Qasem Khan left Constantinople with the signed and sealed copy of the Treaty of Erzurum. See Busse (1972: 169).

10   From 1816 to the End of the Turco-Persian War (1816–1825)

10.323 'Foreign,' *Catskill Recorder* (Friday, 19 November, 1824): 'It is said that a new war has commenced between Persia and the Pacha of Bagdad.[559] The former power, at the head of 25,000 men, has seized on a part of the territories of the latter.'

10.324 'Foreign Intelligence,' *New-York Evening Post* (Tuesday, 23 November, 1824), 'Untitled,' *National Advocate* (Tuesday, 23 November, 1824), 'Postscript. Latest from Europe,' *New-York Spectator* (Tuesday, 23 November, 1824; with minor variations) and from 'According:' 'Paris, Oct. 14,' *The Statesman* (Friday, 26 November, 1824), 'Paris, Oct. 8,' *Independent Chronicle and Boston Patriot* (Saturday, 27 November, 1824), 'Latest Foreign News. From the N.Y. Statesman of Tuesday. Europe,' *Centinel of Freedom* (Tuesday, 30 November, 1824), 'Foreign. Latest from Europe,' *Richmond Enquirer* (Tuesday, 30 November, 1824) and 'Madrid, Sept. 30,' *New-Hampshire Gazette* (Tuesday, 30 November, 1824): 'Accounts from Constantinople of the 11th September, state, that. . . . war had recommenced with the Persians. According to official intelligence, Prince Mehemet Ali had become master of Sullimania,[560] and threatened Bagdad.—The Persian army was more numerous than ever, and this fresh storm could not fail to increase the embarrassment of the Porte.'

10.325 'Foreign. Latest from Europe,' *Catskill Recorder* (Friday, 26 November, 1824) and 'Late from Europe,' *The Schenectady Cabinet* (Tuesday, 30 November, 1824): 'Persia has commenced hostilities against Turkey.'

10.326 'Foreign News,' *Saratoga Sentinel* (Wednesday, 1 December, 1824): 'The Turks, indeed, appear to suffer disasters in every quarter; and, as an addition to their misfortunes, it is said that the Persians have re-commenced hostilities against the Porte, with a more numerous army than ever.'

10.327 'Latest Foreign News. Turkey,' *The Mohawk Sentinel* (Thursday, 9 December, 1824): 'The "Algerine [sic, Allgemeine] Zeitung" of the seventh instant, states that Hostilities had really commenced between Turkey and Persia, and that the army of the Persian prince, Mehemet Ali,[561] threatened Bagdad.'

10.328 'From the N.Y. National Advocate. From Europe,' *Dutchess Observer* (Wednesday, 19 January, 1825) and 'Persia,' *New-York Spectator* (Friday, 21 January,

---

[559] Daud Pasha.

[560] This report seems to conflate the late Mohammad 'Ali Mirza, who did threaten Baghdad before he died, with Mahmud Pasha Baban, the Kurdish chieftain, who 'by a bold march and a costly battle, regained Sulaimaniyyah.' See Longrigg (1925: 246).

[561] Mahmud Pasha Baban. Cf. 10.324.

1825): 'The Schah of Persia[562] has left Teheran for Sultanea,[563] to attend the marriage of his grand daughter, the daughter of Abbas Mirza, with Prince Kermanchah[564]; from there he will organize his army, and attack the Pachalik of Bagdat. The Charge des Affair [sic] of Russia, at Persia,[565] is to be relieved by an ambassador.[566] Persia has in its employ a number of French officers to discipline her troops.'

10.329 'Marseilles, Feb. 10,' *National Advocate* (Thursday, 7 April, 1825), 'Postscript. Latest from England. Marseilles, Feb. 10,' *New-York Spectator* (Friday, 8 April, 1825), 'From England. Marseilles, Feb. 10,' *The Schenectady Cabinet* (Wednesday, 13 April, 1825), 'Thirteen Days Later from England. Marseilles, Feb. 10,' *City Gazette and Commercial Daily Advertiser* (Friday, 15 April, 1825) and 'Latest from Liverpool. Marseilles, Feb. 10,' *The Southern Chronicle and Camden Literary and Political Register* (Saturday, 16 April, 1825): 'Mercantile letters have been received from Aleppo, containing some information respecting the present relations between Persia and the Porte, which do not agree with the reports that have been for some time in circulation. These reports affirmed that hostilities had lately taken place between the Turks and the Persians, and that a new war was at hand. Of this they knew nothing at Aleppo, where they must have better information respecting the state of things. Our letters state, on the contrary, that the negociations respecting the disputed points on the frontiers, which by the last treaty, were to be terminated as soon as possible by an amicable convention, had taken a favourable turn since the arrival of the Turkish Ambassador at Teheran,[567] and that it was expected that the intended demarcation of the frontier line would soon be completed, by which future differences will be prevented....But the strongest proof how little the Porte apprehends from that quarter, is the fact that Turkish troops are ordered from the remote parts of Asiatic Turkey, even from the Pachalic of Bagdad, to march to Asia Minor, to await the further orders of the Porte. According to all appearance, these troops are destined for the next campaign against the Greeks; and they would hardly have been employed in this manner if there were any thing to be feared from Persia.'

---

[562] Fath 'Ali Shah.

[563] Cf. 9.26.

[564] Mohammad Hoseyn Mirza Heshmat od-Doula, who succeeded his father 'Mohammad 'Ali Mirza after the latter's death. See Longrigg (1925: 246). Cf. Busse (1972: 116, 199). Cf. 10.364. For the death of the new bride only two weeks later see 11.43.

[565] Mazarovich.

[566] This did not happen until after the conclusion of the Second Russo-Persian War in 1828 (see below). When he went on leave, Mazarovich was relieved by Andreas Amburger, beginning in September, 1825, who had come with Mazarovich and remained in Tabriz until July, 1826. See Markham (1874: 557) and 1826.45 below with more information on him.

[567] Najib Efendi arrived in Tehran on 16 February 1824. See Busse (1972: 169).

10.1 Miscellaneous

10.330 'From Europe,' *New-York Evening Post* (Wednesday, 10 August, 1825), 'Foreign Summary,' *The Truth Teller* (Saturday, 13 August, 1825) and 'Foreign News,' *Rochester Telegraph* (Tuesday, 23 August, 1825): 'Recent letters from Ispahan announce, that the King of Persia[568] has abdicated the throne in favour of his eldest son, Abbas Mirza.[569] It is said that he proposes to visit the ruins of Shiraz, and intends to employ his leisure moments in rebuilding that city,[570] and restoring it to its former splendour.'[571]

10.1 Miscellaneous

A Brief Review of Morier's Travels

10.331 'Morier's Travels in Persia, &c.,' *The Geneva Gazette* (Wednesday, 15 July, 1818): 'Mr. Morier's work[572] is written without any more art than is necessary to perspicuity. It comprises the remarks of a candid sensible gentleman, made from actual observations, upon the present state of a nation, distinguished, in different periods of antiquity, for supporting the interests of the "Chosen People," and we find with wonder, that neither the lapse of twenty-three hundred years, nor Mohamedism, the great destroyer, have been able to effect any considerable change in the social state of Persia. Her present King[573] cannot conceive the possibility of any restriction upon regal power; though his personal qualities, both of the head and heart, are respectable. It is evident that he occupies the very throne of "that Ahasueres who reigned from India even unto Ethiopia, over an hundred and seven and twenty provinces,"[574] and the description of the present court of Persia, and of the laws of the kingdom and their execution, present a lively picture of that prince, while they show the natural effects of despotic power combined with unbounded wealth. Abundant, interesting and important information is contained in this work; and

---

[568] Fath 'Ali Shah.

[569] 'Abbas Mirza was not Fath 'Ali Shah's eldest son. Tancoigne (1820: 72) and Buckingham (1830: 415, n). * identified him as his third son, Hasan-e Fasa'i (Busse 1972: 36) and Eichwald (1837: 551) as his fourth. Exceptionally, Anonymous (1873a: 715) identified 'Abbas Mirza as Fath 'Ali Shah's eldest son whereas von Hammer (1819: 281), on the authority of Johnson (1818: 169), and Anonymous (1834a: 322), insisted that he was Fath 'Ali Shah's second son. Fath 'Ali Shah did not abdicate his throne.

[570] After the devastating earthquake in June, 1825, noted above.

[571] This rumor first appeared in the *Bombay Gazette* on 29 December 1824. See Anonymous (1825d: 854).

[572] Referring to A second journey through Persia, Armenia, and Asia Minor, to Constantinople, in the years 1810 and 1816, Morier (1818).

[573] Fath 'Ali Shah.

[574] Esther 1: 1.

such as, I venture to say, cannot be found in any other; and could never have been obtained, but by a visit to Persia.'

Persian Wheat in New York

10.332 'Agricultural,' *Otsego Herald* (Monday, 11 May, 1818): 'The Society for the promotion of useful arts of the state of New-York,[575] have obtained a small quantity of Persian Wheat, which they intend distributing to agriculturists who may apply. This Grain originated in Persia, and was sent by a French agent at the Persian court[576] to the garden of plants in Paris,[577] from whence it was received into this country. It is described as a very superior grain[578] to the wheat or rye of Europe or America. It was supposed to be winter grain by the gentleman who received it in this country, and was tried as such by several agriculturalists, but failed in every instance. Three grains were given to a gentleman, who, by accident, having overlooked it, did not sow it till the spring following—the three grains did remarkably well, and produced heads different from any that had ever before appeared in this country.—By careful attention, the fifth year produced twelve bushels and thirteen quarts, of the largest and best grain ever obtained in America....Samples of the grain put up in half pint parcels, may be had on application made to the Recording Secretary, No. 78 North Pearl street, Albany,[579] or to S. De Witt & G. Clarke, Esquires, Mr. James Rogers and Mr. Wm. Mayell.'

---

[575] The Society for the Promotion of Agriculture, Arts and Manufactures was chartered in 1793. In 1823 the Albany Lyceum of Natural History was incorporated and the Society for the Promotion of Useful Arts merged with it. In 1824 the Albany Institute of History and Art was formed. See See Reynolds (1906: 383, 439).

[576] This could have come from any of several French scholars. The botanist André Michaux collected plants in Iran in 1782 and 1783 and 'en avait rapporté un herbier magnifique et une nombreuse collection de graines.' See Brunet (1863: 8). Hamy (1911: 30–34). Michaux would not be considered a 'French agent at the Persian court,' however. Guilaume-Antoine Olivier and his companion Jean Guillaume Bruguière were in Tehran in 1796, during the reign of Agha Mohammad Shah, and amassed 'une importante collection de graines, notamment de plantes d'Orient' which went, in the first instance, to the Jardin des Plantes. See Bonnet (1905: 696). See e.g. Alternatively, it may refer to a member of Gardane's mission. Gardane himself wrote of the non-diplomatic activities of his group, 'Chacun travaille dans la Légation...M.^{r} le Docteur Salvatori fait un Mémoire sur le climat et les maladies.' See Gardane (1809a: 73). Thus it is possible that he sent botanical samples to Paris.

[577] Jardin des Plantes.

[578] Tancoigne (1820: 151–152) remarked upon 'the excellent quality of the wheat of this country.' J.-M. Tancoigne was not listed by Gardane himself in the list of the members, but in his son's later publication on the mission he was described as 'jeune de langue de l'école de Constantinople, attaché à la légation par S.A.S. le prince de Bénévent.' See Gardane 1865: 104.

[579] Dr. Jonathan Eights. He had been elected to the council of the Society for the Promotion of Useful Arts in Albany in 1816 and later became its Secretary. See McKinley (2005: 9).

Persian Rice in New England

10.333 'Untitled,' *Otsego Herald* (Monday, 28 December, 1818): 'Dr. Benjamin Waterhouse,[580] of Cambridge, Mass. has communicated a paper to the Boston Palladium,[581] on the subject of the culture of Rice in New England. He states that there is a kind of mountain rice (the Oriza Mutica) that will grow on high grounds with no more water than the common rains, which he has no doubt would grow to advantage in New England.—Some 8 or 10 years ago, Dr. W. obtained some of this rice, originally brought from Persia, and sowed half of it in Massachusetts, and sent the rest of it to president Jefferson[582]....Dr. W. does not give the result of his experiments.'

Mirza Abu'l Hasan Khan Shirazi in England

10.334 'Persians in England,' *Connecticut Courant* (Tuesday, 5 January, 1819), 'Persians in England,' *National Messenger* (Wednesday, 13 January, 1819), 'Persians in England,' *Christian Messenger* (Wednesday, 20 January, 1819), 'Miscellaneous. Persians in England,' *City Gazette and Daily Advertiser* (Friday, 30 June, 1820), 'Miscellaneous. Persians in England,' *Carolina Gazette* (Saturday, 1 July, 1820), 'Persians in England,' *New-York American* (Friday, 7 July, 1820), 'Persians in England,' *Poulson's American Daily Advertiser* (Wednesday, 12 July, 1820), 'Selected. Persians in England,' *Daily National Intelligencer* (Thursday, 13 July, 1820), 'Persians in England,' *Alexandria Gazette & Daily Advertiser* (Saturday, 15 July, 1820) and 'Persians in England,' *Boston Intelligencer & Evening Gazette* (Saturday, 22 July, 1820): 'For the following account of the impressions made on the minds of Mirza Abul Hassan, ambassador from Persia to this country, and his suite, during the nine months' residence in England, (we believe in the year 1810)[583]—we are indebted to the last number of the Literary Gazette: it is extracted from Morier's Second Journey through Persia, &c. Lond. 1818.

---

[580] Benjamin Waterhouse (1754–1846) was professor of medicine at Harvard, a correspondent of John Adams and Thomas Jefferson, and a leading exponent of the smallpox vaccine. For his life see Cash (2006).

[581] New-England Palladium.

[582] See also Jefferson's letter of 1 December, 1808, to Waterhouse 'on the subject of upland or mountain rice, Oryza Mutica.' Bergh (1907: 204–205).

[583] Cf. 9.98. The ambassador arrived at Plymouth on 30 November 1809. See Toone (1834: 455). He left together with Sir Gore Ouseley and other members of his mission in July, 1810. See Reynolds (1846: xlviii-xlix).

"As the Persian Ambassador attracted much interest in England it may be gratifying to his friends, and not unacceptable to others, to receive some account of his residence in this country.

"His first surprise on reaching England, was at the caravanserais, (for so though no contrast can be greater, he called our hotels.)—We were lodged in a gay apartment at Plymouth, richly ornamented with looking-glasses, which are so esteemed in Persia, that they are held to be fittings for royal apartments only:—and our dinners were served up with such quantities of plate, and of glass ware, as brought forth repeated expressions of surprise every time he was told that they were the common caravanserais. The good folks of the inn, who, like most people in England, look upon it as a matter of course that nothing can be too hot for Asiatics, so loaded the ambassador's bed with warm covering, that he had scarcely been in bed anhour, before he was obliged to get out of it; for having during all his life slept on nothing but a mattrass on the bare ground, he found the heat insupportable, and in this state he walked about the greatest part of the night, with all the people of the inn following him in procession, and unable to divine what could be his wishes.

"One of the public coaches was hired to convey his servants to London; and when four of them had got inside, having seated themselves cross legged, they would not allow that there could be room for more although the coach was calculated to take six.—They armed themselves from head to foot with swords, pistols, and each a musket in his hand, as if they were about to make a journey in their own country; and thus encumbered, notwithstanding every assurance was given them that nothing could happen to them, they got into the coach. His Excellency himself greatly enjoyed the novelty of a carriage, and was delighted at the speed with which we travelled, particularly at night, when he perceived no diminution of it, although he was surprised that all this was done without a guide. We were met at two different posts from London by two gentlemen of the Foreign Office, who greeted him on the arrival; but he grew very anxious as we proceeded, and seemed to be looking out for an Istakhad, or a deputation headed by a man of distinction, which, after the manner of his own country, he expected would be sent to meet him. In vain we assured him that no disrespect was intended, and that our modes of doing honor to ambassadors were different from those of Persia; our excuses seemed to grieve him more; and although to a foreigner the interest of the road greatly increased as we approached the city, yet he requested to have both the windows of the carriage drawn up, for he said he did not understand the nature of such an entry which appeared more like smuggling a bale of goods into a town, than the reception of a public envoy. As for three of his servants who followed us in a chaise behind, they had nearly suffocated themselves: for, by way of experiment, they had put up all the glasses, and then when they wished it, could not put them down, so that they were quite exhausted for want of fresh air.

"He who had witness'd the manner in which our ambassadors had been received in Persia, particularly the hevec en masse of the inhabitants who were sent out to meet him at every place where he stopped, was surprised to see the little notice that he himself, in the same situation in England, had attracted, and the total independence of all ranks of people.

10.1 Miscellaneous

"His first object was to deliver his credentials to the King[584] [as soon as possible, because in Persia it is esteemed a slight if that ceremony be delayed. In this also he was disappointed: for, on the first Wednesday, the usual levee day, his Majesty happened to be unwell, and consequently there was a delay of more than ten days before he could be presented.[585] He bitterly lamented his fate, and daily affirmed, that for this he should lose his head on his return to Persia. When the day came, he was naturally anxious about the reception which he was to find: he had formed his ideas of our court from what he recollected of his own, where the King's person is held so sacred, that few have the privilege of approaching it. He had a private audience at the Queen's House,[586] and from the manner in which he expressed himself after it was over, it appeared the respect which he had hitherto felt towards our monarch was diminished. There are many ceremonies exacted upon approaching the Shah of Persia. He is seen at a great distance; he is approached with great caution, and with many profound inclinations of the body. In his immediate vicinity, the shoes are taken off and none enter the room in which he himself is seated, without a special command from him. Here the Persian entered at once into the same room where his Majesty was standing. He made no inclination of the body; he did not even take his shoes off; and what is more, he put his credentials into his Majesty's own hands. He said, that he had expected to have seen our King seated on a throne at a distance, and that he could not have approached within many paces of him. His surprise then may be conceived, when, on entering a small room, he was taken to a person whom he took to be a capijee, or porter, and was informed that this was the King of England. He said, that if any blame was imputed to him for not having delivered his credentials immediately on arrival, that all would be pardoned him, when he should assure the Shah[587] that he was not desired to take off his shoes as he approached our monarch. These circumstances will perhaps show of what importance it is, upon the introduction of an Oriental minister to the King, that care should be taken to show him the court in its greatest splendour.

"It was surprising to observe with what ease he acquired our habits of life, how soon he used himself to our furniture, our modes of eating, our hours, our forms and ceremonies, and even our language, though indeed, perhaps with respect to the latter acquirement, it

---

[584] George III.

[585] The ambassador presented his credentials to George III on 20 December 1809, three weeks after landing in Plymouth. See Toone (1834: 455).

[586] As Fitzgerald (1899: 48) noted, 'At the end of the [Pall] Mall there stood a fine old brick mansion which had been built by Sheffield, Duke of Buckingham, in 1703. It was of the style and character of Marlborough House, and was joined by semicircular colonnades to two pavilions. This the king purchased for the moderate sum of £21,000 and fitted up as a dower house for the queen. It henceforth becomes very familiar to us through the reign as "The Queen's House," and many interesting transactions occurred there. When the regent came to the throne [William IV], growing tired of Carlton House, he levelled the Queen's House and erected a substantial portion of the present Buckingham Palace.'

[587] Fath 'Ali Khan.

might rather be observed that he soon learnt sufficient just to misunderstand every thing that was said.[588]—He who had sat upon his heels on the ground all his life, here was quite at his ease on chairs and sofas; he who before never eat but with his fingers, now used knives and forks without inconvenience.

"On his being taken to hear a debate at the House of Commons, he immediately sided with a young orator, who gained him over by his earnest manner and the vehemence of his action; and at the House of Lords, the great object of his remark was the Lord Chancellor,[589] whose enormous wig, which he compared to a sheep skin, awoke all his curiosity.[590]

"He frequently walked in Kensington Gardens by himself. As he was one day seated on a bench, an old gentleman and lady, taking him for one of his own attendants, accosted him—How does your master like this, and how does he like that? and so on.—Tired with being questioned, he said, 'He like all very well, but one thing he not like—old man ask too many questions.' Upon this he got up laughing, leaving the old gentleman to find out that he had been speaking to the ambassador in person.

"It may be proper to add that Mirza Abul Hassan, the ambassador and his suite, were finally at the end of their nine months' residence delighted with our island,[591] and that the ambassador was exalted to the dignity of a Khan on his return home.

"They all left London (says our author) with lively emotions of grief; many of them shed tears as they took leave of their English friends, who on their part, appeared to be equally effected. Several would willingly have remained in England; and one in particular, who had been struck with the quiet and security of an Englishman's life compared to that of a Persian, exclaimed that he would not wish for a better Paradise than Chelsea Hospital,

---

[588] At the time of Mirza Abu'l Hasan Khan's second visit to Britain in 1819/1820 a description of his first visit was published by Admiral William Waldegrave (Baron Radstock) who wrote, 'let it be remembered that I do not understand one syllable of the Persian language, and that the Mirza's knowledge of our's extends not beyond a few familiar phrases which he learnt during his passage to England.' On the other hand, he also recorded, 'On the third or fourth day of the ambassador's arrival, the Turkish Ambassador paid him a visit. "What are you about?" cries the Turk. "I am writing English!" "Writing English! why you have scarcely been here three days, whilst I have been in England seven years, and I know not a syllable of the language, or how to form even a single letter." Thanks to Mr. J. Morier's kind attention and instruction, the Mirza writes daily copies that would do credit to any boy of twelve or fourteen.' See Waldegrave (1820: 35). His English seems to have improved greatly by the time of his second visit to Britain.

[589] John Scott, first Earl of Eldon (1751–1838). Scott became Lord Chancellor in 1801 and served, with a hiatus in 1806/7, until 1827.

[590] Surtees (1846: 172) referred to 'the bushy honours of his flowing wig.'

[591] On June 14, 1810, shortly before Mirza Abu'l Hassan left England, 'There was a grand meeting of Freemasons at the Thatched-house Tavern, the Earl of Moira, the vice grand master, in the chair, when the Persian ambassador was introduced and made a mason.' See Anonymous (1810).

10.1 Miscellaneous

Fig. 10.2 Mirza Abu'l Hasan Khan Shirazi, by Sir Thomas Lawrence, 1810. Oil on canvas. Harvard Art Museums/Fogg Museum, Bequest of William M. Chadbourne, CC0 1.0 Universal

where for the remainder of his days he could sit under the trees,[592] do nothing, and drink as much porter as he pleased."' (Fig. 10.2).

Persian War Trophies in St. Petersburg

10.335 'Interesting extracts from letters addressed by a gentleman on board of the United States frigate Guerriere, then in the north of Europe, to his friend, a member of congress,' *New-York Evening Post* (Saturday, 13 February, 1819): 'United State frigate Guerriere, off Cape Trafalgar, November 5, 1818. My last two letters contained some general remarks on

---

[592] The grounds of Chelsea Hospital comprised 'an enclosure of about fourteen acres, planted with avenues of lime and horse-chesnut trees. The ground on the south side of the building [the hospital] is laid out in gardens, which extend to the river [Thames], where they finish wth an elevated terrace.' See Shoberl (1835: 107). In addition, the grounds also had a row of plane trees. See Anonymous (1845c: lxi). Iran is well-known for its plane trees, examples of which have often been described by travellers. See Potts (2018b).

Petersburg—in this I[593] will speak of some of its monuments and edifices....In the church of St. Alexander Newsky, the protecting saint of the empire, are deposited his relics...And the Casan church, built by the present emperor,[594] and intended as a rival of St. Peters, of Rome....From the walls of the churches are suspended the standards taken from France, Turkey and Persia, by the Russian army,[595] and the keys of many fortresses and cities.'[596]

'Abbas Mirza and the Garden Wall

10.336 'Anecdote of Abbas Mirza, Crown Prince of Persia,' *The Repertory* (Saturday, 12 June, 1819), 'Anecdote of Abbas Mirza, Crown Prince of Persia,' *Boston Weekly Messenger* (Thursday, 17 June, 1819), 'Anecdote of Abbas Mirza, Crown Prince of Persia,' *Boston Intelligencer & Evening Gazette* (Saturday, 3 July, 1819) and 'Anecdote of Abbas Mirza, Crown Prince of Persia,' *The Berks and Schuylkill Journal* (Saturday, 10 July, 1819): 'Abbas Mirza, Crown Prince of Persia, is one of the most remarkable men of our times. He was born in the year 1782 and every one expects great changes when he ascends his father's[597] throne. His intercourse with learned Europeans; his speaking the English and French languages very fluently; his introduction of the European military system and discipline, and forming on that system a body of 10,000 infantry, and a considerable corps of artillery, and other measures, display a mind of no common order. Abbas Mirza is not a mere soldier, but his finer qualities render him still more worthy of the throne. Moritz

---

[593] The writer was Dr. Usher Parsons (1788–1868) of Providence, Rhode Island. 'In July, 1818, he sailed from Boston as surgeon of the U.S. Navy frigate Guerrière, Captain Thomas Macdonough, for St. Petersburg, carrying out Mr. George W. Campbell, minister to Russia. He spent about ten days in St. Petersburg, and wrote very full accounts of remarkable objects in that city, and of peculiar customs.' See Parsons (1870: 16). Cf. Pleadwell (1922: 436).

[594] Emperor Alexander I, of Russia. The Kazan Church is located in the Nevski Prospekt in St. Petersburg and was 'built by Alexander I., at a cost of three millions of dollars, and to which the royal family repair for special religious services.' See Butterworth (1882: 306–307).

[595] Cf. Beable (1910: 106), who called 'the Cathedral of the Transfiguration, one of the most important churches in Petrograd. In the court, surrounded by a railing, are twelve Turkish guns and in the interior of the church are numerous Turkish and Persian standards.

[596] Cf. Fetridge (1874: 855), 'The cathedral more resembles an arsenal than a place of worship. On every side are hung military trophies taken from various nations in Europe—Turkish standards, surrendered without a struggle; French colors, in shreds and tatters; Marshal Davoust's baton of office; and keys of surrendered cities—Dresden, Leipsic, Hamburg, Utrecht, Rheims, and Breda.' Cf. the cathedral of St. Peter and St. Paul in St. Petersburg, where, 'Many hundreds of flags—Persian, Turkish, Swedish, French, and Prussian—and the keys of Paris and other European cities, are suspended along the walls.' See Anonymous (1870b: 673).

[597] Fath 'Ali Shah.

Von Kotzebue relates the following honourable anecdote of him: "The Russian Ambassador,"[598] says he, "perceived in the garden belonging to the Prince, a projecting corner of an old wall, which made a very ugly contrast with the rest, and disfigured the prospect. He asked Abbas Mirza why he did not have it pulled down? "Only think," replied the Prince, "I have bought this garden from several proprietors in order to make something magnificent; the proprietor of the place where the wall projects is an old peasant, the only person who positively refused to sell me his piece of land as he would not part with it at any price, it being an old family possession. I must confess it is very vexatious, but notwithstanding, I honour him for his attachment to his forefathers, and still more for his boldness in refusing it me: but I will wait till an heir of his shall be more reasonable."'[599]

Persian Manners Described by J.J. Morier

10.337 'Persian Manners, &c. Entry of the King into Teheran,' *Daily National Intelligencer* (Thursday, 29 July, 1819): 'As in ancient times,[600] almost the whole of the male population of the city was ordered to meet the King, and very early in the morning of the day of the entry, the environs on the road to Khorassen were covered with people. We were summoned by the prime minister[601] in person, who was so anxious that we should be at our post at the earliest moment, that he came almost unattended to us; and, having marshalled our procession, he led the way, and served us as a guide through the streets and bazars. The activity and vivacity of this old man are as amiable as they are extraordinary in his advanced age.—We went in our smartest uniforms, and on our most lively horses; the body guard in their handsome Indian dresses, created a great clang; and, together with the numerous servants and attendants attachedto the mission, we added greatly to the general bustle. The old visier at our head, apparently all the time in great trepidation lest he should be too late, put his horse at the full trot, and at this rate we dashed through the great crowd of horse and foot passengers who had already thronged the road. When we had travelled

---

[598] Ermolov.

[599] Cf. Kotzebue (1819a: 158), 'The Ambassador observed in the garden a projecting corner of an old wall, which spoiled the beauty of the surrounding objects, and disfigured the prospect. His Excellency asked the Prince why he did not order the wall to be pulled down? "Only conceive," replied His Highness ['Abbas Mirza], ["]with a view of forming gardens on a grand scale, I purchased the grounds of several proprietors. The owner of that where the wall stands, is an old peasant, who has absolutely refused to sell his property to me, because he will not part for any price with an ancient patrimonial possession of his family. I must allow, his obstinacy vexes me exceedingly, and yet I cannot but honour him for his attachment to his forefathers, and still more for his boldness in denying me his ground. I must wait until the time when his heir will, perhaps, be more reasonable." Who would have expected to find so much feeling in despotic Asia?'

[600] This is an excerpt from Morier (1818: 385–388).

[601] Mirza Shafi'-e Mazandarani. Cf. 9.4, 9.85, 9.89, 9.93, 9.103.

about two miles from the town, we were placed at our post by some of the officers of Hossein Ali Mirza, one of the princes,[602] governor of Teheran, when we dismounted, smoked, and seated ourselves on the ground, until his majesty should appear. In the mean time the track of his route was distinguishable over the mountains and along the plain by a long line of dust, created by his procession. His baggage and equipages were continually passing, until we heard the *Zumburck* or camel artillery that at intervals fired vollies in advance.[603] As they approached, the order of procession became more distinct. His more immediate arrival was marked by the drums and trumpets of his Nokara,[604] the performers of which were mounted on gaudy dressed camels; then a long row of shatirs, then the king, totally insulated, a speck in the plain; behind him the princes, his sons, with their suites, then the courtiers and officers of *Defter Khoneh*[605] (as we might say, the chief of the public officers,) and the whole was filled up by an immense *tip*, or body of cavalry. As the king drew near, Mirza Sheffea marshalled us about one hundred yards from the road side, and when his majesty beckoned to us, we went forward in hasty strides, which the old vizier was anxious we should increase into a trot, it being the etiquette on these occasions, as we afterwards learnt, to run: our conductor himself was running as fast as he could. The king having given us his *Khosh Amedee*,[606] ordered us to mount our horses, and then requested me to ride near him: whilst Mirza Sheffea dropt in the rear of the king about twenty paces, where was also Hossein Khan Mervi.[607] He had the condescension to converse very familiarly, and his remarks and manners are ever those of a highly polished man; he

---

[602] Hoseyn 'Ali Mirza, fifth son of Fath 'Ali Shah. See Anonymous (1873a: 715); Busse (1972: 461) for numerous refs.

[603] Term used in Arabic, Turkish and Persian for a falconet, i.e. a swivel gun mounted on the saddle of a camel, *zamburak/zanburak*. Cf. Colombari (1853). For the term see Yule and Burnell (1903: 751), s.v. 'Zumbooruck.'

[604] Royal band. Cf. Fraser (1825: Appendix B, 30).

[605] Persian *daftar-khana*, 'office.'

[606] Persian *khosh-amade*, a phrase of welcome.

[607] Mohammad Hoseyn Khan Mervi. Morier (1818: 379) called 'Mahomed Hossein Khan Mervi, one of the principal noblemen of the Persian court.' In a letter to Pierre Ruffin dated 19 January 1809, Jean Raymond, a member of Gardane's mission, called him 'le favori du roi et son *courtisan* Hadji Muhammed Hussein Khan Mervi.' See Dehérain (1930: 60). Writing of his second mission to Persia, Malcolm (1827/2: 189) observed, 'Among the acquaintances I formed at this second visit, there was none that interested me in any degree so much as Mahomed Hoosein Khan of Merv.' Captured by the Uzbeks, he had been taken as a prisoner to Bukhara. He managed to escape to Kabul, reached Kandahar and eventually Tehran. 'The forlorn and fugitive chief of Merv was received at the court of Persia with every mark of regard and honor,' and when Haji Ibrahim died, Fath 'Ali Shah 'is said to have desired to raise Mahomed Hoosein Khan to the rank of prime minister, but he declined the dangerous dignity, declaring he had made a vow never again to enter upon affairs of state, unless an opportunity was afforded him of wreaking his vengeance on the merciless ruler of Bokhara, by sacking that capital. . . . His ostensible station is that of the Nedeem, or chosen companion of the sovereign, and as such he is almost in constant attendance upon the king's person, whose whole conduct towards this unfortunate chief does equal honour to his head and heart.' See Malcolm (1827/

seemed also anxious to give us a public mark of his attention, for as we rode along at two different intervals, he was presented with bowls filled with sugar candy, of which he first took a piece himself, and then ordered that it should be given to me, and to the gentlemen of the mission and our attendants.—This among the Persians is esteemed a very high mark of favor; and whilst we could not refrain from smiling at the strange custom that embarrassed our hands with large pieces of sugar candy on horseback, there was scarcely a Persian around us that would not willingly have given his beard for a similar distinction.

During all this time I had an opportunity of observing the king, and remarking the different stages of the procession. His majesty was gaily dressed in a white close vest, embroidered with spangles. His sword, his dagger, and other ornaments, were entirely inlaid with precious stones. The bridle, crupper, breast plate, were all either rubies, diamonds, or emeralds, whilst a long thick tassel of pearls was suspended under the horse's throat by a cordon that went round his neck. At different intervals he called for his Kalioun[608] (the water pipe,) which was brought to him by his Shatir Bashi, or head of the running footmen,[609] from which he took not more than one whiff, which was afterwards emitted in one long white stream of smoke, which he managed to conduct over his beard as a perfume. He was dignified in all he did, and seemed very attentive to all that was going on. As he approached the town, long rows of well dressed men, at some distance from the road, made low bows, and whenever he called one near to him, he came running with great eagerness, and received whatever he had to say with the greatest devotedness. He was then received by a corps of Mollashs [sic, mollahs] and Peishnamez, (priests) who chaunted forth the Khotbeh* [This is an oration delivered every Friday, after the forenoon service, in the principal mosques, in which the Mahometans praise God, bless Mahomet and his descendants, and pray for the king.] with all their might. Then oxen and sheep were sacrificed in great numbers just as he passed, and their heads thrown under his horse's feet. Many glass vases, filled with sugar, were broken before him, and their contents strewed on his road. Every where dervices were making loud exclamations for his prosperity, whilst a band of wrestlers and dancers were twirling about the mils (clubs) and performing all sorts of antics, to the sound of the copper drums of Looties.[610] Nothing could be more striking

---

2: 203–204). Malcolm noted that, by the time his work was published in 1827, Mohammad Hoseyn Khan Mervi had died.

[608] Persian *qalyan*. For its use and smoking culture in Iran more generally see Floor (2002).

[609] Persian *shater bashi*, chief groom. See Busse (1972: 493).

[610] Wilkes (1823: 718) wrote, 'there is a class of people called looties, who go from house to house, amusing their auditors with relating numerless stories, either true or fictitious, but always grossly indecent. They also perform a variety of tricks similar to those of our jugglers and tumblers.' Chodzko (1842: 52, n). * observed. '*Looty*, a notorious name in Persia: it keeps a medium between the Venetian *bravo* and the French *chevalier d'industrie*. Many travellers have described the Looty-bazaar of Kazvin. Three years ago, the Persian clergy at Ispahan, anxious to shake off the authority of the Shah, secretly kept and protected a very numerous band of Looties. The now reigning Mohamed Shah was obliged to go to Ispahan in 1840 with some troops and artillery, to put down their insolence. The

than the variety of the scene that surrounded the king. Amongst the crowd, I perceived the whole of the Armenians, headed by their clergy, bearing crosses, painted banners, the gospel, and long candles. They all began to chaunt psalms as his majesty drew near, and their zeal was only surpassed by that of the Jews, who also had collected themselves into a body, conducted by their Rabbis, who raised on high a carved representation on wood of the tabernacle, and made the most outrageous cries of devotion, accompanied by the most extravagant gestures of humiliation, determined that they at least should not pass unnoticed by the monarch. On coming close to the walls of the city, the crowd of horsemen and people increased to an extraordinary degree, and where they were confined in some places by the walls of gardens, became quite stationary. In all the bustle I perceived the king constantly looking at a watch carried by Shatir Bashi, anxious that he should enter the gates exactly at the time prescribed by the astrologers.—*Morier*'.

Rev. Henry Martyn's Persian Translations of Scripture

10.338 'From the London Evangelical Magazine.[611] Memoir of the Rev. Henry Martyn, D.D. Late Chaplain, to the Hon. East-India Company, and Missionary to India and Persia,' *Boston Recorder* (Saturday, 20 May, 1820), 'From the London Evangelical Magazine. Memoir of the Rev. Henry Martyn, D.D. Late Chaplain, to the Hon. East-India Company, and Missionary to India and Persia,' *Concord Observer* (Monday, 19 June, 1820) and 'Biographical. From the London Evangelical Magazine. Memoir of the Rev. Henry Martyn, D.D. Late Chaplain, to the Hon. East-India Company, and Missionary to India and Persia,' *Religious Reporter* (Saturday, 1 July, 1820): 'On the 22d of May [1808] he landed at Bushire, in the Persian dominions, and on the 30th set out for Shiraz.* [Shiraz is the second city of Persia, situated in a fertile valley, about twenty-six miles in length, and twelve in breadth, bounded on all sides with lofty mountains. The circuit of the city is about four miles, surrounded with a wall twenty-five feet high and ten thick, with numerous towers.]. . . .On the ninth of June he arrived at the celebrated seat of Persian literature, and immediately commenced, with proper assitants, another version of the New Testament.

---

corporation of Looties infests Persia till now, and keeps secret correspondence with many influential persons at the court. Perhaps they are the remains of the sect of the Assassins.' Referring to their infestation of Isfahan, Fraser (1840: 283) wrote, 'That city, ever since the King's [Fath 'Ali Shah's] death, had been a prey to the utmost confusion and disorder. The *looties*—that is, the rogues and vagabonds of the place—a large body, had commenced a systematic plunder of the inhabitants, and had made the great mosque one of their chief storehouses of the spoil.'

[611] According to Anonymous (1820b: 1, n). *, the article 'is chiefly an Abstract from "Memoirs of the Rev. Henry Martyn, B.C." &c. written, as we understand, by the Rev. Mr. Sargent, to which we beg leave to refer our readers.' See Sargent (1819) and notes below pointing out the derivation of some paragraphs in the present article from that work.

10.1 Miscellaneous

During Mr. Martyn's residence here, he had frequent opportunities of conversing with learned natives, who were accustomed to try him with hard questions; Mr. Martyn's answers were dictated by sound wisdom, singular discretion, and deep piety. His frequent disputations with the leading teachers of the Mohammedan faith excited much attention, and even alarm, so that a defence of Islamism was speedily published,[612] to which Mr. Martyn replied in the Persian language.[613]

Towards the end of November great progress had been made in the translation; Mr. Martyn, therefore, ordered two splendid copies of it to be prepared, designing to present one to the king of Persia[614] and the other to the prince Abbas Mirza, his son....

During his eleven months abode at Shiraz, Mr. Martin was so far from shrinking from any fair opportunity of confessing Christ before men, that he sought out, and gladly embraced every fair occasion of avowing "whose he was, and whom he served."[615] One public argument he held with the chief professor of Mohammedan Law; and another discussion held in the palace of one of the Persian princes, where a numerous body of Mollahs were collected....

On the 24th of May, one year after entering Persia, Mr. Martyn left Shiraz, intending to lay before the king his translation of the New Testament; but, finding, that without an introductory letter from the British ambassador he could not be admitted into the royal presence, he determined to proceed to Tebriz, where the ambassador, Sir Gore Ousely, then resided.[616] His journey, of 8 weeks, to this place, was extremely harrassing; he suffered much, especially by a fever which then attacked him with great severity; the pain in his head, was at times, almost insupportable, and he was scarcely able to proceed; and when he arrived at Tebriz, he appeared to be in the last stages of debility and exhaustion.

The following extract is from the last letter he ever wrote, addressed to a beloved friend in England...."In three days I intend setting my horse's head towards Constantinople,

---

[612] Sargent (1819: 401–402), 'So universal a spirit of inquiry had been excited in the city of Shiraz, by Mr. Martyn's frequent disputations, as well as by the notoriety of his being engaged in a translation of the New Testament into Persian, that the Preceptor of all the Moollahs began greatly to "fear whereunto this would grow." On the 26th of July, therefore, an Arabic defence of Mahometanism made its appearance from his pen. A considerable time had been spent in its preparation, and on its seeing the light, it obtained the credit of surpassing all former treatises upon Islam....a translation, discovered amongst Mr. Martyn's papers, is written with much temper and moderation, and with as much candour as is consistent with that degree of subtlety which is indispensable in an apology for so glaring an imposture as Mahometanism.'

[613] Sargent (1819: 403), 'His answer was divided into two parts: the first was devoted principally to an attack upon Mahometanism: the second was intended to display the evidences and establish the authority of the Christian faith. It was written in Persian, and from a translation of the first part, which has been found, we perceive that Mr. Martyn, "having such hope, used great plainness of speech," whilst, at the same time, he treated his opponent with meekness and courtesy.'

[614] Fath 'Ali Shah.

[615] A direct quote from Sargent (1819: 456).

[616] Almost verbatim from Sargent (1819: 462–463).

distant about 1300 miles....The ambassador and his suite are still here; his & Lady Ouseley's[617] attention to me, during my illness, have been unremitted."* [*Sir Gore Ouseley presented Mr. Martyn's New Testament to the King of Persia, who, in a public rescript, expressed his approbation of the work. He also carried the MS. to St. Petersburgh, where, under his superintendence, it was printed and put into circulation. Public curiosity about the Gospel, now for the first time, in the memory of the Modern Persians, introduced into the country, is a good deal excited here and at Shiraz, and at other places; so that, upon the whole, I am thankful at having been led hither and detained, though my residence in this country has been attended with many unpleasant circumstances. The way of the Kings of the East is preparing: thus much may be said with safety, but little more. The Persians also will probably take the lead in the march to Sion.][618]

On the 2d of Sept. Mr. Martyn commenced his formidable journey to Constantinople....his sufferings were greatly augmented by the unfeeling haste and cruelty of Hasan Aga, a Tartar, to whose guidance he was unhappily consigned....A few days after he writes:—.

"I was pretty well lodged, and tolerably well till a little after sunset, when the ague came on with a violence I never before experienced. I felt as if in a palsy, my teeth chattering, and my whole frame violently shaken. Aga Hosyn and another Persian, on their way here from Constantinople, going to Abbas Mirza, whom I had just before been visiting, came hastily to render me assistance if they could. These Persians appear quite brotherly, after the Turks.'[619]

The Persian Gulf and its Principal Islands

10.339 'Foreign Intelligence. Calcutta, April 1,' *Boston Daily Advertiser and Repertory* (Friday, 15 September, 1820), 'Foreign Intelligence. Calcutta, April 1,' *The Repertory* (Saturday, 16 September, 1820), 'Foreign Intelligence. From papers received at the office of the Boston Daily Advertiser. Calcutta, April 1,' *The American* (Wednesday,

---

[617] Harriet Georgina Whitelock. Cf. 9.109.

[618] Taken from Sargent (1819: 491–492).

[619] This last extract from Martyn's diary appears in Sargent (1832: 415) (cf. Rhea 1888: 44) but is dated 5 October, hence not 'a few days after.' Cf. the account in Anonymous (1854a: 168), 'Early in the present century, Henry Martyn had his attention called to the state of existing Persian versions, and undertook, with the help of ['Nathaniel' Jawad ibn] Sabat [1774–1827; for his career see Green 2012: 120–121], to produce an improved translation. His work he completed in 1808. It was found, however, to be so full of Arabic and foreign terms, that it was unintelligible to the common people. Henry Martyn, therefore, resolved to visit Persia himself, that he might obtain the means of correcting it. In 1811, he reached Shiraz, the seat of Persian literature, and there he remained nearly a year. As soon as his work was completed, the translator was compelled, by shattered health, to leave the country, on his way to England. He died the same year at Tocat, in Asiatic Turkey.' His death occurred on 16 October 1812. See Rhea (1888: 45).

10.1 Miscellaneous

20 September, 1820), 'Calcutta, April 1,' *The Weekly Messenger* (Thursday, 21 September, 1820), 'Calcutta, April 1. Extract of a letter from an intelligent friend attached to the expedition in the Persian gulf, dated on board H M S Liverpool, off the island of Kenn, on the 22d of Feb 1820,' *Aurora General Advertiser* (Thursday, 12 October, 1820; para. 3–7) and 'Calcutta, April 1. Extract of a letter from an intelligent friend attached to the expedition in the Persian gulf, dated on board H M S Liverpool, off the island of Kenn, on the 22d of Feb 1820,' *Weekly Aurora* (Monday, 16 October, 1820): 'One of the most interesting communications,[620] which we have this day to make to our readers, is an extract, at some length, of a letter from an intelligent Friend and Correspondent, attached to the Expedition in the Persian Gulf, dated on board H.M.S. Liverpool, off the Island of Kenn,[621] on the 22d of Feb. 1820,[622] and containing very valuable and judicious remarks on some of the principal stations in the Gulf, with observations on the causes of their decline, and speculations on their probable restoration as a consequence of the Expedition thus sent to extirpate a race of Pirates, first by force of arms, and next by the establishment of an Entrepot among them, not only to keep them in check but to introduce among them all the blessings of commerce and consequent civilization, in lieu of a life of plunder and barbarism.

---

[620] Originally published in the *Calcutta Journal* and reprinted in Anonymous (1820c). For some reason the paragraph about 'the island of Kenn' was not included but appears as 1820.7. The letter may have been written by either Lieut. John H. Grubb (Bombay Marine) or Capt. Thomas Remon (Bombay Engineers) who submitted a report on Kenn to the Bombay Government in 1822 which was reprinted as Grubb and Remon (1856).

[621] Kish or Jazirat al-Qeys. See Horsburgh (1817: 414). As Low (1877/1: 365), at the conclusion of the expedition to suppress the pirates of the lower Persian Gulf, 'In February the fleet, consisting of seven men-of-war and fourteen transports, proceeded across the Gulf to the island of Kenn to water, and here the Expeditionary force was broken up.'

[622] 'H.M.S. "Liverpool," fifty guns, Captain F.A. Collier, C.B.' was one of three ships of war that took part in the expedition, commanded by Major-General Sir William Grant Keir, to destroy the pirates of the lower Persian Gulf in 1819. As Low (1877/1: 351–352) noted, the *Liverpool* set sail from Bombay on 3 November 1819 and 'The divisional staff consisted of Major E.G. Stannus, Assistant Adjutant-General; Captain D. Wilson, Assistant Quartermaster-General; and Captain G.F. Sadleir, of the 47th Regiment, Interpreter.' According to Miles (1919: 324–325), H.M.S. *Liverpool* returned to Bombay in March, 1820. Also present were Capt. William Bruce, the Resident at Bušehr. Dr. Jukes came on the cruiser Benares with a letter for the governor of Fars. See Low (1877/1: 352–353). Low quoted extensively from accounts written by an unnamed officer who seems likely to have been the author of the letters quoted here. Considering the fact that Bruce was the writer of a letter published in 1819 describing cow pox (Bruce 1819), it is plausible to suggest that he was the writer of the accounts quoted in the present article. Moreover, the very pointed remarks in the article about the advantages and disadvantages of Bandar-e Bushehr, and of having the Residency there, also suggest that Bruce, the Resident there, was indeed the writer.

Persian Gulph.—The Letter to which we before alluded as having reached us by the Dawk[623] via Bombay, from a Correspondent attached to the Expedition in the Persian Gulph, is dated from His Majesty's Ship Liverpool, at anchor off the Island of Kenn, February 22, 1820, and contains the following passages:—.

"This service has been productive of more interest to me than I expected could have arisen from it. I feel that it has also been productive of good to mankind in a higher degree than I at all anticipated; and the result to us nationally, may be more important than those politicians, who estimate things from their incipient magnitude, are likely to imagine....I have lately visited the site of former commercial opulence, at Ormuz and Gambroon, both now fallen to decay and desolation, from the decline of those principles that fostered their prosperity in former days, and from the growth and protection of these principles elsewhere. A friend of mine, in conversation with an old patriarchal looking Arab at Gambroon, 'the sad historian of the pensive plain,'[624] lamented to him the ruin that had fallen on that once celebrated Emporium.—'It is your fault,' the man replied, 'Europeans came here and it flourished, they withdrew and it declined; let them return to us and prosperity will again be ours.' This is no bad encomium upon the principles for which we still have credit throughout these countries.

Gambroon is a heap of ruins; the British and Danish [sic, Dutch] Factories are still to be traced, in the mouldering walls, which in a few years will cease to be distinguishable above the drifted sands. Ormuz or *Haramooz*, is a more remarkable place; a sterile rock, tenanted by a few wretched fishermen, who quaintly allege that it yields only '*Nimuk* and *Gilluk*,'* [*Salt,[625] and *Red ochre* from *Iron ore*,[626] so called.] is all that remains of that once-celebrated seat of opulence and empire, which subsisted from the 11th to the 17th centuries, and of which we read such glowing descriptions.—The Portuguese Fort still stands on a small isthmus projecting from the Isle, which has no water but what is collected during the scanty rains that annually fall.

The situation we have now chosen for an establishment is certainly better calculated than any other in the Gulf, not only for our immediate purposes, but also with reference to commercial convenience, should it be the design of Providence that we are to found a new Emporium, through the confidence inspired by our power and our principles. If Ormuz, a

---

[623] 'transport by relays of men and horses, and thence "the mail" or letter-post, as well as any arrangement for travelling, or for transmitting articles by such relays.' See Yule and Burnell (1903: 299).

[624] From the poem 'The deserted village' by Oliver Goldsmith (1770).

[625] *namak*. Pilgrim (1903: 130 and 132) wrote, 'It would be hard to find any place presenting a more singular appearance than do these barren salt hills which cover nearly the whole of the island....The salt occurs in beds as much as 2 feet thick, but is exceedingly impure.'

[626] As Pilgrim (1903: 157) observed, 'Iron oxide or red ochre occurs in large deposits in various islands in the Persian Gulf among the Hormuz series, resulting from the decomposition of the hæmatite....The chief places where these pure deposits of red ochre are found are in the islands of Hormuz, Bu Musa and Hálul.'

sterile rock, could attain to such splendour, from the incidental circumstances of its situation in the channel of trade between the East and West, why should not Kenn, at present do the same?[527] since it has no competition, and as it is quite as conveniently situated with respect to the modern line of intercourse. Bussora and Bagdad have for years comprised the whole commercial industry and opulence of this neighbourhood, and the ancient route by Gambroon, like a deserted channel of the Ganges is never likely to be fertilized again by the reflux of commerce, were it even as convenient as a port, as we have found it the reverse.

Were I to offer a conjecture as to the probable effect of our interference, it would be, that an Establishment on this Island would render it in a short time, like Sincapore, the home of an industrious population, and ultimately the Entrepot of all the maritime Commerce of the Gulf; that the trade of Shiraz carried on by the high road from Bushire would not be disturbed, as the journey is accomplished in a much shorter time than from any other of the ports, being direct, and the road convenient. From Charack,[628] the port immediately opposite to Kenn, the journey occupies 20 days, and from Gambroon, or Bunder Abassi, the old route, 25 days. If therefore Bushire were abandoned, the route by Charak, already frequented by commercial people, would supercede the ancient one.

With Bushire under our influence, we may continue to occupy the channels of trade by sea and land. I should have no objection to our abandonment of Bushire in the fulness of time: if it is destined to decline from the superior attractions of a neighbouring establishment, time will give indications of its approach that will soon become manifest, and our Residency there, may be reduced to correspond with the extent of the interests requiring to be watched over; but I am in all cases inclined to prefer these natural changes to abrupt ones which disturb long existing interests and long confirmed relations; much individual distress and injury is the consequence, and the confidence reposed in us nationally is impaired. In the present instance, it is peculiarly important to us, that this should not happen, since the success of all our hopes, depends on the reliance placed on our professions.

I enclosed to you in my last, a botanical specimen of the Island of Kenn,[629] which as usual is a name of *our own*; the Arabs recognize it by no other name than *Khess* or

---

[627] Anonymous (1892a: 232), 'In consequence of the whole being quite an open and exposed shore, without any harbours to shelter boats or ships, great inconvenience is likely to arise from the difficulty of communication during strong or even moderate breezes blowing directly on the shore, which would cause much surf on it, and considering the badness of the anchorage ground, would also often oblige them to take shelter under the lee-sides of the island.'

[628] Khark.

[629] The origin of this corruption of the name is unclear. Niebuhr (1772: 338) called it, 'Die Insel Kenn,' but in 1797 Vincent wrote, 'Keish, written Kenn in several charts, but I believe always improperly.' See Vincent (1797: 347, n. 188).

Kaeese.[630] I send you some others now; they are two kinds of heath, common upon the Island; there is also a rich trefoil grass, and a description of clover, on both of which the cattle thrive well. The milk and butter here are excellent, and here is also a small shrub, which the Arabs are fond of; when boiled it is a good vegetable. It is too watery to admit of my sending a specimen, it has some slight resemblance to the *milk hedge* in appearance, but much smaller; I consider it quite peculiar.

This Island is of marine formation; coral, rock and sea shells are found in all parts of it, and afford a rich calcareous basis for the soil. That it should be so much better watered[631] than the other Islands of the Gulf, must be attributed to the filtration of the waters of the sea, through these straits. Ormuz, Larak, and most of the other Islands are of volcanic origin, and are sterile to the last degree, from the want of water; they abound with iron ore, and the substrata are probably too compact to admit of the filtration of which I speak while the rains are not sufficiently copious to form a vegetatiod on the external surfaces, which are primitive and barren. The loose sands collected around rocks which form the basis of other Islands in the Gulf, and much of the shores on both sides, admits the sea water, with its saline impregnation, to which I attribute the prevalence of brackish water throughout these coasts and countries. The Gulf Sea, I must inform you, is peculiarly salt, as I believe are most narrow seas.'

10.340 'Calcutta, April 4,' *Weekly Aurora* (Monday, 25 September, 1820): 'The island of Kenn, which is said to be an European corruption of its real name Kaeese,[632] is described by a correspondent of the Calcutta Journal,[633] and by the editor himself, as well adapted to the purposes of becoming an entrepot for all the maritime commerce of the Persian Gulf, and likely, under proper management, to succeed in due time to the departed greatness of Ormuz and Gambroon. Its situation is considered equally advantageous with those of the above settlements for becoming the emporium of a lucrative trade with the surrounding

---

[630] Horsburgh (1817: 414), 'Guase, or Kenn, called also Keish by the inhabitants.' Berghaus (1832: 43) gives the variants 'Käs, Kaise, Kaez, Kenn, Kyen; Keisch...Guess, Queche, Zeits.'

[631] Kempthorne (1835: 281), however, noted, 'Water may be also had at it [Kenn], but the quality is indifferent; it is obtained by digging a hole four or five feet deep in the sand, a short way from the beach.' Similarly Anonymous (1892a: 231–232), 'These villages [on the northwest and southwest sides of the island] are provided with wells, which supply the population, and also irrigate the grain fields and date trees. Some of the water is good, the remainder is indifferent and mostly brackish.... There are a few wells at these two places [ruins on the south side of the island], owing, probably, to its not having been much drawn, there being no irrigation carried on, and the cattle therefore alone supplied with it....Having experienced, during our stay at the island, the variable quality of the water in the wells, we feel a doubt whether any of it would continue good during the whole season.'

[632] Cf. Anonymous (1823f: 472), 'Diesen Namen haben die Europäer der Insel gegeben, denn die Araber nennen sie *Khess*.'

[633] An excerpt, missing from 1820.6, from Anonymous (1820c), citing a letter of 22 February 1820 from 'a correspondent attached to the expedition in the Persian Gulph,' and written on H.M.S. *Liverpool*.

nations, and infinitely superior to either in regard to its convenience as a sea port. We hope therefore that the selection of this place for a British establishment[634] may prove both conducive to the mercantile interests of the nation, and the ultimate happiness of the natives, with whom a closer intercourse will thus be entertained.—The editor of the Journal describes it as about four miles in length, and two in breadth, and inhabited by about fifty families, for whom it produces little more than sufficient sustenance.'

Oil on the Absheron Peninsula near Baku

10.341 'Perpetual Fire,' *New-York Spectator* (after 7 November, 1820), 'Perpetual Fire,' *Auburn Free Press* (Wednesday, 20 July, 1831) and 'Perpetual Fire,' *Black River Gazette* (Wednesday, 7 September, 1831): 'In the peninsula of Abeheron, in the province of Schirwan, formerly belonging to Persia, but now to Russia, there is found a perpetual, or, as it is there called, an eternal fire. It rises or has risen from time immemorable from an irregular orifice of about twelve feet in depth, and 120 feet in width, with a constant flame. The flame rises to the height of from six to eight feet, it is unattended with smoke, and yields no smell. The finest turf grows about the borders, and at the distance of two toises are two springs of water. The inhabitants have a veneration for this fire; and celebrate it with religious ceremonies.'[635]

---

[634] Anonymous (1821b) reported, 'Die Präsidentschaft Bombay hat beschlossen die Insel Kenn oder Kaeese im Persischen Meerbusen zu einem Waffenplatze une einer Waarenniederlage zu machen. Es ist etwa vier engl. Meilen lang und zwey breit. Bey Arrian heißt es Kataca.'

[635] This paragraph first appeared in Anonymous (1821a: 42–43). Malte-Brun (1822: 60) gives a fuller account of the same phenomena: 'An extensive neck of land shoots into the Caspian sea, called the Peninsula of Apsheron, or of Okoressa, whose saline and clayey soil is covered with a languishing vegetation, but whose celebrated springs of naphtha form a source of inexhaustible wealth to the petty sovereign of the town of Bakou. The principal springs are at Balaghan, one of them furnishes 500 pounds a-day. Not far from thence is the *field of fire*, about a square verst in extent, and continually emitting an inflammable gas. The Guebres, or worshippers of fire, have built several small temples there. . . .Not far from thence are two springs of hot water, which bubble up like the naphtha; the water is impregnated with a bluish clay, which renders it thick, but it becomes clear by standing, the clay falling to the bottom. Bathing in it braces the system, and improves the appetite. The khan of Bakou derives from the naphtha a revenue of 14,000 rubles, (or L.2100.).' One of the earliest references to the naphtha springs here is Stöcklein (1729: 13–14), which begins, 'doch besteht der Reichthum von Bazu [sic, Baku] größten Theils in Stein-Oehl, welches in unglaublicher Menge aus tieffen Södbrünnen samt dem mitgemengtem Wasser geschöpft wird. Man sagt, daß der König in Persien von besagtem Stein-Oehl zu seinem Antheil 12. tausend Toman oder sechs mal hundert tausend Abassi, das ist, jährlich drey mal hundert tausend Gulden Rheinisch einnehme.' Cf. Hanway (1753/1: 379–384) and the exhaustive discussion of later literature in Eichwald 1834: 217–237; Jackson (1911: 46–57).

10.342 'The temple of fire in Persia. Extract from the Manuscript Notes of an American Traveller,' *Nashville Clarion* (Wednesday, 20 June, 1821) and 'The temple of fire in Persia. Extract from the Manuscript Notes of an American Traveller,' *Daily National Intelligencer* (Friday, 27 July, 1821): 'The Company of horsemen assembled in the principal square of Baku to accompany us[636] on an excursion to Afsharon exhibited a strange mixture of European and Asiatic costumes.

The Russian Commandant with his officers in full uniform, the Persian Beg and his attendants in splendid robes girded round their loins with Cashmeer shawls, Tartars with their short loose cloaks, thrown gracefully over their shoulders, and Cossacks in their loose trowsers, close jacket, and lofty cap, and feathers, formed a gay and highly picturesque groupe.

As we moved forward, the narrow street forced them into some sort of order, and they moved slowly round the defiles formed by the ancient and modern fortifications, which surrounded Baku; but no sooner had they passed the outer gate, than the scene was suddenly changed. The persians and Tartars darted from the ranks and with loud shouts scoured the plains. Some threw the *djerred*,[637] and others loudly daged [sic, dared] the whole party to touch them, flying, wheeling, & avoiding those who persued [sic] them, with admirable dexterity.

In this joyous manner we passed over a barren plain until we reached the sources of Naphtha, the principle article of commerce between Baku and the interior of Persia. The pits that had been opened did not appear to be more than twenty or thirty feet deep, yet so imperfect is the machinery, that with difficulty they furnish a sufficient supply. Two clumsy buckets made of hide, are alternately fastened to a large wheel, worked by oxen, and the contents are poured by the attendants, into a trough, which conveys the naphtha to the vats. The naphtha undergoes no purification, but is sold on the spot to peasants, who convey it on camels and asses into the intrior. The Persians entertain an opinion that to light the buildings containing silk worms by means of tallow or oil, would destroy the worms. This prejudice occasions a great consumption of naphtha.

The best quality of naphtha emits, in burning, a dense black smoke and a disagreeable odour; that used generally by the peasants would be intolerable, were it not for their habits of living outside of their houses. The lamp in common use is a shallow cup of earthenware placed upon a wooden column and furnished with a coarse cotton wick.

From the Naphtha pits we directed our course to Afsharon, to the temple of Eternal Fire still the object of the veneration of the exiled and persecuted Guebres.[638] As we approached

---

[636] The dateline on the article describes the writer as an 'American Traveller.'

[637] A short spear. For a detailed description of the 'military game of Djerred' see Spencer (1854: 215–219).

[638] Described by many travellers. According to Kinneir (1813: 360), 'About seven *versts* East of the *naptha* springs, the attention is arrested by the *Atash Kudda* or fire temple of the Guebres, a remarkable spot, something less than a mile in circumference, from the centre of which a bluish

10.1 Miscellaneous

the Temple the country became more rugged and covered with scattered fragments of secondary limestone, but not a tree or a shrub to be seen. In the midst of this desolate spot stands a low quadrangular building occupying a space of about one hundred yards square, the walls not more than fourteen feet high. On the flat roof near the gate sate two squalid, meagre figures, their bodies swathed in dirty brown linen, and their dark swarthy faces partly concealed by woolen caps shaped somewhat like our hats.

We alighted at the entrance, which is an elliptic arch of stone highly ornamented, and stopped to look at an inscription in characters with which none of us were acquainted, and of which I have since regretted not having taken a facsimile.

On entering we saw issuing from the earth a bright bluish flame about two feet in diameter, not rising high, but flickering on the surface; which, on examination, we found to be carburetted hydrogen gas. The interior of the quadrangle is furnished with cells about ten feet long by eight wide, the side next the wall raised a foot high so as to serve for a couch.

At each extremity of the cell canes are inserted, two feet into the ground, the upper part coated with clay: a bright flame issued from each of these which is kept constantly burning, so that in the event of the large flame in the court yard, being extinguished, as it sometimes is by violent showers of rain, the Pilgrims may rekindle it from the same holy fire. Five of these cells were occupied: fourmen and one woman were the only ilgrims then at this shrine of the fire worshippers—a spot singularly calculated to nourish the superstition and excite the veneration of this sect—This is probably the province called by the ancient Persians, Azerbeyan, or country of fire, the existence of which has been doubted by many writers.

The Pilgrims, informed us, as well as we could comprehend them through the medium of three interpreters, that they came from the banks of the Indus[639] and intended to remain

---

flame is seen to arise. Here some small houses have been erected; and the inhabitants, in order to smother the flame, have covered the space enclosed by the walls in a thick loam of earth. When fire is, therefore, required for any culinary purpose, an incisionis made in the floor, and on a light being produced, the flame immediately arises, and when necessary is again suppressed by closing the aperture.' This treatment of sacred fire sounds remarkably un-Zoroastrian. On the other hand, the Zoroastrian association of the fire temple may be apocryphal.

[639] Cf. Keppel (1827/1: 300–302), 'Sixteen miles north-east of the town, on the extremity of the peninsula of Abosharon, I came, after ascending a hill, in sight of the object of my curiosity. The country around is an arid rock. Enclosed within a pentagonal wall, and standing nearly in the centre of the court, is the fire-temple, a small square building, with three steps leading up to it from each face. Three bells of different sizes are suspended from the roof. At each corner is a hollow column, higher than the surrounding buildings from the top of which issues a bright flame; a large fire of ignited naptha is burning in the middle of the court, and outside several places are in flames. The pentagon, which on the outside forms the wall, comprises in the interior nineteen small cells, each inhabited by a devotee. On approaching the temple, I immediaetly recognized, by the features of the pilgrims, that they were Hindoos, and not Persian fire-worshippers, as I had been taught to expect....I was much amused at the surprise they showed on hearing me converse in Hindostanee....I followed one of the pilgrims, who first took me into a cell where a Brahmin, for so his thread proclaimed him, was engaged in prayer....My first acquaintance and the Brahmin then accompanied me round the other cells...In one of them was the officiating priest of the Viragee caste....In a small recess stood a figure

at Afsharon until relieved by others. Their religion enjoins them not to abandon the sacred fire to unbelievers. The last party of pilgrims consisting of four men and two women had departed after a residence of two years in the temple.

The term Geubre [sic] by which we distinguish the ancient Parsees, is applied generaly by the Persians to all infidels, and is probably derived from the same Aribic [sic, Arabic] word as the Giaour of the Turks. They are called by the Persians Guebres Atechperes,[640] Infidels, fire worshippers—.

After the conquest of Persia by the Arabs, under the Mahometan leader Omar, these people were sorely oppressed, and took refuge in the most desert parts of Persia, and in western India.[641] In Persia they inhabit the desert of Kerman[642] and the borders of the Persian Gulf. About four thousand families remained at Yezd[643] under a solemn promise of having their civil and religious liberties secured to them, a promise, which has been frequently violated; and this unfortunate race of men were almost exterminated by Shah Abbas the Great[644]. . . .

---

of Vishnoo, and near it one of Hunoomaun. . .Of the pilgrims present, five were Brahmins, seven Viragees, five Sunapeys, and two Yogees.'

[640] Persian *atash-parast*, 'A worshipper of fire, a guebre, one of the sect of the Magi.' See Shakespear (1817: 14).

[641] A reference to the Parsi community of Bombay. Cf. Grose (1766: 123), 'the Parsees, or the race of Persian refugees. . .some centuries ago, fled from the face of the Mahometan persecution, then invaders and conquerors of the Persian dominions. They were brought to these parts [Bombay] where they and their race have ever since continued.' Cf. Menant (1902: 11ff).

[642] For the post-Islamic conquest Zoroastrian community of Kerman see Boyce (1966). Houtum-Schindler (1882: 54) estimated the total population of Zoroastrians in Kerman and three nearby villages in 1879 at 1756 in 412 households.

[643] For the Zoroastrians of Yazd see Browne (1893: 362–393); Jackson (1906: 353–400). Houtum-Schindler (1882: 54) put the total population of Zoroastrians in Yazd and in 22 nearby villages in 1879 at 6483 in 1650 households. Estimates for both Kerman and Yazd, dating back to 1807, were collected by Houtum-Schindler (1882: 56).

[644] Cf. Smith (1811: 798), 'The Mahometans are the declared enemies of the Gaurs [Zoroastrians], who were banished out of Persia by Shah Abbas.' This may reflect a confusion with 'Abbasids,' for it was variously reported that Shah 'Abbas had intentionally established the Zoroastrian community at Julfa (Wicqfort 1667: 176–180; Menant 1902: 42, n. 1). In January, 1707, Cornelis de Bruyn wrote of the Zoroastrians of Julfa, 'Ces *Guébres* ont été chassez de leur païs par les fatalitez de la guerre, & ne consistent plus qu'en un petit nombre, qui sont dispersez en plusieurs Villes de Perse, où ils ont plus de liberté qu'à Ispahan, où l'on a obligé ceux qui étoient établis à Julfa, à embrasser le Mahométisme, au lieu qu'ils joüissoient, sous le Régne du Roy Abas, de la même liberté dont joüissent les Arméniens & les Chrétiens, ce qu'on leur avoit accordé pour les empêcher d'aller habiter sur les Frontieres de Turquie. On leur avoit même donné quelques terres à cultiver, aux environs de cette Capitale, aussi-bien qu'en d'autres lieux.' See Le Bruyn (1725: 170–171). Cf. Ringer (2011: 21) who noted that, 'Persecution of the Zoroastrians intensified with the accession of Shah Sultan Hosayn to the Safavid throne in 1699. The shah signed a decree of forcible conversion of the Zoroastrians in Isfahan, who were subsequently converted to Islam or massacred for refusing.'

10.1 Miscellaneous

The country for more than a mile round the temple, presents the same natural phenomenon we observed within its walls. Wherever we opened the ground to the depth of two feet, and applied a lighted taper, a flame arose, the size of the excavation. The inhabitants burn their lime by means of this gas.—They make an excavation, and pile over it the limestone, which is abundantly scattered over this spot, the gas is then ignited, and burns until extinguised [sic, extinguished] by a shower of rain, or by smothering the flame with earth.'

Résumé of Diplomatic Relations with Persia

10.343 'Literary Selections, for the National Gazette. Persia. From a late British Publication,' *The National Gazette and Literary Register* (Monday, 20 December, 1820) and 'Persia,' *Commercial Advertiser* (Saturday, 20 January, 1821; from 'One necessary preparation'): 'Persia has been from the earliest ages exposed in a peculiar degree to the evils of foreign and domestic war.[645] The seventeenth [sic, eighteenth] century, beyond any former era, presented a series of uninterrupted calamity, under which scarcely any other nation ever groaned. In an early part of it the inroad of the Afghans carried fire and sword to its remotest extremities, and reduced many of its proudest capitals to heaps of ruins. The bloody reaction produced by Nadir Shah, though it vindicated the independence of his country, scarcely induced a pause in the progress of its miseries. Even the lustre thrown around Persia by his foreign victories was only like a flash of lightning through the darkness, which instantly returned deeper than before. After his assassination, Persia had two disputed successions; one of eleven, and the other of fourteen years; during all which periods this great empire continued incessantly tearing its own vitals. It only enjoyed repose, when a daring usurper, after wading to the throne through oceans of blood, held it during his life-time with a firm and vigorous hand. The last of these was Aga mahommed, an eunuch, who saved himself by his energy and cruelty from the contempt which his condition would have inspired; and not only held the throne during his life, but transmitted it to his nephew, Futteh Ali Khan [sic, Shah], the present sovereign.

Persia, buried in these intestine dissensions, was almost lost to the recollection of Europe, unless when occasionally a Russian gazette announced a triumph on the Araxes and the Kur. From this obscurity it was drawn by a series of political events either felt or dreaded. The French revolutionary government, inspired with the most imbittered enmity against England, conceived the hope of striking a blow against her through the medium of her Eastern possessions. This could only be hoped by an overland expedition, in reference to which the state of the Persian empire was an object of primary importance. The Directory sent a mission under Olivier and Brugniere to ascertain the precise state of that empire; but they were too busily employed in Europe to take any measures in consequence. The

---

[645] This long selection is an almost verbatim extract from Murray (1820: 82–92).

attention of our Indian government was first drawn by events occurring within its own sphere. When it was discovered that Tippoo had sent an embassy to the Shah, another became expedient to counteract it. It was conducted by a native Indian; but neither party drew any result from these negociations. After the subversion of the power of Tippoo,[646] India was thrown into alarm by the irruption of Zemaun Shah, king of the Afghans.[647] This was a power against which Persia was well fitted to create a diversion; with a view to which Colonel Malcolm[648] was dispatched in 1801 on an embassy to Futteh Ali Shah. This mission fulfilled all its objects: the Shah gladly embraced the opportunity to invade Khorassan, and conquered a large portion of it; while his invasion had the effect of recalling this barbarous chief from his Indian expedition. The Persian, on this occasion, concluded a treaty, which was to be binding on himself and his posterity while the world existed; and by which all Frenchmen, under pain of death, were prohibited from entering Persia.[649] Many years however, had not elapsed when it was learned, that without any regard to the stipulations of this eternal treaty, a French agent called Jouannin,[650] had been allowed to

---

[646] Cf. 8.13, 8.15, 8.57.

[647] Cf. 8.14, 8.19, 8.20, 8.37.

[648] Cf. 8.17, 8.18, 8.19, 8.20, 8.22, 8.23, 8.29, 8.33, 8.36, 8.52. 8.70.

[649] In discussing Malcolm's 'Gallophobia,' Rawlinson (1849: 7–8) wrote, 'At this time a Gallophobia reigned rampant in India. Napoleon was the "bête noire" of Lord Wellesley's dreams; and thus...Captain Malcolm was...empowered to contract engagements with the Shah, in regard to the French nation, of so stringent—nay, of so vindictive—a nature, that they have been characterized by one of our ablest, as well as most impartial, political writers, as "an eternal disgrace to our Indian diplomacy." [citing Sutherland (1837: 30)]...Captain Malcom...persuaded the Shah to issue a Firman to the provincial Governors, which directed that "you shall expel and extirpate the French, and never allow them to obtain a footing in any place," and added that "you are at full liberty to disgrace and slay the intruders."' Further, Rawlinson (1849: 10) noted on Malcolm's thinking, 'He seems to have had a sad misgiving that the French—notwithstanding that they were subjected by his treaty to a perpetual ostracism from the Persian soil—would still establish themselves on the shores of the Gulf, and would thence launch their victorious navies against the coasts of India.'

[650] Joseph-Marie Jouannin (1783–1844). As Cordier (1911: 340–341) noted, after returning to Constantinople in September, 1804, 'Jouannin fut nommé Jeune de langues du première classe...Ayant fait une étude spéciale de la langue persane, vers la fin de 1805, il fut expédié en Perse avec le chancelier-interprète de la mission de France à la cour de Tehran. Il arriva à la frontière persane en septembre, et le 13 octobre il était présenté au prince Abbas Mirza. Il atteignit Tehràn le 7 novembre 1816 [sic, 1806], où il résida seule comme agent de France auprès de roi de Perse jusqu'au 22 mai 1807, époque à laquelle il fut mis sous les ordres de M. de la Blanche, premier secrétaire de l'ambassade à Constantinople, chargé d'une mission qui finit le 7 novembre suivant. Le 15 mai de la même année, lors de la formation de l'ambassade du général Gardane, Jouannin fut nommé premier drogman de cette légation; le 20 décembre, le roi de Perse, Feth-Ali Chah, le décora de l'ordre du Soleil de seconde classe, en témoignage de sa satisfaction, et en mai 1808, Sa Hautesse lui délivra le diplôme de Mirza, titre qui l'admettait au nombre des lettrés de l'Empire. Le 13 février 1809, le général Gardane, retournant en France, remit à Jouannin la gestion des affaires de la légation, fonction que ce dermier remplit à Tehràn et à Tauris, au milieu de dangers de toute espèce, jusqu'au 27 janvier 1810, jour de sa sortie du territoire persan.'

settle at the Persian court, where he enjoyed the highest favour, and was employed in disciplining the troops after the European manner.[651] It was soon added, that in 1808 the Shah had sent an embassy to Paris. Bonaparte, wholly intent upon foreign conquest, courted this oriental potentate, partly as an auxiliary against Russia, and partly, it is supposed, with a remote view to some future operations against British India. He returned the embassy of Futteh Ali with a very splendid one under General Gardanne, which obtained a distinguished reception, and acquired the entire confidence of the Persian court.

This was a state of things which it behoved Britain, by every expedient, to counteract. Colonel (now General) Malcolm, who had so happily conducted the former mission, was sent again to renew, if possible, the ties which he had then formed. General Malcolm, however, on his arrival at Bushire, found that the French influence was quite paramount in the court of Persia, and that he could not be allowed to proceed to court in the manner which was suitable to the dignity of his official character. He proceeded, therefore, no further than Bushire; and returning to India, suggested to the government there the plan of overawing Persia, by occupying with a military force the Island of Kishme,[652] which might command in a great measure the navigation of the Gulf. A force of 2000 men was accordingly placed under his command for this purpose. Meantime a great revolution had taken place in Persian politics. The entire failure of the French in their promises to procure the evacuation of Georgia, the news of the Spanish revolution, and perhaps the natural caprice of an absolute monarch, had deeply shaken French influence at the court of Teheran. The moment was favourable to Sir Harford Jones,[653] who came out from Britain on a direct mission from the King; and who conceived himself justified in proceeding notwithstanding the failure of General Malcolm. This mission has been well narrated by Mr. Morier, and has been improved by Mr. Macdonald Kinneir,[654] as the means of collecting much geographical information; so that it has greatly refreshed our decaying knowledge of the state of Western Asia.

The embassy landed at Bushire, and proceeded by the usual route to Shiras. This celebrated capital of southern Persia does not seem to have excited in them quite the usual enthusiasm. It is represented as rather pleasing than grand; and the first impression which the view of it produced was much impaired by the meanness of its streets and ordinary houses. The fineness of its climate, and the beauty of its gardens, are fully admitted. It suffered like the rest amid the desolations of Persia; but its trade has of late considerably increased; and it contains a most magnificent bazaar, a quarter of a mile in

---

[651] It is highly unlikely that, as a linguist and interpreter, Jouannin was ever involved in 'disciplining the troops.'

[652] Malcolm's plan had been to occupy Khark, not Qeshm. See e.g. Kaye (1856/2: 432ff); Kynynmound (1880: 123).

[653] Cf. 9.93, 9.95, 9.103, 9.105, 9.110.

[654] Cf. 11.127, 11.182, 11.203, 11.218.

length, built by Kurreem Khan,[655] during the time he made it his residence. The population is estimated at 40,000. In this journey the embassy not only examined the ruins of Persepolis, but discovered those of Shapoor, the ancient palace of Sapor, which had escaped the research of former European travellers. The view of Ispahan from the distance of five miles, with its palaces, spires, and magnificent environs, appeared to them one of the most magnificent prospects in the world, and conveyed no tidings of the dire vicissitudes through which it had passed. These, however, became fully visible when they entered the city and compared it with the description given by Chardin. Its walls were levelled with the ground; its vast suburbs were almost deserted, and a traveller might ride through its circuit for miles, and see nothing but ruins. The principal mosques and palaces, however, are still standing, and have a magnificent appearance, though in decay. Aga Mahommed Hussein,[656] whose talents have raised him to the place of prime minister, being a native of Ispahan, has erected there a splendid new palace, and has enlarged and beautified many of the former edifices; so that Ispahan is beginning to recover from its downfal [sic]. After all it has lost, it is still supposed to contain a population of 200,000 souls. The English passed next through Kashan, one of the many cities which have had their turn as the capital of Persia. Though the greater part is now in ruins, it is still very large and populous, and carries on a great trade with Ghilan. Koom, entirely destroyed by the Afghans in 1722, has been in part rebuilt, but bears still the appearance of a vast ruin.

From Koom the mission proceeded to Teheran, which, so far as the royal residence is concerned, forms the present capital of Persia. It scarcely possesses as yet any grandeur or magnificence worthy of the name. Entirely destroyed by the Afghans, it was rebuilt by Aga Mahommed, who was induced, by strong political considerations, to make it his residence. Without being absolutely a frontier town, its situation was convenient for war against the Russians, now the most formidable foes of Persia; and it placed him in themidst of the wandering tribes from whom he sprung, and who formed the main strength of his armies. Teheran, however, has still the aspect of a new city, and contains no edifice of importance except the *ark*, which combines the character of citadel and royal palace. One great obstacle to its extension is the unehalthiness of the air, which prevails generally through the provinces on or near the Caspian, and is so extreme, that few of the inhabitants remain in the city during the summer months. Teheran, therefore, does not contain a permanent

---

[655] Cf. 6.93ff.

[656] Mohammad Hoseyn Khan Nezam od-Doula Isfahani, who became prime minister in 1819 on the death of Mirza Shafi'. As Hasan-e Fasa'i noted, 'He was an offspring of the Kadkhodā family from Esfahan. By reason of his sagacity and ingenuity in the handling of affairs and in bargaining with the landowners and his capacity to derive advantage from everything, he was superior to most learned men. Although he could neither read nor write, he was not in need of a scribe or accountant in his transactions and administrative affairs. Step by step he advanced: he was appointed lord mayor of Esfahan; then he advanced further and became beglerbegi of that province; next he was promoted to the governorship of the same region; later he became minister of finance of the empire; finally the office of prime minister of the Persian empire was bestowed upon him.' See Busse (1972: 167–168).

populationof more than 10 or 15,000, though the military array of the empire, when present, raises it to 60,000.

The reception of the embassy from the time of its entrance into Persia, had been very distinguished. Sir Harford had made a skilful display of that magnificence which is peculiarly calculated to dazzle the eyes of this oriental people. He wore a robe appropriated only to princes; and suffered to be seen, on proper occasions, the picture of the king set with diamonds, and other splendid presents which he was bearing to the court. At Teheran his reception was more than every flattering, though in its narrow streets and miserable buildings he saw nothing indicative of royalty. Every thing rich or splendid seemed collected round the throne, while all around was poverty, either real or affected. The house in which they were lodged, though that of the second minister, afforded accomodations inferior to those obtained at Shiras or Ispahan. The minister soon waited upon him, attended by a person who, in Europe, does not usually adhere so closely to public functionaries—the royal poet. A great part of the conversation consisted in loading this personage with the most extravagant praises, which seem to have been given and received alike without scruple or reserve. All agreed that he was superior to every other bard of the age, and had no equal on earth; while some hesitated not to exalt him above Hafiz and Ferdusi. The king owned his merits in a more solid manner, by giving him a gold toman, or upwards of a guinea, for every couplet; which, after all, does not perhaps exceed what the booksellers of London or Edinburgh have paid to some of our popular poets.

In this friendly disposition between the parties, the ceremonies of introduction at court were easily arranged. One necessary preparation was, that the mission should be arrayed in green slippers and red stockings. The narrow streets, as they passed through, were crowded with spectators. On entering the royal hall, they were led between files of troops disciplined in the European manner, who performed the platoon exercise as they passed. At the end of the hall was a small and mean door, which being opened, introduced them into a dark and narrow passage, terminating in another door worse than that of any English stable. This ushered them, however, into a very handsome court, adorned with canals and fountains bordered with trees, at the end of which sat the king richly dressed. The presents were then delivered to the prime minister, and the ambassador began a speech in English, the sound of which seemed a good deal to startle the monarch; but on a translation being given, his surprise was changed into pleasure. He then inquired for the king of England, and whether he was son to him who had reigned at the time of the last embassy. On being assured that the very same king was now reigning, he was heard to remark, that in this point also the French had told lies; for it seems they had circulated a report of the king of England's death. The Shah was about forty-five; and beneath a large black beard and mustachios, rather an agreeable countenance appeared. He entered into a pretty long conversation on literary subjects, being himself a professed patron of learning.

After this interview, the ambassador began to treat with the ministers relative to the terms of the proposed treaty. This negociation was conducted in a manner very remote from European ideas of decorum. The discussions were sometimes accompanied with violent contention, and at other times were interrupted by loud bursts of laughter. Once, amid the most serious deliberation, the minister broke off by asking the ambassador to tell the history of the world from the creation. Afterwards, when he had promised to send a copy of the treaty fully written out, the ambassador received instead of it alarge citron. When this treaty was at length produced, the secretary, who valued himself on being the finest writer in Persia, had so filled it with oriental figures and conceits, that it no longer retained any intelligible meaning. Sir Harford having declared it, in this condition, to bear no official value, the secretary was most reluctantly induced to prune it into something more level to an European capacity. When that minister came finally to apply the seals, the Premier called out, "Strike! Strike!" while all the Persians present were exclaiming, "God grant the friendship between the two nations may be lasting! God grant it! God grant it!"

Irregularly as the negociation had been conducted, its result was completely auspicious. The British obtained all their demands; while Gardanne received his dismissal, being prohibited at the same time to go by the way of Georgia, lest he should hold communication with Russia. A few days after, his whole train received instructions to follow their chief; and Persia remained entirely subject to English influence. After the departure of Sir Harford, Sir Gore Ouseley went thither as a permanent resident.'

Excerpts from Morier, et al.

10.344 'Literary Selections, for the National Gazette. Persia. From a late British Publication,' *The National Gazette and Literary Register* (Thursday, 23 December, 1820) = Murray 1820: 92–104 (on various cultural aspects, including antiquities and wine prohibition).

Captain Gordon in Russia

10.345 'Foreign Missionary Intelligence. From the London Missionary Chronicle. Russia. Letter from the Rev. Dr. Henderson. St. Petersburg, Oct. 18, 1820,' *Boston Recorder* (Saturday, 28 April, 1821), 'Foreign. From the Rev. Dr. Henderson. St. Petersburg, Oct. 18, 1820,' *Commercial Advertiser* (Saturday, 23 June, 1821), 'British and Foreign Bible Society. Extracts of Correspondence. From the Rev. Dr. Henderson. St. Petersburg, Oct. 18, 1821 [sic, 1820],' *Religious Intelligencer* [New Haven] (Saturday, 30 June, 1821; from 'A Russian captain'), 'From the Rev. Dr. Henderson. St. Petersburg, Oct. 18, 1820,' *Hampden Federalist and Public Journal* (Wednesday, 27 June, 1821), 'Inquiries after Christianity in Persia,' *Essex Patriot* (Saturday, 7 July, 1821; to 'mercy and love') and 'Untitled,' *Plattsburgh Republican* (Saturday, 21 July, 1821; last two paragraphs only): 'It is a pleasing fact, that when an enquiry was instituted at Okotsk by the Governor, respecting the want of the Holy Scriptures, copies were found in quarters where they were least expected[657]; which is attributed to the zealous and indefatigable exertions of our countryman, Captain Gordon,[658] whose track from Okotsk, the whole way through Siberia to Astrachan, and thence through Persia to India, is marked by the most tender solicitude for the welfare of the inhabitants, a diligent investigation of their spiritual wants, and an ad.. tion of such measures for their relief as the circumstances of his immense journey would allow.

From the accounts recently transmitted by this singularly zealous traveller, the most encouraging prospects are opening for the dissemination of divine truth in the Persian empire.

A Russian captain, lately returned from Persia, mentioned to a friend in Astrachan, that when he was in that country, he happened one day to go into the house of a native, when he was surprised to find between twenty and thirty Persians assembled, and listening with attention to one who was reading a book. They no sooner noticed the stranger than the book was laid aside and concealed, and it was with some difficulty that he could prevail upon them to tell him what book it was.

At last they informed him that it was the *New Testament*; and said, that the reason why they endeavoured to conceal it was, that they were not permitted to read it publicly. How

---

[657] The article originally appeared in *The Christian Guardian, and Church of England Magazine* of 1 February 1821. See Anonymous (1821c). The author of the letter, Ebenezer Henderson (1784–1856), was a Scottish missionary who was very active in Russia. See Henderson (1826).

[658] Captain Peter Gordon, who sailed in a schooner from Calcutta to Siberia and back in 1817, and then on a second journey, travelled overland from Siberia to Astrakhan, which he reached on 1 March 1820, and from there to Bandar-e Bushehr. See Anonymous (1833c). According to O'Flynn (2017: 431), 'Nothing is known of the family origins or personal background of Captain Peter Gordon, an adventurous Scottish sea captain, entrepreneur and freelance missionary in the first decades of the nineteenth century.' His journal of a tour through Persia was published as Gordon 1820. Lumsden (1822: 125) described meeting him not far from Kashan on 3 June 1820, 'On the march we met Captain Gordon on his way from Ockotsk *via* Siberia, through which and other parts of the Russian Empire, he had been travelling since the month of October last; he had come about eleven thousand miles, sometimes at the rapid rate of two thousand five hundred miles in fourteen days, over the snow, and dragged by post-horses in sledges. Captain Gordon went from Calcutta to Ochotsk on a trading speculation, which had entirely failed; and, as his ship had returned to India, and he had no prospect of a passage back by sea, he formed the bold resolution of returning as I have stated. He had been repeatedly detained, and carried far out of his way to the different Russian authorities, before he was permitted to proceed.' The author of Anonymous (1824f: 590) called him 'a gentleman in Calcutta, who...has crossed the Russian empire from the eastern sea to Astracan...The individual I allude to is Capt. Peter Gordon, of the ship (or brig) Brothers, who, three years ago, made a voyage from Calcutta to Okotsk, and travelled overland to Irkutsk. He came here to visit Brother Stallybrass, with whom he had carried on a most interesting correspondence from the time of his arrival at Okotsk. He spent here five or six weeks, and again went to Irkutsk, and from thence to Astrachan.' By the time of the marriage of his daughter Margaret, on 3 June 1824, to Robert Bell, Esq. at Islington Church, Gorson had died and was referred to as 'the late Capt. Peter Gordon, of the Wellesley East Indiaman.' See Anonymous (1824e: 99).

pleasing the idea, that many of the other copies which have been introduced into that empire, may also have their select circles to which they are proclaiming the glad tidings of redeeming mercy and love, and that here and there may be a Nicodemus inquiring, under the shade of concealment, *How can these things be?*'[659]

10.346 'Foreign Intelligence. Persia,' *Christian Watchman* (Saturday, 28 December, 1822), 'Religious Intelligence. Persia,' *Essex Patriot* (Saturday, 4 January, 1823) and 'From the Religious Intelligencer. Persia,' *The Columbian Star* (Saturday, 4 January, 1823; minus the text from 'There are difficulties' to 'reception of the Gospel'): 'The Scottish Missionary Society[660] have in contemplation a mission in this interesting country [Persia], having obtained a knowledge of its condition, by means of their stations on the Caspian. Their Missionaries at Astrachan received some time since, letters from Capt. Gordon,[661] a truly Christian Traveller, which contain some useful information concerning Persia. We call Capt. Gordon, *a truly Christian Traveller*, because at every stage of his progress he seems to have been desirous of doing something for the advancement of Christ's kingdom.—Dr. [Ebenezer] Henderson,[662] who in 1820 travelled as an agent of the British and Foreign Bible Society, writes thus respecting him—.

....The following extracts are from Capt. Gordon's Letters to the Missionaries at Astrachan. From Tebols [sic, Tabriz],[663] May 13, (O.S.) 1820, he writes:

As to the Persians, if you will come among them, do not stop half way. Do not halt in the plains of Daghestan. Come up, and possess the land. It is all before you. The enemy has such complete sway, that his subjects cannot but be weary of his yoke.

The Russian Minister has just been with me. It is his most decided opinion, that you may come here and enjoy every protection; and more than every facility, for the Persians will themselves begin the subject of your Mission. He thinks that you will not fail of great success. He advises you to come quietly; not as avowed Missionaries to the Persians, but on the same footing as you came to Astrachan. The Prince he speaks of as open and free in his discourse, though some of the Priests and more aged Persians are bigotted. If any thing can be done with the Mahomedans, he thinks the Persians the most hopeful.

Abbas Mirza, the Crown Prince and heir to the throne, received copies of Mr. Martyn's Translation of the Testament, as well as his father. An answer has been attempted to this

---

[659] Cf. John 3: 9.
[660] Cf. 10.289.
[661] Cf. 10.345.
[662] Cf. 10.345.
[663] *The Columbian Star* has 'Teboiz.' Given what follows in this article, e.g. a reference to meeting Capt. Hart, as well as the date of the letter referred to (13 May 1820), 'Tebols/Teboiz' must be Tabriz, which Gordon reached in the latter half of April. See Anonymous (1833f: 536).

10.1 Miscellaneous

work at Teheran, with which the Persians are not satisfied. The Prime Minister here is occupied in preparing another.

I tell Capt. Harl [sic, Hart],[664] with whom I have met here, that I am calling you over. He says, "Come along. The Persians desire nothing more than to talk about this *strange thing*, as they did with Mr. [Henry] Martyn, who resided here three months." Had he been much longer at Shiraz, they say that he would have converted half the town. The Mollah who used to dispute constantly with him, now says that he ought not to be spoken of among mortals!

From Ispahan, June 11th, 1820, Captain Gordon adds:

I hope that ere long, you will set out on a twelve month's tour through this country. I feel confident that you would be able to sow much good seed, both by teaching and distributing the Scriptures and Tracts; and do more good, perhaps than Persia has received since its subjection to the Arabian.

Since Martyn's time, the English character has continued to rise in the esteem of the Persians; chiefly from the excellent character of the English officers who have been with them of late who are universally beloved and respected.

There are difficulties, however, enough in your way. These same officers, who will, I am sure, shew you every kindness and attention, as they have done to myself, utterly disapprove of attempting "to convert the Persians; [???], you may follow, with propriety, the example of Martyn—*dwell in your own hired house, and receive all that come to you; teaching those things which concern the Lord Jesus Christ, with all confidence, no man forbidding you.*" This, they said, he did; but never attemppted to convert them.

You would not be under greater restraint here, in Ispahan, than you are now at Astrachan; acting with the same circumspection, you would be equally secure. Here are three thousand Armenians and fifteen hundred Jews, worshipping as publicly as they choose. I take the most public occasions of shewing and distributing your books—only avoiding a crowd: Having given two or three Tracts away in the Bazar, I was beset the next day for more; and retreating, distributed as many as I could spare.

This place contains upwards of one hundred thousand souls, perishing for want of the Light, which you may very probably be the means of causing to arise and shine upon them.

---

[664] Captain, later Major Isaac Hart (d. 1830), 65th or second Yorkshire North Riding Regiment of Foot, who had gone from service in India to train 'Abbas Mirza's forces and was acknowledged as 'generalissimo of the prince's army. See Alexander (1827: 80). Hart was universally praised for his work. See e.g. Mignan (1839: 147); Curzon (1892/1: 578); Potts (2017a: 4); Potts (2017b: 258–259), n. 117. Cf. 11.14, 14.31. Mignan (1839: 155, n). †, wrote, 'With good talents, he combined an invincible perseverance, a masculine understanding, and great energy of mind. These gifts were accompanied by qualities of far greater value—a generosity of spirit, a purity of principle, and a most affectionate temperament of heart, which secured him the respect of every individual (both Persian and European) of his acquaintance.' In 1828 he was awarded the Order of the Lion and the Sun, first Class, 'in testimony of His Majesty The Shah of Persia's approbation of his distinguished conduct, while in the actual Service of that Sovereign.' See Carlisle (1839: 219–220).

I occupy a delightful, retired quadrangle of the palace of Schah Abbas; which is the usual abode of the English who pass through this place. It surely will not be long before you are seated on this carpet, with a company of Priests hearing you and asking you questions. They will not avoid you: only perhaps an English Hakeem (Physician) would have more visitors than an English Mollah. It is, indeed, to our Medical Gentlemen that we owe a great deal of our reputation in Persia;—so that you see the healing of diseases has in a great degree, prepared the people for the reception of the Gospel.

You little think how generally the English Molleh Martyn of Shiraz, is known throughout Persia; and with what affection his memory is cherished.

Yet, of course, there must be a dark side. The Great Enemy, in reliance on the fidelity of the Moslems may have been off his guard for a moment; but will not give them up without a struggle. It would not be surprising, were an active Missionary, zealously engaged in his work, to receive a stab from some fanatic, as soon as his success became apparent; that stab would pierce the heart of Mahomet! The Persians are not without a witness to their own minds; they know how to discern between good and evil.'

Rev. Henry Martyn in Shiraz

10.347 'Happy Allusion to Henry Martyn,' *Pittsfield Sun* (Wednesday, 23 January, 1822): 'Sir Robert Ker Porter, in his travels to Persia, &c.[665] in a description of Shiraz, in that country, makes "a transient but honorable mention of HENRY MARTYN, a name which will never fade from pious memory, so long as unwearied ardour in the cause of the gospel, and the greatest and purest virtues of the heart, shall retain their reverence amongst us.

"Shiraz stood," says our Author,[666] "in an extensive plain, at the foot of the height we were descending, and seemed a place of great consequence and extent, from the mosques and other lofty buildings which towered above the flat roofs of the vast expanse of dwelling-houses. Gardens stretched on all sides of the fortified walls; and, faint with sickness and fatigue, I felt a momentary reviving pleasure in the sight of a hospitable city, and the cheerful beauty of the view. As I drew near, the image of my exemplary countryman, Henry Martyn, rose in my thoughts, seeming to sanctify the shelter to which I was hastening. He had approached Shiraz much about the same season of the year, A.D. 1811, and like myself, was gasping for life under the double pressure of an inward fire, and outward burning sun. He dwelt there nearly a year; and on leaving its walls, the apostle of Christianity found no cause for "shaking off the dust of his feet" against the Mahomedan city. The inhabitants had received, cherished, and listened to him; and he departed thence amidst the blessings and tears of many a Persian friend. Through his

---

[665] Ker Porter (1821).

[666] Nearly a verbatim extract of Ker Porter (1821/1: 687–689).

10.1 Miscellaneous

means, the Gospel had then found its way into Persia; and as it appears to have been sown in kindly hearts, the gradual effect hereafter, may be like the harvest to the seedling. But, whatever be the issue, the liberality with which his doctrines were permitted to be discussed, and the hospitality with which their promulgator was received by the learned, the nobles, and persons of all ranks, cannot but reflect lasting honour on the government, and command our respect for the people at large. Besides, to a person who thinks at all on these subjects, the circumstances of the first correct Persian translation of the Holy Scriptures being made at Shiraz, and thence put into the royal hands, and disseminated through the empire, cannot but give an almost prophetic emphasis to the transaction, as arising from the very native country (Persia Proper) of the founder of the empire, who first bade the temple of Jerusalem be rebuilt who returned her sons from capitivity, and who was called by name to the divine commission."

"The son of the late Jaffer Ali Khan came out to meet me; and received me, more like an old friend than a *frangeh* stranger; and received myself and people into his house with every cordial hospitality our situation needed. My fever had gained an alarming height; and one of my European servants, a Russian, was in an unmanageable state, having become delirious. Repose seemed the first point, to give some check, if possible to the advance of our disorder; and when too ill almost to thank our kind host, I found cool apartments prepared and every comfort he could command, even to a physician, if I would have trusted myself and faithful follower to Asiatic medical skill.

The attentions of my host were so unwearied, that I never could forget I was in the house of the near kinsman of the two noble Persians, Jaffer Ali Khan and Mirza Seid Ali, who had shewn the warmest personal friendship to our "Man of God!" for so they designated Henry Martyn. When the weather became too intense for his enfeebled frame to bear the extreme heat of the city, Jaffer Ali Khan pitched a tent for him in a most delightful garden beyond the walls, there he pursued his Asiatic translation of the Scriptures; or sometimes in the cool of the evening, he sat under the shade of an orange tree, by the side of a clear stream, holding that style of conversation with the two admirable brothers, which caused their pious guest to say, 'That the bed of roses on which he reclined, and the notes of the nightingales which warbled above him, were not so sweet as such discourse from Persian lips.' The land in which he so expressed himself, is indeed that of the bulbul and the rose; the poet Hafix [sic, Hafez] having sung of their charms till he identified their names with that of his native city."[667]

The Alleged Conversion of Fath 'Ali Shah

10.348 'Foreign News,' *The Onondaga Register* (Wednesday, 2 October, 1822) and 'Foreign Intelligence. Latest from Europe,' *The Long Island Farmer* (Thursday, 3 October,

---

[667] This long quotation is taken from Ker Porter (1821/1: 687–689).

1822): 'There have been several arrivals at New-York, from Europe, since our last, the latest of which is the ship Amity, which has brought London dates to the 14th of August and Liverpool to the 15th. We are indebted to the New-York Spectator for the following items.... The King of Persia, it is said, has been recently converted to Christianity by the arguments of the celebrated missionary, Mr. Martin [sic, Martyn].[668] Such a conversion must have an important effect in spreading the lights of the Gospel thro' regions of darkness, ignorance, and idolatry.'

A Scottish Cloak (Tartan?) for Fath 'Ali Shah

10.349 'Liverpool, Jan. 19,' *The Georgian* (Monday, 4 March, 1822), 'Liverpool, Jan. 19,' *Baltimore Patriot & Mercantile Advertiser* (Saturday, 9 March, 1822), 'Liverpool, Jan. 19,' *Augusta Chronicle & Georgia* Gazette (Monday, 11 March, 1822), 'Postscript. Latest from England,' The National Advocate (Monday, 11 March, 1822), 'Latest from England,' *Baltimore Patriot & Mercantile Advertiser* (Wednesday, 13 March, 1822), 'Liverpool, Jan. 19,' *Boston Daily Advertiser* (Wednesday, 13 March, 1822), 'French Affairs,' *Boston Commercial Gazette* (Thursday, 14 March, 1822), 'Latest from England,' *Nantucket Inquirer* (Thursday, 14 March, 1822), 'Liverpool, Jan. 19,' *The Repertory* (Thursdays, 14 March, 1822), 'Liverpool, Jan. 19,' *Boston Weekly Messenger* Thursday, 14 March, 1822), 'Latest from England,' *New-York Spectator* (Tuesday, 19 March, 1822), 'Latest from England,' *The Delaware Gazette* (Wednesday, 20 March, 1822), 'Untitled,' *The Long Island Farmer* (Thursday, 21 March, 1822), 'Foreign Intelligence. Great Britain,' *The Eastern Argus* (Tuesday, 26 March, 1822) and 'Foreign. From Europe. Ireland,' *Augusta Chronicle & Georgia Gazette* (Monday, 1 April, 1822): 'A superb cloak, of the Highland costume, is stated to be preparing in Edinburgh for the King of Persia,[669] by direct orders, from that monarch.'

Missionaries from Basel

10.350 'Basle Evangelical Missionary Society,' *Religious Intelligencer* (Friday, 1 August, 1823), 'Basle Evangelical Missionary Society,' *Boston Recorder* (Saturday, 27 September, 1823) and 'Basle Evangelical Missionary Society,' *New-Hampshire Repository* (Monday, 29 September, 1823): 'This new society [Basel Evangelical Missionary Society], has already sent six missionaries to the shores of the Caspian. They intend to settle on the

---

[668] Rev. Henry Martyn (1781–1812). Needless to say this was a false rumor.
[669] Fath 'Ali Shah.

borders of Persia,[670] where they will find their arduous enterprise not a little facilitated, by the honoured labours of Martyn, whose memory is still gratefully cherished by the Persians—and whom they usually style "*the Man of God*."'

The Danish Orientalist Rasmus Rask

10.351 'Return of Mr. Rask from Asia,' *New-York Evening Post* (Wednesday, 17 September, 1823): 'Professor Rask, of the University of Copenhagen,[671] set out on a journey to Asia six years ago, chiefly with the intention of investigating the relations which exist, or which have existed, between the languages of India and Persia on the one hand, and those of the Gothic and Germanic nations on the other. Mr. Rask has brought with him a great many manuscripts in Sanscrit, Zend, Bengall, and Persian, among which are four copies of the Zendavesta, very different from that which M. Anquetil[672] translated. He has made researches in Buli writing[673] as well as into the Cuneform writing of Babylon and Persepolis.'

The Destruction of Kermanshah by Earthquake

10.352 'Untitled,' *The Hampden Patriot and Liberal Recorder* (Wednesday, 18 September, 1822): 'A letter from Constantinople, dated June 10, asserts that the wrath of heaven had visited the Persian town of Kermanchah with a tremendous earthquake, in which 30,000 inhabitants had perished.'[674]

---

[670] On the early activities of the Basel missionaries see Hoffmann (1842: 42–51). Cf. in general Waldburger (1983); C'Flynn (2017: 475–488).

[671] Rasmus Kristian Rask (1787–1832), renowned philologist and linguist whose career in Denmark was spent principally in the library of the University of Copenhagen.

[672] The eminent French scholar Abraham Hyacinthe Anquetil-Duperron (1731–1805). For Rask's publication on the Avesta, containing also insights into the identification of the values of selected Old Persian cuneiform signs, see Rask (1826).

[673] Almost certainly not Chatgaiyan Buli, or Chittagonian, an Indo-European language spoken in the area of Chittagong, Bangladesh, on which see Hoque (2015). Rather, given that he collected manuscripts in this language (Wolf 1998: 114), Buli is probably a corruption of 'Pali.'

[674] As Anonymous (1822h) wrote, 'der Zorn des Himmels habe die persische Stadt Kermanschah durch ein fürchterlichtes Erdbeben heimgesucht, wobey 30,000 Menschen zu Grunde gegangen wären.'

The Persian Language

10.353 'Persian language,' *Hampshire Gazette* (Wednesday, 1 October, 1823): 'The Persian language is generally understood from the Mediterranean to the Ganges. It is spoken at all the Mahommedan courts in India, & is the usual language of judicial proceedings under the British government in Hindoostan. It excels all the eastern languages in strength, beauty, and melody. The Persians have some celebrated poets, with which all classes are acquainted from the highest to the lowest. They have schools and colleges for language, moral philosophy, and the Mahommedan religion; but they have little knowledge of the sciences.'

Marble from Azerbaijan

10.354 'Marble ponds in Persia,' *Geneva Palladium* (Wednesday, 26 November, 1823): 'This natural curiosity consists of certain pools, or splashes, whose indolent waters, by a slow and regular process, stagnate, concrete, and petrify, producing that beautiful transparent stone, commonly called Tabris marble, much used in the burial places of Persia, and in their best edifices.[675] The ponds are contained within the circumference of half a mile; and their position is distinguished by heaps of stone, which have accumulated as the excavations have increased. The petrifactive process can be traced from its commencement to its termination, in one part the water is clear; in a second, it appears thick and stagnant; in a third, quite black; and in its last stage it is white like a hoar frost. Where the operation is complete, a stone is thrown on its surface which makes no impression, and a man may walk over it without wetting his shoes. Such is the constant tendency of this water to become stone, that, when it exudes from the ground in bubbles, the petrifaction assumes a globular shape, as if the bubbles of a spring, by a stroke of magic, had been arrested in their play, and metamorphosed into stone. The substance thus produced is brittle and transparent, and sometimes richly streaked over with green, red, and copper colored veins. It admits of being cut into very large slabs, and takes a good polish. So much is this stone looked on as

---

[675] A quarry for Tabriz marble was located near Maragha but, according to Kinneir (1813: 157), 'It has not been worked since the death of Nadir Shah, who transported quantities of it into the *Khorassan*, for the embellishment of his palace at *Kelat*.' Francklin (1788: 31) described a bath built by Karim Khan in Shiraz, in which 'the inner appartment is lined throughout with Tauris marble.' As Lumsden (1822: 96) noted, the tomb of Hafiz in Shiraz 'is a single block of Tabreez marble.' Perkins (1843: 196–197) described seeing 'soda springs, boiling up from small orifices in the road, with an effervescence almost as vivid and perfect as can be produced in a chemical laboratory. Is it not from the incrustations of the overflowing water of these fountains, that the beautiful Tabréez marble is formed around and near them? We passed one great quarry, within a few rods of a spring, from which vast quantities of this marble have been taken,' about half a mile from the eastern shore of Lake Urmia.

10.1 Miscellaneous

an article of luxury, that none but the king, his sons, and persons privileged by special firman, are permitted to take it.'[676]

A Persian Meal

10.355 'A Persian Dinner,' *Trenton Federalist* (Monday, 19 April, 1824): 'We take the following description of a Persian entertainment from a volume of Letters by a Madame Freygan [sic, Freygang],[677] wife to the son of a German physician[678] in the service of the Emperor of Russia[679]: who having been educated for the diplomatic profession, was despatched from Triflis, in 1812, as *Counsellor de Cour*, during a period of great anxiety for Russia, in consequence of the recent French invasion, upon a mission to the Court of Abbas Mirza, the hereditary Prince Royal of Persia, at Tabriz.[680] We do not presume to conjecture how far Dr. Kitchener may consider the Persian pilaw and *bonne-bouche* worthy of his attention.[681]

[N.Y. Daily Advertiser.

"A few days ago,[682] Jaffier Kooli Khan[683] invited the Governor General's wife to dinner, and I was of the party. He showed us the attention of providing plates, knives and forks, with which he dispensed himself, eating according to the Persian custom. A flat cake of bread, as large as the table upon which it laid, served for the table cloth and napkins. The Khan made use of a smaller cake of the same description, for the purpose of plate and napkin. We were first helped to sweetmeats, and then to the Persian soup *boobach*. I was curious to see how the Khan might manage his soup, and would have wagered that he could not have gotten through it: but I was mistaken. His bread plate answered as a spoon; he dropped a piece of it into the bowl before him took it out with his fingers and swallowed it?

---

[676] The text is a slightly edited version of the description given in Morier (1818: 284–285).

[677] Frederika Afanasyevna von Freygang (1790–1863), née Kudryavskaya, born in Vienna and married to the Russian diplomat Wilhelm von Freygang (1783–1849). See Colbert (2020). The French novelist Alexandre Dumas met her during his Caucasian travels while he was in Baku, noting that she spoke French very well. See Dumas (1859: 95–96).

[678] Wilhelm von Freygang (1782–1849).

[679] Alexander I.

[680] For the original publication referred to here, see von Freygang and Freygang 1816. An English translation was published in Freygang and Freygang 1823.

[681] Dr. William Kitchener (1775–1827), author of *The Cook's Oracle*. See Kitchener (1817).

[682] This is a long, verbatim excerpt from Letter XXX in Freygang and Freygang (1823: 163–167).

[683] Von Freygang and Freygang (1823: 162) called him 'a Persian khan, Jaffier Kooli, khan of Scheki, who is at present a Lieutenant-General in the service of Russia. He has just arrived to pay his respects to the new Governor-General [of Georgia].'

he had even finished his portion before us, who had plates and spoons. The mode of eating appeared to me still less inviting, as the Persian gentry have their hands died yellow as saffron, and their nails of a deep red. After the soup we had other dishes, sweetened with a great deal of sugar; these were followed by ragouts, highly seasoned with pepper and saffron; then appeared at least six different kinds of pilaw, the favorite dish of Asiatics, and the only one, in my opinion, that is eatable. One of these pilaws was, to my taste, delicious; they were all of different colours; some were made of mutton and chicken, some with chesnuts, others with meat roasted on a wooden spit, from which it acquired rather a smoky flavour; this excepted, the roast is a good thing—they call it *schichlich*.[684] The pilaws are dressed in more than twenty various ways. I here give you one of the recipies[685]:—.

"Cut into slices six or seven pounds of mutton and boil it with one or two fowls; then take the whole of the meat and broth out of the saucepan, and at the bottom of it put some butter, upon which, when warm, a layer of rice about the thickness of an inch, is to be added; then throw in chesnuts, peeled almonds cut in two, some of those small raisins without seeds, which they call *kischmisch*,[686] cloves, cinnamon, and cardamons. The meat is then placed upon all this, and the saucepan filled with rice, pouring on it the broth until the whole be quite covered; a quarter of an hour is sufficient to boil the rice, by which time it will be dry and have absorbed the broth. Then butter is melted and put over the rice, after which the sauce pan should be well covered, underneath the lid with a cloth dipped in hot water, that the rice may be kept moist; it is thus left to soak until served up.

"Our drink consisted of different kinds of sherbet[687] and *airan*.[688] To form a just idea of the Persian method of eating, you ought to see one of them helping himself to a dish of pilaw. The Persian plunges his fingers into the mess, stirs it about, squeezes it within his

---

[684] At Bakhchysarai in Crimea Koch (1855: 71) described 'roasted meat—"shishlik"—prepared in the same manner...as in the East. The wooden spit, entirely covered with small pieces of meat, was turned by boys, over a coal fire, without smoke.'

[685] This recipe is reproduced verbatim, without attribution, in Murray (1860: 331).

[686] A type of grape and raisin. See Adams (1898: 90); Floor (2003c: 326). Wills (1891: 159) wrote, 'The Kishmish grape is the smallest in Persia; it is a bright yellow colour, and very sweet; it is, when dried, what we call the Sultana raisin. The wine is a golden yellow, delicious when quite new, but terribly heady. It is a great favourite with the Armenians, as it is quickly intoxicating. As a rule it will not keep well, but when it does is not to be despised.' Wills experienced kishmish wine while visiting Julfa in Isfahan.

[687] Bailey (1759 s.v.) SHERBET, defined it as 'a pleasant Liquor much in Use, among the *Turks,* and *Persians*, who make theirs generally of Violet Vinegar, and the Juice of Pomegranates, and these with Sugar they form into a king of spungy Loaves which almost immediately dissolve in Water. It is a *Persian* Word, whence the Italian [serbetto] is borrowed as well as our Mixture of Water, Lemons and Sugar, design'd for Punch.'

[688] Pers. *dugh,* a drink consisting of yoghurt, water and salt, served cold. Wilson (1895a: 249) called it 'a kind of buttermilk.' Hedin (1898: 423) noted that, among the Kirgyz, 'The drink chiefly in favour is *ayran* (boiled milk diluted with water, and left to become sour), a particularly refreshing drink in the summer.'

hand, which having filled he conveys to his mouth, and swallows the contents. Not knowing how to use either a knife or fork he wipes his disgustingly greasy hand upon his napkin—that is to say upon the bread which covers his table; and finishes the meal by eating his napkin. While at dinner the Khan made use of his right hand only, the left always resting on his girdle, according to the fashion of the country.

The Persians are extremely fond of fat and of sweets, and particularly of saffron. The Khan, in order that he might not fail in politeness, seated himself like us upon a chair, although the Persians do not use either tables or chairs; they sit always on the floor, upon which a carpet is spread and their dishes are placed before them on large trays. They have a curious manner of sitting with their legs folded under them so as not to be seen—a posture to which one must have been accustomed before it can be maintained for any length of time. After dinner a kalcoore[689] was brought in; this was first smoked by the Khan, and then given by him, with the same tube, to the person he wished to distinguish. The Persians have another strange mode of doing honor to their guests, but it is really so far from inviting that I am half unwilling to relate it. While at meals, they will sometimes take a dainty bit, invariably a greasy morsel, and hold it for some time, kneading it, as it were, in the hand, after which they put it into the mouth of the person who may be the object of their peculiar regard. Fortunately the Khan did not show us this mark of politeness. The ball he gave us was not so splendid as it was amusing: he went through several polonaises, and for a Persian, danced them tolerably well. I saw upon this occasion various oriental dances, such as the Georgian, the Lesghee, and the Persian. But what contortions! The music is as wild as the figure; and now, indeed, I can form some notion of the dance of *Bajaderes*."'[690]

Morier's Quarters in Tabriz

10.356 'Miscellany. The Persians,' *Salem Observer* (Saturday, 1 May, 1824): 'M. Morier, in his "Journey through Persia,"[691] gives the following description of his lodgings at Tabriz, and of the domestic habits of the natives. His habitation belonged to an Armenian family, the head of which was a *Keshish* or priest[692]: it contsisted of several rooms built upon elevated terraces, looking upon two sides of a square, besides sevearl other small unconnected rooms, situated here and there. A garden was attached to it, in which were apple, pear, cherry, walnut, and jujube trees, besides rose trees. "Beneath my chambers were two under-ground rooms, where lived one of the priest's sons & his wife. One of the

---

[689] Pers. *qalyan*, water pipe.

[690] *Bajaderes*, meaning 'Indian dancing girls,' is a corruption of Portuguese *bailadeira*. See Brande and Cox (1867: 219).

[691] The following long excerpt comes from Morier's account of his second mission. See Morier (1818: 228–230).

[692] Cf. the two seals with the inscription *Armen keshish masihi*, 'Armen the Christian priest.' See Sanjian (1999: 303, 325).

rooms was a magazine for arrack, of which the husband was both a drinker and a vender. But, as the prince had prohibited the sale of this liquor, and of wine, under very heavy penalties, none was sold except in a clandestine manner, and that to persons well known. The noises that issued from the adjoining houses were quite characteristic of Persian domestic life. In my immediate vicinity lived an old morose Persian, who daily quarrelled with his women; and I could distinguish the voice of one particular female, whose answers, made in a taunting querulous tone, did not fail to throw him into passions so violent, that they generally terminated in blows, the noise of which, accompanied by corresponding lamentations, I could distinctly hear. Then bordering on the garden wall, scarce twenty yards from where I usually sat, was a society of women, five or six in number, the wives and slaves of a Mussulman, who were either dissolved in tears, sobbing like children, or entranced in the most indecent and outrageous merriment. Sometimes they sung in the loudest tone accompanied by a tambourine; and then quarrelled among themselves, using expressions of no ordinary indelicacy. Accident once gave me a view into their yard, where I saw three women surrounded with children, seated on the bare stones, smoking the *kaleon*.[693] They wore a large black silk handkerchief round their heads, a chemise which descended as low as the middle, a pair of loose trowsers, and green high heeled slippers; and this I believe, may be considered as a sketch of every Persian woman's dress within the harem, in hot weather. But there are noises peculiar to every city and country; and none are more distinct and characteristic than those of Persia. First, at the dawn of the day the *muezzins* are heard in great variety of tones, calling the people to prayers, from the top of the mosques; these are mixed with the sounds of cow-horns, blown by the keepers of the *hummums*, to inform the women who bathe before the men, that the baths are heated, and ready for their reception.[694] The cow horns set all the dogs howling in a frightful manner; the asses of the town generally begin to bray about the same time, and are answered by all those in the neighbourhood; a thousand cocks then intrude their shrill voices, which with other subsidiary noises, of persons calling to each other, knocking at doors, and cries of children, complete a din very unusual to the ears of a European. In the summer season, as the operations of domestic life are mostly performed in the open air, every noise is heard.

---

[693] Pers. *qalyan*, water pipe.

[694] Turkish *hammam*, bath or bath-house. See Petersen (1996: 107–108). As Wills (1891: 334) noted, 'The great amusement of the Persian women of every rank is the bath. Generally three or four hours in the week are passed by the very poorest in the "hammām." As for the wealthier, they have baths in their own houses, and use them almost daily. The middle classes make parties to go to the hammam, and assist each other in the various processes of shampooing, washing with the "keesa," or rough glove, and washing the hair with pipe-clay of Shiraz.' Cf. Malcolm (1827: 72), 'These baths are always good, and often splendid buildings. They are sought by the lower classes as essential to health in persons who seldom wear, and when they do, seldomer change, their under garments. The higher ranks indulge in them to still greater excess, and in their progress through the various apartments of graduated heat, from the outer saloon to the houz or fountain of the inner bath, they are waited upon by different domestics, who, besides aiding to undress and dress them, serve them with every species of refreshment.'

At night, all sleep on the top of their houses, their beds being spread upon their terraces, with no other covering than the vault of heaven. The poor seldom have a screen to keep them from the gaze of passengers and as we generally rode out on horseback at a very early hour, we perceived on the tops of the houses people either still in bed, or just getting up, and certainly no sight was ever stranger."'

Lancashire Meets Persia

10.357 'Letters from the East. Alexandria,' *The Freeman's Journal* (Monday, 21 June, 1824): 'We sailed from Constantinople on board an English vessel bound to Smyrna. . . .On board were two natives of the northern part of England, who had gone to Persia with the hope of getting rich by engaging in a cotton manufactory, set on at Tebriz by a young English merchant. The latter had lost all his little property in the attempt, having been deluded, he said, by false representations; and at last after a long and difficult journey over land with the two natives of Lancashire, had succeeded in reaching Constantinople. To hear the latter, in their broad provincial dialect, relate their adventures in Persia; their passage over mountains covered with snow, and plains parched with heat, half starved at one time and abused or pursued at another, was very amusing.'[695]

Fath 'Ali Shah's Questions for Sir Harford Jones

10.358 'Extracts from late English Papers,' *The Geneva Gazette* (Wednesday, 13 October, 1824) and 'Royal Learning,' *The Catskill Recorder and Greene County Republican* (Thursday, 14 May, 1829): 'The present King of Persia made many inquiries of Sir H. Jones respecting America, saying, What sort of a place is it? How do you get at it? Is it under ground or how?'[696]

---

[695] This excerpt is from John Carne's (1789–1844) Letter III, originally published in the *New Monthly Magazine and Literary Journal* 10 in 1824. See Carne (1824). His collected letters were subsequently published as a volume. See Carne (1826: 46–47).

[696] As Sir Harford Jones Brydges later wrote, 'Finding that I had been in America, he [Fath 'Ali Shah] asked me a great many droll questions about that country, of which, the public have already been told, the Persians have very absurd ideas.' See Brydges (1834/1: 300).

Fath 'Ali Shah's Family

10.359 'Untitled,' *The Catskill Recorder* (Friday, 3 December, 1824), 'Summary,' *The Mohawk Sentinel* (Thursday, 9 December, 1824; only this paper contains the second sentence), 'Summary,' *Onondaga Register* (Wednesday, 15 December, 1824), 'Married,' *The Corrector* (Saturday, 18 December, 1824) and 'Untitled,' *The Delaware Gazette* (Wednesday, 29 December, 1824): 'The present King of Persia has 39 sons and 140 daughters.[697] His family picture, observes one must be bigger than that of the Vicar of Wakefield.'[698]

The Destruction of Shiraz and Kazerun by Earthquake

10.360 'Foreign Summary,' *Salem Observer* (Saturday, 8 January, 1825): 'The city of Schiraz, on the Persian Gulf, has been almost entirely destroyed by an earthquake.'[699]

10.361 'From Europe,' *New-York Evening Post* (Monday, 17 January, 1825): 'In the month of April last [sic, June], the city of Kazroon in Persia, was destroyed, and all the mountains around it levelled to the ground, by an earthquake.'[700]

10.362 'News from Persia,' *National Advocate* (Monday, 17 January, 1825), 'News from Persia,' *New-York Commercial Advertiser* (Monday, 17 January, 1825), 'News from Persia,' *The Statesman* (Tuesday, 18 January, 1825), 'Foreign Intelligence. Persia,' *The Long Island Farmer* (Thursday, 20 January, 1825), '[From the New-York Gazette, Jan. 17.] Latest from Europe,' *Alexandria Gazette* (Thursday, 20 January, 1825; with minor variations, e.g. 'Chiras,' 'Kazroon'), 'Persia,' *New-York Spectator* (Friday, 21 January, 1825), 'News from Persia,' *The Corrector* (Saturday, 22 January, 1825; omits the second paragraph) and 'News from Persia,' *Ithaca Journal* (Wednesday, 26 January, 1825):

---

[697] By the time of his death, Fath 'Ali Shah had had 265 children, 'Of these children 159 died in infancy, and 106 reached mature age; 101 survived him, viz. 55 sons and 46 daughters.' See Anonymous (1873a: 714).

[698] In Goldsmith's popular novel, *The Vicar of Wakefield,* Dr. Primrose and his wife have six children. See Goldsmith (1803: 6–7).

[699] Probably a reference to the earthquake that commenced on 25 June, 1824. According to Wilson (1930: 118), 'A violent shock, followed by many slighter ones for six days and nights. The principal damage was done by the first and three others that followed it before 10 a.m. A part of Shiraz was almost completely destroyed and swallowed up.' Another earthquake struck on 2 June. See Berberian (2014: 64).

[700] As Wilson (1930: 118) noted of the earthquake that shook Shiraz in 1824, 'Kazrun also suffered severely and some mountains in the neighbourhood of Kazrun were levelled (27th Shawal, 1239).' Cf. Ambraseys and Melville (2005: 57).

'Letters from Shiras announce, that in the month of April, 1824, there had been an earthquake which lasted six days and six nights without intermission,[701] and which had swallowed up more than half of that unfortunate city, and overthrew the other, as was the case at Aleppo. Nearly all the inhabitants fell victims to the catastrophe; scarcely five hundred persons could save themselves. Other letters from Aborkoh announce that the same shock, but less violent, had been felt there. Razroon, a city between Aborkoh and Shiras was swallowed up with almost the whole of the inhabitants, in consequence of the same earthquake. All the mountains surrounding Razroon were levelled by it, and no trace of them now remains.'

10.363 'Untitled,' *New-London Gazette* (Wednesday, 19 January, 1825) and 'Untitled,' *Middlesex Gazette* (Wednesday, 19 January, 1825): 'A dreadful Earthquake occurred in Persia in the month of April. Kazroon, a city between Aborkoh, and Shiras, was swallowed up, with the whole of its inhabitants. All the mountains surrounding Kazroon, were levelled by it, and no trace remains of them.'

10.364 '[From the N.Y. National Advocate.] From Europe,' *The Wayne Sentinel* (Thursday, 20 January, 1825): 'Accounts from Bagdad state that the city of Schiras has been entirely destroyed by an earthquake. The Schah of Persia[702] has left Teheran for Sultanea, to attend the marriage of his grand daughter, the daughter of Abbas Mirza, with Prince Kermanchab [sic, Kermanshah][703]; from there he will organize his army, and attack the Pachalick of Bagdat. The Charge des Affair [sic] of Russia, at Persia, is to be relieved by an ambassador. Persia has in its employ a number of French officers to discipline her troops.'

10.365 'From Europe,' *The Rochester Telegraph* (Tuesday, 25 January, 1825) and 'From Europe,' *Plattsburgh Republican* (Saturday, 29 January, 1825): 'Letters from Chiras Persia, state that in the month of August, 1824,[704] there was an earthquake which continued without intermission for six days and nights, and swallowed up more than one half of that unfortunate city, and not more than 500 persons were saved. Other letters mention that the same shock was experienced at Aborkoh, but not as violently.'

---

[701] No April earthquake is recorded by Wilson (1930) or Berberian (2014), but Ambraseys and Melville (2005: 57) do. Given that it lasted six days and six nights this is probably a mis-dated reference to the earthquake that commenced on 23 or 25 June (see above). See Anonymous (1825a) = 1825.11 below. Cf. Patterson (1869: 802).

[702] Fath 'Ali Shah.

[703] Mohammad Hoseyn Mirza. Cf. 10.328, 11.43 who had succeeded his late father Mohammad 'Ali Mirza as governor of Kermanshah after the latter succumbed to cholera. See Longrigg (1925: 246).

[704] Cf. Ambraseys and Melville (2005: 58), 'A shock on 28 August caused additional damage near Shiraz.'

10.366 'Latest from England,' *Mohawk Sentinel* (Thursday, 3 February, 1825): 'The city of Seraz in Persia was destroyed by an earthquake June 20,[705] and it is said, scarcely 500 persons escaped.'

10.367 'Foreign News,' *Oswego Palladium* (Saturday, 5 February, 1825):'An Earthquake, it is stated in letters received at New-York, took place at Chiras, (Persia) in the month of August last [sic, June], which continued for six days and nights, and swallowed up more than one half of that unfortunate city, and not more than 500 persons were saved. The city of Kazroon, between Chiras and Alvorkoh,[706] was totally swallowed up with nearly all the inhabitants, by the same earthquake. All the mountains in the neighborhood were levelled.'

10.368 'The late Earthquake in Persia,' *The Corrector* (Saturday, 12 March, 1825) and 'The late Earthquake in Persia,' *Oswego Palladium* (Saturday, 26 March, 1825): 'We are indebted to a correspondent in Persia, who was an eye witness, for the following account of the dreadful earthquake that has devastated so much of what is interesting in that ill-fated country.—*Bombay Gazette.*[707]

"Jehan Numah,[708] *Near Shiraz,*

June 25, 1824.

"This morning,[709] about half past 5, I was disturbed out of a sound sleep[710] by the violent commotion of an earthquake, of much greater force than the one I sent you an

---

[705] Correctly 25 June as the letter cited above confirms. Cf. Ambraseys and Melville (2005: 57).

[706] Abarquh.

[707] This article was also reprinted as Anonymous (1825a).

[708] The Baghi Jahan Numa, 'a fine garden and palace' in Shiraz, close to the tomb of Hafiz. See Bicknell (1875): Explanation of Plate (unpaginated). Claudius Rich is buried here.

[709] Although Wilson (1930: 118) suggested the earthquake began on 23 or 25 June this letter clearly dates it to the early morning of 25 June, 1824.

[710] Money (1828: 37) identified the writer of this letter when he wrote, 'Captain J. was sleeping at the time of the earthquake (June 25) in a room in one of the most beautiful gardens here, Jehan Nemah. At half past five in the morning he was suddenly roused by a most curious sensation, and on starting on his feet saw the whole house rocking, and the stones, and rafters, and dust pouring down in profusion. He luckily escaped into the garden.' Captain J. must be Capt. Evan Jervis who is listed as belonging to the Third Regiment Light Cavalry with the remark 'Persia' in the *East-India Register and Directory, for 1825*. See Mason, Owen and Brown (1825: 295). In June, 1826, he carved his initials in the palace of Darius at Persepolis. See Simpson (2005: 35). 'It is but a few months since a Captain Jervis was stationed on some government business at Shiraz. He was living in one of the gardens near the town.' See Anonymous (1857c: 200). Jervis was a member of the suite of Colonel Macdonald, the new envoy to Persia. Alexander (1827: 126) wrote, 'The party now consisted of the Envoy and his lady, Major [Henry] Willock, Captain Campbell, Captain Jarvis [sic], agent for horses, Sir Keith Jackson, Bart. H.M. fourth Dragoons, Military Secretary to the Governor of Bombay, Dr. Reoch [Riach],

10.1 Miscellaneous

account of from Khonartueta[711] on the 2d inst.[712] My first object was to move out of the house; but to accomplish it was difficult and dangerous, owing to the number of large bricks, pieces of wood, and mortar, falling from the roof all round the outside of the house, and a few stones and chanam[713] from the ceiling inside that had been previously injured. Having happily effected my escape without injury to myself or servants, I walked out of the garden to see what damage Shiraz had suffered: the first sad effects that I observed was the complete destruction of the Shaw Meez Ally Ebna Hoonza, a beautiful mosque[714] about 400 yards in front of this garden, and perhaps the same distance from Shiraz; its finely ornamented cupola had fallen in and the body of the building was rent in every part. Shiraz itself was enveloped in dust, nor could I for many minutes see anything else; but this sad sight was enough to show that it had suffered severely. As the dust cleared away, it was truly awful and distressing to see the ruins of the fine stately mosques and minarets, a few minuts before the chief ornaments of the town, but now a shapeless mass, and each succeeding minute, as it vanished, some fresh object presented its shattered form. The eastern side of the wall that surrounded the town, and the only face discernible from hence, has fallen in, and most of the towers were laid level with the ground, and the remainder much injured.

But melancholy and distressing as what I have attempted to describe may be, what is it compared to the surferings of the unfortunate inhabitants? The cries and lamentations of thousands, bewailing the loss of relations, friends, and every thing dear, resounded in the air, and were enough to soften the hardest heart; you may then easily conceive what my feelings were, indeed are, at this moment, hearing dismal cries and mournful lamentations in every quarter. To get any thing like an accurate account of the sufferers will take some days. Since the first great shock, and between that time and ten o'clock, there has been three shocks, though smart, nothing compared to the first. I have pitched my teent in the garden, and intend occupying it; the comparative degree of safety will more than compensate for the comforts of the house. The inhabitants have quitted the town, and are living in tents,

---

Mr. George Malcolm, Lieutenant McDonald commanding escort, Lieutenant Strong, and myself.' Jervis retired on 9 November 1837 as a Lieutenant-Colonel. See Anonymous (1838c). In August, 1820, he was Acting Paymaster in the Persian Gulf. See Jervis (1820), Price (1820).

[711] Presumably the 'Khonar Tackta' between Daliki and Kazerun on the route from Bushehr to Shiraz. See Morier (1812: 410). Cf. Gobineau (1905: 136), who calls it Khonar-Takhteh; MacGregor (1887: 143), 'Konartakteh....a very small village and caravanserai.'

[712] Wilson (1930: 118) described the earthquake at Shiraz that occurred on 2 June, 1824, 'Some slight motion premonitory of the great earthquake of 23rd-25th June.'

[713] Lime plaster. See Yule and Burnell (1903: 218), s.v. 'chunám.'

[714] This seems to be a confusion of names. According to Razani and Lee (1973: 131), Table 2, 'In Shīrāz most of the mosques, shrines, important buildings and the adobe city wall were destroyed, notably the shrine of Shahe-Cheragh, Ali-ibn-Hamzah, Seid-mir-Ahmad, and the College of Khan.' Hasan-e Fasa'i referred to the 'shrine of Emāmzāda Seiyid 'Alā al-Din Ḥosein.' See Busse (1972: 224).

routies,[715] and under cumlies[716] outside. Merza Ally Acbor,[717] (our agent) poor fellow, and his whole family, are living with me; his house is completely destroyed; and Zakee Khan's (the minister)[718] quite in ruins; the Prince's state room destroyed, and every part of the palace has been much injured; to be short, I believe not a house has escaped without some injury, and most of them in ruins; the fine bazaar is still standing, but much shaken and injured. The exact number of those who have perished in the ruins I cannot ascertain. Merza Ally Acbor assures me that 2000 is under the number, but receive this as mere conjecture and report only; I should think half the number nearer the mark.'"

10.369 'Foreign Intelligence,' *The Geneva Gazette and General Advertiser* (Wednesday, 23 August, 1826): 'Towards the end of October there was at Shirauz, in Persia, an earthquake,[719] which destroyed several buildings, and, among other national monuments, the celebrated tombs of Hafez and Saadi.'[720]

---

[715] 'These tents are routies. They are large double-poled tents, single, but lined with blue bunting. The tents, like the English bell-tents, reach nearly to the ground, with only a wall of about eighteen inches in height. The opening is at one end, and extends from the pole downwards.' See Henty (1868: 123).

[716] A coarse woollen blanket; also cumbly, cummul. See Yule and Burnell (1903: 279).

[717] Mirza 'Ali Akbar, the 'lord mayor of Shiraz.' See Busse (1972: 172). Baron de Bode, who visited Shiraz in 1841, called him the 'Kalentar [*kalāntar*] or Civil Governor of the city.' See de Bode (1845: 181).

[718] Mohammad Zaki Khan-e Nuri, the 'vizier of Fars.' See Busse (1972: 173). Money (1828: 31 and 47) called him 'the prince's minister' and 'the prime minister.'

[719] Cf. Wilson (1930: 119), on 24 October, 1825, Shiraz suffered 'a shock almost as severe as that of the year before; numbers of buildings were reduced to ruins.' Ambraseys and Melville (2005: 59), 'October Shiraz. A strong shock ruined a number of buildings in Shiraz.'

[720] According to Anonymous (1827a), 'The following letter communicates the particulars of this calamity:—"Bushire, Nov. 10, 1825.—I am sorry to inform you, that a shock of an earthquake was felt at Shiraz at the end of last month [October, 1825], almost equal to that of last year. A great number of buildings have been thrown down, and much property destroyed; I am, however, happy to say, that few have lost their lives on this dreadful occasion. If you should ever revisit Shiraz, the changes that these dreadful visitations have made in it will fill you with grief and astonishment. The tombs of Hafiz and Saadi, the boast and glory of Shiraz, are now heaps of ruins. If these great men were now to rise from their graves, they would find ample subject for the employment of their pens in the spectacle of the almost entire ruin of that city whose former magnificence they have sung in numbers destined never to be forgotten."' According to Blake (1859: 548), 'The monument erected to him [Hafiz] by his countrymen was destroyed by an earthquake in 1825.' Goldsmid (1884: 792) wrote, 'Although the loftier structure erected in commemoration of Háfiz by the Zend king Karm [sic, Karim] Khan was long since destroyed by an earthquake, the poet's tomb remains intact and is well known to travellers in Southern Persia.'

The Plague

10.370 'Greece and Turkey,' *New-York Evening Post* (Wednesday, 2 March, 1825): 'Notwithstanding the winter season, the plague continued its ravages in different quarters of Constantinople. The whole Persian Legation[721] had been carried off.'

Christian Jews

10.371 'Christian Jews,' *New-York Evening Post* (Monday, 4 April, 1825) and 'Christian Jews,' *Oswego Palladium* (Saturday, 16 April, 1825): 'A community of christians has lately been discovered in Persia, who occupy a small town near Tabreez, and have churches and bishops at Jerusalem, Diarbeker, and Mousel.—They are distinguished from other oriental christians by their professing to be of Jewish descent, and by their forming an independent community, regulated by a patriarch and bishops, unconnected with any other establishments.'[722]

Persians at the Leipzig Messe

10.372 'Untitled,' *New-York American* (Friday, 29 April, 1825) and 'Untitled,' *New-York Spectator* (Friday, 6 May, 1825): 'A German Paper contains the following interesting

---

[721]This is likely to be a mistake for 'Prussian,' given the reaction of the Prussian Legation to the outbreak of plague in 1824. See Walsh (1836: 259–260).

[722]This is an abbreviated version of a notice that appeared in *The Gospel Advocate* (Anonymous (1825g: 266–267): 'At a late meeting of the Calcutta Asiatic Society....the Rev. Mr. Mill communicated a notice of a Christian community, in Persia, which is stated to have escaped the observation of European travellers. These Christians are said to occupy a small town near Tabreez, called Khosraven [Khosrava, mod Khosrowabad, near Salmas], but have Churches and Bishops at Jerusalem, Diarbeker, and Mousel. They are distinguished from other oriental Christians by their professing to be of Jewish descent, and by their forming an independent community, regulated by a Patriarch and Bishops unconnected with any other establishments.' The Rev. William Hodge Mill, D.D. (c. 1792–1853) was Principal of Bishop's College, Calcutta, and later Regius Professor of Hebrew at Cambridge University. See Anonymous (1856b: iv). Khosrava had a population of Persian Chaldeans, many of whom were converted to Roman Catholicism. See Badger (1852: 165), 175 who noted that Khosrawa had two churches, three priests and 150 families; Heazell and Margoliouth (1913: 95).

observations on the trade with Persia, as it is conducted by the Persian merchants, who attend the great fair at Leipsic[723]: "The Persians[724] who were here at the Easter Fair were here again at the close of the last fair, and gave us some hopes for the approaching Easter fair. They are men who are extremely well versed in trade and business, who are now visiting the manufactories in Germany and Alsace, in order to see what goods may be suitable for their own country, and which, according to the present Russian system, can pass in transit at the least expense by way of Leipsic. In future they will bring hither silk and Cachmere wool, and as they say, and give us reason to hope, will make considerable purchases: but the ornaments must be more in the oriental style than is usual in our goods. Those which they want will go farther into the interior of Asia, where German, English and French goods have not yet found their way; they also study the predominant taste at the Leipsic fair with respect to the manufactures of their own country, which may meet with a ready sale at Leipsic. The low duty on the transit of goods through Russia facilitates the trade by this channel, which may in time become important. On the other hand, the trade with Russian Poland is subject to many difficulties, but this is attended with the disadvantages to Russia, that its furs must be sold in the China market much lower than formerly, while ordinary Canada furs meet with a sale in Leipsic."'

'Abbas Mirza's Horsemanship

10.373 'Persian Horsemanship,' *Charleston Courier* (Tuesday, 24 May, 1825), 'Persian Horsemanship,' *Salem Observer* (Saturday, 28 May, 1825) and 'Persian Horsemanship,'

---

[723] A reference to the Leipziger Ostermesse of 1825. According to Anonymous (1825b), 'Schon am Ende voriger Messe fanden sich die Perser der letzten Ostermesse wieder ein und gaben Leipzig einige Hoffnung für die kommende Messe. Es sind Orientalen von seltener Handels- und Geschäftskenntniß, die jetzt in Deutschland und im Elsaß [Alsace] Fabriken bereisen und die Fabrikatur und Manufaktur beobachten, um daraus zu benutzen, was ihr Vaterland bedarf, und bei dem jetzigen russischen Zollsysteme am wohlfeilsten über Leipzig durch Rußland transitiren kann. Es werden solche künftig Seide und Kaschemirwolle hierher bringen, und, wie sie sagen und hoffen lassen, sehr bedeutende Einkäufe machen, aber manche Verzierungen müssen orientalischer ausfallen, als die hiesigen Waaren bisher sind. Die Waaren, die sie bedürfen, gehen noch weiter ins innere Asien, wohen deutsche, englische und französische Waaren bisher nicht kamen, auch studieren sie den Leipziger Meßgeschmack über Waaren ihres Vaterlandes, die in Leipzig gangbar werden konnten. Der niedrige Trasitzoll [Transitzoll] durch Rußland erleichtert diesen vielleicht sehr bedeutend werdenden Waarenzug.' Note however, regarding the presence of Persian traders at Tiflis during the war with Turkey, and their subsequent absence, that Bélanger (1838: 426) wrote, 'les marchandises achetées par les Arméniens à Leipzig, leur étant revenues, pour la plupart, à un prix très élevé, rien ne pouvait alors attirer de nouveau les marchands persans.'

[724] Anonymous (1825c) reported, 'In der Nähe von Brünn kam in der ersten Woche des Juni in einem Dorfe Feuer aus, welches auch den Gasthof ergriff, wo 2 Knechte, 12 Pferde und 2 von der Leipziger Messe kommende Frachtwagen, meistens mit Gütern von Tifliser, persischen Kaufleuten beladen, verbrannten.'

Portland Advertiser (Tuesday, 28 June, 1825): 'In Morier's Journey through Persia,[725] he thus speaks of the present king [sic, Crown Prince] of Persia's Horsemanship:—.

"At full gallop the prince[726] could shoot a deer with a single ball, or with the arrow from his bow hit a bird on the wing. He combines indeed the three great qualities of the ancient Persians, which Zenophon [sic, Xenophon] enumerates—riding, shooting with the bow, and speaking truth. His countrymen however are, in general, less severe in their estimate of the requisites of a great character, and are content to omit the last trait of excellence; but they never praise any one without placing in the foremost of his virtues his horsemanship, in which alone perhaps they possess any national pride. I once in fact was in some danger of a serious dispute, by hazarding a doubt, that the Turks rode better than the Persians. It is quite ridiculous to hear them boast of their own feats on horseback, and despise the cavalry of every other nation. They always said, "Perhaps your infantry may surpass ours; but our horsemen are the first in the world: nothing can stand before their activity and impetuosity." In fact they have courage—one of the first qualities of a horseman; they ride without the least apprehension over any country, climb the most dangerous steeps over rock and shrub, and keep their way in defiance of every obstacle of ground. They have also a firm seat; and that on a saddle which, among an hundred different sorts, would be called the least commodious. But that is all: they understand nothing of a fine hand, nor indeed with their bridles can they learn; for they use only a strong snaffle, fastened to the reign by an immense ring on each side, which they place indifferently in the strongest or weakest mouths; nor do they know how to spare their horses and save them unnecessary fatigue, for their pace is either a gallop on full stretch, or a walk."'

Persian Women and Infants

10.374 'Domestic life in Persia,' *National Gazette and Literary Register* (Tuesday, 18 April, 1826), 'Domestic life in Persia,' *Berks and Schuylkill Journal* (Saturday, 22 April, 1826), 'Domestic life in Persia,' *American and Commercial Daily Advertiser* (Wednesday, 26 April, 1826), 'Domestic life in Persia,' *American Traveller* (Friday, 28 April, 1826), 'Domestic life in Persia,' *Eastern Argus* (Friday, 5 May, 1826), 'Domestic life in Persia,' *The Wilmingtonian, and Delaware Advertiser* (Thursday, 15 June, 1826), 'Domestick Life in Persia,' *American Masonick Record and Albany Literary Journal* (Saturday, 11 October, 1828), 'Domestic life in Persia,' *Spirit of the Times & People's Press* (Tuesday, 19 April, 1831), 'Untitled,' *Boston Masonic Mirror* (Saturday, 11 June, 1831; last paragraph only) and 'Untitled,' *Auburn Free Press* (Wednesday, 8 August,

---

[725] Quoted verbatim from Morier (1812: 280–281).

[726] 'Abbas Mirza.

1832; last paragraph only): 'The ladies of Persia are very ignorant.[727] It is not customary to teach them even to read, and still less to sew. The exceptions to this rule are extremely rare. I should be greatly puzzled to describe their occupation until they become mothers. I know of none, but the toilet on which, though less complex than that of our ladies, they manage to spend as much time. The remainder of the day they commonly spend seated on beautiful carpets opposite to the window overlooking a fountain or piece of water. Here they smoke cailleau,[728] drink coffee, and pay or receive visits until the cool of evening, of which they immediately avail themselves to walk in the gardens without the town, where they frequently stop till night.—The most mistaken notions prevail in Europe as to the degree of liberty enjoyed by the women of Persia; in no country with which I am acquainted are they more perfect mistresses of their actions.

I must add, that when they become mothers few fulfil the maternal duties more seduously; they never suffer their children to be attended, or educated by strangers; they keep them under their own immediate care and superintendence until the age of eleven, or twelve, when the boys leave the harem to be circumcised, and the girls to be married, given away, or sold.

There are few countries in which infants undergo such tortures as in Persia, in spite of which, deformity is very rare.—The moment an infant of either sex sees the light, it is plunged repeatedly into cold water; it is enveloped in swathings, which are bound so tight as nearly to stifle it. It is then laid on a cradle without any sort of matress, the bottom of which is formed of leather, stretched like a drum, and perforated in order that no wet may accumulate. The unhappy babe is fastened down in his cradle with bandages of cotton about eight inches long, which are wound over the child and under the cradle. They are in such a state of compression that it is marvelous to me that one survives. Nevertheless, in this state the unfortunate little creature remains twelve hours at a time. Let what will happen, it is never freed from its bonds except morning and evening, and then only just long enough to change its linen.'

A New School for Tabriz

10.375 'Summary,' *Cortland Observer* (Wednesday, 19 April, 1826): "The Christian Observer for January, 1825 [sic, 1826],[729] contains a decree of Prince Abbas Mirza, of

---

[727] English translation of Drouville (1825: 89–91). This also appeared in *The London Magazine* (Anonymous 1826c).

[728] Pers. *qalyān*, water pipe.

[729] The date is incorrect and should read 1826. See Anonymous (1826a).

Persia, authorizing Mr. Wolf [sic, Wolff], the Jewish missionary,[730] to establish a college in the royal residence of Tabriz, where English professors may fix their residence, in order to instruct and give lessons to children."[731]

---

[730] Joseph Wolff (1795–1862) was an Anglicized German Jew who converted to Christianity and missionized widely in the Near East from the 1820s to the 1840s, often enduring extraordinary privations and trials. For accounts of his journeys and mishaps see e.g. Wolff (1833, 1835, 1848 and 1861). O'Flynn (2017: 799) called him, 'The first modern publicist of the plight of oppressed Persian Jews, indigenous Christians and other minority groupings.'

[731] According to O'Flynn (2017: 808), Wolff met 'Abbas Mirza on 1 May 1825. The history of 'Abbas Mirza's decree is more interesting than indicated in the *Christian Observer* (Anonymous 1826a). At the meeting of the Société Asiatique in Paris on 3 October 1825, 'M. Amédée Jaubert communicated a letter from M. Desbassayns de Richemont, dated Tabriz, relating particularly to the state of instruction in the countries which he has visited, and also two letters, written in Persian, by Prince Abbas Mirza, one of which, addressed to Mr. Wolf, is as follows:—"Since the very exalted, very learned, and very virtuous, the chosen of Christian scholars, Mr. Joseph Wolf, of England, has been admitted into our august presence, and has presented to us, in the name of the very noble lord, the model of the great ones of Christianity, the honourable Henry Drummond, a request tending to obtain the institution of a college in the royal residence of Tabriz, where English professors may fix their residence in order to instruct and give lessons to children: and whereas the moral dispositions of persons high in rank ought always to be favourable to what is good and useful; and whereas there exists between this power (Persia)—the duration of which may God prolong!—and that of England, no difference of views or interests, this request has been agreeable to us. We have, therefore, permitted the aforesaid person to establish the said school: we direct that a house be appropriated to this object, and this present has emanated to show our consent. If it please God, the establishment, which is the object of this person's solicitude, shall attain all the perfection desired; and English scholars may devote themselves to the exercise of instruction, under the shadow of our favour and protection. Whatever is necessary to them shall be granted."' See Anonymous (1826b). Travelling overland to India, the Viscount Desbassayns de Richemont, governor of the French colony at Pondicherry, and Charles Paulus Bélanger (1803–1881), who had been charged with the establishment of a botanical garden there, visited Tabriz in May, 1825, where they were guests of 'Abbas Mirza. See Anonymous (1825g: 300–301); Bélanger (1838); Anonymous (1882a: 156–157). For 'Abbas Mirza's choice of a suitable house for Wolff's college and the discussions surrounding this project see O'Flynn (2017: 809–810).

The Second Russo-Persian War and the Treaty of Torkmanchay (1826–1828)

In April, 1826, reports spread that Fath 'Ali Shah had ordered several of his sons to gather troops in their respective provinces and join him in Tehran. By July Hoseyn Qoli Khan Qazvini, 'Abbas Mirza and Allah Yar Khan Qajar Devehlu had crossed the Aras river, inaugurating the Second Russo-Persian War. Various justifications were offered for the attack, ranging from the restoration of the former boundaries of the Safavid empire, prior to Peter the Great's Caucasian campaign, to retaliation over a boundary violation near Lake Sevan (Gökçe) by Russian forces, and offenses against Muslims in Russia's Caucasian provinces prompting a call for a *jihad* by the religious leaders of Karbala which was embraced by Fath 'Ali Shah. By the time the Russian envoy, Prince Menshikov, had arrived at Fath 'Ali Shah's Soltaniyeh camp, ostensibly to announce Nicholas I's accession to the Russian throne but in reality to address several outstanding border issues, the dye was already cast, as he wrote in a dispatch dated 3 July. General Ermolov's notification of the Persian invasion reached St. Petersburg just as festivities in celebration of Emperor Nicholas I's coronation were in progress. Russian sentiments were inflamed by reports that, after quitting Fath 'Ali Shah's camp, Prince Menshikov and his suite were forcibly detained and mistreated on their return to Russia. In September Nicholas issued a declaration of war in a manifesto that was widely reprinted in the press. Some writers speculated that the Russians had intentionally sparked the conflict in the hope of expanding their domains all the way to the Aras river.

Due to Britain's amicable relations with Russia, all British officers involved in training 'Abbas Mirza's forces were forbidden from engaging in the hostilities. As in the First Russo-Persian War, Russian bulletins full of detail vied with misinformation and/or disinformation containing wildly exaggerated figures in the press. While the Porte, which would soon find itself fighting Russia, hoped for Persian success, it stopped short of actively supporting the Persians.

One year into the conflict Nicholas conferred command of the Russian forces on his close confidant, Adjutant General Ivan Feodorovich Paskevich. Nicholas resented Ermolov, and felt he had been over-cautious in response to Persian aggression. Persian hopes of a general rising by the Muslim populations of Qarabagh, Armenia, Shirvan and Georgia against their Russian overlords went unfulfilled. Both Prince Valerian Grigoryevich Madatov, a Qarabagh Armenian, and Paskevich enjoyed victories over the Persian forces led by 'Abbas Mirza and his eldest son, Mohammad Mirza (the future Mohammad Shah). In Washington DC, Franz Friedrich Freiherr von Maltitz, the Russian ambassador, briefed Henry Clay, the American Secretary of State, on the causes and progress of the war.

By early 1827 reports circulated that Persia had solicited Britain's aid in brokering peace. By March Russian forces had crossed the Aras and soon captured 'Abbas Mirza's capital, Tabriz, forcing him to sue for peace. In this way, all formerly Persian territory as far south as the Aras river, as well as an enormous indemnity, were exacted, and Persia's overly optimistic attempt to regain territory lost in previous encounters with Russia ended in abject failure, sealed by the Treaty of Torkmanchay. Although Fath 'Ali Shah initially balked at ratifying the treaty, the threat of renewed Russian campaigning soon convinced him otherwise. The writer and diplomat Alexander Sergeyevich Griboyedov, a member of Paskevich's staff who had played an important role in the peace negotiations, travelled to St. Petersburg with a copy of the signed treaty.

11.1 'Persia,' *Evening Post* (Friday, 15 September 1826): 'Bombay, (India,) April 12. Persia.—Intelligence has arrived, of an order having been issued by the King of Persia,[1] to In- [sic, his] sons, who are in different provinces requiring their attendance at the capital, accompanied by 25,000 men each, which will concentrate an army of 100,000. Abbas Mirza was also summoned to the same rendezvous. The object of this preparation has not yet transpired.'

11.2 'From Late London Papers, received at the Office of the Commercial Advertiser. Persia,' *New-York Commercial Advertiser* (Friday, 20 October, 1826) and 'Persia,' *New-York Spectator* (Friday, 27 October, 1826): 'The Persians residing at Constantinople, wait with patience and anxiety the arrival of a Tartar messenger, who brings intelligence of what passes on the frontiers of Georgia. The King of Persia[2] arrived in the course of the month of

---

[1] Fath 'Ali Shah.
[2] Fath 'Ali Shah.

11 The Second Russo-Persian War and the Treaty of Torkmanchay (1826–1828)   1117

June at the Camp of Oudian,[3] ten leagues southeast of Tauris,[4] while his Royal Highness Prince Abbas Mirza was marching with his troops on Nakhtchiwan on the banks of the Araxes,[5] and Hussein Khan Seidar,[6] and Governor of Irewan, was already stationed on the confines of both Empires. If the Persians at Constantinople were to be believed, the English are not strangers to the determination of claiming by force of arms, the provinces of Aghistan,[7] Chirwan, &c. which were before subjected to the Crown of the Sofis,[8] and of which the Russians have made themselves masters for the last 40 years.'

11.3 'Latest from England,' *New-York Spectator* (Friday, 27 October 1826), 'Untitled,' *The Corrector* (Saturday, 4 November 1826), 'Late from England,' *Genius of Liberty* (Tuesday, 7 November, 1826), 'Latest Foreign News. Russia,' *St. Lawrence Gazette* (Tuesday, 7 November, 1826), 'Foreign. Latest from Europe. By an arrival at New-York. Russia,' *The Fredonian* (Wednesday, 8 November 1826), 'Latest Foreign News,' *Geneva*

---

[3] Cf. Awjan/Ujan, the summer residence of Abbas Mirza,' mentioned by Lyall (1825/2: 114–115); 'the camp in the Chemen Oujàn,' mentioned by Brydges (1834/1: 253).

[4] This seems to be a garbled reference to Fath 'Ali Shah's arrival at Soltaniyeh which he did in fact reach in June, 1826. See Busse (1972: 175).

[5] According to Hasan-e Fasa'i, 'Abbas Mirza joined his father at Soltaniyeh at this time. See Busse (1972: 175). He returned to Tabriz on 10 July 1826. See Busse (1972: 176).

[6] Hoseyn Qoli Khan Qazvini, 'the *Sardar* of the Erevan khanate.' See Williamson (2008: 95). He was a Qajar 'by birth.' See Chodzko (1842: 37). Alexander (1827: 202) noted, 'we paid a visit to the Saliar (or Mahomed Hussein Khan), the son of the Asuff ud Dowlah, or Prime Minister,' and described him as 'a proud-looking young man.' Elsewhere Alexander (1827: 78) wrote, 'Hussun Khan, is a brave and enterprizing chief, who repelled the Russians when they attempted to invade the province [Yerevan] in the last war.' The Second Russo-Persian War began in July, 1826 when Hoseyn Qoli Khan Qazvini 'crossed into Georgia with around 4000 infantrymen (both regular and irregular) and 8000 irregular cavalrymen. A few days later the combined forces of Abbas Mirza and Allah Yar crossed the Arax into Karabakh with their entourage of exiled khans and noblemen. The army numbered around 33,000 men and included up to 29 regular infantry battalions (22,000 men) and over 30 guns.' See Bitis (2006: 14). As Stcherbatow (1890: 25) noted, when Ermolov tried to impose Russian civil administration in the former khanates acquired as a result of the First Russo-Persian War, 'Les Khans dépossédés retirés en Perse entouraient Abbas-Mirza. Leur violence et leur cupidité furent bientôt effacées du souvenir des habitants, tandis que les liens de sang, de la religion et de la tradition s'affermirent encore davantage par l'exil, l'ignorance du peuple et par les malversations de l'administration russe. Les exilés entretenaient des relations constantes avec leurs anciens sujets et fomentaient activement la révolte; ils recherchaient de nouveau la domination de la Perse et la population, mécontente du gouvernement russe, se soumettait à leur influence. C'était ces mêmes Khans, ou leur fils, qui, s'étant révoltés contre la Perse au commencement de ce siècle, avaient lutté contre les innombrables troupes de ce même Abbas-Mirza, aujourd'hui leur protecteur et leur chef dans leur futur conflit avec l'Empire de Russie. Tel était le cas des Khans de Karabagh, de Shirvan et de Talich.' Hoseyn Qoli Khan Qazvini bore the epithet *Sari Aslan*, 'the yellow lion.' See Amanat (1993: 44).

[7] Daghestan.

[8] Safavids.

Palladium (Wednesday, 8 November 1826), 'Foreign Intelligence. Russia,' *Delaware Gazette* (Wednesday, 8 November 1826) and 'Russia,' *Republican Monitor* (Wednesday, 8 November 1826): 'A letter from Constantinople, of Aug. 21st, states that hostilities had commenced beteween Russia and Persia,[9] in the direction of Tiflis, and it is added that the Prince Abbas Mirza has a secret treaty with Russia against his father.[10]

Official accounts have been received at St. Petersburg that the Persians have made irruptions into several parts of Russia.'[11]

---

[9] Cf. Lee (1854: 178), '14th August [1826].—A war has actually broken out between Russia and Persia. The dispute arose about the frontier line. The Persians commenced the war by passing this line, and attacking a Russian regiment and seizing all the baggage.' The period just prior to the outbreak of war is depicted in a dispatch from the Russian ambassador Prince Prince Alexander Sergeyevich Menshikov [Александр Сергеевич Меншиков] (1787–1869), dated Soltaniyeh, 3 July, 1826. According to these, the religious leaders of Karbala urged Fath 'Ali Shah to declare a *jihad* against the Russians. See Anonymous (1826n: 731). In his diary the future commander in the Caucasus, Gen. Paskevich wrote, 'Au mois d'août 1826 nous étions à Moscou à l'occasion du couronnement de l'Empereur, lorsqu'un soir, quelques jours auparavant, je reçus un mot de l'aide de camp général baron Dibitch qui m'informait que l'Empereur m'ordonnait de me rendre chez lui le lendemain et me priait si je le trouvais bon d'aller le voir auparavant. Ne sachant pas pourquoi l'Empereur me faisait venir je vais chez Dibitch, qui me dit, "L'Empereur a reçu du commandant en chef du Caucase, géneral Yermolow, un rapport l'informant que les Persans ont fait irruption dans nos provinces transcaucasiennes et ont occupé le Lankoran et le Karabag, qu'ils s'avancent avec 60,000 hommes de troupes régulières, 60,000 irréguliers et à peu près 80 pièces d'artillerie, qu'il n'a pas de forces suffisantes à opposer aux Persans et qu'il ne réppond pas de conserver le pays si on ne lui envoie pas comme renfort deux divisions d'infanterie et une de cavalerie."' See Stcherbatow (1888: 251).

[10] Fath 'Ali Shah. Alexander (1827: 275) gives a hint of how this idea of a 'secret treaty' may have arisen. He wrote, 'It had been a great object of the Emperor Alexander's crafty policy to secure the Heir Apparent to the Persian throne in his interests, in order to facilitate his designs of pushing the Russian frontier to the Arras [Araxes river]. With this view he consented to a stipulation in the treaty of Gulistan, which, though it merely bound Russia to recognize as the lawful heir to the throne of Persia that son of the Shah whom his Majesty should appoint as his successor, was in effect (as secretly understood) a guarantee that Prince Abbas Mirza should be supported by Russia to the prejudice of his elder brother; and upon his nomination by the Shah as Heir Apparent, he was so recognized by the Court of St. Petersburgh. By the death of that brother, Abbas Mirza's right to the succession became indisputable.' On the other hand, it is also known that Ermolov had a secret understanding with Mohammad 'Ali Mirza, prior to his death and, animated in large part by his hatred of 'Abbas Mirza, Ermolov was prepared to invade Azerbaijan upon Fath 'Ali Shah's death and help install his brother on the throne. Nesselrode, however, informed Ermolov that the Czar would not countenance such a secret relationship. See Stcherbatow (1890: 16–17).

[11] As Stcherbatow (1890: 30–31) wrote, Menshikov 'était à peine arrivé à Sultaniéh qu'Abbas-Mirza, en juin même et durant le séjour de l'ambassadeur à Tauris, avait déjà eu recours aux mesures énergiques qui avaient entraîné le consentement du Schah à la guerre....A l'arrivée de Menchikow à Sultaniéh, la guerre était déjà décidée.' 'Abbas Mirza left Soltaniyeh on 17 July (5 July O.S.). When Eichwald arrived at Tiflis in mid-July, 1826, 'die Truppen trafen von allen Seiten ein, um nach Elisabethopol zu marschiren, wo sich Abbas Mirsa...mit einem großen Corps Truppen gezeit, und zuvor Schuscha, in Karabagh, mit einem andern Corps belagert und von allen Seiten eingeschlossen

11.4 'Untitled,' *New-York Evening Post* (Friday, 27 October, 1826): 'Despatches have been received by the Russian government from General Yermaloff, who commands in Georgia, announcing an invasion of the frontier by several Persian armies. Whether the irruptions complained of were acts of individual misconduct, or encroachments deliberately resolved upon by the monarch of Persia, do not at present appear. General Yermaloff professes himself unable to account for the manifestation of hostility, but suggests that it may be "the effect of the fanatical proceedings that have for a long time taken place in Persia."[12] The Emperor,[13] naturally indignant at the outrage, has ordered Gen. Yermaloff to repel force by force, and to clear the Russian frontier of the hordes that have presumed to pass it; and, at the same time, he has demanded solemn satisfaction of the Schah of Persia,[14] who is required, within 5 days, to depose, and inflict the most exemplary punishment on the Chief who first violated the Russian frontier. Should this demand not be complied with, the General was immediately to advance and commence offensive operations.'[15]

11.5 'Latest from England,' *The New-York Spectator* (Friday, 27 October, 1826), 'Latest from England,' *The Schenectady Cabinet* (Friday, 27 October, 1826), 'Persia and Russia. Constantinople, Aug. 24,' *The Baltimore Gazette and Daily Advertiser* (Monday, 30 October, 1826), 'Russia and Persia,' *New-Bedford Mercury* (Friday, 3 November, 1826), 'Foreign Intelligence,' *The Geneva Gazette and General Advertiser* (Monday, 8 November, 1826) and 'Russia,' *The Western Star* (Saturday, 11 November, 1826): 'The news here is certain that a war has broken out between Russia and Persia; and according to the present report, Russia seems to have sought this opportunity of employing

---

hatte.' See Eichwald (1837: 550–552). Menshikov, however, was delayed through various stratagems at both Tabriz and Yerevan and did not arrive in Tiflis until early September.

[12] The 'fanatical proceedings' may be a reference to the arrival in June, 1826, of 'un scheik de Kerbelaï...nommé Myr-Séid-Mahomed, lequel au nom du prophète prêcha ouvertement le "djakhat" [*jihad*, i.e. holy war]. Ce scheik présentait en même temps au Schah de nombreuses pétitions du clergé et des habitants de nos khanats frontières qui soi-disant le suppliaient de les délivrer des mains des infidèles.' See Stcherbatow (1890: 31). On the other hand, Lee (1854: 179) suggested, 'All believe that General Yermoloff, by his irritating conduct during the last 10 years, has excited this war, that he might have an opportunity of displaying his great military talents. These are represented to be of the first order. He and Count Woronzow are considered the greatest military geniuses of this country.' Writing of Prince Mikhail Semyonovich Vorontsov, Wagner (1856/2: 72–73), noted, 'The prevailing opinion was, that Count Woronzoff was only tolerated at his post, because no plausible reason could be adduced for removing him, and because even an autocrat [Emperor Nicholas] was obliged to spare a servant of such distinguished talents, and character, of such reputation and wealth, and of such great popularity.'

[13] Nicholas I (r. 1825–1855).

[14] Fath 'Ali Shah.

[15] As Christmas (1854: 65) noted, 'hardly was the coronation [of Nicholas I] over, when, by an imperial manifesto, war against Persia was declared, in consequence of Abbas Mirza, who was the heir to the crown of Persia, having invaded the province of Elizabethpal.' War was declared on 28 September 1826. See Hertslet (1891: 117).

her military. The court of Persia did everything to defer the blow, but ineffectually. It has produced considerable sensation here, in consequence of the connection between the Grand Seignor[16] & the Courts of Persia; & several persons anticipate that it will lead to a rupture between this country [England] and Russia. This notion has become the more current in consequence of the bustle of the political departments, and certain interviews between the Russian envoy[17] and the Grand Vizier,[18] which is said to have terminated angrily.—At present however, all is conjecture, excepting the fact of hostilities having commenced between Russia and Persia.'

11.6 'Foreign Advices,' *Boston Patriot and Mercantile Advertiser* (Monday, 30 October, 1826) and 'Russia,' *The Western Star* (Saturday, 11 November, 1826): 'Official accounts have been received at St. Petersburg, that the Persians have made irruptions into several parts of Russia. It is said the Russian cabinet had been intriguing with the heir apparent,[19] which being found out produced a rupture.

The London Globe and Traveller publishes a very brief extract from Constantinople relative to the hostilities which have been commenced between Russia and Persia.'

11.7 'Persia and Russia,' *The Baltimore Gazette and Daily Advertiser* (Monday, 30 October, 1826), 'Latest from England. New-York, October 27,' *Manufacturers & Farmers Journal and Providence and Pawtucket Advertiser* (Monday, 30 October, 1826; first paragraph only), 'Latest from England. Russia,' *Albany Argus & City Gazette* (Tuesday, 31 October, 1826; first two paragraphs, reversed), 'Foreign,' *American Traveller* (Tuesday, 31 October, 1826; first paragraph only), 'New-York, Oct. 27. Latest from England. Russia,' *Connecticut Herald,* (Tuesday, 31 October, 1826; first paragraph only), 'Foreign Intelligence Continued,' *Daily Georgian* (Tuesday, 7 November, 1826; first paragraph only), 'Latest Foreign News. New-York, Oct. 23. Latest from England. Russia,' *Sentinel of Freedom* (Tuesday, 31 October, 1826; first and second paragraphs only, reversed), 'Latest from England. Russia,' *New-York Spectator* (Tuesday, 31 October,

---

[16] Mahmud II (r. 1808–1839).

[17] Matei Minciacky. Cf. 10.309.

[18] Benderli Mehmed Selim Pasha (in office 1824–1828). See Jouannin and van Gaver (1840: 402); Somel (2003: lxxvi). At the time of his appointment he was governor of Silistre (mod. Silistra, Bulgaria). See Smiley (2014: 73). Jones (1829: 120–121) described coming upon him unintentionally when he was incognito noting, 'we…saw a countenance such as would be set down, at once, as that of a "master spirit;" and such he is. His age, I should judge to be about 50: his person is above the middle size, stout and powerful; while black hair, and a black beard, give a character of sterness to features, naturally drark, and expressing boldness and decision. His looks are altogether superior to those of the Sultan; and, among those who speak freely here, he stands higher, though his name is scarcely heard abroad. He has been longer in power, than is usual with Grand Viziers, and it is said, that the successes attendant on the late revolutions in the Capital, are owing principally to him. His name is Mehmed Selim Pasha.'

[19] 'Abbas Mirza.

11 The Second Russo-Persian War and the Treaty of Torkmanchay (1826–1828)   1121

1826; first and second paragraphs only, reversed), 'Foreign. From the N.Y. Com. Advertiser. Latest from England. Russia,' *The Fredonian* (Wednesday, 1 November, 1826; first and second paragraphs only, reversed), 'From the N.Y. Commercial Advertiser. Latest from Europe. Russia,' *Hampshire Gazette* (Wednesday, 1 November, 1826; first and second paragraphs only, reversed), 'Latest from England. New York, Oct. 27. Russia,' *The Virginia Herald* (Wednesday, 1 November, 1826; first and second paragraphs only, reversed), 'Foreign. Latest from Europe. New-York, October 27. Russia,' *Rhode Island Republican* (Thursday, 2 November, 1826; first paragraph only), 'Foreign. Latest from England. Russia,' *Easton Gazette* (Saturday, 4 November, 1826; first and second paragraphs, reversed), 'From the New York Com. Advertiser, Oct. 27. Latest from England. Russia,' *City Gazette and Commercial Daily Advertiser* (Monday, 6 November, 1826; first and second paragraphs, reversed), 'Foreign. Latest from England. Russia,' *Saratoga Sentinel* (Tuesday, 7 November, 1826; first and second paragraphs, reversed), 'Russia,' *The Pittsfield Sun* (Thursday, 9 November, 1826; first and second paragraphs, reversed) and 'Foreign Intelligence. Russia,' *Arkansas Gazette* (Tuesday, 5 December, 1826; first and second paragraphs, reversed): 'Official accounts have been received at St. Petersburg, that the Persians have made irruptions into several parts of Russia.

A letter from Constantinople of Aug. 21st states that hostilities had commenced between Russia and Persia, in the direction of Tiffes [sic, Tiflis], and it is added that the Prince Abbas Mirza has a secret treaty with Russia against his father[20]. . .

The intelligence contained in the Russian Journals, of an excursion of the Persians into the Russian territory, gives rise very naturally to a wish to know, with precision, the limits of the two Empires. By the peace of Seiva, of the 12th of October, 1813,[21] confirmed on the 15th of September following, by the treaty of Tifflis, the Persians gave up to the Russians, Daghestan Schirwan Derbent, and generally speaking, the whole of the western coasts of the Caspian Sea. From these treaties, it follows, that Russia is in actual possession of all the east coast of the Black Sea, as far as the mouth of the Phasis,[22] a position which, in case of a war with Turkey, lays open to her attacks the frontiers of Armenia, and allows her armies to march at once upon Erzeroum and Trebizond. As a consequence of the same treaties Russia is mistress of the western coasts of the Caspian Sea, for an extent of 250 leagues, from the

---

[20] Fath 'Ali Shah.

[21] For 'Seiva' note the French version of the Treaty of Gulistan, dated 12 October 1813, which was concluded 'dans le Camp Russe, sur la Rivière de Siewa dans le Gulistan.' See Hertslet (1891: 115). In English this reads, 'at the Russian camp on the banks of Zuivan near Gulistan in the district of Karabagh.' See Aitchison (1933, Appendix V, xv. Cf. 11.82).

[22] Ancient name, attested in Herodotus, Arrian and other sources, for the Rion river in Georgia. For the Classical refs. See Forbiger (1844/2: 39). It provided an outlet to the Black Sea. See Eichwald (1837: 185).

mouth of Oural,[23] beyond that of the Kour.[24] Her frontiers on that side are contiguous to those of Persia, from which Teheran, the present capital, is distant only 70 leagues.'

11.8 'New York, October 27. Latest from Europe,' *American Watchman & Delaware Advertiser* (Tuesday, 31 October, 1826), 'Foreign Intelligence. Latest from England,' *The Observer* (Wednesday, 8 November, 1826), 'Foreign Intelligence,' *The Geneva Gazette and General Advertiser* (Monday, 8 November, 1826) and 'Russia,' *The Western Star* (Saturday, 11 November, 1826): 'War has been declared between Persia and Russia. It is said the Russian cabinet had been intriguing with the heir apparent,[25] which being found out produced a rupture.'

11.9 'From Late Foreign Journals, Received at this Office. Russia and Persia,' *The Baltimore Gazette and Daily Advertiser* (Tuesday, 31 October, 1826), 'From English Papers. Invasion of Russia by the Persians,' *Daily National Intelligencer* (Tuesday, 14 November, 1826; first paragraph only, from 'While' = Lyall 1826a) and 'Foreign News. Russia and Persia,' *Ohio Monitor* (2 December, 1826; from 'Despatches from General Yermoloff' with variations): 'We have received the *St. Petersburgh Journal*, to the 3rd September, from which we have made extracts. While all minds in the metropolis of Russia seem to have been wholly occupied with scenes of festivity,[26] intelligence of no common importance had been received from the Persian frontier. General Yermoloff, who commands in Georgia, had sent despatches to his Government, to announce that the Russian territory had, in several parts, been suddenly invaded by the Persians.[27]

---

[23] The Ural river. As Chopin (1840: 12) noted, 'L'Oural tient le premier rang, après le Volga, parmi les affluents de la Caspienne; il portait autrefois le nom d'Yaïk, qui se rattachait à des souvenirs d'indépendance, et que, pour cette raison, le gouvernement a changé en celui d'Oural, après une insurrection dont ses bords furent le théâtre.' It discharges into the Caspian Sea below Atyrau, Kazakhstan, c. 360 km. East of Astrakhan.

[24] The Kur river.

[25] 'Abbas Mirza.

[26] Nicholas I became Emperor on 1 December 1825, but, 'For various reasons, the important ceremony of his coronation was postponed for some months. At length this imposing ceremony took place at Moscow, on the 3rd of September, 1826, amid such pomp and splendour as to have exceeded any thing recorded in the previous history of the nation.' See Smucker (1856: 102). Cf. Christmas (1854: 123).

[27] As Ermolov informed Nicholas in a dispatch dated 3 August (22 July O.S.), 1826, 'le serdar d'Erivan [Hoseyn Qoli Khan Qazvini] avait franchi notre frontière le 16 (28) [i.e. 16 July O.S., or 28 July 1826] avec un corps de 5000 hommes, qu'il avait forcé le Prince Sévarzemidzé, commandant du régiment d'infanterie de Tiflis, à abandonner le camp de Alirak-frontière et de se replier à Goumli. Pendant ce temps l'armée persane ayant ravagé le village du Petit-Karakliss, "avait fait prisonniers plus de 150 habitants en se livrant sur eux à des cruautés épouvantables". Ce même 16 (28) juillet la cavalerie ennemie avait fait son apparition sur la rivière Gamza-Tchémène, chassé les chevaux du régiment de Tiflis et massacré la petite escorte qui les gardait. Sur un autre point, à Sadagh-Khatch, un avant-poste fut défait tandis que sur la frontière du Karabagh se concentrait une nombreuse armée de

Whether the irruptions complained of were acts of individual misconduct, or encroachments deliberately resolved upon by the monarch of Persia, do not at present appeare. The best understanding, till very lately, subsisted between the Courts of Persia and Russia, and such, we believe, has been the case, with very slight exceptions, ever since the year 1812, when at the period of the invasion of Russia by Bonaparte, the war then in progress, between Russia and Persia, was happily brought to a conclusion by the good offices of the British Government.

The conduct of the Emperor Nicholas[28] on this occasion has been marked by great promptness of decision. Indignant at the outrage he has sustained, General Yermoloff has been at once directed to clear the Russian frontier by force of the hordes by which it has been overrun, and at the same time he has demanded solemn satisfaction of the Schah of Persia,[29] who is required within 5 days, to depose, and inflict the most exemplary punishment on the Chief who first entered the Russian dominions.

"St. Petersburg, Aug. 18, (30.)

"Despatches from General Yermoloff, who commands in Georgia, have brought accounts of an irruption made by the Persians, into several parts of the Russian territory.

"These first accounts transmitted in haste, do not enable us to understand the character of this aggression. Is it an effort of the fanatical preachings, which have for a long time past taken place in Persia, and which seems to have caused a great fermentation in that country? Have the tribes near our frontier yielded to that inclination to plunder and rapine which constantly animates them? Have their chiefs favoured their proceedings? Have they been unable to sustain them? Or, lastly, are we to ascribe so unjust, so sudden an invasion to the Court of Persia itself? Can that Court have violated in such a degree the peace and the treaties which guarantee it? Can it all at once have taken a resolution to attack us without motive, and without object? Such are the questions which occur, but which the Government is not yet able to answer.

"The reciprocal advantages secured to Russia and to Persia, by the treaty of Gulistan; the friendly relations between them since the conclusion of that treaty; the absence of all grounds for a serious difference; the mission of Major Prince Menzikow[30] to the Schah, to announce to him the Accession of his Majesty the Emperor to the Throne, and to confirm

---

30,000 hommes, qui s'apprêtait à franchir l'Araxe sous le commandement d'Abbas-Mirza.' See Stcherbatow (1890: 32).

[28] Nicholas I.

[29] Fath 'Ali Shah.

[30] Alexander Sergeyevich Menshikov (1787–1869). As Alexander (1827: 275) noted, 'At this critical period, a new turn was given to affairs by the death of the Emperor Alexander, and by the appointment of Prince Menzikoff, by the reigning Emperor [Nicholas I], on a special mission to the Court of Tehran, ostensibly to announce the succession of the Emperor Nicholas, but authorized (in the language of the Russian declaration) "to conclude an agreement respecting the *only* point which delayed the demarcation of the frontiers, to renew the proposal for an exchange of territory, or, *in order to consult still more the interest of Persia, and to place the views of Russia in their true light*, to add to the territory already occupied by the Persians a part of the district of Talychyne."'

and strengthen the friendship and good understanding between the two States; the reception he met with on his arrival in the Persian territory, the attention paid to him, the friendly assurances lavished on him, by the Presumptive Heir to the Crown Prince[31]; every thing, gave reason to preserve the stability and duration of the peace.[32] That the Court of Teheran should reply to this mission by a sudden attack; that it should immediately follow up these assurances by war, without explanation, and without any previous declaration, even without any pretext that might justify it, is an event so strange, that the Imperial Government cannot credit it, till it has received entire confirmation and authentic proofs of it. Accordingly, while General Yermoloff has received orders to repel force by force, and to clear our frontiers of the hordes that have dared to pass them, on the other hand, solemn satisfaction has been demanded of the Schah of Persia. Russia has demanded from that Sovereign the immediate deposition and exemplary punishment (within the term of 5 days) of the Chief who first violated our frontiers.[33] If, contrary to all expectation, this satisfaction should not be given, Gen. Yermoloff was immediately to advance, and commence offensive operations; the justice of our cause would ensure to our arms the Divine protection, and the chastisements would be as exemplary as the attack has been presumptuous and perfidious.

"The public will be regularly and accurately informed of everything relative to the state of affairs on the frontiers of Persia."'

11.10 'From the N.Y. Daily Advertiser, Oct. 27. Latest from England,' *Norwich Courier* (Wednesday, 1 November, 1826), 'Foreign. Russia,' *Boston Recorder* (Friday, 3 November, 1826), 'New-York, October 27. Latest from England,' *Charleston Courier* (Monday, 6 November, 1826), 'From the New-York Daily Advertiser, Oct. 27. Latest from England,' *Augusta Chronicle and Georgia Advertiser* (Wednesday, 8 November, 1826): 'It is said that the Persians have made an incursion over the Russian frontier.'

---

[31] The wording here is confusing since 'Presumptive Heir to the Crown Prince' suggests the heir of 'Abbas Mirza, not that of Fath 'Ali Shah, but this is surely an error. As Alexander (1827: 277) observed, 'Upon the arrival of Prince Menzikoff on the Persian frontier, he was received with great respect, and experienced a friendly reception from Prince Abbas Mirza at Tabreez. He proceeded from thence to the royal camp at Sultania, where he was treated with distinction.' Similarly Eichwald (1837: 559) noted, 'Der Thronfolger Abbas Mirsa empfing den Botschafter in Tauris auf eine sehr ausgezeichnete Art, da der Schach selbst in seinem Sommeraufenthalte Sultania war, wohin auch Fürst Menschikoff zu kommen eingeladen wurde.'

[32] This did not last long, however. As Stcherbatow (1890: 31) observed, 'Au commencement de juillet à Sultaniéh, à la réception publique de l'ambassadeur on fut grossier avec lui et le cérémonial d'usage adopté à l'égard des envoyés des grandes puissances ne fut point observé. Le Schah refusa de recevoir en mains propres la lettre de notre Souverain et ordonna au Prince Menchikow de la déposer sur le coussin; c'était, selong l'usage oriental, un manque de respect du Schah à l'égard de l'Empereur de Russie.'

[33] Hoseyn Qoli Khan Qazvini, military commander in Yerevan.

11 The Second Russo-Persian War and the Treaty of Torkmanchay (1826–1828)   1125

11.11 'Late from England. Russia,' *The Farmer* (Thursday, 2 November, 1826): 'A letter from Constantinople of Aug. 21st, states that hostilities had commenced between Russia and Persia, in the direction of Tiffes.'

11.12 'Russia,' *Kinderhook Herald* (Thursday, 2 November, 1826), 'Latest Foreign News,' *Geneva Palladium* (Wednesday, 8 November, 1826), 'Foreign Intelligence, *Geneva Gazette, and General Advertiser* (Wednesday, 8 November, 1826) and 'Foreign Intelligence. Russia,' *Delaware Gazette* (Wednesday, 8 November, 1826): 'The coronation of the Emperor Nicholas took place on the 3rd of September. . . .A letter from Moscow of the 4th, said to be from a person who has access to the best information, contains the following paragraph: "The new Emperor[34] shows a disposition to deviate very much from the European policy of his defunct brother,[35] wishing thereby to become popular, and to nationalize himself as much as possible. The storm that menaced on the side of Turkey is not yet dissipated, and another is rising on the side of Persia. . . ." Official accounts have been received at St. Petersburgh, that the Persians have made irruptions into several parts of Russia.'

11.13 'Russia and Persia,' *New-Bedford Mercury* (Friday, 3 November, 1826) and 'Constantinople, Aug. 24,' *New-Hampshire Patriot & State Gazette* (Monday, 6 November, 1826; third paragraph only): 'Official accounts have been received at St. Petersburg, that the Persians have made irruptions into several parts of Russia. It is said the Russian cabinet had been intriguing with the heir apparent, which being found out produced a rupture.

A letter received in London from Constantinople, dated Aug. 24th contains the following addition to the above intelligence. . . .

"The news here is certain that a war has broken out between Russia and Persia; and according to the present report, Russia seems to have sought this opportunity of employing her military. The court of Persia did everything to defer the blow, but ineffectually. It has produced considerable sensation here, in consequence of the connection between the Grand Seignor[36] & the Courts of Persia[37]; & several persons anticipate that it will lead to a rupture

---

[34] Nicholas I.

[35] Alexander I (r. 1801–1825).

[36] Mahmud II.

[37] Accounts of contemporary political events, whether from the Ottoman perspective, e.g. Jouannin and van Gaver (1840) and Creasy (1856/2), make no mention of Ottoman-Persian collusion at this time, and this may be an anachronistic and wishful allusion to the Treaty of Erzurum, concluded in 1823 which, however, certainly did not lead to closer ties between Persia and the Porte or cooperation against Russia. Rather, as Moltke (1845: 6) observed, it was the accession of Nicholas I and the change in Russian policy that proved most destructive to Ottoman-Russian peace. 'Mit der Thronbesteigung Kaiser Nicolaus war eine wesentliche Veränderung in der friedlichen Politik des Petersburger Cabinets eingetreten. Seit der furchtbaren Entladung der Unzufriedenheit bei Kaiser

between this country and Russia. This notion has become the more current in consequence of the bustle of the political departments, and certain interviews between the Russian envoy[38] and the Grand Vizier,[39] which is said to have terminated angrily.—At present however, all is conjecture, excepting the fact of hostilities having commenced between Russia and Persia."'

11.14 'From Europe,' *New-York Evening Post* (Monday, 6 November, 1826) and 'Untitled,' *Alexandria Gazette* (Thursday, 9 November, 1826): 'It was reported that the war between the Persians and Russians had been instigated by foreign influence, and that a large army of Persians commanded by English and French officers[40] were marching towards the Russian frontiers. A division of the army of 10,000 men[41] had already made

---

Alexanders Tode, welche nur durch die persönliche Festigkeit und Entschlossenheit des neuen Herrschers bewältigt worden war, betrachtete man den Krieg gegen den Erb- und Glaubensfeind [Turkey] als einen Abzugskanal für das Mißvergnügen der Soldaten-Aristocratie.'

[38] Minciacky.

[39] Benderli Mehmed Selim Pasha.

[40] By this time the French officers in 'Abbas Mirza's service had long since been replaced by English ones, but they were proscribed from accompanying the invading Persian forces. As the Russian ambassador Menshikov wrote in a letter dated from Soltaniyeh of 21 July, 1826, only an Italian artillery officer named Bernardi and a former English artillery serjeant paid directly by 'Abbas Mirza, served in the Persian forces that invaded the Russian provinces. See Anonymous (1826n: 732), Anonymous (1848: 1052). The Englishman was actually a Scot named James Dawson (1785–1865), 'originally a blacksmith at Carron [Scotland],' who 'could read and write tolerably well, but was otherwise a plain, uneducated man,' He had 'accompanied the embassy under Sir Gore Ouseley, and had returned to England with Colonel D'Arcy, subsequently purchased his discharge, and entered the Persian service,' according to Monteith (1856: 128–129). Baddeley (1908: 158, n. 1) wrote that Dawson 'saved 14 of the guns after the defeat of the Persian army and flight of several of the artillery officers.' For his life see Mathews (2013). Regarding the replacement of French by British officers, de Warren (1857: 31) noted, 'les changements merveilleux opérés en très peu de temps dans la force militaire de la Perse par les officiers français de l'ambassade de M. Gardanne....Par un revirement soudain, les Anglais se décidèrent à acheter à tout prix l'alliance persane; et ils usèrent immédiatement de tous les moyens possibles pour couper court à une éducation militaire qui allait trop vite à leur gré. On sait comment ils réussirent à faire éconduire l'ambassade française de 1809, et tous les officiers qui y étaient attachés, en persuadant à Fatteh-Ali-Shah que des officiers anglais remplaceraient avantageusement ceux de Napoléon. Il est vrai que, pour le décider à cette substitution, ils employèrent un argument irrésistible, l'offre d'un subside annuel de 200,000 £ sterling pour la levée et l'entretien d'un corps régulier de douze mille hommes d'infanterie avec vingt-cinq pièces de canon.' As Ferrier (1856: 24) noted, 'the troops of Abbas Mirza...were trained by English officers sent to him by the East India Company,' and in a note, he wrote, 'The English officers principally employed in disciplining the Persian troops under Abbas Mirza were Sir Henry Lindsay Bethune, Capt. Christie, Major Hart, and Colonel Shee. The two first have left an enduring reputation through the country, and a few years ago the traveller was still often asked in the villages of Georgia and Armenia whether Lindsay Sahib was still alive and well.' This note was written either by Capt. William Jesse, who translated Ferrier's manuscript, or H.D. Seymour, who edited the publication.

[41] Cf. Eichwald (1837: 570), Cazalès (1838: 618).

11 The Second Russo-Persian War and the Treaty of Torkmanchay (1826–1828)   1127

an incursion in the Emperor's territories, burned several villages and carried off a number of the inhabitants.'

11.15 'Latest from France,' *National Advocate* (Monday, 6 November, 1826; to 'frontiers'), 'Latest from France,' *New-York Advertiser* (Tuesday, 7 November, 1826), 'Latest from France,' *New-York Spectator* (Tuesday, 7 November, 1826; to 'frontiers'), 'Latest from France,' *The Lyons Advertiser* (after 7 November, 1826; first paragraph only), 'From the N.Y. Daily Adv. Nov. 8 [sic, 7],' *Norwich Courier* (Wednesday, 8 November, 1826; second paragraph only), 'New-York, Nov. 6. Latest from France,' *American Sentinel* (Wednesday, 8 November, 1826; to 'frontiers'), 'Foreign. Europe,' *The Kinderhook Herald* (Thursday, 9 November, 1826; to 'frontiers'), 'Foreign. From France,' *The American Traveller* (Friday, 10 November, 1826; to 'frontiers'), 'Foreign. Latest from France. New York, Nov. 6,' *Richmond Enquirer* (Friday, 10 November, 1826; second paragraph only), 'Foreign Intelligence. Russia,' *Salem Gazette* (Friday, 10 November, 1826; second paragraph only), 'Russia,' *The Corrector* (Saturday, 11 November, 1826), 'General Intelligence. Latest from France. Russia,' *Christian Secretary* (Saturday, 11 November, 1826; first paragraph only), 'Foreign. Russia,' *Columbian Star* (Saturday, 11 November, 1826; second paragraph only), 'Latest from France,' *Black River Gazette* (Tuesday, 14 November, 1826; to 'frontiers'), 'From France,' *American Mercury* (Tuesday, 14 November, 1826; first paragraph only), 'Latest Foreign News. From the Statesman. Latest from France,' *Sentinel of Freedom* (Tuesday, 14 November, 1826; second paragraph only), 'Foreign Intelligence. Russia.' *The Geneva Gazette, and General Advertiser* (Wednesday, 15 November, 1826; first paragraph only), 'Late from Europe. Russia,' *The Cabinet* (Wednesday, 15 November, 1826; first paragraph only), 'Untitled,' *Middlesex Gazette* (Wednesday, 15 November, 1826; second paragraph only), 'General Intelligence. Foreign,' *Zion's Herald* (Wednesday, 15 November, 1826; to 'frontiers'), 'Foreign Extracts,' *Christian Watchman* (Friday, 17 November, 1826; first paragraph only), 'Foreign. Russia,' *New-Hampshire Sentinel* (Friday, 17 November, 1826; second paragraph only), 'Latest from France,' *Augusta Chronicle and Georgia Advertiser* (Saturday, 18 November, 1826; second paragraph only), 'From the New York Statesman. Foreign. Latest from France. Russia,' *Repository and Observer* (Saturday, 18 November, 1826; first paragraph only), 'Latest from France. New-York, November 6,' *Ohio Monitor* (Saturday, 18 November, 1826; second paragraph only) and 'Foreign Intelligence. Latest from France. New-York, November 6,' *Illinois Intelligencer* (Saturday, 2 December, 1826; second paragraph only): 'The differences between Russia and Persia assume a delicate aspect. It seems that the Persians, without any previous indications of hostility, had made an incursion into Russia with 10,000 men, and had burned several villages and carried off a number of persons. Many of the Persian soldiers were dressed in English uniforms.[42] A further report adds, that

---

[42] According to a Russian report published in September, 1826, and republished in abbreviated form in France, 'Abbas Mirza himself was obliged to wear a European uniform and to learn European

the war has been pushed on by foreign influence, and that 200,000 Persians, commanded by English and French officers, were on their march to the Russian frontiers.[43] Some detachments of Russian troops were marching for the frontiers of Persia.[44]

The Persians are said to have invaded the frontiers of Russia with a powerful army from Georgia, and Russian troops have marched from the Crimea.[45] 45,000 men are also ready to cross the Pruth,[46] and 100,000 more are on their way.[47] The boundary line is ill-defined/

---

military exercises in order to counter the hatred of his troops towards the innovations he was attempting to implement. 'Les troupes qu'il avait levées refusaient obstinément de ressembler aux Frendgici, et en particulier, aux Russes qu'elles craignaient et détestaient plus que tous les autres peuples européens. Pour vaincre ces obstacles et affaiblir la haine de ses soldats contre les innovations qu'il méditait, il fut obligé de prendre lui-même l'uniforme et d'apprendre l'exercice militaire. . . .des officiers français et anglais lui furent d'un grand secours dans l'exécution de ce projet, qui, du reste, est restée très-imparfaite, en raison de l'intelligence peu étendue de ce prince, auquel la subordination des officiers et soldats a toujours paru impossible.' See A.J. (1826: 228).

[43] A huge exaggeration of numbers and a false statement with respect to the presence of English and French officers. According to Alexander (1827: 281–282), 'The army under the orders of the Prince Royal ['Abbas Mirza] which took the field against the Russians amounted in number (including irregulars) to forty-five or fifty thousand men. The *Surbaz* (resolute), or disciplined battalions, were twelve thousand strong; there were also a few companies of foot artillery, and several hundreds of Russian deserters. The Shah's military force, except ten or twelve thousand disciplined *Janbaz* (contemners of life), is but an untrained rabble.'

[44] In a dispatch dated 11 August (30 July O.S.), 1826, Ermolov informed Nicholas I that 'le khanat de Karabagh était occupé par 9 à 10 compagnies du 42e chasseurs avec 6 pièces d'artillerie légère; un régiment de cosaques, dont 3 compagnies avec 2 pièces et une partie des cosaques, se trouvaient à Karabagh-les-Monts pour protéger les populations nomades. Le colonel Réouth, commandant du 42e chasseurs, reçut l'ordre de rassembler tout son détachement au village de Tchinaktchi, quartier du régiment, et, à la première apparition de l'ennemi, d'évacuer le khanat en se retirant sans hâte. Il ne réussit pas à s'adjoindre les compagnies du Karabagh, car celles-ci, entourées par la cavalerie persane, se défendirent toute la journée, mais à la fin durent se rendre prisonnières avec 2 bouches à feu. Réouth en reçut la nouvelle très tard; les cosaques envoyés en reconnaissance dans la direction de l'Araxe tombèrent aux mains des ennemies. Cinq d'entre eux parvinrent avec peine à se sauver, et à informer Réouth du sort des trois compagnies et de l'attaque des Persans; il n'eut que le temps de se réfugier avec 5 compagnies et 4 pièces de canon dans la forteresse de Schoucha, où se trouvait déjà la 9e compagnie.' See Stcherbatow (1890: 35–36).

[45] As Baddeley (1908: 156) noted, following the Persian invasion of Qarabagh, Ermolov transmitted to the Czar 'the urgent necessity of reinforcements. Nicholas I., who was in Moscow for his coronation, found it impossible to comply with the demand for two divisions of infantry, but sent one, the 20th, from the Crimea, and six regiments of Don Cossack cavalry.'

[46] In his critique of imperial expansion, Passmore Edwards (1855: 15) wrote, 'The French cross the Mediterranean, the British cross the Atlantic, the Russians cross the Pruth.' As the Pruth River runs between Moldova and Romania, however, the expression 'to cross the Pruth' generally referred to the outbreak of war between Russia and the Ottoman empire, not Persia. Thus, Dirom (1828: 58) wrote, 'Russia may, therefore, resolve upon waging a separate war with the Ottoman Porte, and in ordering her army of 80,000 men to cross the Pruth.'

[47] When war broke out, Alexander (1827: 282) estimated the Russian forces in the southern Caucasus at 'thirty-two thousand infantry, twelve hundred dragoons, six thousand Cossacks, and two battalions

divided—having neither river, mountain, forest, nor city; and it is suspected by some that Russia makes pretence of an aggression for an excuse to advance her line from Gomeri[48] to Araxe, and bring it up with that of Turkey, thus being able to invade Erzeroum and Trebizons/di.'

11.16 'Untitled,' *New-York American* (Tuesday, 7 November, 1826), 'Latest Foreign News. Russia,' *St. Lawrence Gazette* (Tuesday, 7 November, 1826) and 'Foreign Intelligence. Spain,' *Geneva Paladium* (Wednesday, 15 November, 1826): 'Russia in another quarter is said to have been invaded by the Persians; though some suppose and perhaps not unwisely, that this invasion is a mere pretext of the Russian General Yermoloff to invade Persia.[49] The immense armed force of Russia is only then harmless to its own country, when it can be employed in subjugating or desolating other lands; and the present tranquility of Nicholas', as yet unconsolidated throne, requires perhaps that Persia, and perhaps Turkey, should be made the theatre of employment.'

11.17 'New-York, October 27. Latest from England. London, Sept. 23,' *Charleston Courier* (Monday, 6 November, 1826) and 'From the New-York Daily Advertiser, Oct. 27. Latest from England,' *Augusta Chronicle and Georgia Advertiser* (Wednesday, 8 November, 1826): 'We have received this morning the St. Petersburgh Journal to the 20th inst. It is silent respecting the late irruptions of the Persians, and contains no political intelligence.'

---

of artillery; but they were mostly dispersed in detachments throughout Georgia.' Although Eichwald (1837: 568–569) put the total number of Russian troops in Georgia at 34,150 he qualified this by noting that less than half that number were available to repulse the Persian invasion: 'nehmen wir von jenen 34,000 M. die im Laufe des Jahres 1825 Gestorbenen, Erkrankten, die vielen Invaliden und daher zur Garnison der einzelnen Städte gerechneten Soldaten aus, und rechnen wir von dieser Anzahl auch die nothwendig in den einzelnen Kreisen zurückbleibende Besatzung zur Aufrechterhaltung der Ruhe und Beobachtung der Bergvölker ab, so konnte Georgien etwa 15,000 M. gegen Abas Mirsa's weit überlegene Scharen nach Elisabethopol schicken, während dagegen die Gränzen von Karabagh und Schirvan, so wie Talysch, offen und unbesetzt blieben.'

[48] Gyumri, Armenia.

[49] Considering the state of Ermolov's forces, and his repeated requests for more troops, this is certainly untrue. Nikolai Nikolaevich Muraviev/Murav'ev (1794–1866)] observed, 'Abbas Mirza 'connaissait parfaitement la désorganisation qui régnait dans nos troupes,' of which he was kept regularly informed by Qajar informants in Qarabagh. Instead of maintaining military discipline and preparedness, for example, 'un des plus sincères admirateurs de Yermolow...nous dit qu'en 1826, au commencement de notre campagne contre la Perse, les sapeurs, dont les quartiers étaient à Tiflis, travaillaient exclusivement à la construction de maisons dans la ville et étaient absolument ignorants des premières règles de leur arme....On cite...le 41ᵉ chasseurs (colonel Réouth) employé presqu'en entier dans le Karabagh à la construction d'une habitation privée dans la propriété du Prince Madatow et le 7ᵉ carabiniers (colonel Ladinsky) qui bâtissait à Tiflis une maison pour la maîtresse de son commandant. Enfin le Prince Sévarzémidzé, chef du 3ᵉ carabiniers, s'occupait à défricher la terre et à l'ensemencer à l'aide des soldats qu'il commandait.' See Stcherbatow (1890: 27–28).

11.18 'Russia,' *The Baltimore Gazette and Daily Advertiser* (Wednesday, 8 November, 1826), 'Russia,' *The Baltimore Patriot and Mercantile Advertiser* (Wednesday, 8 November, 1826), 'Foreign. Latest from Europe. By an arrival at New-York. Russia,' *New Brunswick Fredonian* (Wednesday, 8 November, 1826), 'Latest from Europe. Russia,' *Daily National Intelligencer* (Thursday, 9 November, 1826), 'Foreign Intelligence. [Paris dates to the 20th September.] Russia,' *The National Gazette and Literary Register* (Thursday, 9 November, 1826), 'Latest from Europe. Russia,' *Albany Argus* (Friday, 10 November, 1826), 'Foreign. Latest from Europe,' *Saratoga Sentinel* (Tuesday, 14 November, 1826), 'Foreign Intelligence. Russia,' *Geneva Paladium* (Wednesday, 15 November, 1826; first sentence only), 'New-York, November 6. Latest from Europe. Russia,' *Charleston Courier* (Wednesday, 15 November, 1826), 'Foreign. Latest from Europe. Russia,' *Farmers' Repository* (Wednesday, 15 November, 1826), 'Foreign. New York, November 9. Latest from Europe. Russia,' *The Torch Light and Public Advertiser* (Thursday, 16 November, 1826), 'Russia,' *Christian Register* (Saturday, 18 November, 1826) and 'Russia,' *The Commentator* (Saturday, 25 November, 1826): 'The Persians are said to have invaded the frontiers of Russia with a powerful army from Georgia, and Russian troops have marched from the Crimea. Forty-five thousand men, are ready to cross the Pruth, and one hundred thousand are on their way to reinforce.'[50]

11.19 'Untitled,' *Boston Commercial Gazette* (Thursday, 9 November, 1826), 'Latest from Europe,' *Boston Recorder* (Friday, 10 November, 1826) and 'Important News,' *Eastport Sentinel* (Saturday, 18 November, 1826): 'War has already began [sic] by the Persians on Russia: 10,000 troops had marched into the Russian territory, and plundered and captured the inhabitants. Several English and French officers were in the Persian army. A Persian army of 200,000 was said to be marching to the frontiers of Russia.'

11.20 'New-York, Nov. 5. Latest from France,' *Essex Register* (Thursday, 9 November, 1826), 'Foreign Items. Latest from France,' *Vermont Watchman and State Gazette* (Tuesday, 14 November, 1826; first paragraph only) and 'Latest from Europe. Russia,' *Daily Georgian* (Thursday, 16 November, 1826): 'The differences beteween Russia and Persia assume a delicate aspect. It seems that the Persians, without any previous indications

---

[50]This was most assuredly not the case. As Hans Karl Graf von Diebitsch (1785–1831), Chief of the General Staff, wrote to Ermolov on 12 August (31 July O.S.), 1826, 'Vous avez 30,000 hommes d'infanterie sur le versant opposé de la chaîne du Caucase, dont 15,000 hommes se trouvent aux environs de Tiflis et près de la frontière d'Erivan. En laissant 2000 hommes pour protéger Tiflis, vous pouvez sans retard réunir en un seul corps 13,000 hommes: ce corps complété par de l'artillerie et de la cavalerie peut sans faute être porté à 15,000 hommes. Sa Majesté Impériale est parfaitement assurée que ce chiffre de troupes sous le commandement d'un chef aussi parfait, aussi expérimenté et possédant à un si haut degré la confiance de ses subordonnés, comme c'est le cas de Votre Excellence, que ces troups, dis-je, suffiront parfaitement à détruire les forces ennemies.' See Stcherbatow (1890: 38).

of hostility, had made an incursion into Russia with 10,000 men, and had burned several villages and carried off a number of persons. Many of the Persian soldiers were dressed in English uniforms. A further report adds, that the war has been pushed on by foreign influence, and that 200,000 Persians, commanded by English and French officers, were on their march to the Russian frontiers.

In case of a rupture England will it is supposed be placed in a delicate situation, as she has always watched with a jealous eye the conquests of Russia over Persia.'

11.21 'Translations from French papers. [From the Paris Etoile of 24th Sept.],' *New-York American* (Friday, 10 November, 1826), 'Translations from French papers. [From the Paris Etoile of 24th Sept.],' *New-York Commercial Advertiser* (Tuesday, 14 November, 1826) and 'Translations from French Papers. From the Paris Etoile of 20th September,' *Ohio Monitor* (Saturday, 25 November, 1826): 'The attack of the frontiers of the Russian empire by the Persians, was an event to which little attention was paid at Odessa. The report circulated for several days, that a division of the second army was to march for the Caucasus. To day we learn in a positive manner that the 20th division of infantry, cantoned until now in the Crimea, is in motion to traverse the strait of Kertch, and directing its march against Georgia, by the line of the Couban. It is to be replaced in Crimea, by battalions from the neighbouring governments. It is believed that other troops will be sent to reinforce the army of Georgia. This news will certainly not fail to have a due influence on the conferences at Akerman, which still continue.'[51]

11.22 '45, Haymarket, Sept. 19, 1826,' *The Baltimore Gazette and Daily Advertiser* (Friday, 10 November, 1826 = [Lyall 1826a]); ['We publish in another column, a letter respecting the rupture between the Persians and Russians, addressed to the Editors of the London Courier, by Robert Lyall.[52] It is rather a curious article and comes from a man who was once badly treated by the Russian government, and who does not seem disposed to put a very favorable construction upon the motives which induced the Russians so readily to take up arms. England must be deeply interested in the result of the contest, and should it take a turn unfavorable to the Persians, the British possessions in the East, might sensibly feel the effects of a power which seems to grasp at universal dominion.]), 'The Persian invasion of the Russian Provinces. To the Editor of the London Courier,' *Richmond Enquirer* (Tuesday, 14 November, 1826 = [Lyall 1826b]), 'Persian Invasion of the Russian Provinces. To the Editor of the London Courier,' *Daily National Journal* (Friday,

---

[51] The original French article on which this was based dates to 20 September 1826, hence a little over two weeks before the Convention of Akkerman was signed (7 October 1826) by Russia and the Porte, regarding the status of Serbia, Moldavia and Wallachia. For the text of the Convention see Noradounghian (1900: 116–121).

[52] The British botanist, physician and diplomat Robert Lyall (1790–1831). He practiced in Russia, serving a number of noble families. For his life see Oliver (1900). He was a prolific writer. See e.g. Lyall (1825, 1826a, b).

17 November, 1826), 'Persian Invasion of the Russian Provinces. To the Editor of the London Courier,' *American Watchman and Daily Advertiser* (Friday, 17 November, 1826), 'Persian Invasion of the Russian Provinces. To the Editor of the London Courier,' *National Journal* (Saturday, 18 November, 1826), 'The Persian Invasion of the Russian Provinces,' *Boston Courier* (Friday, 24 November, 1826), 'The Persian Invasion of the Russian Provinces,' *Boston Patriot and Mercantile Advertiser* (Friday, 24 November, 1826) and 'Russia and Persia. The Persian Invasion of the Russian Provinces,' *Eastern Argus*: 'Sir:—I again take the liberty of requesting a place in your columns, for some remarks which have been suggested by the most recent intelligence from St. Petersburg. I remain, Sir, your very ob't serv't. Robert Lyall. 45, Haymarket, Sept. 19, 1826]: 'Any individual ignorant of the Russian empire, of the character of its natives, of the perfidious policy of the autocrat cabinet, and of the unbounded ambition of the Tsars might justly suppose that this nation was deeply aggrieved by the "irruption made by the Persians into several parts of the Russian territory;" and the cant in which we are informed "that the *justice of their cause* would ensure to their arms the Divine protection," while it is a profanation of words, and an insult to the Deity, might lead a just person to infer that Persia had acted with the greatest wantonness, deceit and treachery. Yet such is the language of Russia—a nation whose double headed eagle has stretched forth her talons to the north and to the south, to the east and to the west—has pounced upon her prey, and has held it fast in the iron grasp of despotism—of a nation which, for hundreds of years, has never been at rest, except for a period suitable to prepare her future means of attack, and to await her projected aggrandizement—of a nation which has added province to province, principality to principality, and kingdom to kingdom—in a word of a nation which has engulphed every territory which bordered its ancient frontiers.

With respect to Persia facts tell us that Russia has been insidiously seizing upon her best provinces in regular succession: that Gen. Yermolof, (who though but the representative of the autocrat, may be almost reckoned an absolute sovereign of the Caucaso-Georgian provinces, entertains the meanest opinions of Persia and of the Persians, as well as of their power—that in the character of Ambassador to the Court of the Shach,[53] he behaved with the greatest arrogance, pride & contempt towards all the constituted authorities; that he boasted he was "*the Ambassador of the most powerful nation of the world*"—no doubt forgetting that there was such an *insignificant* empire as that of Great Britain)—that in an animated discussion he disdainfully threatened Mirza Abdool Wehab, the Prime Minister[54]

---

[53] Fath 'Ali Shah.

[54] 'Abd ol-Vahhab-e Isfahani Mo'tamad od-Doula. When Ermolov came to Persia in 1817 on his diplomatic mission, he 'was sent to the province of Khamsa to prepare lodgings upon the Russian ambassador's arrival, a parasang from the pasture of Solṭāniya, and to entertain him and inquire into his opinions.' See Busse (1972: 152). Ermolov called him 'a minister who possesses the complete confidence of the Shach, and is reckoned the best informed of the nobles.' See Lyall (1825/2: 118). In 1826 John McNeill wrote, 'Mirza Abdul Wahab, Moatamed ud Dowlah (Faithful of the State), is a man of talent and learning, of pleasing manners, and even of delicate sentiments of honour. He has

of the Persian monarch, with the capture of all the Persian territory as far as the Araxes;—and that he scornfully remarked, that he could even fix the day when he and his army should be at Tabreez—In a word, the tenor of the General's sentiments amounted to a declaration of his capability to annihilate the kingdom of Persia, and the dynasty of the Shach, on receiving the permission or the command of his imperial master.* [*In the 2nd vol. of my Travels in Russia, the Crimea, the Caucasus, and Georgia, is contained an abridged translation of Gen. Yermolof's Private Journal of his Embassy to Persia—a journal which he most impolitely allowed to be copied by a number of officers, From one of them, now beyond the reach of despotic power, I borrowed his copy, from which my transcript was made. All the above particulars are contained in the said Journal.][55] Till further and more authentic details arrive, I may, therefore, be allowed to state my opinion with respect to the present *irruption*, as it is called of the Persian territory. The subject presents itself under two views.

1st. As mutual and bitter hatred has long separated Russia and Persia,[56] and as Abbaz Mirza, the brave and enlightened heir presumptive of the Persian Crown, has most eagerly awaited a favourable opportunity to attack the Russians, and to drive them from the Persian provinces, which have been wrested from his Royal Father,[57] by craft, violence and policy, as well as by good fortune—(as, for example, in 1812, when England assisted Russia's ambitious views, because it was then the interest of the cabinet of St. James, that the Russian army should be left at ease upon its southern flank, so as the better to resist the

---

lost his influence with the Shah. A man whom everyone must like, a delightful companion, but so indolent that there is no getting him to set seriously about any business.' See MacAlister (1910: 75). The ambassador John Macdonald Kinneir referred to him as 'Meerza Abdool Wahab, the Moatumud-oo-Dowleh and principal adviser of His Majesty in great affairs of state is a poor, infirm, slumbering dotard, painted and tinctured by a spirit of bigotry, proud of his descent from the royal house of Sefi, a Syed by birth, a secret enemy of the Kujer [Qajar] family, and one of those intolerant Mahomedans, who deem it pollution to hold communion with infidels.' Cited in Lang (1948: 326). Nevertheless, he was one of the few advisers of Fath 'Ali Shah to oppose a new war with Russia. See Kneip (1976: 102–103).

[55] Lyall (1825/2: 87ff).

[56] As Stcherbatow (1890: 32) wrote of 'Abbas Mirza, 'Il ne songeait qu'à détruire toute trace du traité de Gulistan qu'il abhorrait.' Ermolov entertained a low opinion of 'Abbas Mirza. As Stcherbatow observed, 'Yermolow, revenue de Perse en 1817, écrivait qu'il était parfaitement convaincu de l'hostilité d'Abbas-Mirza, et qu'il ne croyait décidément pas aux sentiments pacifiques de la Perse.' He wrote to Count Nesselrode, 'De toute part je reçois des informations qu'il se forme en Perse une puissante armée, et que les forteresses se garnissent. Le fils favori du Schah, le grand homme présumé, Abbas-Mirza, dissimulé comme tous les Persans, fait semblant de nous être dévoué et, sous prétexte de félicitations, leurs agents nous arrivent de tous les côtés pour tâcher de découvrir si nous nous préparons également à la guerre.' And as Stcherbatow concluded, 'La conduite conciliante du Schah Feth-Ali-Khan rassurait quelque peu Yermolow, mais en revanche, à son retour pendant son séjour à Tauris, ses relations avec Abbas-Mirza prirent un caractère ouvertement hostile.' See Stcherbatow (1890: 16–17).

[57] Fath 'Ali Shah.

wanton encroachment of the formidable, and hitherto almost irresistible Napoleon)—and, as he now deeply feels his country's wrongs, it seems probable that he, having heard of the late rebellion at St. Petersburg,[58] by some circuitous route—for the news of no such event would be allowed to pass the Caucasus, at least for a time—and not then having been informed of the *apparent* restoration of tranquility in the North, from such an authority as he deemed authentic—thinking that the propitious moment had arrived for offensive operations, once more resolved to trust his cause to the force of arms,[59] and has, in reality, made an irruption into those provinces which were once the property of his progenitors.

2ndly. As the Russian cabinet has always evinced the strongest disposition to strengthen and to extend its Trans-Caucassian possessions, and as General Yermolof most ardently burns with the desire to give a demonstration of the overwhelming force of the Russian army in that quarter,[60] it may be asked, whether, upon some trifling pretext, this cunning politician has not gladly seized an occasion to talk of *an irruption of the Persians*, so as to throw a veil over his real intentions, and to assign a plausible reason for a quarrel and another extension of the Russian territory! It is possible that some wandering, dissatisfied Persians—easily magnified into *hordes* by a mind which wishes others to believe them so—without the knowledge of the Government, may have been guilty of an indiscretion, and thus incurred General Yermolof's apparent displeasure. While the circumstances may be a source of secret joy to him, it opens the way to Russian aggrandizement.

Whichever of these views may prove correct, since the Russians have resolved to "repel force by force," and that, unless the Chief—perhaps some marauder—who first *violated* the

---

[58]The Decembrist revolt of 26 December 1825. Cf. 11.95.

[59]Cf. Eichwald (1837: 558), who noted that news of the Decembrist revolt 'auch zu den Persern gelangte davon, wiewohl eine sehr entstellte und verspätete Kunde; sie selbst mochten sie im morgenländischen Geschmack ausschmücken und vergrößern, und daher Abbas Mirsa glauben, daß jetzt ganzRußland, wenigstens das ganze Militär, im Aufstande sey. Daher eilte er, seinen längst gehegten Plan, an Rußland Rache zu üben, auszuführen, und bestürmte den alten Feth Ali Schach so lange mit seinen Vorstellungen, jetzt den günstigen Zeitpunkt, das Verlorne wieder zu erlangen, nicht fahren zu lassen, bis der Schach endlich seine Einwilligung zum Einmarsche der Truppen in die russischen Gränzen gab.'

[60]This speculation is flatly contradicted by Ermolov's staggered retreat of his forces in the face of much greater numbers of Persians, e.g. his orders to evacuate Qarabagh, Shirvan and Talysh. Thus in his dispatch of 10 August (30 July O.S.) he noted 'qu'il évacuait de Shirvan et de Talich en répétant sa demande du 12 juillet au sujet d'un prompt envoi de renforts (2 divisions d'infanterie et 4 régiments de cavalerie), sans lesquels il ne saurait prendre l'offensive.' See Stcherbatow (1890: 36). Moreover, as Yermolov wrote to the Czar on 16 September 1826, 'Dans mon dernier rapport je me suis étendu sur les motifs qui devaient mettre obstacle à une action offensive, car elle nous forcerait à faire la guerre sur le territoire ennemi…mais je n'ai cessé, malgré cela, de me rendre compte de la nécessité d'agir contre Abbas-Mirza afin d'alléger dans le Karabagh la situation de la forteresse de Schoucha. C'est ce que j'ai entrepris, encore avant l'arrivée de l'aide de camp général Paskévitsch, le Prince Madatow [Prince Valerian Grigoryevich Madatov (1782–1829)] ayant reçu de moi l'ordre d'attaquer, avec un détachement des troupes cantonnées dans la circonscription de Kasak, l'ennemi qui avait fait son apparition sur la rivière Schamkhor et de pousser plus loin sur Elisabethpol.'

frontiers of the Russian Territory, does not meet with exemplary punishment within the dictated term of five days, General Yermolow was immediately to commence offensive operations. I fear that the result will be highly disadvantageous to Persia, which is unable to resist a spirited attack, and, consequently, may strengthen the preposterous ideas of the Russians with respect to the possibility of a successful irruption into India. It is well known, that under the reign of that Prince of Madmen, Paul,[61] an army, in which were ten thousand Konoks,[62] was designed for the invasion of Hindostan;[63] but it is not so well known that the same idea was revived, in serious interest, in the time of the late autocrat, and that many of his officers were, and still are, sanguine, in the highest degree, as to the result. Indeed, but a few years ago, although the *ostensible object* of an expedition, including a number of Kozacks, between the eastern shores of the Caspian Sea, and the western frontiers of Eastern Tartary towards the Indus, was the discovery of a *new channel of commerce, its real and secret motive* was to examine the route and to ascertain the supplies of wood and water, &c. which that route would yield to a large army. May the Russians long have such innocent amusements. As I have said elsewhere, "if Russia were even in possession of Persia, in my opinion, she could only think of such a plan, in order to find a sepulchre for her troops. The warm climate would sweep them off by thousands and tens of thousands," as is proved by the immense mortality of the troops in Georgia. Besides the genius, the wisdom, the policy, and the enormous influence of the British cabinet aided by solid gold, will always be able to call up armies to resist the forces of Russia, where they double what they are in reality, and in whatever quarter of the globe they may become the enemies of England. Our statesmens and our heroes, who laid prostrate the unparalleled power of the Emperor of the French, may laugh, indeed, at the pretensions of Russia; and pity her weakness,—Since the campaign of 1821–15, the self-conceit, the pride, and the ambition

---

[61] Emperor Paul I, of Russia (r. 1796–1801).

[62] Circassian *konak* signifies a chief or elder who offers protection to a non-Circassian. See e.g. von Klaproth (1827: 102), Spencer (1837: 325), Sheil (1856: 57). It can also have the more general meaning of 'ally.' See Khodarkovsky (1999: 408). *Konok* cannot be the Turkish word for a house or an inn/wayside stop for a courier or resting place. See e.g. Reineggs (1796/1: 9), Rich (1836: 161). Holthaus (1844: 121) described 'the herberges of travellers, the Turkish inns, called Haans, or, when they are smaller, Kanaks. They are very pious foundations of the richer Turks, and give to travellers a free and gratuitous lodging.' As Tancoigne (1820: 3) explained, while the mehmandar was an officer appointed to conduct a party, e.g. a diplomatic mission, 'and to take care that it shall be properly supplied with provisions...a konaktchi-bachi, under the orders of the former,' travelled 'one day's journey in advance, to prepare accomodations, &c.' This is almost certainly an error for 'Kozacks,' i.e. Cossacks, which appears later in the sentence.

[63] As Baddeley (1908: 22, n. 1) noted, in 1801 'Paul decided to take the offensive, and on the 12th January 1801 gave the Ataman of the Don, General Orloff, orders to march on India with all his troops. A little more than a month later (27th February) the Cossacks to the number of 22,507 men, with 24 guns, without transport, stores, or maps, began the campaign....The Cossacks, who suffered great privations, had only crossed the Volga (18th March) when they received notice of the Emperor's death.'

of her natives, and especially of the officers of the army, have become quite unbounded. While with just feelings of exultation, they loudly talk of Borodino, where Buonapart first learned that he had soldiers and not boors to contend with, they seem altogether to forget Waterloo, or that it was the Duke of Wellington[64] who vanquished "the god-like Napoleon."

While we bear in mind, however, our own greatness, immense resources, and unexampled power, it must not be forgotten that General Yermolof is a man of great natural and acquired talents, a brave and energetic soldier—a most active, enterprising and able Governor-General—and a leader who, as well as his officers and his men, have long idly luxuriated in Georgia, most anxiously wish to shake the dust from their arms and have a chance of promotion, besides their share of spoils. Nor should we forget that Persia is a most useful ally, both in respect to Russia and Turkey, and, therefore, that she deserves our interference and assistance to prevent Russia from swallowing her up in her insatiable vortex. We are informed that "the chastisement" of the Persians will "be as exemplary as the attack has been presumptuous and perfidious." It is Russia that dares thus speak—Russia, which has scarcely held any treaty sacred—whose Tsar rules by an absolute despotism, which crushes in the bud the sparks of liberality and the noblest passions of the mind—which holds at nought the rights of man—which makes a mockery of human language in his critical phrases and mystical allusions, and which offends the Divine Laws, by the attempted delusions of the people of the north, and indeed, of the world!

May some guardian angel protect the Persians against the powerful and cunning procedure of the haughty Russians, and may England early consult her interests by the support of a useful ally.'

11.23 'Foreign News. Latest from France. Russia and Persia,' *Newburyport Herald* (Friday, 10 November, 1826) and 'Russia & Persia,' *Saratoga Sentinel* (Tuesday, 14 November, 1826): 'In the midst of the Coronation festivities at Moscow,[65] news arrived, says the Petersburgh (Russian) Journal, of Sept. 3, of the hostile entrance of the Persians into the Russian territory, at several points. The intelligence came from Gen. Yermoloff, who commands in Georgia. It was not known whether it was an authorized invasion, or a border irruption, for the purpose of plunder. The Emperor[66] has sent Major Prince Menzikow to demand reparation,[67] and the punishment of the chief who headed the attack,

---

[64] Arthur Wellesley, first Duke of Wellington (1769–1852).

[65] The coronation of Nicholas I on 3 September 1826. Cf. 11.9.

[66] Nicholas I.

[67] As noted above, Menshikov was sent to announce the accession of Nicholas I, not to demand reparations. In fact, the first incursion took place while he was still in Iran, as noted above (11.3). According to Monteith (1856: 123), 'Before Prince Menschikoff left the royal camp, news was received that the chief of Talisch [Mir Hoseyn Khan] had expelled the Russians from Lankeran.'

11   The Second Russo-Persian War and the Treaty of Torkmanchay (1826–1828)   1137

within five days, and upon a failure to comply with this demand, General Yermoloff was to advance and commence offensive operations.'

11.24 'Foreign News. [From the National Journal.] Latest from England,' *Ohio Monitor* (Saturday, 11 November, 1826): 'Hostilities have commenced between Russia and Persia, it is said that Prince Abbas Mirza has a secret treaty with Russia against his father[68]....It is said the Persians have made irruptions into Russia.'

11.25 'Untitled,' *American Statesman and City Register* (Saturday, 11 November, 1826): 'The Turks express their hopes in strong terms for the success of the Persians over the Russians. They had circulated a report that Tefflis had been taken by the former.'

11.26 'Foreign News,' *New-York Evening Post* (Tuesday, 14 November, 1826) and 'From England,' *Black River Gazette* (Tuesday, 21 November, 1826; close paraphrase): 'The news of the commencement of hostilities between Persia and Russia is confirmed. Persia is clearly the aggressor in this case, and it will probably pay very dear for its temerity. The only point of view in which the struggle is of any consequence or interest to this country, is in relation to our East India possessions.'

11.27 'Foreign News,' *Franklin Post & Christian Freeman* (Tuesday, 14 November, 1826): 'The war between Russia and Persia, is assuming a serious aspect. An army of ten thousand Persians has entered Russia and burned several villages. It is reported that the war is urged on by foreign influence,[69] and that 200,000 Persians, commanded by English and French officers were on their march to the Russian frontiers.'

11.28 'Foreign. St. Petersburgh, Sept. 8,' *Gazette of Maine* (Tuesday, 14 November, 1826) and 'Foreign. St. Petersburgh, Sept. 8,' *Portland Advertiser* (Tuesday, 14 November, 1826): 'The news from the South is of a warlike nature. The Persians have actually committed depredations on the new Imperial domains in Georgia; and a powerful *corps d'armee* was marching to drive them back.'

11.29 'Very Late from England,' *New-York Spectator* (Wednesday, 15 November 1826), 'Very Late from England. Russia,' *Baltimore Patriot & Mercantile Advertiser* (Friday, 17 November, 1826), 'Foreign Intelligence. Russia,' *Poulson's American Daily Advertiser* (Friday, 17 November, 1826), 'Very Late from England. Russia,' *New-York Spectator* (Friday, 17 November, 1826), 'October 11. (From the Etoile of Monday,) Odessa, Sept. 19,' *City Gazette and Commercial Daily Advertiser* (Friday, 17 November, 1826; third paragraph, from 'the irruption'), 'Very Late from England,' *The National Intelligencer*

---

[68] Fath 'Ali Shah.
[69] In this case, the Shi'ite *mollahs* of Karbala could be considered a 'foreign influence.'

(Saturday, 18 November, 1826), 'Very Late from England. Russia,' *American and Commercial Daily Advertiser,* (Saturday, 18 November, 1826), 'Very Late from England. Russia,' *Daily National Intelligencer* (Saturday, 18 November, 1826), 'Odessa, Sept. 19,' *National Journal* (Saturday, 18 November, 1826), 'New-York, Nov. 16. Very Late from Europe. Russia,' *Newport Mercury* (Saturday, 18 November, 1826), 'Foreign. From England. Russia,' *Pawtucket Chronicle* (Saturday, 18 November, 1826; first and second paragraphs), 'Foreign. From the N.Y. Com. Adv. Nov. 14. Very Late from England. Russia,' *Richmond Enquirer* (Tuesday, 21 November, 1826), 'Untitled,' *New London Gazette* (Wednesday, 22 November, 1826; third paragraph only), 'From Europe,' *Norwalk Gazette* (Tuesday, 21 November, 1826), 'Russia and Persia,' *Hampshire Gazette* (Wednesday, 22 November, 1826; from 'letter from the frontiers,' with slight variations), 'Very late from Europe. New-York, Nov. 15,' *The Virginia Herald* (Wednesday, 22 November, 1826), 'Foreign,' *Kinderhook Herald* (Thursday, 23 November, 1826; first paragraph only), 'Untitled,' *The Western Star* (Saturday, 25 November, 1826; second paragraph only), 'Latest from England,' *Black River Gazette* (Tuesday, 28 November, 1826; first paragraph only), 'Foreign Intelligence. Latest from Europe. Moscow, Sept. 12,' *Vermont Watchman and State Gazette* (Tuesday, 28 November, 1826) and 'Foreign Intelligence. Russia,' *Arkansas Gazette* (Tuesday, 26 December, 1826): 'The account of hostilities between Persia and Russia, is confirmed. It is stated from Moscow, Sept. 22, that Gen. Paskewitsch[70] with two divisions of infantry and Gen. Illowaisky,[71] with 20,000 Cossacks, are ordered to the frontiers of Persia.[72]

A letter from Moscow of September 14, says, ["] doubts were some time entertained at the Court of St. Petersburgh, whether the hostilities committed upon the frontiers of Persia

---

[70] Ivan Feodorovich Paskevich (1782–1856), close confidant of Nicholas I and, at this time, Adjutant General of infantry. For his life see Stcherbatow (1888, 1890, 1891a, b). On 9 April 1827 he took command of the Russian forces in the Caucasus. See Mikaberidze (2005: 297). As Eichwald (1837: 579) noted, 'Unterdessen hatten sich immer mehr Truppen in Tiflis versammelt; doch waren wegen der großen Entfernung im Ganzen nur erst 15 Bataillone angelangt. Auf allerhöchsten Befehl traf auch der Generaladjutant Diebitsch mit dem Generallieutenant Paskewitsch in Tiflis ein, um dem Oberbefehlshaber Jermoloff beim beginnenden Feldzuge Hülfe zu leisten, und das Commando der thätigen Armee dem General Paskewitsch zu übergeben.'

[71] Vasily Dmitryevich Ilovaysky (1788–1860), highly decorated officer who enlisted in the Ataman Cossack Regiment in 1792 and rose to be supreme commander of the Don Cossacks in the Caucasus. See Baddeley (1908: 45). Previously he had fought against Napoleon in 1812. See Ségur and Gourgaud (1825: 73), Lyall (1825/2: 194–195), with an account of Lyall's visit to Ilovaysky's house in Novocherkassk, north of Rostov-on-Don. As Lieutenant-General under Paskevich he was involved in many actions, particularly in 1827. See Mikaberidze (2005: 164–165). In 1828–1829 he fought in the Russo-Turkish War as well. See Uschakoff (1838: 221).

[72] According to a report of 24 September from Ermolov to Nicholas I, after Maj. Gen. Prince Madatov learned that the forces of 'Abbas Mirza and Allah Yar Khan had united, he 'immediately sent notice to General Paskevitsch, who joined him on the night of the 21st, at Elizabethopol. These joint forces amounted to 8000 infantry, 15,000 tolerable cavalry, as many more badly armed, and twenty-five pieces of cannon.' See Anonymous (1826n: 730).

11 The Second Russo-Persian War and the Treaty of Torkmanchay (1826–1828)

were to be attributed to the restless and turbulent spirit of the hordes which dwell in those countries, or to a positive intention on the part of the Schah[73]; but intelligence brought by a courier that arrived here yesterday, has set the question at rest, and our Cabinet considers itself decidedly in a state of formal war with Persia." Another letter, from the frontiers of Russia, confirms the intelligence of a formal declaration of war by Russia, in consequence of the incursions of the Persians; the march of troops to reinforce the Russian army in Georgia; and the revolt of some of the frontier provinces. A letter, under the date of St. Petersburgh, the Sept. 21st states, in reference to this Persian irruption, that numerous bodies of troops have received orders to the Caucasus to reinforce the army of Georgia. The Persians, on their side are said not to be idle. They have advanced still further and in greater force, into the Russian territory, and have excited a rebellion in two out of the three Mussleman provinces belonging to Russia.[74] According to the barbarous custom of the Orientals, Prince Menzikoff[75] and his officers, who composed the Russian Embassy at the Court of Schah, have been retained as prisoners.[76] It is not however, supposed that hostilities can be continued with any vigour on either side before the winter.

---

[73] Fath 'Ali Shah.

[74] Qarabagh, Shirvan and Talysh. See Cazalès (1838: 618).

[75] Cf. 11.9.

[76] This seems to be a confusion with the 25 day-long detention of Menshikov and his escort by the Sardar of Erivan [Hoseyn Qoli Khan Qazvini] that began on 16 August. For Menshikov's own account of his detention, contained in a letter written at Tiflis after his release, see Anonymous (1826n: 733 = 11.132). According to Eichwald (1837: 559–560), after Menshikov's arrival at Tabriz, he departed for Soltaniyeh to meet Fath 'Ali Shah, but 'Unterwegs hatte der Fürst überall auffallende Rüstungen zum Kriege bemerkt, und in Tauris konnten die Perser nicht mehr gegen ihn verbergen, wem dieselben galten....Der Fürst Menschikoff, davon unterrichtet, hielt es daher fürs Beste, Persien zu verlassen, wurde aber in Erivan verrätherischer Weise zurückgehalten; man schloß ihn ein, und erlaubte keinem den Zutritt zu ihm; ja der Sserdar hatte sogar die Absicht, über ihn unterwegs auf seiner weitern Reise herzufallen, und die Schuld der Ermordung auf die Kurden zu schieben; daher schlug er dem Fürsten einen Weg vor, auf welchem er zurückkreisen sollte. Allein der Fürst war nicht minder schlau, wählte einen andern Weg, und entkam glücklich auf die russische Gränze.' This ruse was not noted by Menshikov who, in his letter of 24 September, written at Tibilisi, said, 'Seeing the time pass away, and the answers to my letters not arriving, and learning that the English mission had left the camp of the Shah to go to meet Mr. Macdonald, I persuaded my Mehmander to oppose the pretensions of the Serdar of Erivan, and to insinuate to the principal minister, whose creature he is, that considering the antipathy of the Shah to the war, the enemies of Alaiar [Allah Yar] Khan would seize the first opportunity that a doubtful battle would furnish to ruin him, if he did not think beforehand of peace; and the only means to conclude it on advantageous terms were, to let me depart as soon as possible, because I was personally interested in inducing our cabinet to an accomodation. This means succeeded, and I owe to it my liberation, after twenty five days' detention in the most unhealthy place in the environs of Erivan.' Monteith (1856: 125–126) gave a different version of events, noting that, 'while Prince Menschikoff was still at Tabreez...it began to be rumoured that the Persians intended to detain the Russian mission; a request was therefore made by the ambassador [John Macdonald Kinneir] that I should be charged with the duty of conducting the embassy to the frontier; but his request was refused by the authorities at Tabreez, though they did not exactly venture

Accounts from Odessa of September 19, state that the irruption of the Persians has been a signal for an almost general insurrection in their favor. Among the Tartars are Carabat,[77] Schirwan, Chesis,[78] and Elisabethpol.[79] The Russians have evacuated these provinces, as well as a part of Sounketre.[80] The people of the mountains are acting with violence. On the side of the Caspian Sea, the enemy has penetrated as far as Coubla,[81] in the neighbourhood of Derbent, which he is blockading. The Russians will not act on the offensive, as it appears, till after the arrival of the reinforcements, but in the mean time the country is ravaged. The consternation amongst the Armenian merchants is very great; they have suspended all their business and all payments. Teflis the entrepot for the merchandize consumed in Georgia, or sent into Persia, loses its most important market by the irruption of the Persians into the frontier provinces.'

11.30 'Untitled,' *Greene County Republican* (Wednesday, 15 November, 1826): 'London, Sept. 26. From the accounts received this morning, it would appear that war was almost inevitable between Russia and Persia.'

---

to arrest the Prince and his suite there, but gave orders that he should be detained at Erivan, which was accordingly done. He was well treated, and the whole mission were lodged in the garden-house of the Sirdar, surrounded with vineyards and fruit-gardens, a pleasant, but at this season an unhealthy, locality. During this time Sir John M'Donald, the newly appointed envoy, arrived; and as soon as he reached the King's camp, I was despatched to see the ambassador set at liberty, and conducted in safety to the Russian outposts: I found, however, on my arrival, that he had been already released, so I had only to follow him, until assured he was threatened with no further danger.' Alexander (1827: 281) speculated 'that the cause of this detention of the Russian Envoy was owing to a rumour that General Yermoloff had been removed from his office of Governor-General, and that Prince Menzikoff was appointed his successor; the Persian Court therefore thought, that if the Envoy was detained, the troops in Georgia would be left without a head.' Menshikov himself noted, however, that his detention was done in retaliation for the fact that the wife of the rebellious Khan of Talysh had been held 'hostage' by the Russians. See Anonymous (1826n: 733 = 11.132). McNeill (1836: 85), on the other hand, suggested that Menshikov was detained, 'as some military movements were in progress on the frontier when he arrived in its vicinity, he was detained for some time at Erivan, that he might not convey to his countrymen intelligence of the march and distribution of troops which he had seen. No other indignity was offered him, and as soon as intimation of his detention by the frontier authorities reached the Court, orders were issued to permit him to proceed.'

[77] Qarabagh.

[78] In light of the text in Brosset (1857: 322), 'Chesis' is probably a corruption of 'Chaki,' i.e. Sheki in what is today Azerbaijan.

[79] Ganja. It was renamed Elizabethpol by Tsitsianov, in honor of Empress Elizabeth, wife of Alexander I. The name change was approved on 5 February 1805. See von Freygang and Freygang (1823: 160), Brosset (1857: 280, n. 2). The name has since reverted to Ganja.

[80] Syunik/Zangezur/Shoregel?

[81] Qobba, southeast of Darband and northwest of Baku, on the Qudiyal river. See Minorsky (1953: 7, n. ****). In 1796 both Darband and Qobba were governed by one Khan. See Minorsky (1958: 7).

11.31 'Untitled,' *New-York Evening Post* (Wednesday, 15 November, 1826): 'London, Oct. 9. We have received this morning, the St. Petersburg Journal to the 24th of Sept. The differences bewteen Russia and Persia are not alluded to.'

11.32 'Postscript. Very Late from Europe,' *National Advocate* (Wednesday, 15 November, 1826), 'Foreign Intelligence,' *American Statesman and City Register* (Saturday, 18 November, 1826), 'Foreign Intelligence,' *Boston Daily American Statesman* (Saturday, 18 November, 1826), 'The Foreign Gleaner. "News from all Nations,"' *The Emporium* (Saturday. 25 November, 1826) and 'Foreign News. From England,' *The Farmers' Cabinet* (Saturday, 25 November, 1826): 'The French papers state that the Persians have made considerable advances towards the Russian frontiers, and succeeded in exciting revolt in two out of three Musselman provinces belonging to Russia. The Persian invasion was assuming a more formidable appearance than was expected, and in consequence the Emperor Nicholas was making preparations for carrying on the campaign vigorously.'

11.33 'Untitled,' *The Virginia Herald* (Wednesday, 15 November, 1826) and 'Untitled,' *Charleston Courier* (Thursday, 16 November, 1826): 'The Persians, to the number of 10,000 who have invaded the Russian frontiers, are said to have made captives of a great many women and children, and carried away many cattle.'

11.34 'Untitled,' *The National Gazette and Literary Register* (Thursday, 16 November, 1826), 'October 13,' *New-York American* (Wednesday, 15 November, 1826; second and third paragraphs), 'London, Oct. 13,' *Poulson's American Daily Advertiser* (Thursday, 16 November, 1826; second paragraph only), 'London, Oct. 13,' *Boston Daily Advertiser* (Saturday, 18 November, 1826; second and third paragraphs), 'Untitled,' *The National Gazette and Literary Register* (Saturday, 18 November, 1826), 'New-York, Nov. 15. Late from Europe,' *Essex Register* (Monday, 20 November, 1826; second and third paragraphs), 'Russia and Persia,' *Eastern Argus* (Tuesday, 21 November, 1826; second and third paragraphs with minor variations), 'Russia and Persia,' *National Aegis* (Wednesday, 22 November, 1826; with minor variations), 'From Europe,' *St. Lawrence Gazette* (Tuesday, 28 November, 1826; second and third paragraphs), 'Foreign Intelligence. Latest from Europe. Russia,' *Vermont Patriot and State Gazette* (Tuesday, 28 November, 1826; second and with minor variations) and 'Foreign News. October 13,' *Ohio Monitor* (Saturday, 2 December, 1826; second and third paragraphs): 'The London Courier has taken the alarm for the East, in relation to the Russian movements against the Persians. The following is the leading article of that paper of the 13th ult.

"The Paris Etoile of Wednesday, which, with the Paris papers of Tuesday, has arrived in due course, contains a rather important article from St. Petersburg, in relation to the rupture between Russia and Persia. The Emperor, we are told, has ordered large reinforcements of troops to the Caucasus, in order to strengthen the army under the command of General Yermoloff. The necessity for this energy is sufficiently obvious, if it be true, that the

Persians continue to advance, and that they have already caused an insurrection in "two of the three Musselmen Provinces belonging to Russia, which border their frontier."

"Some months must elapse, however, in preparation; for physical and political causes alike interpose to prevent an immediate conflict. There are vast deserts to cross—rivers to pass, which are without bridges—a wide space of country destitute of roads—and equally without the means supplying sustenance for a numerous army: there are formidable obstacles which will have to be surmounted, and which will render it impossible for the troops to make rapid advances, even supposing they encountered no resistance from the enemy. When the armies of Russia, is just observed in the article referred to, pass over the European frontiers, they find numerous facilities for subsistence and conveyance; but beyond the Asiatic frontier, every thing must be created, and every thing must be paid for. If, however, the Emperor be reduced to the necessity of making all these sacrifices—if he be compelled to assemble an effective army on the Persian frontier, we may expect he will not march a man back again till he obtains full indemnity for the past, and ample security for the future. In what way both these objects will be accomplished, need not be told to any observer of Russian policy.'"

11.35 'Russia and Persia. Extract of a Private Letter—Sultania, July 28,' *The National Gazette and Literary Register* (Thursday, 16 and Saturday, 18 November, 1826; without the first paragraph), 'Russia and Persia,' *Daily National Journal* (Monday, 20 November, 1826), 'Russia and Persia,' *National Journal* (Tuesday, 21 November, 1826), 'London, September 26, 1826,' *Louisiana Advertiser* (Thursday, 23 November, 1826): 'The following letter contains some further and interesting details of the situation of Persia, and the causes of the present critical condition of the relations between that country and Russia;' 'London, September 26, 1826,' *Louisiana Advertiser* (Thursday, 23 November, 1826) and 'Foreign News. Russia and Persia,' *Ohio Monitor* (2 December, 1826): 'We lay before our readers the following important communication from Persia: its accuracy may be relied upon':

'Extract of a private letter—Sultania, July 28.
By the last Tartar I gave you an account of Prince Menzikoff's mission to the date of his departure for Sultania.[82] You will be astonished to hear that the fair prospects we then had

---

[82] The author is not identified, but the letter was quoted and paraphrased in Anonymous (1826m) which cited recently arrived (in London) papers from Bombay and Calcutta. Thus it appears that the author, who was at Soltaniyeh, sent the letter to a correspondent in the EIC, probably in either Bombay or Calcutta. The critical description of 'Abbas Mirza makes it probable that the writer was John McNeill, at the time secretary to the Ambassador John Macdonald Kinneir. McNeill wrote of 'Abbas Mirza, 'For some time the Prince will treat the Envoy in the most distinguished and flattering manner; he will then make propositions for their assistance from the Indian Government in maintaining troops, and if his wishes are not complied with to the fullest extent, he will commence a system of petty intrigue and annoyance. . . .In short, in every communication with Abbas Mirza on

11 The Second Russo-Persian War and the Treaty of Torkmanchay (1826–1828)

of a final arrangement between this Court and Russia are now nearly at an end, and there is every probability of immediate hostilities, but, threatening as the appearances are, so perfectly unprepared is this Court for a contest of such magnitude, as well as the natural pacific disposition of the king,[83] I cannot believe there will be war, till I actually hear of an action between their troops.

Abbas Mirza, with his usual deceit and want of stability of character, made all at Tabriez suppose he was, in reality, desirous of peace; but, obliged to assume a contrary appearance since his arrival here, he has not only been the most active instigator of war, but the immediate cause of the present impolitic and premature proceedings. Alisar Khan[84] and Sied Mahomed, the Mushtakeid of Kubela,[85] have been the principal cause of this change.[86] They represented to him how much he would gain in the opinion of all Mahomedans, if he became the champion of their religion, and the loss of character he must sustain by refusing to aid his brethren of Kara Bang[87] Shekey,[88] and Shirwan, now groaning under an infidel yoke, which they were unable longer to bear. The enthusiasm of the people had been much excited by supplications and letters from these provinces, complaining of the daily outrages they suffered from the Russians, and the Persian army had only to appear, when a general insurrection would take place.

Abbas Mirza is accused of having, in the first instance, excited this spirit, which neither he nor his father is now able to control. The king was, and is, most anxious to maintain peace; but having pledged himself either to obtain the restitution of Goukcha,[89] or declare

---

every subject the Envoy must be prepared for every description of meanness, deceit, and treachery, which is made most dangerous by a manner calculated to win everyone, and a plausible, unaffected, and fluent style of conversation fitted to inspire the fullest confidence.' See MacAlister (1910: 74).

[83] Fath 'Ali Shah.

[84] Allah Yar Khan-e Qajar Devehlu, Fath 'Ali Shah's son-in-law, appointed prime minister in 1825. See Busse (1972: 172). He was also 'Abbas Mirza's father-in-law. See Eichwald (1837: 559). Cf. 11.35.

[85] Mojtahed Aqa Seyyid Mohammad of Karbala, son of the late *mojtahed* from Isfahan, Aqa Seiyed 'Ali. See Busse (1972: 174). For the position of *mojtahed* see Zysow (1998/2011).

[86] Seyyid Mohammad 'considered the Holy War with the Russians a duty incumbent upon the Moslems according to the laws of the Sharia.' See Busse (1972: 174).

[87] Qarabagh.

[88] Sheki.

[89] Gökçe, the Turkish name of Lake Sevan, hence a reference to Ermolov's occupation of the northern perimeter of the lake. As Alexander (1827: 271) noted, 'The Russian Government...established posts upon a strip of country which extends along the north and north-east shores of Lake Gokcha, and upon a district situated on the borders of Karabaugh, between the Capan and Mogree [Meghri] rivers. The former territory was uninhabited; but it belonged indisputably to Persia....It is impossible to discover the grounds upon which the Russians could lay claim to the Gokcha territory....General Yermoloff...acknowledged that it was an infringement of the treaty, but excused the proceeding, on account of the district being uninhabited, alleging that it was equally to the advantage of both empires. What is still more to the point, the Russian declaration of war states that the Emperor did not dispute the right of Persia to the Gokcha territory, and required only that the district of Capan should be given

war, he is afraid to retract. A proposal was made to Prince Menzikoff, that the land in question should remain unoccupied, till such time as a reference was made to the Emperor,[90] during which period he might visit the frontier, and report himself on the points in dispute. To this he replied, his instructions had been founded on the proposals made by Abbas Mirza, regarding an exchange for some lands of greater value in Kara Bang, Mogan,[91] and Talish; but since the king did not confirm this proceeding, he was willing to await a reference, but could not evacuate a place they had occupied for twelve years, by permission, and which, from the constant intrigues of the Surdar of Erivan,[92] would compromise the safety of twelve thousand families of their Mahomedan subjects. He afterwards agreed that the Persians should also have a detachment in the same place, and that the stay of the Russians during the next two months should not be considered to give them any additional claim to its possession. This was not accepted, and Abbas Mirza sent for Mr. Amburger, the Russian Chargé d'Affaires,[93] of whom he took leave, and stated his intention of proceeding to the frontier and expelling the Russians from his dominions; and at the same time troops have been sent in different directions, with the ostensible object of invading the Russian territories. They may certainly do much mischief, by a sudden

---

up by Persia, which the document alleges was expressly assigned to Russia by the treaty. The acknowledgement of General Yermoloff was singularly at variance with the statement of General Wilheminoff, the Lieutenant-Governor of Georgia, who at a later period declared, in a letter to the Shah, that Russia had been in possession of the territory in question ever since the peace of Gulistan. It may be here necessary to explain, that though the district of Gokcha is waste and unfertile, yet it commands the pass of Ganja, affording to Persia an easy entrance to Georgia, and to Russia the means of rapidly overrunning the province of Erivan; therefore the one power was as reluctant to give it up, as the other was eager to seize upon it.' As Wilbraham (1839: 104–105) noted, 'The possession of a worthless tract of land which borders on this lake was the ostensible cause of the late war between Persia and Russia.'

[90] Nicholas I.

[91] Mughan.

[92] Hoseyn Qoli Khan Qazvini.

[93] Andreas [Andrei Karlovich] Amburger (incorrectly Amburgherr) [Амбургер Андрей Карлович] (1794–1830; for the date see Amburger [1986: 85], Kantarbaeva-Bill [2010: 209]), from a German family settled in St. Petersburg. Twenty-four years old and, since 1818 an actuary in the Foreign Ministry (Amburger 1986: 85), he was part of Mazarovich's legation and remained in Tabriz until July, 1826. Alexander (1827: 275–276) opined that 'Abbas Mirza felt so much his dependency upon the Russian Emperor, that the latter [Amburger] acquired such an influence at the Court of Tabreez as was viewed by the Shah's Ministers with considerable jealousy and alarm. The intrigues carried on at that Court, under the able management of the Russian Minister, M. Amburger, were of the most deep and dangerous character.' In April 1828 he was appointed 'to be head of Chancery,' returning to Iran with Griboyedov in the latter's new capacity as Minister. See Harden (1979a: 255), Kelly (2006: 41). According to Keçeci (2016: 189), 'when Ermolov was absent from the Caucasus, Amburgherr was a man of integrity and pursued a more moderate line of policy; he was not always in sympathy with the provocative attitude adopted by Ermolov towards Iran. It is not surprising then, that Ermolov preferred Mazarovich and defended him from criticism by St. Petersburg but often disliked and ignored Amburgherr's views.'

11 The Second Russo-Persian War and the Treaty of Torkmanchay (1826–1828)   1145

irruption into the country, while the Ambassador is still here, and the Russians ignorant of the existence of war, but its ultimate result cannot be doubtful.

The Russians at the present moment have at least 40,000 regular troops in Georgia, half of whom are disposable, and these can be augmented at pleasure. General Yermoloff is considered the best officer in the Russian army, but has certainly done less during his Government than was to have been expected from his great character. As a Governor of Georgia, he has much improved the country, but by a number of harassing regulations has rendered the people dissatisfied with the Russian Government, to which they were once much attached.[94] The Chiefs of the Mahomedan tribes and provinces have, under one pretext or other, been expelled or sent to Russia. But I can say, from having travelled through every part of those countries, the people are richer and less oppressed than in any part of Persia. The dissatisfaction so much exaggerated by the Persians, is confined to the Chiefs; the inferior classes, though they complain of the conduct of the inferior Russian Agents, are not disaffected to the Government, except in Kara Bang, where the bad conduct of the Officer commanding,[95] and the licence he allows the troops, have highly exasperated all classes. We understand here (but I will not answer for the truth,) a Russian Major and a

---

[94] For a more sober assessment of Ermolov's achievements in the civil arena, see Stcherbatow (1890: 24–26): 'L'administration de Yermolow posa les fondements du gouvernement civil et de l'union complète de la Russie avec les populations des plus riches province du Transcaucase. Mais à l'époque où cette œuvre importante s'organisait, les circonstances ne pouvaient encore favoriser son développement. Après l'expulsion des Khans dépossédés, Yermolow introduisit l'administration russe dans les khanats frontières et, prévoyant l'avenir, il travailla pour le bien des générations futurs. Mais détruire les abus, selons nous inévitables, qui s'étaient enracinés dans le pays à cette époque, fut au-dessus de ses forces. . . .l'établissement dans ces provinces d'une administration russe quelque peu stable, régulière et morale, était une tâche par trop ardue. . . .L'état de choses dans les provinces limitrophes était à ce point affligeant, que le général Yermolow se vit forcé de décréter certaines mesures répressives contre les constantes désertions des indigènes qui se réfugiaient en Perse. . . .Il est évident que les premiers pas tentés dans le but de russifier le pays ne furent point heureux et qu'ils encouragèrent les plans belliqueux d'Abbas-Mirza.'

[95] This is presumably a reference to Major-General Prince Valerian Grigoryevich Madatov (1782–1829), 'Russian commander in the former khanates of Shakī, Shirvān and Qarahbāgh.' See Keçeci (2016: 209). Thus, according to Stcherbatow (1890: 26), 'Dans la ville de Noukha [Nukhi], le Prince Madatow, qui avait pris la part la plus active à l'exil des Khans, empoisonnait le dernier Khan de Shékin, Ismaïl, et forçait en même temps celui de Karabagh, Mechti Kouli, "a lui abandonner la possession des terres et des villages appartenant au Khan de Khazar." S'étant fait livrer ces biens, Madatow persuada le Khan de fuir en Perse et lui-même agrandit ses nouveaux domaines en expulsant trois cent familles du Karabagh dans le Shirvan.' It is unlikely to refer to Colonel I.A. Reutt (Reutte/Reout/Riout), commander of the 42nd Jäger Regiment (Eichwald 1837: 571), whom Monteith (1856: 125) called 'a Polish officer of talent and resolution.' His second-in-command was the very able Austrian, Maj. Kluke von Klugenau. See Baddeley (1908: 155).

party of soldiers have been cut to pieces in Shirwan, in consequence of the former having taken some Mahomedan women by force.[96]

It is more than probable the precipitate folly of Abbas Mirza will bring things to a crisis, when it might be avoided. One good will arise from it, by leaving the British Government perfectly free in the conduct they may think proper to pursue; the forcible occupation of Goukha is an aggression on the part of Russia. Hostilities will have been commenced by Persia; besides Prince Menzikoff's couriers have been detained at Erivan,[97] and numerous letters from Abbas Mirza, exciting the inhabitants of the Mahommedan provinces to revolt, have been intercepted. What good result can be expected from a war conducted by so weak a character as the Prince Royal, or any of the chiefs who now command the Persian troops. With the exception of the new regiment of guards, none of the Azudbejan troops have even been assembled since 1822; at the present moment they are deficient in every necessary equipment, and he has long ceased to have any European officer in his service.

The present Rusian [sic] Ambassador[98] has had the good fortune or conduct, while not granting a single point, to gain the personal good-will of every individual with whom he has been engaged, and has shewn temper beyond human nature. A few days ago the Koem Makem[99] entered his tent, pretending great fatigue, and saying he could hardly get through

---

[96] This may be a reference to a rising of Lezgins in 1825. According to Brosset (1857: 322), 'en l'année 1825 les Lesguis, de nouveau soulevés, entrèrent dans le Chignith-Cakheth, ravagèrent Enisel, Grem et d'autres petits villages. Il parut aussi chez les Tchétchenses un imposteur, chéikh ou chef de la religion chez ce peuple, qui rassembla jusqu'à 30,000 hommes de milices et fondit sur une nouvelle citadelle construite par les Russes, sur la Soundja. Il la prit, extermina la garnison russe, enleva même les canons qui s'y trouvaient. Il chargea un de ses mollahs d'aller, comme député, auprès du général-lieutenant Lisanévitch, qu'il perça d'un coup de poignard, lui et le général Aghrékof. Tous deux moururent.'

[97] In a letter written at Tibilisi on 24 September 1826, Menshikov wrote that the couriers he had sent on 14 July had been stopped at Ahar, c. 150 mi. west of Ardabil (Le Strange 1905: 169), and that his interpreter, Shah Nazaroff, and staff member, Ivanov, were under arrest in Tabriz, while two couriers sent to him had been arrested in Tiflis and had had their papers taken away from. See Anonymous (1826n: 733 = 11.132 below).

[98] Menshikov.

[99] Mirza Abu'l Qasem Qa'em Maqam who, several years earlier, had succeeded his father Mirza Bozorg when the latter died of the plague. See Busse (1972: 166). Cf. 10.244. According to Fraser (1826: 306), 'All petitions were, by the prince's ['Abbas Mirza] order, brought to the caimookan, and he decided on them without appeal. The quantity of business which he got through was astonishing; but he still had enough to struggle with in the fickle temper of the prince, which being worked upon by flatterers and ill-disposed advisers, often thwarted the good which the minister had been labouring to produce.' Lal (1834: 177) called him 'the prime minister of H.R.H. Abbás Mírzá...a man of small dim eyes,' who 'is accustomed to shake his head always, which shows the people that he is always in deep thought and meditation. He has great influence at Abbás Mírzá's court, and at the same time is believed to be a magician. He does what he wants, and it is impossible to succeed in any business without giving him some present. He sleeps all day, and sits up all night; a more cunning and avaricious man never existed in Persia.'

the troops who were marching to the frontier; and in a few days he hoped to tell him that Kara Bang was in the possession of Persia. He merely smiled, and answered, he was happy to find they had the consideration to leave them in Tiflis during the winter. His presents have been few, and of small value. Pray excuse this. As usual I have delayed writing till the package is closing.

All hopes of peace are now at an end. The envoy left camp this morning. A large Persian force has entered the Russian territory to aid the insurgents of Talish.[100] One hundred Russians have been killed in this place; the aggression clearly on the side of Persia. Alli Yar Khan, the Assadou Doulah,[101] is head of the war faction, supported by Abbas Mirza.

Before I had finished this letter, the king had requested—to speak to Prince Menzikoff, and beg him to point out some means of avoiding war, without sacrificing his character. A speech made by Karang Choush[102] made great noise in camp. He addressed the king (Kishey)—"Man, do you call yourself king of the Mahommedans, and idly pass your time in the harem, when Mussulmen are daily abused by Infidels. I was obliged to look on while five Russian soldiers violated my wife at Karabang.[103] I spit at your beard.'"[104]

---

[100] As von Bernhardi (1877: 241–242) noted, 'Die Unterhandlungen mit Rußland wollte Abbas Mirza eigentlich nur benützen, um zunächst das Chanat Talysch, das sich im Süden des Araxes an der Küste des Kaspischen Meeres entlang dahin zieht, in eine unmittelbare Provinz des persischen Reichs zu verwandeln, wie etwas früher das Gebiet von Eriwan, und er durfte dabei auf die Bevölkerung rechnen. Der Chan dieses Gebiets hatte sich nämlich, obgleich dem Recht nach, gleich allen mohamedanischen Fürsten dieser Region, persischer Oberhoheit unterworfen, während des ganzen Kriegs, wie der unabhängige Herr eines neutralen Landes, jeder Theilnahme an dem Kampfe enthalten, und sogar mit den Waffen der Perser erwehrt, als sie ihn zur Heerfolge zwingen wollten. Seit einiger Zeit endlich weilte ein russischer Agent bei ihm, ein Capitain der kaiserlichen Marine, Namens Wesselágo, der, wie es scheint, von einer kleinen bewaffneten Abtheilung, wahrscheinlich Matrosen, begleitet war. Ob der Chan ausdrücklich und förmlich in die Zahl der russischen Schutzbefohlenen aufgenommen worden war, darüber geben die bekannt gewordenen Quellen keine Auskunft.—Abbas Mirza's Plan soll gewesen sein, nach der Unterwerfung des Gebiets von Talysch, nahe an der Mündung des Araxes über diesen Strom zu gehen, und über die Halbinsel Salian in das schekinsche Chanat nach Nucha am Fuß des Kaukasus vorzudringen, um sich dort mit dem, von dem Russen aus seinem Lande vertriebenen, Selim-Chan von Scheki zu vereinigen, und mit den Bergvölkern, die der Zarëwitsch Alexander [of Georgia] in Bewegung zu erhalten wußte.'

[101] Asaf od-Doula, lit. 'counsellor of the empire.' See Busse (1972: 448). As Hasan-e Fasa'i noted, in 1825, 'For the administration of important affairs, Allāh Yār Khān-e Qājār Devehlu, a mighty emir and distinguished by being the son-in-law of the shah, was appointed prime minister. He was addressed by the title "Āṣaf od-Doula."' See Busse (1972: 172).

[102] A Chousk of Karabang. Anonymous (1827c: 285, n. *) has 'In the Persian camp at Sultania, a Chousk of Karabang [Qarabagh] made the following speech to the Shah.' Chousk is a corruption of Turkic *chaush*, 'sergeant-at-arms, herald.' See Yule and Burnell (1903: 212), s.v. 'chouse.' The precise rank of this officer varied. Evliya Efendi, for example, refers to 'a Chaúsh of high authority' as one of the 'commanding officers and magistrates of Trebisonde,' See von Hammer (1850: 43). Brant (1840: 350) wrote of 'the Chaúsh Báshí (head messenger) of the Páshá.'

[103] According to Hasan-e Fasa'i, 'The Russian troops who were occupying the provinces of Ganja, Karabagh and Shirvan, raped some Moslem women.' See Busse (1972: 174).

[104] This speech is quoted in Anonymous (1827c: 285, n. *) and Walworth (1871: 155).

11.36 'St. Petersburgh, Sept. 21,' *The Baltimore Gazette and Daily Advertiser* (Friday, 17 November, 1826; from 'The Emperor') and 'From our late English papers,' *New-York Evening Post* (Friday, 17 November, 1826; 'We received last night, the Paris Papers of Tuesday, and the Etoile, dated Wednesday. From the latter we extract some rather important intelligence, with respect to the preparations making by Russia to repel the aggressions of the Persians. From the nature of these preparations, we must suppose, either that the incursion is of a more formidable character than has hitherto been admitted—or, that Russia is determined not to content herself with merely expelling the invaders from her territory.: "The Emperor has ordered new and numerous troops to the Caucasus, to reinforce the army of Georgia. The Persians upon their part, have advanced and caused an insurrection in two of the three Mussulman Provinces belonging to Russia, which border their frontier; they are, doubtless, those beyond the Kour, which waters Tiflis, and passes through all Georgia. That which was least reckoned upon has remained faithful. Agreeably to the barbarous custom of the Orientals, Prince Menzikoff and his officers are kept prisoners in Persia.[105]

"Every thing however, is opposed to the idea of a vigorous campaign on the side of Georgia at the commencement of winter. Immense steppes, numerous rivers without bridges, impassable roads and the general poverty of the country, form insurmountable obstacles to the rapid march of an army, even though no resistance should be offered. The Persians, may, therefore, maintain themselves for some time in the countries in which the insurrection prevails, but they will make no progress, nor will they be able to pass the Caucasus; and if Mingrelia, Imeritia, and a part of the Georgian Provinces remain faithful as it appears they will, the Russians may push forward troops by the Black Sea, and threaten the Persians in flank.

A war with Persia, however, is exceedingly troublesome to Russia, whatever be its issue, by the derangement in her finances which it will necessarily produce. When her armies pass over the European frontiers, they find numerous facilities for subsistence and conveyance; but beyond the Asiatic frontier, every thing must be created, and every thing must be paid for. In making war in Georgia, moreover, Russia makes it in in her own territory, and victory brings with it no advantage. Besides, the Emperor, who, from private feeling and military ardour, might feel inclined to put himself at the head of his army, and, to give vigourand activity to its operations, cannot, under present circumstances, withdraw from his European states; and notwithstanding the energy and talents of Generals Yermolof and Paskewitch, we cannot look for that combination and rapidity of movement which the presence of the Emperor would naturally give to the forces."'

---

[105] In a letter written at Tiflis on 24 September, 1826, Menshikov detailed his 25 day long detention at Yerevan, which began on 16 August 1826, by Hoseyn Qoli Khan Qazvini. See Anonymous (1826n: 733 = 11.132 below).

11 The Second Russo-Persian War and the Treaty of Torkmanchay (1826–1828) 1149

11.37 'Foreign. Russia,' *New-Hampshire Sentinel* (Friday, 17 November, 1826) and 'Russia,' *Augusta Chronicle and Georgia Advertiser* (Saturday, 18 November, 1826; 'Russia'): 'Gen. Yermaloff has been ordered to oppose the Persian army, said to be 80,000 strong; and the army of Pruth is to be kept in readiness to march.'

11.38 'Untitled,' *The Western Star* (Saturday, 18 November, 1826): 'Late accounts from Russia make it appear that a war between that country and Persia is inevitable.'

11.39 'Persia and Russia,' *The Evening Gazette* (Saturday, 18 November, 1826), 'Very Late from England,' *Providence Patriot & Columbian Phenix* (Saturday, 18 November, 1826) and '[By the line ship Othello, and Brig Elba.] New York, November 15. [Postscript] Eleven Days Later from England,' *City Gazette and Commercial Daily Advertiser* (Tuesday, 21 November, 1826): 'The war between the Persians and Russians, according to the latest French papers, has actually begun—the Persians having excited an insurrection in the Russian Mahomedan provinces, which they have aided by an army of their own. From the nature of the country, it is not imagined that the Russians can make any rapid advance, while any considerable progress is still more improbable on the part of the Persians, who do not seem to have yet found all the success they calculated upon in stirring up the Mahomedan subjects of Russia.'

11.40 'Russian Affairs. London, Oct. 9,' *Columbian Centinel* (Saturday, 18 November, 1826): 'We have Russian advices to the 24th September, which make no mention of the difficulties with Persia.

Paris accounts say, that the Persians were on the march in the Russian dominions, and had found two provinces in revolt; and that the Emperor Nicholas had ordered an army to march against them. The *Etoile* discredits the reports.'

11.41 'London Papers,' *Columbian Centinel* (Saturday, 18 November, 1826) and 'Latest from England,' *Columbian Reporter* (Wednesday, 22 November, 1826): 'The reports of the incursions of the Persians into Russia, appeared to have been discredited in St. Petersburgh and Paris.'

11.42 'Untitled,' *Washington Review and Examiner* (Saturday, 18 November, 1826): 'The Persians are said to have invaded the frontiers of Russia with a powerful army, and that Russian troops are upon the march.'

11.43 'Foreign Intelligence,' *Poulson's American Daily Advertiser* (Saturday, 18 November, 1826), 'Deplorable State of the Spaniards,' *Connecticut Courant* (Monday, 20 November, 1826), 'Foreign,' *The Corrector* (Saturday, 25 November, 1826) and 'Deplorable state of the Spaniards,' *The Freeman's Journal* (Monday, 27 November, 1826): 'A letter from Bagdad mentions the death of a Persian Princes [sic, Princess], the daughter of Abbas Mirza, 15 days after her marriage with the Prince of Kirmanshah.[106] It is generally believed some rivals in the Harem, jealous of her beauty and engaging manners, destroyed her by means of poison. The funeral was attended by a nephew of the King of Persia,[107] and many nobles of high rank, in consequence of the great respect in which she was held. The marriage of the unfortunate lady was celebrated in a style of grandeur and magnificence seldom witnessed by the Persians. From her father's residence, the procession passed through a double line of troops, extending two leagues consisting of about 12,000 [32,000 in the *Freeman's Journal*] men.'

11.44 'Untitled,' *Boston Commercial Gazette* (Monday, 20 November, 1826), 'From Europe,' *Village Register and Norfolk County Advertiser* (Thursday, 23 November, 1826), 'Secular Summary. Foreign. Greece,' *Boston Recorder* (Friday, 24 November, 1826), 'Foreign News. From England,' *The Farmers' Cabinet* (Saturday, 25 November, 1826) and 'Foreign Items,' *North Star* (Tuesday, 28 November, 1826): 'A large body of Russian troops has been lately ordered to the Persian frontiers, to reinforce the former military in that quarter. The persians have advanced into the Russian territory; and great consternation followed among the merchants and other inhabitants of Armenia. The Russian Envoy and Secretary at the Court (Persian) of *Schah*[108] were imprisoned.'[109]

11.45 'Weekly Summary. Foreign,' *Daily National Journal* (Monday, 20 November, 1826) and 'Weekly Summary. Foreign,' *National Journal* (Tuesday, 21 November, 1826): 'In our paper of Saturday we published an article on the subject of the pending dispute beetween Russia and Persia. According to the tenor of that publication, the Russian Court was at a loss whether to attribute the incursions into the Russian territory to the unauthorized violence of the frontier hordes, or to a settled disposition of hostility on the part of Persia herself. A letter from Moscow of the 14th of September, seems to put this doubt to flight: as it states that "intelligence brought by a courier that arrived here yesterday, has set the question at rest, and our Cabinet considers itself decidedly in a state of formal war with Persia." This statement is confirmed by other letters from Russia, which furnish the additional information of the march of troops to reinforce the Russian army in Georgia, and the revolt of some of the frontier provinces. A letter from St. Petersburg of the 21st of September contains this information. The Persians, on the other side, are not idle. They have pushed forward, in still increasing force, into the Russian dominions. Prince Menzikoff and his officers, who composed the Russian Embassy to Persia, having, according to Oriental custom, been detained as prisoners. A general insurrection has taken place among the Tartars in favor of Persia; and Russia is said to

---

[106] Mohammad Hoseyn Mirza. For a report of the wedding see 10.328, 10.364.
[107] Fath 'Ali Shah.
[108] Fath 'Ali Shah.
[109] Presumably a reference to the detention of Menshikov and his legation at Yerevan.

11   The Second Russo-Persian War and the Treaty of Torkmanchay (1826–1828)   1151

have abandoned Carabat,[110] Schirwan, Chesis,[111] Elisabethpol, and a part of Sounketre.[112] On the side of the Caspian the Persians have penetrated as far as Coubla,[113] near Derbent, and has [sic] blockaded the latter place. The American merchants, in a state of alarm, have suspended all their business and payments; and every thing indicates the bustle and approaching dangers of a state of war.'

11.46 'Paris, Oct. 12,' *National Advocate* (Monday, 20 November, 1826) and 'Paris, Oct. 12,' *Alexandria Gazette* (Thursday, 23 November, 1826): 'Extract of a private letter of the 19th ult. [August] from Moscow:—"For some time doubts were entertained at the court of St. Petersburgh, whether the hostilities committed upon the frontiers of Persia were to be attributed to the restless and turbulent spirits of the hordes which dwell in those countries or to a positive intention on the part of the Schah[114]; but intelligence brought by a courier that arrived here yesterday has set the question at rest, and our Cabinet considers itself decidedly in a state of formal war with Persia. Our Ambassador[115] is believed to be detained at the Schah's camp, near Su-leimanin/Su-Icimania."[116] Another letter from the frontiers of Russia, confirms the intelligence of a formal declaration of war by Russia in consequence of the incursions of the Persians; the march of troops to reinforce the Russian army in Georgia; and the revolt of some [of] the frontier provinces.'

11.47 'Paris, Oct. 1,' *Columbian Centinel* (Wednesday, 22 November, 1826) and 'Foreign Intelligence. Paris, Oct. 1,' *Christian Register* (Saturday, 25 November, 1826): 'The glaring contradictions which daily appear in some Journals, particularly the *Journal des Débats*, the *Courier Francaise*, and *Constitutionelle*, on the distant affairs of Persia and Russia, the Russians and Turks, and the Janizaries, afford the best proof not only of their domestic origin, but the wretched ignorance of the Novelists of the nature of the materials of which their tales are composed. They appear to be ignorant of what has long been well known, that a definitive Convention has been concluded,[117] ratified and exchanged by Russia and Turkey on all the great differences which have existed between them for years. . . .The tales of incursions of the Persians are equally as absurd. We have disdained to copy any part of these crudities, and merely notice them to prevent the public credulity

---

[110] Qarabagh.

[111] Sheki.

[112] Syunik/Zangezur/Shoregel? 'The border provinces, Bombak [Pambak] and Shouraghel, were overrun by the hordes of Eriván, Karabágh by the army of Abbas Mirza.' See Baddeley (1908: 155). According to Alexander (1827: 169–170), the boundary of the Russian and Persian frontier, according to the Treaty of Gulistan, ran 'along the limits of Shuragil.'

[113] Qobba.

[114] Fath 'Ali Shah.

[115] Menshikov.

[116] Here Soltaniyeh has been confused with Sulaimaniyah in Kurdistan.

[117] The Treaty of Akkerman.

from being imposed upon by fabrications the objects of the circulators of which are as detestable as their ingredients are vile.'

11.48 'Foreign News. Europe,' *Hallowell Gazette* (Wednesday, 22 November, 1826): 'The reports as to the differences between Russia and Turkey, and the invasion of Russia by the Persians, are perfectly contradictory.'

11.49 'Untitled,' *Louisiana Advertiser* (Thursday, 23 November, 1826): 'It had been officially stated that whilst Gen. Yermoloff [sic, Prince Menshikov] was negociating with the Persian envoys on the frontiers, upon a difference which had arisen relative to the boundaries, the Persian army made an eruption upon the Russian territory. Hostilities ensued and had taken an unfavorable turn for the Persians. Russian troops had consequently been put in motion and were on their march to Georgia.'[118]

11.50 'From the Bombay Courier of May 10,' *The National Gazette and Literary Register* (Thursday, 23 November, 1826), 'From the Bombay Courier of May 10,' *Poulson's American Daily Advertiser* (Friday, 24 November, 1826) and 'From the Bombay Courier of May 10,' *The National Gazette and Literary Register* (Saturday, 25 November, 1826): 'The north eastern frontier of Persia is at present the seat of war, having been violated by an Usbeck force, under Rehman Kuli Khan[119] of Khiwa. He entered Khorasan in January, at the head of thirty thousand men, and attacked and took Ak Derbend, a fortress commanding an important pass.[120] It was bravely defended by the troops of Seid Mohammed Khan,[121] but was obliged to yield to the superior number of assailants. The male prisoners

---

[118] This report telescopes the true events of this period. The Persian envoys had long since left Ermolov and Tiflis, and the war commenced soon after Menshikov left Soltaniyeh on 26 July 1826. See Alexander (1827: 279).

[119] Although Anonymous (1830b: 72) said that 'Rahman-Kouli-Khan succède à son père *Mohammed-Rahim-Khan* en 1826. Le titre de ces princes d'origine Ouzbeke est *Taksir-Khan;* ils résident à Khiwa,' this is incorrect. Mohammad Rahim Khan was succceeded by Allah Qoli Khan, an elder brother of Rahman's. See Vambéry (1865: 403–404). According to Howorth (1880: 934), 'The Khan's brother, Rahman Kuli, held the office of Inak of Hazarasp. He was a tall and powerful person with a vigorous mind and much consulted by his brother.' The original report on the action reported here specified that Rahman Qoli was the 'second son of the late Raheem Khán of Khiwa.' See Anonymous (1826e: 482).

[120] Not Darband in Daghestan. Schefer (1879: 90, n. 1), described, 'Aq Derbend, post frontière sur la route de Serakhs à Mechhed. Il se compose de onze tours bâties sur la crête d'une chaîne de montagnes à l'entrée du défilé qui conduit en Perse.' Cf. Curzon (1892/1: 176). Fraser (1825: 54), referred to one of the openings of the Kalat valley north of Mashhad, near the modern border with Turkmenistan, as 'the *gates* of the fortress…built up and fortified in such a manner, that it is impossible to force an entrance: on these fortified gateways there are towers, where watchmen continually are posted, to give warnings of approachers.'

[121] Describing the Kalat valley, Fraser (1825: 54–55) wrote there were 'fifteen or twenty fine villages; in one of which…of considerable size and well fortified, Seyed Mahomed Khan the present possessor

11   The Second Russo-Persian War and the Treaty of Torkmanchay (1826–1828)   1153

were put to death, the females sent into captivity. The force with which Rehman Kuli Khan left Khiwa is said not to have exceeded twelve thousand men, but it was swelled rapidly to the amount above stated, by the accession of Turcoman adventurers from all directions.

After the capture of Ak Derbend, the Khan advanced to Meshed, and made demonstrations of its siege. The place was crowded with people, who had sought refuge within its gates from the devastating bands of Turcomans, who spread through the country, and advanced even to Nishapoor.

At the date of the late advices, Rehman Kuli Khan was at Serekha,[122] and was engaged in erecting a fortress on the banks of the Tejan,[123] in the vicinity. It was fully expected that he would advance again in the spring.'

11.51 'Continuation of extracts from foreign papers, received at this Office,' *Louisiana Advertiser* (Saturday, 25 November, 1826): 'Letters from Constantinople state that as soon as the Hon. Stratford Canning[124] received intelligence of the rupture between the Persians and the Russians, he sent off a courier to London.—They mention a rumor of Tiflis having been taken by the Persians, and add that Mr. S. Canning does not appear upon very friendly terms with the Porte, as lately he has had very little communication with the Reis Effendi.'[125]

11.52 'From the Connecticut Journal. War between Russia and Persia,' *Christian Secretary* (Saturday, 25 November, 1826): 'A body of Persians consisting of 10,000 men, have burned a number of Russian villages and led away some of the peasants into captivity. A large army of Persians headed by English and French officers is said to be on the march to

---

of this strong hold resides.... Seyed Mahomed Khan is of the Jalloyer [Jalayer; for the tribe see Potts (2014: 250] tribe...He has neither the reputation of much talent or judgement; and indeed, he chiefly acts under the guidance of Reza Koolee Khan of Cochoon [Quchan]. He can with ease muster a thousand good horse, and two thousand foot soldiers, or by raising his Eels [Pers. *īl*, pl. *īlāt*, 'tribe'] and male villagers, a considerably greater number; besides which he always keeps on good terms with the Toorkomans of the desert, and can thus at a very short notice command a large force of their cavalry.'

[122] Sarakhs, Khorasan.

[123] Tejen/Tedžen or Tajand river in Turkmenistan and Khorasan. As Le Strange (1905: 395–396) wrote, 'The city of Sarakhs lies on the...right, or eastern bank of the Mashhad river, which is now known as the Tajand. This river does not appear to be named by any of the medieval geographers; it rises...in the marshes near Kûchân, and at first flows south-east, passing Mashhad.'

[124] Sir Stratford Canning (1786–1880). The British Minister in Constantinople. Cf. 9.113.

[125] This was during Canning's second stint as Minister in Constantinople (1826–1828). He arrived at the ambassador's residence in Constantinople on 27 February 1826. See Lane-Poole (1888/1: 391). Interestingly, Persia does not feature at all in Canning's notes on events in 1826, as given in Lane-Poole (1888/1). Instead, the situation in Greece and the threat of another Russo-Turkish war were of paramount significance.

the Emperor's[126] dominions. He has also ordered 20,000 Cossacks to the frontiers of Persia.'

11.53 'Baltimore, Nov. 9,' *Ohio Monitor* (Saturday, 25 November, 1826; 'Baltimore): 'The Persians are said to have passed the frontier of Russia in force, and Russian troops have marched from the Crimea.'

11.54 'From Europe,' *New-York Evening Post* (Monday, 27 November, 1826), 'From the N. York Evening Post, Nov. 27. From Europe,' *Connecticut Courant* (Wednesday, 4 December, 1826) and 'Latest from Europe,' *The Schenectady Cabinet* (Friday, 6 December, 1826): 'The Emperor of Russia[127] has issued a formal declaration of war against Persia. A battle had been fought in which the Persians were defeated with considerable loss, and obliged to retreat towards their own dominions.'[128]

11.55 'Foreign News. Russia,' *Franklin Post and Christian Freeman* (Tuesday, 28 November, 1826): 'The Emperor[129] has ordered two divisions of infantry, and 20,000 Cossacks to the frontiers of Persia, for the reinforcement of the army under Gen. Yermoloff. The Persians continued to advance, and had excited an insurrection in two of the Mahometan provinces belonging to Russia. Though Russia and Persia are in a state of war, some months must elapse before the armies can meet. Great deserts are to be crossed, large rivers without bridges to pass, a wide region destitute of roads, and without the means of furnishing subsistence for a numerous army, to be traversed. The preparations for the campaign must therefore be enormous, and it is probable that the result of the war will be commensurate with the difficulties of carrying it on. We might think that nations, between whom so many physical barriers are interposed, need not be at so much pains to surmount them for the sake of cutting each other's throats.'

11.56 'New-York, Nov. 27. Latest from Europe,' *Middlesex Gazette* (Tuesday, 28 November, 1826), 'New-York, Nov. 27. Latest from Europe,' *American Sentinel* (Wednesday, 29 November, 1826), 'Foreign. Russia,' *Boston Patriot and Mercantile Advertiser* (Thursday, 30 November, 1826; with minor variations), 'Foreign News. New York, Nov. 27. Late from Europe,' *Essex Register* (Thursday, 30 November, 1826; with minor variations, first paragraph only), 'New York, November 27,' *American Mercury* (Tuesday, 5 December, 1826), 'Foreign. Russia,' *New Hampshire Republican* (Tuesday, 5 December, 1826; first two paragraphs only) and 'General Summary. Foreign.

---

[126] Nicholas I.

[127] Nicholas I.

[128] As this is the first notice of a Russian victory in the newspapers, it probably refers to the battle near the Shamkir (Shamkirçay) river on 14 (2 O.S) September, reported on in multiple news entries below.

[129] Nicholas I.

11   The Second Russo-Persian War and the Treaty of Torkmanchay (1826–1828)   1155

New York, Nov. 27. Latest from Europe,' *Repository and Observer* (Saturday, 9 December, 1826): 'Russia declared War against Persia on the 28th Sept. and hostilities had commenced. On the 2nd Sept. the Russian General Prince Modatow[130] attacked a large Persian force, who were forced to retreat with great confusion, leaving two Kahns/Khans and 1000 men on the field.[131] The Russian General Yermohoff, with another division was driving the Persians before him.[132]

The manifesto of the Emperor intimates his determination to wage war until indemnity shall be had for past aggressions, and security for the future.

It is thought this war will tend to facilitate the negotiations between Russia and Turkey.'

11.57 'Foreign Intelligence. Further Extracts from Paris papers to the 24th October. Russia and Persia,' *The National Gazette and Literary Register* (Tuesday, 28 November, 1826), 'Latest from France. New York, November 27,' *Poulson's American Daily*

---

[130] Prince Valerian Grigoryevich Madatov (1782–1829). Eichwald (1837: 579) called him an 'Armenier aus Karabagh.'

[131] As Eichwald (1837: 580–582) recounted the story of this action, after the capture of Elizabethopol by the Persian forces, Paskevich ordered Madatov to move out against them, but then changed his mind after realizing the numerical superiority of the Persians, and 'rieth zum Rückzug, aber Madatoff, der die Kriegskunst der Perser genau kannte, zum augenblicklichen Angriff, weil die Perser durch einen Rückzug der Russen nur viel kühner werden und über sie mit ihrer ganzen Macht herfallen würden, und selbst Tiflis dadurch in Gefahr kommen könnte, während ein vortheilhafter Sieg über die Perser sie gleich muthlos machen und zum Weichen bringen würde. Durch ein geschickt ausgeführtes Manöver gelang dem Fürsten Madatoff der Angriff vollkommen, und der Feind wurde am 2 September [O.S., 14 September] zuerst völlig geschlagen. Die Perser hatten in dieser Schlacht 2000 M. regulären Fußvolks mit 4 Kanonen und 20 Falconets auf Kamelen und 8000 Mann Reiterei, unter der Anführung des Mahmed Mirsa [later Mohammad Shah], des Sohns des Thronfolgers Abbas Mirsa, und des Oheims dieses letztern, des Amir Chan Saerdar, eines der Brüder des Feth Ali Schach....In der Schlacht am Fluß Schamchor blieben von den Persern mehr als 1000 M. todt auf dem Schlachtfelde liegen...unter den Getödteten befanden sich auch zwei Chane, deren einer der Bruder des Schachs, der Amir Chan, war.' Using Georgian sources, Brosset (1857: 323) gave a somewhat different version: 'De Chamchadin le général Madatof, avec 2000 hommes, 4 canons et 300 cavaliers géorgiens, alla du côté de Gandja, alors occupé par les Persans, et où se trouvaient avec le sardar Amir-Khan, son oncle, Mahmad-Mirza fils du chah-zadeh Abaz-Mirza. Madatof étant arrivé à Chamkor, Mahmad-Mirza sortit de Gandja avec 4000 hommes, 4 canons et 20 fauconneaux. La cavalerie était composé de 8000 hommes. Dans une bataille qui eut lieu à Chamkor, les Persans furent vaincus et perdirent beaucoup de monde. Les Russes eurent à regretter la mort du brave colonel Grékof, deux officiers et 200 soldats. Les Persans avaient eu 4 khans tués, 1000 blessés et environ 1000 morts. Un canon et 11 fauconneaux restèrent aux mains des Russes. La bataille eut lieu le 2 septembre.' Stcherbatow (1890: 46), for some reason, dated Madatov's attack to the morning of 15 September (3 Sept. O.S.), noting 'La cavalerie irrégulière persane, entraîné par la pusillanimité de Mahommed-Mirza, prit la fuite après les premières décharges de l'artillerie russe; aussitôt l'infanterie régulière (les Sarbases) battirent en retraite. L'avant-garde d'Abbas-Mirza fut poursuivie pendant dix verstes.'

[132] Ermolov was not involved in this action.

Advertiser (Tuesday, 28 November, 1826; to 'obtained'), 'Russia and Persia,' *Baltimore Gazette and Daily Advertiser* (Wednesday, 29 November, 1826), 'Foreign Intelligence,' *Poulson's American Daily Advertiser* (Wednesday, 29 November, 1826; second paragraph only), 'Russia and Persia,' *Long Island Farmer and Queens County Advertiser* (Thursday, 30 November, 1826; first two sentences only), 'From the New-York Commercial Advertiser, Nov. 27. Latest from Europe. Russia and Persia,' *Alexandria Gazette* (Thursday, 30 November, 1826), 'Latest from Europe. Russia and Persia,' *American and Commercial Daily Advertiser* (Thursday, 30 November, 1826), 'War betwixt Russia and Persia,' *American Statesman and City Register* (Thursday, 30 November, 1826), 'From Europe,' *Daily National Journal* (Thursday, 30 November, 1826; with minor variations), 'Untitled,' *The National Gazette and Literary Register* (Thursday, 30 November, 1826; second paragraph only), 'Latest from France. New York, Nov. 27,' *The Pittsfield Sun* (Thursday, 30 November, 1826; to 'obtained'), 'Latest from Europe,' *Salem Gazette* (Thursday, 30 November, 1826; to 'obtained'), 'Untitled,' *Literary Cadet, and Saturday Evening Bulletin* (Saturday, 2 December, 1826; to 'obtained'), 'War between Russia and Persia,' *New-York Observer & Chronicle* (Saturday, 2 December, 1826; to '1000'), 'Latest from Europe,' *The Portsmouth Journal of Literature and Politics* (Saturday, 2 December, 1826; to 'obtained'), 'Latest from Europe. Russia and Persia,' *The Virginia Herald* (Saturday, 2 December, 1826), 'Foreign. [From the New York Daily Advertiser.] Latest from France,' *Eastern Argus* (Tuesday, 5 December, 1826; to 'obtained'), 'Foreign. Russia,' *New Hampshire Republican* (Tuesday, 5 December, 1826; second paragraph), 'Russia and Persia,' *Republican Star and General Advertiser* (Tuesday, 5 December, 1826), 'Foreign. Latest from Europe. Russia & Persia,' *Saratoga Sentinel* (Tuesday, 5 December, 1826; to 'obtained'), 'Late Foreign News. Russia and Persia,' *The Onondaga Register* (Wednesday, 6 December, 1826; to 'obtained'), 'From Europe,' *Daily Georgian* (Wednesday, 6 December, 1826; second paragraph), 'Russia and Persia,' *Hampshire Gazette* (Wednesday, 6 December, 1826; to 'Persia'), 'Untitled,' *Zion's Herald* (Wednesday, 6 December, 1826; second paragraph), 'Latest from Europe. Russia and Persia,' *Berkshire Star* (Thursday, 7 December, 1826), 'Russia and Persia,' *The Torch Light and Public Advertiser* (Thursday, 7 December, 1826), 'Russia and Persia,' *American Patriot* (Friday, 8 December, 1826; to 'dominions'), 'Secular Summary. Foreign,' *Boston Recorder* (Friday, 8 December, 1826; to 'obtained'), 'Foreign. From the Boston Palladium, Nov. 21. Russia and Persia,' *The Commentator* (Wednesday, 13 December, 1826), 'Foreign News. From the Democratic Press. Latest from Europe. Russia and Persia,' *Western Reserve Chronicle* (Thursday, 14 December, 1826), 'Foreign News. From Europe,' *Ohio Monitor* (Saturday, 16 December, 1826; with minor variations, e.g. 'killed 100'), 'Latest from Europe. New-York, Nov. 27. Russia and Persia,' *Vermont Watchman and State Gazette* (Tuesday, 19 December, 1826) and 'Foreign Items,' *Kentucky Gazette* (Friday, 22 December, 1826; to 'obtained'): 'The Emperor of Russia[133] published a formal declaration of war against Persia on the 28th September, but a battle had previously occurred on

---

[133] Nicholas I.

11 The Second Russo-Persian War and the Treaty of Torkmanchay (1826–1828)   1157

the 2nd, in which the former were victorious. The Russians attacked the Persians at the Chamora,[134] 10,000 strong, and killed 1000. Gen. Yermaloff, in an order of the day, says—The Persian court has been treacherous—and the Russian Manifesto intimates that war will be carried on till security and indemity [sic, indemnity] shall be obtained.—Hence it may be concluded that he will use every possible exertion to secure some of the frontier provinces and strongholds of Persia, and thus throw every possible obstacle in the way of future irruptions of his enemies into his own dominions.

A letter from St. Petersburg has the following passage:—"The Persian war with this country resembles the Burmese war,[135] the Persians having taken a fancy to conquer Russia with 20,000 men. The result of such affairs with the Persians is generally the loss of a few heads and noses among the unlucky counsellors.'"

11.58 'Foreign Intelligence. Latest from Europe. Moscow, Sept. 12,' *Vermont Patriot & State Gazette* (Tuesday, 28 November, 1826): 'General Paskewitsch, with two divisions of infantry, & General Illowwaisky,[136] with 20,000 Cossacks, are ordered to the frontiers of Persia, there to receive further orders.'

11.59 'Russia and Turkey,' *Baltimore Gazette and Daily Advertiser* (Wednesday, 29 November, 1826), 'Russia and Turkey,' *Poulson's American Daily Advertiser* (Wednesday, 29 November, 1826), 'War betwixt Russia and Persia,' *Essex Register* (Thursday, 30 November, 1826), 'Russia and Turkey,' *New-York Spectator* (Friday, 1 December, 1826), 'New-York, Nov. 27. Latest from Europe. Russia and Turkey,' *Charleston Courier* (Wednesday, 6 December, 1826) and 'Latest from Europe. Russia and Turkey,' *Berkshire Star* (Thursday, 7 December, 1826): 'It's/It is probable that the negotiations now pending betwixt the Courts of St. Petersburg and Constantinople, may be facilitated by the present movements of the Persians. The Russian autocrat[137] may be anxious to avoid the embarrassments in which he would necessarily be involved by a war with two distinct nations,[138] whose armies, operating in distinct places would compel him to divide his forces, and would harrass him in various directions.—Hence he will probably be induced to grant milder terms to the Turks than those on which he would have insisted, under other circumstances.'

---

[134] Shamkirçay.

[135] The First Burmese War (1824–1826). As Low (1877/1: 410) noted, 'In 1824, war broke out between the Indian Government and the King of Burmah…Early in 1824, orders were given for the equipment of a military force of from eight thousand to nine thousand men, which was drawn from the Presidencies of Calcutta and Madras.' Anonymous (1827c: 207) noted that 'the whole army of Ava [Burma], nearly sixty thousand strong,' contrasted with 'the six thousand British and native Indian troops by whom' Burma was occupied.

[136] Cf. 11.29.

[137] Nicholas I.

[138] Notes made by one of Canning's translators, Mr. Wood, for 11 September state, 'People in general apprehensive of Russian war. Sultan is for war, ministers for peace.' See Lane-Poole (1888/1: 434).

11.60 'Foreign News,' *Hallowell Gazette* (Wednesday, 29 November, 1826): 'According to the last Paris accounts. . . .The invasion of Russia by the Persians is positively denied.'

11.61 'From the N.Y. Daily Adv. Nov. 27. Latest from France,' *Norwich Courier* (Wednesday, 29 November, 1826; first paragraph only), '[From the New York Daily Advertiser.] Latest from France,' *Boston Courier* (Thursday, 30 November, 1826; first paragraph only), 'Untitled,' *The Albany Argus & City Gazette* (Friday, 1 December, 1826; second paragraph only), 'Foreign Compendium. Russia and Persia,' *The Evening Gazette* (Saturday, 2 December, 1826; order of paragraphs reversed), 'Foreign and Domestic. From the New-York Spectator. War between Persia and Russia,' *Connecticut Observer* (Wednesday, 4 December, 1826; first paragraph only), 'Russia and Persia,' *The Geneva Palladium* (Friday, 6 December, 1826; first paragraph only), 'Russia and Persia,' *The Massachusetts Spy, and Worcester County Advertiser* (Friday, 6 December, 1826; paragraphs in reverse order) and 'Foreign. Russia and Persia,' *The Kinderhook Herald* (Thursday, 7 December 1826): 'The Emperor of Russia[139] published a formal declaration of war against Persia on the 28th September, but a battle had previously occurred on the 2nd [September], in which the former were victorious. The Russians attacked the Persians at the Chamora,[140] 10,000 strong, and killed 1000. Gen. Yermoloff, in an order of the day says—The Persian court has been treacherous, and the Russian manifesto intimates that war will be carried on till security and indemnity shall be obtained.

The general opinion is that the Russian war with Persia will not be of long duration. Great preparations were making by Russia. The army of the Don[141] was distant only a few days march from that of Georgia. General Yermoloff was advancing with fifty thousand men. The Georgian Prince Alexander,[142] who deserted the Russian standard for that of Persia, is supposed to be one of the principal instigators of this idle war.'

---

[139] Nicholas I.

[140] Shamkir (Shamkirçay).

[141] Cf. the reference to Gen. Ilovaysky's Cossacks in 11.29.

[142] In the summer of 1800 Alexander, the brother of the Georgian King Giorgi XI, 'turned traitor and fled, an event of no little importance, for during many subsequent years...the fugitive prince was the arch-enemy of Russia, continually stirring up Persia and the smaller native States to attack Georgia, or the latter to revolt against its new masters.' See Baddeley (1908: 60–61). In 1826 he returned to Georgia with 'Abbas Mirza, who sent him to Kakhetia, 'um überall Aufruhr anzustiften.' As Eichwald (1837: 570) noted, 'auch kam der flüchtige georgische Zarewitsch Alexander mit Abbas Mirsa und begab sich nach Kachetian, um hier die Georgier aufzuwiegeln.' According to Brosset (1857: 322), in late August, 1826, Hoseyn Qoli Khan Qazvini, *sardar* of Erivan, 'envoya le tsarévitch Alexandre, avec 2000 Persans, pour occuper le Cakheth. Les Lesguis du Bélakan se joignirent à ce prince au pays de Kisiq et y poussèrent leurs incursions jusqu'à Garesdja. Grâce à la résistance de la ville de Sighnakh, dans le Kisiq, Alexandre se retira, sans avoir pris cette forteresse, et alla rejoindre le sardar dans le Chamchadin. Madatof, qui était dans le Qazakh, ayant battu les Persans et passé dans le Chamchadin, le sardar partit delà et se porta à l'entrée de Zagam, où il s'arrêta.'

11 The Second Russo-Persian War and the Treaty of Torkmanchay (1826–1828) 1159

11.62 'Foreign Intelligence,' *American Sentinel* (Wednesday, 29 November, 1826): 'The Russians have commenced a war with the Persians, which it is said will have a tendency to promote peace between Russia and Turkey.'

11.63 'War betwixt Russia and Persia,' *Boston Daily American Statesman* (Thursday, 30 November, 1826; from 'Russia' and without the final paragraph), 'Foreign News. New York, Nov. 27. Late from Europe,' *Essex Register* (Thursday, 30 November, 1826; 'War,' from 'Russia,' with minor variations), 'Russia,' *Rhode-Island American and Providence Gazette* (Thursday, 30 November, 1826; first and third paragraphs only), 'From the New York Statesman of Nov. 27. Latest from Europe. Russia,' *United States' Telegraph and Commercial Herald* (Thursday, 30 November, 1826), 'From the New-York Statesman. Latest from Europe. Russia,' *Brattleboro Messenger* (Thursday, 30 November, 1826; first and third paragraphs), 'Russia and Persia,' *New-York Spectator* (Friday, 1 December, 1826; first two paragraphs), 'Foreign. Russia,' *The Corrector* (Saturday, 2 December 1826), 'Russia,' *Christian Secretary* (Saturday, 2 December 1826), 'War betwixt Russia and Persia,' *Old Colony Memorial* (Saturday, 2 December, 1826; from 'Russia' to 'counsellors'), 'Foreign. Russia,' *Pawtucket Chronicle* (Saturday, 2 December, 1826; first and third paragraphs), 'New-York, Nov. 27. Latest from France. Russia,' *New-Hampshire Patriot & State Gazette* (Monday, 4 December, 1826; third paragraph only), 'Untitled,' *The Watch-Tower* (Monday, 4 December, 1826; first paragraph only), 'Foreign News. From the N.Y. Enquirer, of November 27. Latest from France. Russia,' *The Watch-Tower* (Monday, 4 December, 1826; third paragraph only), 'Latest from Europe. Russia,' *The Cortland Observer* (on or after Wednesday, 4 December, 1826; third and first paragraphs only, in that order), 'Foreign Intelligence. From the N.Y. Statesman. Latest from Europe. Russia,' *Vermont Patriot & State Gazette* (Thursday, 5 December, 1826; with another paragraph between the first and second), 'Russia,' *The Schenectady Cabinet* (Wednesday, 6 December, 1826; first and third paragraphs, reversed, minus second paragraph); 'Foreign. From the N.Y. Statesman. Latest from Europe. Russia,' *New-Hampshire Sentinel* (Friday, 8 December, 1826; with another paragraph between the first and second), 'Latest from Europe. Russia,' *The Western Star* (Saturday, 9 December, 1826), 'Foreign. From the N.Y. Statesman. Latest from Europe. Russia,' *New-Hampshire Statesman and Concord Register* (Saturday, 9 December, 1826; first paragraph only) and 'New-York, Nov. 27. Latest from Europe. Russia,' *Arkansas Gazette* (Tuesday, 2 January, 1827): 'The Belfast News Letter of October 21, says, Russia has issued a formal declaration of war against Persia; but, prior to the promulgation of this document, hostilities had commenced: a mode of procedure by no means uncommon in similar cases. On the 2nd ult. [September] the hostile armies met, a conflict ensued, and the Russians were victorious. In an order of the day, issued by Gen. Yermoloff, he accuses the Persian court of treachery, and exhorts his soldiers to prove themselves worthy of their former glory. The manifesto of the Russian sovereign broadly intimates his determination to wage war until security shall be obtained for the future and indemnity for the past. Hence it may be concuded that he will use every possible exertion to secure some of the frontier provinces and strong holds of Persia, and

Fig. 11.1 Prince Valerian Grigoryevich Madatov, by George Dawe, 1820. Oil on canvas. Military Gallery of the Winter Palace, CC0 1.0 Universal

thus throw every possible obstacle in the way of future irruptions of his enemies into his own dominions. . . .

A letter from St. Petersburgh, has the following passage:—The Persian war with this country resembles the Burmese war, the Persians having taken a fancy to conquer Russia with 30,000 men. The result of such affairs with the Persians is generally the loss of a few heads and noses among the unlucky counsellors.

Gen. Yermoloff [sic, Madatov] has gained a great victory over the Persians. 8000 of the latter were killed in battle.' (Fig. 11.1).

11.64 'Untitled,' *Daily National Intelligencer* (Thursday, 30 November, 1826) and 'Foreign Intelligence,' *The Geneva Gazette and General Advertiser* (Wednesday, 6 December, 1826; with minor variations): 'From the Frontier of Russia, we hear that General Yermoloff [sic, Madatov], at the head of the Russiam Army, had gained a great victory over the Persians. Eight thousand of the latter were killed in the battle.'

11.65 'Untitled,' *The Supporter, and Scioto Gazette* (Thursday, 30 November, 1826): 'The Russian papers. . .confirm the accounts previously received of the irruption of the Persians into the Russian territory, but no battle of importance had taken place at the latest dates.'

11 The Second Russo-Persian War and the Treaty of Torkmanchay (1826–1828)   1161

11.66 'Foreign. Turkey,' *The Corrector* (Saturday, 2 December 1826): 'Turkey.—'A letter of the 25th says that the Porte persists in the plan of reforming the army with unabating obstinacy.[143] A new ambassador had arrived from Persia within a few days. His name is Dand-Aga,[144] & he comes with the official news of the commencement of

---

[143] As Jouannin and van Gaver (1840: 402) noted, the stubborn Greek resistance displayed against the Ottoman forces, among other things, convinced Sultan Mahmud that military reform was necessary. 'Pour remédier à ce mal invétéré, source de tous les revers des armes ottomanes, il résolut de mettre enfin à exécution le plan qu'il nourrissait depuis plus de quinze années...Il s'agissait de changer tout le système militaire, et de soumettre l'armée, et principalement les janissaires, à la tactique européenne, seul moyen de résister à des voisins aguerris et dont les forces étaient doublées par l'emploi des habiles manœuvres de la stratégie moderne.' For the text of the Sultan's firman announcing the abolition of the Janissaries, dated 16 June 1826, see Lesur (1827: 97–100).

[144] This was Dawud Khan Malekshah Nazar (Mir Dawud-Zadur or Mir Dawoud-Zadour de Melik Chah-Nazar), who had previously served Fath 'Ali Shah in Paris in 1816 as his ambassador to Louis XVIII. Cf. 10.3 and Anonymous (1826o: 734), 'Extract of a letter dated "Constantinople, Oct. 14:"— The Armenian-Persian Daoud Zadnur, now Daoud Khan, the same who in 1816 went to Paris with letters from the Shah to Louis XVIII, has just arrived at Constantinople. It is reported that the object of his mission is to induce the Porte to join Persia against Russia. He is lodged at Kadkenei (the ancient Chaledon), and is said to have solicited permission to reside in Constantinople."—[*Paris Paper*.' We can get a picture of Daud Aga's time in Constantinople from German, French and Belgian newspapers. According to a bulletin dated 25 September, 1826, in *L'Étoile* (Anonymous 1826g): 'Il y a quelques jours qu'on a vu arriver ici un nouvel ambassadeur persan, nommé Daud-Aga. Il a apporté la nouvelle officielle du commencement des hostilités entre la Perse et la Russie. Il assure que les montagnards du Caucase doivent se soulever en masse contre les Russes. Cette nouvelle, par des motifs très-faciles à comprendre, trouve pleine croyance parmi les Turcs. On prétend qu'il vient demander des secours à la Porte.' A bulletin from 16 October in the *Journal de la Belgique* (Anonymous 1826i) wrote: 'L'agent de Perse Daud Aga a déjà eu quelques conférences avec le Kiaja Bey.' A later bulletin from 18 October (Anonymous 1826h) observed: 'Daoud-Aga, agent de Perse, arménien de naissance, a fait le 28 septembre sa visite aux ministres de la Porte.' Interestingly, an undated bulletin in *L'Étoile* (Anonymous 1826j) noted, 'La *Gazette d'Augsbourg* dit que Daoud aga, agent de Perse à Constantinople, avait cherché à faire une visite à M. de Minciaky, et fait demander un passeport pour la Russie. On regarde comme assez vraisemblable que la réception des bulletins de l'armée russe l'aura porté à ces démarches conciliatoires: au reste, M. de Minciaky lui a refusé l'entrevue et le passeport.' Finally, a bulletin from 26 October in Anonymous (1826l) noted, 'Le reiss-effendi, qui bravait encore dernièrement M. de Minciaky, est tout-à-fait changé; il est entré en communications avec lui, et lui a fait déclarer que la Porte, désirant rétablir les relations les plus amicales avec la Russie, avait rompu toute relation avec l'agent de Perse, Daoud-Aga. Le sultan déteste naturellement l'agent persan parce qu'il est chrétien, et parce qu'il a apporté des instructions ou pleins-pouvoirs, dans lesquels le schah de Perse prend le titre de Padichah. Le reiss-effendi ne l'a donc plus revu depuis quelques jours. Il faut remarquer que la Porte a reçu l'avis que les choses allaient mal pour la Perse en Géorgie, et elle est très-contente d'avoir accepté l'*ultimatum*, et d'avoir échappé aux armes de la Russie. On croit que Daoud-aga quittera bientôt Constantinople pour retourner à Téhéran. Toutes ses démarches pour voir M. de Minciaky, ou d'avoir un passeport pour St-Pétersbourg, ont été infructueuses. M. Stratford-Canning a reçu deux fois ses visites, mais il ne les a pas rendues. Le consul-général d'Angleterre lui donna un déjeuner à Péra; mais aucune personne diplomatique n'y assista. Cette conduite changée de la Porte envers M. de Minciaky et Daoud-pacha

hostilities with Russia. He declares that the mountaineers of Caucasus will rise in a mass against Russia, and the Turks believe it. It is rumoured that this envoy comes to ask help from the Port [sic].'

11.67 'Russia and Persia,' *Columbian Centinel* (Saturday, 2 December, 1826), 'Russia and Persia,' *National Aegis* (Friday, 6 December, 1826) and 'Russia and Persia,' *The Farmers' Cabinet* (Saturday, 9 December, 1826): 'Official papers announce, that a formal declaration of war was made by Russia against Persia on the 28th Sept.; but that a battle had been fought on the 2nd [O.S. September] on the Chamora,[145] in which 1000 of the Persians were killed. The Russian army was 10,000 strong, and commanded by Gen. Yermoloff [sic, Madatov]; who, in a bulletin, has declared, that the war shall be carried on till indemnity for the past, and security for the future, shall be obtained. The Persians are stated to have been the aggressors.'

11.68 'From Europe,' *The Commentator* (Saturday, 2 December, 1826): 'The accounts of a war between Persia and Russia are confirmed. It was some time doubtful whether the irruptions of the Persians upon the Russian frontier were authorized by the government, or were mere plundering expeditions. It is now ascertained that the Shah[146] (sovereign) of Persia authorized the war to be levied. Several of the border provinces of Russia have taken advantage of the occurrence to revolt.'

11.69 'Russia and Persia,' *American Advocate* (Saturday, 2 December, 1826) and 'Foreign News. Russia and Persia,' *Ohio Monitor* (Saturday, 2 December, 1826): 'One of the last French papers which have been received, contains an extract from the Journal of St. Petersburgh, which affords more specific information relative to the grounds of dispute between Russia and Persia, than any which has previously reached us. We have accordingly made the following translation of the article to which we refer.—*Nat. Journ.*

We find the following article in the Journal of St. Petersburgh, of the 30th of August:—

The reports of General Yermoloff, who commands in Georgia, have given us the news of an irruption made by the Persians in several points of the Russian Territory.

The first accounts transmitted in haste, will not permit us, as yet, to discover the character of this aggression. Is it the effect of the fanatic discourses which have been circulating in Persia for some time past, and which appear to have excited there a considerable effervescence? Have the different colonies bordering on our frontiers yielded themselves to such a life of robbery and outrage, that they are incessantly carried away

---

[sic, Aga], en conséquence de la tournure des affaires sur le Caucase, est vraiment un trait caractéristique des Orientaux. (*Gazette d'Augusbourg.*).' The Sultan's dislike of Daud Aga because of the fact that he was a Christian, and his anger at Fath 'Ali Shah's use of the title *padishah*, are also mentioned in Anonymous (1826l).

[145] Shamkirçay.

[146] Fath 'Ali Shah.

by it? Have their chiefs encouraged these movements, or are they unable to restrain them? In short, are we not bound to attribute an invasion so unjust, so unexpected, to the disposition of Persia herself? Has this disposition led her, at this moment, to violate the peace and the faith of treaties which she has guaranteed? Has she taken, all at once, the resolution to attack us without notice, and without an object? Such are the questions which present themselves, but which the Government is not yet in a state to answer.

The reciprocal benefits assured to Russia and to Persia by the treaty of Gailistan[147]; the relations of mutual kindness which are established between them since the conclusion of that act; the absence of every subject of serious difference; the mission with which Major General Prince Menchikoff has been charged to the Shah,[148] to announce to him the accession of his Majesty the Emperor[149] to the throne, and to contract and consolidate between the two nations relations of amity and good neighborhood; the entertainment which he received on his arrival in the Persian territory; the respects which have been tendered to him; the amicable assurances which have been so lavishly made by the presumptive heir to the Persian crown; all secured to predict confirmation and continuance. But that to this mission the Court of Teheran should respond by a sudden attack; that these assurances should be immediately followed up by war, without explanation, without prevous declaration, without one pretext by which it could be justified[150]; this is a circumstance so strange, that the Imperial Government cannot give credit to it, until it shall receive full confirmation, and have proved its authenticity.

While, therefore, General Yermoloff is ordered to repel force by force, and to purge our frontiers of the hordes which have dared to overstep them, on the other hand, a solemn satisfaction will be demanded of the Shah of Persia. Russia will demand of this Prince the immediate degradation, and exemplary punishment, within five days, of the commander who first violated her limits. If, contrary to all hope, this satisfaction should not be granted, General Yermoloff will forthwith move forward; offensive operations will be commenced; the justice of our cause will guarantee the divine protection to our arms; and the chastisement will be signal, as the perfidy and rashness of the crime.

The public will be regularly informed, with scrupulous precision, of all which may be communicated relative to the state of things on the Persian side.'

11.70 '4 Days Later from England,' *The Southern Patriot* (Saturday, 2 December, 1826), 'Late from Europe,' *City Gazette and Commercial Daily Advertiser* (Wednesday, 4 December, 1826) and 'From Liverpool,' *Daily Georgian* (Wednesday, 6 December, 1826; second paragraph): 'The most important item of intelligence is the Declaration of War by Russia against Persia.

---

[147] Gulistan.

[148] Fath 'Ali Shah.

[149] Nicholas I.

[150] Omitting, of course, any mention of the contentious occupation of Gokcha (Gökçe).

The Russian General Prince Madatow, with his advance guard, had beat the Persians, commanded by Abbas Mirza,[151] whose army lost 2000 men and several standards. The Persians were on the retreat in great disorder. The first act of war was committed by the Persians. The English had withdrawn all their officers from the Persian army.'[152]

11.71 'Latest from England,' *Charleston Courier* (Wednesday, 4 December, 1826): 'we have received from our correspondents extensive and complete files of London papers to the 19th, and Liverpool papers to the 21st October. What is in them of importance, we have extracted. The commencement of hostilities between the *Russians* and *Persians* is politically the most important. The advance of the *Persians* was succeeded by a formal declaration of WAR by Russia.[153] Already they have had one battle, in which the latter were successful.'

11.72 'Untitled,' *The Watch-Tower* (Monday, 4 December, 1826) and 'Foreign. Late from Europe,' *New-Hampshire Statesman & Concord Register* (Saturday, 9 December, 1826): 'A probability is expressed that the negociations now pending between the courts of Petersburgh and Constantinople may be facilitated, by the present movement of the Persians.'

11.73 'Latest from Europe,' *The St. Lawrence Gazette* (Tuesday, 5 December 1826), 'Latest from Europe,' *The Schenectady Cabinet* (Wednesday, 6 December 1826) and 'Latest from Europe. Russia,' *The Palmyra Sentinel* (Friday, 8 December 1826; from 'Gen. Yermoloff'): 'The Emperor of Russia has issued a formal declaration of war against Persia. A battle had been fought in which the Persians were defeated with considerable loss, and obliged to retreat towards their own dominions....

Gen. Yermoloff [sic, Madatov] has gained a great victory over the Persians. 8000 of the latter were killed in battle.

The Belfast News Letter of Oct. 21, says, Russia has issued a formal declaration of war against Persia; but, prior to the promulgation of this document, hostilities had commenced—a mode of procedure by no means uncommon in similar cases. On the 2nd ult. [September] the hostile armies met, a conflict ensued, and the Russians were victorious. In an order of the day, issued by Gen. Yermoloff, he accuses the Persian court of treachery, and exhorts his soldiers to prove themselves worthy of their former glory. The manifesto of the Russian sovereign broadly intimates his determination to wage war until security shall

---

[151] This is incorrect, for the forces opposing Madatov were commanded by Mohammad Mirza (later Mohammad Shah, 'Abbas Mirza's son) and 'Abbas Mirza's uncle Amir Khan. See Eichwald (1837: 581), Brosset (1857: 323).

[152] As noted above, Henry Willock had ordered the British officers to remain at Tabriz and not to accompany the Persian forces into the field. The only foreign soldiers involved were the Italian Lt. Bernardi and the Scotsman Dawson. Cf. 11.14, 11.132.

[153] This was issued on 16 September 1826, according to Eichwald (1837: 583).

11   The Second Russo-Persian War and the Treaty of Torkmanchay (1826–1828)

be obtained for the future and indemnity for the past. Hence it may be concluded that he will use every possible exertion to secure some of the frontier provinces and strong holds of Persia, and thus throw every possible obstacle in the way of future irruptions of his enemies into his own dominions.

11.74 'Foreign News. Russia,' *Franklin Post and Christian Freeman* (Tuesday, 5 December, 1826): 'The Emperor[154] has issued a formal declaration of war against Persia. Hostilities had commenced before the publication of this document. A battle was fought on the 2nd Sept. in which the Russians, under Gen. Yermoloff [sic, Madatov] were victorious, the Persians losing 8000 men.'

11.75 'French Papers,' *Gazette of Maine* (Tuesday, 5 December, 1826), 'French Papers,' *Portland Advertiser* (Tuesday, 5 December, 1826), 'Secular Summary. Foreign,' *Boston Recorder* (Friday, 8 December, 1826) and' French Papers,' *The Farmers' Cabinet* (Saturday, 9 December, 1826): 'Alluding to the existing war between Russia and Persia, one of the [French] papers asserts that the Persians have demanded succors of the Turks; and that the mountaineers of the Caucasus have risen *en masse* against the Russians.'[155]

11.76 'Weekly Summary. Foreign,' *National Journal* (Tuesday, 5 December, 1826): 'Turkey, having agreed to the ultimatum of Russia,[156] has left her unfettered to carry on the war which she has just declared against Persia. One battle has taken place, in which the Persians are said to have been defeated. The Russian troops are marching to the seat of war in very considerable numbers: and it is said to be the general opinion that the conflict will be but short in its duration.'

11.77 'Intelligence. From the N.Y. American,' *Woodstock Observer, and Windsor & Orange County Gazette* (Tuesday, 5 December, 1826): 'The war between Persia and Turkey had fairly commenced, and a battle fought in which the Persians are said to have lost 1000 men.'

11.78 'Late from England. Russia,' *New-York Commercial Advertiser* (Wednesday, 6 December 1826), 'Russia,' *Baltimore Gazette and Daily Advertiser* (Friday, 8 December, 1826), 'Russia,' *Baltimore Patriot & Mercantile Advertiser* (Friday, 8 December, 1826), 'Russia,' *Rhode-Island American and Providence Gazette* (Friday, 8 December, 1826), 'Late from England. Russia,' *New-York Spectator* (Friday, 8 December, 1826), 'Latest from Europe,' *Washington National Intelligencer* (Saturday, 9 December, 1826), 'Late

---

[154] Nicholas I.

[155] A reference to Dawud Khan Malekshah Nazar's mission to Constantinople and his assertion that the mountain tribes of the Caucasus would rise up against Russia. Cf. 11.66.

[156] A reference to the Convention of Akkerman.

from England. Russia,' *American and Commercial Daily Advertiser* (Saturday, 9 December, 1826), 'Foreign. Latest from Europe. Russia,' *Pawtucket Chronicle* (Saturday, 9 December, 1826), 'Late from England. Russia,' *Saratoga Sentinel* (Tuesday, 12 December, 1826), 'Late from England. Russia,' *Berkshire Star* (Thursday, 14 December, 1826) and '[From the N. York Com. Advertiser, Dec. 6.] Late from England. Russia,' *Charleston Courier* (Friday, 15 December, 1826): 'It appears that General Yermoloff [sic, Madatov] has gained a victory of some importance, which has been celebrated by illuminations and public rejoicing at St. Petersburg. From the official report of General Y. it seems that Abbas Mirza, after the defeat on the Clanhora,[157] had been joined by Allair Khan son-in-law to the Schah,[158] and with their united forces, amounting to 8000 regular infantry, 15,000 regular, and as many irregular cavalry, and 25 pieces of cannon, had again passed the Terter.[159] General Madstoff[160] had, upon this, joined, in the night of the 21st [September], Adjutant General Paskevitch, in consequence of which the

---

[157] Shamkirçay.

[158] Allah Yar Khan was both Fath 'Ali Shah's son-in-law and 'Abbas Mirza's father-in-law. Monteith (1856: 146) called him wrote, 'a Kadjar nobleman unknown to the people or army of Azerdbijan, and remarkable only for excessive vanity and pride.' According to John McNeill, 'He is a man of little talent, but having been brought up entirely at Court and much about the King's person, he has acquired a knowledge of the Shah's feelings which enables him to make himself acceptable.' See MacAlister (1910: 74).

[159] The Terter (Тертеръ), or Terterçay, a tributary of the Kur river. See Radde (1901: 38), Hübschmann (1904: 349). It is located close to Gülüstan [Gulistan] in mod. Azerbaijan where the treaty of 1813 was signed. See Montpéreux (1839: 105). As Brosset (1857: 323) noted, 'Le 12 septembre [O.S.] 1826, le chah-zadeh Abaz-Mirza, qui était sur les bords de la rivière Tartar, avec une armée considérable, ayant appris l'échec de son fils [Mohammad Mirza] et la réoccupation de Gandja par les Russes, se mit en mouvement, à la tête de forces considérables. Ala-Iar-Khan Qadjar, gendre du chah, vint également le trouver avec de puissants renforts. Cependant le général Madatof avait été rejoint à Gandja, dès le 9 de septembre, par le général-adjudant Paskévitch, avec quelques troupes et de l'artillerie. Tous deux se portèrent sur la Kouraq-Tchaï, où ils rencontrèrent l'ennemi. Il se livra en ce lieu un rude et sanglant combat, qui dura huit heures, et dans lequel un millier de Géorgiens, mêlés aux Russes, déployèrent leur valeur. Le chah-zadeh fut vaincu. Son armée se composait de 4000 soldats réguliers, de 8000 hommes, la fleur de la cavalerie, et de 25 canons d'artillerie régulière. Le sardar persan Amir-Khan et 2000 hommes périrent dans cette affaire. Le chah-zadeh, dans sa retraite, entraîna les troupes qui assiégeaient la citadelle de Choucha et, ayant fait évacuer les travaux, alla se poster sur l'Araxe. Les Russes restèrent maîtres de 3 canons, de deux grands camps, de quatre *fourgons* [meaning of the Georgian word used here unknown to Brosset] tout remplis, d'un étendard, de 80 fauconneaux, et des caissons de plomb et de poudre. Ils eurent 240 officiers et soldats blessées ou tués.'

[160] Madatov.

11 The Second Russo-Persian War and the Treaty of Torkmanchay (1826–1828)

Persians contented themselves with taking a position on the left bank of the above mentioned river, and were obliged to raise the blockade of Schouchi.[161]

---

[161] Shusha [Шуша], capital of the khanate of Qarabagh. As Eichwald (1837: 571) noted, 'Der Obrist Reutt, Commandeur des 42sten Jägerregiments, berichtete zuerst dem Oberbefehlshaber, General Jermoloff, über den Einfall der Perser, und er hielt von ihm den Befehl, sich so lange wie möglich in Tschinachtschai zu halten; aber dies war in dem unbefestigten Dorf unmöglich; er entschloß sich daher, nach der Festung Schuscha zu eilen, und befahl dem in Gerüssi befindlichen Bataillon, ihm dorthin zu folgen. Aber die überall aufstehenden Bewohner Karabagh's verfolgten ihn beständig und griffen ihn von allen Seiten an, so daß er nur mit Mühe Schuscha erreichte, das gleich darauf von Abbas Mirsa mit seinen 40,000 Persern eingeschlossen wurde.' Cf. Brosset (1857: 324, n. 1), 'Le 25 juillet, le colonel Réout se renferma dans Choucha, qu'il défendit avec courage durant 48 jours, étant entièrement coupé de la Géorgie, par l'interposition des forces persanes dans le Qarabagh, qui déjà avaient occupé Gandja, sous la conduite de Mahmad-Mirza, fils ainé d'Abaz-Mirza.' In the words of Balleydier (1857/1: 253), writing of 'Abbas Mirza and the siege of Shusha, 'Sur son passage, dans le khanat de Karabagh, était la forteresse de Choucha, que le prince royal ne pouvait pas laisser sur ses derrières. Il espérait d'autant plus l'emporter sans coup férir, que ses émissaires l'avaient renseigné sur la position de cette place, défendue seulement par six compagnies du 42e des chasseurs à pied et quatre bouches à feu; mais le courage de son commandant, le colonel Réout, décidé à s'ensevelir sous les ruines de la forteresse plutôt que de l'abandonner à l'ennemi, la rendait presque inexpugnable. Abbas-Mirza somma ce brave officier de livrer la place confiée à sa valeur. "Viens la prendre!" répondit Réout; et le prince royal, espérant l'écraser par le nombre, l'attaqua aussitôt avec la plus grande partie de son armée....Mais la forteresse de Choucha continuait à résister avec l'énergie du désespoir à toutes les attaques de l'ennemi. Ni les fatigues de la garnison combattant nuit et jour sur les remparts, ni le manque de vivres et de munitions, ne purent ébranler le courage du colonel Réout. Cette héroïque résistance, retenant pendant plus de six semaines le principal corps de l'armée persane sous les murs de la place, donna le temps à quelques bataillons de ligne des frontières du Caucase de rejoindre le général en chef à Tiflis.' Cazalès (1838: 618–619) offered some details about the fortress itself, noting, 'La forteresse était en très mauvais état, elle n'avait qu'un très faible garnison, et il ne s'y trouvait que quatre pièces de canon, dont deux, du temps des khans, étaient à peu près hors de service....Il fallut d'abord réparer les fortifications, et les assiégés y travaillèrent activement sous le feu continuel de l'ennemi. Le 30 juillet, les Persans attaquèrent la place de deux côtés à la fois; mais ils furent repoussés avec perte et ne purent pas livrer l'assaut. Le manque de vivres se fit bientôt sentir dans la ville, et le colonel Reutt fit sortir tous les Tartares sur lesquels on ne pouvait pas compter. Ils purent donner aux Persans des renseignemens exacts sur l'état de la forteresse; ils leur annoncèrent aussi que les plus distingués d'entre leurs compatriotes étaient tenus en prison pour avoir essayé d'exciter un soulèvement en faveur de la Perse, et que le commandant menaçait de les faire périr si Abbas-Mirza tentait de donner l'assaut. Peutêtre ces Tartares arrêtèrent-ils le prince héréditaire en lui représentant la triste position de leurs amis; au moins peut-on croire que cette circonstance ajouta à son indécision et à sa négligence. Ce qu'il y a de sûr, c'est qu'il laissa aux Russes le temps de se rassembler à Tiflis et de venir à sa rencontre avec des forces assez imposantes.' On 5 September, after learning of the defeat of the Persian forces at Shamkir, 'Abbas Mirza lifted the siege of Shusha after 47 days and left with the bulk of his army to join Allah Yar Khan at Elizabethpol/Ganja . See Eichwald (1837: 578). According to Ustrjalow (1857: 82), when Paskevich was on his way from Tiflis to meet up with Madatov's forces, in order to relieve Col. Reutt at Shusha, 'Bei Anbruch des Tages [13 O. S./25 September 1826] erschienen bei ihm zwei Armenier mit der Nachricht, daß Abbas-Mirza, durch die Niederlage seines Sohnes am Flüßchen Schamchoras [Shamkirçay] beunruhigt, die Belagerung der Festung Schuscha aufgehoben hätte und mit seiner ganzen Armee (35,000 M.) eilig gegen Jelisawetpolj zöge.' Note that, while the dates given are often slightly divergent, e.g. 12 vs 13 September, when they diverge by a larger number, e.g. 13 vs 25 September, this is due to the fact that some writers were using Old Style (O.S.) dates, e.g. 13 September, while others employed New Style, hence 25 September.

From another report of Gen. Paskeetch[162] it appears that he was attacked on the 25th of September, by the Persians, to the number of 35,000 men, commanded by Abbas Mirza in person and three of his sons; but that the assailants, after a short engagement, fled in disorder, leaving behind 1100 prisoners, eighty caissons, and a quantity of baggage.[163] The loss of the Russians was fifty killed, among whom is Col. Gretoff,[164] and two hundred and fifty wounded. The enemy was pursued in his flight, and when the latest report was sent off, it was thought that the whole province of Karabosch[165] was already delivered from the

---

[162] Paskevich. Cf. 11.29.

[163] The instigator of the attack is disputed. According to Anonymous (1847d: 592), the Russians attacked a Persian force of 60,000 men (18–20,000 regular infantry; 24 cannon), not vice versa. Balleydier (1857/1: 253) put Paskevich's forces at '6000 hommes d'infanterie, 3000 cavaliers et quelques pièces de canon, tandis que le prince royal comptait sous ses drapeaux 24,000 fantassins réguliers, 8000 hommes de troupes diverses, 12,000 cavaliers et une nombreuse artillerie.' The battle took less than one hour. According to Eichwald (1837: 582–583), Paskevich had 15,000 infantry and 20,000 cavalry as well as 25 cannon. He put the Persian losses at 1100 prisoners, including 9 officers; two standards, three cannon, 1 falconet [small swivel gun carried on a camel] and 80 cases of gunpowder. On the other hand, according to Balleydier (1857/1: 253), 'Les Persans attaquèrent les premiers avec assez de résolutions, mais l'action fut de courte durée: les carrés d'infanterie persane, foudroyés par le feu de l'artillerie russe, furent mis en déroute. La victoire de Paskevitch fut complète; 1120 prisonniers, 2 khans, 3 drapeaux, 3 bouches à feu, 1 falconet et 80 caissons, tombèrent en son pouvoir. Ainsi battus, dispersés et mis en fuite, les Persans se hâtèrent de repasser l'Araxe.' For a detailed analysis of the battle, as well as a plan showing the disposition of the Persian and Russian forces, see Ustrjalow (1857: 83–84) and Schlachetenplan V.

[164] Mikaberidze (2005: 138–141) provides biographies of six Don Cossack officers and indicates the existence of at least eighteen Grekovs in the Russian military. According to Stcherbatow (1890: 61), Grekov commanded a batallion of 400 Cossacks in this engagement. As Anonymous (1847d: 591–593) noted, 'Le prince Madatoff commandait toute l'infanterie; la première ligne était sous les ordres du colonel Avenarious, du 41e des chasseurs; la deuxième, commandée par le lieutenant-colonel comte Simonich, des grenadiers de Géorgie; la cavalerie, sous les ordres du colonel Sabelsky, des dragons de Nijni-Novogorod; la troisième ligne enfin, commandée par le colonel Popoff, des grenadiers de Kherson. C'étaient tous des officiers distingués, tels encore le lieutenant-colonel Grekoff, du régiment de Schirvan, et le major Klüke, du 42e, alors attaché au 7e des carabiniers.... De son coup d'œil prompt et sûr, Paskevitsch reconnut le côté faible de l'ennemi, et ordonna la charge pour enfoncer le centre de sa ligne....Pendant cette charge, et presqu'au même moment, le comte Simonich tomba grièvement blessé, et Grekoff mort.' As Paskevich wrote to the Czar, 'Le lieutenant-colonel Grékow, excellent officier du régiment de Shirvan, a malheureusement été tué en menant son bataillon à la baïonnette.' See Stcherbatow (1890: 64). In 1815 a Lieutenant-Colonel Grekoff, who may have been the same individual, commanded a regiment of Don Cossacks. See Anonymous (1829i: 131). A namesake, also a Col. Grekov, commanded a Cossack regiment in the Russo-Turkish War of 1828–1829, perhaps a brother? See Eichwald (1837: 629), Uschakoff (1838: 281). In addition, a General Grekov served against Napoleon and under Ermolov in 1818 against the Chechens. See Weil (1886: 111), Mackenzie (1854: 60), Brosset (1857: 322, n. 1). Lyall (1825/2: 277) noted that Major-General Grékof 'has no children,' hence he could not have been our Col. Grekov's father.

[165] Qarabagh.

11 The Second Russo-Persian War and the Treaty of Torkmanchay (1826–1828) 1169

Persians. This victory was considered as so important, that the guns were fired at St. Petersburgh, and the city illuminated on the occasion.'

11.79 'Liverpool, Oct 21,' *Daily Georgian* (Wednesday, 6 December, 1826): 'The formal declaration of war against Persia by the Emperor Nicholas, has been issued. It is dated Moscow, the 28th September. Hostilities have commenced. The hostile armies met on the 2nd ult. [O.S. September]. The issue of this first encounter [the battle of Shamkir] was in favor of the Russian army, and the advantage was quickly followed up. The Russians were under the command of Major-General Prince Madatow.—The seat of this war is so little known, we may presume, to our readers, that we need not trace the progress of the Russians from place to place. The Russian ambassador,[166] and his official attendants at the court of Persia, have been kept prisoners there since the commencement of hostilities. The Commander in Chief in Georgia, Gen. Yermoloff, addressed the army in spirited language, in an order of the day, dated September 30, pointedly condemning as treacherous the invasion of the Russian territory by the Persians, and exhorting the soldiers to courage and loyalty.'

11.80 'Russian Declaration of War,' *Poulson's American Daily Advertiser* (Wednesday, 6 December, 1826; from 'The doubts'), 'Russian Declaration of War Against Persia,' *The National Gazette and Literary Register* (Thursday, 7 December, 1826; from 'The doubts'), 'War between Russia and Persia. Hamburg, Oct. 12,' *Washington National Intelligencer* (Saturday, 9 December 1826),[167] 'Hamburgh, Oct. 13,' *Alexandria Gazette* (Saturday, 9 December, 1826; beginning 'The Russian Declaration of War against Persia is as follows,' and then from 'Hamburgh, Oct. 13'), 'Untitled,' *The New-York American* (Monday, 11 December 1826), 'From a Late London Paper. War with Russia. Hamburgh, Oct. 13' *Boston Daily Advertiser* (Tuesday, 12 December, 1826) and 'Hamburg, Oct. 13,' *New-York Commercial Advertiser* (Friday, 15 December, 1826; from 'The Russian declaration'): 'By the packet ship Julius Caesar, Capt. West, arrived at Philadelphia, London papers have been received to the 18th of October, and Liverpool to the 20th.

The most important articles they contain are the official declaration of war against Persia by Russia, with a statement of the successes that have attended the Russian arms at the first outset. The British Press says—"It is in vain to attempt to disguise the question concerning this war. The interest of Persia is scarcely more compromised by it than that of Great Britain; and settled *it must be* without further encroachment on the part of Russia, or England must at least obtain some advantages equivalent to that of Russia, and sufficient to render her successive acquirements of no importance as points of attack on our Indian

---

[166] Menshikov.

[167] The front page is signed R. H. Walworth (Mansfield Tracy Walworth's father), Saratoga Springs, N.Y., showing us at least one potential source of intelligence on the Second Russo-Persian that appears in Walworth (1871).

possessions. The spirit of conquest has infected the whole nation of Russia, and, disguise it as we may, something must be done, in the only practicable way, to check her career."

It is not likely that the general peace of Europe will remain uninterrupted for many years longer.... [*Washington National Intelligencer* only].

Hamburg, Oct. 13.—The Russian Declaration of War against Persia is as follows:

"The doubts which Russia entertained respecting the nature of a sudden and unjust attack, are now removed. For a whole month Russia was willing to consider it as impossible that the Sovereign of Persia,[168] in a time of profound peace, and in the midst of an amicable negotiation, should, without any ground or serious difference—nay, even without a pretext for complaint, and without any previous declaration—have ordered his troops to invade the Russian territory, and at the same time to make it the theatre of insurrection and war. This opinion, however natural, was a mistake. It is not one of the barbarous tribes, dwelling on our frontiers, that has unexpectedly invaded them, as Russia, in its moderation and good will, supposed; no, it is the Persian army itself that has attacked our posts, and advanced towards the interior of our frontier provinces. Nor is it a restless Chief, who, in spite of the command of the Schah, leads them on; it is his own son,[169] the presumptive heir of his throne, that directs this invasion, and accompanies it with invitations to revolt. Compelled to oppose force to force, and war to war, Russia would consider it as a duty to refute, in the presence of Europe, the accusations upon which Persia founded the necessity of these extraordinary measures, if it were acquainted with the grievances of that State, or could even divine them. But though Russia is ignorant of the object and the causes of the contest, which must be now decided by arms, it will, however, confining itself to a sketch of its relations to the Government by which it is attacked, show whether it had reason to expect such a breach of treaties, and of all the principles of the law of nations.

At the time when memorable triumphs crowned that noble alliance which saved the European Continent, and gave peace to the world, it had pleased Divine Providence to bless the efforts of Russia in its contest with Persia. Several Persian Provinces were conquered by the Russian armies, and as, in consequence of their victories, Persia had solicited peace, a convention between the two Powers was signed at Gulistan, on the 12th October, 1813. It is stipulated on the principle of the *status quo ad presentem*—the state of the possessions of both parties—and imposed upon Russia only two essential obligations towards the Court of Teheran, viz.: to recognize as the lawful heir to the Persian throne that son of the Schah whom he should appoint as his heir; and, in concert with Persian commissioners, to settle the new demarcation of the frontiers, which were assigned by the treaty of Gulistan to the Provinces which are annexed to the Russian empire. The first of these obligations was most punctually performed by Russia, and as soon as the Cabinet of St. Petersburg learned that Feth-Aly had designated his son Abbas Mirza for his successor, he hastened to recognize his rights as presumptive heir, with which his father's decision invested him. The second

---

[168] Fath 'Ali Shah.
[169] 'Abbas Mirza.

11 The Second Russo-Persian War and the Treaty of Torkmanchay (1826–1828)

has given rise to some difficulties, and the principal was not yet removed when Russia had the misfortune to lose the great Prince who had carried to so high a pitch its prosperity and its glory. Meantime the negotiations, which related to the more important difficulties, gave continued proof of the moderation and frankness which characterised the policy of the Emperor Alexander. In conformity with his orders, the system of peace, friendship, and reciprocal good will, which his Cabinet observed towards all foreign Powers, should be also extended to his relations with Persia.

These orders prescribed to the Ambassadors and agents at the Court of Teheran the mode of conduct which was best calculated to convince the Schah, his heir,[170] and his Ministers, that Russia had no thought whatever of conquest—that it wished only for repose, and required nothing but the execution of the treaties. They enjoined all the Russian authorities to observe the most conciliatory conduct and measures, which could never tend to give to Persia just grounds for suspicion or complaint.—Lastly, in the difference which had arisen between the two States, because Persia, after the cessation of hostilities, had occupied a tract of country between the rivers of Tschuw and Kapanakushan,[171] which, by the treaty of Gulistan, was expressly assigned to Russia; and because, on the other hand, Russia had placed posts on a strip of country which divides to the Northwest the waters of Lake Goktscha[172] from the mountains that run along it: The Emperor Alexander, far from disputing the rights of Persia on this point, required no more for giving it up than that the district belonging to him should be given up at the same time, or he proposed to exchange this rich and fertile tract for that bank of the Goktscha which is of far less importance, and whose dry and poor soil offered no compensation but the vicinity of the lake.[173] A project of demarcation, conformable to these proposals, was presented to the Persian Court. After long discussions, in which, however, nothing unpleasant intervened, the two parties appeared to be coming to an understanding, in March, 1825; and when God called the Emperor Alexander to himself, every thing seemed to indicate that this amicable discussion was drawing to a conclusion.

---

[170] 'Abbas Mirza.

[171] Alexander (1827: 272) noted, 'With respect to the Capan [Kapan] territory, the Russians assert that the river running in the neighbourhood of Mogree [Meghri] is called *Capanek*, and forms the boundary; and that Persia exceeds her limits, as defined in the treaty, if she occupies the country as far as *Capan*. The Persians, on the other hand, maintain that there is no river called *Capanek*; that the river running in the neighbourhood of Mogree is called *Mogree Chai*; that the Capan Chai forms the true boundary; and that the country between these two rivers has been in the possession of Persia since the termination of the war. The statements of the Persian government are fully warranted by a map of Georgia, published by authority of the Russian government in the year 1819. In this official document, the Capan forms the actual boundary of the two empires, and no river named *Capanek* is laid down. The claim of Russia, therefore, which was not set up till some time after the treaty, is destroyed by her own evidence.' Also Kapanakçay.

[172] Gökçe (Sevan).

[173] This discussion, and some of the wording, is closely mirrored by Alexander (1827: 271) in his discussion of the causes of the Second Russo-Persian War.

The Emperor Nicholas, inheriting the principles of his august predecessor, hastened to tread in his footsteps. In the month of January, he confided to Major General Prince Menzikoff an extraordinary mission to Persia. He commissioned him to announce to the Schah, and to Prince Abbas Mirza, his accession to the throne; and, to this end, addressed autograph letters to them, the friendly expression of which only announced the desire to see the existing frontiers observed and peace consolidated. The full purpose of Prince Menzikoff even authorized him to conclude an agreement respecting the very point which delayed the de. . . He was further instructed to convince the Schah and the Hereditary Prince, of the uprightness of the views of his Imperial Majesty; to show them power combined with justice and moderation; to prove to them that it was the common interest of both empires to strengthen the ties of peace between them; to destroy all their suspicions; and lastly, to convince them that the Emperor Nicholas desired nothing more than the accurate and scrupulous observance of the treaty of Gulistan." This is the mission in which Persia has answered with war. The principal events that followed are well known.

Prince Menzikoff, serving on the frontiers of Persia, was received with great respect at Tauris, Abbas Mirza loaded him with honors and the most friendly assurances. He was soon invited to the camp of Sultania, to execute the mission of the Emperor to the Schah. At the same moment, a sudden movement begins in Persia. Abbas Mirza, anticipating the Ambassador of his Imperial Majesty, repairs in the greatest haste to Sultania; the Persian troops advanced to our frontiers; the posts stationed there are attacked, and compelled to retreat; the Russian territory is occupied.

The Emperor Nicholas, being informed of these hostilities, was at first disposed to ascribe them only to the disobedience of some Persian Commander, who had disregarded the intentions of his Sovereign, and he demanded nothing more than the immediate removal and exemplary punishment of the Surder of Erivan,[174] whom he considered to be the first aggressor. But when his orders arrived in Georgia, it was no longer possible to execute them, and the affair was decided. Abbas Mirza having returned from the camp of Sultania, took, in person, the command of the Persian forces. He has already occupied a part of the provinces of Karabasch,[175] belonging to Russia. He has excited rebellion there. His emissaries encourage the Mahomedan subjects of his Majesty in the frontier provinces to revolt. The Proclamations announce a religious war.

Such proceedings cannot remain unpunished. Russia declares war against Persia. It declares that, as the Treaty of Gulistan is broken, it will not lay down its arms till it has obtained guaranties for perfect security for the future, and a just indemnity, by an honorable and solid peace.

Given at Moscow, the 16th (28th,) of September, 1826.'''

---

[174] Hoseyn Qoli Khan Qazvini.

[175] Qarabagh.

11 The Second Russo-Persian War and the Treaty of Torkmanchay (1826–1828)   1173

11.81 'Persian War,' *Republican Farmer* [Bridgeport CT] (Wednesday, 6 December, 1826): 'The defeat of the Persians with the loss of 1000 killed, gives much satisfaction at St. Petersburg. The Russians talk of taking some of the frontier provinces and strong holds of Persia, so as to prevent future eruptions from that quarter.'

11.82 'War with Russia. Hamburgh, Oct. 12,' *Poulson's American Daily Advertiser* (Wednesday, 6 December, 1826), 'War with Russia,' *Albany Argus & City Gazette* (Friday, 8 December 1826; altered first sentence; to 'provisions'), 'War between Russia and Persia. Hamburg, Oct. 12,' *Washington National Intelligencer* (Saturday, 9 December, 1826), 'War with Russia. Hamburgh, Oct. 12,' *United States' Telegraph and Commercial Herald* (Saturday, 9 December, 1826), 'War with Russia. Hamburgh, Oct. 12,' *New-York American* (Saturday, 9 December 1826; altered first sentence; to 'provisions'), 'Latest from Europe,' *The National Intelligencer* (Saturday, 9 December 1826; altered first sentence; to 'provisions'), 'War with Russia. Hamburgh, Oct. 12,' *The Berks and Schuylkill Journal* (Saturday, 9 December, 1826; 'To day we received the official news that Russia declared war with Persia on the 28th of last month [September]. The manifesto fills several pages. At the same time we have received the following accounts, dated the 7th September, of victories gained by the Russians on the frontiers of Persia,' and then from 'Major-General' to 'provisions'), 'Latest from England. War with Russia,' *Albany Argus* (Tuesday, 12 December, 1826; with minor variations), 'From a Late London Paper. War with Russia. Hamburgh, Oct. 12,' *Boston Daily Advertiser* (Tuesday, 12 December, 1826), 'War with Russia,' *Republican Monitor* (Wednesday, 13 December 1826; altered first sentence; to 'provisions'), 'War with Russia,' *Onondaga Register* (Wednesday, 13 December 1826; altered first sentence; to 'provisions') and 'Russia and Persia,' *Kinderhook Herald* (Thursday, 14 December 1826; altered first sentence; to 'provisions'): 'To-day we have received the official news that Russia declared war against Persia on the 28th of last month. The Manifesto fills several pages. At the same time we have received the following accounts, dated the 7th Sept. of victories gained by the Russians on the frontiers of Persia.

"Major-General Prince Madatow attacked the Persians on the 2nd of September, who occupied a strong position on the right bank to the river Chamhora.[176] The enemy had 2000 regular infantry, eight pieces of cannon, twenty falconets, carried by camels,[177] and 8000 cavalry. Mehmed Mirza,[178] son of Prince Abbas Mirza, and grandson of the Emperor, as well as the Surdar of Merchan [sic, Amir Khan], brother of the Emperor,[179] and other

---

[176] Shamkirçay.

[177] A *zamburak/zanburak*. Cf. Colombari (1853).

[178] The future Mohammad Shah.

[179] Amir Khan Qajar, uncle of 'Abbas Mirza. Although Cazalès (1838: 621) and this article him as Fath 'Ali Shah's brother, Alexander (1827: 284) and Conder (1827: 240) both said he was 'Abbas Mirza's maternal uncle, hence a brother of his mother, not his father. Sheil (1838: 55) called him simply 'a relation of Fath 'Alí Sháh' and attributed the foundation of Dilaman, near Salmas, to him.

Persian great men, were at the head of them. The advance of our army was given notice of at a distance by the outposts of the enemy, who were drawn up in order of battle and awaited our approach. The fire of four Persian cannon, accompanied with musketry, was pretty violent. But some artillery placed in a battery on our side soon silenced the guns of the enemy. Our artillery was especially directed against the enemy's cavalry, which soon followed the example of the commander Mehmed Mirza, who sought safety in flight. The Persian infantry were thus deprived of its support, and our cavalry, consisting of 800 Cossacks, the Georgia militia, and some Tartars from the district of Kazasch,[180] pursued the fugitives briskly, and cut off their retreat. Terror and confusion seized the Persians; they made but a faint resistance, and were pursued for ten wersts.

The enemy lost in this engagement two cannon, and above 1000 men were left on the field of battle. We took one cannon, eleven falconets, and several powder wagons. After these advantages, Major Gen. Prince Madatow advanced to Elizabethpol, which he took without opposition on the 4th of September; but though this advance after the victory at Chamhora[181] was made with incredible rapidity, 1500 Persian infantry, who were in the citadel, succeeded in leaving it before our troops arrived. The enemy not only did not halt under the walls of the city, but were even seen to fly in the greatest disorder on the other bank of the Zeyva,[182] beyond Elizabethpol. Our cavalry, which advanced 20 wersts, did not meet with a single Persian. At Elizabethpol, we took possession of the enemy's camp, with large magazines of provisions. In the citadel we found great quantities of flour, powder, and lead.[183] Gen. Yermoloff adds to these accounts, that Mahometans and Armenians had already arrived from Karabasch,[184] who affirm that since the appearance of the Russian Troops, the inhabitants of those parts were become sensible of their treason,

---

Monteith (1856: 125) called him 'a most timid and incompetent chief.' According to Anonymous (1826n: 730), he was killed on 15 September, less than two weeks after the action reported here. Cf. 11.97.

[180] Kasatcha/Kazachia [Казачья], in the Crimean peninsula. See Krasinski (1848: 275). In the tenth century the area of the lower Don River was known as Kazachia. See Czaplicka (1918: 44). Contrary to some scholars, e.g. Lawson 1900: 134, the term Cossack is not derived from Kazachia. See Pritsak (2006).

[181] Shamkirçay.

[182] River north of Gulistan [mod. Gülüstan] where the treaty of 1813 was signed. See Brosset (1857: 304, n. 1). According to Montpéreux (1839: 105), the stations of Terter, Zeïva and Kouraktchaï preceded Elizabethpol [Ganja]. Cf. 11.7.

[183] Cf. Eichwald (1837: 582), 'Der Furst Madatoff eilte sofort nach Elisabethopol, das er auch ohne Schwertschlag einnahm, den 4 Septbr.; die 1500 M. regulärer Truppen der Perser, die in der Stadt waren, erwarteten nicht Madatoff's Ankunft, sondern flohen noch vorher in der größten Eile davon. Der Feind verließ überhaupt in der größten Unordnung die von ihm besetzten Gegenden, setzte über den Fluß Seiwa, und die nachsetzende russische Reiterei fand 20 Werst weit keinen Perser mehr. In Elisabethopol wurde das feindliche Lager, das mit den besten Lebensmitteln versehen war, genommen; auch in der Festung fand sich viel Proviant, Pulver und Blei.'

[184] Qarabagh.

11   The Second Russo-Persian War and the Treaty of Torkmanchay (1826–1828)   1175

and are ready to atone for it by immediate submission. On this intelligence General Yermoloff ordered the Adjutant General Paskewitch to effect, as soon as possible, his junction with Major General Prince Madatow, and to march to Karabasch."'

11.83 'Official Papers. [The Letters and Papers of which the following are Translations, have been officially communicated to the Department of State, by Baron de Maltitz, Charge d'Affaires from Russia.]. Baron de Molitz, Charge d'Affairs [sic] from Russia, to Mr. Clay,[185] Secretary of State. [Translation.],' *Daily National Journal* (Thursday, 7 December, 1826): 'Monsieur the Secretary of State—I addressed to you, recently, a communication relative to the unexpected invasion which has disturbed the tranquility of the Russian frontiers on the side of Persia.

Subsequent intelligence which I have just received from the Imperial Ministry states, that the hope which was entertained by the government of his Majesty of being able to avoid war, has been destroyed—and that it has been compelled to issue the declaration which, in compliance with the orders from my Court, I have now the honor of communicating to the government of the United States of America. I profit by the occasion, Monsieur the Secretary of State, to join with it the Bulletin of the first events of this war, and to express to you a conviction that the Cabinet of Washington will partake of the indignation which must be excited by an attack so perfidious, a violation so flagrant, of all the principles of the laws of nations.

I have the honor to be, with very high consideration,
    Monsieur the Secretary of State,
        Your very humble and very obedient servant,
            The Baron de Maltitz[186]
Washington, the 18 (30) Nov. 1826.
            [Translation.]
            Declaration

The doubt which Russia still entertained with regard to the nature of a sudden and unjust aggression, are removed. For a month, she was willing to look upon it as impossible that, in

---

[185] Henry Clay (1777–1852), American Secretary of State (1825–1829). Clay was kept abreast of developments in the Russo-Persian war from multiple State Department sources, including Henry Middleton in Moscow, who commented on the weakness of Persia (dispatch of 17 September, received 1 December, 1826) and predicted the Persian adventure 'will cost them dear' (dispatch of 21 October 1826, received 26 December, 1826); James Brown in Paris, who cited erroneous accounts in Russian newspapers alleging that Menshikov had been assassinated in Persia (dispatch of 23 September, received 8 November, 1826); and Christopher Hughes in Brussels, who wrote of 'excitement among the Diplomatists, and politicians in general,' generated by 'the war between Russia & Persia' (dispatch received 10 December, 1826). See Hopkins and Hargreaves (1973: 691, 708, 801, 812).

[186] Franz Friedrich Freiherr von Maltitz (1794–1857), Chargé d'Affaires *ad interim* in the Russian embassay in Washington, 14 March 1826–20 December, 1827. See Anonymous (1866b: 789), Lanman (1876: 621. Cf. 11.113).

profound peace, in the midst of an amicable negotiation, without any serious cause of dispute, without even the pretext of complaint, without previous declaration, the sovereign of Persia had commanded his troops to violate the Russian territory, to invade it, and to carry into it at the same time war and insurrection. This opinion, so natural, was nevertheless erroneous. It is not, as Russia in her charity and moderation supposed it, one of those barbarous hordes residing near our frontiers which has suddenly crossed them; it is the Persian army itself, that has unexpectedly attacked our posts, and advanced towards the interior of our frontier provinces. It is no longer a turbulent chief, who heads it in despite of the orders of the Schah[187]; it is his own son, it is the heir presumptive to his throne who commands it, who directs this invasion, who accompanies it with incentives to revolt. Compelled to oppose force to force, and war to war, Russia would consider it her duty to repel, in the face of Europe, the accusations upon which Persia may have founded the necessity of these violent measures, if she knew the complaints of that State, or if she could even divine them. But, although she is ignorant both of the subject and the causes of the difference which is about to be decided by her arms, Russia, in restricting herself to giving a rapid view of her relations with the government which attacks her, will show whether she ought to have expected such an infraction of treaties, and of all the principles of National Law.

At the time when memorable triumphs were crowning that noble union which saved the continent of Europe, and pacified the world, Divine Providence deigned also to prosper the efforts of Russia, in the war which she was carrying on against Persia. Many Persian provinces were conquered by the Russian arms, and Persia having, in consequence of these victories, sued for peace, a Treaty between the two Powers was signed at Gulistan, on the 12th of October, 1813. From that epoch, this treaty constituted the rule of their mutual relations. It defined, according to the basis of *status quo ad præsentem*, the state of their respective possessions: and imposed upon Russia only two essential obligations towards the court of Teheran—that of recognising, as the legitimate heir, to the crown of Persia, the son of the Schah, to whom that monarch himself should secure his heritage, and that of effecting, in concert with Persian Commissioners, the demarkation of the new limits which the Treaty of Gulistan assigned to the provinces which had been annexed to the Russian empire. The *first* of these obligations was fulfilled by Russia with the most scrupulous exactness, and as soon as the Cabinet of St. Petersburgh was informed that Feth Aly had designated as his successor, his son Abbas Mirza, it hastened to acknowledge in him the rights which the decision of his father had vested in him as heir presumptive. The *second* gave rise to some difficulties, and the chief of them was not yet adjusted when Russia had the misfortune to lose the great Prince who had carried to such a height her glory and prosperity. However, the negotiations relative to these trifling difficulties did not cease to give evidences of that moderation, of that good faith, which characterized the general policy of the Emperor Alexander. His orders concerning his relations with Persia, were

---

[187] Fath 'Ali Shah.

11 The Second Russo-Persian War and the Treaty of Torkmanchay (1826–1828)

uniformly in accordance with that system of peace, friendship and reciprocal good will, which his cabinet pursued towards all Foreign Powers. They prescribed, to his ambassadors and agents at the court of Teheran, that line of conduct best adapted to convince the Schah, his heir and his ministers, that Russia entertained no ideas of conquest; that she wished only for tranquility, and demanded nothing but the performance of treaties. They prescribed to all the Russian authorities in Georgia, the most conciliatory modes of proceeding, and measures, the result of which might never afford to Persia any just grounds for suspicion or complaint. Finally, in the difference which arose between the two states, because Persia had, after the cessation of hostilities, occupied a tract of territory between the rivers Tchoudouv[188] and Kapanaktchay,[189] which the treaty of Gulistan assigned expressly to Russia; and because, in her turn, Russia had established ports on the strip of land which separates, to the North West, the waters of Lake Goktcha[190] from the mountains by which they are bordered, the Emperor Alexander, far from disputing the right of the Persians to this point, demanded only, in order to restore it, the simultaneous restitution of the district which belonged to him, or proposed the exchange of that rich and fertile district for the said shore of the Goctcha, which is much less considerable in extent, and of which, the soil, poor and arid, offered no other compensation than its vicinity to the lake. Projects of demarcation to this effect were transmitted to the Court of Persia. After prolonged discussions, unmarked, however, by any impleasant occurrence, in the month of March, 1826, opinions were about coinciding, and, when God called to himself the Emperor Alexander, every thing seemed to indicate, that this peaceable discussion was drawing to a close. Heir to the principles of his august predecessor, the Emperor Nicholas hastened to follow in his footsteps. In the month of January, he confided to the Major General, Prince Menchikoff, an extraordinary mission to Persia: He directed him to notify to the Schah, and to Abbas Mirza, his accession to the throne: and he himself addressed to them, to this end, autograph letters, of which the kindly expressions manifested only a desire to see the existing treaties observed, and peace established. The powers of Prince Menchikoff authorized him also to effect an agreement relative to the only question which retarded the demarcation of limits, to reiterate the proposition of exchange mentioned above; or, in order still further to contribute to the interests of Persia, and to exhibit, in their true light, the intentions of Russia, to join to, the points already occupied by the Persians, a portion of the District of Talyschyne.[191] The instructions desired him, moreover, "to persuade the Schah

---

[188] Eichwald (1837: 570) noted that, 'Es war etwa in der Mitte des Juliusmonats, als Abbas Mirsa, dem der Schach in Sultanie den Oberbefehl über die ganze active Armee ertheilt hatte, in die Gränze von Karabagh mit einem Corps von 40,000 M. einbrach; es war auf der chudoperin'schen Brücke, im Süden von Schuscha, 90 Werst von hier entfernt, über den Araxes gegangen.' 'Chudoperin' is a corruption of Khoda Afarin.

[189] Kapanakçay. Cf. 11.80.

[190] Gökçe (Sevan).

[191] Talysh. As Le Strange (1905: 173) noted, 'The narrow strip of shore and mountain slope, running north from the south-west corner of the Caspian, and facing east over that sea, is the Ṭâlish country, a name which Yâḳût gives under the plural form Ṭâlishân or Ṭîlshân.'

and the hereditary prince, of the uprightness of his imperial majesty's views; to show them power, united with justice and moderation; to prove to them, that it is the common interest of the two emperors, to tighten the bonds which peace may have created between them; to do away all their suspicions, and, finally, to convince them, that the Emperor Nicholas, following the example of his august brother, desires only the exact and religious observance of the Treaty of Gulistan." Such is the mission, which the Court of Teheran has answered by war. The principal events which have followed, are already known. Arrived at the frontiers of Persia, the Prince Menchikoff is there received with marks of great respect. At Tauris, Abbas Mirza lavishes upon him demonstrations of honor, and the most pacific assurances. Shortly after, he is sent to the camp of Soultanieh, in order to fulfill towards the Schah the orders of the Emperor. At the same moment, a sudden movement manifests itself in Persia. Abbas Mirza makes all haste to reach Soultanieh before the envoy of his emperial majesty. The Persian troops march towards our frontiers; the posts which guard them are surprised, and compelled to fall back; the Russian territory is invaded. Informed of these acts of hostility, the Emperor, at first, is disposed to attribute them solely to the disobedience of some Persian chief, pretending ignorance of his sovereign's orders; and he demands only the immediate deposition, and exemplary punishment of the Sardar of Erivan,[192] who appeared to him to be the first aggressor. But, when these orders reach Georgia, the execution of them is no longer possible, and the affair is decided. Abbas Mirza having returned from the camp of Soultanieh, takes command in person of the Persian forces. He has already occupied a portion of the Province of Carabak,[193] belonging to Russia; he has there excited a revolt;—his emissaries foment it in all the adjoining countries, among the Mahometan subjects of his majesty;—the proclamations announce a religious war. Proceedings of this nature must not remain unpunished. Russia declares war against Persia. She declares, that the Treaty of Gulistan being violated, she will not lay down her arms until she is assured of pledges of the most complete security for the future, and of just indemnifications, by an honorable and solid peace.

Given at Moscow, on the 16th Sept. 1826.

[Translation.]

News from the Army of Georgia, under date 29th August, (O.S.)

The Persian army under the orders of Abbas Mirza, heir presumptive to the crown of Persia, had invaded the district, of [sic, or] Kannat,[194] of Talychine, and that of Carabah, and had advanced even to the environs of Elisabethpol. Its strength was estimated at 30 or 40 thousand men. Abbas Mirza stirred up to rebellion against Russia the mussulman population of the provinces which he occupied. With the same object, his emissaries traversed the adjoining countries, and excited them to revolt, in the name of the religion of Mahomet.

---

[192] Hoseyn Qoli Khan Qazvini.

[193] Qarabagh.

[194] Khanate, district ruled by a Khan, as shown below where reference is made to the 'Kannat or district of Chirvan.'

11 The Second Russo-Persian War and the Treaty of Torkmanchay (1826–1828)

This invasion having taken place during profound peace; found our frontiers almost unprovided with troops. The posts which guarded them were too weak to resist the efforts of the Persian army. They were compelled to fall back as the enemy advanced.

In consequence of this same state of peace, the army of Georgia was distributed in its cantonments. General Yermoloff was concentrating it around Tiflis; but, on account of the distances, time was requisite to effect the junction of the different corps, and the commander in chief had not yet left that town, although he had assembled 15 batallions. However, by his orders, the Major General Prince Madatoff had marched to meet the Persian army. The latter had just brought from the environs of Elizabethpol, into the district of Cuamchalil,[195] a corps of about two thousand men, augmented by a body of the insurgent population and by some cavalry from Erivan; which had served as an escort to the ci-devant prince Alexander of Georgia, a refugee sent by Abbas Mirza into Cachetie[196] in order to excite an insurrection there. The prince Madatoff, who occupied the banks of the river Akstapha, being informed of this movement of the enemy, made a night march in order to surprise him, but at the break of day, he found the camp raised and the enemy ranged in battle order on the heights. A batallion which was sustaining the *tirailleurs*,[197] sent in advance, immediately attacked these hills. The enemy broke, and a few cannon shots sufficed to put them into complete rout. The want of cavalry saved them from being overtaken in their flight. But some Armenians from a neighboring village having perceived a party in flight, killed a good many of them, made some prisoners, and carried off some horses.

In the Kannat or district of Chirvan, the former Khan of that country, named Moustapha, at the head of a numerous troop of insurgents, and a large body of Persian cavalry, had occupied the village of Aksa.[198] The Major general de Krabbe[199] attacked him, drove him

---

[195] Shamshedil, area north of Lake Sevan (Gökçe), bordering the former khanate of Erivan. Bournoutian (1982: 77, r. 9) noted, 'The Russian Shamshedil or Shamshadin, in fact, was more accurately known by the name of the Turkic tribe living there as Shams od-Dinlu.' 'Schamschadilu' was separated from Kakheti by the Kur river. See Klaproth (1814: 47).

[196] Kakheti, region northeast of Tiflis noted for its wine. See e.g. Gamba (1826/2: 217ff), Ussher (1865: 95). Minorsky (1953: 27). For a detailed geographical description see Klaproth (1814: 46–70).

[197] Light infantry sent in advance of the main body of an army, to engage the enemy in skirmishes. On their deployment in nineteenth century warfare see e.g. Hartwig (1841: 15–16, 21–22, 24–25).

[198] In 1821, 'les Russes chassèrent de Chamakhi Moustafa, khan de Chaki, et organisèrent à Chaki une administration russe, en remplacement des khans indigènes, qui avaient gouverné jusqu'alors.' See Brosset (1857: 317). Prior to the action described here, as Eichwald (1837: 578) noted, 'Mustapha Chan von Schirwan nach Schamachie eilte, die Stadt besetzte und an allen den Tartaren, welche den Russen treu geblieben waren, die größten Grausamkeiten, vorzüglich an den Begs einiger reichen Familien, beging.' This makes it likely that Aksa is mod. Agsu, c. 36 km southwest of Shamakhi. It was also referred to as Akssu. See Eichwald (1837: 579).

[199] Major General Karl Karlovich von Krabbe [Карл Карлович фон Кръъе (1781–1854)] was described by Eichwald (1834: 111) who noted that, 'dem als Militärbefehlshaber von Schirvan, Baku, Kuba, Derbend und Tarki diese Provinz Daghestan unter specielle Aufsicht anvertraut ist; unter ihm

from his position, and caused him to suffer a very considerable loss.[200] Abbas Mirza had engaged the inhabitants of the province of Chekiue to march to the aid of Moustapha, but it is stated that they were also dispersed, and that they lost a considerable number of men. Abbas Mirza had likewise attempted to excite an insurrection in Dagestan, and had sent there, for that purpose, a former Khan of Kachum,[201] named Sourkay.[202] The Major General Aslau [sic, Aslan] Khan, whose zeal and fidelity are well tried, did not suffer him to fulfil his mission.—Aslau Khan has sent to the army of General Yermoloff his own son with 200 cavalry.[203]

---

stehen die Commandanten der Einzelnen Städte und müssen ihm beständig berichten.' He commanded the 'détachement du Kouban posté à Staraïa-Schémakha.' See Stcherbatow (1890: 76). Bournoutian (1998: 525) noted that von Krabbe, a German, entered the Russian military in 1798 and fought in the Napoleonic wars. He was the father of Nikolai Karlovich Krabbe (1814–1876), an admiral in the Russian navy. For a brief life history see http://necropolural.narod.ru/index/0-395

[200] According to Brosset (1857: 326), 'Le colonel Menchicof [sic Mitchenko, commanding the Absheron Regiment; see Stcherbatow (1890: 76)] arrivé de Qouba [Qobba], le 7 septembre, avec ses troupes, consistant en un régiment, attaqua Moustapha, khan de Chirwan [Shirwan], qui était au Vieux-Chamakhi avec ses forces considérables, le battit et le força à s'en-aller du côté de Moughan [Mughan]. Les Russes l'ayant poursuivi et atteint au bord du Mtcouar, il y eut un second engagement, où les Persans furent encore vaincus, mais conservèrent le pont de Djichir. Moustapha-Khan déploya tant de bravoure que les Persans passèrent ici le Mtcouar, après s'être emparés de quelques caissons d'artillerie, renfermant du plomb et de la poudre. Pour les Russes, ils traversèrent aussi le fleuve et allèrent du côté du Qarabagh.'

[201] According to Zonn et al. (2010: 267–268), 'The dwellers of Kazikumukh Village [in Daghestan], when invaded by the Arabs, accepted Islam and began to spread it so enthusiastically that they were given an honorable name of Kazikumukhs by the Arabs (*kazi*—"one fighting for one's faith").'

[202] Sorkhay of Qazi Qomuq. One of the most famous Lezgin figures in Daghestan, 'Surchai Chan [II] von Kasikumük.' See Koch (1847: 419). Active in the First Russo-Persian War, Schlechta-Wssehrd (1864b: 16) called him Surchai Chan the 'lezghischer Stammhaupt' while Aytberov (2014: 383) observed that 'the most trusted person of the Qajar dynasty in Daghestan was Surkhay, the ruler of Kazikumukh, whose mother, by the way, came from the famous Ustajlu Qizilbash tribe...Due to this distinguished person an actively working line of the intercourse was set between the Dagestani leaders and Tehran.' He was the father-in-law of Mustafa Khan of Sheki and took refuge with him when he was ousted by the Russians. See Brosset (1857: 317, n. 2). As Gammer (2003: 179) noted, in reaction to Ermolov's efforts to solidify the Russian presence in Daghestan in 1818, 'The rulers of Avaria, Kazi-Kumukh, Mekhtuli, Karakaytag and Tabasaran and the confederation of Akusha formed an alliance against the Russians.' Not to be confused with 'Surchai Chan [I] der Kasikumüken' who attacked Shamaki in Shirvan in 1721. See Dorn (1845: 408).

[203] As Eichwald (1837: 579–580) described these events 'In der schirvan'schen Provinz nahm Mustapha Chan mit einem zahlreichen Heer Aufrührer und einem großen Corps persischer Reiterei das Dorf Akssu ein; der Generalmajor v. Krabbe vertrieb ihn zwar aus diesem Ort, verlor aber viele Truppen. Die von Abbas Mirsa aufgeregten Bewohner der scheki'schen Provinz kamen dem Mustapha Chan zu Hülfe, wurden aber auch geschlagen und mußten sich nach einem großen Verlust nach allen Seiten zerstreuen. Auch Dagestan suchte Abbas Mirsa durch den früheren kasikumük'schen Chan Ssurchai aufzuwiegeln; doch ließ ihn der jetzige Chan, Generalmajor Asslan

11 The Second Russo-Persian War and the Treaty of Torkmanchay (1826–1828) 1181

The inhabitants of Akoucha,[204] having received from Abbas Mirza an incendiary proclamation, transmitted it immediately to Chanhal of Taiquie,[205] a Lieutenant General, with a request to communicate it to the General in Chief Yermoloff. The devotion of this brave and numerous tribe ensures the tranquility of Dagestan.

The Sardar of Erivan[206] had as yet undertaken nothing.—He was waiting, it was said, the arrival of Abbas Mirza, at Elizabethpol, with a considerable force. The General in Chief Yermoloff, profited by the inaction of this Chief, to erect intrenchments in the steppe of Lory,[207] which will stop the Persians on that side, and leave the rest of the army at liberty to pursue their operations.

From the news of the 2nd of August, there was reason to suppose that the Major General Prince Menchikoff, was detained under the walls of Erivan. Subsequent intelligence affords the happy certainty of his arrival in the Russian territory with all his suite. He was expected every moment at Tiflis.[208]

[Translation.]

News from the Army of Georgia of the 7th of September.

On the second September, the Major General, Prince Madatoff, attacked the Persians, who had taken a position on the right bank of the river Chamhora. The enemy counted 2000 regular Infantry, 4 cannons, 20 falconets mounted on camels, and near 8000 cavalry. They were commanded by Mehmet Mirza, the son of Abbas Mirza, by the Serdar Amir Chan, the uncle of the latter, and by several other Persian Chiefs of distinction. A signal of the approach of our troops at a distance was given by the advanced guards of the enemy, who

---

Chan, nicht bis dahin kommen, ja er schickte sogar seinen Sohn mit 300 M. Reiterei dem General Jermoloff zu Hülfe, und zeichnete sich bei jeder Gelegenheit durch Eifer und Ergebenheit an Rußland aus.'

[204] A town in Daghestan. See e.g. Eichwald (1837: 735), Koch (1847: 363), Monteith (1856: 114), Blaramberg (1872: 258). According to Reineggs (1796/1: 100), 'Akuscha ist das letzte Volk, welches zu Ghazi-Kumuk gerechnet wird. Seine Stärke und guter Ruf, so wie desselben überall bekannte Tapferkeit, ist dem ganzen Kaukasus und allen angränzenden Fürsten sehr wohl bewust; selbst die Lesghä fürchten desselben Macht, da der Stamm 18,000 Familien zählt, und bisher das Gleichgewicht zwischen allen Kaukasiern erhielt.'

[205] Shamkhal of Tarki. Cf. Eichwald (1837: 580), 'Um dieselbe Zeit hatten auch die Akuschen eine schriftliche Aufforderung zum Aufstande von Abbas Mirsa erhalten; aber sie stellten sie durch den Generallieutenant Schamchal von Tarki dem Corpscommandeur zu und blieben treu; so daß aus dieser Anhänglichkeit eines so zahlreichen und kriegerischen Volks an Rußland auf eine fortdauernde Ruhe in Dagestan geschlossen werden konnte.' For the title *shamkhal* see Floor (2010a: 342ff.).

[206] Hoseyn Qoli Khan Qazvini.

[207] Lori. As Fonton (1840: 45) noted, 'La rive droite de la vallée de la Kura, comprenant les distances de Bortchala, de Bambaki, de Kasakhi et de Chamchadil, coupée par les rameaux de la chaîne de l'Alaghèz, n'est pas, beaucoup s'en faut, aussi productive, soit à cause de la qualité du sol, ou bien à cause du manque de bras. On y rencontre des parties absolument désertes et incultes, comme par exemple la steppe de Lory.'

[208] As noted in 11.130 Menshikov arrived at Erivan on 16 (4 O.S.) August 1826 and was detained there 20 September. His account of the detention in Yerevan was written at Tiflis on 24 September.

awaited us, ranged in order of battle. The fire of the four pieces of the Persian artillery was tolerably brisk, and accompanied by discharges of musketry; but a few cannon brought into battery on our side, soon silenced those of the enemy. Above all, they made great havoc in the ranks of his cavalry, which was soon compelled to follow the example of Mehmet Mirza, who had already sought safety in flight. The Persian Infantry was then left without support; and our cavalry, composed of eight hundred Cossacks of Georgian militia, and some Tartars from the district of Kazask, having briskly charged the fugitives, cut off their retreat. They could oppose but a very feeble resistance, and for more than ten versts they were pursued with great slaughter.

The enemy lost, in this affair, two Chans and more than a thousand men left on the field of battle. We took from them a cannon, several caissons, and eleven falconets.

After this success, the Major-General, Price Madatoff, advanced towards the town of Elizabethpol, and took possession of it on the 4th September without resistance. But notwithstanding the rapidity of his march after the victory of the Chamhora,[209] 1500 of the regular Persian Infantry had evacuated the citadel without waiting the arrival of our troops. After being routed on the 2nd, the enemy not only did not stop under the walls of that town, but they were even seen flying in the greatest disorder on the other bank of the Zeyva, beyond Elizabethpol. Our cavalry, which was sent twenty versts in advance, did not meet with a single Persian. In the environs of Elizabethpol, we took possession of the enemy's camp, which was well stocked with provisions of all kinds. In the citadel we found a large quantity of flour, powder, and lead.

In addition to this news, General Yermoloff states, that some Mahometans and Armenians had already arrived from the Karabak,[210] who assure him, that on the appearance of the Russian troops, the population of those districts, who are sensible of all the guilt of their treason, will be eager to make amends for it. In consequence of the information, General Yermoloff had ordered the Aide-de-Camp, General Paskeritch [sic, Paskevich], to hasten his junction with the Major-General, Prince Madatoff, and to march towards the Karabak.'

11.84 'London, Oct. 18,' *Charleston Courier* (Thursday, 7 December, 1826): 'Frankfort Papers, to the 12th instant [October], have been received this morning. Under date of St. Petersburgh, September 30, we find the following Order of the Day, issued by Gen. Yermoloff, on the subject of the recent invasion of the Russian territory, in which he pointedly condemns the treachery of the Persians, and exhorts the soldiers under his command, to exert themselves in a manner worthy of their former renown, by proving themselves zealous in the cause of their new Emperor.

---

[209] Shamkirçay.

[210] Qarabagh.

"St. Petersburgh, Sept. 30.—General Yermoloff, Commander in Georgia and the Caucasus, has issued the following Order of the Day respecting the invasion of the Persians:—

"I lately returned from the line of the Caucasus, where I chastised the rebellious Tschetschenzes[211]; but the Persians, with much more insolence and treasury, have dared to make attacks on our army. They have broken the peace, while, on our parts, every means were employed to preserve a good understanding; they broke it at the moment when the Ambassador[212] sent by his Majesty the Emperor[213] to arrange the demarcation of the frontiers was in Persia, and was graciously received by the Schah[214] himself. The Sardar of Erivan[215] has entered our territory with a corps of troops; they plunder and murder, like robbers, the peaceable inhabitants, the subjects of our great Emperor, while others are excited by them to rebellion and treachery. Persian troops have entered Karabasch,[216] and one of the sons of the Schah, Abbas Mirza, receives with kindness the Chans and other traitors who have fled from us, brings them in his train, and promises to reinstate them in their former possessions. I will not speak to you of your valour and intrepidity; you constantly give proofs of them, and when did Russians ever do otherwise? You have, at all times, distinguished yourselves by fidelity to the Emperor, and I now call upon you to give an example, and to display new zeal for your new Sovereign. Have patience, and defend yourselves with firmness. I shall point out to you, brave comrades, the moment when you shall attack the enemies of the Emperor. The Emperor shall be made acquainted with your merits and services, and there are already many in the corps of the Caucasus who have been generously recompensed by the favors of the Emperor.'"

11.85 'Untitled,' *The National Gazette and Literary Register* (Thursday, 7 December, 1826), *The Republican Advocate* (after 14 December, 1826): 'The prompt successes of the Russians in the new war with Persia, animated the attention of the British politicians, to the potency and designs of the colossal Northern power. Bell's Messenger[217] dwells on the subject thus—

"The foreign intelligence of the week embraces some points of particular interest. It appears that Russia has actively engaged in warfare against the Persians; and although it is difficult to understand the nature of the quarrel, and the results to which it may lead, one thing is certain, that the Russian armies are now advancing into the provinces of Persia, and

---

[211] Chechens.

[212] Menshikov.

[213] Nicholas I.

[214] Fath 'Ali Shah.

[215] Hoseyn Qoli Khan Qazvini.

[216] Qarabagh.

[217] *Bell's Weekly Messenger*, a popular British newspaper founded in 1796, partly popular in Britain for its agricultural content. See Goddard (1983).

fighting battles in barbarous places, the names of which we shall not venture to pronounce.'"

11.86 'Latest from England,' *Albany Argus & City Gazette* (Friday, 8 December, 1826) and 'Russia and Persia,' *The Kinderhook Herald* (Thursday, 14 December, 1826): 'The war between Russia and Persia may, it is hinted in one of the London papers, occasion some uneasiness to England. Of this we do not think much.—The ambition of Russia is indeed great as is its military force, which latter must be employed, but Russia, as yet, will not provoke the hostility of England.'

11.87 'Untitled,' *Baltimore Gazette and Daily Advertiser* (Friday, 8 December, 1826) and 'Foreign. From the Baltimore Gazette of Friday,' *The Torch Light and Public Advertiser* (Thursday, 14 December, 1826): 'The Russians have gained another victory over the Persians, and there is little hazard in venturing the prediction that the latter will soon be ready to accept any conditions which may be offered by the former, whether founded in justice or not—The total deficiency of Persia in all those requisites necessary to maintain a war against her powerful opponent, shews a degree of temerity in this aggression not easily accounted for upon the principal of selfpreservation. With the awful example of the ill-fated Poland, standing in bold relief upon the page of history, it seems somewhat surprizing that Persia, single handed, would unnecessarily provoke a power which can annihilate her in a moment—As to the sympathies of mankind on such occasions, it answers but little purpose, being seldom felt and known until the last hope of an expiring nation is crushed by the overwhelming power of its oppressor.'

11.88 'Berlin, Oct. 24,' *The National Gazette and Literary Register* (Friday, 8 and Saturday, 9 December, 1826), 'Berlin, Oct. 24,' *New-York Commercial Advertiser* (Friday, 8 December, 1826), 'Foreign Intelligence. Berlin, Oct. 24,' *Boston Courier* (Saturday, 9 December, 1826), 'Latest from Europe. Berlin, Oct. 24,' *Boston Daily Advertiser* (Saturday, 9 December, 1826), 'Prussia. Berlin, Oct. 24,' *Massachusetts Journal* (Saturday, 9 December, 1826; with minor variations), 'Foreign News. Russia and Persia,' *New-York Observer & Chronicle* (Saturday, 9 December, 1826; to 'river,' and continuing 'From another report'), 'Foreign Intelligence. Russia and Persia,' *Christian Register* (Saturday, 16 December, 1826; to 'river,' and then 'From another report...,' omitting second paragraph) and 'Foreign Items. Berlin, Oct. 24th,' *Vermont Watchman and State Gazette* (Tuesday, 19 December, 1826): 'From a report of General Yermoloff, dated the 24th of September, it seems that Abbas Mirza, after the defeat on the Clanhora, had been joined by Al-Khae [sic, Allah Yar Khan], son-in-law to the Schah,[218] and, with their united forces, amounting to 8000 [9000, *Christian Register*] regular infantry, 15,000 regular, and as many irregular cavalry, and 25 pieces of cannon, had again passed the Terter. Gen.

---

[218] Fath 'Ali Shah.

11 The Second Russo-Persian War and the Treaty of Torkmanchay (1826–1828)   1185

Madatoff had, upon this, joined, in the night of the 21st, Adj.-Gen. Paskevitch, in consequence of which the Persians contented themselves with taking a position on the left bank of the above mentioned river, and were obliged to raise the blockade of Shouchi.

At the same time the brother[219] of the Serdar of Erivan[220] had made an incursion with 3000 cavalry into the plain of Poloria,[221] and driven off a great quantity of cattle; but the troops stationed in those parts recovered the greater part of the booty.[222] The Serdar himself had gone towards Schamshadil,[223] and threatened Kazask, which induced General Yermoloff, as all was quiet on the line of the Caucasus and in the province of Daghestan, to march with three battalions; one of which consisted of Soldiers of the Guard who mutinied,[224] and 400 Cossacks, towards Kazask, in order to protect that district.

From another report of General Yermoloff, it appears that General Paskevitsch was attacked on the 25th of September, by the Persians, to the number of 35,000 men, commanded by Abbas Mirza in person and three of his Sons[225]; but that the assailants, after a short engagement, fled in disorder, leaving behind eleven hundred prisoners, eighty caissons, and a quantity of baggage. The loss of the Russians was fifty killed, among whom is colonel Gretoff,[226] and two hundred and fifty wounded. The enemy was pursued in his flight, and when the latest report was sent off, it was thought that the whole province of Karabasch[227] was already delivered from the Persians. This victory was considered as so important, that the guns were fired at St. Petersburg, and the city illuminated on the occasion.'

---

[219] Hasan Khan.

[220] Hoseyn Qoli Khan Qazvini.

[221] Lori, south of Tiflis.

[222] As Eichwald (1837: 584) wrote, 'Der Generalmajor Dawidoff, der auf der rechten Flanke die Truppen, welche auf der Straße nach Erivan aufgestellt waren, commandirte, griff hier den 21 September die Perser unter Anführung des Hassan Chan, des Bruders des erivan'schen Sserdars, der mit 3000 Reitern in die Steppe von Lori vorgedrungen war, und dort alles Vieh weggetrieben hatte, beim Orte Mirak an, brachte ihnen einen bedeutenden Nachtheil bei, und zerstreute sie nach allen Seiten; hierauf verfolgte er sie noch weiter nach dem Orte Sudagent, 2 kleine Märsche von Erivan entfernt, wo sich der Sserdar einschloß, und seinen Bruder ohne Hülfe ließ; der Sserdar war nämlich gleichzeitig mit ihm in die schamschadil'sche Distanz eingefallen, um dort die Bewohner gegenn die Russen unter die Waffen zu bringen, mußte aber bald unverrichteter Sache in die Festung zurückkehren, um nicht vom General Dawidoff abgeschnitten zu werden.'

[223] Cf. 11.83.

[224] Those guards, mentioned above, who had not initially sworn allegiance to Nicholas I after Alexander's death. Cf. 11.95.

[225] According to Brosset (1857: 324, n. 1), 'Abaz-Mirza, son fils aîné Mahmad-Mirza et son second fils Ismaïl-Mirza, avec Alla-Iar-Khan, commandaient les troupes persanes au nombre de 60,000 hommes; les troupes russes étaient seulement au nombre de 8000 hommes. La victoire fut complète, l'artillerie et les camps ennemis tombèrent au pouvoir du vanqueur.'

[226] Grekov.

[227] Qarabagh.

11.89 'Latest from England,' *New-York Commercial Advertiser* (Friday, 8 December, 1826) and 'Latest from England,' *The Southern Patriot* (Thursday, 14 December, 1826): 'The papers contain accounts of some advantages gained by the Russian General Yermoloff over the Persians. The probability from present appearances is, that the war between those powers will last but a short time.'

11.90 'Latest from England,' *Columbian Centinel* (Saturday, 9 December, 1826): 'A serious war appeared to be raging between Russia and Persia, and a victory over the Persians had been celebrated at St. Petersburg.'

11.91 'Latest from France. Russia,' *Albany Argus* (Monday, 11 December 1826), 'Untitled,' *New-York American* (Tuesday, 12 December, 1826), 'Latest from France. Russia,' *Albany Argus* (Tuesday, 12 December, 1826; '1100' instead of '11,000' privates; cf. 11.97, 11.100), 'Latest from France,' *Boston Courier* (Tuesday, 12 December, 1826; '1100' instead of '11,000' privates; cf. 11.97, 11.100), 'Latest from France. Russia,' *Daily National Journal* (Tuesday, 12 December, 1826; '1100' instead of '11,000' privates; cf. 11.97, 11.100), 'Latest from France,' *Middlesex Gazette* (Wednesday, 13 December, 1826), 'Late from Europe,' *American Sentinel* (Wednesday, 13 December, 1826), 'Latest from France,' *The Virginia Herald* (Wednesday, 13 December, 1826) and 'Foreign. Latest from Continental Europe. From Paris Papers to the 2nd of November, received at New York,' *The Maysville Eagle* (Wednesday, 27 December, 1826): 'Another action took place between the Persians and Russians on the 25th Sept. The latter were attacked near Elizabethpol by the Persians under the command of Abbas Mirza, and his two sons. Their army consisted of 14,000 infantry, about 20,000 cavalry, and 26 pieces of artillery, but after a short action they were completely routed, with the loss of 11,000 privates and a number of officers, and abandoned their baggage.—The Russians had a Cossack Col.,[228] 2 other officers, and 48 privates killed, and 250 wounded. A dispatch from Gen. Yermoloff, announcing this event was received at St. Petersburgh 14th Oct. when an illumination and rejoicings took place.'[229]

11.92 'Foreign Intelligence. [Paris dates to the second November.],' *National Gazette and Literary Register* (Monday, 11 December, 1826), 'Latest from France,' *Alexandria Gazette* (Tuesday, 12 December, 1826), 'Latest from France,' *New-York Commercial Advertiser* (Tuesday, 12 December, 1826), 'Latest from France,' *Rhode-Island American and Providence Gazette* (Tuesday, 12 December, 1826), 'From France,' *Salem Gazette* (Tuesday, 12 December, 1826), 'Latest from France,' *New-York Spectator* (Tuesday, 12 December,

---

[228] Col. Grekov.

[229] This is presumably the engagement about which Lee heard on 9 October, 1826, while in Odessa. 'News of a considerable victory over the Persians, near Hanja [sic, Ganja], and their complete route [sic, rout]. They behaved in the most cowardly manner.' See Lee (1854: 182).

1826), 'London, Tuesday Evening, Nov. 7,' *Boston Commercial Gazette* (Thursday, 14 December, 1826), 'Latest from France,' *American Patriot* (Friday, 15 December, 1826; with minor variations), 'Foreign,' *Portland Advertiser* (Friday, 15 December, 1826; with minor variations), 'Latest from France,' *Charleston Courier* (Saturday, 16 December, 1826; with minor variations), 'Foreign. Latest from France,' *New-Hampshire Statesman* (Saturday, 16 December, 1826; with minor variations), 'Foreign Compendium,' *The Evening Gazette* (Saturday, 16 December, 1826; with minor variations), 'Foreign and Domestic,' *Connecticut Observer* (Monday, 18 December, 1826; with minor variations), 'From France,' *Daily Georgian* (Monday, 18 December, 1826; with minor variations), 'Foreign. Russia,' *Gazette of Maine* (Tuesday, 19 December, 1826; with minor variations), 'From Europe,' *New-Hampshire Republican* (Tuesday, 19 December, 1826), 'Secular Summary. Foreign,' *Boston Recorder* (Friday, 22 December, 1826; with minor variations) and 'Latest from France,' *Augusta Chronicle and Georgia Advertiser* (Saturday, 23 December, 1826; with minor variations): 'Russian Gazettes are filled with accounts of advantages gained by the Russians over the Persians.'

11.93 'Russia and Persia,' *The Freeman's Journal* (Monday, 11 December, 1826) and 'Russia and Persia,' *The Delaware Gazette* (Wednesday, 20 December, 1826): 'The last foreign intelligence having confirmed the report of the commencement of hostilities between Russia and Persia, the following statement of the military force at the disposal of the Emperor Nicholas, may prove of some interest to the reader. The prospect is, that the war will be one of conquest, and that the fair and sunny plains of Persia are destined to be [?] by the hordes of the Autocrat. The military force of Russia, at the death of Alexander, in December last [1825], consisted of the following divisions

Army of the Centre,	240,000
Advanced Guard,	80,000
Army of the Right,	80,000
Army of the Left,	80,000
Garrison Troops,	70,000
Military Colonies,	67,000
Corps of the Caucasus,	65,000
Detailed, Corps of Finland, &c.	45,000
Grand Total,	727,000

With this military force, and a revenue sufficient to maintain it, there is nothing surprising in the jealousy which has arisen in other parts of Europe concerning the future measures of the new Emperor.'

11.94 'From England,' *Baltimore Patriot & Mercantile Advertiser* (Monday 11 December, 1826): 'The Russian Government is taking great pains to prove, by the publication of various official documents, that the war between it and Persia, is entirely the fault of the latter.'

11.95 'Russia and Persia,' *Boston Daily American Statesman* (Monday, 11 December, 1826) and 'Russia and Persia,' *American Statesman and City Register* (Tuesday, 12 December, 1826; 'Russia'): 'Under date of Berlin, Oct. 24, it is stated that Gen. Yermoloff had gained another victory of some importance over the Persians. According to this account, the victory of the Russians was of a most decisive character; but it seems that a battalion of the guards which was sent against the Persians mutinied. Nothing is said of the course adopted to prevent other troops from following the example.'[230]

11.96 'Latest from France,' *Poulson's American Daily Advertiser* (Monday, 11 December, 1826), 'Latest from France,' *Alexandria Gazette* (Tuesday, 12 December, 1826), 'From France,' *Salem Gazette* (Tuesday, 12 December, 1826), 'London, Tuesday Evening, Nov. 7,' *Boston Commercial Gazette* (Thursday, 14 December, 1826) and 'Latest from France,' *Saratoga Sentinel* (Tuesday, 19 December, 1826): 'By advices of the 14th. inst. from St. Petersburgh, we have the following intelligence of the army of Georgia:—Gen. Yermoloff has received a report from Gen. Paskewitch, stating that on the 25th ult. he was attacked at seven wersts from Elizabethpol by the Persians under the command of Abbas Mirza, his two sons[231] and his son-in-law.[232] Their army consisted of 15,000 men of regular infantry, about 20,000 of regular cavalry and irregular infantry, and 26 pieces of artillery [but?] after a short action they were completely routed. The enemy lost 1100 privates and officers made prisoners, 2 khans, 4 colors, 3 cannon, 17 alcones [sic, falconets], and 80 caisons. On our side we had a heretan colonel,[233] two other officers and 43 privates killed, and 9 officers and 240 privates wounded. The enemy abandoned their baggage, and are closely pursued. This intelligence was announced at St. Petersburgh by the ringing of bells and a general illumination. In the action fought on the 14th Sept. [O. S.] Amir Khan, uncle of Abbas Mirza, was killed.'[234]

---

[230] This is a misunderstanding of the guards from St. Petersburg who had participated in the Decembrist revolt against the succession of Nicholas upon Alexander's death, but went on to serve in the Russo-Persian war with distinction. See e.g. Baddeley (1908: 169). Cf. 11.22.

[231] The Persians were commanded on this occasion by 'Abbas Mirza and his sons, Mohammad Mirza and Isma'il Mirza, along with Allah Yar Khan. See Brosset (1857: 324, n. 1).

[232] Fath 'Ali Shah's son-in-law, Allah Yar Khan Qajar Devehlu, not 'Abbas Mirza's. Cf. 11.35, 11.78, 11.88.

[233] 'Heretan' is almost certainly a corruption of the Cossack title *ataman*. See Périn (1820: 180). Cf. the Ukrainian Cossack title *hetman* (see Wagner 1810: 9). The likelihood of such a meaning is increased by the fact that all of the Grekovs listed by Mikaberidze (2005: 138–141) were Don Cossacks. Moreover, an 'Ataman Cossack' regiment was also comprised of Don Cossacks. See Valentini (1829: 389), von Dewall (1885: 464). Hence 'Ataman [heretan] Colonel' would suggest that Grekov commanded a unit of Ataman Cossacks.

[234] Amir Khan Qajar. Brosset (1857: 323) noted that in the defeat of 'Abbas Mirza on 12 O.S./ 24 September 1826, 'Le sardar persan Amir-Khan et 2000 hommes périrent.' According to Eichwald (1837: 582), 'man fand bei ihm [Amir Khan Qajar] einen Koran, in grünen Sammet [velvet] gebunden, 3 schöne Smaragdpetschafte [emerald signets] mit seinem Namenszug und einen schach'schen Firman, 100 schöne Mädchen und 100 Knaben aus Elisabethopol nach Teheran an den Hof des Schachs zu senden.'

11.97 'From France,' *Boston Daily American Statesman and City Register* (Tuesday, 12 December, 1826), 'London, Tuesday Evening, Nov. 7,' *Boston Commercial Gazette* (Thursday, 14 December, 1826) and 'From France,' *Haverhill Gazette & Essex Patriot* (Saturday, 16 December, 1826): 'The Journal de Paris of the 1st of Nov. contains extracts from a private letter from St. Petersburgh, in which it is stated, that an armistice was immediately to take place between the Russians and Persians.[235] It was said that Abbas Mirza, in order to keep up the courage of his soldiers, had circulated the false report that an Ottoman army of 200,000 men had been collected in the plains of Adrianople, and commanded by the Vizier[236] in person, had attacked the Russians [sic] armies of the Danube.'[237]

11.98 'From Late Foreign Journals, Received at this Office. Persia,' *Baltimore Gazette and Daily Advertiser* (Tuesday, 12 December, 1826): 'The Russian army of the Caucassus [sic] is under the command of the General Yermoloff, a brave and indefatigable officer, and who has, for his second in command, a General Williaminoff.[238] The head-quarters of the army is at the city of Tiflis, the ancient capital of Georgia, and the government of which city is administered by an officer by the name of Von Howen, a German by birth, and who is a general officer in the Russian service.[239] The army of the Caucassus [sic] is variously stated in regard to numbers, but may, probably, be set down as amounting to 30,000 men; and they are certainly among the finest troops in the Russian service, being for the greatest part composed of the troops that were at Paris with the Emperor Alexander, and who,

---

[235] This was certainly a false rumor as Russian troop movements and occasional skirmishes, particularly with the Shahsevan nomads, took place in December, 1826, and January, 1827. See Eichwald (1837: 586–590). Cf. Brosset (1857: 325–328).

[236] Benderli Mehmed Selim Pasha.

[237] This, too, was a false rumor.

[238] Alexei Alexandrovich Velyaminov (1785–1838). There were in fact two Velyaminov brothers (the other was Ivan Alexandrovich Velyaminov [1771–1837]), both of whom were generals. As Gamba (1826/2: 145–146) wrote in discussing Ermolov's arrival in the Caucasus, 'il arrivoit en Géorgie précédé d'une haute réputation, et entouré d'un grand nombre d'officiers de mérite. Les deux généraux Williaminoff qui l'accompagnoient, étoient des hommes distingués, l'un dans l'administration militaire, l'autre comme chef d'état-major.' Cf. Gutierrez (1827: 187) who noted that, when Ermolov left Tibilisi to campaign against the rebellious Chechens prior to the outbreak of the Second Russo-Persian War, 'he left his second in command Lieutenant-general Williaminoff, brother to the chief of the staff, intrusted with the care of this province.'

[239] Reinhold Johann Freiherr von der Howen (1775–1861), Lord of Neuhof (Kurland), Major-General in the Russian Imperial Army and father-in-law of Moritz von Kotzebue. See Kotzebue (1984: 253), O'Flynn (2017: 492, n. 61). Gamba (1826/2: 176) wrote, 'Le gouvernement de Tiflis est confié au général Vanhœven, Livonien. Il se distingue par un caractère de bonté et d'affabilité, et accueille de la manière la plus aimable les étrangers qui passent par cette ville, ou qui s'y fixent.' Eichwald (1837: 190), called him the 'Civilgouverneur' von der Howen. In 1836 the Russian Lieutenant-General Johann von Blaramberg met 'den Ober-Quartiermeister Oberst Baron von der Howen' in Tiflis. See Blaramberg (1874: 30).

conceiving most probably that they had imbibed, during their residence in France, *two* [sic] *many free ideas*, sent them to Georgia, to be as much as possible out of the way. Though the pay of the officers is much superior to that of the rest of the Russian army they are very far from being satisfied, as they look on their service as a kind of banishment. The chief of the Etat-Major[240] is Colonel Kotzebue,[241] an officer of Engineers, and son of the celebrated German author.[242] The staff of the army is very numerous, and among it is a number of Georgian Princes, and men of rank of that country, whom the Russian Government are particularly careful of attaching to its interests, and who are often intrusted with the command of the most important posts on the frontiers of the Russian and Persian dominions.

That part of Persia nearest to the Russian possessions, is the province of Erivan, which is under the dominion of an officer named the Sardar[243]—a powerful and warlike Prince, as he may be justly considered, and who, though in a manner subject to and tributary, to, the Schah or King of Persia, is of a very independent and spirited character, and can be just barely said to acknowledge the Persian monarch as his master.

The Sardar of Erivan resides at the town of the same name, a strongly fortified place, and which the Russians will long have cause to remember with regret, they having in former wars been several times repulsed in their attacks on it with heavy losses........

The present Schah or King of Persia is named Futty Ali Schah, a middle-aged man, but much debilitated in health and constitution: his eldest son,[244] and who may be considered as Prince Royal, which title is often given to him, is named Prince Abbas Mirza, a sensible, and, for a Persian, a well informed and liberal thinking man, and possessed of a warlike and matchless spirit; the usual residence of the Prince is at Tabreez, or Tauris, a strongly fortified town, and whose population is stated at 70,000 or 80,000 souls.

It may be remarked here, that the name of Mirza is very differently understood, according as it is placed before or after a name; in the latter case it signifies a prince of the blood royal; and placed before a name signifies nothing more than the English appellation of Mister, or the French Monsieur.

The Persian Ambassador Abool Hassan, who was in England some years since, was, by the Persians called Mirza Abool Hassan; but since his return to Persia the King honoured

---

[240] Chief-of-staff.

[241] Moritz von Kotzebue (1789–1861). Cf. 10.19. See Kotzebue (1819a, b). Eichwald (1834: xvii) thanked him for providing his plan of the fortress of Derbend, 'die er meist selbst während seines Aufenthalts im Kaukasus...an Ort und Stelle aufnahm.'

[242] August von Kotzebue (1761–1819). For his life see von Kotzebue (1827), von Kotzebue (1984). Cf. 11.99.

[243] Hoseyn Qoli Khan Qazvini.

[244] According to Hasan-e Fasa'i 'Abbas Mirza was the fourth son of Fath 'Ali Shah. See Busse (1972: 36).

11   The Second Russo-Persian War and the Treaty of Torkmanchay (1826–1828)   1191

him with the title of Khan, or General[245]; he therefore has dropped the title of Mirza, and is called Abool Hassan Khan, the title in that country being invariably placed after name. This personage is now in a high confidential situation near the King's person, who appears to hold him in great estimation.

Some Italian officers[246] are with the army of the Prince Abbas Mirza, and not a few Russians are also in the ranks of the army; who, preferring the religion of Mahomet to that of the Greek church, and the indulgence of having *more wives* than they could have at home, have thought fit to change both their allegiance and their religion.

The Persians are, in appearance, attached to the English, and dislike the French nation. A Dr. Schultz is now in Persia, on a four years' residence, having been sent out by the French Government for that length of time, at its expense. He is a Prussian [sic, Hessian][247] by birth, and his object, at least his real one, for visiting that country, is not accurately ascertained.[248]

A Major Monteith, of the Madras Engineers, is also at this time in Persia, which he is making extensive surveys of, for the information of the East India Company.'[249] (Fig. 11.2).

11.99 'Latest from France,' *Boston Courier* (Tuesday, 12 December, 1826), 'Foreign Compendium,' *The Evening Gazette* (Saturday, 16 December, 1826), 'From Europe,' *New-Hampshire Republican* (Tuesday, 19 December, 1826; with minor variations), 'Untitled,' *Hampshire Sentinel* (Wednesday, 20 December, 1826; with minor variations), 'Secular Summary. Foreign,' *Boston Recorder* (Friday, 22 December, 1826; with minor variations, omitting words from 'cannon' to 'by') and 'Weekly Compendium. Foreign,' *Columbian Star* (Saturday, 30 December, 1826; with minor variations, to 'route'): 'Letters from Petersburg, of Oct. 14, mention, that cannon were fired, and the city was illuminated, on occasion of a new advantage obtained on the 25th September, by Gen. Paskevitch, who, at the distance of a few leagues from Elizabethpol, beat the Persian army, commanded by Abbas Mirza, 15,000 men strong of regular infantry, about 20,000 irregular cavalry and

---

[245] As Hasan-e Fasa'i noted, in 1825, 'Haji Mirzā Abu'l-Ḥasan Khān, the ambassador, was granted the title "minister of the foreign powers" (vazir-e doval-e khāreja).' See Busse (1972: 172).

[246] According to Anonymous (1826n: 732) = Anonymous (1848: 1052 = 11.132 below). Lt. Bernardi, cf. 11.14, was the only Italian in 'Abbas Mirza's service after the departure of Rubino (Gian Battista) Ventura. Cf. Anonymous (1826d).

[247] Friedrich Eduard Schulz (1799–1829) was born in Gießen, in Hesse, and educated in Göttingen, in Lower Saxony (Niedersachsen), and Paris. See Potts (2017b: 249).

[248] German philologist who is mainly remembered for his documentation of Urartian inscriptions. For his career and achievements see Potts (2017b).

[249] William Monteith (1790–1864), long-serving officer in the Madras Engineers whose Persian service began in 1809/10 with Malcolm's first mission. Thereafter he stayed to help train 'Abbas Mirza's army, fought in the First Russo-Persian War and fulfilled various other roles as well. See Chichester (1894).

Fig. 11.2 'Capt.ⁿ Monteith, of the E.C. Artillery serving in Persia. 1813,' by James Justinian Morier. Pencil on paper. Balliol College Archives Morier-N03-04-051

infantry, and 26 pieces of artillery. According to the report of Gen. Yermaloff, after a short engagement, the Persians were completely defeated and put to route [sic]. They lost 1100 soldiers and officers prisoners, 2 khans, 4 standards, 3 cannon, 1 falconet and 80 caissons. The Russians lost 43 soldiers killed, and 240 officers and soldiers wounded. The Persians, who had abandoned their baggage, were closely pursued, and there was reason to believe that the entire province of Carabagh was delivered from invasion.'

11.100 'Latest from England,' *New-Hampshire Gazette* (Tuesday, 12 December, 1826): 'The papers contain the Russian official declaration of war against Persia; and also a statement of the successes of the former against the latter. The victory had been celebrated by a fete at St. Petersburg. The Persians were commanded by Abbot [sic, 'Abbas] Mirza, the son, and Alliar Khan, the son-in-law, of the Persian King[250]; and the Russian corps commanded by Generals Yermoloff, Madstoff [sic, Madatov] and Paskevitch. The report of the victory states, that Gen. Paskevitch was attacked on the 25th September, by 35,000 Persians under Prince Mirza, but that after a short conflict, the latter fled in disorder, 1100 men taken prisoners, and loosing 80 waggons; and that the Russians had pursued the enemy thrugh the province of Karabosch.[251] The Russian loss is stated to have been Col. Grotoff [sic, Grekov], and 50 others killed, and 250 wounded.'

11.101 'Latest from Europe. Russia and Persia,' *Columbian Centinel* (Wednesday, 13 December, 1826) and 'Later. Turkey and Russia,' *The Farmers' Cabinet* (Saturday, 16 December, 1826): 'The accounts of the success of the Russians in the new war with the Persians, are confirmed in these papers, with reports of the continued triumph of the Russian arms, and the prospect that the war will be a short one, and the fruits of it be the addition of a number of the fair and fertile provinces of Persia, to the overgrown Empire of the Czars. Rejoicings had taken place at Moscow and St. Petersburgh, on account of the successes.'

11.102 'Summary,' *Hallowell Gazette* (Wednesday, 13 December, 1826): 'The Russian generals Yermoloff, Madstoff, and Paskevitch had gained a victory over Abbot Mirza, the son, and Alliar Khan, the son-in-law of the Persian king.[252] 1100 Persians were made prisoners. The Russians had 50 killed and 250 wounded.'

11.103 'Latest from Europe,' *Massachusetts Spy* (Wednesday, 13 December, 1826): 'The Russian papers are filled with accounts of new successes gained by their army over the Persians.'

11.104 'Russia and Persia,' *Massachusetts Spy* (Wednesday, 13 December, 1826): 'The Continental papers afford numerous articles of war-events in the rupture between Persia and Russia, and that the news of a victory by the troops of the latter had been celebrated by a fete in St. Petersburgh.—The Persians, they say, were commanded by Abbas Mirza, the son, and Alliar Khan, the son-in-law, of the Persian King[253]; and the Russian corps commanded by Generals Yermoloff, Madstoff and Paskevitch. The report of the victory states, that Gen. Paskevitch was attacked on the 25th September, by 35,000 Persians under Prince Mirza, but that after a short conflict the latter fled in disorder, 1100 men taken prisoners, and losing 80 wagons; and that the Russians had pursued their enemy through

---

[250] Fath 'Ali Shah.
[251] Qarabagh.
[252] Fath 'Ali Shah.
[253] Fath 'Ali Shah.

the province of Karabosch. The Russian loss is stated to have been Col. Grotoff [sic, Grekov], and 50 others killed, and 250 wounded.'

11.105 'Russia and Persia,' *National Aegis* (Wednesday, 13 December, 1826) and 'Russia and Persia,' *The Republican Monitor* (Wednesday, 3 January, 1827): 'Official information of the declaration of war, by the Emperor of Russia[254] against the Persians has been communicated to the Government of the United States.[255] The cause of the commencement of hostilities is said to be, the invasion of the Russian empire by an army commanded by the heir apparent of the crown of Persia. The troubles following the death of the late Alexander and the accession of the reigning prince, present an occasion for making or attempting, a dismemberment of the great empire of the North which was treacherously embraced. The disturbances in Russia were quenched by the effusion of a little blood, and the suppression of a powerful conspiracy, and her almost numberless armies were left at liberty to fall on the assailant. Intelligence has been received of several battles, but the claims of the warriors are beyond the power of expression, unless they are contained in the lamentation of the noble poet of England.'[256]

11.106 'Foreign. England,' *Norwich Courier* (Wednesday, 13 December, 1826): 'Commercial letters from Tiflis, in Georgia, of Sept. last, received at Moscow, mention a report in circulation, that an armistice would shortly be concluded between the Russians and Turks. If this be true it must be through fear, and then the Persians will doubtless soon offer terms of peace. It is said that the Abbas Mirza has spread a rumor that 200,000 Turks, commanded by the Grand Vizier[257] at Adrianople, have attacked the Russians.'

11.107 'Latest from France. Russia,' *Richmond Enquirer* (Thursday, 14 December, 1826): 'General Yermoloff has gained two splendid victories over the Persians. Amir Khan, the uncle of Abbas Mirza, was killed in a battle on the 14th Sept. The Persians loss was considerable. On the 25th Sept. another victory was gained over the Persians, commanded by Abbas Mirza, and his two sons.'[258]

11.108 'Untitled,' *The Republican Advocate* (after 14 December, 1826), 'Latest from Europe,' *New-York Commercial Advertiser* (Tuesday, 19 December, 1826), 'Latest from Europe,' *National Advocate* (Wednesday, 20 December, 1826), 'Foreign Intelligence.

---

[254] Nicholas I.

[255] As noted above, by a note from the Russian chargé d'affaires, Baron von Maltitz, to Henry Clay, Secretary of State. Cf. 11.83.

[256] There follows a seemingly bowdlerized version of verses 14–15 of Canto VII from Byron's *Don Juan*, clearly diverging from the main text.

[257] Benderli Mehmed Selim Pasha.

[258] Mohammad Mirza and Isma'il Mirza. Cf. 11.96.

From Paris Papers received at this Office,' *National Gazette and Literary Register* (Wednesday, 20 December, 1826; with minor variations), 'By Last Evening's Mail. From the New-York Commercial Advertiser, Dec. 19. Latest from Europe,' *Alexandria Gazette* (Friday, 22 December, 1826), 'Latest from Europe,' *New-York Spectator* (Friday, 22 December, 1826), 'Latest from France,' *The National Intelligencer* (Saturday, 23 December, 1826), 'Constantinople, Oct. 16,' *American and Commercial Daily Advertiser* (Saturday, 23 December, 1826), 'Translated from the Constitutionnel, of November 15,' *Newport Mercury* (Saturday, 23 December, 1826), 'Foreign. Europe. Constantinople, Oct. 16,' *Boston Commercial Gazette* (Saturday, 23 December, 1826), 'Latest from Europe,' *American Mercury* (Tuesday, 26 December, 1826), 'Translated from the Constitutionnel of Nov. 15,' *The Cayuga Patriot* (Wednesday, 27 December, 1826) and 'Latest from France Constantinople, Oct. 16,' *Charleston Courier* (Thursday, 27 December, 1826): 'The Nuremberg Correspondent announces that, independently of the Infantry Division, & the 20,000 Cossacks, which marched at the news of the attack by the Persians, several other corps of the First Army, under the command of Gen. Sacken,[259] had set out for the theatre of war.'

11.109 'Late from France,' *Essex Register* (Thursday, 14 December, 1826): 'The Russian Gazettes are filled with accounts of advantages gained by the Russians over the Persians. On the 25th Sept. a severe action was fought. The Persians lost 1100 prisoners, 4 colors, 3 cannon and 80 caissons. Their army consisted of 15,000 infantry and 20,000 cavalry. The Russians lost, by their official report, 43 privates killed, and 9 officers and 240 privates wounded. The Persians abandoned their baggage, and were closely pursued.'

11.110 'Latest from Europe. Russia and Persia,' *American Traveller* (Friday, 15 December, 1826): 'The accounts of the success of the Russians in the new war with the Persians, are confirmed in these papers, with reports of the continued triumph of the Russian arms, and the prospect that the war will be a short one, and the fruits of it be the addition of a number of fair and fertile provinces to the overgrown Empire of the Czars. Rejoicings had taken place at Moscow and St. Petersburgh, on account of the success.'

---

[259] Major General Dmitry Yerofeyevich Freiherr von der Osten-Sacken (1789–1881). A highly decorated, long-serving Russian-Baltic German cavalry officer. Anonymous (1855a: 281) reported, 'Als Paskewitsch in dem Kriege gegen Persien an die Spitze der russischen Truppen gestellt wurde, machte er Osten-Sacken zu seinem Stabschef. Dieser erhielt auch selbstständige Kommando's im Felde, wie er namentlich Achalkalaki und eine minder bedeutende Festung einnahm. In der entscheidenden Schlacht am Araxes, welche das persische Heer vernichtete, stand der link russische Flügel unter seiner Obhut.' Moreover, when 'Abbas Mirza eventually sued for peace, 'wurde eine interimistische Regierung für die Provinz Adsherbidsan, unter dem Vorsitze des Generalmajors Barons Ostensacken unter anderer Personen, niedergesetzt.' See Eichwald (1837: 605). He later served in the Russo-Turkish War of 1828–1829, though he was relieved of his command for failing to pursue the retreating Ottoman forces after the battle of Milli-diouz. See Baddeley (1908: 191, 219).

11.111 'Russia and Persia,' *Eastern Argus* (Friday, 15 December, 1826): 'The Russian minister at Washington, the Baron de Maltitz,[260] has transmitted to the Secretary of State,[261] the Russian Declaration of War, against the Persians, together with the first bulletin of the army, with which his excellency expressed a conviction "that the cabinet of Washington will partake of the indignation which must be excited by an attack so perfidious, a violation so flagrant, of all the principles of the laws of nations."'

11.112 'Specks of War,' *Yeoman's Gazette* (Saturday, 16 December 1826): 'The most important recent foreign news is the formal declaration of War between Russia and Persia, which took place on the 28th September. It seems that good friendship has not for some time past existed between these nations, and that the latter has become treacherous. A formal battle was fought on the 24th Sept. and a decided victory obtained by the Russian General, Yermaloff, over the Persian commander, Abbas Mirza.—The Russian loss was 50 killed and 250 wounded, and they took upwards of 1000 Persians, prisoners. This war is considered, among the politicians of Europe, an important occurrence. Should Russia push her conquests through Persia, as she is sufficiently able to do, it will introduce her hardy sons into a country, having a luxuriant soil and mild climate, and which they will not willingly give up. In the event of a war with England, she might easily become master of the wealth of the Indies which is now in the possession of the British government.—The great military and political power of Russia is looked upon by the European powers with jealousy, and an increase of it, with alarm.'

11.113 'Russia and Persia,' *The Corrector* (Saturday, 16 December, 1826): 'The accounts from St. Petersburgh, relative to the war with Persia, speak with confidence of the Russian armies. Under date of Berlin, Oct. 24, we find that Gen. Yermoloff has gained a victory of some importance, which has been celebrated by illuminations and rejoicings at St. Petersburgh.'

11.114 'Foreign News,' *Nantucket Inquirer* (Saturday, 16 December, 1826): 'Great rejoicings took place in the latter city [St. Petersburg] on the 14th Oct. in consequence of a victory gained by the Russian army over the Persians on the 25th September.'

11.115 'Foreign. Latest from France,' *New-Hampshire Statesman* (Saturday, 16 December, 1826), 'Foreign and Domestic,' *Connecticut Observer* (Monday, 18 December, 1826) and 'Latest from France,' *Augusta Chronicle and Georgia Advertiser* (Saturday, 23 December, 1826): 'The Russian papers are filled with accounts of fresh advantages gained by the Russians over the Persians.'

---

[260] Cf. 11.83.

[261] Henry Clay. Cf. 11.83.

11 The Second Russo-Persian War and the Treaty of Torkmanchay (1826–1828)

11.116 'Foreign Intelligence. Constantinople, Oct. 17,' *Poulson's American Daily Advertiser* (Saturday, 16 December, 1826; with minor variations), 'Very Late from England. Constantinople, Oct. 17,' *Alexandria Gazette* (Monday, 18 December, 1826), 'Constantinople, Oct. 17,' *Charleston Courier* (Saturday, 23 December, 1826), 'Constantinople, Oct. 17,' *The Charleston Mercury, and Morning Advertiser* (Saturday, 23 December, 1826) and 'Very Late from England. New York, December 14. Constantinople, October 17,' *Macon Telegraph* (Tuesday, 2 January, 1827): 'The Envoy of Persia, Dand-Aga,[262] publishes daily the most favorable news respecting the Persians. They are up to the 12th of September. He announces among other things, though not at all likely, that desertion has been very general among the Cossacks.'[263]

11.117 'From France,' *Southern Patriot* (Saturday, 16 December, 1826): 'Accounts from St. Petersburg state, the Russians have obtained a victory over the Persians. A force of 25,000 men under Abbas Merza had been defeated by the Russian Gen. Paskevitch, near Elizabethpol.'

11.118 'Foreign Intelligence,' *The Greene County Republican* (Wednesday, 20 December, 1826): 'The Armenian Persian, David Zadour,[264] had arrived at Constantinople. The object of his mission is said to be to induce the Porte to join Persia against Russia.

11.119 'Europe,' *Hallowell Gazette* (Wednesday, 20 December, 1826): 'The Russian papers are filled with accounts of their victories over the Persians.'

11.120 'Foreign Intelligence. From Paris Papers received at this Office,' *National Gazette and Literary Register* (Wednesday, 20 December, 1826): 'The Journal du Commerce of the 14th has the following paragraph:—Unfavorable reports are circulating at Constantinople, as to the attempts of the Russians in their quarrels with Persia.'

11.121 'Latest from Europe,' *Baltimore Gazette and Daily Advertiser* (Thursday, 21 December, 1826), 'Latest from France,' *Poulson's American Daily Advertiser* (Thursday, 21 December, 1826), 'Foreign Compendium,' *The Evening Gazette* (Saturday, 23 December, 1826; to 'enemy'), 'Latest from France,' *Providence Patriot & Columbian Phenix* (Saturday, 23 December, 1826; to 'enemy'), 'Russia,' *Massachusetts Journal* (Saturday, 23 December, 1826; 'with minor variations), 'Foreign News. Russia and Persia,' *New-York Observer & Chronicle* (Saturday, 23 December, 1826; with minor variations, to 'enemies' rather than 'enemy'), 'Foreign and Domestic,' *Connecticut Observer* (Monday, 25 December, 1826; to 'enemies' rather than 'enemy'), 'Latest from France,' *Centinel of*

---

[262] Cf. 11.66. This is Dawud Khan Malekshh Nazar, known as Daud Agha or Daud Khan.
[263] A completely false rumor.
[264] Cf. 11.66, 11.119.

Freedom (Tuesday, 26 December, 1826), 'By the Mails. Foreign News,' *Massachusetts Spy* (Wednesday, 27 December, 1826; to 'enemy'), 'Latest from France,' *Southern Patriot* (Wednesday, 27 December, 1826; to 'enemy'), 'Foreign. From Europe. Russia,' *Rhode Island Republican* (Thursday, 28 December, 1826), 'From France,' *Daily Georgian* (Friday, 29 December, 1826; to 'enemy') and 'Foreign News,' *The Free Press* (Wednesday, 3 January, 1826 [sic, 1827]): 'Accounts from the frontiers of Poland of 26th [25th, *Free Press*] October, state that besides the 20,000 Cossacks, and the division of infantry which have proceeded to the frontiers of Persia, many other corps have received orders to place themselves under the command of Field Marshal Sacken.[265] It is the intention of the Emperor of Russia[266] to settle matters with the Persians in one battle; but it is thought that it will take two campaigns, as the season has so far advanced. It is also said that the Russian soldiers have more to struggle against, from the want of provisions, than from the enemy....Reports were current at Constantinople unfavourable to the Russians in their contest with Persia. The captain Pacha arrived there on the 17th of October.'

11.122 'Russia and Persia,' *Christian Mirror* (Friday, 22 December, 1826): 'The National Journal contains a communication from the Baron de Malttitz, Russian minister at Washington, to the Secretary of State,[267] in which are several documents, and among them a manifesto, setting forth the causes of declaration of war by Russia against Persia. From this it appears that in the last war between Russia and Persia, several Persian provinces, inhabited by Mahometans, were conquered by Russia, and finally ceded to her by the treaty of Gulistan, in 1813. It is said that the Persians have never fully complied with the terms of this treaty, though they professed to do so; and the recent invasion of these provinces by Abbas Mirza, the heir to the Persian throne, is represented to be unprovoked by Russia, and a wanton violation of the treaty of Gulistan. From other sources, however, we learn that the Mahometan population of these provinces disliked their Christian masters, complained of the aggression and insults of the Russian soldiery, and caused such an excitement among the Mussulmans, that the court of Teheran, contrary to its inclinations, and to a prudent policy, permitted an army, animated by hatred to the Russians, to march into the ceded provinces. This was enough for Russia—the Persians were met and defeated; the war has been carried in their own territory; and another large slice of the Persian king's dominions will probably pay the forfeit of his temerity.'

---

[265] Cf. 11.109.
[266] Nicholas I.
[267] Henry Clay. Cf. 11.83.

11 The Second Russo-Persian War and the Treaty of Torkmanchay (1826–1828)

11.123 'Constantinople, Oct. 16,' *The National Intelligencer* (Saturday, 23 December 1826), 'Turkey. Constantinople, Oct. 16,' *Massachusetts Journal* (Saturday, 23 December, 1826; 'Turkey') and 'Latest from France. Constantinople, Oct. 16,' *Charleston Courier* (Thursday, 27 December, 1826): 'The Persian Envoy[268] constantly sets abroad reports favorable to the Persian troops.'

11.124 'Gleanings from Late English Papers. With Passing Comments. The Russo-Persian Army,' *The National Intelligencer* (Saturday, 23 December, 1826), 'From Late English Papers. The Russo-Persian Army,' *Poulson's American Daily Advertiser* (Tuesday, 26 December, 1826) and 'From Late English Papers. The Russo-Persian Army,' *Connecticut Mirror* (1 January, 1827): 'The Army of the Caucasus is commanded by General Yermoloff, a skilful officer, whose second in command is General Williaminoff. The number of the army is stated at 30,000 men. Its head quarters is Tiflis, the ancient Capital of Georgia. This army is composed of the best troops in the Russian service, chiefly consisting of the troops who accompanied the Emperor Alexander to Paris, who, it is supposed, sent them to Georgia, in order that the new ideas and manners which they had acquired in their expedition to France, might not make them troublesome. The officers are said not to be satisfied with their banishment, although their pay is somewhat higher than the other officers of the Russian army. The chief of the *Etat Major* is Col. Kotzebue, son of the German Dramatist,[269] and, we believe, the author of an interesting volume of Travels through Persia.[270] The Staff of the army comprises many Georgian Princes, with whom it has always been the policy of the Emperor Alexander to be on harmonious terms, and to whom are often entrusted important commands.'

11.125 'Gleanings from Late English Papers. With Passing Comments. Persia,' *The National Intelligencer* (Saturday, 23 December, 1826), 'From Late English Papers. Persia,' *Poulson's American Daily Advertiser* (Tuesday, 26 December, 1826), 'From Late English Papers. Persia,' *Connecticut Mirror* (1 January, 1827) and 'From the New York American: Persia,' *The Genius of Liberty* (Tuesday, 9 January 1827): 'The Schah, or King of Persia, is named Futty Ali Schah. He is an aged and decrepid monarch. His son, who is looked upon in the light of a Prince Royal, is named Abbas Mirza. He is a shrewd and discerning personage; very warlike in his dispositions; and has introduced, or endeavored to introduce, the European mode of warfare among the Persians. To this end he employs a Persian named Mahomet Ally,[271] who was sent to England, many years since, to gain instruction in the

---

[268] Dawud Khan Malekshah Nazar. Cf. 11.66.
[269] August von Kotzebue.
[270] Kotzebue (1819a, b).
[271] Mohammad 'Ali Chakhmaqsaz. For his full name see Atai (1992: 23).

Mechanic Arts.[272] This man has the charge of the Royal Arsenal at Tabreez,[273] a fortified

---

[272] Anonymous (1826p: 627) wrote, 'At Tabreez, also, resides an Englishwoman, a native of London, the daughter of an eminent gun-maker, who is married to a Persian of the name of Mahomet Ali, who was sent to England some years since by Prince Abbas Mirza, to learn some of the English mechanical arts, and who since his return to Persia has been intrusted with the superintendence of the arsenal of the Prince, who has also in his employ a Scotsman, formerly a private in the royal artillery, who accompanied Sir Gore Ouseley in his embassy to Persia, and who superintends the construction of the carriages for the artillery, and the casting of brass ordnance.' Capt. Joseph D'Arcy (1780–1848), who in 1815 accompanied Mohammad 'Ali and five other Persian students sent to England by 'Abbas Mirza, called him 'a smith, to learn to make locks.' See Green (2016: 3). As Atai (1992: 45) noted, 'Muhammad 'Ali Chakhmaqsaz, who was an artisan and had the lowest social background in the group, learned locksmithing and gunsmithing. He took an English bride and thus became the first Iranian student to do so. Upon return, he was granted the title of *Khan* in part thanks to his wife who was allowed by the king to mix with the ladies of the court. Later he was put in charge of the royal foundry in Tehran.' Floor (2003b: 260) called him 'the only real artisan (he was a gun-smith) among the students whom 'Abbas Mirza had sent to Europe.'

[273] Fraser (1826: 309) described the condition of the armory noting, 'The operations we saw in progress were not calculated to inspire more respect. In one place we observed two men casting musket-bullets; in another, about a hundred muskets in preparation…In the chief room there were a few hundred rounds of cannister-shot, with some English shrapnel and other shells. The whole bore a greater resemblance to a gentleman's shooting-closet, furnished with specimens of various warlike instruments, than to the arsenal of a prince carrying on war against a powerful neighbour. It would indeed have been unreasonable to expect more important results from the limited means that were applied to these operations. As an instance, I may mention that we heard the chief of the gunsmith's department, requiring money, was furnished with four hundred tomauns, or about 220*l*. sterling, for the purpose of expediting a certain number of fire-arms. The whole sum was quickly expended in materials. A short time afterwards, he was called upon to deliver all the arms that were ready. The chief gunsmith himself waited on the prince to inform him, not only that none were ready, but that none could be furnished until more money should be supplied. "More money!" exclaimed the prince; "why, what have you done with all that great sum I gave you the other day?"' Perkins (1843: 149) noted, 'There is an armory in the citadel at Tabréez, where small arms and cannon are very well manufactured. The Persians may in general be said to be enterprising and imitative, though not very inventive. Their skill in imitation may be illustrated by an instance. On a fine brace of pistols being shown at Tabréez, by an English officer, a Persian gunsmith (who had visited England) declared that he could make as good pistols, and those so nearly resembling the Englishman's, that the latter would be unable to point out the difference. A wager was laid; the Persian took one of the pistols home with him as a model, and not long afterwards brought back *two*, and presented them to the officer, who, to be sure, could not tell which was his own, until he found on one of them a small Roman *letter*, in the name of the English artizan, *inverted*. The Persian, not knowing the meaning or the use of the *mark*, had made that slight mistake, in his effort at imitation.' This facility for imitation was not solely a function of the Mohammad 'Ali's having learned his trade in England. Scott Waring (1807: 32) remarked on 'a very able gun-smith, who made pistols nearly equal to those in Europe,' when he visited Shiraz who was later visited by Sir William Ouseley who wrote, 'I went to see the manufactory of fire-arms at the house of *Badr*…famous throughout Persia for his skill in imitating the guns and pistols made by our most excellent European artists. Some of the fowling-pieces which he had just finished, bore every appearance of admirable English workmanship. But his ingenuity only served to impoverish him; for he was chiefly employed by the very great men, whose orders he dared not refuse, yet from whom he found it difficult to obtain, and impossible to enforce, payment.' See Ouseley (1821: 58).

town, containing 80,000 inhabitants, the residence of Abbas Mirza. There is also a Scotchman in the employment of the Prince, who was formerly a private in the English Artillery service.[274] There are many Italian[275] and Russian Officers in the Persian army.[276] The Ambassador Aboul Hassan, who was in England several years since, has since been advanced to the rank of Khan,[277] or General, is a great favorite of the King, and holds a situation of great importance about the person of his Majesty.'

11.126 'Latest from France,' *New-Hampshire Gazette* (Tuesday, 26 December, 1826): 'Letters from Bucharest of Oct. 22, state, that Constantinople, at the last accounts was tranquil…Reports were in circulation that the Russians had been defeated several times by the Persians. This was doubted.'

11.127 'London, Oct. 9. Russia and Persia,' *Boston Daily Advertiser* (Wednesday, 27 December, 1826): 'We have received the following important official intelligence from St. Petersburgh, relative to the war now subsisting between Russia and Persia:

Official Article.
St. Petersburgh. Oct. 4 (16).—The accounts received from Major General Prince Menzikoff, since his return to Tiflis, furnish highly interesting information respecting the circumstances which induced the Court of Teheran suddenly to attack Russia. We annex these accounts as the Prince has given them: and if the declaration of the Cabinet of St. Petersburgh had not already proved that the aggression of the Persians is distinguished by a degree of injustice and perfidy of which it would be difficult to find a more melancholy example, the following details would suffice to make Europe appreciate the generous frankness with which Russia has constantly acted towards Persia, and the entirely foreign and deplorable causes which have drawn the Schah[278] into a war, at a moment when, on the one hand, the most friendly policy, and, on the other, the great interests of his Empire, imperiously called on him to maintain peace. We have had occasion to announce, that after having been received and treated with great respect at Tauris by Prince Abbas Mirza, Prince Menzikoff left that city to proceed to the camp of the Schah, at Sultania. On the road he was suddenly passed by Abbas Mirza, who proceeded thither with all possible speed. This unexpected journey, the haste with which it was made, the reports of war with which it was accompanied, could not but strike Prince Menzikoff. In fact, when he reached Sultania, he found that war was resolved upon. We annex his despatches.* [* Prince Menzikoff's

---

[274] James Dawson. Cf. 11.14, 11.132.
[275] Only Bernardi. Cf. 11.14, 11.132.
[276] Cf. 10.205 for the presence of a few Russian officers in 'Abbas Mirza's forces. Most of the deserters were common soldiers, however, not officers.
[277] Cf. 11.99.
[278] Fath 'Ali Shah.

couriers were stopped by the Persian Government, and he could not send the series of his despatches till he reached Tiflis.]

"Sultania, July 3 (15).—The principal Minister of the Schah is Alaiar Khan,[279] by birth a Kadjar, the son in law of his Sovereign, and brother in law of Abbas Mirza, who has married his sister. He bears the title of Assefout-Dovle, which title was created for him.[280] The other Ministers are dependent on him, and all the decisions of the Schah pass through his hands.

"However, Alaiar Khan's want of knowledge in business has obliged him to have recourse to the other ministers, in the transactions with Foreign Powers; and they, especially Mirza-Aboul Hassan-Khan, and Mirza Abdoul-Wehab,[281] have attempted to profit by this circumstance, to ruin him, by proving to the Sultan[282] his incapacity, and offering at the same time to prove that he had robbed the Exchequer of 30,000 tomans. The ruin of Alaiar Khan was about to be decided, when he found a resource in extreme measures; war afforded them. He joined with the Seid of Kerbelay,[283] in whom he found a supporter. On the other hand, he sent for Abbas Mirza, who repaired, full gallop, to Sultania, to support his brother in law. The Mollahs preached a religious war, and inflamed the people; and Alaiar Kahn [sic, Khan] produced pretended petitions from the discontented in our provinces, inviting the Persians to their assistance; and Abbas Mirza insisted on the opportunity for war. The Schah, fearing his sons, the Mollahs, and the people, yielded, notwithstanding his aversion to war; and Alaiar Khan is at the height of his power.

"The troops were ordered to march towards our frontiers, and the appeal of the Mollahs to the people was despatched to all the provinces, to be read in the Mosques.

"All these resolutions were taken and executed during my journey from Tauris to Sultania, where I arrived under very unfavorable auspices.

"In these circumstances, the only useful end I can aim at is to gain time, that the Authorities in Georgia may be able to repulse [?] aggression; but I have little hope of protracting the negociation about the frontiers for they are here resolved to continue it merely for form's sake, to make extravagant pretensions, and to break it off when I reject what cannot be accepted.

"Sultania, July 3 (15).—My arrival at Sultania has terminated the civilities of the Persians towards me. My tent is surrounded with guards, who prevent all communication. At the public audience which the Schah granted me, they affected not to pay me the honours which are usually shown [?] to the Charge d'Affaires who reside at this Court,

---

[279] Allah Yar Khan Qajar Devehlu.

[280] As Hasan-e Fasaʻi noted, 'For the administration of important affairs, Allah Yar Khan-e Qājār Devehlu, a mighty emir and distinguished by being the son-in-law of the shah, was appointed prime minister. He was addressed by the title "Āsaf od-Doula."' See Busse (1972: 172).

[281] Cf. 11.22. Chancellor (Moʻtammad od-Doula) since 1809 and, like Mirza Abu'l Hassan Khan, an opponent of the Second Russo-Persian War. See Busse (1972: 131, 175–176).

[282] Mahmud II.

[283] Mojtahed Aqa Seiyed Mohammad of Karbala'. Cf. 11.35.

though the ceremony of my reception was regulated beforehand. According to this, the Schah was to take from my hands the Emperor's[284] letter, and I had positive assurance, twice repeated, that he would do so; yet, when I presented it to him, he would not take it, but made a sign with his hand that I should lay it on a cushion. Now, according to the custom of the country, this was want of respect to the Emperor. This proceeding was excused on the pretext of misunderstanding, but was done at the instigation of Abbas Mirza, who, always yielding to the impulse of the moment, wishes, in his warlike ardour, to push things to extremity.

"Sultania, July 5 (17.)—This morning I had a conference with the Ministers of the Schah, in which Alaiar Khan presided, and he alone spoke. He renewed strange pretensions, particularly insisting on the restoration of the Coast of Lake Goktcha.[285] I opposed to this the letter of the Prince Royal to General Yermoloff, by which he consented to give up this coast to us, in exchange for the track between the Kapan and the Kapanktchay. He answered that the Schah had never given his consent or approbation to such an exchange, and that it was inadmissible.

"I observed that this change of intention was not known to the Emperor when I left St. Petersburgh, and, consequently, my instructions could not mention a fact of later note, but that I would immediately apply to my Government for new orders. The Minister found nothing to object, and only said, that as the Schah was going to set out for Ardebil, I should be furnished with means to return to Tiflis, and the negociations might be continued in some frontier town which should be agreed upon for holding [the?] conferences.

"The Prince Royal is gone this morning to assemble troops on our frontiers of Karabag. He fancies himself already in possession of Tiflis, and dictating terms to Russia. Indulging in the most flattering hopes, his presumption is quite childish. He compares himself to Tamerlane, and Nadir Schah.

"Sultania, July 9 (21.)—The Prince Royal sent a courier from Mina[286] to his brother-in-law, Alaiar Khan, to desire him to save the appearance of a first aggression. It has consequently been decided, in a Meeting held at the Minister's, to propose to me to terminate the differences respecting the frontiers, according to the stipulations of the Treaty of Gulistan, giving them a meaning which I could not adopt.

"This resolution being adopted, Alaiar Khan transmitted to me the annexed note, passing over the proposal I had made to him on the 5th and without mentioning the resumption of the negociations in a frontier town, to which he had before assented. My answer is also enclosed. † [† In the conference of the 5th (17th), Prince Menzikoff, knowing that war was resolved upon, and not willing that the absolute rejection of even an inadmissable proposal should afford Persia a pretext for hostilities, declared, as he says, that he would ask for fresh instructions, and would agree to Alaiar Khan's proposal, to

---

[284] Nicholas I.

[285] Gökçe (Sevan). Cf. Alexander (1827: 271).

[286] Mianeh, roughly halfway between Tabriz and Zanjan.

resume the negotiations in a frontier town. Yet, on the 7th (19th) Alaiar Khan sent him a note, in which, passing over all that had preceded, or supporting by any proofs the vague accusation which he made against the authorities on the frontiers of Georgia, of not having shewn a conciliatory spirit in the differences between the two States, he declared that the Schah would never resume the negotiations, except on the basis of the treaty of Gulestan, haughtily requiring Prince Menzikof to say whether Russia would agree to this, adding, that if it did not, the Court of St. Petersburgh could not justly complain of what Persia might in the sequel resolve.

Prince Menzikoff's answer was very simple and judicious. He merely recapitulated what had been done by the Emperor of Russia—the consent given by Persia to the exchange of territory (mentioned in the Russian declaration of war)—and the wish of his Majesty the Emperor to maintain peace, and to consult the interest of Persia. The Persian Minister did not receive this note till the 30th of Aug. (11th Sept.) when Prince Menzikoff was mounting his horse to leave the territory occupied by the enemy, and to join our troops. In his answer the Persian Minister held out a hope of the acceptance of the proposal to negotiate in a frontier town, and says not a word of six weeks' flagrant hostilities and open war—of the violation of our territory by an armed force—of the invasion of our provinces beyond Elizabethpol—and of the insurrection excited in all the neighbouring countries among the Mahometan subjects of the Emperor. It would be difficult to imagine a more flagrant instance of bad faith.]

"I have sent a copy to Aboul Hassan-Khan, that he may communicate the contents to the Schah.

"Sultania, July 8 (21).—Mr. Willock, the English Charge d'Affaires,[287] came to see me this evening, and told me the Schah had sent to him to ask him to speak to me on the means of avoiding a rupture between the two states, and that he had chosen him, because he could not trust any of his ministers, who were divided in opinions and interests. Mr. Willock added, he had charged himself with this message, not officially, but from his personal wish to see the differences between Russia and Persia arranged, and that, before entering on particulars, he asked my permission to speak on the object of his visit. I answered that I received his proposal with infinite pleasure, and I assured him that the policy of the Emperor was too frank and too upright for me to conceal my proceedings from the agent of an allied power, and that I accepted his good offices, without admitting his intervention. After saying that this was his own meaning, and after a long discussion, he proposed to me to take with me to Tiflis a Persian negotiator, whose proceedings I should second, and who should endeavour to obtain from Gen. Yermoloff the evacuation of the coast of the Goktcha during the next winter, which should be employed in arranging the points in dispute respecting the frontiers.

---

[287] Henry Willock. Cf. 10.15. For his career see Anonymous (1842a).

"I immediately assented to this proposal, which Mr. Willock thinks will afford the Schah a pretext to stop the march of the troops, and which, besides, is absolutely conformable to the spirit of the note which I have written today to Alaiar Khan.

"The English officers and sergeants who exercise the Persian troops, have received orders from Mr. Willock not to follow them, but to remain at Tauris. Mr. Cormick, the Prince's English physician,[288] has also refused to accompany him, and Abbas Mirza will have no Europeans in his army, except an Italian named Bernardi, who has served as a subaltern in the French artillery, and, perhaps, an ex-sergeant of the English artillery,[289] now in the pay of the Prince, and, consequently, independent of the Charge d'Affaires of his government.

"Mr. Willock intends to follow the court to Ardebil, but declared to the Schah, that if he should approach our frontiers nearer than that point, he should be obliged to leave him.

"Sultania, July 11 (23).—The proposal of Mr. Willock, mentioned in my preceding, had just been acceded to by the Schah, and the Kaimacan[290] was chosen to accompany me to Tiflis, when an unexpected event defeated all the plans for an arrangement. This is, the revolt of the Khan of Talyche,[291] who, after having massacred the little Russian

---

[288] John Cormick (d. 1833), an Irishman from Cussane, Tullahought, County Kilkenny (Flannery 2004: 24; not County Tipperary as stated by Ekbal and Richter-Bernburg 1993/2011), entered the medical establishment of the East India Company in 1800 as Assistant Surgeon and arrived in Madras in February, 1802 (Montgomery 1865: 125). In 1809 he went to Persia as 'Mr. Surgeon Cormick' in Malcolm's second mission. See Kaye (1856: 512, n. *). There he remained, becoming personal physician to 'Abbas Mirza in Tabriz, where he was known as *Hakim bozorg*, 'great doctor.' See Fontanier (1844: 222). He also served as physician to the Ouseley embassy. See Ouseley (1821: 453). For his journal of a journey in Kurdistan to treat the sick Wali of Senna, which included a visit to Karafto cave, see Ker Porter (1821/2: 563–568). According to Elgood (1951: 464), 'Cormick had announced his intention of retiring in the winter of 1830, but was still at work in Tabris' in 1832. He died of cholera at Nishapur in early October, 1833, *en route* to joining 'Abbas Mirza and was buried at St. Mary's Church in Tabriz. See MacAlister (1910: 168), Wright (1998: 170). As McNeill wrote on 11 November 1833, 'He had wealth and honour and the favour of princes...The loss of so benevolent and useful a person will be sensibly felt at Tabreez where he did much good with little ostentation.' See Elgood (1951: 467). For his paper on cholera in Persia in 1822 see Cormick (1823).

[289] James Dawson.

[290] Mirza Abu'l Qasem Qa'em Maqam, 'Abbas Mirza's first minister. Cf. 11.35.

[291] Eichwald (1837: 590) called him 'Mirás Chan von Talysch, der in Lenkoran bisher residirt hatte,' but he was in fact Mir Hasan Khan. See Fath 'Ali Shah's firman of September, 1826, giving him and other local khans instructions. See Lesur (1827: 92–93).

garrison at Arkevan,[292] asked assistance of Persia, to make himself master of Lenkoran.[293]

"Alaiar Khan has taken advantage of this event to influence the Schah, who has resolved on war, and sets out tomorrow for Ardebil, where he will arrive on the 18th (30th) of this month. All the troops are in the camp at Sultania.

"This determination having been taken, I have every thing ready for my departure.

"Tauris, July 20 (Aug. 1.)—On arriving at Tauris, I learned that the couriers whom I dispatched on the 2nd (14th) from Sultania were detained at Ahar.[294] I found M. Ivanoff[295]

---

[292] Erkivan, in the Masalli district of Azerbaijan, c. 40–42 km northwest of Lenkoran. As Hagemeister (1851: 339) noted, 'Die nördliche Hälfte der Ebene am Meere bildet den Kreis Arkewan, die südliche den von Lenkoran. Der erste theilt sich in ein Steppenland, ein nördliches und ein bergisges. Das Steppenland besteht aus sehr fruchtbarer Dammerde, wo das Getreide, ohne Wässerung und ohne Erholung, alle Jahr an einer und derselben Stelle wächst.' According to Brosset (1857: 303, n. 2), 'la citadelle d'Arkévan' was 'construite par les Anglais sur les ruines d'un ancien fort du même nom.' Some sources confuse Arkevan with *Askeran*, e.g. Alexander (1827: 279), but this, as Monteith (1856: 44) noted, was located near Shusha, almost 300 km inland from Lenkoran.

[293] As Alexander (1827: 279–280) noted, 'In Talish the people rose and cut off the detachments dispersed throughout the country; they then took Askeran [sic, Arkevan], and in concert with a Persian army laid siege to Lankeran on the Caspian, which had been taken by the Russians in the last war. It was now garrisoned by a weak battalion of regulars, who, alarmed probably by the massacre of the troops in Askeran, withdrew in the night to the island of Sari, leaving in the fort six pieces of cannon, military stores, and provisions in abundance.' Brosset (1857: 324, n. 1) observed, 'la garnison russe d'Arkévan, dans le district de Thalych, avait été surprise et massacrée, et le gouverneur de ce pays menaçait déjà la forteresse de Lenkoran.' According to Stcherbatow (1890: 43–44), 'La population du khanat de Talich s'était soulevée en masse, et son Khan, tout dévoué jusque-là à la Russie [Baddeley 1908: 144 noted that, 'Of all the khanates, Talish, the most distant, alone remained independent, for the reason that its rulers were implacably hostile to Persia.'], s'était placé à la tête de la rébellion. "Le Khan de Talich, écrit un Russe, activement employé à cette époque dans le Transcaucase, redoutait de partager tôt ou tard le sort de ses voisins: de plus, les abus et les brigandages du commandant russe du Lenkoran (son administrateur en même temps), lui firent perdre patience". Ce commandant, et major Ilinski, qui avait sous ses ordres le bataillon des marins de la mer Caspienne cantonné dans le khanat, ne parvint pas à le réunir à temps, ce qui exposa ce bataillon à des pertes très sensibles dans les postes détachés qu'il gardait. Ilinski se retira du Lenkoran avec ces débris sur l'île de Sara.'

[294] As Le Strange (1905: 169) noted, 'Âhar, which lies 150 miles west of Ardabîl, on the Âhar river, is named in the lists of the earlier Arab geographers, and described by Yâḳût as a well-built city.'

[295] Kelly (2006: 167) notes that when Andreas Amburger became Consul General in Tabriz, he had 'an assistant called Ivanov.' A 'Colonel Iwanoff' accompanied Ermolov on his embassy to Fath 'Ali Shah in 1817. See von Kotzebue (1819a: 250). It is unclear whether he was related to Theodore Ivanov, Counsellor of Legation in the Russian embassy in Washington DC in 1820 and Russian Consul General in Philadelphia in 1822. See (1820d: 192), Anonymous (1822l: 39). Similarly, in and around 1840 the Chevalier Fedor A. Ivanoff was Russian consul general at Smyrna [Izmir] where he amassed an important coin collection. See e.g. Newton (1865: 46), Frary (2015b: 195).

and the Dragoman, Chah-Nazaroff,[296] attached to our mission, under arrest and guarded in their respective lodgings. Two couriers sent to me from Tiflis have also been stopped, and their papers seized. All these shameful proceedings are by order of Abbas Mirza. I have demanded my papers, which have just been given up to me. M. Ivanoff and Chah Nazaroff are set at liberty, but the hotel of the mission is surrounded by guards, and nobody dares to go out without being accompanied by some soldiers, with their arms.

"Tiflis, Sept. 12 (24).—I arrived on the 4th (16th) Aug. at Erivan, where the Serdar[297] caused me to be detained, under various pretexts, till the 9th (21st), and afterwards let me know that he could not permit me to join the Russian troops, but that he would have me escorted to the frontiers of Turkey; and if I did not agree to this he could not assign me any other route, but that through our Tartar province at Kagah, the fidelity of which, at that time, was, at least, suspicious. I was warned at the same time that the delay which I experienced arose from the measures which the Serdar was taking to plunder my baggage, and to seize upon my person, as soon as we should be one day's journey beyond the frontiers of Persia; and I was informed, at the same time, who the individuals were that were commissioned to execute these outrages.

"During the discussions concerning my departure, Mirza Ismael, my Mehmander, received orders from Alaiar Khan to detain me at Erivan till further orders, under the specious pretext that it was necessary I should wait for the answer which it was intended to make to my note of the 9th (21st) July.

"I protested against so manifest a violation of the law of nations, writing both to Abbas Mirza and to the principal Minister; and I informed the English Mission of the situation in which I was.

"During this time every day of my detention was marked by some new insult. It was insinuated to me from Alaiar Khan, that the wife of the Khan of Talyche[298] having been kept as hostage at the time of his revolt, I should be detained at Erivan till she should be set at liberty; but that I might ransom myself by giving up to the Chief Minister my plate, and the presents not yet distributed, which I had in my possession.

"They endeavoured, but in vain, to bribe my Dragomans. The Serdar desired my Mehmandar to require of me the payment of a parcel of cotton, which he had sent to Russia before the commencement of hostilities, or to keep some persons of my suite as hostages.

"Being unable to bribe my Dragomans, the Serdar expressed his intention to keep them by force, as being both natives of the province of Karabag, which he already considered as a conquered province, and a part of Persia.

---

[296] Melik-Shahnazar was a well-known 'Armenian noble house' to which Daud Aga, Fath 'Ali Shah's emissary to Constantinople, belonged. See Keçeci (2016: 204, n. 47). Presumably Menshikov's translator was part of the same family. In Griboyedov's correspondence he is referred to as Mirza Neriman Melik Shah Nazarov. See Harden (1971a: 88, n. 43).

[297] Hoseyn Qoli Khan Qazvini.

[298] Mirza Hasan Khan.

"I should write a volume if I were to give your Excellency an account of all the vexatious attempts which I have been obliged to resist, and to which the inventive genius of my gaolers every day gave a new form, but always with a view to extort money or effects. Seeing the time pass away, and the answers to my letters not arriving, and learning that the English mission had left the camp of the Schah, to go to meet Mr. M'Donald,[299] I persuaded my Mehmendar to oppose the pretensions of the Serdar of Erivan, and to insinuate to the principal Minister, whose creature he is, that, considering the antipathy of the Schah to the war, the enemies of Alaiar Khan would seize the first opportunity that a doubtful battle would furnish to ruin him, if he did not think beforehand of peace, and, the only means to conclude it on advantageous terms were, to let me depart as soon as possible, because I was personally interested in inducing our Cabinet to an accomodation.

"This means succeeded, and I owe it to my liberation, after 25 days' detention, in the most unhealthy place in the environs of Erivan, which has severely affected all the individuals of the Mission, both masters and servants, including the Physician and his Assistants, so that Lieut. Count Tolstoy[300] has been obliged to act as doctor, and have to let blood, in order to assist the sick.

"Mr. Macdonald, the new English Minister at the Court of Teheran, learnt on his arrival at the camp of the Schah, that orders had already been given to let me pass freely; but fearing some new act of perfidy on the part of the Persians, he thought it advisable to demand new firmans, and to send Major Monteith to see that they were carried into execution: however, I had already reached Tiflis when that officer arrived at the camp of the Serdar of Erivan.'"

11.128 'From Late Foreign Journals, Received at this Office. Russia and Persia. By Dr. Lyall,' *Baltimore Gazette and Daily Advertiser* (Saturday, 30 December, 1826) and 'From the London Morning Chronicle. Russia and Persia. By Dr. Lyall,' *Boston Daily Advertiser* (Saturday, 30 December, 1826): 'In the declaration of war issued by the Emperor Nicholas, his Imperial Majesty declares, that in the "orders prescribed to his (Alexander's) ambassadors and agents at the Court of Teheran, relative to the mode of conduct which was best calculated to convince the Schach, his heir, and his Ministers, *that Russia had no thought whatever of conquest, that it wished only for repose, and required nothing but the execution of the treaties*, they enjoined all the Russian authorities to observe the *most conciliatory conduct*, and measures which could never tend to give to Persia just ground for suspicion or complaint."—Indeed, the councillors of the Autocrat make out an

---

[299] Lieutenant-Colonel John Macdonald Kinneir (1782–1830), British envoy to Persia from September, 1826 to June, 1830. See Markham (1874: 556). He was referred to as 'Colonel Macdonald' and signed his letters 'J. Macdonald.' See MacAlister (1910: 70).

[300] In 1839 Lt. Count Yegor Petrovich Tolstoy (1802–1874) met Sir John McNeill and received from him an account of Griboyedov's murder (cf. 12.2). See Kelly (2006: 209–210). When McNeill's wife travelled back to Persia from Scotland in 1829 she received friendly assistance along the way from Tolstoy. See MacAlister (1910: 130).

excellent case for his Imperial Majesty, who has been all along studying the "interest of Persia." Therefore, he complains of violated treaties—unprovoked injustice—sudden invasion—excitement to revolt—and total want of good faith on the side of the Persians; while he attributes to the Russians immaculate rectitude—amicable discussion—conciliatory conduct—apathy of conquest—desire of repose—necessity of self-defence—indemnity for past aggressions, and security for futurepeace.

In the same strain, the active, the brave, the intelligent, but the somewhat savage agent of the Autocrat, in the South, General Yermoloff, complains of the measures of the Serdar of Erivan,[301] who, forthwith, must be chastised for his insolence.

The escape of the Armenian Patriarch,[302] and the Monks, from the Monastery at Etchmiadsin, and their *sejour* in an adjoining district, under the protection of Russia[303]—the mal-administration of the Persian provinces over which Russia now sways her sceptre—the violation of female chastity—and religious fanaticism—have, by turns, been assigned as the cause of the irruption of the Persians into the territories of the Autocrat; and, beyond doubt, they all have had their share in influencing the resolutions of the

---

[301] Hoseyn Qoli Khan Qazvini.

[302] Yeprem (Estremus) I.

[303] This account credits the patriarch with deeds performed by the leading bishop of Echmiadzin. As Sargent (1819: 504–505) noted, 'The monastery, and consequently the whole of the Armenians, are under the direction of Nestus [sic, Nerses V Ashtaraketsi (1770–1857)], one of the bishops; for the patriarch Ephraim is a mere cypher, and passes most of his time in bed.' As Tololyan (2001: 88) observed, Nerses 'in 1826–1827, as a bishop...had helped to raise, had blessed, and then accompanied a column of ten thousand Armenians who fought with the Czar's troops against the Persians during the Russian conquest of the Transcaucasus.' Gamba (1826/2: 194–195) described this episode as follows: 'J'ai déjà parlé de l'arrivé successive d'un grand nombre d'Arméniens dans les provinces Russes au-delà du Caucase; mais, de toutes les migrations, la plus remarquable et la plus importante dans ses résultats, est celle du patriarche des Arméniens, échappé, en 1822, avec presque tout son clergé, du couvent d'Etchmiadzin, situé en Perse, dans la province d'Erivan, à peu de distance du mont Ararat. Pour rendre raison de cet événement extraordinaire, il est bon de rappeler que, depuis près de trois ans que la guerre dure entre la Perse et la Turquie, les Kourdes, placés sur l'extrême frontière, et qui, au milieu des désordres inséparables des hostilités entre barbares, ne respectoient ni amis ni ennemis, étoient venus plusieurs fois insulter le couvent des Arméniens, en avoient exigé des contributions, et même, dit-on, avoient tué deux religieux. Cette raison étoit plus que suffisante pour justifier le patriarche arménien d'être venue chercher un asile chez une nation capable de le faire respecter. La Turquie ni la Perse ne purent voir avec indifférence le patriarche, ou plutôt l'âme et le chef de la nation Arménienne, établir désormais sa résidence chez un peuple qui, pour l'une des nations, est un objet de haine implacable, et pour toutes les deux un sujet de terreur. Quoi qu'il en soit, le général en chef donna ordre d'accueillir avec distinction le patriarche, qui choisit son domicile au couvent de Sanain en Somkéthie.' In 1812 von Freygang 'alighted at the house of the Patriarch Efreme, a respectable old man, who received me in the most obliging manner.' See von Freygang and Freygang (1823: 276). On his way to Tehran in 1817 Ermolov and his delegation met 'the venerable patriarch Efremkam, surrounded by the priesthood' upon their arrival at Echmiadzin. See von Kotzebue (1819a: 96).

Shach[304] and Abbaz Mirza. But, in my opinion, the principal cause of the present invasion, is to be found in the deep hatred and the unbounded indignation—aided by traitors—which have been long rankling in the hearts of the Persians, in consequence of the avaricious, arrogant, and dictatorial measures of the Russian Cabinet, and the haughty, insolent, and tyrannical conduct of General Yermolof, during his Embassy to the Courts of the Shach, and of Abbaz Mirza, in the year 1817.

I[305] have been accused of partiality towards Russia but I hope without cause. At all events, the present remarks will not come under that censure, because they are chiefly founded upon the documents of the Russian Ambassador, and of one of his attaches, and upon the report of a gentleman who was sent by the late Autocrat [Alexander] on a special mission to Teheran. These documents are—First, The abridged translation of General Yermolof's "*Private Journal of his Embassy to the Court of Persia, in the year* 1817," contained in the second volume of my "Travels in Russia, the Krimea, the Caucasus, and Georgia," which was published nearly two years ago,[306] and which, as it throws much light upon the conduct of Persia and Russia toward each other, may be reckoned a very important political paper at the present juncture. Secondly, Upon the "Voyage en Perse à la suite de l'Ambassade en 1817 par Maurice de Kotzebue,[307] one of the sons of the late and celebrated dramatic writer[308]; and, thirdly, upon "Letteres sur la Caucase et la Georgie suivie d'une relation d'un Voyage en Perse en 1812," of which Mr. Freyganch[309] an employee of Russia, and his Lady,[310] were the Authors.* [*A translation of this work was lately published by Mr. Murray, accompanied by valuable Notes.][311]

In 1812–13, "Russia was peculiarly anxious to be at peace both with Turkey and Persia, and this object was accomplished by the assistance of the British Government, through our Ambassadors at the Courts of those States. Mr. Freyganch was sent by Russia, on a special mission to the court of Abbaz Mirza, to conclude a peace, and Sir Gore Ousely [sic, Ouseley], who had arrived in that country, from India, was very desirous to further his object."[312]—The result of the measures adopted was the *convention* of Goulestan. By it the Russians pretend that the provinces of Karabaugh and Talish were *ceded* to them, whereas I have been informed that they *were only to be held possession of for a limited time*, as a guarantee for the ratification of a future treaty.—"This was dangerous policy," said one of

---

[304] Fath 'Ali Shah.

[305] Robert Lyall.

[306] Lyall (1825/2).

[307] von Kotzebue (1819b).

[308] August von Kotzebue.

[309] Wilhelm von Freygang (1782–1849).

[310] Frederika Afanasyevna von Freygang (1790–1863).

[311] Von Freygang and Freygang (1816, 1823).

[312] This and subsequent quotations are from Lyall (1825/2). Here the reference is Lyall (1825/2: 88–89).

my friends, who was well acquainted with political affairs, "and both the Persians and the English were *gulled*. These provinces, once under the claws of the Imperial Eagle, were never intended to be restored to Persia; and the general and favourable change in the aspect of the affairs of Russia by the defeat and downfall of Napoleon, soon enabled her to assume a dictatorial tone towards Persia."[313]

In the year 1815, the well known Abool Hassan Khan was sent by the Shach to Petersburgh, with magnificent presents for the Emperor Alexander, and to solict [sic] the restoration of what he esteemed the *pledged*, and what the Russians now call the *conquered* or *ceded* provinces. After the lapse of some months, Alexander gave the Persian Ambassador his leave, and said that his opinions would be more fully made known at the Court of Teheran, by a special embassy. Whether, from misrepresentation or deception, agreeably to General Yermolof, the Shach, even during the negociations in Persia, in 1817, remained, "in full assurance, agreeably to the representation of his Ambassador at Petersburg, that all the territory occupied by Russia would be restored."[314] Therefore, by General Yermolof's own showing, it seems that the treaty of Gulestan, in 1813, was merely a conditional, or preparatory measure—a *convention*, as the Emperor Nicholas himself calls it, or the basis of a definitive treaty. That basis the Shach most anxiously, but vainly, endeavored to get modified in the treaty of Teheran, or rather of Sultania—a treaty to which the autocrat of Russia makes no allusion in his declaration of war, although concluded four years after that of Gulestan.

General Yermolof, in his preface to the report of his embassy, says—"Through reciprocity of friendship I was sent as Ambassador to his Persian Majesty, confidently charged to communicate the opinions of the Emperor upon the subject in question."[315] The details of the General's progress, of the measures he pursued at the Courts of Abbaz Mirza and of the Shach, and of his return to Tiflis, are all triumphantly detailed, with much minuteness, in his own words, as well as the haughty and contemptuous manner in which he conducted himself toward the Serdar of Erivan,[316] towards Abbaz Mirza and his courtiers, and even towards the Shach himself and the Persian Ministers, which begat him the hatred of the nation, and justly roused general indignation.

The Persian Ministers, during many meetings at Sultania, made the utmost efforts to get General Yermolof to consent to the restitution of the provinces of Karabagh and Talish, but without any success. The Ambassador's own *ultimatum* was, "I told them (the Ministers) for the last time, that I myself, as Commander-in-Chief in Georgia, upon whom devolved the care of the frontier, had informed the Emperor that *it was not possible to make the smallest cession*, and that this Sovereign *gave me leave to speak in his name*."[317]

---

[313] Lyall (1825/2: 90).

[314] Lyall (1825/2: 125).

[315] Lyall (1825/2: 88).

[316] Hoseyn Qoli Khan Qazvini.

[317] Lyall (1825/2: 147–148).

A treaty of peace between Russia and Persia being concluded and signed at Sultania, on the 27th August (8th Sept) 1817, General Yermolof returned to Tiflis.

According to the Emperor Nicholas's justification of his declaration of war, the differences of the Courts of Persia and Russia had never ceased, respecting *the line of demarcation between their territories*. The grand point then is, to ascertain which of the Powers is in the fault; i.e. which gave the first provocation, made the first encroachment, or first violated the other's territory. By the incontrovertible report of General Yermolof himself, the Russians are highly to blame for willingly having provoked the retaliation of the Persians, and I have received the following statement of the disputes regarding the respective territories of the two Powers:—

After the Convention of 1813, and the fixture of the line of demarcation between the Persian and the Russian territories in the Province of Karabah, the Russians continued to feed their flocks and herds on the plain beyond their own frontier. As the plain was extensive, and of no great value, the Persians paid little attention to this infringement of the treaty, till some years afterwards, when a general survey of the whole frontier was made, and the Russians wished to include the part of the plain alluded to in their dominions;—alleging as a proof that it belonged to them, the fact that the Persians had not before claimed it, and that they had long appropriated it to their use. To this the Persians keenly objected, and hence arose the dispute about the territory of the two contending Powers.

Let us now illustrate some of the foregoing assertions by facts.

M. Freyganch, who seems to have been well treated by the Persians, and who frequently expresses his gratitude, thus expresses himself in 1812: "Hassan [sic, Hoseyn] Kouli-Khan is the hero of Persia: by his bravery and his audacity the present Shach ascended the throne.[318] He is the chief of the Persian army, and possesses the entire confidence of the Prince. War is his element: he rejects peace with Russia, and neglects nothing to excite the Shach and Abbaz Mirza to the continuation of war." In fact, this Khan, who has the title of Serdar of Erivan,[319] is a very powerful and almost an independent Prince. General Yermolof, being well aware of the Serdar's character, it was to be expected, though only for political reasons, would have known that it was of some importance to conciliate such an influential person, or at least not to incur his hatred. On the contrary, on approaching Erivan, the Ambassador absolutely constrained the haughty Serdar to come out of the town to meet him. The General himself thus reports the affair: "The Serdar himself came out on a visit to meet me; and calling to his assistance that dissimulation which is coeval with a

---

[318] Von Freygang and Freygang (1823: 391–392) wrote, 'Baba Khan [Fath 'Ali Shah], seconded by Hadjee Ibrahim, and Houssein Kooli Khan, the present Sardar of Erivan, mounted the throne of Persia in 1798, under the title of Futteh Ali Shah, and is the present monarch.' Here Hassan, 'brother to the commander of the province,' as noted by von Kotzebue (1819a: 103), has been confused with his brother.

[319] Hoseyn Qoli Khan Qazvini.

Persian's birth, he endeavoured as much as possible to conceal his disagreeable feelings."[320]

Respecting the same ceremony, Kotzebue, who every where admires Gen. Yermolof's measures, remarks, "that the inhabitants could not conceal their surprise at seeing so proud a man set out from the fortress, and go to meet us. It was a homage which he only renders to the Sovereign himself; but the Ambassador had insisted upon this part of the ceremonial, *et pour surcroit de contrariete*, the Serdar, perhaps, for the first time in his life, *fut trompe par la pluie jusqu'aux os*.[321] Is this a proof of the "most conciliatory conduct" enjoined by the Emperor Alexander, towards the Persians?

It has been the immemorial usage at the Persian Court, that all admitted to public audiences should appear in *Red Slippers*.—Mr. Freyganch, who complied with this ceremony, states, that "far from affecting any superiority by this ceremony, or exacting it from mere ostentation, the Court of Persia only adheres strongly to this formality, because introduced by the Persian religion, it is very ancient and preserves the superb carpets, which are the greatest ornaments of the Persian habitations."[322] General Yermolof, however, refused to comply with this usage, both at the Court of the Shach, and at that of the Crown Prince; and hence he was not received in the usual hall of audience. Indeed, this account of the *Red Stockings*, which he, for the sake of greater ridicule, regularly calls the *red slippers* in his journal, is quite amusing, and he has been well seconded by Kotzeube [sic]. With much self-congratulation, says this author, "telle est la delicatesse du Prince hereditaire, qui'l [sic] ne permet pas que les officiers Aglais [sic] foulent ses tapis autrement qu'avec des chaussures legeres de morroquin a la botte du pays; tandis que nos boites a talons ferres y fasoient un vacarme affreux. N'oublions pas, que le seul aspect d'hommes bottes suffit pour choquer les regards et revolter l'orgueil de la nation entiere."[323] Was this conciliatory conduct, or is it the boast of a barbarian?

On this presentation to the Shach, General Yermolof says, "All preceding Foreign Ambassadors had put on *Red Stockings*. I entered in ordinary boots."[324] And Kotzeube

---

[320] Lyall (1825/2: 96). Note the original says 'came out a verst to meet me,' not 'came out on a visit to meet me.' The Russian term *verst* (верста) was presumably unintelligible to an American typesetter and possibly interpreted as a typographical error.

[321] The text from the opening quotation mark to '*jusqu'aux os*,' is a quotation from Lyall (1825/2: 96), but although Lyall puts von Kotzebue's remark in quotation marks, he has only paraphrased the following: 'The inhabitants were all surprised, that this haughty man should have condescended to advance out of the walls of the fortress, to meet any individual but the King [Fath 'Ali Shah] himself.' See von Kotzebue (1819a: 106).

[322] Von Freygang and Freygang (1823: 313) where 'houses' is the last word in the sentence, rather than 'habitations.'

[323] Kotzebue (1819b: 143)

[324] Lyall (1825/2: 141).

[sic] triumphantly remarks, in allusion to the same event, "nous y avions ajoute l'innovation hardie de paroitre en bottes."[325]

It is the custom of the King of Persia to present Ambassadors and distinguished personages with *khalats*, or dresses of honour, in the form of a *robe de chambre*, in which they appear at their farewell audience. "Gen. Yermolof," says Kotzebue, "declared that he would not submit to this ceremonial, and that a Russian would offend his Sovereign if he put on another dress above his uniform. The King admitted this excuse, and made in our favour this first, and perhaps, last, derogation from etiquette."†[326] [† I believe Kotzebue is mistaken here.—General Gardanne refused to comply with the same usage when sent to Persia by Napoleon in 1807.]

The following narrative, from the *Private Journal* is, perhaps, the best proof of the *conciliatory conduct* of the Russian negociators.

Mr. Mirshe, a French officer in the service of Abbaz Mirza,[327] had conducted himself improperly towards the Russian Embassy at Tabreez, and because he was not punished exactly according to General Yermolof's wishes, this brave man sent his Adjutant and six of his grenadiers, who laid the French officer prostrate by a blow, opened his clothes and

---

[325] von Kotzebue (1819b: 231).

[326] Lyall (1825/2: 152), paraphrasing von Kotzebue (1819a: 303–304).

[327] Mirshé. According to Lyall (1825/2: 154–155), 'Mr. Mirshé, a French officer, who called himself a colonel of Napoleon's guards, and a chevalier of the Legion of Honour, would not permit the musicians to take up their quarters in a house destined for them. According to Yermólof, he not only endeavoured to drive them away by bawling, but even struck one of them two blows with his sabre. General Yermólof sent to inform Abbas Mirza of the affair, and to demand satisfaction. The Prince immediately sent an officer to assure the General that the Frenchman should be punished; but when the ambassador asked leave to be a witness of the action, he perceived that there was a design to deceive him. Perhaps forgetting his proper place, or acting *à la Russe*, the General immediately sent his adjutant and six grenadiers to take the delinquent under arrest; and if they did not find him at home, to wait for him. Those musicians whom he had struck were ordered, besides, to employ the castigation of the pleti, or whips. When Mr. Mirshé arrived at his quarters, he wished to defend his conduct by new iimpertinences, but a gentle blow laid him prostrate. His clothes were then opened, and the flagellation was effectually bestowed. His sabre, which had been taken from him, was sent by the General to Abbas Mirza; thereby signifying that it was to be hoped he would not have such a rascal in his service. The answer was, that he should be chased away from the town. The sabre, however, was not received; because foreseeing the future, Abbas Mirza locked himself up in the *harem*; so that the messenger might not be admitted. That prudent prince, however, by this conduct, showed his evident and well-merited displeasure at the illegal, dictatorial, and even tyrranical proceeding of General Yermólof. It was an act worthy of a tyrant, after the gentle procedure of Abbas Mirza; and is no doubt well-remembered.' The name is more likely to be Mircher, an originally Luxembourgeois family (Mersher, from the town of Mersch), that settled in France in the early eighteenth century. It is tempting to associate him with Guillaume Mircher (1785–), son of Pierre Mircher, who indeed fought with Napoleon, although he never rose to the rank of Colonel and, after being captured by the Russians, returned to live in Strasbourg, where he had a son named Hippolyte Mircher (1820–1878) who became a renowned general. See Furia (2008: 11–18). Possibly the Mirshé in 'Abbas Mirza's service came from the same family.

chastised him with rods like a child, while they sent his sabre to Abbaz Mirza. At this unwarranted and arbitrary procedure, an angel must have felt indignant, yet the Prince of Persia behaved with much circumspection.

After treating of the Georgian army, of the means taken for hemming in the mountain tribes of the Caucasus, and of the horrid and barbarous manner in which the Russians pretend *"to civilize"* these tribes by fire and sword, indeed by *total extermination of themselves and their villages*,‡ [‡ Troops surround the villages, the signal is given, and they are soon in a blaize. They commenced the general massacre.—At times all perish— young and old—men, women, and children, between the flames and the sword. The accuracy of this account was doubted, when first made public nearly three years ago. I am horrified in being obliged to add, that additional facts have only shown me that my expressions were not exaggerations. There are now other travellers in London who have heard the same details from the Russians themselves.] I have made the following deductions in my *Travels*:—

"From all I have read, heard, and seen, of General Yermolof's plans, of course sanctioned by his Government, I should suppose that his great objects are, 1st. To have a very powerful and hardy army in the Caucasus and Georgia, to be employed according to circumstances. 2nd. To diminish, by all possible means, the power of the inhabitants of the mountains. 3rd. To extend, in the meantime, the dominions of Georgia, by encroachments upon Persia; and, 4thly, To take advantage of a favourable opportunity to attempt the conquest of Persia."[328]

I fear that the consummation of most of these objects is but too near at hand, and I doubt not that Russia will be gainer in territory by the war, and the terms of the consequent peace to which Persia is likely to be forced into compliance, unless powerfully aided in her diplomacy by the influence of her ally, Great Britain. Even in the former case, however, we shall have the satisfaction of knowing, that another increase of territory will only be the addition of another restless member to her overgrown body—in fact, a diminution of the force of Russia.'

11.129 'General Summary. Foreign. Russia,' *The Miner's Journal, and Schuylkill Coal & Navigation Register* (Saturday, 30 December, 1826): 'Rumor assigns important victories to the Russians, and also to the Persians. The former is most probable, and of this the English papers are aware, and talk of taking measures for opposing the course of Russia; or of being put in possession of equal advantages. And add that the general peace of Europe cannot long remain.'

11.130 'Untitled,' *New-York Evening Post* (Tuesday, 2 January, 1827): 'Paris, November 17, Five o'clock....A letter of the 26th ult. from Warsaw, says—"From the strength of the forces sent against Persia, it would seem that the project of Russia is to finish at a blow, and

---
[328] Lyall (1825/2: 57).

in the least time possible, a campaign into which she was forced by the most unjust aggression. Nevertheless, it is to be feared that a single campaign will be insufficient, particularly as the season is too far advanced for great progress to be made during the winter in the inhospitable countries that form the theatre of war.—Besides, the Russians will probably find more to struggle with in the difficulty of obtaining provisions, than in the strength of the enemy, especially as the inhabitants of the country, rude and Mahometan for the most part, do not entertain very favorable dispositions towards their masters."'

11.131 'Foreign Intelligence. [Paris dates to the 19th November.] Paris, Nov. 18,' *National Gazette and Literary Register* (Wednesday, 3 January, 1827): 'The emperor of Russia[329] has sent to Gen. Paskewitch, who *gained* a victory near Elisabethpol, a sword of honor, with the inscription—To the Conqueror of the Persians.

A German Journal gives the following as a list of the troops which compose the Persian Army that invaded the Russian Territory—Guards of the King[330] and Princes[331] of the royal family, 4000 men; Nomade troops, 80,000; militia, 150,000; cavalry, artillery and infantry, trained à l'Europeenne, 20,000, of which 9000 form the king's supplementary guard.

A letter of the 26th ultimo, from Warsaw, says—"From the strength of the forces sent against Persia, it would seem that the project of Russia is to finish at a blow, and in the least time possible, a campaign into which she was forced by the most unjust aggression. Nevertheless, it is to be feared, that a single campaign will be insufficient, particularly as the season is too far advanced for great progress to be made during the winter, in the inhospitable countries that form the theatre of war."'

11.132 'Continuation of Foreign Extracts,' *New-York Spectator* (Friday, 12 January 1827) and 'Foreign Compendium,' *The Evening Gazette* (Saturday, 13 January, 1827; 'Journal…of Nov. 4th'): 'The Journal of St. Petersburgh of to-day contains the following article, under the name of "News from the Army in Georgia, of 30th Sept. (12th Oct.):—

"After Abbas Mirza had suffered a total defeat on the 13th (25th) September, near Elizabethpol, he left the Russian territory, raised the blockade of the fortress of Schuscha, and on the 18th (30th) retreated over the Araxes. After our victory of the 13th (25th) the enemy fled with such precipitation that Lieutenant-General Prince Madatow found it impossible to overtake him. A part of the Persian cavalry has followed Abbas Mirza over the Araxes. The infantry has dispersed, fled into the mountains, and was endeavouring with all speed to reach the Persian frontier. Adjutant-General Paskewitsch has received orders to leave some troops in Schirwan, in order to drive out the Persians who have remained there, as well as in the south of Daghestun. On the 21st September (3rd October) General

---

[329] Nicholas I.
[330] Fath 'Ali Shah.
[331] 'Abbas Mirza, Mohammad Mirza and Isma'il Mirza.

11 The Second Russo-Persian War and the Treaty of Torkmanchay (1826–1828)

Davidow,[332] who commands towards Eviran [sic, Erivan], attacked the enemy, commanded by Hassan Khan, brother of the Sardar[333] of that Province. The Persians were totally routed, and General Davidow, after having caused them a very great loss, pursued them to the little town of Sudharent, two short days journey from Erivan, where the Sardar has shut himself up, without affording the smallest assistance to his brother. The son of the former Khan of Elizabethpol, Zguria Khan, who has been taken prisoner,[334] has declared that, in the battle of the 13th (25th,) the army of Abbas Mirza consisted of twenty-four battalions, each consisting of 800 to 1000 men, 24 cannon, 12,000 cavalry, and 8000 troops of various descriptions. The head quarters of Gen. Paskewitsch were at Kendolan,[335] not far from Schuscha, and those of Gen. Yermoloff at Hassan See, in the district of Schamshadil.[336]—Abbas Mirza has repassed the Araxes, at Aslangas.[337] According to the latest accounts, he was, on the 20th of September, (2nd Oct.) at Mailian,[338] to the left of the Asfangas, in the vicinity of the mountains, and the Schah of Persia[339] himself at Agar.'"[340]

11.133 'Still later from Europe,' *The Freeman's Journal* (Monday, 15 January, 1827): 'Major Willock arrived in London on the 25th, over land from India,[341] with the long

---

[332] Major General Denis Vasilyevich Davydov (1784–1839). Poet and cavalry officer who fought in numerous wars, including the Finnish, Russo-Turkish, Napoleonic and Second Russo-Persian. See Eichwald (1837: 584), Tucker (2013).

[333] Hoseyn Qoli Khan Qazvini.

[334] Ugurlu Khan. According to Eichwald (1837: 583), 'unter den Gefangenen befand sich auch der Ugurlu Chan von Choi [Khoy], der Sohn des letzten Herrschers von Gändsha [Elizabethpol], Dshawat [Javad] Chan, der bei der Einnahme von Gändsha durch den tapfern Zizianoff niedergestoßen wurde. Nach der Schlacht bei Elisabethopol, wo die Perser in der größten Verwirrung flohen, fanden die russischen Soldaten den Ugurlu Chan im Gebüsch am Ufer des Karatschai, von armenischen Armeniern halb entkleidet und beraubt, liegen; sie nahmen ihn gefangen, da er sich zu erkennen gab, und er wurde späterhin nach Stavropol mit 210 M. Sarbasen [*sarbaz*] gebracht, wo er zwei Jahre lebte und Russisch schreiben und sprechen lernte.' Cf. Bitis (2006: 20).

[335] Khaldan. Roughly 90 km east of Elizabethpol/Ganja.

[336] Former khanate joined to the newly constituted Georgian province by Alexander I in 1801, northwest of Elizabethpol/Ganja. See Swietochowski (1995: 4), Bournoutian (2016, Map 1).

[337] Aslanduz.

[338] Mod. Maralyan. Eichwald (1837: 587) wrote of 'Das Corps, das den 25 October bei Dorfe Marljan über den seichten, aber an 50 Faden breiten Fluß ging.'

[339] Fath 'Ali Shah.

[340] Mod. Agarak. For the name see Hübschmann (1904: 375 and 378), '*agarak* "Grundstück, Acker, Hof, Landgut."' Agarak is located just north of the Araxes river in modern Armenia.

[341] George Willock. Cf. 10.40. He had gone to Calcutta in July, 1826, before proceeding to England. As Alexander (1827: 79) noted, 'In July, Major George Willock, brother to the late *chargé d'affaires* in Persia, arrived at Calcutta on a private mission from the court of Tehran respecting the arrears of subsidy. The subject of the Persian mission had, it appears, undergone much discussion in the council of the Supreme Government of India; and in August the Envoy was informed, by a letter from the Secretary to Government in the Political Department, that the mission was suspended until the receipt

pending treaty between England and Persia. According to his account, the Persians claim some advantages over the Russians.'

11.134 'Russia,' *Greenfield Gazette & Franklin Herald* (Tuesday, 16 January 1827): 'The Russian belligerent operations against Persia are suspended by the accounts from Odessa. Nothing will be done till next spring. The Russians have great deserts and mountains to cross before they can reach the Persians. Abbas Mirza was defeated on the 13th of September.'

11.135 'Latest from Europe,' *The Geneva Gazette and General Advertiser* (Wednesday, 17 January, 1827): 'The journals say that Persia has solicited the mediation of England in the existing war with Russia. According to the Russian accounts, the Persian army was retreating from the Russian territory in disorder, and in want of provisions.'

11.136 'Foreign News,' *The Onondaga Register* (Wednesday, 17 January, 1827): 'Several vessels have arrived at New-York from Europe, with later dates than any we have heretofore given. The packet-ship Corinthian brings London papers to the 25th of November....The war between Russia and Persia is not carried on with a great deal of vigour; but Russia is making preparation to open the campaign in the spring with a large force.'

11.137 'Foreign,' *The Kinderhook Herald* (after 18 January 1827): 'Despatches received in London from the Persian government, of Sept. 19th, request the mediation of England with Russia. The Persians say they were driven to an invasion by the repeated aggressions of the Russians; and that at the above date they had suffered no reverses.'[342]

11.138 'Extract of a letter from St. Petersburgh, to a gentleman of Washington, dated 6th October, 1826,' *Rochester Telegraph* (Saturday, 20 January, 1827): 'The war against Persia is drawing to a close. The Persians have already been beaten, and driven back into their territory.'

11.139 'Foreign Extracts—Continued. Russia and Persia,' *New-York Spectator* (Tuesday, 23 January 1827): 'Accounts from Georgia, of 26th October, afford no important

---

of advices from England. The Envoy was directed to remain at Bombay on the salary attached to his rank, with a table allowance of a thousand rupees per mensem.'

[342] A case of complete disinformation which only ceased in October, 1827, when the Persians suffered the loss of their 'impregnable' fortress of Sardarabad, Armenian Sardarapat (see 11.192 below). As Lacroix (1866: 76) observed, it was only with this defeat that 'tous les bruits fâcheux que des nouvelles mensongères, venues de Tehéran et de Constantinople, répétées, avec malveillance, dans les journaux de Londres, avaient propagés en Europe et même en Russie, au sujet des échecs que l'armée russe aurait éprouvés en Géorgie,' finally stopped.

11 The Second Russo-Persian War and the Treaty of Torkmanchay (1826–1828) 1219

intelligence. The Schah of Persia[343] has gone from Agar[344] to Tauris, and left the troops he had with him at the disposal of Abbas Mirza. The latter, notwithstanding the difficulty of finding provisions in Kaabasch, has not withdrawn from the Araxes, for fear that Gen. Paskewitsch might employ his troops against the Persians, who still remain in Schirwan under Shah Aly Mirza.[345] General Yermoloff, with the detachment that he has assembled, has proceeded from Kaketia to Tschari,[346] and intended to cross the river Alazan,[347] on the 29th of October.[348]

The *Journal of St. Petersburgh* gives the following further accounts from Georgia of the 21st of October:—

"The Persians have evacuated the province of Schirwan, and Major-General Von Krabbe, who was at Kuba, has already advanced to Staraja.—Schamakha[349] Mustapha, formerly Khan of Schirwan, had here received orders from the Schah, to send Schaksadi Schekali Mirza[350] back to Persia, to keep the Persian infantry with him, and to remain himself in Schirwan, but; as soon as Mustapha learnt that Gen. Krabbe was advancing to Staraja Schamokha, he hastened to cross the Kurat [sic, Kur at] Dschajawak,[351]

---

[343] Fath 'Ali Shah.

[344] Agarak. Cf. 11.135.

[345] 'Ali Shah Mirza, Fath 'Ali Shah's tenth son according to Anonymous (1873a: 716).

[346] A Lezgin district. See Klaproth (1815: 90).

[347] Principal tributary of the Kur river in Georgia. See e.g. Klaproth (1824: 299), Bélanger (1838: 115), Boyes (1877: lxiv). Also 'Alasani.' See Klaproth (1814: 48).

[348] As Eichwald (1837: 585) noted, 'Da sich jedoch der Sohn des Schachs, Ali Naki Mirsa, noch im Hochgebirge des Kaukasus befand, um dort die Lesghier aufzuwiegeln, die an die schirvan'sche Provinz gränzen, so marschirte General Jermoloff nunmehr, da die Ruhe im südlichen Theile Georgiens und in Karabagh wieder hergestellt war, mit einem am Arpatschai versammelten Corps durch Kachetien, Dschari und Nucha nach der schekischen Provinz, um diese gänzlich vom Feinde zu reinigen, und überall die frühere Ruhe und Ordnung wiederherzustellen; er schlug sein Lager beim Dorfe Chaldan in dieser Provinz auf, und glaubte so durch seine Gegenwart in der Mitte der muselmänn'schen Provinzen diese in dem gehörigen Gehorsam erhalten zu können.'

[349] Despite the punctuation the Russian topoonym 'Staraja Schamakha' is meant here, i.e. 'Old [*staraya*] Shamakhi.' Klaproth (1814: 206) distinguished Old and New Shamakhi, noting, 'Neu-Schamachi an der Linken des Ack-ßu, erhebt sich erst langsam aus seinen Ruinen, dennoch haben sich die reicheren Einwohner wieder angesiedelt und die Stadt hat die Hoffnung, nun unter Russischem Schutze, bald wieder zu ihrem vorigen Wohlstand zurückzukommen, weil der Handel weder durch Rebellen noch durch Kriege gestört wird.—Alt-Schamachi an einem Bache, der zum Pirsahat-tschai fließt, ist ganz von Gebirgen eingeschlossen und jetzt nur spärlich bewohnt.' The town had been intentionally destroyed by Mustafa Khan in 1795 as retribution against those residents who supported Agha Mohammad Shah, from whom Mustafa fled, rather than swear fealty. See Klaproth (1814: 205).

[350] *shahzadeh* 'Ali Shah Mirza, Fath 'Ali Shah's tenth son, mentioned above.

[351] A reference to the bridge of boats at Javad, near the confluence of the Kur and Araxes rivers. See Minorsky (1958: 77, 165 and n. 3), Minorsky (1937: 398). In the eighteenth century a toll for crossing was collected. As Klaproth (1814: 208–209) wrote, 'der Hauptort Dshawat wird von Armeniern und

endeavouring, however, to get the inhabitants of the country, especially the Nomades, to accompany him in his flight. They, however, being informed of his intention, had dispersed. The few whom he compelled to follow him were soon set at liberty by Mustapha Khan's brother, Gaschim Khan,[352] who, with the other chief men of the country, was with Gen. Krabbe, and who, at the head of the cavalry of Schirwan, pursued Mustapha to Dschawat. The enemy fled in such confusion that they left behind, untouched, the magazines of provisions found in the villages of Lacki[353] and Nuwaga."[354]

"Accounts from Persia say, that the Schah, on his interview with Abbas Mirza, at Agar, bitterly reproached him and threatened to declare him deprived of his right of succession to the throne, and to have his eyes put out; but that, yielding to the entreaties and assurances of his son, he had consented to give him fresh troops. Having received these reinforcements, Abbas Mirza has pitched his camp near a place called Makiszlou, (Makrisla,)[355] a few wersts from the bridge of Khudaperim,[356] and spread a report that he was going to repass

---

Tataren gemischt, bewohnt. Er liegt zwischen dem Ufer des Kur und einem kleinen See und hatte sonst einen eigenen Beg, der unter dem Chan von Schamachi stand. Der Name dieses Orts bedeutet Uebergang, weil eine Schiffsbrücke über den Kur, der hier auf 70 Faden breit ist, führt, die im Frühlinge bei großern Wasser abgebrochen wird, weil dann der Strom austritt und die Ebene auf eine Meile weit überschwemmt.'

[352] Qasem Khan. Russian sources called him 'Kasim (Казымъ – Chassem).' See Dorn (1845: 422). There is some confusion in Dorn (1845: 422–423, n. 5), however, who referred to him as both Vetter (cousin) and Bruder (brother) of Mustafa Khan. Thus, 'als im J. 1796 die Russen sich Schamachi näherten, Mustafa Chan sich auf die Gebirge zurückzog, und Ursache an seiner Freundschaft zu zweifeln gab, worauf sein Vetter *Kasim* als Chan von Schamachi bestätigt ward. Nach dem Rückzuge der Russen verjagte aber Mustafa seinen Bruder, und bemächtigte sich wieder Schamachis.' Klaproth (1814: 205) very clearly identified him as Mustafa Khan's brother. Eichwald (1837: 586) called him 'Haschim Chan.'

[353] Cf. the Armenian villages of 'Groß-Lack' and 'Klein-Lack' in the Kobustan district. See Klaproth (1814: 208).

[354] Cf. Eichwald (1837: 586), 'Der frühere Chan von Schirvan, Mustapha, hatte zwar, als er von Cuba nach Alt-Schamachie gekommen war, den Befehl vom Schach erhalten, den Schach Sade, Schich Ali Mirsa, unter sicherer Bedeckung nach Persien zu schaffen, bei sich die Sarbasen zurückzulassen, und selbst in Schirvan zu bleiben; allein Mustapha Chan überzeugte sich bald von der Annäherung des Generals von Krabbe, verließ Alt-Schamachie, und setzte über den Kur bei der Ueberfahrt Dshawat, nachdem er eine Menge schirvan'scher Bewohner mit sich fortgezogen hatte; doch suchten die meisten, die sein Vorhaben merkten, von ihm sich loszumachen, und flohen in ihre Heimath zurück; andere wurden von dem Bruder des Mustapha Chan, Haschim Chan, befreit, der zugleich mit andern an Rußland ergebenen Begs, die sich beim General Krabbe befanden, und mit einem Theil der schirwan'schen Reiterei, den Mustapha bis zur Ueberfahrt Dshawat verfolgte, und dabei seine Proviantmagazine in den Dörfern Lakki und Navage wegnahm, da er in der Eile seiner Flucht diese vergessen hatte.'

[355] Anonymous (1826q) has 'Maksizlu (Machrisla).' Anonymous (1826r) has only 'Maksizlu.' This is the village of Mafruzlu c. 7.5 km west of Khoda Afarin. See Adamec (1976: 421).

[356] Khoda Afarin. Several bridges have stood here. Le Strange (1905: 167) noted, 'lower down the Aras lay the town of Zangiyân in the Murdân Na'îm district, where a...bridge, still in existence,

the Araxes. Should he do this, he will meet with the corps of General Paskewitsch, which is between the Araxes and the Akh-Uglan,[357] on the little river Tscheraken.'"[358]

11.140 'Russia and Persia,' *The New-York Evening Post* (Wednesday, 7 March, 1827; first three paras. only), 'Russia and Persia,' *Eastern Argus* (Tuesday, 13 March, 1827), 'England and Persia,' *New-York American* (Tuesday, 13 March, 1827) and 'Foreign. England and Persia,' *The Western Star* (Friday, 30 March, 1827; with minor variations, and all paras. after para. three): 'From the London New Times....Some paragraphs have appeared lately in several of the Paris papers, respecting Persia and Russia, and the ineffectual attempts of mediation, on the part of England, to terminate the war between these countries, which a series of circumstances conspire to invest with a significant character. An article in the Quotidienne, which we can hardly persuade ourselves has been put forth, at this particular juncture, as a piece of mere ordinary intelligence. The apparent object of this article is, to recall the military project of Bonaparte, in conjunction with Russia and Persia, to invade and revolutionize our East India possessions; the real object, we believe, is conveyed in the following concluding sentences:—

"It is of some consequence that the British Cabinet should know how possible it is to raise against it the discontented population of India; it is good that it should know that, if its policy should create uneasiness in Europe, the latter has merely to frame the wish, in order to snatch from Great Britain those possessions whence her commerce derives all its prosperity, and her policy all its arrogance."....

It is thus we feel inclined to interpret the ambiguous allusions to the Persian war, in the Paris papers, the repeated assertion of the determination of the Emperor Nicholas to prosecute that war to extremity; and lastly, the not ambiguous insinuation that our

---

crosses the Araxes. This is called the Pûl-i-Khudâ-Âfarîn in Persian, "the Bridge of Praising God," which Mustawfī says had been built by one of the Companions of the prophet Muḥammad in the year 15 (636).' Dubois de Montpéreux (1840: 57) wrote of 'le pont de Khoudapérim, si remarquable, que les habitants du pays croient que Dieu l'a construit de ses mains.' Another bridge was built here in 1030 by 'Fadlun the Kurd,' or Fadl I, 'a symbol either of his solicitude for the development of trade, or more probably of his designs against Azarbayjan.' See Minorsky (1953: 44). According to MacGregor (1871: 249), s.v. Khuda Afrīd, 'There are two bridges here close to each other, one of which is very ancient, the other modern, but both are partially ruined, some of the arches having been at different times destroyed, but they are occasionally repaired by trees being thrown.' According to Kleiss (1986: 330) the younger bridge dates to the Qajar era.

[357] Mod. Akoglan. Anonymous (1859b: 121) has 'Akuglan, a town in Persia, in the prov. of Azerbijan, 105 m. ENE of Nakchivan, in a rich and fertile district.' Cf. Bitis (2006: 26), 'Akhuglan in the Karabakh [Qarabagh].' Stcherbatow (1890: 175) called it 'Agh-Oglou, au passage même de la rivière.'

[358] According to Eichwald (1837: 585), 'Der Generaladjutant Paskewitsch befand sich im Lager beim Dorfe Tscherakan in der karabagh'schen Provinz, in der Nähe der chudoperin'schen Brücke, um den Feind gehörig zu beobachten, der vor ihm über den Araxes gegangen war.' This is probably Shirakan.

European policy may be kept in check, by the fear of seeing our Empire in the East subverted.—New Times

We draw these conclusions from no hasty premises.....Let us see how this feeling connects itself with the hope of arresting our progress, by aiming a blow at our East India possessions, and how existing circumstances between this country and Persia are supposed to furnish the contemplated means.

The political relations between this country and Persia, from their peculiarity, and the remote influence they are considered to exercise upon the more important interests of Great Britain, have been matters rather of secret diplomatick negociation, than of publick inquiry. It is only when, in consequence of the link which binds them with interests nearer home, that they are calculated to awaken a more lively anxiety.

Our readers are aware that hostilities have broken out between Russia and Persia—that the war is now carrying on—and that the Cabinet of St Petersburgh is bilieved [sic] to cherish views of aggrandisement in that quarter, which the present quarrel, on whichever side it may have originated, will afford facilities for accomplishing.

It is equally notorious that the general policy of England is opposed to the principal of territorial aggrandisement by any of the Allied Powers, as tending to disturb that balance of power, which was deliberately fixed at the Congresses of Vienna[359] and Aix-la-Chapelle,[360] when, out of the ruins and scattered elements of the Continental Thrones, crippled, subverted, or shaken by the wars consequent upon the French Revolution, the present political edifice was constructed.

Among these events which which mainly contributed to the overthrow of Napoleon, after his fatal invasion of Russia, were the successful negotiations entered into by England at Teheran, to terminate the war then carrying on between Russia and Persia, and thus to concentrate the military energies of the former power, in her retaliatory invasion of France.

These negociations ended in the signing of a definitive Treaty of Friendship between Great Britain and Persia, on the 25th of Nov. 1814, at Teheran. This treaty was signed, on the part of Great Britain, by James Eorie [sic, Morier], Esq. and Henry Ellis, Esq.[361] on the

---

[359] Peace conference held in Vienna from November, 1814, to June, 1815, after Napoleon's defeat. See Chapman (1998). As de Pradt (1815: 4), wrote, 'The Congress of Vienna will stop these invasions of force; it will banish these Roman practices; it will re-establish those humane habits that have governed Europe; and, in the silence of arms, reason will be heard.'

[360] Also known by its German name Aachen. This refers to the congress held in the autumn of 1818 when France was received again as one of the five great powers, along with Britain, Russia, Prussia and Austria, following the Napoleonic wars and the French payment of reparations. See de Pradt (1820).

[361] Bindoff et al. (1934: 85) noted that he 'arrived at Kinakir, where he met Morier, 14 Aug. 1814 and accompanied him to Tehran *via* Tabriz, arriving at Tehran mid-Nov. 1814. With Morier...negotiated and signed the treaty of 25 Nov. 1814 with Persia, and left Tehran for England early Dec. 1814 bearing the treaty.' As Ingram (1981: 305) wrote, 'Ellis, the bastard son of the earl of Buckinghamshire, and brother-in-law of Viscount Goderich, had begun his career as a "Malcolmite." He had been attached to Malcolm's mission to Persia in 1808 and had then accompanied another of

part of Persia, by Mirza Mahommed Sheffi,[362] Mirza Buzurk Caimaquam,[363] and Mirza Abdul Wahab.[364]

By this treaty, it is understood that Great Britain guaranteed to Persia, in case of invasion by Russia, not only military support but a subsidy of £200,000, a year, so long as the war should continue. With respect to the first point, that of military aid, no difference of opinion, we believe exists; but upon the second, we understand doubts were raised by Persia, whether the subsidy was to be constructed as a war contribution only, or whether it was not to become a permanent charge, in consideration of certain commercial privileges conceded to us, and as a means of keeping Persia always in a condition to resist any aggression from her powerful and ambitious neighbour. If we are not mis-informed, England did consent to pay it for a short period after the actual termination of hostilities, but without by so doing, recognizing the claim advanced by Persia.

The question has been repeatedly agitated since the year 1814, and, at one period, with so much warmth, by the Persian government, that our then Charge'd Affaires [sic] at the Court of Persia (Mr. Willock)[365] found himself in a position of some personal danger even.

Recent events have revived both these questions, with increased vehemence of discussion. Mr. Willock has arrived in this country[366] to represent to his Majesty's Government the full reliance of Persia upon, as well as the absolute necessity of, its aid, at the present moment. The demand, we believe, is urgent and unqualified, inasmuch, as without it, Persia must submit to whatever terms her gigantick adversary may choose to impose.

Malcolm's admirers on a mission to Sind. While acting as a private secretary to his father, who was president of the board of control in the earl of Liverpool's government from its formation in 1812 until 1816, Ellis was sent to Teheran to negotiate the final terms of the treaty of Teheran. Although Ellis had warned Castlereagh that the British would have to find a way to prevent the transformation of Persia into a protectorate of Russia, until he joined the board of control in 1830 he shared the assumption of the "Malcolmites" that the Persian Connection was the best way to defend British India. Ellis had supported Canning's decision to put the Persian Mission back under the control of the government of India in the hope that the British would then be able to act in Persia with greater vigour. The terms of the treaty of Torkmanchay showed that this was a forlorn hope. During his four years at the board of control Ellis transferred himself, as it were, from the Bombay to the Ludhiana School of Indian defence. His strategy for propping up Persia as a buffer state devoted more attention to holding back Russia than regaining Great Britain's former influence.'

[362] Mirza Shafi'-e Mazandarani. Cf. 9.93.

[363] Mirza 'Isa-ye Farahani or Mirza Bozorg Qa'em Maqam-e Sadarat-e Ozma. Cf. 10.244.

[364] Mirza 'Abd ol-Vahhab-e Isfahani. Cf. 10.15, 11.22, 11.127.

[365] Henry Willock is meant here, not George.

[366] According to Anonymous (1842a: 81), 'After having honourably discharged the duties of chargé d'affaires for nearly twelve years, Mr. [Henry] Willock retired from the office, on the 5th January, 1827, and came over to England.' In fact, he resigned when, on 27 August 1826, the senior diplomatic post in Persia was transferred from Whitehall to the East India Company by the Foreign Secretary George Canning (Ingram 1981, 1984: 181) and Macdonald Kinneir became Envoy to the Court of Persia. See Harden (1971a: 80).

Here commence all the difficulties of the question; and these difficulties may be said to divide themselves into two branches; first as relates to the obligations imposed upon us by the faith of treaties; secondly, as relates to the obvious delicacy of our position with regard to Russia.

In reference to the first of these difficulties, Persia may be regarded as the Portugal of the East. The basis of our connexion with her is strikingly analogous. A similar cause being established, would exact from us similar interference. Persia, too, like Portugal, has been threatened of political intrigues and pretensions (wherein a marked resemblance may be traced) to subvert the ascendancy of England; while the interests at stake are of incalculably greater magnitude.

So important, indeed, are these latter, that it is not hazarding too much to affirm, the general policy of the country would step in to protect Persia from becoming a Province, or Pachalick, as it were, of Russia, even if it were possible to show that she was not the original aggressor. But these, and other considerations, connected with all the details of this momentous subject, would lead us too far at present.'

11.141 'Latest from Europe,' Onondaga *Register* (Wednesday, 14 March, 1827), 'Late from Europe,' *The Geneva Gazette* (Wednesday, 14 March, 1827; with minor variations), "Late from Europe,' *Catskill Recorder* (Wednesday, 14 March, 1827), 'Foreign,' *Kinderhook Herald* (Thursday, 15 March, 1827; with minor variations), 'Late from Europe. Paris,' *The Freeman's Journal* (Tuesday, 19 March, 1827), 'Late from Europe. Paris,' *St. Lawrence Gazette* (Wednesday, 20 March, 1827) and 'Untitled,' *Plattsburgh Republican* (Saturday, 31 March, 1827; with minor variations): 'It is said that Persia had applied to England for assistance in the war with Russia.'

11.142 'Persia,' *Eastern Argus* (Tuesday, 13 March, 1827), 'Late Foreign News. Persia,' *The Geneva Gazette* (Thursday, 21 March, 1827) and 'Late Foreign News. Persia,' *Catskill Recorder* (Thursday, 21 March, 1827): 'The packet ship Robert Fulton, arrived in New-York on the 13th, bringing London papers to the 7th, and Liverpool to the 9th of February, inclusive.... It is said that the secret treaty between Great Britain and Persia, signed about the year 1814, binding this country to the payment of an annual subsidy of £200,000 to the Schah of Persia,[367] and the latter Prince to the maintenance of a stipulated body of men, is still in existence.—What operation this compact may have on the present crisis of the war with Russia is a difficult, and no doubt, a very serious question.'[368]

---

[367] Fath 'Ali Shah.

[368] As Markham (1874: 379–380) noted, 'In 1814, Mr. Ellis, in conjunction with Mr. Morier, was deputed to negotiate a finally definitive Treaty between Great Britain and Persia. Mîrza Shafy, the Prime Minister, and another statesman, named 'Abdu'l-Wahhâb, were appointed to treat on the part of the Shâh. The principal articles of this Treaty were that England agreed to supply aid in troops, or a subsidy of 200,000 tomâns annually, in case of the invasion of Persia, provided that the Shâh was not the aggressor: that if any European power, at peace with England, made war on Persia, England is still

11   The Second Russo-Persian War and the Treaty of Torkmanchay (1826–1828)   1225

11.143 'From the Quotidienne,' *New-York American (for the Country),* (Tuesday, 13 March, 1827) and 'From the Quotidienne—a Paris Paper,' *The Freeman's Journal* (Monday, 2 April, 1827): 'A great deal was said at one period of a military expedition to India, of which Bonaparte had conceived the idea, & in which Russia and Persia were to concur. Some persons have been inclined to cast doubts upon the project. ...Whatever doubts may be entertained of the practicability of this bold project, there are none entertained at present of its having been contemplated. We ourselves saw, in 1815, a Memorial at that time deposited in the State Paper Office of the Minister of War, entitled "The Campaign of Indostan."[369] We are rather inclined to believe that the declaration of war made in 1812 by Bonaparte against Russia, principally arose from the refusal of the Emperor Alexander to participate in an enterprise, the object of which was, the ruin of the Power which, at that time, formed the sole counterpoise to the great Empire. If there was any necessity for recurring to proofs, which attest the reality of this project, we should find, at least, one in the mission with which General Gardanne was charged to the Sovereign of Persia. That Ambassador went to Teheran, accompanied by a great number of officers, intended, without doubt, to organize and discipline the Persian army. But the most authentic proof is to be found in the Memorial which we have just mentioned, which is probably the same that was recently published, and which contains, not only the plan of the expedition, but the route of the forces that were to carry it into execution; the means of providing for their subsistence, &c.; all of which are detailed with a military precision, the merit of which soldiers only can appreciate. According to this Memorial, the expedition was to set out from Aster-Abad, a city situated at the southern extremity of the Caspian Sea. ...It is of some consequence that the British Cabinet should know how possible it is to raise against it the discontented population of India; it is good that it should know that if its policy should create uneasiness in Europe, the latter has merely to frame the wish, in order to snatch from Great-Britain those possessions whence her commerce derives all its prosperity, and her policy all its arrogance.'

11.144 'Persia,' *New-York Evening Post* (Friday, 23 March, 1827): 'The British Ministry is said to be actively employed in bringing the quarrel between Russia and Persia to a close

---

bound to assist Persia by troops or by a subsidy: that if the Afghans invaded India, Persia was to send an army against them: and Persian rebels were to be expelled from British territory, and, if they refused to leave it, they were to be seized and sent to Persia. This treaty, usually known as the Treaty of Tehran, was signed by Mr. Morier and Mr. Ellis on the part of England: and by Mîrza Shafy (Prime Minister), 'Abdu'l-Wahhâb (Secretary of State), and Mîrza Bûzûrg (Kâim-Makân), on the part of Persia, on November 25, 1814; and continued in force until the war between Persia and England in 1856–1857.' The 'serious question' was whether or not Britain was obliged to keep paying the subsidy if Persia, as alleged, initiated the conflict.

[369] This may be a document drafted by General Gardane, entitled 'Idées du général Gardane sur une expédition dans l'Inde par Delhi et Patna en traversant la Turquie et la Perse' with 'Notes sur certains détails faisant suite aux idées sur une expédition dans l'Inde, adressées par le général Gardane, le 24 décembre 1807, à S. Exc. le Ministre des relations extérieures.' See Gardane (1865: 111–144).

by mediation. Our treaty with Persia does not, it seems, bind us to commit ourselves to war with any power by which she may be attacked but to afford her aid in money, should our moderation fail. This need not, necessarily, embroil us with Russia, in case she persists in her aggressions against Persia, but to a captious power would prove somewhat an embarrassing state of things, and might lead a predisposed court to an open rupture.'

11.145 'Latest from Europe. Russia and Persia,' *New-York Spectator* (Friday, 23 March, 1827): 'The Journal de St. Petersburgh, of January 26th, contains some account of the proceedings of General Yermoloff, in Georgia, but they are not of much importance. We quote the following. . . .

Tranquility prevails on the frontiers of Persia. A detachment of Persian cavalry, which attacked one of the Nomade camps, near the Araxes, could not do any injury to the inhabitants, and was even repulsed with loss. In order to prevent similar attempts, part of the van-guard had gone from Akouglane[370] towards the bridge of Koupoperinisk,[371] to be better able to protect the banks of the Araxes. Towards the steppe of Mongan[372] the inspection of the frontier is confided to the detachment of Colonel Mistchenko,[373] placed near the ford of Djavat,[374] and on the Koura.'

11.146 'Latest from Europe. Russia,' *The Schenectady Cabinet* (Wednesday, 28 March, 1827), 'Foreign News. Persia,' *The Yeoman's Gazette* (Saturday, 31 March, 1827), 'Russia,' *The Freeman's Journal* (Monday, 2 April, 1827) and 'Foreign. Latest from Europe. Russia,' *The Western Star* (Friday, 6 April, 1827): 'Hostilities have been suspended between Persia and Russia, by the season; and it is supposed they will not be resumed.'

11.147 'Latest from England,' *The Schenectady Cabinet* (Wednesday, 4 April, 1827), 'Latest from England,' *Kinderhook Herald* (Thursday, 5 April, 1827) and 'Late Foreign News. Late from Europe,' *Onondaga Register* (Wednesday, 11 April, 1827): 'There had

---

[370] Cf. 11.142.

[371] Khoda Afarin.

[372] Mughan.

[373] Also spelled Mitchenko/Mitschenko/Mistschenko/Mitzchenko/Mistchenkow. As Stcherbatow used the form Mitchenko in his study of Paskevich, this will be adopted here. In 1825, in the wake of the Decembrist rebellion, Mitchenko was ordered to arrest Griboyedov. See Kelly (2006: 131–132). According to Eichwald (1837: 584) 'Obrist Mischtschenko I' was 'Commandeur des apscheron'schen Fußregiments.' Stcherbatow (1890: 44) wrote that he commanded the Kura regiment. Previously and subsequently he served in Daghestan (Gammer 1994: 32, 52) and played an active part in the Russo-Turkish War of 1828–1829. See Bourde (1878: 170–171). An infantry colonel named Konstantin Ivanovich Mitchenko was at Jassy in 1841. See Jelavich and Jelavich (1962: 136).

[374] Javad. Cf. 11.139.

been frequent meetings of the Divan at Constantinople, supposed to be respecting the advance of the Russian armies into Persia. The Turkish government was alarmed at being nearly surrounded by the armies of Russia.'

11.148 'St. Petersburg, Feb. 21,' *National Gazette and Literary Register* (Monday, 16 and Tuesday 17 April, 1827), 'St. Petersburg, Feb. 21,' *Eastern Argus* (Tuesday, 24 April, 1827) and 'St. Petersburg, Feb. 21,' *The Charleston Courier* (Wednesday, 25 April, 1827): 'News[375] from the army in Georgia of 24th January. Lieutenant General Prince Madatoff, after having passed the Araxes, on the 28th December, effected his junction with the detachment of Colonel Mitzchenke, commanding the regiment of infantry of Apcheron, which had come from Djavat. The troops then advanced rapidly by the defile of Daraourte[376] to the little river Zambour,[377] near which was encamped a part of the Nomade tribes of Sekaksevan,[378] Adjaline[379] and others. The sudden appearance of our troops threw these tribes into great confusion. The cavalry of Karabagh and Schirwan, reinforced by the Armenians of Karabagh, suddenly attacked their camp with success, and took from them 15,000 sheep, besides a considerable number of camels and horses. About 500 Nomade families of Karapagh, who had been carried beyond the frontiers of the Persians, came and offered their submission, and were put back into that province.

Lieutenant General Prince Madatoff having caused a report to be spread that he intended to advance into the Chenate of Talyche, slowly continued his march in order to induce the Nomade tribes on the borders of Talyche to take refuge in the district of Meschkine,[380] where it was more easy to attack them; this plan perfectly succeeded.

On entering into the district of Meschkine, during the night of the 1st of January, Prince Madatoff learnt of the arrival of these Nomades, and immediately detached his light cavalry and the Armenian infantry to attack them. The enemy being taken by surprise, made but a faint and short resistance; they had 18 men killed, and some wounded; on our side we did not lose a single man; and we took from the several Nomade tribes of Sekaksevan[381] 2000 camels, 10,000 head of horned cattle and 60,000 sheep.[382] Prince Madatoff occupied the

---

[375] The account given in this article is identical to that found in Eichwald (1837: 589–590).

[376] Tapper (1997: 162). Brosset (1857: 327) has 'la montagne de Daraoud.'

[377] Brosset (1857: 327) has 'la rivière de Zabour.'

[378] Shahsevan. Cf. Tapper (1997).

[379] Tapper (1997: 59).

[380] Area between Ahar and Ardabil, traditional territory of part of the Shahsevan. See Tapper (1988: 87, 1997: 134). Cf. Brosset (1857: 327), 'Metnic' who wrote, in n. 2, 'Au lieu de Metnik, on lit "le district de Mechkin, Мешкинскій округъ," chez Zoubof…Ce qui me fait croire que notre historien aura puisé à une source russe et lu le nom du pays comme s'il était écrit Метниксій, différence très minime, pour qui ne sait pas la vraie orthographe du nom.'

[381] Shahsevan.

[382] Brosset (1857: 327, n. 3) noted that, according to Zubov, 200, rather than 2000 camels, were seized.

little town of Lahar or Lori, in the District of Meschkine. Ala Khan, governor of this District, and his brother Schon Kour Khan,[383] came and solicited the protection of Prince Madatoff, who received them with kindness. The terror inspired by the appearance of our troops has spread as far as the city of Ahar Emi Zade Seifoumouleck. Mirza,[384] who occupied it, has fled to Tauris with his family, and the 1500 regular troops under his command, have disbanded themselves. Prince Madatoff writes, that the road leading to the town of Lahar[385] and the passage of Mount Salvate[386] Hiadytchi[387] are rather difficult The corps under his command amounts to 11,000 troops of different descriptions, with thirty-five pieces of artillery.'

11.149 'London, March 8.—City, Quarter past Two,' *Savannah Georgian* (Monday, 16 April, 1827) and 'From the Savannah Georgian, April 16. Twenty days later from Liverpool,' *Louisiana Advertiser* (Saturday, 5 May, 1827): 'Advices from Tifles, of the 24th January, mention, that on the 9th of that month, Lieut.-General Prince Madatoff had passed the Araxis, and having formed a junction on the other side with Col. Mitzchenko, they had vigorously attacked the tribes cantoned along the Samboor.'[388]

11.150 'Untitled,' *National Gazette and Literary Register* (Tuesday, 17 April, 1827) and 'Untitled,' *The Freeman's Journal* (Monday, 23 April, 1827): 'The Paris Constitutionel of the 17th Feb. mentions that a peace had been concluded between Russia and Persia. Russia,

---

[383] 'Ata Khan. Similarly, Eichwald (1837: 590) wrote, 'Ata Chan, Verwalter dieses Kreises, und sein Bruder Schukur Chan, erschienen vor ihm, und baten um Schutz; Madatoff nahm sie gern auf.' Tapper (1997: 128) called 'Ata Khan 'a legendary figure among the Meshkin tribes,' who was 'said to have been blinded by Agha Mohammad Qajar.' This, Tapper has suggested, could explain why he and his brother welcomed the Russians. See Tapper (1997: 151). According to Brosset (1857: 327), Shükür Khan ('Choukour-Khan') was 'Ata Khan's father, not his brother.

[384] This appears to be a corrupted reference to *amir-zadeh*, 'son of commander' or 'descendant of an amir,' Seif ol-Moluk Mirza, a nephew of 'Abbas Mirza's, for whom see Busse (1972: 200). Brosset (1857: 327) has 'le chah-zadeh Seïf-oul-Mirza.' For the title see Sparroy (1902: 104), Floor (2010a: 370).

[385] Lahar was located on the route from Aslanduz to Ardabil. See Morier (1818: 251), MacGregor (1871: 616).

[386] Salavat (S'alawat; Салаватыs), a mountain in Daghestan, north of Nucha, has been confused here with Sav/balan (Саваланъ), an extinct volcano in Azerbaijan, visible from Ardabil .See Radde (1901: 31, 38) in the 'Verzeichnis der Namen aller Sammelplätze, die im Herbarium caucasicum vertreten sind, mit den angewendeten Abkürzungen.' Cf. Radde (1885). Tapper (1997: 235, 301) seems to have accepted 'Salavat' but geographically this is clearly not the toponym being referred to here. For the exploration of Savalan cf. Potts (2017a).

[387] The meaning of 'Hiadytchi' is unclear. It looks like a corruption of the name Hidayat and may relate to the legend of a 'prophet' buried atop Savelan. See Potts (2017a). Brosset (1857: 327) had 'Salawad-Ghritchi,' and in n. 5 noted, 'Chez Zoubof. . .Savad-Gliaditch. . . .C'est le Savalan.'

[388] Given as 'Zambour' in 1827.19 above. Cf. Eichwald (1837: 589), 'Flüßchen Sambura;' Brosset (1857: 327), 'Zabour.'

it is said, was to obtain to the fortress of Erivan, and thus her frontiers would extend to the Araxes.'

11.151 'London, March 8' *National Gazette and Literary Register* (Tuesday, 17 April, 1827): 'Accounts from Madras have been received to the 17th Oct. A great sensation appears to have been produced by the transpiring of the dispatches to the Indian Government from Persia, in which details were given of the war with Russia, and the advance of the armies of the North into the Persian territory.... Bengal papers and letters to the 8th of November have been received. The good people at Calcutta appear sadly alarmed at the advance of the Russians into Persia; and the government papers in particular give long details on the subject; they recommend caution to the Indian government, and that a survey should be made of the frontiers, &c. that in case of hostilities being necessary, the English army may not be sacrificed as in Ava, through ignorance of the country. The Gazette of the 23rd October, in a lengthened paper on this subject, says, "For the present we must rest contented, and not disturb the eagle of Russia in her quarry."'

11.152 'Russian and Persian War,' *The Geneva Palladium* (Wednesday, 18 April, 1827): 'From the New-York Albion, of March 31.

The remote situation of the theatre of these hostilities, and the little that is known of the country in which the conflicting armies are engaged, seem to place the subject almost without the sphere of newspaper investigation. Little therefore, comes to our knowledge except what is derived from the Russian statements, or when we hear of a battle fought, the favorable issue of which is generally claimed by the Autocrat.[389] The imperfection of our geographical knowledge of that part of the world, the inaccuracy of maps, and the egregiously undefined state of the boundary in dispute, render it an almost hopeless task to comprehend the precise nature of the question, more more to convey a knowledge of it to others. Still, as there is an importance attached to this question from the supposed influence that an acquisition of power on the part of Russia in Persia may have over the British power in India, the subject is worthy of consideration. Some of the English journals and periodicals have lately taken the subject in hand, and to them, chiefly, we are indebted for a few facts which may not be uninteresting to our readers.[390]

All the accounts we have hitherto received describe the war as being an unprovoked aggression on the part of Persia. General Yermaloff, in his proclamation to the Georgians, says,—"The Persians, who have long been known to you by their hostile dispositions and base insolence, have unexpectedly entered our territories with their forces;" and the Emperor Nicholas charitably considered the invasion the unauthorized act of some lawless or subordinate chief, until he learnt that the Persian army was commanded by the Prince Abbas Mirza in person. We shall endeavor to ascertain the extent of the Persian guilt, so far

---

[389] Nicholas I.

[390] Much of what follows is taken verbatim, without attribution, from McNeill (1827).

as our limited means will permit us in doing, which it may illustrate the subject if we take a brief view of the historical relations of the two countries.

It seems to be now conceded on all hands, that Russia has a steady, hereditary, and unconquerable desire to extend her power in the east, particularly on the side of Persia. This feeling began with the Great Peter, and has been constantly followed up by his successors, and by none more than Catherine—who, next to the planting of her imperial eagles on the walls of Byantium, held this as the most cherished object of her policy. The difficulty, however, of passing the great geographical boundaries which nature had given the two countries, was formidable, for it was not easy to conceive a stronger or clearer line of demarkation than nature herself has erected. The black sea on the one side, and the Caspian on the other, connected by the stupendous range of the Caucasian mountains, seemed to fix the limits which the Almighty has given to man. This line can be traced in a moment on almost any map. Yet did Peter pass this barrier, and establish himself beyond it, and although he acquired thereby, only a few trifling and badly protected districts, it is certain, that that profound politician had some ulterior object, of much higher importance, in view.

Peter in pursuance of his darling scheme, to open a trade with India, let no opportunity escape to mix in the affairs of the intermediate countries, and as early as 1717 sent an embassy under Prince Bekewick[391] to the Khan of Khiva.[392] This embassy was accompanied by a military force, which had orders to seize any gold mines that lay in their way, but the Prince and his army were cut to pieces. Such was the predatory nature of this embassy. The descent of a body of Lesgees in 1719, from the Caucasus to the province of Sheerwan, on the Persian side of the range, when among other atrocities they put to death a number of Russian merchants; the inability of the resident chief to avenge the outrage; and the apathy of the Persian Government on the subject, afforded Peter an opportunity to interfere, and finally to establish himself on the south side of the Caucasian range. In 1722 he fitted out his famous expedition from Astrachan, consisting of 100,000 men, for the avowed purpose of punishing the Lesgees. With this army he entered the Persian territory with professions of amity for that power, and took possession of the fortress of Derbend, the key of the Persian provinces, bordering on the Caspian. Here he, partly by force, and partly cajolery, induced the Persian Envoy, who was in his camp, to sign a treaty, by which Persia ceded to Russia the provinces of Gilan, Mazanderan, and Astrabad, with the town of Shamakhoo as soon as it should be recovered from the Turks. Thus by force and fraud Peter obtained possession of all the shores on that part of the Caspian which belonged to Persia. The Sha, however, refused to ratify the treaty and sent an army against the Russians, which for the time kept them in check.

---

[391] Alexander Bekovich-Cherkassky (d. 1717). Cf. 1.11.

[392] Shir Ghazi Khan (r. 1715–1728). 'The last effective Yadigarid khan,' and 'a patron of learning and literature' who repulsed Peter the Great's attempt to take possession of Khiva but who was murdered in 1728 as a result of 'internecine tribal struggle between the Kongrat and Manghit tribes.' See Soucek (2000: 186).

Things remained many years in an unsettled state, and the Turks at length attacked the northern and western part of Persia, over-ran many provinces, and pushed their conquests all over Georgia; but an energetic Prince, Nadir Sha, rose to retrieve the character of his country. By a series of brillian military achievements he drove the Turks from all their newly conquered territory, cleared Georgia, and expelled the Russians from all their country so treacherously usurped by Czar Peter, and re-established the ancient boundary of Persia on the ridge of the Caucasian mountains. It is said that this great warrior never lost but one battle.

Nadir Sha, to confirm his power on the Caspian, and to reward his faithful adherents, raised the ancient family of the Wallees of Georgia to the dependent throne of that country, and in order to hold this family more effectually in his power, divided Georgia into two kingdoms, giving one to Heraclius who had attended him in his wars, and the other to Tamras, the head and representative of the Wallee family. But on the death of Nadir, Persia was torn by internal commotions, and the kings of Georgia finding themselves, after the death of their master, unable to check the predatory incursions of the Caucasian Mountaineers, and forgetting the injunction of their benefactor, made a formal application for assistance to Russia. This happened in 1752, and from that period may be dated the possession of Georgia by Muscovites.

In 1781, a treaty with the Oss,[393] a pagan tribe inhabiting the Caucasus, opened to Russia the defiles leading into Georgia; and in a treaty made in 1783, the Wallees acknowledged the paramount sovereignty of Russia. The Empress Catharine 3rd [sic], on her part promising the Wallees the perpetual possession of their own territories, and any other they might happen to conquer elsewhere. Paul Potemkin,[394] in 1785, constructed a military road across the mountains. And thus secured a good highway for the readier prosecution of her future schemes. Georgia then became a dependency of Russia, without regard to the rights of Persia, and Potemkin had orders to receive, under a promise of protection, any other nation that might think proper to desert its own legitimate sovereign.

A series of wars then ensued with various success between Persia and her revolted provinces, for a number of years, when, in 1800, the Emperor Paul incorporated Georgia

---

[393] Ossetians.

[394] Count Pavel Sergeyevich Potemkin (1743–1796). Cousin of Catherine the Great's favorite Prince Potemkin and 'commander of Russian forces in the northern Caucasus.' See Atkin (1980: 38). One contemporary referred to him as 'prince Paul Sergiéitch Potemkin, commandant de la ligne du Caucase, qui tenait en bride les peuples sauvages de ces contrées.' See Brosset (1857: 399). As Durand (1857: 34–35) observed, 'il fallait faire franchir les monts à un matériel de guerre considérable, et les défilés étaient presque infranchissables; celui de Dariel, déjà exploré, n'avait encore reçu que de légères améliorations, et de grands travaux restaient à faire pour le rendre praticable à l'artillerie. Paul Potemkin fut chargé de hâter l'exécution de cette route militaire.' Writing of the rulers of Georgia and the Tartars of the Crimea, Dulaurier (1861: 963) said, 'La création de la grande route militaire par le général Paul Potemkin les plaça sous la main des Russes.' As Atkin (1980: 44) noted, 'There was an overland route linking Tbilisi and the Caucasian Line, but it was narrow and steep even after Paul Potemkin made improvements since it crossed the high Caucasus.'

with the Russian empire. This act, which Paul asserted was done to compose all differences, was not likely to have any such salutary consequences, and, accordingly a number of battles was continued to be fought between the Persian and Russian troops until 1814, when England, by great exertion happily brought about a peace, by her mediation.— By the treaty made on this occasion, Persia surrendered all right to the conquests of Russia south of the Caucasus, and engaged not to maintain a navy on the Caspian sea. For these humiliating concessions, Russia agreed to support the Crown Prince against all competitors; and England engaged to pay a subsidy to Persia of 200,000 tomans annually to support troops whenever the latter might be attacked by any power at war with England: and in case the power so attacking Persia should not be at war with England, then England was bound to use her best efforts to bring about an accomodation, and if she failed in her efforts to do so, then 200,000 tomans were still to be paid. The delicate situation of England at this moment under such circumstances is very obvious. It was a strange bargain certainly, but John Bull[395] is apt to make such blunders; he was at that time closely grappling with his great enemy, Bonaparte, and therefore did not stand upon trifles.'

11.153 'Russia,' *The Western Star* (Friday, 20 April, 1827): 'No details of the advance of the Russian armies into Persia are mentioned; but only the main fact of great success, and the probability of that country being occupied by a Russian force for a lengthened period.'

11.154 'Untitled,' *The Geneva Gazette and General Advertiser* (Wednesday, 25 April, 1827) and 'Foreign. Late from Europe,' *The Corrector* (Saturday, 5 May, 1827): ['London, March 12....] The Russian government were making the greatest preparations for vigorously prosecuting the war against Persia.'

11.155 'Foreign,' *The Kinderhook Herald* (Thursday, 26 April, 1827): '[By the packet ship Columbia, bringing London papers to the 12th March.] 'Official accounts from Persia to the 17th of January, mention some further military successes obtained by the Russians over the Persians.'

[By the Edward Quesnel, bringing Paris papers to the 9th March.] 'The Constitutionel mentions that peace had been concluded between Russia and Persia. Russia, it is said, was to obtain the fortress of Erivan, and thus her frontiers would extend to the Araxes.'

11.156 '*From Blackwood's Magazine.* Greece—No. III,' *New-York Spectator* (after 30 April, 1827): 'In the cessation of European war, Russia has habitually prepared for hostility by the double measure of keeping a vast army in the exercise of war, and pressing down her frontier towards the empire of the Sultan.[396] In the gradual seizure of the northern

---

[395] Cf. 10.33.
[396] Mahmud II.

provinces of Persia, and even in the establishment of a corps of troops on the shores of the Aral, it is impossible to conceive that her romance should have extended to the conquest even of Persia. India must be altogether beyond her grasp as a permanent possession. She has a more solid and splendid treasure nearer home. But Persia, as an ally, might operate a most powerful part in the fall of Turkey....On the late menace of Russian war, the Sultan was startled on his throne by the trampling of the Persian cavalry....But the Russian diplomacy at the Porte was checked by a superior influence. England had interposed—a feeble and dubious treaty was made—and the Persian auxiliaries submissively turned their bridles back to Teheran.'

11.157 'Interesting Foreign News,' *The Geneva Gazette and General Advertiser* (Wednesday, 16 May, 1827): ['The ship Dalhousie Castle brings London papers to the 14th and Liverpool to the 17th April]....The prospect of peace between Russia and Persia is favorable.'

11.158 'From Europe,' *The Schenectady Cabinet* (Wednesday, 16 May, 1827), 'Foreign News. France,' *Onondaga Register* (Wednesday, 16 May, 1827) and 'Russia,' *The Western Star* (Friday, 18 May, 1827): ['By the arrival at New-York, of the ships Pacific and Great Britain, from Liverpool, and Henry IV, from Havre, English papers to the 12th, and French to the 16th, have been received]....Peace is about to take place between Russia and Persia.'

11.159 'Russia and Persia,' *National Intelligencer* (Thursday, 31 May, 1827; minus paragraph beginning 'We have understood'), 'From Calcutta,' *Republican Monitor* (Wednesday, 6 June 1827), 'From the Salem Gazette. From Calcutta,' *Geneva Palladium* (Wednesday, 6 June 1827; from 'Persia'), 'Russia and Persia,' *Western Star and Lebanon Gazette* (Saturday, 16 June, 1827), 'Russia and Persia,' *Georgia Courier* (Wednesday, 21 June, 1827) and 'Russia and Persia,' *Western Sun & General Advertiser* (Friday, 23 June, 1827): 'The following intelligence from Asia is of much interest, because we have for a long time considered the war, which Russia wages with Persia, pregnant with consequences much more important than the mere fate of a Persian dynasty, or the integrity of the Persian possessions. Every move that Russia makes in the East brings her nearer to British India; and England must view with the deepest interest, if not with apprehension, the progress of the Russian power in that quarter. She can, in fact, not remain much longer an inactive spectator of the war, and it is in the fields of Persia that we may expect to see the peace of Europe broken, and the conflict renewed between two of her greatest Powers.
From Calcutta.
Salem, May 25.

Through the politeness of Capt. Endicott, of the ship George,[397] arrived at this port, we have received copious files of the India Gazette,[398] and the Bengal Hurkaru,[399] to the 27th January.

Persia.

"We understand, says the Editor of the Bombay Gazette,[400] by a letter from the Gulf, of a recent date, that a Persian Chief, named Mostopha Khan,[401] brother-in-law to the King of Persia,[402] at the head of six thousand troops, was marching towards Triflees, (in Ganjah) and, meeting an encampment by the way, approached it, in order to reconnoitre and pillage it, if deserted; no sooner had he entered it, however, than suddenly a troop of russians sallied forth from different directions and put to the sword the whole of the army, with the exception of the leader and a few follows [sic, followers], who narrowly escaped and took refuge at the head quarters of Abbas Meerza, who at the same time was engaged in battle with the inhabitants of Shoosh, (a city in Arminia.)[403] The Russian troops closely pursuing the enemy, met the grand army of Abbas Meerza, and fought them with great slaughter in such a manner that Abbas Meerza was obliged to ask an immediate succor of the troops that

---

[397] Samuel Endicott (1792–1872). The *George* was a fabled ship, built in 1814, 'one of the finest vessels that ever sailed out of Salem—remarkably fast sailing, lucky under all commanders, always arriving with her cargo of Calcutta goods in just the nick of time, when the market for such goods was at the highest rate and the goods in great demand.' Samuel Endicott of Beverly, Massachusetts, sailed on her maiden voyage in May, 1815, as Clerk; on her second voyage as Second Mate; on her third and fourth voyages as First Mate; and from her fifth through eighth voyage as Master, i.e. Captain. See Putnam (1924: 1–12). The newspapers used in the preparation of this article were obtained when Endicott commanded the *George* on her eleventh voyage, departing Salem for Calcutta on 6 August, 1826, and arriving 126 days later, and returning on 23 May, 1827, '107 days from Calcutta.' See Putnam (1924: 18).

[398] Calcutta newspaper that ran from 1780 to 1834, when it was absorbed by the *Bengal Hurkaru*. Originally it was 'the arm of the Governor-General Warren Hastings.' See Codell (2004: 109).

[399] Established in January, 1795, as a weekly, this was 'the senior journal of India,' and became a daily on 29 April 1819. On 1 October 1834 it merged with the *India Gazette*, and in 1844 the *Bengal Herald* and *Calcutta Literary Gazette* were merged with it. See Smith (1851: 1).

[400] Founded in 1789 as the *Bombay Herald*. The name was changed in 1791 and the paper continued until 1914. For some historical anecdotes on the *Bombay Gazette* see Douglas (1893), Sanyal (1894: 165–166), Lovett (1926).

[401] Cf. 11.83, 11.139, variously identified as the khan of Sheki, Shirvan and/or Shamakhi. As noted frequently above, he was 'der letzte persische Herrscher Schirvans, der erst vor Kurzem nach Persien floh, und sein Chanat den Russen überließ.' See Eichwald (1834: 432). Further, as Eichwald (1837: 31) noted, 'Mustapha Chan von Schirvan erhielt den 25 Mai 1806 noch vor dem schekin'schen Chane die allerhöchste Bestätigung seiner Herrschaft. Er floh aber...als Verräther Rußlands, schon im Jahr 1819 nach Persien, und 1820 wurde sein Chanat mit Rußland vereinigt.'

[402] Fath 'Ali Shah.

[403] A reference to 'Abbas Mirza's long and eventually abandoned siege of Shusha. Cf. 11.78.

were stationed at Ganjah, who immediately came to the assistance of the Prince Royal. The Persians at last giving way to the conqueror, dispersed and Abbas Meerza, after leaving the enemy sole master of his garrison and twenty pieces of cannon, made his escape. The Russians finding the city of Ganjah wholly deserted, entered it without the least bloodshed."

Later accounts from Bombay, given in the India Gazette, offer the following confirmation of this account:

"A despatch from our resident in Persia, came in this morning, announcing the total defeat of the grand Persian army by the Russian General Helmadoff,[404] with a force of ten thousand men, and that he had employed his artillery alone, making his adversaries scamper off with great loss and slaughter. He is expected soon to be at Tabriz, and General Yermaloff has got as far as Tehran.[405] No doubt was entertained but the Russians would overrun Persia: the consequence it is not easy to fortel but the correctness of the above may be depended upon."

The editor of the Gazette says:—

"We have understood that the King is personally quite opposed to the war, and that it may be considered as the result of a popular clamor, by the circumstance of the King having in general terms stated, that the Russians ought not to remain in possession of the ground they occupied before the war, being taken up and fully commented upon by the Mualeyees and Moollas. These generally bigoted persons fostered the wishes of the malcontents, who were also excited by Prince Abbas Mirza, who panted for war and glory like a second Hotspur.[406] The King, in the end, although aware of the impolicy of the war, and although anxious to manage affairs prudently and cautiously so as to avoid a rupture with a powerful foe, found himself unable to resist the war faction, who accordingly carried on matters their own way.

"The result, we fear, is likely to prove disastrous to the independence of the Persian Monarchy. Should the Russians reach our frontiers, as the Cossacks have but an undefined idea, we believe, of right and wrong, and stimulated perhaps by success, they may encroach and give rise to measures on our part.'"

---

[404] No Russian general by this name is attested, and Helmadoff looks like a confusion with Yermaloff.

[405] The commander in the action described in this article was Madatov and, needless to say, Ermolov never 'got as far as Tehran.'

[406] Henry Percy (1364–1403), eldest son of the 1st Earl of Northumberland, nicknamed 'Hotspur' for his speed and aggression, particularly during the Hundred Years War when he commandeered a vessel at Yarmouth, sailed to France, and 'made such ridings into the quarters about Calles [Calais], that they never wish a worse neighbour.' As Brennan (1902: 38) noted, 'His quickness of action on this occasion made him more of a hero than ever; and "Hotspur" was his name thenceforward, first among his own soldiery, and afterwards throughout the length and breadth of England.' He was immortalized by Shakespeare in *The Historie of Henry IV* [part 1] subtitled, 'With the Battell at Shrewsbury, betweene the King, and Lord Henry Percy, surnamed Henry Hotspur of the North.'

11.160 'From Calcutta,' *The Freeman's Journal* (Monday, 4 June, 1827), 'From Calcutta,' *St. Lawrence Gazette* (Tuesday, 5 June, 1827) and 'From Calcutta,' *Geneva Gazette and General Advertiser* (Wednesday, 6 June 1827): 'Capt. Endicott, arrived in Salem from Calcutta, has furnished the Editor of the *Salem Gazette* with India papers to 27th January.] Of the extracts, are advices received at Bombay, from *Persia*, communicated by the British President,[407] announcing the total defeat of the Persian army by the Russians; that Gen. Yermaloff had got as far as Teheran, and that no doubt was entertained, but the Russians would overrun Persia. The war (as our accounts from Russia have stated) was excited by the Prince Abbas Mirza, a second *Hotspur*; the aged King, his father, although opposed to the war, being led away by the war faction. "The Result," adds the *Bombay Gazette*, "we fear, is likely to prove disastrous to the Persian Monarchy. Should the Russians reach our frontiers, as the Cossacks have but an undefined idea, we believe, of right and wrong, and stimulated by success, they may encroach, and give rise to some measures on our part."'

11.161 'Russia and Persia,' *The Delaware Gazette* (Wednesday, 13 June, 1827): 'Captain Edicott [sic, Endicott], of the ship George, arrived at Salem, (Mass.) from Calcutta, has brought files of the India Gazette, to the 27th of January, containing an account of a battle between the Persian army, 6000 strong, headed by the brother in-law to the king of Persia, and 10,000 Russians, commanded by the Russian Gen. Helmandoff [sic, Ermolov], in which the former were entirely defeated, the whole of the Persian army, with the exception of their commander, having been put to the sword by the Russians. The India Gazette says:

"No doubt was entertained but the Russians would overrun Persia, and the result we fear, is likely to prove disastrous to the independence of the Persian monarchy."

The National Intelligencer speaking on this subject, remarks:

"The following intelligence from Asia is of much interest, because we have for a long time considered the war, which Russia wages with Persia, pregnant with consequences much more important than the mere fate of a Persian dynasty, or the integrity of the Persian possessions. Every move that Russia makes in the east, brings her nearer to British India; and England must view with the deepest interest, if not with apprehension, the progress of the Russian power in that quarter. She can, in fact, not remain much longer an inactive spectator of the war, and it is on the fields of Persia that we may expect to see the peace of Europe broken, and the conflict renewed between two of her greatest powers."'

11.162 'From Late London Papers,' *New-York Advertiser* (Friday, 10 August, 1827) and 'Foreign and Domestic News,' *Onondaga Register* (Wednesday, 15 August 1827): 'The war between the Russians and the Prussians (sic, Persians) has not yet, it appears, been

---

[407] Mountstuart Elphinstone (1779–1859), who arrived in India in 1796, served as President and Governor of Bombay from 1819 to 1827, when he was succeeded by Sir John Malcolm. See Colebrooke (1884: 100ff.).

bro't to a close. We have, this morning, received the Extraordinary Supplement to the St. Petersburgh Journal, of the 19th ult., from which it appears there had been some sharp fighting. The result is described to have been decidedly in favour of the Russians:—

St. Petersburgh, May 7.

News from the Army in Georgia.

General Paskevitsch having assumed, on the 29th of March, the chief command of the corps of the Caucasins [sic],[408] immediately ordered the necessary measures to accelerate the march of the vanguard, which was to get into the province of Erivan, under the command of Gen. Benkendoff.[409] Notwithstanding the numerous obstacles caused by the heavy falls of snow, and copious rains, the vanguard, composed of seven battalions of Infantry, a company of Light Artillery, and two Regiments of Cossacks, succeeded in passing, on the 6th April, Mounts Akziuk and Bozobdal.[410] Gen. Benkendoff, proceeded towards Etchmaidzine, and occupied it without having experienced any resistance, having met with no enemy except in the vicinity of the villages Aiglanlon, where the Persians, covered by their walls, opened a well sustained fire on the detachment of the head of the column; but a few cannon shot, and a decisive charge, executed by Major Youdine, with two companies of the Infantry regiment of Schirvan, put the enemy to flight, and the villages were immediately occupied. The Kurdise [sic, Kurdish] cavalry, dismounted, opened a fire of small arms on the reinforcement sent to support the head of the column, but was every[411] where repulsed by the arms of the Regiment of Carbineers.

---

[408] The long, drawn-out replacement of Ermolov by Paskevich, despite the explicit orders issued by the Czar, is detailed in Stcherbatow (1890). The appointment of Paskevich dated to 27 March 1827. As Brosset (1857: 328) noted, 'Au mois d'avril de l'année 1827, le commandant en chef de la Géorgie, Iermolof, fut révoqué et le général-adjudant Ivan Féodorovitch Paskévitch désigné pour le remplacer.'

[409] Konstantin Khristoforovich von Benckendorff (1785–1828). Fom a noble Livonian family, Benckendorff was a highly decorated Russian general and diplomat who distinguished himself in the Napoleonic and Second Russo-Persian wars, and served as Russian ambassador in Württemberg and Baden. He died of typhus in Bulgaria during the Russo-Turkish War. He was buried in a circular mausoleum resembling a Greek temple outside of Stuttgart which he had had built for his wife, who predeceased him in 1824. See Wege et al. (2007: 181).

[410] Besobdal is located 'auf der Straße, die von Eriwan grade nach Tiflis führt.' See von Bernhardi (1877: 226). In the Russo-Turkish war that followed, the Russian cavalry and artillery returning from Erzurum to Georgia also had to cross 'die Gebirge, Saganlug, Aksibijuk und Besobdall.' See Uschakoff (1838: 210).

[411] Also Judin. See Anonymous (1827e: 169), Eichwald (1837: 587). In 1835 a Lieutenant-Colonel Youdine 2 (indicating there was another officer by the same name) commanded the light artillery battery of the Don. See Anonymous (1837d: 74).

The charge of our irregular cavalry, in which Gen. Benkendorff gave fresh proofs of brilliant courage, is the more remarkable, as it has proved to our Cossacks with what advantage they could engage the Kurds.[412]

The following officers particularly distingused [sic, distinguished] themselves on this occasion:—Colonel Karpoff, 2nd,[413] Count Jolstoy [sic, Tolstoy], Captain of Cavalry and Aide-de-Camp to the Emperor, and the Aid [sic] de-Camp of Gen. Benkendorff,[414] as well as the Georgian Prince, Meli Koff,[415] who has brought to his Majesty,[416] the present report from the Commander in Chief of the army of the Caucasus.

The Georgians in general behaved with much intrepidity in this affair.

On the same day, at 7 in the evening, Gen. Benkendorff having made his detachments halt three wersts from Sardar Abad,[417] advanced in person with five companies and four pieces of cannon, towards that fortress, which he approached within musket shot, opened a fire with shells, which damaged several buildings in the place and caused great confusion. Colonel Gourko [sic, Grekov],[418] and Lieut. Kotzebue,[419] distinguished themselves in this attack by their able arrangements.—After having reconnoitered Sardar Abad, Gen. Benkendorf returned the following day to Etchmiadzine.

---

[412] As Eichwald (1837: 591) wrote, 'Ungeachtet des sehr beschwerlichen Ueberganges über den Besobdal und Achsebiuk, unter heftigem Schneegestöber und Regengüssen, erreichte Benkendorf das Kloster Etschmiadsin, wo es den 15 April zu einem heftigen Gefechte mit den Persern kam, die sich beim Dorf Aglenlu, von der kurdischen Reiterei verstärkt, aufgestellt hatten. Die Folge des Gefechts war die Eroberung des Klosters, wo die Russen ansehnliche Vorräthe fanden.'

[413] Karpoff 2nd or Karpov II as Russians sources referred to him was Akim [Yekim] Akimovich [Yekimovich] Karpov who later servied under Paskevich in the Russo-Turkish war. See Fonton (1840: 427). Karpov commanded a Cossack regiment under Lieutenant-General Ilovaisky. See Stcherbatow (1890: 205).

[414] When Moritz Wagner visited Tabriz in 1845 he commented on the plethora of European and Russian goods in the bazaar. 'Even the portraits of Benkendorf, Paskiewitsch, and other Russian Generals were offered for sale in the Armenian shops.' See Wagner (1856/3: 103).

[415] Russified version of the Georgian family name Melikichvili (of Somketia). Of the family Toumanoff (1983: 51) noted, 'Race dynastique régnant dans la ppté [principauté] de Siounie...qui paraît historiquement en 314....Inscription dans la Liste des Princes (en Ibérie) 24 juill. 1783 sous le nom de Mélikischvili.—Reconnaissance russe du titre de Prince ou Princess Melikoff 30 oct. 1816 et 2 févr. 1824 et confirmation 6 déc. 1850—à base du traité de 1783.' As Gamba (1826/2: 316) wrote, during his stay in Baku, 'les attentions de M. le colonel Melikoff pour nous ne sont pas démenties un instant: il les prolongea même au-delà de notre départ.'

[416] Nicholas I.

[417] Boyes (1877: 81) described Sardarabad as 'an old and very considerable mud fortress, situated about 5 or 6 miles from the Turkish frontier, from which it is divided by the Arpachi.'

[418] Cf. 11.78, 11.88, 11.91, 11.100, 11.104.

[419] Paul Demetrius von Kotzebue (1801–1884), younger brother of Col. Moritz von Kotzebue. For the former's participation see Mikaberidze (2011: 3).

11   The Second Russo-Persian War and the Treaty of Torkmanchay (1826–1828)   1239

The baggage of the vanguard arrived on the 15th without accident at Etchmiadzine, though the enemy attempted several times to attack it; but the measures taken by Majors Mitchenko and Belfort[420] baffled all their attempts.

In the Monastery of Etchmiadzine a supply of provisions was found sufficient for the whole detachment for five or six days. The venerable Narses, Archbishop of the Armenians,[421] notwithstanding his great age, followed the army, and by his conduct gave the best example to his countrymen.[422]

Leaving at Etchmiadzine the 2nd battalion of the Infantry Regiment of Schirvan, two cannon, and a company of Cossacks under the command of Lieut. Colonel Voliensky,[423] Gen. Benkendorff marched on the 16th April to reconnoitre Sardar Abad, a new Persian fortress, situated twenty wersts from Etchmiadzine, on the left of the road of Talyne.[424] At

---

[420] In December, 1797 Jan Potocki had a memorable encounter with Belfort (or his father?) at Mozdok in northern Ossetia. He wrote, 'Le major de place à Mozdok est un comte *de Belfort*; il parle *cinq* langues, a été étudier dans *cinq* académies, mais son éducation a été gâtée, à ce qu'il dit, par cinq impératrices, dont deux russes et trois allemandes. Il a pour femme une Italienne, autrefois danseuse de corde, qu'il n'appelle jamais autrement que *la comtesse*, malgré sa mise dégoûtante. La connaissance de cet aventurier mérite seule un voyage au Caucase.' See Potocki (1829: 145). Potocki sent a portrait sketch of Belfort to his friend Stanislaus August in January, 1798, with the words, 'Pour me faire pardonner tant d'ennui j'envoye ci joint le portrait du Comte de Belfort.' See Rosset and Triaire (2006: 56).

[421] Nerses V Ashtaraketsi. Cf. 11.128. When Gamba was in Tiflis Nerses V was the Armenian Archbishop there. See Gamba (1826/2: 157). For his life, see von Haxthausen (1854: 300–303). As Barratt (1972: 394) noted, 'In Narzez…the Russian General Staff found an essential ally. Without his help, indeed, it may be questioned if Paskevich could have wrung such favourable terms from the shah as were elicited the following spring. For conquest of Armenia and Nakhichevan made possible direct raids on Tabriz and the surrounding area.'

[422] As Lacroix (1866: 2) noted, 'Ce vénérable prélat, malgré son âge avancé, avait voulu suivre l'avant-garde russe, pour donner l'exemple à ses compatriotes et pour justifier, par son dévouement, la confiance personnelle que le tzar venait de lui témoigner en lui adressant ce rescrit si flatteur et si bien mérité: "La violation de la paix par les Persans et leur invasion inattendue dans nos provinces ont donné aux Arméniens qui habitent en Géorgie l'occasion de signaler le dévouement et la gratitude sincère qui les attachent à Notre personne. Ils ont prouvé, dans cette circonstance, qu'ils savaient apprécier la bienfaisante sollicitude du Gouvernement à leur égard, et qu'ils reconnaissaient combien leur condition était préférable à celle de leurs coreligionnaires dispersés dans d'autres contrées. Nous vous chargeons de témoigner Notre entière satisfaction à tous les Arméniens qui se trouvent sous votre administration spirituelle, et de les assurer, en Notre nom impérial, qu'ils continueront à être l'objet de Notre sollicitude. Tant que votre nation, qui a trouvé un refuge assuré sous l'égide du Gouvernement russe, Nous conservera cette inviolable fidélité, Nous Nous ferons un devoir de Nous occuper constamment de son bonheur et de sa tranquillité. Attribuant aussi la conduite louable des Arméniens de votre diocèse à l'influence de vos exhortations pastorales, Nous vous en témoignons ici personnellement Notre reconnaissance, et vous adressons l'assurance de Notre bienveillance impériale. Nicolas."'

[423] Presumably a Polish officer in Russian service, the name might also be V/Wolensky, Wollensky or Walensky.

[424] A 'fort between Ssardarabad and Gümri [Alexandropol],' as Mackenzie (1854: 187) noted, and the third stage out from Echmiadzin on the road to Alexandropol [mod. Gyumri, Armenia]. See Boyes (1877: 83).

the same time he detached three companies of the Regiment of Schirvan towards Erivan, with a view to draw off the attention of the enemy, and particularly to fatigue the Kurdise [Kurdish] cavalry, which occupied the road of Sardar Abad. In fact, this cavalry marched towards Erivan, and there was some skirmishing between it and the three companies above mentioned. At one in the afternoon, Gen. Benkendorff met with the Kurds, to the number of 10,000 horse,[425] commanded by Hassan Khan, a famous partisan, brother of the Sardar of Erivan.[426] Three companies of the Regiment of Kardoff 2nd, and two companies of that of Andriff,[427] supported by our cannon, and two companies of the Regiment of Infantry of Tiflis, followed the example set them by their officers, rushed upon the enemy with extraordinary intrepidity. In a moment the Kurdise [Kurdish] cavalry was put to flight, and pursued for seven wersts with much loss.[428] Among the killed are found the nephew of Hussein, Aga Kurdestan[429]; among the prisoners is Ismael, Khan of Arderum,[430] one of the confidential officers of the Sardar.—The enemy lost in this affair 86 horseman, and for the first time since the beginning of the war, had not time to carry the killed from the field of battle. The loss on our side was very considerable. The wounds received by the Cossacks are chiefly from spears and sabres.'

---

[425] According to Eichwald (1837: 591) and Lacroix (1866: 3) it was a body of 1000 cavalry, not 10,000.

[426] Hoseyn Qoli Khan Qazvini.

[427] Andreof, mod. Endirey, Daghestan.

[428] Eichwald (1837: 591) noted that Benckendorff left a batallion in the cloister, 'während er selbst nach der Festung Sserdar-Abad marschierte, um ihre Recognoscirung vorzunehmen; unterwegs hatte er einige heftige Gefechte mit der kurdischen, ihn immerfort verfolgenden Reiterei zu bestehen; diese wurde vom Hassan Chan selbst angeführt, und bestand aus wenigstens 1000 der verwegensten Kurden; Benkendorf schickte gegen sie 500 don'sche Kasaken, die von 2 Compagnien Fußvolk und einer Kanone unterstützt wurden, und trieb sie nach einer verzweifelten Gegenwehr in die Flucht; hier hatten sich zum erstenmale die Kasaken so vortheilhaft mit den Kurden gemessen, und ihnen ihre Ueberlegenheit gezeigt. Benkendorf ließ darauf 5 Compagnien Fußvolk mit 4 Kanonen sich der Festung nähern, und sie mit Granaten beschießen, während er selbst ihre Recognoscirung beendigte.'

[429] 'Hussein Agha' who 'commanded the Kurds of Erivan' during the Russian campaign against Turkey that followed the conclusion of the Russo-Persian War. Cf. Eppel (2008: 247). According to Monteith (1856: 221), he 'had been outlawed, and for many years the tribes had remained under the Persian government; but he was never cordial in his submission, though his daughter was married to Hussein Khan [Hoseyn Qoli Khan Qazvini], the Persian Sirdar. He could command the services of 3000 excellent cavalry.' Without explanation Williamson (2008: 93) estimated the size of 'Kurdish Cavalry (led by Hussein Aga)' at only 2000. In 1808, when Ermolov undertook his mission to Fath 'Ali Shah, 'Hussein Aga' and 'Abdul Aga' were the 'two principal chiefs under' the Kurdish chief Timur Bey. See Tancoigne (1820: 322).

[430] Arderum is a corruption of 'Arzerum,' i.e. Erzurum. Cf. Fonton (1840: 219).

11.163 'Untitled,' *New-York Evening Post* (Monday, 20 August, 1827): 'Extract of a private letter of the 20th from Berlin:—"The peace with Persia, which Gen. Diebitsch[431] was authorised to negotiate, seems to have met with insurmountable obstacles in the obstinacy of the Court of Teheran, which, through the influence, it is said, of a foreign Court,[432] refuses to submit to the least sacrifice. It does not appear, however, that the Russian forces make very rapid progress in these distant and barbarous countries, where it is extremely difficult to act with a considerable army, seeing that here the necessary subsistencies would soon fail, and the bad roads do not allow them to be transported in a sufficient quantity.'

11.164 'Latest from Europe,' *The Geneva Gazette and General Advertiser* (Wednesday, 5 September 1827): 'Letters from Odessa of the 24th of July, say that peace is on the point of being concluded between Persia and Russia.—The Schah,[433] they say, is to cede to the Emperor of Russia[434] the whole country as far as the Araxes, including the fortress of Erivan. The annual revenue of the country is estimated at 50,000,000 of francs.'

11.165 'Russia and Persia,' *The Corrector* (Saturday, 8 September 1827): 'It would seem, from our latest European papers, that the war with Persia was undertaken by the emperor of Russia,[435] for the purpose of extending his frontier to the river Araxus. This was a favourite object with his predecessor, and appears to be in a fair way of being obtained, as accounts from Odessa represent the Persians willing to make great sacrifices for peace. It is asserted, also, that Russia will demand the cession of the province of Talidje[436] and the Steppes on

---

[431] Hans Karl Friedrich Anton Graf von Diebitsch and Narten (1785–1831), highly decorated Russian officer who won particular renown in the Russo-Turkish War (1828–1829). As Monteith (1856: 127) noted, 'General Diebitch had been despatched to Georgia with authority to displace General Yermoloff, or at all events to place General Paskiewitch in command of the advanced army.' According to Bitis (2006: 22), 'Diebitsch was also to ascertain whether Ermolov had been guilty of negligence regarding the gathering of supplies in 1826; whether the alleged disorder in the Corps threatened the observance of discipline; and, in particular, whether Ermolov's secret aim was "to prolong the war rather than hasten its conclusion". Nicholas was interested not so much in the mistakes themselves but rather in whether they resulted from the wilful and "harmful obstinacy" of Ermolov. Should, on this score, the latter be proved innocent, then Diebitsch was either to reconcile him with Paskevich or should that prove impossible, to decide which of the two was to be recalled.' In Gammer's words, 'the Emperor sent Count Diebitsch, officially to investigate the relationship between the two [Ermolov and Paskevich], in fact to depose Yermolov...On 9 April 1827 Yermolov left the Caucasus and official service never to return.'

[432] Only England wielded any significant influence at this point. It is not likely, however, that Henry Willock or Sir John Macdonald advised against making sacrifices for the sake of peace.

[433] Fath 'Ali Shah.

[434] Nicholas I.

[435] Nicholas I.

[436] Talysh.

the right of the Araxus, which would go far to secure the command of the Caspian sea. In urging her demands, Russia might plausibly state that Georgia, although protected on other sides, is exposed towards the south to the incursions of the Turcomans, Kurds, and other co-religionists of Persia; while the establishment of the proposed line on the river would protect that country, and enable Russia to avail herself of the advantages of that remarkable commercial position, Tiflis. The commercial importance of these countries will be principally derived from their productions of silk.'

11.166 'Latest from Europe. Russia,' *The Rochester Daily Telegraph* (Monday, 10 September, 1827): 'Advices have been received by Tartar from Persia at Constantinople, which states that the discomfiture of the Russian army was of such a nature that it was falling back in every direction, or in other words evacuating the Persian Territory, and re-entering Georgia.'

11.167 'Latest from London,' *The Rochester Daily Telegraph* (Tuesday, 11 September, 1827), 'Untitled,' *The Schenectady Cabinet* (Wednesday, 12 September, 1827), 'Foreign Intelligence,' *Geneva Gazette and General Advertiser* (Wednesday, 12 September, 1827) and 'Foreign and Domestic News,' *Onondaga Register* (Wednesday, 12 September, 1827): 'It was whispered at Constantinople, that a secret messenger had been despatched to Teheran, with a view of concluding an alliance, offensive and defensive, between Turkey and Persia.'

11.168 'Late from England. Turkey. Foreign News,' *New-York Evening Post* (Friday, 14 September 1827; minus second paragraph) and 'From papers received by later arrivals,' *Geneva Gazette and General Advertiser* (Wednesday, 26 September 1827; minus last two sentences of first paragraph): 'Letters of the 25th of July from St. Petersburgh say, that so far from there being any truth in the rumour that a peace had been concluded between Russia and Persia, preparations were making to prosecute hostilities with vigor. The unimportant results as yet obtained, are attributed to the negligence of Gen. Yermoloff,[437] who established no magazines and disgusted the inhabitants by his arbitrary acts. The measures of Gen. Debitsch[438] it is said has [sic, have] bettered the state of affairs and success is confidently anticipated.

Accounts from Frankfort of the 10th of August state that there was a secret understanding between Prince Abbas Mirza, of Persia, and the Pacha of Alkalsike, (Turkish Georgia,)

---

[437] By July 25, when the letters cited here were written, Ermolov had been superseded by Paskevich for four months.
[438] Cf. 11.163.

and it is said, the Pacha had by order of the Porte, furnished provisions and munitions of war to the Persian troops.'[439]

11.169 'Turkey,' *The Albany Argus & City Gazette* (Tuesday, 18 September, 1827): 'Petersburgh letters of the 21st July contradict the rumors of an early peace between Persia and Russia. Extensive preparations are making by the latter power, to carry on the war vigorously.'

11.170 'Germany,' *The Albany Argus & City Gazette* (Tuesday, 18 September, 1827) and 'Late from England. Germany,' *The Freeman's Journal* (Monday, 24 September, 1827): 'An article from Odessa, dated the 6th July, affirms, that peace was on the point of being concluded between Persia and Russia, and that the Schah[440] was to cede all the country as far as the Araxes, a tract which is stated to produce in silk alone to the amount of fifty millions of francs.'

11.171 'Russia,' *Ithaca Journal & General Advertiser* (Wednesday, 19 September, 1827): 'Letters of the 25th ult. from St. Petersburgh contradict the rumours of an early conclusion of peace between Russia and Persia, and add that the extensive preparations made by the former power, and the manner in which the war has been hitherto followed up, indicate the contrary. The unimportant results as yet obtained are attributed to the negligence of Gen. Bermoloff [sic, Ermolov], who established no magazines, and created dissatisfaction among the inhabitants and authorities of the provinces by different arbitrary acts. The measures of Gen. Mebitsch [sic, Diebitsch],[441] it is added, and the new clerk, in the commissariat department, sent into the provinces beyond the Caucasus, have bettered the state of affairs, and final success is fully anticipated. These letters conclude by expressing an expectation that upon peace being concluded, the town and province of Erivan will be ceded to Russia. The inhabitants, we are told, eagerly implore the protection of the Emperour.'[442]

---

[439] As von Haxthausen (1854: 101, n. *) noted, 'Akhalzik was a point of the greatest importance to the Turks: established here, they ruled and plundered all the districts south of the western Caucasus, and issuing from hence their emissaries sustained the warlike spirit of the Circasians and Lesghis. Rallying under the standard of the Pasha of Akhalzik, the Lesghis robbed and devastated the rich country of Georgia....Kidnapped boys and girls were at that time a sort of merchandize in request, and were brought to Akhalzik, where the great fair for this traffic was held. From this place the boys and girls were transported to Erzeroum, Trebizond, Teheran, and Constantinople. The Armenians had an especial privilege for this trade, and Akhalzik was of equal importance to the Russians, who, after a sanguinary defence, took the fortress. The Turks had held possession of this important place for two centuries and a half....The town is said to contain sixteen thousand inhabitants, eight churches, a synagogue of the Jews, and a Mohammedan mosque.'

[440] Fath 'Ali Shah.

[441] Cf. 11.163, 11.168.

[442] Nicholas I.

11.172 'Late from England. Turkey,' *The Freeman's Journal* (Monday, 24 September, 1827): 'Petersburgh letters of the 21st July, contradict the rumors of an early peace between Persia and Russia. Extensive preparations are making by the latter Power to carry on the war vigorously.'

11.173 'Russia and Persia,' *The Yeoman's Gazette* (after 6 October, 1827): 'The accounts of a reverse experienced at Erivan by the Russian army invading Persia, appears to be corroborated; but they come through Turkish channels.'

11.174 'From England,' *New-York Evening Post* (Monday, 8 October 1827): 'The ship Antioch arrived yesterday afternoon from Liverpool, and brought a London paper of the 3rd ult. . . .The Russians gained a victory on the 17th of July over the Persians, on the banks of the Araxes.'[443]

11.175 'Foreign Intelligence. Latest from England,' *Greene County Republican* (Wednesday, 10 October, 1827): '[The ship Olive Branch, Captain Harding, arrived at Boston on Tuesday from Liverpool, whence she sailed 2nd Sept.]. . . .By an overland despatch from India, information had been received. . . .The messenger passed through Constantinople Aug. 3rd, and confirms previous accounts of the arming of the Turks and defeat of the Russians near Erivan.'

11.176 'Aspect of Affairs in the East,' *New-York Spectator* (Friday, 12 October 1827), 'Russia and Persia,' *Albany Argus & City Gazette* (Monday, 15 October 1827) and 'Foreign Intelligence,' *Greene County Republican* (Wednesday, 17 October 1827; from 'Instead of' to 'Abbas-Abad'): 'A letter from Smyrna, of August 4, which appears in the Gazette of France, says: "Since yesterday our city has been in an agitation which may give every unprejudiced observer a correct notion of the irritation of the Turks towards the Christian Powers, and particularly Russia. In the market places, the streets and coffee-houses, we hear only the joyful exclamation, 'Victory of the Persians over the Russians!' People cordially shake hands with each other, as if the Porte had gained a victory; a lively interset in the public events hitherto unknown among the nations of the East, manifests

---

[443] As Eichwald (1837: 596–597) wrote, 'Die irregulären Perserschaaren, von ihrer schlecht bedienten Artillerie nur schwach beschützt, wurden bald zersprengt, und suchten ihr Heil in der Flucht zugleich mit dem in Unordnung gebrachten Centrum der Perser, während das persische reguläre Fußvolk gar keinen Antheil am Gefechte genommen, und ruhig im Lager stehen geblieben war; die Russen verfolgten die fliehende Reiterei bis an das Flüßchen Dschewanbulak. An diesem Tage (dem 5 Juli) [O.S. = 17 July N.S.] hatte Abbas Mirsa in eigener Person mit seinen beiden Brüdern, Melich Kassum Mirsa und Ali Naki Mirsa, nebst dem Alajar Chan und den Sserdaren Ibrahim Chan und Hassan Chan den Oberbefehl der persischen Truppen geführt; Abbas Mirsa konnte sich kaum durch die Flucht retten, und seine kostbare Flinte, so wie der sie tragende Pisch Chadmet, fielen in die Hände der Sieger außer hundert andern Gefangenen, worunter mehrere vornehme Officiere waren. Dieser glänzende Sieg verschaffte den Russen auch die Schlüssel von Abbasabad.'

itself among all classes of the people. It appears that news arrived yesterday morning from Bagdad, that the Russians had been completely beaten on the 12th July, by the Persians under the walls of Erivan. To give more appearance of authenticity to this news, which is very improbable, it is added, that several English travellers, who left Erivan on the 16th of July, had confirmed this news at the office of the Consulata, and that they asserted that about 50,000 Persians were in pursuit of the Russians, who were retreating by forced marches. Nothing can be compared with the joy manifested by the Turks at these reports. The Christians who live at Smyrna see but two [sic, too] clearly what threatens them if the Porte should suffer any reverse from their christian brethren."

The accounts from St. Petersburgh, however, give an account of an engagement on the 17th of July, in which the tables were turned.

"Instead of the Russians having experienced a defeat in the vicinity of Erivan, we find, by an extract from the St. Petersburgh Gazette, that a solemn Te Deum had been sung in the chapel of the Emperor's palace, and in the presence of his Imperial Majesty himself,[444] of his mother,[445] and his brother, the Grand Duke Michael,[446] in honor of a great victory gained by General Paskewitch, on the 12th July, over a body of 16,000 cavalry, commanded by the Schah's[447] favorite son, Prince Abbas Mirza, in person. The triumph is said to have been so complete, that Abbas Mirza had a narrow escape from being taken by the Russian Dragoons; and that his own gun-bearer fell into the hands of the conquerors. The first result of this victory was, the immediate surrender of the fortress of Abbas-Abad,[448] the garrison of which had made a desperate but unavailing sortie during the battle.

---

[444] Nicholas I.

[445] Empress Maria Feodorovna, née Sophie Dorothea von Württemberg (1759–1828).

[446] Grand Duke Michael Pavlovich (1798–1849).

[447] Fath 'Ali Shah.

[448] A fortress 'die, auf europäische Art befestigt, am linken Ufer des Araxes, südostwärts von Nachetschivan liegt.' See Eichwald (1837: 594). Cf. McNeill (1836: 100), Ekbal (1982/2011). It was described in Anonymous (1831c: 60) as 'nach fränkischem Mußter.' As Ker Porter (1821/1: 616) noted, 'About 6 miles south-west of Nackshivan, and close to the bank of the Aras, stands the fort of Abbas-abad; first constructed under the direction of General Gardanne, when the French embassy was in the country; and since improved by Captain Monteith.' The actual architect of 'Abbasabad was Captain Armand-François Lamy (spelled variously Lami, Lamie and by Gardane [1809a: 2] as Lamy). Vibart (1883: 114) noted that the fortress was 'rendered capable of defence according to a plan traced out by captain Lamie, a French officer,' whom Monteith (1856: 81) called 'a French officer of great talent.' On his career see Sarrut and Saint-Edmé (1835: 112–114). Bélanger (1838: 270) described the fortress as 'construit par Abbas-Mira, sur les dessins des officiers du génie français attachés à l'ambassade du général Gardanne. Les Persans tiennent une petite garnison dans ce fort, que défendent une vingtaine de pièces de canon de différens calibres.' The influence of Lamy on 'Abbas Mirza was enormous. As Drouville (1819: 5) observed, 'Plusieurs officiers de mérite étaient attachés à la suite de l'Ambassade française, entr'autres un capitaine du génie nommé Lami. Le Prince ['Abbas Mirza] prit de lui des leçons de mathématiques et fit des progrès rapides. Il se fit traduire les œuvres militaires de Guibert ainsi que les règlements des manœuvres d'infanterie. Il apprit assez de dessin pour lever correctement un plan, mais il sentit qu'il ne pourrait pas

Four Persian standards, captured on this occasion, were carried in triumph through the principal streets of St. Petersburgh, and all the members of the Great Council of the Empire, the Generals, the Court, and the Diplomatic Body, were present in the chapel when Te Deum was sung.'"[449]

11.177 'Foreign,' *The Corrector* (Saturday, 13 October 1827) and 'Foreign: Late from England,' *The Western Star* (Friday, 19 October, 1827): 'An overland despatch had arrived at London from India, with information of the death of the celebrated Chief Runjeet Sing.[450] The messenger passed through Constantinople on the third of August, and brought letters fully confirming the previous accounts of the arming of the Turks and the defeat of the Russians near Erivan. The Russian Cavalry had been particularly unsuccessful. In two engagements with the Persians they were defeated and cut down in great numbers.'

11.178 'Untitled,' *The Geneva Gazette and General Advertiser* (Wednesday, 17 October 1827): 'The Russian forces had obtained a victory over the Persians, on the banks of the Araxes. The Persians lost 400 killed, 100 prisoners and two standards.'

11.179 'Foreign,' *Kinderhook Herald* (Thursday, 18 October, 1827) and 'Latest from England,' *Black River Gazette* (Wednesday, 24 October, 1827): ['The packet ship Birmingham, capt. Harris, arrived at New-York on the 11st inst. bringing London dates to the 6th, and Liverpool to the 8th September. . . .] The Morning Herald speculates on the rumour that Russia intended to apply to England for a new loan, which the war with Persia, and preparations for enforcing the demands made on the Porte, have rendered necessary. This journal expresses its surprise that no great sensation has been created in England by the attempt of the Russians on Persia, the ally of Great Britain, and the great barrier between its East India possessions and Russia.'

---

communiquer lui-même ces connaissances à d'autres, et il engagea le capitaine Lami à former seize élèves pris parmi les officiers; il suivait les leçons et stimulait l'émulation de ces jeunes gens, autant par son exemple que par ses exhortations. Il partageait ainsi son temps entre l'étude et les manœuvres des troupes d'infanterie et d'artillerie, qu'il faisait instruire par des officiers français.' On 10 February 1828 the fortress was surrendered to the Russians according to Article 4 of the Treaty of Torkmanchay. See Hurewitz (1956: 96).

[449] From 1826 to 1836 the Court Kapella was directed by Feodor L'vov. See Dunlop (2013: 10). However, it is also possible that the Te Deum was sung by the priests present. Ritchie (1836: 137–138) described witnessing a similar event in 1835 in which the 'priests then thundered forth the Te Deum; and emperor, empress, court, soldiers, spectators—every living soul in that mighty concourse of human beings—sunk upon their knees.'

[450] Maharaja Ranjit Singh (1780–1839). Cf. 13.68, 15.3. The founder of the Sikh kingdom of the Punjab, he did not die until 1839, although he did become seriously ill in late 1826. See Cunningham (1849: 194). This may have given rise to a rumor of his death.

11 The Second Russo-Persian War and the Treaty of Torkmanchay (1826–1828)

11.180 'Foreign. Late from England,' *The Western Star* (Friday, 19 October 1827): 'By the arrival at Boston of the Olive Branch, Capt. Harding, who sailed from Liverpool Sept. 2, we have received advices 1 day later than those by the Canada.

An overland despatch had arrived from India…The messenger passed through Constantinople on the 3rd of August, and brought letters, fully confirming the previous accounts of the arming of the Turks and the defeat of the Russians neaer Erivan. The Russian cavalry had been particularly unsuccessful. In two engagements with the Persians they were defeated and cut down in great numbers….

Three days Later from England.—The ship Antioch, Capt. Rich, arrived at New-York on Saturday, from Liverpool, whence she sailed on the 4th ult. The Editors of the Gazette are indebted to Capt. Rich for a Liverpool paper of the 4th, and the London Morning Chronicle of the 3rd ult. from which they have extracted every thing of moment….The Russian force under Gen. Packewitsch obtained a considerable victory on the 17th of July over the Persians, on the banks of the Araxes.—The latter lost 400 killed 100 prisoners and two standards; the Russians had 9 killed and 29 wounded.'

11.181 'Foreign News.' *New-York Evening Post* (Wednesday, 24 October 1827): 'By the arrival of the packet ship Cadmus, Captain Allyn, arrived at this port yesterday from Havre, we have received files of Galignani's Paris Messenger[451] up to the 15th of September…. Letters from Odessa announce the retrograde march of the Russians on this side the Araxes. It seems even that one of the divisions of the Georgian army has returned as far as Lahar,[452] passage of Mount Salvate.'[453]

11.182 'Very Late from England,' *The New-York Spectator* (Tuesday, 30 October 1827), 'Foreign Intelligence. [London dates to the 29th September.],' *The National Gazette and Literary Register* (Wednesday, 31 October, 1827), 'Tuesday (Evening) October 30. Very late from England,' *New-York Spectator* (Friday, 2 November, 1827), 'Very late from Europe,' *American and Commercial Daily Advertiser* (Friday, 2 November, 1827), 'From the Commercial Advertiser. New-York, Oct. 30,' *Connecticut Mirror* (Monday, 5 November, 1827), 'Latest from England,' *The Freeman's Journal* (Monday, 5 November, 1827; with a slight difference in last sentence), 'From the N.Y. Advocate. Latest from Europe,' *American Mercury* (Tuesday, 6 November, 1827), 'Foreign. Latest from Europe,'

---

[451] English-language newspaper, founded by Giovanni Antonio Galignani (1757–1822), proprietor of the Bibliothèque Anglaise in Paris. Published from 1814 to 1895, *Galignani's Messenger* was 'a household word' to 'generations of English-speaking visitors to Paris in particular, and to France in general.' Its creation 'was the natural outcome of the great influx of English visitors to Paris after the downfall of Napoleon.' See Roberts (1904).

[452] A town close to the Kara Su, just west of the Talysh mountains, and northwest of Ardabil. See Morier (1818): map of 'Routes through Aderbigian, the most northern province of Persia, including part of Armenia.'

[453] Cf. 11.151.

The Schenectady Cabinet (Wednesday, 7 November, 1827), 'Foreign News. Russia,' *Republican Farmer* [Bridgeport CT] (Wednesday, 7 November, 1827), 'Foreign Intelligence. New-York, Nov. 2. Turkey and Greece,' *American Sentinel* (Wednesday, 7 November, 1827), 'Latest from Europe. Russia and Persia,' *The Geneva Gazette and General Advertiser* (Wednesday, 7 November 1827), 'Very Late from England,' *The Geneva Palladium* (Wednesday, 7 November 1827), 'From the Baltimore Patriot. Very late from England,' *South-Carolina State Gazette and Columbia Advertiser* (Saturday, 10 November, 1827), 'Foreign. Latest from Europe,' *The Western Star* (Friday, 16 November 1827), 'New-York, Oct. 31. Latest from Europe,' *Kentucky Reporter* (Saturday, 17 November, 1827) and 'New-York, Oct. 31. Latest from Europe,' *Michigan Herald* (Wednesday, 21 November, 1827): 'A despatch from the British envoy at the court of Persia,[454] to Mr. Stratford Canning,[455] transmitted the news of a great victory gained by the Russians on the right bank of the Araxes. The Augsburgh Gazette[456] says, that the loss of 40,000 men by the Persians, and of 11,000 by the victors, is probably an exaggeration.'[457]

11.183 'Foreign Affairs,' *New-York Spectator* (Friday, 16 November 1827): 'Russia continues to prosecute a languid war with the effeminate Persians, while her eye is fixed steadily upon the shores of the Bosphorus, and the ancient capital of the Greek Empire.... Great Britain is not sure—and the Russian war with Persia renders her less so—that Russia may not one day be disposed to stretch her giant arms across central Asia to the Indies,'

11.184 'Foreign Intelligence,' *New-York Spectator* (Friday, 16 November 1827), 'Untitled,' *The Schenectady Cabinet* (Wednesday, 21 November, 1821), 'Foreign Intelligence. From France,' *Greene County Republican* (Wednesday, 21 November, 1827), 'Foreign News,' *Kinderhook Herald* (Thursday, 29 November, 1827) and 'Foreign. Europe,' *The Western Star* (Friday, 30 November, 1827): ['The Edward Quesnel, Capt. Hawkins, arrived

---

[454] John Macdonald Kinneir.

[455] Stratford Canning (1786–1880). British Minister in Constantinople. Cf. 9.113, 11.51.

[456] According to Anonymous (1839f), 'The *Augsburg Gazette* may be said to be the representative of all Germany. It does not confine itself to the advocacy of any one set of opinions, but opens its columns as an arena for them all....This journal has the advantage of being in semi-official connexion with most of the Governments of Europe, which adds great weight to the influence of certain communications which appear from time to time in its columns...This system, and its concomitant advantages, give the *Augsburg Gazette* a character distinct from every other journal in Europe.'

[457] This cannot refer to the Russian capture of Yerevan that began with an assault on 1 October 1827, since the papers cited are from 1 and 2 October. It is more likely to refer to Lieutenant General Afanasy Ivanovich Krasovsky's (1781–1843) victory, after a ten hour battle, on 17 August, in which the Persians are said to have suffered over 3000 dead and wounded, and the Russians 6 officers and 679 soldiers dead, and 17 officers and 318 soldiers wounded. See Anonymous (1827b), Eichwald (1837: 599–600), and Barratt (1972) for the campaign.

11 The Second Russo-Persian War and the Treaty of Torkmanchay (1826–1828)   1249

last night from Havre, and brings Paris papers to the 2nd of October—up to which day inclusive, we have already received French advices through the English papers....] With regard to Russia, she is represented as about to conclude a peace on one side, and to threaten a speedy war on the other.[458] Accounts from Odessa of Sept. 10th say, that it is believed hostilities are to cease with Persia; while affairs are assuming a very martial aspect on the frontiers of Turkey.'

11.185 'Foreign News,' *New-York Evening Post* (Wednesday, 28 November, 1827), 'Foreign,' *Kinderhook Herald* (Wednesday, 6 December 1827) and 'Russia and Persia,' *The Western Star* (Friday, 14 December 1827): ['By the James Cropper, from Liverpool, London dates to the 16th of October are received....] An article from Tiflis states, that Prince Abbas Mirza had sent an ambassador[459] to the Russian head quarters[460] to treat of peace, and that there was a strong probability of an adjustment of the differences between the two governments. It is said, however, that Russia is not to be appeased without some sacrifices on the part of Persia. It is expected that she will demand and obtain the cession of all the conquered territory up to the Araxes, and the payment of expenses of the war. It is also said that Tiflis is to be made one of the principal markets of Asia.'

---

[458] In other words, to conclude peace on the Persian side, and threaten a new war on the Turkish side.

[459] Fath 'Ali Khan-e Rashti, Governor-General (*beglerbegi*) of Tabriz. For his identity see 11.197.

[460] At Deh Kurgan, described as a 'village in Azarbījān, Persia, on the east shore of lake Ūrūmia, 35 miles south-south-west of Tabrez....It was the scene of a conference between Count Paskewitz and the Prince Royal of Persia after the occupation of Tabrez by the Russians [Tabriz fell on 10 October (O.S.), 1827, according to Markham (1874: 396); 13 October (O.S.?) according to Brosset (1857: 330, n. 1), Baddeley (1908: 174), or 26 October according to Lacroix (1866: 89) whose claim is bolstered by the fact that the date was the birthday of the Czarina's mother and Eristov's division celebrated a mass in her honor 'en présence du chef et du corps des mollahs et des membres du consulat anglais, qui adressèrent leurs félicitations au général russe et lui demandèrent l'autorisation de rester à leur poste, quoique Tauris ne fut plus au pouvoir du schah de Perse.'], during the War of 1826, and the district formed the head-quarters of the Russian cavalry.' See MacGregor (1871: 122). Brosset (1857: 330, n. 1), however, noted that 'le 4 novembre le prince ['Abbas Mirza] eut une entrevue avec le général Benkendorf, au village de Tchévister.' Lacroix (1866: 89) noted that, 'Le 2 novembre, les conférences pour la paix s'ouvraient dans un village situé à deux lieues de Tauris.' According to Morteith (1856: 148), 'The Prince Royal gave himself up at Ali Shah, a village about twenty-five miles from Tabreez, and proceeded to Dokhergan a small town thirty miles from his capital.' Rawlinson, however, said the conference took place at Gogān, '30 miles south of Tabrez, 5 miles from Deh Kūrgān.' See MacGregor (1871: 166). Eichwald (1837: 606) called the place 'Deikargan'; cf. Stcherbatow (1891a: 22), 'Deï-Kargan,' while MacAlister (1910: 94, 100, 104 and 119) called it 'Deheragon,' 'Deheraghon,' and 'Dekhurgaum.' Hasan-e Fasa'i called it 'Khārqān.' See Busse (1972: 182). Terms were agreed on 9 November 1827. See Markham (1874: 396). McNeill, in Tehran, heard of the peace on 30 November. See MacAlister (1910: 95).

11.186 'Foreign Affairs,' *Cayuga Republican* (after 28 November 1827): 'An article from Tiflis states that Prince Abbas Mirza had sent an ambassador[461] to the Russian headquarters to treat of peace, and that it was likely it would soon be made. The conditions which is expected Russia will demand and obtain are the cession of all the conquered territory up to the Araxes, and the payment of expenses of the war. It is also said that Tiflis is to be made one of the principal markets of Asia.'

11.187 'Russia & Persia,' *New-York Spectator* (Tuesday, 5 December 1827), 'Foreign: Russia & Persia,' *New-York Evening Post* (Saturday, 8 December 1827) and 'Russia & Persia,' *The Corrector* (Saturday, 8 December 1827): 'Russia & Persia.—The Journal of St. Petersburg of Sept. 26th, contains more news of the army in Georgia. It appears that a desperate battle took place between a division of the Russian army which advanced to the relief of the convent of Etchmiadzine which was besieged by the Persian army of 25,000 men—10,000 infantry, with a battery of 22 pieces of artillery, and 15,000 cavalry— commanded by Abbas Mirza. The Russians claim the victory, saying that the enemy lost three thousand men, while their own loss was very severe. The enemy attacked the Russians on all sides, and their cannon battery did much damage to the Equipages; considerable bodies of infantry and cavalry charged them with impetuosity, but were always repulsed at the point of the bayonet, and the Russian artillery, ably directed, did them considerable injury. The ravage which the Russian artillery made in the ranks of Abbas Mirza was enormous. in many places the ground was literally covered with their dead, up to the mouths of the Russian cannon. The battle lasted from 7 o'clock in the morning till 4 o'clock in the afternoon.'

11.188 'Foreign News,' *Onondaga Register* (Tuesday, 5 December 1827): 'Persia is making overtures of peace with Russia.'[462]

11.189 'Foreign,' *Kinderhook Herald* (Wednesday, 6 December 1827): 'Russia and Persia.—An article from Tiflis states, that Prince Abbas Mirza had sent an ambassador[463]

---

[461] Fath 'Ali Khan-e Rashti. Cf. 11.197.

[462] These began immediately after the surrender of Tabriz on 13 October and Paskevich's arrival there three days later. See Baddeley (1908: 174). According to MacAlister (1910: 92), 'By the month of October the Shah began to realize that the feeble resistance he was able to make was quite insufficient to save his country, and he gave Abbas Mirza instructions to conclude peace on any terms. An earnest request was made to Colonel Macdonald to assist in these negotiations. At the same time the Shah proposed sending Mirza Abdul [Abu'l] Hassan Khan on a Mission to St. Petersburg by the route of Constantinople, Vienna, Paris, and London, to all of which courts he would be accredited. Fetteh Ali Shah sent for John McNeill on 15th October to ask his advice about this. McNeill approved, but the project was not then carried out, probably because the Shah's attention was soon entirely taken up with his troubles in his own country.'

[463] Fath 'Ali Khan-e Rashti.

11 The Second Russo-Persian War and the Treaty of Torkmanchay (1826–1828)   1251

to the Russian head quarters to treat of peace, and that there was a strong probability of an adjustment of the differences between the two governments. It is said, however, that Russia is not to be appeased without some sacrifices on the part of Persia. It is expected that she will demand and obtain the cession of all the conquered territory up to the Araxes, and the payment of expenses of the war. It is also said that Tiflis is to be made one of the principal markets of Asia.'

11.190 'Foreign,' *The Corrector* (Saturday, 15 December, 1827): 'Letters have been received from Persia, dated the 5th of Sept, which state that Abbas Mirza had defeated a Russian corps, consisting of 3000 infantry of the Moscow regiment of Imperial Guards, 30 Hutans [?], and 1000 Cossacks, with several guns.—The Persian army consisted of 5000 regular infantry, 5000 horse, and 23 pieces of cannon.

The battle took place about six miles from the fort Eutch Relaser [sic, Echmiadzin], and lasted from dawn till evening. The Russians lost 1600 men, killed or taken prisoners, and the remainder took shelter in the above named fort, which is closely invested by the Persian army. During the engagement, the following remarkable circumstance took place:—Two battallions of the Persian army gallantly charged two battallions of the Imperial Guards, and after a long, sanguinary, and obstinate conflict, completely routed, with great loss the Russian battallions.'[464]

11.191 'Foreign. Latest from England,' *Newburyport Herald* (Friday, 14 December, 1827) and 'Foreign Intelligence,' *Greene County Republican* (Wednesday, 19 December 1827): 'St. Petersburg papers contain detailed accounts of the operations of the army of Georgia to the 27th of Sept. from which it appears that the Russian army had advanced with little opposition as far as Sardar Abad, the siege of which place commenced on that day. Erivan was not to be besieged till the surrender of the former fortress.[465] Abbas Mirza is said to have continued his retreat along the right bank of the Araxes.'

11.192 'Continuation of Foreign News, by the late Packets: Russia,' *New-York Spectator* (Thursday, 20 December 1827) and 'Russia,' *The Freeman's Journal* (Monday, 24 December 1827): 'The St. Petersburgh Journal of the 24th of October, contains intelligence of the war in Georgia. The fortress of Sardar Abad had fallen. The place was defended by Hassan Khan,[466] who effected his escape with 1500 troops. They were

---

[464] An example of the disinformation which Lacroix (1866: 76) deplored.

[465] As Monteith (1856: 137) noted, in discussing the Russian capture of Sardarabad, 'General Paskiewitch was enabled, by the stock of provisions taken in the place, to lay immediate siege to Erivan.'

[466] Cf. 11.88.

partially overtaken, and 500 are said to have been killed and 200 made prisoners.[467] The Russians were reaping further conquests over the Persians. Abbas Mirza had been again defeated, and was still on the retreat. Preparations were making to attack Erivan.'

11.193 'Untitled,' *The Lyons Advertiser* (after 21 December 1827), 'Untitled,' *New-York Evening Post* (Wednesday, 26 December 1827), 'Latest from England,' *The Palladium* (Wednesday, 2 January 1828) and 'Foreign,' *The Kinderhook Herald* (Thursday, 3 January 1828): 'The St. Petersburgh Journal of the 31st of October, intimates that negociations are going on between Russia and Persia, and that England is acting as a mediator/medium

---

[467] It was constructed by Hoseyn Qoli Khan Qazvini. Monteith (1856: 136–137) called it 'a large fortified village, inhabited principally by Armenians. It stands on the banks of a canal which I had been employed in planning. This was fed by a great dam thrown across the Arras, and watered a fine tract of country…it was surrounded with a rampart of rough stone only cemented with clay, and with bastions at short intervals, but no ditch. I had strongly objected to the work, as being incapable of resisting the fire of artillery for any length of time; but Hussein Khan [Hoseyn Qoli Khan Qazvini] appeared very proud of his proficiency in the art of fortification, and determined to stand a siege. The Russians commenced operations by throwing a quantity of shells into the village,—a mode of proceeding which merely destroyed some of the stores, that would later have fallen into their hands, besides expending much valuable ammunition. The walls, however, soon began to give way, and the splinters from the stone did more execution than the shot. After a few days the garrison, principally Mazanderanee and Arab irregulars, attempted to leave the place, but nearly 2000 of them were killed by the Russian cavalry; though their commander Hussein [sic, Hasan] Khan, about the worst officer that could have been entrusted with such a duty, succeeded in escaping to his brother the Sirdar.' According to Eichwald (1837: 601–602), the Russian artillery began a heavy bombardment of Sardarabad on 19 September. 'Dadurch stürzte nun nach einer halben Stunde der Thurm über dem Thore zusammen, und die Mauer selbst wurde stark beschädigt. Unterdessen hatte sich aber Hassan Chan mit einigen Truppen in die Festung geworfen, und feuerte den Muth der Besatzung an. Als aber das Feuer der russischen Breschbatterien eine starke Bresche in der Mauer gemacht, und die russischen Wurfgeschütze Brand und Verheerung in der Stadt selbst angerichtet hatten, so verlangte Hassan Chan zur Unterhandlung wegen der Uebergabe einen Waffenstillstand auf 3 Tage. Hierauf erwiederte Paskewitsch, daß wenn innerhalb 24 Stunden die Festung nicht übergeben werden würde, so solle die ganze Besatzung über die Klinge springen. Da flüchtete Hassan Chan, der die Unmöglichkeit sah, sich länger halten zu können, bei dunkler Nacht mit der etwa aus 1500 M. bestehenden Besatzung aus der am wenigsten beobachteten Nordseite der Festung und wollte nach Erivan eilen, wurde aber von der russischen Reiterei entdeckt und sofort hartnäckig verfolgt; sie verursachte ihm einen bedeutenden Nachtheil; er verlor dabei an 250 M. gefangene. Die Folge davon war, daß die Russen die Festung nahmen und in ihr 13 bronzene Kanonen, 14,000 Tschetwert Weizen und vielen andern Kriegs- und Mundvorrath fanden.' As Paskevich noted in his dispatch of 22 October [O.S., 3 November N.S.], 1827, to Czar Nicholas, 'la soumission inattendue de Sardar-Abad a terrifié le Schah. Il a aussitôt ordonné à Abbaz-Mirza de signer la paix sans retard, et de nous céder les provinces d'Erivan et de Nakhitchevan.' See Stcherbatow (1891a: 249).

11 The Second Russo-Persian War and the Treaty of Torkmanchay (1826–1828)   1253

between the two powers.[468] The *Charge d'affaires* of his Brittanic Majesty at the Court of Persia,[469] has been presented to the Emperor[470] and the Empress mother.'[471]

11.194 'Latest from England. St. Petersburgh, Nov. 4,' *The Schenectady Cabinet* (Wednesday 16 January 1828): 'News has just arrived that the important fortress of Erivan had surrendered to the Russian troops, and that the garrison, consisting of 3000 men, with Hassan Khan, the commander, were prisoners of war.'[472]

---

[468] As Paskevich wrote to Nicholas from Tabriz on 29 (O.S.) October, 1827, 'Le Caïmacan m'ayant déclaré que sans l'intervention de l'ambassadeur d'Agleterre [sic, Angleterre] il serait impossible d'obtenir du Schah le payement des millions exigés dans un si court délai, je lui accordai l'autorisation de voir Mr. Macdonald et j'insinuai à ce dernier que dans le cas présent son intervention ne pouvait être que bienfaisante pour la Perse, vu u'il devait mieux se rendre compte du danger qui menaçait l'État que le Schah lui-même et ses conseillers. Il se rendit volontiers chez le Caïmacan et après sa conversation avec lui il écrivit une lettre à son chargé d'affaires à Téhéran, par laquelle il l'invitait à ouvrir les yeux au Schah sur sa situation désespérée dans l'Aderbaïdjan et qu'elle s'aggraverait encore s'il refusait satisfaction à la Russie.' See Stcherbatow (1891a: 253–254). Cf. Monteith (1856: 148), after the fall of Tabriz, 'Negotiations were now entered into, and Abbas Mirza was entrusted with the duty of conducting them, under the guarantee of the British Minister, Col. M'Donald Kinneir.' According to Baddeley (1908: 174–175), however, that, after the fall of Tabriz, 'negotiations for peace were at once set on foot, and carried on through the intermediary of Dr. (afterwards Sir John) McNeil, who enjoyed the full confidence of the Shah.'

[469] This refers to Henry Willock on his return journey, via St. Petersburg, to Persia. As Harden (1971a: 80–81) noted, 'in 1828, while stopping in St. Petersburg on his way back to Persia, he passed himself off to Count Nesselrode, the minister of foreign affairs, as the chargé d'affaires of the British mission to the Persian court, apparently indicating that he was Macdonald's successor.' Ingram (1984: 186) wrote that 'Willock was sent to St. Petersburg…to find out what terms of peace would satisfy Russia and to persuade the Persians to agree to them.'

[470] Nicholas I.

[471] It was probably due to Willock's absence that John McNeill became the principal negotiator in Tehran, while Macdonald remained at Tabriz. See MacAlister (1910: 94ff.).

[472] According to Eichwald (1837: 602–603) the Persian garrison at Yerevan was 5000 men strong, 'und unter ihren Befehlshabern befand sich auch Hassan Chan nebst sieben andern ausgezeichneten Chans. Ein Theil der Sarbasen hatte sich mit Hassan Chan in die Mesdsched [mosque] geflüchtet, um sich da noch zu vertheidigen; aber dieser ergab sich sofort mit ihnen zu Gefangenen, als sich zwei Compagnien des vereinigten Leibgarderegiments mit dem Generaladjutanten Grafen Suchtelen [Adjutant General Paul Petrovich Suchtelen (1788–1833)] dorthin genähert hatten. Außerdem fielen in die Hände der Sieger die 3000 M. starke Besatzung mit Kassum Chan, Ali Mardan Chan, Aßlan Chan, dem Chef der Artillerie Feth Ali Chan, und dem Commandanten der Festung Ssuwan Kuli Chan; ferner 4 Fahnen, 35 Kanonen, 2 Haubitzen und 8 Mörser, nebst 1500 Pf. Pulver, 10 Millionen Tschetwert Getreides und bedeutenden Schätzen des Sserdars von Erivan.' Cf. Lacroix (1866: 83) who noted that, as Russian forces entered Erivan and the garrison began to disperse in flight, 'Hassan-Khan s'était réfugié dans une mosquée, avec ses officiers et deux cents hommes déterminés à s'y défendre jusqu'à la dernière extrémité; mais le lieutenant-général comte Suchtelen ne leur donna pas le temps de préparer leur défense: on cerna la mosquée et l'on braqua contre la porte une pièce de

11.195 'Foreign News. Russia,' *Ithaca Journal & General Advertiser* (Wednesday, 6 February, 1828): 'The Russians are making a good deal of progress in Persia, as we learn from some Armenians from that quarter; but they do it very quietly; at least it appears the attention of Europe is not directed there.'

11.196 'Latest from Europe,' *The Freeman's Journal* (Monday, 25 February 1828) and 'Foreign. Latest from England,' *The Western Star* (Friday, 29 February 1828): 'Peace had been concluded between the Russians and the Persians. The Russians retain all the territory lying north of Araxes, and a small portion of that to the southward[473]—the Persians to pay all the expenses of the war.[474] The treaty leaves Russia at liberty to pursue her measures against Turkey.'[475]

---

canon; il n'en fallut pas davantage, pour que Hassan-Khan et ses compagnons se décidassent à mettre bas les armes. Le comte Suchtelen désarma lui-même son illustre adversaire.'

[473] As Paskevich wrote to Nicholas I on 22 October, 1827, 'j'ai envoyé au village de Karamélik le conseiller d'État actuel Obreskow, auquel j'ai confié le soin de mener les négociations sur les bases suivantes: (1) Cession à l'Empire de Russie des khanats d'Erivan situés sur les deux rives de l'Araxe et de Nakhitchevan, de sorte qu'à partir des limites du dit khanat jusqu'au gué d'Ediboul. l'Araxe devra servir de frontière entre les deux puissances. (2) Restitution à la Russie du khanat de Talisch, qui lui appartient en vertu du traité de Gulistan, et qui est occupé aujourd'hui par les troupes persanes depuis leur invasion dans cette province avant l'ouverture de la guerre actuelle.' See Stcherbatow (1891a: 252).

[474] Initially the sum demanded by Paskevich was 'Payement de 15 kourours [crore] de tomans (monnaie courante, autrement dit 30 millions de roubles argent) comme compensation pour les frais de guerre et les pertes causées par elle aux sujets russes. Cinq kourours de la somme stipulée doivent être versés 30 jours après la date inscrite ci-dessous; pour le payement des dix autres kourours, une période de deux mois est accordée à dater du versement de la première partie, en y ajoutant la condition que l'Aderbaïdjan, considéré comme gage du payement du reliquat, sera maintenu dans la pleine et entière dépendance de l'administration russe. Après le payement des 15 kourours au terme indiqué, ou avant ce terme, les troupes russes évacueront l'Aderbaïdjan et cette province fera retour au gouvernement persan. Si par contre les 10 derniers kourours ne sont pas payés au teme indiqué, cette province sera détachée du royaume de Perse, et des khanats indépendants y seront organisés sous la protection de la Russie, les 5 kourours versés à la Russie ne seront pas restitués.' See Stcherbatow (1891a: 252–253). The amount eventually agreed upon between 'Abbas Mirza and Paskevich was 10 crore [10 × 10,000,000] toman. See MacAlister (1910: 95). In the end Fath 'Ali Shah insisted on paying only 5 crore, three in gold and two in silver. McNeill urged that, if Mirza Abu'l Hasan Khan could be sent with a further 3 crore, the Russians would probably be satisfied and would withdraw from Tabriz to the north side of the Aras, but Fath 'Ali Shah was unwilling and said anything above 5 crore must be provided by 'Abbas Mirza. According to MacAlister (1910: 101), 'The next step in advance was that Mirza Abdul Hassan Khan was despatched with the 5 crores. Men were kept at work night and day packing the money, which took some 1600 mules to carry it. It was counted into bags, and these bags were, again, put into sacks; and on 27th December, to John McNeill's intense relief, the first detachment of the convoy started.'

[475] As Paskevich wrote to Nicholas on 28 January 1818 from his camp at Deh Kurgan, 'Les résultats de nos négociations avec les Persans deviennent d'heur en heure plus incertains. Les renseignements ci-joints, envoyés de Téhéran, permettront à Votre Majesté Impériale de se rendre compte des

11 The Second Russo-Persian War and the Treaty of Torkmanchay (1826–1828)

11.197 'Peace between Russia and Persia,' *Charleston Courier* (Monday, 25 February 1828): 'The Gazette de France gives the following details of the preliminary conditions of peace between Russia and Persia. The terms are considered humilating to Persia.

Paris, Dec. 26.—Official accounts from St. Petersburgh, dated the 6th of December, announce the following details:—

Immediately after the taking of Tauris, Feth Ali Khan[476] who had held the office of Governor-General of that city, had been commissioned by Abbas Mirza to carry proposals of peace to Gen. Paskewitsch. The latter took advantage of this mission, to make Feth Ali Khan the organ of his answer, and to acquaint the Persian Prince with the conditions upon which peace would be granted. A few days afterwards, he received by the same officer the assurance of the entire adherence of Abbas Mirza, the news of the sending of a Persian Plenipotentiary in the person of his Caimacan, or Principal Minister,[477] and an urgent request to fix as soon as possible the time and place for an interview, which the Prince himself asked of the General-in-Chief. In consequence, M. Obesnoff, Councillor of State,[478] met the Persian Plenipotentiary on the 2nd of November, in a village beyond Tauris, where they agreed the next day on the following preliminaries:—

1. That the Schah of Persia should entirely cede to us the whole of the Khanate of Erivan both on this and the other side of the Araxes, as well as the Khanate of Nakhitchevan.
2. That the Russian part of Talyche, which had been occupied by the Persians, should be restored to us immediately after the conclusion of the peace.
3. That a pecuniary indemnity should be paid to us for the expenses of the war, and the injury done by the invasion of the enemy.
4. That a part of this indemnity should be paid immediately on the signature of the peace and the remainder in short intervals.

---

dispositions du Schah. Les Persans ont reçu des informations encourageantes de Turquie, où le bruit d'une guerre avec la Russie s'est répandu dans le peuple. Le séraskier d'Erzeroum communique secrètement aux provinces persanes limitrophes les nouvelles de l'arrivée prochaine de 15,000 hommes d'élite, de l'armement des forteresses, et de l'organisation des dépôts sur différents points. En outre, un fonctionnaire du Schah et quelques marchands venus ici de Constantinople, disent avoir quitté cette ville le jour même où les ambassadeurs des trois puissances alliées se préparaient au départ. Le ministre d'Angleterre a reçu la confirmation de ce fait. Bien que toutes mes mesures soient prises pour que ces informations ne parviennent pas à Abbas-Mirza, et que dans mes entretiens avec lui je ne manifeste aucune inquiétude par rapport à la Turquie, je ne saurais l'empêcher de recevoir des communications secrètes; d'autant plus qu'à Téhéran on se leurre de l'espoir que cette puissance [Turkey] viendra au secours de ses coreligionnaires.' See Stcherbatow (1891a: 258–159).

[476] Fath 'Ali Khan-e Rashti, Governor-General (*beglerbegi*) of Tabriz. See Busse (1972: 183). For his career see Werner (2000: 162–167).

[477] Mirza Abu'l Qasem.

[478] Alexander Mikhailovich Obrescov (1793–1885). Together with Paskevich and 'Abbas Mirza, he was the third signatory to the Treaty of Torkmanchay. See Martens (1829: 564), Hertslet (1835: 597).

5. That, till the whole is paid, our troops should occupy, by way of security, the whole of the province of Adzerbidjan.

"The Plenipotentiaries having at the same time fixed the term of six days, dating from the 5th of November, to wait for the categorical assent of Abbas Mirza to these preliminaries, Gen. Paskewitsch received from him, on the 9th of November, an answer, by which he declares, that he entirely assents to them. In consequence, the interview was to take place, on the 16th of Nov. at Dekhargane,[479] a village between Tauris and Masagha [sic, Maragha],[480] so that we have every reason to believe that peace is now actually signed."

11.198 'Untitled,' *Geneva Palladium* (Wednesday, 27 February, 1828): '*Russia* has dictated peace to Persia, much in the same manner and upon the same terms, as we terminate hostilities occasionally against the Indians—by taking a considerable slice of their territory as the price of peace. In like manner Russia has consented to lay down her arms, for value received in an extension of her frontier.'

11.199 'Foreign Intelligence,' *Augusta Chronicle & Georgia Advertiser* (Friday, 29 February, 1828): 'The Persians are making a very disgraceful peace with the Russians—upon the following preliminaries:

"1. That the Schah of Persia should entirely cede to us the whole of the Khanate of Erivan both on this and the other side of the Araxes, as well as the Khanate of Nakhitchevan. 2. That the Russian part of Talyche, which had been occupied by the Persians, should be restored to us immediately after the conclusion of the peace. 3. That a pecuniary indemnity should be paid to us for the expenses of the war, and the injury done by the invasion of the enemy. 4. That a part of this indemnity should be paid immediately on the signature of the peace and the remainder in short intervals. 5. That, till the whole is paid, our troops should occupy, by way of security, the whole of the province of Adzerbidjan."'

11.200 'Russia and Persia,' *Commercial Advertiser* (Friday, 29 February, 1828): 'The occupation of Tauris by the Russian army was followed by a treaty of peace; and this being ratified, a provisional Russian Administration met, for a final adjustment, on the 2nd of November, in a village beyond Tauris, and the next day they agreed on the following preliminaries:

1. That the Schah of Persia should entirely cede to us the whole of the Khanate of Erivan both on this and the other side of the Araxes, as well as the Khanate of Nakhitchevan.

---

[479] Cf. Stcherbatow (1891a: 127), 'Dey-Kargan.' MacGregor (1871: 122) called 'the scene of a conference between Count Paskewitz and the Prince Royal of Persia after the occupation of Tabrez by the Russians, during the War of 1826,' by the name of 'Deh Kūrāng…A village in Azarbījān, Persia, on the east shore of lake Ūrūmīa, 35 miles south-south-west of Tabrez.'

[480] Maragha.

1 [sic, 2]. That the Russian part of Talyche, which had been occupied by the Persians, should be restored to us immediately after the conclusion of the peace.

3. That a pecuniary indemnity should be paid to us for the expenses of the war, and the injury done by the invasion of the enemy.

4. That a part of this indemnity should be paid immediately on the signature of the peace and the remainder in short intervals.

5. That, till the whole is paid, our troops should occupy, by way of security, the whole of the province of Adzerbidjan.

The assent of Abbas Mirza to these terms was received by General Paskewitsch on the 9th of November; and an interview, for the settlement of the terms of the conclusive treaty, was to take place on the 16th of November, at Dekhargane, a village between Tauris and Massagna.'

11.201 'Londres, 4 Janvier,' *New-Orleans Argus* (Thursday, 6 March, 1828): 'La rivière Araxès, qui se décharge dans la mer Gaspienne [sic, Caspienne] doit être à l'avenir, la limite entre la Russie et la Perse. Cependant la Russie a retenu un petit morceau dans la Perse au Sud de l'Araxès; ce qui lui donnera par la suite l'occasion de pousser la Perse, en devenant de manière ou autre l'agresseur, à une autre guerre où elle sera encore victorieuse, sera encore la paix en prenant encore un autre morceau de son territoire. C'est ainsi qu'en agissaient les Romains avec toutes les nations auxquelles il fesaient la guerre; et c'est ainsi qu'on fait dans l'Inde. La Russie par cette guerre et ce traité s'est mise dans le voisinage de Teheran, la ville principale au Nord d'Ispahan la capital, qui n'en est éloignée que de 300 milles. La première guerre et le premier traité, à ce que nous pensons, la mettra en contact avec Hispahan; alors nous commencerons à songer à nous mêmes, et peut-être pas avant, c'est alors que nos papiers ministériels commenceront à parler des empiétemens de la Russie, de son manque de bonne foi &c.

Nous commencerons à songer à envoyer des troupes pour aider la Perse. Mais alors la question que l'on se fera sera comme suit: Faut-il 5000 hommes comme dans le cas de Lisbonne; ou 10,000 ou même 20,000, et s'il le fallait nous pourrions rassembler ce dernier nombre (car en Angleterre il n'y a pas plus de 20,000 hommes de troupes, et encore Mr. Hune [sic, Hume][481] grogne-t-il de ce petit nombre) Quelles seraient les dépenses! Pour entretenir une armée de 20,000 hommes dans un tel endroit et à une telle distance, il en conterait au moins 20 millions par an. Le pays consentirait-il à une augmentation de taxes jusques à ce montant? Ou nos ministres croiront-ils qu'il serait sage d'emprunter tous les ans 20 millions et d'augmenter les taxes d'un million tous les ans pour payer l'intérêt, ou diraient-ils Nous avons assez tâté du système d'emprunts? [London Herald.]'

---

[481] Abraham Hume (1703–1772). He was deeply involved in solving problems of military logistics in the mid-eighteenth century. See Bannerman (2014). On 1 February 1746 he was appointed 'commissary general of stores, provisions and forage, to all his majesty's forces at home and abroad.' See Anonymous (1746).

11.202 'Foreign Intelligence,' *The Freeman's Journal* (Monday, 17 March, 1828), 'Russia and Persia,' *Black River Gazette* (Wednesday, 19 March, 1828) and 'Latest from England. Russia and Persia,' *The Western Star* (Friday, 21 March, 1828): ['London papers to the 15th January, have been received at Charleston, from which the following intelligence is gleaned. . . .] It is stated that Russia had received from Persia a million and a half of specie for indemnity in the last war, and that three and a half millions more were to be paid by installments.'[482]

11.203 'Russia and Persia,' *Geneva Gazette & General Advertiser* (after 7 April 1828), 'Latest from England. Russia & Persia' *New-York Spectator* (after 5 May 1828), 'Russia and Persia,' *The Freeman's Journal* (Thursday, 12 May, 1828) and 'Russia and Persia,' *The Western Star* (Monday, 16 May 1828): 'Official despatches received at St. Petersburgh on the 10th March, confirmed the satisfactory account of the termination of difficulties with Persia. The sons of Abbas Mirza[483] delivered up the fortress of Ardebil,[484] after the

---

[482] According to Monteith (1856: 148–150), after the treaty was signed, 'Sir John MacNeill, then attached to the British embassy, with a Russian commissioner, now proceeded to Teheran, where the preliminary articles of the treaty were agreed upon, but were not acted upon by the King. The leading article was one which the natural avarice of Futteh Ali Shah rendered it difficult for him to bring himself to comply with, for it stipulated the immediate payment of the sum of 2000,000 l. sterling [3000,000 tomans]; and he continually interposed delays in making over the money to the Russian government. . . .Prince Paskiewitch at last became uneasy at the frequent excuses and delays which occurred in the stipulated payment; and in the month of January [1828] the conference at Dokhergan was declared to be at an end, and preparations were made for an advance upon Teheran.' After losing Ardabil, Khoi, Salmas and several other towns, 'The King was now fairly alarmed, and in great haste forwarded the first instalment of the contribution levied upon him. . . .The district and fortified town of Khoey was held in deposit for the payment of the second instalment; but nearly 2000,000 of tomaums had been paid over in gold before General Paskiewitch left Tabreez, and this sum was conveyed principally on the cavalry horses.' MacAlister (1910: 105) put the total paid at 10 crore = £2000,000 in gold and silver. In fact there were further abrogations of the agreement and complications involving Macdonald and McNeill, both of whom had to stand guarantor for parts of the sum as described in MacAlister (1910: 106–116). In the end, the Russians agreed to leave Azerbaijan upon payment of 6.5 crores of tomans.

[483] Jahangir Mirza and Mohammad Mirza. See Eichwald (1837: 607). For the involvement of the two brothers around this time see Tapper (1997: 181). For more on Jahangir Mirza see Werner (2000: 199–200).

[484] According to Eichwald (1837: 607), because Fath 'Ali Shah initially refused to pay reparations to the Russians until they had left Azerbaijan, hostilities were resumed, even though it was winter and the snow was already deep. 'Den 15 Januar [1828] nahm hierauf der Generalmajor Pankratjeff mit seinem Corps die Stadt Urmiu ein, und der Generallieutenant Graf Suchtelen bewegte sich nach Ardebil, welches den 25 January seine Thore öffnete, um die Russen in die Stadt zu lassen. Abbas Mirsa's Söhne, Mahmed Mirsa [Mohammad Mirza] und Dshihangir Mirsa [Jahangir Mirza, governor of Ardebil and Meshkin] wollten sich in der Stadt vertheidigen, aber bald ergaben sie sich und die Citadelle den Russen mit der Bedingung, unter ihrem Schutze zu bleiben. der persischen Besatzung wurde jedoch ein freier Abzug gestattet.' As Monteith (1856: 150) noted, after Fath 'Ali Shah's

11 The Second Russo-Persian War and the Treaty of Torkmanchay (1826–1828)   1259

discharge of a few Congreve rockets,[485] and the garrison retired with arms and baggage. The British minister, Mr. M'Donald, had succeeded in persuading the Schah to except [sic, accept] all the terms of peace proposed by the Russian plenipotentiaries.'[486]

11.204 'Persia,' *American and Commercial Daily Advertiser* (Monday, 14 April, 1828): 'Abbas Mirza, the heir of the throne, who has just concluded an unsuccessful campaign against the Russians, is about forty-six years of age. He is a person of great dignity of deportment, and when ten or eleven years younger, possessed a handsome person. His conversation is sensible, and, says our authority, "his smile well timed."[487] His eye is full of goodness: he is also just, and never sanctions the cruelties authorized by the Persian laws. ["] Notwithstanding his long beard and terrific moustaches," adds our author, "Abbas Mirza won the hearts of us all." He is highly courteous, dresses plainly, and is averse to all pomp.

The last campaign is not the only one in which Abbas Mirza has contended against Russia, and with like ill fortune. In 1805 he commanded an army of thirty thousand men; and the poor state of Persian tactics may be estimated, when we are told, (on Russian authority indeed,) that a Russian colonel, with six hundred men and a single field piece, made good his defence during three days, against this great force, led on by Abbas Mirza in person.[488] The Russians fought under no other cover than some tombs and high grave-

---

apparent refusal to ratify the treaty, and following Gen. Paskevich's loss of patience, 'Count Suchtelen marched to Ardebil* [*Though the city had capitulated, the beautiful and extensive library belonging to the mosque and tomb of Shah Sefi was packed up and despatched to Russia.], which fortress surrendered, and his division was to unite with the troops of Shah Suoand [Shahsevan] and Shekakie [Shakaki Kurds].'

[485] Rocket invented by Sir William Congreve (1772–1828). See Werrett (2009). According to Gorton (1828, s.v. Congreve), 'The Congreve rockets are of various dimensions, and are differently armed according to the purposes for which they are designed, whether for the field or bombardment. Those of the first kind carry shells or case-shot; the others are armed with highly combustible materials, and are called carcass rockets. Their form is cylindrical, and they are partly composed of strong metallic cases, with sticks attached of varioius lengths according to the size of the rocket. The carcass rockets are armed with strong iron conical heads pierced with holes, and containing a substance as hard and solid as iron itself, which when once inflamed is inextinguishable, and scatters its burning particles in every direction. When this substance is consumed the ball explodes like a grenade. The rocket is projected horizontally, and whizzes loudly as it flies through the air. The ammunition is divided into three clases, heavy, medium, and light; the heavy including all above forty-two pounds weight; the medium those between forty-two and twenty-four pounds; and the light from eighteen to six pounds. . . .Their composition has not been kept a secret from foreigners, as appears from their having been used in the Austrian, Saxon, and other services, with improvements on the original invention.'

[486] Paskevich and Obrescov.

[487] This and the following quote are taken from Kotzebue (1819a: 153).

[488] A reference to the action described by Baddeley (1908: 69–70) as follows: 'A Persian army of 20,000 men led by Abbas Mirza entered the first-named khanate [Qarabagh], but wasted its strength in the vain effort to overcome the resistance of a mere handful of Russians under the leadership of the

stones, the battle being fought in the church-yard of a village. To crown this enterprise, a Russian general, with twelve hundred men, and a few guns, marched against Abbas Mirza, and totally defeated him. The king, who was near with a large army, retreated with precipitation. After this, it is not surprising that a war with Persia, is generally equivalent to the acquisition of territory. The province of Erivan, so often spoken of, is watered by the Araxes, which winds along the base of Mount Ararat. Here, the Armenians say, Noah[489] built his first dwelling. Numerous villages lie scattered about. The country is intersected by numberless canals, which irrigate the rice and cotton fields, but emit disagreeable and unwholesome vapours. It is a curious fact, however, which is somewhat contradictory of the commonly supposed contagiousness of the plague, that though that pestilence rages with violence in the neighbouring Ottoman possessions, it has never extended its ravages beyond the line of the Araxes, and this though there is a continual trade with Turkey, and the Persian government never adopts the slightest precautionarymeasures against its introduction.—This fact corresponds with others which have been observed in Europe, relative to this dreadful malady, one of whose chief mischiefs is the delay it causes to commerce by the quarantine system. The advocates of the free trade system in Europe, could not better subserve the interests of commerce than by promoting more extensive inquiries into the true nature of this disease, whose contagiousness has been doubted.

Of Abbas Mirza the following story[490] is related in Kotzebue's Narrative of the Russian Embassy into Persia. "The Embassador[491] discovered in his garden a projecting corner of an old wall, which spoiled the beauty of the surrounding objects, and disfigured the propsect. His Excellency asked the Prince why he did not order the wall to be pulled down? "Only conceive," replied the Prince; "with a view of forming gardens on a grand scale, I purchased the grounds of several proprietors. The owner of that where the wall stands, is an old peasant, who has absolutely refused to sell his property to me, because he will not part for any price with an ancient patrimonial possession of his family. I must allow, his obstinacy vexes me exceedingly, and yet I cannot but honour him for his attachment to his forefathers, and still more for his boldness in denying me his ground. I must wait till the time when his heir will, perhaps, be more reasonable."[492] With this story

---

heroic Kariághin, with Kotliarévsky to help him, whose feats of arms sound truly legendary. For three weeks, though frequently surrounded, he defied the whole Persian army, defeating it in pitched battles on three separate occasions; not only that, he stormed and captured various fortified places, and finally, with a force reduced to 100 men, cut his way through to the commander-in-chief [Tsitsianov], on whose approach the Persians beat a hasty retreat....So ended the campaign of 1805, noted in Russian military history for the valiant and almost incredible deeds performed by handfuls of men opposed to whole armies.'

[489] Genesis 6–9.
[490] Cf. 10.336.
[491] Ermolov.
[492] Quotation taken directly from Kotzebue (1819a: 168).

attached to it, the old wall would, to our view, have been the best point of view in Abbas Mirza's garden.'

11.205 'Foreign & Domestic News. Fifteen days later from England. War between Russia and Turkey,' *The Fredonia Censor* (after 18 April, 1828), 'Foreign News,' *Ithaca Journal & General Advertiser* (Wednesday, 30 April, 1828; 'hostilities were to be re-commenced') and 'Foreign News. Latest from England,' *Republican Monitor* (Tuesday, 6 May, 1828): 'Letters from Persia announce that peace between Persia and Russia had not been concluded,[493] and that hostilities would recommence.'

11.206 'Important from Europe. Russia and Turkey,' *The New-York Spectator* (Friday, 25 April, 1828), 'Important from Europe,' *The Schenectady Cabinet* (Wednesday, 30 April, 1828), 'Russia and Turkey,' *The Geneva Gazette and General Advertiser* (Wednesday, 30 April, 1828), 'Russia and Turkey,' *Lyons Advertiser* (Wednesday, 7 May, 1828) and 'Russia and Turkey,' *The Western Star* (Friday, 9 May, 1828): 'From the London Courier of March 15. . . .From the regret and surprise expressed by the Porte at the manner in which its manifesto[494] has been viewed by foreign powers, it is inferred that the Divan is inclined to yield. But Russia would now exact considerable sacrifices, particularly as in addition to the offensive manifesto, she charges Turkey with having excited Persia to make war, and recently with having instigated her to refuse ratifying the treaty of peace. The letters from Vienna impute the conduct of the Porte to the belief, that not only she would be seconded by Persia in a war against Russia [but that discord would dissolve the alliance between Russia; correctly in the *Schenectady Cabinet, The Geneva Gazette and General Advertiser* (only this last sentence) and the *Western Star*, omitted in the others; both contain only this first paragraph], Great Britain and France.'

---

[493] In fact, the treaty was signed on 23 February but Fath 'Ali Shah and 'Abbas Mirza did not ratify it until 24 August 1828. See MacAlister (1910: 105, 116).

[494] The 'manifesto' referred to is probably the Sultan's edict [*hatt-i şerîf*] of 20 December 1827 'which was sent to the Pashas and Ayans of the provinces, in order to prepare them for' war. As Chesney (1854: 17–18) noted, 'One part of this remarkable document was so incautiously worded that it seemed to impugn the well-known fidelity of the Turks to their engagements; for amongst other alleged grievances against Russia, it was stated, "that the treaty of Akkerman having been unjustly extorted, ought not to be considered binding;" and that, "as the object of the enemy was to annihilate Islamism and to tread Muhammedanism under foot, the faithful, rich and poor, high and low, should recollect that it is a duty to fight for their religion, and even willingly to sacrifice property and life in this vital struggle." It is not surprising that such a document should have had a prominent place amongst the justificatory reasons set forth by Russia for declaring war upon Turkey; which took place accordingly, without any reference to the other contracting powers.' As Moltke (1845: 226) noted, 'Das türkische Kriegs-Manifest war noch vor Ablauf des Jahres 1827 erschienen. Dennoch beschränkten sich die russischen Operationen bis Ende Mai des folgenden Jahres [1828] auf die Besetzung der Donau-Fürstenthümer, eine einleitende Maßregel, bei deren Ausführung man auf feindlichen Widerstand nicht zu rechnen hatte.'

'Paris, March 13.—The news which has been received to-day from St. Petersburgh, justifies the apprehensions which were naturally conceived on the effect which the Turkish manifesto would excite in that capital. This document, by whatever name it may have been called, has been considered by the Russian Cabinet as a real declaration of war,[495] with the more reason as repeated acts of hostility accompanied the publication of it. The Bosphorus entirely closed against navigation—Russian vessels confiscated—the influence of the Porte easily recognised in the rupture of a treaty which Russia was on the point of concluding with Persia[496]. . . .The same letters announce, that the treaty between Persia and Russia has not been signed,[497] and that hostilities were going to recommence.'

11.207 'Russia and Turkey,' *New-York Spectator* (Saturday, 26 April, 1828): 'Russia also complains. . .last, though not least, that the Sultan has been intriguing with, and holding out to, the Schah of Persia,[498] promises of men and money, to prevent him from ratifying the treaty of peace.'

11.208 'The Greeks,' *New-York Spectator* (Monday, 28 April, 1828) and 'Foreign,' *The Corrector* (Saturday, 3 May, 1828): 'Odessa. Feb. 12. We have long been without any direct news from Persia. According to the reports which we receive from Moscow, they must be very interesting. A report is spread that Abbas Mirza is on his way to St. Petersburgh, not in the character of a negotiator, but as a fugitive. It is said that he has fled to avoid the anger of his Sovereign, who considers him as a traitor.[499]—It is also asserted that the Schah[500] has united all his troops with those of his son, and is preparing to open the campaign anew. If these accounts should be true, they will render the affairs of Turkey still more delicate, for they are calculated to confirm the Divan in the opinion that it may resist the Powers.—*Gazette de Augsburg*.'

---

[495] According to Baddeley (1908: 176), 'On the 20th March Paskiévitch, then within one day's march of Eriván, received despatches from St. Petersburg informing him that war had been declared against Turkey.'

[496] In Count Nesselrode's replies of 13 and 25 April 1828 to the Reis Effendi and the edict of the Sultan, which reached Constantinople on 15 May along with a Russian manifesto declaring war, 'proceedings which virtually annulled the existing treaties with Russia' were cited, including the facts that, 'The trade of the Black Sea was impeded by searching the vessels so employed; Russian subjects were attacked, and Turkey even went so far as to announce to all Muslims her determination to return evil for good, war for peace, and not to fulfil solemn conventions.' See Chesney (1854: 19).

[497] Given that the dateline of the article cited here is Paris, 13 March, it would have been based on intelligence that predated the signing of the treaty on 23 February (MacAlister 1910: 105).

[498] Fath 'Ali Shah.

[499] There is no truth to this rumor.

[500] Fath 'Ali Shah.

11   The Second Russo-Persian War and the Treaty of Torkmanchay (1826–1828)   1263

11.209 'Russia and Persia,' *Syracuse Gazette & General Advertiser* (after 28 April, 1828): '(From the Liverpool Chronicle, of March 28.)....Hostilities have again commenced between these two countries, in consequence, as it is said, of the latter power having refused to ratify the late treaty, the provisions of which were so manifestly to her disadvantage.'

11.210 'From the Moniteur,' *Cayuga Patriot* (Wednesday, 30 April, 1828), 'Late and Important from Europe,' *The Kinderhook Herald* (Thursday, 1 May, 1828) and 'Latest from England. War between Russia & Turkey,' *The Freeman's Journal* (Monday, 5 May, 1828): 'The same letters announce, that the treaty between Persia and Russia has not been signed and that hostilities were going to recommence. The Russian army, at the moment of passing the Pruth, is abundantly supplied with all necessary resources.'[501]

11.211 'Untitled,' *Genius of Liberty* (after 1 May, 1828): 'An extraordinary supplement to the Journal of St. Petersburg of the 4th inst. contains the important fact of hostilities having been commenced between Russia and Persia, in consequence of the latter having refused to ratify the provisions of the treaty.'

11.212 'Foreign News. Latest from England,' *Republican Monitor* (Tuesday, 6 May, 1828): 'Russia considers herself at war with Turkey on her own account....she accuses Turkey of having instigated Persia to make war upon her....All the grounds of war which she enumerates are Russian grounds, and it belongs only to herself to do herself justice. But the conduct of Turkey with regard to Persia is the prominent grievance.'

11.213 'Russia and Persia,' *Ithaca Journal & General Advertiser* (Wednesday, 7 May, 1828), 'Russia and Persia,' *Greene County Republican* (Wednesday, 7 May, 1828; first paragraph only), 'Russia and Persia,' *The Geneva Gazette and General Advertiser* (Wednesday, 7 May, 1828; first paragraph only), 'Foreign' *The Kinderhook Herald* (Thursday, 8 May, 1828; first paragraph only) and 'Russia and Persia,' *The Corrector* (Saturday, 10 May, 1828; first paragraph only): 'Hostilities have again commenced between these two countries, in consequence, as it is said, of the latter power having refused to ratify the late treaty,[502] the provisions of which were so manifestly to her advantage.

---

[501] Although Nesselrode's reply to the edict of the Ottoman Sultan did not reach Constantinople until 15 May 1828, 'the Sultan had already heard on the 12th of the advance of the Russians from the Governor of Brailow [Brailov, Ukraine].' See Chesney (1854: 22). Further, he noted that, 'In explanation of that part of the Hatti Scheriff which attributed hostile designs to Russia, it was affirmed that war had evidently been contemplated by that power for several years; with which view an army had been for some time assembled in Bessarabia, ready to cross the Pruth.' See Chesney (1854: 20–21).

[502] As noted above, the treaty was not ratified until 24 August 1828. Cf. MacAlister (1910: 116).

The renewal of hostilities between Russia and Persia, if it be true, is calculated to embarrass the Russians in some measure, in their controversy with the Grand Seignior.[503] It is probable that this event may have been brought about by the interference of the Sublime Porte. Russia has men enough to fight both nations; but it is doubtful whether she has money enough. War in Persia must be expensive to the Russians. All their supplies must be drawn from a great distance, and at great cost. This, added to the other difficulties in the way of her going on alone in the warfare with Turkey, may have some tendency to prevent vigorous hostilities.'

11.214 'Latest from England,' *The New-York Evening Post* (Thursday, 8 May, 1828): 'What may grow out of the separate difference between Russia and the Porte, it is impossible to say—but we do not see that any cause of quarrel exists which might not be settled by negotiation. The complaint that the influence of the Porte had prevented the conclusion of a treaty between Russia and Persia, is now at an end, as the treaty has at length been made in spite of this supposed influence.'

11.215 'From the Aurora and Pennsylvania Gazette,' *New-York Evening Post* (Friday, 9 May, 1828) and 'From the Aurora & Pennsylvania Gazette,' *Delaware Gazette* (Wednesday, 21 May, 1828): 'An intelligent correspondent has suggested as there is now a prospect of war in Europe, it would be interesting to our readers, to have brought into one view, the population and strength of the several nations likely to be involved in it. The following is the result of what we have been enabled to collect from the most authentic sources within our reach. . . .Persia, now at war with Russia, has a territory of 1,500,000 square miles, a population of 24,000,000, an Army of 250,000 men, but no Navy.'

11.216 'Very Late from Europe,' *New-York Evening Post* (Monday, 12 May, 1828), 'Foreign Intelligence,' *Geneva Gazette and General Advertiser* (Wednesday, 21 May, 1828) and 'Foreign. Affairs of the East,' *The Western Star* (Friday, 23 May, 1828; 'eighty' instead of 'eight' millions of rubles): 'Whatever may be the designs of Russia in her differences with Turkey, it is certain she has profited by her late war with Persia, to extend her dominions in that quarter. Public rejoicings have been ordered at St. Petersburgh on account of the conclusion of the treaty which has extorted an additional indemnity from Persia for having broken off the negotiations after they were declared to be concluded, and which adds to the Asiatic dominions of Russia two provinces, the Khanats of Erivan and Nakhetchevan. These will henceforth bear the name of the province of Armenia. Russia is also put in possession of the main chain of the Ararat Mountains, with its rich salt mines.[504]

---

[503] Mahmud II.

[504] For salt in the Armenian region see e.g. Abich (1858: 32, 33, 58, 149). Cf. Parrot (1834: 188) who noted that Karl Schiemann, a medical student, and Maximilian Behaghel von Adlerskron, a student of

11   The Second Russo-Persian War and the Treaty of Torkmanchay (1826–1828)   1265

The amount of indemnity to be paid by the Schah[505] is stated at eight millions of rubles.'[506]

11.217 'Foreign news Russia and Persia,' *Auburn Free Press* (Wednesday, 14 May, 1828): 'Official news from St. Petersburgh of the 8th March, received at Paris on the 24th announces that at the moment when Gen. Paskewitch was preparing to recommence hostilities, the Schah[507] addressed him a communication with the most prompt despatch, to assure him of his pacifick disposition, and announcing that the sums were on their way, destined for the payment of the pecuniary indemnity. The Schah at the same time invited in the most pressing manner the intercession of Albas [sic, 'Abbas] Mirza, to bring to a conclusion the work of pacification[508]; authorising him to remit the sums agreed upon, one half of which had already arrived at Miana, near Tauris.[509] When the courier departed, a place was about to be fixed upon, where the respective Plenipotentiaries were again to meet, for the definitive signature of the treaty of peace.'[510]

11.218 'Foreign News,' *The Schenectady Cabinet* (Wednesday, 14 May, 1828): 'There is little doubt of peace having been concluded between Persia and Russia. The Russians made

---

mineralogy, made 'eine kleine Excursion nach einem in ganz Armenien und bis Tiflis berühmten Salzbergwerke...''Wir hatten so viel von den Salzbergen bei dem Dorfe Kulpe gehört...daß wir beschlossen, sie selbst in Augenschein zu nehmen,' and Parrot (1834: 193), 'Die Salzberge (es sind wirkliche Salzberge, denn unter einer nicht beträchtlichen Lage von Thon und Gyps kommt man gleich auf Steinsalz) sind sehr ergiebig. Die Berge, aus denen das Salz gewonnen wird, haben über 15 Werst im Umkreise. Das Salz wird in großen viereckigen Stücken von 2–3 Pud (80–120 Pfd.) gehauen.—300 Menschen sind fast täglich dabei beschäftigt....Es wird weißes und rothes Salz gewonnen. Seit einigen Jahren sind diese Bergwerke an einen armenischen Kaufmann aus Erivan für 12,000 R°. S.M. verpachtet.'

[505] Fath 'Ali Shah.

[506] Eichwald (1837: 608) put the final sum at 18,000,000 rubles. According to Macdonald's diary entry of 16 March 1828, the exchange rate agreed upon was 'four silver roubles to the tomân, according to the terms of the Treaty of Turkomanchai.' See MacAlister (1910: 112–113).

[507] Fath 'Ali Shah.

[508] 'Abbas Mirza's authority is confirmed by a letter from Macdonald to McNeill, dated 29 March 1828, which refers to 'the full powers vested in him by the Shah on all matters touching the foreign relations of Persia.' See MacAlister (1910: 114).

[509] On 18 January 1828 'John McNeill...started from Teheran to accompany the 6 crores from Casveen [Qazvin] to Tabreez....In passing through Meanna McNeill called on Baron Rosen, the General commanding the division....This news had the effect of stopping the renewed hostilities, and shortly it was arranged that a further conference should be held at Turkomanchai. McNeill returned to Teheran, trying to work further on the feelings or fears of the King.' See MacAlister (1910: 104).

[510] The treaty was signed at Torkmanchay on 23 February 1828 by 'General Paskevitch, M. D'Obrescoff, the Crown Prince Abbas Mirza, the Persian Prime Minister (who had been a prisoner in the hands of Russia, but was liberated to take part), the Minister of Foreign Affairs (i.e., "Fatty" [Mirza Abu'l Hassan Khan]), the Kaim Makam (Viceroy), and Manoocher Khan (Chief Eunuch). See MacAlister (1910: 105). Hurewitz (1956: 96) gives the date as 10/22 February.

themselves masters of the fortress of Ardebil,[511] which seems to have quickened the pacific intentions of the Schah.[512] Part of the money to be paid by Persia had arrived, and been deposited in the hands of the British Minister, Mr. M'Donald.[513] The remainder was on its way.[514] The Petersburgh Gazette avails itself of this occasion to speak highly of Mr. M'Donald's conduct, who strongly advised the Schah to make peace, thus proving the good understanding that subsists between the courts of St. Petersburgh and London.'[515]

11.219 'Foreign News. Affairs of the East,' *Greene County Republican* (Wednesday, 14 May, 1828): 'The Gazette of Augsburgh, of the 25th March, says:—"A Russian courier, who left St. Petersburgh on the 12th of March, brings the communication of the Russian Cabinet, according to which the Emperor of Russia[516] is resolved to put his army in motion, and to march against the Porte. The manner in which this power has acted latterly, particularly in endeavoring to employ its influence to prolong the misunderstanding between Russia and Persia, that in which it not only insulted the Russian nation in its manifesto, but also plainly intimated that it did not intend to remain faithful to the most faithful engagements...seemed to have been the principal motives which have induced the Russian Cabinet to make war upon the Porte....There was a general illumination at St. Petersburgh on account of the peace with Persia."'

11.220 'Foreign News. Russia,' *Ithaca Journal & General Advertiser* (Wednesday, 14 May, 1828): 'By the packet ship John Jay, Capt. Holdredge arrived at New-York on the 7th May, London dates to the 7th, and Liverpool to the 8th of April received....We

---

[511] As Stcherbatow (1891a: 53) noted, 'Les amas de neige n'avaient pas empêché Souchtelen d'occuper Ardebil le 25 janvier (6 février); pour ce qui est de la forteresse, elle ne s'était pas encore rendue. Il semblait même que les deux Princes [Jahangir Mirza and Mohammad Mirza] fussent décidés à la défendre malgré les injonctions contraires de leur père.'

[512] Fath 'Ali Shah.

[513] This happened on 28 January 1828 when McNeill 'and Colonel Macdonald met at the village of Turkomanchai.' See MacAlister (1910: 104).

[514] As MacAlister (1910: 106) noted, 'The treaty was signed, but the trouble about the money was by no means over. Four of the 10 crores stipulated had still to be arranged for; one payment had to be made before the troops were withdrawn from Azerbijan, another in two months, and a third in January, 1830.'

[515] As MacAlister (1910: 106) observed, 'Colonel Macdonald persuaded General Paskovitch to undertake to evacuate Azerbijan immediately on the payment of one half-crore in addition to the 6 crores he had already received....To complete the half-crore, Colonel Macdonald raised the necessary 50,000 by accepting a personal bond from Abbas Mirza, payable in two months. Thus the evacuation was purchased.' Evidence of the high esteem in which the Czar held Macdonald is demonstrated by the fact that, 'The Czar wished to confer upon him the Cross of the Second Class of the Order of St. Anne, which, however, he was not allowed to accept, and presented him with a gold snuffbox set with diamonds, worth £1500.' See MacAlister (1910: 118–119).

[516] Nicholas I.

11   The Second Russo-Persian War and the Treaty of Torkmanchay (1826–1828)   1267

received this morning the Journal of St. Petersburgh, of the 11th inst. which contains two important articles; the first being the declaration of the Emperour's[517] opinion upon the memorable manifesto of the Porte. . . .The other article refers to the progress of the Russian arms against the Persians, and the speedy submission of the Schah.'[518]

11.221 'Peace between Persia and Russia,' Poulson's American Daily Advertiser (Wednesday, 14 May, 1828), 'Peace between Persia and Russia,' New-York Spectator (Friday, 16 May, 1828; ends before 'St. Petersburg') and 'Peace between Persia & Russia, Pennsylvania Intelligencer (Tuesday, 20 May, 1828; ends before 'St. Petersburg'): 'St. Petersburg, March 27. From the Journal de St. Petersburgh, March 29.) (Extraordinary Supplement.) Yesterday, the 26th, Counsellor Griboyedoff[519] arrived here [St. Petersburg] with the treaty concluded and signed with Persia, on the 22nd of February, at Tourkmantschai.[520]

A salute of 201 guns, fired from the ramparts of the citadel,[521] announced to the public this happy event, brought about by glorious exploits, and by a negotiation fruitful in results equally brilliant.

To-day a solemn *Te Deum* has been performed in the Winter Palace.[522]

How many motives are there in fact to render thanks to the Almighty for the issue of a war crowned by a glorious peace, the conditions of which repair all the losses caused by an unforseen aggression, and prevent the return of it.

The addition which the Russian territory obtains by this treaty, offers all desirable security for the maintenance of our pacific relations with the Persian Government.

We shall shortly be able to communicate to the public all the clauses of this important treaty.'

---

[517] Nicholas I.

[518] Fath 'Ali Shah.

[519] Alexander Sergeyevich Griboyedov (1795–1829). Russian writer and diplomat, 'was chosen by the commander in chief of Russian forces in the Caucasus, General Ivan Fedorovich Paskevich, to bring the treaty to St. Petersburg, where he arrived in March, 1828.' See Harden (1971a: 75). In the letter to Nesselrode given to Griboyedov when he left with the treaty, Paskevich wrote, 'I am trusting the Despatch and Treaty to Griboyedov as a major contributor to the recent negotiations. Your Excellency can learn from him every detail. He, better than any other, can explain to you all the complications and problems encountered. May I recommend Griboyedov to your Excellency as a first-class, totally dedicated and experienced official in these matters. He entirely deserved the confidence of his Imperial Majesty.' See Kelly (2006: 161).

[520] Village c. 64 mi. southeast of Tabriz. See MacGregor (1871: 597). Vambéry (1867: 68) described being shown the house and the actual room in which the treaty was signed in 1862.

[521] Founded in 1703 by Peter the Great. For a description see Georgi (1793: 106).

[522] The 'Palais d'hiver impérial,' completed in 1754, for which, see Georgi (1793: 51).

St. Petersburg. March 28.

Rescript of his Majesty the Emperor to the Governor-General of St. Petersburg.[523]

The treaty of perpetual peace between Russia and Persia was concluded and signed at Tourkmantchai on the 22nd February last.

This treaty guarantees to Russia a new and secure position, besides a complete indemnity for all its losses; it acquires an increase of territory, by the union to its dominions of the Khanats of Erivan and Nakhetchevan, which will henceforth bear the name of the Province of Armenia. Thus, this war caused by an unexpected invasion, has been terminated by a peace equally advantageous and glorious.

Thanking God, who always protects the good cause, and who has crowned our arms with new glory, we hasten to acquaint you with this happy event, persuaded that our faithful subjects will join their thanksgivings to those which we offer to the Almighty.

The treaty of peace will soon be made public by a special manifest.

I remain, &c.   NICHOLAS

St. Petersburgh, (15th) 27th March, 1828

Berlin, April 8.

The Prussian State Gazette of this date, after giving, under the head of St. Petersburgh, 29th March, the Supplement and the rescript of the Emperor adds—

"As far as the stipulations of the defensive treaty are yet known, the indemnity to be paid by the Schah is increased, on account of the breach of the negotiations, which were already concluded, to 80 millions of rubles,[524] and Russia obtains besides the above mentioned provinces of Erivan and Nakhitchevan, the Mount Cerarat [sic, Ararat], with its rich salt mines.

A grand entertainment was given yesterday at Court in honor of this happy event, to which three hundred persons were invited.'"

11.222 'Nine Days later from Europe: Russia and Persia,' *New-York Spectator* (Friday, 16 May, 1828) and 'Foreign. Russia and Persia,' *Pennsylvania Intelligencer* (Tuesday, 20 May, 1828): 'At length, we have official advices of the Peace between Russia and Persia. The St. Petersburgh Gazettes of March 27th and 28th, are engrossed with the glad tidings of this event, which has put money into the coffers and added two Provinces to the

---

[523] Pavel Vasiliyevich Golenischev-Kutuzov (1772–1843), was military general of the St. Petersburg Governate from 1825 to 1830. He had fought in the Napoleonic wars with distinction and brought the news of Napoleon's defeat from Paris to St. Petersburg after the Battle of the Nations at Leipzig in 1813. See Plokhy (2012: 16). For George Dawe's (1781–1829) portrait of him in the Hermitage, see https://www.hermitagemuseum.org/wps/portal/hermitage/digital-collection/01.+Paintings/39193/

[524] As noted above, Eichwald (1837: 608) put the final sum at 18,000,000 rubles. Baddeley (1908: 176) gave the sum as 20,000,000 rubles which is the correct figure as shown in Article 6 of the treaty (Hurewitz 1956: 97). The figure of 80,000,000 is obviously wildly inflated.

vast Empire of Russia.[525] They are to be called the Province of Armenia—Russia has also the main claim of the Ararat Mountains, and all the rich Salt Mines. How valuable an acquisition this is to Russia may be seen by one glance at the Map; and if extensive Empire be desirable, well indeed may she rejoice!'

11.223 'From Europe,' *Lansingburgh Gazette* (Tuesday, 20 May, 1828): 'St. Petersburgh, March 27.

His Majesty the Emperor has conferred on General Paskiwitsch the title of Count Paskiwitsch, of Erivan.[526]

The treaty of peace with Persia arrived here yesterday. *Te Deum* was performed to day in the church of this city, in commemoration of that important event. . . .

Warsaw, March 21.

Several German Journals have published statements respecting the military force of Russia, which are more or less inaccurate. . . .The army of Georgia, or of the Caucasus, had suffered at the very beginning of the war against the Persians, considerable losses, caused by the insalubrity of the climate, but by the reinforcements which it received in July and August last [1827], it has been completed to 75,000 men.'

St. Petersburg. March 28.

Rescript of his Majesty the Emperor to the Governor-General of St. Petersburg.[527]

The treaty of perpetual peace between Russia and Persia was concluded and signed at Tourkmantchai on the 22nd February last.

This treaty guarantees to Russia a new and secure position, besides a complete indemnity for all its losses; it acquires an increase of territory, by the union to its dominions of the Khanats of Erivan and Nakhetchevan, which will henceforth bear the name of the Province of Armenia. Thus, this war caused by an unexpected invasion, has been terminated by a peace equally advantageous and glorious.

Thanking God, who always protects the good cause, and who has crowned our arms with new glory, we hasten to acquaint you with this happy event, persuaded that our faithful subjects will join their thanksgivings to those which we offer to the Almighty.

The treaty of peace will soon be made public by a special manifest.

I remain, &c. NICHOLAS

St. Petersburgh, (15th) 27th March, 1828

Berlin, April 8.

---

[525] As noted above, the former Khanats of Erivan and Nakhchivan.

[526] Or 'Erivansky,' in honor of his capture of Erivan. See e.g. Müller-Simonis (1892: 60), Barratt (1972: 409), Bitis (2006: 49).

[527] Pavel Vasiliyevich Golenischev-Kutuzov. Cf. 11.221.

The Prussian State Gazette of this date, after giving, under the head of St. Petersburgh, 29th March, the Supplement and the rescript of the Emperor adds—

"As far as the stipulations of the defensive treaty are yet known, the indemnity to be paid by the Schah is increased, on account of the breach of the negotiations, which were already concluded, to eighty millions of rubles,[528] and Russia obtains besides the above mentioned provinces of Erivan and Nakhitchevan, the Mount Cerarat [sic, Ararat], with its rich salt mines.

A grand entertainment was given yesterday at Court in honor of this happy event, to which three hundred persons were invited.'"

11.224 'Foreign Compendium,' *The Evening Gazette* (Saturday, 17 May, 1828), 'Foreign Summary. From the London Corrier [sic], April, 15,' *Christian Register* (Saturday, 17 May, 1828): 'We have received this morning the St. Petersburgh Gazette of March 27th and 28th. They are engrossed by the glad tidings of the peace with Persia, which has put money into the coffers, and added two Provinces to the vast Empire of Russia. They are to be called the Province of Armenia. Russia has also the main chain of the Ararat Mountains, and all the rich Salt Mines. How valuable an acquisition this is to Russia may be seen by one glance at the map; and if extensive Empire be desirable, well indeed may she rejoice.—*London Courier, April* 15.'

11.225 'From Europe,' *Lansingburgh Gazette* (Tuesday, 20 May, 1828): 'St. Petersburgh, March 27.

His Majesty the Emperor has conferred on General Paskiwitsch the title of Count Paskiwitsch, of Erivan.

The treaty of peace with Persia arrived here yesterday. *Te Deum* was performed to day in the church of this city, in commemoration of that important event....

Warsaw, March 21.

Several German Journals have published statements respecting the military force of Russia, which are more or less inaccurate....The army of Georgia, or of the Caucasus, had suffered at the very beginning of the war against the Persians, considerable losses, caused by the insalubrity of the climate, but by the reinforcements which it received in July and August last [1827], it has been completed to 75,000 men.'

11.226 'From Europe,' *Lansingburgh Gazette* (Tuesday, 20 May, 1828; minus the last sentence) and 'From Europe,' *The Schenectady Cabinet* (Wednesday, 21 May, 1828): 'The London Courier of the 15th says....Peace has been most advantageously concluded between Russia and Persia. In addition to a large sum of money the Russians have gained

---

[528] As noted above, Eichwald (1837: 608) put the final sum at 18,000,000 rubles. Baddeley (1908: 176) gave the sum as 20,000,000 rubles which is the correct figure as shown in Article 6 of the treaty (Hurewitz 1956: 97). The figure of 80,000,000 is obviously wildly inflated.

two Provinces. They are to be called the Province of Armenia. Russia has also the main chain of the Ararat Mountains, and all the Salt Mines. How valuable an acquisition this is to Russia may be seen by one glance at the map; and if extesive empire be desirable, well indeed may she rejoice! On the arrival of this intelligence at St. Petersburgh, a salute of 121 guns was fired and a solemn Te Deum was performed.'

11.227 'Foreign Intelligence. Very late from Europe,' *The Boston Statesman* (Saturday, 17 May, 1828) and 'Foreign. Affairs of the East,' *The Western Star* (Friday, 23 May, 1828): 'Whatever may be the designs of Russia in her difference with Turkey, it is certain she has profited by her late war with Persia, to extend her dominions in that quarter. Publick rejoicings have been ordered at St. Petersburgh on account of the concusion of the treaty which has extorted an additional indemnity from Persia for having broken off the negotiations after they were declared to be concluded, and which adds to the Asiatick dominions of Russia two provinces, the Khanhts [sic, Khanates] of Erivan and Nakhetchevan. These will henceforth bear the name of the province of Armenia. Russia is also put in possession of the main chain of the Arrarat Mountains, with its rich salt mines.—The amount of indemnity to be paid by the Schah is stated at eighty millions of rubles.'

11.228 'Very late from Europe,' *Vermont Watchman and State Gazette* (Thursday, 27 May, 1828) and 'Foreign & Domestic Intelligence. [From the Boston Traveller.] Late from Europe,' *Woodstock Observer* (Thursday, 27 May, 1828): 'The peace between Russia and Persia has put money into the coffers and added two provinces to the vast empire of the former power. They are to be called the province of Armenia. Russia has also the main chance of the Ararat Mountains, and all the rich salt mines.'

11.229 'Russia and Persia,' *The Rochester Album* (Thursday, 27 May, 1828): 'Peace is officially announced between these two nations, in the St. Petersburg Gazettes of 27th and 28th March. After a short quarrel, Russia has indemnified herself by a round sum of money (only 80,000,000 rubles) and a huge slice of territory, as will be perceived by the following document, the promulgation of which was the signal for all manner of rejoicings and thanksgivings.

Rescript of His Majesty the Emperor to the Governor-General of St. Petersburg.[529]

The treaty of perpetual peace between Russia and Persia was concluded and signed at Tourkmantchai on the 22nd February last.

This treaty guarantees to Russia a new and secure position, besides a complete indemnity for all its losses; it acquires an increase of territory, by the union to its dominions of the Khanats of Erivan and Nakhetchevan, which will henceforth bear the name of the Province

---

[529] Pavel Vasiliyevich Golenischev-Kutuzov. Cf. 11.221, 11.223.

of Armenai. Thus, this war caused by an unexpected invasion, has been terminated by a peace, equally advantageous and glorious.

Thanking God, who always protects the good cause, and who has crowned our arms with new glory, we hasten to acquaint you with this happy event, persuaded that our faithful subjects will join their thanksgivings to those which we offer to the Almighty.

The treaty of peace will soon be made public by a special manifest.

I remain, &c.   NICHOLAS
St. Petersburgh, (15th) 27th March, 1828.'

11.230 'Extraordinary Supplement to the Journal of St. Petersburgh, of the 5th of April,' *Commercial Advertiser* (Wednesday 28 May, 1828; minus first para), 'Russia and Persia [From the London Times of April 22.],' *National Journal* (Saturday, 31 May, 1828), 'Extraordinary Supplement to the Journal of St. Petersburgh, of the 5th of April,' *Boston Daily Advertiser* (Saturday, 31 May, 1828) and 'Extraordinary Supplement to the Journal of St. Petersburgh, of the 5th of April,' *The Freeman's Journal* (Monday, 16 June, 1828; minus first para.): 'The Extraordinary Gazette of St. Petersburgh of the 5th instant [April, 1828], contains a Manifesto of the Emperor, imbodying the treaty of peace with Persia. The conclusion of the treaty and its chief conditions had been already known, though they are now published for the first time in official form. The advantages which Russia reaps from her recent victories are immense, and, without strong proofs to the contrary, might be reckoned the motives for a contest of which they seemed from the beginning the evident results. A great extension of teerritory, a secure frontier, and a weighty indemnity for the expenses of the conquest may well satisfy the young Czar with his first military exploits and armed negotiations. The Sultan at Constantinople[530] would do well to take warning from the fate of his brother Sovereign in Persia, and not tempt an invasion to the west, which may terminate in a new conquest and a fresh indemnity.

The following is the declaration alluded to:

[Extraordinary supplement to the Journal of St. Petersburgh of April 5]

Manifesto of His Majesty the Emperor.

By the Grace of God, We, Nicholas I., Emperor and Autocrat of the Russias, &c. &c. &c.

The Almighty has again poured down blessings on Russia, by terminating by a glorious peace the war with Persia, the commencement of which gave reason to apprehend that it would be of long duration.

It was in the midst of friendly negotiations and when positive assurances gave us the hope of preserving the relations of good neighbourhood with Persia, that the tranquility of our people was disturbed on the frontiers of Caucasus, and that a sudden invasion violated the territory of the Emperor, in contempt of solemn treaties. It was then necessary to repel force by force.—Obliged to pursue the enemy through a country without roads, laid waste

---

[530] Mahmud II.

by the troops which were to have defended it – often opposed by nature itself – exposed to the burning sun of summer, and the rigours of winter – our brave army, after unparalleled efforts, succeeded in conquering Erivan, which was reported impregnable.—It passed the Araxes, planted its standards on the top of Ararat, and, penetrating further and further into the interior of Persia, it occupied Tabriz itself, with the country depending on it.—The Khanate of Erivan, on both sides of the Araxes, and the Khanate of Nakhitchevan, a part of the ancient Armenia, fell into the hands of the conquerors.

But in the course of these rapid conquests the Russians acquired glory of another kind. In the midst of a war, the enemy's country became the theatre of their valour, and the safety of persons, and all kinds of property remained as sacred and inviolable to them as if they had been in profound peace in the country of an ally. Humane, mild, and generous, their conduct has surrounded the Russian name with a splendour superior to that which victory bestows.

It is thus that in eight months, after the entrance of our troops into the Persian territory, decisive exploits and important results have crowned our arms; their success has demonstrated that Providence defended our just cause. Covered by its mighty eyes, and considering peace as the greatest of blessings, Russia will never suffer it to be disturbed without inflicting on the aggressor just and severe chastisement. The road to new triumphs was open before us, but the moment that peace which we so highly value was possible, our only wish was to conclude.

Our object was to secure to the empire a natural and strong barrier on the side of Persia; to obtain a complete indemnity for all the losses occasioned by the war, and thus to remove all the causes which might lead to its return.

Such, in fact, are the bases on which a Treaty of Perpetual Peace was concluded and signed on the 10th (22nd) February at Tourkmantchaï, between Russia and Persia, the publication of which accompanies this Manifesto.

For us, one of the principal results of this peace consists in the security which it gives to one part of our frontiers. It is solely in this light that we consider the utility of the new countries which Russia has just acquired. Every part of our conquests that did not tend to this end was restored, by our orders, as soon as the conditions of the treaty were published.

Other essential advantages result from the stipulations in favour of commerce, the free development of which we have always considered as one of the most influential causes of industry; and, at the same time, as the true guarantee of a solid peace, founded on an entire reciprocity of wants and interests.

To him who regulates the fates of empires the humble tribute of our profound gratitude belongs. Let all our dear and faithful subjects, after acknowledging the striking proofs of the favour and protection of the Most High in the events of this war, offer up their most fervent prayers at the foot of the altars. May this peace—the work of Providence—be firm and durable; and may His holy will assist us in preserving tranquility on the frontiers of our dominions! Given at St. Petersburgh, March 21, (April 2,) in the year of our Lord 1828, and in the 3rd of our reign.

Signed,	NICHOLAS
Countersigned	Count de NESSELRODE[531]

Here follows the Treaty of Peace, in 16 articles,[532] the preamble of which recites the reciprocal wishes of the Emperor of Russia and the Padischah of Persia for the restoration of peace, and for which end Plenipotentiaries are named—viz. Gen. Paskewitsch and the Councillor of State Alexander Obrescoff on the part of Russia, and Prince Abbas Mirza on the part of Persia:—

1st. There shall be perpetual peace, friendship, &c.
2nd. The Treaty of Gulestan to be dissolved, and replaced by the present.
3rd. Persia cedes the Khanate of Erivan, on either side of the Araxes, and the Khanate of Nakhitchevan; and all the public documents connected with these two provinces shall be delivered within six months.
4th. Details, with great minuteness, the future frontier line between the two empires. It begins at the point of the Ottoman States, the nearest to Little Ararat, and crosses that mountain to the source of the Lower Karassou, follows the source of that river, till it falls into the Araxes opposite Chorour,[533] and then follows the course of the latter river as far as the fortress Abbas-Abad.

This fortress, situated on the right bank, together with the surrounding coiuntry to the extent of three wersts and a half, is to belong to Russia. The frontier line then again follows the course of the Araxes as far as twenty-one wersts beyond the ford of JedibouIouk, from which point a straight line is to be drawn across the plain of Monghaw[534] to the bed of the river Bolgarou,[535] twenty-one wersts above the point of confluence of the two rivers Odinabazar and Sarakamyche. The line then passes across the summit of Djikoir, so that all waters falling into the Caspian belong to Russia;[536] and continues to cross the summit of

---

[531] Karl Robert Reichsgraf von Nesselrode-Ehreshoven, Foreign Minister of the Russian Empire. For the record of his ministry at this time see Nesselrode (1904/7). Cf. 10.197.

[532] The following is only a summary of the actual treaty for the text of which see e.g. Markham (1874: 552–554) (abridged) and Hurewitz (1956: 96–102) (complete).

[533] As MacGregor (1871: 221) noted of the Kara Su: 'A river of Azarbījān, Persia, which rises in the rocks of Boralan in the plain facing Little and Great Ararat, and falls into the Aras opposite Shārūr Dāgh. It forms the boundary between Persia and Russia in this part.'

[534] Mughan.

[535] The Bolgaruçay. As Dorn (1875: xxi) noted, 'Der Bolgaru-tschai entströmt von der Quelle Chilchan; bis zum Dorfe Burawar...heisst er Schamba-tschai...bis zu dem Schirin-Su..., d.i. Süsses Wasser genannten Ort, ist er unter dem Namen Adina-Bašar-tschai...bekannt und erst weiter heisst er Bolgara. Dieser kleine Fluss ist bloss im Winter da, verläuft sich aber auch zu dieser Zeit in der Steppe, indem er sich in Rohrdickichten und verschiedenen niedrigen Stellen verliert.' According to Petzholdt (1866: 121), the Bolgaru 'sich nach und nach in der Mugan'schen Steppe verliert.'

[536] The hydrology of this whole passage, with the corrected toponyms, is fully explicated in MacGregor (1871: 363–364).

other mountains, observing the above principle, relative to rivers falling into the Caspian, to the source of the river Artara, the course of which, as it falls into the Caspian, completes the whole line of frontier.

5th. The Shah[537] confirms the above line of frontier.
6th. Persia to pay an indemnity of 20,000,000 rubles.
7th. Prince Abbas Mirza is recognized as heir apparent to the throne of Persia.
8th. The Russians to enjoy the free navigation of the Caspian. The Persians to enjoy the same *sur l'ancien pied*; Russia alone to have armed vessels on the same.
9th. Ambassadors to be received by both parties with all due honors.
10th, 11th, 12th, and 13th, regulate the nomination of Consuls, and the transfer of private property, as also a mutual enlargement of prisoners.
14th. No deserters to be given up by either party.
15th. An amnesty to be awarded by Persia to the inhabitants of the province of Adzerbaldjane, and, if they should be inclined to emigrate into Russia, a period of one year is to be allowed them for the disposal of all moveable property, and a period of five years for the disposal of lands.
16th. The ratificaction of this treaty to be exchanged within the space of four months.'

11.231 'From England,' *The Schenectady Cabinet* (Wednesday, 4 June, 1828): 'The Emperor of Russia has ordered a medal to be given to, and worn by all his troops engaged in the war with Persia.[538] A military spirit and taste will probably spread in Russia.'

11.232 'Untitled,' *The Corrector* (Saturday, 7 June, 1828): 'A Paris paper of April 22, says the treaty of the 22nd February, between Russia and Persia, is about to augment

---

[537] Fath 'Ali Shah.
[538] According to Eichwald (1837: 609–610), 'In dem am 15 März 1828 allerhöchst ertheilten Armeebefehl gab der Kaiser den tapfern russischen Kriegern für die Beendigung dieses blutigen Perserkrieges seine volle Zufriedenheit zu erkennen, da es ihnen gelungen war, innerhalb 8 Monate diesen durch so viele wichtige Thaten ausgezeichneten Feldzug zu beendigen, und nicht nur die unerträgliche Hitze des Sommers und die Rauhigkeit des Winters, sondern auch alle Beschwerden des Feldzugs zu überwinden, die ihnen die zahlreichen Haufen des Feindes und die Natur selbst durch wilde unersteigliche Bergpässe und schroffe Felsengegenden in den Weg gelegt hatten; dafür wurde für alle, die an den Gefechten der denkwürdigen Jahre 1826, 1827 und 1828 Theil genommen hatten, eine besondere silberne Medaille mit der Aufschrift: für den persischen Krieg, gestiftet, um sie an dem vereinigten Bande des Wladimir- und Georgenordens zu tragen.' Schulze (1853: 890) described it as follows: 'une médaille en argent qui se porte à la boutonnière à un ruban partagé en deux moitiés égales, dont l'une a les couleurs de l'Ordre de St. George et l'autre celles de l'Ordre de St. Wladimir. L'empereur *Nicolas* la fonda l'an 1828 pour tous les militaires, qui avaient pris part à la campagne contre les Perses. D'un côté on voit au-dessus l'œil du monde, au-dessous 1826, 1827, 1828, lesquels chiffres sont entourés d'une couronne de laurier ouverte en haut. L'autre côté porte l'inscription: "ЗА ПЕРСИДСКУЮ ВОЙНУ." c'est-à-dire: "Pour la campagne de Perse."

the embarrassments and fears of England.—For a long time the progressive march of a great power towards the Black Sea, and its establishments in the Crimea had made her suspect projects calculated to disturb her. They are no longer doubtful, as the Roulan[539] has ceased to serve as a barrier.[540]—Since the Russians have arrived at the sources of the Cyrus,[541] and have solidly established themselves beyond Mount Caucasus, they have become masters of Georgia and the whole coast of the Caspian Sea, from the mouth of the Wolga to the Gulf of Ghilan. Ispahan[542] has long wavered between the Russian and English influence.'

11.233 'Postscript,' *New-York Evening Post* (Monday, 16 June, 1828), 'Extraordinary Supplement to the Prussian State Gazette,' *The Delaware Gazette* (Wednesday, 18 June, 1828), 'Extraordinary Supplement to the Prussian State Gazette,' *The Corrector* (Saturday, 21 June, 1828), 'Russian Declaration of War. Extraordinary Supplement to the Prussian State Gazette,' *Genius of Liberty* (after 21 June, 1828), 'Extraordinary Supplement to the Russian State Gazette,' *The Schenectady Cabinet* (Wednesday, 25 June, 1828), 'Foreign News. Late and Important from England,' *Greene County Republican* (Wednesday, 25 June, 1828), 'Late and Important from Europe. Russian Declaration of War,' *The Cayuga Patriot* (Wednesday, 25 June, 1828), 'Foreign & Domestic. Russian Declaration of War Against Turkey. Extraordinary Supplement to the Prussian State Gazette,' *The Gazette* [Syracuse NY], 'War—At last!,' *The Geneva Gazette and General Advertiser* (Wednesday, 25 June, 1828), 'Foreign,' *The Kinderhook Herald* (Thursday, 26 June, 1828) and 'Extraordinary Supplement to the Russian State Gazette. Berlin, May 4,' *The Republican Monitor* (Tuesday, 1 July, 1828): 'At the moment when the negociations between Russia and Persia are nearly concluded, a sudden change on the part of the Persian government checks the course of them. It soon appears that the Ottoman Porte exerts himself to make Persia waver, by promising powerful aid, arming in haste the troops in the adjoining provinces, and preparing to support by a threatening attack this treacherous hostile language.'[543]

---

[539] Probably the 'Rione or Phasis' river in Georgia. See Malte-Brun (1822: 37).

[540] On the matter of Russia not exciting the European powers to fear Russian expansion, Baddeley (1908: 176) noted, 'Paskiévitch had recommended the retention of Azerbijan, saying that in that event the English might as well take ship at Bushire and retire to India. But the Emperor preferred, if the renewal of the war made it impossible to restore the province to Persia, to divide it into several independent khanates, lest the European Powers should suspect, and justly, that Russia aimed at exclusive domination in Asia.'

[541] Kur river.

[542] An obvious anachronism since Isfahan, the Safavid capital, had long since been superseded by Tehran, the Qajar capital.

[543] As McNeill (1836: 105) noted, 'Another ground of complaint against Turkey was, that she had endeavoured to impede or prevent the conclusion of peace between Russia and Persia. This charge, which is supported by no evidence, was certainly not one which could in justice be urged by a government that had a few years before instigated these same Persians to attack Turkey.'

11.234 'Continuation of Foreign News. Berlin, May 5. Explanatory Remarks,' *Commercial Advertiser* (Tuesday, 17 June 1828), 'Russian Declaration of War.. Berlin, May 5. Explanatory Remarks,' *The National Gazette and Literary Register* (Thursday, 19 June, 1828), 'Russian Declaration of War against Turkey. Extraordinary Supplement to the Prussian State Gazette. Berlin, May 5. Explanatory Remarks,' *Poulson's American Daily Advertiser* (Thursday, 19 June, 1828), 'From the Supplement to the Prussian State Gazette, of April 6. Berlin, May 5. Explanatory Remarks,' *United States' Telegraph* (Saturday, 21 June, 1828), 'From the Supplement to the Prussian State Gazette, of April 6. Berlin, May 5. Explanatory Remarks,' *United States' Telegraph* (Monday, 23 June, 1828), 'Foreign. Russian Declaration of War against Turkey,' *Richmond Enquirer* (Tuesday, 24 June, 1828), 'Foreign & Domestic. Russian Declaration of War Against Turkey. Extraordinary Supplement to the Prussian State Gazette,' *The Gazette* [Syracuse NY] (Wednesday, 25 June, 1828) and 'Late and Important. Extraordinary Supplement to the Russian State Gazette. Berlin, May 5. Explanatory Remarks,' *Schenectady Cabinet* (Wednesday, 25 June, 1828): 'In 1821, when the Emperor Alexander had good reason to complain of the Porte, and a breach seemed to be at hand, Persia declared war against Turkey; but the Emperor,[544] far from taking advantage of the opportunity, far from engaging Persia, Russia declared it had not cause to make war, and wished to see it ended. In 1828, when peace was on the point of being concluded between Russia and Persia, Turkey assured the latter, through the Pacha of Van,[545] that war between Russia and Turkey was at hand,[546] and invited Persia not to make peace with us, promising the assistance of the Ottoman troops.'

11.235 'Late and Important from Europe,' *The Albany Argus* (Friday, 20 June, 1828), 'Extraordinary Supplement to the Russian State Gazette. Berlin, May 4. Manifesto of His Majesty the Emperor.' *The Albion* (Saturday, 21 June, 1828), 'Russian Declaration of War

---

[544] Nicholas I.

[545] This allegation arose from a letter, intercepted by Paskievich, 'dans laquelle le pacha de *Van* doit avoir informé Abbas Mirza, *au mois de décembre*, que la guerre étant déclarée entre la Russie et la Porte, il enverrait 100C hommes (*mille* hommes!) sur les frontières, qui seraient à la disposition du prince! Et ce qu'il y a de plus plaisant, c'est que, dans cette même lettre incendiaire, le même pacha doit avoir avoué que, *depuis deux mois*, il manquait de toutes nouvelles de Constantinople!' See Prokesch-Osten (1877: 452). Anonymous (1828c: 254) identified the Pasha of Van as 'Bekri Mehemed.'

[546] According to McNeill (1836: 104–105), 'Russia had...no separate ground of complaint, except the declaration of the Forte contained in the letter to the Pashas, that it had concluded the Convention of Akerman only to gain time: a declaration which the Turkish government evinced a distinct inclination to retract: and which, if even it had been unexplained, was not more inexcusable than the mental reservation of Russia in concluding the same convention on the express condition that she should not interfere in the Greek question,—an engagement which she contracted without any intention to fulfil it, whereas the Porte had adopted that convention sincerely, and in good faith, though it afterwards falsely accused itself of an insincerity it had not felt.'

against Turkey,' *National Journal* (Saturday, 21 June, 1828), 'War declared against Turkey' *New-York Observer and Religious Chronicle* (Saturday, 21 June, 1828), 'Continuation of Foreign News, by the Pacific. Russian Declaration of War against Turkey,' *City Gazette and Commercial Daily Advertiser* (Thursday, 26 June, 1828), 'Extraordinary Supplement to the Russian Gaz. Manifesto of his Majesty the Emperor,' *The Pittsfield Sun* (Thursday, 26 June, 1828), '(Continuation of foreign news.) Declaration,' *The Watch-Tower* (Monday, 30 June, 1828), 'Foreign & Domestic News. Extraordinary Supplement to the Prussian State Gazette,' *Vermont Watchman and State Gazette* (Tuesday, 1 July, 1828), 'Extraordinary Supplement to the Russian State Gazette. Berlin, May 4. Manifesto of His Majesty the Emperor,' *Republican Monitor* (Tuesday, 1 July, 1828), 'Late and Important from Europe. Russian Declaration of War,' *Michigan Herald* (Thursday, 3 July, 1828) and 'Late and Important from Europe. Russian Declaration of War,' *The Commentator* (Saturday, 5 July, 1828): 'General Paskewitsch, after the conclusion of a glorious campaign, was negociating a treaty of peace with Persia, the conditions of which were already accepted by the count [sic, court at] Teheran. On a sudden, lukewarmness succeeded to the eagerness which had hitherto been shown for the conclusion of a convention which was already approved by both parties in all its particulars. These delays were followed by difficulties, and then by an evidently hostile tendency; and while on the one hand, the conduct of the neighboring Pachas, who hastily armed, manifested this tendency, on the other hand, authentic information and positive confessions revealed the secret of the promise of a diversion which was to oblige us to make new efforts.'

11.236 'Russian Declaration of War against Turkey,' *Republican Monitor* (Saturday, 21 June, 1828) and 'Russian Declaration of War against Turkey,' *Onondaga Register* (Wednesday, 25 June, 1828): 'Russia has, at length, declared her intention of seeking, and obtaining satisfaction for all the injuries, and insults received from the Porte. On the 4th inst. two official documents, dated St. Petersburgh, April 14th, (26) were received in Berlin. One is termed a Manifesto of the Emperor, and the other a Declaration. In the first, the Emperor complains...of the intrigues of Turkey to prolong the war in Persia.... The declaration describes, at much greater length, the causes which render an appeal to arms indispensably necessary. It reproaches the Porte with....its endeavors to cause a renewal of the war in Persia.'

11.237 'St. Petersburgh, May 3. Order of the Day of His Majesty the Emperor,' *Commercial Advertiser* (Monday, 30 June, 1828; second para. only), 'St. Petersburgh, May 3. Order of the Day of His Majesty the Emperor,' *The Daily Chronicle* (Tuesday, 1 July, 1828; second para. only), 'Russia and Preparations for opening the Campaign,' *Poulson's American Daily Advertiser* (Wednesday, 2 July, 1828), 'Russia and Preparations for opening the Campaign,' *Baltimore Gazette and Daily Advertiser* (Wednesday, 2 July, 1828), 'Russia and Preparations for opening the Campaign,' *Phenix Gazette* (Thursday, 3 July, 1828), 'Continuation of Foreign News. Russia and Preparations for opening the Campaign,' *New-York Spectator* (Friday, 4 July, 1828) and 'Russia and preparations for opening the Campaign,' *City Gazette and Commercial Daily Advertiser* (Wednesday, 9 July, 1828): 'We have given below two interesting documents, which probably complete the series of official papers published by that court in consequence of the declaration of war against Turkey. One of these is an order of the Day of the Emperor Nicholas to his troops, in which, after announcing the termination of the war against Persia, he tells them that it has not yet "set bounds to the brilliant deeds of the Russian armies." After this flourish, the subject of the Turkish war is introduced. The peace with Persia is denominated "glorious and advantageous;" and it is stated that the object of the war against Turkey is to put an end to the troubles and massacres in that country, and to establish the peace, which that power is charged with having violated, "on solid foundations."....This document bears the same date as the Declaration of War, which we published some days since....

St. Petersburgh, May 3. Order of the Day of His Majesty the Emperor.[547]

The glorious and advantageous peace with Persia has not yet set bounds to the brilliant deeds of the Russian armies. We terminate a just war, but on another side an equal struggle awaits us for the defence of our honor, and of the rights purchased with Russian blood. The hostile proceedings of the Turkish Government had already exhausted the generous forbearance of the Emperor Alexander, of glorious memory; that Government has now filled up the measure; scarcely had it confirmed the peace by the most solemn oaths, when it openly threw off the mask of friendship which it had assumed.'

11.238 'From the New-York Enquirer,' *The Freeman's Journal* (Monday, 7 July, 1828) and 'Foreign News. Latest from England,' *Greene County Republican* (Wednesday, 9 July, 1828): 'It appears, by intelligence from Teflis, of the 15th of March, that part of the Russian army, which was employed against Persia, is to be detached against Turkish Georgia,[548] the Pacha of which favoured the operations of the Persians.'[549]

11.239 'Nuremburg. May 7,' *New-York Spectator* (Tuesday, 8 July, 1828): 'The territory and the population which Russia has acquired by its late treaty with Persia, appear in themselves of trifling importance. The two khanats [sic, khanates] of Erivan and Fahetchivan [sic, Nakhchivan], which, under the name of the province of Aran,[550] formerly made the extreme northwest corner of the Persian empire, are scarcely 400 geographical square miles in superficial extent,[551] or about equal to the kingdom of Wurtemberg. The

---

[547] Nicholas I.

[548] According to Malte-Brun (1822: 33), 'Imeritia has sometimes been known under the name of Turkish Georgia, and the remainder has been called Persian Georgia.' Klaproth (1827: 93) ascribed to Turkish Georgia the pashaliks of 'Akhal-tsikhé, Gouria, Djavakhéthi et Narimani.'

[549] As von Haxthausen (1854: 101, n. *) noted, the pasha of Akhalzik had raided Georgia repeatedly and was hostile towards the Russians.

[550] See e.g. Minorsky (1937: 142–144).

[551] This is a gross understimation. Nakhchivan alone is over 2000 sq. mi. and, with the addition of Erivan, comprising much of modern Armenia, the Russian territorial gain would have been much larger. 11.241 put it at over 100,000 sq. mi.

population is said not to exceed 150,000 souls; so that this new Russian province has about as many inhabitants as the grand duchy of Weimar. If these numerical data afford but little matter for particular observation, this cannot be said of these provinces in other points of view. The most important, perhaps, is the circumstance of religion. With the climate of Erivan, Russia has obtained possession of the monastery of Etchmiadzine, the residence of the Chief Patriarch of the Catholic Armenians,[552] who enjoy extraordinary respect in the East. This monastery is also in great esteem as a place of pilgrimage, and is considered to be equally holy with Jerusalem. In Asiatic Turkey there are at least a million and a half of Armenian Christians, and we have lately seen what attention the cession of Etchmiadzine to Russia excited in Constantinople, and what rigorous measures towards the Armenians of the capital the Sultan Mahmoud was induced to adopt, in concert with the Patriarch of the opposite party. In a military point of view, the cession of this territory is, perhaps, equally important. Russia having obtained possession of both banks of the Araxes, and surrounding Mount Ararat on three sides, a Russian army may, if circumstances should require it, march in three columns upon Erzerum, without touching the Persian territory. The first way is from Tiflis, through Kars; the middle one, into the vale of the Araxes, by Kagzetnan, or Kaghizmann[553]; the third by Bajazid,[554] Kara-Kelissiah,[555] and Tobrao-Kelah,[556] through extremely fertile countries.'

11.240 'Items,' *The Kinderhook Herald* (Thursday, 17 July, 1828), 'Untitled,' *Lansingburgh Gazette* (Tuesday, 22 July, 1828), 'Items,' *Onondaga Register* (Wednesday, 23 July, 1828), 'Untitled,' *Christian Mirror* (Friday, 25 July, 1828) and 'Untitled,' *The Geneva Gazette and General Advertiser* (Wednesday, 30 July, 1828): 'Russia has acquired, by her late treaty with Persia, Mount Arrarat, where Noah's ark rested after the flood.'[557]

---

[552] This is incorrect. As Butin (1913: 454) noted, following a series of prior schisms in the Armenian church, 'In 1441 another schism occurred, and a catholicos was elected in Etchmiadzin in Greater Armenia. To-day he bears the title of "Supreme Patriarch and Catholicos of all Armenians", and, at least theoretically, is considered the principal catholicos by all non-Catholic Armenians.'

[553] Cf. Mostras (1873: 141), 'dans l'eyalet d'Erzeroum, liva de Kars, sur l'Aras.' Abbott (1842: 220) called it 'Kurghesman' and in 1837 travelled from Erzurum to Toprakkale via this town.

[554] Mod. Doğubayazit.

[555] Abbott (1842: 220) called it 'Kara Klissia.' The name means 'Black Church.' Morier (1818: 328) called 'Kara Klisseh…the chief military post of the Russians on this frontier.' Johnson (1818: 238) said it was 'a miserable village, and of no importance except as a station for Russian troops; they consist of one brigade of the line, and a small body of Cossacks. The place is low and muddy; all the houses are built of timber, so mortised as to form strong walls, and their roofs are covered with earth.'

[556] Toprakkale.

[557] Genesis 8:4, 'And the ark rested in the seventh month, on the seventeenth day of the month, upon the mountains of Ararat [Heb. ărārāṭ, Gk. Ἀραράτ].' Ararat here almost certainly denotes the broader region known in antiquity as Urartu rather than the specific oronym known today as Mt. Ararat. See e.g. Day (2013: 65–66) with earlier lit.

11 The Second Russo-Persian War and the Treaty of Torkmanchay (1826–1828)

11.241 'Peace between Russia and Turkey [sic, Persia],' *City Gazette and Commercial Daily Advertiser* (Wednesday, 23 July, 1828): 'We have read the extraordinary articles of this Treaty—*extraordinary* because Greece is not even mentioned!! We had believed in the Declarations of Nicholas, and are in perfect amazement at the result. An acquisition of Territory seems to have governed the policy of the Emperor of All the Russias. We shall have occasion to notice this Treaty more at length; in the mean time, we give the following from the Boston Evening Bulletin, of the 12th inst. for the gratification of our readers.

Treaty between Russia and Turkey [sic, Persia], and territorial acquisition by Russia— The Gibraltar Chronicle gives the articles of the treaty between Russia and Persia at full length, from which we extract the most material parts. It was signed at the village of Tourkmantchai, Feb 22nd, 1828, and was to be ratified by the Emperor of Russia, and Schah[558] of Persia within four months.

Art. 1. There shall be peace, &c.

2. Hostilities having cancelled the stipulations of the former treaty, that of Gulistan, the parties propose to substitute new stipulations.

[Then follows, the most essential part of the treaty]

3. His Majesty the Schah, as well in his own name as in that of his heirs and successors, unreservedly cedes to the Empire of Russia the Khanat of Erivan, as well within as without the Araxes, and the Khanat of Nakhitchevan. In consequence of this cession, his Majesty the Schah engages to have delivered up to the Russian authorities, within six months after the truce of the present Treaty, all the archives and public documents concerning the administration of the two Khanats aforesaid.

[This Khanat of Erivan, also called Persian Armenia, Greater Armenia, and Eastern Armenia, thus transferred by these few lines, is only about the extent of all New-England and New-York, being about 600 miles in length, and 180 in breadth, and containing accordingly, more than 100,000 square miles. Its extent is just about equal to that of Great Britain and Ireland. It seems, therefore, that while the war with Turkey has been fomenting, Russia has not lost the time, but has been advancing with gigantic strides in territorial acquisition. Notwithstanding the declarations of the Emperor Nicholas, disclaiming all projects of aggrandizement in Europe, if the next peace with Turkey does not include at least the Turkish part of Moldavia and the whole of Walachia within the Russian boundaries, it will indicate a change in the character and policy of that government]

4. This article defines the boundaries of the two empires according to the above session, beginning at the point in the Turkish frontier nearest to the Little Ararat, extending across the summit of that mountain, and terminating at the mouth of the river Astara, where it discharges itself into the Caspian Sea.

---

[558] Fath 'Ali Shah.

5. This article is a solemn acknowledgement of the above cession of territory by the Schah of Persia for himself, his heirs, successors, &c. '*in testimony of his sincere friendship for his Majesty the Emperor of all the Russias*"

[The next article is an additional testimony of the sincere friendship of the Schah, as it provides for an indemnification of Russia by the payment of about ten millions of dollars towards defraying the expense of making this immense acquisition. The article is as follows]

6. With a view to make compensation for the considerable sacrifices that the war which broke out between the two States, occasioned to the Russian Empire, as well as the loss and damage which Russian subjects have suffered therefore, his Majesty the Schah of Persia engages to make up for them by means of paying a pecuniary indemnity. It is agreed between the two High contracting Parties that the amount of this indemnity shall be fixed at ten kurours of tomans raidje,[559] or 20 millions of silver rubles; and that the mode, terms, and guarantees for the payment of this sum shall be regulated by a special arrangement which shall have the same force and value as if it were inserted, word for word, in this present Treaty.

7. Article 7th is an acknowledgement on the part of Russia of the right of the Schah's son, Prince Abbas Mirza, to succeed to the Persian empire on the death of his father.

[It does not appear whether this stipulation is intended as a pledge on the part of Russia not to attempt further acquisition on the decease of the Schah, or as a guaranty against domestic factions and civil war in Persia]

8. Russian merchant vessels shall enjoy, as in time past, the right of navigating freely on the Caspian Sea, and along its coasts, and to trade there. They shall find in Persia succor an assistance in case of shipwreck. The same right granted to Persian merchant vessels to navigate upon the ancient footing, in the Caspian Sea, to touch at the Russian shores; and, in case of shipwreck, the Persians shall receive reciprocal succor and assistance. As to the armed vessels such as bear the navy flag of Russia, being 'ab antiquo,' the only ships which had the exclusive right to navigate in the Caspian Sea, the said exclusive privilege is, for that reason, in like manner reserved and secured now; so that, with the exception of Russia, no Power can have armed vessels in the Caspian Sea.

9. Article 9, is a stipulation on the subject of receiving ambassadors.

10. The parties agree to make a common treaty and each is to recognize and protect the consuls of the other, together with their attendants and suits to consist, however, of not more than ten persons.

---

[559] *raij*. Discussing the copper coins of the Mughal emperor Jahangir (r. 1605–1627), Frey (1917: 236) noted, 'On the copper coins of Jahangir, the son of Akbar, are to be found the words RAWANI and RAIJ, both meaning "current coin," and corresponding in weight with the Tankah,' which was a 'standard in both gold and silver, of about one hundred and seventy-four grains in each metal, introduced by the kings of Delhi. The Tankah was divided into sixty-four parts, each called a Kani, and equal to four Falus.' Cf. Codrington (1904: 119).

11. The debts and claims of the subjects of the two powers shall not be extinguished by the war, but may be prosecuted and settled as if peace had not been interrupted.

12. Persons holding real estate in the ceded territory, shall have three years to dispose of it. These individuals, former officers of this province, are excepted from the provisions of this article.

[This stipulation seems to be, that any Persian who is not transferred with the territory, (the peasants are expressly transferred) but continues to be a Persian subject, shall have three years in which to sell his estates.—If he cannot dispose of them within that period they become forfeited.

14. Provisions respecting captives and deserters.

[The next article provides for the safety of those Persians who have joined or assisted the Russians during the war, and is as follows—]

15. With the beneficence and salutary view of restoring tranquility in his states, and removing from his subjects whatever might aggravate evils that have already been brought upon them by the war so happily terminated by the present treaty, his Majesty the Schah, grants full and complete amnesty to all the inhabitants functionaries of the province of Adzerbaidjane. Not one of them without exception of category shall be liable to be prosecuted or molested for his exploits during the war, or during the temporary occupation of the said province by the Russian troops. There shall be moreover granted to them the space of one year, from this day to remove freely with their families from the Persian states into the Russian states, and to transport or sell their movable property, without the Governments or local authorities being able to throw any obstacle in their way, or to levy any duty or intrusion upon the property or effects sold or exported by them. As to their real property, the term of five years shall be granted to them to sell or dispose of it at their pleasure. From this amnesty such persons are excepted as may be guilty within the space of the said year, of any crime or offence liable to penalties pronounced by the Tribunals.

16. Orders shall be given for the cessation of hostilities.

[Such are the material provisions of this treaty, an instrument evidently dictated by Russia]

11.242 'Foreign News,' *Auburn Free Press* (Wednesday, 20 August, 1828): 'If we are to believe the Augsburg Gazette, Prince Abbas Mirza has invaded the Turkish territories from Persia. It may be so, but an alliance between Persia and Russia is a most unnatural thing; circumstances may have rendered it a matter of necessity on the part of Persia, but we doubt it very much.'

11.243 'Answer of the Porte to the Russian Manifesto,' *Baltimore Patriot & Mercantile Advertiser* (Wednesday, 27 August, 1828), 'Continuation of Foreign News. Answer of the Porte to the Russian Manifesto,' *The New-York Spectator* (Friday, 29 August, 1828), 'Answer of the Porte to the Russian Manifesto,' *The National Gazette and Literary Register* (Friday, 29 August, 1828) and 'Answer of the Porte to the Russian Manifesto,' *New-York Advertiser* (Friday, 29 August, 1828): 'The Court of Russia has...without any motive, disturbed the existing peace—has declared war, and invaded the territory of the Sublime Porte. Russia alledges that the Sublime Porte has caused this war, and has published a manifesto, in which she accuses the Porte of not having executed the conditions of the treaties of Bucharest and Ackermann....and instigated the Court of Persia to make war upon Russia. ...As to the reproach of having excited Persia against Russia, it is a pure calumny. Never did the Sublime Porte think it consistent with its dignity to instigate one nation against another. Far from exciting Persia, the Sublime Porte observed the strictest neutrality, neither mixing itself up with the origin or the issue of the war or the peace between the two empires. If some neighbouring Pachas made preparations, they were only measures of precaution usual to every State bordering upon two other nations at war. It thus clearly appears that the endeavour of Russia to ascribe these preparations to hostile intentions towards herself, has as little foundation as the rest.'

11.244 'Continuation of Extracts from French Papers, to the 18th and English to the 14th of August,' *City Gazette and Commercial Daily Advertiser* (Monday, 24 September, 1828): 'Petersburgh letters of the 21st July contradict the rumors of an early peace between Persia and Russia. Extensive preparations are making by the latter power to carry on the war vigorously.'

11.245 'Late from Europe. From Smyrna,' *Alexandria Gazette* (Thursday, 25 September, 1828) and 'Continuation of Foreign News: From Smyrna,' *New-York Spectator* (Friday, 26 September, 1828): 'It is...stated, on the authority of letters from Aleppo, of April 1, giving the following information from Bagdad of the 1st of March, that the Scah[560] of Persia had refused peremptorily to ratify the treaty concluded by the Prince Abbas Mirza with General Paskewitch; that the cession of two provinces had particularly irritated the King, who suspected his son of having done it to obtain, from the Russians, the formal acknowledgement of his own right to the succession to the throne of Persia;[561] and that in consequence the King had abdicated in favor of another of his sons,[562] who had assembled a considerable army, to attack the Russians anew, and to recover the provinces occupied by them. This news does not appear very probable.'

11.246 'Latest from Europe,' *The Kinderhook Herald* (Thursday, 9 October, 1828): ['By the packet ship Florida, arrived at New-York, from Liverpool, London papers to the 31st August and Liverpool to the 1st Sept. have been received....*Constantinople July 28....*]

---

[560] Fath 'Ali Shah.

[561] This had been obtained fifteen years earlier in the 1813 treaty of Gulistan with Russia where (Art.4) we read, 'His Majesty the Emperor of Russia...engages for himself and heirs to recognise the Prince who shall be nominated heir-apparent, and to afford him assistance in case he should require it to suppress any opposing party.' See Hurewitz (1956: 85).

[562] Clearly a baseless rumor.

11.1 Miscellaneous

For the last two days a report has been current here that hostilities had commenced between Russia and Persia.'

11.1 Miscellaneous

Persian trade

11.247 'Trade with Persia,' *The New-York Evening Post* (Thursday, 14 December 1826): 'Trade with Persia.[563]—Notwithstanding the importance of trade with Persia, it has been little understood up to this time in Europe. The merchants of Constantinople know little of the market. The English is the only nation which trades direct with Persia, by the port of Bonderburkhur[564] in the Gulf of Persia, where they sell their merchandize either for ready mony, or barter it against silk; and the English trade is considerable. The festival called Nourouz, which is celebrated at Tauris, Teheran, and in all parts of Persia at the end of February [sic, March], is the most proper time for the sale of European merchandise. The fair, which takes place at this time continues a whole month. It is necessary to arrive at Sulta in [sic, Soltaniyeh] in the month of June, during the annual stay there of the Shach.[565] This is the only town in Persia where goods are sold for cash, because there is no barter trade; at Tauris, on the contrary, the principal transactions are by barter; nevertheless, European cloth, of gold and silver, as also a small assortment of other goods, are bought for ready money. Persia receives from Constantinople manufactured silk, cloth of gold and silver, and other French manufactures, for the purchase of which 300 merchants of Tauris make the journey annually; the Prince Abbas-Mirza ordinarily [sic] devotes 20,000 tomans in this sort of speculation. The distance from Teflis[566] to Tauris is about 600 versts [660 km]. This journey, which is made with convoys of merchndise in about 22 to 30 days, and which may be made on horse back from 6 to 10, is traversed by an infinity of rivulets, and must be forded, which occasions many difficulties, at the time of the mountain thaw. At all times

---

[563] This is the text of a letter with the dateline 'St. Petersburg, Aug. 17 (29), 1826,' hence, written just as hostilities were beginning in the Second Russo-Persian War. See Anonymous (1826f).

[564] Bandar Bushehr.

[565] Fath 'Ali Shah.

[566] The sudden introduction of Tiflis here suggests that the data was drawn from sources used by Gamba (1826) and Bélanger (1838) which examine the role of Tiflis in commerce, particularly in relation to Russia, Persia, England, India and Turkey. As Gamba (1826/2: 215) noted, 'Dans la situation actuelle de l'empire Ottoman, le marché de Tiflis est devenu d'un intérêt général pour toute l'Europe. Les négociants qui viendront s'y fixer jouiront, dans la Perse, d'un grand avantage, celui d'une sûreté entière.' Cf. Bélanger (1838: 425), 'J'ai dit, dans mon rapport précédent, comment la route de Constantinople ayant été fermée au commerce pendant la guerre avec la Turquie, les marchands persans étaient allés faire leurs achats à Tiflis, et comment, aussitôt après le rétablissement de la paix, ils avaient quitté cette ville pour reprendre la route de l'Asie-Mineure et revenir à leurs anciennes relations.'

this road is free from danger, and provisions may be procured every where. The caravans consume ten in going from Tauris to Sultani, at which place a person on horseback may arrive in 3. At this present time the Armenians send by way of Teflis & Ghilan, to the amount of 1,600,000 Russian merchandise, the chief of which are glassware and crystals, coarse calicoes, refined sugar, nankeens, printed calicoes, common cloths, and such like. This trade from Astrachan is carried on by sea to Lenkoran, from whence the merchandise, is forwarded to Tauris by horses. At Tauris there is an unusual arrival, by the way of Erzerum of ten to twelve caravans from Constantinople.—According to the Persian Custom house registers, Persia imports by this road to the amount of four or five hundred thousand tomans of English and French goods, and gives in return raw silk, Cachemere and Kerman shawls, tobacco, indigo, and pepper. Very little is brought from Smyrna because the goods must be bought with ready money. Two hundred to three hundred horses bring annually from Trebizond to Tauris, glassware, pottery, porcelain, and ordinary cloths; from Benderbukhir are brought sugar, coffee, indigo, printed cottons, coverlets, and English cotton goods to a considerable amount. The value of the imports at Teheran and Tauris by this road is reckoned at about a million of tomans. The shawls of Cachemere are also brought by the way of Benderbukhir, because the road by land is dangerous.[567] Lastly, by the way of Bagdad many English and French goods are brought & by this road, at least to the amount of 100,000 tomans, goods are brought to Tauris.—*Petersburgh Journal.*'

Chevalier Gamba's Travels

11.248 'Voyages and Travels,' *National Gazette and Literary Register* (Saturday, 30 December, 1826) and 'Voyages and Travels,' *New-York American* (Tuesday, 6 March 1827): 'We commence with a recent account of a region rendered peculiarly interesting at this time from having become the seat of war between Russia and Persia. The Chevalier Gamba,[568] who has been travelling over Russia, from the Baltic Sea, to the frontiers of

---

[567] Cf. Bélanger (1838: 437), citing Éduard Desbayssayns de Richemont, who noted, 'les marchands qui faisaient le commerce de Kaboul et de Cachemire, se voyant continuellement exposés à être pillés en traversant le Khorassân et l'Afghanistân, préfèrent à présent passer par Bombay et le golfe Persique. Cette voie est plus longue, mais elle est beaucoup plus sûre; aussi presque tous les châles que la Perse reçoit aujourdh'hui sont-ils importés par Bouchehr.'

[568] Jean-François/Jacques-François Gamba (1763–1833) came from an Italian background and was born in Dunkerque. He travelled extensively through the Caucasus in 1817–1819. Appointed the first French consul in Tiflis in 1820, he was recalled to Paris for consultations in 1824, but returned in 1826 and served in Georgia until his death in 1833. See Gamba (1819, 1826), Michaud (1870: 492–493). As O'Flynn (2017: 350, n. 75) observed, 'Gamba had been charged by the Duc de Richelieu to develop Black Sea and trans-Caucasus trade routes,' and 'considered Tiflis to be well situated for the resumption of trade under the protecting auspices of the Russian government.' When Alexandre Dumas visited the Caucasus in 1858–1859 Gamba's sister was still alive and 'possède de grands biens en Mingrélie.' See Dumas (1859: 241).

Persia, from the Sea of Azof to the Wolga, and from the Euxine[569] to the Caspian, considers the provinces beyond Mount Caucasus to be an admirable position for the establishment of the entrepôt of an immense commerce....M. Gamba, (who was French consul at Tiflis, and) who shares with General Yermoloff the honor of having proposed this freedom of trade, has now been for two years at Paris....M. Gamba's work cannot fail powerfully to attract the attention of merchants, and even of the governments of Europe towards Asia.... The Persian, for more than a century, has been accustomed to see his country overrun; and yielding passive obedience to Tartar, Turcoman, or Affghan chiefs, considers himself destined by Providence to slavery and oppression; he blushes for the history of the past. Resistance has always been in vain. He has witnessed the destruction and pillage of his cities, the massacre of all dear to him; despoiled of his property, condemned to a precarious existence, to preserve it he has had recourse to extreme and debasing means....It is with regret that I paint the Persians under such unfavourable colours, and I am anxious to state some splendid exceptions. Amongst these, it is delightful for humanity to be able to cite the hereditary Prince Abbas Mirza, whose noble intentions continually tend to ameliorate the manners and the condition of the nation he is destined to govern.'

A Prince Prepares for Blindness

11.249 'Eastern Despotism,' *Rochester Telegraph* (Friday, 31 August, 1827): 'The lady of Dr. Macneil,[570] the physician to the mission, was one day in the Zenanah,[571] (in Persia) when she observed one of the princes, a boy of ten years of age, with a handkerchief tied over his eyes, groping about the apartment. Upon enquiring what he was doing, he said that as he knew that when the Shah his father died, he should have his eyes put out, he was now trying how he could do without them.—*Alexandria's* [sic, Alexander's] *Travels*.'[572]

---

[569] The Black Sea.

[570] Elizabeth (Eliza) Wilson McNeill (1792–1868), wife of John McNeill. For her life see MacAlister (1910).

[571] Fraser (1826: 60, n. *) identified 'zenanah' as 'seraglio, female establishment,' i.e. the harem.

[572] Taken verbatim from Alexander (1827: 210). Fraser (1825: 204) recounted an almost identical story: 'An English gentleman, attached to the court of Abbass Meerza, was witness to a curious and melancholy illustration of this feeling [jealousy of male relatives who may contest the crown]; he went to visit one of the princes, then a young lad, and found him strangely employed. Seated on his cushion, and with his eyes shut, he was feeling with both hands, like a blind person, for his calleeoon [water pipe], which his servant was presenting to him. After a moment, the gentleman asked, "What are you doing, prince? is there any thing the matter with your eyes?" "Oh no," said the boy "nothing; but I am practising blindness; you know that when my father dies we shall all be put to death, or have our eyes put out, and I am trying how I shall be able to manage without them."' Both stories are related in Conder (1827: 230).

Uniting the Atlantic Ocean and the Black Sea

11.250 'Union of the Atlantic and the Black Sea,' *Geneva Palladium* (Wednesday, 12 December 1827): 'The project of uniting the Rhine and the Danube, which was conceived and even commenced by Charlemagne, and submitted by General Dessoles [sic, Dessolles][573] to the attention of Bonaparte, when First Consul, is now reviving on the Continent.—By the assistance of Canals a water communication would be opened, by the accomplishment of this project, between the countries of France, Germany, Holland, &c. and Persia, by means of canals between the Black Sea and the Caspian.—The canal is proposed to be begin [sic] at Kelhem [sic, Kelheim], on the Danube, near Ratisbone,[574] where the Altmuni [sic, Altmühl] falls into the river, at right angles, and will form the bed of the canal.—*New Liverpool Gazette*.'

---

[573] Jean Joseph Paul Augustin marquis Dessolles. Cf. 10.28.

[574] Regensburg, Germany.

From the Murder of Griboyedov to the Death of Fath 'Ali Shah (1829–1835)

In the spring of 1829 a shocking story appeared in the press. Alexander Sergeyevich Griboyedov, the former member of Paskevich's staff who had delivered the signed copy of the Treaty of Torkmanchay to Nicholas I, and was then sent back to Tehran as Russia's ambassador, was brutally murdered, along with almost all of the members of his legation, by an angry mob. Only Ivan Sergeyevich Maltzov survived. Like the murder in 1802 of Haji Khalil Khan-e Koroghlu Qazvini, Fath 'Ali Shah's ambassador to the EIC, the story of Griboyedov's death garnered extensive coverage in the international press as the circumstances leading up to the mob's attack and the official government response to it were outlined in minute detail. Although it was initially thought that 'Abbas Mirza and his prime minister, Mirza Abu'l-Qasem, would travel to Tibilisi in order to offer an official apology to General Paskevich, it was later decided that this would be too risky, should the pair be held hostage until Persia remitted in full the indemnity it still owed Russia according to the terms of the Treaty of Torkmanchay. Instead, 'Abbas Mirza's 16 year old (seventh) son, Khosrow Mirza, was dispatched with a number of senior advisers to make the apology. When the young Persian envoy reached Tibilisi, however, Paskevich recommended that he proceed onwards to deliver his apology to the Russian Emperor in person.

Khosrow Mirza's embassy was followed closely in the press. His reception by high-ranking Russian military officers and governors along the way was reported in detail, as were the events held in his honor, the sites that he visited and his audience and speech to Nicholas I who, along with the court, was charmed by the elegant and affable young Persian envoy. In fact, the impression made was so favorable that the Emperor forgave a portion of the outstanding debt owed to Russia by Persia.

Meanwhile, Russian forces, again led by Paskevich, had beaten Turkey in a war that began almost immediately after the Persian campaign had concluded. In Persia, rebellions broke out in the south, causing Fath 'Ali Shah to send 'Abbas Mirza to quell disturbances at Yazd and Shiraz. From there 'Abbas Mirza proceeded to Khorasan where the local chiefs had long been in a state of open rebellion. His reputation dented by his defeat at the hands of the Russians, 'Abbas Mirza looked to repair his image with a victory over the rebels in Khorasan. At the same time, Russian overtures were made to Fath 'Ali Shah to conduct joint operations against the Khan of Khiva with a view to opening up a passage to Herat, previously a Persian possession, the reconquest of which was earnestly desired by the Qajars. Britain was naturally alarmed at these developments for, if successful, they paved the way for a Russian assault on India, a prospect that had long since replaced Napoleon's much vaunted plan of attacking British interests there with Persian assistance, whether passive or active, in British minds.

Then, in October, 1833, Persian plans were thrown into disarray by the sudden death of 'Abbas Mirza. This prompted a flurry of British and Russian diplomatic activity to secure the succession of Fath 'Ali Shah whose own health was poor. The Shah had chosen Mohammad Mirza, 'Abbas Mirza's eldest son, as his successor, and given him a *farman* confirming this, rather than Hoseyn 'Ali Mirza Farman-Farma, 'the prince of Shiraz,' governor of Fars and Fath 'Ali Shah's fifth son. In October, 1834, almost exactly one year after 'Abbas Mirza's death, Fath 'Ali Shah finally died in Isfahan. As one report noted, since Mohammad Mirza had 'about 60 uncles' (55 in fact), a contest for the Persian throne was virtually a certainty.

12.1 'Foreign News,' *Ithaca Journal & General Advertiser* (Wednesday, 1 April, 1829): '[From the Constitutionel] Widdin, Jan. 3. Very disadvantageous reports are afloat respecting the Russians, which we will repeat, without, however, giving implicit belief to them.... We are assured that the two provinces conquered in Persia by the Russians have rebelled.'

12.2 'Assassination of a Russian Minister. St. Ptersburgh, March 27,' *Saratoga Sentinel* (Tuesday, 12 May, 1829), 'Assassination of a Russian Minister. St. Ptersburgh, March 27,' *Commercial Advertiser* (Wednesday, 13 May, 1829)' 'St. Petersburg, March 27.—Assassination of the Russian Ambassador in Persia,' *New-York American* (Wednesday, 13 May, 1829), 'St. Petersburg, March 27. Assassination of the Russian Ambassador in Persia,' *The National Gazette and Literary Register* (Thursday, 14 May, 1829), 'Assassination of the Russian Ambassador in Persia. St. Petersburg, March 27,' *Poulson's American Daily Advertiser* (Thursday, 14 May, 1829), 'Assassination of a Russian Minister. St. Ptersburgh, March 27,' *The Daily Chronicle* (Thursday, 14 May, 1829), 'Assassination of the Russian Ambassador in Persia,' *Albany Argus* (Friday, 15 May, 1829; 'A St. Petersburgh date of May 27th says,' appears before 'Letters'), 'St. Petersburg, March

27. Assassination of the Russian Ambassador in Persia,' *Baltimore Patriot* (Friday, 15 May, 1829), 'Foreign. Assassination of the Russian Embassy in Persia,' *Christian Watchman* (Friday, 15 May, 1829), 'Asia. Persia. Assassination of the Russian Ambassador,' *The Atlas* (Saturday, 16 May, 1829), Assassination of a Russian Minister. St. Ptersburgh, March 27,' *Baltimore Gazette and Daily Advertiser* (Saturday, 16 May, 1829), 'Assassination of the Russian Ambassador in Persia. St Petersburg March 27,' *The Berks and Schuylkill Journal* (Saturday, 16 May, 1829), 'Important from England. Assassination of the Russian Ambassador to Persia,' *The Freeman's Journal* (Monday, 18 May, 1829; first paragraph only), 'Important from England. Assassination of the Russian Ambassador to Persia,' *The Schenectady Cabinet* (Wednesday, 20 May, 1829; 'A St. Petersburgh date of May 27th says,' appears before 'Letters'), 'Assassination of the Russian Ambassador to Persia,' *Black River Gazette* (Wednesday, 20 May, 1829) first paragraph only], 'Assassination of a Russian Minister,' *Ithaca Journal & General Advertiser* (Wednesday, 20 May, 1829), 'Assassination of the Russian Ambassador to Persia,' *The Schenectady Cabinet* (Tuesday, 20 May, 1829), 'Assassination of a Russian Minister. St. Ptersburgh, March 27,' *The Charleston Courier* (Wednesday, 21 May, 1829), 'Persia,' *The Kinderhook Herald* (Wednesday, 21 May, 1829), 'Latest from Europe. St. Petersburg, March 27.—Assassination of the Russian Ambassador in Persia,' *The Lynchburg Virginian* (Wednesday, 21 May, 1829), 'From the Boston Commercial Gazette, May 13. Latest from Europe. Persia. Assassination of the Russian Embassy. St. Petersburg, March 27,' *Brattleboro Messenger* (Thursday, 22 May, 1829; first paragraph only), 'Assassination of the Russian Ambassador in Persia,' *The Corrector* (Friday 23 May, 1829), 'Assassination of the Russian Ambassador to Persia,' *The Wayne Sentinel* (Friday 23 May, 1829), 'Late and important from Europe. St. Petersburg, March 27. Assassination of the Russian Ambassador in Persia,' *Daily Georgian* (Friday 23 May, 1829), 'Late from Europe. St. Petersburg, March 27. Assassination of the Russian Ambassador in Persia,' *The National Republican, and Ohio Political Register* (Monday, 26 May, 1829), 'New-York, May 12. Latest from England. Assassination of the Russian Ambassador to Persia,' *The Courier* [New Orleans LA] (Friday, 5 June, 1829), 'Foreign. Very late from England. Assassination of the Russian Embassy. St. Petersburg, March 27,' *Pensacola Gazette* (Tuesday, 9 June, 1829): 'Letters from Teheran informs [sic] us of a horrible catastrophe which took place in that city on the 31st of January, (12th February,) in consequence of a violent quarrel between the suit [sic, suite] of M. Gribjedoff,[1] our Minister at that court, and some of the populace. Some idlers having assembled before the Ministers [sic] house during the quarrel, thought fit to take part in it, and some of them were soon killed, an immense crowd hastened from the Bazar to avenge their countrymen, forced the gate of the hotel, and in spite of the resistance of our cossacks, and of the Persian guards, four of whom were killed, succeeded in penetrating to the inner apartments, where all that came in their way was sacrificed to their rage. In vain the Schah himself accompanied by his son Selou

---

[1] Alexander Sergeyevich Griboyedov. Cf. 11.221.

Sultan Governor General of Teheran,[2] came with a considerable force to check the rioters.[3]—It was too late—M. Gribojedoff and his suit [sic, suite] had already fallen victims to the rage of the assassins. Only M. Melzoff, the first Secretary of Legation,[4] and three other persons escaped the carnage.

---

[2] Appointed in 1817, the governor of Tehran was Fath 'Ali Shah's tenth son, 'Ali Shah Mirza Zell os-Soltan. See Anonymous (1873a: 715), Pakdaman and Royce (1973: 149, n. 35). Additionally, he was a full brother of 'Abbas Mirza's. See Hagigi (2012: 58). The title *Zill al-Sultan*, 'shadow of the king,' given to a son of the Shah's who closely resembled his father (Kneip 1976: 260, n. 68), was often mistaken for a proper name. As we can see from the case of 'Ali Shah Mirza, who was Fath 'Ali Shah's tenth son, it was not the case that, 'The eldest son of the Shah...is known, and is always spoken of, by the title "Zil-i-Sultan",' who, 'though first-born,' is not necessarily Crown Prince, as Arnold (1877: 253) claimed.

[3] As MacGregor (1871: 500) noted, 'The governor of Tehrān and commander of the forces endeavoured to quell the disturbances, but were set at defiance by the mob and compelled to take refuge in the citadel.'

[4] Ivan Sergeyevich Maltzov (1807–1880), Иван Сергеевич Мальцов. As Griboyedov's Persian secretary (Kelly 2006: 179 stressed that his name is unknown) noted after the attack, 'It was after mid-day that I reached my own quarters. Our servants, by explaining that the apartments were occupied by Mahomedans only, prevented the populace from breaking into them. They served also for a place of refuge to M. Maltzoff, the first secretary. His own rooms were widely separated from M. Grebayedoff's, and when the house was forcibly entered, he was unable to join his companioins....By dint of entreaties, and the distribution of a large sum of money, M. Maltzoff induced some of the Shah's ferashes [tent-pitchers], and a small party of the Furuhan infantry that had retired into our quarters, to attend to his safety. When the commotion had somewhat subsided, we sent information to the Prince Alli Shah ['Ali Shah Mirza, prince-governor of Tehran, brother of 'Abbas Mirza] that M. Maltzoff was alive. A company of infantry was in consequence ordered up to the house, under the pretext of taking charge of it; and, late in the evening, M. Maltzoff was dressed in the uniform of a Persian soldier, and marched in their ranks to the palace. This disguise was thought necessary to preserve him from the still unappeased fury of the populace. His situation had been most perilous, since every corner and nook of the house, even by the light of candles, had been searched, which could have served as a place of concealment to any individual of the Russian Mission. The system of extermination was so closely adhered to, that the mob invaded the premises of the British palace; they murdered there seven or eight Russians, lodged in the stables, and carried off the whole of the horses belonging to the envoy.' See G. Willock (1830: 511) (that Willock translated the unnamed Persian secretary's text is confirmed by a letter of J.B. Fraser's to the editor of *Blackwood's Magazine*; see Harden 1971a: 77, n. 9). Macdonald wrote, however, 'M. Maltzoff himself, the First Secretary of Legation, whose life was saved by the fidelity of those around him, freely acquits the Government from further blame in the affair, than that necessarily arising from a neglect in the adoption of those precautionary measures, which under existing circumstances ought certainly to have been taken on the preceding evening. The deed was done by the people, and the priesthood animated by a spirit of fanaticism, and conceiving that their civil and religious usages had been wounded by the strangers.' See Lang (1948: 333). On 25 March 1829 Macdonald wrote, 'M. Maltzoff, for whose safety I have adopted the requisite precautions, left this City [Tabriz] yesterday for Nukshiwan [Nakhchivan/Naxçivan] having previous to his departure accepted a gift of 700 Ducats from Abbas Meerza by way of remuneration for his losses.' See Lang (1948: 333). Later, in a letter to Paskevich regarding the aftermath of the affair, Nesselrode wrote, 'Veuillez, mon cher Comte, nous

Fig. 12.1 Alexander Sergeyevich Griboyedov, by Ivan Kramskoy, 1873. Oil on canvas. Tretyakov Gallery, CC0 1.0 Universal

The Schah[5] Abbas Mirza, and the whole court are in the greatest consternation; the latter has gone into mourning for 8 days. Eager to give us all the satisfaction we have a right to demand, he intends to send his eldest son with the Caimacan[6] to Gen. Paskewitsch,[7] to communicate to him all the particulars and explanations which the General-in-chief may desire respecting this dreadful event.' (Fig. 12.1).

12.3 'Late from England,' *New-York Evening Post* (Wednesday, 13 May 1829), 'Untitled,' *The Lansingburgh Gazette* (Tuesday, 19 May, 1829) and 'Foreign. From England,' *The Catskill Recorder and Greene County Republican.* (Thursday, 21 May, 1829): 'Gribojedoff, the Russian Ambassador at the court of Persia, was assassinated in the city of Teheran, on the 12th of February. A quarrel took place before the door of the Russian

---

envoyer Malzoff à Pétersbourg, il reçoit double récompense que sa conduite mérite à tous égards. C'est un jeune homme qui pourra devenir tres distingué lorsque l'âge et l'expérience auront un peu mûri ses idées et calmé ses passions.' See Stcherbatow (1891a: 265). As Paskevich wrote to Nesselrode on 13 April 1829, 'la conduite de Maltzoff mérite des éloges.' See Stcherbatow (1891a: 271).

[5] Fath 'Ali Shah. A comma is missing after 'The Shah,' but it is unlikely that this should be read as 'The Shah Abbas Mirza.'

[6] Mirza Abu'l-Qasem. Cf. 11.35.

[7] Ivan Fedorovich Paskevich. Cf. 11.29ff.

Minister, between his suite and the populace, in which some of the latter were killed. On the news being spread, an immense crowd hastened from the bazaar to avenge the death of their countrymen.—They forced the gate of the hotel, beat down the Cossacks, and killed four of the Persian guards, and penetrating to the inner apartments, sacrificed to their rage every thing that came in their way. The Russian Minister was butchered, with his whole suite, excepting M. Melzoff, first Secretary of Legation, and three other persons. The Schah,[8] who put himself at the head of a considerable force, to disperse the rioters, came too late. His court has gone into mourning for 8 days.'[9]

12.4 'Assassination of the Russian Embassy in Persia,' *Columbian Centinel* (Wednesday, 13 May, 1829) 'Assassination of the Russian Embassy in Persia,' *New-Bedford Mercury* (Friday, 15 May, 1829), 'Assassination of the Russian Embassy in Persia,' *Newburyport Herald* (Friday, 15 May, 1829), 'Assassination of the Russian Embassy in Persia,' *Salem Gazette* (Friday, 15 May, 1829), 'Assassination of the Russian Embassy in Persia,' *Farmer's Cabinet* (Saturday, 16 May, 1829), 'Assassination of the Russian Embassy in Persia,' *Essex Gazette* (Saturday, 16 May, 1829), 'Assassination of the Russian Embassy in Persia,' *Trumpet and Universalist Magazine* (Saturday, 16 May, 1829), and 'Assassination of the Russian Embassy in Persia,' *Greenfield Gazette & Herald* (Tuesday, 19 May, 1829), 'Assassination of the Russian Embassy in Persia,' *New-Hampshire Gazette* (Tuesday, 19 May, 1829), 'Assassination of the Russian Embassy in Persia,' *The Times and Dover Enquirer* (Tuesday, 19 May, 1829), 'Assassination of the Russian Embassy in Persia,' *The Connecticut Courant* (Tuesday, 19 May, 1829), 'Assassination of the Russian Embassy in Persia,' *New London Gazette* (Wednesday, 20 May, 1829), 'Assassination of the Russian Embassy in Persia,' *Connecticut Gazette* (Wednesday, 20 May, 1829), 'Foreign News. Persia. Assassination of the Russian Embassy in Persia,' *Massachusetts Spy* (Wednesday, 20 May, 1829), 'Secular Summary. Foreign. Assassination of the Russian Embassy in Persia,' *Boston Recorder* (Thursday, 21 May, 1829): 'Accounts via St. Petersburg, state that M. Gribojedoff the Russian Ambassador in Persia and his suite had been assassinated at Teheran, a capitol of Persia. A quarrel commenced between some of his followers and the populace of the city, in which some of the latter were killed. An immense crowd then hastened from the Grand Bazaar on [sic, or] market place and forced the Ambassadors residence. He and his whole suite, excepting one Secretary[10] and three servants were murdered. The Schah,[11] and the whole court, were in the greatest consternation, and had

---

[8] Fath 'Ali Shah.

[9] Neither Hasan-e Fasa'i (Busse 1972: 187–190) nor Willock (1830) makes any mention of either the personal intervention by Fath 'Ali Shah, beyond sending two of his sons to try to quell the riot (Harden 1979b: 47), or an 8 day period of mourning. In fact, as Kelly (2006: 194) noted, 'It was 4 days before order could be restored in the city [Tehran], during which the Shah and his court were virtually prisoners behind the locked gates of the citadel.'

[10] Mal'tzov.

[11] Fath 'Ali Shah.

gone into mourning for 8 days on this melancholy event. The Schah had sent his son with an interpreter to the Russian General Paskewitch to make the explanation on this dreadful event.'[12]

12.5 'Very late from Europe,' *Pawtucket Chronicle and Rhode-Island and Massachusetts Register* (Saturday, 16 May, 1829), 'Foreign Intelligence. Very late from Europe,' *New-Hampshire Patriot and State Gazette* (Monday, 18 May, 1829) and 'Foreign & Domestic Intelligence. Very late from Europe,' *Woodstock Observer. Windsor & Orange County Gazette* (Tuesday, 19 May, 1829): 'In consequence of a quarrel between some of the populace of Teheran and the suite of M. Gribojidoff, the Russian Ambassador, the latter gentleman was attacked in his hotel, and with his followers, except two or three, put to death. The Schah[13] and his son[14] attempted to stop the rioters, but too late.'[15]

12.6 'Persia. Assassination of the Russian Ambassador,' *Daily National Journal* (Saturday, 16 May, 1829), 'Persia. Assassination of the Russian Ambassador,' *National Journal* (Saturday, 16 May, 1829; first two paragraphs only), 'Assassination of the Russian Ambassador,' *Oneida Observer* (after 18 April 1829; first two paragraphs only) and 'Persia. Assassination of the Russian Ambassador,' *Vermont Gazette* (Tuesday, 19 May, 1829): 'An event has occurred in Persia which may have a considerable effect upon the relations between that country and Russia. In some riot, the causes of which are not yet accurately known, the populace of Teheran and the suite of M. Gibojidoff, the Russian Minister, quarrelled.—Some of the populace having been killed, a crowd hastened from the Bazaar to avenge their countrymen, forced the hotel and put to death the Minister and all his suite, three or four only excepted.

The Schah[16] himself and his son attempted to check the rioters, but too late. Abbas Mirza, with the Cairnacan,[17] are to be sent to General Paskewitsch to communicate the particulars of this event.'[18]

---

[12] In the end Fath 'Ali Shah sent his grandson Khosrow Mirza, not one of his sons. See below.

[13] Fath 'Ali Shah.

[14] 'Ali Shah Mirza Zell os-Soltan.

[15] Fath 'Ali Shah only learned of the massacre after the fact and 'Abbas Mirza was in Tabriz at the time. See Kneip (1976: 262). He did, however, send 'Ali Shah Mirza, prince-governor of Tehran, and another son, 'Imam Wurdee Meerza Commander of the Forces,' i.e. Imam Verdi Mirza, Fath 'Ali Shah's twelfth son, along with 'Ali Shah Mirza's vizir, to try to put down the riot. See Harden (1979b: 47–48).

[16] Fath 'Alli Shah.

[17] Mirza Abu'l-Qasem.

[18] In fact, 'Abbas Mirza sent his secretary-interpreter, Mirza Mas'ud, along with another secretary, Mirza Mustafa, and several other retainers to Tibilisi where they arrived on 18 March, 1829. Along with Mirza Saleh, who acted as an Iranian diplomatic representative in Tibilisi, they went to Paskevich and told him that a high-ranking delegation led by 'Abbas Mirza's eldest son, Mohammad

Letters from Jassy[19] state that there has been a great change in Persia; that the old king has abdicated the crown; that Abbas Mirza has taken the reins of Government, and has declared war against Russia. It is reported that several English officers from the British army in India had entered the service of the Schah.'

12.7 'Untitled,' *Baltimore Gazette and Daily Advertiser* (Wednesday, 27 May, 1829): 'Some of the French papers, recently received, encourage the idea that the Persians may yet endeavour to make a stand against the encroachments of Russia, and enter the field for the purpose of regaining their lost possessions. Such an attempt at this moment might promise success, should the people united under capable and experienced leaders, as it would be impossible for Russia to detach from her forces, on the march to Turkey, any thing like an adequate number of men to subdue a nation determined to be free.—The present Schah,[20] a despotic ruler of Persia, has given every indication of imbecility in the administration of his government, and there is no one instance more striking in this characteristic than his tame submission to the all grasping and unjust demands of Russia at the close of the late war.

The assassination of the Russian Ambassador[21] and suite at Teheran, is now ascertained to have been occasioned by the hatred of the Persians, in consequence of the exactions made by the Schah to pay the amount of the contribution imposed by Russia at the conclusion of the late Peace, and such is said to be the rage of the Persians, notwithstanding their habit of submission to despotic authority, that they are clamorous for war with Russia.

Mirza, and the Qe'em Maqam would be arriving soon. See Orouji (2014: 198). As Alexander (1830: 160) noted, 'At first he [Fath 'Ali Shah] thought of sending the heir-apparent, Abbas Mirza, to Tiflis, to explain the real state of the case; but it was at last determined that one of the sons of the Prince should be despatched on this errand: accordingly, Khoosroo [Khosrow] Mirza, 16 years of age only, but the son of the favourite wife, left Persia with a numerous suite, intending to proceed no further than Tiflis: but the Governor-General of Georgia [Paskevich], (acting probably under the authority of the Emperor,) thought it advisable that the young Prince should proceed to St. Petersburgh; and, in his way to the capital, he passed through Moscow, and remained there for several days.' Cf. Idesbald (1833: 8), Lang (1948: 335), Kneip (1976: 261), Bournoutian (2014). As for the Qa'em Maqam, he 'feared that he would be held as a hostage and feigned illness.' See Orouji (2014: 198). In a letter to the Foreign Minister Count Nesselrode, dated 2 May 1829, Paskevich wrote, 'Je m'empresse d'informer Votre Excellence, que Khosrew-Mirza arrivera sous peu à Tiflis....J'ignore s'il a l'autorisation d'aller à St.-Pétersbourg. J'ai exposé franchement mon opinion à Mirza-Massoud et à Mirza-Salé sur l'urgence de ce voyage...Ces deux employés...connaissant parfaitement sa position et ses intérêts personnels, sont tombés, autant qu'on peut croire aux paroles des Persans, d'accord avec moi sur la nécessité de faire continuer à Khosrew-Mirza son voyage pour la capitale, mais ils m'ont en même temps exposé leurs doutes sur cet objet, vu que le Schah consentirait difficilement à y envoyer son petit-fils, et qu'Abbas-Mirza n'agirait pas arbitrairement pour ne pas déplaire à son père, qui se défie de lui.' See Stcherbatow (1891a: 282).

[19] Iaşi, Romania.
[20] Fath 'Ali Shah.
[21] Griboyedov.

The Persians accuse their Government, and justly too, of having basely abandoned the Turks, who are of the same religious faith, and of having lost the best opportunity of throwing off the ignominious Russian yoke. The Schah, it is thought will find it difficult to resist the popular feeling; and should he be compelled to submit to the unanimous voice of the nation, the most important results must necessarily follow any diversion of the Russian forces from their original destination, to attempt the re-conquest of Persia.'

12.8 'Persia, Turkey, and Russia,' *Oneida Observer* (after 25 May 1829), 'Foreign News. Russia and Turkey, &c.,' *Niles' Weekly Register* (Saturday, 30 May, 1829), 'Persia, Turkey, and Russia,' *The Catskill Recorder* (Thursday, 4 June 1829) and 'Persia, Turkey, and Russia,' *The Hartford Times* (Monday, 8 June, 1829): 'The Baltimore Gazette states that the assassination of the Russian Ambassador[22] at Teheran, was caused by the hatred of the Persians in consequence of the exactions made by the Schah[23] to pay the amount of the contribution imposed by Russia at the conclusion of the late Peace,[24] and that such is the rage of the Persians, notwithstanding their habit of submission to despotic authority, that they are clamorous for war with Russia.

Now is the time most assuredly, for Persia to retaliate on the spoiler of her fairest provinces, and although the *Schah* is truly described by the Baltimore Editor as an imbecile and timid ruler, yet in Prince Abbas Mirza his country has a brave, talented and persevering champion—Should Persia put herself in hostile array, the Russian-Asiatic Army will have rather an unpleasant campaign.'

12.9 'Postscript. From the Mercantile Advertiser of Monday,' *The Pittsfield Sun* (Thursday, 28 May, 1829) and 'From the Mercantile Advertiser of the 25th ult.,' *Vermont Gazette* (Tuesday, 9 June, 1829): 'The assassination of the Russian Ambassador[25] and suite at Teheran, is said to have been occasioned by the hatred of the Persians, in consequence of the exactions made by the Schah[26] to pay the amount of the contribution imposed by Russia

---

[22] Griboyedov.

[23] Fath 'Ali Shah.

[24] Fath 'Ali Shah expressed his fear of widespread anti-Russian sentiment in conversation with Macdonald. See Harden (1979b: 37–38). The proximate trigger for the riot, however, was Khoja Mirza Yakub Markarian's allegation that Allah Yar Khan was holding two Christian Armenian women captive in his harem. They were interrogated at the Russian Mission, to determine whether they wished to leave their 'captivity' in Tehran. Although they declined his assistance (one of them was engaged to an Iranian), Griboyedov insisted that they be held to see whether they changed their minds, at which point the rumor spread that they were being forcibly held by the Russians for some nefarious, sexual purpose. A meeting of mollas decided they must be surrendered, incited a mob, and the attack ensued. See the various summaries of the episode in e.g. Idesbald (1833), G. Willock (1830), Algar (1980: 95–97) and Kelly (2006).

[25] Griboyedov.

[26] Fath 'Ali Shah.

Fig. 12.2 'Mirza Buzurk, Minister to Abbas Mirza,' by James Justinian Morier. Pencil on paper. Balliol College Archives Morier-N03-04-119

at the conclusion of the late Peace, and such is said to be the rage of the Persians, notwithstanding their habit of submission to despotic authority, that they are clamorous for war with Russia. Should this be determined on, it will divert part of the Russian troops from their march to Constantinople.

The Persians accuse their Government of having basely abandoned the Turks, who are of the same religious faith, of having lost the best opportunity of throwing off the ignominious Russian yoke, and of re-conquering the lost provinces of Persia. The Schah it is thought will find it difficult to resist the popular feeling.'

12.10 'Perse. Assassinat du ministre de Russie et de toute sa suite,' *L'Abeille* (Tuesday, 2 June, 1829): 'Le Journal de St. Pétersbourg parle d'un évenement arrivé en Perse, qui peut avoir beaucoup d'effet sur les relations de ce pays avec la Russie. Dans une émeute, dans [dont] la cause n'est pas encore bien connue, la populace de Teheran et la suite de M. Gribojidoff, ministre russe, se disputaient. Quelques individus de la populace ayant été tués, la foule se pourta au Bazar pour les venger, força l'hotel, et mit à mort le ministre et toute sa suite, à l'exception de trois ou quatre personnes. Le Schah[27] lui-même et son fils tentèrent d'arrêter le carnage, mais sans succès. Abbas Mirza et le Caìmacan[28] doivent être dépêchés auprès du gen. Paskewitsch, pour lui communiquer les particularités de cet événement malheureux.' (Fig. 12.2).

---

[27] Fath 'Ali Shah.
[28] Mirza Abu'l-Qasem.

12.11 'Late from Constantinople,' *New-York Spectator* (Wednesday, 10 June, 1829), 'Late from Constantinople,' *Baltimore Gazette and Daily Advertiser* (Friday, 12 June, 1829), 'Late from Constantinople,' *Poulson's American Daily Advertiser* (Friday, 12 June, 1829), 'Late from Constantinople,' *The Repertory* (Thursday, 18 June, 1829), 'Foreign Intelligence. Late from Constantinople,' *The Southern Patriot* (Thursday, 18 June, 1829), 'Foreign & Domestic News. Late from Constantinople,' *Vermont Watchman and State Gazette* (Tuesday, 23 June, 1829): 'The Augsburgh Gazette contains the following intelligence of the 12th of April from Constantinople: "A Tartar, sent off from Teheran by the British Charge d'Affaires, has brought intelligence that the Russian Embassy, and all the Russians who were in Persia, have been massacred,[29] and the Schah[30] himself is in danger if he does not suspend the payment of the war contribution to Russia. All the foreigners at Teheran are in dread, and the English Charge d'Affaires[31] has addressed to the Persian Government a note,[32] in which he declares that he shall consider it responsible for any act of violence that may be exercised against British subjects; and at the same time demands the punishment of those persons who are guilty of the massacre of the Russians. The latter point it would be very difficult to accomplish, as the whole nation took part in the massacre....According to private accounts from St. Petersburg, the lady of the Russian Ambassador[33] in Persia was still at Tauris,[34] with one officer of the

---

[29] This account seems to telescope events and confuses the question of who was in Tehran at the time of the massacre. Both Macdonald (ambassador, not Chargé d'Affaires) and McNeill were in Tabriz. See MacAlister (1910: 128), Lang (1948: 329). Macdonald first became aware of the incident on the night of 18 February, when he was summoned by 'Abbas Mirza who had just received a *firman* from Fath 'Ali Shah informing him of the whole affair. For a French translation of the *firman* see Stcherbatow (1891b: 70–73). Thereafter Macdonald sent his nephew Capt. R.D.H. Macdonald, 'to Tehran to receive such documents and statements as the Persian Government may be prepared to give,' as the ambassador said in a note addressed to Mirza Abu'l Hasan Khan Shirazi, Fath 'Ali Shah's foreign minister, dated 21 February 1829. See Lang (1948: 331–332), Kelly (2006: 198. Cf. 12.17).

[30] Fath 'Ali Shah.

[31] John Macdonald Kinneir. Cf. 11.127.

[32] See Lang (1948: 330–332) for the text of Macdonald's note to Mirza Abu'l Hassan Khan, which was taken to Tehran from Tabriz and delivered by the ambassador's brother, Capt. Macdonald. The Russian consul Andreas Amburger apparently also 'wrote a Note of Protest to Mirza Abul Hassan Khan,' although no copy of it has survived. See Harden (1979b: 53).

[33] Griboyedov.

[34] Nina Alexandrovna Griboyedova, née Chavchavadze (1812–1857), a Georgian princess. She and Griboyedov had married on 3 September 1828. See Harden (1971b: 439). As Kneip noted, 'it required considerable resourcefulness on Macdonald's part to persuade Nina to leave Persia, since she was unwilling to do so without her husband's permission. Only after she had returned safely to her parents in Tiflis was the news broken to her. The trauma of the occasion caused her to give premature birth to a son, named Aleksandr, who lived only an hour, long enough to be baptised. Although only a teenager when widowed, the beautiful Princess preferred never again to remarry and won universal respect by her fidelity to Griboedov's memory. She died of cholera in 1857, at the age

Embassy,[35] at the time the catastrophe took place at Teheran, by which means she fortunately escaped the carnage.

[Tauris is situated at the north-east [sic, north-west] frontiers of Persia, several hundred miles distant from Teheran, which lies south-west of Tauris.]

12.12 'From the East,' *Morning Courier and New-York Enquirer* (after 10 June, 1829), 'Foreign News. Latest from France. From the East,' *The People's Friend & Gazette* (Thursday, 11 June, 1829), 'Latest from France,' *The Freeman's Journal* (Monday, 15 June, 1829), 'Latest from France,' *Onondaga Register & Syracuse Gazette* (Monday, 15 June, 1829), 'Foreign News. Russia,' *Ithaca Journal & General Advertiser* (Wednesday, 17 June, 1829), 'Latest from France. From the East,' *Onondaga Register & Syracuse Gazette* (Wednesday, 17 June, 1829) and 'Very Late from England. From the East,' *Black River Gazette* (Wednesday, 17 June, 1829): ['By the packet ship Montgomery, Capt. Sise, from Havre, whence she sailed on the 10th of May, we have received our regular files of Paris papers from 1st to 9th May inclusive, from which we translate the following intelligence of the affairs of Europe....] Letters from Smyrna, of April 5th, say that a War between Persia and Russia is inevitable.[36] These letters say nothing about the 400,000 Russians, and the poor dogs that are starving at Constantinople.'

12.13 'Very late from England. Russia and Persia,' *Commercial Advertiser* (Monday, 8 June, 1829), 'Late Foreign Intelligence. Russia and Persia,' *Poulson's American Daily Advertiser* (Wednesday, 10 June, 1829), 'Russia and Persia,' *New-York Spectator* (Friday, 12 June, 1829) and 'Very late from England. Russia and Persia,' *The Virginia Herald* (Saturday, 13 June, 1829): 'The only article we find respecting the relations between Russia and Persia, the harmony of which may possibly be interrupted by the assassination of the Russian Minister[37] at the Persian Court, is the following, from St. Petersburgh, March

---

of 45.' See Kneip (1976: 267–268). When Griboyedov and his suite left Tabriz for Tehran she remained behind, as a guest of the British ambassador Macdonald and his wife, because she was pregnant. See Harden (1971b: 440).

[35] The Consul General in Tabriz, Andreas Amburger. See Harden (1971b: 441). He was actually in Nakhchivan/Naxçivan at the time of the attack. See Kelly (2006: 197). Amburger and Griboyedov's widow were accompanied by Dr. Cormick. See Harden (1971b: 441).

[36] As Lang (1948: 334) noted, 'Paskevič...wrote to Abbas Mirza protesting Griboedov's murder and the warlike rumors emanating from Persian headquarters, as well as the intrigues which Persia was reported to be carrying on with the Ottoman Porte.' Further, on 4 May 1829 Macdonald wrote, 'The Priests and several other leading men of the Court, would seem anxious for a rupture [with Russia], but the King is himself inclined to offer every atonement in his power for the murder of Monsieur Grebayedof save the disbursement of his money....Sensible of the weakness of Persia and of the fatal consequences that must attend another war with Russia from the feeling of disaffection towards the Kujer [Qajar] family throughout the Kingdom, I have hitherto exerted the whole of my influence to prevent such a catastrophe.' See Lang (1948: 334).

[37] Griboyedov.

12 From the Murder of Griboyedov to the Death of Fath 'Ali Shah (1829–1835)   1301

29:—The melancholy events of Teheran incessantly occupy the public mind. People are lost in speculations respecting the origin and motives of this unfortunate, and, perhaps, eventful occurrence. Many individuals well acquainted with politics consider this as an ebulition of embittered feelings on the part of the Persians and a consequence of that animosity when, after a disgraceful peace seeks to find vent, as similar scenes are not unfrequently observed amongst people wholly or partly barbarous. Others are of opinion that, under the circumstances of the offended national feelings of the Persians, not much consequence ought to be attached to the same; and that the populace of Teheran has been seduced solely by the money of foreign emissaries to commit so wanton an act. Be this as it may, it is not probable that a fresh Ambassador is likely to be sent to the Persian Court, on the part of Russia, until the Shah[38] proceeds to give ample satisfaction, as well as sufficient security for the future.'[39]

12.14 'Untitled,' *The National Gazette and Literary Register* (Thursday, 11 June, and Saturday, 13 June, 1829): 'The Augsburg Gazette contains a letter from Constantinople of the 12th of April, in which it is stated that the intelligence of the assassination of the Russian Ambassador[40] at Teheran had caused much joy at Constantinople,[41] and it was generally believed it would be the means of a rupture between Russia and Persia.[42]

It appears from a Petersburgh paper of April 20, that this murder had excited considerable sensation, but the Persian Government had used great exertions to make every reparation, by sending envoys to Gen. Count Paskewitch, at Teflis, to explain the affair.'

12.15 'Constantinople, 26th March,' *New-York American* (Friday, 12 June, 1829), 'Foreign Intelligence. Constantinople, 20th March,' *The Southern Patriot* (Thursday, 18 June, 1829) and 'Continuation of Extracts from French Papers, per ship Montgomery, at New-York. Turkey. Constantinople, 26th March,' *Charleston Courier* (Friday, 19 June,

---

[38] Fath 'Ali Shah.

[39] Major-General Prince Nikolai Andreyevich Dolgorukov left Tiflis to take up his appointment as Griboyedov's replacement on 30 June, 1829. See Anonymous (1829e), Amburger (1986: 95).

[40] Griboyedov.

[41] This was not a view shared by *Le Courrier de Smyrne* where we read, 'On a lieu de supposer que ce personnage vient pour solliciter une alliance; mais il est aussi à présumer que le fait qui donne lieu à cette démarche et qui a inspiré à la Porte la meme horreur qu'à tous les cabinets de l'Europe, le massacre de la légation russe à Téhéran, la détournera d'une alliance que dans d'autres circonstances la politique lui aurait conseillée.' See Anonymous (1829c).

[42] According to Jouannin and van Gaver (1840: 417), the commencement of the Russian campaign against Turkey 'avait été retardée, de la part des Russes, par suite de la crainte d'une rupture avec la Perse, à l'occasion d'un attentat commis par la population de Tèhèran sur la légation moscovite. Mais cette déplorable affaire ayant été étouffée par les satisfactions qu'offrirent le châh et le prince héréditaire Abbas-Mirza, le comte Paskewitch reprit l'offensive contre les Ottomans, qui avaient profité du moment d'hésitation qu'il montra.'

1829): 'We have received news of the assassination of the Russian Ambassador,[43] and of all the members of the Legation at Teheram [sic, Teheran], Persia. It may be supposed that under the circumstances, this news causes great discontentment and gives birth to the hope of a new war between Russia and Perssia [sic]—a war which will make a powerful diversion in favor of the Turkish army.'

12.16 'Turkey. Constantinople, 12th April,' *New-York American* (Friday, 12 June, 1829), Turkey. Constantinople, 12th April,' *The Southern Patriot* (Thursday, 18 June, 1829) and 'Continuation of Extracts from French Papers, per ship Montgomery, at New-York. Turkey. Constantinople, 12th April,' *Charleston Courier* (Friday, 19 June, 1829): 'There is no longer any doubt here that the Persians will not take up arms against the Russians, since the assassination of the Russian Ambassador[44] at Theran.'

12.17 'Untitled,' *New-York Evening Post* (Friday, 12 June, 1829) and 'From England,' *The Catskill Recorder and Greene County Republican* (Thursday, 18 June, 1829; first paragraph only): 'The packet ship Pacific, Captain Crocker, arrived last evening bringing us our files of London and Liverpool papers to 16th May....A letter from St. Petersburgh of the 20th of April, in relation to the assassination of the Russian Minister[45] and his officers at Teheran, says that there is every reason to believe the Persian government had no part in it, and that it eagerly offers the most complete satisfaction that the case will admit of. A person in the confidence of Abbas Mirza has been sent to Gen. Paskewitsch at Teflis, to make the necessary explanations,[46] and one of his sons[47] will soon follow on a similar mission. The letter proceeds to say:

"As soon as Mr. Mcdonald, the English Envoy at Tauris, was informed of this melancholy event, he sent to Mirza Hassan Khan[48] the Schah's[49] Minister of Foreign Affairs, a despatch, of which the following are the principle points. He observes that, in consequence of this catastrophe, all confidence is destroyed, and that it would be in vain to pretend that the representative of any Power can henceforth think himself safe in Persia; that it is not enough that the Government disavows proceedings the consequences of which, perhaps, it fears itself, but that it must offer complete satisfaction; that the instigators of the massacre, and those who perpetrated it, must be given up, wherever they may be; that no rank ought to protect them, no sanctuary serve them as an asylum, no subterfuge be employed to screen

---

[43] Griboyedov.

[44] Griboyedov.

[45] Griboyedov.

[46] A note from 'Abbas Mirza to Gen. Paskevich informed him that 'en vous envoyant notre honoré secrétaire d'Etat Mirza-Salegh [Mirza Saleh Shirazi], j'ai cru devoir vous faire parvenir par son entremise, avec le très gracieux firman d'accompagnement de Sa Majesté le Schah, Souverain de la Perse.' See Stcherbatow (1891a: 266).

[47] Khosrow Mirza (1813–1875). For his life see Bournoutian (2015).

[48] Mirza Abu'l Hasan Khan Shirazi.

[49] Fath 'Ali Shah.

them from the punishment which they have merited; and that if the Government is not able to clear itself completely from the suspicion of any participation whatever in the crime which has just been committed, not only Russia, but the whole civilised world will become its enemy.

"It is Captain Macdonald, brother [sic, nephew] to the Envoy,[50] who has been sent with this note to Teheran. He had orders to take under his special protection the officers and individuals of the Russian Legation, who had survived the massacre, and to conduct them to Tauris.—He has besides declared, that the slightest insult or violence towards them would cause him, and the British subjects placed under his orders, immediately to quit the Persian territory.[51]

"All the members of the English Legation, as well as the subjects of his Britannic Majesty at Tauris, have gone into mourning for 3 months,[52] as a mark of their profound affliction at the sad event which has taken place.'"

12.18 'Foreign Intelligence. Continuation of Extracts from Papers received by the Silas Richards,' *New-York Spectator* (after 13 June, 1829): 'The following letter, which appears in the *Hereford Journal* of Wednesday, contains a fuller account than any yet published of the catastrophe which befel the Russian embassy at the Court of Teheran, with the causes which led to it. It is said to have been written by a Persian nobleman, and addressed to a gentleman of rank in this country[53]:

"Tabreez, Feb. 20, 1829.

---

[50] Captain (later Major) Ranald Dugald Harcourt Macdonald (c. 1800–1848) of the 8th Light Cavalry. According to MacAlister (1910: 131), Yapp (1980: 138) and Wright (1998: 171) Capt. Macdonald was John Macdonald's nephew, not his brother. 'In February 1826...on the question of the despatch of a Mission to Persia being again taken into consideration, he was ordered to Bombay to assume command of the escort of the British Envoy, and proceeding then to Persia he continued attached to the British Embassy in that country for 10 years. He returned to India in October 1836....on the 21st November 1848,—he died at Anarkalli, Lahore,' and was buried in Lahore. See Irving and de Rhé-Philipe (1910: 90), de Rhé-Philipe (1912: 217). Cf. Harden (1979b: 2).

[51] In Macdonald's official letter of protest to the Persian government we read, 'Captain Macdonald is also directed to receive charge of the survivors of the Russian Mission, and conduct them to Tabreez. The Undersigned would be unwilling to believe that they are in any danger of being subjected to further insult or violence, but it is his duty to state, that if a single hair of their heads should be injured, he will instantly withdraw from the Persian Territories, with the whole of the British Subjects under his orders.' See Lang (1948: 331).

[52] According to Lang (1948: 330) the 'British community was to observe 2 months of mourning.'

[53] Given that the original version of this article was published in the *Oriental Herald and Journal of General Literature*, edited by J.S. Buckingham (Anonymous 1829j: 146–148), and given Buckingham's travels in Persia and the book resulting from them, it is probable that he was the recipient of this letter, although who its noble Persian author may have been is unknown. It clearly differs from the account given by the secretary of the Russian Embassy's *mehmendar* as given in G. Willock (1830). Letters from Mirza 'Abd ol-Vahhab-e Isfahani, Fath 'Ali Shah's principal adviser (*Moatamad-ud-Dow'leh*; see Lang 1948: 326) and his Foreign Minister Abu'l Hassan Khan describing the events are known to exist (Kelly 2006: 214) but were not available to me.

Knowing you to be interested in Persian affairs, and a circumstance of great political importance having occurred of [sic] Teheran 10 days ago, I thought I would have the pleasure to communicate it to you myself, and shall be glad if it renders my letter acceptable to you. Mr. Grybydoff, the Russian Ambassador with his suite and guard of Cossacks, in all I believe 35 people, left this place for the Court of Teheran, about 2 months ago on a mission, from the Emperor,[54] of congratulation to the King,[55] on the late treaty of peace between this country and Russia. This treaty which you have no doubt seen grants a power to the subjects of the respective kingdoms to go to and fro unmolested; but the Ambassador on his way thought fit to collect all the Armenians he could find,[56] even such as were slaves at the time of Aga Mahmoud Khan.[57] At Casbine[58] he interfered in those matters so much as to give great offence amongst the people, by punishing very severely a Mahomedan who was the neighbor merely of a person who had bought an Armenian slave, of which he was accused of being the accessory, although he was perfectly guiltless: this excited the indignation of the people so much, that he was seriously advised to depart, or they would not answer for his personal safety.[59] Arrived at Teheran, every attention was paid him, a guard of honour being appointed him, and greater respect shown,[60] I understand, than even to the splendid mission of General Yermouloff.[61] But he chose to raise every

---

[54] Nicholas I.

[55] Fath 'Ali Shah.

[56] As G. Willock (1830: 502) noted, 'He [Griboyedov] had been accompanied from Tabreez by nine or ten Armenians, whose relations had been carried into captivity. These people continually pestered him by entreaties to rescue the captives. He could not leave his chamber for a moment, without being importuned by them on this subject. No sooner was one slave released, than she gave information respecting several others. The slaves were never given up, without kindling considerable angry feelings.'

[57] Agha Mohammad Shah, Fath 'Ali Shah's uncle and predecessor on the Qajar throne.

[58] Qazvin.

[59] This story is not recounted by Willock who, however, told the story of a German woman who had been taken as a captive by a groom of Hoseyn Qoli Khan Qazvini, former governor of Yerevan, and brought to Qazvin, where she was sold to a merchant who in turn sold her to a *seyyid* named Shaykh 'Abdul 'Aziz, cousin of the chief mollah of Qazvin. In the end the German woman preferred to remain with her husband by whom she had had two children. See G. Willock (1830: 498–499).

[60] As G. Willock (1830: 501) observed, 'A series of grand entertainments were given to the Mission at the houses of the Ummeen-ed-Dowleh [Amin od-Doula], Meerza Abul Hussan Khan [Mirza Abu'l Hasan Khan Shirazi], and Meerza Mahomed Alli Khan. A spirit of emulation prevailed between these personages; each endeavoured to gratify their guests by unbounded attention, by the excellence of the repast, display of their choicest services of china, glass-ware, and household apparatus, by illuminations and by fireworks.' Cf. Lang (1948: 326) who noted, 'The princes and notables of Teheran at first vied with one another in giving lavish entertainments to the Envoy.'

[61] Ermolov. Cf. 10.8ff.

12 From the Murder of Griboyedov to the Death of Fath 'Ali Shah (1829–1835) 1305

possible grievance respecting those claims of the Armenian and Georgian subjects. The King's eunuch, Aga Yacoub, formerly an Armenian, but now a Mahomedan more than twenty years, having plundered the King to the amount of 40,000 or 50,000 tomauns, fled to the Russian Ambassador's for refuge, and he protected him against the claims of the King, and in contempt of his authority.[62] He also granted refuge to two Armenians, who had murdered a Mahomedan; but even this the Government overlooked, and compromised the affair with the relatives of the deceased.[63] Many other instances I could name of his interfering in the affairs of the Georgians and Armenians, even in contempt of the Persian Government; amongst others, he required two Armenian women being given up to him belonging to Allaya Khan,[64] who were formerly Turkish slaves, brought from Van during the last war between this country and Turkey[65]; these women did not seek his protection, but on the contrary wished to remain at Teheran, but he chose to consider them as Armenian subjects, and that they should return to their country. The King remonstrated, and even condescended to send the women to the Ambassador's residence, under the charge of one of his eunuchs, in order that they might be questioned by him as to the fact alludeded to; but he refused to question them in the presence of the eunuch, whom he very ill treated and sent away, detaining the women by force, and contrary to the King's orders. From what I can learn by the accounts already received, these women were treated very barbarously by the Russians. In the morning they made their escape, and ran through the

---

[62] G. Willock (1830: 504) called Khoja Mirza Yakub Markarian 'a native of Erivan, where his relations still resided. His father, an Armenian, was gardener to Mahomed Khan, hereditary chief of Erivan province. He had been carried into slavery about the time Erivan was besieged by General Sisianaff [Tsitsianov], in the year 1226 (1808), and had been brought up as an attendant on the seraglio of the famous Golden [Gol'den] Ismael Khan. On this chieftain's disgrace, he became, after a lapse of some years, the property of the Shah. For a long period he had enjoyed his majesty's peculiar favour and confidence, as a domestic of the seraglio; and, at the moment of relinquishing the Shah's service, held the responsible appointment of treasurer, and superintendent of the jewellery of the harem.' The day after Khoja Mirza Yakub's first visit to Griboyedov, 'it was officially notified to the envoy, that the refugee had unsettled accounts to the amount of 30 or 40,000 tomans.' See G. Willock (1830: 505). There were several stories of his origins. As Harden (1971a: 75, n. 7) noted, 'He eventually became one of the shah's three chief eunuchs, the other two of whom had been taken prisoner with him. He was taught Persian, Arabic, and bookkeeping. He soon made himself valuable to the shah by bringing order to the royal accounts and several several times as the shah's treasurer. Together with his two companions, Khoja Mirza Yakub formed a company for supplying goods to the women of the shah's harem. With his earnings he helped his family in Erivan, built up a library, and continued to study. He remained secretly Orthodox in his religion and hoped 1 day to return home.'

[63] No alleged murder is recorded in the other extant sources, only the story of Khodja Mirza Yakub Markarian and the two Armenian women.

[64] Allah Yar Khan Qajar Devehlu. Cf. 11.35.

[65] G. Willock (1830: 506) described them as 'a young woman, and a girl of thirteen or fourteen..... the youngest was under engagements of marriage' to 'a Mahomed Tahur Beg,' and 'on being questioned by M. Grebayedoff, explicitly mentioned that they were not solicitous to leave Tehran.'

streets crying aloud for vengeance. This excited the indignation of the populace, who advanced with menacing threats to the residence of the Ambassador. His house was then protected by about 100 of the King's Guards, and from 20 to 30 Cossacks. These were ordered to fire upon the populace, and they killed six men. This exasperated the mob to the greatest height. The bodies of these men were then exposed in six different mosques, and the moolahs excited the people to fury, calling upon them for revenge on the murderers. The populace was then increased to about 30,000,[66] inflamed by strong religious feeling of the sacrifice of six Mussulmans by the Muscovite Infidels; nothing could stem their rage, and they went forward resolved upon their utter destruction. The King, in the mean time hearing of the tumult, ordered out 2000 of the troops, or Tonbosses,[67] to the rescue of the Russians, and sent his son, Alli Shah,[68] to their personal assistance. The Prince, at the risk of his life, succeeded in saving one of the Ambassador's Secretaries[69] and two Cossacks; with these exceptions the whole of the Russians were massacred, the exact number of which I cannot ascertain, but they are estimated to be 30 at least.[70] Such was the violence of the mob, that to save young Maltzoff they were obliged to carry him in a box through the street for protection, to the Palace.[71] Mr. Grybydoff, it is said, was killed by a blow from a stone in the temple:[72] the people seeing him fall, then rushed into the house and murdered every Russian they could meet with. This horrible event has caused great consternation in the two Governments, both here and at Teheran. The king has sent to say that he will offer every indemnity to Russia, which she may require for so horrible an outrage, over which he had no controul, and did his utmost to prevent.[73]—His Majesty overlooked many

---

[66] G. Willock (1830: 508), on the other hand, wrote, 'A crowd of four or five hundred persons, preceded by boys, and some worthless desperate men, who, with frantic genstures, brandished their clubs and naked swords in the air, had advanced from the mosque to the envoy's habitation.'

[67] *tofangchi*, the common Persian term for a matchlockman or musketeer, i.e. riflemen. See e.g. Ouseley (1823: 294).

[68] 'Ali Shah Mirza, governor of Tehran. Cf. 12.2.

[69] Maltsov.

[70] Willock (1830: 512) put the figure at 'about twenty-six or twenty-seven...killed and wounded.'

[71] This is incorrect. As noted above, the First Secretary was disguised 'in the uniform of a Persian soldier, and marched in their ranks to the palace.' See Willock (1830: 511).

[72] According to Willock (1830: 510), 'The envoy had been pierced through and through by a blow on the left breast with a knife; and an athletic phalwan [*pahlavān*], or public wrestler, named—, in the service of a citizen of Tehran, was shewn to me as the person who had inflicted it.'

[73] In fact, as Macdonald noted in August, more than 6 months after the massacre, 'No steps have yet been taken by the Shah to p unish any of those concerned in the massacre of M. Gebayedof and his suite, nor until this is done can we venture to look upon the question at issue with Russia as finally settled. His Majesty in so far as he himself is concerned manifests every inclination to comply with the just demands of the Emperor [Nicholas], but the Prime Minister, the Priesthood, and the Kujer Nobles are opposed to the act and continue to exercise the whole of their power and influence in order to prevent or retard it.' Eventually, Fath 'Ali Shah dismissed and imprisoned the chief of the Tehran police; banished the chief mollah, Mirza Messeh, although it caused 'a tumult like the day of

provocations of the Ambassador, that nothing might occur to disturb the peace with Russia, and so tamely did he submit to them, that it excited great indignation amongst the people, and it is a general opinion, that had the King gone into the midst of them during this insurrection, they would have sacrificed him to their fury; as it was, he was obliged to keep the door of his ark* [*The fortified part of the Palace] shut. That the Russians brought upon themselves this horrid catastrophe, there can be no doubt—not that this is offered as an excuse for one of the most barbarous and outrageous deeds which has ever disgraced the annals of this or any other country. Messengers are immediately going off to the Court of St. Petersburgh, and it will soon be seen what steps they take to revenge this outrage on the dignity of the sovereign and the murder of his people; but I hope this deplorable event will not involve this country in any costly consequences though the result of it can be by no means anticipated. His Royal Highness is plunged in the deepest grief on the ocasion [sic], and has ordered a general mourning amongst his people, and I never saw him so deeply afflicted. I had the honor of an audience with him yesterday, and mentioned my intention of writing to you, which he particularly wished me to do. You had heard, perhaps of his Royal Highness's intention to vist St. Petersburgh this spring, which I need not say is for a time postponed.'"

12.19 'Latest from Europe. London, May 12,' *Saratoga Sentinel* (Tuesday, 16 June, 1829; minus last sentence), 'Gleanings. Foreign,' *The Kinderhook Herald* (Thursday, 18 June, 1829; minus 'which we have extracted…*Chambres*') and 'London May, 12,' *Vermont Gazette* (Tuesday, 23 June, 1829): 'We have not yet heard of any movements on the part of the Persians to justify the speculations of a renewal of the war with Russia.[74] The Petersburgh version of the massacre at Teheran, which we have extracted from the French Ministerial Paper the *Messager des Chambres*, gives a different account from that which we inserted from Constantinople. The Petersburgh statement declares that the Persian government had no hand in it, but that it expressed great abhorrence, and a desire to afford

---

judgement,' according to the Shah himself; and had the noses, ears and tongues cut off of 'a number of habitual offenders, though to have been involved in Griboedov's murder.' See Lang (1948: 337).

[74] Regarding speculations of Persia's renewal of the war with Russia, despite the calamitous state of its finances, it is important to note that, 'On June 19, Macdonald called on Abbas Mirza's Minister, the Kaim Makam, whom he found in his dressing gown, sitting under a cherry tree with the sweat trickling down his face, trying to draft a letter to General Paskevič. He told Macdonald that in a moment of panic after Griboedov's death, the Shah had made an offensive coalition with the Turkomans of Khiva and Bokhara, Afghanistan, and the Ottoman Porte against Russia….War now seemed unlikely. How, asked the Kaim Makam, was he to explain all this to Paskevič, conciliate both Russia and the Ottoman Empire, and restrain the Turkomans?' See Lang (1948: 335–336).

the fullest satisfaction. The conduct of the British Legation is highly, and of course justly spoken of in this unhappy affair.'[75]

12.20 'Massacre of the Russian Ambassador,' *The Ithaca Journal & General Advertiser* (Wednesday, 1 July, 1829) and 'Things in General. The Massacre of the Russian Ambassador and Suite at Teheran,' *The Kinderhook Herald* (Thursday, 2 July, 1829): 'We gather from the Baltimore Gazette some further particulars of the late events in Persia, which we did not find in our own foreign papers. M. Geybydoff (the Russian Ambassador) had been at the Court of Teheran for 2 months past, to carry into effect some articles of the late treaty between Russia and Persia respecting the Armenian and Georgian subjects of Russia, whom he claimed to return to their country.—Amongst these claims was that of two Armenian women,[76] belonging to Alluya Khan,[77] who did not seek protection from the Russian Ambassador, since they were slaves from Turkey, and brought from Van during the last war between Persia and Turkey; but the Ambassador chose to consider them as belonging to Russia. The King[78] ordered the women to be sent to him under the charge of his eunuch, in order that they might be questioned as to the fact alluded to. But the Ambassador refused to question them in the presence of the eunuch, whom he very ill-treated and sent away, detaining the women all night in his house by force. Here they were most barbarously used by the Russians.

They made their escape in the morning, crying loudly through the streets for revenge. This instigated the populace to hasten towards the Ambassador's, from when the Cossacks fired upon them, and killed six men. The bodies of those men were then taken to the mosques, and exposed by the Moolahs, calling aloud for vengeance on their murderers, which excited the most ungovernable fury in the minds of the people, 30,000 of whom assembled and surrounded the residence of the Ambassador with the utmost fury. The King in the meantime, hearing of the tumult, sent his guards to protect the Russians, who behaved nobly in their defence, and it is said that 100 of them were destroyed by the populace; his son, Alli Shah,[79] went to their assistance, and at the risk of his life, with the

---

[75] On 4 April 1829 the British ambassador in St. Petersburg, Lord Heytesbury, wrote to the Foreign Secretary, the Earl of Aberdeen, 'The conduct of Colonel Macdonald upon this melancholy occasion has given great satisfaction to the Emperor, and I have been requested by Count Nesselrode to convey to the King our Master, thro' Your Lordship, the expression of His Imperial Majesty's gratitude.' See Lang (1948: 333–334).

[76] The translator of Fath 'Ali Shah's *firman* describing the events leading up to the massacre called them 'deux femmes Khardos de Moosh,' i.e. referring to Kardu and the Karduchians, a Classical toponym covering part of Armenia first encoiuntered in Xenophon's Anabasis (Nöldeke 1898: 73), and identifying Muş, in eastern Turkey, which had a large Armenian population, as their original home.

[77] Allah Yar Khan Qajar Devehlu.

[78] Fath 'Ali Shah.

[79] 'Ali Shah Mirza, governor of Tehran.

12 From the Murder of Griboyedov to the Death of Fath 'Ali Shah (1829–1835)

means of saving one of the Ambassador's secretaries,[80] and two Cossacks, but nothing could stem the violence of the enraged multitude, who massacred all the Russians, (with these exceptions,) estimated to be about 30 people, including the Cossack guard.

It thus appears that a wanton aggression was committed upon the right of hospitality, and the known prejudices of the Persians regarding their females, which was followed up by the murder of unarmed citizens, circumstances which we should think were calculated to rouse the feelings of a population much more phlegmatic than the Persian.'

12.21 'From Europe,' *New-York Evening Post* (Tuesday, 7 July, 1829): 'There is a general expectation in the Turkish army in Asia, that Persia will resume hostilities against Russia; the Kourds, the Circassians, and the Lasians,[81] are said to be already in arms, and the Khans of Tartary are ready to declare in favour of the Turks.'

12.22 'Latest from Europe,' *The Freeman's Journal* (Monday, 20 July, 1829) and 'Foreign. Russia and Persia,' *The Kinderhook Herald* (Thursday, 23 July, 1829; with minor variations, e.g. packet ship 'Bully,' '27th of May'): '[By the packet ship Sally, Capt. R.L. Macy, arrived at N.Y. on the 14th inst. files of Paris papers have been received, to the first of June inclusive....The Constitutionel contains a Frankfort article of the 17th May, stating that according to late letters from Vienna, there was a rumor on Change in that city, of an irruption made by the Persians on the Russian territory. It was even said that the Persians had succeeded in taking by assault several strong places, making a part of those which, by a treaty of peace the Shah[82] had ceded to the Muscovites. The news had an effect on the funds....Letters from Vienna announce again that Persia has declared war against Russia, and that hostilities have commenced by the taking of two fortresses.'[83]

12.23 *Morning Courier and New-York Enquirer* (Monday, 27 July, 1829; from 'The latest accounts...'), 'Untitled,' *New-York Spectator* (Tuesday, 28 July, 1829), 'Extracts from German papers,' *New-York American for the Country* (Friday, 31 July, 1829) and 'From the Theatre of War,' *The Herald* [Sandy-Hill NY] (Tuesday, 4 August, 1829): '*Persia* has made common cause with *Turkey*.[84] This will render Gen. Paskewitz's progress to Erzeroum a little more uncomfortable than he expected....The latest accounts from Constantinople of the 12th of May say, that the extraordinary Ambassador from Persia[85]

---

[80] Maltzov.
[81] Lezgins.
[82] Fath 'Ali Shah.
[83] These are all false rumors.
[84] A false rumor.
[85] According to Anonymous (1829c), the ambassador was Mohammad Sharif Mirza Khan. As Stcherbatow (1891b: 123) wrote, 'à la première nouvelle de l'assassinat de Griboïédow, Abbas affolé avait, du consentement du Schah, envoyé Mollah-Schérif à Constantinople, muni d'un plein pouvoir pour la conclusion d'une alliance avec la Turquie. Cette alliance fut conclue et tenue secrète. Mais

immediately after the first visit to the Reis Effendi,[86] dispatched couriers to Teheran.[87] The dispatches of which they are the bearers are said to give the most satisfactory account of this first conference. All the great men of the Empire have visited the Ambassador.'

12.24 'Foreign,' *The Greenfield Gazette & Franklin Herald* (Tuesday, 28 July 1829): 'Paris papers to the 2nd June have been received at New York. At Vienna it was reported that a rupture between Persia and Russia had broken out, and that Persia had captured all the fortified places ceded to Russia by the last treaty.'[88]

12.25 'Important Foreign News,' *The Schenectady Cabinet* (Wednesday, 29 July, 1829), 'Foreign News. Russia and Turkey,' *Ithaca Journal & General Advertiser* (Wednesday, 5 August, 1829) and 'Latest from Europe,' *The Corrector* (Saturday, 8 August, 1829): '[At a late hour this morning, we heard of the arrival of a vessel from Greenock [Scotland], bringing papers to the 15th of June, containing London advices to the 13th, and Paris of the 10th. . . .] Important accounts may be expected from Asia, as it appears by advices from Constantinople, that Persia is about to make common cause with Turkey,[89] and that Gen.

---

lorsque Maltzew, retournant de Tauris à Tiflis, se trouva de passage à Téhéran, Abbas l'informa de l'arrivée de plénipotentiaires ottomans. Il s'étendit sur leurs propositions, que le Schah refusait soi-disant d'accepter, sans toutefoirs faire la moindre allusion à la mission confidentielle de Mollah-Schérif.' On June 18, 1829, Nesselrode reported to the Russian ambassador in London (1812–1834), Prince Christoph Heinrich von Lieven, 'Les dernières nouvelles de Constantinople annoncent l'apparition dans cette capitale d'un Envoyé du Schah de Perse, et les feuilles publiques lui attribuent la mission de proposer au Sultan une alliance offensive et défensive contre nous.'

[86] Pertev Pasha (1785–1837), Reis Efendi from 1827 to 1830. See Çakir (2013: 95).

[87] In a letter to Nesselrode dated 8 September 1829, Paskevich reported, 'Le courrier dirigé tout récemment à Tauris par l'ambassade anglaise de Constantinople a passé il y a peu de jours par Erzeroum. Les papiers dont cet individu était porteur consistaient: (1) En un firman du Sultan, pour un voyage à Van et dans les environs. (2) En plusieurs lettres particulières fraîchement datées de Constantinople, et contenant des renseignements sur la marche des armées russes et sur la sensation que nos succés produisent dans la capitale de l'Empire Ottoman.' See Stcherbatow (1891a: 285).

[88] A wildly incorrect rumor.

[89] Letters obtained by Paskevich's forces after the fall of Akhalzikh included one (undated) sent by the Turkish military commander to the *kahya*, or chief minister, of the province which said, 'Avant l'arrivée de l'ambassadeur persan, Mollah Chérif, à Constantinople, la Porte a envoyé en Perse, en qualité de plénipotentiaire, un de ses ministres, appelé Tibi-Effendi; et, afin que sa mission ne fût pas connue, jusqu'à son arrivée à Erzeroum, on l'a fait partir de Constantinople, comme chargé d'inspecter les munitions de guerre de l'armée orientale. Cet Effendi est maintenant en route; et, dans cet intervalle, l'ambassadeur Persan, Mollah Chérif, est arrivé à Constantinople. Quoique par ce courrier nous ne sachions pas encore la décision de l'alliance, nous espérons cependant que dans peu nous en aurons des nouvelles. Malgré cela, nous avons su qu'Abbas-Myrza avait envoyé à Tiflis son fils comme ôtage, après y avoir expédié deux personnes de distinction: il paraît donc qu'Abbas-Myrza flatte d'un côté la Porte, et de l'autre la Russie, pour mettre en exécution ce qui lui sera le plus avantageux. A second letter from the Turkish military commander to his *kahya*, dated 25 May, said, 'L'affaire de l'alliance avec l'ambassadeur Persan qui était allé à Constantinople, est arrangée; nous

12 From the Murder of Griboyedov to the Death of Fath 'Ali Shah (1829–1835)

Paskewitch having received large reinforcements of men, and supplies of artillery, was preparing to advance upon Erzerum.'[90]

12.26 'Latest from France,' *The Daily Chronicle* (Friday, 31 July, 1829), 'Latest from France,' *Baltimore Gazette and Daily Advertiser* (Saturday, 1 August, 1829), 'Latest from France,' *Baltimore Patriot & Mercantile Advertiser* (Saturday, 1 August, 1829), 'Latest from France,' *Baltimore Republican and Commercial Advertiser* (Saturday, 1 August, 1829), 'Late Foreign Intelligence. Latest from France,' *Poulson's American Daily Advertiser* (Saturday, 1 August, 1829), 'Latest from France,' *Daily National Intelligencer* (Monday, 3 August, 1829), 'From the East,' *Rhode Island American, Statesman and Providence Gazette* (Tuesday, 4 August, 1829), 'From France,' *The Schenectady Cabinet* (Wednesday, 5 August, 1829), 'From the East,' *American Sentinel* (Wednesday, 5 August, 1829) and 'Foreign. Latest from France,' *Greensburgh Gazette* (Friday, 7 August, 1829): 'Advices from Constantinople of the 14th May, represent that the Porte felt less apprehension as to the integrity of the empire, from supposing it certain that England and France wished to treat directly with them; and were, in consequence, less active in preparing for defence....The arrival of the Persian Ambassador[91] also gives rise to many reflections.—It is said that after he has concluded his negotiations here he will go to London.[92]—Although the Persian does not inspire the Porte with much confidence, yet it seems disposed to treat with him, without committing itself, and sent commissioners to give him a formal reception. The Persian nation seems violently irritated against the Russians.'

12.27 'Latest from France,' *Morning Courier and New-York Enquirer* (Thursday, 6 August, 1829), 'Postscript. Latest from France,' *Baltimore Republican and Commercial Advertiser* (Monday, 10 August, 1829), 'Foreign Intelligence. Latest from France,' *United States' Telegraph* (Monday, 10 August, 1829), 'Untitled,' *National Ægis* (Wednesday, 12 August, 1829) and 'Foreign Intelligence. Latest from France,' *United States' Weekly Telegraph* (Saturday, 15 August, 1829): 'Extract of a letter of the 2rd ult. from St. Petersburg: "We learn from Tiflis, under date of May 14, that accounts had just been

---

en avons reçu la nouvelle que nous avons fait parvenir à Abbas-Myrza. Mais les Persans, d'après leurs démarches, et d'après les renseignemens que nous avons, ne prendront aucune mesure hostile contre les Russes.' For both see Stcherbatow (1891b: 74–75).

[90] The advance on Erzurum is described in detail by Monteith (1856: 263ff), who was an eyewitness. As he noted, 'The Russians followed the two great routes; General Bourtsoff took the one by Zavinn and Ardos with one battalion of Sappers, two battalions of Chasseurs, one regiment of Cossacks, and 12 pieces of artillery. Prince Bekowitch Tcherkaskoi followed the route of Medginghert, and was to unite with General Bourtsoff at the village of Khorassan [mod. Horasan]....On the 21st [July, 1829] Prince Paskiewitch followed the road opened by General Bourtsoff....On the 22nd all the flanking columns united at Ardos, where the army encamped.' Erzurum was occupied by the Russians by 6 pm on 27 July. See Monteith (1856: 273).

[91] Mohammad Sharif Mirza Khan. Cf. 12.23.

[92] If ever contemplated, this certainly did not eventuate.

received there, stating that Hosreff Mirza, eldest son of Abbas Mirza,[93] sent by the Persian government with explanations relative to the disastrous affair which proved so fatal to our mission at Teheran, had passed the Araxa, and was then on the frontiers of the Empire.'[94]

12.28 'One day later from England,' *New-York Spectator* (Friday, 7 August, 1829), 'Frontiers of Wallachia, May 22,' *New-York Amercan for the Country* (Friday, 7 August, 1829) and 'One day later,' *Savannah Georgian* (Thursday, 13 August, 1829): 'President Salsuchin[95] is gone to the head quarters at Kallarasch, in company with col. Rusche.[96] Count Salsuchin was mentioned, some time ago, as successor of the murdered ambassador in Persia; but the present occurrences of the army seem to require his presence here, and contradict the above report.'

12.29 'Supplementary Intelligence. London, Monday, June 22,' *The Atlas* (Saturday, 8 August, 1829): Letters from St. Petersburg, dated the 10th inst. state, that the grandson of the King of Persia,[97] Hosreff-Mirza, had left Teheran for St. Petersburg, to offer apologies and reparation to the Russian court on the late disastrous event, by which the Russian ambassador[98] and others of his suite fell victims to the popular fury at Teheran.'

12.30 'Extracts from Late Foreign Papers,' *Commercial Advertiser* (Thursday, 20 August, 1829), 'London, July 2,' *Boston Weekly Messenger* (Thursday, 20 August, 1829), 'Persia,' *Christian Register* (Saturday, 22 August, 1829; beginning second para.), 'London, July 2,'

---

[93] Sixteen-year old Khosrow Mirza was 'Abbas Mirza's seventh son in a family comprising 25 sons and 25 daughters at the time. See Idesbald (1833: 9). As Orouji (2014: 197–198) noted, 'Abbas Mirza feared that Russia might keep his eldest son as a hostage until the full payment of the remaining indemnity. He, therefore, decided to send his seventh son, the 16-year-old Khosrow Mirza, who had made a favorable impression on Paskevich during the peace negotiations.' In addition, as Idesbald (1833: 10) noted, 'Khosrev s'était déjà occupé, avant son voyage, de l'étude de la langue française, et commençait à en prononcer quelques mots. Il a composé un discours sur l'éloquence, que l'on assure être semé d'idées ingénieuses.'

[94] According to Idesbald (1833: 10), 'Khosrev-Mirza voyagea à cheval jusqu'à Tiflis.' Eichwald (1837: 643) dated Khosrow Mirza's entry into Tiflis to 2 May [O.S], 1829 but this is contradicted by Stcherbatow (1891a: 130) who noted, 'Le 2 (14) mai on apprit à Tiflis que Khozrew-Mirza, le second [sic seventh] fils d'Abbas, avait déjà franchi notre frontière.'

[95] Adjutant General Pavel Petrovich Suchtelen (1788–1833)]. During the recently concluded war with Persia Count Suchtelen had occupied Ardabil. See Monteith (1856: 150). For his role in the Russo-Turkish War of 1828–1829 to which this article refers see von Moltke (1845: 98, 108, 109, 114 and 139).

[96] Possibly Colonel I.A. Reutt/Reutte/Reout/Riout, commander of the 42nd Jäger Regiment (Eichwald 1837: 571), whom Monteith (1856: 125) called 'a Polish officer of talent and resolution.' For his involvement in the Russo-Turkish War of 1828–1829 see Uschakoff (1838: 190, 205, 269, 293 and 294).

[97] Fath 'Ali Shah.

[98] Griboyedov.

12 From the Murder of Griboyedov to the Death of Fath 'Ali Shah (1829–1835)   1313

The Portsmouth Journal and Rockingham Gazette (Saturday, 22 August, 1829) and 'Persia. London, July 2,' *The Massachusetts Spy and Worcester County Advertiser* (Wednesday, 26 August, 1829): 'There is some information relative to Persia in the late London papers. She sent her Ambassador to Scutaria[99] in the greatest haste, the Schah and his subjects being dissatisfied with the peace with Russia.—The Divan, though of course not averse to a connection which would give it a new ally, is said to have declined giving a final answer until the arrival of the French and British Ministers. In the mean time, our readers may wish to have some information respecting this Persian Ambassador.

Sedi-Khann, or Sidy-Khan, the Persian Envoy to Constantinople,[100] and the Diplomatist whose daily interviews (of late) with the Turkish Reis Effendi,[101] have awakened attention and interest, is the person alluded to in a recent publication, (M'Farlane's[102] Constantinople in 1828.)[103] The author, who was intimately acquainted with him at the Turkish capital during the summer and autumn of last year, describes him as a most gentlemanly and intelligent Oriental—as one who speaks the English language with fluency and purity, whilst he is well informed on all matters connected with England, and our vast connections in India, and passionately fond of every thing that has the merit of being English. These acquirements and predilections are attributable to the circumstances of his having been educated in his youth at a British school in India—to his having visited our country as Agent of the Persian Prince, Abbas Mirza—and to his friendly relations with many distinguished Englishmen, here, in India, and in Persia.

---

[99] Üsküdar, near Constantinople.

[100] In a letter to Count Nesselrode of 1 July 1829, Paskevich wrote, 'Sadich-Khan, émissaire expédié par Abbas-Mirza à Constantinople, vient d'arriver, avec un agent de la mission anglaise qui lui a été donné pour adjoint, à Melez-Ghird, petit fort situé non loin de Toprakh-Kalé, d'où il s'est vu contraint de m'adresser la lettre ci-jointe en original, pour me demander secours et protection contre les Kurdes...Cette lettre, écrite d'un style barbare, me paraît avoir été évidemment écrite et signée, non par le personnage par lequel elle m'a été adressée, mais par l'agent anglais qui l'accompagne.' See Stcherbatow (1891a: 284). Cf. Anonymous (1829d), 'Nous avons reçu un courier de Smyrne qui nous a apporté les nouvelles suivantes: Constantinople, 12 mai. Le nom de l'ambassadeur persan est Sidy-Khan, prince arménien, en service de la cour de Téhéran. Les Persans craignant la colère de l'empereur de Russie, font de grande préparatifs de guerre, et envoient cet ambassadeur pour obtenir un allié.' This report was corrected by intelligence from 23 May, however. According to Anonymous (1829c), 'L'ambassadeur persan n'est-pas, comme on l'avait dit d'abord, Siddi Khan, mais Méhémet Sheriff Mirza Khan.' The same article refers to a Persian chargé d'affaires who resided permanently in Constantinople, but it is unclear if this was Siddi [sic, Sadeq] Khan.

[101] Pertev Pasha. Cf. 12.23.

[102] Charles MacFarlane (1799–1858), prolific Scottish historian, biographer and novelist. For his life see Goodwin (1900).

[103] The following lines on Sadeq Khan are a paraphrase of those found in MacFarlane (1829: 298–299).

Sedi-Khann is an Armenian and a Christian, and by birth a subject of the Persian Monarchy.[104] When he was in London (about a year and a half back) he was known as Sedi-Bey; he has since been made a Khanu [sic, Khan], or Lord of the Empire, and has been honored with the Persian Order of the Lion and Sun.[105] His influence over the mind of the hereditary Prince of Persia[106] is said to be unbounded; and we may dwell on the circumstance with satisfaction, as the enlightened European ideas which he is known to entertain cannot but be advantageous in counsels and suggestions addressed to a comparatively uninformed and semi-barbarous ruler.

Sedi-Khann is a man about 45 years of age, extremely active and persevering, even if compared with Englishmen or Frenchmen, or any other of the nations of Europe, and miraculously so if contrasted with his sluggish brethren of the East. Since his departure from England, he has twice performed the harassing journey to and from Constantinople and the Persian capital. The precise object of his present mission to the Ottoman Porte remains as yet in mystery.'

12.31 'St. Petersburg, July 15,' *Commercial Advertiser* (Tuesday, 8 September, 1829), 'St. Petersburg, July 15,' *New-York Spectator* (Friday, 11 September, 1829) and 'St. Petersburg, July 15,' *The Schenectady Cabinet* (Wednesday, 16 September, 1829): 'His Highness Chosrew Mirza, Prince of Persia, arrived on the 10th of June, at midnight in the fortress of Wladikawkask, accompanied by a numerous suite,[107] by Major General

---

[104] In a letter to Nesselrode dated Erzurum, 10 July 1829, Paskevich described 'Sadich-Khan, émissaire expédié par Abbas-Mirza à Constantinople,' who had just arrived, requesting protection from the Kurds, as 'un renégat arménien et un homme vénal.' See Stcherbatow (1891a: 284).

[105] For this order given to foreigners who performed a particular service and which had been established in 1808 by Fath 'Ali Shah, see Wright (1979, 1981), Potts (2017a: 13, n. 138).

[106] 'Abbas Mirza.

[107] According to Idesbald (1833: 10), Khosrow Mirza's suite consisted of 40–50 'personnes de tous grades.' Five of these were particularly important. These were a khan, 'ou prince suzerain, l'un des premiers chefs de l'armée. Agé de cinquante ans environ, il était grave et avait l'air fin et spirituel, mais il ne parlai aucune langue de l'Europe. On l'avait adjoint à l'ambassade pour servir de conseil et même de guide au jeune prince, qui le traitait avec beaucoup d'égards. Un autre conseiller, Mirza Babba, d'une figure assez insignifiante, et ne sachant que quelques mots d'anglais, ne jouait dans le monde qu'un rôle fort secondaire. Les trois hommes les plus remarquables de cette suite et sur lesquels il peut être intéressant d'entrer dans quelques détails étaient Mirza-Saleh, Mirza-Massoud et le capitaine Séminneau.' The unnamed khan described by Idesbald was identified in Anonymous (1829h) as the 'Ober-Befehlshaber der persischen regulären Truppen Machmed-Chan-Emir-Nisam,' whom Hasan-e Fasa'i called 'Amir-e Nezam Mohammad Khan-e Zangana, a shrewd man,' otherwise known simply as Mohammad Khan. See Busse (1972: 190). 'Mirsa-Baba' is listed in Anonymous (1829h) as Khosrow Mirza's personal physician ('Leibarzt'). In contrast Idesbald (1833: 81) wrote, 'Mirza-Saleh était le médecin du prince....Il paraissait avoir quarante ans environ; sa taille était élevée, ses traits durs, son ensemble avait même quelque chose de grossier; cependant ses yeux vifs annonçaient beaucoup d'intelligence. Dans sa jeunesse, il avait été envoyé par son gouvernement, et par l'entremise de la compagnie des Indes orientales, à l'université d'Édimbourg pour y étudier la

Rennenkamp,[108] of the suite of his Imperial Majesty,[109] and other Russian officers. A Guard of Honor was sent to meet him 12 wersts from the fortress; without the gates he was received of Major General Skworzolo,[110] the Governor, and other officers, who accompanied his Highness to the residence prepared for him, before which a guard of honor was ready to receive him with military honour as he alighted from his carriage. On the 12th, being the Persian festival of the Couram Beiram,[111] the Prince received the

---

médecine. Il y passa quatre ans avec deux ou trois de ses compatriotes, et il parlait l'anglais avec aisance.' This seems to be an error since, according to Anonymous (1829h) 'Mirsa-Sale' was Khosrow Mirza's 'Secretär' and his life is well-documented. Mirza Saleh Shirazi was one of the Persian students who was sent to England and it was he who set up a printing press in Tabriz. See Kelly (2006: 267–268), Green (2016: 2–3). Cf. 13.105, 14.134. Anonymous (1829h) identified 'Mirsa-Massud' as 'Staats-Secretär.' The Franco-Sardinian officer Barthélémy Semino was Khosrow Mirza's aide-de-camp or 'Adjutantant des persischen Erbprinzen.' After Khosrow Mirza's audience with Nicholas I, Idesbald (1833: 80) described Semino as 'un aide-de-camp du prince portant un uniforme de fantaisie, bleu de ciel et argent, et la tête couverte d'un bonnet d'astrakan; celui-là avait la barbe rasée. C'était un Français fort embarrassé de son costume et de sa contenance.' Idesbald (1833: 84–86) gave considerable detail about his career in the Napoleonic wars and how he ended up working for 'Abbas Mirza. Cf. Anonymous (1829k). Semino rose to the rank of general and in 1837 served under Mohammad Shah in the siege of Herat. Ferrier (1858: 221) described him as 'Colonel of Engineers, a Sardinian subject, and an old officer of the Empire, serving in the Shah's army as a Frenchman—his mother was French and born at St. Tropez, his father at Nice.' He was a friend of Ferrier's. The two saw each other in Tehran in 1839. See Ferrier (1856: 51). In a letter to Palmerston sent from Tabriz on 26 December 1838, John McNeill, who certainly had his sources, wrote, 'M. Semino is of French origin, but was born in one of the Greek islands, of which I believe his mother was a native. His first employment in Persia was as a draftsman to Colonel Monteith, was then employed in preparing his map of Azerbijan. From the service of Colonel Monteith, M. Semino passed into that of Abbas Meerza, and has latterly been employed by the Shah as a military engineer.' See Anonymous (1841a: 1). For his career see Mahdavi (2012). Khosrow Mirza's suite also included an executioner and a poet who wished to claim asylum in Russia but was refused by the Czar so as not to offend Fath 'Ali Shah. See Idesbald (1833: 81, 91–92).

[108] Pavel Yakovlevich Rennenkampf (1790–1857). Rennenkampf had been a member of Ermolov's mission to Fath 'Ali Shah in 1817. See Kotzebue (1819a: 68). His rank at the time of Khosrow Mirza's arrival in Tiflis was, however, that of colonel, as proven by a letter from Paskevich to Nesselrode of 2 May, 1829, in which he noted, 'J'ai envoyé à sa rencontre le colonel Rennenkampf, qui restera auprès de lui pendant tout son séjour ici.' See Stcherbatow (1891a: 282), Stcherbatow (1891b: 100). Later, following the Second Russo-Persian War, Paskevich appointed him, per a letter of 17 December, 1828, 'to determine the boundary between Persia and Russia according to the Treaty of Turkmanchai.' See Harden (1971a: 78, n. 11), Harden (1979a: 257). He stood very high in Czar Nicholas' estimation, as seen from a letter written by the Czar to Diebitsch of 12 March, 1827, in which he mentioned Rennenkampf as a potential chief-of-staff for Paskevich. See Stcherbatow (1890: 302). Khosrow Mirza presented Rennenkampf with a stallion when he was promoted to general. See Melville (2013: 89, n. 76).

[109] Nicholas I.

[110] Major-General Skworzow (Skvortsov/Skvorzov) was the Commandant of Vladikavkaz. For the correct name see e.g. Anonymous (1829f).

[111] *Kurban bayrami*. Cf. 1.155.

compliments of his suite, and of the Russian generals and officers. While his Highness stayed there, the band of the regiment played every evening under his window.[112] On the 14th [June] he proceeded on his journey to St. Petersburg, after thanking the governor, in the most flattering terms, for the hospitable reception he had met with.'

12.32 'Still later from England,' *New-York Evening Post* (Saturday, 19 September, 1829) and 'Foreign. Still later from England. New-York, Sept. 13,' *Richmond Enquirer* (Friday, 25 September, 1829): 'The Bucharest accounts, of July 14th, represent the Russians as marching upon Adrianople[113]....The apprehensions of a war between Russia and Persia have subsided, say the French papers, in consequence of the Schah[114] having sent his son [sic, grandson][115] to give satisfaction to the Emperor Nicholas for the assassination of the Russian Ambassador.'[116]

12.33 'Late from Europe,' *Boston Patriot & Mercantile Advertiser* (Thursday, 24 September, 1829), 'Foreign. Late from Europe,' *New-Hampshire Patriot and State Gazette* (Monday, 28 September, 1829),'Late from Europe,' *Eastern Argus* (Tuesday, 29 September, 1829), 'Foreign. Late from Europe,' *The Pittsfield Sun* (Thursday, 1 October, 1829), 'Latest from England,' *The Southern Patriot* (Thursday, 1 October, 1829) and 'Latest from England,' *The Charleston Courier* (Friday, 2 October, 1829), 'Untitled,' *L'Abeille* (Tuesday, 20 October, 1829): 'Prince Chosrew Mirza, the new Persian Ambassador, arrived at Moscow 25th July, and was received with the greatest honors.'

12.34 'Foreign News. Passage of the Balkan,' *New-York Observer* (Saturday, 26 September, 1829), 'Latest Foreign News. Passage of the Balkan,' *The Phenix* [Westfield NY] (Wednesday, 30 September, 1829) and 'Foreign News. Passage of the Balkan,' *Western Intelligencer* (Tuesday, 20 October, 1829): 'The French papers state, that all apprehension of war between Russia and Persia had ceased, in consequence of the

---

[112] As Mohammadi (2016: 63) noted, 'The band of the "soldats"...welcomed the Persian delegation in Vladikavkaz on June 10...On June 11, 1829, at around sunset time, the Russian "soldats" marched in front of the Prince's residence in Vladikavkaz, then performed the prayers with "the melancholy sound of muzekān", which Mostafā Afshār [Khosrow Mirza's secretary] found it being affective.'

[113] In European Turkey, close to the Bulgarian border, a 5–6 day caravan journey from Constantinople, according to Valentini (1829: 43–44). By 19 August the relatively modest Russian forces consisting of 4500 cavalry, 12,200 infantry and 100 pieces of artillery stood before Adrianople.' See Schiemann (1908: 348). Their mere presence, however, represented such a threat to Constantinople itself that the Porte capitulated. The Ottoman plenipotentiaries arrived at Adrianople on 28 August 1829 and after the signing of the Treaty of Adrianople on 2 September the Russian forces there remained until 20 November. See Moltke (1854: 445).

[114] Fath 'Ali Shah.

[115] Khosrow Mirza.

[116] Griboyedov.

Schah[117] having sent his grandson[118] to give satisfaction to the Emperor Nicholas, for the assassination of the Russian Ambassador[119] and suite. The young prince was expected in the course of last month at St. Petersburgh.'[120]

12.35 'Untitled,' *The Atlas* (Saturday, 26 September, 1829): 'The latest French papers affirm that there was no cause of further apprehension of war between Russia and Persia, the Schah[121] having sent his grandson to the Emperor[122] to give satisfaction for the assassination of the Russian Ambassador.[123] The young Prince was expected to arrive at St. Petersburg in the month of July, where he would be received in a manner worthy of his rank and the objects of his mission. These statements correspond with former advices. A later account informs us that Prince Chosrew Mirza, the new Persian Ambassador arrived at Moscow, on the 25th of July, and was received with the greatest honours.'

12.36 'St. Petersburg, Aug. 7,' *The Daily Chronicle* (Monday, 28 September, 1829): 'Prince Chosrew Mirza arrived at Moscow on the 25th of July, and was received with great honors. The Vice Chamberlain, A.V. Bulgakow, went to Kolomenskoi[124] to visit the

---

[117] Fath 'Ali Shah.

[118] Khosrow Mirza.

[119] Griboyedov.

[120] Originally, Khosrow Mirza only expected to travel to Tibilisi, the headquarters of Gen. Paskevich. As Idesbald (1833: 11–12) noted, 'la preuve, c'est qu'il y arriva avec très-peu de bagages, que les effets qu'il fit venir en suite ne le rejoignirent qu'á Moscou. Le schah n'avait pas jugé nécessaire d'envoyer un prince de son sang juqu'à Saint-Pétersbourg même, et c'était un seigneur de sa suite, Mirza-Massoud, qui devait s'y rendre en qualité d'envoyé extraordinaire. Le comte d'Érivan [Paskevich] et le prince Nicolas Dolgoroucky, qui était en route pour Téhéran avec une mission de l'empereur, déterminèrent habilement Son Altesse à se rendre jusqu'à la capital de la Russie, en lui faisant entendre que Sa Majesté Impériale avait besoin de cete acte de déférence pour croire à la sincérité du repentir du schah; et pour se laisser fléchir, après l'horrible violation du droit des gens dont son peuple s'était rendu coupable enversa sa légation, Paskéwitch lui recommanda bien expressément de n'aborder l'empereur qu'en s'agenouillant devant lui; il le répéta même à Son Altesse Royale, au moment où il prenait congé d'elle, croyant nécessaire de bien pénétrer ce prince de vénération et de crainte pour la grandeur du monarque chrétien qu'il allait visiter, et de frapper son esprit du caractère expiatoire de sa mission.' As Paskevich himself wrote to Nesselrode on 2 May from Tiflis, 'J'ignore s'il a l'autorisation d'aller à St. Pétersbourg. J'ai exposé franchement mon opinion à Mirza-Massoud et à Mirza-Salé [who accompanied Khosrow Mirza] sur l'urgence de ce voyage et c'est dans le même sens qu'est conçue ma lettre à Abbaas-Mirza, que j'ai cru devoir lui adresser itérativement et dont copie ci-jointe.' The prince reached St. Petersburg on 16 August 1829. See Lang (1948: 336).

[121] Fath 'Ali Shah.

[122] Nicholas I.

[123] Griboyedov.

[124] Estate located close to Moscow where, in 1768, Catherine the Great rebuilt the wooden summer palace originally erected in 1672 by Czar Alexis I (r. 1645–1676). Khosrow Mirza must have been

Prince, who declared he should never find words to express to the Schah[125] and the Emperor his gratitude for the attention shown him in Russia. At Moscow, the Palace of the Countess of Rosamowsky[126] was prepared for his reception. At the gate of the hotel he was received by the Commandant of Moscow[127] with a guard of honour. The Civil Governor received him at the head of the Magistrates, and the chief merchants of the city presented him with bread, salt, fruit and flowers. The arrival of Prince Gallitzin being announced, he went to meet him, shook hands with him, conversed a quarter of an hour standing, and expressed his pleasure at the good understanding that prevailed between the two Sovereigns. The next day the Prince held a grand levee, and there was afterwards a dinner for 100 persons at the Military Governor's. The healths of the Schah, of Prince Abbas Mirza and the Royal Family of Persia, of their Majesties the Emperor[128] and Empress,[129] and the Imperial Family, were drank [sic] to the sound of trumpets. Prince Chosrew Mirza joined in every toast, drinking mead. Before rising from the table, he took Prince and Princess Gallitzin[130] by the hand, begging them to stop a little, that he might drink the health of the master and mistress of the house. The Prince visited the armory,[131] where Prince Jusapow[132] showed him the sailor's dress that Peter I. wore while working as

---

impressed by his quarters there for, as Réau (1921: 265–266) wrote, 'Le palais de Kolomenskoe passait pour la huitième merveille du monde. Les voyagers étrangers étaient séduits par sa saisissante originalité.'

[125] Fath 'Ali Shah.

[126] Konstanze Dominika Razumovska, née von Thürheim (1785–1867). Second wife of Count (later Prince) Andrey Kyrillovich Razumovsky (1752–1836), Russian diplomat who was Russian ambassador to Venice, Naples, Copenhagen, Stockholm and, from 1792 to 1807 (minus the period 1799–1801), Austria where he remained, in a renowned Viennese palace, for rest of his life. A violinist, he was an intimate of Beethoven's. Konstanze von Thürheim married the 64-year old widower, who was over twice her age, on 10 February 1816. See Kleinschmidt (1877: 477–480), Clive (2001: 277–278). Built in 1819, Countess Razumovsky's palace was known as 'Perovsky House,' after the Perovko district in which it was located. See Semler (1999: 184).

[127] Dmitry Vladimirovich Golitsyn (1771–1844). Military Governor-General of Moscow from 1820 to 1844. See Bradley (2009: 58). He played an active role in the Napoleonic wars. For a summary of his military career see Mikaberidze (2005: 128).

[128] Nicholas I.

[129] Alexandra Feodorovna, née Charlotte of Prussia (1798–1860).

[130] Tatiana Vasilyevna Golitsyna, née Vasilchikova (1783–1841).

[131] The Kremlin Armoury.

[132] Prince Nikolai Borisovich Yusupov (1750–1831), 'Commander of the Moscow Expedition for Building of the Kremlin and the Workshop of the Armoury.' See Piotrovsky (2000: 56). As Idesbald (1833: 12–13) noted, 'Ce dernier, mort en 1831, était connu de tous les étrangers qui ont fait le voyage de cette ancienne résidence des czars. Possesseur d'une immense fortune, ce prince, un des derniers débris de la cour de Catherine II, aimait à exercer l'hospitalité et à faire admirer ses jardins et ses palais. D'origine tartare, il avait conservé dans ses goûts toute la pompe et toute la mollesse des Orientaux.'

a shipwright at Zaardam.[133] He took it in his hand, and looked at it with admiration. One of the suite laughing at the Emperor of Russia having worn such a coarse dress, the Prince looked sternly at him and said, "If Peter had not worn that dress, Russia would have no navy, and not be what it is." He afterwards visited the theatre, which was crowded, and surprised him by its size; he was particularly pleased with the ballet.[134] The Prince is of middle size, and well made; he has fine eyes and an agreeable smile, much dignity in his deportment, and great vivacity in conversation. He is extremely affable to all around him.'

12.37 'St. Petersburgh, August 15,' *Poulson's American Daily Advertiser* (Tuesday, 13 October, 1829): 'Prince Chosrew Mirza arrived at Zarskojasselo[135] on the 11th [August] where he was received with all due honor.[136] His highness intended to remain at Zarskojesselo on the 12th. to see all that is curious, and to go to Peterhof.[137]—Prussian State Gazette, Aug. 12.'

12.38 'Foreign Intelligence. Continuation of Extracts from French and English papers,' *New-York Spectator* (Tuesday, 20 October, and Friday, 23 October, 1829) 'Foreign

---

[133] In 1697 Peter travelled to the Netherlands. 'Mit zehn Edelleuten aus dem Gesandtschaftsgefolge, worunter sich auch sein Lieblingsadjutant Menschikow befand, erschien er in dem Städtchen Zaardam als Schiffszimmermann mit der Art in der Hand, und machte sich auf der Werste von Zaardam ohne Verzug an die Arbeit. Seine Fortschriftte im Schiffsbau waren so rasch, daß er in zwei Wochen den Rang eines Meisters erhielt.' See Ustrialow (1840: 37).

[134] None of the European newspaper accounts on which this is based mention the name of the ballet seen by Khosrow Mirza.. However, on 28 and 31 August Khosrow Mirza again visited the theater. 'Am Abend desselben Tages [31 Aug.] geruhete S[r.] Hoheit in der kaiserlichen Hauptloge des großen Theaters, der Teutschen Vorstellung des "Freischütz", bis zum Schluß der Oper, beizuwohnen. Am Freitage [28 Aug.] hatte der Prinz der Aufführung des Ballets "Zephyr und Flora" seine Gegenwart geschenkt.' See Anonymous (1829j). This is 'Zéphire et Flore, ballet anacréontique,' in two acts, choreography by Charles Louis Didelot, music by Frédéric Marc Antoine Venua that premiered on 12 December 1813. This was a reworked version of an earlier work by Didelot entitled 'Flore et Zéphire.' See Chouquet (1873: 386).

[135] Lit. the 'Czar's village,' c. 22 mi. outside of St. Petersburg, was described as 'the unique locus and laboratory of new ideas in Russian eighteenth-century architecture…No other ensemble of palaces and parks has such importance for Russian culture as Tsarskoye Selo.' See Shvidkovsky (1996: 41). Cf. Brumfield (1997: 154–156).

[136] Khosrow Mirza was received by the Grand Master of Ceremonies, Count Stanislas Potocki. See Idesbald (1833: 14). A.B. Granville said of Count Potocki, 'This nobleman is well and advantageously known by most of the people of rank in England. Attached to him are five Masters of Ceremonies.' See Granville (1829: 38). He functioned as 'maître des cérémonies suprême du couronnement' at the coronation of Czar Nicholas. See Schnitzler (1854: 456), Balleydier (1857/2: 403). Potocki died in 1831 of the cholera outbreak in St. Petersburg. See Lacroix (1868: 439).

[137] Imposing palace of Peter the Great rebuilt between 1752 and 1755 by the Italian architect Bartolomeo Francesco Rastrelli who also supervised work on Catherine the Great's palace at Tsarskoye Selo. See Brumfield (1997: 153–154). Here Khosrow Mirza was met by Nesselrode. See Idesbald (1833: 14).

Intelligence. Continuation of Extracts from French and English papers. Russia & Turkey,' *Commercial Advertiser* (Tuesday, 20 October 1829; from 'On the 22nd') and 'Untitled,' *The Delaware Register* (Saturday, 24 October, 1829; first paragraph only): 'The following account from St. Petersburgh shows that there is no danger of any breach of peace between Russia and Persia, on account of the assassination of the Russian Ambassador and suite, at Teheran, in a popular tumult:—

St. Petersburgh, Aug. 26

On the 22nd of August Prince Chosrew Mirza had his first audience of the Emperor, on which occasion he made the following speech in the Persian language[138]:—

"Most Mighty Emperor[139]—The re-establishment of the tranquility and prosperity of Persia, the cordial union which the peace between your Imperial Majesty and the great Ruler of Iram, my Sovereign and beloved Grandfather, had confirmed, irritated the demon of evil; misled by his fatal influence, a body of furious madmen ventured, at Teheran, to commit an unheard of crime, of which the Russian Legation became the victims. This deplorable event threw a veil of mourning and profound affliction over the royal house and its faithful subjects. Feth-Ali's just and noble heart so shuddered at the thought that a band of wretches had, with impious hands, torn the bonds of peace and union which he had just renewed with the great Sovereign of Russia. He chose me among the Princes of the house, and commanded me to hasten without loss of time to the capital of your Empire, convinced that my voice, faithful to truth, would be heard with kindness by your Imperial Majesty, and that my words might serve to maintain unimpaired the friendship which unites the two greatest and most powerful Sovereigns of the earth.

These are the wishes of what my august Sovereign has commanded me to be the organ.

Deign, most magnanimous Emperor, to devote to oblivion, an event which has afflicted Persia no less than Russia itself. May the world learn how, in the midst of an unparalleled crisis, the wisdom of the two Sovereigns and their reciprocal confidence succeeded in averting all dangers, in dispelling all suspicion and ... a result agreeable to the wishes of all parties.

As for myself, chosen for this mission on so remarkable an occasion, I consider myself at the summit of happiness in appearing before your Imperial Majesty, and according to the orders of my Sovereign, in exerting all my efforts to consolidate constant union between

---

[138] According to Idesbald (1833: 79), 'le prince de Perse lut un discours écrit sur une feuille de parchemin, posée au-dessus des lettres dont il était porteur. Il prononça ce discours assez étendu d'une voix assurée, mais sa diction monotone et nasale ressemblait à une psalmodie juive, dont les sons, tantôt traînans, tantôt enflés, étaient remarquables par la répétition des même consonnances. Cette déclamation, par son étrangeté, appelait involontairement le sourir, et il était temps que Son Altesse se tût, malgré le décorum de cette cérémonie. Quand l'ambassadeur eut cessé de parler, M. Rodofinikin [Konstantin Rodofinikin (1760–1838)], chef de l'institut asiatique, du département des affaires étrangères, lut, en russe, une traduction de son discours.'

[139] Nicholas I.

two great nations, which Providence itself destines to maintain a reciprocal and unalterable friendship."

The Vice-Chancellor,[140] in his Majesty's name, replied as follows[141]:—

"His Majesty the Emperor, my august Sovereign, commissions me to assure your Royal Highness that he receives with the greatest satisfaction the expressions of sorrow which you announce in the name of your sovereign. His generous heart could not but be struck with horror at a crime committed with the wretched intention of renewing the differences between two neighboring nations, but just reconciled with each other. The mission which he has given you is a fresh proof of this truth. It dispels all the clouds with which so lamentable a catastrophe might threaten the relations between Russia and Persia.—Your Royal Highness will convey these assurances to his majesty the Schah. You will convince him of the decided will of his Imperial Majesty to maintain peace, and confirm the relations of friendship and good neighborhood so happily restored by the Treaty of Turkmantschi.

The Emperor commands me to add, that the Schah could not have made a choice more agreeable to him than by giving this mission to your Highness. I hope you will find the confermation [sic] of this assurance in the feeling which I hear [sic] express to you in the name of my august master."

Letters from Tiflis of the 30th of July, say, that the body of the late Russian Ambassador, Gibojadow, had been brought to that city, and interred with all the honour due to his rank.[142]—*Hamburgh Papers*, Sept. 5.'

12.39 'Untitled,' *The National Gazette and Literary Register* (Friday, 23 October and Saturday, 24 October, 1829): 'The Persian Prince Chosrew Mirza, whose arrival at St. Petersburgh we recently mentioned, had the honor of an audience of the Emperor Nicholas on the 22nd ult. to whom he was introduced with the usual ceremony. His Highness addressed the Emperor, in the Persian tongue, to the following effect:—

"The concord and peace so happily established between your Imperial Majesty and the Prince of Iran, my Master and Grandfather, excited the indignation of the demon of evil. It was by his inspiration that a party of brigands committed a horrible crime at Teheran, of which the Russian Embassy was the victim. This deplorable event filled the royal house

---

[140] Count Karl Robert von Nesselrode. After becoming Vice-Chancellor and State Chancellor of the Russian empire, Nesselrode retained his foreign ministry portfolio. See Riasanovsky (1959: 45).

[141] As Idesbald (1833: 79) noted, 'le comte de Nesselrode fit également en russe, à Son Altesse, une réponse dont un interprète récita la traduction en persan. Une différance très-sensible existait entre sa prononciation et celle du prince, qui, dès que cet interprète eut achevé sa lecture, s'approcha de l'empereur, en s'inclinant, et lui remit les lettres du schah, au nombre de trois, que le vice-chancelier prit des mains de Sa Majesté, et déposa sur une petite table.'

[142] As Kelly (2006: 200) noted, Griboyedov's body, in a coffin, arrived in Tibilisi on 17 July 1829 and, 'The next day, the Military Governor of Tiflis attended the requiem mass in Sion Cathedral sung by the Exarch of Georgia, the Metropolitan John. His mutilated body was finally laid to rest in the monastery of Saint David on the hillside above Tiflis.'

with mourning, as well as its faithful subjects. The noble and upright heart of Feth Ali Schah shuddered with terror in thinking that a band of miscreants might have broken the bonds of peace and union which he had just formed with the great Monarch of Russia. He chose me from among the Princes of his House, commanding me to proceed without delay to the capital of your Empire, under the firm persuasion that my voice, faithful to the truth, would be kindly listened to by your Imperial Majesty, and that my words would serve to render for ever unalterable the friendship that unites the two greatest and most powerful masters of the earth. Such are the wishes of which my gracious master has rendered me the organ. Condescend, generous Emperor, to bury in oblivion a catastrophe that Persia has felt no less than Russia herself. Let the whole world learn how much the wisdom and mutual confidence of two Monarchs have succeeded, amidst the greatest crisis, and the most perplexing circumstances,—to avert all danger, to dissipate all suspicions, to remove all uncertainty, and produce a result which answers the wishes of all. As to myself, who have been honoured with so important a mission, I consider it the height of my happiness to have been admitted to appear before your Majesty, and devote my utmost solicitude to the continuance of an Alliance between two great nations whom Providence has itself destined to an eternal friendship."

The Vice-Chancellor[143] replied as follows, in the name of the Emperor:—

The Emperor, my sovereign master, has charged me to assure your royal highness that it is with sentiments of the greatest satisfaction, that he receives the expression of regret that you transmit him in the name of your powerful master. His generous heart would have shuddered with horror if such a crime had been committed with a view again to divide two neighbouring states but just reconciled. The step you have taken will disperse all the clouds with which this catastrophe seemed to threaten our two empires. Your royal highness will convey this assurance to the Schah, and express to him the firm determination of his imperial majesty to maintain the relations of friendship, peace, and good neighbourhood, which were so happily established at the treaty of Turkmantschai. The Emperor has, moreover, commanded me to say to you that the Schah could not have made a choice more agreeable to his heart, than in charging your highness with this noble mission. I hope that this assurance will now be confirmed, in your eyes, by the sentiments which I now express to you in the name of my sovereign master.'

12.40 'Extracts from English Papers. From the London Morning Chronicle of Nov. 30. Berlin, Nov. 13,' *New-York Spectator* (12 January, 1830): 'The differences with Persia are entirely arranged. The Emperor[144] has granted to the Schah[145] a reduction of several

---

[143] Nesselrode. Cf. 12.38.

[144] Nicholas I.

[145] Fath 'Ali Shah.

12 From the Murder of Griboyedov to the Death of Fath 'Ali Shah (1829–1835) 1323

millions of silver rubles of the contribution remaining to be paid[146]; and the Persian Prince[147] has left St. Petersburg to return to Teheran.'

12.41 'Asiatic Turkey,' *The Schenectady Cabinet* (Wednesday, 27 January, 1830): 'The news of the peace with the Porte,[148] was announced at Tiflis, on the 29th of October. The account before us says—

"The impression made by this happy and glorious event on the inhabitants of the territory of the Caucasus was the more lively, in proportion to the injurious effects of a war with the neighbouring States. The din of war has lasted 3 years, and we have a lively recollection the dangers and pillages which we escaped by the memorable battle of Selissawatopol.[149] The peace with Persia was a subject of great rejoicing to us, but it was followed by a war with an equal Power, and much more warlike people."'

12.42 'Untitled,' *The National Gazette and Literary Register* (Monday, 1 February, 1830), 'Late from Europe,' *Newburyport Herald* (Tuesday, 2 February, 1830), 'Constantinople, Nov. 27,' *Columbian Centinel* (Wednesday, 3 February, 1830), 'Foreign Summary. From Europe,' *Christian Register* (Saturday, 6 February, 1830), 'Foreign. Late from England,' *Farmers' Cabinet* (Saturday, 6 February, 1830), 'Foreign News. Late from England,' *Pensacola Gazette and Florida Advertiser* (Saturday, 27 February, 1830): 'The Persian Prince Chosrew-Mirza has arrived at Moscow, where brilliant entertainments were given in his honor. The Prince seemed delighted with the city, and displayed remarkable politeness and gallantry towards the ladies. He is stated to have demanded in marriage three young ladies at a time, whom he would have taken with him to Persia as his legitimate wives. When it was represented to him that such a demand was contrary to European customs and could not be complied with, he alleged ignorance as an excuse.'[150]

---

[146] As Idesbald (1833: 88) noted, 'Le principal objet de cette mission, après le pardon à implorer, c'était d'obtenir une diminution sur le troisième et dernier paiement du tribut à fournir à la Russie, en indemnité de la dernière guerre.' Furtherore, as Idesbald (1833: 91) observed, Khosrow Mirza spent nearly 2 months in St. Petersburg at a high cost borne by the Russians and, 'Pour se fair quitte de ces hôtes, le meilleur moyen était de leur accorder une partie de leurs demandes. Après de longs pourparlers, le cabinet russe consentit à abandonner la moitié du troisième et dernier paiement de l'indemnité. Ce sacrifice s'élevait à environ 2,500,000 francs.' According to Hasan-e Fasa'i, As has been reported, the sum to be paid to the Russians was fixed at 10 crore, according to the peace treaty, of which 8 crore had been paid. Of the 2-crore balance the emperor gave Prince Khosrou Mirzā 1 crore for his endeavors, and prolonged the term of payment of the other crore by 5 years.' See Busse (1972: 190).

[147] Khosrow Mirza.

[148] The Treaty of Adrianople, signed on 2/14 September 1829. Cf. Noradounghian (1900: 166–173).

[149] Elizabethpol (Ganja).

[150] Describing Khosrow Mirza's eye for women, Idesbald (1833: 13–14) wrote, 'il prit part, dans les bals, aux polonaises (promenades), que l'on rendit fréquentes pour lui, et parut très-satisfait de l'usage européen qui le plaçait dans la compagnie des dames. Il distingua particulièrement la jeune

12.43 'Foreign. Turkey,' *Kinderhook Herald* (Thursday, 11 March, 1830): 'The latest intelligence from Odessa (28th December) is, that "Halil Pacha, Ambassador Extraordinary of the Porte, has not yet received his passports for St. Petersburgh, and some persons are of opinion that he will not yet proceed thither. General astonishment is excited by the numerous and costly presents which the Ambassador is charged to deliver to the Emperor, and many believe that the Porte hopes by this means to free itself from the contribution under which it has been laid.[151]—Letters from Constantinople frankly avow this intention, and mention it as a reason for the Sultan rejecting the offer of a loan. When it is considered, however, what immense sacrifices Russia has made in this war, and their disproportion with the indemnity stipulated by the treaty of Adrianople,[152] it is not probable that the

princesse T***, et au milieu d'une fête, pour lui donner une preuve du prix qu'il attachait à son souvenir, il tira son poignard, vint à petits pas derrière cette demoiselle, et lui coupa subtilement un morceau de sa ceinture. On lui fit probablement entendre que la galanterie n'exigeait pas de tels escamotages, car depis il ne s'est plus montré aussi démonstratif. La comtesse P***, fort jolie aussi, et désirant lui être agréable, avait appris quelques mots persans dont le sens était un compliment pour le prince auquel elle les adressa. "En ce moment, madame, lui répondit celui-ci avec beaucoup de grâce, mes oreilles sont étonnées de ce qu'elles entendent, mais mes yeux le sont encore plus de ce qu'ils voient." Il prouva, dans une autre occasion, qu'il n'avait qu'une idée bien confuse de nos mœurs. Étant allé visiter, à Moscou, l'institut de Saint-Cathérine, pensionnat pour les demoiselles nobles, il fut tellement frappé de la beauté de quelques jeunes élèves, qu'en sortant il demanda à l'officier qui l'accompagnait si l'on ne pourrait pas lui en faire présent. Ce dernier, ne se souciant pas d'expliquer au prince ce que son désir avait d'irrégulier, se contenta de répondre que cela ne le regardait pas, que Son Altesse devait en parler à l'empereur.'

[151] As Schiemann (1908: 369–370) explained, shortly after the end of hostilities, the Sultan decided to send 'Halil Pascha, den Adoptivsohn seines Günstlings, des Seraskiers Chosrew Pascha, in außerordentlicher Gesandtschaft, wie der Reis-Efendi und [the Prussian General Philipp Friedrich Carl Ferdinand Freiherr von] Müffling [1775–1851] geraten hatten, nach Petersburg.' The purpose of this was to reduce the amount of war compensation demanded of the Porte. However, 'Dem Kaiser sowohl wie Nesselrode war der neu angekündigte Besuch nicht genehm.' Not only would the costs incurred by Russia by large, but the Czar wanted all of the arrangements of the peace and financial indemnity to be settled at Constantinople. Despite Russian objections to Halil Pasha's proposed visit, he arrived in Odessa in mid-November. There he was to be delayed on grounds of quarantine for as long as possible. See Schiemann (1908: 376). 'Als dann Anfang Februar [1830] endlich Halil Pascha eintraf, war der Kaiser bereits soweit, ihn am 11. in feierlicher Audienz im Georgssaal empfangen zu können. Man war sichtlich bemüht, den Türken durch Entfaltung großen Prunkes und militärischer Schaustellungen zu imponieren, und dieser Zweck ist auch erreicht worden.'

[152] Article 8 of the Treaty stipulated, 'le commerce russe ayant, depuis la conclusion de la Convention précitéee [Convention of Akerman], éprouvé de nouveaux dommages considérables par suite des mesures adoptées, touchant la navigation du Bosphore, il est convenu et arrêté que la Porte Ottomane, en réparation de ces dommages et pertes, payera à la Cour Impériale de Russie, dans le courant de dix-huit mois, à des termes qui seront réglés ultérieurement, la somme de 1500,000 ducats de Hollande, en sorte que l'acquittement de cette somme mettra fin à toute réclamation ou prétension réciproque des deux Puissances contractantes, du chef des circonstances mentionnées ci-dessus.' See Noradounghian (1900: 170–171).

Emperor Nicholas will make further concessions.[153] The contribution under which Persia was laid, was much more considerable although the sacrifices of Russia in the war with Persia were small in proportion; and the Emperor only granted to Persia a slight reduction upon the contribution, although that power made much greater cessions of territory.'"

12.44 'Latest from Europe. Paris, Feb. 18,' *Commercial Advertiser* (Wednesday, 31 March, 1830), 'Latest from France,' *New-York Evening Post* (Wednesday, 31 March, 1830), 'Latest from France. Paris, Feb. 18,' *The New-York Morning Herald* (Thursday, 1 April, 1830), 'Latest from France,' *The Pennsylvania Inquirer* (Thursday, 1 April, 1830) 'Latest from France,' *Baltimore Patriot & Mercantile Advertiser* (Friday, 2 April, 1830), 'Latest from Europe. Paris, Feb. 18,' *Phenix Gazette* (Saturday, 3 April, 1830), 'Foreign News. Latest from France,' *The Norwich Republican and Stonington Telegraph* (Saturday, 3 April, 1830), 'Latest from France,' *Richmond Enquirer* (Tuesday, 6 April, 1830), 'Latest from Europe,' *Ithaca Journal & General Advertiser* (Wednesday, 7 April, 1830), 'Foreign. Latest from France,' *Hampden Whig* (Wednesday, 7 April, 1830), 'Foreign News. Paris, Feb. 18,' *The Massachusetts Spy and Worcester County Advertiser* (Wednesday, 7 April, 1830), 'Paris, February 18,' *Norwich Courier* (Wednesday, 7 April, 1830), 'By Yesterday's Mails. Latest from Europe. Paris, Feb. 18,' *The Charleston Courier* (Thursday, 8 April, 1830), 'Latest from France,' *City Gazette & Commercial Daily Advertiser* (Thursday, 8 April, 1830) and 'From England,' *Vermont Gazette* (Tuesday, 13 April, 1830; with minor variations): 'Advices from Frankfort of the 31st inst. state after private letters from Constantinople, that an agent,[154] charged with a secret mission to the Schah of Persia,[155] has quitted that capital for Teheran.'

12.45 'St. Petersburg, Feb. 6,' *The Daily Chronicle* (Monday, 5 April, 1830): 'Prince Chosrew Mirza arrived at Tiflis on the 13th of January.'

---

[153] According to Schiemann (1908: 389) Nicholas I and his cabinet decided that, 'Von der Kriegskontribution sollten zwei Millionen Dukaten erlassen werden, eine weitere Million, wenn die Pforte ohne jede Zögerung die Entscheidungen der Londoner Konferenz in den griechischen Angelegenheiten anerkenne. Von den acht Millionen Dukaten sollten zwei sofort bezahlt werden, die übrigen in jährlichen Raten von je einer Million von Neujahr 1831 ab....Diese als äußerstes Zugeständnis bezeichneten russischen Vorschläge wurden von den türkischen Bevollmächtigten durch ein Gegenprojekt beantwortet, das als Maximum vier Millionen Dukaten bot, wobei in diese Summe auch die Entschädigung der vom russischen Handel erlittenen Verluste mit einbegriffen werden sollte. Außerdem aber forderten sie sofortige Räumung aller türkischen Provinzen. Sie erklärten sich bereit 1,600,000 Dukaten gleich zu zahlen, wollten jedoch den Rest in Jahresraten von nur 400,000 Dukaten tilgen. Aber schon nach wenigen Tagen mußte sich Halil davon überzeugen, daß der russische Vorschlag in der Tat ein Ultimatum war.'

[154] This was presumably Tibi Efendi mentioned by Stcherbatow (1891b: 75).

[155] Fath 'Ali Shah.

12.46 'Foreign,' *Kinderhook Herald* (Thursday, 15 April, 1830) and 'Foreign,' *Mechanics' Press* (Saturday, 17 April, 1830): 'Abbas [sic, Khosrow] Mirza, son [sic, grandson] of the king of Persia,[156] was making a very favorable impression on the Russian court. His appearance is elegant; he made a brief and frank address to the Emperor in apology for the massacre of the late Russian ministers; and he is very profuse with his rich presents.'[157]

12.47 'Mild and Merciful,' *Baltimore Patriot & Mercantile Advertiser* (Saturday, 7 August, 1830), 'Foreign News, from France,' *Newburyport Herald* (Saturday, 7 August, 1830), 'Foreign,' *The Portsmouth Journal and Rockingham Gazette* (Saturday, 7 August, 1830), 'Foreign. From the N.Y. Gazette. From France,' *The Corrector* (Saturday, 7 August, 1830; minus the last part beginning 'none'), 'Miscellaneous Items. Retributive Justice,' *The Massachusetts Spy* (Wednesday, 11 August, 1830; minus the preamble and the last part beginning 'none'), 'Summary,' *Augusta Chronicle and Georgia Advertiser* (Saturday, 14 August, 1830), 'Items. Retributive Justice,' *Greenfield Gazette & Franklin Herald* (Tuesday, 24 August, 1830; minus the preamble and the last part beginning 'none'), 'Summary,' *Auburn Free Press* (Wednesday, 8 September, 1830; minus the preamble), 'Mild and Merciful,' *Republican Star and General Advertiser* (28 September, 1830; minus the preamble and the last part beginning 'none'): 'The Journal de Gand [Gent] gives the following as an act of retributive justice:—"The ambassador of Russia[158] in Persia having been assassinated, the Emperor Nicholas demanded a signal reparation. The Schah[159] in compliance, banished the High Priest,[160] and ordered the noses, ears and tongues of 1500 men[161] to be cut off after they had undergone the bastionnade [var. bastinado], none of whom were guilty of the deed. Quite a mild punishment this!'

12.48 'Russia and Persia,' *New-York Spectator* (Thursday, 13 August 1830): 'Advices from St. Petersburgh, June 13, announce the departure of General Potemkin,[162] to the army on the Caucasus. It is added—Prince Chosereff, and Mirza [sic], son of Abbas Mirza, arrived at Tiflis on the 19th of May, when he was received at the gate by a detachment of

---

[156] Fath 'Ali Shah.

[157] According to Idesbald (1833: 91), 'Son Altesse...distribua des plaques de l'ordre du Soleil aux grands de la cour, offrit à l'impératrice des perles, des pierres précieuses et des cachemires d'un grand prix. Plusieurs dames eurent également des châles en souvenir.'

[158] Griboyedov.

[159] Fath 'Ali Shah.

[160] Identified by Kelly (2006: 213) as *mojtahed* 'Mirza Mesikh, the chief mulla-imam,' called one of the 'spiritual leaders of the mob in Tehran.'

[161] Similarly, in discussing the riot and murder of the Russian delegation, Stcherbatow (1891b: 123) wrote, '1500 hommes furent bientôt rassemblés, attaquèrent le palais, massacrèrent les deux filles, l'ambassadeur et tout son monde.'

[162] Count Pavel Sergeyevich Potemkin (1743–1796), 'Commander of Russian forces in the northern Caucasus.' See Atkin (1980: 38).

12 From the Murder of Griboyedov to the Death of Fath 'Ali Shah (1829–1835)

Russian troops, and conducted to the residence of Count Paskiewitsch where our Generals and the Persian Mirzas,[163] Massoud[164] and Salek [sic, Saleh],[165] who had preceded the Prince, were waiting for him. Nizim Emir,[166] a Chief of the Staff of Abbas Mirza, accompanies the Prince. The Commander-in-Chief took Prince Chosereff in his own carriage to the residence prepared for him.'

12.49 'From the Boston Daily Advertiser, June 9. Further from Turkey,' *New-York Evening Post* (Friday, 10 September, 1830): 'The Ambassador of Persia arrived at Constantinople, June 14th, with a brilliant suite.'[167]

12.50 'Late from France,' *The New-York Evening Post* (Monday, 21 February, 1831), 'Foreign News. From the Commercial Advertiser of Feb. 21. Latest from Europe. Paris, January 9,' *Chittenango Herald* (after Monday, 21 February, 1831), 'Thirteen days later from Europe. Persia,' *Albany Evening Journal* (Thursday 24 February 1831), 'Foreign,' *The Corrector* (Saturday 26 February 1831), *Greenfield Gazette & Franklin Herald* (Tuesday, 1 March 1831; first four sentences only) and 'Untitled,' *Auburn Free Press* (Wednesday, 2 March 1831): 'The St. Petersburgh Gazette of Dec. 21 [1830], contains the following: –. . . . "Persia is at this moment a prey to a horrible civil war. The eldest son[168] of the Shah[169] has raised the standard of rebellion, and marched against his father.[170] Prince

---

[163] The writer here has confused the name Mirza, as the first part of a name, with the title Mirza that follows a name, e.g. 'Abbas Mirza.

[164] Mirza Mas'ud. According to Idesbald (1833: 81), 'Mirza-Massoud avait une cinquantaine d'années; il était d'une taille moyenne, et sa physionomie expressive décelait un esprit hors du commun. Tout son extérieur était prévenant, toutes ses manières affables; quand on rencontrait son regard, on y trouvait une sorte de sympathie, ou plutôt un sentiment d'intelligence, qui semblait indiquer à une longue similitude de goûts, d'usages de pensées; on se serait cru dans la compagnie d'un homme du monde de Paris, de Vienne ou de Londres, et l'illusion devenait complète quand on l'entendait s'exprimer facilement en français avec un accent étranger assez piquant et une grande finesse de reparties.'

[165] Mirza Saleh Shirazi, Khosrow Mirza's secretary. Cf. 12.31. See Kelly (2006: 147–148 and 201) where he is described as 'the Crown Prince's ['Abbas Mirza] diplomatic adviser.'

[166] Amir-e Nezam Mohammad Khan-e Zangana. Busse (1972: 190).

[167] Mohammad Sharif Mirza Khan. Cf. 12.23.

[168] Hasan 'Ali Mirza, governor of Kerman, According to Anonymous (1873a: 715) he was Fath 'Ali Shah's sixth son. In 1824 he had been made governor of Kerman after a failed uprising by 'Abbas Qoli Mirza, who had launched an unsuccessful attack on Yazd. See Sykes (1902: 69).

[169] Fath 'Ali Shah.

[170] He 'was in a state of open rebellion.' See Gibbons (1841: 136). As Lal (1834: 178) noted, 'H.R.H. ['Abbas Mirza] hurried down to Kirmán, which was ruled by Hasan Alí Mírzá, who resided at Mashad a few years ago. He wished to wage war with Abbás Mírzá, who in the mean time frustrated his designs by sending friendly words through his cunning minister Qáim Moqám. Hasan Ali Mírzá, having trusted to the faith of Abbás Mírzá, came two days journey, received him respectfully, and conducted him to Kirman with all sorts of honor and triumph. After a few days, Abbás Mírzá (or the

Abbas Mirza hastened to the succour of his father, and is fighting against his brother. A great part of his army is organised and trained upon the European principle. The inhabitants of the caucasus [sic], habitually impatient at the yoke of Russia, have also risen in insurrection in some parts near the black [sic] and Caspian Seas. A detachment of the Russian Army has been attacked on the road to Tiflis, where it lost two pieces of cannon.[171] Marechal Paskewitz d'Erivan[172] has orders to employ considerable force, in order to subdue and punish the rebels".'[173]

12.51 'From the Journal des Debats, Feb. 8,' *Baltimore Patriot & Mercantile Advertiser* (Wednesday, 23 February, 1831), '[From the Journal des Debats.],' *Phenix Gazette* (Thursday, 24 February, 1831), 'From the Journal des Debats, Jan. 8.,' *Daily National Intelligencer* (Friday, 25 February, 1831), '[From the Journal des Debats, Feb. 8,]' *The New-London Gazette, and General Advertiser* (Wednesday, 2 March, 1831) and 'From the Journal des Debats, Feb. 8,' *Norwich Courier* (Wednesday, 2 March, 1831): 'Persia is a prey to a horrible civil war. The eldest son[174] of the Schah[175] has revolted, and marched against his father. Prince Abas Mirza has flown to the assistance of his father. A great part of his army is instructed in European tactics.

---

unfaithful Prince, as he is nominated by the conquered people), took hold of Hasan Alí Mírzá, and sent him to Tehrán, where he lives now, as a prisoner.' He rebelled again after Fath 'Ali Shah's death, contesting the succession of Mohammad Shah. Cf. de Bode (1845: 60). For his career see also Busse (1972: 459–460).

[171] Shortly after Paskevich and his army returned from their Turkish expedition, a general uprising began in the Caucasus, inflamed greatly by one Kazi Molla. The action referred to here is probably the attack c. 30 May 1830 by the inhabitants of Gyumri on General Rosen's forces as they tried to ascend a narrow defile, carrying their cannon. See Stcherbatow (1891a: 202–203). Soon after the reduction of Gyumri, Paskevich departed for St. Petersburg.

[172] The title Count Paskevich of Erivan was conferred by Nicholas I on the general after his return from Tabriz to Tiflis. A letter of 18 March 1828, written by Nicholas in his own hand was addressed to 'Comte Ivan Féodorovitch Paskévitsch d'Erivan.' In it the Emperor noted, 'Désirant que dans votre descendance se perpétue, indissolublement lié à votre nom, le souvenir de la conquête dont la Russie vous est redevable, j'ai joint à votre nom de famille celui de la redoutable place forte dont la prise a imprimé à la campagne une direction si décisive.' See Stcherbatow (1891a: 80). Cf. Christmas (1854: 42), 'he had the title of d'Erivansky conferred on him for having taken the city of Erivan;' and Müller-Simonis (1892: 60), 'Paskievitch qui emporta la ville, reçut le titre d'Erivanski.'

[173] As Czar Nicholas I wrote to Paskevich on 25 September 1829, following the war with Turkey, 'Ayant ainsi terminé une glorieuse entreprise, il vous en reste à accomplir une autre, non moins glorieuse, à mes yeux, et qui, par rapport à ses avantages directs, est infiniment plus important, c'est la pacification, à tout jamais, des tribus montagnardes, ou la destruction des rebelles. Il n'est pas indispensable d'aborder cette affaire immédiatement, mais elle doit être accomplie mûrement et très résolument, dès que j'aurai été informé de votre plan.' See Stcherbatow (1891a: 178).

[174] Hasan 'Ali Mirza.

[175] Fath 'Ali Shah.

12 From the Murder of Griboyedov to the Death of Fath 'Ali Shah (1829–1835)

The inhabitants of the Caucasus, habitually little subordinate to Russia, have raised the standard of revolt in a great number of the vallies. A detachment of the Russian army was attacked on the route to Tiflis, and lost two pieces of cannon. Marshal Paschewitz Erivan is ordered to deploy considerable forces against these insurgents.'

12.52 'Hague, January 10,' *Farmers' Cabinet* (Saturday, 26 February, 1831), 'Foreign,' *Essex Gazette* (Saturday, 26 February, 1831), 'Foreign News,' *Portland Advertiser and Gazette of Maine* (Tuesday, 1 March, 1831): 'Persia is said to be involved in a horrible civil war, the eldest son[176] of the Schah[177] having revolted.'

12.53 'Latest from Europe,' *The Liberator* (Saturday, 26 February, 1831): 'Persia is delivered up to a horric civil war. The eldest son[178] of the Schah[179] has revolted.'

12.54 'Later from Europe,' *Jamestown Journal* [Chautauqua NY] (Tuesday, 1 March, 1831) and 'Interesting Foreign News. Twelve Days Later from Europe,' *The Geneva Gazette and Mercantile Advertiser* (Wednesday, 2 March, 1831): 'Poland was exerting every nerve in preparation for the contest [with Russia]; and if the insurrection in the Caucasian department, and the civil war in Persia, which may require Russian intervention, shall extend, "powerful Russia" may find herself more fully employed than at the first outbreaking of the Polish insurrection she thought for.'[180]

12.55 'Turkey and Russia,' *Kinderhook Herald* (Thursday, 7 April, 1831): 'the Sultan,[181] it is said, is endeavoring to induce the Persians to act, so as to give employment to the Russians on that frontier.'

12.56 'Russia,' *New-York Evening Post* (Monday, 16 May, 1831) and 'Foreign Intelligence. Russia and Poland,' *Geneva Courier* (Wednesday, 25 May, 1831): 'A letter from Frankfort states that the inhabitants of the Caucasus, who have never been able to reconcile themselves to the yoke of Russia, and have seized every opportunity to get rid of the garrisons which the Russian Government keep up amongst them at a very heavy expense, upon finding that the Emperor Nicholas was drawing all his forces towards the west, have

---

[176] Hasan 'Ali Mirza.
[177] Fath 'Ali Shah.
[178] Hasan 'Ali Mirza.
[179] Fath 'Ali Shah.
[180] Paskevich was in fact reassigned from the Caucasus to Poland in late March, 1831. See Stcherbatow (1891a: 212–213).
[181] Mahmud II.

risen in insurrection, and already obtained some advantages.[182] The writer of the letter adds—"It is also currently reported that Persia has declared war against Russia;[183] and that if the [East India] Company, with whom the Porte contracted to furnish 40,000 muskets, and as many sabres, had fulfilled their engagement,[184] Turkey also, in all probability, would have come to a rupture. Of all the Powers engaged in the new coalition against France, Russia, perhaps, is the least to be feared, on account of the embarrassments created by her neighbors."—*Tribune.*'

12.57 'Still Later from Europe, *Kinderhook Herald* (Thursday, 19 May, 1831; first two sentences only) and 'Foreign Intelligence,' *Geneva Courier* (Wednesday, 25 May, 1831; first two sentences only) and 'Eight days later from England,' *The Schenectady Cabinet*

---

[182] As Brosset (1857: 331) noted, 'En 1831, il y eut de nouveau un soulèvement général des peuples du Caucase, qui se portèrent en masse sur Qizlar et sur les villages des environs: tout fut ravagé jusqu'à Stavropol. Le commandant en chef des Russes, le général en chef Emmanuel, leur ayant livré bataille en ce lieu, fut vaincu et périt lui-même dans cette affaire.'

[183] Urquhart (1863: 16) noted, with respect to Georgia, 'it was not till the Polish war of 1830–1831 that any specific plan of emancipation seems to have been formed in Georgia. The occasion was again lost between the delay and the uncertainty of information from the West, and the waiting upon movements from the East. No Polish emissaries came to them, and the Persian army, which they expected, and which, under the Crown Prince, Abbas Mirza, was actually on its march, was pursued by the Secretary of the British Legation, and forced, under a threat of war from England, to halt and to retire.' Cf. Cargill (1840: 17) who observed that the Polish revolution of 1830 had 'cast a thrill of hope throughout the nations in the East which has [sic, have] been enslaved by Russia, and among others there was a movement for liberty in Georgia. "Under the influence of this event, a conspiracy had been framed, which included almost the totality of the chief men of the country, and was favoured by the then Prince Royal of Persia, if not undertaken at his suggestion: for Abbas Mirza had so fully made up his mind upon this event, that he had already put in motion the whole of his disposable troops in Azerbigan, with the intention of marching into Russia herself; and had already been 3 days on his march when he was overtaken by a member of the British mission at Teheran, and persuaded to return."'

[184] This appears to have originated in Daud Pasha's request in late 1827 to Sir John Malcolm, then recently appointed Governor of Bombay, 'for assistance in military personnel and matériel, basing his application upon orders that he had lately received from Constantinople to organize an army of regular troops.' Included in that request were '3000 muskets and sets of infantry equipment and 400 barrels of gunpowder....The Pasha's application, which may have been prompted by the well known connection of Sir J. Malcolm with a former loan of British officers to the Persian army, as well as by the proximity of Russian forces to the northern frontier of the Pāshaliq, was strongly supported by the Government of Bombay, Mr. F. Warden, a Member of Council, alone dissenting on the ground of the disputatious and unprofitable course in the past of the British relations with Turkish 'Irāq. In May 1828, however, the Government of India decided that a courteous negative should be returned to the Pasha's request, one reason for this decision being a mistaken impression on their part that war between Britain and Turkey was not improbable in the near future, while another was a notion that the Pāsha might employ his new resources to rebel against his master the Sultān; but they authorised the purchase by an agent whom the Pāsha had deputed to Bombay of whatever military stores the Baghdād Government might require.' See Lorimer (1915: 1330–1331).

(Wednesday, 25 May, 1831): ['By the arrival of the Charlemagne, Capt. Robinson, from Liverpool on the 9th of April, we have London dates to the 8th and Liverpool to the 9th inclusive.]. . . .it is rumoured that Persia and Turkey are about to proceed against Russia. Whether this be true or not, there can be but little doubt, that these powers will avail themselves of the success of the Poles,[185] to retrieve from Russia their losses in the late wars with that power. . . .A letter from Frankfort states that the inhabitants of the Caucisus [sic], who have never been able to reconcile themselves to the yoke of Russia, and have seized every opportunity to get rid of the garrisons which the Russian Government keep up amongst them at a very heavy expense, upon finding that the Emperor Nicholas was drawing all his forces towards the west, have risen in insurrection, and already obtained some advantages. The writer of the letter adds—"It is also currently reported that Persia has declared war against Russia. . . ."[186]

12.58 'European Intelligence,' *Salem Gazette* (Friday, 20 May, 1831): 'A report is mentioned, derived from the Warsaw Journal, which does not appear to be entitled to the least credit, that the Turkish Sultan,[187] in conjunction with the Schah[188] of Persia, had declared war against Russia.'

12.59 'Russia,' *Vermont Gazette* (Tuesday, 24 May, 1831), 'Russia,' *Delaware Gazette* (Wednesday, 25 May, 1831), 'Eight days later from England,' *The Schenectady Cabinet* (Wednesday, 25 May, 1831), 'Russia,' *Washington Review and Examiner* (Saturday, 28 May, 1831), 'Russia,' *Miners' and Farmers' Journal* (Wednesday, 1 June, 1831) and 'Russia,' *Liberty Hall and Cincinnati Gazette* (Thursday, 2 June, 1831; with final sentence, 'There is nothing authentic in regard to these rumors; either of which should it be confirmed, would be of great moment in creating a diversion in favor of the Poles.'): 'Rumors were still rife that the Turkish Sultan[189] and Persia had declared war against Russia, and that Gen. Sermoloff [sic, Ermolov] who had been dismissed from the Russian service,[190] had issued a

---

[185] For the extraordinary string of Polish victories over numerically far superior Russian forces during the Polish insurrection in 1831, see e.g. Cushing (1833: 125–156).

[186] Cf. 12.56.

[187] Mahmud II.

[188] Fath 'Ali Shah.

[189] Mahmud II.

[190] As Barratt (1972: 387–389) noted, 'Nicholas I's decision to remove A.P. Yermolov from his posts as governor of Georgia and the Caucasus, commander of the Caucasian Corps of the Imperial Army and, since 1817, unofficial ambassador to Transcaucasia, is explicable only in terms of the tsar's own character. . . .Yermolov had, since becoming head of staff to Barclay de Tolly (1805–1807), pursued a brilliant military career. Supported by Alexander, who approved his plan of campaign in Dagestan (1817–1819), he had added two khanates to the Empire. . .His administrative achievements were remarkable. . .In Petersburg he was regarded as the victor of Georgia and Dagestan....Nicholas chose, perhaps unconsciously, to belittle Yermolov's achievement. . .he found Yermolov's repeated requests

proclamation from Samarad, on the banks of the Wolga, calling on all Russians to resist the despotism of Nicholas.'[191]

12.60 'Latest from Europe,' *New-York Morning Courier and Enquirer* (Tuesday, 28 June, 1831) and 'Latest from Europe,' *Rochester Republican* (after 5 July, 1831): 'A Persian Envoy, Syiad Khan, had arrived at London.'[192]

12.61 'Persia and Arabia,' *Greenfield Gazette & Franklin Herald* (after 29 November 1831): 'A foreign journal gives the following news. According to accounts from Persia, it appears that Abbas Mirza has actually marched a large force for the province of Yezd, for the purpose of securing his present ascendancy over his brother[193] on Futteh Ali Shah's

---

for reinforcements tiresome. Certain letters to Benkendorf of 1825 suggest that he suspected, or wished to be thought to suspect, Yermolov's reasons for wishing to increase the size of an army which was already large, devoted to its commander and conscious of numerous signal victories. Reinforcements were refused. When, therefore, the Mohammedan populace of Nagorno-Karabag rose en masse, on the apparent instigation of Abbas-Mirza, the Russians repulsed and suppressed them with difficulty. Yermolov had predicted such a rising. Nicholas found the news from Georgia "unsatisfactory", and resolved to replace the governor, "without noise, without scandal, and without insult."' As Gammer (2003: 181–182) noted, 'On 9 April 1827 Yermolov left the Caucasus and official service never to return. He stayed in his house in Moscow and on his estate for the last 34 years of his life never being officially involved but always up to date on events in the Caucasus.'

[191] As Anonymous (1831a), signed 'H.B. & Co.,' noted, 'the Times Newspaper has published a proclamation from Count Yermoloff to the Russian nation. This may not be the genuine proclamation of the General, and we are inclined to think it is not.' The author went on to quote the original *Times* article: 'we received, at a late hour last night, the Warsaw *State Gazette* of the 29th ult., containing the following remarkable proclamation, addressed to the Russian nation by General Yermoloff. This General, it will be remembered, distinguished himself in the Persian war, and has since been disgraced by the Court, but still possesses great influence among his countrymen. He must have himself raised the standard of revolt on the banks of the Wolga, though we have not heard of his operations, and must have sent agents to distribute this moving appeal over the rest of the empire.' The proclamation, dated 'Samarad, Jan. 29, on the banks of the Wolga,' allegedly became known when it was 'found on an officer, decorated with the order of St. George, who was killed in a recent affair.' The incendiary language in the proclamation included the lines, 'We must be free: rise, and the throne will tremble; but if the despot will arrest our enterprise, and that by the aid of those accomplices on whom he bestows all favours, in forgetting that he is our monarch and not theirs,—in forgetting that he is the father of all the Russians,—then the whole world will see that the Russians are not made for slavery,—that they must have their liberty: they can be free, and they will be free. General Jermoloff.'

[192] No ambassador from Persia was accredited in 1831, and no Persian diplomat visited Britain between Sadegh Bey, in 1826–1827, and Hoseyn Khan in 1839. See Hertslet (1891: 222). Cf. Volodarsky (1985).

[193] Hasan 'Ali Mirza. Cf. 12.50.

12   From the Murder of Griboyedov to the Death of Fath 'Ali Shah (1829–1835)   1333

death.[194] It is also reported that a considerable number of Russians had joined his forces,[195] and it was feared, should this prove true, it would be the means of placing our political relations with that country in an embarrassing situation.'

12.62 'Rebellion in Persia,' *Albany Evening Journal* (Friday, 20 January, 1832) and 'Rebellion in Persia,' *Northern Light* (Thursday, 26 January, 1832): 'We have advices from Persia which mention the commencement of the civil war in that country, to which we have before adverted. Abbas Mirza has laid siege to Shiraz, having previously made prisoner his brother, Hassed Ulie Mirza,[196] late Governor of Kerman, and all his sons, except one, who succeeded in reaching Shiraz. The south of Persia is said to be in a most dreadful state.'

12.63 'Persia. London, Jan. 14,' *The New-York Evening Post* (Wednesday, 29 February, 1832), 'London, Jan. 14,' *The Daily Chronicle* (Wednesday, 29 February, 1832; first two paras. only), 'London, Jan. 14,' *The United States Gazette* (Friday, 2 March, 1832; first two paras. only), 'London, Jan. 14,' *Newport Mercury* (Saturday, 3 March, 1832; first two paras. only) and 'London, Jan. 14,' *Richmond Enquirer* (Tuesday, 6 March, 1832; first two paras. only): 'We have advices from Persia, which contain some farther intelligence respecting the civil war, already noticed as having broken out. It appears that Abdul Rezek Khan[197] came

---

[194] Although Fath 'Ali Shah did not die until October, 1834, Hasan 'Ali Mirza rebelled in 1831. Cf. 12.50.

[195] This may be an allusion to Russian deserters who fought in 'Abbas Mirza's army.

[196] Hasan 'Ali Mirza.

[197] 'Abdul Razzaq Khan. In a letter dated 30 September, 1830, to George Swinton, Chief Secretary of Government, in India, John McNeill wrote, 'Three years ago the inhabitants of Yezd, headed by one of their hereditary chiefs, Abdul Rezak Khan, drove from the province the King's son, Md. Wullee Mirza [Mohammad Vali Mirza, Fath 'Ali Shah's fourth son; see Anonymous (1873a: 715)], whose oppressions had become intolerable. The Shah, finding that it would be difficult to reduce the country to obedience, and Abdul Rezak Khan, having tendered his submission and sent his son as a hostage, was confirmed in the government under a promise that he would deliver up the treasure amassed by Md. Wullee Mirza, which has been seized by the Khan when the Prince fled. Part of this treasure only had been surrendered, and the Prince Royal had, at the Shah's instigation, taken some steps to enforce the payment of the remainder when Hassan Ali Mirza, Governor of Kerman, sent a force against Yezd, under the command of Zekie Khan, formerly Vizier of Fars and now Minister of Kerman. A report has just reached us that Yezd has surrendered to this officer, and though it still requires confirmation, there seems to be no sufficient reason to doubt its accuracy.' See MacAlister (1910: 146–147). Cf. Watson (1866: 266–268) who noted that, before his death, when 'Abbas Mirza returned from Afghanistan to Tehran, he 'brought with him Abdul Rezak Khan of Yezd, who had risen in rebellion against the Shah during the occupation of Azerbaeejan by the Russians, and who had forced the governor of Yezd, Mahomed Veli Meerza, to make his escape from that place. This Khan had also insulted and ill-used the family of the prince, and had expelled the members of his harem from Yezd. Abbass Meerza had promised to intercede with the Shah for the pardon of these prisoners of rank; but Abdul Rezak Khan so much dreaded the effects of the revenge of

two stages to meet the Prince Royal, on his march to the city of Yezd,[198] which place he entered on the 22nd.[199]

Ramazyance[200] Hassan Allee Meerza had some time before obeyed the Shah's orders to retire, and had moved towards Kerman. After the surrender of Yezd, however, the people refused to receive him at Kerman, and his army having gradually melted away, he was not in a situation to use force against them.

Mahomed Veli Meerza, that, ere reaching Tehran, he twice attempted to commit suicide,—in the first instance by taking a large quantity of opium, and afterwards by inflicting upon himself a wound with his dagger. In this state he was brought before the Shah, and having been, along with the other wo captives, severely reprimanded, he was made over to the custody of Mahomed Veli Meerza, with the distinct understanding that, though he was to be disgraced, his life would not be taken, and that he was to receive no bodily injury. . . .The prince [Mohammad Veli Mirza] was beset by the women of his family who had been ill-treated by Abdul Rezak, and, no longer able to restrain his desire for the blood of his foe, he entered the apartment where the Khan was being attended by doctors, who were endeavouring to bandage the wound which his own hand had inflicted on his person. These were ordered to retire, and Mahomed Veli nearly severed the Khan's head from his body with one blow of his sabre. Upon this the women of his family rushed into the apartment, and after having mangled the body, caused it to be thrown out into the street.' A different version of events is given in Goldsmid (1867: 277), 'During the reign of Fath Ali Shah. . .Yezd was governed by one of his numerous sons, Mohamed Wali Mirza, who, in course of years, had amassed an unusually large fortune, even for a prince. Called, probably on this account, to Teheran by his father, he left his government, his harem, and his money in charge of his Vizier Mirza Abdul Rezak, who, during the absence of the Prince took possession for himself of all that had been entrusted to him, raised an army, and became Yaghi or rebellious. The Shahzadeh [Mohammad Vali Mirza] on his return from Teheran being refused entrance, brought a force and besieged the city. After a long defence, during which the city was almost destroyed, Abdul Rezak was forced to flee, first to Kirman and then to Meshed, where he took *bust* or sanctuary in the sacred shrine of the Imam Reza. Here, of course, he might have remained in safety, but he was induced by Abbas Mirza, the heir apparent to the throne, to leave his refuge and throw himself at the feet of the King. Disregarding the promises of forgiveness held forth by his son, the Shah ordered the wretched Vizier to be given over to the vengeance of the harem he had dishonoured; when the women, armed with bodkins and scissors, speedily put him to an ignominious death.'

[198] As Lal (1834: 177) noted, 'H.R.H. Abbás Mírzá set out from Tabrez towards Yazd, the ruler of which place, Abdul Razá Khán, came out and acknowledged obedience to Abbás Mírzá, who appointed his nephew, Saif Malik Mírzá, governor of Yazd.

[199] According to Markham (1874: 400), 'In March 1831, 'Abbas Mîrzâ commenced his advance towards Yezd and Kirmân, to reduce the Governor, who was in a state of open rebellion, and to restore order. He crossed the desert from Kashân and occupied Yezd on the 25th, Kirmân falling into his hands on the 5th of the following month.' In discussing the superiority of 'Abbas Mirza's forces, thanks to his employment of English military officers, Stocqueler (1832: 172) observed that, 'During the past year (1831) they took the fort of Baft near Yezd, unaided by artillery, and opposed to a body of defenders far superior to them in numerical strength.'

[200] 'Ramazyance' is a corruption of the name of the ninth month in the Islamic calendar, Ramadan. Hence the meaning of the sentence has been distorted by the full stop after '22nd,' and the date '22 Ramadan,' when 'Abbas Mirza is meant to have entered Yazd, i.e. 6 March 1831.

He therefore proceeded to Sherei Baee,[201] where he was in like manner refused admittance, and was understood to be, with a few followers, at a village on Fars. The Shah had issued a firman, addressed to Abbas Meerez [sic, Mirza], directing him to collect and transmit to the Royal Treasury the arrears of revenue due by Yezd and Kerman, and, as this afforded a good pretext for interfering with the latter province, there was no doubt but Abbas Meerez would eventually establish his ascendancy in the southern portion of the empire. The early settlement of the dispute had proved very fortunate, for the Uzbecks had invaded the province of Khorassan, with an army of 40,000 men and 40 guns, under the command of one of the sons of the late Mahomed Rahun Khan, Khiva,[202] who had been invited there by the refractory Chiefs of Kala[203] and Tarbut.[204] The Uzbecks, by the same accounts, had reached Radean [sic, Radkan], two stages from Meshed, for the safety of which city great apprehensions were entertained. These invaders had frequently entered Khorassan before, but hitherto the object has been merely plunder, but, from the present preparation, and the magnitude of their force, it was feared they meditated a permanent conquest. It was, therefore, supposed, that Attabas [sic, 'Abbas] Meerza would [be] compelled to march to Khorassan.[205] These advices state that Russia had agreed to

---

[201] Shahr-e Babak, located roughly equidistant between Kerman, Yazd and Shiraz. See MacGregor (1871: 546), Le Strange (1905: 286–287).

[202] Mohammad Rahim, Khan of Khiva (r. 1806–1825). He was described as 'a man as much favoured as enterprising, and who has succeeded in subjecting several Turcoman hordes in the south-east and west. His territory extends from the Caspian Sea to the frontier of Bokhara....The avaricious Mahomed Rahim appears to be pleased when he hears of the plundering of Russian and Bokharian caravans, and the Khivans often make raids into the heart of the Bokharian country, although they dare not take the field openly, for Bokhara contains six times the population of Khiva.' See Meyendorf (1870: Appendix 3, v). On the submission of the Tekke Türkmen to him see Fraser (1825: 259). According to Muraviev (1823: 231, n. 1), 'Les vues ambitieuses de Mohamed-Rahim, khan actuel de Khiva, ont fixé son attention sur ces Kirghis. Durant mont séjour dans ses états, il projetait d'occuper l'embouchure du Sir-Déria: il y envoya des troupes, le bruit courait qu'il voulait construire un fort sur ses rives, pour tenir en respect les hordes des Kirghis qui s'y trouvaient, et menacer les caravanes qui faisaient le commerce de la Boukharie avec Orenburg. Sie ce plan s'exécute, la Khivie sera bornée au nord par l'embouchure du Sir, qui court de l'est à l'ouest, et se jette dans le lac Aral; et l'influence de cet état s'étendra sur les tribus kirghis, contiguës à celles qui sont sous la protection de la Russie.' Mohammad Rahim is buried in the Palvan-Ata mosque at Khiva which he built in 1811. See MacGahan (1874: 297).

[203] Kalat, Khorasan.

[204] Torbat-e Heydari, Khorasan.

[205] As Markham (1874: 402) noted, after restoring order at Yazd and Kerman, 'Abbas Mirza 'marched with his army towards Khurâsân, taking the road by Isfahân and Kâshân to Samnân. He was accompanied by his son Muhammad Mirza, the Kâïm-Makâm, Colonel Shee [Potts 2017a: 6], who had long been employed in disciplining the troops in Azerbaijan, and some English drill serjeants. He reached Mâsh-had on January 12, 1832, and commenced a campaign against the turbulent and almost independent chiefs of Khurâsân.' Markham (1874: 407) was of the belief that 'Abbas Mirza 'undertook his campaign in Khurâsân, not to put an end to...Turkmân atrocities [treatment of slaves], or to destroy the vile slave markets of Khiva, but to reduce the hereditary

abandon her claim of 1 crore of tomauns, still due from the indemnity stipulated in the last treaty, on condition that Persia would unite with her in an attack on Khiva,[206] the avowed object of which is to put down the slave-trade in that country, where there were 10,000 Russian, and twice the number of Persian, slaves.[207] It is said that there was good reason to suppose that the Persian Government had already taken steps for securing the advance of Russian troops towards Khiva, or that they had made proposals to that effect, which, if acceded to, must have the effect of giving that country a preponderating influence with the

---

nobility of an important Persian province, and to extend the dominion of the Shâh to the banks of the Oxus. These were the avowed objects.'

[206] In 1833 Chesney wrote, 'Scarcely was the ink dry after Hussein [sic, Khosrow] Meerza's return from St. Petersburg, when the object of the article of the treaty became apparent, by the demand of Russia to be allowed to punish the Usbecks, separately or conjointly with Persia. Finding herself thus committed, Persia, instead of endeavouring to extricate herself, got deeper into the trammels, by discussions on the subject, during which it was broadly hinted by her late enemy, that she might indemnify herself to the eastward for the loss of Georgia, and that Russia was ready to assist her with officers and arms, and would furnish and pay from two thousand to four thousand body guards for the Prince; and, if the same report be true, by the remission of the last crore for the Russian army. These offers are said to have proved too tempting for the Prince Royal ['Abbas Mirza], who consented to the combined movement, and he had already received twelve field-pieces, two thousand stand of arms, and an officer of the Etat Major, Baron d'Aube, to march on Khiva and Bockhara, when the well-timed interference of the British mission....More recently, according to report, the Emperor of Russia has written to the Shah and Prince Royal, offering to contribute towards the expences of the Khorassan campaign.' See Chesney (1836: 497–498).

[207] In a study drawn up in 1833, Chesney (1836: 499–501) wrote, 'The design against Khiva became known by pure accident. Yalantoosh Khan was about to proceed thither on a special mission from the Prince, to demand the restitution of all the Russian and Persian slaves, with a future annual tribute of 1000 tomauns. The Envoy was provided with letters from the Russian officer, Baron d'Aube, which, in case of a refusal, he was to give to a Russian agent, pointed out at Khiva, who was to forward them to a sea-port on the Aral, so as to reach Count Suchtelen, the Governor of Orenburg, who would in consequence have put troops in march to meet them, and effect the demand by force of arms. This was to have taken place in April, as was admitted by the Minister of Abbas Meerza, who had ineffectually opposed Abbas Meerza's present understanding with Russia, being quite aware that a march on Bokhara would end by placing that country at the feet of Russia: because, after once obtaining a footing on any pretext, such as repressing the Uzbeck's slavery, Russia would always have the same motives to urge as excuses to continue to maintain her ground. During the discussions which followed the discovery of tthe Khiva mission, Abbas Meerza admitted that *the Russians watched his progress eastward with the greatest anxiety and interest*, but that he had not asked assistance since last year, when it was opposed by our Envoy; and that the offers on the present occasion were made by the Russian Government spontaneously, to relieve the Prince's difficulties, and see him through them without humiliation. Thus the Russians pursue one steady course of policy, in order to gain all the influence possible in the Persian councils—doubtless with a fiew to the East, which Yermoloff has been heard to say should be the real policy, giving up European affairs.'

Court of Persia,[208] which, in its present weak and distracted state, appears scarcely capable of maintaining a perfectly independent position with regard to its formidable neighbors.'

12.64 'Persia,' *New-York Spectator* (Friday, 2 March, 1832): 'The latest advices received in England from Persia represent that the civil war had been nearly quelled. The Prince Royal had entered the city of Yezd, being met on his way by Abdul Rezek Khan, at two stages from the city. Hassan Allee Meerza had retired, pursuant to the Shah's order, and moved towards Kerman, where, as well as in other towns, the people refused to receive him; and he was left at the last accounts with a few followers, at a village on [in] Fars. This was effected in good time, as the Usbecks had invaded Khorassan, with a force of 40,000 men and 40 guns, not, apparently, with more predatory views, but to make a permanent conquest.

It was supposed that the Prince Royal, Abbas Meerza, would march to Khorassan. It is intimated that the Court of Persia, in its present weak state, is pretty much under the management of Russia, which power had agreed to abandon her claim for 1 crore of tomauns, still due, by the last treaty, on condition that Persia would join in the attack on Khiva, where the slave trade is carried on, and where 10,000 Russians, and twice as many Persians, are in bondage.'

12.65 'From Europe,' *American Traveller* (Tuesday, 6 March, 1832), 'Untitled,' *New-York Evening Post* (Wednesday, 7 March, 1832), 'Latest from England,' *Phenix Gazette* (Friday, 9 March, 1832), Latest from England,' *New-York Spectator* (Friday, 9 March, 1832), 'Still later from Europe,' *The Albany Argus* (Tuesday, 13 March, 1832), 'Still later from Europe,' *The Geneva Gazette and Mercantile Advertiser* (Wednesday, 14 March, 1832), 'Latest from England,' *Spirit of the Times* (Wednesday, 14 March, 1832), and

---

[208] As Chesney (1836: 473–474) wrote, 'it is…no very difficult task for such a cunning, calculating power as Russia to gain a very commanding interest [in Persia], for which purpose she has only to espouse the cause of any one of the Princes, whose success must then be certain, distracted as the country is. Thus placed on the throne at the expence of a heavy load of debt, in gratitude and cash, he must in spite of himself become the mere tool of Russia, which power would in this way succeed in obtaining the real disposal of all the resources of Persia.' Further, Chesney (1836: 498–499) noted, 'it is but too apparent that there is an understanding with Russia in the movements eastward; whether it be sincere on the part of Abbas Meerza, or merely a temporary expedition to get out of the debt, without foreseeing the evils of calling in foreign assistance against the Khan of Khiva and others.' When Rev. Joseph Wolff visited 'Abbas Mirza on 19 July, 1831, in his tent outside Tabriz (where he and his entourage had gone because of the cholera outbreak in the city), he observed, 'the Russian Secretary, who was writing a letter, took no notice of the prince. I felt much for his Royal Highness to be treated thus,' but 'as he associates much with the Russians, and courts them, they treat him without respect.…When the Russians approached Tabreez, Abbas Mirza fled with 20 men from Salmoot. When Dr. came to him, and told him that Paskewitsh had arrived at Tabreez, Abbas Mirza said, "My father has money enough. Let their father be burnt (the Russians). Let the rascals take money, and go about their business (Pool begherand rah berawand), for they know that they can take the country whenever they please "' See Wolff (1833: 35).

'Foreign Intelligence. Still Later,' *Delaware Gazette* (Wednesday, 14 March, 1832): 'A Paris paper states, it does not appear on what authority, that Russia has formed an alliance with the Schah of Persia,[209] to reconquer Khiva, and was negotiating for a free passage to Herat, on the road to Cabul. It is alleged that Russia has offered to repay to Persia the expenses of the last war, on condition of being permitted to have a free passage through the North of Persia.'[210]

12.66 'Persia,' *New-York Evening Post* (Monday, 11 February, 1833): 'The last accounts from Bombay state that some sensation had been created by the receipt of letters from Persia, announcing that Prince Abbas Mirza had ordered 30,000 men to march upon Hirat,[211] and that this movement was only preparatory to an advance upon India, in conjunction with Russia.'[212]

12.67 'Turkey,' *New-York Evening Post* (Monday, 25 March, 1833): 'Extract of a letter from Constantinople, dated the 16th Jan.: "The arrival of the Persian Ambassador created a powerful sensation here, particularly when it was asserted that he came to offer essential assistance to the Porte[213]; but on its becoming known that

---

[209] Fath 'Ali Shah.

[210] As Chesney (1836: 500–501) noted, 'from all accounts Dolgorouky's chief occupation (when at Ispahan 2 years ago [1829]) was in making inquiries about the practicability of the different routes towards the Indus through Herat, Cabool, &c.; and it is to be feared that the communication which must, in all human probability, follow the King's death, will give Russia such a commanding influence in Persia, that she can easily make the country a stepping-stone onwards, since whatever Prince may be placed on the throne by her support will naturally become her willing instrument, and through him, and his nominal Government, the resources of the kingdom would in reality be more effectually at command, than if it were an open conquest: and as Russia probably looks before her in this way, she is naturally willing to sacrifice the remainder of the debt, and give up other points, perhaps Georgia itself, to urge Persia onwards in the east, where she knows the Prince must fail, *unless he calls in her assistance*, or receives our's in sufficient time.' Cf. Lang (1948: 335–336).

[211] Herat. 'Abbas Mirza confided to McNeill 'that he felt his military reputation had suffered by his being defeated by an enemy too strong for him—Russia, and that his brothers would therefore entertain hopes of opposing him with success. He, on this account, sought for a field in which to employ his army, and proposed the subjugation of Khorassan, which had long been in a state of nearly open rebellion, his ulterior object being an attack upon Herat, which at one time had formed part of Persia, as it was under the sufawi dynasty.' 'Abbas Mirza deparPrimary> early in 1832. See MacAlister (1910: 154–155).

[212] In fact, 'Abbas Mirza used his alleged 'Russian collaboration' as a means of extracting a 100,000 toman subsidy from the British 'in return for the abandonment of the Khivan embassy, the rejection of the alleged Russian aid, and the expulsion of two so-called Russian observers from the Iranian camp.....Far and wide went the impression that Britain feared a Russian attack on India and that she connected this menace with the Iranian threat to Afghanistan.' See Yapp (1980: 115).

[213] The Porte was under tremendous pressure. Daud, the pasha of Baghdad, had withheld forces demanded during the Russo-Turkish war and was declared a rebel by the Sultan. Then, in October,

the Schah[214] required the cession of the pachalich of Bagdad[215] as the price of his succour, the affair was considered in a very different light.'

12.68 'Turkey and Egypt,' *New-York Evening Post* (Monday, 8 April, 1833), *Evening Journal* (Monday, 8 April, 1833), 'Latest from Europe,' *New-York Spectator* (Monday, 8 April, 1833), 'Turkey & Egypt,' *Utica Sentinel & Gazette* (Tuesday, 9 April, 1833) and 'Latest from Europe,' *The Schenectady Cabinet* (Wednesday, 10 April, 1833): Paris, Feb. 22.—The Augsburgh Gazette of the 19th inst. states that...the Persian Envoy has frequent conferences with the Reis Effendi.'[216]

12.69 'From the New York Gazette,' *Pennsylvania Inquirer and Morning Journal* (Tuesday, 25 February, 1834), 'Latest from France,' *The United States Gazette* (Wednesday, 26 February, 1834), 'From France,' *American & Commercial Daily Advertiser* (Thursday, 27 February, 1834) and 'Foreign Intelligence,' *Eastern Argus* (Friday, 28 February, 1834): 'Letters from Tiflis mention the death of the celebrated Persian Prince Abbas Mirza.'[217]

1832, the Porte suffered a heavy defeat at Konya at the hands of Mehemet 'Ali Pasha's Egyptian forces. See Longrigg (1925: 262, 274). Fath 'Ali Shah presumably saw an opportunity here that he hoped to exploit.

[214] Fath 'Ali Shah.

[215] According to McNeill (1836: 108), 'Tymour, Pasha of Van, on the approach of the Russians [before the end of the Russo-Turkish War], sent a message to the Prince Royal of Persia ['Abbas Mirza], offering to deliver up his Pashalic into His Royal Highness's hands, if he would engage to protect it from the Russians, and surrender it to the Porte at the termination of the war.' On the other hand, 'The Pasha of Bagdad, when the Russians invaded Turkish Armenia, was a Georgian of the name of Daud or David, a man of much energy and ambition, who aimed at establishing his own independence. A brother of the Pasha, who had continued to reside in his native country, and was now therefore a Russian subject, carried on a petty trade between Tiflis and Bagdad, and became the medium of communication between his masters and his brother. Almost all the offices of trust in the Pashalic were held by Georgians, and they all had connexions in their native country,—many of their nearest relatives were in the Russian service. The influence of the government of Georgia in Bagdad began to be felt, and when General Paskevitch found himself at Erzeroom, on the banks of a branch of the Euphrates, and not far from the stream of the Tigris, he conceived the project of descending these rivers, and occupying the modern capital of Assyria and Mesopotamia. But the successes of General Diebitch on the Balkan had placed Russia in so advantageous a position, with means so inadequate to maintain it, that it was considered imprudent to hazard a failure on the side of Asia, and the Emperor therefore abandoned the enterprise, for a time.' For Ottoman attempts to rein in Daud Pasha's authority see Venturini (1833: 595–596).

[216] 'Akif Pasha (1787–1845), a writer who became Reis Efendi in 1832. See Wasti (2014: 502, n. 18).

[217] This occurred on 21 October, 1833. See MacAlister (1910: 168).

1340　　　12　From the Murder of Griboyedov to the Death of Fath 'Ali Shah (1829–1835)

12.70 'Latest from England,' *Pennsylvania Inquirer and Morning Journal* (Wednesday, 12 March, 1834), 'Latest from England,' *The United States Gazette* (Saturday, 15 March, 1834) and 'Untitled,' *The Charleston Courier* (Thursday, 20 March, 1834): 'Accounts from Constantinople to Dec. 31, confirm the death of the Persian Prince Abbas Mirza, and that the Schah himself[218] was dangerously ill. In the event of his death the son of Abbas Mirza,[219] it was supposed, would succeed to the throne of Persia without opposition.'

12.71 'Persia,' *New York Spectator* (Wednesday, 12 March 1834): 'Commercial letters from Bagdad states [sic] that Persia is in a state of insurrection, and Mirza Momammed [sic] Khan, son of Abbas Mirza, had applied for the assistance of Russia[220] against four or five of his brothers,[221] who dispute his right of succession to the throne.—According to some versions, a corps of the Russian army in Grusia (Georgia) has marched to the frontier of Persia; according to others, troops have already passed the frontier.'

12.72 'Persia,' *National Gazette and Literary Register* (Thursday, 13 March, 1834), 'Persia, *Vermont Gazette* (Tuesday, 18 March, 1834), 'Persia,' *Cortland Advocate* (Thursday, 20 March, 1834): 'The death of the Persian prince, Abbas Mirza, is not only

---

[218] Fath 'Ali Shah.

[219] Mohammad Mirza.

[220] After the death of 'Abbas Mirza, Mohammad Mirza, who was at the time campaigning with his father in Khorasan, was appointed governor of Azerbaijan and Khorasan. See Anonymous (1839b: 1), an extract of a letter from the British Secretary of Embassy and briefly (3 September-30 October 1832) Acting Minister Plenipotentiary at the Court of Russia in St. Petersburg (Cook and Keith 1975: 167), John Duncan Bligh (1798–1872), to Palmerston, dated 3 January 1834; this is confirmed by von Tornau (1848: 408). Later in the year, when Fath 'Ali Shah died, the Russian ambassador, Count Ivan Osipovich Simonich (1794–1851; in office 1832–1838), was with Mohammad Mirza in Tabriz. See Brosset (1857: 332). As Fraser (1840/2: 257) noted, although the English officers and diplomats in Iran were actively involved in advancing Mohammad Mirza's succession, 'the Russians offered troops to put the Shah upon the throne, without expense or trouble.' Nevertheless, Fontanier (1844: 345) quoted Col. Passmore as saying, 'si le schah se laisse guider par la Russie, nous donnerons de l'argent à son cousin pour qu'il le renverse, et lui fournirons des officiers pour l'aider.' In the end Mahomed Mirza was chosen, with the approval of both Powers' [i.e. England and Russia]. See MacAlister (1910: 170).

[221] According to von Tornau (1849: 408), 'die wichtigsten der Thron-Prätendenten waren die Prinzen von Kermanschahon, Schiraz, Mazenderan, und der Zelli-Sultan, Gouverneur der Stadt Teheran.' However, Fath 'Ali Shah did not die until October, 1834. Perkins (1834) wrote hyperbolically, '*Persia* is now the scene of great political commotion. Abbas Mirza, the heir apparent to the throne, is dead; and his father, the king, is apparently near his end. On the demise of the latter, about *three hundred* and *seventy sons* will contest, with the sword, if need be, their conflicting claims to the crown.'

12 From the Murder of Griboyedov to the Death of Fath 'Ali Shah (1829–1835)

confirmed, but in addition it is added, that the Shah[222] himself is dangerously ill. His death is daily expected,[223] and in that the son of Abbas Mirza,[224] it was supposed, would succeed to the throne.'

12.73 'Russia and Turkey,' *The Schenectady Cabinet* (Wednesday, 30 July, 1834) and Russia and Turkey,' *Long Island Farmer and Queens County Advertiser* (Wednesday, 30 July, 1834): 'There are some accounts of difficulties having arisen between Russia and Turkey, in relation to the frontiers which are to divide the two countries, and Russian troops have, it is said, advanced beyond the line stipulated by the late treaty.—There are also rumors of war between Russia and Persia.'[225]

12.74 'Constantinople. June 17,' *Long Island Farmer and Queens County Advertiser* (Wednesday, 20 August, 1834): 'A treaty is said to have been formed between England and Persia, on the same basis as that between Persia and Russia.'

12.75 'From Canton,' *New York Daily Advertiser* (Monday, 20 October, 1834): 'The Prince Royal of Persia, Abbas Merza, died at Meshed, where his R.H.[226] was engaged in carrying on the war against Herat.'

12.76 'Persia,' Boston Recorder (14 November, 1834): 'By private letters from Bushire, we understand, that it is intended by the Persian Court, to send an embassy to London, relative to the question of accession to the throne of Futtee Ali Shah. The matter of dispute is whether Ali Mahummed Mirza, a youth of 21 years of age, and son to the late Abbas Mirza, will succeed the old King, or whether the Prince of Schiraz, now the eldest son of

---

[222] Fath 'Ali Shah.

[223] As Fraser (1838b/1: 405–406) noted, 'Every one is looking out for the death of the Shah, whose health, we learn, has long been precarious, and a general scramble is almost daily expected. Even a few days before we reached Câsveen, in consequence of a strong report of the King's death having prevailed, the chiefs of the Eeliaut tribes, living within the walls, rose with their people and shut the gates, with the intention, no doubt, of a regular pillage, or something of the kind. The shops were shut, the people took to hiding their property, and all was in the greatest confusion: when the arrival of a chupper from Tehran, with tidings that the King was not only alive, but that he had gone out to hunt, a day's journey from the capital, dissipated the hopes of the turbulent, and restored order in the city.' Fath 'Ali died on 23 October 1834. See MacAlister (1910: 168).

[224] Mohammad Mirza.

[225] After 'Abbas Mirza's death, 'Russia, to whom a crore of tomâns was still due of the war indemnity, hoped to place the weight of her power and influence so that whoever was chosen would appear to owe the throne to her.' See MacAlister (1910: 170).

[226] His Royal Highness.

the King,[227] will be preferred to that dignity and power.[228] It is generally however, expected that the settlement of the question will lead to much bloodshed. A report is current, that Bassora is occupied by Mahommed Ali Pacha.[229] Two American ships of war, named the "*Peacock*" and the "*Boxer*," were a few months since at Muscat, proposing to the Imaum[230] a treaty of peace and commerce, which has been graciously accepted and entered into.[231] In consequence of this, His Majesty's Frigate *Imogene* has been dispatched

---

[227] Hoseyn 'Ali Mirza Farman-Farma, governor of Fars and fifth son of Fath 'Ali Shah. See Anonymous (1873a: 715), Busse (1972: 233).

[228] Shoberl (1828: 32–33) wrote, 'Hussain Ali Mirza, governor of Shiraz, is next to Abbas the greatest favourite with his father. His person and manners are dignified, but his disposition is very different from that of his brother Abbas. Pleasure is the sole occupation of Ali Mirza, who divides his time between the chase and his harem. The revenues of his province are squandered in silly expenses, in magnificent hunting equipages, splendid dresses, and the purchase of beautiful women. This prodigality pleases the Persians, and those people, who love to find defects in their superiors and to reveal them, speak of the prince with commendation only. He has none of those sanguinary inclinations inherent in despotism: he has never caused ears or noses to be cut off or eyes to be put out: the bastinado is the only punishment inflicted by his command.'

[229] Haji Mohammad 'Ali Ridha Pasha, commonly known as 'Ali Pasha, he had been sent in February, 1831, to remove the recalcitrant Daud Pasha. The occupation of Basra refers to the short-lived rebellion there of 'Abd al-'Aziz, the former governor, in 1833, which was put down by 'Ali Pasha's troops. See Longrigg (1925: 282), Khayyat (1976–1977: 132).

[230] Seyyid Sa'id (d. 1856). For his life see Badger (1871: lxxxi–xcvi).

[231] For the account of this embassy see Roberts (1837: 5–6) who noted that 'our government...resolved to despatch the United States' sloop-of-war *Peacock* and schooner *Boxer*...to convey to the courts of Cochin-China, Siam and Muscat, a mission charged to effect, if practicable, treaties with those respective powers which would place American commerce on a surer basis, and on an equality with that of the most favoured nations trading to those kingdoms.' According to Ross (1884: 30), 'The arrival at Muscat...of the United States sloop-of-war *Peacock* with Mr. Roberts, who had been appointed Plenipotentiary to negociate a treaty of amity and commerce with the kingdom of 'Oman, was a notable event in the life of Sa'eed. The growing importance of Muscat and Zanzibar as commercial depôts had begun to attract foreign merchants, and improvements in the customs regulations soon became a necessity. The chief part of the trade and customs farm was still, as it had been for centuries, in the hands of Indian traders, whose position was well known and assured, and in whose favour no cause had arisen for England to interfere. The American merchants, however, were in a different position. They had only begun to trade at Zanzibar some 10 or 12 years before, and the heavy exactions and constant annoyances to which they were subjected by the Customs House farmer and Indian traders, who were jealous of interlopers, compelled them to make representations to their Governments, which thus took the lead in entering into engagements with 'Oman to remove grievances and place its commerce on a secure and satisfactory basis. The treaty which was concluded in September 1833 was of a comprehensive character and well considered in its details, and formed the prototype on which the English and French treaties were subsequently drafted.' Cf. Kelly (1968: 236). For the text of the American-Omani treaty see Anonymous (1856d), Hurewitz (1956: 208).

to Zanzibar, where the Imaum is at present residing.[232] Several of the Company's Cruizers have gone to Bahrem,[233] a flourishing island on the Arabian side of the Persian Gulph, in order to blockade the place, in the event of redress being refused for a gross outrage committed on the Company's Agent there.[234] It appears that he has been bastinadoed, and a considerable sum of money extorted from him.[235] The Resident at

---

[232] Anonymous (1834d) added, 'A private letter says:—"Capt. Hart, in the *Imogene,* has recently been sent to the Persian Gulf, on a mission to the Imaum of Muscat, relative to a treaty which his highness has recently concluded with the American government, by which they would be entitled to make a settlement at Zanzibar, or on any other part of his coast. The result of the missiion has granted to England the same indulgence, should it become requisite. The Imaum testified his perfect satisfaction in the sought arrangement. He presented to Capt. Hart a Persian horse of the pure breed. His highness's squadron was at sea, consisting of one line-of-battle ship, two frigates, two corvettes, and two brigs. The *Imogene,* a command of Capt. Blackwood (he having been restored to health), has since been despatched to China."' According to Ross (1884: 30), 'It was not in accordance with Sa'eed's character that he should allow the opportunity to slip without intriguing to gain some advantage for himself, and, as the conquest of Mombasa was the matter now uppermost in his mind, he offered to allow the Americans to erect factories where they pleased, at Zanzibar or on the East African coast, on condition of their rendering him armed assistance in the prosecution of his plans. It does not appear that the United States Government reciprocated Sa'eed's views, nor is it likely they would have consented to engage in such an enterprise, but the news of the proposal was received in India with the reverse of pleasure, and Her Majesty's ship *Imogene* was soon despatched to observe the state of affairs. Captain Hart reached Zanzibar in 1834 and was able, not only to frustrate the proposed scheme, but to obtain Sa'eed's consent to the negociation of a similar treaty with England.' For his visit to Zanzibar see Hart (1856). Cf. Miles (1919/2: 335–336). As Badger (1871: lxxxiii), 'From 1829 to 1844 the Seyyid Sa'id was engaged in consolidating his territories on the east coast of Africa,' while 'the frequent absence of the Seyyid at Zanzibar, which he eventually made his principal residence, produced a succession of intestine disorders in 'Omân and greatly weakened his authority in that quarter.'

[233] Bahrain.

[234] Khushal was a Sindhi Hindu serving as Acting Agent on Bahrain during his brother Chandu's absence in India. Chandu had been appointed in 1829 or 1830 by the Resident at Bušehr, Capt. David Wilson. See Onley (2007: 140). He was assaulted by three men in 1834.

[235] According to Kemball (1856: 383), 'At this time a gross insult was offered to the British Government in the person of its Native Agent, by the sons of Shaikh Abdoolla bin Ahmed. The cause of dispute would appear to have been a sum of money due by the Agent, on account of some mercantile transactions, to the Shaikh himself, which his sons were desirous of possessing, in opposition to their father's wishes. They demanded, and by abuse and ill-treatment enforced, payment of certain large sums of money; nor would the old Shaikh either settle the matter with them, or protect the Agent against their extortion. The offence was aggravated by a repetition of the ill-treatment while the Agent was actually employed in his official duties, having left his concealment for the purpose of going on board a British vessel then in the harbour. This, and the failure of early remonstrances in obtaining redress, rendered it imperative that some public and undeniable reparation should be insisted upon. The appearance of a respectable force, and the threat of resorting to coercive measures, at length induced the Shaikh to comply with the demand upon him, that his son, or, in the event of his failing to do so, he himself, should come on board the senior officer's vessel, with a Khelut or dress of honour for the Agent, and that the persons who had been instrumental in the ill-treatment should be

Bushire[236] dispatched these vessels, from which it would seem he is invested with power to declare war against these Arabian tribes, *ad libitum*, or according to his own discretion.

The old King of Persia, Futteh Ali, is now on the verge of his grave, and cannot be expected to live much longer. His sons, who are in various commands in the country, are all anxious for the supreme command, and it was naturally supposed that his death would be the signal of war between them. The eldest son, Abbas Mirza, had been acknowledged the heir to the throne both by the Russian and the English Court, and he entertained sanguine hopes that through their united influence he might obtain the succession. Last year the prince died, leaving with his army his son, Mahomed Shah. According to European notions, he, as being the eldest son of the eldest son, has the fairest title to the throne; but according to the ideas prevalent in Persia and generally in the East, the second son of the reigning monarch, Hoosein Ali Mirza, generally known as the prince of Shiraz, has a prior right. The struggle on the death of the old Shah will therefore be between the eldest son, and the brother of the deceased Abbas Mirza.'

12.77 'From London Papers received at Boston,' *National Gazette and Literary Register* (Saturday, 24 January, 1835): 'Official intelligence had reached England, by way of Russia, of the death of Feeth Ali Schah, the sovereign of Persia.[237] This event had been for a long time expected and there has been a good deal of uncertainty in relation to his successors. The death of the Prince Royal Abbas Mirza, which took place more than a year ago, left the Schah for some time in doubt on whom he would confer the succession, for it seems to have depended on his nomination. He has recently designated Mahomed Mirza, the eldest son of Abbas Mirza, as the heir apparent. This selection is said to have been produced by English interference. As the new sovereign is said to have about 60 uncles, many of whom are governors of provinces, and have considerable bodies of troops at their command, it is supposed that he may stand in need of foreign assistance in the preservation of his throne. Russia, it is supposed may favor the pretensions of some competitor. It is under these circumstances that the new minister has been appointed to congratulate the young prince on his accession.'

---

flogged, either on board the ship, or alongside in one of his own boats, in presence of the crew.' Cf. Onley (2007: 141) who wrote, the junior Bahrain shaykhs had begun to extort money at will from the island's inhabitants, and 'Khushal himself had been threatened, assaulted, and robbed, forcing him to go into hiding. In early February 1834, David Blane received word of the dire situation in Bahrain. He sent a sloop-of-war across to rescue Khushal and deliver a stern letter to Shaikh 'Abd Allah [Al Khalifah] demanding immediate reparation. When the ship arrived on 9 February, Khushal came out of hiding to meet it and was assaulted and robbed once again. The commander of the ship delivered the letter to Shaikh 'Abd Allah and returned to Bushire with the Agent.' 'By late March,' after the ruler of Bahrain failed to give satisfaction to Blane's remonstrance, 'Blane had run out of patience and dispatched two sloops-of-war to Bahrain.'

[236] David Anderson Blane (1801–1879). Blane was Resident from January, 1832 to June, 1834. See Tuson (1979: 184).

[237] Fath 'Ali Shah died on 23 October 1834 at Isfahan. See Anonymous (1873a: 715).

12.78 'Foreign News. Persia,' *Alexandria Gazette* (Wednesday, 4 February, 1835): 'Futteh Ali, Shah of Persia, is dead. He has left 60 sons[238]—some of whom will certainly "do battle" for the crown.'

12.1 Miscellaneous

A Persian translation of Herodotus

12.79 'Herodotus in Persian,' *New-York Evening Post* (Thursday, 20 August, 1829): 'We observe, by an announcement in one of the last London literary magazines, that Mirza Mahommed Ibrahim, a Persian gentleman, resident in England, and attached to the East India College,[239] is employed, and has already made much progress, in translating Herodotus, from an English version, into the Persian language. Thus, after a lapse of twenty-two centuries, says the periodical whence we derive this information, the earliest account of Persia which Europe received, and of the dynasty which was overthrown by

---

[238] Actually 55 sons and 46 daughters who survived him. See Anonymous (1873a: 714).

[239] Mirza Mohammad Ibrahim (c. 1800–1857). Well-known thanks to H.L. Fleischer's 1847 (2nd ed. 1875) *Grammatik der lebenden persischen Sprache nach Mirza Mohammed Ibrahim's Grammar of the Persian Language* (Fleischer 1875; Ibraheem 1841), Ibrahim was professor of Arabic and Persian at East-India College in Haileybury, Hertfordshire, from 1826 to 1844, the first 3 years of which was as assistant to the Rev. H.G. Keene (Monier-Williams 1894: 186). He was described by Sir Monier Monier-Williams (1819–1899) as 'a very able, clever, and resolute man, with an iron will and a vindictive temper, qualified by much latent good nature, which occasionally showed itself in an unexpected manner. He came from Persia knowing little of English, and yet in a short time mastered our language so thoroughly that he was able to speak it correctly and fluently, and with scarcely any accent.' He possessed 'qualities which enabled him to maintain order and enforce attention. His classroom was at the end of the passage, on the right of the gateway as you entered the college, and the most rowdy students were like lambs in his presence. Yet his method of teaching had no particular merit. He would simply hear us translate the portion of the test [sic, text] appointed to be prepared for the day, and would launch out into a torrent of angry invectives if anyone—especially any pupil to whom he had taken a dislike—made bad mistakes. Then, after listening to and correcting our *vivâ voce* translations, he would proceed to translate the passage which had to be prepared for the next day's lecture, and his utterance would be so rapid that only the best men could follow him. Still, to me it was always a treat to hear him read his own language. In teaching grammar, the Mirza of course made use of his own Persian Grammar, for writing which the East-India Company—so at least it was commonly reported—paid him 1000 pounds. It was an expensively printed book, and the ability of the writer was conspicuous in its composition; but, like all works by natives of the East, it contained many inaccuracies. In the dialogues at the end, English idioms were very cleverly rendered into Persian, and I recollect that we had to learn these as part of our first Term's test.' See Monier-Williams (1894: 73–74).

Alexander, is now about to be returned to the occupiers of that country in their present vernacular tongue.'[240]

Caspian Sea trade

12.80 'Commerce on the Caspian,' *The Atlas* (Saturday, 26 September, 1829): 'A letter froim Astrachan, of July 24, says—"Last year a manufacturer of Schuja sent printed calicoes and nankeens to the value of 300,000 rubles to the Persian port Zinzili,[241] on the Caspian. Part of his goods was sent to Tauris,[242] where they were sold at 30 per ct. profit; the remainder was sold to advantage at Zinzili. The clerk who was sent with them is expected in a short time at Bacow,[243] to receive another consignment of the same value."'

General Devaux, in the service of Mohammad 'Ali Mirza

12.81 'Translated from the French. General Devaux,' *City Gazette & Commercial Daily Advertiser* (15 January, 1830): 'One of the gallant officers of our old army *General Devaux*, has profited by the voluntary exile to which he submitted in 1815, to exalt the French name among the Persians.[244] Having taken refuge in a province of that empire then

---

[240] Ibrahim was a member of the Oriental Translation Committee, chaired by Sir Gore Ouseley, the Second Report of which, dated 30 May 1829, stated, 'The Committee now incidentally notice a fact which, it is thought, will be interesting to the admirers of the early Greek historians. Through the residence in this country of Mirza Mohammed Ibrahim, a Persian gentleman who is attached to the East-India College, the earliest accounts Europe received of his country, and the dynasty which was overthrown by Alexander, are, after the lapse of twenty-two centuries, likely to be given back to its present occupiers in their vernacular tongue, as he has considerably advanced in the translation of Herodotus into Persian from an English version. His work, when finished, however the egotism of the Greeks may wound the vanity of the Persians, will be a noble and unique present to his sovereign and his country.' See Anonymous (1829a: 17) ['Second Report']. In a letter to Augustus de Morgan of 27 October 1829, John Briggs of the Madras Army asked, 'Are you aware that Mirza Ibrahim, the Persian Professor at Haileybury College, is translating Beloe's *Herodotus* into Persian.' See Bell (1885: 107). The Oriental Translation Fund report was presumably Briggs' source. Fisher (2001: 28) noted that Ibrahim 'cotranslated liturgies, Anglican Common Prayers, and sections of the Christian Bible into Persian' but makes no mention of a translation of Herodotus. Ibrahim's translation, if it was ever completed, was apparently never published.

[241] Bandar-e Anzali.

[242] Tabriz.

[243] Baku.

[244] Cf. 10.71. For his life see also Belge (1829), Bran (1829), Anonymous (1830a).

under the government of a son of the Schah,[245] he obtained permission to train six batallions of the troops in the European mode. The young prince some time after declared war against the Turks, without the consent of his father. Very soon however, he found cause to repent of this rash measure, by learning that an army of 22,000 was advancing against him, to oppose which he had only 14,000 men. Devaux however animated his courage; and when the two armies came in sight of each other, formed the whole mass of irregular troops with the artillery into one body, and advised the Prince not to attack the enemy, but merely to return their fire. He then ordered three of his battalions to make a vigorous charge on the enemy in front, while he with the other three should at the same time assail their flank. This bold manœuvre alarmed the Prince, who did not foresee its effect; and he exclaimed, "Devaux you will certainly ruin us." The Turks were then making a tremendous fire, which concealed from their observation the movement of the Persians. Devaux continued to advance—and the Turks finding themselves attacked on different sides soon gave way. They were pursued and cut to pieces, leaving their camp with immense booty to be despoiled by the Persians. The Prince on reaching the field of battle, found Devaux seated on one of the enemy's cannon; After a cordial embrace, he immediately decorated him with the distinguished orders of the Lion, and the Sun.

Devaux after this astonished the Persians still more by taking a strong fortress by storm, during the intense heat of summer, and at the time a pestilential wind was blowing. The report of this last exploit, caused him to be summoned to the Schah's[246] Court, where he was received with the highest honors. Poets made him the theme of their praise, and orders were given by the Schah to his principal artist to prepare a painting, representing him at the moment of rushing into the midst of the enemy. This picture has been placed in the great gallery of the palace: and the General has moreover the power of cutting off as many heads as he pleases—a distinguished privilege among these barbarous people.

For some time past however Devaux has wished to leave Persia,[247] which circumstance was a subject of general regret at Court, where he is regarded as one of the firmest supports of the throne. The Schah has prevailed upon him to remain, but his heart is with France; and should she ever have need of his services, he would fly to her assistance.'[248]

---

[245] Mohammad 'Ali Mirza. Cf. 10.65ff.

[246] Fath 'Ali Shah.

[247] In fact, after the death of Mohammad 'Ali, Devaux remained in the service of his son for only a short time before abandoning an earlier desire to ply his trade in Lahore and accepting an offer from his erstwhile opponent, Daud Pasha of Baghdad. 'Bei seiner Ankunft wurde er zum Generalissimus der Armee ernannt, und im Jahre 1828 zum Gouverneur von Hella...Nach dem Pascha genießt er der höchsten Gewalt, und hat sich ihrer schon oft bedient, um Europäern nützlich su seyn.' See Bran (1829: 461).

[248] As Bran (1829: 461–462) wrote, 'Allein, obgleich es scheint, daß er ein neues Vaterland adopdirt hat, so bleibt ihm Frankreich immer theuer, und wenn einst Gefahr eintreten sollte, würde es an ihm einen seiner eifrigsten Vertheidiger finden.'

A Persian poet

12.82 'Untitled,' *New-York Commercial Advertiser* (Wednesday, 14 April, 1830), 'Untitled,' *Baltimore Patriot & Mercantile Advertiser* (Friday, 16 April, 1830), 'Untitled,' *National Gazette and Literary Register* (Saturday, 17 April, 1830), 'Untitled,' *New-York Spectator* (Tuesday, 20 April, 1830) and 'Untitled,' *American Sentinel* (Wednesday, 28 April, 1830): 'The Persian poet, Mirzagul, having composed some verses in honour of the Schah's birth-day, received from his Majesty the present of a pair of breeches without a seam, the skin of an hyppopotamus. The buttons are topazes. To this *indispensable* accoutrement was added a pair of boots of rat skin, with heels of massive gold.'

Members of Fath 'Ali Shah's family make a pilgrimage to Mecca

12.83 'From England,' *Broome Republican* (Thursday, 15 July 1830): 'Odessa, April 21. A letter from Erzeroum, of March 8th, says: "A few days ago, a caravan of pilgrims, on their way to Mecca, arrived here from Persia. It consists of 500 persons, among whom is Mirza Mussan Khan,[249] brother of the Caimacan of Tauris, with his wife, the daughter of the Shah,[250] also one of the principal wives of the Shah himself, and one of the wives of Abbas Mirza. The suite of the persons consists of several Khans and Beys from Tauris and Khoi. The caravan takes the road to Aleppo.'

12.84 'Pilgrims,' *New-York Commercial Advertiser* (Wednesday, 4 August, 1830), 'Pilgrims,' *New-York Spectator* (Friday, 6 August, 1830): 'A caravan of pilgrims, on their way from Persia to Mecca, arrived early in March last at Erzeroum. It consisted of 500 persons; among whom were a wife of the schah,[251] one of abbas mirza's, and many of the khans and beys of Tauris and Choi.[252] The caravan proceeded to Aleppo.'

---

[249] Haji Mirza Musa Khan, son of Mirza Bozorg Qa'em Maqam, and brother of Mirza Abu'l-Qasem. As Werner noted, 'After the death of Mīrzā Buzurg in 1237/1822, there seems to have been a certain animosity between his sons, Abū al-Qāsim and Mīrzā Mūsā, on the succession of their father's unofficial position and his title. At first, Abū al-Qāsim was assigned the title of Qā'im-Maqām, while Mūsā became the vazīr of the prince. For some years, however, it is not clear who acted as the actual head of 'Abbās Mīrzā's administration and his court....A letter to his brother Mīrzā Mūsā Khān in Tabriz, dated 1243/1828 and written in Tehran, shows both the continuing, albeit less pronounced, involvement of Mūsā Khān with the affairs of Azerbaijan and the role played by Abū al-Qāsim as the agent or representative of 'Abbās Mīrzā at the court in Tehran.' See Werner (2000: 197).

[250] Fath 'Ali Shah.

[251] Fath 'Ali Shah.

[252] Khoy.

Sir John Malcolm and Madame de Staël

12.85 'Destiny,' *The Freeman's Journal* (Monday, 6 December, 1830): 'When Major General Sir John Malcolm[253] returned the first time from Persia, at a fashionable and crowded ball "at home," he met Madame de Stael.[254] After being introduced to Madam, and she informed of his late arrival from the Persian court, "Sare John," said she, "you must inform me all about Persia, and every thing about it, and all worth notice; and to begin at the top of all, what is the king of Persia like? what does he look like?" "Madame,' replied Sir John, "he looks like a man worthy of his destiny." "Ah, what is his destiny?" entreated Madame. "He has," replied Sir John, "five hundred wives."'[255]

Rumored visit of Mirza Abu'l Hasan Khan Shirazi to the United States

12.86 'Untitled,' *The New-York Evening Post* (Saturday 18 December, 1830), 'Untitled,' *Delaware Gazette* [Delhi NY] (Wednesday, 29 December, 1830) and 'Unitled,' *The Geneva Gazette and Mercantile Advertiser* (Wednesday, 19 January, 1831): 'We learn from a distinguished friend abroad, that the United States will shortly be honored by a visit from an illustrious traveller, who cannot but excite as much interest and curiosity among us, as he will feel, himself, in the novelties of our western republic. This is no other than the accomplished Persian, whose long residence in England, as Ambassador from his Persian Majesty, formed the basis of the amusing volumes of Haji Baba,[256] and other works of satire and light literature.—He has since resided, as the representative of his sovereign, at Constantinople.[257] The curiosity of the Persian court has been excited by our fine ships, our commerce, and the occasional presence of an American traveller to learn something official

---

[253] Cf. 8.17 ff.

[254] Anne Louise Germaine Necker, Baronne de Staël-Holstein (1766–1817). A major Swiss literary, political and social figure of the late 18th/early 19th century. As Harrington (2010: 31) noted, Malcolm accompanied Sir Walter Scott on a trip to Paris in 1815 where 'he joined in the great social events of Allied-occupied Paris, rubbing shoulders with the tsar and Madame De Stael; introducing Sir Walter Scott to his old friend the Duke of Wellington; and making contact with such luminaries of European orientalism as Sylvester De Sacy.'

[255] This is a great exaggeration. According to Anonymous (1873a: 715) Fath 'Ali Shah had '158 wives and 265 children, of which 106 reached mature age. His 60 sons had 670 children.'

[256] Morier (1824). According to Javadi (1983/2011), Mirza Abu'l Hasan Khan Shirazi wrote a work entitled *Ḥayrat-nāma-ye sofarā* 'in the usual florid style of the period' which 'illustrates many of the incidents that are humorously described in Hajji Baba and its sequel.'

[257] Mirza Abu'l Hassan Khan was in Constantinople briefly in 1818–1819 on his way to France and England. See Busse (1972: 155).

about the *Yanzee Duneea*, or new world.[258] This gentleman, whose residence at Paris and London has given him an acquaintance with the languages and manners of Europe unrivalled in the higher circles of the east, has been selected for this purpose. He does not, however, come in an official, public character, though, in fact, sent by his court to see the whole length and breadth of the land, which he will do with the eyes of a good traveller, as well as a good Persian. He will probably be here, by the way of England, some time next fall.'[259]

Cholera and plague

12.87 'Progress of the Indian Cholera,' *Delaware Gazette* (Wednesday, 3 August, 1831): 'After the first invasion, Persia had several returns of the Cholera. In October, 1829, a very serious inroad commenced in Teheran, the royal residence. But the occurrence of winter stopped its progress for the time. The contagion, however, was again resuscitated towards the middle of June, 1830, in the provinces of Mazanderan and Shirvan, upon the southern shore of the Caspian Sea.—From the latter, it passed through the town of Tauris, and destroyed 5000 of its inhabitants. Crossing the Russian frontier, it rapidly advanced towards the interior. In two provinces 4557 persons were seized with the malady, of wom more than a third died. The 8th of August it entered Tiflis. The population was soon diminished from 30,000 to 80,000, by deaths, and emigration to avoid the distemper. To avert the spreading mortality, the inhabitants had recourse to religious ceremonies and processions, which, by collecting crowds, only served to extend the disease.'[260]

12.88 'From the Boston Medical Journal of July 19. Cholera Morbus,' *Jamestown Journal* (Wednesday, 17 August, 1831): 'In 1822 it ravaged Cochin China...In its westerly course, it appeared to take routes the one leading through the Arabian Sea & up the Persian Gulf the

---

[258] Turkish *yeni dünya*, 'new world.' Discussing the disputed etymology of 'Yankee,' Goadby (1860: 51), noted, 'The old Persian term for the inhabitants of a new world was Yanhi-dooniah, and their name for America, Yanghi-duina.' Cf. Layard (1873: 107), 'Yenghi Dunia (America).' Pers. *dunya'*, 'world.'

[259] Mirza Abu'l Hassan Khan never travelled to the United States. For his career see Javadi (1983/2011).

[260] For this outbreak see e.g. Macnamara (1876: 88–89), on 'the progress of the epidemic from India directly westward into Persia...the advance of cholera from Herat to Teheran in 1829....we may assume cholera to have existed at Teheran during the time of its outbreak in Orenburg in the autumn of 1829. It would appear, also, that the disease had subsided in Persia throughout the winter of 1829–1830, for Sir W. Crichton informs us that, *in the spring of* 1830, the cholera broke out in the province of Khorasan, and appeared at Tabreez, and in the seaport towns of Reshd and Bakou on the Caspian. In July it was generated at Tiflis; it soon after appeared in Astrakhan, and here "the stream of cholera, which entered Russia from the northern provinces of Persia, formed a junction with that which flowed through Orenburg."'

12.1 Miscellaneous

other across the immense territory of Persia itself....With a still more rapid course, it passed north, ravaged the cities of Teheran and Tauris in Persia, gained the Persian Gulf, and in September of the year just named had appeared in Astrachan in Asiatic Russia.'[261]

12.89 'Cholera,' *New-York Spectator* (Friday, 30 September 1831) and 'Cholera,' *Albany Evening Journal* (Monday, 3 October 1831): 'Bender-Abouschir...through which it was introduced into Persia, lost a sixth of its population. At Schiraz out of 45,000, 7000 were carried off in the space of 16 or 18 days. At Yerd [sic, Yezd], the number who died was 4500 out of 25,000. But a part of the population of these towns had fled, on the first appearance of the disorder. The emigration was immense from Tauris, where 4800 died in 25 days. The number of deaths in Ispahan, Cachan, Koom and Carbin [sic, Kazvin] is not known, nor the total mortality in the camp before Erzeroum; but it is asserted that 2000 soldiers died during one day's march; and we must believe that the troops suffered severely from the malady, since Prince Abbas Mirza, the Schah's[262] eldest son, was compelled to raise the siege at the moment when the place was about to surrender; and, notwithstanding his previous successes, could not continue to carry on the campaign against the Turks.'[263]

12.90 'From the Journal of Health. History of the Indian Cholera,' *Jamestown Journal* (Wednesday, 28 September, 1831): 'In 1821, is said to have destroyed 60,000 subjects of the prince of Oman, round Muscat[264]; during this year, it reached Baherin [sic, Bahrein], Bassora, Bagdad, Bushire, and Shiraz. In this latter city the population of which is 40,000

---

[261] For the outbreak of 1822 see Macnamara (1876: 63). This was the episode which forced 'Abbas Mirza to retreat from Erzurum and eventually killed his brother, Mohammad 'Ali Mirza.

[262] Fath 'Ali Shah.

[263] This last remark about lifting the seige of Erzurum due to the cholera outbreak among 'Abbas Mirza's army refers to an incident in 1822 (see above).

[264] According to the Omani historian Salil ibn Razik, 'This year, A.H. 1236 [A.D. 1820–1] a plague [the Asiatic cholera] broke out in 'Omân and proved fatal to a great many. This plague differed from that which occurs at Constantinople, at Damascus, Baghdâd, and el-Básrah. It first attacks a man's abdomen, and then matter is ejected from the mouth and anus until he dies. Some who are seized die at once; others after 2 or 3 days; and only a few survive. God preserve us from so dire a disease! Great numbers in 'Omân fell victims to it...It also spread over Persia, and el-Kuwait, and el-Bahrein, and ezh-Zhâhirah, and the district of et-Tawwâm, and carried off, God the Creator alone knows how many.' See Badger (1871: 344–345). J.B. Fraser, who landed at Muscat on 8 July 1821, reported that the Imam 'confirmed a report which had before reached us, of the epidemic cholera having visited Muscat, where it had committed considerable ravages. His highness informed us that he had lost by the disease at least 10,000 of his subjects; that Muscat had by no means suffered the most, as it had extended over the most part of Omaun. It had broken out spontaneously, first at Rooee [Ruwi], a village 3 or 4 miles from Muttra, without any known means by which contagion could have been conveyed. A ship with slaves from Zanguebar, which had lost a number on the passage, had, it is true, come to Muscat, but not until after the disease had appeared there; at the time we were here it had entirely ceased.' See Fraser (1825: 21).

there shed 16,000 in the first few days.[265]....During the succeeding winter, the disease became dormant, both in Persia and Syria. In 1822, it spread to Ispahan, Teheran, and Tabriz...and reached, in 1823...to Astrachan, in Asiatic Russia.'

12.91 'Cholera,' *The Freeman's Journal* (Monday, 30 January, 1832): 'The disease was abating at Constantinople. It was making great ravages in Persia.'[266]

12.92 'Cholera in Persia,' *New-York Evening Post* (Tuesday, 1 May, 1832; minus last two sentences), 'Cholera in Persia,' *Lansingburgh Gazette* (Tuesday, 8 May, 1832), 'Foreign News,' *Geneva Courier* (Wednesday, 9 May, 1832), 'Cholera in Persia,' *The Schenectady Cabinet* (Wednesday, 9 May, 1832), 'The Cholera in Persia,' *Delaware Gazette* (Wednesday, 9 May, 1832) and 'The Plague and Cholera in Russia,' *The Oswego Palladium and Republican Chronicle* (Wednesday, 9 May, 1832): 'According to accounts from the frontiers of Persia, the plague and cholera had hardly begun to subside in that country. In some provinces those formidable diseases had carried off more than two-thirds of the population. The province of Ghillan appears to have been among the greatest sufferers. Out of a population of 300,000, only 60,000 men and 40,000 women and children remained.[267] The eggs of the silk worms have been completely destroyed there, and it was calculated that it would take 7 years to produce the same quantity of worms as formerly. Before the arrival of these diseases, the revenues of Ghillan were usually framed at 350,000 tomauns. Since then, no more than 80,000 tomauns could be obtained.'[268]

---

[265] According to Macnamara (1876: 62), 'On the 20th of August it [cholera] broke out at Bushire; and on the 29th was heard of at Cauzeroon (Kazerun) and Sheerauz (Shiraz), in which latter place it first appeared in the prince's harem. The disease was very severe in this locality, and our author's companion, Mr. [Claucius] Rich, here died of cholera. From Shiraz it was carried north to Jedz [sic, Yazd] and Teheran, and from thence to Resht, at the foot of the Caspian Sea.'

[266] The year 1832 was particularly memorable in the annals of cholera worldwide and numerous works have been devoted to it. See e.g. Rosenberg (1962), Morris (1976), Kotar and Gessler (2014). De Kay (1833: 134–135) related that a young Englishman, arrived at Bandar-e Bushehr from Calcutta, 'traversed Persia by the way of Tabriz, Ispahan or Teheran, Ararat, and Erzeroom....He describes the panic occasioned by the cholera to be so great throughout Persia that many towns refused to permit him to enter, and he was consequently compelled to bivouac frequently in the open fields. Bands of robbers were roaming about the country, and taking advantage of the general consternation, would knock at the door of a house at midnight, and in answer to the demand of who they were, would reply, "I am cholera." The affrighted inmates would immediately take to their heels, and leave their houses to be pillaged by these ingenious miscreants.'

[267] At Bandar-e Anzali Holmes (1845: 71) described seeing 'a number of grave-stones, marking the burial-place of those who fell victims to the dreadful plague which visited the whole of this coast in 1830–1831, and destroyed here about two-thirds of the population.'

[268] By 1843 Holmes (1845: 99) reported that the 'total revenue on the production of silk in Gheelaun amounts to between 140,000 and 150,000 tomauns (70,000*l.* and 75,000*l.*).'

12.1 Miscellaneous

12.93 'Untitled,' *The Schenectady Cabinet* (Wednesday, 27 June, 1832): 'In another part of this paper will be found an interesting account of the place of origin and progress of the Spasmodic Cholera, through Asia, till its introduction into Europe. It is extracted from the London Quarterly Review for November, 1831....To prove the contagious character of the disease, and that by strict quarantine regulations it may be avoided by thickly populated places, we here quote the following paragraphs, extracted by the review from a report on the subject by M. de Jonnes[269]: "In Persia, when the malady was attacking the large towns on the high roads, the caravans were forbidden to pass through Teheran, the residence of the Shah.[270] This measure was adopted on the recommendation of Dr. Martinengo.[271] This capital remained free from 1821 to 1829, after which it was attacked, owing to a neglect of the means which had hitherto preserved it."'

12.94 'The Cholera,' *Delaware Gazette* (Wednesday, 8 August, 1832): 'After the first attack, Persia was visited several times by the cholera; in October, 1829, it appeared very seriously at Teheran, at the residence of the King,[272] but the winter arrested its progress for some time; it however reappeared in the middle of June, 1830, in the province of Mazanderan and Shirvin, on the southern coast of the Caspian sea. From this latter province it passed through the city of Tauris from which it swept off 5000 inhabitants,[273] and arriving at the frontiers of Russia it rapidly advanced toward the interior of this empire. In two provinces, 4557 persons were infected, and more than a third of them died. On the 8th of August [1830] it appeared at Tiflis,[274] the population of which was soon reduced by death and emigration from 30,000 to 8000. The inhabitants wishing to stop the mortality,

---

[269] Alexandre Moreau de Jonnès (1778–1870). French physician who in 1831 wrote of himself, 'Chargé depuis treize ans, en qualité de rapporteur de la Commission sanitaire centrale et du Conseil supérieur de santé, de recueillir les faits qui peuvent faire connaître la nature du choléra pestilentiel, sa marche ses progrès et les moyens de les arrêter.' See Moreau de Jonnès (1831: 4). Kennedy (1832: 247, n. *), described him as 'An able foreigner...who has been long engaged in observing the phenomena of cholera.' Moreau de Jonnès (1831) is an important study on cholera.

[270] Fath 'Ali Shah.

[271] Moreau de Jonnès (1831: 60) called him 'médecin de Turin, employé à cette époque à la cour du Schah.' Discussing the cholera outbreak of 1822, Sterling (1832: 103–104) noted, 'The city of Tehèran remained entirely exempt from it. The Schah, from the advice of Dr. Martinengo, interdicted all communication between this city and the environs; he especially forbade the entrance of caravans into it.' This is an English translation of Anonymous (1831d: 89).

[272] Fath 'Ali Shah.

[273] On 30 September 1830 McNeill wrote, 'The Cholera Morbus still prevails in some parts of this province [Azerbaijan], and has a second time this year committed ravages at Teheran and Ispahan, in the former of which cities it has caused a great mortality. The plague has reappeared at Tabreez, and has extended to many of the villages in the vicinity....The deaths caused by the Cholera and plague up to the present time are estimated in the most statements at more than thirty thousand.' See MacAlister (1910: 147).

[274] On 5 May 1830 according to Anonymous (1849a).

which rapidly increased, had recourse to processions and religious ceremonies. This disease, however, was only extended by these assemblies. At the same time, the cholera arrived in Astracan the 1st of July [1829].[275] In 10 days 1229 inhabitants were attacked, one third of whom died.'[276]

12.95 'Untitled,' *The Geneva Gazette and Mercantile Advertiser* (Wednesday, 26 December, 1832): 'The plague is making most awful progress in Persia: nearly two-thirds of the population of *Bushire* have perished.'[277]

---

[275] On 21 June 1830 according to Anonymous (1849a).

[276] According to Anonymous (1875: 548), the cholera outbreak at Astrakhan discussed here occurred in 1829, not 1830. 'In all there were twelve hundred and twenty-nine attacks and about five hundred deaths in Astrakan, including the chief magistrate and many of the police. By August 8, villages from two to four miles distant began to be involved, to which many families had fled from the city.'

[277] According to Anonymous (1832b), 'Bombay papers contain accounts from Bushire of the 20th of May, describing a fearful mortality in that place from the plague. It originally broke out there early in February, when most of the European residents removed to an island [Khark; see Anonymous (1832d: 182), referring to letters received by the Honourable Company's schooner *Frolic*, 'from the resident and party on the island of Corgo, stating that the plague at Bushire was gradually abating.'] in the Persian Gulf; and all communication with the infected district was carefully guarded against. Towards the end of April, two of them were despatched to Bushire, to ascertain the state of the place, as no information had been received from the natives who were left in charge of it. On arriving, they were all found to have fallen victims to the disease. The mortality in the town itself had been frightful; an immense number of small families had been entirely destroyed, while in those of from twenty to thirty individuals, rarely more than two or three had escaped. The bodies, being piled up in heaps, for the survivors were unable to otherwise dispose of them, had further infected the atmosphere. Of one hundred men, who were induced by the high wages offered by the Shaik, to attempt removing them, four only survived, and it was found impossible to continue the work. In the town, famine was adding to the horrors of the scene. Children, who had lost their parents, were to be seen wandering about in a state of starvation, and the price of articles of subsistence had risen in some instances a hundred fold. Those who had fled into the interor had spread the contagion in every direction, and the mortality in the districts round the town is stated to have been as great as in the town itself.' When Lieut. D'Arcy Todd arrived at Bušehr in December, 1833, he wrote, 'Plague and famine have depopulated the town: out of twenty thousand inhabitants, which it contained 12 months ago, there are not more than fifteen hundred remaining.' See Kaye (1869b: 11). Colvill (1872: 48) noted that, after decimating Baghdad and Basra, 'The disease appears to have taken a south-easterly direction, for on the 10th of May 1832 it was reported that Bushire had been devastated by it, not one-tenth...of the inhabitants being left.' Cf. Tholozan (1874: 21), Khan (1908: 44).

Rev. Joseph Wolff

12.96 'Rev. Joseph Wolffe,'[278] *New-York Spectator* (Tuesday, 28 February, 1832), 'Rev. Joseph Wolffe,' *Connecticut Observer* (Monday, 5 March, 1832), 'Rev. Joseph Wolffe,' *Auburn Free Press* (Wednesday, 7 March, 1832): 'Letters from this eccentrick missionary from Persia, have been received. He was at Tabrez, on his way to Tartary and the borders of India, for the avowed purpose of preaching christianity to the heathens in those countries. The Persian government, though Mahomedan, was affording every necessary facility for his mission, giving him letters of friendship, passports, &c.[279] It is well that Mr. Wolffe has selected those barbarous regions, for the theatre of his missionary labors. Were he in some parts of the United States, he might be in danger of chains and imprisonment.'

A 'Persian' ambassador and the Reform Bill

12.97 'Foreign Intelligence,' *The Schenectady Cabinet* (Wednesday, 30 May, 1832) and 'Latest from Europe,' *The Oswego Palladium and Republican Chronicle* (Wednesday, 30 May, 1832): 'The debate on the question of ordering the Reform Bill to a second reading in the Lords, had not terminated on the 13th, but was to be renewed on that evening....Our accounts come down to the evening editions of the papers of the 13th, by which we learn that in anticipation of this most important debate, the galleries were crowded before 3 o'clock. The Persian [sic, Mughal] Ambassador, Ram Mohun Roy,[280] was early in the seats allotted to the Ambassadors.'

---

[278] Cf. 10.375.

[279] Wolff's diary entry for 29 June 1831, written at 'Abbas Mirza's camp outside of Tabriz, noted, 'Captain Campbell has already written to Abbas Mirza for letters to Khorassan and Bokhara; Dr. M'Neill also give me letters for these places. From Tabreez to Bokhara a caravan went, with stoppages, seventy days. I leave Tabreez, if the Lord please, in the middle of August, so that I may be at Bokhara in the month of October: I stop, *im sha Allah* (i.e. "if it please God"), till December: go on to Cabul and Calcutta, and hope to be at Tabreez in May next year.' See Wolff (1833: 32).

[280] Raja Rammohun Roy (1772–1833). Mughal ambassador to the Court of St. James and an important Indian intellectual. For a contemporary perspective on his life and achievements see Carpenter (1833). For modern perspectives see e.g. Zastoupil (2010), Sen (2012). For his urgent desire to be present at the readings of the Reform Bill see Carpenter (1866: 75–77).

Seeds of Persian cultivars sent to America

12.98 'For Evening Post,' *New-York Evening Post* (Friday, 15 June, 1832): 'Horticultural Society[281] Rooms, 601 Broadway, Tuesday evening, June 12th....The Society was honored with a communication from Sir Henry Willock,[282] of London, accompanied by a collection of the seeds of trees, shrubs and plants brought by him from Persia and Turkey. They are stated to be natives of a climate varied as our own, being subject to occasional severe cold in winter, and excessive heat in summer. Among them is the seed of the much celebrated *Sheraz Tobacco*, from the South of Persia,[283] the high and delicate perfume of which is so much appreciated in Constantinople, that the article is conveyed to that market on camels, a distance of 2500 miles. The value of this donation is greatly enhanced by a memoir on the mode of its cultivation and preparation, drawn up at the request of Sir Henry by Dr. Riach, of the Hon. East India Company's medical service.[284] This variety, if introduced into our Southern States, may prove a valuable acquisition.

---

[281] The New-York Horticultural Society was founded in 1818, incorporated by the New York state legislature on 22 March, 1822, and terminated in 1844. See https://www.nybg.org/library/finding_guide/archv/NYHS_RAf.html. For the act of incorporation and a list of the members in 1822 see Anonymous (1822m: 79–80).

[282] Former *chargé d'affaires* in Persia. Cf. 10.15, 10.166–10.167, 10.197–10.199, 10.204. Willock made other botanical donations to the London Horticultural Society, e.g. melon seeds in 1824 (Lindley and Moore 1866: 357) and 1826 (Lindley 1826); seeds of the humble plant (*Mimosa pudica*), sometime before 1825 (Edwards 1825: 941); Crimson mountain tulip (*Tulipa montana*) in 1826 (Edwards 1827: 1106); *Rosa berberifolia*, sometime before 1828 (Lindley 1829: 1261); Berberry-leaved Lowea, *Lowea beberifolia*), sometime before 1829; Shiraz tobacco in 1831 (Lindley 1833, s.v. 1592; Bentham 1842: 418); and Dalmatian toad-flax in 1832 (Maund 1835–1836, s.v. Lina'ria Dalma'tica No. 570). Hooker 1890, s.v. Tab. 7096 wrote, regarding the rose that flowered in 1828 and had been 'raised from seed sent by Sir Henry Willock from Persia,' that, 'Of all the numerous seedlings that were raised from Sir H. Willock's seeds and distributed, scarcely a plant remains alive. Two are still growing in a peat border in the Chiswick Garden; but they are languishing and unhealthy; and we confess that observation of them in a living state, for nearly 4 years, has not suggested a single method of improving the cultivation of the species.' Sometime between 1 May 1826 and 1 May 1827 Willock was awarded one of eight 'Large Silver Medals presented by Order of the Council of the Horticultural Society of London...for having successfully transmitted from Persia, seeds of several varieties of Melons of great excellence.' See Anonymous (1830c).

[283] For a colored illustration of *Nicotiana persica* which was published shortly after Willock's communication was read to the Horticultural Society, see Lindley (1833: Fig. 1592). Anonymous (1891b).

[284] Dr. James Pringle Riach (1797–1865), a Scot from Perth where his father had been a teacher in the Academy (Anonymous 1838a: 13). He was commissioned Assistant Surgeon in the Medical Establishment of the East India Company on 4 January 1821 (Anonymous 1822g: 495). This is identical to the text later published as Riach (1835). He first went to Iran in Macdonald's mission, and is attested in a grafitto in the palace of Darius at Persepolis from June, 1826. See Simpson (2005: 53). Cf. MacAlister (1910: 82). In 1832 Riach was given the Order of the Lion and the Sun (Crawford 1914: 211), the highest Persian order of merit, created originally by Fath 'Ali Shah. He succeeded Dr. Cormick in his duties. See MacAlister 1910: 177. In 1836 he went as First Medical Officer in

12.1 Miscellaneous

Among the seeds presented are those of a number of culinary vegetables—the Pea, Melon, Pumpkin, Gourd, &c. of that country. Also a collection of flowering and aromatic plants from mountains in the vicinity of Tabriz in Persia, most of them entirely new in English Botanists and all of them quite hardy. A disposition of these seeds will be made at a special meeting of the society, to be held next Tuesday evening the 19th instant, when the members are respectfully invited to attend.'

12.99 'For Evening Post,' *New-York Evening Post* (Saturday, 23 June, 1832) and 'N.Y. Horticultural Society,' *The Geensee* [sic, *Genesee*] *Farmer* (Saturday, 7 July, 1832): 'Horticultural Society—Special Meeting—Tuesday, June 19th—Jacob Lorillard, Esq,[285] President, in the Chair—A letter from Sir Henry Willock of London was read. This was accompanied by a box of seeds brought by him from Persia and Turkey. They are described as the seeds of trees, shrubs and plants, suited to the climate of the United States, many of them having been collected in the mountainous parts of Persia, where they were covered with snow 4 months of the year, and all of them are deemed *hardy*. The following are described:

The Paper Almond,[286] or Badaam Kaghizee,[287] of Persia.

The Laurel of Trebizond—grows to the size of a forest tree, and its fruit eatable.[288]

McNeill's mission. See MacAlister (1910: 188). Laurie (1855: 73) considered him a 'canny Scot.' The American missionaries who arrived in Urmia in 1834, considered him 'the beloved physician' (Perkins 1843: 260) and 'a tried friend of our mission' (Grant 1841: 105). Read (1850: 343) considered Riach, Sir John Campbell, Lord Ponsonby, Commodore Porter and Colonel Sheil, 'not to mention others of like noble character and expansive philanthropy, to whom Providence had, at this time, given power and influence at the courts of Persia, and of the Sublime Porte. It was through the very timely instrumentality of these men that our mission found such ready access to the Nestorians in Persia and among the Koordish mountains.' He retired as Surgeon in the Bombay Establishment on 16 December 1839. See Clark (1842: 84).

[285] Jacob Lorillard (1774–1838), a wealthy tanner, banker and prominent New Yorker. For a brief sketch of his life see Norcross (1901: 60–62).

[286] More commonly 'paper-shelled almond,' denoting *Prunus amygdalus* var. *fragilis*. See Wood et al. (1885: 183). They are described as 'a choice variety, with very thin shell.' See Rusby (1921: 189).

[287] *badami kaghizi*. Steingass (1963: 137), 'Jordan almond.' Cf. Laufer (1919: 406).

[288] The reference to edible fruit suggests this is the so-called cherry-laurel or 'laurel cherry…the common Laurel of gardens…They are all, so far as we know, seedlings of one species, the *Prunus lauro-cerasus*, an evergreen shrub, native of the Levant and Caucasus. This was introduced into English gardens about 1576 from Trebizond.' See Anonymous (1889: 620). As Flückiger and Hanbury (1874: 226) noted, 'Pierre Belon [1517–1564], the French naturalist, who travelled in the East between 1546 and 1550, is stated by Clusius [Carolus Clusius/Charles de l'Écluse (1526–1609)] to have discovered the cherry-laurel in the nieghbourhood of Trebizond. Thirty years later, Clusius himself obtained the plant through the Imperial ambassador at Constantinople, and distributed it from Vienna to the gardens of Germany. Since it is mentioned by Gerarde [John Gerard/e (c. 1545–1612)] as a choice garden shrub, it must have been cultivated in England prior to 1597.'

The Senjeèd, a hardy tree, grows to the size of the willow, and in similar soil. Its flowers are so odoriferous that their fragrance may be observed the distance of a mile; and its fruit is also eatable.[289]

The Persian Rose Tree, or Nasteran,[290] grows to the height of 20 feet, its top depending gracefully like that of the weeping willow; its flowers very odoriferous, of a pale amber colour, and the branches entirely covered with the blossoms.

Fourteen varieties of ornamental and aromatic plants gathered on the mountains near Tabriz, not named, and most of them new to English Botanists.

A species of Broom, the Persian Pea "Nakhood,"[291] Melons,[292] Gourds, Pumpkins, &c.

Nine species of hardy trees and ornamental shrubs growing near Constantinople, all of which were distributed among the members present.

In addition to the above, Sir Henry has sent a packet containing seed of the celebrated *Sheraz Tobacco*, so celebrated in the markets of the East for its delicate perfume. This was accompanied by a memoir prepared at the request of the philanthropic donor by Dr. Riach[293]; and as this seed will be distributed, and a part of it sent by the Society to their correspondents in the Southern States, they deem it advisable to publish Dr. R's remarks on its cultivation and preparation.

On the cultivation of Tobacco in the Persian Province of Fars, commonly called the Sheraz Tobacco[294]—by Dr. Riach, of the Honorable East India Company's Medical Service.

---

[289] Fraser (1840/2: 50) identified the *sinjeed* as jujube, *Ziziphus jujuba* Miller, which produces an edible drupe with 'a thin, wrinkled, red skin over the whitish, rather sweet flesh around a single hard stone.' See A'lam (2000/2017). According to Harlan (1862: 531), 'The *singid,* or *sinijid*, is more a subject of novel admiration than utility. Its fruit when dry (and it is not used in its recent state) is of an oval form, about an inch in length and half an inch in its shortest diameter. It very nearly resembles in appearance the date, when that fruit assumes a red color in its unripe condition....The tree is ornamental, and I think belongs to the class of willow, of which it resembles the swamp species. It is cultivated chiefly for the fragrance of its blossoms, the odor of which is intense....I have no doubt this tree would be much approved with us for its cool shade, the scent of its flowers, and its ornamental adaptability. It grows to the size of our swamp willow, and would be useful in parks and for other similar purposes.'

[290] *nastaran, Rosa moschata* (var. *R. nastarana*), musk rose. See A'lam (2012).

[291] *Cicer arietinum*, chickpea (Pers. *fal-e nokhod, noql-e nokhodi*). See Watson (1866: 394).

[292] Lindley (1826: 553) wrote an account of ten varieties of Persian melons grown from seed at the Garden of the Horticultural Society in Chiswick, England, from 'two parcels of seeds transmitted to the Society by Henry Willock, Esq....one in the year 1824, the other in the spring of the present year.' Note that Sir Harford Jones had also brought seeds of a melon to England where the fruit was christened 'Sweet Ispahan Melon.' See Knight (1830: 586).

[293] Cf. 12.98.

[294] Pottinger (1816: 235) noted, at Robat, on the western edge of Kerman province, 'The tobacco of this and the neighbouring districts is the mildest and best in the world: it is usually sold under the name of Sheeraz tobacco, from an erroneous idea that it grows at that city; but what is produced there, is not comparable in flavour or delicacy.' According to Watt (1908: 795), 'Sheeraz Tobacco' is *Nicotiniana*

In December, (which is about the middle of winter here) the seed is sown in a dark soil which has been slightly manured (red clayey soil does not do).[295] To protect the seed and to keep it warm, the ground is covered with light thorny bushes, which are removed when the plants are 3 or 4 inches high, and during this period the plants are watered every 4 or 5 days—only, however, in the event of sufficient rain to keep the soil well moistened, not falling. The ground must be kept wet until the plants are 6 or 8 inches high,[296] when they are transplanted into a well moistened soil which has been made into trenches for them; the plants of being put on the tops of the ridges 10 to 12 inches apart, while the trenched plots are made so as to retain the water given. The day they are transplanted water must be given to them, and also every 5 or 6 days subsequently, unless rain enough falls to render this unnecessary. When the plants have become 2 1/2 to 3 1/2 feet high, the leaves will be from 3 to 15 inches long. At this period, or when the flowers are forming, all the flower capsules are pinched or twisted off; after this operation and watering being continued (and irrigation is the system universally employed throughout) the leaves increase in size and thickness until the month of August or September, when each plant is cut off close to the root, and agin stuck firmly into the ground. At this season of the year heavy dews fall during the night; when exposed to these the color of the leaves changes from green to the desired yellow. During this stage, of course no water is given to the soil. When the leaves are sufficiently yellow, the plants are taken from the earth early in the morning, and while they are yet wet from the dew, are heaped on each other in a high Kupper house, (a shed, the walls of which are made with light thorny bushes or such like)[297] where they are freely exposed to the wind. While there, and generally in 4 or 5 days, those leaves which are still green, become of the desired pale yellow colour. The stalks and centre stem of each leaf are now removed and thrown away—the leaves are heaped together in the drying house for

---

alata and was a 'native of Brazil.' The author of Anonymous (1891b: 78) noted, '*N. persica* is precisely the same as *N. alata*,' and was 'certainly Brazilian...I am unable to offer an opinion as to how this species has been introduced into Persia.' In fact, Chardin already referred to the presence of 'Tobacco of *Brazil*, which they call *Tombacou Inglesi*, or *English* Tobacco, because the first *European* takers of Tobacco, with whom they had any Commerce, were the *English*. The *English* us'd to bring this Tobacco from *Brazil*, and sell it in *Persia*, about 50 years ago.' See Floor (2002: 56–57). There were no fewer than 13 different types of Shiraz tobacco (*tambaku-ye Shirazi*) at the turn of the twentieth century, defined largely on their place of origin. See Floor (2003c: 461). According to Consul Dennis, Shiraz tobacco was 'much stronger than ordinary tobacco, and cannot be smoked in the usual way,' and was therefore reserved for water pipes. See Anonymous (1891b: 80). Cf. Floor (2002: 74), who noted that Shiraz tobacco was known for its high nicotine content. Investigations undertaken in the late nineteenth century, however, showed that 'the plant of the Shiraz *tunbaku* was nothing more, as had indeed been expected, than ordinary *Nicotiana Tabacum*.'

[295] In 1890, by contrast, according to a very similar description provided by 'Haider 'Ali Khan, British agent at Shiraz,' the sowing was done in early February. See Anonymous (1891b: 82).

[296] According to Haider 'Ali Khan, 'When the plants begin to show above ground they must be watered once a week, so that the ground remains slightly moist.' See Anonymous (1891b: 82).

[297] Anglo-Indian *chopper*, Hindi *chhappar*, huts or houses with thatched roofs. See Yule and Burnell (1903: 209).

3 or 4 days more, when they are in a fit state for packing. For this operation the leaves are carefully spread on each other and formed into sorts of cakes the circumference 4 to 5 feet, perhaps, of the bag, and 3 to 4 inches thick, great care being taken not to break or injure the leaves.

Bags made of strong cloth, but thin and very open at the sides are filled with these cakes and pressed very strongly down on each other—the leaves would be broken if this were not attended to. When the bags are filled they are placed separately in a drying house, and turned daily until tey are transported, when a second bag like the first is sometimes put on. If the leaves be so dry that there would be a risk of their breaking during the operation of packing, a very slight sprinkling of water is given to them, to enable them to withstand it without injury. The leaf is valued for being thick, tough, and of a uniform light yellow color, and of an agreeable aromatic smell.

In the vicinity of Sheraz, November and December are cool; January and February more so; these may be considered the winter months. In December and January snow falls not unfrequently; the hills are covered with it some months, but it seldom lies any considerable time on the plains. March and April may be considered the spring. (though then the sun during several hours of the day is extremely powerful) and the remaining months till November again, ere the very hot summer and warm autumn of these parts.

The crops of wheat are generally cut down in July, or even as late as August.

Sheraz, April 7, 1831.

Dr. Riach to Sir Henry Willock.

The thanks of the New York Horticultural Society, and of the whole community, are due to Sir Henry Willock for this valuable communication: and those who have it in their power will confer a particular favor on the Society by forwarding to the care of its President the seeds of any rare, useful or ornamental plants, natives of this continent, to be transmitted to Sir Henry in return.'

12.100 'Untitled,' *The Freeman's Journal* (Monday, 13 August, 1832), 'Selected Items,' *The Schenectady Cabinet* (Wednesday, 15 August, 1832) and 'Untitled,' *Lansingburgh Gazette* (Tuesday, 28 August, 1832): 'Commodore Porter[298] has sent from Constantinople to Mr. Skinner, of Baltimore,[299] the seed of the Cuula-ghad, or rare apple tree, completely covered with dark pink flowers of delightful fragrance. It is a native of Persia.'[300]

---

[298] David Porter (1780–1843). U.S. naval officer, commander-in-chief of the Mexican navy and, from 1830 to 1843, American ambassador in Constantinople. For his experiences there see Porter (1835).

[299] John Stuart Skinner (1788–1851), Porter's 'friend, was the editor of an agricultural paper.' See Porter (1875: 269). Originally a postmaster in Baltimore, Skinner was a prolific author of manuals on all manner of agricultural topics. In 1819 he founded *The American Farmer*, the first agricultural journal in the United States.

[300] The account of the tree here is quite garbled. An accurate recounting in Buckingham and Buckingham (1832: 174–175), reads, 'The American Farmer announces the receipt of the seed mentioned in the following extract of a letter from Commodore Porter, to J.S. Skinner, Esq. of

12.1 Miscellaneous

Cashmere shawls

12.101 'Cachemire Shawls,'[301] *The Daily Chronicle* (Wednesday, 27 June, 1832): 'The Boghdscha, or square shawl, with the flower-basket in the centre,[302] may here take precedence of the other kinds, from the superiority of its original destination, rather than from its commercial value; for, in this respect, it is usually surpassed by the long scarf shawls. These, when they have a deep border, are commonly denominated Risaji...the striped shawls, and such as have large patterns, are called Fermaisch[303]....The name Risaji, seems to have some relation to the name of Risa,[304] the eighth of the twelve Imauns, who is much revered in Persia....The word *Fermaisch* which is not to be found in the Persian dictionaries, is derived from *fermuden* to command[305]; what reference the parallel

---

Baltimore, dated Constantinople, Feb. 16, 1832. "I now send you what will be a curiosity in the United States, the seed of the Guul-aghad, or the rare tree. It is the most beautiful thing of the kind I have ever seen. It grows to the size of an ordinary orchard apple-tree, throws out many branches extending horizontally, and affords a most delightful shade. It is literally covered with flowers of a dark pink color, and from the smell, though not from any resemblance, I should suppose it to be of the family of the Acacia, which is of the nature of the locust. This tree in no wise resembles the locust, except in the seedpod and the seed. The bean is precisely that of the locust bean, and if the planting and treatment should be the same as would be practised in the planting and treatment of the locust, you cannot go far wrong. The tree is a rare tree here, and I was informed by the Armenian from whom I obtained the seeds, that it was a native of Persia. Its name in Turkish is Guul, (rare) Aghadj, (tree) and is pronounced Goclagadegh.'" Mallouf's French-Turkish dictionary gives 'Rosier' for *gul aghadji*. See Mallouf (1856: 735).

[301] This is a combination of two articles published in *The World of Fashion, and Continental Feuilletons* (London, 1 November, 1831). See D.V. (1831a, b). Only those parts pertaining to Iran are excerpted here.

[302] Cf. von Hammer (1835b: 368), '*Boghdscha*, viereckig, mit einem Blumenkorb in der Mitte.' As McClellan (1910: 194) wrote, 'The original meaning of the wreaths and bunches of flowers woven in the middle of the square shawl pieces, and which so greatly enhance their value, is full of significance. The Turkish and Persian name of these shawls is Boghdscha; the origin of the word is, however, neither Turkish nor Persian, but Indian, from Pudscha [Anglo-Indian *pooja,/pujah* Skt. *pūjā*, 'Hindu ceremonies in idol-worship;' see Yule and Burnell (1903: 722)] which means a flower offering. When the season of the year will not afford the flowers which the Hindoos offer to their gods, the women spread out shawls, in the middle of which the embroidered basket of flowers supplies the place of fresh blossoms....The Boghdscha, or square shawl, with the flower-basket in the centre, may here take precedence of the other kinds, from the superiority of its original destination, rather than from its commercial value; for, in this respect, it is usually surpassed by the long scarf shawls, which are commonly denominated Risajii.'

[303] *farmaish*. According to von Hammer (1835b: 368), '*Shawl* ist die angenommene Schreibweise des türkischen Shawl, deren vorzüglichste Arten: 1) *Fermaisch*, d. i. die gestreiften.'

[304] Floor (1999: 304), '*shal-e reza'i*.'

[305] *farmudan*. The verb from which the noun *farman*, 'an order, patent, passport,' is derived. See Clarke (1878: 73).

stripes, or the patterns have to the orders of a commander, it is not easy to guess.[306] A very beautiful Fermaisch, striped with red and yellow, was presented by the Persian ambassador, Mirza Abul Hassan Khan, in 1819, to the court interpreter[307] at Vienna, together with a very lean Persian steed, on which a wit observed, "*Que l'ambassadeur avait regale un cheval maigre et un shawl gras.*"

....As a further elucidation of the subject, we subjoin a translation of the list sent with 12 shawls, which Mirza Abul Hassan Khan presented, in the name of the Schah of Persia,[308] to her Majesty, the Empress of Austria.[309]

1. Kaschmire shawl, Tirmeh,[310] i.e. Moondart.
2. Risagt, white, with a wide border; from the manufactory of Dervish Mohammed.
3. Tirmeh, resembling linen. Moondart, or summer month, (for Tirmeh, or Tirmah, is the name of the first Persian summer month)[311] with an apricot border.
4. White Risaji, with a chain border.
5. Musk-coloured Risaji, with leaves and chain.
6. Risaji, of the colour of the heavenly water, with a chain border.
7. Emerald Risaji, with roses in the corners.
8. Ditto.
9. White Risaji, with roses in the corners.
10. Garlick-coloured Risaji, bordered.
11. White shawl (Abreh.)
12. Ditto, with willow branches.

In conclusion, we give the explanation of the word shawl, from the Persian dictionary, Fesheng Schuri,[312] which illustrates every article with a Persian verse, and the following one, by a distich of Mir Rasim Schal, is the well-known dress piece, woven of wool, as are the carpet and Aba, (in contradistinction to the richer silk and gold stuffs.)

"I long not for rich silks or satins,
My mind is contented with the schal and woollen stuff.'"

---

[306] Irvine (1897: 181), wrote that in Bengal *farmaish* denoted '"requisition," for it means the order sent to an official to supply a superior with goods, which latterly were very seldom paid for, though in earlier days their cost was allowed as a debit against the revenue collections.'

[307] Joseph von Hammer (1774–1856), eminent Austrian Orientalist. For his memoirs see Bachofen von Echt (1940).

[308] Fath 'Ali Shah.

[309] Empress Caroline Augusta of Bavaria (r. 1816–1835), wife of Francis I.

[310] Floor (1999: 305, 312–313).

[311] *Tir*. 22 June-22 July. See Balland (1990: Table 37).

[312] *Farhang-e Shuri*. See Suûri (1742–1743).

Hydraulic works at Shushtar

12.102 'Scraps,' *The Daily Chronicle* (Wednesday, 1 August, 1832), 'Untitled,' *Long Island Farmer and Queens County Advertiser* (Thursday, 9 August, 1832) and 'Persian Sam Pachism,'[313] *Vermont Patriot and State Gazette* (Monday, 27 August, 1832): 'At Shuster, a city at the foot of the Bucktiari[314] range of mountains, in Persia, there is a bridge 80 feet above the waters of the river Karoon.[315] From the summit of this bridge, the Persians throw themselves in sport, and with impunity, into the river below.'

Lithography in Persia

12.103 'Extracts from Foreign Papers. Lithographic Press at Sheraz,' *New-York Commercial Advertiser* (Tuesday, 2 October, 1832), 'Lithographic Press at Sheraz,' *New-York Spectator* (Thursday, 4 October, 1832) and 'Lithographic Press at Sheraz,' *Plattsburgh Republican* (Saturday, 10 November, 1832): 'A letter from a gentleman in Persia mentions the establishment of a lithographic press at Sheraz. A native of that place named Mirza Ahmed,[316] who was some time employed as Khoosh Nuwees[317] in the government lithographic establishment under Captain Jervis,[318] is the enterprising individual who has

---

[313] Sam Patch (1799–1829), 'America's first professional daredevil' (Johnson 2003: ix), whose jump from a platform into Niagara Falls in 1829 earned him instant fame and made his name a byword for daring stunts.

[314] Bakhtiyari.

[315] Karun. This seems to be a reference to the Shadorwan weir-bridge which spans the Karun river at Shushtar. It rises, however, only 4–5 m. above the Shotayt, as the branch of the Karun river here is called. It has been described many times, e.g. Ouseley (1819: 357–358), Curzon (1892/2: 374). According to Houtum-Schindler (1880: 321), the bridge was 'partly destroyed in 1832, and repaired by Muḥammed 'Alí Mírzá some years later.'

[316] Probably the same Mirza Ahmed met by Wolff in 1825 when he visited Shiraz and who had formerly been in Calcutta. See Wolff (1829: 60). Vosoughi (2016: 1267) mentions no Mirza Ahmad Shirazi, but rather Mirza Saleh Shirazi and Mirza Asadollah Shirazi. The latter had learned lithography in St. Petersburg.

[317] *khush-nawis*, 'writingmaster.' See Shakespear (1817: 366). Cf. Gilchrist (1808: 83), 'clerk,' Gilchrist (1820: xx), 'writing master' and Thompson (1838: 231), 'writer.'

[318] George Ritso Jervis (1794–1851). Later Colonel Jervis, at one time Chief Engineer, Bombay Presidency. According to Anonymous (1851a: 418), 'To use the words of a Bombay newspaper... "it is to Colonel Jervis entirely we are indebted for the earliest successful efforts made to introduce a correct system of education among the natives [of India]....before the dream of colleges and professors had entered our heads, Captain (now Colonel) Jervis laboured without intermission to obtain translations, and have men taught to read and write, and reason and reflect."' Jervis (1853: 79) wrote, 'My honoured brother, Colonel Jervis, founded the first lithographic press in Western India, in 1825 (from whence he sent forth a beautiful copy of the Gospel of St. Luke in Persian); and contributed largely to the instruction of the natives by the translation into several languages of

introduced this valuable improvement into Persia. He has already printed a few of the smaller elementary works usually made use of in schools of that country, and has commenced printing the Koran, the first sheet of which has been forwarded here as a specimen. As a proof of the spirit with which the work is carried on, it is only necessary to say that the sum of 500 romandus [sic, *tomans*], or about 3500 rupees, has been given to a celebrated Persian writer who is to furnish the copy and we suppose correct the proof sheet.'

12.104 'Untitled,' *Boston Daily Advertiser & Patriot* (Friday, 5 October, 1832), 'Untitled,' *The National Ægis & General Advertiser* (Wednesday, 10 October, 1832) and 'Lithographic Press in Persia,' *Christian Register* (Saturday, 13 October, 1832): 'A lithographic press has been established at Schiraz in Persia by Mirza Ahmed, an inhabitant of that city. Some elementary works have been already printed for the use of schools, and the publication of the Koran has been commenced.'

Philosophy

12.105 *New-York Mirror* (Saturday, 23 March, 1833) and 'Persian Story,' *Plattsburgh Republican* (Monday, 8 November, 1834): 'Saadi the Persian[319] tells a Story of three sages, a Greek, an Indian, and a Persian, who is [sic, in] the presence of a King of Persia, debated on this question: "of all the evils which is the greatest?" The Grecian said, "Old age oppressed with poverty;" the Indian answered, "Pain with impatience;" the Persian pronounced it to be,—Death without good works before it."'[320]

Byron's brass buttons

12.106 'Anecdotes of Byron,' New-*York Evening Post* (Wednesday, 31 July, 1833): 'Nothing of this alustrious [sic, illustrious] poet, however trivial, can be otherwise than

---

scientific and other books, which he likewise lithographed and published. In these laborious and remarkable services he often called on me to take a part, and was open to every suggestion.' For a sketch of his life see Anonymous (1852a: 106–109).

[319] Musharrifu'd-Din ibn Muslihu'd-Din 'Abdullah, better known as Sa'di Shirazi (1213–1291), renowned mystical Persian poet. See Browne (1906: 526ff). Jackson and Yohannan (1914: 101) noted that he was 'generally conceded to be the most popular writer in Persian literature.'

[320] Cf. Anonymous (1815).

12.1 Miscellaneous

interesting. We knew him well. At Mr. Murray's[321] dinner-table, the annotator[322] met him and Sir John Malcolm. Lord Byron talked of intending to travel in Persia.[323] "What must I do when I set off?" said he to Sir John. "Cut off your buttons!" "My buttons!" what these metal ones?" "Yes; the Persians are in the main very honest fellows; but if you go thus bedaened [sic, bedizened], you will infallibly be murdered for your buttons."'[324]

The Death of Sir John Malcolm

12.107 'Sir John Malcolm,' *New-York Evening Post* (Saturday, 3 August, 1833): 'It is with much pain we state that Sir John Malcolm died after a short but severe illness, at his house in Princes street, on the 30th May,[325] in the sixty-fifth year of his age; he was all but recovered from a paralytic stroke when he ventured out in an east wind; was attacked with influenza and hurried to the grave. His loss will be felt by his countrymen, more particularly by persons connected with India: to worth he was kind and friendly, and to genius he ever lent, without solicitation, a helping hand. He was much beloved in Bombay, and during his lifetime, his comrades in council and in arms, ordered his statue as a companion to that of Elphinstone.[326] He abounded in anecdote; his happy gaiety of nature and unrestrained

---

[321] John Murray II (1808–1892), eminent publisher, intimate friend of Sir Walter Scott, Lord Byron, A.H. Layard and many other luminaries of nineteenth century letters. Murray published Malcolm's *Sketch of the Sikhs* in 1812 and 3 years later his *History of Persia* (1st ed. 1815, 2nd ed. 1829) followed by *Sketches of Persia* (1827). See Smiles (1891: 236).

[322] James Smith (1775–1839) who, with his younger brother Horace (1779–1849), published an enormously popular volume of parodies of famous contemporary poets (e.g. Wordsworth, Coleridge, Byron, Southey) in 1812 entitled *Rejected Addresses*. See Smith and Smith (1812). James was the author of the 'Notes' subjoined to each poem. There he referred to himself as 'the annotator.' See Smith and Smith (1888: xviii, n. *).

[323] As John Murray's son noted in an account published in Smiles (1891: 268) (= Anonymous 1892b: 406), 'Lord Byron dined several times at Albemarle Street. On one of these occasions he met Sir John Malcolm—a most agreeable and accomplished man—who was all the more interesting to Lord Byron because of his intimate knowledge of Persia and India. After dinner Sir John observed to Lord Byron how much gratified he had been to meet him, and how surprised he was to find him so full of gaiety and entertaining conversation. Byron replied, "Perhaps you see me now at my best."'

[324] This entirely apocryphal anecdote was in fact the work of James Smith and had only just appeared in the 18th edition of *Rejected Addresses*. See Smith and Smith (1833/1: 18).

[325] As Kaye (1856/2: 607–608), Malcolm had been suffering from influenza since February and on 28 April suffered a stroke ('paralysis') while being driven in his coach. By mid-May he seemed to be recovering but on 25 May he suffered a setback. 'It is supposed that, having been taken out on that day [in his carriage], although an extremely ungenial one, by the special direction of his chief medical attendant, the keen air smote him, and that the shock was greater than his shattered constitution could sustain. All the worst symptoms of his malady reappeared; and from that time he never rallied..' See Kaye (1856/2: 611).

[326] Cf. 11.160.

kindliness of heart, made his company acceptable to the most fastidious; nor did we ever meet with a man, who, like him, could pass so readily from the comic to the serious—could smooth his brow in the midst of the most joyous laughter, and give wholesome council and solemn advice. He was known and beloved from the centre of Persia to the frontiers of the Birman [Burman] Empire; he spoke the languages of the East with fluency, and was intimate with the natures and social manners of all the tribes of the East. His history works will continue his memory with honour among us: his "History of Central India;"[327] his "Political History of the East;"[328] his "Persian Sketches;"[329] his "Account of John Leyden;"[330] and lastly, his "Life of Lord Clive," unpublished,[331] but completed in the last chapter, are works that cannot soon die; they show a skilful scholar, a shrewd biographer, and an accurate and eloquent historian. The close of his life may be reckoned unfortunate. Relying on the influence of his talents, the good deeds he had done, and, moreover, on his right of birth, he offered himself as a member of the Dumfries Boroughs, and was rejected. He was received in the place on which his genius and worth must shed lasting honor, with respect, indeed, by some, but with much disrespect by others, and returned to London, sorrowful, but not incensed; nay, he came and told the writer of this very brief and imperfect sketch, of his ill success in "bonnie Dumfries," and dwelt with much good humour on the virulence of a shoemaker, named Wilson. "I wish," said he, "you had but seen the damned birsing [angry] body coming against him who had thrashen Holkar,[332] with a bantam-cock strut, and all his inseam awls, outseam awls, pegging awls, and closing awls—Lord how the creature crew!" It may be some time before Dumfries will have an opportunity of rejecting a genius of her own blood again. The last time we saw Sir John was at the Abbotsford subscription meeting[333]: he looked pale and exhausted—we sill think we

---

[327] Malcolm (1832).

[328] Malcolm never published a work entitled Political History of the East. The author here is presumably referring to Malcolm (1826).

[329] Actually *Sketches of Persia*. See Malcolm (1827).

[330] A reference to the Scottish Orientalist and poet John Casper Leyden (1775–1811) who died on Java while on an expedition with Lord Minto. This may be a reference to the eulogy delivered at Leyden's funeral in Bombay which appeared in the *Bombay Courier*. See Bayne (1893: 216). Malcolm sent a copy to Sir Walter Scott. See Koditschek (2011: 57 and n. 1). Malcolm also composed 'Verses to the memory of Leyden.' See Malcolm (1813). For the friendship between Leyden and Malcolm see Morton (1819: xxxvii–xl, lxxvi–lxxxi).

[331] Published posthumously as Malcolm (1836).

[332] At the battle of Mahidpur, on 6 January 1818, Malcolm led a Sepoy force commanded by British officers to victory over the Mahratha chief Malhar Rao Holkar II. See Kaye (1856/2: 208–211), Beale (1881: 167), Balfour (1885: 94).

[333] At the first 'Abbotsford subscription' meeting, held on 9 November 1832 and attended by Malcolm, 'it was resolved that a subscription should be forthwith opened for the purpose of securing Abbotsford with all its literary and other treasures, to the family of Sir Walter Scott' who had died on 21 September 1832. See Anonymous (1832c). A subsequent meeting, at which Malcolm was again present, was held on 27 April 1833, just over a month before his death. See Anonymous (1833c).

hear him saying, "And should all our endeavours fail—and they surely cannot—it will be a consolation to think, that when on some distant day my son passes along the Tweed, and Abbotsford in ruins, he can truly say, 'My father tried to save you from destruction, but was not seconded by his country.'" Nor shall we soon forget the anecdote he told us of Lord Clive.[334] "When Clide [sic, Clive][335] was a young man a friend called on him 1 day, and found him sitting with books and a pistol on the table. 'Take that pistol,' said Clive to his visitor, 'and fire it out at the window:' he did so at once: before the smoke subsided, and while the room rung with the report, Clide sprung to his feet, exclaiming, 'God has something for me to do yet—I snapped that pistol twice to my head before you came in—yet it did not go off—God has work for me yet."[336] We hope a full and ample memoir will be written of this distinguished man."—*London Athenæum*.'

Descriptions of Isfahan

12.108 'Ispahan,'[337] *St. Lawrence Republican* (Tuesday, 6 August, 1833): 'On the southern boundary of Persia we find the remains of Ispahan, that immense city, to which Chardin[338] gives 33 miles in circumference, and which, when he visited it, contained from 6 to 700,000 inhabitants.[339] This superb capital, which the Persians considered as one half of the world, has now left a mere shadow of its former grandeur. The large spaces which served as pleasure grounds to the avenues, are now converted into common gardens. We may travel for 3 h on country roads, which were formerly streets leading to the centre of the city. Still, however, according to the account of M. Olivier,[340] the bazars constructed by ShaAbbis [sic, Shah 'Abbas], which was covered in with vaults, and lighted by numerous domes, are of prodigious extent and proclaim the former magnificence of the city.[341] Sir

---

[334] Malcolm once referred to Clive as 'my hero.' See Kaye (1856/2: 476).

[335] Robert Clive, 1st Baron Clive (1725–1774), first Governor of the Bengal Presidency and a key figure in the early years of the East India Company. For his life see Malcolm (1836).

[336] The anecdote appears, with slightly different wording, in Malcolm (1836/3: 45). Kaye (1856/2: 587, n. *), noted that, on his way to Scotland in August, 1832, Malcolm 'passed the night at the house, near Watford, of his old friend, Mr. Halyburton, from whom he derived some anecdotes of Clive to be inserted in his biography.'

[337] The entire text of this article was drawn discontinuously from Malte-Brun (1822: 246–252).

[338] Jean Chardin. Cf. 1.190, 1.196.

[339] According to Chardin (1711/8: 3–4), 'Plusieurs gens font monter le nombre de ses *habitans* à onze cens mille ames. Ceux cui en mettent le moins, assurent qu'il y en a six cens mille. Les mémoires qu'on m'avoit donnez étoient fort differens sur cela....Après tout, je crois *Ispahan* autant peuplée que *Londres*, qui est la ville la plus peuplée de l'*Europe*.'

[340] Guillaume-Antoine Olivier (1756–1814). For his significance cf. Bernard (1997).

[341] The long description of Isfahan's buildings and other architecture in Olivier (1807/5: 177–186) mentions neither vaults nor domes.

R.K. Porter says he travelled under its massy arches considerable more than a mile, to where they terminate at the northern angle of the Royal Square, and that, after crossing the square, the bazar is continued at the opposite angle.[342]

This vast square called the Maiden Shah,[343] one of the most extensive in the world, was formerly one of the chief ornaments of Ispahan; enriched with shops, where every commodity of luxury and splendid manufactory was exposed. Here also the troops were exercised, and the nobility exhibited their Asiatic tournaments before their king. In the centre of each side of this immense area, stands some edifice, remarkable for grandeur or for character. In the northwest is the great gate of entrance to the bazar, on which, in former times, stood the celebrated clock of Ispahan. The south eastern side shows the Meshed-Shah,[344] a superb mosque, built by Shah-Abbas, and dedicated to Mehedi 1 of the 12 Imans. On the northeast is the mosque of Looft Ullah[345]; and on the southwest the Ali Kapi,[346] or gate of Ali, forms a majestic parallel to the bazar porch on the opposite side. The length of the square is about 2000 feet, and its breadth 700. Each face presents a double range of arches, the one above the other, the longest range consisting of 86, and the shortest of 30. At a few paces from these arcades there is a constant supply of water, running through a canal of black marble, and opening into a variety of basins of the same substance, which are constantly full, and rendered more cool and refreshing by a close shade of elegant trees. The Sefi, or Ali Kapi gate, is described as one of the most perfect pieces of brick work to be found in the Persian empire. Over the great entrance it rises into several stories, and the flights of steps which lead to them are formed of the most beautiful variegated porcelain. The roof of the large chamber over the gate is sumptuously gilt and carved, and supported by 18 lofty octagonal pillars, once richly emblazoned in gold, but now faded. It is open on all sides but one. On the side nearest the balustrade facing the square, a round platform marks the spot on which Shah-Abbas used to sit, and from whence he reviewed his chivalry, galloping & skirmishing beneath, or witnessed the combats of wild animals. The freshness of all the buildings is particularly striking to a European, or the inhabitants of any comparatively humid country, in which the atmosphere cherishes a vegetation of mosses, linchens [sic], and other cryptogamous plants, which we particularly associate in our minds with the spectacle of decay. Above this there is a numerous range of small rooms, some of them evidently appropriated to purposes of carousal.—From the roof of the building an extensive view of the city is obtained. In former times this was

---

[342] Ker Porter (1821/2: 38) described the 'great bazar of Shah Abbas; the whole of which enormous length of building is vaulted above, to exclude heat, yet admit air and light. Hundreds of shops, without inhabitant, filled the sides of this epitome of a deserted mercantile world; and having traversed their untrodden labyrinths for an extent of nearly two miles, we entered the Maidan Shah, another spacious soundless theatre of departed grandeur.'

[343] Meydan-e Naqsh-e Jahan.

[344] Masjed-e Shah.

[345] Lotf-Allah.

[346] 'Ali Qapu.

undoubtedly splendid, but at present, with the exception of the palaces in the gardens, the whole mass below is one mouldering succession of ruinous houses, mosques, and shapeless structures, which had formerly been the mansions of the nobility, broken by groups or lines of various tall trees, which once made part of the gardens of the houses now in ruins.—Ispahan, though two-thirds of it are in ruins, contains more than 200,000 inhabitants.

At present, Ispahan is in some degree recovering from its state of abject decay.—Mohammed Hussein, whose talents have raised him to the place of Ameen-a-Doolah, or second minister of the king, being a native of Ispahan,[347] has erected in it a splendid new palace, and enlarged and beautified many of the former edifices. Having, in the faithful discharge of his public duty, encouraged agriculture, and recolonized many deserted villages in the country, he has used similar means to populate the habitable streets of this city, by promoting the old manufactures, and striving to attract commerce back to its ancient channels."

Astrologers

12.109 'Persian Astrologers,' *Long Island Farmer and Queens County Advertiser* (Wednesday, 14 August, 1833): 'There is nothing whatever done in Persia without an Astrologer first gives his opinion respecting it.—Sir John Malcolm relates that a certain Persian Ambassador[348] was once about to set out for India on a mission.[349] His astrologer told him that he must not leave his house by the ordinary door, for that there was an evil star in the heavens which shed a malignant influence upon the house in that direction.—The Ambassador then, in order to leave the premises, had a hole made in one of the walls at the side of his mansion, but he found when he passed through it that he had got into the residence of a neighbor; in short, his Excellency had to make breaches in five succeeding walls in order to pass into the street, in a quarter which was shut out from the power of the evil constellation.—In the street, however, a fresh obstacle presented itself for he had

---

[347] Haji Mohammad Hoseyn Khan Amir-od Doula (1758–1823). Curzon (1895: xv), recognized that, in Morier's *Hajji Baba of Ispahan* (1824), 'The Amin-ed-Dowleh, or Lord High Treasurer, "a large coarse man, and the son of a greengrocer of Ispahan," was Mohammed Hussein Khan, the second personage of the Court.' Hasan-e Fasa'i wrote of him that, 'By reason of his sagacity and ingenuity in the handling of affairs and in bargaining with the landowners and his capacity to derive advantage from everything, he was superior to most learned men. Although he could neither read nor write, he was not in need of a scribe or accountant in his transactions and administrative affairs. Step by step he advanced: he was appointed lord mayor of Esfahan; then he advanced further and became begler-begi of that province; next he was promoted to the governorship of the same region; later he became minister of finance of the empire; finally the office of prime minister of the Persian empire was bestowed upon him.' See Busse (1972: 167–168).

[348] Haji Khalil Khan-e Koroghlu Qazvini. Cf. 8.46.

[349] This is a paraphrase of a story related in Malcolm (1815/2: 577–578).

already ascertained that the mischievous influence presided as much on the gate of his fort as upon the door of his house. Under these circumstances, not being able to proceed by land in the natural road, he took a boat in order to land and pursue his journey to India 2 miles off. But the roughness of the sea forbade the experiment, and it is an actual fact, that permission was granted by the Governor of the town to the Ambassador to throw down a part of its wall, in order to let out the gallant diplomatist by a passage that was luckily deserted by the ill-omened star.'[350]

Fath 'Ali Shah's crystal bed

12.110 'Splendid Bedstead,' *Phenix Gazette* (Tuesday, 20 August, 1833), 'Splendid Bedstead,' *Newburyport Herald* (Tuesday, 20 August, 1833), 'Splendid Bedstead,' *Nantucket Inquirer* (Saturday, 24 August, 1833), 'Splendid Bedstead,' *Richmond Enquirer* (Tuesday, 10 September, 1833) and 'Splendid Bedstead,' *Middlesex Gazette* (Wednesday, 18 September, 1833): 'There has been lately exhibited in the palace of the Tamedo, at St. Petersburgh,[351] a state bed, constructed at the royal manufactory[352] by order of the emperor, to be sent as a present to the Schah of Persia. It is formed of solid crystal, resplendent with silver ornaments. It is ascended by steps of blue glass, and has a fountain underneath so contrived as to throw out on each side, jets of odoriferous waters. The effect when the chamber is lighted up is absolutely dazzling, as it has the appearance of myriads of diamonds.[353]—*Galignani's Messenger*.'

---

[350] The paraphrase was taken from a review of Atkinson (1832) published in Anonymous (1833b: 494–495).

[351] No palace by this name is known in St. Petersburg, suggesting it is a misprint or mistranscription of 'Tauride' or Tavricheskiy Palace. Built by Catherine the Great in 1783, it was later given to Potemkin, the hero of 'Tauride,' after the conquest of the Crimea. At certain points in its history, some of the rooms were used to display paintings, sculpture and other types of art objects. See Bædeker (1883: 176).

[352] Founded in 1792, the Imperial Glass Works 'was established, like the porcelain works, with a view of supplying with its wares the numerous Imperial palaces, and on a similar basis. These works are now unrivalled in Russia for the perfection of the articles turned out, and the fine quality of crystal glass.' See Anonymous (1881a: 498).

[353] Granville (1829: 317) wrote, 'In November 1825, the people of St. Petersburgh had an opportunity of viewing, at this Imperial manufactory, perhaps the most singular piece of workmanship, in crystal, that has ever been exhibited to public curiosity. This consisted of a large bedstead in cut crystal, wrought at the Imperial manufactory, made entirely by Russian artists, from a design of Monsieur Ivanoff [I.A. Ivanov (1779–1848)], by order of the late Emperor, and intended as a present to the Shah of Persia. It is reported to have been magnificent in the extreme. It has not proved a bed of roses to that Sovereign, and the chances of war have made him pay pretty dearly for the splendid present.' This 'Glass Manufactory, belonging to the government,' had produced, 'A glass bed, of great value, presented by the emperor to the king of Persia, the enormous mirror presented to the sultan, and the glass railings of the church of Smolna.' See Anonymous (1839a: 209). According to Anonymous

12.1 Miscellaneous

Fath 'Ali Shah's plate

12.111 'The Shah of Persia's *Plate,*' *Long Island Farmer and Queens County Advertiser* (Wednesday, 9 October, 1833), 'Untitled,' *The Corrector* (Saturday, 12 October, 1833; first paragraph only), 'Untitled,' *The Schenectady Cabinet* (Wednesday, 23 October, 1833; first two sentences only), 'The Shah of Persia's Plate,' *The Freeman's Journal* (Monday, 18 November, 1833), 'The Schah of Persia's Plate,' *The Portsmouth Journal of Literature & Politics* (Saturday, 7 December, 1833; to 'ground') and 'The Schah of Persia'a Plate,' *Saturday Morning Transcript* (Saturday, 14 December, 1833; to 'ground'): 'The Shah of Persia possesses the most magnificent collection of plate in the world. It consists of upwards of 4.000 utensils of gold, most of which are set with precious stones or pearls. Among them are sets of spoons, vases, cups, jugs, basins, dishes, &c.;—some of the cups are so heavy that when filled they cannot be lifted with one hand.—Perhaps the most remarkable portion of the collection is a set of spoons, each a foot long. The bowls of these spoons are of wrought gold, and the handles are richly set with rubies, and terminated by large diamonds. The immense size of these spoons is occasioned by the Oriental custom of eating, seated on the ground.

Foreigners are permitted to see this splendid and unique collection of plate, and also the crystal bedstead, lately presented by the Emperor of Russia[354] to the Shah of Persia.'[355]

(1866c: 109), the bed was 'formed of crystal glass, resplendent with silver ornaments. It was ascended by steps of blue glass, and had a fountain for scented water attached to it. When the chamber in which it stood was lit up the bedstead presented the appearance of countless diamond sparks.' In fact, the crystal fountain was intended as a gift to Khosrow Mirza but its transport was cancelled after Griboyedov's death. It was, instead, on its way to Charles II of France when he was deposed, and it ended up being given to the Czar's brother-in-law. A.I. Ivanov, who designed the bed for Fath 'Ali Shah, had joined the Imperial Glass Works in 1806. As Shelkovnikov (1967: 124) noted, 'The Art Academy Report for 1836 states that Academician I. Ivanov designed vases and candelabra which were executed under his surveillance. It seems clear that the majority of decorative pieces produced by the manufactory from 1820 on were designed by Ivanov.' More recently, a thorough account of the crystal bed (*khrustal'naia krovat'*), with an illustration of it, has been given in Chadaga (2014: 100–106) who noted that, already in 1819, Alexander I had given Fath 'Ali Shah a crystal swimming pool from the Imperial Glass Works, which prompted the Shah to request a crystal bed. The request was approved in April, 1824, and in February, 1826, shortly before the start of the Second Russo-Persian War, Lt I. Noskov and two glass artisans were sent to Tehran with the disassembled bed. After a harrowing journey, and the deaths of the two artisans to disease, the bed was delivered by Noskov who, 'fulfilled the shah's wish and set up this infinitely complicated thing, putting into proper order its parts, not a single one of which was damaged, neither during the journey nor during the assembly.' Although Noskov declined the Shah's offer of the Order of the Lion and Son, money and shawls, he did accept the release of 250 Russian prisoners-of-war who had been captured several months earlier. Cf. Andreeva (2018: 60–61, 69–70), Spillman (2006: 12).

[354] Nicholas I.
[355] From Anonymous (1833e: 457).

The Persian discovery of wine

12.112 'Wine,' *Long Island Farmer and Queens County Advertiser* (Wednesday, 16 April, 1834), 'Important Discovery,' *Long Island Farmer and Queens County Advertiser* (Wednesday, 27 November, 1839), 'Discovery of Wine,' *New-York Evening Post* (Thursday, 28 May, 1846), 'Discovery of Wine,' *Daily Evening Transcript* (Friday, 29 May, 1846) and 'Discovery of Wine,' *The Newport Mercury* (Saturday, 20 June, 1846) and 'The Origin of Wine,' *Richmond Enquirer* (Friday, 30 July, 1847): 'Jemished, the founder of Persepolis,[356] is, by Persian writers, said to have been the first who invented wine. He was immoderately fond of grapes, and desiring to preserve some, they were placed for this purpose in a large vessel, and lodged in a vault for future use. When the vessel was opened, the grapes had fermented; and their juice in this state was so acid, that the king believed it must be poisonous. He had some vessels filled with it, and *poison* written upon each; they were placed in his room.—It happened that one of his favorite ladies was affected with a nervous headache (Hyphas) and the pain distracted her so much, that she desired death. Observing a vessel with *poison* written on it, she took it and swallowed its contents. The wine, for such it had become, overpowered the lady, who fell down into a sound sleep, and awoke much refreshed. Delighted with the remedy, she repeated the dose so often, that the monarch's poison was all drunk. He soon discovered this, and forced the lady to confess what she had done. A quantity of wine was made, and Jemsheed and all his court drank of the new beverage; which from the circumstance that led to its discovery, is this day known in Persia by the name of Zeber-e-Kooshon,[357] the *delightful poison.—English paper.*'

The Dasht-e Kavir

12.113 'The Kuveer or Salt Desert,' *New-York Evening Post* (Friday, 6 June, 1834): 'A picturesque and very eastern story, full of hair-breadth 'scapes, battle, murder, and sudden death, all arranged by one evidently quite at home with the materials which he employs. The heroine, Guleyaz, is a beautiful and spirited creature, and in good contrast to the more timid and yielding Leilah; while the hero is as brave and as much in love as any reader of

---

[356] The Persian name of the site is Takht-e Jamshid, 'the throne of Jamshid.' He is the Avestan Yima. According to Mirkhond, 'Jamšid moved his residence from Sejestān to Fārs at the beginning of his reign and...built the palace now called Čehel Menār (i.e., Persepolis).' See Skjærvø (2012).

[357] *zeher-e-khoosh*. This is taken almost verbatim from Malcolm (1815/1: 16), where it is attributed to 'Moullah Ackber's MSS.' In 1817 it was reproduced as one of a series of 'Anecdotes...taken promiscuously from Sir John Malcolm's History of Persia.' See Anonymous (1817b: 295). Cf. Morewood (1838: 86–87) and Birdwood (1862: 202–203) with only slight variations.

romance could desire. We have spoken of hair-breadth escapes, and cannot do better than give one of them.'[358]

Raiding in Persia

12.114 'Chappows,' *Geneva Gazette* (Wednesday, 25 June, 1834): 'The works of Sir Walter Scott have made most readers well acquainted with the "forays," or predatory incursions, by which the borders of England and Scotland were so much disturbed previously to the union of the two crowns. From the Tigris to the Indus, transactions very similar to such forays are known by the name of "Chappows;"[359] and we imagine that a short account of them will not be without interest, as affording materials for a comparison between the state of this country in the sixteenth and preceding countries, and a considerable part of Asia in the nineteenth.

Besides the towns and villages which this extent of country, under different rulers, contains, it is abundantly spotted with the encampments of wandering tribes, who, under different names, are probably all members of the same great Turkish family, which has extended its ramifications so much farther westward than the limits we have assigned to the *chappow* in the form we purpose to describe it. This restriction is necessary, for the foray in some form or other, diversified only by the peculiar habits of a people, exists wherever a government is weak and a frontier much exposed. As we have to consider these tribes only with regard to the *chappow*, in which their usages differ very little, it will not be necessary to quote their specific denominations, although we would be understood as speaking generally of the people called Turkomans, who live chiefly in the country to the east of Persia, and who differ little, except in a dash of character more wild and savage, from the nomades (Eelaut) who wander in Persia itself[360]; and who, although much under the control of the government, still cherish their lawless habits, and are always ready to avail themselves of any opportunity to indulge them, which the weakness or supineness of that government may afford.

Their habits of life make the Turkomans more than usually attentive to the breed and management of their horses, with a particular regard to those qualities which are of most importance to them in their *chappows*. The horses bred and reared by them are so highly esteemed in Persia, and fetch such good prices, that some of the tribes, compelled by the

---

[358] Here follows a long excerpt from Fraser (1833: 28–32) which, however, was probably taken from a review in the *London Literary Gazette* of 17 August, 1833, where it had been excerpted. See Anonymous (1833d: 521–522). Cf. Anonymous (1834b).

[359] *chapaw*. Cannon and Kaye (2001: 75) note the use of 'chappow/chupow' meaning 'raid, foray, plundering expedition,' in English for the first time in Kinneir (1813: 26–27) who wrote of Georgian slaves in Persia that 'the greater part of them are carried away by the Persian armies, in their *chupows*, or predatory incursions into Georgia.'

[360] *ilat*, sing. *il*, 'tribe,' used of pastoral nomad tribes in Iran. See Potts (2014: 247).

strength or contrivance of the Persian government to forego their chappows, employ themselves very profitably in rearing horses for sale. They do not relish this employment, however; but look forward in sanguine expectation that such stupid times will not last forever. "If matters go on in this way," said a member of one such tribe to Sir John Malcolm, "our sons will become a set of blackguard horsedealers, instead of gallant warriors, and their children will be instructed in the art of cheating unwary citizens, instead of the manly occupation of plundering a rich traveller. We shall no more have fine Persian girls to keep our tents clean and dress our victuals, nor active fellows to rule our horses and attend our flocks.—What a sad change! And as to our profits in breeding and selling horses, I have known more money given, in one day, for the ransom of a nobleman or a wealthy merchant, than our whole tribe can now make by trafficking in cattle for a twelvemonth."[361]

These so much prized horses are considerably beyond the average size of the animal in Persia. They measure from 15 to 16 hands high, and in shape resemble an English carriage horse of the highest breed. Their unusual size is attributed to the fine pasture lands on which they are reared; and the astonishing capability of bearing fatigue which they exhibit, to their high blood and the manner in which they are trained. The Turkomans ride them with snaffles, and allow them to go slouching along with their necks loose. These plunderers train their horses as much as we do our racers or hunters; and before they begin their expeditions, they put them in complete condition. They have been known to go 140 miles in 24 h; and their predatory parties have been ascertained to march, without halting, from 80 to 110 miles daily, for a fortnight together.

Before proceeding on a *chappow*, the Turkomans prepare some hard balls of barley-meal, which equally serve for the subsistence of themselves and their cattle, being, when wanted, soaked in water to fit them for use. It is said to be customary with them in crossing the desert of Kerman, and other deserts in which no water can be obtained, to open a vein in the shoulder of the horse and drink a little of his blood. They consider this to be as beneficial to the animal which loses the blood as to the rider who imbibes it.

The number of persons engaged in a chappow varies greatly. From 30 to 50 mounted robbers, with about half the number of led horses, destined to bring away the spoil, is perhaps a fair average estimate.—They do not hesitate to make a bold dash into large towns, occasionally, but more frequently some flourishing village is the object of attack. This is sometimes made in the open day; and in an inconceivably short time the dwellings are pillaged, the fields often laid waste, the finest of the young men, women, and children, made slaves, and the whole party is on its homeward flight. The least resistance to them is fatal. The houses are then burnt, the old and feeble murdered, and all the property that cannot be carried away, destroyed. Their principal weapon is a spear, rudely formed, with a small piece of steel at the point, and generally from 10 to 12 feet long. This is in their hands, so very effective a weapon, that they hold all others in light estimation. "We were one day,"

---

[361] The quotation is from Malcolm (1827/2: 14–15).

says Sir John Malcolm, "looking at a party of the king's guards, each of whom was armed with a sword, a spear, a pair of pistols and a dagger. Raham [sic, Rahman] Beg (the Turkoman mentioned before) tossed up his head in contempt, exclaiming,—'What is the good of all this arsenal?—What can a soldier want beyond a spear and a heart!'"[362] Nevertheless, the Turkomans have the bow and arrow also in use, but fire-arms are very sparingly employed.

Their treatment of the prisoners they take in their *chappows* is, in the first instance, terribly severe. A very recent traveller* [*Lieut. Burnes. The writer of this article met that gentleman in Persia, and feels pleasure in recording that to his skill, experience, and kindness, he is probably indebted for the preservation of a life which he hopes to render useful.] in these countries relates that he sometimes met them returning from their chappows, and dragging their captives after their horses by a cord, at the end of which was a hook so inserted through the flesh as to embrace the collarbone. This savage process, however, seems to be only resorted to in order to subdue the spirits of the more refractory prisoners, who are thus made to keep up on foot with the beast to which they are attached, until quite exhausted, when they are placed on the back of a horse. Capt. Christie's[363] account, in Pottinger's Travels,[364] of the manner in which the Belochees treat the victims of their *chappows*, so well illustrates the subject, that we shall make use of his statement. When first taken, the prisoners regard themselves as the most unfortunate beings in existences [sic] and, indeed, the treatment they then experience is of the harshest and most discouraging description. They are blindfolded, and tied on camels, and in that manner transported, to prevent the possibility of their knowing how to return; and, to deter them from even wishing to revisit their native soil, the hair of the women and the beards of the men are cut off, and the roots totally destroyed by a preparation of quick-lime. But they are soon reconciled to their fate, and become attached and faithful servants. Capt. Christie expressed his surprise to the *sirdar* of Nooshky,[365] that his numerous slaves should work so dilligently without any person to oversee them. "Why not?" he replied, "they are clothed, fed, and treated like the other members of my family; and if they do not labor, they are well aware that bread will be scarce, and that they must suffer as well as ourselves. It is their interest to produce plenty, for they know that they get their share of whatever falls to my lot."—Capt. Christie assented to the justness of his observation, but added that he should have thought them likely to run away.—"Nothing of the kind!" replied the old sirdar, "they are too wise to attempt it. In the first place, they do not know the way to their own country; and even admitting that they did, and that they wished to return, they are

---

[362] Taken from Malcolm (1827/2: 16).

[363] Captain Charles Christie (d. 1812), 5th Bombay Native Infantry. Cf. 9.112.

[364] Lieutenant Henry Pottinger (1789–1856). Cf. 9.112. The reference is to Pottinger (1816).

[365] Nushki in western Pakistani Baluchistan, on the edge of the Helmand desert. See Balfour (1885: 1113). The *sirdar* was identified by Christie as Eidel [Adel] Khan Rukhshanee [Rakshani/Rashkani]. See Pottinger (1816: 64).

much happier here, and have less to care for. Were they at home, they must toil fully as hard as they do now; besides which, they would have to think of their clothes, their houses, and their food. Now they look to me for all their necessaries; and, in short, that you may judge of their feelings, I need only inform you that the greatest punishment we can inflict upon them is to send them about their business."[366] We think it very likely that the slaves themselves would not have spoken in a tone very different from that of their master. Slavery, in Mahomedan countries, as compared with the general condition of the people, is far from presenting a disadvantageous contrast. It is there but a name, and a name of which no man is or need be ashamed.

Persons of such apparent consideration as to warrant the captors in expecting a good ransom, are, until that expectation is relinquished, more favorably treated, in the first instance and afterwards, than those who are designed for permanent slavery. About 2 years since, the uncle of the king of Oude was taken prisoner by the Turkomans, while proceeding on a pilgrimage to Mushed.[367]—Notwithstanding the plainness of his appearance, they discovered from the softness and clearness of his hands and feet, that he was not accustomed to work or exposure, and therefore reserved him for ransom. He used to speak of his residence among them without indignation or complaint. His master, indeed, was somewhat of a churl; but his mistress was very kind. They obtained no good thing of which he did not get a share; and although they would not allow him to be idle, he was put only to easy work, such as disengaging cotton from the pods, mending clothes, and, occasionally, washing. His superiority in the latter accomplishment is within our personal knowledge; and he confessed that he was proud to know something which would render him useful among the Turkomans.'[368]

Execution

12.115 'Execution of a Female in Persia,' *Farmer's Gazette* (Friday, 11 July, 1834), 'Execution of a Female in Persia,' *Long Island Farmer and Queens County Advertiser* (Wednesday, 16 July, 1834), Execution of a Female in Persia: By an Eye-Witness,' *Norfolk Advertiser and Independent Politician* (Saturday, 19 July, 1834): 'A considerable crowd assembled before I arrived at the place of execution.[369] In the center was a brazen mortar, placed on a piece of rising ground—a match communicating with the interior of the mortar was at some distance, andnot far from it was a fire-brand ready lighted. I took my place with a heavy heart in the midst of the crows, and I chose it at that distance which placed me out of all probability of danger. Scarce had I stopped when I saw the officer of justice approach,

---

[366] Most of this is taken verbatim from Pottinger (1816: 64).
[367] Mashhad.
[368] Taken from Anonymous (1834b).
[369] Probably taken from Anonymous (1831b: 226) or Anonymous (1833c).

for whom the guards opened a passage with difficulty and not without dealing some blows among the throng. Between two of them advanced the condemned person. From her head to her feet she was covered with a thick black veil to hide her face. Her step was firm, and her expressive countenance seemed unmoved. She often spoke to an eunuch who accompanied her, but the noise around prevented my hearing a word she uttered. However, as she drew near to the place of punishment, the spectators became profoundly silent; and when she arrived at the mortar not a breath was heard. She took the advantage of the silence to raise her voice and address the multitude, with a precision and clearness which excited universal astonishment. But the officers, perceiving the impression that she produced on the standers by, soon interrupted her. She made no effort to continue, and suffered herself to be taken close to the mortar; her step was firm, she did not pray, she did not speak, but appeared more resigned than many would be in the same situation, she did not even shed a tear. She was told to kneel down, and lean her head against themouth of the mortar. She obeyed. Her wrists were bound with a cord, & they were firmly tied to some pickets that had been purposely placed there. In the meantime she did not discover the least emotion. She leaned her head on the mortar, and awaited her fate with the calmness that the bravest soldier might envy. At length the signal was given. A man armed with the fire-brand, bent it slowly to the match and just as it was about to take fire, a shudder took place among the crowd. The match was lighted; a dead groan issued from every bosom; the smoke disappeared; there was no explosion; and the unhappy creature raised her head to see what had happened. A rapid beam of hope shot across my breast; I thought it was meant that she should be saved. Scarce had this idea entered my mind, when another brand was lighted. The victim raised her head a second time, and gave a deep sigh, as if her soul had just taken its flight; this long, this dreadful sigh, had scarcely finished, when the explosion took place, and the smoke of the powder hid every object from sight. The fatal cloud, however, was soon dispersed; the explosion had finished, all was annihilated, except a few shreds of her garments, and the bones of her arms. Two women rushed forward at the fatal moment towards the scene of punishment, seized the remains, and hiding them with their veils, hastily returned to their haram, carrying off those [?] testimonies of the fulfilment of a sanguinary judgment.—*By an Eye Witness*.'

The security of Persian pilgrims

12.116 'Aleppo, May 18,' *New-York Commercial Advertiser* (Thursday, 21 August, 1834): 'Ibrahim Pacha[370] is occupied at this moment in bringing the Arabs of the Desert to reason. Those of Koram and Zara have been completely beaten, and are entirely dispersed. These last especially, who comprise nearly 3000 families, after having defended

---

[370] Ibrahim Pasha (1789–1848), son of Mohammad 'Ali of Egypt. He led the invasion of Syria in 1831. See Venturini (1833: 600), Burns (2017: 254).

themselves in a wood against 1500 irregular cavalry, have been cut in pieces by a reinforcement of 400 regular infantry, who came to join the former.—The sudden increase of the waters in the woods where these Arabs were, assisted to hasten their ruin. Forty thousand head of cattle, and considerable booty have been the fruit of this attack, provoked by the complaints made by the Schah of Persia to Mehemet Ali, on the subject of a caravan of Persian pilgrims, who, on their return from Mecca, had been plundered. The damage is estimated at more than 2000 purses, [200,000 francs,] as well in goods as specie. Ibrahim Pacha, by the orders of his father, after having in vain employed all mild means, resolved to attack them. This General has taken for his share of the booty, 8000 sheep, and 1600 oxen.—The troops shared the remainder, which they are selling at low prices. It is said that a great deal of specie was found in the tents of these Arabs. The wandering hordes which have been thus destroyed, are the same who pillaged about a year ago a caravan coming from Lattaquie, and in which the European merchants in Syria suffered a loss of nearly 400,000 francs. A few days ago an expedition was made against the Anezian Arabs, who occupy all the desert between Damascus & Bagdad. We flatter ourselves that it will also be attended with complete success.'

James Baillie Fraser on Persian history

12.117 'Untitled,' *American & Commercial Daily Advertiser* (Wednesday, 27 August, 1834): 'The power of Russia is the dread of modern Europe. On every side she has been making steady and prodigious advances during the last half century, constantly extending her already immense territories on the East—rounding and consolidating her western frontier by the subjugation of Poland—and with unerring sagacity marching onward to the conquest of Turkey. The preponderating influence she has acquired in European politics has, however, been the principal point of view in which Russian affairs have been regarded on this side of the Atlantic. Few have even cast a thought upon the extension of Russian power in Asia. But in England, the eyes of politicans have been turned anxiously in that direction. So much of British commerce and grandeur, speaking politically, is derived from the British possessions in the Indies, that the approaches of such a power as Russia, in that quarter, have been watched with jealousy and alarm.—Hence the zeal with which the politics of the Asiatic courts have been studied, and the missions, political and commercial, that have been sent into Persia, which forms as it were a frontier kingdom between the Russians and the British. The former have established a decided predominance by arms, and pushed forward their position into the Persian territories, on the high road, so to term it, to India. The British, with astute policy, have been conciliating the Persians, and anticipating the death of the present monarch and the fall of his dynasty, when the various tribes may imitate their Hindostanee neighbors, and put themselves under the British protection. Such an expectation is distinctly expressed, in the late History of Persia, prepared by Mr. Fraser,[371] who was himself a diplomatic agent of the British government in Persia.

From his work we extract an account of the present monarch of Persia, and a summary account of the leading events of his reign. He succeeded his uncle *Aga Mohammed*, the closing events of whose reign were made the ground work of the splendid romance of '*Zohrab*,'[372] also written by Mr. Fraser [sic, J.J. Morier]. The character of the tyrant, and the manner of his death, are faithfully described in *Zohrab*[373]:

The firmness and temperate management of Hajji Ibrahim[374] secured the throne to the deceased monarch's nephew, who assumed the ensigns of royalty by the name of Futeh Ali Shah; and though Saduk Khan[375] quitted the camp with his numerous followers, the rest of the army marched at the command of the minister to the capital, which was kept by Mirza Mohammed Khan Kujur[376] for the heir of Aga Mohammed. Saduk made a feeble effort at opposition, but was defeated.—Two similar attempts, by Hussein Kouli Khan, brother of the king, and by a son of Zukee Khan Zund,[377] were subdued with equal facility; and since that time the internal tranquility of the kingdom has been little disturbed.

By nature unwarlike, and succeeding to an almost undisputed throne, the reign of Futeh Ali has been marked by few remarkable events. The most important are those connected with the progress of the Russian arms, which was equally rapid and decisive. In 1800, Georgia was finally incorporated with the empire of the czar. In 1803, Mingrelia submitted to the same power,—Ganjah was taken, and Erivan invested, although the invaders were forced to raise the siege for want of stores, and from sickness. Daghistan and Shirwan had been overrun: and, in 1805, Karabaug voluntarily submitted to their sway. The tide of conquest proceeded with various fluctuations until checked by British interference, though the treaty of Goolistan, in October, 1813, fixed the boundaries so indifinitely [sic] as to give rise to much fruitless negotiation, and finally to a fresh war.

One part of the policy of the government of St. Petersburg in regard to Persia has been to acquire an influence over the heir-apparent, by promising to assist him in the struggle which is anticipated at the death of his father; and the agents of that ambitious power had actually established this dangerous ascendancy, when the threatening attitude and language

---

[371] James Baillie Fraser (1783–1856). For his life see Anonymous (1856f), Wright (1994), Farmanfarmaian (1996), Wright (2000/2012).

[372] Morier's novel *Zohrab the hostage*. See Morier (1832).

[373] From here to the end of the article the text is taken verbatim from Fraser (1834: 232–237), not from Morier (1832).

[374] Cf. 8.36.

[375] Sadeq Khan Shaqaqi. Cf. 8.1, 8.3.

[376] Mirza Mohammad Khan Rokn od-Doula, father of Allah Yar Khan. See Natchkebia (2012: 208, n. 5).

[377] Mohammad Khan. Cf. Shoberl (1828: 25) noted that, after Agha Mohammad Shah's assasination, 'Three other competitors...entered the lists,' including 'Mohammad Khan, son of Zeki Khan, successor to Kerim.'

adopted by the Russian authorities, no less than his regard for the British, disposed Prince Abbas Mirza to break the bonds that were fastening him, and to trust once more to the interposition of the latter nation.—This, however, as well as remonstrances from the courts of Teheran and Tabriz, having failed, the Shah reluctantly resolved to seek redress for past encroachments, and a security from farther loss, by force of arms. In this measure he was supported by the unanimous voice of the religious order, who called for "war against the infidels," and many of the frontier tribes, who had been exasperated by the cruelties inflicted by the invaders, rejoiced in the prospect of revenge.

Hostilities commenced with a massacre of all the Russian detachments and garrisons which could be overpowered. And the prince-royal,[378] in July, 1826, took the field with an army of 40,000 men, about 12,000 of whom were regulars, together with a few companies of foot-artillery, and deserters from the enemy. The Muscovite troops on the south of the Caucasus have been estimated at the same amount, including 6000 Cossacks and some dragoons. The opening of the campaign was favorable to Persia. Gokchah, Balikloo,[379] and Aberan were recovered,—Kareklissia was evacuated,—the country ravaged almost to the gates of Teflis,—Karabaug overrun,—Sheesha taken, and its strong castle invested.

But the flattering hopes awakened by these successes were speedily dissipated. Early in September, Mohammed Mirza, son of Abbas, sustained a repulse at Shamkoor, near Ganjah; and, on the 25th of the same month, the prince himself, having rashly engaged the force under General Paskewitch in the open field, was defeated with the loss of 1200 men. He fled with a few attendants, and his army dispersed, after having plundered his own camp.

Abbas repaired to court, and by much exertion another army was collected, with which, however, nothing was effected; and during the winter several ineffectual attempts were made to accommodate matters by British mediation. The war recommenced in the spring of 1827: Erivan was invested by General Benkendorff,[380] who, however, raised the siege on the approach of the shah towards Khoi; but the good effects of this movement were counterbalanced by a check which the prince sustained before Abbasabad, and the treacherous surrender of that town, which soon followed.

The defeat of 4000 Russian infantry and 2000 cavalry, with twenty field-pieces, at Abaran, in August, 1827, again encouraged the hopes of Abbas; but the advance of Paskewitch, with strong reinforcements and a battering train, put an end to the delusion, and the Persians had few other advantages to boast of during the continuance of the contest. In January, 1828, the king, seeing no prospect of maintaining the war with success, and

---

[378] 'Abbas Mirza.

[379] Schlechta-Wssehrd (1866: 293) wrote of 'den dortigen befestigten Flecken von Baliklu und die beiden Territorien von Gunoi und Goktscha, nördlich von dem gleichnamigen Binnensee im armenischen Hochland.'

[380] Konstantin Khristoforovich von Benckendorff. Cf. 11.162.

12.1 Miscellaneous

anxious to avoid further loss, accepted once more the aid of the British minister[381] at his court to procure a peace; which the enemy, who had attained many of their objects, did not now decline. The terms proposed by the latter were humiliating enough; and the ineffectual remonstrances and reluctance of the Shah and his ministers protracted the negotiations until the 21st February, when a treaty was signed at Turkomanshaee, of which the principal conditions were as follows—

By the first article, the treaty of Goolisten[382] is annulled, and a new arrangement settled. By the third article, Persia cedes the Khanat of Erivan and that of Nakshivan. By the fourth, the boundary line is described as drawn from that of the Ottoman states, passing over the summit of Little Ararat, and down the Lower Karasu to the Aras, then proceeding in the bed of that river to Abbasabad and Yedibouloob,[383] traversing the plain of Mogan to Adina Bazaar,[384] ascending the current of that name to its source, and thence running along the west of the Elburz or Caucasian Mountains to the source of the Ashtara, which it follows to the sea; thus ceding the greater part of Tallish[385] to Russia, and including all the islands of the Caspian Sea that fall within its direction. The sixth article stipulates for the payment of 10 crores (of 500,000 each) of tomans by Persia, as indemnification for the expenses of the war; and these are followed by a variety of provisions for the regulation of commerce, for the government of the ceded provinces, and the management of the migratory population, with other necessary precautionary clauses.

Since the signature of this treaty the peace has remained undisturbed, although an event which occurred at Teheran in February, 1829, might have furnished [sic] an excuse for further exactions. In that month, Mr. Grebayadoff, the Russian envoy at the court of Shah, and 44 individuals belonging to his suite, fell victims to the popular phrenzy, being massacred in his official dwelling. The king, equally shocked and alarmed at an outrage which he could not prevent, despatched a mission charged with an explanation to the court of St. Petersburg, which was graciously received, and harmony has since been preserved.

After the termination of this war, the prince-royal had time to attend to the interests of his future kingdom, and has made some progress in reducing the rebellious chiefs of Khorason. Assisted by the science and valour of a Polish gentleman, who is now at the head of his army,[386] he possessed himself of Yezd, took Toorhish[387] and Khaboosdan[388]

---

[381] John Macdonald Kinneir. Cf. 11.127.

[382] Gulistan.

[383] A corruption of Yazdabad, the former name of 'Abbasabad. See Ekbal (1982b/2011).

[384] For Monteith's 1828 description of the Russo-Persian boundary following the Second Russo-Persian War, which ran through Udinabazaar, see MacGregor (1871: 363).

[385] Talysh.

[386] Isidor/Izydor Borowski (1803–1837). Polish soldier-of-fortune who had previously served under 'Abbas Mirza. See Spitz (1960), Potts (2017a).

[387] Torshiz, mod. Kashmar, Khorasan.

[388] Khabushan, Khorasan.

by storm, and reduced the other chieftains in that quarter to an acknowledgement of fealty and submission. But these, it is obvious, are temporary advantages that can only be maintained by a firm control, supported by a well organized force, and directed by a judicious system of government, which are scarcely to be expected from the present royal family.

It is indeed sufficiently manifest that the downfall of the Kujur dynasty, short as their reign has been, is fast approaching, and that if the heir-apparent succeed in preserving his crown for a season, it will be more from the operation of foreign influence and political jealousy, than by the exertion of any power or popularity that he is likely to acquire. The very name of the Kujurs is detested throughout the kingdom; and it is notorious that pressing petitions have been made on the part of the greater number of the chiefs and nobles, backed by the earnest wishes of all ranks, for permission to throw themselves upon British protection; declaring that all they look for is peace and security; and protesting that, should their application be rejected, they will rather submit to Russia than continue any longer subject to the misrule and extortion of their present masters.'

12.118 'History of Persia,' *New-York Commercial Advertiser* (Thursday, 28 August, 1834), 'Extract from Frazer's [sic, Fraser] History of Persia,' *Long Island Farmer and Queens County Advertiser* (Wednesday, 3 September, 1834; second and third paras. only) and 'History of Persia,' *The Catskill Recorder* (Thursday, 6 November, 1834; paras. 1, to 'writer,' and 9–13 only): 'Harper's Family Library, No. 70, contains the history of Persia, from the latest ages down to the present time, written by James B. Frazer [sic, Fraser], Esq. a highly accomplished and popular writer. It is embellished with a map of Persia, and with a number of interesting views and portraits. Frazer's long residence in the country of which he treats, and his extensive travels in Asia, have given him important advantages in the preparation of this history. He has, besides availed himself of the remarks and observations of other authors, with the view of rendering his historical sketches as perfect as possible. The manners and character of the people, their laws, religion and literature, and the productions, manufactures, and geographical features of the country, are clearly and fully described in this work.—We have derived much gratification from the volume, and furnish a few extracts to show its style and character.

Nothing[389] more strikingly illustrates the demoralizing influence of the system of Government in Persa, than the insensibility to disgrace which it produces among all classes of the people,—a callousness that is most remarkable among courtiers. A minister or governor offends the king, or is made the object of accusation, justly or unjustly. He is condemned, perhaps unheard, his property is confiscated, his slaves are given to others, his family and wives are insulted, perhaps delivered over to the brutality of grooms and feroshes, and his person is maltreated with blows or mutilated by the executioner's knife. Nothing can be imagined more complete than such a degradation; nothing, one would

---

[389]The first two paragraphs here, to 'calleeon,' are taken verbatim from Fraser (1834: 296–298).

imagine, could be more poignant than his anguish, or more deep and deadly than his hatred and thirst for revenge. Yet these reverses are considered merely as among the casualties of service, as clouds obscuring for a while the splendour of courtly fortune, but which will soon pass away, and permit the sun of prosperity to shine again in its fullest lustre; and experience proves tlmt [sic, that] these calculations are correct, for the storm often blows by as rapidly as it comes on. Royal caprice receives the sufferer again into favour; his family is sent back to him, with such of his slaves as can be recovered; and his property pruned of all dangerous exuberance, is returned. A bath mollifies his bruised feet,[390]—a cap conceals his cropped ears,—a khelut covers the multitude of sins and stains, and proves a sovereign remedy for all his misfortunes—and tho [sic, the] whitewashed culprit is often reinstated in the very government he had lost, perhaps carrying with him a sentence of disgrace to his successor, to whose intrigues he owed his temporary fall. It is indeed surprising to see how improvidently the king and his ministers bestow situations of confidence on strangers, or on men who, from having been the objects of such injustice as we have described as their bitterest enemies; yet the management of a conquered state is frequently intrusted to the khan or prince who before possessed it in his own right. The pardoned rebel of one province is appointed to the supreme command in another; and the disgraced noble or governor is sent to take charge of a district where the utmost fidelity and zeal are required.

Yet, severe as the procedure towards faulty or suspected servants too often is, capital punishments are comparatively rare. We do not speak of the times of a Nadir or an Aga Mohammed Khan, when no man's life was for a moment secure, but of the ordinary administration of such kings as the Suffees, and the princes who succeeded them. This fact is remarked by Chardin, and confirmed by Sir John Malcolm. But when sentence of death is passed against the governor of a province or a nobleman residing at court, the method of putting it in execution is as follows:—An order made out by the prime minister and under the royal seal, together with that of one of the civil or ecclesiastical magistrates, is placed in the hands of an officer appointed for the purpose, commonly a nassakchee or a gholam. This man rides post, pressing horses as he requires them. Then presenting himself to the principal person of the place, he shows the royal mandate, and forces that individual to accompany him and lend his assistance. He enters the house of the condemned, booted, armed and travel-stained; walks straight up to his victim, takes the warrant from his bosom, and places it in the hands of his witness; then, drawing his scimitar, he rushes on the unfortunate criminal, exclaiming, "It is the king's command," cuts him down, and strikes off his head. Resistance is seldom offered: for were the delinquent powerful enough for the attempt, the messenger of death would never arrive to execute the decree; and there have been instances, even when the person proscribed was not in actual rebellion, of his causing the fatal officer to be robbed of the warrant, thus gaining time until interest could be made for his pardon. But when once his destination is reached, escape is scarcely possible; for terror of the royal name, arms every one against him who is denounced—even in his own

---

[390] A reference to the soles of the feet having been beaten with a long stake, i.e. the *bastinado*.

house he is viewed as an excommunicated wretch, whom to assist or to touch were ruin. Should the sentence only imply disgrace, or when its extent is yet unknown, it is melancholy to see how the object of kingly displeasure is instantaneously forsaken like an infected creature. "All nature," says Chardin, "seems roused against him;" and the man, a glance of whose eye but a moment before would have shed delight on thousands of dependents, might then in vain solicit a cup of water or the use of a calleeon.

In every mosque[391] of consequence, and at every considerable shrine, there are at least three regular ecclesiastical officers: the Mootwullee, who manages its temporal affairs[392]; the Muezzin, or Crier to Prayers; and the Mollah, who conducts the ceremonial. If the establishment is rich, there are several of the last mentioned order, from among whom is selected a Peish Namaz, who recited the prayers and goes through the motions and genuflexions to guide the congregation.[393] They also occasionally preach a sort of sermon on texts from the Koran. Besides there are in every city, and connected with all seminaries of learning, a crowd of mollahs, who live by their wits, and have little of the priest but the name. They practise astrology, write letters and contract for those who are ignorant of penmanship, and contrive by these means to prolong a miserable existence. Nothing can be lower than the character of these people; their hypocrisy, profligacy, and want of principle, are the subject of stories, epigrams, and proverbs without end. "Take care," says one adage, "of the face of a woman and the heels of a mule; but with a mollah be on your guard at all points." "To hate like a mollah," and "to cheat like a mollah," are sayings of equal frequency in the mouth of a Persian.

The Seyeds or descendants of the Prophet notwithstanding their origin, deservedly share in this obloquy; and should one of them have become a hajji,—that is, have made the pilgrimage to Mecca,—his reputation as a rogue is fully established. The correctness of this severe remark is illustrated by innumerable stories. One of these relates, that a man having bought a fine-looking bunch of grapes from a person who sat behind a window, paid his money and laid hold of the end to pull it towards him; but every one of the grapes, which had been artificially fastened on, fell in the inside, leaving him nothing but the bare stalk. "Oh seyed! oh mollah' oh hajji!" exclaimed the disappointed purchaser. 'You know me then?' said the seller, opening his door and coming out. "I never saw you in my life before," returned the other; "but I was quite convinced that no one could have played me such a trick who had not a right to all these holy titles."* [Malcolm's Persia, vol. ii. p. 574.] It is unnecessary to add, that cazees and other officers connected with the law come in for their full portion of satirical abuse, and not without cause. Every popular tale is full of their corrupt and shameless venality. When men possessing stations so highly responsible, and

---

[391] The next three paragraphs are taken verbatim from Fraser (1834: 300–303).

[392] The manager or caretaker of a mosque or religious endowment (*waqf*). Acording to Wright (1899: 859), 'the mu'azzin (crier for prayers), and sometimes the Mutavalli (guardian of the mosque)...need not necessarily be a priest.

[393] *pishnamaz*, 'prayer leader.' See Halm (2004: 86).

in general liberally paid by government, are guilty of such malpractices, what can be expected from the inferior orders, who in misery and want are exposed to a thousand temptations, while their very existence depends on a sanctimonious exterior? Demoralized in the earlier stage of their career, is it to be imagined, that in their rise to the higher ranks of the priesthood or the law, they can avoid becoming hypocrites and profligates? The very extent of ascetic self-denial which they are obliged to observe, whether congenial to their dispositions or otherwise, produces deceit and concealment. "It is with these holy tricks," says Kæmpfer, speaking of many of the priests, "that they captivate men's affections, establish a reputation for sanctity, and obtain from the silent suffrages of the people a species of supreme pontificate." Sir John Malcolm, who quotes this passage, thinks the censure too strong; yet it is much to be feared that the conduct even of the higher classes of the priesthood has divested them as a body of the right of just compliment.† [† The writer of these pages was acquainted with a highly esteemed mooshtehed[394] at Mushed,[395] who was, doubtless, in most respects, an amiable and worthy, as well as a learned man; but, instead of being in reality the sincere and orthodox Mussulman which the nation believed him, he frankly confessed himself in private a decided freethinker, and smiled at the absurd superstitions of his professed creed.] That there are many bright exceptions, is a fact not less unquestionable than the general truth of the allegation; and the author just named relates a striking instance of the worth of one of these holy persons, and of the consideration which even the most powerful monarchs have testified for their virtues.

An individual once complained to Mollah Ahmed, mooshtebed of Ardebil, that Abbas the great had taken away his sister, and shut her up by force in his harem. The holy man immediately gave him a note for the king, to the following effect:—"Brother Abbas, restore to the bearer his sister." The monarch commanded the woman immediately to be given up, and showing his courtiers the note, said aloud, "Let this be put into my shroud, for in the day of judgment, having been called brother by Mollah Ahmed will avail me more than all actions of my life."

"The seraglio of the king," says he,[396] "is most commonly a perpetual prison, from whence scarce one female in six or seven ever has the good luck to escape: for women who have once become the mothers of living children are provided with a small establishment within the walls, and are never suffered to leave them.—But privation of liberty is by no means the worst evil that exists in these melancholy abodes. Except to that wife who is so fortunate as to produce the first born son, to become a mother is the most dreaded event that can happen to the wretched favorites of the king.—When this occurs, no only do the

---

[394] *mojtahed*. For this class of much esteemed Islamic jurists see Zysow (1998/2011).

[395] Mashhad.

[396] Although this paragraph is taken from Fraser (1834: 304–305), it is in fact a quote from Jean (John) Chardin, for Fraser prefaced it by writing, 'an Eastern harem must ever be the abode of discontent and intrigue, and consequently of misery and crime. No one has painted the horrors of such a prison in more lively colours than Chardin, while describing what he had seen and heard concerning the harem of the shah.'

mothers see their last chance of liberty and marriage cut off from them, but they live in the dreadful anticipation of seeing their children deprived of life or of sight when the death of their lord shall call a new tyrant in the person of his son, tho brother of their offspring, to the throne. Should they avoid the misfortune of having children, by an assiduous court paid to the king's mother, or to the mother of his eldest son, it sometimes happens that they attain the good fortune of being bestowed upon some of the officers about the court; for the ministers and grandees, who are always intriguing with these influential ladies, seldom fail of soliciting a female of the royal harem, either for themselves or their sons. Indeed, it is no uncommon thing for the king himself to bestow one of these fair captives upon his favorites or his courtiers, and sometimes when the harem gets crowded, this is done to a great extent, as a measure of economical expediency.—Happy is she that is thus freed from her prison, for she at once exchanges the situation of a slave for that of a legitimate and influential wife, and the head of a domestic establishment, when she is ever treated with the attention due to one who ahs been the favorite of a king."

The bath[397] is of all others the luxury most extensively enjoyed; for a few copper coins enable the poorest to avail themselves of this healthful pleasure, so necessary to a people who are not over-nice in the use of their linen. The bath is, in fact, the lounge of the Persians, as the ale-house is in England, or the coffee-houses in Turkey; for as the operation of bathing, which includes that of kneading the muscles, cracking the joints, shaving the head, trimming and dying the beard, and tinging the hands and feet with henna, occupies from 2 to 3 h at least, during great part of which the patient lies stretched on his back to permit the dyes to fix, he employs the time in hearing the news, in smoking, drinking coffee, or in sleeping. The public baths are open 2 days of the week exclusively for women, and the remaining five for men. They are frequented as early as 3 or 4 in the morning, and continue so for the greater part of the day, and sometimes of the night. People of rank usually have baths attached to their houses, which, however, they occasionally let out to the public, with the reserve of certain days for their own use.

Marriages[398] in Persia are occasions of great and almost ruinous display. The period of feasting occupies from 3 to 40 days, according to the condition of the parties. These are necessary for observing the established forms. On the first, company are assembled; on the second, the bride's hands are stained with henna; on the third, the rite takes place. Perhaps an account of a marriage in middle life, as it actually occurred, may explain the nature of the ceremonies better than any detail. As the men have (the bridegroom in this instance was a widower of advanced age) seldom an opportunity of choosing a wife by sight, they are forced to employ some female friend to select a suitable partner; and to her they must trust for all that appertains to mental or personal charms. The choice being made, and the gentleman satisfied, he sends a formal proposal, together with a present of sweetmeats, to the lady; both of which, it is previously understood, will be accepted. This point being

---

[397] This paragraph on bathing is taken verbatim from Fraser (1834: 333).

[398] The text from here to the end of the article is taken verbatim from Fraser (1834: 339–342).

gained, he next forwards an assortment of fine clothes, shawls, and handkerchiefs, bed-clothes, and bedding, looking glasses, glass and china ware, bathing and cooking apparatus, henna for her hands, sugar and confits; in short, a complete domestic outfit: of all which it is understood, the bride's family will double, and return to the future husband. A day is fixed for fetching home the bride; when a crowd of people collect at both houses—the gentlemen at the bridegroom's, the lady's at that of the bride. The latter next proceed to complete the duties of their office, by conducting the young lady to the bath, where, after a thorough ablution, she is then decked in her finest attire. As soon as it is dark, the bridegroom's party proceed to bring her to her new habitation: and much discussion sometimes arises at this stage of the business, as to the number of lanterns, of fiddlers, and guests that are to marshal the procession.

On reaching the bride's house, it is usual, before she mounts, to wrap her in a shawl provided by the husband. This, again, is often a point of dispute; on the present occasion, the lady's friends objected to the indifferent quality of the shawl; those of the gentleman's party, on the other hand, swore that it was excellent.—Neither would give in; the guests were all waiting, and the affair assumed a serious aspect: when one of the visitors stepped forward, and volunteered his own. It was accepted, and the cavalcade proceeded—the bride being accompanied by a great number of persons, and attended by a boy bearing a looking-glass. At intervals on the road, bridges are made in the following manner for her to step over; gentlemen of the husband's party are called upon by name and must place themselves on their hands and knees on the ground, before her horse; and the choice generally falling on corpulent awkward individuals, much mirth is excited.—In this way the party proceeds, with fiddling, drums beating, tamborine playing, and lanterns flourishing, till they meet the bridegroom who comes to a certain distance in advance—and this distance is the subject of another very serious discussion.—As soon as he sees his lady, he throws an orange or some other fruit at her with all his force, and then off he goes towards his house. This is the signal of a general scamper after him, and whoever can catch him, is entitled to his horse and clothes, or ransom in lieu of them.

When the bride arrives at the door, a man of either party jumps up behind her, and seizing her by the waist, carries her within. Should this be done by one of the bridegroom's attendants, it is an omen of his maintaining in future, a due authority over his wife; but, on the contrary, should one of her friends succeed in performing the duty—and it is always the subject of a sharp contest—it augers that she will in future "keep her own side of the house." Another effort at insuring the continuance of his own supremacy is often made by the gentleman, who, on reaching his own domicile after throwing the orange, takes a station over the portal, that the lady on entering may pass under his feet, and thereby become subject to him; but if discovered in this ungallant attempt, he is instantly pelted from his post.

When at length, she has allotted for her reception, the husband makes his appearance, and a looking-glass is immediately help up in such a position as to reflect the face of his bride, whom he now for the first time, sees unveiled. It is a critical and anxious moment, for it is that in which the fidelity of his agents is to be proved, and the charms of his beloved to be compared with those pictured by him in his ardent imagination; while the young ladies in attendance, as well as the gossiping old ones, are eager to catch the first glimpse, and communicate to all the world their opinion of her claims to beauty. After this, the bridegroom takes a bit of sugar-candy, and, biting it in two halves, eats one himself, and presents the other to his bride; on the present occasion he had no teeth to bite with, and so he broke the sugar with his fingers, which offended the young woman so much that she cast her portion away. He then takes her stockings, throws one over her left shoulder, places the other under the right foot, and orders all the spectators to withdraw. They retire accordingly, and the happy couple are left alone.

Such are the honors [sic, humours] of a Persian wedding in middle life, and they are varied no doubt, by the circumstances or disposition of the parties; but the expense is always great, and as we have said, sometimes ruinous.'

A Persian view of the West

12.119 'Ignorance and Pride go together,' *Long Island Farmer and Queens County Advertiser* (Wednesday, 3 September, 1834), 'Ignorance and Pride go together,' *The Jeffersonian* (Monday, 20 October, 1834) and 'Ignorance and Pride go together,' *The Pittsfield Sun* (Thursday, 13 November, 1834): 'It is with nations as with individuals; those who know the least of others, think the highest of themselves....The Persians think that European and American merchants, who come to them to trade, live on a small barren island in the northern waters; for why should they come to us, say they, to buy things, if they can get them at home?'

Index-2

A
Abaran, 1380
Abarkuh, 1105
Abazadze, David, 790
Abazes, *see* Abkhazians
Abbas ('Abbas) I, Shah, 752, 763, 863, 872, 922, 1084, 1094, 1367
Abbas ('Abbas) Mirza, 773, 776, 780, 803, 810, 813, 816, 817, 819, 822, 832, 845, 853, 857, 858, 868, 874, 875, 877–880, 893, 900, 903, 905, 907, 910, 913, 918, 920, 957, 961, 963, 964, 966, 971, 974, 977–981, 983, 985, 988, 990, 992, 999, 1002, 1003, 1008, 1010, 1014, 1015, 1017, 1018, 1021, 1026, 1030, 1032, 1034, 1035, 1044–1046, 1058, 1063, 1070, 1075, 1076, 1086, 1092, 1105, 1111, 1113, 1115, 1116, 1118, 1119, 1122, 1124, 1126, 1127, 1129, 1133, 1134, 1137, 1138, 1143, 1144, 1146, 1147, 1150, 1155, 1158, 1164, 1166, 1167, 1170–1172, 1177, 1178, 1180, 1181, 1185, 1186, 1188, 1190, 1191, 1193, 1194, 1196, 1198, 1199, 1201, 1205, 1207, 1210, 1211, 1214–1218, 1220, 1229, 1234, 1236, 1242, 1244, 1245, 1249–1251, 1254–1260, 1262, 1265, 1275, 1277, 1282–1285, 1287, 1289, 1290, 1292, 1293, 1295–1300, 1302, 1307, 1312–1315, 1318, 1326–1328, 1330, 1332–1341, 1344, 1348, 1351, 1355, 1380, 1381
Abbas ('Abbas) Qoli Mirza, 1327
Abbasabad ('Abbasabad), 1244, 1245, 1274, 1380, 1381
Abbot, Charles, 950
Abd ('Abd) al-Rahman Pasha, 794, 802, 877
Abdollah ('Abdollah) Khan. 722
Abdollah ('Abdollah) Khan Damavandi, 971
Abdollah ('Abdollah) Mirza, 922
Abdollah ('Abdollah) Pasha Baban, 1004, 1024
Abdul ('Abdul) 'Aziz, Shaykh, 1304
Abdul ('Abdul) Razzaq Khan, 1333
Abdul Mirza, *see* 'Abdollah Mirza
Abdurrahim/Abdurrahman Pasha, 1039, 1040
Abeleaise, *see* Abkhazia
Abishgar, 971
Abkhazia, 882, 883
Aborkoh, *see* Abarkuh
Abosharon, *see* Absheron
Absheron, 1081
Abu Musa, 1078
Abu Sherer, *see* Bandar-e Bushehr
Abu Shiher, *see* Bandar-e Bushehr
Abu Talib Khan, 730
Abzirhijan, *see* Azerbaijan
Achsebiuk, *see* Akziuk
Adams, John, 1065
Adams, John Quincy, 1056
Adams Smith, John, 949
Aderbidjan, *see* Azerbaijan
Adiljavas, 971
Adjaline, *see* Ajerlu
Adrianople, *see* Edirne
Adzerbijan, *see* Azerbaijan
Afghanistan, 814
Afghans, 781, 1088
Afshars, 916
Aga Abd al Nubby, *see* Mohammad Nabi Khan
Aga Nubber Khaun, *see* Mohammad Nabi Khan
Aga Yhacoub, *see* Khoja Mirza Yakub Markarian
Agar, *see* Agarak
Agarak, 1217, 1219, 1220

Agha Baba, *see* Eristov, Giorgi Evseevich
Agha Hoseyn, 1076
Agha Mohammad Hoseyn, 730, 737, 740, 741, 743
Agha Mohammad Shah, 699–701, 707, 711, 723, 724, 808, 815, 826, 889, 916, 1064, 1088, 1304, 1379
Aghistan, *see* Daghestan
Aghrékof, *see* Grekov, Nikolai
Aglenlu, 1238
Agra, 781
Agsu, 1179
Ahar, 1018, 1146, 1206, 1228
Ahmed Efendi, 965, 966
Ahmed Khan, 818, 819
Aiglanlon, 1237
Aislie, Robert, 876
Ajerlu, 1227
Ak Darband, 1153
Akbar Shah II, Mughal emperor, 836
Akhalkalaki, 879, 1195
Akhalzikh/Akhaltsikhe, 745, 1242, 1279
Akh-Uglan, *see* Akoglan
Akif ('Akif) Pasha, 1339
Aklot, 971
Akoglan, 1221
Akoucha, *see* Akusha
Aksa, *see* Agsu
Aksaray, 1059
Akstapha, *see* Aghstafa
Akusha, 1181
Akziuk, 1237
Alaiar Khan, *see* Allah Yar Khan Qajar Devehlu
Ala Khan, *see* Ata ('Ata) Khan
Alasani, *see* Alazan
Alazan, 1219
Alborz, 1381
Albuquerque, Afonso de, 752
Aleppo, 786, 877, 1036, 1062, 1348
Alexander, *see* Gruzinsky, Alexander Irakliyevich
Alexander I, of Russia, 718, 727, 745, 786, 787, 804, 807, 817, 826, 829, 833, 867, 868, 879, 903, 906, 908, 909, 925, 932, 955, 956, 964, 978, 986, 988, 996, 997, 999, 1002, 1011, 1016, 1052, 1070, 1099, 1118, 1125, 1171, 1176, 1189, 1199, 1210, 1211, 1217, 1277
Alexander, James Edward, 936
Alí ('Ali) Beg, 966
Ali ('Ali) Khan Qutub, 1033
Ali ('Ali) Mardan Khan, 889, 1253
Ali ('Ali) Naki Mirza, 1244
Ali ('Ali) Pasha, 794, 802
Ali ('Ali) Qoli Khan, 889
Ali ('Ali) Qoli Khan-e Shahsevan, 788
Ali ('Ali) Shah, 1249

Ali ('Ali) Shah Mirza, 1219, 1292, 1295, 1306, 1308
Alirak, 1122
Alisar Khan, *see* Allah Yar Khan Qajar Devehlu
Al Jazirah, 767
Allah Qoli Khan, 1152
Allah Yar Khan Qajar Devehlu, 1115, 1117, 1138, 1139, 1147, 1166, 1167, 1185, 1188, 1193, 1202, 1203, 1205–1208, 1244, 1297, 1305, 1308, 1379
Allard, Jean-François, 912, 913
Allracan, *see* Astrakhan
Altmühl, 1288
Altun Kupri, 794
Alvand, 830
Ambourger, *see* Amburger, Andreas
Amburger, Andreas, 965, 1062, 1144, 1206, 1299
Amir Khan Qajar, 1155, 1164, 1166, 1173, 1181, 1188, 1194
Anatolia, 789, 1022
Andréossy, Antoine François, 877
Andriff, *see* Endirey
Angoulême, Louis Antoine d, 938
Angoulême, Marie-Thérèse d, 938
Anquetil-Duperron, Abraham Hyacinthe, 1097
Anselly, *see* Bandar-e Anzali
Antakya, 1002
Antioch, *see* Antakya
Anton II, Catholicos, 868
Apsheron, *see* Absheron
Aq Qöyunlü, 767
Araks, *see* Aras
Aral Sea, 830
Ararat, Mt., 798, 929, 965, 1264, 1268, 1270, 1280, 1381
Aras, 754, 776, 779, 780, 784, 798, 803, 821, 832, 852, 878, 879, 881, 893, 1018, 1115, 1117, 1129, 1133, 1147, 1177, 1195, 1216, 1217, 1219, 1221, 1226, 1227, 1229, 1232, 1243, 1246–1249, 1251, 1254–1257, 1260, 1273, 1274, 1281, 1312, 1381
Araxes, *see* Aras
Archis, 971
Ardabil, 1146, 1203, 1205, 1206, 1258, 1312
Ardalan, 794, 1024
Arden, Lady, 947
Arderum, *see* Erzurum
Ardos, 1311
Arkevan, *see* Erkivan
Armenia, 767, 776, 780, 789, 801, 816, 857, 885, 887, 927, 966, 976, 993, 1008, 1011, 1012, 1022, 1029, 1039, 1041, 1116, 1150, 1268, 1269, 1271, 1272, 1281
Armenians, 700, 790, 967, 1174

Aroomee, *see* Urmia
Arpaçay, 840
Arran, 885, 887
Artara, *see* Astara
Arzab, 797
Ashpukhdar, *see* Tsitsianov, Pavel Dmitryevich
Askar ('Askar) Khan-e Afshar Urumi, 824, 826, 916
Askaran, 803
Askeran, 1206
Aslan Khan, 865, 971, 1180, 1253
Aslanduz, 879, 1217
Aslangas, *see* Aslanduz
Asof, *see* Azov
Asov, 717
Astara, 1275, 1281
Astarabad, 717, 726, 807, 830, 886, 960, 961, 1230
Asterbat, *see* Astarabad
Astrakhan, 716, 717, 727, 768, 833, 888, 900, 926, 1091, 1230, 1286, 1350, 1354
Ata ('Ata) Khan, 1228
Attoobees, *see* Utub ('Utub)
Aube, Baron d, 1336
Aubrélique, Louis-Philippe, 912, 974
Australia, 1045
Avadh/Awadh, 735
Avaria, 886
Avaristan, 886
Avdula-Mirza, *see* Abdollah ('Abdollah) Mirza
Awjan/Ujan, 920, 1117
Aydın, 1058
Azerbaijan, 728, 767, 784, 802, 885, 965, 1018, 1030, 1044, 1060, 1098–1099, 1118, 1254, 1256, 1258, 1275, 1283, 1353
Azudbejan, *see* Azerbaijan
Azzaroom, *see* Erzurum

B

Baba Khan, *see* Fath 'Ali Shah
Baban, 794, 877, 1024
Babylon, 749
Baccow, *see* Baku
Backus, Elijah, 759, 761
Bactra, 765
Bactriana, 765
Badakhshan, 767, 908
Bagh, 725
Baghdad, 719, 727, 748, 749, 781, 788, 794, 801, 802, 838, 844, 847, 849, 903, 904, 907, 963, 966, 968, 970, 971, 975–979, 981, 982, 985–988, 991, 992, 994–996, 999, 1001–1005, 1008, 1012, 1013, 1020, 1024, 1025, 1027, 1029, 1031, 1034–1037, 1039–1043, 1048, 1049, 1051, 1055, 1057, 1059, 1061, 1079, 1286, 1330, 1351
Bagot, Charles, 1014
Bagration, Peter Ivanovich, 779
Baha'-al-Din Ayaz, 766
Bahlul Pasha, 971
Bahrain, 755, 1343, 1351
Bahram Mohammad Pasha, 1036
Bahrem, *see* Bahrain
Baird, David, 741
Bajazed, *see* Doğubayazit
Bajazid, *see* Doğubayazit
Bakhchysarai, 1050, 1100
Bakhtiyari, 1363
Baku, 703, 726, 753, 767, 773, 803, 804, 821, 882, 883, 887, 1081, 1082, 1099, 1179, 1346, 1350
Bala Hisar, 725
Balaghan, 1081
Balhern, *see* Bahrain
Balkh, 708, 765
Baltic Sea, 926
Baluchis, 749
Baluchistan, 1375
Bambaki, *see* Pambak
Bamian, 766
Bandar 'Abbas, 713, 717, 752, 766, 829, 841, 850, 891, 904, 1078, 1079
Bandar-e Anzali, 703, 837, 1346, 1352
Bandar-e Bushehr, 700, 712, 714, 718, 729, 744, 771, 808, 849, 851, 859, 876, 896, 905, 1002, 1034, 1035, 1077, 1087, 1091, 1285, 1286, 1351
Banks, Joseph, 1043
Banu Na'im, 713
Barakzai, 934
Bareck, *see* Khark
Barlow, George, 809
Barnett, George Henry, 877
Barrie, Robert, 866
Bashire, *see* Bandar-e Bushehr
Basra, 730, 748, 764, 767, 770, 788, 802, 808, 849, 894, 1002, 1020, 1034, 1035, 1039, 1079, 1351
Bassano, *see* Maret, Hugues-Bernard
Bathurst, Henry, 936
Bavan, 765
Báyazíd, *see* Doğubayazit
Bayzaid, *see* Doğubayazit
Bazu, *see* Baku
Beauchamp, Joseph de, 801
Behaghel von Adlerskron, Maximilian, 1264
Behbehan, 894
Bekovich-Cherkasky, General, 1311

Bekovich-Cherkassky, Alexander, 1230
Bélanger, Charles Paulus, 1113
Belfort, Major, 1239
Benares, *see* Varanasi
Benckendorff, Konstantin Khristoforovich von, 1237, 1239, 1240, 1249, 1332, 1380
Bender/y, 811
Benderbukhir, *see* Bandar-e Bushehr
Benderli, Mehmed Selim Pasha, 1120, 1126, 1189, 1194
Bengal, 782, 801
Beni Naeem, *see* Banu Na'im
Benkendoff, *see* Benckendorff, Konstantin Khristoforovich; Benckendorff, Konstantin Khristoforovich von
Benkendorff, *see* Benckendorff, Konstantin Khristoforovich von
Benu-Mâîn, *see* Banu Ma'in
Bernard, Lieutenant, 829
Bernardi, Lieutenant, 1126, 1164, 1191, 1201
Berry, Marie-Caroline de Bourbon-Sicile de, 938
Berthier, Louis-Alexandre, 809, 811, 823
Besobdal, 1237, 1254
Bessarabia, 806, 811, 1263
Bethune, Henry Lindsay, 879, 881, 919, 974, 1126
Bhag, *see* Bagh
Birecik, 1037
Biri, *see* Birecik
Bishapur, 871, 1088
Bitlis, 971
Black Sea, 728, 737, 764, 790, 801, 816, 829, 830, 867, 981–983, 986, 990, 1001, 1022, 1026, 1029, 1121, 1148, 1276, 1286, 1288
Blacque, Alexander, 993
Blair, Archibald, 830
Blane, David Anderson, 1344
Blanquet du Chayla, Armand Simon Marie, 705
Blaramberg, Johann von, 1189
Bligh, John Duncan, 1340
Bogle, Archibald, 713
Boigne, Benoît de, 781
Bokhara, 818, 1307, 1335, 1336, 1355
Bolgaruçay, 1274
Bombak, *see* Pambak
Bombay, 699, 709, 710, 712, 717, 729–732, 735, 736, 739, 740, 742, 743, 808, 814, 836, 859, 861, 1077, 1303, 1330
Bonaparte, Joseph, 715, 719
Bonaparte, Napoleon, *see* Napoleon
Bonderburkhur, *see* Bandar-e Bushehr
Bontems-Lefort, Auguste de, 822, 823
Borowski, Isidor/Izydor, 1381
Bosphorus, 787
Boulgákoff, *see* Bulgakov, Yakov Ivanovich

Bourtsoff, *see* Burtsov, Ivan Grigoryevich
Boutin, *see* Bontems-Lefort, Auguste de
Bouvet de Maisonneuve, Pierre François Étienne, 850
Bozobdal, *see* Besobdal
Bradbury, Robert, 958
Brailov, 1263
Brande, George William, 837, 840
Brazil, 859, 873
Briggs, Gilbert, 709
Briggs, John, 1346
Brougham, Lord, 833
Bruce, Thomas, 727, 738
Bruce, William, 862, 1077
Bruguière, Jean Guillaume, 1064
Brune, Guillaume Marie-Anne, 737, 784, 912
Bruyn, Cornelis de, 871, 1084
Buckingham, James Silk, 1303
Bulgakov, A.V., 1317
Bulgakov, Yakov Ivanovich, 804, 821, 891
Buravar, 1274
Burton, Isabel, 953
Burton, Richard, 953
Burtsov, Ivan Girgoryevich, 1311
Bushira, *see* Bandar-e Bushehr
Bushire, *see* Bandar-e Bushehr
Bussora, *see* Basra
Bussorah, *see* Basra
Byazeed, *see* Doğubayazit
Byron, George Gordon, 1364
Byzied, *see* Doğubayazit

C

Cabool, *see* Kabul
Cabul, *see* Kabul
Cachetie, *see* Kakheti
Caffa, *see* Feodosia
Calcutta, 712, 729, 731, 732, 801, 808, 836, 849, 852, 1091
Campbell, George W., 1070
Campbell, James Drummond, 878, 900, 919, 924, 1106, 1355
Campbell, John, 1357
Campbell, William, 709
Candia, *see* Heraklion
Canning, Elizabeth, 877
Canning, George, 1034, 1223
Canning, Harriet Raikes, 877
Canning, Stratford, 869, 876, 877, 1153, 1161, 1248
Canning, William, 876, 896
Caplantic, *see* Kaflankuh
Carabak, *see* Qarabagh

Carabat, *see* Qarabagh
Carajular, 935
Caroline Augusta, of Bavaria, 1362
Carosman Oglu, *see* Karaosmanoğlu
Carrack, *see* Khark
Carro, Jean de, 770
Casbin, *see* Qazvin
Casbine, *see* Qazvin
Caspian Sea, 703, 717, 727, 754, 756, 764, 767, 768, 774, 776, 780, 782, 790, 798, 801, 804, 807, 809, 810, 825, 829–831, 833, 834, 836–838, 840, 866, 867, 870, 878, 882–887, 906, 911, 913, 926, 960, 961, 1001, 1035, 1088, 1096, 1121, 1135, 1140, 1147, 1206, 1230, 1257, 1274, 1275, 1281, 1282, 1288, 1328, 1346, 1350
Castlereagh, Lord, 726, 874, 875, 936, 937, 950, 976
Caswin, *see* Qazvin
Cathcart, William, 878, 911
Catherine II, of Russia, 860, 867, 1230, 1231, 1318, 1370
Caucasus, 699, 704, 726, 727, 774, 786, 804, 810, 816, 818, 830, 850, 857, 879, 898, 911, 961, 1118, 1128, 1131, 1133, 1134, 1138, 1139, 1144, 1147, 1148, 1162, 1183, 1185, 1215, 1232, 1241, 1267, 1272, 1328, 1329, 1331
Cavakert, *see* Kavakert
Cazeroon, *see* Kazerun
Cazvin, *see* Qazvin
Celaleddin Pasha, 1016
Chabahar, 713
Chah-Nazaroff, *see* Nazarov, Mirza Neriman Malik Shah
Chahrokh, *see* Shahrokh, Shah
Chalderan, 966
Chalis, *see* Khalis
Chamkor, *see* Shamkirçay
Chamora, *see* Shamkirçay
Champagny, Jean-Baptiste de Nompère de, 819, 845, 857
Chandu, 1343
Chapanoğlu, 844
Charack, *see* Khark
Charagh 'Ali Khan-e Nava'i, 743
Chardin, Jean, 810, 831, 871, 913, 1088, 1367
Charlotte, of Great Britain and Ireland, 860
Charok Shaw, *see* Shahrokh, Shah
Chattanuttee, 729
Chatul, *see* Shatt al-'Arab
Chechens, 1146, 1183, 1189
Chekiue, *see* Sheki

Chennai, 731
Chernihiv, 1016
Cherry, John Hector, 731, 742
Chesis, *see* Sheki
Chester, Robert, 936, 948
Chilchan, 1274
Chirvan, *see* Shirvan
Chirwan, *see* Shirvan
Chmpagny, Jean-Baptiste de Nompère de, 828
Choczim, *see* Khotyn
Choiseul-Gouffier, Marie Gabriel Florent Auguste de, 891
Chorassan, *see* Khorasan
Chorour, *see* Sharur Dagh
Chosrew Mirza, *see* Khosrow Mirza
Christian VII, of Denmark and Norway, 835
Christie, Charles, 879–881, 1126, 1375
Chudoperin, *see* Khoda Afarin
Churegel, *see* Shoregel/Shuragel
Circassia, 940
St. Clair, Arthur, 758
Clanhora, *see* Shamkirçay
Clay, Henry, 1116, 1175, 1194, 1196, 1198
Clive, Robert, 836, 963, 1367
Close, Barry, 710
Colchester, *see* Abbot, Charles
Colchis, 816
Colebrooke, John, 709
Collier, Francis Augustus, 1077
Congreve, William, 859, 1259
Consalvi, Ercole, 867
Contarini, Ambrogio, 753
Cook, James, 1043
Cormick, John, 881, 919, 1205, 1337
Cosmas Indicopleustes, 831
Cossacks, 777, 803, 1128, 1135, 1138, 1157, 1174, 1182, 1185, 1188, 1195, 1236, 1237, 1240, 1294, 1306
Cosseim Beg, *see* Qasem Khan
Couban, *see* Kuban
Coubla, *see* Qobba
Court, Claude Auguste, 974
Court, William à, 1308
Crimea, 806, 814, 816, 982, 986, 1050, 1100, 1128, 1130, 1131, 1133, 1276
Cuamchalil, *see* Shamshedil
Cuban, *see* Kuban
Cuillier-Perron, Pierre, 781
Curdistan, *see* Kurdistan
Cuvier, Georges, 1043
Cyrus, *see* Kur
Czizianow, *see* Tsitsianov, Pavel Dmitryevich

D

Dadiani, Darejan, 868
Daghestan, 700, 745, 767, 882, 883, 885, 911, 1045, 1121, 1179–1181, 1185, 1216, 1331, 1379
Daghestanis, 960
Daglostan, *see* Daghestan
Dalrymple, Alexander, 830
Dand-Aga, *see* Nazar, Dawud Khan Malekshah
Dantzig, *see* Gdansk
Dara, 860
Daraoud, 1227
Daraourte, 1227
Darband, 703, 726, 767, 794, 803, 821, 867, 883, 884, 886, 887, 900, 1121, 1140, 1179, 1190, 1230
Darband, Kurdistan, 794
D'Arcy, Joseph, 878, 1126, 1200
Darial, 790
Dasht-e Kavir, 1372
Daud Khan, 904
Daud Pasha, 963, 968, 974, 989, 996, 999, 1000, 1004, 1007, 1009, 1012, 1013, 1020, 1024, 1048, 1051, 1061, 1330, 1338, 1347
Davidow, *see* Davydov, Denis Vasilyevich
Davydov, Denis Vasilyevich, 1217
Davy, Humphrey, 1043
Dawson, James, 1126, 1164, 1200, 1201, 1205
Dawud Khan Malekshah Nazar, 905, 1197
Dayadin, 971
Daylam, 767
Decaen, Charles Mathieu Isidore, 738, 740, 850
Deccan, 830
Deheragon, *see* Deh Kurgan
Dekhargane, *see* Deh Kurgan
Deh Kurgan, 1249, 1254, 1256, 1258
Delhi, 781, 836
Della Valle, Pietro, 763, 897–898
Desbassayns de Richemont, Eugène, 1060, 1113
Dessolles, Jean-Joseph Paul Augustin, 938, 1288
Devaux, Charles, 903, 912, 968, 970, 974, 1005, 1009, 1037, 1346, 1347
De Wint, Peter, 870
Dibitch, *see* Diebitsch, Hans Karl Graf von
Dickson, David, 900
Didelot, Charles Louis, 1319
Diebitsch, Hans Karl Graf von, 1118, 1130, 1138, 1241, 1243, 1315, 1339
Dilaman, 1173
Dilaram, 935, 939
Diyarbakir, 801, 1109
Djaro-Bielokani, 745
Djezan, *see* Qeshm
Djichir, 1180

Dniestr, 816
Doğubayazit, 795, 797, 799, 829, 965, 966, 971, 1032, 1033, 1280
Dokhergan, *see* Deh Kurgan
Dolgoronsky, *see* Dolgorukov, Peter Petrovich
Dolgorukov, Nikolai Andreyevich, 1301, 1317, 1338
Dolgorukov, Peter Petrovich, 806
Downshire, Lord, 958
Dschajawak, *see* Javad
Dublin, 958
Duckworth, John, 813
Dufresne, Guillaume, 739
Dumas, Alexandre, 1099
Duncan, Jonathan, 710, 713, 718, 740, 741, 814, 850
Dundas, Henry, 719
Dupré, Adrien, 829, 864, 865
Durrani, Firuz Shah, 707
Durrani, Homayun, 725
Durrani, Hyder, 725
Durrani, Kamran Shah, 934
Durrani, Mahmud, 725
Durrani, Mahmud Shah, 725, 934, 949, 951
Durrani, Nasir, 725
Durrani, Shuja' Shah, 744
Durrani, Timur Shah, 725
Durrani, Zaman Shah, 702, 707–710, 725, 744, 745, 814, 934
Dwight, Timothy, IV, 700, 758, 759

E

Eazerum, *see* Erzurum
Echmiadzin, 776, 777, 785, 916, 1209, 1237–1239, 1250, 1251, 1380
Ediboul, *see* Besobdal
Edinburgh, 958
Edirne, 1189, 1194, 1316
Edmonstone, Neil Benjamin, 731
Egypt, 736, 737, 801, 984, 1040, 1042, 1043
Eights, Jonathan, 1064
Elbing, *see* Elbląg
Elbląg, 821
Elgin, *see* Bruce, Thomas
Elishar, 803
Elizabethpol, *see* Ganja
Ellis, Henry, 870, 894, 931, 1222, 1225
Elphinstone, Mountstuart, 1236
Elwind, *see* Alvand
Emin Vahid Efendi, 809, 811
Emmanuel, Giorgi Arsenyevich, 1330
Endicott, Samuel, 1234
Engleheart, George, 860

Index-2 1395

English East India Company, 699, 714, 773, 814, 860, 912, 963, 1191
English, George Bethune, 1056
Enisel, 1146
Enzellee, *see* Bandar-e Anzali
Ephraim, Patriarch, 868
Erekle II, 728, 790, 868, 1231
Ergerumon, *see* Erzurum
Eristov, Giorgi Evseevich, 803, 804
Erivan, *see* Yerevan
Erkivan, 1206
Ermolov, Alexei Petrovich, 863, 903, 907, 908, 910, 911, 913, 916, 917, 920, 923–925, 928, 929, 932, 957, 960, 967, 969, 973, 975, 978, 981, 984, 985, 1018, 1071, 1116–1119, 1122–1124, 1128, 1129, 1132, 1134, 1136, 1140, 1141, 1143–1145, 1148, 1152, 1154, 1157–1160, 1162–1164, 1167, 1169, 1174, 1179–1186, 1188, 1189, 1192–1194, 1196, 1199, 1203, 1204, 1209–1215, 1217, 1219, 1226, 1235, 1236, 1240–1243, 1260, 1287, 1331
Ertz Roum, *see* Erzurum
Erwan, *see* Yerevan
Erzurum, 789, 796, 806, 819, 843, 853, 904, 965–967, 971, 976–979, 981, 983, 986, 988, 989, 991, 992, 995, 996, 999, 1001–1003, 1007, 1012, 1014, 1016, 1019, 1020, 1023, 1025, 1026, 1030, 1034, 1036, 1039, 1047, 1051, 1056, 1060, 1121, 1129, 1309, 1311, 1339, 1348, 1351
Escars, *see* Pérusse des Cars, Jean-François de
Este, Augusta Emma d', 947
Etchmiadsian, *see* Echmiadzin
Eton, William, 750
Etzerum, *see* Erzurum
Etzmiadzin, *see* Echmiadzin
Euphrates, 748, 767, 983, 984, 1040
Euxine, *see* Black Sea

F

Fabvier, Charles Nicolas, 827, 832, 864, 865, 945
Farahabad, 754
Fars, 765, 784, 821, 1290, 1333, 1335, 1337, 1342, 1358
Fathali Char, *see* Fath 'Ali Shah
Fath 'Ali Khan, 699, 858, 896, 1067
Fath 'Ali Khan-e Rashti, 1249, 1250, 1253, 1255
Fath 'Ali Shah, 701, 707, 709, 711, 715, 717–719, 723, 724, 726, 728, 732, 733, 735, 740, 744, 756, 764, 773, 775, 776, 780, 782, 784, 785, 788, 790, 791, 793, 795, 800, 802, 804, 808, 809, 813, 815, 817, 819, 821, 823, 826, 832, 840, 841, 850, 851, 854, 861, 863, 864, 866, 867, 870, 877, 890, 892, 893, 896, 903–905, 908–910, 912–914, 916, 919, 922–925, 934, 938, 939, 944, 945, 949, 951, 956, 957, 959–961, 963–965, 971, 974–977, 982, 984–987, 992, 994, 999, 1002, 1005–1009, 1013, 1018, 1021, 1026, 1027, 1046, 1047, 1054, 1058–1060, 1062, 1063, 1070, 1072, 1074, 1075, 1085, 1086, 1095–1096, 1103–1105, 1115, 1116, 1118, 1123, 1126, 1132, 1133, 1139, 1143, 1150, 1151, 1161, 1162, 1166, 1170, 1176, 1177, 1183, 1184, 1190, 1193, 1199, 1201, 1205, 1210–1212, 1216, 1217, 1219, 1220, 1224, 1234, 1240, 1241, 1243, 1245, 1250, 1254, 1258, 1262, 1265–1267, 1275, 1281–1284, 1289–1388
Fath Khan Barakzai, 725, 934, 935
Feodorovna, Alexandra, of Russia, 1318
Feodosia, 717
Ferdowsi, 1089
Ferrier, John, 841
Ferrières-Sauvebœuf, Louis François de, 891
Feth-Ali-Chah, *see* Fath 'Ali Shah
Finkenstein, 812, 821, 822, 825, 829
Firuz Eddin, *see* Firuzuddin, Haji
Firuzabad, 765
Firuzuddin, Haji, 934, 935
Flacourt, Étienne de, 739
Forster, George, 801
Foster, *see* Forster, George
Francis I, of Austria, 939, 964, 970, 1052, 1362
Fraser, James Baillie, 770, 1292, 1382
Frederick William III, of Prussia, 807
Freygang, Frederika Afanasyevna von, 1099, 1210
Freygang, Wilhelm von, 1099, 1210, 1212

G

Gabarabad, 763
Gaghma-Mkhar, 728
Gallitzin, *see* Golitsyn, Dmitry Vladimirovich
Gamba, Jean-François, 919, 1286
Gambier, James, 869, 872, 873
Gambier, Lady, *see* Snell, Jemina
Gambroon, *see* Bandar 'Abbas
Gamza-Tchémène, 1122
Gandja, *see* Ganja
Gändsha, *see* Ganja
Ganges, 781
Gangi, *see* Ganja
Gangia, *see* Ganja
Ganja, 723, 726, 728, 775, 780, 818, 821, 857, 882, 883, 887, 1129, 1134, 1140, 1144, 1147, 1151, 1155, 1166, 1167, 1174, 1178, 1181,

1182, 1186, 1197, 1204, 1216, 1217, 1234, 1323, 1379
Gannshiu, *see* Ganja
Gardane, Ange de, brother of Claude Mathieu, 846
Gardane, Ange de, grandson of Louis, 843
Gardane, Ange-Nicolas de, 843
Gardane, Ange Nicolas de, brother of Claude Mathieu, 842
Gardane, Ange Paul Louis de, 843
Gardane, Claude Mathieu de, 773, 812, 819, 821, 822, 824–827, 832, 833, 838, 840–845, 850, 851, 854, 856, 857, 862, 867, 910, 912, 932, 945, 1064, 1072, 1086, 1087, 1126, 1214, 1225, 1245
Gardane, Louis de, 843
Gardane, Louis de, nephew of Louis, 843
Gareja, 1158
Gaschim Khan, *see* Qasem Khan
Gdansk, 821
Gebayedof, *see* Griboyedov, Alexander Sergeyevich
Gelae, 767
George III, of Great Britain and Ireland, 839, 860, 863, 864, 970, 1067
George IV, of the United Kingdom, 859, 873, 875, 883, 936, 944, 948, 950, 952–954, 959, 1047
Georgia, 726, 728, 745, 775, 776, 780, 782, 787, 788, 790, 796, 803, 806, 809, 816, 818, 819, 823, 850, 852, 857, 868, 881, 883, 884, 900, 903, 906, 907, 909, 911, 916, 921, 925, 941, 947, 952, 960–962, 973, 999, 1000, 1018, 1019, 1027, 1035, 1038, 1042, 1043, 1045, 1058, 1087, 1090, 1096, 1099, 1116, 1117, 1121–1123, 1128–1131, 1133, 1136, 1137, 1139, 1140, 1144, 1145, 1148, 1151, 1158, 1161, 1162, 1169, 1172, 1177–1179, 1183, 1194, 1199, 1204, 1211, 1218, 1219, 1226, 1231, 1242, 1250, 1276, 1279, 1330, 1331, 1379
Georgians, 700, 763, 791, 792, 1018, 1238
Geybydoff, *see* Griboyedov, Alexander Sergeyevich
Ghalib Sharif, 748
Ghazna/h, 766
Ghilan, *see* Gilan
Gibojadow, *see* Griboyedov, Alexander Sergeyevich
Gibojidoff, *see* Griboyedov, Alexander Sergeyevich
Gilan, 711, 726, 754, 767, 780, 807, 1088, 1230, 1276, 1286
Giorgi XI, of Georgia, 1158
Giorgi XII, of Georgia, 728

Glasenapp, Georg Johann von, 803, 821
Gökçe, *see* Sevan (Gökçe)
Goktcha, *see* Sevan (Gökçe)
Goktscha, *see* Sevan (Gökçe)
Golenischev-Kutuzov, Pavel Vasiliyevich, 1268, 1269, 1271
Golitsyn, Alexander Nikolaievich, 899
Golitsyn, Dmitry Vladimirovich, 1318
Golitsyna, Tatiana Vasilyevna, 1318
Gombroon, *see* Bandar 'Abbas
Gomeri, *see* Gyumri
Gomron, *see* Bandar 'Abbas
Gordon, Peter, 1091, 1092
Gorgan, 886
Gori, 792
Goudowitch, *see* Gudovich, Ivan Vasilyevich
Goukcha, *see* Sevan (Gökçe)
Goukha, *see* Sevan (Gökçe)
Goumli, *see* Gyumri
Govindapur, 729
Grebayedoff, *see* Griboyedov, Alexander Sergeyevich
Grekov, Colonel, 1168, 1186, 1193, 1194, 1238
Grekov, Nikolai, 1146
Grem, 1146
Gretoff, *see* Grekov, Colonel
Greville, Charles C.F., 953
Grey, Charles, 833
Griboyedoff, *see* Griboyedov, Alexander Sergeyevich
Griboyedov, Alexander Sergeyevich, 909, 1116, 1144, 1208, 1267, 1289–1388
Griboyedova, Nina Alexandrovna, 1299
Grigol, Dadian, 745
Griscom, John, 1043
Grotoff, *see* Grekov, Colonel
Grubb, John H., 1077
Grusia, *see* Georgia
Grusien, *see* Georgia
Grusija, *see* Georgia
Grusinie, *see* Georgia
Grussinie, *see* Georgia
Gruzinsky, Alexander Iraklievich, 915
Gruzinsky, Alexander Irakliyevich, 783, 790, 1147, 1158
Gruzinsky, Iulon Irakliyevich, 783, 790
Gruzinsky, Levan Iulonovich, 790, 868
Gruzinsky, Luarsab Iulonovich, 790
Gruzinsky, Parnaos Irakliyevich, 783, 790
Grybydoff, *see* Griboyedov, Alexander Sergeyevich
Guase, *see* Kish
Gudovich, Ivan Vasilyevich, 817, 819, 840, 853, 857

Guenge, *see* Ganja
Guilan, *see* Gilan
Gujarat, 725
Gulistan, 882, 883, 1166
Guria, 728, 882, 883, 1279
Guriel, *see* Guria
Guriev, 780
Gustav IV Adolf, of Sweden, 771
Güzelhisar, *see* Aydın
Gwalior, 781
Gyumri, 777, 817, 840, 1122, 1129, 1328

H

Hafez, 751, 861, 1089, 1095
Hafez 'Ali Pasha, 1030
Hafez Mohammad Pasha, 966
Haider 'Ali Khan, 1359
Haileybury College, 1346
Haji Baba, 1043
Halil Pasha, 1324
Halul, 1078
Hamayoon, *see* Durrani, Homayun
Hamid Bey, 977
Hamilton, William Rowan, 958
Hammer(-Purgstall), Joseph von, 935, 937, 944, 1362
Hanja, *see* Ganja
Hanjam, 713
Hart, Henry, 1343
Hart, Isaac, 919, 974, 1093, 1126
Hasan 'Ali Mirza, 861, 1327, 1328, 1332, 1333
Hasan Khan, 971, 1185, 1217, 1240, 1244, 1251, 1253, 1254
Hasanabad, 763
Hasan-e Fasa'i, 724, 729, 730, 734, 736, 783, 784, 857, 862, 889, 923, 965, 1034, 1063, 1117, 1190, 1294, 1323
Hastings, Warren, 836, 1234
Haujee Khuleel Khann, *see* Khalil Khan-e Koroghlu Qazvini, Haji
Headfort, Lord, 948
Heideranlu, 966, 1017
Helmadoff, *see* Ermolov, Alexei Petrovich
Henry VIII, of England, 959
Heraclius, *see* Erekle II
Heraklion, 1027
Herat, 707, 725, 765, 891, 908, 934, 935, 1315, 1338
Heytesbury, *see* Court, William à
Hillsborough, 958
Hindley, John Haddon, 751
Hine, W. John, 838
Holkar, Yashwant Rao, 781

Holland, New, 1045
Hollingbery, William, 709, 720, 751
Holmes, George, 741
Hooghly, 729
Horasan, 1311
Hormuz, 712–714, 717, 751, 752, 766, 841, 850, 904, 1078
Hornby, William, 740
Hoseyn Agha, 1240
Hoseyn 'Ali Mirza, 721, 756, 791, 861, 934, 1072, 1290, 1342, 1344
Hoseyn Khan, Haji, 802
Hoseyn Qoli Khan, 724, 728, 803, 893
    See also Vakhtang VI, of Kartli
Hoseyn Qoli Khan, of Baku, 803
Hoseyn Qoli Khan Qajar, 1379
Hoseyn Qoli Khan Qazvini, 917, 929, 965, 966, 1017, 1030, 1032, 1115, 1117, 1122, 1124, 1139, 1144, 1148, 1158, 1172, 1178, 1181, 1183, 1185, 1190, 1207–1209, 1211, 1212, 1217, 1240, 1252, 1304
Hosreff Mirza, *see* Khosrow Mirza
Howard, Fulk(e) Southwell Greville, 869, 870, 872
Howard, Mary, 869, 870
Howard, Richard, 869
Howen, Reinhold Johann Freiherr von der, 1189
Hrazdan, 776, 778
Hüe de la Blanche, Xavier Olympe, 823, 945, 1086
Hughes, Christopher, 1175
Hume, Abraham, 1257
Hüseyin Aga, 1035
Husrev Mehmed Pasha, *see* Khosrow Mohammad Pasha
Hussein Kuli Mirza, *see* Hoseyn 'Ali Mirza
Hyder 'Ali, 814
Hyderanloo, *see* Heideranlu

I

Iași, 811
Ibrahim Beg, 803
Ibrahim Bey, 799
Ibrahim Khan, 1244
Ibrahim Khan, Haji, 724, 764, 776
Ibrahim Pasha, 1377
Ibrahim, Haji, 1379
Iermolof, *see* Ermolov, Alexei Petrovich
Ilinski, Major, 1206
Illowaisky, *see* Ilovaysky, Vasily Dmitryevich
Illowwaisky, *see* Ilovaysky, Vasily Dmitryevich
Ilovaysky, Vasily Dmitryevich, 1138, 1157
Imam Verdi Mirza, 1295
Imeritia, 745, 790, 792, 882, 883, 900, 1148
Immanetta, *see* Imeritia

Iraq ('Iraq) 'Ajami, 728, 767, 995
Irewan, *see* Yerevan
Isfahan, 722, 762, 763, 767, 770, 801, 802, 804, 807, 847, 862, 865, 889, 900, 905, 908, 945, 1044, 1074, 1084, 1088, 1089, 1257, 1276, 1290, 1335, 1338, 1344, 1351, 1352, 1367, 1369
Isle de France, 739
Isma'il Khan, 1240, 1305
Isma'il Mirza, 1185, 1188, 1194, 1216
Ivanov, A.I., 1371
Ivanov, assistant to Amburger, 1206
İzmit, 843

J

Ja'far 'Ali Khan, 863, 1095
Ja'far Khan Zand, 889
Ja'far Qoli Khan, 889
Jackson, Francis James, 858
Jackson, George, 858
Jackson, John, 801
Jackson, Keith, 1106
Jacquemont, Victor, 912
Jahan Numa, 721
Jahangir Mirza, 1258, 1266
Jalaladdin Pacha, *see* Celaleddin Pasha
Jalayer, 1153
Jari, 1219
Jarun, *see* Hormuz
Jassy, *see* Iaşi
Jatshmiasin, *see* Echmiadzin
Jaubert, Pierre Amédée, 795, 799, 805, 808, 810
Javad, 1219, 1220, 1226, 1227
Javad Khan, 1217
Javakheti, 1279
Jazirat al-Qeys, *see* Kish
Jefferson, Thomas, 945, 1065
Jermoloff, *see* Ermolov, Alexei Petrovich
Jerusalem, 1109
Jervis, Evan, 1106
Jervis, George Ritso, 1363
Jesse, William, 1126
Johnson, John, 974
Jones, Harford, 710, 719, 727, 770, 774, 808, 849, 850, 854–856, 858, 862–866, 869, 875, 924, 928, 1087, 1089, 1090, 1103
Jones, William, 700, 750, 764, 807, 835, 850, 886
Jonnès, Alexandre Moreau de, 1353
Jouannin, Joseph-Marie, 862, 1086
Juchereau de Saint-Denys, Antoine, 813
Jukes, Andrew, 770, 808, 1077
Julfa, 763, 770, 1084
Julfa, on the Aras, 917
Julon, *see* Gruzinsky, Iulon Irakliyevich
Jumna, 781
Jusef Bey, *see* Yusuf Pasha

K

Kabul, 707, 708, 725, 766, 782, 801, 818, 906, 1072, 1338
Kachum, *see* Qazi Qomuq
Kaeese, *see* Kish
Kaempfer, Engelbert, 871
Kaflankuh, 922
Kagah, 1207
Kakheti, 728, 790, 1146, 1158, 1179, 1219
Kalat, 1152, 1335
Kallarman Oglou, *see* Karaosmanoğlu
Kaluga, 1009
Kanagria, *see* Kanakir
Kanakir, 778, 852
Kandahar, 708, 725, 767, 781, 801, 818, 831, 1072
Kandeish, 706
Kapan, 1171, 1203
Kapanakçay, 1171, 1177, 1203
Kapanaktchay, *see* Kapanakçay
Kapchak, 886
Kara 'Ali, *see* Nasuhzade, 'Ali
Karabag, *see* Qarabagh
Karabagh, *see* Qarabagh
Karabak, *see* Qarabagh
Kara Bang, *see* Qarabagh
Karabog, *see* Qarabagh
Karabosch, *see* Qarabagh
Karaçay, 1217
Karafto, 1205
Karakepek, 803
Kara Kilise, 792, 1280
Karaklis, *see* Vandzor
Karaklis, Little, 1122
Karamallik, 1254
Karaosmanoğlu, 788, 789, 844
Karapagh, *see* Qarabagh
Karass, 898, 1050
Kara Su, 1274, 1381
Karbala, 748, 1020, 1115, 1118, 1137, 1143, 1202
Karbuli, 778
Kardu, 1308
Karduchians, 1308
Kariaghin, 803
Kariagin, Pavel Mikhailovich, 818, 1260
Karim Khan Zand, 814, 1088, 1108
Karnataka, 708
Karoon, *see* Karun
Karpoff, *see* Karpov, Akim Akimovich
Karpov, Akim Akimovich, 1238

Karrack, *see* Khark
Kars, 727, 817, 966, 971, 981, 984, 1012, 1025
Kartli, 779
Karun, 1363
Kasak, 1134
Kasatcha/Kazachia, 1174, 1182, 1185
Kashan, 764, 895, 1088, 1325, 1351
Kashgar, 708
Kashmar, 1381
Kasikumük, *see* Qazi Qomuq
Kasim Khan, *see* Qasem Khan
Kásum, *see* Qeshm
Kattı Giray, 909
Kavagera, *see* Kavakert
Kavakert, 776, 778
Kavalali Mehmed 'Ali Pasha, of Egypt, 913
Kawkert, *see* Kavakert
Kazasch, *see* Kasatcha/Kazachia
Kazask, *see* Kasatcha/Kazachia
Kazerun, 765, 1104, 1105
Kazi Molla, 1328
Kazikumukh, *see* Qazi Qomuq
Kazroon, *see* Kazerun
Keir, William Grant, 894, 1077
Kelly, Richard J., 756
Kendolan, *see* Khaldan
Kenn, *see* Kish
Ker Porter, Robert, 876, 935, 1094, 1368
Kerch, 1018, 1131
Kerend, 968, 989
Kerkuk, 989, 991, 1004, 1024
Kerman, 766, 916, 1084, 1327, 1333, 1334, 1358
Kermanshah, 821, 857, 877, 903, 912, 963, 974, 989, 1003, 1004, 1025, 1097, 1105
Kertch, *see* Kerch
Khabushan, 1381
Khaldan, 1217
Khalid Baban, 794
Khalil Khan-e Koroghlu Qazvini, Haji, 699, 729, 732, 735, 737, 740, 743, 745, 808, 851, 891, 1289, 1369
Khalis, 1020, 1039, 1040
Khamir, 752
Khamsa, 923, 1132
Khan Khouim, 886
Khanashin, 803
Khark, 714, 848, 850, 861, 1079, 1087
Kharqan, *see* Deh Kurgan
Khess, *see* Kish
Khindis, 971
Khiva, 960, 1152, 1230, 1290, 1307, 1335–1338
Khoda Afarin, 1177, 1220, 1226
Khoja Mirza Yakub Markarian, 1297, 1305
Khokhalooya, *see* Kuhgiluyeh

Khonar Takhteh, 1107
Khorasan, 701, 702, 707, 711, 723, 745, 765, 817, 819, 820, 908, 934, 1086, 1098, 1152, 1153, 1290, 1335, 1340, 1350, 1355, 1381
Khos/zrek, 886
Khosrow Mirza, 909, 1289, 1295, 1296, 1302, 1312, 1314–1317, 1319, 1321, 1323, 1326, 1327, 1371
Khosrow Mohammad Pasha, 965, 966, 971, 1030, 1060
Khosrowabad, 1109
Khotyn, 811
Khoy, 700, 822, 829, 965, 966, 1024, 1030, 1033, 1217, 1258
Khudaperim, *see* Khofa Afarin
Khushal, 1343
Khuzestan, 766
Khyvah, *see* Khiva
Kiagar, *see* Qajar
Kinneir, John Macdonald, 893, 894, 1034, 1087, 1106, 1139, 1142, 1208, 1223, 1248, 1250, 1253, 1258, 1259, 1265, 1266, 1299, 1303, 1306, 1381
Kirghiz, 1335
Kirkpatrick, James Achilles, 710
Kischme, *see* Qeshm
Kish, 1077–1079
Kishm, *see* Qeshm
Kisil-osun, *see* Kizil Uzun
Kisiqi, 1158
Kislar, *see* Kizlyar
Kizil Uzun, 922
Kizl Ozan, *see* Kizil Uzun
Kizlyar, 780, 890, 1330
Kléber, Jean-Baptiste, 819
Kluky von Klugenau, Franz, 1145, 1168
Kohraisan, *see* Khorasan
Kol-Sanschak, *see* Koysinjaq
Konoks, *see* Cossacks
Koslofski, *see* Kozlovsky, Platon Timofeyevich
Koslowsky, *see* Kozlovsky, Platon Timofeyevich
Kotlärewsky, *see* Kotlyarevsky, Peter Stepanovich
Kotlérowski, *see* Kotlyarevsky, Peter Stepanovich
Kotlyarevsky, Peter Stepanovich, 803, 879, 881, 1260
Kotzebue, August von, 913, 1190, 1199
Kotzebue, Moritz von, 903, 911, 913–917, 921, 922, 924, 925, 928, 931, 957, 1070, 1071, 1189, 1199, 1210, 1213, 1260
Kotzebue, Otto von, 925, 1052
Kotzebue, Paul Demetrius von, 1238
Koupoperinisk, *see* Khoda Afarin
Kour, *see* Kur
Koysinjaq, 1004

Kozacks, *see* Cossacks
Kozaks, *see* Cossacks
Kozlovsky, Platon Timofeyevich, 779
Krabbe, Karl Karlovich von, 1179, 1180, 1219, 1220
Krabbe, Nikolai Karlovich, 1180
Krasovsky, Afanasy Ivanovich, 1248
Kremlin, 1318
Krusemark, Friedrich Wilhelm Ludwig von, 867
Krusenstern, Adam Johann von, 925
Kuban, 882, 883, 911, 1131
Kubela, *see* Karbala
Kufa, 1020
Kuhgiluyeh, 854
Kuhistan, 767
Kuoth, *see* Qobba
Kur, 703, 704, 754, 867, 887, 1122, 1148, 1166, 1219, 1226, 1276
Kurakçay, 1166
Kurakin, Alexander Borisovich, 867
Kurdistan, 963, 978, 1020, 1024, 1060, 1205
Kurds, 844, 916, 918, 924, 964, 974, 1017, 1023, 1139, 1240, 1242, 1259, 1313
Kurge, 886
Kusakin, *see* Kurakin, Alexander Borisovich
Kussan, 935
Kutatis, 745

L
Lablanche, *see* Hüe de la Blanche, Xavier Olympe
Lacki, 1220
Lahar, 1228, 1247
Lahore, 725, 744, 781, 912, 1303
Lallemand, Charles François Antoine, 905
Lallemand, Henri, 905
Lallemant, *see* Lallemand, Charles François Antoine
Lamy, Armand-François, 832, 1245
Larak, 717
Layard, Austen Henry, 1365
Lenkoran, 753, 882, 1118, 1206
Leo X, 959
Letchkhum, 745
Leyden, John Casper, 1366
Lezgins, 1146, 1158, 1230, 1309
Lieven, Christoph Heinrich von, 943, 954, 975, 1310
Lindsey, *see* Bethune, Henry Lindsay
Linois, Charles Alexandre Léon Durand, 738
Lisanevich, Dmitry Tikhonovich, 1146
Lisanievich, 803
Liston, Robert, 876, 877, 936
Londonderry, Lord, 958, 1015

Loodhianah, *see* Ludhiana
Lori, 915, 1181, 1185, 1228
Lorillard, Jacob, 1357
Lory, *see* Lori
Lotf 'Ali Khan, 889
Louis XIV, of France, 785
Louis XV, of France, 739
Louis XVI, of France, 938
Louis XVIII, of France, 912, 937, 938, 1047, 1161
Lovett, Jonathan Henry, 743
Ludhiana, 725
Lutis, 1074
Lützow, Rudolf Graf von, 970
L'vov, Feodor, 1246
Lyall, Robert, 1131, 1208, 1210

M
Macdonald, Ranald Dugald Harcourt, 1299, 1303
Macdonough, Thomas, 1070
MacFarlane, Charles, 1313
Mackintosh, James, 741, 742
Mackintosh, Major, 919
Macquarie, Elizabeth, 872
Macquarie, Lachlan, 837–839, 872
Madatov, Valerian Grigoryevich, 886, 1116, 1134, 1138, 1145, 1155, 1160, 1162, 1164–1167, 1169, 1173–1175, 1179, 1181, 1184, 1193, 1216, 1227, 1235
Madatow, *see* Madatov, Valerian Grigoryevich
Madras, *see* Chennai
Madstoff, *see* Madatov, Valerian Grigoryevich
Mafruzlu, 1220
Magallon, François Louis, 740
Mahidpur, 1366
Mahmud Durrani, 707
Mahmud II, Ottoman sultan, 962, 969, 975, 978, 979, 988, 990, 991, 994, 997, 1000, 1010, 1012, 1021, 1023, 1026, 1035, 1039, 1042, 1043, 1050, 1054, 1057, 1120, 1125, 1161, 1202, 1232, 1264, 1272, 1329, 1331
Mahmud Pasha, 797, 799
Mahmud Pasha Baban, 1004, 1024, 1061
Mahmud Shah, *see* Durrani, Mahmud Shah
Mahrattas, 739, 745, 781, 835
Mailian, *see* Maralyan
Majoribanks, Catherine Jane, 948
Makintsev, Samson Iakovlev, 1018
Makiszlou, *see* Mafruzlu
Makran, 766
Makrisla, *see* Mafruzlu
Malasgird, *see* Malazgirt
Malazgirt, 971
Malcolm, George, 1107

Malcolm, John, 699, 708–711, 713, 714, 717, 718, 720, 724, 729, 735, 737, 743, 744, 751, 756, 764, 774, 849, 850, 855, 861, 862, 866, 880, 892, 919, 1086, 1087, 1236, 1330, 1349, 1365, 1369, 1385
Malik Qasem Mirza, 1244
Malthus, Thomas Robert, 833
Maltitz, Franz Friedrich Freiherr von, 1116, 1175, 1194, 1196
Maltzew, see Maltzov, Ivan Sergeyevich
Maltzov, Ivan Sergeyevich, 1292, 1293, 1306, 1309
Mandali, 1020, 1037, 1039, 1040, 1048–1051
Manesty, Samuel, 710, 891
Manisa, 1038
Manuchehr Khan, 1265
Maraga, 881
Maragha, 1098, 1256
Maralyan, 1217
Marand, 917, 1032
Maratha, 781
Maret, Hugues-Bernard, 812, 821
Maria Feodorovna, of Russia, 1245
Marljan, see Maralyan
Marmont, Auguste de, 809, 812
Martyn, Henry, 873, 896, 899, 901, 985, 1003, 1075, 1076, 1093–1095, 1097
Mascall, Joseph, 830
Mashhad, 711, 723, 766, 814, 1153, 1334, 1335, 1341, 1376, 1385
Mashhad-e Murghab, 871
Máskat, see Muscat
Massagong, see Mazagaon
Masshad, see Mashhad
Mauritius, 739
Mazagaon, 730, 732, 735
Mazandaran, 754, 780, 870. 1230, 1350
Mazarovich, Semyon Ivanovich, 903, 922, 957, 960, 961, 974, 978, 983, 987, 1010, 1017, 1018, 1062, 1144
McNeill, Elizabeth Wilson, 1287
McNeill, John, 1132, 1142, 1166, 1250, 1253, 1254, 1265, 1266, 1315, 1333, 1355
Mecca, 964
Medginghert, 1311
Media, 754, 767
Meghri, 1143
Mehdi Ali Khan, see Mirza Mehdi 'Ali Khan Bahadur
Mehdi Qoli Khan, 1145
Mehemet 'Ali Pasha, 1027. 1036, 1040, 1042, 1043, 1052, 1056, 1339
Méhémet Sheriff Mirza Khan, see Mohammad Sharif Mirza Khan

Mehmed Mirza, see Mohammad Mirza
Mehnide Ali Khan, see Mirza Mehdi 'Ali Khan Bahadur
Meli Koff, see Melikishvili/Melikov, Colonel
Melich Kassum Mirsa, see Malik Qasem Mirza
Melikishvili/Melikov, Colonel, 1238
Melzoff, see Maltzov, Ivan Sergeyevich
Menchikoff, see Menshikov, Alexander Sergeyevich
Mendeli, see Mandali
Menduli, see Mandali
Menouli, see Mandali
Menshikov, Alexander Sergeyevich, 1115, 1118, 1119, 1123, 1124, 1126, 1136, 1139, 1140, 1142, 1144, 1146, 1148, 1150–1152, 1163, 1169, 1172, 1175, 1177, 1181, 1183, 1201, 1207
Menshikov, Valerian Grigoryevich, 1203
Menzikoff, see Menshikov, Alexander Sergeyevich
Meranda, see Marand
Mériage, Louis-Auguste-François, 815
Merv, 708, 818, 1072
Merv Shahjan, 765
Meshkin, 1227, 1228
Mesopotamia, 812, 1022, 1029
Messagong, see Mazagaon
Metternich, Klemens von, 867, 936, 937, 1052, 1057
Meudoli, see Mandali
Mian Gholam Mohammad, 725
Miana, see Mianeh
Mianeh, 922, 1203, 1265
Michael Pavlovich, of Russia, 1245
Michaux, André, 1064
Michelsen, see Michelsohnen, Johann von
Michelsohnen, Johann von, 806, 807, 811, 816
Middleton, Henry, 1175
Mikhelson, see Michelsohnen, Johann von
Mill, William Hodge, 1109
Milne, John, 770
Minciacky, Matei, 1057, 1120, 1126, 1161
Mingrelia, 726, 728, 745, 789, 882, 883, 900, 1148, 1379
Minto, Lord, 849, 855, 861
Mir Abdul Latif Khan Shushtari, 742
Mir-Daoud-Zadour-el-Melik, see Dawud Khan Malekshah Nazar
Mirez Mahommed Saulit, see Mirza Saleh Shirazi
Mir Hasan Khan, 1205
Mir Hoseyn Khan, 1136
Mir Mahmud Ghalza'i, 807
Mir Qasem, 831
Mir Sa'id Mohammad, 1119
Mirshé, Monsieur, 1214

Mirza Abu'l Hasan Khan Shirazi, 774, 856, 857, 859, 899, 903, 907, 909, 911, 935–940, 944, 946–948, 950, 952–954, 958, 959, 1065–1069, 1190, 1201, 1202, 1204, 1211, 1250, 1254, 1265, 1299, 1302, 1304, 1362
Mirza 'Abd ol-Vahhab-e Isfahani, 923, 1132, 1202, 1223, 1224, 1303
Mirza Abu'l-Qasem, 1034, 1146, 1205, 1255, 1265, 1289, 1293, 1295, 1298, 1348
Mirza Ahmed, 1363
Mirza 'Ali Akbar, 1108
Mirza Asadollah Shirazi, 1363
Mirza Baba, 1314
Mirza Bozorg, 858, 863, 893, 919, 921, 1033, 1223, 1225, 1348
Mirza Hasan Khan, 1207
Mirza Ibrahim, 901
Mirza Isma'il, 1207
Mirza Ja'far, 899
Mirza Mahomed Sauhl, *see* Mirza Saleh Shirazi
Mirza Mas'ud, 1295, 1314, 1317, 1327
Mirza Mehdi 'Ali Khan Khorasani, 707, 709, 710
Mirza Mohammad 'Ali Khan, 1304
Mirza Mohammad Ibrahim, 1345
Mirza Mohammad Khan Qajar Devehlu, 1379
Mirza Mohammad Reza Qazvini, 805, 809, 811, 812, 817, 821, 822, 828, 841
Mirza Morteza, 781
Mirza Musa Khan, Haji, 1348
Mirza Mustafa, 1295
Mirza Reza, 1043
Mirza Safi'-e Mazandarani, 855
Mirza Sa'id 'Ali, 1095
Mirza Saleh Shirazi, 904, 1016, 1034, 1044, 1046, 1047, 1295, 1314, 1317, 1327, 1363
Mirza Shafi'-e Mazandarani, 776, 838, 839, 844, 850, 853, 862, 864, 920, 923, 1071, 1223, 1224
Mirza Turki, 1034
Mistchenko, *see* Mitchenko
Mitchenko, Colonel, 1180, 1226–1228
Mitchenko, Major, 1239
Mitzchenke, *see* Mitchenko, Colonel
Modatow, *see* Madatov, Valerian Grigoryevich
Moghaddam, 818
Mohammad Agha, 989, 1013
Mohammad 'Ali Chakhmaqsaz, 1199, 1200
Mohammad 'Ali Khan, 1027
Mohammad 'Ali Mirza, 821, 857, 877, 903, 904, 912, 924, 963, 964, 966, 968, 970, 971, 974, 976, 978, 980, 983, 986, 988, 989, 992–994, 999, 1002–1005, 1007–1009, 1012, 1020, 1021, 1024, 1030, 1037, 1061, 1105, 1118, 1347
Mohammad 'Ali Ridha Pasha, Haji, 1342
Mohammad Beg, 971
Mohammad Emin Rauf Pasha, 1026, 1033
Mohammad Faiz Allah Efendi, 816
Mohammad Hoseyn Beg, 793
Mohammad Hoseyn Khan, 1117
Mohammad Hoseyn Khan, Haji, 722, 1369
Mohammad Hoseyn Khan Isfahani, 1088
Mohammad Hoseyn Khan Mervi, 1072
Mohammad Hoseyn Khan Qajar, 852
Mohammad Hoseyn Khan Qajar Qoyunlu, 728
Mohammad Hoseyn Mirza, 1009, 1013, 1020, 1105, 1150
Mohammad Isma'il Khan, 699, 733, 734
Mohammad Karim Khan Afshar, 853
Mohammad Khan Qajar, 775, 783
Mohammad Khan-e Zangana, 1314, 1327
Mohammad Mirza, 1116, 1155, 1164, 1167, 1173, 1182, 1185, 1188, 1194, 1216, 1258, 1266, 1290, 1295, 1335, 1340, 1341, 1380
Mohammad Nabi Khan, 730, 851, 854
Mohammad Qasem, 875
Mohammad Rahim Khan, 1152
Mohammad Rahim Khan, of Khiva, 960
Mohammad Rahim, of Khiva, 1335
Mohammad Shah, 1073, 1116, 1155, 1164, 1173, 1315, 1328
Mohammad Sharif Mirza Khan, 1309, 1311, 1327
Mohammad Tahur Beg, 1305
Mohammad Vali Mirza, 817, 1333
Mohammad Zaki Khan-e Nuri, 1108
Mohammad Zaman Khan, 971
Mohammed Ruza, 901
Moldavia, 806, 807, 840, 906, 969, 1055, 1057, 1131, 1281
Mongan, *see* Mughan
Monghaw, *see* Mughan
Monroe, James, 1056
Monteith, William, 818, 893, 919, 972, 1191, 1208, 1245, 1315
Montrésor, James, 914
Montrésor, John, 914
Montrésor, Joseph (Jozef) Antonovich, 914, 915
Montrose, Duke of, 959
Moore, Thomas, 958
Moravioff, *see* Muraviev/Murav'ev, Nikolai Nikolaevich
Morea, 969, 983, 984, 1018, 1019, 1022, 1051, 1058
Morgan, Augustus de, 1346
Morier, James Justinian, 821, 855, 858, 859, 861, 863, 870, 873, 947, 949, 955, 1068, 1087, 1101, 1222, 1224, 1379
Morier, John Philip, 858

Morra, *see* Morran
Morran, 783
Moscow, 1316, 1317
Mosul, 801, 907, 982, 984, 1001, 1037, 1109
Mtkvar, 1180
Müffling, Philipp Friedrich Carl Ferdinand Freiherr von, 1324
Mughan, 792, 818, 1144, 1180, 1226, 1274, 1381
Muhammad b. 'Abd al-Wahhab, 747, 748
Mukud, 725
Mukudum, *see* Moghaddam
Müller, Dr., 925, 929
Multan, 725, 766, 801, 888
Munro, Thomas, 710
Murad IV, Ottoman sultan, 749, 767
Muraviev/Murav'ev, Nikolai Nikolaevich, 960, 1129
Murray, Augusta, 947
Murray, John, II, 1365
Mursa Selagio, *see* Mirza Saleh Shirazi
Muş, 971, 989, 991, 1017, 1308
Muscat, 708, 712, 713, 717, 752, 831, 848, 850, 1034, 1342, 1351
Mustafa Afshar, 1316
Mustafa Khan, of Sheki/Shirvan, 1179, 1180, 1219, 1220, 1234
Mustafa Pasha, of Aleppo, 1036
Myan Ghulam Mahammed, *see* Mian Gholam Mohammad
Mysore, *see* Mysuru
Mysuru, 706, 710, 814

N

Nackshewan, *see* Nakhchivan/Naxçivan
Nader Mirza, 711
Nader Shah, 765, 767, 807, 835, 886, 1098, 1231
Najib Efendi, 965, 1054, 1062
Nakhchivan/Naxçivan, 780, 832, 1117, 1254–1256, 1264, 1268, 1269, 1271, 1273, 1274, 1279, 1281, 1292, 1300, 1381
Napier, William, 972
Napoleon, 699, 704, 705, 708, 715, 737, 738, 746, 773, 781, 784, 785, 787, 795, 798, 800, 807, 809–811, 814–817, 819–821, 823, 826, 827, 829, 832, 834, 840, 845, 850, 856, 879, 901, 905, 910, 912, 932, 938, 943, 945, 1086, 1087, 1126, 1134, 1136, 1214, 1232, 1288
Narimani, 1279
Narses, Archbishop, 868
Naser od-Din Shah, 904
Nasuhzade, 'Ali, 980
Nauhivan, *see* Nakhchivan/Naxçivan
Nawbandajan/Nubandagan, 765

Nazar, Dawud Khan Malekshah, 1161, 1165, 1199
Nazarov, Mirza Neriman Malik Shah, 1207
Nebolsin, Peter Feodorovich, 803
Nerciat, Georges Philippe Auguste Andréa de, 822, 823, 865, 935, 945, 952
Nerses V Ashtaraketsi, 1209, 1239
Nesselrode, Karl Robert von, 904, 997, 1014, 1057, 1118, 1133, 1253, 1262, 1263, 1274, 1293, 1310, 1314, 1315, 1317, 1321
Nesvetaev, Peter Danilovich, 817
Névétaïef, *see* Nesvetaev, Peter Danilovich
Nicholas I, of Russia, 1115, 1119, 1122, 1123, 1125, 1128, 1136, 1138, 1144, 1149, 1154, 1156–1158, 1163, 1165, 1177, 1183, 1185, 1187, 1194, 1198, 1203, 1208, 1211, 1216, 1229, 1238, 1241, 1243, 1245, 1253, 1254, 1266, 1269–1272, 1277, 1279, 1281, 1289, 1304, 1306, 1315–1318, 1320, 1322, 1325, 1328, 1331, 1371
Nicomedia, *see* İzmit
Niebolseen, *see* Nebolsin, Peter Feodorovich
Niebuhr, Carsten, 749
Nieuhoff, John, 753
Nishapur, 711, 765, 1153, 1205
Noskov, I., 1371
Noukha, *see* Nukhi
Novosiltsev, Nikolai Nikolaievich, 786
Novosiltzoff, *see* Novosiltsev, Nikolai Nikolaievich
Nukha, 803
Nukhi, 1145, 1147
Nurabad-e Mamasani, 765
Nushki, 1375
Nuwaga, 1220

O

Obesnoff, *see* Obrescov, Alexander Mikhailovich
Obrescov, Alexander Mikhailovich, 1254, 1255, 1259, 1265
Odich, 745
Odinabazar, *see* Udinabazaar
Odschan, *see* Awjan/Ujan
Ohsson, Mouradgrad d', 771
Okhotsk, 1091
Olivier, Guillaume-Antoine, 746, 1064, 1367
O'Neil, Robert, 837–839
O'Neill, Eliza, 958
Oojaun, *see* Awjan/Ujan
Orbelian, Stephanos, 778
Orenburg, 900, 1350
Orsa, *see* Urfa
Osipov, Major, 779
Osman Paswan Oğlu, 769

Ossetians, 868, 1231
Ossifof, *see* Osipov, Major
Osten-Sacken, Dmitry Yerofeyevich Freiherr von der, 1195, 1198
Oudh, *see* Avadh/Awadh
Oudian, *see* Awjan/Ujan
Oudinot, Nicolas Charles, 833
Ouoskherdjan, Jean, 778
Oural, *see* Ural
Ouseley, Eliza Shirin, 872
Ouseley, Gore, 756, 774, 858, 859, 868, 872, 875–879, 881, 883, 893, 896, 899, 901, 907, 909, 924, 928, 936, 950, 955, 1065, 1075, 1090, 1126, 1200, 1205, 1210, 1346
Ouseley, Harriet Georgina Whitelock, 872, 1076
Ouseley, William, 700, 751, 755–757, 858, 870, 873, 884, 895, 1200
Outrey, Georges, 805
Oxus, 765, 818, 1336

P

Pagès, Pierre Marie François de, 801
Painda Khan, 725, 934
Pallas, Peter Simon, 753, 888
Palmerston, Lord, 1315, 1340
Palowitsch, *see* Pavlovich, Constantine
Pambak, 728, 790, 792, 914, 1151
Panckoucke, Charles-Joseph, 783
Pankratiev, Nikita Petrovich, 1258
Pankratjeff, *see* Pankratiev, Nikita Petrovich
Parell House, 742
Parnaos, *see* Gruzinsky, Parnaoz Irakliyevich
Parsons, Usher, 1070
Pasargadae, 871
Paskevich, Ivan Feodorovich, 1116, 1118, 1138, 1155, 1166–1168, 1175, 1185, 1188, 1191, 1193, 1197, 1216, 1217, 1219, 1221, 1237, 1241, 1247, 1249, 1251, 1253–1259, 1262, 1265–1267, 1270, 1276, 1278, 1284, 1289, 1292, 1293, 1295, 1296, 1301, 1302, 1309, 1310, 1312–1315, 1317, 1328, 1329, 1339, 1380
Paskewitsch, *see* Paskevich, Ivan Feodorovich
Pasley, Charles William, 709, 743
Patna, 781
Patras, 996
Patrick, Mehitabel, 877
Paul I, of Russia, 703, 716, 718, 719, 727, 728, 1135, 1231
Paulucci delle Roncole, Filippo, 879
Pavlovich, Constantine, 906
Pelenk, 792, 793
Penda Khan, *see* Durrani, Painda Khan

Perron, *see* Cuillier-Perron, Pierre
Persepolis, 722, 770, 871, 923, 1088, 1106, 1356
Persian Gulf, 700, 704, 746, 747, 749, 765, 766, 782, 788, 801, 809, 830, 849, 850, 862, 913, 927, 1039, 1077, 1078, 1080, 1285, 1343, 1351
Persis, 765
Pérusse des Cars (née de Laborde), Pauline Louise Joséphine, 939
Pérusse des Cars, Jean-François de, 939
Peshawar, 725
Peshbulak, 725
St. Petersburg, 1317, 1319, 1381
Peterhof, 1319
Peter I, of Russia, 779, 831, 867, 955, 1230, 1318
Phasis, 787, 789
   See also Rion
Pinkerton, Robert, 898, 899, 902
Pir Qoli Khan Qajar Shambayati, 788, 790, 792, 803, 915
Planta, Joseph, 936
Plessis, Armand Emmanuel Sophie Septimanie de Vignerot du, 826
Pol-e Dokhtar, 922
Pol-e Kaflankuh, *see* Pol-e Dokhtar
Poloria, *see* Lori
Porter, David, 1360
Porter, John, 830
Portnagene, *see* Portnyagin, Semen Andreyevich
Portnyagin, Semen Andreyevich, 852
Potemkin, Pavel Sergeyevich, 1231, 1326
Potocki, Jan, 1239
Potocki, Stanislas, 1319
Pottinger, Henry, 1375
Pozzo di Borgo, Carlo Andrea, 904
Price, William, 871
Pruth, 968, 979, 983, 996, 1128, 1130, 1149, 1263
Punjab, 725, 744, 913, 1246

Q

Qaleh Dokhtar, 922
Qara Qöyunlü, 767
Qarabagh, 775, 818, 821, 857, 878, 882, 883, 1116, 1117, 1122, 1128, 1129, 1134, 1139, 1143–1145, 1147, 1151, 1155, 1167, 1172, 1174, 1177, 1182, 1185, 1192, 1194, 1203, 1207, 1210, 1211, 1219, 1227, 1259, 1379
Qaraklis, *see* Kara Kilise
Qasem Khan, 1032, 1054, 1060, 1220, 1253
Qazakh, 1158
Qazi-Qomuq, 886, 1180
Qazvin, 700, 701, 768, 783, 785, 1304, 1351
Qeshm, 712, 717, 752, 850, 1040, 1087

Qizil Rabat, 1020
Qizlar, *see* Kizlyar
Qobba, 1140, 1151, 1179
Qom, 895, 1088
Quchan, 1153

R
Radstock, Lady, 947
Radstock, Lord, 859, 947, 1068
Raffanel, Monsieur, 993
Rageia, *see* Rayy
Raglan, *see* Somerset, FitzRoy
Rahman Qoli Khan, 1153
Rahmatullah Khan, 725
Ram Homuz, 894
Raminis-Chwili, *see* Ramishvili, Gogia
Ramishvili, Gogia, 790
Rasht, 726, 807, 830, 1350
Rask, Rasmus Kristian, 1097
Rawlinson, Henry Creswicke, 972
Raymond, Jean, 1072
Rayy, 871
Razroon, *see* Kazerun
Razumovsky, Andrey Kyrilovich, 1318
Razumovskya, Konstanze Dominika, 1318
Reboul, Lieutenant, 832, 864, 865
Regensburg, 1288
Remon, Thomas, 1077
Rennell, James, 801, 835
Rennenkampf, Pavel Yakovlevich, 1315
Réouth, *see* Reutt, I.A.
Rescht, *see* Rasht
Reshd, *see* Rasht
Retsch, *see* Rasht
Reutt, I.A., 1128, 1129, 1167, 1312
Reza Qoli Khan, 1153
Reza Qoli Mirza, 711
Ria, *see* Rayy
Riach, James Pringle, 1106, 1356, 1358, 1360
Rion, 728, 789, 1121, 1276
Ritescheff, *see* Rtishchev, Nikolai Feodorovich
Robat, 1358
Robinson, William, 830
Rodofinikin, Konstantin, 1320
Romieu, Antoine Alexandre, 781, 784, 800, 805
Rosen, Georg Andreas von, 1265, 1328
Roulan, *see* Rion
Rousseau, Jean-Baptiste Louis Jacques Joseph, 877
Rousseau, Jean-François Xavier, 781, 800
Roy, Raja Rammohun, 1355
Rtishchev, Nikolai Feodorovich, 879, 907, 909
Ruffin, Pierre, 784, 796, 805, 823, 1072
Rumbec, *see* Pambak

Runjeet Singh, *see* Singh, Ranjit
Rush, Richard, 949, 954

S
Sabat, Nathaniel (Jawad ibn) Sabat, 1076
Sacken, *see* Osten-Sacken, Dmitry Yerofeyevich Freiherr von der
Sadagh-Khatch, 1122
Sadatabad, 763
Sadeq Efendi, 977, 997, 1057
Sadeq Khan, 1313
Sadeq Khan Qajar Devehlu, 699–701
Sadeq Khan Shaqaqi, 701, 1379
Sa'di, 861, 1364
Sadi-Chan, *see* Sadeq Khan Qajar Devehlu
Sadleir, George Forster, 1077
Salavat, 1228
Salil bin Raziq, 713, 1351
Salisbury, Lady, 953
Sallian, *see* Salyan
Salmas, 1109, 1173, 1258
Salvatori, Dr., 1064
Salyan, 753, 1147
Samboor, *see* Zambur
Samoiloff, *see* Samoilov, Nikolai Alexandrovich
Samoilov, Alexander Nikolayevich, 925
Samoilov, Nikolai Alexandrovich, 925
Sanain, 1209
Sanandaj, 794, 1205
Sanga, *see* Hrazdan
Sangan, *see* Zanjan
Sannah, *see* Sanandaj
Sanson, Nicolas Antoine, 829
Sarafraz Khan, 725
Saragarta, *see* Kavakert
Sarakamysh, 1274
Sarakhs, 1153
Sardarabad, 1218, 1238, 1239, 1251
Sargent, John, 1074
Sari, 803, 1206
Sauvidgebaulogh, *see* Savojbolagh
Savalan, 1247
Savary, Anne Jean Marie René, 905
Savojbolagh, 1045
Sayf bin Mohammad, 712
Schamchora, *see* Shamkirçay
Schamsadil, 1185
Schiemann, Karl, 1264
Schultz, *see* Schulz, Friedrich Eduard
Schulz, Friedrich Eduard, 1191
Schwechat, 935
Schyras, *see* Shiraz
Scindea, *see* Sindhia, Daulat Rao

Scott Waring, Edward, 832
Scott, John, 1068
Scott, Walter, 1349, 1365
Scutari, *see* Üsküdar
Sébastiani de la Porta, Horace François Bastien, 737, 805–807, 813, 823, 828, 841, 945
Sebekee, *see* Shakaki
Sedi-Chan, *see* Sadeq Khan Qajar Devehlu
Sedi-Khann, *see* Sadeq Khan
Sefid Rud, 754
Seif ol-Moluk Mirza, 1228
Seiks, *see* Sikhs
Seistan, 708, 766
Seiva, *see* Zuivan
Sekaksevan, *see* Shahsevan
Selby, William, 710, 712
Selim III, Ottoman sultan, 787, 788, 795, 807, 809, 811, 824
Selim Pasha, 966, 967, 971, 1017, 1022, 1023, 1026
Semino, Barthélémy, 1315
Semlin, 826
Semnan, 1335
Sengilabat, *see* Zanjilabad
Senna, *see* Sanandaj
Serbia, 1131
Serir, 886
Sevan (Gökçe) Lake, 776, 1115, 1171, 1177, 1179, 1204, 1380
Sévarzémidzé, Prince, 1122, 1129
Sevastopol, 986
Seychelles, 729
Seymour, H.D., 1126
Seyyid Mohammad, 1143, 1202
Seyyid Mohammad Khan, 1153
Seyyid Morad Khan, 889
Seyyid Sa'id, 1342
Seyyid Sultan bin Ahmed, 712, 713, 717, 718, 752, 755
Shabankara, 908
Shah 'Abdul Azim, 922
Shah 'Alam II, Mughal emperor, 760, 836
Shah Nazaroff, 1146
Shahr-e Babak, 1335
Shahrizor, 1003, 1024
Shahroban, 1020
Shahrokh, Shah, 711, 807, 835
Shahsevan, 1227, 1259
Shakaki, 1017, 1259
Shamakhi, 767, 887, 1179, 1219, 1234
Shamkir, 887, 1169
Shamkirçay, 1134, 1154, 1155, 1157, 1158, 1162, 1166, 1173, 1174, 1181, 1182, 1380
Shammar, 1020

Shamshedil, 1179, 1181, 1217
Shapoor, *see* Bishapur
Sharur Dagh, 1274
Shatt al-'Arab, 1040
Shee, Benjamin Basil, 1126, 1335
Sheffield, Lord, 950
Sheil, Justin, 1357
Shekey, *see* Sheki
Sheki, 728, 803, 821, 882, 883, 1140, 1143, 1145, 1147, 1151, 1179
Shelley, Frances, 939
Sheridan, Thomas Henry, 858, 860, 862, 863
Shir Ghazi Khan, 1230
Shirakan, 1221
Shirakavan, *see* Shoregel/Shuragel
Shiraz, 699, 701, 717, 720, 765, 832, 849, 860, 862, 873, 889, 894, 896, 904, 1034, 1063, 1075, 1076, 1079, 1087, 1089, 1094, 1095, 1104, 1105, 1107, 1108, 1290, 1333, 1335, 1342, 1344, 1351, 1352, 1356, 1359, 1360, 1363
Shirvan, 728, 767, 792, 803, 821, 882, 883, 887, 900, 911, 1081, 1116, 1117, 1121, 1129, 1134, 1139, 1140, 1143, 1145–1147, 1151, 1179, 1216, 1219, 1220, 1227, 1234, 1350, 1379
Shore, John, 725
Shoregel/Shuragel, 818, 882, 883
Shouchi, *see* Shusha
Shusha, 700, 775, 878, 1118, 1128, 1134, 1166, 1167, 1177, 1185, 1206, 1217, 1234, 1380
Shushtar, 767, 893, 1363
Siberia, 1091
Sidy-Khan, *see* Sadeq Khan
Sighnaghi, 1158
Sikhs, 725, 726, 912, 1246
Silvestre de Sacy, Antoine-Isaac, 715, 871
Simolin, Ivan Matveyevich, 891
Simonich, Ivan Osipovich, 1340
Sindhia, Daulat Rao, 781
Singh, Ranjit, 744, 888, 912, 1246
Sirehgheran, 885
Sirfraz Khan, *see* Sarafraz Khan
Sirjan, 766
Sisakan, 778
Sivas, 977
Sizianoff, *see* Tsitsianov, Pavel Dmitryevich
Skinner, John Stuart, 1360
Skvortsov/Skvorzov, Major-General, 1315
Smith, L.F., 860
Snell, Jemima, 872
Solayman Küçük, 844
Solomon I, of Imeritia, 745
Soltan Hoseyn, Shah, 807, 1084

Soltaniyeh, 791, 845, 907, 910, 920, 923, 924, 1062, 1115, 1117, 1118, 1124, 1126, 1139, 1142, 1151, 1172, 1177, 1178, 1201, 1202, 1205, 1206, 1211, 1285, 1286
Somerset, FitzRoy, 940
Somerset, Lady, 940
Somketia, 915, 1140, 1151, 1209
Soojah-ool-Moolk, *see* Durrani, Shah Shuja'
Sorkhay Khan, 886, 1180
Soundja, *see* Sunzha
Sounketre, *see* Somketia
Sourkay, *see* Sorkhay Khan
Staël, Madame de, 1349
Stannus, Ephraim Gerrish, 1077
Stavropol, 1330
Strachey, Richard, 709
Strangford, Lord, 904, 966, 969, 970, 972–974, 976, 1014, 1041, 1051, 1053, 1055, 1057
Stroganov, Grigori Alexandrovich, 972
Strong, Lieutenant, 1107
Stuart, Charles, 959
Stuart, Henry, 729
Suchtelen, Pavel Petrovich, 1258, 1312, 1336
Sudharent, 1217
Suez, 736
Sulaimaniyah, 794, 802, 877, 1004, 1024, 1025, 1061
Sulayman Pasha, *see* Büyük Solayman Pasha
Sultanbud, 878
Sultania, *see* Soltaniyeh
Sunzha, 1146
Suram, 790
Surchai, *see* Sorkhay Khan
Susa, 767
Susiana, 766
Sutherland, James, 860, 875
Suvan Qoli Khan, 1253
Suvorov, Alexander Vasilyevich, 780
Suwarow, *see* Suvorov, Alexander Vasilyevich
Switzerland, 1047
Syer, William, 741
Syiad Khan, 1332
Syr Darya, 1335

T
Tabaris, *see* Tabriz
Tabaristan, 886
Taberseran, 885
Tabran, *see* Tehran
Tabreez, *see* Tabriz
Tabriez, *see* Tabriz
Tabriz, 701, 753, 758, 780, 783, 818, 845, 853, 857, 858, 878, 888, 896, 903, 910, 917, 918, 920–922, 957, 960, 965, 966, 971, 974, 976, 1003, 1018, 1030–1032, 1034, 1035, 1044, 1045, 1060, 1062, 1075, 1092, 1098, 1099, 1101–1103, 1112–1113, 1116, 1117, 1119, 1124, 1133, 1139, 1164, 1178, 1190, 1200, 1201, 1205, 1206, 1214, 1219, 1228, 1235, 1249, 1250, 1253, 1255, 1256, 1258, 1285, 1292, 1295, 1299, 1300, 1302, 1303, 1310, 1315, 1328, 1334, 1337, 1340, 1346, 1348, 1350–1353, 1355, 1357, 1358, 1380
Tahiran, *see* Tehran
Taiquie, *see* Tarki/u
Tairan, *see* Tehran
Tajand, 1153
Tajar Pasha, 788
Talib Agha, Haji, 1013, 1020, 1048
Talidje, *see* Talysh
Talleyrand-Périgord, Charles Maurice de, 781, 800, 806, 812, 821, 823, 834
Talyne, *see* Talysh
Talysh, 882, 883, 907, 1117, 1123, 1134, 1136, 1144, 1147, 1177, 1178, 1205, 1206, 1210, 1211, 1227, 1241, 1254, 1255, 1257, 1381
Tamras, *see* Teimuraz II
Tancoigne, Joseph Michel, 1064
Tarki/u, 1179
Tartars, 819, 1140
Tasman, Abel, 1045
Tatishchev, Dmitry Pavlovich, 1057
Tauris, *see* Tabriz
Taurus, *see* Tabriz
Tbilisi, 703, 723, 727, 777, 782, 785, 790, 791, 804, 818, 830, 853, 857, 868, 878, 886, 887, 900, 904, 906, 911, 912, 914, 919, 921, 957, 973, 1060, 1118, 1121, 1125, 1129, 1137–1139, 1146, 1148, 1167, 1179, 1181, 1189, 1194, 1199, 1201, 1204, 1205, 1207, 1208, 1211, 1234, 1239, 1249, 1279, 1285, 1287, 1289, 1295, 1296, 1299, 1301, 1302, 1310–1312, 1315, 1317, 1321, 1323, 1325, 1326, 1328, 1329, 1339, 1350, 1353, 1380
Tchévister, 1249
Tchinaktchi, 1128
Tchoudouv, *see* Khoda Afarin
Teffis, *see* Tbilisi
Teffleez, *see* Tbilisi
Tehran, 701, 702, 708, 723, 756, 774, 781, 783, 791, 800, 804, 808, 814, 817, 821, 826, 841, 845, 850, 862, 864, 873, 876, 878, 883, 896, 901, 903–905, 909, 911, 912, 920, 924, 926, 936, 957, 960, 961, 965, 972, 974, 996, 1001, 1034, 1057, 1062, 1064, 1072, 1086, 1088, 1089, 1122, 1161, 1235, 1257, 1285, 1289, 1291–1308, 1310, 1312, 1315, 1320,

1321, 1323, 1325, 1326, 1330, 1333, 1334, 1340, 1341, 1348, 1350–1353, 1371, 1380, 1381
Teimuraz II, 1231
Teixeira, Pedro, 713
Telavi, 728
Terseran, 885
Terterçay, 1166, 1184
Teslis, *see* Tbilisi
Thebisand, *see* Trabzon
Théimouraz, *see* Gruzinsky, Teimuraz
Thélaw, *see* Telavi
Thomas, William, 837, 840
Tibet, 708
Tibi Efendi, 1325
Tiffes, *see* Tbilisi
Tiflis, *see* Tbilisi
Tigris, 705, 748, 749, 767, 983, 984, 986, 1040
Timoor Shah, *see* Durrani, Timur Shah
Timur Bey, 1240
Timur Pasha, 1339
Tipu Sultan, 706, 708, 713, 731, 739, 814, 828, 831, 1086
Tiutschkof, *see* Tuchkov, Sergey Alexeyevich
Tobrao-Kelah, *see* Toprakkale
Tokat, 1076
Tokharestan, 767
Tolstoy, Yegor Petrovich, 1208, 1238
Toopruck Kullat, *see* Toprakkale
Topliff, Samuel, 993
Toprák Kil'ah, *see* Toprakkale
Toprakkale, 965, 966, 971, 977, 1032, 1313
Torbat-e Heydari, 1335
Torbat-e Jam, 711
Torkmanchay, 1115–1288
Tormasov, Alexander, 857
Tormesoff, *see* Tormasov, Alexander
Torshiz, *see* Kashmar
Tostar, *see* Shushtar
Tourkmantschai, *see* Torkmanchay
Trabzon, 788, 789, 891, 971, 976, 982, 984, 986, 988, 990, 1013, 1022, 1029, 1121, 1129
Trapezunt, *see* Trabzon
Trebisonde, *see* Trabzon
Trézel, Camille Alphonse, 829, 864
Triflees, *see* Tbilisi
Truilhier, Hilarion, 830
Tschari, *see* Jari
Tscheraken, *see* Shirakan
Tsereteli, Zorab, 790
Tsitsianoff, *see* Tsitsianov, Pavel Dmitryevich
Tsitsianov, Pavel Dmitriyevich, 727, 745, 773, 776, 779, 782, 790, 803–805, 914, 1217, 1260, 1305

Tsitsishvili, *see* Tsitsianov, Pavel Dmitryevich
Tuchkov, Sergey Alexeyevich, 777
Turbat, *see* Torbat-e Jam
Turcomans, 767, 960, 1153, 1242, 1335, 1373
Tus, 766
Tzitzichvili, Giorgi, 728
Tzitzichwili, *see* Tsitsianov, Pavel Dmitryevich

U
Üç-Kilise, *see* Echmiadzin
Udgani, *see* Awjan/Ujan
Udinabazaar, 1274, 1381
Udjani, *see* Awjan/Ujan
Ugurlu Khan, 1217
Upton, John Henry, 872
Ural, 1122
Urfa, 1037
Urmia, 853, 917, 1098, 1357
Üsküdar, 1313
Utub ('Utub), 712
Uzbeks, 1072, 1152, 1335

V
Vakhtang VI, of Kartli, 779
Van, 817, 965, 971, 1305
Vanadzor, 914, 915
Varanasi, 718, 740, 781
Vassilovitz, Ossip, 784, 785
Velyaminov, Alexei Alexandrovich, 973, 1144, 1189
Velyaminov, Ivan Alexandrovich, 1189
Ventura, Rubino (Gian Battista), 912, 913, 1191
Venua, Frédéric Marc Antoine, 1319
Verdier, Aymard Philippe Joseph, 832
Veselago, Captain, 1147
Viefville des Essarts, Monsieur, 823
Vieuzac, Bertrand Barère de, 805
Vincent, William, 830
Vistula, 976, 984, 998
Vladikavkaz, 1314, 1316
Voliensky, Lieutenant-Colonel, 1239
Vorontsov, Mikhail Semyonovich, 779, 1119

W
Wahhabis, 1027
Wallachia, 816, 906, 1055, 1057, 1131, 1281
Walpole, George, 936
Walworth, Mansfield Tracy, 1169
Walworth, Reuben Hyde, 1169
Warden, Francis, 1330
Waterhouse, Benjamin, 1065

Webster, Noah, 759
Weljaminow, *see* Velyaminov, Alexei Alexandrovich
Wellesley, Henry, 735
Wellesley, Richard, 699, 729, 732, 735, 741, 743, 745
Wellington, Duke of, 710, 725, 828, 884, 892, 939, 940, 954, 1086, 1136
Wesselágo, *see* Veselago, Captain
Westmeath, Countess, 948
Whitworth, Charles, 867
William, Fort, 729, 731, 735, 743, 808
Williaminoff, *see* Velyaminov, Alexei Alexandrovich
Willock, George, 919, 936, 950, 958, 1217, 1292
Willock, Henry, 770, 860, 919, 924, 957, 960, 972, 975, 1006, 1015, 1017, 1034, 1106, 1164, 1204, 1205, 1223, 1253, 1356, 1357, 1360
Wilson, D., 1077
Wilson, Lieutenant-Colonel, 808
Wilson, Robert Thomas, 909
Wittishendst, Alexander, 943
Wladikawkask, *see* Vladikavkaz
Wolff, Joseph, 1113, 1337, 1355
Woronzow, *see* Vorontsov, Mikhail Semyonovich
Wrede, Karl Philipp Josef von, 857
Wright, George, 1027

Y

Yalantush Khan, 1336
Yazd, 765, 1084, 1290, 1327, 1332, 1334, 1335, 1351, 1352
Yazdabad, *see* Abbasabad ('Abbasabad)
Yedi Buluk, 1274
Yeprem (Estremus) I, Patriarch, 916, 1209
Yerevan, 728, 773, 775–777, 780, 782, 785, 789–791, 793, 793, 819, 830, 852, 857, 884, 887, 893, 904, 914, 915, 917, 928, 1032, 1034, 1117, 1119, 1140, 1146, 1147, 1179, 1181, 1190, 1207, 1212, 1217, 1240, 1244–1247, 1252, 1254–1256, 1260, 1262, 1264, 1268, 1269, 1271, 1273, 1274, 1279, 1281, 1304, 1381
Yermoloff, *see* Ermolov, Alexei Petrovich
Yermolow, *see* Ermolov, Alexei Petrovich

Youdine, *see* Yudin, Major
Yozgat, 844
Ypsilanti, Alexander, 969
Yudin, Major, 1237
Yusuf Bey, 828, 830
Yusuf Khan, 1018
Yusuf Pasha, 773, 789, 796, 800, 815, 816, 819, 843
Yusupov, Nikolai Borisovich, 1318

Z

Zabulestan, 766
Zabur, 1227
Zadour, David, *see* Nazar, Dawud Khan Malekshah
Zagam, 1158
Zainderood, *see* Zayandarud
Zaki Khan Zand, 890, 1333, 1379
Zambur, 1227, 1228
Zanga/i/u, *see* Hrazdan
Zanjan, 845, 922
Zanjilabad, 921
Zanzibar, 1343
Zarand, 766
Zaranj, 766
Zarskojesselo, 1319
Zavaleeshin, *see* Zavalishin, Irinarkh Ivanovich
Zavalishin, Irinarkh Ivanovich, 804
Zavinn, 1311
Zayandarud, 722, 762, 905
Zebreez, *see* Tabriz
Zechanskoy, Colonel, 779
Zechansky, *see* Zechanskoy, Colonel
Zeiva, 1174, 1182
Zell os-Soltan, *see* Ali ('Ali) Shah Mirza
Zenderhend, *see* Zayandarud
Zengy, *see* Hrazdan
Zguria Khan, *see* Ugurlu Khan
Zinzili, *see* Bandar-e Anzali
Zizianoff, *see* Tsitsianov, Pavel Dimitriyevich
Zizianow, *see* Tsitsianov, Pavel Dmitryevich
Zohab, 1020
Zoprak-Kaleh, *see* Toprakkale
Zoroaster, 831, 979
Zubov, Valerian Alexandrovich, 890
Zuivan, 1121